DICTIONARY OF LITERARY THEMES AND MOTIFS

DICTIONARY OF LITERARY THEMES AND MOTIFS

L – Z

JEAN-CHARLES SEIGNEURET,

EDITOR

A. Owen Aldridge, Armin Arnold, and
Peter H. Lee,

EDITORIAL BOARD

Madeleine G. Demers,
RESEARCH CONSULTANT

Kabimbi John Kalubi,
EDITORIAL ASSISTANT

GREENWOOD PRESS
NEW YORK • WESTPORT, CONNECTICUT • LONDON

Library of Congress Cataloging-in-Publication Data

Dictionary of literary themes and motifs.

Includes indexes.
1. Literature, Comparative—Themes, motives—
Dictionaries. I. Seigneuret, Jean-Charles.
PN43.D48   1988   809'.933'0321   87–12004
ISBN 0–313–22943–0 (lib. bdg. : alk. paper)
ISBN 0–313–26396–5 (lib. bdg. : alk. paper: vol. 1)
ISBN 0–313–26397-3 (lib. bdg. : alk. paper: vol. 2)

British Library Cataloguing in Publication Data is available.

Library of Congress Catalog Card Number: 87–12004
ISBN 0–313–22943–0 (set)
ISBN 0–313–26396–5 (v.1)
ISBN 0–313–26397–3 (v.2)

First published in 1988

Greenwood Press, Inc.
88 Post Road West, Westport, Connecticut 06881

Printed in the United States of America

∞™

The paper used in this book complies with the
Permanent Paper Standard issued by the National
Information Standards Organization (Z39.48–1984).

10   9   8   7   6   5   4   3   2   1

CONTENTS

//

PREFACE

//

When a *Survey of Research Tool Needs in French Language and Literature*, which I conducted for the National Endowment for the Humanities in 1977–1978, revealed that the need for a thematic dictionary of European literature ranked third among twenty-one essential research tools listed in an interdisciplinary section, I offered to assist my colleague at Washington State University, Professor Lester Shepard, an expert in comparative literature, in producing a dictionary of themes and motifs in world literature. After much preliminary work, a contract was signed with Greenwood Press in 1980. By examining recent bibliographical references, we were able to identify more than 600 scholars who had written articles or books of thematic significance. They were contacted and invited to contribute entries to the future *Dictionary of Literary Themes and Motifs*. Faced with the need to expand their expertise to world literature, many potential contributors turned us down. Others had made previous commitments for the near future. Approximately one hundred scholars accepted our invitation, but even those who declined welcomed our proposed endeavor.

To assist our collaborators, Madeleine G. Demers, Lester Shepard, and I read summaries of more than 4,500 works of literature and identified three or four major themes per work. In addition, another 600 Slavic works were examined by Eva Kagan-Kans, Associate Professor of Slavic Languages and Literatures at Indiana University, and her team of colleagues and graduate students, Maria Carlson, Henry Cooper, Andrew Durkin, Steve Gititsky, Joanne Innis, Irene Kiedrowski, Tim Larson, Ronald Meyer, Nadia Peterson, Teddy Robertson, Andrea Rogers, and Eric Stinebring. Printouts by keywords were made available and were meant to assist, not to replace, conventional research. We asked that authors approach their topics, whenever possible, in a historical manner and that efforts should be made to include discussion of non-Western literatures. A number of entries included such discussion; others did not, primarily because the authors involved felt that these literatures were outside their expertise. Our work therefore stresses Western literatures with a special emphasis on England and the United States. There is an obvious need for a thematic dictionary devoted exclusively to the non-Western world.

In 1982, as entries began to arrive, Lester Shepard had to withdraw from the project and I decided, with great trepidation, to take it over and bring it to fruition. I was extremely fortunate to obtain the services of three internationally known experts in comparative literature who would form an editorial board. The board was small enough to facilitate speedy evaluation of manuscripts, yet representative of both Western and Eastern literatures. To Professors A. Owen Aldridge, University of Illinois; Armin Arnold, McGill University; and Peter H. Lee, University of California, Los Angeles, go my deepest thanks. I was fully guided by their comments as far as content is concerned, and contributors were strongly encouraged to revise their entries accordingly. The final responsibility for content of the entries remains, of course, with the authors.

During the next two years, entries continued to trickle in, though as often happens with a work dependent on the voluntary contributions of a large number of scholars, many entries were abandoned along the way, and suitable replacement authors had to be found, mostly by seeking nominations from active participants. Beginning in 1984 a concerted effort was made to secure entries on topics considered essential, with the final outcome being 143 entries written by 98 scholars. Most major themes are included directly or indirectly, along with a number of minor topics that reflect the expertise of some of our contributors and serve as examples of a broad range of narrower themes that could not, at this time, be covered to any extent (e.g., Bear, Butterflies, Lion, and Unicorn representing the animal and insect worlds; Philately and Mountaineering serving to illustrate hobbies and sports).

The word "dictionary" in our title should not be construed as implying completeness. Far from it. Our work is meant to grow over the years and to reflect current research interests while filling out the gaps of this first edition. It contains almost three times the number of entries of Elisabeth Frenzel's *Motive der Weltliteratur* (1962, rev. ed. 1980), yet does not pretend to replace it but to expand on it. There is no question that authors writing on themes also found in Frenzel's work are extremely indebted to her previous research. Following Frenzel's examples, we decided to limit the topics of this present work to concrete and abstract common nouns. Proper nouns, such as literary characters, persons, and places, merit separate treatment.

There are at least as many potential themes and motifs in literature as angels on the head of a pin. Hence, this "dictionary" will remain in a constant state of being. For an expert discussion of themes, motifs, and thematology, the reader is invited to turn to the Introduction, written by Professor François Jost of the University of Illinois, whose work on comparative literature has achieved world recognition. Other important sources on this subject are listed in the bibliography appended to Jost's Introduction.

Readers seeking information on a particular theme or motif in these volumes should first ascertain if the topic is listed in the table of contents as an entry. If the topic is not listed, or for additional information, the reader is invited to consult the Cross-Index to Themes and Motifs following the last entry. Whenever an entry discusses, in a meaningful way, a secondary theme or motif, this related "keyword" can be found in the Cross-Index. Keywords are listed there in alphabetical order and are followed by the titles of the entries in which they are illustrated or discussed.

Entries begin, in general, with a short definition of the headword and, when appropriate, briefly sketch in the origin and historical background of the theme or motif involved. For the most part, the approach is chronological but, when the logic of the subject so requires, the material is grouped according to geographical area, genre, style, or a combination of these. Analysis and interpretation are allotted space and presented depending on the contributor's perception of the significance and character of the topic. Each entry concludes with cross-references to related entries, where appropriate, and a brief bibliography (three or four items at the most, with the exception of lengthy entries such as Travel).

Bibliographical and literary references follow the format recommended by the Modern Language Association of America (1984). Foreign titles alluded to in the entries are transliterated when appropriate and, when first mentioned, are followed by their English titles or the titles they are known by in English. None is listed if the title is identical in both languages or if no English title exists. I chose to transliterate Greek titles rather than give only their Latin titles, as is common practice among classicists, for the sake of consistency and because recent reference works follow this practice. Subsequent references within the same entry may list foreign works by their English translations or their original titles. The traditional spellings of Russian authors have been used. Genre and date of publication (sometimes performance in the case of plays) are given in parentheses if they are not explicit in context. Rather than decide which works did not require notification of genre (Shakespeare's *Hamlet*, for example), I chose to treat all literary works equally: better to sin by commission than by omission. The most time-consuming editorial task undertaken in the preparation of this dictionary was the checking of all titles and dates for accuracy. For the sake of consistency, I chose to normalize dates (known or assumed) and titles of English translations throughout the work, and I take full responsibility for changes made to contributors' entries. When faced with an approximate date (noted as "c." for *circa*) the reader should not assume that *all* scholars agree with it. It represents my considered judgment. Preparing the index and verifying titles and dates were facilitated by my editorial assistant, Kabimbi John Kalubi, a doctoral candidate in French literature, to whom I am very grateful.

I am also indebted to the Department of Foreign Languages and Literatures at Washington State University and the Department of Romance Languages and Literatures at the University of Cincinnati for supplies and clerical assistance. Most of all, I wish to thank the members of my editorial board and my contributors, many of whom must have wondered if the work would ever go to press; my mother, Madeleine G. Demers, research consultant par excellence;

my wife, Sue Seigneuret, who assisted me and encouraged me when I was ready to give up; and my children, Bernard, Hélène, and Madeleine, who kept asking me, as the years went by, "Are you not finished yet?"

JEAN-CHARLES SEIGNEURET

INTRODUCTION

—————————— // ——————————

The history of literary motifs and themes is an essential part of a contemporary academic discipline known as thematology or thematics. This Dictionary meets an urgent need of the literary-oriented world at large, and especially of the English-speaking community, which has been deprived so far of authoritative reference books in this domain. Some twenty years ago, it is true, Sith Thompson completed his related six volume *Motif-Index of Folk Literature*, which may have encouraged, if not inspired, present-day critical endeavors. The work renders mainly ancillary services, however, to researchers engaged in the study of letters. Closer to our concerns are Elisabeth Frenzel's two books, *Stoffe der Weltliteratur* and *Motive der Weltliteratur*. Although directly accessible only to German-speaking scholars, they are valuable and have been consulted by some of the contributors to the present publication. Individual studies on various themes have also been systematically pursued during the last fifty years. Hundreds of monographs and articles about multifarious motifs and themes, from Potiphar's wife to the Flying Dutchman, have found their way to the shelves of academic and public libraries and enriched the cash registers of various publishing houses and bookstores. The entries of this Dictionary, however, do not reproduce indiscriminately reference cards stocked in the Library of Congress. A choice had to be made among thousands of theoretically eligible items. The criteria for selection were their relevance to a broad and prominent body of literary works, their significance for the evolution of cultural history, and their vitality as measured by the interest shown by presently active researchers. The focus points to the West, although scores of entries reveal the universal interests of their authors.

Two factors may explain the rise of the thematological method: its interpretive potentialities and its intrinsic congruency with the history of ideas. Influential literary authorities, moreover, have considered it an efficient antidote against primarily aesthetic movements such as "progressive Universalpoesie," a formula first used in 1800 by Friedrich von Schlegel in the *Athenäum* which he published with his brother August Wilhelm. The concept has been revamped by Verlaine with his dedication to "De la musique avant toute chose," [Music before everything], the first line of his famous "Art poétique," [The Art of Poetry] written in 1874. For centuries, literature has been considered a compound of two elements, form and substance, words and thoughts, just as water is composed of oxygen and hydrogen. In literature the two ingredients, obviously, are not measured by definite proportions like atomic weights in chemistry. While quality remains an obligatory constituent of any product of art, science is uniquely based on quantities. The autopsy of some defunct critical theories of temporary vogue sadly reveals the cause of their demise. An overdose of form has to be blamed for the fatal anemia. The anatomy of long-lived practices, on the contrary, testifies to the fact that only a balance of values between flesh and spirit can guarantee intellectual health. Recent German criticism has overreacted to aestheticism by creating and propagating the word and the notion of "Literatur-*wissenschaft*" (science), although "Literatur*kunde*" (knowledge) would be a more appropriate expression. Indeed intuition and sensibility may prevail over, or at least challenge, historical data and controllable events.

Literary lexicographers seek to list appropriately selected keywords accompanied by adequate commentaries concerning related developments and opinions. Transcending the notion of bare inventory, the present volumes contain or suggest conclusive judgments. The bringing together of similar topics in various cultures and in diverse circumstances provides insight not only into the mechanism of the literary clockwork, but also into the process of establishing and defining aesthetic values. The reader is invited to examine the function and artistic significance of textual elements within the overall framework of different, but factually and intellectually kindred writings. A straight enumeration might occasionally be necessary in order to demonstrate and illustrate briefly the diffusion or popularity of specific motifs and themes. Characteristic prototypes, "proto-motifs" and "protothemes," preferably identified in masterpieces, are here assigned their proper role in literary history and criticism. Nonetheless this publication is primarily intended to serve as a thesaurus of reference.

German critics have been most concrete and specific in defining the various components of thematology. Their views are widely adopted in the West and tend to prevail over all other suggestions. They use the term *Stoff* for logically or chronologically arranged parts of literary matter pertaining to human existence or fragments of events. In narrative genres, *Stoff* consists of a self-sufficient story or meaningful episode; it constitutes a rationally comprehensible whole born out of an organizing principle. In Flaubert's novel *Madame Bovary* (1856) the diverse incidents are logically and psychologically tied together; in the *Life* (1791) of Johnson they are cemented primarily by chronology. The intelligibility of these and similar works is based on a cause-effect or past-present relationship. Obviously a drama and a poem also have a theme since both are usually treating a more or less precisely delineated topic or plot. Thus *Stoff* is the intelligible subject matter of a literary work of fiction. Indeed *Stoff* and theme are identical.

Beyond the facts and feelings and their narrative or poetic expressions endowed with their intrinsic value and meaning, there mignt loom a fundamental problem of which one specific work is just one single and unique illustration. This all-pervading, deeper meaning (which may be psychological, philosophical, political, moral, sociological, or religious in nature) is precisely the thematological element that we call *"motif."* Flaubert delivers a clear message: romantic dreamers are marked for decline and fall. Boswell, in the preface to the second edition of his biography of Johnson, compares his work to Homer's and quotes the following lines from Horace: "To show wisdom and what sense can do / The Poet sets Ulysses in our view." The task of identifying thematical and motival aspects in a work devolves upon the reader. At one place in one of Tolstoy's novels, the nephews of Anna Karenina are playing with little boxes representing cars in a train. The episode has tragic overtones for the critic who knows the outcome of the novel. It is, at least indirectly, affiliated with one of the virtual motifs of the story—adultery does not pay—since Anna quits her lover forever by committing suicide by throwing herself under the wheels of a locomotive. Events sometimes carry several issues expounded on different levels; thus, often more than one lesson is dispensed. The Russian novel embodies at *least* two other motifs. Society crushes whoever defies its rules; whoever yields to the spell of a femme fatale or of an "homme fatal" sadly seals his destiny forever.

The rationale of the system may be easily comprehended, though the proposed terminology has not been so far universally adopted. There is no international consensus—there is no Parliament in the Republic of Letters—to regulate the vocabulary of thematics. One critic may call *motif* what another designates as *theme*. Both words are occasionally used interchangeably, and some examples of this synonymity are given in this Dictionary. We should remember, however, that contributors may deal with works in which the two concepts overlap; furthermore, they are conscious of the fact that they have to be concerned with themes as defined here, and only indirectly with motifs. The difference between the two notions cannot be specified in the individual articles and thus is taken up in this Introduction.

Common sense combined with elementary philosophy and simple semantics often proves to be a wise and accurate judge in disputes over terminology. This is the case of "motif" as a thematological concept. It has developed from the Latin *movere*, to set forth ideationally, not factually, to stimulate and spur, prompt and urge, or to cause something to happen and to move forward. It explains or justifies a motion or a development on a theoretical level. It is *Beweggrund*. According to a growing number of scholars, the motif is intellectual by nature; it expresses a process of reasoning about men's conduct of life and, as a consequence, does not concern itself with the analysis of individual characters or extraordinary happenings. An unspecified agent is engaged in a certain type of action and similar results are achieved, thanks to similar conditions and circumstances—one of the meanings of agency. The motif, therefore, represents what Ernst Robert Curtius calls "Urbedingungen des Daseins" ("Prime conditions of existence"). Gottfried Keller states in his novelle *Romeo und Julia auf dem Dorfe* (*The Village Romeo and Juliet*, 1856) that fables, basic human situations, reappear ceaselessly "in neuem Gewand," and "zwingen alsdann die Hand, sie festzuhalten:" nothing new except the garnment, the theme. Thus a person (agent) living with vain dreams and wishes (agency, instrumentality) brings his own downfall (action and consequence). The motif is abstract and reflects teleological thinking. The theme, on the contrary, is practical and concrete. It represents one out of countless incarnations of the same motif. Emma and Werther as well as an infinity of other fictional characters belong to the same family of themes. Similarly *Don Quijote* (*Don Quixote*, novel, 1605, 1615) remains but one single actualization of innumerable possibilities. Cervantes' hero is unique (theme), while his message (motif) is familiar to readers of every continent. Such types are walking in our streets (motif), where, however, there are no windmills (theme). In short, the theme is a specific expression of a motif, which is universal in essence. Its individualization is the result of the passage from the general to the particular (Raymond Trousson). It is usually embodied in a plot. As far as the motif is concerned, it represents the quintessence of fictional narrative, its soul, its transcendence. The motif bridles and guides the imagination of authors of masterpieces. It is the post to which they tie their capricious fantasy. One may conclude that motifs are subject to be incarnated in universal types.

Half a century ago, Paul Van Tieghem, considered the official godfather of modern comparatism and one of the most apodictic prophets of the discipline which he helped promote, distinguished five sectors in thematology: themes, types, legends, ideas, and sentiments. Strangely enough, some contemporary reflections on thematology do not reach much further than those of the French scholar, even though in recent decades studies in motifs and themes have assumed international and interdisciplinary dimensions. Thematology holds an eminent position not only in comparative literature, but in other areas of the liberal arts such as text interpretation and linguistics, history and musicology. The reason why a discipline that is an integral part of the humanities still suffers from an equivocal terminology may be perceived in the fact that some undisciplined proponents of that discipline delight in exhibiting their intellectual freedom.

A majority of eminent scholars properly identify themalogical concepts. While at work with notions, however, some of them are still at play with words. Yet continuing efforts, although with limited results, are being made in the Anglo-American world specifically, in order to dispel contradiction and confusion. In his essay "Thematics and Criticism" Harry Levin identifies basic aspects of the dichotomy *Stoff-Motif* (*Stoff* meaning "theme"), though without offering clear-cut definitions. "The adjective *thematic*," he writes, "has generally had to do with meaning as distinguished from techniques." True, but hardly a conclusive statement, since both the motif and the theme have in one way or the other to do with meaning. For numerous scholars a theme remains "something named by an abstract noun or phrase: the futility of war, the mutability of joy, heroism, inhumanity" This statement from Monroe C. Beardsley's *Aesthetics* (p. 403) obviously induces the reader to conclude that theme means subject matter. The futility of war, for instance, has been for decades a sterile subject of conversation between superpowers, but the theme, in our thematological sense, that is, a demonstration of how and why wars *actually* are futile, has been treated in *Voĭna i mir* (*War and Peace*, 1865–1869), and in scores of lesser known novels.

Other scholars explain that the theme consists in the ideas that emerge from the particular structure of textual elements such as action, observations revealing states of mind, feelings, or gestures. "Such textual elements I designate by the term *motif*; the idea that emerges from motifs by means of abstraction I call the theme" (Eugene H. Falk). Elsewhere we read: "Discovering themes or meanings in a work involves us in making connections between the work and the world outside it. These connections are meanings" (Robert Scholes). In our language this specific meaning is the motif, provided that the "world outside it" refers to generalization and depersonification. Scholes's views are shared mainly by disciples of what one may call the Anglo-American school of thematics, although other explanations and comments abound in any part of Western criticism. *A Handbook to Literature*, after asserting that *theme* (see entry) is the central or dominating idea in a literary work concludes that "in poetry, drama, and fiction it is the abstract concept which is made concrete through its representation in person, action, and image in the work" (Holman, Thrall, Hibbard). In its first part this ambiguous statement seems to allude to the motif, in the second to the theme. There is a way out of the maze. When we are concerned with ideas and notions, born from human life, and illustrative of anybody's biography, we are in the domain of the motif. Yet with concepts by themselves, good and evil, virtue and vice, prosperity and poverty, happiness and distress, love and death, we are in the realm of simple topics or of metaphysics. Thematics is not primarily concerned with speculative philosophy. Quite a few scholars have grown tired of the semantic bedlam created by a host of individualistically minded thematologists and are tending toward allegiance to a firm system, to a creed professing that the motif remains the permanent and the impersonal, the theme, the transitory and the personal. According to that faith, the motif is the soul that undergoes a continuous thematic metapsychosis passing into countless individual literary bodies, the works. Writers are the midwives in multiple rebirths. Today the list of motifs is probably closed, while that of themes will be open until the universal judgment.

One may ask whether a novelist or a playwright first invents a theme and imposes upon it a motif, or vice versa, just as scholars in operatics are bustled by the dilemma "prima le parole, poi la musica" [first the words, then the music]. The question is perhaps irrelevant for our theoretical discussion, but quite intriguing for the biographer of an author. Why did Melville narrate the destiny of a whale? is an intriguing question. *Moby-Dick* (1851) transcends by far the adventurer's cetacean experiences. It is in part an allegorical account of the author's life—its crucial phase—and he endowed it with a motif. Whoever loves danger, as the Ecclesiast warns, shall perish through danger, or at least run a high risk of perishing through it. This is the motif or one of the plausible motifs of the novel. First, it seems, the actual, immediate motivation for writing the work was Melville's thrilling experiences at sea; then came the philosophical motif endowing the work with a meaning beyond its particular story, beyond the theme.

Why did Samuel Johnson write *Rasselas* (novel, 1759)? He had to foot the bills for the funeral of his mother. Why did Voltaire write *Candide* (novel, 1757)? He wanted to air his wrath against Frederic, his scorn for Rousseau, and his contempt for Leibniz. Here we are concerned with factual motivations, with concrete reasons. Let us return to thematics. If we depersonalize Voltaire's story, we notice that he means to deliver an overall valid message, namely, that whoever organizes his existence according to foolishly optimistic principles ends up by being a fool himself. This very same motif, identifiable only in the abstract and on the ethical level, may be found in a host of novels in universal literature. The theme of each of them, however, is unique. Only in one work may we find a narrative combination involving the rape of Cunégonde, an auto-da-fé at Coimbra, a Jesuit in Paraguay, a garden in Constantinople, and a crop of pistachios, while in hundreds of works we may find types like Candide.

As a consequence of these remarks, we notice that the number of themes is theoretically unlimited, that of motifs, limited. As we read in *Gespräche mit Eckermann* (*Conversations with Eckermann*, 1836–1848), Goethe noticed that the Italian playwright count Carlo Gozzi, who was the first critic to statisticize the basic meanings of European drama, maintained that the tragedy knows only thirty-six primary situations. Goethe reported Gozzi's statement to Schiller, who disagreed. Yet, after some reflection and investigation, Schiller was not even in a position to cite an amount of examples equalling Gozzi's proposed number. The commedia dell'arte offers some twenty motifs and hundreds of themes. Lope de Vega credits himself with 1,500 plays—while Calderón wrote "only" 120. And even a book entitled *Les 200.000 situations dramatiques* (E. Souriau, 1950) has seen the light of day. But the Spanish dramatists were repeating their own motifs, and obviously the French author was alluding to particular circumstances within similar plots. In neither France nor Spain is there a question of producing the suggested abundance of instances revealing a fundamental sense of life, of motifs, but rather of developing illustrations, or individual junctures of various contingencies of themes.

Around the literary stars of first magnitude we have seen glittering in the themalogical firmament, several planets are circling in diverse orbits. The *leitmotiv* illustrates the motif in its thematic materialization. The word was first used by composers. Wagner attached a specific salient musical motif (that is the smallest melodic unit) to some of his major characters. The sound of that motif, which he called "leitmotiv," announces to the audience that the hero is about to appear on stage or refers implicitly to some incident of the plot. In painting, the motif is a striking element identified in several pictures of an individual artist or in a vast collection of works. It may function as leitmotiv, since it can guide and lead through parts of an artist's or of a group of artists' achievements. Literary criticism uses the term leitmotiv almost as a synonym for a recurring image and may also relate it to the objective correlative. Tolstoy and Melville once more provide illustrations. The numerous allusions to the railroad throughout *Anna Karenina* (1877) foreshadow the heroine's suicide, which epitomizes the intellectual substance of the novel, the motif. All references in *Moby-Dick* to Jonas, to sea monsters, to their bones, to endangered species symbolize the whale's and the hero's destiny. Western literatures abound with leitmotivs or comparable thematological components. In Dickens' novel *Bleak House* (1853) all birds belong exclusively to crazy Miss Flite, and in Fielding's novel *Tom Jones* (1749) only Mrs. Western, Sophia's aunt, ceaselessly declares that she "knows the world." The leitmotiv is comparable to, though *not identical* with, the Homeric epithet: only in the *Ilias* (*Iliad*, epic, c. 8th century B.C.) do we find "swift-footed Achilles" and "white-armed Hera," and only in the *Odysseia* (*Odyssey*, epic), "bright-eyed Athene" and "Menelaos dear to Ares." These particular adjectives and phrases are monopolized by individual characters.

The *topos*, on the contrary, that originated with ancient grammarians, is a stock figure or expression, a suggestive cliché that may be found in any context. *Locus amoenus*, for example, designates a place offering well-defined geographical and climatic "amenities." The phrase conveys to the reader the image of a certain landscape, the actual description of which would need considerable space. Finally, if we wish to complete the inventory of the thematological arsenal, we must remember literary types; their two groups consist of the *archetypes*, the prime samples or oldest known representatives of specific human patterns of behaviors, attitudes, or actions, and the *prototypes*, the most prominent model for these deeds or ways of living. We recognize in Tirso de Molina's drama *El burlador de Sevilla* (*The Libertine of Seville*, 1630) the archetype of the Don Juan motif, while Molière's play (1665), Mozart's opera (1787), or Byron's poems (1818–1823) may be considered prototypes—whichever work comes first to the objective critic's mind. Evidently a celebrated archetype may also be a prototype.

The permanent problem criticism has to face is the balance between the two constitutive elements of literature, the idea and its incarnation, the *fond* and the *forme*, The *Gehalt* and the *Gestalt*. It has been explained that the motif represents the abstract substance of a work, while the theme is its concrete treatment, its application to various particulars or striking happenings, its illustration. The former reflects the overall human significance of a work, and the latter, thanks to a series of devices that have just been mentioned, constantly reminds the reader of the ultimate meaning of a specific human situation or events. The motif does not depend upon linguistics or poetics, metaphors or allegories. It concerns itself with intellectual esthetics, that is to say, with the intrinsic beauty of thoughts, of logically verifiable truths, or of intuitively perceived and objectified truths. The theme uses all the resources offered by handbooks of stylistics and semiotics, rhetoric and poetry. It has to generate tangible values by materializing one of the thousand potentialities of the motif with imaginary accounts or with lived experience. Beauty is made flesh. Understood in this manner, thematology represents a compendium of literature itself. Although in theory it distinguishes between the two prime elements, in practice it asserts and confirms their indissoluble alliance, their *indivisa unitas*.

It is not to be expected that the difference between these two literary components be formally made in the individual articles of this Dictionary, since its main purpose is to trace the history and scholarly implications of important themes. The distinction is of prominence, however, even if here and there it is left to the reader to disentangle various notions and concepts. The final purpose of criticism, to be sure, is to help to understand the mechanics or trade secrets of literary beauty. If it is hard labor to detect them, one may find some solace by rereading the last phrase of Plato's second Hippias Dialogue: "for beauty is a difficult thing."

Bibliography

Beardsley, Monroe C. *Aesthetics, Problems in the Philosophy of Criticism*. 2d ed. Indianapolis: Hackett, 1981.

Bisanz, Adam J., and Raymond Trousson. *Elemente der Literatur: Beitrage zur Stoff-, Motiv-, und Themenforschung*. 2 vols. Stuttgart: Kröner, 1980.

Bodkin, Maud. *Archetypal Patterns in Poetry: Psychological Studies of Imagination*. 1934. New York: AMS Press, 1978.

————. *Studies of Type Images in Poetry, Religion, and Philosophy*. London: Oxford University Press, 1951.

Burke, Kenneth. *A Grammar of Motives and a Rhetoric of Motives*. Cleveland: World Publishing Co., 1962.

Calvet, Jean. *Les types universels dans la littérature française*. 1926. 2 vols. Paris: Lanore, 1964.

Clemente, José Edmundo. *Los temas esenciales de la literatura*. Buenos Aires: Emece, 1959.

Curtius, Ernst Robert. *European Literature and the Latin Middle Ages*. Trans. Willard R. Trask. [New York]: Princeton University Press, 1953.

Ehrenpreis, Irvin. *The "Types Approach" to Literature*. New York: King's Crown Press, 1945.

Falk, Eugene H. *Types of Thematic Structure; the Nature and Function of Motifs in Gide, Camus, and Sartre*. Chicago: University of Chicago Press, 1967.

Fokkema, D. W., and Elrud Kunne-Ibsch. *Theories of Literature in the Twentieth Century: Structuralism, Marxism, Aesthetics of Reception, Semiotics*. London: C. Hurst, 1977.

Frenzel, Elisabeth. *Motive der Weltliteratur: ein Lexikon dichtungsgeschichtlicher Längsschnitte*. 2d ed. Stuttgart: Kröner, 1980.

————. *Stoffe der Weltliteratur: ein Lexikon dichtungsgeschichtlicher Längsschnitte*, 6th ed. Stuttgart: Kröner, 1983.

————. *Stoff- und Motivgeschichte*. 2d ed. Berlin: Schmidt, 1974.

Holman, C. Hugh, William Flint Thrall, and Addison Hibbard. *A Handbook to Literature*. 5th ed. New York: Macmillan, 1986.

Jeune, Simon. *Littérature générale et littérature comparée, essai d'orientation*. Paris: Lettres modernes, 1968.

Jost, François. "Grundbegriffe der Thematologie" in *Theorie und Kritik: zur vergleichenden und neueren deutschen Literatur*. Bern: Francke, 1974.

———. *Introduction to Comparative Literature*. Indianapolis: Pegasus, 1974.

Kayser, Wolfgang. *Das sprachliche Kunstwerk*. 1948. Bern: Francke, 1983.

Kohlschmidt, Werner, and Wolfgang Mohr. *Reallexicon der deutschen Literaturgeschichte*. 2d ed. 4 vols. Berlin: De Gruyter, 1958–1984.

Körner, Josef. "Erlebnis, Motiv, Stoff." *Vom Geiste neuer Literaturforschung. Festschrift für O. Walzel*. Ed. Julius Wahle and Victor Klemperer. Potsdam: Akademische Verlagsgesellschaft Athenaion, 1924, 80–90.

Levin, Harry. "Thematics and Criticism." *The Disciplines of Criticism*. Ed. Peter Demetz et al. New Haven: Yale University Press, 1968: 125–145.

Marino, Adrian. *Kritik der literarischen Begriffe*. Trans. Bernd Kolf. Cluj: Dacia Verlag, 1976.

Muschg, Walter. *Tragische Literaturgeschichte*. 1948. München: Francke, 1983.

Pickett, Ralph E. *Recurring Themes in Art, Literature, Music, Drama, and the Dance as Found in Various Episodes of Classical Mythology, Religion, and History*. Rev. ed. [New York]: R. E. Pickett, 1961.

Scholes, Robert, ed. Introduction. *Elements of Fiction. An Anthology*. By Scholes. Rev. ed. New York: Oxford University Press, 1982.

Sperber, Hans, and Leo Spitzer. *Motiv und Wort, Studien zur Literatur-und Sprachpsychologie*. Leipzig: O. R. Reisland, 1918.

Stanzel, Franz. *Narrative Situations in the Novel*. Trans. James P. Pusack. Bloomington: Indiana University Press, 1971.

Thompson, Stith. *Motiv-Index of Folk Literature*. Rev. ed. 6 vols. Bloomington: Indiana University Press, 1955–1958.

Trousson, Raymond. *Un problème de littérature comparée: les études de thèmes; essai de méthodologie*. Paris: Minard, 1965.

Van Tieghem, Paul. *La littérature comparée*. 4th ed. Paris: A. Colin, 1951.

Weber, Jean-Paul. *Domaines thématiques*. Paris: Gallimard, 1963.

Weisstein, Ulrich. *Comparative Literature and Literary Theory, Survey and Introduction*. Bloomington: Indiana University Press, 1973.

Wilpert, Gero von. *Sachwörterbuch der Literatur*. 6th ed. Stuttgart: Kröner, 1979.

FRANÇOIS JOST

DICTIONARY OF
LITERARY
THEMES
AND MOTIFS

L
//

LABYRINTH

The word "labyrinth" designates both a general configuration and a specific design. In the most general terms, a labyrinth is a complicated structure in which one becomes lost. More specifically, the particular labyrinth design, which is thought to have originated in the classical world, consists of a regularly patterned path that frequently forms concentric circles or squares about a central point, or enclosure, and is often divided in half or in four by lines that shift direction along one or two axes. The meanders of the design impede progress toward the central enclosure. While in visual representations it is possible to distinguish between multicursal and unicursal labyrinths (between paths that present choices at forks and those that do not), this distinction largely disappears in the literary symbol. The more general sense of a formalized design within which a wanderer can lose his way remains as a constant. The labyrinth may thus be classified as a motif of quest. It is used primarily as a metaphor in literary texts, though a few works explore the structure at greater length. It has appeared consistently since classical times and has been especially popular in titles from the Renaissance onward, presumably because it serves as a kind of emblem. Though emphasis shifts in different periods, the labyrinth persistently encapsulates visions of the world, the mind, or art.

Classical Sources

The earliest known man-made labyrinth was located in Egypt; Herodotus claimed to have been more impressed by it than by the pyramids. This structure seems to have been the model for the Grecian labyrinth. Pliny maintains that Daedalus took from this Egyptian labyrinth the pattern of the one he made in Crete, "although he only copied the hundredth part of it, since it contained winding ways and bewildering twists and turns . . . with many entrances designed to produce misleading goings and comings." Perhaps the most significant record

of the Cretan labyrinth is Ovid's description of its construction in his epic poem
Metamorphoses (c. A.D. 2–17). King Minos of Crete has not sacrificed the divine
white bull to Neptune as he should have, and thus the god has taken his revenge
by making his queen Pasiphaë desire the bull and conceive a child by it, thanks
to an ingenious mating device designed by Daedalus. When the hybrid child,
the minotaur, is born, Minos has Daedalus build a "labyrinthine enclosure with
blind passages" to house it. Ovid adds a significant twist to the labyrinth symbol
when he says that Daedalus himself was scarcely able to find his way back out
of this labyrinth. The labyrinth here represents an ingenious—an almost too
ingenious—work of art, as well as a place where an explorer may become lost.
The most complete early narration of the explorer in the labyrinth is Plutarch's
Thēseus (*Life of Theseus of Athens*, 2nd century); Theseus entered the labyrinth,
guided by the princess Ariadne's ball of string, killed the minotaur, and returned.
To triumph over the labyrinth requires not brute force but astuteness and often
outside aid.

Psychological interpretations of this myth, particularly those of C. G. Jung
and his followers, stress the labyrinth as a structure of initiation, where a young
man enters the domain of the terrible earth mother, triumphs over her forces,
represented by the minotaur, and exits a mature man. In this task he is aided by
the anima, or sister side of woman, represented by Ariadne. The ancient writers
themselves, however, concentrated on the physical properties of the structure
rather than its symbolic resonances.

Medieval and Renaissance Examples

Medieval adaptations of the classical image of the labyrinth developed a
number of symbolic resonances that expressed Christian doctrine. Many of these
Christian interpretations explicitly elaborated the difference between the Thesean
explorer and the Daedalian architect as an analogy for the different positions of
man and God with reference to the universe. In these versions the labyrinth
represents the entangling layers of worldly sin surrounding man; God perceives
order in the design and may endow man with the Ariadne's thread of grace he
needs to reach the divine center of the pattern. In medieval manuscripts the
visual and the verbal often come together. Labyrinth designs, some of them with
captions, accompany religious texts, particularly those that speak of man's wanderings and temptations. A German translation of Boethius (c. 1085) contains
a design of a labyrinth with a center containing the figures of the world and of
the devil, with an inscription that points out the minotaur who will devour
everyone who enters the labyrinth; this center represents not heaven but hell,
but the implication is still that man needs God's help to find his way out. Slightly
later on, the notion of complications that the labyrinth suggested made it a
metaphor for elaborate doctrine or rhetoric. Evarardus Alemannus, for example,
in the thirteenth century, entitled his book of rhetoric *Laborintus*. This idea may
have been based on the false etymology of *labor intus*, but it seems to have
persisted, because in 1538 the Swiss scientist Paracelsus criticized medieval

scholasticism and warned against attempts at supernatural cures in a work called *Labyrinthus medicorum errantium.*

Chaucer and Boccaccio use the labyrinth symbol in essentially the same way, though in different sorts of books. Chaucer compares it to his own intricate *House of Fame* (poem, c. 1379), emphasizing the presumptuous cleverness of Daedalus the designer of so elaborate a house, in the end a tawdry and dangerous place to tarry. A similar feeling, though in a lighter vein, is implied by Boccaccio's use of the symbol in the title for his complicated love story, *Il Corbaccio* or *Laberinto d'amore* (*The Corbaccio*, 1354–1355). The labyrinth here becomes symbolic not only of the world or of society in general, but more specifically, of the relationships between men and women.

The Spaniard Juan de Mena and the Frenchman Jean Bouchet both wrote works entitled *Labyrinth[s] of Fortune.* In Juan de Mena's poem (*Laberinto de fortuna*, completed in 1444) the narrator is guided by Providence through Fortune's house. From there he can look down on the world—the *mundana machina.* At one point he says that Fortune's certain order is disorder. The willful creation of disorder is Fortune's great power—and a continuing fascination of the labyrinth symbol. Jean Bouchet's work (*Le labirynth de Fortune*, 1524) is a dream vision where the labyrinth appears as a backdrop for a moral dialogue between Human Discipline, Happiness, Unhappiness, and True Doctrine. Like Chaucer's and Boccaccio's, this labyrinth of fortune is a worldly city, richly decorated and well protected, but dangerous. Similarly, near the end of the sixteenth century, the labyrinth is associated with Spenser's wandering wood, the den of Errour (*The Faerie Queen*, epic poem, 1590–1596). It is the worldly space, in contrast to the divine temple, which may, in fact, as we have noted earlier, exist at its very center. Thus the labyrinth here, as before and after, holds out alternate possibilities for man's interaction with it: wandering or rest; damnation or salvation; human error or heroic act.

Originally incorporated into church architecture in early Christian times as mosaic pavements on floors, the labyrinth became increasingly secularized and was extremely popular as a design for gardens, a kind of formalized game. This is the version of the labyrinth that appears in the stories of the "Bower of Rosamond," which tell of King Henry II and his lover Rosamond. The *Complaint of Rosamond* (poem, 1592), by Samuel Daniel, recounts how the king woos Rosamond, and after she falls to him, builds a palace—really a garden–with intricate passages, where she becomes "the minotaure of shame."

Seventeenth, Eighteenth, and Nineteenth Centuries

The concentration on the world as confusing labyrinth continues into the seventeenth century. John Norden the Elder's *Labyrinth of Man's Life* (poem, 1614) pictures the labyrinth of the world as a "fatall *Desert of changes,* and *miseries,*" its hidden minotaurs being vice or envy. Virtue is here the divine Ariadne who gives prudent men the line of right reason to help them find their way through life. Calderón de la Barca's play, *La vida es sueño* (*Life is a Dream*,

1635) puts greater emphasis on divine love or grace as the Ariadne's string that will lead man out of the fearful and dark labyrinthine political and social world. The Czech writer John Comenius continues in this same tradition in his *Labyrint světa a ráj srdce* (*The Labyrinth of the World and the Paradise of the Heart*, 1631); in doing so he develops another resonance of the labyrinth as it symbolizes the world: the labyrinthine city. Comenius' traveller first sees a town "seeming fine and beautiful," but then perceives that it was "crowded with people as if with insects." As he looks down from above, he notes that the streets are broken through in many places, suggesting confusion and even decay. Children howl as they are about to be born. The traditional center of the labyrinth, the restful uncomplicated holy space, cannot be reached by traversing the labyrinthine city; Comenius locates his Paradise of the Heart in a separate coda at the end of the text. A similar labyrinthine city appears in Baltasar Gracián's allegorical novel *El Criticón* (1651–1657). The same overtones of vain human endeavor and decadence dominate this view of the capital of a declining power. It is a perfect labyrinth, with false entryways and numerous towers. Like the youth in Comenius' tale, who must remove his glasses at last to exit from the labyrinth of the world to the paradise of the heart, we are told that we must look at the things of this world upside down in order to see them truly. These quests for a restful sacred center apart from the labyrinthine city of the world recall many myths of paradise.

In addition to these religious treatments, the secular labyrinths of love continue as well, particularly in the drama. Characters pass through complications to the happy space of love at the end of a comedy or a romance. They contrast with Comenius' dreamer in that the disentanglement may be achieved in the world. But the connotations of trouble, danger, and frustration remain. Cervantes echoes Boccaccio in giving the title *El laberinto de amor* (*The Labyrinth of Love*) to one of his comedies (1615). Lope de Vega and Sor Juana Inés de la Cruz (in Mexico) both base love comedies on the Cretan story (*El laberinto de Creta* [*The Cretan Labyrinth*, 1621] and *Amor es más laberinto* [*Love Is the Greatest Labyrinth*, in collaboration with Juan de Guevara, 1693]). Similarly, Daedalus the wise temporarily combines what are often inharmonious elements in the labyrinthine dances of Ben Jonson's masque *Pleasure Reconcil'd to Vertue* (1618). With his help the Princes of Virtue and the Ladies of Pleasure "may securely prove then, any laborinth, though it be of love." The ancient notion of an initiation pattern persists in this highly formalized genre.

In the eighteenth and nineteenth centuries the popularity of the labyrinth as a symbolic title seems to decline; perhaps because of a greater degree of realism in fiction, labyrinthine structures appear as forests or cellars with particular names. Horace Walpole's novel *Castle of Otranto* (1764) is a well-known example of the latter, where strange encounters take place in dark passageways. It, like many of the nineteenth century examples that follow it, emphasizes the dark, hidden aspects of the design, causing it to suggest not political or social life so much as the hidden emotional, even unconscious, life of individuals.

From the labyrinth of the world we move to the labyrinth of the mind, with an emphasis on its unconscious rather than its artistic functions. In his *Tanglewood Tales* (1853), Hawthorne, in describing the labyrinth of Crete, maintains that it is not nearly so intricate as the brain of a man like Daedalus, who built it, or the heart of any ordinary man, "which last, to be sure, is ten times as great a mystery as the labyrinth of Crete." More concretely, the narrator of Poe's "The Fall of the House of Usher" (1839) goes through many dark and intricate passages on his way to the studio of Roderick Usher. Injun Joe's frightening cave in Twain's novel *Tom Sawyer* (1876) is called a labyrinth. In Victor Hugo's novel *Les misérables* (1862), the sewers of Paris are described as a dark labyrinthine double to the city's labyrinth above the ground. In his treatment of the labyrinth in late nineteenth- and early twentieth-century literature, Gaston Bachelard situates the pattern in the domain of the unconscious rather than the conscious mind, in his *La terre et les rêveries du repos* (1948).

The Twentieth Century

In the twentieth century, the labyrinth continues to symbolize the world's complications, but in keeping with the increasingly self-reflective nature of modern writing, it is often used to suggest the intricacies of thought and of writing itself. In Joyce's autobiographical *Portrait of the Artist as a Young Man* (1916) Stephen Dedalus' escape from his maternal Dublin, pictured as a labyrinth, leads him toward an identification with his namesake, the Greek Daedalus, and suggests that he, like Joyce, may one day create a labyrinthine text to portray the city and its inhabitants. It is difficult to divide works that use the labyrinth primarily as a symbol for the mind from those that employ the pattern principally as a symbol for art or for writing. This is because, just as the labyrinthine mind resembles the labyrinthine world it inhabits, so the labyrinthine mind creates labyrinthine fictions. Nevertheless, under the rubric of the labyrinth of the mind one can group the following works.

Frank Kafka's unfinished story "Der Bau" ("The Burrow," c. 1924; published 1931) dramatizes the labyrinth's capacity to represent both protection and prison. The narrator, the inhabitant of a burrow, continually tunnels back and forth into a hillside, worrying about being discovered, yet suffering from enclosure, lost "in a maze of technical speculations." André Gide's novel *Thésée* (*Theseus*, 1946) stands out because it is a retelling of the original myth. There, Daedalus has built a kind of magical chameleon labyrinth, one that entraps different people differently: "each is led on by the complexities in his own mind to lose himself . . . in a labyrinth of his own devising." For this Theseus, the danger is that he will be overcome by sensuous vapors and not return to his thread of duty. For him, Ariadne's love is an additional danger rather than a saving power. Lawrence Durrell centers his novel *The Dark Labyrinth* (1947) around a tour to a series of caverns in Crete. Since the tourists all experience varying degrees of self-revelation in the caverns, exploration of the physical labyrinth symbolizes psychological exploration. Like Gide and Durrell, Anaïs

Nin, in her novel *Seduction of the Minotaur* (1961) uses the labyrinth as a symbolic landscape, a setting for a voyage to an inner self. A woman travels to a "primitive" labyrinthine jungle, hoping to escape her labyrinthine city life. But in the end she learns that it is this civilized labyrinth that she must inhabit. The minotaur she confronts is "the hidden masked part of herself unknown to her"; she perceives it on exploring "the detours of the labyrinth" of her own mind.

In his essay *Le Minotaure ou la halte d'Oran* (1950), Albert Camus creates a sense of existential anguish and alienation by presenting the city of Oran as a labyrinth turned in on itself. Nevertheless, he maintains that for an artist this solitary labyrinth can serve as a necessary stage of hermetic concentration before he creates his works. Less voluntary entrapments in the labyrinth of art are more characteristic of contemporary literature. Labyrinths appear with an almost obsessive frequency in the short stories and poems of the Argentine Jorge Luis Borges (*Laberintos* [*Labyrinths, 1962*]). These labyrinths symbolize both the world and the artificial systems—including the art of fiction—that men create in attempting to understand, or at least to order, that world. Borges pictures the idea of a Daedalus figure trapped inside a labyrinth of his own devising in an image that forms the epilogue to *El hacedor* (*Dreamtigers*, stories and poems, 1960); a writer who proposes to portray the world through his works discovers just before his death that the labyrinth of lines he has created in those works traces the features of his own face. Julio Cortázar's novel *Rayuela* (*Hopscotch,* 1963) and José Donoso's *El obsceno pájaro de la noche* (*The Obscene Bird of Night*, novel, 1970) build from this same idea. Their protagonists construct elaborate labyrinths of words around themselves; these labyrinths are both protection and prison, reflecting the city or the house of their inhabitant.

The novels *L'emploi du temps* (*Passing Time*, 1957) by Michel Butor and *Dans le labyrinthe* (*In the Labyrinth*, 1959) by Alain Robbe-Grillet, in attempting to construct texts that are labyrinthine in shape, carry this symbolic identification of labyrinth and art one step further. In both novels, we follow the peregrinations of characters in a city at the same time as we participate with a narrator in the construction of a story about those characters. Since we are "in the labyrinths" rather than above them, the stories are incomplete; we experience dead ends, sharp turns, backtracking, and repetitions of scene or event. The three entities the labyrinth has come most frequently to represent, the world, the mind, and art, are thus merged, and the reader's experience of them intensified.

See also: Cave.

Selected Bibliography

Bachelard, Gaston. *La terre et les rêveries du repos*. Paris: Corti, 1948.

Knight, W. F. Jackson. *Cumaean Gates: A Reference of the Sixth Aeneid to the Intiatio Pattern*. Oxford: Basil Blackwell, 1936.

Matthews, W. H. *Mazes and Labyrinths: Their History and Development*. New York Dover, 1970.

Santarcangeli, Paolo. *Il libro dei labirinti: Storia di un mito e di un simbolo*. Florence: Vallechi, 1970.

WENDY B. FARIS

LAMENESS

Lameness (or lame, limping, maimed, deformed or crippled; "handicapped" seems used primarily by contemporary social welfare agencies) can be symbolic or may not. It is a more apparent deformity than loss of sight or hearing, and thus its removal is visually noticeable. That Jesus can cure paralysis is similar to his cures for leprosy, hemorrhaging, blindness, and muteness, and even to his cure for the ultimate affliction of death (Matt. 9:18–25 and John 11:1–44, in the famous case of Lazarus). These symbolize his power and his divinity, but the afflictions themselves have no symbolic freight; rather, they attest to lives of hardship and the physical calamities that hardship produces. Literature is replete with the crippled survivors of hardship—famine, plague, storm, and war—but, for the most part, these lame individuals are like stage backdrops or props. They remind us of the natural and social conditions that are the literary work's setting, that poverty cripples (Tiny Tim in Dickens' novel *A Christmas Carol,* 1843), that war maims (Johnny Boyle in O'Casey's play *Juno and the Paycock,* 1924), and that industry has its accidents (Jurgis Rudkus in Sinclair's novel *The Jungle,* 1906).

Some writers, however, go beyond the mere depiction of maimed figures as a realistic part of the landscape, by using deformed characters as symbolic expressions. Thus, particularly since T.S. Eliot's poem *The Waste Land* (1922) and World War I, crippling often reflects on both the individual and the surrounding society. Laurence Stallings' work provides examples of the difference. In the romantic war play he wrote with Maxwell Anderson, *What Price Glory* (1924), Stallings has Sergeant Quirt wounded in the leg. It is not a serious wound, and it figures both as a piece of realistic business and as a plot device; it has no symbolic significance. But in the same year, Stallings, who lost a leg in the battle for Chateau-Thierry, published a novel, *Plumes*. The protagonist Richard Plume is descended from generations of warriors; his surname suggests a military crest, a panache. Richard returns from World War I on crutches, wearing braces to support his wounded legs. But his wounds are not just physical. He must readjust to a society that is not hospitable to cripples, to a family tradition of militarism that he no longer believes in, and to a self no longer innocent nor able to believe in unlimited possibility.

Most symbolic limpers seem to fall into one of three categories: fertility, sterility, or—as with Richard Plume above—human limitation. The apparently odd use of someone lamed, crippled, to suggest fertility goes back to prehistoric fertility rites, which are confusedly preserved in both the Bible and various

Mediterranean myths. The basic principle would seem to have been homeopathic magic—the interrelationship of like entities. If the ruler of a land was healthy, potent, or fecund, the land would flourish, crops grow, herds multiply, number of children increase. If the king were not physically and sexually competent, his land would suffer. Testing the king and replacing him occurred in the annual contests described by Frazer in *The Golden Bough* (essay, 1890–1915), the rivalry between old winter and young spring kings described by the Cambridge anthropologists where an established ruler is replaced by a younger, more virile one. Analogues may be seen in the rivalry between the Egyptian deities Set and Osiris or even perhaps figured in the conflict between mature Goliath and stripling David. Thus there was generational strife, elder overthrown by younger—whether an actual son or symbolic one: Uranus, Chronus, then Zeus; Saul, David, then Absalom's rebellion; Oedipus killed Laius and rules after him; Theseus caused his father Aegeus' death and succeeds him, as Perseus killed Acrisius, and Jason brought back to Iolcus his wife Medea, who is responsible for the death of Pelias, Jason's uncle. Heroes all, yet all involved in patricide or something near it—and frequently known by their feet: Oedipus' name (by conventional translation) is swollen foot; Aegeus recognized Theseus by his sandals; and Jason limps into Iolcus, having lost one sandal fording the Anaurus river while carrying Hera in disguise.

The ancients believed the brain, spinal fluid, marrow, and semen to be one life-rich substance. Injuries to brain and spine were usually fatal; injury sufficiently serious to spill marrow from the bones, equally life threatening. Since castration was not fatal, the testes were considered semen reservoirs, not the producers of this life fluid. The presumed manufacturers of this precious substance—the marrow bones of the knee and thigh—were considered more sacred, more central to procreation, in fact, than the testes, hence the traditional sacrifice of thigh bones in Greek ritual. Language itself attests to the special nature of marrow bones: the Hebrew *barekh,* "knee," is cognate with *barukh,* "bless." Greek and Latin for "knee," *gonu* and *genu,* are the roots of gonad, generate, genital, genus, germ, germinate, genesis, gender, kind, and even king. The "thigh" in Latin, *femur, femora,* is cognate with feminine, female, fecund, and fetus. Similar relationships between knee and generation occur in Assyrian-Babylonian *birku,* Russian *koleno,* and Finnish *polvi.*

A king who had to be sacrificed before his potency waned, so that the land would not suffer, was frequently castrated before his death, not to deprive him of sexuality, since the testes were not considered the manufacturers of sperm, but to prevent any further discharge of his potency, so that his successor would inherit that potency undiminished. Such ritual castration probably underlies Crunus' castration of Uranus; Set's rending of Osiris and the recovery by Isis of all but the genitals; and the castration of Attis, the Phrygian Adonis, whose worship included the priests' self-mutilation. Frequently the conflict was portrayed in animal form; thus Set is represented by a donkey, the enemy of Ancaeus, and Adonis as a boar.

When kings were able to resist being sacrificed, or when their cultures had evolved beyond live sacrifice to symbolic acts of castration (which circumcision may be) and/or laming, we then have individuals who survive the wound but whose nature as sacred kings is marked by it. Odysseus survives his encounter with the boar to rule Ithaca; Oedipus survives his pierced feet to rule Thebes; Theseus and Jason are marked by their sandals and become kings; Anchises is lamed but fathers Aeneas, who has his hip broken but founds what will be Rome. Greek characters notably leg or foot wounded include Achilles, Paris, Philoctetes, Cheiron, Hephaestus, and the god Zeus himself; and from Zeus's thigh was reborn Dionysus, whose name means "lame god." In the Bible, there is Jacob, patriarch of Israel, whose thigh is dislocated in a wrestling match with an angel (Gen. 30:24–31) and whose name means to catch by the heel. The knees—as sources of life—were clutched in supplication throughout early literature; Homer speaks metaphorically of death as "loosing of the knees" (*Ilias* [4.313; 19.354, *Iliad,* epic poem, c. 8th century]), adoption of a child was formalized by placing it on one's knees (Gen. 30:3, 48:12, 50:23) and birth could be prevented, in folklore, by crossing the knees or lacing fingers around them (Ovid, *Metamorphoses,* 9.298–311, epic poem, c. A.D. 2–17).

Thus a leg or foot wound—as in the cases of the various figures mentioned in the paragraphs above—designated the individual as a sacred ruler—one whose fertility was vital for the land. Modern authors familiar with this classical background have used limpers to designate fertility; among examples that could be cited are D. H. Lawrence's *The Man Who Died* (novel, 1929); Tennessee Williams' *Cat on a Hot Tin Roof* (play, 1955); Bernard Malamud's *The Assistant* (novel, 1957) and *A New Life* (novel, 1961); Saul Bellow's *Henderson the Rain King* (novel, 1959), whose very title indicates the use of fertility myth (Bellow has a degree in anthropology); and Robert Penn Warren's *Wilderness* (novel, 1961).

The next category, sterility, is obvious in its symbolism. Eliot's Fisher King in *The Waste Land* is wounded sexually—as we are told by Jessie Weston in *From Ritual to Romance* (1920)—and his land suffers for it. Maimed offspring of this maimed progenitor include Ernest Hemingway's Jake Barnes in *The Sun Also Rises* (novel, 1926), the unnamed boy in "God Rest You Merry, Gentlemen" (1933), and Harry in "The Snows of Kilimanjaro" (1938); Philip Quarles in Aldous Huxley's *Point Counter Point* (novel, 1928); and Clifford Chatterley in Lawrence's *Lady Chatterley's Lover* (novel, 1928). Thomas Sutpen's groin wound in Faulkner's novel, *Absalom, Absalom!* (1936) presages the ultimate futility of his desire to found a dynasty. Nathanael West's characters Peter Doyle in *Miss Lonelyhearts* (novel, 1933), Lemuel Pitkin in *A Cool Million* (novel, 1934), and Tod Hackett in *The Day of the Locust* (novel, 1939) all live in the waste land, and all are crippled, as is Laura Wingfield in Tennessee Williams' *The Glass Menagerie* (play, 1944). The effects of industrialization are seen in the wounds and prostheses of Claire Zachanassian (*Der Besuch der alten Dame* [*The Visit*, play, 1956]) by Friedrich Dürrenmatt and of V, in Thomas Pynchon's novel *V* (1963).

European literature similarly used lame and/or impotent characters to comment on the postwar wasteland; for example, Ernst Toller's *Hinkemann* (play, 1922), and in several of the stories of Heinrich Böll. In addition, European authors have used lameness as an objective correlative for inner sterility, as a sign of the wasteland within. Christian Buddenbrooks in Thomas Mann's *Buddenbrooks* (novel, 1901), a member of a decaying burgher class, limps from neuritis and is ultimately confined to a mental institution, the inabilities of the individual reflecting those of his class. Perken's inner corruption is emblematized by his gangrenous leg in André Malraux's *La voie royale* (*The Royal Way*, novel, 1930), a use Hemingway imitates in *The Snows of Kilimanjaro*.

The link between wickedness and lameness probably owes something to the folk-tradition that the devil cannot completely conceal his hooves when he takes human form and so limps. Thus Goethe has Mephisto questioned about his walk in the play *Faust* (pt. 1, sc. 5, 1808); Shakespeare adds lameness to Richard III's deformities, a disability not mentioned by Holinshed, Shakespeare's source. Diabolical lameness is also present in Dickens with Quilp of *The Old Curiosity Shop* (novel, 1840) and Rigaud of *Little Dorrit* (novel, 1855–1857), and in James Thurber's murderous duke of *The 13 Clocks* (novel, 1950).

The final, largest category of limpers are those whose authors maimed them as a sign of their imperfect, fragile, limited humanness. When Adam and Eve are expelled from earthly paradise, the Garden of Eden, to earn their bread by the sweat of their brows, God said to the serpent (Gen. 3), man "shall bruise your head, and you shall bruise his heel." Oedipus' lameness may mark his humanity, a correction to his hubris that he refuses to recognize, as he refuses to listen to Tiresias' warning. The cry of Herman Melville's Ahab (*Moby-Dick*, novel, 1851)—"Accursed fate! that the unconquerable captain in the soul should have such a craven mate!" "Sir!" "My body, man . . . " (ch. 134)—is the plaint of all of us whose reach exceeds our grasp and whose dreams remain unrealized or unrealizable. Further, Ahab's dismasting has social implications too, an echo of sterility. Leaving wife and child to hunt Moby Dick once again, he uses the crew as pawns in his pursuit, spurns Pip at the end lest Pip's humanity cure him, and sacrifices the entire crew—save one—for his revenge. To assert his own humanity, he denies others theirs. We admire his courage, his effort to impress the natural universe with man's place in it, but Melville's lesson is that hubris is mad and that "in all cases man must eventually lower . . . his conceit of attainable felicity" (ch. 94). Peachey Carnehan survives crucifixion in Rudyard Kipling's "The Man Who Would Be King" (story, 1888) to haltingly embody a similar lesson.

Many of Hemingway's protagonists are wounded in the leg, as he was in the First World War. I have spoken of phallic-injured Jake Barnes as an example of sterility, but Jake and other of Hemingway's heroes—Frederic Henry, Nick Adams—are, like Ahab and Richard Plume, socially wounded as well. They must not only lower their expectations for "attainable felicity," but they must adjust to a society whose values are not theirs, whose hypocrisies have wounded them, and they must gain what satisfactions they can, circumscribed as they are.

The limitations of modern man are particularly apparent in the crippled or im-
mobile characters of Samuel Beckett's plays. Estragon with too-tight boots and
a kicked and bleeding shin in *En attendant Godot* (*Waiting for Godot*, 1952)
becomes paralyzed; wheelchair-bound Hamm in *Fin de partie* (*Endgame*, 1957),
watched over by his parents, Nag and Nell, stuffed into two ash cans, having
lost their legs in a tandem bicycle accident. In *Happy Days* (1961), Winnie is
buried in sand, to her breasts in the first act, to her neck in the second; and in
Comédie (*Play*, 1963), the characters' heads only emerge from grey urns. In
Beckett's novels, too, the same lack of free movement is apparent. Molloy, in
the novel that bears his name (1951), suffers stiffening in one leg, shortening
of the other, and a loss of toes; Moran, who searches for Molloy, is also crippled.
In *L'innommable* (*The Unnamable*, 1953), Mahood is a one-legged dervish; in
Malone meurt (*Malone Dies*, 1951), Malone is bedridden, but clutches half a
crutch.

For this last group of characters, their author shows (through maimed individuals) that the human condition is one of limitations; for these people, their
physical imperfections reflect an unjust, absurd universe, a world whose satisfactions will also be limited.

See also: Crippling.

Selected Bilbiography

Hays, Peter L. *The Limping Hero*. New York: New York University Press, 1971.

PETER L. HAYS

LANGUAGE

The basic and important necessities of human life and activity, food, shelter,
clothing, sex, family, love, money, responsibilities and others appear frequently
in world literature. From time to time, a topic, theme, or motif of language may
also occur in works of literature, religion, history, fiction, drama, and poetry
from earliest times to the present. Language is always a vehicle of communication, but is not often itself the subject or theme. Instead, broader areas, the
word, or communication, form the object of discourse. Playwrights, for instance,
are fond of putting characters in tense, lifelike situations where communication
between generations, classes, or opposing groups must resolve conflict, display
emotion, or make statements. The novelist and poet no less use language for
their purposes. To put it another way, everyone is using language, many in a
most masterful way, but hardly anyone makes it a proper theme or subject instead
of a means to an end or a subsidiary issue.

Language thus cuts across the whole of human activity (indeed, makes much
of it possible) and consequently, one cannot hope, in this small essay, to discuss
all occurrences and references to language in all works of literary art in all times

and places. Hence, here the focus will be on language qua language when occurring as a relevant theme, motif, or necessary mode in literary works, and typical selections that are both representative and subjective from the vast canvas of recorded compositions will be discussed. Many individual studies can and should be written about the use of language in the works of specific world-famous authors and poets.

The Ancient Origins

As the history of early man clearly begins more than a million years ago, it follows that the development of the complex symbolic and grammatical structures that every known language of past and present shows must likewise be very ancient and must antedate all written materials with their graphs and symbols. A clear proof of this central concern of man for interpretation are early bilingual dictionaries on clay tablets of languages like Akkadian and Babylonian for the use of students, scribes, and traders. The separate stories of decipherment of cuneiform inscriptions, Egyptian hieroglyphics, Old Persian, Runic Turkic, Cretan Greek, and other languages make marvelous reading about language and its early records—some of which embrace literary efforts. Hence, language and its use precedes us in our furthest quest into ancient records.

Man and Animal in Fable Cycles

Man is distinguished from all other creatures by his faculty of language (this is an Aristotelian principle, too). Animals are certainly highly intelligent and are often strikingly adapted to their environment and can also be trained to do surprising things. They definitely have systems of communication, coding, and signalling, some of which are very complex. Humans, however, with their verbal language, their immensely developed systems of philosophy, technology, and symbolism, and the fact that they alone record through writing, art and music, and literature, their history, feelings, and knowledge, stand unquestioned as a class of being well beyond the animal kingdom.

Many, perhaps all, animals communicate; the higher primates seem able to use symbols; the mimicry of dolphins may reflect a system virtually a match for language. The mere mechanical repetition of words or sentences as parrots do, even if clever and appropriate at times, cannot be an instance of language. Man is quick to ascribe his own emotions, practices, and social organizations to animals, and among early literary collections are various cycles of animal fables, in which dogs, foxes, birds, and others freely make use of language (and in particular, communicate with each other across species lines), thus effectively mirroring human foibles to point up moral ethic, provide a comment on humanity and society, and generally be instructive and even humorous.

In Aesop's fables, we see the fox musing to himself about the grapes that are probably no good anyway, dialogues between such unlikely pairs as the wolf and the lamb, the flea and the ox, and numerous others. Very many of these are found in Indian and Central Asian story cycles, such as the *Panchatantra (Five*

Books, c. A.D. 300–500), and found their way ultimately to storytellers and fabulists of recent centuries, including the Grimm Brothers, La Fontaine, and others. The native traditions of countless preliterate tribes have similar tales.

Language as a part of Religion, Nation, Philosophy

Man looks below himself and applies his use of language to animals; he also looks above himself and uses language to look to his God, gods, creators, magical controllers of his fate, environment, and affairs, by projecting in similar fashion his society and mores onto supernatural beings in more powerful and awesome form. God's creation, *adam* (Hebrew, "man," both as a generic and as a personal name), immediately sets about naming things, thus making use of language; soon thereafter, the serpent uses language to beguile Eve into sin, giving impetus to the Downfall. God communicates the Ten Commandments, the written word; God speaks to Moses from the burning bush; we have even an explanation of the multiplicity of world languages in the account of the Tower of Babel. In the New Testament, on the Day of Pentecost the tongues of fire made men speak other languages, and this transcendent use of language, or of a meta-language, is a vital part of some Christian practices today.

The *locus classicus* for expression of the holy nature of language surely is John 1:1, where the *Logos,* the Word, is linked with the creator and the redeemer. Man must use language to extol the deity, to communicate with God through prayer; the theologian must master ancient languages to read his sacred scriptures in their originals (except for the Book of Mormon), to get closer to their root meanings, and to aid him in interpreting them for daily practice. On a purely popular level one can still find persons who feel that ancient Hebrew is somehow God's language. Many religionists fail to see how central language is to the interpretation of their faith and its principles or dogma; if we translate the Greek noun applied to Mary not as "virgin," but simply as "girl," as Koinē scholars contend, it could rob Christianity of a major pillar. Thus one can see that the issue of language in religious literature can be an especially crucial matter and is perhaps best set aside from language in belles-lettres.

Men are gregarious and never existed in isolation; they formed larger and larger groups, until the nation or state came into being. This entity is often identified with or defined by the use of a single shared speech. Thus, literary matters can also become political matters, when poets or writers plead for their native language or revel in its glories. The poet, to be sure, often praises speech or his specific language as a tool to admire his beloved damsel, his deity, the beauties of nature. This is no dead issue; even recent decades have seen riots and political oppression originate from issues of language rivalry, whether in Belgium, Pakistan, African nations or Hispanics in Texas. Hardly a finer example can be found than the poignant story of Alphonse Daudet, "La dernière classe" ("The Last Class," 1873), referring to the 1871 German occupation of Alsace-Lorraine and the resultant mandated change from French to German in the public schools.

Sometimes there are language issues concealed in the biography of a given writer; to know this fact may help evaluate features of his or her work. Instances that come to mind are the dilemma faced by Conrad Ferdinand Meyer in having to choose between French and German; the stories of Karen Blixen (appearing as Isak Dinesen), many originally written in English instead of her native Danish; and the impressive level of English literary mastery attained by such writers as Joseph Conrad and Vladimir Nabokov, whose native languages were Polish and Russian, respectively. Today, as a result of changed political circumstances, Norway claims as its own those Danish authors born on Norwegian territory who wrote in the literary Dano-Norwegian, for example, Ludvig Holberg. Many provincial authors have had to shift to the standard literary style of the capital or court in their time and country.

The question of language lies at the heart of some philosophers, who wonder whether the nature of our speech reflects our systems of thinking, or whether the ways of thought have influenced the structure of our language. If language is the first human and social institution, then a study of speech will teach us about our nature and our past. The Greek philosophers speculated about the entire world, including language, but the greatest classical writers were more a product of a tradition emphasizing rhetoric and poetry. The famous orations of Cicero include one, *De oratore* (*On the Orator*, 55 B.C.), which gives much advice on the employ of language. This essay also incorporates quite a long illustrative sequence (about chapters 52 to 80) on the use of humor, jests, puns, and anecdotes, and why they are pertinent, effective, and funny.

Among the classic early English philosophers, John Locke (*Essay Concerning Human Understanding,* 1690) can be understood as advancing a theory of language. The origins of language become a central concern, and J. Herder's famous prize essay of 1770 profoundly affected the rise of philology as the study of language. Modern philosophers, such as Ludwig Wittgenstein, have given weight to language and its interplay with thought, but these issues better belong to philosophy and its history than to literature.

Use of Language versus Language as Theme

The linguistic genius shown by the ancient bards, scops, and troubadors, in the fashioning of the Homeric heroic epithets, the Anglo-Saxon kennings, and other formulaic expressions, is certainly great. Similarly, nearly all poets (remember, it is Greek *poiētēs,* the maker, creator) are language masters and sensitive commanders of their craft. Thus, to say that (to choose only American poets as examples) Emily Dickinson, Walt Whitman, Marianne Moore, Archibald MacLeish, or Wallace Stevens were great poets and great masters of language is a commonplace, but to find specific passages where language as such is a theme requires an individual analysis of each poet's output. In like fashion, choosing names of worldwide masters of language in prose or drama, whether Dante, Shakespeare, Milton, or Molière, we know the facts about their accomplishments and background in language, but separate essays must be devoted to the theme of language in Shakespeare, Goethe, Shaw, or others.

To be sure, individual scenes and occurrences, some quite pertinent and useful, come to mind. In Walter Scott's *Ivanhoe* (novel, 1819) there is a memorable passage where the peasants shrewdly observe that the good Anglo-Saxon language is fine to use for animals when herded or tended, but that words of Norman-French origin replace these homely names when the viands are placed on the tables of the nobility. In the classic English drama, one thinks at once of an endearing characer whose sprightly use and misuse of language gave her name to the malaproprism, namely, Mrs. Malaprop (c'est mal à propos) herself (Richard B. Sheridan's *The Rivals*, play, 1775). Indeed, a later relative of hers is H. G. Wells's shop assistant Mr. Polly, who delights in long words that he often misuses and massacres.

Playwrights in particular deal in communication; hence, language questions more readily come to the fore. T. Bernard's light-hearted farce, *L'anglais tel qu'on le parle* (*English as She Is Spoke*, 1899), so popular with high-school French classes, is just a vaudeville exercise in stringing together puns and plays on idioms. Everyone is vastly entertained, but it is hardly a critique of language. Far more serious in mien is William Gibson's *Miracle Worker* (1957, originally a TV drama, later a play and movie), the story of Helen Keller, who underwent a slow transformation into a user of language, though she was deaf, dumb, and blind. Imprisoned in her world, little Helen had to be made to see the connection between symbols and things. In act 1, at the first encounter of the despairing parents with the new teacher (Anne Sullivan), they ask, "What will you teach her first?" Anne (who herself was formerly blind) replies, "Language I hope. . . . Language is to the mind more than light is to the eye." In the final act occurs the marvelous scene at the pump, where the miracle is wrought, and the child sees the link between the water and the symbol. The world of the sound-handicapped, the deaf who are denied some use of language, is also an effective theme in the 1980 award-winning play by Mark Medoff, *Children of a Lesser God*.

Imaginary Voyages and Utopias

Quite apart from the actual role played by language in any account or description of a journey to places on Earth, there is a definite place for use of language in accounts of lunar journeys or visits to imaginary lands and utopias. One would think it indispensible to solve the problem of language and communication, but this feature is often neglected, for instance, in Plato's account of the Atlantis legend. Atlantis has later echoes in Sir Francis Bacon's *A New Atlantis* (novel, 1627) and in Arthur C. Doyle's *Adventure of the Maracot Deep* (story, 1927) where exploration of a surviving underwater Atlantis reveals a Greek derivative still being spoken.

Alēthēs historia (A True Story) by Lucian of Samosata (A.D. 115–200?) is often anthologized as the first science-fiction story. It reports a voyage through the atmosphere to the moon, with a sort of Swiftian satire on the inhabitants and their practices. Greek is the language employed. Sir Thomas More's famed *Utopia* (political romance, 1516) gave rise to many later ones, and the theme of utopia has been well explored, though language played no role in the original.

The world-renowned astronomer Johannes Kepler also wrote an early science-fiction story, *Somnium sive astronomia lunaris (Somnium or the Astronomy of the Moon),* printed 1634, though the language issue does not emerge. However, a work of similar date, Bishop Francis Godwin's *The Man in the Moone* (1638), is quite remarkable for its approach to language. The moon language is tonal, that is, words occur as tunes and notes (examples are given of words like notes on a staff). This led to the proposal by Bishop John Wilkins (in the *Mercury, or the Secret and Swift Messenger,* 1641) that an international language or a universal language could be formed by using musical notes for things and notions instead of words and letters. In turn, this seems to have influenced development of modern international languages such as Esperanto. Last, we may cite Cyrano de Bergerac's use of the lunar voyage theme in his twin works, *Histoire comique des états et empires de la lune (The Comical History of the States and Empires of the Moon,* 1657) and *Histoire comique des états et empires du soleil (The Comical History of the States and Empires of the Sun,* 1662). In the moon, the nobility employs a language of music and tones, and the people a language of movement and gesture. In the sun, the hero learns a language of truth, a kind of mother-tongue of nature, which he intuits.

Surely one of the most famous stories of all time is Jonathan Swift's *Gulliver's Travels* (1726), and one might easily dwell on it at length. Suffice it to say that Swift deals realistically with the problems of language and communication in each of his voyages. Gulliver must actually spend effort mastering the language in question, and examples of native words and phrases abound.

He copes first with the language of Lilliput, with many words and phrases from daily use cited; and much the same applies to his second voyage, to Brobdingnag, the land of giants. In the city of Lagado, Gulliver visits the Academy, where a scheme is projected to abolish words altogether, and instead carry about the actual objects for which the words stand. Finally, in the equine land of the Houyhnhnms, Gulliver masters the whinny-language, all the while giving satirical observations on the superiority of horse-society to that of man.

However, in Defoe's novel, *Robinson Crusoe* (1719), the language issue is minimal, since the hero instructs his man-servant, Friday, in English.

Examples in the mid-nineteenth and late nineteenth century may be multiplied, and here only Edgar Allen Poe's moon-tale, *The Unparalleled Adventure of Hans Pfaall* (1837) will be mentioned. This Rotterdam native contrives a balloon and goes to the moon, but leaves our curiosity mightily piqued with his reference to the "substitute for speech, in a singular method of inter-communication," which the lunar inhabitants employ. H. G. Wells's *First Men in the Moon* (novel, 1901) has his two travellers, Bedford and Cavor, teach English to the insectlike creatures there. In *The Time Machine* (novel, 1895), however, the hero makes progress rapidly in the simplified structure of the future language.

A Theme in Works of Science Fiction

One of the important devices of science fiction is that of convention. As applied to language, it means that one presumes by convention a mode of communication was developed without the reader needing to be informed of the technical details. Another all-too-frequent technique is that of ignoring the problem, unbelievable though it seems, by never actually explaining how the earthmen or space travellers land on Arcturus IV and immediately begin talking to the inhabitants or fellow-scientists there. More realistic approaches are those in which aliens learn our language, or the reverse, we learn the alien speech, sometimes with ample examples, and sometimes compressed into a side-remark, "When I had learned the language after six weeks." Since science fiction delights in the employ of technology that has not yet been invented (how else can we travel faster than light?), it is no great matter to invent an interpreting machine to handle communications. Sometimes these show a woeful lack of understanding of any linguistic principles by the authors.

Time-travel, past and future, is a commonplace of science fiction, consequently, one can encounter ancient languages of earth, or future forms of English as it may develop, as well as numerous universal or at least interplanetary and galactic languages of widest use. Communication with other worlds may involve languages of animals, insects, birds, and all sorts of nonearthly sentients of weird appearance and speech organs. Some of these are also naturally telepathic, a skill at which all writers agree Earthmen are most deficient.

There are also a few science-fiction novels or stories that actually have language as the main and dominant theme of the entire narration, but these are very few. Philip J. Farmer's *Tongues of the Moon* (1964) relates how the surviving humans on the moon solve the problem of a common or universal language for their new society. Another is Jack Vance's *The Languages of Pao* (novel, 1958), a planet where the three social classes have each their own tongue and an Interpreters Corps to serve their linguistic needs.

The novels of J.R.R. Tolkien laid in Middle Earth create the Elvish and Elderin languages with considerable realistic detail, aided by the author's professional background in Germanic philology. Both *Lord of the Rings* (1954–1956) and *Silmarillion* (1977) create elaborate naming schemes too. Much special work on these topics is called for.

A Theme in Some Twentieth-Century Works

Bearing in mind again that individual authors of fame merit separate treatment of the language theme in their works, a few highpoints and selected examples will be mentioned here. For instance, George B. Shaw, as is well known, took such interest in linguistic questions that much of his fortune was left to promote a phonemic alphabet for English, and *Androcles and the Lion* (play, 1916) has been printed in a bilingual version. The famous and complex works of James Joyce certainly raised the use of language to new levels and deserve the detailed study that scholars have given them. Joyce strove to have multilayered allusions, puns and words with double and triple meanings, sometimes almost tortured in conception. Since the subconscious of Bloom was to symbolize the mind of man, his stream of discourse has to represent possible solutions deriving from any earthly language. In point of fact, Joyce knew, used, and had studied quite a few languages; as a result, it is not beyond plausibility to feel he did intend some of the obscure usages and parallels that he employs. According to one scholar, material from twenty-seven languages can be identified in the works of Joyce.

The Christian author C. S. Lewis has given a most realistic and thoughtful depiction of language and communication problems in his memorable trilogy of Christianity, disguised as science fiction (*Out of the Silent Planet* [1938], *Perelandra* [1943], *That Hideous Strength* [1945]). The Cambridge don, Ransom, is abducted by a mad scientist to Mars, where he discovers a society of several races and laboriously works his way into their language system. In the second novel, Ransom plays a Jesus-like role in the allegory in which he is pitted against the mad scientist (a devil image) to redeem the primeval Man and Woman. Here he is able to use his Malacandrian, a kind of Old Solar. In the third part, a commentary on modern university involvement with bureaucracy and technology, Ransom, as the Arthurian Pendragon, deals with the revived Merlin by first using Latin and then to convince him, the Old Tongue itself. He has a powerful passage:

"What shall I say in the Great Tongue?" . . . [He] raised his head, and great syllables of words came out of his mouth. . . . For this was the language spoken before the Fall and beyond the Moon. Language herself, as she first sprang out of the molten quick-silver of . . . Deep Heaven.

Another of similar force is the following.

For Ransom, whose study had been for many years in the realm of words, it was heavenly pleasure. He found himself sitting within the very heart of language, in the white-hot furnace of essential speech. . . . For the lord of Meaning himself . . . was with them.

Vladimir Nabokov, in his novel *Pale Fire* (1962), invents Zemblan, a language seemingly of mixed Scandinavian and Slavic antecedents, as a byway of the commentary on Shade's 999–verse poem. The novel relates Kinbote's friendship with poet John Shade, gives the text of Shade's oeuvre, and then, through Kinbote's detailed commentary, reveals the commentator's Zemblan background and politics, frequently quoting the original Zemblan words—to the point that it was virtually possible to analyze the Zemblan language.

A remarkable work of the last decade is Robert Merle's much-acclaimed novel, *Un animal doué de raison* (*The Day of the Dolphin*, 1967). Set in Florida, the novel details the experiences of a scientist working with dolphins who succeeds in teaching them to communicate in English. The construction of the book carefully leads up to the high scene, when, prepared by prior episodes in which the dolphins speak words (nouns, verbs, or adjective plus noun in noun phrases, or verbs and verb phrases were accurately if elementarily used by the mammals), the breakthrough occurs. The dolphins create whole sentences with subjects and predicates. Of course, this is the "gimmick" (suspension of disbelief) without which the rest of the story becomes impossible. The dolphins then move rapidly into a most complex use of fairly abstract language. In the end, the treachery of Man and the Establishment bureaucracy of intelligence agencies prove the downfall of the man-animal link.

Mass-Market Literature

There is a huge realm of widely sold literature, such as Gothic romances, detective stories, spy thrillers, Westerns, and other profitable fiction. None of these employ even brief reference to language, beyond occasional encounters with foreign agents, Latin lovers, Indian scouts, or versatile heroes who speak several relevant languages for the story purposes. There are some language references in the Sherlock Holmes stories of A. C. Doyle; Holmes had some acquaintance with Italian and was able to point out that the murderer who scrawled *Rache* was not referring to Rachel, but "revenge" in German. One whole story revolves around language: the adventure of the Greek Interpreter. Mr. Melas, an interpreter of Greek and other languages, is abducted to interrogate a captive held by kidnappers. He manages to interpolate additional inquiries amidst the required questions in the foreign language, learns the plight of the victim, and summons Sherlock to the rescue.

In 1982 Penguin Books released a clever murder mystery by David Carkeet, *Double Negative*. The story is laid in an Indiana nursery, where six linguists are studying children's speech patterns. A bizarre murder is solved by a linguistic clue from one of the babes.

Edgar R. Burroughs, author of the widely selling Tarzan novels and other Mars and Venus adventures, has quite a bit of realistic language material in his prodigious output. For use on Venus, Burroughs created the language of Amtor, complete with a Venusian alphabet, in the *Pirates of Venus* (1932). His most famous character, Tarzan, grew up knowing French and English, and for the story *Tarzan and the Lost Empire* (1929), learns to speak Latin to an enclave of Romans in a lost valley.

Memoirs of Interpreters; Biographies of Linguists

A tiny subclass of literature contains a few works by interpreters and translators, whose major task it was to render orally or in writing speech or documents from one language to others. Of considerable political and anecdotal interest is A. H. Birse, *Memoirs of an Interpreter* (1967). It is largely a personal account of his experiences with Stalin, Churchill, Roosevelt, and others, with a minimum on the niceties of translation. A most remarkable book has been devoted to the thirty-year relationship between Thomas Mann and his English translator, Helen Tracy Lowe-Porter, *In Another Language* (1966). Mann's German style was difficult and involved, and Lowe-Porter spent her entire career on his works. Perhaps the only book that really comes to grips with the problems of rendering one language into another is Col. Robert B. Ekvall's *Faithful Echo* (1960). Ekvall was American Interpreter for Chinese to high-ranking military officials, and for the Korean peace-talk conferences in 1953. He portrays excellently the day-to-day difficulties of interpreting, recounting both his failures and triumphs. There have also been popular accounts of experiences of simultaneous inter- preters, as at the United Nations, but these lie largely outside the realm of literature.

There is some biographical material about great linguists (i.e., polyglots, persons with wide practical mastery of many languages). Chief among these must be Charles W. Russell's *The Life of Cardinal Mezzofanti* (1858). This remarkable figure never left Italy but spoke dozens and dozens of languages, securing certificates of attestation from travelling native speakers. He gave Lord Byron his first lessons in Modern Greek. Heinrich Schliemann, the famed amateur archaeologist and discoverer of multilayered Troy, was a great practical linguist. One of his learning techniques, as reported in various biographies, was to mem- orize long passages from famous novels in the new language. America's answer to Mezzofanti must be the diplomat Jeremiah Curtin, who knew between thirty and sixty languages (*Memoirs of Jeremiah Curtin*, 1940), as is evident from his many published translations. Curtin was the translator of Henryk Sienkiewicz (*Quo Vadis?* [1897] and others).

Authors and Characters as Linguists

The fact that proficiency in a given language may be among the accomplish- ments of an author perhaps makes it more likely that he will employ language as a theme. This topic deserves additional investigation, and here we can only dwell briefly on a few obvious examples. Byron includes a verse in Greek as part of his poem, *Maid of Athens, Ere we Part* (1830). Chaucer's knowledge of French is quite marked and evident from the vocabulary used in his works. Benjamin Franklin, along with many other figures of our Revolutionary times, knew and used French. Rudyard Kipling grew up in India, where he spoke Punjabi, and included the Punjabi names of animals in his *Jungle Books* (stories, 1894–1895). Ernest Hemingway's mastery of Spanish and his long residence in Cuba is clear from his works, and Longfellow not only was Professor of Romance Languages at Harvard, he also translated from Scandinavian and other languages. *See also:* Travel, Utopia.

Selected Bibliography

Cornelius, Paul. *Languages in Seventeenth and Early Eighteenth Century Imaginary Voyages*. Geneva: Droz, 1965.

Knowlson, James R. "Communication with Other Worlds in Fiction." *The Philosophical Journal* 5 (1968): 61–74.
Krueger, John R. "Language and Techniques of Communication as Theme or Tool in Science-Fiction." *Linguistics* 39 (1968): 68–86.

JOHN R. KRUEGER

LAUGHTER

A commonplace human physiological response, laughter is a product not only of physical stimuli like tickling but also of intellectual ones like one's own perception of incongruities and the appreciation of others' wit and humor. It is, as critic Northrop Frye observes, a miniature earthquake that rolls through the body and affects various parts, sometimes for a long while. Laughter is one of the traits that, as Aristotle first indicated, differentiates man from animal, and it has been the subject of frequent albeit brief comment and literary portrayal. There are many kinds of laughter, ranging from the quotidian (whether in reaction to pratfalls or jokes) to the philosophical, the laughter that springs from a sense of the absurdity of life (or even from defiance of and despair over it) or from an acceptance and celebration of human experience.

Antiquity and the Middle Ages

Like its accomplice, comedy, laughter is usually associated with irreverence, irresponsibility, and, intellectually, a perception of something amiss in the universe. It therefore does not appear much in Scripture, where the emphasis is on the serious design of a life created by God. God does not normally laugh—except when he is said to deride the heathens who contend against him and his anointed—nor do his prophets, angels, votaries. Though the author of Ecclesiastes acknowledges that there is a time to laugh, he hastens to add that laughter is mad, foolish, vain. One of the few occasions for laughter in the Bible exemplifies the negative principle, for when Sarah hears that she will bear a child in very old age, she laughs, and her reaction is clearly an expression of human overconfidence, limited vision, and lack of trust in God. In the same spirit in the New Testament, when news comes of the death of someone's daughter and Jesus promises a miracle, the family laughs scornfully but is proved wrong. Jesus himself in fact never laughed, and that set Christians such as the church father St. Basil against laughter.

In Homeric epic, by contrast, laughter is not incompatible with divinity. In a fit of what has come to be known as "Homeric laughter," the gods laugh long and hard in the *Ilias* (*Iliad*, c. 8th century B.C.) on seeing Hephaistos limping about and in the *Odysseia* (*Odyssey*, c. 8th century B.C.) on watching the trap Hephaistos sets for his adulterous wife Aphrodite and Ares. It has been suggested that in this scene Homer, no doubt unconsciously, provided a rationale for levity and comedy (traits absent in the Judeo-Christian tradition) by showing even the gods capable of incongruous behavior and of consequent laughter. Aphrodite is also given the epithet of "lover of laughter," as if to intimate that levity and lovemaking go together.

As a psychologist, Plato indicates in his dialogue *Philēbos* (*Philebus*, 4th century B.C.) that laughter comes when well-endowed people whom one envies are seen to be in some way weak and vulnerable, but as a moralist and lawgiver (*Politeia* [*The Republic*, dialogue, c. 380 B.C.]) he, with the severity of a Puritan, worries over laughter's disruptive power and therefore bans it, along with most fiction, from the ideal society. Poets are not to be allowed to show prominent men, let alone gods, mastered by (or perhaps even the subject of) laughter. Aristotle (*Politika* [*Politics*, essays, 4th century B.C.]) somewhat agrees and would allow only those who are of age to drink strong wines to watch comedy. (Some of these strictures seem less extreme when one considers the tradition that the ancient comic writer Philemon died of a fit of uncontrollable laughter.) In the *Peri poiētikēs* (*Poetics*, essays, 4th century B.C.), Aristotle speaks of the moderately ugly, flawed, deficient as the causes of laughter.

Xenophon (*Kyrou paideia* [*The Education of Cyrus*, historical novel, 4th century B.C.]) portrays the urbane Cyrus as defending someone who through wit makes people laugh rather than weep. More puritanical was the government of republican Rome, which according to Livy (*Ab urbe condita libri* [*History of Rome*, c. 27 B.C.–A.D. 14]) tried and rebuked one of the vestal virgins for wittiness and jesting. Livy also tells of the time that Hannibal laughed while Carthaginian senators were weeping over the plight of their city; the general defended himself by saying that his laughter sprang from misery and not joy. In *De oratore* (*On the Orator*, 55 B.C.) Cicero accepts laughter as something that the orator should make use of for comic relief. It is best aimed at blemishes and not at the wicked, who should arouse disgust, nor at the wretched, who should arouse sympathy. It is caused either by facts (when the wording is inconsequential) or by language (when the risible element disappears with alteration in the wording). The former is the heartier, the latter the more scholarly and cerebral. What excites laughter is the disappointment of expectations and the ridiculing of others' character. Since wit cannot be taught, theoretical books on the laughable are themselves laughable.

The comic writer Lucian (2d century) often invokes the laughing philosophers, Diogenes the Cynic and Democritus, who think that all human affairs, especially those of great men and of quack philosophers, are a joke and not, as for Heracleitus, a subject for tears. In that spirit of acknowledging the relevance of mirth, Lycurgus, according to Plutarch (*Kleomenēs* [*Cleomenes*, biography, 2d century]), dedicated a statue to Laughter, and the Spartans dedicated a sacred place to that divine principle. Perhaps one of the most curious early exhibitions of the legitimate role of laughter appears in Apuleius' *Metamorphoses* (*The Golden Ass*, novel, c. 150), in which the story is told of the town that celebrated Laughter Day. The hero Lucius finds himself the butt of a huge practical joke that is part of the celebration in honor of the best of all gods and that dissolves the town into laughter wherever he then goes.

St. Augustine notes (*Confessiones* [*Confessions*, c. 397–400]) that a youthful incident of stealing pears gave many satisfactions at the time, one of which was laughter over not being found out and another was not doing so alone because "we do not easily laugh when we are alone." In *De civitate Dei* (*The City of God*, treatise, 413–26) he adverts to the Sarah episode and speaks of the laughter of Abraham as originating "in wondering delight" and not in scorn and mistrust; with the birth and naming of Isaac (= "laughter") even Sarah was confirmed in faith as she showed that her laugh "was not that of scornful reproach but that of joyful praise." Yet that this is a vale of tears is proved by the fact that we are born "not with laughter but with tears," and Zoroaster alone is said to have laughed when he was born, an unnatural omen portending no good to him.

The Renaissance and Seventeenth Century

That laughter can express pain and hysteria rather than joy or insight is brought out by the ballad "Sir Patrick Spence" (15th century); ordered out on a doomed sea trip, "a loud lauch lauched he," and then he wept. In fact, if the medieval period shed little new light on laughter, the Renaissance more than made up for this omission. Castiglione (*Il Cortegiano* [*The Courtier*, treatise, 1528]) noted that laughter pleases everyone, restores the spirit, and distracts from troubles. Its origin is in deformity, incongruity, and things seeming amiss. Yet what it is and how it takes control is beyond explanation. Erasmus (*Moriae encomium* [*The Praise of Folly*, essay, 1511]) observed that folly is so common as to require a thousand Democrituses to laugh at it and some to laugh at the laughers. He concedes though that sometimes laughter accomplishes what reason and argument cannot. Rabelais (*Gargantua et Pantagruel* [*Gargantua and Pantagruel*, novels, 1532–1564]) put into currency the phrase "Rabelaisian laughter" by his celebration of the human body with broad, coarse humor. Socrates, he says in the preface, always laughed, and the rest of the book follows in the spirit of that blithe oversimplification. Montaigne (*Essais* [*Essays*, 1580–1588]) preferred Democritus and his laughter over Heracleitus and his tears, not because laughing is better but because the things we laugh at we consider worthless, which is what the human race is. He then added something to the truism about laughter being an exclusively human trait: "Our own peculiar condition is that we are as fit to be laughed at as able to laugh."

If Tasso articulates the traditional Platonic-Christian view—in *Gerusalemme liberata* (*Jerusalem Delivered*, epic poem, 1581), the fountain of laughter is associated with Armida's Bower of Bliss, with self indulgence and sexual wantonness—Donne ("Paradox X," poem, c. 1600) subscribes to the Democritean-Erasmic position: laughter is a sign of wisdom. Fools laugh least and are the most laughed at. We laugh at both witty and absurd things; many would even laugh at Heracleitus weeping. The wise man knows what to laugh at; even Donne and his Paradox X can be laughed at. In the incident of the wine skins, Cervantes

(*Don Quijote* [*Don Quixote,* novel, 1605, 1615]) presents through dramatization
instead of theory three sources of laughter: "Who would not have laughed at
hearing the nonsense the two of them talked, master and man? And laugh they
all did with the exception of mine host, who was roundly cursing himself." That
is, one cause of laughter is the Don's bizarre fantasy; another is Sancho's credulity
and stupidity; and a third is the host, discomfited by the incursions of this strange
duo and beset by quotidian worries about nonpaying customers. Webster's *The
Duchess of Malfi* (play, 1613) contains a scene that describes what is no doubt
understood implicitly at many centers of political power, especially when an
authoritarian ruler is surrounded by sycophants and fearful servants: the duke
takes umbrage at someone laughing out of turn and says that courtiers should
take fire only when he does, no matter how funny the situation. Laughter apparently can manifest dangerous independence and superior insight.

Though his comedies clearly aim to arouse laughter, when Jonson turns to
theory in his prose *Timber* (essay, 1640), he (influenced by a misinterpretation
of Aristotle's *Poetics*) curiously denies that the moving of laughter is the end
of comedy, laughter being "a kind of turpitude" depraving a part of man's
nature. Since it can be generated by a wry face, a deformed mask, or a man in
drag, the ancient philosophers correctly thought it indecorous for a wise man.
The laughter of the multitude is seldom raised by truth or nature but by depravity,
insolence, obscenity, scurrility; such was the case with Aristophanes' presentation of Socrates, a slander on an honest man. On the other hand, Milton in
his prose defends his use of grim laughter as part of a noble tradition of teaching
and confuting and as not originating in mere levity or insolence. Certainly in
"L'Allegro" (1632) "Laughter holding both his sides" is invoked, and the
poem celebrates those deeds that conduce to jollity. Yet *Paradise Lost* (poem,
1667) offers little laughter: for man, only in the prelapsarian state, as the elephant
entertains Adam and Eve; for Satan, only in the brief period in which he thinks
he has defeated God; for God, when poor, deluded man is lost in the mazes of
thought, in quaint astronomical theories, or in futile attempts to build the Tower
of Babel, or when Satan and his crew hatch vain designs and tumults against
heaven; for the reader, no laughter at all.

The pious but genial Sir Thomas Browne (*Pseudodoxia epidemica,* treatise,
1646) dismissed as ridiculous Heracleitus and men reputed never to laugh. He
then disposed of the venerable Christian prejudice against laughter stemming
from the fact that Jesus in the Gospels weeps but never laughs: (1) Jesus must
at least have smiled, as part of his humanity during the Incarnation, for even
God is said to laugh; (2) the laughter of "contempt or indignation" differs from
that of "mirth and jocosity" and must have come into play in his anger against
the money changers in the Temple; (3) many other things may be presumed to
have taken place even though not mentioned in Scripture, and so is it with
laughter. His conclusion is that it is false to condemn all laughter, to discipline
man out of his nature, to banish urbanity and harmless mirth, which is consistent
with religion and inoffensive to God.

Hobbes (*Human Nature*, 1650, and *Leviathan*, 1651) was one of the first thinkers to arrive at an original new idea on the subject when he said that "those grimaces called laughter" are caused by "sudden glory arising from some sudden conception of some eminency in ourselves by comparison with the infirmity of others or with our own formerly;" that is, laughter comports with malice, sadism, superiority feelings. Dryden follows Hobbes in noting in the *Essay of Dramatic Poesy* (1668) that the lively and accurate representation of a person's idiosyncracy, like all deviations from custom, "begets that malicious pleasure in the audience which is testified to by laughter" and which springs from the imitation of nature. But in the *Mock Astrologer* (play, 1671) he reverts to the old moral outlook. Laughter exposes the audience to deformities and shames it thereby into a cure, delight coming before instruction. Molière's *L'avare* (*The Miser*, play, 1668) contains a particularly witty contrivance in having the protagonist whose money hoard has disappeared suspect everyone; noticing the audience laughing at his paranoia, he takes the laughter as a sign that they are a party to the theft, thereby ironically increasing the laughter and in turn his suspicions.

The Eighteenth Century to Modern Period

The Christian hostility to laughter—expressed, for example, in Bossuet's *Maximes et réflexions sur la comédie* (*Maxims and Reflections upon Plays*, 1694)—began to be replaced in the later seventeenth and the eighteenth centuries by a new prejudice based on refinement, gentility, good taste. Congreve (*The Double Dealer*, play, 1694) makes fun of that hauteur when he has an aristocratic comic character say that laughter is the most unbecoming thing for a "man of quality," it being a vulgar expression of the passions that anybody can resort to. Addison (*The Spectator*, essays, 1711–1712), recalling a theologian who noted that laughter is the "effect of original sin and that Adam could not laugh before the fall," adds that, though providing relief and being perhaps necessary, laughter is associated with slackness, dissolution of the soul, and human weakness. Instead of being laughed out of vice and folly, men are often laughed out of virtue and sense by attacks on the solemn, decent, and praiseworthy. Dr. Johnson, noting that Swift resisted any tendency to laughter and that Pope was never seen to laugh—even as in ancient Rome Crassus was legendary for having laughed only once in his life—quotes their friend Dr. Arbuthnot to the effect that neighing is more noble than laughing. (Johnson himself thought laughter acceptable only within bounds; it has its moral uses, for spending some time with "laughters" enables one to correct one's own faults.) For Voltaire (who allegedly boasted that he "never made ha-ha") laughter is (*Candide*, novel, 1759) compromised by the company it keeps. Paris is the place where people always laugh, even when they do the most detestable things. Lord Chesterfield (*Letters to His Son*, 1774) also shows an aristocratic severity to laughter: True wit pleases and smiling is acceptable, but laughter is a sign of folly and ill manners; excited by buffoonery, it is beneath well-bred people. Though neither melancholy nor cynical, he himself had never, since he learned the use of reason, been heard to laugh. In the light of all these refined and haughty utterances, one hardly wonders that poor Molière had complained in *La critique de l'école des femmes* (*Criticism of the School for Wives,* play, 1663) that making people of breeding laugh is a hardy undertaking.

Bernard Mandeville (*The Fable of the Bees,* poem, 1714) is a Hobbesian in his belief that laughter springs from envy and malice; he himself would laugh at the spectacle of man, full of deceit and self-deceit, priding himself on being superior to "other animals." Sterne (*Tristram Shandy,* novel, 1759–1767) insists that he writes against spleen, which is routed by the physiological reaction called laughter (the technical details of which he, like a good Rabelaisian, gives). But for amatory matters, books that excite laughter are not to be given to the ladies, as lust is the most serious passion. In Gibbon (*Decline and Fall of the Roman Empire,* 1776–1788) a captured and exhausted king, when at long last meeting his conqueror, burst into laughter; the many witnesses of the spectacle might believe that grief had maddened him, but Gibbon surmises that it was a philosophic laughter at "the vain and transitory scene of human greatness." Such philosophic laughter others noted: The King of Brobdingnag's laughter (Swift's *Gulliver's Travels,* satire, 1726) at Gulliver's description of English society alternates with astonishment and revulsion; when, in the same spirit, Byron (*Don Juan,* epic poem, 1819–1824) remarked that "I laugh that I may not weep," he but echoed Pascal's observation (*Pensées* [*Thoughts,* 1670]) that, depending on our moods, we laugh and weep at the same things and paralleled Coleridge's idea that laughter expresses anguish and horror as well as joy.

Laughter was becoming more subject to philosophic scrutiny and consequently emerged, especially in the nineteenth century, with heightened respectability. If Hobbes thought it to be aggressive, Shaftesbury (*Sensus communis,* essay, 1709) thought it constructive. Coming in reaction to constraint and repression, it ferrets out bad ideas and thereby purifies the truths they are intermingled with. Hegel (1770–1831) thinks that it expresses self-satisfied shrewdness, while Schopenhauer (*Die Welt als Wille und Vorstellung* [*The World As Will and Respresentation,* 1818]) sees it as arising from an imperfect approximation of abstract to sensory knowledge, from the incongruity between the concept and the object it represents. We enjoy having the troublesome governess, Reason, reproved; hence deepest seriousness is at the root of laughter. Kierkegaard (*Enten-eller* [*Either/Or,* 1843]) writes of a vision in which the gods offer him a choice of one blessing from among youth, beauty, power, longevity, love. He chooses rather to have always the laugh on his side. The gods, instead of responding, begin to laugh. He infers not only that his request is granted but that the gods know how to express themselves with taste, for a gravely spoken "granted" would have been unsuitable. In *Gjentagelsen* (*Repetition,* 1843) he speaks of a performance of a farce as providing an opportunity for a pathological study of how laughter is conditioned by differences in social levels and in temperaments. Also, the actors in farce must not be reflective types who study laughter but intuitive geniuses who allow themselves to be swept along by the volcanic natural energy of laughter.

For Carlyle (*Sartor Resartus,* philosophical satire, 1833–1834), no one who has once laughed heartily is all bad; the man who cannot laugh is guilty of strategems and treason. And when it wells up, the laughter reveals a man's character. Emerson ("The Comic," 1840) ascribes laughter to the comparing of fractions with wholes, to separating some items from the interconnectedness of all things, to the nonperformance of what is pretended to be performed, to the pedant's confusion of means and ends. Neither lower (animal) nor higher (angelic) orders have reason—which alone reveals the whole and the discrepancy between is and ought—or laughter. The perception of the comic is an important bond among men and a pledge of sanity. Baudelaire, noting in "De l'essence du rire" ("The Essence of Laughter," 1855), that Jesus, though sometimes angry or tearful, never laughed and that for the omniscient God "the comic does not exist," points to the consequent logical association of laughter with The Fall and with the satanic. As a case in point he cites C. R. Maturin's *Melmoth the Wanderer* (novel, 1820), in which the hero laughs out of despair, rage, pride, and rebellion against God. Laughter, Baudelaire, concludes, results from the clash between the sense of our "infinite grandeur" vis-à-vis the beasts and our "infinite misery" vis-à-vis the divine; it celebrates the joy in one's own superiority and in the superiority of man over nature. The originally Christian association of laughter with Satan is adopted by some romantic sensibilities. In Goethe's play *Faust* (1808) Mephistopheles scoffs at divine dispensation by telling the angels that they would laugh at his rhetoric had not laughter been cast out of heaven long ago. Ivan, in Dostoevsky's *Brat'ia Karamazovy* (*The Brothers Karamazov,* novel, 1880), a rebel and atheist suffering a nervous breakdown and talking with someone who is a seedy-looking petit-bourgeois Satan or his own alter ego, laughs often, like Maturin's Melmoth or Hawthorne's witches.

The iconoclastic Nietzsche was one philosopher who celebrated laughter with abandon. At first, in *Die fröhliche Wissenschaft* (*The Gay Science,* 1882), he accepted Hobbes's analysis of it as a rejoicing at another's expense, albeit, seeing it as done with a good conscience, he added derisively that Hobbes, as a typical Englishman, tried to disgrace it. Though he even subscribed, in *Menschliches, Allzumenschliches* (*Human, All Too Human,* 1878), to the older view that in neighing with laughter man surpasses animals in vulgarity and though he speaks of a spiritual smile replacing loud laughter as a man grows more joyous and certain, he conceded that laughing at something is the first sign of a higher psychic life. It is only in *Also sprach Zarathustra* (*Thus Spoke Zarathustra,* prose poem, 1883–1892) that laughter is wholeheartedly endorsed. Laughter, like beauty, is necessary for the great souled. Every truth is false that is not accompanied by at least one laugh. One kills the spirit of gravity by laughter rather than wrath. One must "learn to laugh," especially at oneself. "All good things laugh.'' When one god insisted that there is only one god and that he is it, the others laughed themselves to death. The greatest sin of Jesus was saying ''Woe unto those who laugh here,'' and, in his hatred of life, he promised howling and gnashing of teeth for laughers, when he should instead have loved those who laugh, there being every reason to laugh here. Nietzsche would in fact rank philosophers by their laughter—all the way up to those capable of ''golden laughter''; and, insofar as the gods philosophize, they also laugh in a superhuman way at the expense of such ''serious'' things as holy religious rites. Laughter is thus for Nietzsche not just a physiological phenomenon but an affirmation of life and a denial of the gravity of soul associated with Christianity.

In nineteenth-century fiction, Hawthorne particularly shows a great curiosity in the working of laughter. In ''The Christmas Banquet'' (1844) a person in frail health who would die if he laughed asks to join in a banquet in order to acquire a life-preserving melancholy. The conversation, however, turns so absurd that he laughs and dies. This anecdote is an updating of the old Democritean sense of the ridiculousness of human existence. The hero of ''Ethan Brand'' (1851), after having looked everywhere for the unpardonable sin, which turns out to be in his own heart after all, breaks into a mirthless laugh of scorn. Such pessimistic laughter, says the narrator, is in fact the ''most terrible modulation of the human voice,'' especially when it is out of place as when coming from a sleeper, a madman, or an idiot. Hence it is thought to be the main form of expression of ''fiends and hobgoblins.'' So also young Goodman Brown's discovery of evil rampant and his loss of faith is accompanied by satanic laughter (story, 1835).

Above all, laughter is central in the great enigmatic short story ''My Kinsman, Major Molineux'' (1851). A young man, Robin, comes to town looking for a prominent relative who would help him rise in the world. After much searching and mystification, he finally sees his relative—a harried old man being tarred and feathered and derided by the townspeople. In confusion, embarrassment, and fear, Robin is caught up by the contagion of laughter, laughing himself even louder than anyone else. Suddenly the procession is gone, and Robin faces the prospect of having to rise in the world on his own. The laugh is one of the richest and most cryptic in all literature. On the part of the mob it is the laughter of anarchy, of rebellion against authority, an early symptom of the coming American Revolution. On the part of Robin it is partly a sign of the herd mentality, of contagious weakness and conformity, like worshipping the golden calf or, with Peter, denying Jesus; partly directed at his folly in wanting to rise and in depending on a prominent person in a world where nothing is certain; partly a psychological joining in to kill the father figure and a rejection of Robin's own virtuous upbringing; partly an initiation into maturity, into a condition of having to forge his own destiny rather than to depend on others, a setting aside of authority, security, and dignity in favor of independence, individuality, and risk taking.

The author of the *Alice* books (1865–1872) was keenly aware that laughter and life, religion and absurdity, are intertwined. In a letter, Lewis Carroll distinguished the laughter of joy, which is in harmony with our deeper life, from the laughter of amusement, which should be kept apart from it because of the danger of bringing mockery and mere wit to bear on solemn things. (Cf. Gogol's view, in *Mërtvye dushi* [*Dead Souls*, novel, 1842], that "the high laughter of delight" is worthy of a place next to "lofty lyrical emotion" and differs greatly from circus clowning.) That religious or appropriate kind of laughter that Carroll is so keen on distinguishing from the more irreverent kind is exactly the one which irritates Paul (Lawrence's *Sons and Lovers*, novel, 1913) when it issues from his first love, Miriam, whose spirituality and distaste for sex troubles their relationship. "You never laugh laughter," he pithily exclaims, meaning no doubt the Rabelaisian, Falstaffian laughter that would offend Carroll. Laughter here, more than elsewhere, has to do with character, morality, even metaphysics; it is, as the old joke has it, serious business.

In the twentieth century, Bergson (*Le rire* [*Laughter*, essay, 1900]) associated laughter with the *élan vital*, the life impulse. Max Beerbohm ("Laughter," 1920) said that laughter (mainly *at* rather than *with*) is an attribute of youth, being directed at people set in authority over us, who are most vulnerable to our sense of the ridiculous. Freud (*Der Witz und seine Beziehung zum Umbewussten* [*Wit and Its Relation to the Unconscious*, 1905]), developing his own theory of laughter by updating Hobbes, distinguished between the harmless wit that produces "a slight ripple of laughter" and the irresistible outburst coming from wit which is hostile or obscene. The latter is a veiled aggression or symbolic seduction made pleasurable by the release of inhibition. Less mired in psychology than in religion is Reinhold Niebuhr's idea that laughter is a no-man's-land between faith and despair. When directed at life's surface absurdities, it is necessary to preserve our sanity, but when addressed to evil and death, it turns to bitterness and mere derision. Laughter therefore exists in the vestibule of the temple; its echo can be heard even in the temple itself; but none of it can be, alongside faith and prayer, in the holy of holies.

The puritanism of Christianity is carried over into modern secular totalitarianism. In Orwell's *1984* (novel, 1949), O'Brien tells the hero that in the future society there will no sex, orgasm, love, art, literature, science, and "no laughter, except the laugh of triumph over a defeated enemy." (The state has obviously replaced God.) Yet even an apolitical modern esthete and agnostic like the young Yeats frowned on laughter, speaking about it with the solemnity of Scripture, Plato, Augustine, Puritans, and totalitarians. His contemporary, Shaw, however, saw its bracing therapeutic value when he said, "He who laughs lasts."

The eerie philosophic laughter of Hawthorne's "Molineux" story seems more frequent in modern fiction. Remaining in cholera-ridden Venice, the amatorily smitten Aschenbach in Mann's *Der Tod in Venedig* (*Death in Venice*, novelle, 1912) watches entertainers whose performance has laughter as its refrain, a mimic laugh with a mocking note that takes possession of everyone in the audience. Its infectious quality therefore makes it analogous to the other two epidemics afflicting even the most stolid individual, love and cholera. That the audience is caught up in the laughter and is oblivious to imminent doom is, moreover, a metaphor for human ignorance and vulnerability. Laughing epidemics are also at the heart of O'Neill's *Lazarus Laughed* (play, 1927). The resurrected Lazarus' declaration of the end of death and fear is signalled by a laugh that quickly spreads. Arrested by the Romans for his subversive activity, he brings his rampant laughter with him to the court of Caesar, debilitating the masses of people and even the soldiers, before dying a martyr's death. Laughter here is curiously bifocal: at once a pious celebration and acceptance of the larger Christian vision of life, according to which everything is in its place and the only reality is "life, eternity and God's eternal laughter"; and, concurrently, the old Democritean response to the absurdity of human beings who are oblivious to these spiritual truths because they are bogged down in such trivia of everyday life as the acquisition of power and the fear of death. The latter kind of laughter, steeped in pessimism, appears at the end of *The Iceman Cometh* (play, 1946), when the Micawberish pipe-dreamers, ridden hard by the activist Hickey, relapse into their sloth with joyous laughter on discovering that the importunate reformer, abruptly arrested for the murder of his wife, has been taken out of their lives. A satanic, mocking, abandoned, unhealthy, aloof laugh characterizes the hermetic, inscrutable hero of Mann's *Doktor Faustus* (novel, 1947), the modern composer Adrian Leverkühn, as well as the climax of one of his major compositions, *Apocalypsis*.

Samuel Beckett, like Hawthorne, is obsessed with laughter. One character, Belacqua (*More Pricks than Kicks,* stories, 1934), with the example of Heracleitus and Democritus before him, chooses the latter's way a few hours before his death. Hamm in *Fin de partie* (*Endgame,* play, 1957), weeps to keep from laughing; another character says that the best way to magnify God is to snigger at his little jokes. In *Watt* (novel, 1953) a distinction is made among three laughs: the bitter or ethical; the hollow or intellectual; and the mirthless—"the laugh of laughs, the laugh laughing at the laugh." As one critic observes, Beckett's laughter is a mask for, not release from, despair. It is in the spirit of Pirandello, who said that the saddest sight is laughter on the face of man, and not quite that of the rabbi in a Babel short story who says that any animal or fool can howl but "only a wise man can tear the veil of existence with his laughter."

A rare and perhaps definitive confrontation between the separate traditions of Platonic-Christian hostility to laughter and Democritean-Nietzschean celebration of it is at the heart of Umberto Eco's *Il nome della rosa* (*The Name of the Rose,* novel, 1980), in which one view is that laughter is the dangerous sower of doubts and the other (and triumphant) view is that laughter stimulates original thought, catalyzes truth, and, by being paradoxically directed at the truth (and even coming from truth itself), liberates from blinding fanaticism.

See also: Comedy, Comic Hero.

Selected Bibliography

Boston, Richard. *An Anatomy of Laughter*. London: Collins, 1974.
Brooke, Nicholas. *Horrid Laughter in Jacobean Tragedy*. New York: Barnes, 1979.

Monro, D.H. *Argument of Laughter*. Carlton: Melbourne University Press, 1951.
Morreall, John. *Taking Laughter Seriously*. Albany: State University of New York Press, 1983.

MANFRED WEIDHORN

LAW

In all societies there exists a set of laws, written or unwritten, that, like the ground rules of any sport, provide a framework within which men can cooperate, a standard by which they can be judged, and a set of penalties they must answer to if they transgress. Aristotle and Montaigne (and, after them, Pascal and Bagehot) observed that society needs only a law that men will subscribe to out of habit, not necessarily a just or rational law. Early societies tried to exact such a fidelity by alleging a divine origin for the laws and adumbrated a set of consequences in the next world for those who eluded the laws in this one. In more modern, advanced, rationalist periods, the attempt is made to exact allegiance not by invoking supernatural forces but by rendering the laws just. The role of the law in human affairs, and particularly the discrepancy between the law and notions of justice or equity, is the theme of many a work of literature.

Antiquity

In a sense, the earliest law is the one constraint placed on Adam at the beginning of the Bible. Adam proceeds to quickly break that law, as his son Cain breaks a different one, and both are duly penalized. Later God makes a covenant with Noah and then another one with Abraham (and, as Aristotle would say, a contract is a law). The latter's descendants are to be His people, chosen as bearers of the moral law and as subjects of refining affliction (the two seeming sometimes indistinguishable). To flesh out that moral law and renew the covenant, God gave the Israelites en route from Egypt to the Promised Land a code—the Mosaic Law, moral and ceremonial—which became the center of their religious and cultural life. (Solomon is one king who stood out by his wise dispensation of legal judgments.) The long story of the Israelites contains many episodes of running after alien gods but always returning to that Law which, unlike the creation of a Hammurabi, Lycurgus, or Solon, is intrinsically linked to a covenant between God and Jew, a vision of a single god, a peculiar reading of history, an ethical strain, and a nebulous vision of eschatology.

The New Testament portrays perhaps the single most important crisis in the history of the Mosaic Law. Jesus appeared at a time when the Law seemed to have lapsed into mechanical, external observance. His acts and sayings (e.g., the sabbath was made for man rather than vice versa, or that he who is sinless should be the first to stone the adulteress) appear to inject a certain leavening into the Law. Whether that injection constituted, as he intimated, not a suspension of the Law but a bringing of people's actions into accord with its original thrust, or a serious defection from the Law altogether is, of course, a matter of vast controversy. His injunction to render unto Caesar what is Caesar's, furthermore, may suggest that the Christian is to abide by the laws and authority of pagan men, at least insofar as these do not violate Christian principles, but it has created another noisy controversy as to just how civilly obedient or socially meliorist a Christian may be. What is crucial is the arraignment and execution of Jesus by the Judaic (and Roman) Law. The people (elders, priests, pharisees, and a portion of the populace) who adhered to the Law feared its putative violation by his ad hoc judgments against it and by his apparent claim to a special status, which permitted such taking of the Law into his own hands.

A basic difference in emphasis between the two testaments, then, is over how the Law is to be regarded. The Christian scripture is a two-edged sword, at once liberal and oppressive. From a legal and political rather than theological standpoint, the God of the New Testament is an enlightened monarch who scraps an old constitution now felt to be archaic and (literally) provincial and replaces it with one that enlarges his kingdom by extending potential citizenship to any individual in the world (rather as the later Roman emperors conferred citizenship on those living in the provinces and colonies outside Italy). And in order to render the novel arrangement attractive, he appoints a popular and (again literally) charismatic new proconsul and intermediary.

Yet that liberalization is balanced by a paradoxical growth in severity. When Jesus said that he who but lusts after a woman is already an adulterer, he made thoughts and intentions as crucial and real as actions; he set up a new—and impossible, for who has clean thoughts?—standard of judgment. Hence, despite the Christian attempt to break away from it, Judaic legalism survives in the Christian belief that history is to end in the big bang of a Last Judgment, a cosmic trial scene to cap all courtroom dramas. To be sure, Paul, the erstwhile zealot against Christians, tried his best to cut the umbilical cord connecting the nascent Christianity to Judaism; by presenting the cancellation of the ceremonial law and the interiorization of the moral law as paradoxically a fulfillment of the Mosaic Law, he would have us see God as a loving and merciful Father rather than as a warrior, moral accountant, and stern judge. But men need judges, want to be judged. Theoretically, at least, the Law had ceased to be carnal, literal, legalistic, technical, external, and written and had become spiritual, invisible, internal, intuitional. In practice, of course, the emergent church found itself letting the legalism and ceremonialism in through the back door as it saw that the end of days was not at hand.

Homer's epic poem *Ilias* (*Iliad,* c. 8th century B.C.) contains no sense of a law. There are, to be sure, unwritten codes; according to one, Paris had sullied Greek honor by seducing and eloping with Helen, and many Greek warlords abided by an earlier agreement in joining Agamemnon in the quest for revenge. Other codes governed the behavior of warriors with each other on the battlefield, the almost commercial relations of gods and men, the behavior of heroes in the face of death. But the absence of a law is marked by the rampant individualism in the Greek camp, of which the defection of Achilles is salient. The hero's grievance, that he does the fighting and Agamemnon does the collecting, suggests that the absence of any ground rule governing work and remuneration is a potential friction point and that the explosion over Bryseis had only been a matter of time. Agamemnon (like Creon in *Antigonē* [play, c. 441 B.C.]) voices a legal issue and indicates that society has a stake in his own position when he intimates that, were Achilles to succeed, others might follow his precedent and show similar insubordination. But no one heeds him.

The closest thing to a law, in fact, is the presence of a consensus, which enables the reader to gauge how to react to the quarrel between king and warrior. That consensus (only partly expressed by the various convocations and assemblies) would have Chryses' daughter ransomed, despite Agamemnon's refusal to do so, and disapproves of his taking Bryseis away from Achilles. It in no way criticizes the warrior for sulking over his diminished dignity and for refraining from combat even while Greeks are falling left and right. Only when Agamemnon publicly confesses his error and offers huge reparation does the consensus, as now articulated by Odysseus, Phoinix, and Aias, turn against Achilles and, even while approving of his stand so far, warn him of hubris. In the same way, an implicit norm in Homer's epic poem *Odysseia* (*Odyssey*, c. 8th century B.C.) arraigns the suitors so that the hero's eventual ruthless handling of them and even of their bedfellows has, in the absence of a law, the imprimatur of both narrator and bystanders.

Aeschylus' *Oresteia* (trilogy of plays, 458 B.C.) dramatizes the evolution, in a community operating on the unwritten *lex talionis*, of an objective, communal law and its important concomitant of a judicial system and a quasi-ritualistic legal proceeding with trial by jury. That breakthrough was necessitated by the clash between the *lex talionis* and another unwritten law, the sacred bond between mother and child. The verdict rendered on Orestes of, in effect, "not guilty but don't do it again," dramatizes the complexity of legal and moral issues, a point also made by the preceding archaic debate over filial propinquity. No trial is offered Prometheus (*Promētheus desmōtēs*, [*Prometheus Bound*, play, c. 450 B.C.]), whom Zeus punishes for helping man. Prometheus has broken no law, only offended the savage and whimsical king of the gods. Nor does the law come directly into play in Sophocles' *Oidipous tyrannos* (*Oedipus Rex*, play, c. 429 B.C.), yet the hero's self-blinding suggests that something must be answered for. That he committed parricide and incest (themselves unwritten taboos) unintentionally is less relevant than that a moral or legal boundary of some sort has been crossed. In the later *Oidipous epi Kolōnō* (*Oedipus Colonus*, play, c. 406 B.C.), however, intention does become an issue, as the aged ex-king and now holy outcast insists repeatedly on the distinction. The *Antigone* is perhaps the first literary work to deal with the vexing question of the relation of man-made law, a creation of time, place, and individual whims, to some unwritten higher, divine, and presumed immutable law. The drama revolves around the conflict of individual or family with city or state, of conscience with duly vested authority. Were Antigone to have her way, society would be threatened by anarchy in the name of a higher law; were Creon to have his way, society would be threatened by tyranny disguised as legality, by the might-makes-right principle. Creon does in fact equate loyalty to the state with loyalty to himself; rebuked by Tiresias and by public opinion, he is punished by events.

The audience's response to Euripides' *Mēdeia* (*Medea,* play, 431 B.C.) parallels its response to the events in the first third of the *Iliad:* the consensus sides with a person who, because of a threefold disability—as a woman, an alien, and a clever person with presumed magical powers—finds the customs and laws of Greece indifferent to her plight as a jilted wife. But, not having an Aeschylean court of law to turn to, she reverts to the *lex talionis,* and, when her striking back takes the extreme form of killing her children, the consensus turns against her. In the *Bakchai* (*The Bacchants,* play, c. 405 B.C.), the tension resembles that in the *Antigone,* as Pentheus, like Creon, stands for the state, the established laws and customs. But instead of Antigone's defiance on behalf of divine law, there is divinity itself, Dionysus, a god and leader of a new cult. The resistance of old law to new vision proves deleterious to both upholders of the old and followers of the new.

Aristophanes (*Sphēkes,* [*The Wasps,* 422 B.C.]) satirizes the Athenian love of litigation and jury duty, and the play is capped with an amusing mock trial. In *Ornithes* (*The Birds,* play, 414 B.C.), that same litigiousness, along with the general turbulence of Athenian civilization, prompts a quest for a rustic utopia; when such a one is established in the remote clouds, it is soon beset by parasitical Athenians bringing with them the very ills the two main characters were fleeing from, including a Lawyer (or Legislator) peddling a basketful of new laws. Herodotus (*Historiai* [*History,* 5th century B.C.]) interprets the Persian War as a struggle of Greek freedom against Oriental despotism but leaves implicit the idea that the difference turns on the rule of law rather than of one man. In Thucydides' *Historiai* (*History,* c. 400 B.C.), when the Athenians propose seizing Melos, the Melians appeal to a just divine law against arbitrary conquest. The Athenians reply that, judging from the course of history (and mythology), might makes right both in human and divine affairs.

This view is eloquently articulated also by the sophist Thrasymachus (Plato's *Politeia* [*The Republic,* dialogue, c. 380 B.C.]) but he is quickly silenced so that Socrates can proceed undistracted in the building of an avowedly utopian society based on justice and reason. This is the first serious attempt (alongside the contemporary comic one in the *Birds)* to make law congruent with justice, to in effect reconstruct society. In his last years, Plato wrote the *Nomoi* (*The Laws,* dialogue, c. 350 B.C.), a more practical version of the ideal state. Among its many legal and political observations is one that belief in the gods is necessary for human allegiance to the laws of society. His *Euthyphrōn* (*Euthyphro,* dialogue, c. 390 B.C.) revolves around a young man who, motivated by justice and piety, takes his father to court for killing a slave. Socrates, not so sure that recourse to the court of law would in this case constitute an act of piety, asks many questions but receives no definitive answer, and the reader is left doubting whether all actions worthy of a citizen are also worthy of a son, whether legality and piety are congruent. Along the way, Socrates also raises the important legal-philosophical-theological question of which has higher priority—the gods or piety, holiness, justness, rationality. Such questions were bound to offend the unenlightened, and eventually Socrates was arraigned on charges of teaching impiety and of corrupting the young. The *Apologia* (*Apology*, dialogue, 4th century B.C.) appears to offer what may be one of the earliest transcripts of an actual trial or at least of Socrates' argument in his own defense. Asserting that his is a life devoted to the gods and to reason and asking for acquittal in a dignified manner, he takes the verdict and the sentence without flinching. The laws of the city may be unjust or mistakenly applied, but he, as a citizen, insists on adhering to them even unto death rather than weaseling out by sycophancy, bribery, or compromise. Manipulated by demagogues and by individuals afraid of the truth, the law has made its first—and not its last—martyr for free inquiry.

Typically empirical rather than idealistic, Aristotle (*Politika* [*Politics*, essays, 4th century B.C.]) studied the legal, political, and historical frameworks of various polities in order to establish principles of political behavior and the governance of states. He also drew (*Ethika Nikomacheia* [*Ethics*, 4th century B.C.]) a distinction between natural and legal justice or between justice and equity, or between universal, natural law, binding on all men (and, he notes, invoked by Antigone), and particular law, peculiar to each community. Ideas of a social contract as an early form of mutual alliance can be found as well in Lucretius (*De rerum natura* [*On the Nature of Things*, 1st century B.C.]), while Catullus speaks of the love between him and Lesbia as a contract—one, he soon realizes, written on water. Virgil's Roman sensibility (*Aeneis* [*Aeneid*, epic poem, 19 B.C.]), while yielding the crown for artistic and astronomical achievements to other peoples, assigns to Rome the credit for "the rulership of nations" and the placing of all earth beneath its laws.

The Middle Ages and the Renaissance

The distinction between the two kinds of law, in the *Antigone* and in Aristotle's works, is reinterpreted by St. Augustine (*De civitate Dei* [*The City of God*, treatise, 413–426]) in terms of the earthly city with its laws and the city of God with a different Law. The *Chanson de Roland* (*Song of Roland*, epic poem, c. 1100) contains (along with the *Wasps*) one of the few early scenes of a fictional trial, as Ganelon is tried and executed for the act of treason that resulted in the defeat and death of Roland. A somewhat different situation is portrayed in Gottfried von Strassburg's *Tristan* (romance, c. 1210); the adulterous love affair gradually coming to the attention of the vacillating King Mark, Queen Isolde is put on trial, and she manages to evade guilt by making her oath turn on a legalistic technicality. The execution of Queen Guinevere, after a similar trial, is foiled (Malory's *Morte d'Arthur*, prose romance, c. 1469) when Lancelot takes the law into his own hand and rescues his beloved by force. The Icelandic classic *Njáls saga* (c. 1280) contains a rich stew of violence and legal actions, warriors and lawyers, acts of revenge and extended court-room drama; the hero is even credited with instituting a Fifth or Appeals Court.

No author has ever portrayed the rule of Law—God's Law governing the universe—as comprehensively and lovingly as Dante (*La divina commedia* [*The Divine Comedy*, epic poem, c. 1320]). The structure of the work and the journey of the pilgrim are shaped by the simultaneously rational and mysterious working of grace. The circles of eternal punishment, temporal purgation, and eternal, blissful contemplation revolve around an all-merciful, all-just God who has calibrated the moral weight of every action. If Jesus found Judaism too mechanical and constraining, he might well have marvelled that a religion developed in his name seemed to have, in Dante's version, outdone Judaism for list making, punctiliousness, fine tuning, and putting everyone literally in his place. Room in all this is yet found for human law, and Justinian, not normally thought of as an exemplary Christian saint, is in Paradise on the basis of his codification of the Roman Law.

The man-made law is the only one in Machiavelli's *Il principe* (*The Prince*, essay, 1532), where it is at the disposal of the ruler, whose task is the preservation of the state. Under normal conditions, though, the ruler, both to set an example and to establish himself in a good light, should, if he can, honor that law. What happens in practice is another matter; the moral ambiguity of many of the laws vexes Thomas More (*Utopia*, political romance, 1516), who points out that the application of the criminal law and of severe punishment cannot cure crime because the latter is caused by social conditions like poverty and inequitable distribution of goods. The enclosure laws, for example, benefit the rich, injure the farmers, and create beggars and thieves, as the rich "arrange for injustice to be legally described as justice." Given the imperfect state of things, it is no wonder that, as part of his satire of many groups and institutions, Rabelais, in his Gargantuan novels (1532–1564), takes aim at lawyers, courts, legal language and proceedings, and, especially, decretals (papal decrees and canon law—already attacked by Dante). And Montaigne (*Essais* [*Essays*, 1580–1588]) more solemnly remarks on a case of men arraigned and subsequently shown to be innocent yet executed all the same by judges intent on saving the face of their profession and on avoiding establishing precedents for the reversal of judgments.

Various individuals find themselves having to take the law into their own hands in Shakespeare's plays. Brutus would have the assassination of Caesar so conducted as to be a disinterested, almost legal, cutting off of the dangerous spirit of Caesarism and not at all aimed at the personable Julius. Hamlet sees himself as the scourge and minister of higher powers, not as one settling personal grudge, despite his disillusionment with his mother and his initially gratuitous dislike of Claudius ("O my prophetic soul!"). Othello, about to kill Desdemona, must control himself so that the act be one of impartial justice, as he thinks, rather than of personal revenge. Prospero administers condign punishment that just stops short of turning into vindictiveness. When Hamlet begs forgiveness of Laertes for the death of Polonius, the latter hides behind a distinction, as if he personally were willing to forgive but honor, the gentleman's code, and even a species of legality will not allow him to do so, at least until some properly accredited committee has passed on the matter.

Great if rigged trials of wives accused of infidelity or barrenness take place in *The Winter's Tale* (1611) and *Henry VIII* (1613). The deranged Lear fantasizes about getting revenge by putting his two malevolent daughters on trial. They escape the court through apparent bribery, as the consciousness of general human corruption and his own past mismanagement of the realm overtake his fantasy. The ineptness of his rule is also marked by his new realization that the laws had favored the wealthy and been severe on the poor and vulnerable (to which inequity Hamlet adds the one about the ''law's delay''). In *Coriolanus* (1607–1608), the hero is arraigned before a tribunal, partly through his own impolitic behavior and partly through the machinations of the tribunes representing the people. His contemptuous ''I banish you!'' hurled at the populace as he is leaving Rome indicates that he hardly acknowledges the legality or moral authority of those judging and exiling him; but, being neither a philosopher nor a martyr, he, more like Achilles than Antigone, has no higher standard to appeal to than the force of his sword.

The two plays in which legality and trials are central are *The Merchant of Venice* (c. 1595) and *Measure for Measure* (c. 1603–1604). In the former, Shylock, always operating within the law, now makes a nonprofitable financial arrangement for reasons that remain ambiguous. Once his daughter absconds with his money and revenge becomes his main purpose in life, he turns to the law as his main weapon. The great trial scene sketches a *Kulturkampf* between Judaism (as Shakespeare understood and misunderstood it) and Christianity (as it has proved to be more in theory than in practice). Shylock is literal-minded, legalistic, tribalistic, and, in the Pauline as well as literal sense, ''fleshly'' carnal; Portia is the exponent of mercy, grace, forgiveness, and human brotherhood. She triumphs over him by a reductio ad absurdum, a hanging of him by his own rope, an adoption of his legalistic premises to show their unworkability. The trial scene thus also becomes a metaphor for the Last Judgment, and Shylock is an Everyman who had better not judge lest he be judged, had better forgive if he expects to be forgiven. His reliance on the laws of Venice is as futile as the Judaic reliance on the Law of Moses; both ignore the Law of Grace. Yet that same Law of Grace is shown willy-nilly by Shakespeare to be applied externally and legalistically, and the mishandling of an unattractive Shylock by the unctuous, intolerant Christians brings out some of the contradictions inherent in the new Law of Christianity, a Law that was, as we saw, at once liberating and confining.

That image of the Last Judgment is also rendered at the end of *Measure for Measure*, as all the main characters are brought before an all-seeing duke aroused over their violations of his laws during his apparent absence. The play is in fact a study of the psychology and the politics of the Law. An ordinance prohibiting extramarital sex having long not been enforced, vice is rampant. The attempt to enforce it anew would be unpopular and may be one reason why the duke, taking a leaf from Machiavelli, withdraws himself and allows a surrogate to function as what we would now call a lightning rod. The revival of the law results in the arrest of individuals like Claudio and Juliet, who are not vice-ridden and who in ordinary circumstances would be let off. (Cf. Gretchen's similar running afoul of the law and suffering execution in Goethe's *Faust* [play, 1808]). But when the majesty of the law must be reasserted, extenuating circumstances are set aside; to exculpate them would be to invite more infractions.

The plight of the otherwise worthy couple is one problem; another has to do with the enforcer of the law. Angelo may seem legalistic and ruthless but is, from his own point of view, a man of integrity given the thankless job of reinstating a law that his predecessor allowed to fall into desuetude. By being strict with Claudio, he is doing a favor to the many others who will thereby be deterred from making the same error; by being soft on Claudio, he would be hard on many others. He embodies the Machiavellian principle that a little bloodshed early will prevent a lot of it later and the corollary that by being severe he is really merciful. Yet the play raises a third question–how much in Angelo's stand is a principled fight on behalf of the integrity of the law and how much is simply an expression of a sour personality draping the law around itself? Pleas for mercy based on the idea that he is a human being who should, through sympathetic identification, be able to see his own fallibility fall on deaf ears. Finally the very poignancy and eloquence of such appeals on behalf of sensual lovers coming from one devoted to a life without sex wounds his stoic armor at the one vulnerable point. He falls prey to the very sin he condemns, and even goes it one better by adding deception and injustice to lust. He would execute a man for the very sin he himself would commit, but the culprit at least was loved and affianced, while he himself uses a form of force and is duplicitous and unfaithful to boot. The reform of the law has, as often happens, fallen into tainted hands, indeed, for (as Jesus and Paul implied) no man is as good as the law he would enforce—on others.

The complex role of the law is also dramatized in Cervantes' novel *Don Quijote* (*Don Quixote*, 1605, 1615). The Don in one of his adventures releases the prisoners of a chain gang simply because every man has a right to be free. He would not stoop from his idealistic perch to inquire if they happened to have done anything evil or illegal to deserve to be put in chains. He has no sense of the necessity of the law of the earthly city, of judgment and punishment for man in his fallen state. In the same way is he blithely oblivious to the consequences of his taking the law into his own hand in the case of the farmer beating the boy. Though he for the moment liberates the victim, as soon as he rides away, the farmer redoubles his severity in caning the boy. By contrast, the down-to-earth, practical Sancho Panza's term in office as governor of an island proves that (as Socrates had suggested) a simple man of the people can dispense justice as well as any legal expert, since (as Aristotle said) equity has more to do with common sense than with legal casebooks.

The Neoclassical Era to the Modern Period

The case that Molière's idealistic Alceste *(Le Misanthrope [The Misanthropist,* play, 1666]) makes against a compromising, corrupt society is defined in part by the litigation he becomes involved in. Similarly, the Lilliputians (Swift's satire, *Gulliver's Travels,* 1726) have excellent laws that, directing their rigor to slander, fraud, rewards, and morality, would put British laws to shame were it not for "scandalous corruptions" that the little people—like the petty human race—have fallen into. Hence employment and promotion at court go by dancing on ropes and leaping over sticks; hence also Gulliver himself falls afoul of intrigue and political manipulation of the law when he is charged with urinating on the palace, an act that actually saved it from combustion but aroused the queen's ire. Despite such politicization, the rule of law (richly intertwined though it be with the rule of custom—meaning mainly Monarchy, Aristocracy, and Church) is eloquently, and at times tearfully, defended by Burke *(Reflections on the Revolution in France,* 1790). The Revolution is indeed in this matter a watershed in the Western consciousness, as the discrepancy between Law and Justice becomes—at least in literary works—wide, ideological, and subject to amelioration. A result is one of the most powerful deplications of the social conflict, in Heinrich von Kleist's Kafkaesque novel *Michael Kohlhaas* (1810). The hero, an injustice done him in connection with his horses, appeals confidently to the authorities only to find one injustice and cover-up piled on top of another. The social system—legal, administrative, governing—acts to protect itself, not to right a wrong, partly because, like Montaigne's judges and Shakespeare's Angelo, it sincerely sees itself having the good of society in its hands, but partly because of greed, selfishness, indifference, and inertia. Nothing less than force will budge it; and a theory based on force or activism was soon developed by Marx. Rousseau *(Du contrat social [The Social Contract,* treatise, 1762]) had discussed how the social contract gave man "equality in the eyes of the law" and how "moral freedom" is obtained by obedience to "the laws laid down by society." But the law had to be in some sense relevant and proper. Montesquieu *(L'esprit des lois* [*The Spirit of the Laws,* essay, 1748]) had seen the law as highly circumstantial, imperfect, mutable; its appropriateness could be ascertained only upon scientific analysis of the epoch, the locale (including the climate), and all other germane facts. And Marx *(Kommunistiches Manifest [The Communist Manifesto,* 1848]) saw the law as merely an illusion, a mask for bourgeois exploitation of society; jurisprudence and social forms under capitalism as but the will of the bourgeoisie "made into a law for all"; private property as a bourgeois legal concept. Such a reading of reality is implicit in Bazarov's radicalism (Turgenev's *Otísy i deti* [*Fathers and Children,* novel, 1862]) and (adulterated with racial notions) in Huck's personal dissent (Twain's novel *Huckleberry Finn,* 1884). Nigger Jim is in the eyes of the law a runaway slave, a piece of property, someone left out of the Declaration of Independence's clarion call for freedom and deemed three-fifths of a person in that influential legal document, the American Constitution. For Huck, who judges by a higher principle, the important thing is that though Jim is black outside he is all white inside.

The "law's delay" has never been so grandly dramatized as in Dickens's *Bleak House* (novel, 1853); cases involving the disposition of property drag on over decades and bankrupt all those seeking justice while enriching the lawyers. From such triumphs of system over human needs emerges the most telling, earthy articulation (in *Oliver Twist*, novel, 1837–1838) of the gap between Law and Justice: "If the law supposes that, the law is a ass!" The majesty of the law is also called into question by the difficulties that the saintly Mr. Pickwick (*Pickwick Papers*, novel, 1836–1837) gets into. Sharp or selfish lawyers like Jaggers or Vholes abound in Dickens' novels. Courtroom scenes are handled with great verisimilitude and drama in such novels as *Pickwick*, *Bleak House*, *A Tale of Two Cities* (1859), and *Great Expectations* (1860–1861).

Dostoevsky's *Prestuplenie i nakazanie* (*Crime and Punishment*, novel, 1866) deals with the criminal justice division's successful trailing and apprehension of the murderer. No such optimism on this theme pervades the *Brat' ia Karamazovy* (*The Brothers Karamazov*, novel, 1880); here the crime hunters close in with great efficiency—on the wrong man. In one of the greatest trial scenes, the defense attorney puts up a moving defense—which, based in part on an articulation of the modern existential view of paternity, is legally a red herring and strategically perhaps a mistake. The dry, methodical prosecutor carries the day with the jury and gets the innocent Dmitri convicted of the murder of his father, thereby unwittingly proving that even a successful legal brief, in rewriting events, may be a work of fiction. The ordeal of the trial and of the sentencing to Siberia, nevertheless, work a moral regeneration in Dmitri, so that the Law, despite its fumbling, has a benign role after all. If it does not capture the culprit, it at least captures the conscience of a sinner. Not only is the human law somehow doing its job amid the confusions of earthly affairs, but, parallel to it, a higher law is exacting divine vengeance. The actual murderer, Smerdyakov, commits suicide because his act of parricide receives no blessing from his atheistic half-brother Ivan, whom he was trying to impress, while Ivan himself, for having merely wished his father's death, undergoes his own inner trial and sentencing in the form of a nervous breakdown.

The law fumbles again in Melville's *Billy Budd* (novella, 1891). An attractive young sailor, the object of Iago-like jealousy on the part of a loser in life, is falsely accused. In his inarticulateness, coupled with his righteous indignation, he kills the villain. The captain must look to the results, not the intentions or causes. That clemency now, in the wake of a recent mutiny, would be accounted weakness and might encourage new mutinies compounds the problem. He therefore reluctantly gives the Law, not Nature or Heart, its sway, and Billy is, like Jesus, a martyr to the Law or at least to a rigorous application of it. The captain is portrayed as a sympathetic figure caught up in a tragic dilemma, unlike his brothers in legal severity—the blinded rabble and the indifferent Pontius Pilate in the New Testament, the vindictive Shylock, the smug and ultimately duplicitous Angelo. The law again is not up to subtle moral discriminations in Ibsen's *Et dukkehjem* (*A Doll's House*, play, 1879), especially when it comes to a virtual legal nonentity like a woman, even if she tries "to spare her old dying father or to save her husband's life." In *Rosmersholm* (play, 1886) and especially in the play *En folkefiende* (*An Enemy of the People*, 1882), the law that impinges on people's lives is, as it had been in the *Iliad*, the consensus, in these cases not of those in an ancient Greek military camp but in a modern Norwegian town, with considerable input from that modern institution, the press.

Two classic modern trials are in Shaw's *Saint Joan* (play, 1923) and Camus's *L'étranger* (*The Stranger*, novel, 1942). In the latter, a man charged with murdering an Arab is found guilty not so much on the basis of the evidence as because he offended local mores by not weeping at the funeral of his mother. He is guilty, in effect, of lacking filial feelings or, more precisely, of not exhibiting such feelings. In the English play, the trial of Joan (like that of Gulliver) shows how psychology and politics distort the legal process. Joan has been the savior of France in its war with England, but the claim of individual conscience that she embodies causes such erstwhile perennial adversaries as Englishman and Frenchman, feudal lord and churchman, to join forces to undo her. She is an innocent "crushed between Church and Law," a "modern" person (Protestant and nationalist) punished by an aroused Catholic and feudal establishment.

The convergence of individual pettiness, pedantry, and vindictiveness with the larger political imperatives is shown by the way in which the small minds at the court, unable to see the broad issues, seem to be trying her mainly for wearing men's clothing and for stealing a horse. Among the many ironies Shaw presents is that the trial that sent Joan to the stake was a legally unexceptional process, observant of the truth and of legal niceties, while the deliberations centuries later, which led to her exoneration and canonization, were an "orgy" of lying, corruption, and calumny. And how easy it is to consign someone to the mercies of the law, but how hard to confront the suffering that execution entails is brought out by one prosecutor's poignant change of mind, in perhaps the first and subtlest literary attack on capital punishment.

Joyce's *Ulysses* (novel, 1922) contains one of the most amusing and surrealist versions of a trial—one that takes place within the self rather than in an actual court of law. Many matters come into this fantasy of Bloom's—he is, for example, accused by various respectable or mythical women of having written obscene letters to them—but basically he is on trial for his thoughts (as every Christian must perpetually be), in the finest (if belated) dramatization of Jesus' idea that he who but lusts after a woman is already an adulterer. Once one begins with the assumption that thoughts are as real as deeds, everyone becomes a prey to the law, and Christianity has no difficulty persuading people of their depravity and of the existence of original sin. The outlook on the verdict is not good, because as Freud (*Das Unbehagen in der Kultur* [*Civilization and Its Discontents*, 1930]) pointed out, a pious Christian is in a hopeless condition; the more devout he becomes, the more offensive do the slightest lapses from purity seem, and the more guilt ridden does he feel under the rigors of such a dispensation. The new inner Law, which was to liberate man from the old external Law ("Love God," as Augustine put it, "and do what you want"), turns out to be curiously confining.

Bloom (or the sensitive Christian whom this lapsed Jew paradoxically represents) at least knew what the charges against him were—lustful thoughts, sending compromising letters, fantasizing about Gerty McDowell and then masturbating, even taking a perverse secret pleasure in the knowledge that his wife was cuckolding him that day. No such balm is available to Joseph K., the hero of Kafka's *Der Prozess* (*The Trial*, novel, 1925). Here is one of the supreme readings of reality in terms of the mysterious workings of the law. Someone is arrested, tried, and executed, without ever knowing what the charges are, who the judges are, what the law is, what reason, cause, or community is served. This haunting tale deals with at least four kinds of trial, judgment, or confinement: (1) personal and psychological—yet another version of a man having to answer to a law in the chambers of his own mind, as in their different ways did Ivan and Bloom (though what illicit thoughts K. harbored is never shown, and the subject is rather what psychologists call "free-floating anxiety"); (2) sociological—man trapped in the mazes of the impersonal bureaucracy that characterize modern life and in which the law is represented or interpreted by files, committees, rigid routines; (3) political—an eerie prophecy of the impending Holocaust and gulags, mind-boggling events in which tens of millions of people were taken away at odd hours by shadowy figures with dubious legality and shipped off to slave-labor or extermination camps for no fathomable reason; (4) cosmic and metaphysical—man brought to life in a universe he never made and cannot comprehend, having to suffer and feel guilty for wrongs that are trivial or nonexistent, and doomed to die without dignity and to be swallowed up in eternal darkness or a barbaric hell. In Kafka's *Das Schloss* (*The Castle*, novel, 1926) the problem is to gain ingress into a place that is a center of power and authority but that has cryptic rules and mysterious functionaries who act arbitrarily and, in the case of Sortini, lustfully and ruthlessly. If the story of the Law begins with the Covenant and the Mosaic Law, Kafka's *Castle* seems to go behind the Bible to a world in which there are many gods and few laws. Like the divinities in Greek mythology, they are capricious, lascivious, brutal; they offer no covenant, revelation, or law, no code of conduct, nor rules for advancement, nor password for ingress.

Dostoevsky's Grand Inquisitor episode had suggested that, for a mankind unable to confront either the living God or the original Jesus, a ruling caste operating in Christ's name was necessary to keep everyone law abiding. (The idea first appeared in Plato's *Republic* and *Laws*.) Huxley's novel *Brave New*

World (1932) offers an optimistic version of this man-made law operating in a society based, in line with modern secular values, on pleasure. Orwell's *1984* (novel, 1949) offers the pessimistic version of a society based not on pleasure but, because man is more depraved than sensual, on fear and terror. The happiness that had been the goal of Jew or Christian in the next world and the fear and trembling he had known in confronting God here and now have been secularized, confined to this world, and turned into the tools of faceless men ruling in the name of hollow platitudes about the dignity and equality of men. In *1984,* the law is what the ruling party says it is. Deprived of both the putative divine origin it once had and the claims to being just later made for it, it is an arbitrary human fabrication. After a century and a half of "progress," it has become part of a thin veil of altruistic rhetoric covering naked power and malice.

Selected Bibliography

Bloch, R.H. *Medieval French Literature and Law.* Berkeley: University of California Press, 1977.

Schwarze, H.W. *Justice, Law and Revenge.* Bonn: Bouvier, 1971.

Weisberg, Richard, *The Failure of the Word: The Protagonist as Lawyer in Modern Fiction.* New Haven, Conn.: Yale University Press, 1984.

Windolph, F.L. *Reflections of the Law in Literature.* Philadelphia: University of Pennsylvania Press, 1956.

MANFRED WEIDHORN

LEADER

A leader is a person who stands at the head of an enterprise or movement (often political or military) and who guides followers toward a goal (social, cultural, ideological, and/or geographical). The leader is always superior to other people in degree (by merit or by status), but not necessarily superior in kind; he is generally a human being, and not a god. Unlike the god, the leader is not superior to the physical world and the order of nature; with abilities and authority greater than those of his followers, he remains nevertheless fallible.

The leader's position does not guarantee virtue; leaders can be evil as well as good, law-breakers as well as law-makers. Nor does the leader's position guarantee the respect of the followers; an incompetent leader may be judged weak, and a forceful leader may be considered dangerous. Often, however, the leader, in literature and life, has achieved leadership by representing the highest aspirations of a group; the followers most admire the person who best exemplifies their idealized view of themselves and their mission. But all leaders, whatever the response they evoke, are judged according to their ability to direct and command the groups at whose head they stand. In this the figure of the leader differs from that of the romantic hero, who is seen most often in splendid isolation. Some romantic heroes, like Goethe's Werther, retreat into a fiercely private state of sensitivity, there to think, love, and create free from the restrictions and diseases of society. Other romantic heroes, like Byron's Childe Harold, set forth on adventurous exploits, on perilous quests, and they too are isolated, in spirit, if not in body. As Kipling says, he travels the fastest who travels alone. Followers, to the romantic hero, are at best superfluous. The hero constantly seeks occasions to display, without interference or distraction, cleverness, bravery, determination, artistic creativity, spiritual perfection, and physical strength and dexterity.

The responsible leader, on the other hand, rarely has the luxury of occupying himself with the solitary search for perfection. The duties of administration may preclude the development of personal prowess. Virgil's Aeneas, whose destiny is more impressive than his achievement, is the classic example. The leader, especially the head of state, often refrains from taking risks, in the interests of protecting the group. His gifts are prudence and justice, safety and survival, prosperity and stability. And if that safety happens to require conquest, and that stability happens to depend on victory, the leader will frequently allow others to assume the more visible roles. The leader directs the actions that are executed by other people, some of whom may be more appealing and glamorous than the leader himself. The paradigm of the ideal leader describes a just governor, all of whose virtues are relevant to his public obligations. By providing a group with a symbol and a clear direction, the leader exemplifies, expresses, and fulfills the public will. The leader is in effect the servant of the followers, at the cost of his own autonomy and glory.

A different sort of leader is the power-mad tyrant, who pursues personal aggrandisement, wealth, and an everwidening control at the expense of his subjects' welfare and often against their will. If the tyrant indeed rules by the consent of the governed, the literary work generally makes evident the ways he has misled the populace about his mission and his concern for their well-being. Occasionally the tyrant himself shares the delusion he projects. The tyrant, however, is always exceptionally threatening as a leader figure. Readers and followers alike depend on the leader for direction and coherence; when the leader represents no one but himself, however, and when he guides people to destruction, he betrays those who rely on him and also jeopardizes the very possibility of sense and order in the world. The attractive qualities of drive, energy, and charisma, ironically, have often made the tyrant appear more interesting than the just, prudent governor who is in fact more capable as a leader. The tyrant, who bears allegiance to no person outside himself and to no cause higher than himself, assumes some of the aura of the romantic hero; his willingness to dispose of the lives of others is oddly similar to the hero's wish to dispense with the presence of others.

The persistent attractiveness of the independent hero may account for his appearance, in numerous literary works, in proximity and in opposition to the responsible leader. In the background we see the leader: older, wiser, less active, more judicious, heavily burdened with anxieties and obligations. In the foreground we see a rebellious follower, perhaps the mightiest warrior: brave, re-splendent, militantly self-willed, and bitterly resentful of anyone who impedes his quest for glory. The conflict between the leader and the hero may become more absorbing than their shared opposition to an external enemy; the classic example is the struggle in Homer's epic poem *Ilias* (*Iliad,* c. 8th century B.C.) between King Agamemnon and Achilles. In plays like Corneille's *Horace* (1640), *Polyeucte* (1641–1642), and *Suréna* (1674), the hero resents submitting to the authority of a weak or conventional leader. Supremacy, it is felt, is a matter of performance, not of position.

The concept of "leader" predates that of "god"; two common forms of the leader (the shepherd who leads animals and the king who rules a body of people) are also common images for gods in myths and the Bible. The concept, which has been used continually, has remained helpful and valid. The patterns of leadership and the types of leaders that have been traced here are found in the literature of all centuries and all nations, yet the concept itself has undergone no systematic development. Although the de jure monarch is rarely the head of a modern state, we still fear, as did the ancients, that power will corrupt our leaders. The positive image of the leader as the standard-bearer, as the crystal-lization of the popular will, is as current as today's best-seller and as old as time. The qualities and contexts assigned to a given leader tend to depend on the writer's views about a particular ruler or captain, or about the nature of leadership itself. Leaders will therefore be classified here not by the natural origin of the works in which they appear, but, in the case of historical leaders, according to the historical personage who served as model (arranged chrono-logically by the dates of that model) and, in the case of fictional leaders, according to the evaluation of the leader's role embodied in the literary figure.

Literary Portrayals of Historical Figures

Political leaders have inspired such varied emotions as admiration, fear, loy-alty, and disdain not only in their subjects, but in writers of their times and later centuries. Literary responses to the historical acts of leaders and to the legends that have grown up around them have tended to convey a judgment, as well as a description, of the historical reality that is recounted.

King David of Israel, one of the first leaders for whom there are solid records, united the twelve tribes of Israel into one nation, made Jerusalem its religious and political capital, expelled the Philistines, and, through conquest, came to rule almost all the territory from Damascus to Aqaba and from the Arabian Desert to the Mediterranean. During the forty years of his reign (c. 1012–c. 972 B.C.), he showed both diplomatic skills and military prowess; as the probable author of at least a few of the psalms with whose authorship he is credited, he may have displayed literary talent as well. The Bible, in the Books of Samuel and Kings, written at least several hundred years after the events, portrayed David as a paradoxical figure: gentle poet and glorious warrior, killer and man of God, savior and adulterer, committed to his family and dynasty, yet reluctant to name his successor. During the Middle Ages, the paradoxes were smoothed over; in the Jewish liturgy, David was the abstract model of the greatest king and the perfect religious figure; in Christian medieval drama, David was an allegorical Messiah figure. Later writers saw him less as a leader than as a man with troubled family relationships: *La venganza de Tamar* (*Tamar's Vengeance,* c. 1623), a play by Tirso de Molina; *Los cabellos de Absalón* (*Absalom's Hair,* c. 1633), a play by Pedro Calderón de la Barca. He appears also as a physically powerful hero in Michael Drayton's *David and Goliath* (poem, 1630) and Abraham Cowley's *Davideis* (epic poem, 1656). In seventeenth-century England, David's story was used as an allegory of contemporary political events: Thomas Fuller's *David's Heinous Sinne, Heartie Repentance,* and *Heavie Punishment* (long poems, 1631); John Dryden's *Absalom and Architophel* (long poem, 1681). In eighteenth-century England, David became the subject of religious controversy. Samuel Chandler's funeral sermon for George II, entitled ''The Character of a Great and Good King Full of Days, Riches, and Honour,'' compared the dead king with King David (October 25, 1760). An anonymous reply, ''The Life of David, or the History of the Man after God's Own Heart,'' was published in February 1761; the author accused David of being a murderer, adulterer, traitor, and hypocrite. Many responses and counter-responses ensued in the pulpits and the popular press. Christopher Smart may have perceived his *Song to David* (long poem, probably completed by 1760, finally published in 1764) as a vindication of a hero with whom he identified. In the United States, during the seventeenth and eighteenth centuries, David was a much less controversial figure. He was presented, in Puritan sermons, as the model of military leadership; his lamentation for Saul and Jonathan (2 Sam. 1:17–27) was cited as an exhortation to military training and preparedness. Later versions of his story, however, have tended to stress his poetic gifts, his ability to cure Saul's depression, his attachment to Jonathan, and his internal contradictions, rather than his performance as a leader: Robert Browning's ''Saul'' (dramatic monologue, 1845), Thomas Hardy's *The Mayor of Casterbridge* (novel, 1886), André Gide's *Saül* (play, 1903), D.H. Lawrence's *David* (play, 1926).

Although there is an enormous body of literature devoted to this great leader, relatively few writers have chosen to deal with his leadership as such. The same pattern holds true for many other historical leaders. Artists often prefer to render the private life and thoughts of a public personage rather than to depict the well-known course of unquestioned and unquestionable events. Leadership, for the most part, becomes aesthetically interesting primarily when the leader is on the verge of establishing his leadership (by force or by persuasion) or losing it (through physical danger or moral attack). The key examples of literary portrayals of historical leaders, therefore, tend to focus on moments of crisis and to ignore the times between.

Alexander the Great (356–323 B.C.), the Greek leader who spread Greek culture by conquering most of the civilized world, is celebrated in medieval romances for his bravery in battle. *Li romans d'Alexandre (The Romance of*

Alexander), a French romance of the late twelfth century by Alexandre de Paris, recounts his heroic deeds. The iambic hexameter line, known as the Alexandrine, became the standard form for French heroic verse; Alexander himself also became the model for the leader in heroic poetry. Centuries later, Jean Racine's *Alexandre le Grand* (*Alexander the Great,* play, 1665) emphasized not the quest for power, but its renunciation; Racine's Alexander surrenders the Indian kingdom because he admires the king he has defeated. Terence Rattigan's *Adventure Story* (play, 1949) portrays Alexander as an appealing, idealistic young man who is corrupted by power because he takes swift, decisive action without sufficient reflection and self-knowledge.

Julius Caesar (102–44 B.C.)—Roman general, conqueror of Gaul, politician of the popular party, tribune, and dictator—appears in literature primarily as a military hero to be admired and as a crafty, ambitious demagogue to be dreaded, not in his more peaceable roles as organizer of the Julian calendar and as agrarian reformer. Although Caesar figures in numerous historical dramas of varying quality, his best-known portrayal is perhaps the least fair. In William Shakespeare's *Julius Caesar* (play, c. 1599) he is neither strong nor noble and seems to court his own assassination by his thoughtless complacency and reckless boasting. In George Bernard Shaw's *Caesar and Cleopatra* (play, 1899), on the other hand, the leader is canny, level-headed, and calmly free of illusions about power or himself. The Caesar of Thornton Wilder's *The Ides of March* (novel, 1948), however, is a figure of tragic nobility, graced by charm and mildness, dignified by fearlessness and impartiality, dedicated to the public responsibilities that confine and isolate him.

Cleopatra (69–30 B.C.), the last Macedonian queen of Egypt, had as her life ambition an alliance between Egypt and Rome. As one of the few female leaders, she is known in literature and in popular mythology more for her affairs with Caesar and Marc Antony than for her diplomatic and military achievements. Condemned by medieval clerics as an embodiment of several of the deadly sins, she was defended by Geoffrey Chaucer, in the long poem *The Legend of Good Women* (1386), as the personification of fidelity, extolled for loving Antony in spite of myriad disasters and, ultimately, at the cost of her life. Shakespeare's mature heroine in *Antony and Cleopatra* (play, c. 1607), on the other hand, is a seductress and a pragmatic politician, a devoted lover and a self-centered seeker of acclaim. John Dryden's Cleopatra in *All for Love, or The World Well Lost* (play, 1678) is, on the last day of her life, similarly devious, if not quite so complex. In *Caesar and Cleopatra,* George Bernard Shaw portrays the young Cleopatra as a pert, kittenish, naive young woman in need of Caesar's mature guidance in political matters.

Jesus Christ, the founder of the Christian religion, is believed by his followers to be the son of God as well as the Messiah whose coming was predicted by the prophets. After being baptized by John the Baptist, he began to proclaim his teachings—salvation through repentance and faith, the power of God's healing love, and the need for humility and self-sacrifice—to his twelve disciples and to the people at large. Although he did not attempt to undermine the Roman state in a direct or concrete way, his immense popular following and his reference to a new Kingdom of God led to his being perceived as a threat and, ultimately, to his crucifixion. The four Gospels and the epistles of the New Testament are the earliest sources of information about Christ's life and teachings. A vast number of other writings came later: theological treatises, reverent biographies, and skeptical analyses, such as *La vie de Je´sus* by Ernest Renan (*The Life of Jesus*, 1863).

Numerous literary works refer to Christ as a theme or motif. Theodore Ziol- kowksi, in *Fictional Transfigurations of Jesus* (1972), has distinguished five major categories. (1) Fictionalizing biographies—such as Nicolas Notovich's *La vie inconnue de Je´sus-Christ* (*The Unknown Life of Jesus Christ*, novel, 1894), Giovanni Papini's *Storia di Cristo* (*Story of Christ*, novel, 1921), and Robert Graves's *King Jesus* (novel, 1946)—attempt to fill in the blanks left in the Gospel stories by supplying additional psychological insights and narrative incidents. (2) Works in the category known as *Jesus redivivus* present Christ in a modern setting. Examples include Honore´ de Balzac's "Je´sus-Christ en Flandre" ("Jesus Christ in Flanders," short story, 1831), Alphonse Louis Constant's *La dernie`re incarnation* (*The Last Incarnation*, collection of legends, 1846), the Grand In- quisitor story in Fedor Dostoevsky's *Brat'ia Karamazovy* (*The Brothers Kara- mazov*, novel, 1880), Rainer Maria Rilke's *Christus: Elf Visionen* (*Visions of Christ*, cycle of poems, 1896–1898), and Richard Voss's *Die Erlo¨sung* (*The Redemption*, novel, 1918). (3) In the genre known as the *imitatio Christi*, a modern character sets out to live as he or she imagines Christ would. Key examples are Mrs. Humphry Ward's *Robert Elsmere* (novel, 1888) and Charles M. Sheldon's *In His Steps* (novel, 1896). (4) In the fourth group, that of the fictional transfigurations of Jesus, the pattern of the protagonist's life corresponds to the significant events in the life of Jesus, events such as baptism, gathering of disciples, undergoing temptation, conveying a message about a new world, suffering betrayal, and undergoing a dramatic death. Among the most interesting examples are Herman Hesse's *Demian* (novel, 1919), Ignazio Silone's *Pane e vino* (*Bread and Wine*, novel, 1937) John Steinbeck's *The Grapes of Wrath* (novel, 1939), Graham Greene's *The Power and the Glory* (novel, 1940), and William Faulkner's *A Fable* (novel, 1954). (5) The final category, broader than the fourth, is that of the "pseudonyms of Christ," works in which the hero is sensed to be somehow Christ-like, although the plot of the work does not cor- respond to the narrative outlined in the Gospels. Examples include Fedor Dos- toevsky's *Idiot* (*The Idiot*, novel, 1868), Joseph Conrad's *Lord Jim* (novel, 1900), Franz Kafka's *Der Prozess* (*The Trial*, novel), Nathanael West's *Miss Lonely- hearts* (novel, 1933), and Albert Camus' *L'e´tranger* (*The Stranger*, novel, 1942).

Hadrian (76–138), who served as emperor of Rome from 117 until his death, demonstrated early his capacity for rigorous administration at home and ruthless aggression abroad. He preferred, nonetheless, to strengthen Rome by means of culture and consolidation rather than through conquest. He is thus known not

only for building Hadrian's Wall in Britain and for quelling the Jewish insurrection of Bar Kochba in Palestine, but also for rebuilding the Pantheon, advocating a general return to Greek culture, writing his own poetry and music,
and sponsoring artists. His hand-picked successors—Antoninus Pius (reigned
138–161) and Marcus Aurelius (reigned 161–180)—followed his example. In
Marguerite Yourcenar's *Mémoires d'Hadrien* (*Memoirs of Hadrian,* novel,
1951), which she calls a "meditation on history," dramatic life is given to the
Spanish and Greek cultures that formed Hadrian, to his appetite for knowledge,
to his love for the young Antinoüs (and his grief at his young lover's incomprehensible suicide), and to his humanistic vision of a world designed to meet
the needs of the spirit. Expounding his thoughts in letters to Marcus Aurelius,
Yourcenar's Hadrian faces death with courage and with the hope that his ideas
will live on in the leaders who follow him. "For my part," he says, "I have
sought liberty more than power, and power only because it can lead to freedom."

Muhammad (c. 570–632), at once a political ruler and a religious leader,
established the Arab Empire and the religion of Islam. After discovering himself
to be a prophet, he began, in about 610, to teach his beliefs to his family, to
the inhabitants of Mecca (who became his opponents), to several clans in Medina
(who became his allies, when he moved to Medina in 622), and ultimately to
tribes throughout the peninsula of Arabia, which he united by conquest. His
political and religious achievements are chronicled and dramatized in several
sources, both religious and secular.

The Qoran (or Koran), the major text of the religion of Islam, consists largely
of moral exhortations, religious teachings, fierce attacks on wrongdoers, and
enthusiastic tributes to God. These materials, all of which were recorded during
Muhammad's lifetime and collected about twenty years after his death, speak
to the substance of Muhammad's leadership (the revelation he wished to impart),
rather than to the narrative history of his life as leader. Later Islamic sources
glorify his military skill and acclaim his saintly character. The earliest biography,
properly speaking, is the *Sīrat Rasūl Allāh (Life of Muhammad, Apostle of Allah),*
by ibn-Iṣḥāq, written about 750; it is accepted as an account of the campaigns,
but not as an authority on religious law. In *Maghāzi (Expeditions),* Wāqidī (747–
823) focuses on both the military exploits and the relationship between Muhammad and the Companions, his immediate followers. The Companions themselves
gave rise to the *Hadīth (Traditions),* which consisted of stories about the Prophet's
wise sayings and their personal experiences of him; the most reliable edition of
the *Hadīth* was compiled by Bukhari and published about 850. In Western
literature, the literary response to Muhammad has often been negative, even
scabrous. Alexandre du Pont's *Li romans de Mahon (The Romance of Muhammad,* long poem, 1258) reflects the image of the Prophet that is also found in
Embricon de Mayence's *Vita Mahumeti (The Life of Muhammad,* biographical
novel, c. 1040–1041) and other works, such as Dante's *Inferno (Hell,* from *La
divina commedia* [*The Divine Comedy*, epic poem, c. 1320]). Muhammad was
seen as a highly unattractive figure: a cynical sensualist, an ambitious charlatan,

and a clever opportunist. Du Pont's Muhammad is greedy for gain and power, gifted in his sensitivity to crowd psychology—and cursed with epilepsy. Later Western views were frequently no more sympathetic. Voltaire's *Mahomet, ou le fanatisme* (play, 1741; translated and substantially revised as *Mahomet the Imposter* the following year, by James Miller) portrays the Prophet as an unscrupulous villain, tricking Séide (whose name has come to mean "fanatical partisan") into murdering the man he loves and respects (and who turns out to be his father). He subordinates loyalty and honesty to his supreme goal: giving the "blind universe" a new strength and unity.

King Arthur of Britain represents the fusion of a mythical figure with a genuine historical personage who probably lived in the sixth century, although records are not complete or clear. A brave, successful general and a primitive chieftain whose exploits are described in the historical writings of Nennius (c. 800), Arthur becomes, in *Historia regum Britanniae* (*The History of the Kings of Britain*, 1137), by Geoffrey of Monmouth, an imperial monarch, a Christian warrior-king, and a world conqueror. The poet Chrétien de Troyes portrays Arthur, in the romances *Lancelot* (c. 1180) and *Li contes del Graal* (*The Story of the Grail*, c. 1190), as the conventional, decorative king who presides as figure-head over a court for which his knights perform deeds of valor. In many of the Arthurian legends, such as *Sir Gawain and the Green Knight* (long poem, c. 1370) by the Pearl Poet, the king himself is in the background. Sir Thomas Malory, however, in the prose romances known collectively as *Morte d'Arthur* (c. 1469), presented Arthur as the moral center of his court, as a thinker, an idealist, and a miraculous being, although not entirely without flaw. Edmund Spenser's Arthur in *The Faerie Queene* (epic poem, 1590–1596) is even less of a military figure and even more of a moral exemplar. In the poems known as *Idylls of the King* (1859–1885), Lord Tennyson offers yet another idealized Arthur: serenely pure, august, and steady, with stains removed and virtues stressed, Arthur guides and guards his subjects. In portraying Arthur as leader in works from the earliest accounts to T. H. White's *The Once and Future King* (novel, 1958), writers have surrounded the kernel (the historical Welsh chieftain) with their own conceptions—moral, religious, military, and political—of the leader.

Charlemagne (742–814), the Frankish king who, after conquering most of France, Spain, Germany, and northern Italy, was crowned Emperor of the West, is similarly the center of a cycle of legends based only loosely on history. *La chanson de Roland* (*The Song of Roland*), a chanson de geste written around 1100, recounts the defeat of Charlemagne's rear guard by a Saracen ambush, a defeat that spurred Charlemagne on to vanquish the pagans. *La chanson de Roland,* beginning with the historical event of a defeat by the Basques in a pass in the Pyrenees, changes the location to Roncevalles and the enemy to the infidel Saracens, enabling the poet to portray Charlemagne as the great Christian king in a holy war; after Roland's death, Charlemagne obtains time for the ensuing battle by praying to the angel Gabriel, who stops the course of the sun. The same material receives burlesque treatment in the final cantos of Luigi Pulci's

Il Morgante maggiore (*The Greater Morgante,* 1470, 1483). There, however, as in Matteo Maria Boiardo's unfinished *Orlando innamorato* (*Roland in Love,* epic poem, 1487) and its completion, Ludovico Ariosto's *Orlando furioso* (1516), Charlemagne appears as the king in the background, in whose name great deeds are done by others.

Joan of Arc (1412–1431) is a rare leader on several counts: a captain whose very leadership is a phenomenon more significant than any victories she achieved, a woman whose power was not inherited or, indeed, granted to her by any man, a leader who was also a martyr and a saint. Inspired by visions and by voices she identified as those of saints, she led French troops to victory against the British at Orleans and then crowned the Dauphin king of France. Literary treatments deal not only with her brief blaze of glory, but also with her subsequent fate: condemned as a heretic by a French ecclesiastical court, burned at the stake through the offices of a British secular justice, officially declared innocent twenty-five years later, and ultimately canonized (1920). Christine de Pisan's "Le dittié de Jeanne d'Arc" ("The Poem of Joan of Arc," 1430) emphasized Joan's patriotism and military valor. Jean Chapelain's *La pucelle, ou la France délivrée* (*The Maid, or France Delivered,* epic poem, 1656) is a reverent treatment, placing Joan in the context of a sacred national mythology; Chapelain's Joan finds her sword hidden behind the altar of St. Catherine, left there for her by Charles Martel, grandfather of Charlemagne. Voltaire's *La pucelle d'Orléans* (*The Maid of Orleans,* poem, 1755, 1762) denigrates Joan's leadership, treating her voices with skepticism and her personal character with exuberant obscenity. Friedrich von Schiller's *Die Jungfrau von Orleans* (*The Maid of Orleans,* play, 1801) portrays Joan as strong and virtuous, triumphing over all earthly temptations, dying (unhistorically) in battle, rather than at the stake. In *Personal Recollections of Joan of Arc* (novel, 1896), Mark Twain presents her leadership as a sort of practical skill, a "natural capacity for business," but he admits that the source of her genius remains a puzzle. Anatole France's *La vie de Jeanne d'Arc* (*The Life of Joan of Arc,* prose narrative, 1908) implies that her leadership depended on decisiveness, on acting without the knowledge that makes one aware of possible risks; Joan's voices seemed to encourage her to dispense with reflection and meditation. George Bernard Shaw's *Saint Joan* (play, 1923) portrays a straightforward, practical young woman whose originality is moral and political, rather than military; her new ideas (which anticipate nationalism and the Protestant Reformation) made her a valuable leader and a dangerous threat.

Peter the Great (1672–1725), was the tsar who built St. Petersburg on the inhospitable marshes at the mouth of the Neva as Russia's "window on the West"; the same stubborn purpose and force are apparent in his efforts to use Western ideas and practices to reform the Russian army, navy, church, alphabet, and class structure. Alexander Pushkin's *Mednyĭ vsadnik* (*The Bronze Horseman,* poem, 1833) describes a statue of Peter. When a poor clerk excoriates Peter for the death of his fiancee (who has drowned because the Neva has flooded its borders), the enraged statue seems to pursue the clerk through the streets of St.

Petersburg. The statue represents the clerk's perception of Peter as a leader insensitive to the welfare of the Russian people, determined at any cost to build his city where he wishes. In an earlier long poem, *Poltava* (1828–1829), Pushkin celebrated Peter's military leadership in the campaign of 1709 against Charles XII of Sweden. In *Arap Petra velikogo* (*The Blackamoor of Peter the Great*, novel, 1828), Pushkin presents Peter as august yet kind, wise yet simple. A similar portrait of Peter as a good man without pretentions appears in the modern Soviet novel, D. I. Petrov-Biryuk's *Kondrat Bulavin* (1946). Aleksei Tolstoy's *Petr Pervyĭ* (*Peter the Great,* novel, 1929–1945) portrays Peter at different stages of his life, from 1682 to 1703, as he develops and displays grandeur and ambition, cruelty and crudity; Tolstoy's Peter is a dictator, but not yet a tyrant, coarse, but not yet grotesque. Boris Pilnyak's *Ego veličestvo Kneeb Piter Komondor* (*His Majesty Kneeb Piter Komondor,* novel, 1919) is a much more hostile portrait: Pilnyak's Peter is indeed an oppressive tyrant, a leader who leads his people nowhere, a hypocrite maddened by his lust for power and his crude passion for women.

Napoleon Bonaparte (1769–1821), the first emperor of France, attempted to form an empire by conquering much of continental Europe; weakened by his disastrous Russian campaign, defeated at Leipzig and again (after exile on Elba) at Waterloo, he died in exile on the island of St. Helena. The subject of more books than any other historical figure (with the exception of Jesus Christ), he appears in literature as ogre and demigod, Prometheus and petty tyrant, messiah and condottiere. Byron's "Ode to Napoleon" (1814) presents Napoleon as an enemy of liberty; however, the third canto of *Childe Harold's Pilgrimage* and "Ode to St. Helena," both of 1816, betray Byron's fascination with the tyrant he fears, respects, and secretly admires. Victor Hugo, once hostile to Napoleon ("Buonaparte," poem, 1822), came to see him as the destined leader of France, as inevitable as the ocean, whatever the defects of his character ("Ode à la colonne" ["Ode to the Column," 1827]; *Les châtiments* [*The Castigations,* poem, 1853]). Honoré de Balzac includes, in the novel *Le médecin de campagne* (*The Country Doctor,* 1833), a folktale, "Le Napoléon du peuple" ("The Napoleon of the People"), which attributes Napoleon's success as a leader to divine protection, as evidenced by Napoleon's perpetual companion, a mysterious "Red Man." Leo Tolstoy's Napoleon, in *Voĭna i mir* (*War and Peace,* novel, 1865–1869), is revealed to be a banal, clumsy, vain, and ineffectual leader; by deft distortion of historical evidence, Tolstoy stresses Napoleon's self-absorption and self-confidence, while denying the possibility that these qualities are justified by a genuine historical significance. George Bernard Shaw's *The Man of Destiny* (play, 1898) portrays Napoleon, at twenty-seven, as a captain who does not understand the art of war; he is ambitious, practical, hard-headed, hard-working, clever at influencing and leading men by projecting illusions—yet still subject to error. Thomas Hardy's *The Dynasts* (epic drama, 1903–1908) presents Napoleon's leadership itself as an illusion; the universe is in fact ruled not by him, but by the Universal Will and by the Spirits Sinister, Ironic, and Pitying.

Psychological portraits of two modern Russian leaders appear in the writings of Alexander Solzhenitsyn. In the chapters "Lenin v T͡Siuikhe" ("Lenin in Zurich"), published separately in 1975 from his work-in-progress on the years 1814–1817, Nikolai Lenin (1870–1929), the leader of the Bolshevik faction of the Social Democratic Party, is seen in the years of his exile, before he led the Bolsheviks to power in the coup d'état of 1917; cautious, suspicious, and disillusioned, Lenin prepares himself and his fellow revolutionaries for a sudden, secret, decisive return to Russia at the outbreak of the First World War. Solzhenitsyn shows Lenin's efforts to control himself; first, by conquering his despair and uncertainty, and, later, by restraining his impatience at the moment of success. This self-control is the prerequisite for the control of others. Solzhenitsyn's portrait of Joseph Stalin (1879–1953), Lenin's successor, in *V kruge pervom (The First Circle,* novel, 1968) is similarly intimate; at seventy, his Stalin is sickly, exhausted, mistrustful, afraid of losing strength and losing face, self-consciously developing and projecting a threatening manner, attempting to terrify others because he is terrified of them and of himself.

More than any leader since Napoleon, Adolf Hitler (1889–1945) has inspired countless historical analyses and literary characterizations. Appointed chancellor (1933) and ultimately adopting the title of "Führer," he attempted to expand Germany by annexing her neighbors and to purify Germany by exterminating non-Aryans; after the collapse of Germany, he is assumed to have committed suicide. During his lifetime, Third Reich "passion plays" like Richard Euringer's *Deutsche Passion: 1933 (German Passion: 1933)* portrayed Hitler as Christ, rescuing and redeeming the Fatherland. In *The Portage to San Cristóbal of A.H.* (novel, 1981), George Steiner creates a nightmare. Adolf Hitler, having escaped to the upper Amazon from the debacle of the Third Reich, is captured, in his nineties, by a small group of Israeli Nazi-hunters. After the disintegration of their radio, which cuts off both the captors and their captive from help and provisions, the young Israelis journey with Hitler back to civilization. The hike through hundreds of miles of swamp exhausts the young raiders, but not the elderly Hitler. His amazing physical fortitude is matched, at the end, by his vehement claims of moral rectitude. Even in captivity, even without followers, he displays the qualities of his leadership: persistence, consistency, and deathless evil.

Several literary treatments of Hitler are not in fact direct portrayals. Bertolt Brecht's *Der aufhaltsame Aufstieg des Arturo Ui (The Resistible Rise of Arturo Ui,* play, 1941) presents Hitler's career as the rise to power of a Chicago gangster; his leadership depends on his speaking skills, on his penchant for dodging accountability, and on the corruption in the economic system that nourishes him. Norman Spinrad's *The Iron Dream* (novel, 1972) presents an alternative history. Instead of becoming chancellor, Hitler emigrated to the United States and became a writer of science fiction. His purported masterpiece, *Lord of the Swastika,* recounts the sword-and-sorcery adventures of a strong, blond giant who takes over the universe by killing all of his genetic inferiors and cloning a genetically pure race; the stages of his triumph—the takeover of a small political party, the arranging of violent demonstrations, and the political alliance with the military— parallel those of the career of the historical Hitler. The fictional hero Feric Jaggar is a device for launching a bitter attack on fascism and militarism as the foundations of Hitler's leadership. The portrayal, although it is indirect, is as pointed and as telling as the direct presentation of historical leaders.

Literary Portrayals of Fictional Leaders

Because Homer's Agamemnon in the *Iliad* is a leader by virtue of his position and not his qualities, his power resides in his scepter and in his sphere of action: battle. He himself, however, is not particularly outstanding on the field of war, nor is he especially wise or diplomatic. Yet, as commander-in-chief of the Greek forces, he has the sole authority to continue or abandon the siege of Troy. In overcoming his whims, his pride, his inclination to despair, he displays loyalty to his cause, his command, and his fellow Greeks—a loyalty noticeably lacking in Achilles, whose brave independence and military prowess spur him to rebel against Agamemnon, without making him fit or entitled to replace his leader. The pattern recurs many times in literature. The leader, bearing with dignity, fatigue, and personal cost the weight of power, is challenged or overshadowed by a hero devoted primarily to honor and glory. Aeneas versus Turnus in Virgil's epic poem, the *Aeneis (Aeneid,* 19 B.C.), Gunnar versus Sigurth in the *Elder Edda* (Icelandic epic poems written in the ninth to twelfth centuries), Hrothgar and Hygelac versus Beowulf in *Beowulf* (Anglo-Saxon epic poem of the early eighth century)—the leader and the hero are presented, as if in juxtaposition, if not in competition. The social contract seems to exact a heavy price from these leaders; they are in effect forced to surrender their freedom, to limit the scope of their actions, and to discipline their inclinations. But they must do so. Leaders are viewed as potentially worthy of great honor, admiration, respect, and gratitude. Although the role may diminish a person's opportunity and capacity for valor and splendor, the leadership is viewed as a positive phenomenon, arousing moral goodness in the leader and providing wise guidance and stability for the followers, including those heroes who are able to exercise the opportunities unavailable to the leader. The dangers of leadership—corruption of the leader, oppression of the followers—are apparent in these cases, yet mostly implicit.

A less sanguine consideration of leadership characterizes several later works. The Satan of John Milton's *Paradise Lost* (epic poem, 1667), who would rather rule in hell than serve in heaven, assumes leadership of the fallen angels after his rebellion against God; expelled from heaven, he vows eternal enmity. Through inducing Eve and Adam to disobey God, Satan brings Sin and Death into God's new world. Although Satan's speeches seem to reveal a grandeur and a nobility of spirit, he has done no good to the legions he leads, nor will his apparent victory be lasting.

To be corrupted in the act of exercising power, however, is not always the same as being corrupted by power. Sometimes, predisposed to corruption, people become leaders in order to dominate and unfairly exploit their followers; at other times the very act of wielding leadership brings out the tyrant in the leader. Both the pursuit and the practice of leadership can entail conduct worthy of condemnation. In Rudyard Kipling's "The Man Who Would Be King" (story, 1888), two British scamps—ignorant, destitute, and disreputable—make a bid for an empire in Kafiristan; one of them pretends to be Alexander's heir in order to become a king. Leadership is another form of the petty dishonesty they have practiced throughout their roguish careers in trade; dethroned by excessive ambition and a weakness for women, Dravot loses his temporary preeminence, without having done significant good or harm. Leadership here is simply a more serious and dangerous variety of the swindle; the leader's divinity is in the eye of the subject, who then destroys the leader when he carelessly exposes the swindle by revealing his vulnerability.

Some leaders, of course, can be worthy of respect. A noble Indian leader is the subject of *Winnetou* (1892), the most popular novel by Karl May, the Zane Grey of Germany. This novel, set in the Western United States not long after the Civil War, is filled with incidents: fights with bears and buffalos, battles with Indians, incredible escapes. A serious underlying theme, however, is the mutual respect that develops between Shatterhand, a German immigrant prospector, and his blood brother Winnetou, son of the Apache chief and eventually himself a chief. May's Indian, even in defeat, represents dignity, innocence, pride, and freedom; he is a "bleeding giant," the victim of enforced (and futile) integration into a world where he does not belong and where he can no longer lead. Winnetou (a character to whom May returned in several other stories and novels) is a sympathetic figure, both great and good—most unlike the leaders generally found in novels of politics.

Political novels often portray the leader as swindler and sometimes also as self-swindled. Robert Penn Warren's *All the King's Men* (1946) chronicles the rise and fall of a power-hungry demagogue whose idealism (genuine, and particularly apparent in the early stages of his career) does not guarantee honesty, or indeed honor in any sense. Edwin O'Connor's *The Last Hurrah* (1956) exposes the delusions of a politician who does not realize that his leadership is no longer inevitable, that his natural constituents have deserted him (geographically and ideologically), that he is not the best man for the job and the time, although he is more humane and charismatic than the politician who defeats him.

In J. M. Barrie's *The Admirable Crichton* (play, 1902), leadership is defined in two ways: as a position in society and as a quality of character. When an earl is shipwrecked on a desert island—together with family, friends, and servants—the proper leader proves to be the butler. His talents, which infinitely exceed those of his social superiors, outweigh the prevailing class system and its attendant hierarchy, which the butler himself endorses when in civilization. In society, says Crichton, leadership depends on position, and it should; in a state of nature, leadership should depend on ability, and it does.

Both literature and history, however, are haunted by the prospect of the leader whose ambition is fueled by lust for power unlimited by scruple. In *It Can't Happen Here* (novel, 1935), Sinclair Lewis traces the transformation of the United States into a fascist dictatorship under the presidency of Berzelius Windrip, a magnetic demagogue bristling with facts and figures. Imposing his will and his vision with the help of the militia and assorted hoodlums, he seizes control of the legislature, judiciary, and labor unions, suppressing all vocal opponents and other minorities. The novel shows how the people's choice could become the people's scourge.

The leader, in popular thrillers and in science fiction, has frequently been a megalomaniac. In Ian Fleming's series of James Bond novels, Sir Hugo Drax (*Moonraker*, 1955) and Dr. No (*Dr. No*, 1958) appear to be more concerned with maintaining control over their underlings and asserting control over the outside world than they are in the ostensible material benefits they are pursuing; power itself—rather than anything one might use power to obtain—seems to be the goal. Fu Manchu, the evil Chinese doctor who wishes to be Emperor of the Underworld, seeks not only personal power, but also the defeat of all other powers; throughout Sax Rohmer's long-running series (more than fifteen novels over the course of more than thirty years, beginning in 1913), the entire white race is under symbolic attack. Fu Manchu, as a would-be alien leader, is a threat in a sense echoed by the famous catch-phrase that was attributed, in cartoons, to the little green men from outer space: "Take us to your leader." To conquer Earth, the aliens would have to find and replace the leader. If there is no existing leader, however, there can be no replacement. In Eric Frank Russell's "And Then There Were None" (story, 1951), the planet Gand proves impregnable and unconquerable when the invaders are unable to locate any leaders. In a political system characterized by benevolent anarchy and free exchange, there is no place for a leader, native or foreign.

Gillian Freeman's *The Leader* (novel, 1966) follows the efforts of a bank clerk, frustrated by the dullness of his work and smothered by his solicitous mother, to initiate and head a neo-Nazi movement in Britain. Appealing to envy and to prejudice against the alien (Jews, blacks, and others who can be defined as not English), he recruits members for his "Britain First" party from the ranks of schoolboys, wastrels, and malcontents, as well as from the members of the middle class who have come to feel dispossessed. His remarkable success in arousing enthusiasm is accompanied by his personal disintegration. Dependent on the advice of a fortune-teller, he begins to behave even more erratically when she disappears: accusing his close supporters of treachery, polarizing his movement, staging purposeless demonstrations, planning "hit lists" for extermination, attempting suicide, and ultimately submitting to his mother's care. The evil he has done lives after him, however, when his followers continue to work for his conception of Britain's future. Leadership can flourish or fester after the leader is gone.

With this anatomy of power turned poisonous, Freeman refers to an enduring fear: that the leader will take advantage of the followers, fighting private battles, seeking private gains, and serving private needs. The expression of this fear is found as early as the first work discussed here. Before the reign of David, Israel's greatest king, there was Saul. Ignoring the warnings of the prophet Samuel (1 Sam. 8), who asked his people not to place themselves under the sway of a king, Israel demanded a ruler, and accepted Saul—who disobeyed the word of God, disregarded the well-being of his people, and yielded to the demons of jealousy and despair. For each leader like David, there are many Sauls.

See also: Birth of Hero, Christian Hero, Social Status of Hero.

Selected Bibliography

Brombert, Victor, ed. *The Hero in Literature*. Greenwich, Conn.: Fawcett, 1969.

Levy, Gertrude Rachel. *The Sword from the Rock: An Investigation into the Origins of Epic Literature and the Development of the Hero*. London: Faber and Faber, 1953.

Moorman, Charles. *Kings and Captains: Variations on a Heroic Theme*. Lexington: University Press of Kentucky, 1971.

Sellier, Philippe. *Le mythe du héros, ou le désir d'être dieu*. Paris: Bordas, 1970.

SHOSHANA KNAPP

LESBIANISM

The term "lesbian" derives from Lesbos, a Greek island on which the woman poet, Sappho, lived in the sixth century B.C. Sappho taught music, dancing, and poetry to young women of wealthy families, and it is to them that many of her love lyrics are written. The less frequently employed term "sapphist," after Sappho, is synonymous with "lesbian." The term "tribade" (which refers specifically to a woman who "rubs" another woman's genitals, thought to be the common lesbian sexual activity) was also used in other centuries. A "lesbian" is a woman who loves other women emotionally and usually, but not always, sexually.

Antiquity

The earliest clear example of lesbianism in extant literature is from the poetry of Sappho, (fl. c. 600 B.C.), although some literary historians have argued that Ruth's speech to Naomi, "Whither thou goest," which has come to be used as part of the heterosexual marriage ceremony, is an example of romantic love between women. It is thought that Sappho wrote about 12,000 lines of verse, but only a few hundred lines survive. Her work was burned by the church, first in A.D. 380, under the command of Gregory Nazianzen on the grounds that she was a *gynaion pornikon erotomanes* (a lewd nymphomaniac), and later in 1073 in both Rome and Constantinople. The lines of her poetry that survive are those that have been quoted by other authors and a few fragments that were discovered in twentieth-century excavations in Egypt. Many of those lines, as in her poem to Aphrodite, show her passionate attachment to young women. One writer of antiquity, Maximus of Tyre, observed that three young women were to her what Alcibiades and other young men were to Socrates. After her death until recent times, most of the extant literature dealing with lesbianism was written by men.

Ovid in his *Sappho Phaoni (Epistle of Sappho to Phaon)* from *Heroides* (n.d.) presents Sappho in her later years, having deserted her girl loves, pining over a young boatman, Phaon, and finally leaping to her death from the Leucadian cliffs because of the agonies of unrequited passion. However, many scholars doubt the accuracy of this story and point to evidence that suggests she died in her own home, an old woman.

Ovid also deals with love between women in his epic poem *Metamorphoses* (c. A.D. 2–17), where he employs a plot device that became popular during subsequent eras in various modifications. Iphis is a girl raised as a boy by her mother to avoid Iphis' father's command that a female baby must be put to death. She is betrothed to another girl, Ianthe, by her unsuspecting father. Iphis comes to love Ianthe passionately, and Ianthe reciprocates, not knowing Iphis' true sex. Iphis laments her impossible love and her realization that she must devise ways to prevent the marriage. Finally, however, she is forced into a marriage ceremony with Ianthe, but the goddess comes to her rescue. At the altar she is metamorphosed into a boy.

Most classical literature shows male intolerance of lesbianism, often coupled with an ambivalent fascination and sometimes a refusal to believe in the efficacy of lesbian sexual activity. In Ovid's story, Iphis' conscience tells her to do "only what is lawful" and love only "within a woman's right." Clearly lesbian love was not "lawful" by the time Ovid wrote, although it appears to have been in Sappho's day, judging from her unself-conscious proclamations.

The Roman writer, Juvenal, in his Satire 6 (*Satirae*, c. A.D. 100–127) presents well-born women competing with prostitutes in lesbian sex orgies, proving their skill and endurance, assisted by *olisbos*, artifical penises. At the end of their lesbian orgy, however, they search frantically for men, having acknowledged that lesbian sexual activity cannot satisfy women.

His Spanish-born, Roman contemporary, Martial, also satirizes lesbianism in his *Epigrammata (Epigrams*, A.D. 86–101). He presents Bassa, who is thought by many to be pure since she will not permit men to come to her home, neither as lovers nor servants. But, in fact, she is a hypocrite. She engages in tribadism with her female servants, having been endowed with a large clitoris. Martial also writes of Philaenis, endowed as is Bassa, who not only has sexual relations with women, but also is the aggressor in sodomy with young boys.

A Greek writer born in Syria, Lucian (117–c. 180 A.D.) demonstrates an antipathy toward lesbianism as well as a fascination. In his *Hetairikoi dialogoi (Dialogues of the Courtesans*, 2d century) he presents Leana, who relates to a courtesan friend how she was seduced by two wealthy women who had hired her to play music at a banquet. The friend demands with relish the details of the seduction. However, Leana stops short of describing the actual physical act, saying, "It was rather disgusting. So, by Aphrodite, I won't tell you anything more about it." These attitudes concerning lesbianism reappeared in literature by men in many subsequent centuries.

The Middle Ages and Renaissance: Transvestite Tales

In *Huon de Bordeaux* (*Huon of Bordeaux*), a thirteenth-century French epic, a woman, Ide, disguises herself as a knight in the service of the Holy Roman Emperor. She is given the emperor's daughter as a bride in recognition of her outstanding service, and to refuse the gift would be to offer great insult. Ide marries her, keeping her gender a secret. She feigns illness as an excuse for not consummating the marriage, although the two exchange embraces and kisses. After two weeks the bride is in great despair, so Ide confesses that she is a woman. The confession is heard by a spy and reported to the ruler, who orders her burned at the stake because "he wolde not suffre suche boggery to be used." Like Iphis, she is rescued at the last minute, metamorphosed into a male.

La fleur lascive orientale (*The Wanton Oriental Flower*, tales), which may have originated in the Orient, appeared in Europe during the Crusades. It was rewritten and published during the sixteenth century. "The Princess Amany" in this work tells of a princess who resists marrying a non-Moslem by disguising herself as a man and running away. Her adventures include intimacy with two women who do not know she is a female. In India she marries one of them, a princess, and they live together in marital bliss after some initial problems. When Amany's original suitor reappears, now converted to Islam, he takes both of them for wives and they learn they prefer intimacy with him rather than with each other.

Canto 25 of the Italian epic *Orlando furioso* (1516), by Ludovico Ariosto, presents Bradamant, dressed (like Ide) as a knight, engaging in knightly exploits. She receives a head wound and her hair is cut while the wound heals. All then mistake her for her twin brother. Fiordispina sees Bradamant asleep in the forest and instantly falls in love with her, waking her with a passionate kiss. Bradamant confesses she is a woman, but Fiordispina continues to love her, lamenting that she is cursed more than any woman has ever been cursed in love because what she desires is impossible, since love between women cannot, she believes, be consummated. Bradamant leaves and tells the story to her twin brother, who then goes to Fiordispina and claims that magic has transformed "her" into a male so that they can consummate their love.

Book 2 of Sir Philip Sidney's prose romance *Arcadia* (1590) is a reversal of the Bradamant story. The hero disguises himself as Zelmane, an Amazon, and is permitted friendly intimacy with Philoclea, daughter of the king, who does not know that Zelmane is a man. Philoclea falls in love with Zelmane, but, like Fiordispina, laments because such a love cannot be consummated. She is delighted when she discovers Zelmane's true sex. In all of these male-authored works, the possibility of a serious love relationship between two womanly females is never entertained.

The Late Sixteenth through the Eighteenth Centuries

Transvestism continued as a theme in the literature of this period. A plot similar to the one in *Arcadia,* in which a male is disguised as a female when another female falls in love with "her" is repeated in Honoré d'Urfé's *Astrée* (*Astrea,* pastoral novel, 1607–1628). Transvestism is also the subject of Dekker and Middleton's *The Roaring Girl* (play, 1611), based on the lowlife figure, Mary Frith, who appeared also in Nathan Field's play *Amends for Ladies* (1618). In the Dekker and Middleton play, Mistress Gallipot observes of her, "Some will not stick to say she's a man, and some both man and woman," to which Laxton responds, "That were excellent, she might first cuckold the husband and then make him do as much for the wife."

The subject of love between women is treated from a somewhat different (though still masculine) perspective in the libertine and erotic literature of the sixteenth, seventeenth, and eighteenth centuries. Frequently lesbian lovemaking is viewed with tolerance, as is almost any sexual act in this genre, but there is still more than a hint that it cannot possibly be sufficient for a woman. The French writer, Pierre de Bourdeille, Seigneur de Brantôme, in *Vies des dames galantes* (*Lives of Fair and Gallant Ladies,* 1665–1666) deals primarily with the amorous exploits of the females of the court of Henri II. He includes a lengthy discussion of *donna con donna* (lesbian lovemaking), in which he points out that many husbands "were right glad their wives did follow after this sort of affection rather than that of men, deeming them to be thus less wild." That he does not take the efficacy of *donna con donna* seriously himself is suggested by his assurance to men that most women who make love with other women will "if they but find a chance and opportunity free from scandal ... straight quit their comrades and go throw their arms around some good man's neck." Such heterosexual preference is depicted in Nicolas Chorier's work *Satyra sotadica* (1617), in which two women arouse each other, first by talk, then by lesbian sexual activity; however, they are soon happy to be joined by men. An adaptation of this work appeared in England under the title *A Dialogue Between a Married Lady and a Maid* (1688). The French libertine poet Denis Sanguin de Saint-Pavin similarly doubts the efficacy of lesbian lovemaking. In Sonnet 33 (1655) he speaks of "These Innocents who deceive themselves, / Searching in vain, in their love, / The pleasure which they refuse us." Pontus de Tyard in "Elégie pour une dame enamourée d'une autre dame" ("Elegy for a Woman Who Loves Another Woman," 1573) shows that lesbian love is ephemeral, but he is not unsympathetic to it. The female speaker of the poem, who claims to have rejected men because they laugh at a woman's honor, is punished by Cupid for her disdain of heterosexuality. He forces her to love another woman, who initially encourages the speaker and then tires of her. The speaker is doomed to misery in her unrequited love.

Similar views of love between women as ephemeral and lesbian lovemaking as inefficacious or poor imitations of heterosexuality continued to the end of the

seventeenth century and into the eighteenth century. The Sappho-Phaon myth
was still very much alive. In one of the first encyclopedias, *Dictionnaire historique et critique* (*Historical and Critical Dictionary,* 1697), author Pierre Bayle
devotes much of the article on Sappho to a discussion of her desertion of women
in favor of Phaon. Lesbian sexual activity was generally seen as attempting to
mirror heterosexuality. Robert James, in his English *Medicinal Dictionary*
(1743), explains that the active partner in a tribadistic relationship stimulates the
passive one with her large clitoris. In another English work, John Cleland's
Fanny Hill or Memoirs of a Woman of Pleasure (novel, 1749), Fanny Hill as a
novice prostitute is initiated into sexuality by Phoebe, a seasoned prostitute who
recognizes that everything is lacking in her lovemaking to Fanny since a penis
is lacking. "Oh! That I were a man for your sake," Phoebe cries. In a French
novel by Mathieu François Mairobert, *L'espion anglois* (1777–1786), a madame
observes of a young girl (by the name of Sapho) who is brought to her house
of prostitution that she "has a diabolical clitoris" and will thus "be better for
women than men." The madame rejoices because "our famous tribades will
pay the girl's weight in gold." In a satirical British work, William King's *The
Toast* (1736), the tribade, Myra, is seen as having been presented by Venus with
a set of male sex organs. She is so sexually voracious, however, that she must
have men as well as women. Both this work and the lesbian portions of Mairobert's *L'espion anglois* appear to be thinly veiled attacks on overly aggressive
acquaintances of the writers.

One of the most infamous treatments of lesbianism in the eighteenth century,
Denis Diderot's *La religieuse* (*The Nun,* novel, 1760) seems also to have been
stimulated by resentment, specifically against Mme. le Gendre, the sister of his
mistress, Sophie Volland, with whom she had a relationship that was, to him,
disconcertingly intimate. *The Nun* was written too out of his anger at the Catholic
church and its system of celibacy (cf. the sixteenth century Italian work by Pietro
Aretino, *I ragionamenti* [dialogues, 1534–1536], in which the nuns indulge in
sexual dalliance with each other). The lesbian mother superior in *The Nun* uses
her authority to obtain sexual favors. Through her the convent is seen as a place
where the depraved lead the innocent to depravity.

The Female Perspective: Middle Ages through the Eighteenth Century

There are few belletristic works about love between women written by women
after the time of Sappho through the period under consideration. Those that exist
generally demonstrate a very different view of female same-sex love from that
which we have seen. The female troubadour Bieris de Romans wrote poems of
praise to a "lovely woman," who is raised "high above all others" through her
"merit and beauty." The speaker begs the beloved to give her "that which hope
promises," and declares, "from you stems all my happiness." In the poetry of
the English writer Katherine Philips (1631–1664) the female speaker proclaims
that she loves Lucasia, who is "all that I can prize, / My Joy, my Life, my
Rest." Philips, who lived most of her life during the reign of the Puritans, does

not dwell on the physical manifestations of her arousal as Sappho sometimes does. Instead, she is much more concerned with the ecstasy of her soul—but it is another woman who brings about this ecstasy and makes her feel complete.

While there were some satirical treatments of lesbianism by women writers, these are rare. The most notable is a work by the first female political journalist in England, Mary Manley, whose satirical *Secret Memoirs and Manners of Several Persons of Quality of Both Sexes from the New Atalantis, an Island in the Mediterranean* (1708–1711) was an exposé of the foibles of members of the opposing Whig party. In one section she speaks of the close relationships of many women of "The Cabal," which would be meritorious if they were limited to "only tender friendship," but are clearly often carried "a length beyond what nature designed."

However, most women writers who dealt with the subject during this era treated love between women as a superior kind of affection. They borrowed from David, who said of Jonathan, "Your love was wonderful to me, passing the love of women," and claimed that their love was "passing the love of men." The term "romantic friendship" came to be widely used in eighteenth-century England to describe such relationships. Romantic friendships may not have been often specifically genital, although many were patently sensual and were love relationships in every other sense. Romantic friends pledged eternal devotion, longed to be together always, claimed to care for each other above any other earthly consideration, slept together, held each other in long embraces. Romantic friendship was a socially accepted institution in eighteenth-century England, France, Germany, and America, perhaps because society believed that love between females fulfilled positive functions such as providing a harmless release for homosocially segregated girls and unhappily married women. The sexual possibilities of such love were either rarely entertained or were generally not considered threatening to society, since women would necessarily marry, for economic survival alone if no other reasons in those times when there were almost no jobs available to women outside of the lower classes. (Also, as this discussion indicates, in a phallocentric society most men would not take lesbian sex seriously.) Literary examples of romantic friendship may be found in a number of novels by eighteenth-century women, and several by men, including Jean-Jacques Rousseau's *La nouvelle Héloïse* (*The New Heloise*, 1761); Sarah Scott's *A Description of Millenium Hall* (1762); Helen Maria Williams' *Anecdotes of a Convent* (1771); *Danebury: or, The Power of Friendship* (1777)— "by a Lady"; Harriet Lee's *The Errors of Innocence* (1786); Mary Wollstonecraft's *Mary: A Fiction* (1788); Anne Hughes's *Henry and Isabella* (1788); Charlotte Lennox's *Euphemia* (1790); and Charles Brockden Brown's *Ormond: or, The Secret Witness* (1799). The most revealing reflections of romantic friendship in eighteenth-century verse are the poems by the English writer, Anna Seward, to and about Honora Sneyd.

Romantic Friendship in the Nineteenth Century

The institution of romantic friendship continued to be socially acceptable through much of the nineteenth century, particularly in America and England, where women moved still further from men as both continued to develop their own, even more distinct, sets of values. In many poems and novels of the nineteenth century women often refer to each other in terms similar to Antonia's address to Lady Dunstane in George Meredith's novel *Diana of the Crossways* (1885): "My beloved! My only truly loved on earth" (cf. Henry Wadsworth Longfellow's *Kavanagh* [1849], Elizabeth Wetherell's *The Wide, Wide World* [1850], Louisa May Alcott's *Work: A Story of Experience* [1873], Oliver Wendell Holmes' *A Mortal Antipathy* [1885], Edith Arnold's *Platonics* [1894], Sarah Orne Jewett's short story "Martha's Lady" [1897], and the poetry of Katharine Bradley and Edith Cooper, who wrote together under the name Michael Field. See also the published letters, journals, and autobiographies of literary figures; for example, Margaret Fuller's journal, Edith Simcox's autobiography, Geraldine Jewsbury's letters to Jane Carlyle, Sarah Orne Jewett's letters to Annie Fields, Emily Dickinson's letters to Sue Gilbert). However, it was not until the end of the century, when many educational and work opportunities had become available to women, that fictional romantic friends were presented as shunning marriage and spending their entire lives together, as in Florence Converse's *Diana Victrix* (1897), although some earlier romantic friends are permitted to live together after they have married men and become widows, as in Louisa May Alcott's *Work*. Henry James, who called his 1886 novel *The Bostonians* (a book that many critics mistakenly see as anti-lesbian), "a very American tale," indicated the connection between new American womanhood (as a result of the feminist movement) and romantic friendship, which became more demanding as women became more autonomous.

Lesbian Exoticism and Lesbian Evil in the Nineteenth Century

Women's growing independence in the nineteenth century meant that romantic friendships, which previously might be seen as harmless to the fabric of society, since women must and would marry had they the opportunity, potentially became threatening to the status quo. The earliest and most violent response seems to have come from France. It is significant that with the first glimmerings of a feminist movement in France during the late 1820s and the 1830s, a new image of love between women appeared (primarily in novels by men) that had been largely absent from earlier literature. The image was that of an exotic, fascinating woman transvestite who, without conscience, claims for herself all manner of male privileges, including the possession of other women's bodies. One of the earliest examples of this image is in Henri de Latouche's *Fragoletta* (1829), about a woman who disguises herself as a man and seduces another woman. This was soon followed by Théophile Gautier's *Mademoiselle de Maupin* (1835) and Honoré de Balzac's *La fille aux yeux d'or* (*The Girl with the Golden Eyes,* 1833). The latter novel became a prototype for the image of the evil lesbian that was so popular in French literature by the end of the century. The androgynous Marquise de St. Réal of this novel buys a twelve-year-old girl, Paquita, from her mother and proceeds to do as she wishes with her, unhampered by the forces of social decency. After violating the girl's body for several years, she brutally murders her when she telepathically discovers that Paquita has been unfaithful with a man.

Subsequent French poets also treated lesbianism as exotic and invariably as unhappy. Charles Baudelaire, for example, in *Les fleurs du mal* (*The Flowers of Evil*, 1857) entitles two of his lesbian poems "Femmes damnées." In a third poem, "Lesbos," he observes that "manful" Sappho is conquered by Phaon and describes the "screams of torment" that rise from Lesbos at night. Paul Verlaine presents similar images in *Les amies: scènes d'amour sapphique* (*The Friends: Scenes of Sapphic Love*, 1867). In his poem "Sappho" the Greek poet is sick with her passion for Phaon, forgetful of the lesbian rites of her cult, and seeking refuge in death. In other poems as well women are tortured by their lesbianism, but Verlaine's attitude, like that of many other writers of this era, is ambivalent. Lesbianism is a twilight love and brings suffering, but it is also exotically lovely. In one poem he calls it "le glorieux stigmate." Later in the century Pierre Louÿs presented a similar ambivalence in his *Chansons de Bilitis* (*Songs of Bilitis*, 1894), in which lesbians are promiscuous, fickle, narcissistic, sado-masochistic, and childish—but they are also intriguing and beautiful. Through the influence of Gautier, Balzac, and Baudelaire, Algernon Swinburne brought such images to English literature, both in the novel *Lesbia Brandon* (1877, posthumous, 1952) and in poems such as "Anactoria" (1906) and "Hermaphroditus" (1863). These images are also present in German literature of the 1890s, particularly in Baroness von Puttkamer's poems, *Auf Kypros* (*On Cypress*, 1898) and in the 1890s poems of Peter Hille, which were posthumously published in 1904.

As the century progressed, so did the literary image of lesbian evil. This was due in part to the general fascination with decadence in the later nineteenth century. Perhaps it was also a reaction to women's growing independence throughout the nineteenth century. In addition, the emergence of the sexologists in the 1870s and 1880s helped cast a suspicious light on the romantic friendships that had earlier been almost universally considered so ennobling. Adolphe Belot's novel *Mademoiselle Giraud, ma femme* (*Miss Giraud, My Wife*, 1870), laughs at husbands who do not understand that intense affection between women is a sign of their corruption. The wife of this novel, Paule, is in emotional and sexual bondage to another woman, Berthe, and cannot free herself, even when she wishes to. Berthe is evil incarnate. She drives Paule to death, apparently through emotional and sexual excess. After Paule's death, Paule's husband manages to kill Berthe, making the murder look like an accident. Berthe's husband writes to him, understanding that he murdered Berthe: "I thank you in my name and in the name of all honest people, for having ridden us of this reptile." Lesbian decadence and corruption are also presented in Emile Zola's novel *Nana* (1880), Guy de Maupassant's short story "La femme de Paul" ("Paul's Mistress") from *La maison Tellier* (*The House of Tellier*, 1881), August Strindberg's autobiographical *Le plaidoyer d'un fou*, written in French (*Diary of a Madman*, 1887), Catulle Mendes' *Méphistophéla* (novel, 1890) and Joséphin Péladan's novel *La*

Gynandre (1891). The latter presents an attitude that was prevalent in the literature about lesbians in earlier centuries—that lesbians would prefer men given the opportunity. The male hero, Tammuz (named after the Babylonian equivalent of Dionysus), succeeds at the conclusion in matching all the salvageable lesbians with eligible bachelors, feeding them aphrodisiacs, lowering the lights, and thus converting them to the joys of marriage and motherhood.

There were relatively few such fiction works of lesbian corruption and disease in nineteenth-century England and America. Of those, the novella *Carmilla* (1872), by the Irish writer Joseph Sheridan Le Fanu, is especially notable because the lesbian of his story is literally a vampire. In many later works lesbians were seen as figurative vampires. George Moore in *A Drama in Muslin* (novel, 1886) presents a romantic friendship gone wrong, which he depicts with a pseudo-sophistication about such matters that was absent in earlier eras. Cecilia, the lover, is a physically deformed young woman whose anatomical twistedness mirrors her emotional twistedness. The "normal" object of her affection responds to Cecilia's passionate avowals, as romantic friends never did in earlier days, "Cecilia dear, you shouldn't talk to me like that; it is absurd. Indeed, I don't think it is quite right." It was not until the mid-1890s that similar negative views of love between women emerged in the United States, in works such as Mary Wilkins Freeman's short story, "The Long Arm" (1895) and Mary Hatch's *The Strange Disappearance of Eugene Comstock* (1895). The former is about a woman who kills the male suitor of her woman companion of forty years. The latter is about a transvestite lesbian villain who corrupts women, leads a band of robbers, and ends by killing herself.

The Twentieth Century

In America and to a lesser extent in England the institution of romantic friendship was not entirely dead by the early twentieth century, according to literature. There were numerous short stories about ennobling love between women that appeared in popular magazines such as *St. Nicholas, Ladies Home Journal, Strand, Century,* and *Harpers,* as well as occasional novels such as Josephine Dodge Daskam's *Smith College Stories* (1900), *The Story of Mary MacLane by Herself* (1902), and Clarissa Dixon's *Janet and her Dear Phebe* (1909). But the change that took place over the ensuing decades is reflected in a comparison of Mary MacLane's 1902 work in which she talks about loving another woman "with a peculiar and vivid intensity, and with all the sincerity and passion that is in me" and wishes only to live with her "anemone lady . . . in some little out-of-the-world place for the rest of my life," and her later work, *I, Mary MacLane: A Diary of Human Days* (1917), in which she declares that "to each other [lesbian] are . . . victims, preyers, masters, slaves," and admits that although "I have lightly kissed and been kissed by Lesbian lips, I am too personally fastidious . . . to walk in direct repellent roads of vice even in freest moods."

As the pseudo-scientific messages of the sexologists such as Krafft-Ebing,

Havelock Ellis, and later Sigmund Freud began to filter more and more into popular consciousness, and as women's continually increasing autonomy made relationships that were once necessarily secondary to women's lives now potentially primary, the positive view of love between women, as seen in society's attitude toward romantic friendship, came to be replaced almost entirely by literature that treated such love as either a medical problem or a vice. Feminism was blamed for the rise of lesbianism early in twentieth-century Germany. Maria Janitschek's heroine in *Mimikry: Ein Stück modernen Lebens* (*Mimicry: A Piece of Modern Life*, novel, 1903) complains that feminism has made women more like men and men more like women. Since women and men no longer complement each other, females have forgotten what they were supposed to look for in a mate. Woman now "finds in woman more what she needs than in man." However, in *Die neue Eva* (*The New Eve,* novel, 1906), Janitschek seems to regard lesbianism as did the predecessors of Freud such as Gley and Arduin, whose work she may have been familiar with through the *Jahrbuch für sexuelle Zwischenstufen* (1899–1923, ed. in 1983 by J. W. Schmidt). She presents the story of Seffi, whose lesbianism is "caused" by a faulty environment that encourages the homosexual side of her natural bisexuality to become dominant. In Aimée Duc's *Sind es Frauen?* (*Are These Women?* 1903), a novel that treats explicit lesbianism with relative sympathy, the blame for lesbianism is laid, as it was in the work of nineteenth-century sexologists, on deformed genes. The lesbians of this novel even call themselves "Krafft-Ebingers," and though they are clearly feminists, they believe they desire intellectual and physical freedom only because they are congenital inverts.

The most famous English novel that treats love between women as a matter of congenital inversion is Radclyffe Hall's *The Well of Loneliness* (1928). The main character, Stephen Gordon, is seen as a man trapped in a woman's body. She falls in love only with feminine women, who are not congenital inverts— and thus she is doomed to failure. When she discovers that her beloved Mary is attracted to a man, she sacrifices her own well-being and sends Mary off to marry him, remaining alone and lonely at the end of the novel. Hall was especially influenced by the theories of the sexologist Havelock Ellis, and it was he who wrote a brief preface to the novel.

Few English and American novels of this era were as sympathetic to lesbianism as Hall's, and despite her sympathy, even that work (by admitted design) serves as a cautionary tale, leading the reader to believe that lesbians see themselves as deformed and are doomed to loneliness. Many novels of the first half of the twentieth century, even those by women writers, present love between women as downright evil, and the lesbian as a vampire, including Clemence Dane's *Regiment of Women* (1925), Naomi Royde-Smith's *The Tortoiseshell Cat* (1925), Dorothy Sayer's *Unnatural Death* (1927), G. Sheila Donisthorpe's *Loveliest of Friends* (1931), Sinclair Lewis' *Ann Vickers* (1923), Francis Brett Young's *White Ladies* (1935), Dorothy Baker's *Trio* (1943), and Arthur Koestler's *Arrival and Departure* (1943). Where the lesbian is not evil in works of this period, she is sick, as in D. H. Lawrence's short story "The Fox" (1921), Naomi Royde-Smith's *The Island: A Love Story* (1930), and Djuna Barnes's *Nightwood* (1936); or she is laughable, as in Compton MacKenzie's *Extraordinary Women* (1928), Georgette Heyer's *Penhallow* (1942), and Mary Stewart's *Wildfire at Midnight* (1956).

Similar images may be found in twentieth-century French literature. In Edouard Bourdet's play *La prisonnière* (*The Captive*, 1926) a young woman tries unsuccessfully to escape from the clutches of an older woman seductress, but she is "fascinated," like the prey of a cobra, and cannot move to safety. The young woman tells her husband that she knows "the place I really belong is here against your shoulder," but when the older woman summons her, a year after marriage, she is helpless to resist. Françoise Mallet's novel *Le rempart des Béguines* (*The Illusionist*, 1957) presents another older woman seductress who is insanely sadistic and enjoys a "wicked delight" in wielding power over her fifteen-year-old victim. Such images are not present in the five insouciant Claudine novels (1900–1907) by Colette, but despite Claudine's numerous involvements with women, the center of her life is her husband, Renaud, and she never really rebels against her position as a wife. However, Colette also wrote a defense of lesbianism in *Ces plaisirs* (*The Pure and the Impure*, 1932) in which, among other things, she attacks Marcel Proust's picture of decadent lesbianism in *A la recherche du temps perdu* (*Remembrance of Things Past*, novels, 1913–1927). Colette observes that Proust endowed the lesbians of his Gomorrah "with shocking desires, customs and language, showing how little he knew her." Critics generally agree that in his depiction of Albertine, Proust was really writing about homosexual men. The life styles of gay men and lesbians in the late teens and the twenties of this century were not interchangeable, as Colette and other women writers of the period such as Natalie Barney point out in their criticism of Proust.

Several women writers of the twentieth century appear to have been quite influenced by the decadent images of lesbianism from French literature of the previous century and even to have internalized those images in their own lives. The most notable poet of this group, Renée Vivien, an Anglo-American who lived in Paris and wrote in French, was especially influenced by Baudelaire and Swinburne in her picture of the lesbian as a social outcast whose forbidden delights are generally outweighted by torments. This image of lesbian decadence seems to have survived well into the twentieth century, as is apparent even in a 1964 autobiographical novel by Violette Leduc, *La bâtarde* (*The Bastard*), in which she calls her erotic life with another woman "the sullies of my flesh." Similar views may be found in the work of the international writer Anaïs Nin. She explains in her prologue to *Ladders of Fire* (1946), in which a main character is a lesbian, "This novel deals with the negative pole, the pole of confused and twisted nature." In Nin's *House of Incest* (1936) the narrator declares to her woman lover, "I will let you carry me into the fecundity of destruction."

There were, however, a number of lesbians writing during the first half of the twentieth century who challenged such images. Natalie Barney, an American expatriate living in Paris, proclaimed the joy and fulfillment of lesbianism, both in her life and in her writing with works such as the novel *Actes et entr'actes (Acts and between Acts,* 1910). Another American expatriate in Paris, Gertrude Stein, also proclaimed the joys of lesbianism, but often in language so abstruse that most readers would have no idea to what she referred (e.g., "Didn't Nelly and Lilly Love You" [1922]). Edmund Wilson has suggested that Stein developed so hermetic a style to disguise her homosexual subject matter (Edmund Wilson, "Books," *The New Yorker,* 15 September 1951:124–31). The American poet Amy Lowell also presents love between women in very positive and romantic terms, but generally the reference to gender in her lesbian poems is so vague that the reader must peruse to understand that both the lover and the beloved are female.

Despite these few (often veiled) positive images, the predominant twentieth-century depiction of the lesbian in literature into the 1960s is aptly summed up in one of the myriad cheap paperback books that flooded the market in the 1950s and 1960s. The lesbian character in Ann Herbert's *Summer Camp* (1966) admits, "I am a genuine lesbian, truly twisted, and I know it."

Lesbian-Feminism in Literature

With the advent of the sexual revolution, the gay liberation movement, and the second wave of feminism, the image of the lesbian in literature began to change by the early 1970s. Lesbian-feminism, which sees lesbianism as a political act, a rejection of patriarchal values and an acceptance of "woman-identification," became a dominant motif in lesbian literature. The emergence of lesbian and feminist presses and their goal of publishing books by and for lesbians and feminists guaranteed that work which did not promulgate the view of lesbian as sickie or sinner would find an audience. Once several of the lesbian-feminist books proved to be commercially successful, a number of the larger "establishment" publishers were willing to accept books with more positive lesbian themes.

One of the earliest and by far the most popular of these lesbian-feminist works was the comic novel *Rubyfruit Jungle* (1973), by an American writer, Rita Mae Brown. Her character, Molly Bolt, a female picaro, is a crusader for justice, an avowed lesbian who is joyous in her lesbianism. She is depicted as being in every way a superior being. This was followed by other American novels in which the protagonist identifies herself as a lesbian-feminist and accepts her lesbianism happily—it is often one of her greatest strengths. The protagonist in many of these novels also grapples with universal problems such as coming of age (Elana Nachman's *Riverfinger Woman* [1974]) and growing old (June Arnold's *Sister Gin* [1975]), which are apart from her lesbian-feminism. The genre has expanded to include lesbian-feminist detective fiction such as Mary F. Beal's *Angel Dance* (1977) and lesbian-feminist gothics such as Victoria Ramstetter's *The Marquise and the Novice* (1981), in which lesbians are always the very admirable protagonists. In poetry also a number of recent authors have written about lesbianism explicitly and from very positive perspectives, including Adrienne Rich, Audre Lorde, and Olga Broumas. Although England, France, and Germany have not yet produced so large a body of lesbian-feminist literature, several notable works that openly celebrate lesbian-feminism have emerged from those countries, including Monique Wittig's prose poem *Le corps lesbien* (*The Lesbian Body,* 1973) and Verena Stefan's autobiographical *Häutungen* (*Shedding,* 1975).

See also: Feminism, Homosexuality, Sex, Vampire.

Selected Bibliography

Faderman, Lillian, *Surpassing the Love of Men: Romantic Friendship and Love Between Women from the Renaissance to the Present.* New York: Morrow, 1981.

Foster, Jeannette. *Sex Variant Women in Literature.* New York: Vantage Press, 1956.

Grier, Barbara. *The Lesbian in Literature.* 3d ed. Tallahassee, Fla.: Naiad Press, 1981.

Rule, Jane. *Lesbian Images.* Garden City, N.Y.: Doubleday, 1975.

LILLIAN FADERMAN

LIBERTINE

A person unfettered by moral or, especially, sexual restraints is defined as a "libertine." The term was also once used to refer to religious freethinkers or atheists, particularly in seventeenth-century France. Pascal decried them; Molière depicted them in his plays *Tartuffe* (1664) and *Dom Juan* (*Don Juan,* 1665). Sexual libertines are a predominant motif from earliest times to the present.

The Ancient Period: Origins

Since libertinism represents a major aspect of erotic love, no wonder the phenomenon should at all times have played such an important role in both Eastern and Western literatures. Many peoples have exalted the concept of eroticism, deities of physical love being found, for instance, in such disparate religions as Greco-Roman (Aphrodite-Venus and Eros-Cupido), Assyro-Babylonian (the Mesopotamian goddess Ishtar, whom the Arabs transformed into the god Athtar), and Hindu (the god Kamadeva and his wife Pleasure). If not as universal as the fecund Earth-Mother, they are indeed common. Glorification of physical sex characterizes much of Asiatic literature and art and permeates Arabic literature. The *Rubá'īyát* of Omar Khayyám (eleventh century A.D.) is strongly hedonistic. The Sanskrit poet Vālmīki's *Rāmāyaṇa* (c. 300 B.C.), inspiration for dance and art all over Southeast Asia, tells of the lecherous Rāvaṇa, kidnapper of Rāma's bride Sītā. The Greek gods and goddesses, so free with their sexual favors, were ruled by Zeus, a model Don Juan. Greek heroes like Theseus and Jason were hardly monogamous. Homer's epics, *Ilias* and *Odysseia* (*Iliad* and *Odyssey,* c. 8th century B.C.) and Hesiod's *Theogonia* (*Theogony,* poem, c. 8th century B.C.) are replete with tales of sexual inconstancy.

Callimachus of Cyrene's (c.305–240 B.C.) little epigram (No. 31, 32, or 33 in most editions) tells of Epicydes the Huntsman chasing prey only to lose interest once caught. How like the hunter am I, says the poet. The fun is all in the pursuit. An ode in the *Anakreontea (Anacreontea),* possibly by Anacreon himself (c. 570–476 B.C.) lists the poet's various amours. Alexander the Great and the degenerate Nero were merely more profligate than most, as Ovid's epic poem *Metamorphoses* (c. A.D. 2–17) makes abundantly clear. Ovid's whole life and works are a paean to hedonism. Catullus (c. 84–54 B.C.) was another Roman poet of the many who burned incense on the altar of love.

Saad Youssef has noted in "Don Juanism in Arabic Literature" (*Comparative Literature Studies* 13 [1976]) an early Don Juan in the Arab Heroic Age poet Imru'-al-Qays (died c. 550) and other similar figures such as 'Umar ibn Abī Rabī 'ah (644–712) and Abū Nuwās (c. 750–815) who spent most their lives pursuing pleasures of the flesh.

But evidence is available elsewhere than in secular literature. The Old Testament, from Adam and Eve's fall to the actions of the aged Solomon and the much later Hellenistic Song of Songs that celebrates the amorous life, to David and Bathsheba, Amnon and Tamar, Noah's children Shem, Ham, and Japheth, the shameless Jezebel and Rahab the Harlot gives ample testimony to the prevalence of biblical libertines, lechery, and adultery.

The Middle Ages

If Christianity strongly reproved sexual infidelity throughout medieval Europe, we may oppose the Japanese Lady Murasaki Shikibu's erotic tenth-century classic novel *Genji monogatari (The Tale of Genji)* about a historical prince. Even in the area of its own influence, the church could not prevent the many tales of immoral, libertine priests in Boccaccio's *Il decamerone (Decameron,* novellas, c. 1350) or Chaucer's *Shipman's Tale* in the *Canterbury Tales* (c. 1380–1400), wherein the priest protagonist is a prototypical Don Juan. Nor the verse fabliaux, short stories that often recount misdeeds of priests and monks. The *Liber lamentationum Matheoli* (1290) by the so-called Matheolus the Bigamist urges readers of his poem to seize not one woman but a hundred. Guillaume de Lorris' *Roman de la rose (Romance of the Rose,* didactic poem, c. 1230) lauds the dominance of love, and Jehan de Meung's continuation (c. 1275) reveals an almost dangerous libertinism, religious as well as erotic. Clearly, Christianity could at best only mitigate the exalting of physical love and even a tolerance for unchastity.

The Renaissance

The tradition begun with the earliest literatures and continuing down through the Middle Ages still strives. One thinks of the bawdy seventeenth-century (?) Chinese classic, *Chin P'ing Mei (The Golden Lotus),* which chronicles the amorous adventures of a twelfth-century lecher named Hsi-men Ch'ing. Spain presents a character like Rodolfo in Cervantes' "Fuerza de la sangre" ("The

Force of Blood''), one of his *Novelas ejemplares* (*Exemplary Novels,* 1613).
Italy affords many examples, such as Lorenzo Valla's *De professione religio-
sorum* (mid-fifteenth century), where the vow of chastity is subjected to ridicule,
or his *De voluptate* (*On Pleasure,* dialogue, 1433), advocating pleasure as the
goal of life. Among humanists he did not stand alone. Machiavelli writes an
erotic novella, *Belfagor* (first printed in 1549). In France there is Rabelais. The
motto ''Fay ce que vouldras'' (''Do what you will'') of his Abbaye de Thélème
in *Gargantua* (novel, 1534) has become almost legendary. Even the advice to
follow nature in Montaigne's *Essais* (*Essays,* 1580–1588) is often interpreted as
an argument against moral shackles.

The Seventeenth Century

John Fletcher's comedy *The Wild Goose Chase* (1621), whose lecherous hero
Mirabell keeps a list of his numerous female conquests, prefigures the many
immoral English Restoration plays soon to follow Cromwell's death in 1658.
Seducer-heroes frequently walk the stage of the great Spanish Golden-Age dramatists such as Lope de Vega's Leonido in *La fianza satisfecha* (*A Bond Honoured,*
c. 1614) and Calderón de la Barca's Ludovico in *El purgatorio de San Patricio*
(*The Purgatory of Saint Patrick,* c. 1628).

Equally Spanish is Miguel de Mañara (1626–1679). Though historical fact
seems inseparably entwined with legend, we know that he repented after a life
of sexual debauchery and died in the odor of sanctity. His nineteenth-century
rebirth as Juan de Mañara will be noted in due course. That such figures as
Mañara, Mateo Vázquez de Leca (1573–1649), the Conde de Villamediana (d.
1622), or Philip IV (1605–1665) actually existed in the Spain of their day as
models of libertinism, and undoubtedly, at least indirectly, influenced dramatic
characters, has some bearing when we chronicle the appearance of the seminal
play and the seminal libertine hero of all time, Don Juan Tenorio of Tirso de
Molina's *Burlador de Sevilla* (*The Libertine of Seville,* written c. 1618, published
1630).

Among half a dozen or so other plays by Tirso with similarly profligate heroes,
El burlador alone enjoys international repute, the only one to have created one
of the most famous characters in any literature. Along with Faust, Hamlet, Don
Quijote, possibly a few more, Don Juan remains supreme, incarnating a basic
human quality. Since the appearance of Tirso's *Burlador,* over 2,500 plays,
novels, poems both lyric and narrative, stories, motion pictures, operas, ballets,
and other works have used the name Don Juan and related various aspects of
his life, character, and ultimate punishment.

The plot of Tirso's drama bears retelling: Don Juan Tenorio, ''El burlador de
Sevilla'' (''The Trickster of Seville''), is a truly Renaissance figure, bursting
with the juices of life. Society cannot bring him to heel (he mocks its rules),
nor can a sense of filial piety (he taunts his own father), nor even loyalty to
crown or God (he fears neither). But by offending the god he does believe in,
he commits a fatal error. Frequently warned to repent his many seductions, he

answers with the haunting refrain, "¡Qué largo me lo fiáis!" ("[O God,] how long you trust me!"). He will repent in his old age, no longer able to sin. But God acts through the statue of the Comendador de Ulloa, a nobleman whom Don Juan had killed when surprised seducing his daughter. The seducer passes by the statue, recognizes it, mocks it, pulls its beard, and invites it to dinner. The stone figure actually appears and invites the seducer-murderer to sup with him in return. This the fearless Don Juan does, only to be seized and carried down to Hell. Thus the author, a monk himself, effects a Christian conclusion for this account of ultimate profligacy. Whence Tirso derived the Tenorio story has never been properly ascertained—from the embarrassment of choices already listed we may surmise that scholars possibly never will—but the odd details of the pulled beard and the invitations to dine come from folktales. The motifs of the dangers attendant upon insulting the dead and even the double invitation are frequently found in European literature then and long before. Tirso's contribution was to motivate the punishment by having it befall someone who had wronged the punisher, an evil man unarguably deserving of his fate.

An interesting sidelight upon this story is Gendarme de Bévotte's theory (*La légende de Don Juan*, 1911) that it cannot antedate the Spanish Renaissance, when the church still had power to condemn profligacy but secular man was now bold enough to defy its authority. If the theory is by its very nature unverifiable, though not untenable, Don Juan did first appear in that country, at that time.

The legend of Don Juan quickly spread to Italy. A 1625 version, possibly Tirso's, has been reported; and there are Giliberto's lost *Convitato di pietra* (1652) and a second play by a pseudo-Cicognini (probably before 1650) with the same title, among others. England saw Shadwell's drama *The Libertine* in 1676, a veritable orgy of Restoration sexual excesses. The legend soon appeared as well in the Netherlands, Germany, and Austria. Italians favored the commedia dell'arte format, emphasizing potentially farcical or burlesque elements: the comic servant, the statue, and soon, and it is through this interpretation that the legend, performed by strolling players, reached France, eventually to be immortalized in Molière's *Dom Juan*, the seducer now become a philosopher of vice and freethinking.

The Eighteenth Century

Don Juan's character underwent several changes at this time. For one, it became a folk and puppet theater staple, especially in Italy and Austria. There was also a London pantomime, *Don Juan, or The Libertine Destroyed*, staged in the late 1770s at the Drury Lane Theatre. Its popularity extended to the newly united states, playing Boston, New York, Washington, D.C., Baltimore, Philadelphia, and other cities, its first printing there (1792; in outline form only). The pantomime, with songs by William Reeve and music by Gluck, produced and possibly even written by David Garrick, appears from the outline to derive from Shadwell's *Libertine*. It remains of interest for having introduced Don Juan to the New World.

The Italian playwright Carlo Goldoni has left us *Don Giovanni Tenorio ossia il dissoluto* (1736); if not among his great dramas, it is intriguing on two counts: first, it purports to depict the true story of its author's cuckolding by his wife and leading man. Goldoni himself played the cuckold's part, his wife that of the faithless woman, and the leading man that of the seducer. Goldoni claimed that the seduction scene gave his wife the very words she used in betraying him, of which fact the audience had already been apprised. The author thus achieved a unique if masochistic revenge. The other point of interest lies in the play's ending. The rationalistic eighteenth century found rather incredible a statue's carrying the hero down to Hell. Goldoni substituted a more realistic denouement: Giovanni is struck by a fatal bolt of lightning—but on a clear day!

Don Juan inspired only one truly great work during the whole century, Mozart's *Don Giovanni* (1787), by many considered the finest of all operas. Lorenzo da Ponte's libretto must share some of that glory, though it owes details to several other eighteenth-century Italian Don Juan operas.

The century had other strings for its bow. The period of the French Regency, 1715–1723, was on the whole a time of loose morality. Regency roués were many; literature reflected the society that spawned them. Actually, all through the century a certain frivolousness has been noted. The fabled Italian Giacomo Casanova, today almost synonymous with Don Juan himself, is typical of his era. His sexual exploits are piquantly related in his *Histoire de ma vie* (*History of My Life*, 1798). A certain story has it that when Casanova first saw the Mozart-Da Ponte opera, he thought that his good friend the librettist had used him as the model. Since Da Ponte himself was a libertine, the story tells us more than a little about both of them and their times as well. Incidentally, another synonym for libertine is Lothario, "the haughty, gallant, gay Lothario" of Nicholas Rowe's tragedy *The Fair Penitent* (1703), adapted by Samuel Richardson into his novel *Clarissa Harlowe* (1748), Lothario becoming the equally famous Lovelace. In its newer avatar the character occurs in some dozen or more imitations (plays, stories, operas, novels) based on it, all in France, from 1783 to 1898.

The eighteenth century was basically a rather frank age. Delicately, tastefully described sex was judged a quite suitable subject for art and literature both. Even the Reverend John Cleland's *Memoirs of a Woman of Pleasure* (sometimes called *Fanny Hill*, 1749), a frankly pornographic novel, portrayed life in a brothel with taste, verve, and considerable style. It deserves the vogue it still enjoys. Something else is the Marquis de Sade's novels, *Justine* (1791; expanded version, 1797), *Juliette* (1797), and especially *Les 120 journées de Sodome* (*The 120 Days of Sodom*, unpublished until 1904, but probably composed in 1785), in which every sexual excess and perversion is catalogued to the point of satiety and eventual burlesque. The evil French lords of the castle where these perversions are carried out are libertines in the truest sense of the word, but restraints normal to the age are quite absent. It might be noted in passing that the Don

Juan theme as a whole even unto our own day has remained relatively free from pornography. Occasional eroticism is its normal limit, even if the same cannot always be said of libertinism in general.

We now come to the century's finest example of the novel of seduction, a masterpiece for any age, Choderlos de Laclos' *Les liaisons dangereuses* (*Dangerous Acquaintances,* 1782). Remarkable for its psychological insight (something the French novel has long considered its special province), it tells of an utterly depraved, cold-blooded seducer, acting almost entirely for the pleasure of domination.

The Nineteenth Century

In a way the nineteenth was the golden age for libertine and seduction literature. Some have argued that repressive English Victorian mores represented the official stance of the time, even for Europe, but that the unofficial outlook, however clandestinely, favored libertinage, hence the prevalence in literature of works depicting what society refused openly to countenance. Whatever the truth of this contention, the age was rich in themes of seduction and kindred subjects. As well, the Don Juan legend took on new vigor, the terrain widening in Western literature to embrace the Americas. Plays and novels concerning professional pleasure seekers—"dandies," *viveurs,* and *viveuses* ("high livers," "swingers," male and female), "lions" (a term referring to rather animalistic male and female sexual proclivities), "libertines," "circes," "sirens," révoltées (women who have cast off moral shackles)—are common throughout the century, especially after 1850, as seen from the titles of a hundred and more examples published or staged in New York, London, Berlin, Madrid, and many other cities, but above all in Paris. The nature of the seducer predictably reflects the theories of morality and literature alike prevalent at the moment. Just as the early Don Juan, for instance, in the orthodox Spain of his day, was a believer, a seventeenth-century skeptic and philosopher with Molière, a feckless courtier in the eighteenth, he is a romanticist, a realist, eventually a social victim in the nineteenth, and will emerge in the present century cuckold or homosexual—a chameleon mirroring the beliefs and prejudices of the times and authors that depict him.

Of all the changes rung by time, the advent of romanticism has probably effected the greatest modification in the concept of the seducer. The romanticist is, above all, a seeker of ideal love. Such perfection being rare, he must go from woman to woman, affair to affair, ever questing, seldom finding. Byron's long, unfinished epic poem *Don Juan* (1819–1824) depicts just such a hero, somewhat fickle but basically good, whose amorous adventures carry him from Spain to Turkey, Russia, and finally England. If he becomes as cynical in the later cantos as he was innocent at the start, he is never evil, and never intended for an afterlife in Hell. He is, of course, the typical Byronic hero, Byron himself, whose concept of love allowed for immense latitude. In its many philosophical asides, the poem also hints at another aspect of so many later nineteenth-century Don Juans. These heroes endlessly rationalize their behavior; donjuanism has become a philosophy. Byron's poem started another vogue as well, that is, continuations and imitations of his epic; in all some hundred are known.

Romanticism has also given us the seminal short story about the new Don Juan, the German writer E.T.A. Hoffmann's "Don Juan" (1813), which already embodies the romantic concept of seeker of ideals. It is widely acclaimed for leading Don Juan in new directions, though arguably if Hoffmann had not written his story, some other author would have. Don Juan was almost predestined to personify the romantics' ideal.

Prosper Mérimée, French master of the novella, wrote another, almost equally seminal work, *Les âmes du purgatoire* (*Souls in Purgatory*, 1834). Far from his best works, such as *Carmen* (1845) or *Mateo Falcone* (1829), its principal virtue remains its combining the legend of Miguel de Mañara (mentioned before and now become that of Juan de Mañara; Mérimée metathesizes the name into Maraña) with that of Juan Tenorio. The vile seducer, finally seeing the error of his ways, will repent, become a monk, and achieve salvation. The romantics liked this concept. Not only is salvation for the truly repentant good Catholic dogma, but it is being offered to those who are not really sinners but rather idealists. Such men, they felt, surely do not deserve eternal damnation. Mérimée's story was taken up by Alexandre Dumas *père* in an extravagant romantic French drama called *Don Juan de Maraña* (1836). Finally, the new Don Juan was immortalized in José Zorrilla's drama *Don Juan Tenorio* (1844). The story is more or less Tirso's, but with admixtures of Dumas-Mérimée. Don Juan is saved for Heaven. The poetry is lofty; actors relish playing the part of Don Juan. The religious message is reassuring to seducers, which may partly explain why the drama has become improbably popular, performed all over the Spanish-speaking world as a sort of miracle play each year on or around November 1, All Souls's Day. Guilty of romantic excesses, it is saved for most viewers and critics by the emotional grandeur of its conception.

We must at least mention a few others of the century's Don Juan works, such as Christian Grabbe's German play *Don Juan und Faust* (1829), one of several versions to attempt a fusion of two famous characters, and the Austro-Hungarian Nikolaus Lenau's dramatic poem *Don Juan* (1844), inspiration for Richard Strauss's still popular tone poem *Don Juan* (1887–1888). Let us add that the romantic tendency to forgive Don Juan's amorous sins is challenged by the new literary theorists of realism. Now he will be shown unhappily married, or an aging failure, or rivaled by a son in actions he has come to consider wrong but remains powerless to prevent in his own offspring, or, finally—an Ibsenian touch—the cause of his son's diseased heredity.

Other libertines are almost Don Juan's clones. Don Félix de Montemar is Don Juan in all but name, in Espronceda's *El estudiante de Salamanca* (*The Student of Salamanca*, 1839–1840), probably the finest of all Spanish narrative romantic poems. The story reflects part of the old Mañara legend, that of the man witnessing his own funeral. Espronceda condemns Montemar, carried to Hell in a version of the Dance of Death.

Flaubert's novel *Madame Bovary* (1856) describes, in the heroine Emma, the folly of the romantic quest for ideal love, and, in Rodolphe, a thoroughly despicable Don Juan. Still another French writer, Pierre Louÿs, combines a new vision of Hellenic beauty with a pandering to hedonism and licentiousness in such novels as *Aphrodite* (1896). The notorious Austrian novelist Leopold von Sacher-Masoch (1836–1895), like the Marquis de Sade before him, was to lend his name to a form of sexual abnormality. The curious are referred to his *Venus im Pelz* (*Venus in Furs,* 1870). The anonymous *My Secret Life* (London, 1888), the endless autobiography of a lecher, has become a sort of déclassé classic. By now we are deep into the territory of uncontested pornography, another facet of the concept of libertinism.

The Twentieth Century

Our current age is again rich in libertine protagonists. With our growing emphasis on the woman's point of view and women's rights, it should come as no surprise to find Bernard Shaw's comedy *Man and Superman* (1903) showing his John Tanner (i.e., Juan Tenorio) victim of a woman's wiles, led by the nose into marriage, overcome by the invincible feminine procreative force. With Freudian psychology and its several successors enjoying strong public acceptance, we should also understand Don Juan analyzed as a neurotic and, especially, as a crypto-homosexual. If he can find no truly lovable woman, it is because subconsciously he seeks male companionship. Lenormand's *L'homme et ses fantômes* (play, 1924) depicts such a Don Juan. And with the modern conviction that there are no longer true heroes, real winners, we should appreciate Edmond Rostand's dramatic poem *La dernière nuit de Don Juan* (*Don Juan's Last Night,* 1921), wherein the "hero" learns that women have always mocked his advances, never really loved him. He is finally reduced to playing the seducer as a mere stage puppet. The drama, like so many modern works, reprises older literature. Incidents recall Tirso, Molière, and others; our enjoyment is sadly dulled if we are unaware of details from the Don Juan canon.

Even Spain, clinging more closely to the ideal of the traditional Don Juan than most other countries—it has been said that every Spaniard at heart longs to play the role of Don Juan—can show us a seducer like Valle-Inclán's Marqués de Bradomín, hero of his novel sequence, the *Sonatas* (1902–1905), a Don Juan "feo, católico y sentimental" ("ugly, Catholic, and sentimental"), in his old age powerless to effect an amorous conquest. Other modern Spanish writers still see Don Juan more traditionally, for instance the philosopher Ortega y Gasset (1883–1955) in his many essays, but Miguel de Unamuno (1864–1936) makes him a sexual criminal.

The Mexican novelist Carlos Fuentes has recently portrayed Don Juan in *Terra nostra* (1975), fusing the fictional character Juan with John the Baptist. Even more incredibly, Cuban novelist Guillermo Cabrera Infante concludes his *La Habana para un infante difunto* (1979) with Don Juan's crawling up inside his current amour's womb. Has not Freud told us that man's natural desire is to return to the place of his origin? Other Latin American nations, the United States, and Canada have seen lyric poetry, novels, plays, a bit of everything, traditional and innovative in turn, devoted to Don Juan.

The silver screen throughout the Western world has been a fertile field for depictions of libertines in general and Don Juan in particular. Over fifty Don Juan films, mainly with more or less traditional scripts, have been shot since 1906, many by prominent writers, with actors like John Barrymore and Errol Flynn playing the leads. William Faulkner tried his hand at one; Ingmar Bergman directed *Djävulens öga* (*The Devil's Eye*) in 1960. Included in the count of fifty are screen versions of Mozart's opera and the Molière and Zorrilla plays.

Frank Harris' *My Life and Loves* (1922–1927) across the Atlantic, and on this side, Henry Miller's various controversial autobiographical novels such as *Tropic of Cancer* (1934) and the *Rosy Crucifixion* trilogy (1949–1960) laud the sexually free life. Anaïs Nin has essayed frankly pornographic tales (e.g., *Delta of Venus*, c. 1940–1941), supposedly written on demand for a rich aficionado; some of the characters are not only libertines but actually called "Don Juans." Then there is Pauline Réage's *L'histoire d'O* (*The Story of O*, 1954), the scandalous pornographic bondage novel that preaches a quite Sadean view of complete sexual freedom for men, though not for women.

These samples represent twenty-five centuries of worship at the shrine of sexuality. In general they give man the right to freedom, but not woman. Women must preserve the sanctity of home and marriage, while to men is granted the boon of infidelity. Until very recently, the chauvinistic Don Juan theme appealed little to women writers. Honors for conceiving the first important, full-fledged version by a woman (George Sand had already devoted chapter 11 of her 1833 novel *Lélia* to Don Juan, and there were other tentative, rather inept works later in the nineteenth and in the early twentieth centuries) should probably go to the Ukrainian Lesya Ukrainka for her 1912 play *Kamenny hospodar*. A fair number of other examples followed, for example, Suzanne Lilar's play *Le Burlador* (1943). To be sure, there are depictions of female libertines, most notably Flaubert's *Madame Bovary*. We could add Anatole France's novel *Thaïs* (1890) and Somerset Maugham's well-known short story "Rain" (1921; very successfully dramatized by other hands; also the subject of a motion picture). We might think, as well, of historical figures such as the nymphomaniacal Catherine the Great, Empress of Russia (1729–1796). They remain in the minority, in any case, and perhaps more significantly, have seemed to writers, and public too, much less forgivable than their male counterparts.

See also: Seduction, Sex.

Selected Bibliography

Mandel, Oscar, ed. *The Theatre of Don Juan: A Collection of Plays and Views, 1630–1963*. Lincoln: University of Nebraska Press, 1963.

Singer, Armand E. *The Don Juan Theme, Versions and Criticism: A Bibliography.*
    Morgantown: West Virginia University, 1965. Supplements, *West Virginia University Philological Papers* 15 (1966), 17 (1970), 20 (1973), 22 (1975), and 26 (1980).
Weinstein, Leo. *The Metamorphoses of Don Juan.* 1959. New York: AMS Press, 1978.
Wittmann, Brigitte, ed. *Don Juan: Darstellung und Deutung.* Darmstadt: Wissenschaft-liche Buchgesellschaft, 1976.

ARMAND E. SINGER

LIEBESTOD

The term *Liebestod* was probably coined by Richard Wagner for his opera *Tristan und Isolde* (*Tristan and Isolde,* 1865), where it occurs in act 2, scene 2. Literally: death-in-love, love-in-death, or love's death *(Liebes-Tod).* As distinct from the English love-death, or French *mort d'amour,* which mean death as a result of (usually unhappy) love, *Liebestod* refers to a situation involving *mutual* love and expresses in one word the idea that *both* lovers prefer union in death to separation in life.

Wagner's opera ends with the practically simultaneous voluntary death of Tristan and Isolde, whose allegiance seems impossible in life and who believe that only in the sweet eternal night of death their love can find its ultimate consummation and fulfillment. Their death is the expression of an extraordinary mutual attachment and functions as the demonstration par excellence of perfect love. By extension, *Liebestod* is used to characterize all plots or plot segments in which both protagonists die as a result of an uncontrollable mutual passion and in this manner achieve exemplary status as ideal lovers.

The pattern involves obstacles preventing the lovers' permanent union, secrecy and deception, transgressions of human and divine laws for the sake of love, and a hostile fate representing reality's revenge of the ideal. In antiquity, the Middle Ages, and the Renaissance the *Liebestod* often follows upon a fatal accident or error of judgment; in the modern period the lovers frequently act upon an avowed death-wish, so that there is no fatal mistake. What distinguishes the *Liebestod* plot in its purest form from other stories of obstructed love is the fixity of the obstacle and the death of both lovers in direct connection with their passion. The suicides can be active or passive, the lovers' deaths physical, emotional, spiritual, or mental. As a rule, the lovers are idealized, each other's perfect match, and the female protagonist has a decisive part in the action. Like other motifs, the pattern is capable of concretization in numerous ways and allows for a wealth of possibilities with regard to characterization, social setting, obstacles, and incidents leading to intrigue and disaster. Certain thematic particularities, however, are constant, embedded in the very sequence of events; passionate love incapable of compromise and therefore in antagonism with society and life, the ideal versus the real.

Humanity's unceasing fascination with *Liebestod* is attested throughout world literature, reflected in numerous folktales: in the stories of the Greek Ceyx and Alcyone, the Scandinavian Hagbard and Sygny, the Irish Deirdre and Noise, Diarmait and Graine, the Persian Khosrow and Shirin, the Japanese Osome and Hisamatsu, the Indian Hir and Ranjhan (protagonists of a legend popular in Punjab), and many others. In Western literature, the *Liebestod* pattern has generated a number of themes with vital traditions, the most persistent of which are the legends of Pyramus and Thisbe, Hero and Leander, Tristan and Isolde, Paolo and Francesca, and Romeo and Juliet, all quintessential *Liebestod* tales. To reassert the validity and continuous appeal of the theme, authors may link it with a tradition and recount the history of unfortunate lovers whose individual characteristics and social and geographical context are given in earlier oral or written versions. Others retain of the classical examples only the basic narrative components to create original characters and new stories frequently set in their own time and milieu. Often the central impediment is inspired by contemporary taboos or codes regulating relations between the sexes: differences in age or class, race or religion. Marriage to a third party is but one among a number of possible obstacles. In almost all earlier instances of *Liebestod,* the agents of the obstacle (parents, spouse, priest, etc.) are figures of authority who represent order and society, moral and religious laws that prove cogent and fatal; the protagonists' conflict with the norms of the community lies at the heart of the tragic action. In the modern period, especially under the influence of Wagner's opera, Freud, and psychoanalysis, the obstacle may be wholly interiorized and need not be socially determined. The question whether fate, society, or the lovers themselves are to blame for the tragic denouement provides a key to each individual treatment. A diachronic account of the most representative examples of *Liebestod* in Western literature reflects attitudes to love and suicide characteristic of each period.

Antiquity

The ancient Greeks and Romans generally rejected voluntary death as a severe fault (Pythagoras, 6th century B.C.), an impious usurpation of the rights of the gods (Plato, c. 429–347B.C.), a cause of impurity of the soul (Plotinus, 3d century A.D.), or an objectionable passionate excess. Only the Stoics thought favorably of suicide, but not if it caused harm to family or society. Yet desperate lovers met with some sympathy, especially those like Alcestis and Achilles, who laid down their lives for the beloved. Plato, in his dialogues, admired the valor that springs from love and held that to die following the lover's death is especially pleasing to the gods *Phaidōn* [*Phaedo,* n.d.] 68A, *Phaidros* [*Phaedrus,* n.d.] 265A ff., *Symposion* [*Symposium,* c. 384 B.C.] 179 ff.). Passionate romantic infatuation, however, was mostly looked upon as a kind of disease or madness.

The oldest literary rendition of *Liebestod* preserved in the West, the verse tale of Pyramus and Thisbe by Ovid (*Metamorphoses* 4.55–167, c. A.D. 2–17), is neither romantic nor tragic. Ovid has no real appreciation for his lovers' predicament. He laces the tale with playful irony, melodramatic cues, and erotic sous-entendres, which deflate their pure aspirations. The social obstacle, parental prohibition, lacks motivation and is mocked in the labored discourses through the chink in the wall, its physical correlative. The lion's mangling of Thisbe's veil having occasioned frantic Pyramus' "fatal mistake," the *Liebestod* indeed proves the intensity of the children's feelings but also their immaturity, blind impetuosity, and foolish romantic notions. There is no triumph in the unification of their ashes in one urn. Ovid's more sympathetic epistolary treatment of the Hero and Leander legend (*Heroides* 18–19, n.d.) focuses on the lovers' longing and fears and develops the tragic opposition between passion and prudence, *amare* and *bene velle,* but does not glorify the passion or the implied *Liebestod.* Nor does the Christian Neoplatonist poet Musaeus make any attempt to sublimate the passion or spiritualize the lesson of the tragedy. The protagonists of his small epic poem *Hērō kai Leandron* (*Hero and Leander,* 5th century) are victims of a delusion that obliterates their sense of responsibility and duty (Hero is a priestess). Leander's death in the waves followed by Hero's fall from her tower are presented as the deserved destiny of maddened love. The poet's sober account of the private wedding, held in secret and sanctioned only by Eros, betrays strong moral reservations. Musaeus deplores the lovers' beguilement but treats them with respect and compassion nevertheless.

The Middle Ages

Early Christian thought was not as radically hostile to suicide as were the ancients, but St. Augustine in *De civitate Dei* (*The City of God,* treatise, 413–426) categorically condemned voluntary death, and medieval penal law judged suicide severely as a sin and a moral wrong. Under the influence of the great love stories of antiquity and increasingly refined mores, however, suicide for love gained acceptance in courtly society and literature along with the idea that loyal love must go as far as death.

The classic *Liebestod* tale of the period is that of Tristan and Isolde, which appeared in numerous versions throughout Europe from the beginning of the twelfth century onward. In the poems of the Anglo-Norman Thomas (c. 1160) and the German Gottfried von Strassburg (c. 1210) romantic passion is glorified as an ennobling and purifying force, a source of virtue, and a supreme good worthy of complete devotion. The lovers are models of constancy and, at the end, martyrs for love. For the first time, the romantic conflict between passion and society is fully developed and the impediment amply motivated. The love philtre, organizing symbol of the tale, excuses the destructive and immoral aspects of the adulterous love and accounts for the strength of the bond at the same time as it illustrates the magical and mystical quality of the relationship. Impelled by never-ending longing, Tristan and Isolde flout society embodied in the person of Isolde's husband Mark, king of Cornwall, yet cannot conceive of a life together outside their social world and try to reconcile one with the other, lying and cheating to achieve this aim. Their *Liebestod,* ultimate evidence of their loyalty, is precipitated by the action of hostile winds delaying Isolde's arrival. In Thomas' version the hero's "fatal mistake" results from a lack of faith in his beloved, and hence the catastrophe has a psychological as well as an external cause. There is no violent suicide here, no conscious attempt to die, but rather a sudden cessation of life following the disappearance (real or imagined) of the other's love. Love is the principal inspiring force of life, the sole source of spiritual development, emotional growth, and personal fulfillment. The *Liebestod* tales of Thomas and Gottfried elevate romantic love to a position it had never held in the West before.

The Renaissance

For medieval readers the philtre was perhaps a necessary device to account for the inordinate passionate attachment of Tristan and Isolde, who sinned against the basic Christian teachings of moderation, restraint of the flesh, and the individual's submission to the will of God, the church, and the community, but in the humanist Renaissance fatal passion had gained sufficient acceptance in the European mind to be treated seriously and realistically. It no longer needed a supernatural justification. The *Liebestod* theme occurs frequently in the literature of this period and figures prominently in the plays of Shakespeare, who treats it comically in the burlesque Pyramus and Thisbe interlude of *A Midsummer Night's Dream* (c. 1595) and with tragic seriousness in *Romeo and Juliet* (c. 1596) and *Antony and Cleopatra* (c. 1607), where he examines the nature of passion in relation to other manifestations of the irrational in human conduct: wild flights of fancy and sentiment unchecked by reason; pride, hate, and greed; lust for power and control. In *A Midsummer Night's Dream* the *Liebestod* of Pyramus and Thisbe, acted out by simple artisans ignorant of the courtly conventions on which the playlet draws, crowns the reductio ad absurdum of Shakespeare's deliberate, systematic parody of every component of the *Liebestod* pattern. His serious treatment of the theme in *Romeo and Juliet,* by contrast, strikes a delicate balance between fate and personal responsibility, outer and inner necessity, sympathy and censure. Linking the uncontrollable passion of the two children with the irrepressible and sociably disruptive mutual hatred of the parents, Shakespeare explores their common source and shows the destructive effects of a rigid sense of honor and of a loyalty disrespectful of the demands of reality. The lovers are victims of chance and only in part of their environment, and could have avoided their untimely death. It is their very refusal and inability to submit to the will of their elders and the dictates of reason, however, that enables the love of Romeo and Juliet to reach the heights of ecstasy and emotional intensity in which alone the beauty and richness of life can be experienced to the full. By the moral standards of the play their intransigeance is objectionable, but Shakespeare does not condemn their idealism and in his compassionate poetic rendering of their suffering, frustration, and exaltation, pays tribute to the tragic reality of pure aspirations. The *Liebestod* is not a mere symbolic representation of the inevitable shortlivedness of youthful passion but a powerful enactment of life cruelly turning against its own most vital and endearing qualities. At the end of *Romeo and Juliet,* a sense of loss and admiration undercuts the contentment with order restored.

Romanticism and the Nineteenth Century

The Age of Reason and neoclassicism, though sensitive to the grandeur of the love myths of antiquity, ostensibly had little use for the emotional paroxysms of rebellious lovers who, to avoid separation, opt for a common death. The only legendary *Liebestod* theme that enjoyed some popularity in this period is that of Pyramus and Thisbe, which was treated almost exclusively comically.

With the advent of romanticism, however, there emerges a new attitude to voluntary death and a different kind of passion that is less marked by primal appetites than by softness and sublimity. A secret malaise of the soul, *taedium vitae* and *mal de vivre*, legitimizes suicide as a sensitive and logical act, enabling the soul's flight from the deadening spiritual miasma of society to purer spheres. *Liebestod,* immensely popular with the romantics, often becomes a conscious choice motivated by the insatiable aspirations of passion itself. The hero and Doña Sol in Victor Hugo's drama *Hernani* (1830) both take poison and confidently await their entrance into a better world where they will be forever together. In Wagner's opera the love that binds the protagonists is a common longing for liberation from the limitations and false truths of life. In *Axël* (drama, 1890) by Villiers de l'Isle-Adam, the lovers eagerly depart to the celestial regions of death to prevent physical desire and consummation from tainting the purity of their attachment.

Not only the romantics but the realists and naturalists as well often used the double death for love, which occurs throughout the late eighteenth and nineteenth centuries as a simple motif or a major theme in numerous works and in all genres: for example, in Schiller's *Kabale und Liebe* (*Love and Intrigue,* drama, 1784), Goethe's novel *Die Wahlverwandtschaften* (*Elective Affinities,* 1809), Kleist's novella *Verlobung in Santo Domingo* (*The Engagement in Santo Domingo,* 1811), Grillparzer's drama *Des Meeres und der Liebe Wellen* (*Hero and Leander,* 1829), Stendhal's novel *Le rouge et le noir* (*The Red and the Black,* 1830), Soumet's opera *Norma* (1831), Dumas' *Antony* (play, 1831), Sand's *Indiana* (novel, 1832), Vigny's drama *Chatterton* (1835), Hugo's *Hernani* and *Ruy Blas* (1838), Gottfried Keller's novelle *Romeo und Julia auf dem Dorfe* (*The Village Romeo and Juliet,* 1856), Zola's tale "Simplice" (1864), Maeterlinck's play *Pelléas et Mélisande* (*Pelleas and Melisande,* 1892), Hardy's novel *Jude the Obscure* (1896), and, besides Wagner's opera, many interpretations of the Tristan and Isolde theme, which experiences a glorious revival. When the death-wish is clearly expressed or an integral part of the lovers' psyche and ideal of love, the obstacle is usually nominal, as in Wagner's *Tristan,* or altogether nonexistent, as in Zola's fairy tale "Simplice." Treatments of the theme concerned with realism and social comment, on the other hand, rely on class distinctions and material circumstances and inequities to account for love's defeat and to justify the lovers' self-immolation.

The Twentieth Century

In the twentieth century these two orientations—the philosophical and psychological, which focuses on thoughts and emotions not necessarily dependent upon external circumstances; and the realist/naturalist approach, which shows love and human potential for happiness thwarted by narrow moral norms, political oppression, or the materialistic values of bourgeois society—continue, incorporating social, moral, and aesthetic preoccupations of our time. Marianne Helldegen, the female protagonist of Hans Erich Nossack's *Liebestod* novel *Spätestens im November* (*No Later than November,* 1955), is comfortably married to a prominent German industrialist. A brief encounter with the prize-winning author Berthold Möncken (little monk), who instantly recognizes in her a kindred soul and potential *Liebestod* partner, reveals to her the complete emptiness of her existence. She leaves her husband and child to live with Möncken in his cell, a cheap, bare room with no space for privacy, where he continues to concentrate entirely on his work and where Marianne feels like a useless intruder. Their cohabitation soon becomes unbearable, and Marianne returns home. Yet, though they do not communicate with each other, the link remains strong, and when Möncken completes his play—on Paolo and Francesca—and after the première walks into her house, Marianne is ready to leave with him. Knowing that their life together will never be satisfying, an endless succession of reunions and separations, yet unable to relinquish the tie or what it represents to them, they joyously meet their death in a deliberate car crash. Interestingly, the entire story is narrated by Marianne herself after she and Möncken have been killed. Edith Wharton's Mattie Silver and her middle-aged New England lover in *Ethan Frome* (novel, 1911) meet a fate far worse than death. They emerge crippled and debilitated from the sled accident that should have killed them and depend for the rest of their life on Ethan's sour wife. Held back by an unduly strict sense of duty to the wife who has never given him affection, Ethan can neither seize on his last chance for happiness and elope with Mattie, nor muster enough courage to steer the sled straight into a tree and die. Albert Camus' guilt-ridden terrorists Dora and Kaliayev in *Les justes* (*The Just Assassins*, drama, 1950) believe that in a world full of injustice and suffering they have no right to love each other and be happy. They adhere to a revolutionary doctrine that requires that each successful attack be paid for with the life of the responsible terrorist. Yet their moral scruples and political zeal seem almost a rationalization of a deep-seated, unavowed longing for death, and the death penalty indeed brings welcome relief. Maggie in Arthur Miller's play *After the Fall* (1964), where the *Liebestod* is but an ancillary motif, wants to commit the suicide that "kills two," because she cannot accept in herself and her lover the evil and guilt that the horrors of Nazi Germany and of McCarthy's witch hunt in America have shown to be irredeemably part even of Western civilized man.

A third orientation is represented by Jean Anouilh's play *Roméo et Jeannette* (*Romeo and Jeannette,* 1945), a sardonic parody of the legend immortalized by Shakespeare. Anouilh ridicules the stupidity of irrational romantic love and presents death-seeking passion as absurd.

Liebestod in Nonwestern Literatures

In Arabic literature the double death for love is relatively rare, though several instances occur in that inexhaustible treasury of folktales *Alf Layla wa-layla* (*The Arabian Nights,* 8th to 17th centuries): in the story of Ali Ben Beccar and Caliph Haroun Alraschid's favorite, Shemsennehar (*Nights* 153–169), on which Goethe drew for his *Elective Affinities; The Lovers of the Benou Tai (Nights* 410–411); *Otbeh and Reyya (Nights* 680–681); and two tales about lovers of the Benou Udreh *(Nights* 383–384; 689–691), the second story being a variation on the Pyramus and Thisbe theme. 'Udhrī love poetry and love tales (Ummayad period, A.D. 661–750) have much in common with Western stories of fatal love; the Ummayad love story is anti-social, a criticism of social norms, and an expression of a longing for individual freedom, but this rejection of society is only partial. As in Western *Liebestod* stories, there is no radical attempt to eliminate the obstacle by killing the adversary, by eloping, or by the girl's refusal to marry someone else. As opposed to the heroines of the Western *Liebestod* tradition, however, the Arabian beloved is mostly passive, accepting love, and suffering for it, but not acting.

In Japan, by contrast, *Liebestod* has been a familiar occurence not only in literature but also in life, especially during the brilliant flowering of Japanese culture in the Genroku era (1680–1703), which produced a large number of plays based on actual love suicides. In the gay quarters of Osaka, Kyoto, and other large cities, townsmen of the merchant class *(chōnin)* could mingle freely with members of other classes and find the romance and excitement unavailable at home. Not infrequently, a townsman would fall in love with a prostitute and, if he desired to live with her, faced conflicting material obligations to his family and to the proprietor of the girl, who had to be ransomed. Inflicting burns and wounds, cutting off fingers, or pulling out nails were prevalent methods by which lovers demonstrated to each other the strength of their love. When the lovers saw no hope for a permanent union, they might perform the supreme act of "sincerity" and commit suicide together. Such love suicides are called *shinjū* (literally sincerity of the heart). The practice was modeled on the *Samurai* tradition of disemboweling oneself when one failed to meet some obligation or showed disagreement with authority. By the end of the seventeenth century, *shinjū* had become amongst the townsmen something of an institution. Love suicides were greeted as the most exciting news of the day and described in full detail in scandal sheets, with particular attention to the conflict of obligations, the weapons used, the contents of suicide notes, and so on. (*Shinjū okagami*

(*The Great Mirror of Shinjū*, 1704) suggests the prevalence of the practice, discussing seventeen recent cases.

Capitalizing on this popular interest, Chikamatsu Monzaemon (1653–1725) wrote some fifteen *Liebestod* dramas, many of them based on fact and written and performed but a few days after the love suicides had happened. Most important are his domestic plays *Sonezaki shinjū* (*The Love Suicides at Sonesaki*, 1703), *Shinjū Mannensō* (*The Love Suicides at the Women's Temple*, 1708), and *Shinjū ten no Amijima* (*The Love Suicides at Amijima*, 1720). Chikamatsu shows courtesans of low rank capable of true feelings and sacrifice, introduces as a high point in the plays a poetic description of the lovers' walk to the place of suicide, and makes the most of the popular Buddhist belief that lovers who died together would be reborn on the same calyx on the lake before Amida's throne.

This sensational and romantic treatment of *shinjū* in literature in turn inspired frustrated lovers and incited those eager to have their death publicized or immortalized in prose and drama. Love suicides became so frequent that in 1722 the officials for a time prohibited the performance of plays on the subject and tried to discourage potential *Liebestod* couples with punitive measures. The practice, however, still continues today.

Whereas in the Christian tradition the *Liebestod* is primarily a narrative device—double suicides for love occur rarely, if ever, in real life—Japanese literature draws on actual fact and gives expression to a cultural reality. But contrary to what is often its explicit narrative intention, the *Liebestod* always illustrates symbolically the very transience and frailty of intense passionate emotions and the inviability of the ideal.

See also: Death and the Individual, Love Triangle, Secret Love.

Selected Bibliography

Bijvoet, Maya C. "*Liebestod:* The Function and Meaning of the Double Love Death in Major Interpretations of Four Western Legends." Ph.D. Diss. University of Illinois, Urbana, 1985.

Fougères, Michel. *La Liebestod dans le roman francais, anglais et allemand au dix-huitième siècle*. Sherbrooke: Naaman, 1974.

Shively, Donald H. *The Love Suicide at Amijima*. Cambridge, Mass.: Harvard University Press, 1953.

MAYA C. BIJVOET

LION

Associations of the lion with royalty, an important source of its literary prestige, were already well established when they began to be exploited spectacularly by Assyrian rulers in the second half of the second millennium B.C. Kings were compared to lions in royal and ritual texts, each having the higest rank in their particular realm. Hunting and killing lions were royal prerogatives and perhaps a ritual obligation. Keeping menageries of lions was a sign of royal power, while sculptured lions guarded the entrance to the palace, supported the throne, and kept watch over royal burials. Divinities were often shown flanked by lions, either dominating the animals or generally associating with their power. The frequent appearance of the lion in such Near Eastern contexts had an early and very strong influence on Greek art, an influence especially remarkable because the animal is not native to Europe. The main gate of the palace at Mycenae in the Greek Argolid is surmounted by a pediment displaying two lions flanking a pillar, an impressive emblem that may be either royal or religious or both. An inlaid dagger-blade from a royal grave at Mycenae shows men hunting lions with spears, and the animal is used as a decorative motif on swords, drinking vessels, and gems recovered from other graves.

The spread of lion-imagery indicated by these artifacts is confirmed by the first great literary exploitation of the animals, in the epics of Homer (c. 8th century B.C.). Both the *Ilias* (*Iliad*) and the *Odysseia* (*Odyssey)* use the lion in similes, although each poem does so in a distinctive way. The similes, a feature of Homeric technique that influenced the entire later tradition of Western epic, are far more numerous in the *Iliad* than in the *Odyssey,* and more of the *Iliad*'s similes refer to lions than to any other animal or activity. In these passages, which are concentrated in the narrative of the battles and individual combats, the lion typically preys on sheep, cattle, or deer. Strength and ferocity in the animal illustrate the corresponding qualities in the warriors. Since the heroes of both armies are aristocrats of divine ancestry, it may be that the royal associations of the lion are being exploited. It is improbable that Homer or his oral epic tradition based these lion similes on actual knowledge of the animal's habits. To prove this lack of first-hand knowledge, it has often been noticed that Homer's lions are never said to roar. The frequency and impressiveness of the *Iliad*'s references to lions are therefore a remarkable exercise in imagination and stylization. In the *Odyssey* a few lion similes occur, attached several times to the figure of Odysseus himself, as, for example, in his meeting with Nausicaä (*Odyssey* 6.130–134).

Homer's authoritative influence assured that the lion would have prominence in classical Greek literature. In Aeschylus' *Oresteia* (458 B.C.) an elaborate simile based on a lion cub raised as a pet (*Agamemnon,* lines 717–736) forms part of the rich imagery of that trilogy of plays. Euripides' vengeful Medea (*Mēdeia* [*Medea,* play, 431 B.C.]) is twice compared to a lioness (lines 187 and 1342), once as she protects her children, the other time after she has taken her revenge against Jason. In Sophocles' *Philoktētēs* (*Philoctetes,* play, 409 B.C.) the older hero, Philoctetes, and the younger, Neoptolemus, will return to the battlefield of Troy and protect each other like a pair of lions (*Philoctetes,* lines 1434–1437). Aristophanes compares Alcibiades to a lion cub in his comedy *Batrachoi* (*Frogs,* 405 B.C., lines 1431–1433), and Perikles' mother is supposed to have dreamed just before he was born that she would give birth to a lion cub (Herodotus, *Historiai*, 6.131 [*History*, 5th century B.C.].

In Greek mythology the lion is preeminently associated with Heracles. The first of his Twelve Labors was to destroy the lion of Nemea, a feat from which he acquired two of his permanent attributes. He cut a club with which to subdue the lion and then skinned the dead animal. On all of his subsequent labors Heracles carried this club and wore the lion's skin. In innumerable representations throughout antiquity he is shown wearing the lion's head over his own, like a helmet, his face framed by the lion's jaws, while the rest of the skin covers his back. Heracles' lion-skin is both a memorial of his first great labor and also a permanent sign of the semidivine strength of the most popular and representative of the heroes of Greek mythology. Pindar in his first Nemean ode (? 476 B.C.) mentions the lion-skin prominently as he narrates the scene in which Heracles predicts the future greatness of the hero Ajax.

Knowledge of the actual physiology and habits of lions was a mixture of truth, tales, and speculation, at least in so far as it is reflected by ancient naturalists from Aristotle onward. The body of beliefs, however, carried over into the medieval physiologists and influenced centuries of allegorical interpretations. The lion, in this tradition, is the sovereign of the animal world. Lions are rare animals, and the reason for their scarcity is that the young destroy their mother's womb at birth. An alternative reason is that the number of cubs diminishes by one each time the mother gives birth. The new-born cubs are not yet alive and the father brings them to life by breathing on them. Mature lions sleep with their eyes open. They erase their tracks by sweeping behind themselves with the tuft of their tail. While the lion is a ferocious and strong predator, it does not attack those who are already dead or who are prostrate. (This last detail of leonine behavior was often understood to mean, "those who prostrate themselves in supplication.") Lions prey upon men rather than women and they attack children only when driven to do so by hunger. Their roar is powerful enough to stop other swift animals in their tracks. Lastly, the lion has no natural enemies, but is afraid of cocks, especially white ones. These assertions about the lion prevailed for centuries and determined the symbolic values that were assigned to the animal.

The ancient writers of fables, Aesop (6th century B.C.), Phaedrus (c. 15 B.C.– c. A.D. 50), and Babrius (c. A.D. 1st century) often include the lion among the animals in their anecdotes. Some of the traits, not always consistent, that the lions of the fables show became firmly established in popular literature of many times and ages. The lion is sometimes shown as the wise ruler of an animal kingdom where the birds and beasts can assemble to consult their king. Natural enmities are suspended; the weaker animals can ask the lion to call the stronger to account. In other fables, however, the King of Beasts is characterized as rapacious and arrogant. When he hunts in the company of other animals he claims the "Lion's Share" when the booty is divided, that is, he takes everything, claiming part because he is king, part because he is the strongest, and the rest because he will attack anyone who touches it. Elsewhere he steals the prey of weaker animals and mocks them when they appeal for justice. The dying lion is helpless, however, and those he has wronged approach him fearlessly with insults.

The lion was common in the Near East in biblical times, so that the numerous references to it in the Old Testament are apparently based on actual experience. Great leaders of the Hebrews are credited with killing lions, the most important being Samson (Judg. 14:5–6) and David (1 Sam. 17:34–36). The prophet Daniel, thrown into a den of lions by King Darius, is delivered safely because of his faith in God (Dan. 6). The animal in the wild was recognized as supremely strong, a predator on flocks, and endowed with a terrifying roar. These characteristics are often used in the Bible in images of divine or royal power and anger. The prophet Isaiah portrayed an age of future peacefulness when the lion would either be absent (Isa. 35:9) or would change from a carnivorous hunter to a harmless grazing beast (Isa. 11.6–7). These and other biblical references contributed greatly to the symbolic importance of the lion.

Composite monsters very frequently have the body of a lion as the most important component. Winged lions guarded the royal palaces of Assyria, and a lion with eagle's wings is the first of the four beasts in Daniel's dream-vision (Dan. 7). This winged lion became identified with St. Mark the Evangelist and, when he became the patron saint of Venice, it also served as the symbol of that city. Other composite beasts derive from Greek mythology. The Sphinx, adopted from Egypt, has a lion's body joined with the torso and head of a woman. Sphinxes occur both with wings and without them. Griffins are winged lions with the heads of eagles. (This is the Gryphon of Lewis Carroll's *Alice in Wonderland* [stories, 1865].) The Chimaera has a lion's body with the foreparts of a goat and a snake added to it. In all these monsters the basic ingredient is the surpassing strength of the lion, augmented by the attributes of the other creatures.

The story of Androcles and the lion has its roots in folklore, but Aulus Gellius (c. A.D. 130–c. 180), in his *Noctes atticae* (*Attic Nights*, 5.14), attributes his version of the story to a certain Apion, a learned writer, who included the tale in a book on the wonders of Egypt and who said that he was an eyewitness to the part of the story that took place at Rome. Androcles, the slave of a Roman proconsul in Africa, escapes from his master to avoid cruel treatment. A lion comes to the cave in the desert where Androcles has taken shelter. It shows Androcles its paw, which is sore because a splinter has entered it and the paw has become infected. Androcles heals the paw and he and the lion, becoming friends, share the cave for three years. But Androcles, tiring of this life, returns to civilization, is returned to his former master, and is condemned to death. In the Circus at Rome he is set to fight a lion, but it refuses to harm him and turns out to be his former African friend. Androcles is set free, is given the lion as a pet, and they travel about enjoying their fame.

A variation of this narrative is attached to St. Jerome (c. 348–420), who is depicted conventionally in the desert with a lion as his companion. The lion is in debt to the saint for having been healed, as in the Androcles story, or is repentant after having killed a donkey that belonged to Jerome and his companions. The charity of the saintly man is able to tame the strongest of the wild animals. Another variation occurs in the French romance of Chrétien de Troyes, *Yvain, ou le chevalier au lion* (*Yvain, or the Knight of the Lion*, c. 1180). After he rescues it from a fight with a dragon, Yvain adopts the lion as his companion in his chivalric adventures. This lion is credited with great strength and intelligence. At the same time, its actions are clearly not based on natural observation, and it often seems more like a pet dog than a lion. The significance of this lion in *Yvain* is much discussed; it seems to be a symbol of the ideal of courtly behavior to which the hero aspires during his trials and adventures.

An episode in the medieval Spanish epic *Poema de mío Cid* (*Poem of the Cid*, 1140) involves a lion kept by the Cid, the leader of the Spaniards against the Arabs. This lion escapes from its nets while the Cid is sleeping in the same room. His retainers bravely stand between him and the lion, while his recently married sons-in-law flee in terror. He later taunts them with this cowardice. The medieval belief that the lion could detect true princes among imposters may underlie this episode.

The lion has a place in English literature because of its royal and allegorical associations accumulated over the centuries. Spenser's references to lions in his epic poem *The Faery Queene* (1590–1596) are remarkably numerous, although they are only one element in an extensive pattern of animal imagery. He uses lions in many similes to illustrate such emotions in his characters as anger, strength, courage, and nobility. Spenser also introduces lions as figures in his allegory. The encounter between Una and the lion in 1.3.5, for example, shows the fierce beast acting with sudden gentleness when he recognizes the virginal beauty and royalty of Una. But Wrath rides on a lion's back later in book 1 (1.4.33), while in book 3 (3.12.22) Cupid rides on a lion to show the power of love. Such multiple aspects of the lion in Spenser are partly inspired by the frequent appearance of the animal in heraldry, in particular the lion's function (from 1603) as a supporter, with the unicorn, of the royal arms. The royal menagerie in the Tower of London was established in 1264, and lions were among the animals regularly exhibited there until the early nineteenth century. Shakespeare's frequent references to lions are usually similes or metaphors of the traditional traits of the animal as they appear in human characters. In the play *As You Like It* (4.3; c. 1599) Orlando fights a lioness (off-stage, of course) that is threatening his brother, a feat that leads to their recognition and reconciliation. Shakespeare's most famous lion is in the play of Pyramus and Thisbe in *A Midsummer Night's Dream* (c. 1595). The plot of this play-within-a-play is derived from Ovid's epic poem, *Metamorphoses* (4.55–166, c. A.D. 2–17), in which the lion is more or less incidental (other predators might have performed its function just as well). Shakespeare's lion, as performed by Snug the joiner, gains a great deal of its charm from the contrast between the savagery of the beast and the naivety of the interpreter, a literary strategy that foreshadows much children's literature.

In literature following the Renaissance, that is, after the crest of the lion's heraldic and emblematic presence, it appears in three main categories. First is the continuation of innumerable and sporadic minor references based on the lion as it occurs in proverbs, fables, popular imagery, and astrology. "Lion" and "lion-hearted" are complimentary sobriquets, as in Richard Coeur de Lion and numerous others. The animal is long associated with England in cartoons, clichés, and many other forms of expression.

Second is the use of the lion as a figure of fantasy and amusement, particularly in literature for children. The outstanding example of this category is the Cowardly Lion in L. Frank Baum's fantasy *The Wizard of Oz* (1900) and its sequels, whose incarnation in the movie rivals the literary original. This genre of lion can perhaps be associated in popular culture with the art and spectacle of the lion-tamer in circuses.

The third category is reserved for lions that appear in literary works that are set in countries where the animal is a native species. It is a natural symbol of the spirit of Africa or of other such ideas in hunter's tales about that continent. The human who lives with lions is now no longer a saint or outcast, but appears as a naturalist, biologist, or ethnologist. Increasing knowledge of the animal in its habitat tends to reduce its power as a symbol, at least in its royal and religious associations. Yet current ecological concern about the survival of the lion, among other such impressive wild animals, has given a fresh impetus to human evaluation of an ancient and powerful symbol.

See also: Bear, Hunt, Monsters.

Selected Bibliography

Friedmann, Herbert. *A Bestiary for Saint Jerome: Animal Symbolism in European Religious Art*. Washington, D.C.: Smithsonian Institution Press, 1980.

Perry, Ben Edwin. *Babrius and Phaedrus*. Cambridge, Mass.: Harvard University Press, 1965.

Physiologus. Trans. Michael J. Curley. Austin: University of Texas Press, 1979.

White, T. H. *The Book of Beasts*. London: Cape, 1954.

HARRY G. EDINGER

LITERATURE WITHIN LITERATURE

Literature is in its beginnings, and remains at its core, simply storytelling. In the process, the teller and his audience are invisible, outside the framework of the story, joint beholders of fictional events that are temporarily indistinguishable from actual happenings observed by God. Perhaps because of this God-like role, writers have sometimes felt that theirs is a peculiar calling, not at all like shoemaking or medicine, and have gone out of their way to draw attention to the anomalies of their craft by contaminating the objectivity of the story with the intrusions of the normally invisible. They have done it in many ways: the story within a story; references to literature as a genre; acknowledgement of indebtedness to other literary men or works; authorial self-reference or the presence of the author as a persona; the assigning of artistic traits to the protagonist; injecting the audience into the tale or play.

Antiquity and the Middle Ages

Take the story within the story. Given the suspicion with which the religious sensibility regards "fiction"—literally "lying"—the author of the Bible feels compelled to legitimate storytelling. Hence he presents the prophet Nathan reproving King David for his sinfulness, not by direct address but by raising a hypothetical case, having David pass judgment on it, and then forcing the king to see that the case is his own. So mere storytelling—as against revelation—has its role to play in bringing sinners closer to God, and Nathan may be considered the Judaic Thespis or Orpheus, the mythological inventor of an artistic genre. So also literature itself portrays the genesis of the literary act.

Nathan addressed his tale to a king, Jesus to the masses. The Nazarene brings storytelling to a high art form, relating numerous parables, some of which, like the one about the talents and the need to make money, require sophistication in interpretation. Shaw went so far as to call Jesus an artist. In this regard, Jesus followed in the footsteps of Moses, who was the reputed author of the first five books of the Bible, in many of which he himself appeared as shepherd, rebel, leader, and lawgiver.

In the *Odysseia* (*Odyssey*, epic poem, c. 8th century B.C.), the figure of the bard is prominent. Agamemnon, conscious of mythology/literature/history, is envious of the noble role the hero's Penelope will play in future storytelling as against the evil role of his own Clytemnestra. Odysseus, on the way back from the Trojan War, is reduced to tears at the Phaiacian court by the bard Demodocus' recital of those wars, for the events already have entered the realm of folklore. Another bard, Phemios, recites at Ithaca for the suitors. But perhaps the greatest bard is that first Renaissance all-round man, the hero Odysseus himself, who enthralls the Phaiacians with the story of his adventures. This exotic romance section of the *Odyssey* may well be a fabrication of his, he having shown himself throughout to be so sly a character, so prolific a teller of tall tales about himself. Then, given high praise by his audience for his narration, he pays tribute to Demodocus and to bards in general as worthy of respect. That this is no mere lip service is proved at the end of the epic, when Odysseus wreaks vengeance and the bard Phemios throws himself at his mercy, asking exemption on the basis of his craft and divine inspiration. As a good storyteller himself and a connoisseur in the craft, Odysseus relents. Thus Homer has the main character of his own story, into whom he has infused life, in turn grant life to an alter ego of himself.

The first writer to parade himself openly in his works (and to make up his own plots) was Aristophanes. Either because of the circumstances of the presentation of Greek comedy, with authors openly canvassing for votes, or because of his innovativeness and supreme self-confidence, he makes the chorus in the middle of many of his plays come forward and, in Pirandello-like fashion, break down the barrier (so recently erected, as it were) between author and audience, fantasy and reality, by speaking of himself—his comic greatness deserving of a prize, his patriotism, and even of his own bald head. And speaking not only of himself, for in the *Hippēs* (*The Knights,* 424 B.C.), *Nephelai* (*The Clouds,* 423 B.C.) and the *Batrachoi* (*The Frogs,* 405 B.C.) the audience is variously described as clever, criminal, homosexual, stupid, and gullible.

Aristophanes also became embroiled in intellectual wars that prompted him to put such literary figures as Aeschylus, Euripides, and Socrates within his plays. These were men, albeit literary men, and antiquity contains only one case of the appearance of a single, influential literary work within another—something that would become an important theme in later literature. That case is bound up with theological significances, as the writers of the New Testament, notably Matthew, continually present the sayings and acts of Jesus in the light of the prophecies and passages of the Old Testament. Jesus operates within Judaism, and his life is seen as the fulfillment of the promises and hopes in the tales of the Jewish Bible.

The narrator as a character in his own work, whether in autobiography or in a first-person narrative, is rare in antiquity. In the Middle Ages, as a result of the interiorization wrought by Christianity, of the emphasis on confession, and of the brief confessional remarks of Paul, the autobiography was virtually invented with St. Augustine's *Confessiones* (*Confessions,* c. 397–400). That work is not, however, overtly a piece of fiction, and a millennium later the genre becomes enmeshed with the genres of dream visions and pilgrimage books to produce what many consider the single greatest literary work, Dante's epic poem *La divina commedia* (*The Divine Comedy,* c. 1320). This survey of the afterworld (and of this world, too) is written not in an impersonal, Michelin-guide fashion but in terms of the spiritual autobiography of one man. Like St. Augustine, Dante—who is called only once, near the center of the work, by his name—is a Christian sinner who drifted until a visionary experience brought him to himself. That the catalyst was, thanks to the courtly love tradition, a woman requires bringing in the main events of his life. Although these autobiographical passages total only five or ten percent of the text, as against nearly the whole of the *Confessions,* they are of central importance, as though the universe revolved metaphysically around God but artistically around the poet Dante.

Dante's character, furthermore, is defined along the way. He is susceptible to some of the sins he sees. He faints with compassion over the adulterous tale of Francesca; he walks bowed down like those guilty of pride; he is not envious; above all, he is a writer. What makes him special is that, besides being a Christian sinner, a lover, a social critic, and political activist, he sees himself as an artist. He is proud enough of craft and self to place the greatest pagan poets in a special limbo free of the discomforts of Hell and then to briefly join them for some shoptalk. No one who has ever appeared at the center of a story—fiction or not—has made such vast claims for himself, least of all a repentant, humbled pilgrim on the way to the beatific vision! Dante's poem is also peculiar in that, besides borrowing important ideas from the *Aeneis* (*Aeneid*, epic poem, 19 B.C.)—for example, the visit to Hell—he singles out Virgil, makes him one of the three central personae of the work, and assigns him the important role of guide for almost two-thirds of the trip. Here is a unique example of the overtly acknowledged influence of one literary masterpiece on another.

Dante had been anticipated in making an artist or semi-artist the central character not only by Homer in the *Odyssey* but also by Gottfried von Strassburg in *Tristan* (c. 1210). Though writing a chivalric romance, Gottfried deviated from the norm by making his Tristan something of a Renaissance man, with intellectual interests and abilities, with powers as a musician that sometimes threaten to turn the obligatory martial exploits into perfunctory matter.

Boccaccio is the narrator of the longer story of *Il decamerone* (*Decameron,* novellas, c. 1350), within which the characters tell their short stories. He intrudes occasionally to defend his subject matter (specifically love and sex) and to present himself as someone who loves the ladies (Gottfried also makes passing references to his own, apparently unsuccessful, experiences as a lover) and who, conscious that his writings will not satisfy the learned as high literature, is nevertheless satisfied with his achievement. The *Decameron* clearly influenced Chaucer's *Canterbury Tales* (c. 1380–1400) but, as in the case of Homer's vast influence on Virgil, the connection is never acknowledged. However, if Boccaccio appears on the fringe of the story frame as narrator only, Chaucer inserts himself into the frame as one of the pilgrims. He is the gregarious one who quickly comes to know all the others at the hotel. He also participates in the storytelling contest set up by the hotelier. But where Dante presents himself as a great writer-prophet undertaking a supremely important journey, Chaucer seems to be a man of limited accomplishment. When it is his turn, his tale of Sir Thopaz is so inept in structure, content, and jingling rhyme that the other pilgrims are bestirred (as in no other case) to stop him before he gets far. In place of Dante's proud self-regard, we have here self-depreciation and irony. The provenance is not Christian humility or psychological insecurity but structural and esthetic considerations. To enhance the authenticity of the pilgrimage and the characters on it, Chaucer presents himself as incapable of inventing a tale. One is to infer that he must have merely recorded what happened, not added or adorned anything—a supposition buttressed by Chaucer's ironic apologies for scabrous language and incidents on the grounds that he may not deviate from what happened. Literature here strives to efface or transcend itself, as the author injects himself into the story in order to prove that this is no story.

The Renaissance

An informal, secular "confessions" is what Montaigne's *Essais* (*Essays, 1580–1588*) are; unstructured and unchronological, they contain more of a depiction of his personality and tastes than of his life and times. But no writer ever insisted—and made the reader feel—that he and his book were consubstantial.

Shakespeare particularly enjoyed toying with his vocation in his plays. In *Julius Caesar* (c. 1599), Cassius, leading the assassination of Caesar, makes a sort of self-fulfilling prophecy (and Shakespeare through him winks at the audience) when he says that their action will be reenacted on the stage in many times and places. Shakespeare also manipulated perspective by means of the play within the play. One work begins with a frame in which a lower-class character, Christopher Sly, is hoodwinked into thinking that he is a nobleman who is having a play performed for him. The play that ensues (actually the play within the play) is the *Taming of the Shrew* (c. 1594), but when it is concluded, nothing more is heard from Sly. (The frame is consistently maintained in Beaumont's *Knight of the Burning Pestle* [1613], with periodic comments from the beholders of the play.) In *Love's Labour's Lost* (c. 1594) and *A Midsummer Night's Dream* (c. 1595), the frame or outer play is the key one and the inner play only a passing interlude—performed ineptly by amateurs when the main action is over and derided by the characters in the main plot.

In *Hamlet* (c. 1600), this literary device is brought to artistic heights. The play within the play is performed—at the mathematical center of the play—by professional actors working with a script commissioned, (apparently) written, and directed by Hamlet. It simultaneously establishes Claudius' guilt and warns him of Hamlet's coming revenge. By reenacting a crime committed, it has something of the psychoanalytical function of forcing a patient to confront a traumatic past. And by doing all these things at once, under the aegis of Hamlet, himself not only the hero and a Renaissance man but also an excellent actor-director-writer-poet performing various roles for the benefit of the key personages at court, it is a great playwright's tribute to his craft. Shakespeare has assigned his own vocation to the noblest of princes and shown it to involve nothing less than the uncovering of truths about the ruling circles of a society, about the mysteries of the complex self, and about man's place in the universe.

The work that contains the richest set of literary self-references is Cervantes's novel *Don Quijote* (*Don Quixote,* 1605, 1615). If the quest for a fulfillment of the Old Testament is the dynamic of the New; if a confessed love of the *Aeneid* shapes the *Divine Comedy*; and if, within that work, the love and damnation of Paolo and Francesca were catalyzed by a reading of chivalric romance, so did an immersion in the same chivalric romance genre propel Don Quixote into a bizarre career of knightly beneficence. Literature is nothing less than transmitted values and romantic dreams, the repository of role models. The literary torch may be passed on by great works (Old to New Testament, Virgil to Dante) or, as here, by bad books: Cervantes started out only to parody meretricious popular books (as had Rabelais and would Fielding) and ended by creating something unprecedented.

Most nearly unique, however, is the way Cervantes toys with the matter of the authorship of his novel. He pretends that he works with a story derived from fragments of several writers, from the "annals of la Mancha," from vague traditions, and, signally, from a translation of an Arabic manuscript written by one Cid Hamete Benengeli and discovered by chance. Half-way through part 2, a comment on structure and technique is attributed to an indefinite "they" with reference to an "original version" which states that the interpreter incorrectly translated a chapter by Cid Hamete. Cervantes has, in short, hidden himself behind layers of mystification about the relation of fiction to reality.

Cervantes even avails himself of the old trick (used by Shakespeare among others) of having a character in the story say that the events are so unheard of that they could not appear in a work of fiction. In part 2, the Don and Sancho are amazed to find themselves known to the world because they have been written up in a book (i.e., part 1). Then the Don worries that the book may have been written by one of his enchanter-foes and therefore is inaccurate. The mystification is enhanced by the fact that part 1 proved so popular that spurious continuations and imitations of it by others were published, and Cervantes was forced in his legitimate continuation to attack the impostures. The result was now a three-fold metaphysical division: "reality"; the "real" work of "fiction" (*Don Quixote*); the "spurious" work of fiction. Not only is there, therefore, ado about the authorship of *Don Quixote,* but the Don himself, who had early on been certain that he would be written about, is presented in part 2 as conscious of the fame that he achieved in part 1 and which is being distorted and sullied in the imitations. So angry is he now that he refuses to do things he is said to do in the spurious book in order to show up its unreliability. Then he runs into a gentleman whom he has read about in part 2, who claims to have been an intimate friend of the Don and Sancho, and who sees no resemblance between the two men before him now and the ones he knew so well—even when the Don insists that he, standing there now, is the "real" Don. The Don's legend has, fortunately or unfortunately, outpaced his corporeal self. In short, not until the literature of the twentieth century was there to be such ingenious tinkering with the curious relations between reality and fantasy and among author, character, and audience.

In the seventeenth century, autobiography was still a rarity. This did not stop Milton—proud, self-righteous, combative—from inserting short autobiographical passages in his prose writings by way of justifying his polemical activities. Less defensive and more poignant are the personal passages that he—in one of his few departures from the epic conventions of Homer and Virgil—inserted in the proems of books 1, 3, 7, and 9 of *Paradise Lost* (poem, 1667).

Molière has his Aristophanic moment when, in *L'avare* (*The Miser,* 1668), the distraught protagonist seeks his stolen hoard and looks accusingly at the members of the audience, whose laughter he takes as proof that they are accomplices in the theft. Furthermore, literature, especially Platonizing books, is shown to have unhinged the women in *Les précieuses ridicules* (*The Ridiculous Snobs,* 1659) and in *Les femmes savantes* (*The Learned Ladies,* 1672) even as it had altered the lives of Francesca and Quixote. In *La critique de l'école des femmes* (*Criticism of the School for Wives,* 1663) and *L'impromptu de Versailles* (*The Impromptu of Versailles,* 1663), Molière did something probably unprecedented. He wrote literary works about the appreciation and criticism of plays, about the intellectual dynamics of comedy and of his own plays in particular, and about playwrighting and rehearsing. In the former, he put the critics of his play on the stage and let them have their say; in the latter, he put himself on the stage rehearsing a play and coping with the multifarious pressures of his vocation.

The Romantic and Modern Periods

The eighteenth century contains one major work filled with self-conscious tinkering with the conventions and forms of a literary genre—Sterne's *Tristram Shandy* (novel 1759–1767). Its narrator is at the center of the narrative, a conscious opaque presence who filters everything through his sensibility. He sees fit to forego the usual presentation of character, dialogue, drama, and working up to a climax; to disavow novelistic intentions; and to tease the reader with such unprecedented devices as offering him a blank or ink-filled page, wrenching typography and chronology, or openly engaging in a colloquy the two presences that in the conventional novel (except perhaps for Fielding's *Tom Jones* [novel, 1749]) were invisible—the narrator and the reader. In the slightly less shapeless epic poem *Don Juan* (1819–1824), Byron comments liberally in spontaneous-sounding lines on poets, contemporaries, the work itself and its structure, and, most of all, his own character—as, for example, his writing certain lines while intoxicated. Something of this romantic irony, this serio-comic treatment of oneself, characterizes also the narrator of the Byron-influenced *Evgeniĭ Onegin* (*Eugene Onegin,* novel, 1823–1831) of Pushkin.

Like the *Divine Comedy, Don Quixote,* and the *Précieuses,* Jane Austen's *Northanger Abbey* (1818) (which also contains the author's spirited defense of novels) is about a literary influence, in this case the then-fashionable gothic novels. The heroine, eager to visit old castles filled with eerie objects and dark traditions, unfortunately keeps on running into the daylight dullness of the quotidian. In France, an infatuation with romantic novels leads a bored doctor's wife (Flaubert's *Madame Bovary,* novel, 1856) to turn to love affairs that she expects will be as grand as the ones in books but that turn out to be increasingly sordid. It is the *Don Quixote* scenario, applied to a woman rather than a man, amatory rather than chivalric, tragic rather than comic, "modern" rather than medieval-Renaissance.

In romantic literature, the artist often becomes the center of attention. Wordsworth's *The Prelude* (1799–1805) is one of the first examples of the *Künstler-roman,* a narrative of the making of the artist. Wordsworth chooses this special theme as the subject for a long poem, aware that, just as Milton had replaced the warrior-heroes of pagan epic with the nonmartial Judeo-Christian Adam, he in turn replaces the Christian hero and mythic first man with that archetypal human being, the poet. Coleridge's "The Rime of the Ancient Mariner" (poem, 1798) is, on one level, a parable of the writer or artist. The mariner, having through adverse experience looked into the heart of darkness and the reality of evil, can obtain temporary relief only by telling his story to others. Like a writer, he tells because he must.

In Shelley's poem "Ode to the West Wind" (1819), the narrator is a poet who parallels his emotional and artistic barrenness with winter and death in nature, hoping that this insight will, like spring and vegetal rebirth, reactivate his poetic inspiration and coincidentally give him a subject to write about. The poet would thus become both the celebrator of nature, which is the source of men's emotional nourishment, and a prophet who reminds people that their own corporal lives and emotional depressions are part of a cycle that, like the seasons and like the poet's creativity, will see revival. Along similar lines, Keats ("Ode on a Grecian Urn," 1819) concludes that the work of art (and by extension the artist) alone deals with reality, alone provides the beauty and the truth that are equivalent and which are—to the implicit exclusion of religion and science—the only intellectual nourishment men need.

The protagonist of Dostoevsky's novel *Zapiski iz podpolïa* (*Notes from Underground,* 1864) is, like Francesca, Quixote, and Emma, aware of himself standing against the background of literary exemplars. More than the others, he consciously wrestles with the ontological problem raised by their careers. Which is more "real," the lived life or the visions of reality presented in books? He senses that people have lost touch with life and get much of their sense of reality from books, a flawed source, especially of such dubious concepts, from Schiller and German Romanticism, as "the sublime and the beautiful." (Byron had remarked in *Childe Harold* [narrative poem, 1812–1818] on the mystery of writing, of black marks on white paper affecting people and altering the world.) Hence, in the midst of confessing all, he expresses distrust of even the most candid autobiography, such as Rousseau's.

He sees himself as an "anti-hero," unable to act or think or feel, yet continuously aware of his audience of readers, including some who might criticize him, he boasts of his superiority over them on the grounds that he alone has carried the hostility latent in everyone into the open and to an extreme; he alone has not deceived himself by calling "common sense" what is actually cowardice about such self-confrontation and -revelation. The final claim is no less than that he is more alive than the reader; as W. H. Auden was to put it, the work of literature reads you.

Henry James in various short stories (e.g., "The Figure in the Carpet," 1896) and Thomas Mann in *Doktor Faustus* (novel, 1947) have dealt at length with the mind of the artist. But the modern epoch stands out for widespread Cervantes-like self-consciousness about the ontology of artistic works and the breaking down of the invisible wall between story and audience, writer and audience. Two major figures on this theme have been Luigi Pirandello and Jorge Luis Borges. In the former's *Sei personaggi in cerca d'autore* (*Six Characters in Search of an Author,* play, 1921), the participants in a putatively real-life situation, with their petty little melodramatic story, are eager (as many people seem to be) to have the world know their turmoil; they seek an author, director, and acting company to depict their tale. Pirandello has thus gone into the workshop of the writer's mind to dramatize one of the ways in which material becomes literature; a story clamors to be converted into art and insists that that be done on its terms—the way it happened, down to the color of the sofa—and not as writer and director, with imperatives of their own, think is most persuasive, moving, esthetic. Metaphysical questions about what is real, relevant, artistic are likewise raised in *Ciascuno a suo modo* (*Each In His Own Way,* 1924), which modernizes and enlarges suggestions in Cervantes and Molière. A play is performed, and then the diverse reactions of the audience are given on stage in act 2, the audience including several people whose scandal-ridden lives formed the basis of the play in act 1. Art and reality here are like two mirrors facing each other.

Borges manipulates in many ways the mystery of literature, reality, and authorship. Thus he supposes in "Pedro Menard, Autor del *Quijote*" ("Pierre Menard, Author of *Don Quixote,*" story, 1944) that parts of *Don Quixote* have been written by a contemporary of William James and Bertrand Russell without any prior knowledge of Cervantes' book. The work turns out to be word for word the same as the earlier version but is said to be "much richer"—because, the reader infers, one reads it (or any book) in the context of the time of its composition.

The conditions of the artist becoming increasingly doubtful in a modern, scientific civilization, art turns hermetic, and writers particularly spend much time in their work mulling over the meaning of their vocation. In Mann's "Tonio Kröger" (story, 1903), for instance, the hero-writer is a marginal man (nearly arrested as a criminal) who envies normal people their physical and emotional health, unself-consciousness, attractiveness, simple-mindedness, conformity, bourgeois life style, and their obliviousness to all matters intellectual. Proust's *A la recherche du temps perdu* (*Remembrance of Things Past,* novels, 1913–1927) contains a close study of the characters, theories, and vocations of artists—painter, composer, writer, actress—especially of the writer Bergotte and the discrepancy between the luminescence of his books and the dark spots in his character and private life. Even that unusual theme is subsidiary to the study of the main character, the narrator Marcel (named only once or twice, as Dante is named only once in the *Divine Comedy*), and how he came to his vocation of writer of these long novels, which are not so much "fictions" as memoirs esthetically reordered.

The other great modern master of the novel, James Joyce, has also as central character in the two most powerful of his novels, *Portrait of the Artist as a*

Young Man (1916) and *Ulysses* (1922), Stephen Dedalus, an artist-poet-intellectual trying to define his identity and establish his vocation as writer. In *Ulysses,* someone remarks that it will take ten years for Stephen to do so, which is exactly the span in Joyce's life between his return from Paris (as, at the beginning of *Ulysses,* Stephen has just returned from there) and the beginning of the composition of *Ulysses*. This is the Chinese box or mirror-facing-mirror effect. Just as Dante tells the story of how his trip through the universe brought him to the point of telling the story of the trip, which has to be told, and so on, and Proust discovers after three thousand pages that he must write three thousand pages about the discovery that he must write, and so on, so Joyce indicates that in ten years he will write the book in which we are told that in ten years, and so on. The circularity is consummated in *Finnegans Wake* (novel, 1939), which ends with the first half of a sentence, the second half of which begins the book. The novel has become its own world, achieved its own orbit.

Moreover, Joyce's experiments with styles and techniques in each chapter of *Ulysses*— predominantly in the second half of the novel, with its informal anthology and parody of the great English styles of the past—give one the sense that literature is a matter of artifice and convention, of time and place, and that there is more to the narrative than merely telling a story, as did Homer in the beginning, or even manipulating the narrator's point of view, as James and Conrad did so conscientiously only the day before. Literature here contemplates its own navel.

Other writers have carried on in this vein, whether by incorporating into the novel a notebook or diary connected with the writing of the novel, as in Gide's *Les faux-monnayeurs (The Counterfeiters,* 1925) and Doris Lessing's *Golden Notebook* (1962), or by having, as in Nabokov's *Pale Fire* (1962), a long pseudo-scholarly commentary and footnoting apparatus appended to a short cryptic pseudo-poetic text. In these, as in numerous experiments by such current writers as Beckett, Barth, Pynchon, Sorrentino, Barthelme, and Calvino, the process has become as interesting as the finished product, the literary act as important as the literary work. Literature, more than ever before gazing at itself in the mirror, is its own subject matter.

See also: Artist in Literature through the Renaissance, Artist/Poet in Drama since the Renaissance, Autobiographical Impulse.

Selected Bibliography

Alter, Robert. *Partial Magic.* Berkeley: University of California Press, 1975.
Nelson, R. J. *Play within a Play.* New Haven, Conn.: Yale University Press, 1958.
Righter, Anne. *Shakespeare and the Idea of the Play.* New York: Barnes & Noble, 1962.
Weidhorn, Manfred. "Why Does Dante Cite Nathan in the 'Paradiso'?" *Philological Quarterly* 61 (1982): 90–91.

MANFRED WEIDHORN

LOVE IN GREEK AND ROMAN LITERATURE

Love is here used in the sense of an affection between two persons, implying some degree of endearment over at least some time. Sexual gratification for its own sake, purely erotic literature, pornography, and sexual humor are not considered. Homosexuality (save for a few instances) is also excluded as being too extensive and too complex a subject for treatment in this entry. Love among the divinities of the Greeks and Romans is also excluded, as belonging properly to mythology.

Aphrodite (Latin Venus) was the Greek goddess of love and a major figure in the Olympian family. Eros (Latin Cupid or Amor), the god of love, was usually less prominent. Both these divinities were anthropomorphic (with one exception), having personalities of their own; they were also frequently personifications of love as a force or emotion. These two aspects cannot always be distinguished. According to Hesiod (probably late 8th century B.C.) in the *Thegonia* (*Theogony,* didactic poem), Eros is one of the great primordial figures that emerged out of Chaos (or the Void) at the beginning of things. He is a cosmic force of generative desire and is not anthropomorphic. Aphrodite is of later origin, having arisen from the genitals of Uranus (Sky) after they had been severed and thrown into the sea. According to Homer (epic poet, probably mid- or late 8th century B.C., but somewhat earlier than Hesiod) Aphrodite is the daughter of Zeus (grandson of Uranus) by Dione, a sky goddess. In most later Greek and Latin literature Eros is the son of Aphrodite. Down into the fourth century B.C. he is represented as an athletic young man; thereafter he becomes softer and progressively younger and smaller, eventually almost a baby.

Greek Literature

The Pre-Classical Period. In the *Ilias* (*Iliad*), although the clearly announced theme of the epic is the wrath of Achilles, love nevertheless plays a prominent role, both in the background and in the forefront of the action. The story of the judgment of Paris lies at the beginning of the whole Trojan War; for, since Paris had awarded the prize for "the fairest" to Aphrodite, he merited the reward promised, Helen, the most beautiful of women. She was, to be sure, already the wife of Menelaus, king of Sparta, but this did not stand in the goddess's way, whence the Greek siege of Troy. In the early books of the *Iliad,* Helen and Paris more than once are shown both separately and together. Helen seems virtually helpless under the influence of Aphrodite, who makes it clear that the pair are enjoying their union owing to her favor. Indeed, at the end of book 3, after Paris has been removed from the scene of his duel with Menelaus by the physical intervention of the goddess and returned to his bedroom, Helen, in initial revulsion from their relationship, threatens to have nothing further to do with Paris; but her brief assertion of independence swiftly collapses before the dread display of divine displeasure. The episode closes with Paris amorously leading a compliant Helen to bed with the declaration that she has never seemed more alluring to him than now. The varying tempers of the lovers are seen now one disenchanted and rejecting the other, now readily yielding, the other now ready to fight his rival and accept the verdict of combat, now evading his earlier commitment and tenderly bent on sexual pleasure. There are also scenes of tender conjugal discourse between Hector and his wife, Andromache (especially in book 6), and a clear portrayal of their parental love for their little son.

Among the Greeks, too, love plays its part, although in book 1, in the scenes between Achilles and Agamemnon, it is not easy to separate the element of the physical attraction of a man to a woman from the influences of pride, ambition, and rage as motivating factors in the quarrel between the two. Suffice it to say that Achilles behaves with real tenderness toward his prize of honor, Briseis, both in the first book, when he must relinquish her, and in the later books of the poem, after she has been restored to him. Indeed, it is even hinted that Achilles intended to make her his lawful wife (9.340ff.; 19.295ff.). There are many other references to the joys of wedded love, but these are close to the center of the plot of the *Iliad*. Close, too, is the love between mother and son, particularly as exemplified in the scenes between Achilles and his mother, Thetis.

In the *Odysseia* (*Odyssey*), too, love is prominent. Odysseus throughout is motivated to pursue his return homeward by his love for his wife and his son; even the blandishments of the goddesses Calypso (5, 12) and Circe (10) could not distract him from his determination to reach home. The noble and licit love between Odysseus and Penelope is sharply contrasted with the illicit couchings of the suitors with the serving girls and their unseemly determination to compel Penelope to marry one of them, and also with Clytemnestra's adulterous union with Aegisthus and her connivance in the assassination of her lawful lord upon his return from Troy.

Archilochus (iambic, elegiac, and other poetic forms, c. 680–c. 640 B.C.) is the earliest Greek poet to set forth in direct and lively fashion his own opinions and highly personal feelings. He covered a wide range of subjects and displayed great metrical variety. Several of the surviving fragments speak of the charms of fair maidens; he was in love with one Cleobule, whose praises he sang, but after her father gave her as wife to another man he was bitter and denounced father and daughter with extreme sarcasm. Callinus and Tyrtaeus (elegiac poets, mid-7th century B.C.) primarily sing of warfare and valor, but refer to the wives and children whom the warriors are protecting. Alcman (choral melic poet, 7th century B.C.) writes with tender sympathy of the beautiful young maidens who dance in the girl's choruses at the festivals and gives evidence that he is susceptible to the delights of love.

Mimnermus (elegiac poet, 7th century B.C., last third) is the first who is avowedly a love poet; love forms the chief constituent of his work. He sang of golden love and the sweet delights of Aphrodite; he lamented the brevity of youth and joy and asserted that when old age approaches, portending the end of love's pleasures, it is better to die than to live. Alcaeus of Lesbos (monodic melic poet, c. 600 B.C.), an aristocrat of stormy career and passionate affections, included the delights of love among his themes, although he seems more interested in the passing dalliance of drinking parties than in matrimony or other union of some duration. Sappho (monodic melic poetess, c. 600 B.C.), an aristocrat of Lesbos, was married and had a daughter, to whom she was devoted. She wrote a beautiful hymn to Aphrodite and several wedding songs, but her most striking and passionate poems are addressed to various young ladies with whom she was associated. She described their charms and their physical beauty in glowing terms and is remarkable among the lyric poets of Greece in portraying realistically the actual physical sensations that love aroused in her. But she went no further than this in her verse.

The poems of Anacreon (monodic melic poet, late 6th–early 5th century B.C.) were almost entirely concerned with the joys of love; he wrote impartially of boys and girls and was noteworthy for his light and playful manner. His poems have neither the direct and personal intensity of Sappho nor the vigor of Alcaeus; they are gentle, sometimes pensive, sometimes mellow, as when he refers with mild regret to his gray hair and advancing age; and they are sophisticated, as becomes a court poet (to Polycrates of Samos and to the Pisistratids in Athens). He was widely imitated in later times. An extensive collection of these, the Anacreontics, survives.

The Classical Period. Aeschylus (525 to 456–55 B.C.) is represented by seven plays, all dating from after the Persian invasion of 480–479 B.C. In the earliest of these (*Persai* [*Persians,* 472 B.C.], and *Hepta epi Thēbas* [*Seven Against Thebes,* 467 B.C.]) love plays only a minor role; the affection of the Persian ladies, wives, sisters, and mothers of the absent warriors, their longing for the return of their men, the desire evident in their eyes, their weeping, all give evidence of their love for their men; and the queen Atossa, mother of Xerxes, clearly expresses her love for her son and her anxiety about his safety. Similarly, in the *Seven Against Thebes* the chorus of Theban women gives utterance to their affectionate feelings and apprehensions concerning their own soldier loved ones. But in both plays these are only incidental results of the action, neither causing it nor determining its course. In the *Seven,* however, the love of the former king Laius for his wife, Jocasta, apparently had been (before the beginning of the play, as narrated by the chorus in the second stasimon, lines 743–761) the cause of his violating the express prohibition, given by Apollo at Delphi, against his leaving any issue. It was his son by Jocasta, Oedipus, who was the agent of the later woes that beset Thebes. There are other complicating factors besides love that dominate the events of the play, but love cannot be ignored.

Hiketides (*Suppliants,* 463 B.C.) is a very different matter, for in this play, alone among the seven that survive, love is the central and dominating issue, whether love accompanied by violence and rightly rejected, or love wrongly rejected but violently pursued. The fifty sons of Aegyptus have (prior to the opening of the action) fallen in love with the fifty daughters of Danaus (their cousins, for all are descendants of Io, an Argive princess) and sought to marry them; but the Danaids have, apparently for no better reason than a willful and perhaps wrongful rejection of love, refused to accept their suit and have fled by ship from Egypt to Argos, the men pursuing. This is one possible interpretation of the drama: the Danaids apparently have an unreasonable revulsion toward any love from men. Another possible interpretation is that the sons of Aegyptus manifested arrogance and violence from the outset, although this is nowhere actually stated in the text of the play, so that the women fled for fear of force. But under either interpretation love and the rejection of love are the prime causes of the action. There is much discussion of love and of marriage and virginity in the play, which ends with the men apparently about to gain the upper hand. The two remaining tragedies of the trilogy (Aeschylus regularly composed in trilogies) presumably tell of the victory of the Egyptians, the enforced marriage, and the vengeance taken by the Danaids, who on their wedding night slew with concealed knives their bridegrooms—all but one, that is, for one of the girls, having fallen in love with her husband, spared him. The final resolution of the situation is either the judgment and condemnation of the forty-nine and the commendation of the one surviving pair, or the opposite. In any case, a fragment survives, usually attributed to the third play (*Danaïdēs* [*Danaids,* c. 463 B.C.]), which contains, it is believed, lines from a speech of Aphrodite, who perhaps appeared at the end in an epiphany. They assert the universally beneficent, fructifying, and generative power of love, which pervades all living things.

The final group of plays is the *Oresteia* (458 B.C.), the only complete trilogy by Aeschylus to survive; it consists of the *Agamemnon,* the *Choēphoroi (Libation Bearers),* and the *Eumenides.* Love is neither prominent nor happy in any of them. The *Agamemnon* is the account of the return of Agamemnon victorious from Troy, only to be murdered upon his arrival by his wife, Clytemnestra, with the connivance of her paramour, Aegisthus. The motive of both is vengeance; on the queen's part for Iphigenia, her daughter, sacrificed at Aulis to obtain safe sailing for the fleet against Troy, and on Aegisthus' part for his older brothers, killed, cooked, and served at dinner by Agamemnon's father, Atreus, to his brother and Aegisthus' father, Thyestes. The queen may once have loved her husband, but at Aulis her love was turned to hate, and this hatred governed the rest of her life. Agamemnon had, indeed, loved his charming daughter, but he feared to spare her lest his allies revolt and his expedition to retrieve Helen perish before its launching. And, of course, behind all this was the love between Helen and Paris, here no longer portrayed in a favorable light, as to some degree in Homer, but plainly condemned as lustful, adulterous, and ruinous. Finally, Apollo had once loved Cassandra, Priam's daughter and Agamemnon's prisoner, slave, and concubine, but her present woe and imminent death are a result of

Apollo's thwarted affection. In brief, what love there may have been in the background of this play has all gone wrong. In neither the *Libation Bearers* nor the *Eumenides* does love play any significant part.

Sophocles (c. 496–406 B.C.), too, is today represented by only seven out of the more than one hundred plays that he wrote. In the *Aias* (*Ajax,* before 441 B.C.) Tecmessa, the hero's prize and concubine, manifests loyalty and affection toward him that may indeed be love; her remarks are slightly reminiscent of Andromache's to Hector in the *Iliad,* although their circumstances are very different. After his death, too, her lament is touching. Teucer, also, is loyal and steadfast, both before and after his half-brother Ajax's death, and may be regarded as an example of brotherly love. But in the main the plot hinges on wholly other matters, and love is not one of the issues of the play. The *Antigone* (c. 441 B.C.) illustrates magnificently the conflict between private and public duty, between divine and human law. But love, though not the cardinal issue, is nevertheless pervasive in feeling and tenderness. Antigone clearly loved both her brothers, although she is concerned about burying only one (Polynices; Eteocles had his proper rites), and her motivation for doing so is as much a sense of family duty as of love. She may be supposed to be in love with Haemon, although there is no scene between them; her feelings for him, however, are referred to by Ismene, her sister, and she most certainly felt deep anguish at having to die unwed and unfulfilled as a woman (note the bridal imagery in several instances). Certainly Haemon was genuinely in love with her, as is shown by his vigorous defense of her to the king, his father, and his desperate suicide at her place of interment. Although harsh and tyrannical, Creon, putting a stern and narrow concept of his royal duty before all other considerations, is not without human feeling, as becomes clear in the poignant passages in which he discovers his son dead and learns of his wife's suicide. In this play love, although subordinate to other themes, greatly helps to evoke sympathy, as well as admiration, for Antigone and serves to demonstrate that Creon, too, is a tragic figure who learns by suffering.

By contrast with the other plays of Sophocles, the *Trachiniai* (*Trachinian Women*, c. 430 B.C.) may be called a love story, albeit a tragic one. Deianira, the heroine and wife of Heracles, having lived with him and endured his long absences for many years and his infidelities on the road as well, is still intensely in love with him. As the action commences, she announces that he has been away now for fifteen months, longer than usual; but what particularly has aroused her anxiety is an oracle that he had entrusted to her before his departure, wherein it was written that this latest was to be the last of his many journeys afar, to last for fifteen months, the end of which should see him relieved of all his many toils, either serenely happy and at rest or dead. Since the ordained time has come, she despatches their son, Hyllus, to find him. And presently news is brought that booty and prisoners sent on ahead by Heracles, while he lingers on Mt. Oeta to make sacrifice, have arrived. Upon receiving the prisoners she learns that one of them, the beautiful Iole, daughter of the king of Euboea, is now her husband's reigning mistress. Deianira, distraught but unwilling to harm Iole and understanding the ways of men, bethinks herself of a tunic, a shirt which the centaur Nessus had once given her (as he lay dying, slain by Heracles on their wedding journey), with the assurance that, bathed in his own (Nessus') blood, it would prove a potent means of recovering her lord's affections, should this be needed. She resolves to avail herself of it now, and entrusts it to a messenger for Heracles, with the instruction that only he must wear it and only when sacrificing. After the messenger's departure, she discloses to the chorus that, of course, Nessus' blood had been infected with the venom of the Lernaean hydra when he had been struck by the poisoned arrows of Heracles, and she is now fearful that the tunic, instead of restoring her spouse's affections, may fatally poison him. Presently Hyllus arrives to report the terrible affliction of his father upon donning the garment. He accuses her of murder, whereupon Deianira departs, and presently it is announced that she has killed herself in remorse. Next, Heracles is carried in wracked with pain. After denouncing his wife, he is informed that she is dead by her own hand. Heracles finally instructs Hyllus to build him a funeral pyre, to place him upon it, and to burn him. This is done. Both have, in a sense, died for love.

Oidipous epi Kolōnō (Oedipus at Colonus, c. 406 B.C.) the last play of Sophocles, an account of the marvelous passage into the other world of the blind and aged Oedipus, now for many years an exile, presents love in striking contrast with hate as creating a chiaroscuro against which the figures of the drama move. The love of Oedipus for his two daughters, Antigone, who attends and guides him, and Ismene, who keeps him informed of what is afoot in Thebes, and their love for him are juxtaposed with the old king's hatred for Creon, his uncle and brother-in-law, who in his turn is harsh and arrogant toward Oedipus and violent toward his daughters, and the even more bitter hatred that exists between Oedipus and his two sons, whom he curses. Creon and Polynices represent discord and conflict, Antigone and Ismene, harmony, and Theseus, serenity.

Euripides (480 or 484–406 B.C.), the third great tragic poet of the Greeks, is today represented by seventeen plays. Three of these require particular attention, a few others brief notice. The *Alkēstis* (*Alcestis,* 438 B.C.) is hardly a tragedy in any but the technical Aristotelian sense, certainly not in the modern; but it is very clearly a love story. King Admetus, who has harbored and treated kindly the god Apollo during the latter's necessary exile in servitude in expiation for a murder, is rewarded by the god, upon the occasion of his release from his punishment, in a somewhat odd fashion. Apollo has learned from the Fates the day on which Admetus is destined to die and has obtained from them a modification, in that, if the king can find someone who willingly will die in his place, he may live on. This information the god gives to the king before departing. The appointed day having arrived, Admetus can find no one who will die in his place, not even either of his parents. Finally his wife, Alcestis, upon being approached, cheerfully agrees to lay down her life for his out of her love for him, and this is done. The depth of her love for her husband is truly moving and beautifully portrayed, and it forms the central theme of the drama. Love here is indeed all. The happy ending is provided by Heracles, who, in gratitude for Admetus' unstinting hospitality even on a day of sorrow, undertakes to wrestle with the god Death and, conquering him, restores Alcestis to her lord.

The *Mēdeia* (*Medea*, 431 B.C.), quite properly a tragedy, is at once very different and more complex in structure and emotional pattern. Medea had, long ago in Colchis, fallen madly in love with the hero Jason and enabled him, by her acumen and magical skills, to obtain the golden fleece. She had accompanied him, after destroying her brother for his sake, and later she had also caused the death of Jason's uncle, who was ill-disposed toward him. They had at length settled in Corinth and have two young sons. Medea is a woman of immense emotional and intellectual power, and she is passionately in love with Jason, who, however, is much more emotionally detached and views love as a force that can be used to his advantage to get him ahead in the world. Accordingly, as the play opens, it is made clear that he has set Medea aside and arranged to marry the daughter of the king of Corinth. Medea is distraught; when she realizes that he has no intention of abandoning his scheme, her passionate love is transformed into equally passionate hate. A proud, determined, and ingenious woman, she devises a plan whereby she can avenge herself upon him without suffering any injury herself. In the end, the king and Jason's new bride expire in terrible torment, and Medea is driven away in a winged chariot provided by her grandfather, the Sun, and carries away with her the bodies of her two children, leaving Jason helpless and utterly desolate. Their sons she had slain, although she loved them dearly, in order to prevent them from falling into their father's hands, whether for his vengeance or his comfort. The scene in which she faces the grim necessity of killing them is one of anguish, for here is a part of the former love that is still alive and has the power to cause her intense pain.

The *Hippolytos* (*Hippolytus*, 428 B.C.), too, has love as its chief and central theme, love of woman for man, but with the focus not on marriage or on tender feeling, but on sexual desire (and adultery, but this aspect is secondary). Of primary interest here, however, is the dramatic framework and the divine role, for the action is a conflict between two goddesses: Aphrodite (love, sexual enjoyment) and Artemis (virginity and hunting). In the prologue Aphrodite appears as a dea ex machina, openly as the goddess of sexual attraction, and announces that since Hippolytus, the youthful son of Theseus by Hippolyta, the Amazon, is devoted to hunting and to Artemis, goddess of the chase, to the point of neglecting her (he insists on preserving his virginity), she is determined to destroy him. To accomplish this she has caused Phaedra, Theseus' present wife, his step-mother, to lust passionately for him. No matter how Hippolytus may respond, he will be ruined, and so, too, will Phaedra, but this consideration will not stand in Aphrodite's way, for she is resolved to even the score with Artemis. The drama, played out between two mortals, is in fact a conflict of power between two divinities. The nature of Aphrodite is here perceptible as the goddess of love and at the same time the embodiment or personification of the sexual urge. But the human agents are real, and their sufferings far too acute for the play to be taken as merely allegory, although it is that in part. The main action of the play simply works out the details of Aphrodite's revenge. Phaedra, helplessly longing for Hippolytus and reduced to a wretched state, nevertheless tries to resist her passion and remain faithful to her husband; but her old serving woman, without the principles of her mistress and seeing no virtue in repression, at length cajoles her into an apparent acquiescence to her making a proposal to Hippolytus on Phaedra's behalf. But the young man is at once shocked and revolted and declines in no uncertain terms to accede to any sexual relation whatever. Phaedra, upon learning of his reaction, is terrified lest he reveal her advance to his father, although he has sworn an oath to secrecy, an oath which in fact, while tempted to disregard, he keeps. Distraught and despairing, unhappy Phaedra hangs herself after leaving a note accusing Hippolytus of violating her. Theseus, upon his return, filled with rage toward his son, curses him with one of the three curses granted him by Posidon, and the young man meets his death as a result of an encounter with a monster from the sea. Only when it is too late to save him does his father learn from Artemis that his son was innocent. Two mortals have perished to satisfy Aphrodite's honor. The role of love in this play, too, is confirmed and embellished by some magnificent choral odes that dwell on the nature of love as at once beguiling with charm and terrible in power (especially lines 525–564).

Old Comedy is, for all practical purposes, represented by Aristophanes. Although his plays refer now and again to marriage and to marital and parental love, these are never developed as major or even minor themes. Given the ithyphallic element in Aristophanic comedy, it is obvious that there will be a large amount of sexual humor and erotic joking, but these are employed for the amusement of the moment rather than as a reflection on the nature of human affection. They are bawdy and very funny, but have little to do with love.

New Comedy (last two decades of the 4th, and the 3d century B.C.) is a very different matter. There apparently was much about love in a fairly serious sense; but owing to the fragmentary nature of what remains of this period (Menander alone is represented by as much as most of one whole play), we shall let our treatment of Latin comedy stand for it. (Note that New Comedy belongs chronologically to the Hellenistic Age.)

The prose writers of Greek literature were historians, orators, and philosophers. While there are many references to women, to marriage, and to extramarital liaisons in these writers, the interest is usually historical, social, or legal, and no great attention is given to love as an emotion. Empedocles (poet-philosopher, 5th century) has an elaborate discussion of love (or attraction) as a cosmic force in nature countervalent to hate (or repulsion), but the treatment is wholly impersonal and physical. Plato has a philosophical treatment of love in his dialogues *Symposion* (*Symposium*, c. 384 B.C.)—see also *Phaidros* (*Phaedrus*), in which the love of one beautiful body will lead the soul through the contemplation of many beautiful bodies, via the concept of physical beauty in general, at length to grasp the idea of beauty. Finally, both Plato (*Nomoi* [*The Laws,* c. 350 B.C.]) and Aristotle (*Politika* [*Politics,* essays, 4th century B.C.]) have elaborate considerations of love, marriage, the family, and the begetting and rearing of children, but these are wholly directed toward the establishment of the best possible form of the state.

The Hellenistic Period. Of Hellenistic poets there are three who merit attention. Menander has been mentioned briefly. Theocritus (c. 300–260 B.C.) is traditionally hailed as the father of bucolic or pastoral poetry. Among his works (called idylls) there are bucolic poems proper (e.g., 1, 3, 7), there are vivid scenes of contemporary life, not necessarily rural (e.g., 2, 15), and there are poems on subjects drawn from mythology (e.g., 11, 18, 22) and some in praise of contemporary princes (e.g., 16, 17). Of the third group, Idyll 11, on the love of the Cyclops for Galatea, though mythological, has genuinely bucolic flavor and is a love song of great appeal. The Cyclops, acknowledging his singularly ugly appearance, yet urges on Galatea his lasting devotion, pointing out that faithfulness is to be preferred to beauty. In the second group, Idyll 2, the *Pharmakeutria* (*The Sorcerer*) is a brilliant and penetrating portrayal of a girl in love attempting by magic to recover the affection of her unfaithful lover. It is one of the finest surviving examples of the intimate analytical treatment of amatory themes, which is the great innovation of the Hellenistic period. The course of the affair is reviewed in detail from the first glimpse that aroused the erotic flame in the girl's bosom through the gloriously blissful consummation to her present lonely desolation. She is divided between praying for the return of her beloved to her and devising injuries that will cause him to suffer in punishment. The idylls of the first group are peopled with rustic swains and country maids and filled with singing contests centering on themes of love, notably on such traditional figures of bucolic passion as Daphnis, with shepherds' reed pipes, with wooden milk bowls, and tender kids as prizes, and abound with allusions to pastoral life and local flora. Although they have their own conventions, they are polished and artful, but totally apolitical.

Apllonius of Rhodes (3d century B.C.) is the only Hellenistic poet to produce an epic, the *Argonautika* (*Argonauts*), in the traditional Homeric meter and dialect. But in style it is far less splendidly heroic, while the manner of presenting the love affair has a romantic coloring. Hera and Athena, eager for the survival and success of Jason, their favorite, prevail on Aphrodite to cause her son, Eros, to make Medea, the Colchian princess and sorceress, fall in love with him. Eros, pictured as a mischievous young boy, shoots one of his little arrows into Medea's heart, whereupon she at once conceives an irresistible passion for Jason. This whole scene, very different from anything known from the Classical Period, is, in fact, typically Hellenistic. What follows, the course of Medea's love and Jason's response, the careful and penetrating attention to the inner motivation of the lovers and the progress of their feelings is, again, unlike anything of the earlier period, but very similar, on a more extended scale, to the study of love as a passion in Theocritus' Idyll 2. It glances backward to the relationship between

Jason and Medea—at a later stage of its development—in Euripides' play and forward to the affair in Virgil's *Aeneis* (*Aeneid*, epic poem, 19 B.C.) between Aeneas and Dido. Medea is throughout the more ardent, the more totally committed, and even the more aggressive of the pair. Jason is responsive and a thoroughly cooperative and satisfactory lover, especially at the outset, but cooler and calculating of his fortune. Late on, in book 4, as they near Greece, Medea is hard put to obtain from him some sort of permanent commitment.

Roman Literature

The Pre-Classical Period. Roman comedy is represented, for practical purposes, by Plautus (c. 250–184 B.C.) and Terence (c. 185–159 B.C.). Both wrote the type of comedy derived from Greek New Comedy; indeed, their plots are derived from those of Menander and others, the characters have Greek names and wear Greek dress, and the action takes place in Greek towns. For all that, they manage (particularly Plautus) to give a Roman air to their productions. Yet an acquaintance with these Latin playwrights is still the best way to grasp what the plays of Greek New Comedy must have been like. Essentially, the plots are always love-stories. The young man falls madly in love with a girl, wants to marry her, and despite all obstacles, at the end succeeds in doing so. The variations are many, the complications formidable, but love and the poets' ingenuity triumph over all. Sometimes the girl is a slave, or seems to be such, sometimes a prostitute, sometimes she is in want, or again, the boy may be out of money. But, after all the adversities have threatened and been surmounted, love triumphs. The girl turns out to be free-born or even an heiress; the boy's family fortune is restored; shipwrecks, pirates, exposures of infants, irascible fathers, conniving pimps, drunken companions, confusions of identity, all finally vanish. To be sure, in some of the plays other aspects of the plot seem to overshadow in interest the basic love affair, as do pairs of identical twins in Plautus' *Menaechmi* (*The Two Menaechmuses*, c. 200 B.C.), the character of the braggart soldier in Plautus' *Miles gloriosus* (*The Braggart Soldier*, c. 204 B.C.), the virtues of lenience in rearing children as opposed to strictness in Terence's *Adelphi* (160 B.C.), the machinations of the witty but unscrupulous parasite in Terence's *Phormio* (161 B.C.); but all is well, provided love is well.

The Early Classical Period. Lucretius (didactic poet, 94–55 B.C.), who wrote in epic hexameters an exposition of Epicurean philosophy, opened his poem *De rerum natura* (*On the Nature of Things*, n.d.) with a brilliant and famous apostrophe of *Alma Venus*, the traditional ancestress of the Roman people, as personifying the generating, life-giving power of love.

Catullus (elegiac, lyric, epigrammatist, 87–58 B.C.) was a poet in the Alexandrian tradition, learned, sophisticated, rich in mythological allusion, and working for the most part in short units. He is also, however, the most intense and personal love poet to emerge in the ancient world. Sappho occasionally and Archilochus perhaps more often were his only close rivals. He is novel in another respect, too, in that he is the first, in his love poetry, to write almost exclusively and quite realistically of his own love affair; his love poems form, more than do those of any earlier poet, an amatory autobiography. He calls his mistress Lesbia; scholars are virtually agreed that she was in fact Clodia, a wealthy and noble woman of few moral inhibitions. The affair began apparently rapidly, moved to a consummation of ecstatic pleasure, waned and waxed again, through a series of suspicions, quarrels, and reconciliations, to a final and irrevocable collapse in intense bitterness. The early playful attention to his mistress's pet sparrow, the joyous fascination of kissing her a thousand times, the assured contempt of censorious disapproval, the rapture of commitment without restraint, contrast sharply with the desolation and disillusion that follow. Catullus also composed a Latin version of Sappho's most physical poem (51, "Ille mi par esse deo videtur ["Then like a God He Seems to Me"]) in Latin Sapphic strophe; noteworthy, too, are his charming poem on Acme and Septimius (45), the Epithalamia or Wedding Songs (56, 62), and the poem on the Marriage of Peleus and Thetis (64); these last three (231, 66, and 408 lines) are longer than his usual love lyrics.

The Classical Period: The Augustan Age. Virgil (70–19 B.C.) is the greatest of all Roman poets and one of the very great poets of all time. His earliest published work is the *Bucolica* (*Eclogues* or *Bucolics,* 42–39 B.C.), ten hexameter poems varying in length from sixty-three to one hundred and eleven lines, dealing with country life and love in the tradition of Theocritus, with, however, important differences. Some have little or nothing about love (e.g., 1, 4), others much (e.g., 2, 8, 10). The countryside is, where identifiable, mainly Italian; there are many themes not found in Theocritus, for example, politics, civil war, rural disorganization, land confiscation, the golden age, and various discussions of literature. The tone is highly sophisticated and the interests of contemporary society conspicuous. In 2, Corydon laments the cruelty and want of faith of Alexis. The psychological depth is Virgilian, the idea of *dives amator* as rival does not reflect a Greek model, and the rapid shift of mood gives a dramatic effect not noted in Theocritus. Eclogue 8 affords a perception of contrast between how two lovers react to infidelity. Eclogue 10 shows Gallus, a Roman and a man of letters, languishing in Arcady, and his idea of rural life contemplates not tending pastures and flocks, but hunting. On the whole the treatment of love is tender, delicate, and discriminating, but a feeling of urbanity is pervasive.

In the *Aeneid* there is more of love. The feeling of affection between mother and son, real although necessarily somewhat remote when the mother is a goddess, becomes evident in book 1 in Venus' solicitude for her son when, disguised as a huntress, she meets Aeneas, tells him where he is, and directs him toward Dido's city, and finally when she causes her son, the boy Cupid, to substitute himself for Ascanius at the initial entertainment in Dido's palace. Again, in book 2, Venus advises Aeneas to leave the fallen Troy, and several times in the next two books she intervenes to aid Aeneas. This same maternal protection and aid is manifested also on several occasions in books 7 through 12, until the ultimate fight has been completed. Aeneas' affection for his son and his reverent duty toward his father, Anchises, are demonstrated on various occasions in books 2, 3, 5, and 6, and later (for Ascanius and Iulus).

But the greatest love story in the *Aeneid,* powerful and carefully wrought, is the love affair between Aeneas and Dido, which is initiated in the closing lines of book 1 and consummated in book 4. It is told with sympathy and understanding for the queen; it probes her passion and her mind with care and precision, tracing the torrential course of her emotions, but the poet leaves no doubt that she is doomed from the beginning. Her passion is mercilessly manipulated by Venus for the safety of her son and frustrated by Jupiter for the accomplishment of the destiny of Aeneas and Rome. As early as book 1, line 712, she is described as "praecipue infelix, pesti devota futurae [And above all, luckless Dido—doomed to face catastrophe]," and again, in line 749, "infelix Dido [luckless Dido]." There is much in the affair that invites comparison with Apollonius' handling of Jason and Medea, and, more significantly, there are important differences. Dido is divinely wounded, Aeneas responds; her emotions are described in detail, his are not. On the morning of the destined day of accomplishment the appearance of both is given in the grand epic manner; both are greater, more glorious, more radiant than ordinary mortals. But how swift and how chilling the climax (4.167–170): "The fires flashed, the sky was aware of the union, and the nymphs shrieked on their peak. That day was first the cause of death, first of evils." From this moment on the narrative moves straight and unrelentingly to doom for Dido. Aeneas departs to his destiny.

Horace (65–8 B.C.), the next great poet of the reign of Augustus, treats love, as he does most aspects of life, with grace, with good humor, and usually with delicacy. His references to his father are fond and grateful (*Satirae* [*Satires* I, 6 (45–86) 4, (105 ff.)], c. 30–37 B.C.) and to women are charming and understanding, but free of entanglement. He is without peer in his portrayals of a young girl's fragrant allure (*Carmina* [*Odes,* c. 23 B.C.] 15), of her timid gracefulness of limb, like a doe (1.23), of her lovely voice, and of her coquettish airs. He can be gently sad, yet hopeful, as age advances (3.26), ready to resume love's intrigues once more (4.1); he can also be mercilessly frank about the fading charms of the aging courtesan (4.13). But he is almost invariably amiable, tolerant, and detached.

Tibullus was the earliest of the major elegists of Augustus' reign; at least he was the earliest to die (19 B.C.), apparently still fairly young. The Roman elegists of this period devote their poetry—to say nothing of themselves—primarily, although not exclusively, to love. They are the love poets par excellence of Latin literature. Tibullus' mistress, whom he addresses in five of the ten elegies of his first book (1.1, 2, 3, 5, 6), was Delia, whose actual name was Plania, a free woman of obscure *gens* (stock), possibly married. He declares his devotion to her, prefers her service to warfare and riches, wants her with him in the quiet life in the country, complains that she is watched by a *custos* (watchman), laments when excluded from her house and company, suspects her of having another lover (a *dives amator*), upon whom he invokes a variety of curses, and recalls that she has made the rites of the Bona Dea an excuse for going out. In book 2 Delia has disappeared, and is replaced by Nemesis (real name unknown), apparently a courtesan. He speaks of the *servitium Amoris* (service or slavery of Love) that binds him in her service (2.4) and describes the scenes of rough, rural abundance where he is detained because of her sojourning there. Finally (2.6) he announces that he will take up the military life, but finds that he cannot bear to tear himself away from her; *acer Amor* (stern Love) tortures him beyond endurance.

Propertius (c. 48–2 B.C., or earlier) is an elegiac poet of considerably greater volume of production, of wider range and variety, more imagination, more enormous learning, and greater poetic power than Tibullus and real and intense feeling. His work may be regarded as the high point in the theme of Love in Roman literature. His first book, which he called the *Monobiblos,* was addressed to his mistress, Cynthia (actual name Hostia), almost certainly a courtesan of beauty, wit, education, experience, and singular attraction for Propertius. She is less prominent in his subsequent books, a little so in book 2, considerably so in book 3, and represented in book 4 in only two poems. The great majority of the poems in the first two books are concerned with love, about half of those in book 3, and in book 4 only three or four. Book 1 was perhaps published in 28 B.C. or shortly before; book 2 in 26 B.C., book 3 in 23 B.C. (or both 2 and 3 perhaps together c. 23 B.C., possibly originally as three books, with 2 divided); and book 4 c. 16 B.C. (not before).

Unlike Catullus certainly, and probably unlike Tibullus, Propertius, although writing with real passion, is not writing autobiography. The incidents described in the poems certainly did not occur in the order arranged, and some or many of them may not be literally accurate, although really felt. Nor need the woman named "Cynthia" be supposed to be the same woman throughout. Propertius clearly applied his considerable intellect as well as his imagination to the theme of love, which fascinated him, and he examines it in every conceivable mode and variation. Exalted and depressed, serene and angry, devoted and disillusioned by turn, he sees love and the beloved in many lights, in many situations, and varying combinations of these, as well as seeing women of somewhat different character and disposition. Cynthia may be present or absent, accessible or not, serene or captious, good-humored or angry, faithful or unfaithful, and all of these in relation to similar shifts in himself. The result is a collection of poems of extraordinary range, variety, and interest. His style is brilliant, now vivid, now mysterious, often epigrammatic, sometimes apparently simple, or again learned and allusive. His appeal is both to the intellect and to the emotions.

Ovid (43 B.C.–A.D. 18) wants the power and the passion of Propertius, but he was extraordinarily inventive, graceful, and smooth in language and witty and totally artificial in his love poems, but always clear and entertaining. The *Amores* (c. 20 B.C., three books) recount with resource and invention his experiences in love, presumably with Corinna, his mistress (but here there seems to be no real person behind the name). The *Heroides* (n.d.) is a series of letters ostensibly written by famous heroines of mythology to their husbands or lovers (twenty-one epistles). The *Ars amatoria* (*Art of love,* c. 1 B.C.) instructs the novice on how to select, court, and enjoy available partners of the opposite sex (books 1 and 2 help men, book 3, women). The *Remedia amoris* (*The Cures for Love,* n.d.) teaches how to reverse the process, fall out of love, and discontinue the affair. Ovid's other works, though varied, ingenious, and informative, do not fall under the rubric of love.

See also: Androgyny, La Belle Dame sans Merci, Homosexuality, Lesbianism, *Liebestod,* Love Triangle, Secret Love, Senex Amator, Sex (Heterosexual, Erotic).

Selected Bibliography

Harsh, Philip Whaley. *A Handbook of Classical Drama.* Stanford, Calif.: Stanford University Press, 1944.
Kenney, E. J., ed. *The Cambridge History of Classical Literature.II. Latin Literature.* Cambridge: Cambridge University Press, 1982.
Lesky, Albin. *A History of Greek Literature.* London: Methuen, 1966.
Luck, G. *The Latin Love Elegy.* 2d ed. London: Methuen, 1969.

CHARLES H. REEVES

LOVE TRIANGLE

Storytellers have always been interested in conflict. From the parting of Light and Dark in Genesis to the sight of protesters clashing on the street with police, the pairing of opposites has excited passion and laid the basis for many of the world's great moral systems. Such a clear dichotomy, however, while satisfying the prescriptive demands of morality, has frequently been modified in the hands of storytellers to fit the richness of experience. Primitive hunters were seldom alone when they cornered the great mastodons. Servants in twelfth-century France did not wait on their masters in empty castles, and lovers of all ages seldom have retreated to desert islands. If the love triangle has such an enduring and universal allurement in literature, it has less to do with the triangle's strength than with man's age-old habit of leaning on other people. To portray individuals in a triangle is to show man as a creature capable of sharing or seeking influence, courting approval, or fleeing from an established alliance. In short, the triangle offers a paradigm not only of the individual's will, but of the ways of the wider society.

The term "love triangle," while coined in twelfth-century Europe, has always been present as a concept in literature. Numerous examples can be found in mythology—the universal illustrations being the Oedipus and Oresteian triangles, or in a collective sense, the tragic triangle. The elements of the tragic triangle are father, mother, and son. Explicit within the triangle are the father's murder and the incestuous union of the mother and son.

The feudal love triangle is comprised of a lord, his lady, and one of his vassals. The lord can count on allegiance from his liege, even as far as the death of his vassal. The bond of love between vassal and lady tends to undermine the rival force, that is, the bond of allegiance. The vassal oscillates between these two forces, and any action by him or the lady can destroy the equilibrium of the triangle. Destructive acts on the part of the vassal invariably abuse civil, religious, and chivalrous codes.

If, however, the triangle were to be composed of two women competing for a man, the forces defined here do not apply. Blind rivalry between the two ladies could degenerate into senseless revenge—such as the death of innocent children in the myth of Medea. In the Tristan myth, women having the same name compete. The wife's deceit kills both her husband and her rival. Such a triangle usually appears only as an appendage to the original love triangle.

The love triangle enjoyed an extended literary vogue between the twelfth and fifteenth centuries. The triangle served as a medium for most works dealing with courtly love, and it was elaborated most conspicuously in the novel. In the sixteenth and seventeenth centuries, it extended its appeal to both the tragic and comic theater. The illicit side of the triangle has since found its way into many epics that have evolved from Genesis, most notably Milton's *Paradise Lost* (1667). In the eighteenth century the prose novel enjoyed a revival. In the nineteenth century it blossomed from the courts of Spain to the palaces of St. Petersburg. By this time, however, the word "love" has disappeared. The compelling force of nineteenth-century society, based essentially on family and marriage, has lessened the traditional sympathy toward the lovers. This is now a society that values husbands above all. They have made him a "jailer" (S. de Beauvoir, *Le deuxième sexe* [*The Second Sex,* essay, 1949]), solely responsible for the conduct of his wife. If he fails to keep her on the straight and narrow path, he is an accessory to her indiscretion. The longevity of the theme is expressed in the newer term—"eternal triangle." The authors of the twentieth century have reached out to all periods in their various triangles, but with particular interest (after Freud) in the Oedipus triangle.

Antiquity

The idea of the triangle in Grecian antiquity is best examplified in the *Oresteia* of Aeschylus (trilogy of plays, 458 B.C.) as well as in Sophocles' *Oidipous tyrannos* (*Oedipus Rex,* play, c. 429 B.C.) and *Oidipous epi Kolōnō* (*Oedipus at Colonus,* play, c. 406 B.C.).

Aeschylus considered the idea of justice to be central to both the definition of drama and the definition of man, because man must choose between the conflicting claims of Apollo and the mother goddesses, in this case the Eumenides. In the triad of the Orestes, after the mother kills the father, she must die for her part in his death. She claims, however, that in killing her husband, she has avenged the death of her daughter. Her son will avenge his father, and crime will go on engendering more crime. Human revenge always compounds the mistakes. Aeschylus' idea that crime will go on engendering more crime appears often in the Elizabethan "tragedy of revenge."

The first of the three plays that form the *Oresteia, Agamemnon,* contains a triangle: Agamemnon, Clytemnestra, and Aegisthus. It resolves into the murder of the king. The second of the trilogy, *Choēphoroi (Libation Bearers)*, contains still another trilogy, Clytemnestra, Aegisthus, and Orestes. The latter will be referred to as the Oresteian triangle. The outcome, consequence of the first triangle, is the murders of Aegisthus and Clytemnestra by Orestes. There is matricide and resulting madness for the avenger of his father's murder.

In Sophocles' *Oedipus Rex,* again the three points of the triangle lie wholly in the family. Sophocles, of course, has simplified the Oresteian situation. In a sophisticated way, wordly power and domestic intimacy have been intermingled. Son and lover have unwittingly become one. The Oedipus triangle will comprise patricide *and* incest.

In the early seventeenth century, Shakespeare's tragedy *Hamlet* (c. 1600) contains elements of the three triangles outlined here. Gertrude, Claudius, and Hamlet reflect fully the Oresteian triangle. The revenge-seeking ghost of King Hamlet, however, recalls the earlier triangle of Agamemnon, Clytemnestra, and Aegisthus. Numerous references by Hamlet to incest bring into the play the main component of the Oedipus triangle. Amidst the pervading struggle for power, Hamlet feigns madness. He becomes a murderer, but will not commit matricide. Finally Hamlet's efforts to thwart Claudius' attempts against his life recall the struggle in *Oedipus Rex* of Tiresias and Creon against Oedipus. Shakespeare has touched upon all the themes comprised into the Oresteian triangle, as well as the Oedipus triangle.

Recurring madness—pain inflicted upon the matricide—prevents Racine's Oreste, in the tragedy *Andromaque* (1667), to complete by his suicide the everlasting triangle, the blood wedding of Pyrrhus whom he has killed, of Hermione whom he has loved, and of himself, the ill-fated avenger.

In choosing the myth of Oedipus for his play, *La machine infernale (The Infernal Machine*, 1934), Cocteau wanted to embody modes of awareness that the seventeenth century only touched upon. He supports beforehand Little's thesis (*Myth and Society in Attic Drama,* 1967), that Athenian playwriting was the vehicle by means of which the popular mind advanced from tribal to city-communal ways of thinking.

Because the town of Thebes is stricken by the plague, King Oedipus seeks to identify the culprit. This leads to a struggle between him and Creon, brother of Queen Jocasta and the intervention of the gods—the infernal machine—through the medium of Tiresias, the seer. This subsequently invites the invasion by society of the triangle that contains forces it cannot tolerate. It expels from its midst the patricide, the incestuous, the scapegoat. In the nineteenth century novel, the lover, the "alienated hero" will be expelled again and again.

In claiming that "King Oedipus, who slew his father Laius and married his mother Jocasta, merely shows us the fulfillment of our own childhood wishes"

(*Die Traumdeutung* [*The Interpretation of Dreams,* 1900]), Freud has lessened the impact of the incest, indispensible component of the Oedipus triangle. He has placed it in the realm of the little boys' fantasies. In the second scene of Cocteau's *La machine infernale,* the cradle lies next to the conjugal bed. The consumation of the marriage is doomed by this proximity. Was incest part of the dreams of little Prince Hamlet?

The best illustration of the Oedipus triangle at this basic level is found in a Japanese epic, Lady Murasaki's *Genji monogatari* (*The Tale of Genji,* novel, 11th century). In a few strokes of the brush, the Lady Murasaki narrates the childhood of Prince Gengi, son of the emperor and of his concubine Kiritsubo. Having lost his mother at an early age, Gengi fantasizes in the company of the new concubine, the Lady Fujitsubo. He was told that the emperor had chosen the lady because of her resemblance to Gengi's dead mother.

The short-lived affair between Gengi and the Lady Fujitsubo has resulted in the birth of a new prince Gengi, whom the emperor recognizes as his own, rendering null and void the incestuous relationship. However, the deep sense of shame felt by the Lady Fujitsubo reminds one of the guilt that led, in the Oedipus myth, to Queen Jocasta's self-destruction.

In antiquity the last fateful heroine of an incestuous triangle is Phaedra, whom Aphrodite caused to love Hippolytus—the son of Theseus. The subject has been treated both by Euripides and by the Roman poet Seneca. In the seventeenth century it will inspire Racine to write the tragedy *Phèdre* (*Phaedra,* 1677).

The Middle Ages

The distinctive kind of relationship called a love triangle arises in the last quarter of the twelfth century. After the Norman occupation, the literary production of France, as well as that of England, evidences a commingling of Greco-Roman and Celtic traditions. The love triangle will make manifest elements of these two cultures. It deeply reflects the feudal system with its notions of landed property and its strict hierarchy. These notions regulate both the roles of lord and vassal, as well as knight and lady.

Two sorts of triangles arise. The first, the Arthurian, is typically composed of the lord—king Arthur, his lady—Guinevere, and the vassal—Lancelot of the Lake. The written source is Geoffrey of Monmouth's *Historia regum Britanniae* (*The History of the Kings of Britain,* c. 1137) itself inspired by Nennius' *Historia Brittonum* (c. 800). The second sort of three-pointed conflict is the Tristan triangle; it reflects even more clearly the influence of the Celtic bards. Its story tells of Mark, king of Cornwall, of his nephew Tristan, and of Iseut, daughter of the queen of Ireland, as well as the wife of King Mark.

Two concepts of love are put forth in the two Anglo-Norman versions of the Tristan triangle, *Le roman de Tristan* (*The Romance of Tristan*), one of Thomas (c. 1170)—the courtly version—one of Béroul (c. 1190)—the common version. In Béroul's poem, the effect of the wayward love potion is temporary. At the end of three years, the lovers part and the common order resumes its tempo. In the Germanic analogs, Eilhart von Oberge's *Tristant and Isalde* (c. 1170) follows this version. Thomas, however, extends the effect of the potion to the grave, and the lovers must carry their impossible love all the way into death. This version influences Gottfried von Strassburg's romance *Tristan* (c. 1210). Gottfried's work will be the source of Wagner's opera *Tristan und Isolde* (*Tristan and Isolde*, 1865).

For more that two centuries, however, King Arthur and the Knights of the Round Table are the main source for the Arthurian romances. Chrétien de Troyes, the most admired writer of the twelfth century, turns from the Greco-Roman inspiration to the Round Table. He carries into his Arthurian romances a study of love that reflects Ovid's works on the subject. Two of Chrétien de Troyes' novels tell of Lancelot's love for Queen Guinevere. In *Lancelot* (romance, c. 1180), Chrétien de Troyes introduces elaborations of the ideas of hesitation and humiliation, the motifs associated with the hero's offense and, therefore, with all stages of its expiation. The major themes are Lancelot's exploits in the great tournament that takes place at King Arthur's court. At first Guinevere has ordered the knight not to do well (faire au pis). Only after three days does the queen order him to do his best (faire au mieux), at which time, Lancelot will display prodigious valor. In this novel, Chrétien de Troyes outlines a principle dear to all women in courtly circles. The perfect lover places himself in a state of total submissiveness to the will of the lady. Her good pleasure is the only law he can obey. Chrétien de Troyes evidently approves a notion of love that involves a reversal of values and a resulting isolation of the lovers from all those around them.

In the fifth canto of Dante's *Inferno (Hell)*, part 1 of the epic poem *La divina commedia* (*The Divine Comedy*, c. 1320), the love triangle that is presented— Paolo and Francesca killed by their brother and husband—is an illustration of the Tristan triangle. The lovers are united in death. The cause of their death, however, was the reading of *Lancelot*, an Arthurian romance. Tristan can be found among the shades with the other sinners of the flesh, notably with Paris and Helen—refugees from one of the most famous triangles.

Yet it is the story of Tristan and Iseult that will be featured most often in literature, all the way to the twentieth century. The reason for this survival is given in Denis de Rougemont's *L'amour et l'occident* (*Love in the Western World*, 1939 and 1956). The story of Tristan is a myth, "a story, a symbolic fable, simple and at the same time striking, summarizing an infinite number of more or less analogous situations. The myth permits one to seize, in one glance, uniform relations and to disengage them from the confusion of daily appearances."

The Indispensability of Keeping Love a Secret. Not only must Tristan and Iseult keep their love secret from the world, they must be assured that the king will not become suspicious. To do so, they are compelled to resort to deceit. This is to be applied to simple, daily occurrences—in the Béroul version, "Le rendez-vous sous l'arbre [meeting under the tree]" or "Le nain et la farine [the dwarf and the flour]''—where the lovers must trick the tricksters, the barons and their hireling, the Dwarf, who spy on the lovers' brief encounters.

The notion that to endure, love must be kept a secret, becomes, as Eileen Power points out in *Medieval Women* (1975), ''a peculiar characteristic of courtly love.'' Marie de France's lay *Lanval* (c. 1170) and *La Châtelaine de Vergi (The Lady of Vergi,* anonymous narrative poem, 13th century) show that it is indeed a sine qua non for survival.

Lanval's love is shrouded in secrecy. A fairy has granted him the power to summon her to his side when he so wishes. However, he will lose this power at the very instant he discloses the secret to anyone.

When the Châtelaine wishes to meet with her lover knight, she sends her emissary, a little dog, to the orchard. The knight knows then that he will meet only the Châtelaine. The author says that this system has worked a long time.

But the display of wealth and radiant happiness proves that Lanval and the knight *(La Châtelaine de Vergi)* are distinguished. Queen Guinevere and the duchess inform them of his fact. Both ladies made overtures to the knights. Both were turned down. Lanval, however, revealed inadvertently the existence of the fairy to Guinevere. Thus he lost the means to prove what he claimed, that this lady love was more beautiful than the queen. No amount of begging will bring back the beautiful fairy. In King Arthur's court, the barons proclaim Lanval guilty of felony. In *La Châtelaine de Vergi,* however, the knight has been discreet. He invokes the bond of allegiance he owes the duchess' husband to turn down her offer. Piqued, she accuses the knight of having tried to seduce her. The duke's wrath deeply grieves the lover of the Châtelaine. His lord gives him the choice of revealing his secret love's name or enduring perpetual banishment. Such banishment would of course prevent him from seeing the Châtelaine ever again. He chooses to reveal to the duke the way he meets his lady love, obtaining from the duke a pledge of secrecy.

The existence of a rival has led in both cases to a triangle where two ladies compete for the love of a knight. This triangle is weaker but potentially filled with dire consequences. The duchess knows her husband will kill her if she reveals the way the knight and the Châtelaine meet. She confronts, however, her rival with her knowledge. The Châtelaine is so grieved that she dies, and the knight stabs himself on her body. The duchess dies at the hands of her husband, but victory over her rival was dearer to her than her own life.

In *Lanval,* however, Guinevere is publicly humiliated. The fairy appears in court and refuses to speak to anybody but the king. As to the accused, he rushes in hot pursuit of his lady love and is never heard of again. On the contrary, in *La Châtelaine de Vergi,* the contrast between the devotion of the lovers and their tragic end raises questions about the absolute nature of love as it is understood by the Châtelaine. Such love cannot stand the exposure to society. Is it therefore impossible to make it fit within its bounds?

Invasion of the Grotesque into the Love Triangle. Of the medieval treatises on casuistic love, André Le Chapelain's *De arte honeste amandi (The Art of*

Courtly Love, 12th century) offers the most thorough codification of courtly love. Some of the dignity of woman in courtly love decays into mere wickedness in Jehan de Meung's didactic poem *Le roman de la rose* (*Romance of the Rose,* part 2, c. 1275), and in the poem *El libro de buen amor* (*The Book of Good Love,* c. 1343) by Juan Ruiz.

In Chaucer's *The Merchant's Tale* (*The Canterbury Tales,* c. 1380–1400), the twenty-year-old maiden who marries the sixty-year-old knight and takes up with the knight's young page receives help from the pagan past. Proserpine bestows on her—as well as all women—the gift of a clever tongue and an irrefutable excuse.

A woman's prerogative is again exemplified by Antoine de La Sale's novel *Le petit Jehan de Saintré* (c. 1450). Here a lady (la Dame des Belles Cousines) has brought a page to knighthood, only to show her favors to a monk. A fight ensues between the monk and the page, in which the page is knocked down. This is also quite a blow to feudalism and the spirit of religion.

But first and foremost, it is obvious that within the triangle, the knight has lost his object. Lancelot, who has forsaken true valor for the love of Guinevere, loses his eligibility to search for the Grail. Instead Perceval, the pure at heart, will qualify for the quest as shown by Chrétien de Troyes in *Li contes del Graal* (*The Story of the Grail,* romance, c. 1190). But such a change in the hero from lover to chaste seeker is relatively rare in Western literature. It resembles much more the Buddhist belief, in which the hero is represented to us as a saint or an ascetic, a world renouncer. It is therefore evident why there are remarkably few love triangles in the literature of the Eastern world of Buddhist tradition.

The Sixteenth and Seventeenth Centuries

In the sixteenth and seventeenth centuries, the Italian Renaissance deeply affects France and Spain. Marguerite de Navarre's *Heptaméron* (tales, 1559) is modeled in form on Boccaccio's *Il decamerone* (*Decameron* novellas, c. 1350) as well as adopting the ideas of love that can be found in Petrarch's *Canzionere* (poetry, begun after 1327).

Neoplatonism, as it is expounded by Leone Ebreo in his treatise *Dialoghi d'amore* (1535) and by Castiglione in *Il cortegiano* (*The Courtier,* 1528), also finds its way north and is praised by Marguerite de Navarre. In this philosophy a woman's physical beauty—clearly emblematic of her beatific moral nature—is supposed to bring man from the world of the flesh to the world of ideas and from his low, carnal state to the airiness of heaven. For the man, this entails a devoted submission to a mistress possessing all of the beauties and virtues as well as all the cruelties of a perfect moral order. Marguerite de Navarre and her disciples apparently believe that this new Neoplatonic kind of courtly love will not cause the same havoc in society that led to the earlier death of *La Châtelaine de Vergi*'s lovers.

The *Heptaméron,* therefore, does not exalt the triangle as more suitable to love than is marriage. Rather, it elaborates on the double standards that govern men and women. Marguerite de Navarre particularly objects to the harsh law of honor that binds the women. Here, it is impossible not to think of the "gloire" to which Corneille's and Racine's heroines will sacrifice their love. Most of the *Heptaméron*'s male characters seek a happy medium between the women-as-enemy found in Jehan de Meung's *Roman de la rose* and the worshipped Platonic idol such as is found in *Il cortegiano*.

The Comic Theater. The triangle does not lend itself well as the main theme of a comedy. An author might project too openly his own feelings of rancor or disappointment. Machiavelli seems to have done this in his *Mandragola* (*The Mandrake,* c. 1512–1520). Molière, too, lets out domestic bile in his comic writing. In *L'école des femmes* (*The School for Wives,* 1662), for instance, the gap separating people is age, as the "Senex Amans" found in this comedy. In *George Dandin* (1668), the poor George marries a lady of noble birth; she takes advantage of their difference in social status, not only to deceive him, but to hold him up to ridicule. Both reflect Molière's unhappy marriage.

From the Epic to the Novel—The Triangular Desire. To illustrate this transition, György Lukács, in *Die Theorie des Romans* (*The Theory of the Novel,* 1920), has picked Cervantes' *Don Quijote* (*Don Quixote,* 1605, 1615) as one of the turning points of this transformation. At the very start of *Don Quixote,* it is the intention of Cervantes to create a mock chivalric triangle, the author, Don Quixote, and Amadis. The object is to show that the chivalric novels, such as *Amadís de Gaula* (*Amadis of Gaul,* complied by Montalvo in 1508) are a decadent imitation of the medieval epics.

Starting from the desire of Don Quixote to emulate Amadis, René Girard has set up in *Deceit, Desire and the Novel* (Y. Freccero, trans., 1965) the triangular desire. If a vain person desires an object, all you need to do is convince him that this object is already coveted by a third prestigious person. The desiring subject is Don Quixote, the mediator. The object of his desire is the one who possesses the epitome of knighthood, that is, Amadis. For him Don Quixote feels the humblest veneration as well as the most intense rancor.

Cervantes must, however, reach another triangle, such as was created by Ariosto in his mock epic, *Orlando furioso* (1516), which is presented in *Don Quixote* as a story within the story, "El curioso impertinente." The composition of this triangle is the following: the husband, Anselmo, whose jealousy will bring about madness and death; his wife, Camilla, who will flee her husband's wrath into a convent; and Lothario, the reluctant lover, who will seek refuge in battle. He is killed subsequently and at that time only will Camilla join the convent.

The transition between the chivalric triangle and "El curioso impertinente" is established by the medium of four people embedded in *Don Quixote*'s plot, Cardenio, Lucinda, Don Fernando, and Dorothea.

The first to meet Don Quixote is Cardenio (1.24). This young man is subject to fits of madness, just as is Don Quixote himself. Cardenio proceeds to tell the errant knight his story, which must resolve itself into a triangle, counterpart of the one found in "El curioso impertinente": Cardenio, Lucinda, and Fernando, friend of Cardenio. But we will not attain the triangle in this particular encounter. Cardenio mentions the fondness of Lucinda for Amadis. This leads us astray from the triangle in formation, resulting in a heated debate on the love affair between the doctor and Queen Madasima in the novel *Amadis of Gaul*. Neither Don Quixote nor Cardenio can stand contradiction, and Cardenio disappears into the mountains. He is found again, however, by the priest and the barber, forever in search of Don Quixote. It becomes clear at that time (1.27) that the mediator Fernando has appropriated Lucinda, the object of Cardenio's desire. Cardenio has witnessed the marriage ceremony and the mock suicide of Lucinda. He has run away without intervening. Cardenio does not know, however, that Fernando cannot attain his end. He really belongs to another lady, Dorothea, whom we meet next (1.28). She presents herself as Micromina, a maiden in distress who calls upon Don Quixote, knight errant, to avenge her from the evil giant (really her seducer Fernando) who has forced her to flee a home she can no longer inhabit while disgraced.

Because Dorothea has entered the world of fantasies of Don Quixote, the normal order is restored, but only two couples are left—Cardenio and Lucinda, Fernando and Dorothea. Some important points have, however, been made.

Unlike Camilla and Lucinda who have sought refuge in a convent in "El curioso impertinente," Dorothea has chosen self-imposed exile, exchanging a comfortable home for the dangers of the wilderness. She becomes, in a way, a counterpart to Don Quixote. She alone of the three women had this option, since she had been seduced but unmarried. The others could only escape their marriage vows by fleeing to a convent. The treacherous aspects of the seduction of Dorothea, the presents flaunted at the object of desire, also exist in both men of "El curioso impertinente." Anselmo and Lotario practice deceit on Camilla. Against all laws of honor, Lotario will betray Camilla to her husband when he has reason to believe she is unfaithful to both lover and husband.

A common element here is a display of the way a woman can deceive when presented with a difficult situation. Both Lucinda, the reason for Cardenio's madness, and Camilla have staged a sham suicide, but neither Anselmo nor Cardenio can bring themselves to intervene. It is not so for the curious impertinent. Anselmo, the first "man of resentment," dies dishonored, since honor cannot stand deceit.

The baroque novel, too rich in anecdotal adventures, does not lend itself to the interpretation of the triangle. We will have to wait until 1678 for a short novel issued from the précieux movement to find a triangle worth studying. In Mme de La Fayette's *La Princesse de Clèves (The Princess of Cleves)*, the husband dies from jealousy. But this feeling was induced in him by his wife's unsolicited confession. Unlike all other women, as stated by the heroine, Mme de Clèves felt that the bond of marriage and the harsh law of honor—*Hepta-*

méron—were never to be violated. On his deathbed, however, her husband reproached her for having revealed to him her love for another man. He would rather have been left in blissful ignorance.

Tragedy and the Triangle. The Elizabethan tragedy of revenge, like its Greek predecessors, extols law and order. In the Attic tradition, it was a son's duty to avenge his father. Orestes, in this view, had acted justly according to the gods. More than two thousand years later, Shakespeare's *Hamlet* (c. 1600) again takes up the question of what a son's duty is.

The notion of incest occupies Hamlet because, like Oedipus, he is plagued by the moral image of his father. He is, of course, the nephew and stepson of the murderer Claudius. The attacks and counterattacks by the antagonist Claudius and the avenger Hamlet both focus on Gertrude, wife of the dead king, mother of Hamlet, and now wife of Claudius. Though Hamlet does not mention the Old Testament, Leviticus 20:21 could be invoked in his accusation against his mother. Perhaps Hamlet's famous hesitation is a metaphor for the incest-derived sterility mentioned in Leviticus. At any rate, both Claudius and Hamlet become rivals for Gertrude—who is torn between the two of them. Another Greek-derived tragedy, Goffe's *Orestes* (1623) shows justice forgotten in Orestes' passion for horrible and purely personal retaliation. *Orestes* also shows, if only by its hollow goriness, with what detail and freshness Shakespeare has brought back to life the Oedipus triangle.

Love triangles figure in many Elizabethan tragedies. In Philip Massinger's *The Roman Actor* (1629), we are taken to a play-within-the-play (called ''The False Servant''), where we view the strange execution of the lover by the husband. In Massinger's *Fatal Dowry* (1619), the author presents the killing of the lover in a duel and the stabbing of the wife by the husband. A judge in the play, acting in the belief that he is applying an unwritten law, acquits the husband. In the course of the play, a friend of the lover kills the husband. That friend in turn is killed by a friend of the deceased husband. Like the contemporary Spanish plays by Lope de Vega (1633) and Calderón (1635) both called *El médico de su honra (The Surgeon of His Honor)*, where the husband has his wife bled to death to cure her of her adulterous disease, Elizabethan tragedy pronounces, as a matter of law, the husband's right to revenge himself on his wife and her lover. In the word of one dramatist, he can even kill her ''with kindness'' (T. Heywood, *A Woman Killed with Kindness,* 1603).

Later in the seventeenth century, Racine often fashions an interesting triangle out of a characteristic trio: a woman, a lover of the Orestes type, and the powerful monarch who is refused love (*Andromaque,* 1667). In *Bérénice* (1670) the Emperor Titus wants to marry Queen Bérénice, but the people as well as the Senate of Rome object in view of the law that forbade an emperor to marry a queen. Antiochus, the unloved, waits in the background, hoping to take advantage of the public dispute. At the end of the tragedy Queen Bérénice suggests that Titus, Antiochus, and she exile themselves in three separate directions. The Queen believes this will serve as an example to all unhappy lovers. In *Phèdre (Phaedra,*

1677), King Thésée chooses to believe his guilty wife and sends his innocent son to a tragic death. In Euripides and Seneca, the king made the same decision. When a dying Phèdre confesses her guilt to her husband, she leaves Thésée to bear forever the guilt of his son's death.

Eighteenth and Nineteenth Centuries

The Modern Alienated Hero and the Wayward Heroine. Eighteenth-century England traces opposing courses for the modern novel. In *Joseph Andrews* (1742) and *Tom Jones* (1749), Fielding values honesty, sincerity, goodness; therefore, there are no triangles. On the contrary, Richardson, so called master of the modern novel, thrives on seduction. His libertine Lovelace *(Clarissa Harlowe,* 1748), however, unlike his model Don Juan, applies his efforts to the seduction of only one woman, Clarissa.

We find in the abbé Prévost's *Manon Lescaut* (novel, 1731) the perfect modern hero of alienation. Indeed, Des Grieux pursues an impossible dream and is unable to reconcile it with his own dual nature. The epoch's thematization of virtue and morality emerges in the hero's dissenting from his social role. He will eventually rejoin it. The end of *Manon Lescaut* shows Des Grieux seeking reconciliation with his brother. There is no indication, however, that he will reenter clerical life. But the young nobleman will refuse the parental choice of a rich wife and enter a monastery, rather than forsake his love for a woman of the lower class. In turn, in *La nouvelle Héloïse (The New Heloise,* novel, 1761), Rousseau creates Saint-Preux, who oscillates between an awareness of transience and a desire to prolong his love eternally. It is, however, up to Julie de Wolmar to define the part Saint-Preux will play in her new-ordered life. She favors making him her children's tutor—as he was once hers. However, by reliving a once shared experience, love is rekindled and time abolished. Stendhal's Julien Sorel (*Le rouge et le noir* [*The Red and the Black,* novel, 1830]) is the sum of Des Grieux and Saint-Preux. He will pay with his life for his denunciation of a society that does not accept any changes in the set composition within social groups. In it the tyranny of wealth is more unyielding now than what was once social rank and inherited privileges.

In Goethe's novel *Die Leiden des jungen Werthers (The Sorrows of Young Werther,* 1774) we find a new sort of love triangle, the Werther-like passion— as it is referred to in Tolstoy's novel *Anna Karenina* (1877)—as well as self-annihilation. A growing awareness of Lotte's husband makes Werther yield finally to the dignity of the husband and to the power of the woman. Unable to bear himself in the end, he commits suicide (as Vronsky, the lover in *Anna Karenina,* attempts to do, feeling that his rival, Anna's husband, has shown himself to be a better man).

We find in Charlotte *(Die Leiden des jungen Werthers)* a growing sense of the role the woman will be called upon to play in the triangle. Charlotte and Werther share many things. They exchange gifts, common to lovers, as well as help to take care of Charlotte's younger, orphaned siblings. Through the medium of art, they become one. However, Lotte can be possessed only on a Platonic level, which Werther cannot accept.

Benjamin Constant's novel *Adolphe* (1816) presents the reader with the hero's perspective on the events by rhetorical questions, conflicting explanations, and shifts in point of view. Reason falls short, and Adolphe loses his identity. Balzac borrows several times from Constant the theme of lassitude that, in a prolonged liaison, eventually overwhelms the lovers. The theme of the chain-gang lovers (les galériens de l'amour) can be found in *Béatrix ou les amours forcés* (*Beatrix*, 1845) and *La muse du département* (*The Muse of the Department*, 1843). Both novels deal with the triangle. Lovers who have defied the laws of society are riveted to one another by gratitude, love, or pity, but neither can initiate a break.

We find Pushkin's *Evgeniĭ Onegin* (*Eugene Onegin*, 1823–1831) in the *Adolphe* tradition. In this novel the hero's deadened sensibilities have rendered him incapable of narrating his own story. He is ultimately overwhelmed by the strong character of the heroine Tatyana. Indeed, in phase 1 of the triangle, Tatyana and Olga compete for the hero, while phase 2 shows the hero and Tatyana's husband competing for her, the result being that Tatyana chooses her husband.

After the Revolution of 1830, it becomes evident in the French novel that an ambitious young man who wants to penetrate the bounds of society, must secure the help of a married woman. In Balzac's *Le Père Goriot* (*Father Goriot*, 1834), Rastignac will make his fortune with the help of a banker's wife. But while entertaining these relations with the married ladies, the young heroes never abandon their prospects for a rich marriage. Those are the elements we find at the end of Flaubert's *L'éducation sentimentale* (*The Sentimental Education*, 1869). The triangular theme of this novel deals with failure. We witness in the novel the formation of three triangles, each new one cancelling the preceding one. The first triangle consists of the Arnoux couple, and Frederic, who, without ever reaping his reward—Mme Arnoux's surrendering—helps the couple financially. The second triangle comes into existence when Frederic can no longer withstand Mme Arnoux's inflexibility. He enters into a rocky liaison with Rosanette, mistress of M. Arnoux. The third triangle appears at the time when Frederic has agreed in principle to marry the rich widow, Mme Dambreuse. It lives its short life at the auction-sale of the Arnoux's household. It consists of Frederic and the two women who compete for his love: Mme Dambreuse and Rosanette. It focuses on an empty antique box that Frederic has seen in the Arnoux's household, but which also has been seen at the home of Rosanette. Mme Dambreuse gets the box but loses Frederic. Rosanette exits, never to reappear as "la maréchale" in Frederic's life.

Between the time *Die Leiden des jungen Werthers* became known to the public (1774) and 1900, the woman occupies more and more the top position in the love triangle. Her escape from her group will have consequences as severe as the worst *derailment*— the metaphor is found in Balzac's *La muse du département*. But what happens if the heroine keeps entering different social circles, as

Sister Carrie does in Dreiser's novel (1900)? None of these moves has any stability; she never marries Drouet. The actual *derailment* is committed by Hurstwood, who takes the central position in the triangle. It is the older, well-established man that will commit a crime—the robbery—and take Sister Carrie to New York toward a new marital-like situation in another town. It is eventually Hurtswood who will endure an ignominious death at his own hands, just like Anna Karenina. Through his flight from his wife, the husband has assumed the part usually played by the wayward heroine. The robbery and flight may have resulted from the triangle formed, for a short while, by the Hurtswood couple and the unaware Sister Carrie.

Theodor Fontane's *Effie Briest* (novel, 1895) never becomes aware of her potential. She is caught in the web of the Prussian honor code, the remains of feudalism. She receives at the hands of her husband the punishment once bestowed on "the woman killed with kindness" of the Elizabethan tragedy.

The Jealous Husband and the "Man of Resentment." Nineteenth-century examples of the triangle particularly develop the figure of the jealous husband, also, in most cases, the "Man of Resentment."

Did King Mark murder Tristan with a poisoned sword? With the king's right of life and death over a vassal, it would have been sanctioned, as Renée L. Curtis points out in *Tristan Studies* (1969). Other commentators, such as the deist M. de Wolmar *(La nouvelle Heloïse)*, preach tolerance and suggest that in the name of forgiveness, the former lover might even be invited into the household. Either way, what becomes of the lover when discovered tells us not only about the author but also the cost of achieving justice in society and sometimes the advantages of keeping dishonor out of public scrutiny

In Hawthorne's novel *The Scarlet Letter* (1850), the husband Roger Chillingworth postpones public justice to wreak his own more fiendish torment on the exposed lover, Arthur Dimmesdale. When Dimmesdale does confess on the scaffold, the public is sympathetic more to the minister than to the reclusive Chillingworth. The erstwhile husband dies soon after the lover has revealed the ancient affair in public. We are left with a great deal of sympathy for the lover and the feeling that the husband has for many years been nourishing himself almost exclusively on resentment.

In Stendhal's *Le rouge et le noir,* M. de Rênal ought to display jealousy upon being made aware of his wife's infidelity. Everything we know of his temperament points in that direction. Stendhal explains that it is the contemporary custom to give the guilty wife the worst type of public exposure, "le pilori de la province [the provincial pillory]," as well as consigning her to outcast status, unless her husband chooses to extend his protection to her. The reason for this is that the group—or the small town, microcosm of society—is a volatile quantity based on kinship or, in the words of Balzac, on two forces—family and marriage. The group cannot, therefore, tolerate the opposing forces contained in the triangle. When an affair is suspected, the usual procedure is the explusion of the lover, which will satisfy the group's anger. The matter of punishing the wife will rest with the husband. But a husband usually wants the least possible public exposure of his dishonor. In Tolstoy's *Anna Karenina,* Karenin goes beyond inviting Anna to remain at home and keeping up appearances. He suggests that both Anna and himself, as well as Vronsky, live under the same roof and keep a "ménage à trois" of vaudevillian proportions. (The influence of Paul de Kock [1793–1871] is very much felt in Russia, and this is especially noticeable in the poignant novel of Dostoevsky, *Vechnyĭ muzh* [*The Eternal Husband,* 1870]. The man with the crape on his hat seems to be in his element only within the triangle.) Yet he has not been able to bear the revelation contained in his dead wife's hidden letter. The eternal husband will behave, in a cruder way, as fiendishly as Roger Chillingworth in *The Scarlet Letter.* The force emanating from the husband's jealousy greatly differs in intensity. If this husband is a "Man of Resentment," his jealousy has been supplanted by the stronger feeling of resentment. He might fear to lose his wife's inheritance (*Le rouge et le noir, La muse du département*), or violently desire children he cannot beget (*La muse du département*), or resent his wife's refusal to complete his work thereby robbing him of possible future acclaim (George Eliot's novel *Middlemarch,* 1871–1872). In all these cases, the group must work to restore the balance of forces, that is, in *Middlemarch,* Casaubon's brother-in-law must follow the "reaching hand" and prevent the union of Dorothea and Ladislaw.

The Twentieth Century

The sentence of death or revenge that was the dues of the Oedipus triangle, as well of the Tristan triangle, has reappeared in the twentieth century, mostly in the theater. Claudel's *Partage de midi* (*Break of Noon,* 1906) has overtones of the Tristan legend, and O'Neill's trilogy of plays *Mourning Becomes Electra* (1931) contains an Oresteian triangle where we leave the hero beset by madness. In *La machine infernale* Cocteau shows, in his adaptation of the Oedipus myth, that the intervention of the gods subsequently invites the invasion by society of the triangle.

The alienated hero reappears within the triangle in Radiguet's novel *Le diable au corps* (*The Devil in the Flesh,* 1923) and in Cocteau's *Les enfants terribles* (*The Holy Terrors,* novel, 1929). The latter contains indications of an incestuous relationship, also existing in Thomas Mann's story "Wälsungenblut" ("Blood of the Walsung," 1921).

As to the jealous husband, the force of expulsion emanating from the group has considerably lessened at the end of the nineteenth century. In the twentieth century, we have in Machado de Assis' novel *Dom Casmurro* (1899) and in Robbe-Grillet's novel *La jalousie* (*Jealousy,* 1957) variations of the husband's jealousy in a real or imaginary triangle. In Robbe-Grillet, the husband's jealousy centers only on objects, in Machado de Assis, on an assumed resemblance.

The study of Marguerite Duras' novels *Moderato cantabile* (1958) and *L'a-*

mour (1971) also shows the woman at the center, directing the other forces. In *L'amour*, however, loneliness has substituted itself for the characters' attachment. The man (l'homme) moves ceaselessly between the man and the woman: "Du fait de l'homme qui marche constamment, avec une lenteur égale, le triangle se déforme, se reforme, sans se briser jamais [Because of the man walking ceaselessly with an even slowness, the triangle loses its shape, assumes it again, without ever breaking up]."

See also: Anxiety, La Belle Dame sans Merci, Jealousy, Love in Greek and Roman Literature, Oedipus Complex, Secret Love.

Selected Bibliography

Bergson, Henri. *Durée et simultanéité*. 1922. Paris: PUF, 1968.
Frye, Northrop. *Spiritus mundi: Essays on Literature, Myth and Society*. Bloomington: Indiana University Press, 1976.
Girard, René. *Violence and the Sacred*. Trans. Patrick Gregory, Baltimore, Md.: Johns Hopkins Press, 1977.

MARIE-HENRIETTE FAILLIE

M
//

MARRIAGE

From the French *mariage* (12th century), marriage is the condition of being united to another person as husband or wife; the relation between married persons. Marriage, in literature, has traditionally supplied the happy ending to comedy, connoting social stability, happiness, and the renewal of life. This is true in such diverse literary forms as fairy tales, sixteenth- and seventeenth-century stage comedy, and the romantic novel from its inception to the present day.

Apart from this fairly universal constant, however, marriage is viewed and treated in widely different ways. On the one hand it is a practical arrangement, a legal contract dealing with financial and social concerns; on the other, it is an idealized union based on love, analogous to such other archetypal relationships as that between body and soul, Christ and the church. At different periods in literary history one or the other of these views or variants on them predominate. At times, as in the Middle Ages, they are separated, with marriage proper concerned with the practicalities, while the ideal aspects of the relationship between man and woman are siphoned off into the courtly love tradition. In more modern works, the attempt to incorporate the two into a single relationship is often the cause of tension and conflict.

The effect of children on the marriage relationship, and the contrary claims of fidelity versus infidelity, romanticism versus cynicism, passion versus reason, and excitement versus contentment are all subsidiary themes.

Classical and Judaeo-Christian Background

The Greek word for marrying, *gameō,* derived from the root *gam* or *gem* (to fit together or pair), defines marriage as the indissoluble union of two people. In the Homeric period monogamy and fidelity, on the part of the wife, at any rate, were the rule; Penelope comes down to us as the pattern of these virtues. The man always had greater freedom than the woman, and in the Hellenistic period morals for the latter became looser as well. At the same time, the appearance of sacred prostitution, introduced through Oriental cults, prepared the way for the idealization of eroticism, which emerges as one strain in early Christian thought and, in the guise of courtly love, survives well into the Middle Ages.

In the Old Testament the archetypal marriage is that between Adam and Eve. It provides a pattern both of an ideal union, with the characteristics of mutual help and sustenance, before the Fall, and also the contrary pattern of futile bickering and enmity after it. Throughout the Old Testament marriage is important primarily for the begetting of children, and while monogamy is the ideal, a man may take a second wife in order to obtain offspring. The wife is the helper of the husband, but subordinate to him. Adultery is severely punished. Hosea's analogy between the breaching of the bond with God by Israel and the breaching of the marriage relationship by his wife, the harlot, reinforces the Hebraic recognition of marriage as a potentially ideal state and its destruction as correspondingly devastating.

In the New Testament the sacrament of marriage is blessed through Christ's presence and the performance of his first miracle at the wedding in Cana. Figuratively, the ideal nature of marriage is emphasized by the frequent description of the church as a bride adorned to receive her husband (Christ). Several parables (for example, that of the wise and foolish virgins) conceive of the final union of the believing soul and Christ as a wedding banquet, an image that persists in literature to find a seventeenth century expression in the final poem of George Herbert's *The Temple* (1633).

Against this is set the celibacy of Christ himself, imitated by many of his followers, and the Pauline warnings against the lusts of the flesh. With Paul, the distinction between *Eros* and *Agapē* comes into Christian theology, and the dangers of the former are reinforced by the personal experience and writings of Saint Augustine. The view of marriage based on these premises is that of a necessary evil, essential only to legitimize both passion and the living products of that passion.

Other Religions

Most Eastern religions had less ambivalent views about marriage and considered it essential to man's present and future happiness. In Hinduism, celibacy was an impiety and a misfortune; happiness in the next world depended on having a continuous line of male descendents to make offerings for the repose of the soul. "Without a wife in the house, the devil will live there," goes an ancient Hindu proverb. Islam saw marriage as the means of perfecting religion; bachelors would find the road to paradise difficult (Edward Westermarck, *A Short History of Marriage*, 1926). In neither case was equality or companionship an important element in the relationship, which was viewed predominantly from the man's point of view.

The Middle Ages

In no other period were marriage as a practical institution and "love" as an ideal and romantic force operating outside that institution more clearly separated than in the Middle Ages. Among the nobility, marriages were contracted for reasons of property, wealth, and power alliances. Marriage was expected to bring little joy to either husband or wife. Rutebeuf, a thirteenth-century jongleur, laments his marriage for money to a fifty-year-old woman "maigre et sèche [skinny and dried up]," who has reduced him to wishing for his own death. And Eustache Deschamps, the French contemporary of Chaucer, is scathing about the institution in his diatribe against women, *Le miroir de mariage* (poem, late 14th century). A woman, for her part, could expect to fare even less well in marriage than a man; she was primarily her husband's property, and he her "lord," demanding fealty and obedience.

Outside the marriage relationship, however, the feudal system operated to make the "lady" the superior partner; the man was her vassal and owed her homage. The same woman, of course, frequently played both roles. There is very little sense of moral outrage when a young woman, married for practical reasons to an old and jealous husband, takes a handsome (and usually noble) young man for her lover, as the *Lais* (verse-narrative romances, c. 1170) of Marie de France illustrate. The Arthurian legends place more emphasis on the moral imperatives of chastity and fidelity, but lapses are treated with some sympathy. It is in Chaucer's *Franklin's Tale* that the elements of marriage and courtly love are first united, when Dorigen takes Aurelius as "hir servant and hir lord, / Servant in love, and lord in mariage" (792–793). The subsidiary theme of "mastery" is one that follows throughout the "marriage group" in the *Canterbury Tales* (c. 1380–1400). Women long for mastery, but they only attain it by vast superiority of intellect and trickery, as in the *Wife of Bath's Tale*, or by the free gift of their husband, as in the *Franklin's Tale*—never by right.

The idealization of woman outside the marriage relationship and her contrasting subjugation within it are illustrated by one of the common literary analogies of the period—that between soul and body, husband and wife. While outside the analogy the soul is often conceived of as a beautiful woman (a concept deriving both from classical sources and the cult of Mary), within it the soul always corresponds to the man and the woman to the body, thus emphasizing her position of subordination.

The Renaissance

In the early Italian Renaissance, a new dimension was added to the idealization of woman prevalent in the courtly love tradition. To Petrarch and Dante, heavily influenced by the cult of the Virgin, their beloved was not only the arbiter of manners and source of "gentillesse," but a semidivine being leading them through earthly to heavenly love. Such relationships could not, by definition, end in sexual consummation or marriage. The early sonnet cycles in France and England imitated much of the Italian idealization of the mistress, but with a greater recognition of the physical imperatives of the relationship. Thus in Sidney's *Astrophil and Stella* (sonnets, written 1580–1584) we find an insupportable conflict between reason and passion, a conflict that is only reconciled through the kind of rational love, directed toward marriage, that is found in the *Amoretti* (sonnets, 1595) of Spenser. In this respect Spenser, in the sixteenth century, consolidates the union of "love" and "marriage" found fleetingly in Chaucer in the fourteenth century.

Marriage as such does not elicit a great deal of attention from sixteenth-century writers. It is the legitimization of desire (Thomas Cranmer [1489–1556] perpetuates St. Augustine's views on the subject) and the happy conclusion to the comedy of life. Love for the opposite sex is not seen as a particularly ennobling passion, and in any case of conflict between "love" and "friendship" (as in Shakespeare's comedy *The Two Gentlemen of Verona* [c. 1594]) it is the latter that normally takes precedence.

Only in the early seventeenth century does a more introspective attitude to the relationship between the sexes and the institution of marriage emerge. Passion is still the motivating force behind marriage (in literature, if not in life, where arranged marriages were still prevalent), but particularly among the emerging middle class a new element comes to be important—compatibility of mind. Milton's *Doctrine and Discipline of Divorce* (1644) gives full expression to this need in marriage but, interestingly, this "modern" view of marriage is notably absent from *Paradise Lost* (poem, 1667). Working here in an imaginative mode, Milton interprets the archetypal marriage relationship between Adam and Eve as one of subordination of wife to husband. Eve takes no part in Adam's rational discourse with the angels, and her disobedience to Adam is analogous to the rebellion of the lower faculties of the soul (appetite united with will) against the higher (reason). The human relationship is a reflection of that between God and man in a universe that is still essentially hierarchical.

The Late Seventeenth and Eighteenth Centuries

In the late seventeenth century, such conceptual models of marriage as those of Milton became increasingly rare. Marriage, in European literature, came to be treated primarily as a human contract. Given that such contracts were still rarely entered into by the mutual consent of the parties involved, once the sacramental elements of the institution were abandoned, marriage could be viewed with extreme cynicism and become the subject of literary satire. Rather than being the pledge of mutual affection, marriage, in this period, is assumed to render such affection unlikely, if not impossible. Thus in Vanbrugh's *The Provoked Wife* (play, 1697), Sir John Brute exclaims, "The woman's well enough; she has no vice that I know of; but she's a wife: and d—n a wife! if I were married to a hogshead of claret, matrimony would make me hate it" (2.1). The marriage contract has no intrinsic validity—only what it is given by the parties involved for as long as passion continues. The plots of comedies of the period are based on the intrigues of husbands and wives deceiving one another without compunction or guilt in the game of married life. Even the selection of an "innocent" (ignorant) wife from the country is no guarantee of immunity from this kind of treatment, as Arnolphe in Molière's *L'école des femmes* (*The School for Wives*, 1662) discovers. The treatment of the theme ranges from biting satire to indifferent cynicism, only occasionally mingled with examples of marriage based on the more traditional values of romantic love and mutual desire.

In the eighteenth-century drama, there is less explicit sexual infidelity and more emphasis on the process of courtship. This is still seen primarily as a game in which the ideal prize combines an attractive physical appearance with financial and social status to match. "Love" is usually said to be present, but there is little exploration of its nature. Young people now expect to have some say in the choice of their partners; indeed, in such a work as Sheridan's *The Rivals* (1775) the *lack* of parental approval appears to be the key factor in precipitating "love," which perhaps says much about its essentially superficial presentation. In Marivaux's light-hearted play, *La double inconstance* (*Double Infidelity*, 1723) the lovers change partners as easily as in a dance, with the "infidelity" excused both because it takes place before marriage and is based on a genuine change of heart.

The Romantic Period

The cynical view of marriage prevalent in the late seventeenth and much of the eighteenth century did at least attempt a certain realism in contrast to the earlier idealism. This prepared the way for a new attitude in the romantic period, which saw marriage very much as a relationship between two individuals founded on mutual consent, but with an added element of idealism based not on religious prototypes but on subjective emotion. In European literature, it was the rise of the novel that provided the literary form ideal for the exploration of these emotional and psychological aspects of the marriage relationship. Marriage without love comes to be unacceptable (as in the novels *Tom Jones* [1749] by H. Fielding and *Clarissa Harlowe* [1748] by S. Richardson), but at the same time the libertine attitudes of the late seventeenth century give way to an extreme emphasis on the virtues of chastity—for women at least—and the necessity of marriage as a preliminary to sexual activity. Indeed, in a novel such as Richardson's *Pamela* (1740), the primary function of marriage seems to be to sanction sex.

By the nineteenth century the purely sexual elements of marriage receded as companionship became more important. While in the novels of Jane Austen (1775–1817) marriage is seen primarily as a desirable social end (daughters *must* be married off, one way or another), heroines such as Emma and Elizabeth Bennett manage to find men with whom they are intellectually compatible as well. Dickens harks back to the companionate ideal of Milton's treatise on divorce when he states in *David Copperfield* (novel, 1850): "There can be no disparity in marriage like unsuitability of mind and purpose." Yet this does not signal a complete reversal in the goals of marriage. In George Eliot's novel *Middlemarch* (1871–1872) the heroine, who believes she is marrying primarily for intellectual companionship, finds only too quickly that her "Milton" is an impossible academic bore, and she is subsequently torn by the conflict between a love that includes both passion and intellectual compatibility and her lifeless marriage.

Middlemarch is, in fact, typical of a new type of novel that, as the century progresses, comes to deal more frequently with the development of a marriage rather than, as in earlier writers, with a courtship that simply uses marriage as the traditional comic ending. Tolstoy, in *Semeĭnoe schastie* (*Family Happiness*, novel, 1859) depicts the development of a young girl's emotions from the first awakening of love and the initial excitement of marriage, through a period of despondency when she believes all "love" has disappeared, swallowed up in the routine of domestic life, to a new plateau where excitement has given way to the felicity of domestic contentment blessed by children. A less happy tracing of the life of a marriage is found in Guy de Maupassant's *Une vie* (*A Life*, novel, 1883). Here the infidelities of the husband prevent the happy reconciliation that takes place in Tolstoy's story, and the heroine ends by focusing her energy and love on her child and eventually her illegitimate grandchild.

It is worth noting that children become an increasingly important element in the marriage relationship during the nineteenth century. Maternity, which almost totally disappeared as an ideal in the cynicism of the late seventeenth and early eighteenth centuries (while Shakespeare's Cleopatra puts the asp to her breast where it "sucks" her asleep, Dryden's simply applies it to her arm), reappeared with the idealization of childhood from the time of Blake and Wordsworth onward.

If the nineteenth century expected more of marriage than any previous age, it is not surprising that many of the "histories" of marriage show the devastating results of trying to meet these expectations within a single institution and with a single partner. Tolstoy's *Anna Karenina* (novel, 1877) is a classic example of the woman who wants marriage to provide security, social respectability, and maternal satisfaction, but also the excitement and passion that she finds only in her lover. The inability to choose between these elements and, especially, the inability to choose between sexual and maternal love eventually destroys her. In general, attitudes toward such infidelity vary from the relative laissez-faire of the French tradition to the more stringent German standards of, for example, Goethe's *Die Wahlverwandtschaften* (*Elective Affinities*, novel, 1809).

Set against the predominantly romantic and idealistic view of marriage are numerous dissenting voices, particularly on the Continent. Balzac, in *Les petites misères de la vie conjugale* (*Pinpricks of Married Life*, novel, 1846) explores the tedium and boredom that, he asserts, are the inner meaning of every marriage. This attitude is not so much a throwback to the previous century as the precursor of a new realism, which is an important strain running through the treatment of marriage in the twentieth century.

The Twentieth Century

The two aspects of marriage—a practical arrangement often full of mundane annoyances, and an ideal relationship between two people—which, in the Middle Ages, were split between the institutions of marriage and courtly love, were both firmly incorporated within marriage by the late nineteenth and early twentieth centuries. The resulting inflated theoretical expectations of marriage, already noted in nineteenth-century literature, continue and increase in the twentieth century. At the same time these expectations, no longer tied to traditional assumptions that saw marriage as the necessary means of sanctifying lust and ensuring the orderly inheritance of property, and as the social goal of every young man and woman (the "happy ending"), are less universal. In general, however, twentieth-century marriage is expected to provide, simultaneously, romantic love, companionship, and the practical framework within which individual happiness and success can be pursued and children reared. Its inevitable failure to provide all these things at once leads very often to a satirical, cynical treatment of the institution similar in some respects to that of the late seventeenth and early eighteenth centuries but rather more bitter because, while the earlier cynicism derived from a total lack of expectation, the twentieth-century cynicism derives from the failure of unrealistically high and diverse expectations. Furthermore, both the expectations and the institution itself exist in a kind of moral vacuum where everything must be self-generated. Whereas in earlier times the social and moral norms of marriage were clearly set out, the duties and expectations of each partner fully known, twentieth-century marriage as portrayed in literature is a kind of ad hoc institution, improvising its own rules and priorities as it goes along.

The combination of romanticism and cynicism within this nihilistic framework is well illustrated in the works of Salacrou. The two strains are divided between the men and the women with the men, for the most part, portrayed as romantic dreamers longing for purity in their relationship with women, while the women are adulterous and choose a mate primarily for sexual gratification. The cause, he argues, is primarily the lack of any firm moral norms. In *Histoire de rire* (*When the Music Stops,* play, 1939) Jules tells his friend,

You talk of betrayal, but you can't betray something which no longer exists. The time has gone when the purpose of marriage was to start a family and a man married his wife forever. Today, my friend, religion means nothing to our wives. . . . And so the only morality left to them is "love," the most uncertain, most ill-defined word in the human vocabulary.

The absence of a clear conceptual framework means not only that such words as "love" are free to take on their own meanings, but that the roles of husband and wife, no longer defined in terms of theological prototypes, are themselves the subject of scrutiny and debate. Ibsen's *Et dukkehjem* (*A Doll's House,* play, 1879), the most famous example of a wife's challenge to her traditional role in marriage, is the precursor of a long line of similar works stretching down to the present day. The tension between the demands of marriage as a social institution and the needs of individual self-fulfillment found in Ibsen is a persistent source of conflict in the modern novel. And new permutations on the old theme of the struggle for dominance within the partnership provide yet another such source. In Strindberg's *Dödsdansen* (*Dance of Death*, play, 1901), for example, this struggle is carried to such an extreme that it appears to be the sole object of the marriage relationship, with each partner deriving a perverse pleasure from torturing and being tortured. Although the explicit use of the analogy would be inappropriate in a twentieth-century context, we have here almost returned to the medieval and Renaissance concept of husband and wife as a warring partnership like soul and body, unable to live either with or without one another. The unhappy results of improper subordination (wife dominating husband) seem, curiously enough, to be borne out in modern writers, from James Thurber in comic vein to Eugene O'Neill in tragic. This traditional stance is balanced by submissive wives, heirs of Nora, who may eventually choose to assert themselves by opting out of marriage altogether.

The role of children in the marriage relationship, which increased in importance in the nineteenth century, often provides another source of conflict if it is not perceived similarly by husband and wife. Thus in García Lorca's tragic play *Yerma* (1934), the heroine marries only to have children; her husband marries only to keep her for himself and his pleasure. When he thwarts her passionate need for a child, she kills him.

Marriage, in modern literature, is no longer an accepted social norm; its failure to fulfill the diverse demands put upon it has led to a fundamental questioning of it as a desirable institution. When a late seventeenth-century playwright asserts that love and marriage, naturally, cannot coexist, it is within a context that assumes the continuance of marriage at least; the institution is strong enough to be the butt of jokes and cynicism. When Salacrou has one of his characters plead, "Marriage and love are not necessarily irreconcilable," it is a plea for an estate under siege. Perhaps the most telling change of all in the present century is that the permanency of the union, originally a defining characteristic, is no longer taken for granted. And since marriage is not seen to be so necessary as a practical arrangement in life as it once was, writers concentrate rather on how well it is fulfilling its ideal functions. Thus marriage is examined as a product on the basis of whether or not it satisfies its partners' needs. The approach is usually realistic, the method psychological, the verdict very much in doubt.

See also: Escape, Feminism, Incest, Love Triangle, Secret Love.

Selected Bibliography

Goody, Jack, *The Development of the Family and Marriage in Europe*. Cambridge: Cambridge University Press, 1983.

Outhwaite, R.B., ed. *Marriage and Society: Studies in the Social History of Marriage*. London: Europa, 1981.

Shorter, Edward. *The Making of the Modern Family*. New York: Basic Books, 1975.
Stone, Lawrence. *The Family, Sex and Marriage in England 1500–1800*. New York: Harper and Row, 1979.

ROSALIE OSMOND

MASQUE OR MASK

A masque was a sophisticated amusement (later a formal theatrical performance) whose essence was the surprise entry of certain persons visored and disguised to dance with each other and with chosen onlookers. A Prologue, Presenter, or "Truchman" explained the allegorical costumes and the slight mythological fable the performers enacted, these motifs having been selected to enhance some courtly compliment. Then came the "taking out" of privileged spectators to the dance floor in order to dance. Although other nations fostered related forms, the masque as such developed in England where, during the Early Stuart period, it attained its highest expression and importance. Once the genre had established these distinctive features in the early seventeenth century, it gained in other literary modes the status of a compelling theme or motif. For poets the masque became a pervasive metaphor and structural model: Milton's *Paradise Lost* (poem, 1667), unfolds its vistas much in the manner of movable perspective scenery, peculiar in his day to masques; the Cavalier poets are also inclined to envision the world as a masque, not as a stage. For dramatists the masque grew into a mandatory, crowd-pleasing motif.

The term "mask" evokes ideas that have little to do with the genre and theme under discussion here. The masque is not synonymous with the visor covering the performer's face; such masks were optional in masques. Thus the masque has distant (if any) ties to Greek and Roman, medieval, commedia dell'arte, Japanese nōh, and Abbey Theater masks. Neither should the masque be confused with masquerades, momeries, medieval disguisings, Carnival, Mardi Gras, or masked balls; such masked entertainments contribute to Verdi's opera, *Un ballo in maschera* (1859), but the masque as defined here does not. Yet the masque did evolve from certain of these traditions.

Background in Pagan Rituals and the Christian Middle Ages

The desire to put on masks for communal rituals has been an abiding one. Critical seasons of the year regularly provoke tribal peoples to conduct rites of death, rebirth, and coming of age. Under masks primitives drive into the woods some grotesque effigy, kill some enemy, or pretend in a mime to slay their leader.

Mimetic sacrifices known to pagan cultures stand behind the medieval Twelfth Night custom of selecting a King of the Bean and a Queen of the Pea; communal disguising, ritual murder, and subsequent rebirth also link the St. George and

Robin Hood plays still performed in parts of England to immemorial pagan habits.

The Greeks and Romans had parallels to the masques in their stage machinery. Vitruvius (1st century B.C.) transmits complete designs for scenic devices later adapted by Serlio, Parigi, and Inigo Jones.

The *scena ductilis* (painted side wings sliding in grooves) and the *scena versatilis* (revolving prisms illustrated differently on each plane) derive in turn from the antique Greek stage, with its *perioktoi* of three-sided rotating pillars. Like classical set design, classical poetry also foretells later masking practices. The stately triumphs for military and Olympic victors celebrated in Pindar's odes, along with the jocund Kalends and Saturnalia that delighted Horace (*Carimina [Odes,* c. 23 B.C.]), anticipate the combined pomp and license found in masques with antimasques. The Romans, with their mummers dressed in skins, beast masks, and women's clothes, and carrying the cervulus or hobby horse, capture the spirit of English morris dances, May Days, and Midsummer Eves. During Saturnalia, for example, Roman masters feasted and played at dice with their slaves; Richard II, in the earliest recorded English mumming, uses loaded dice to win prizes from his mute, masked subjects. Not just the peasantry but even the court continued the pagan masking traditions.

Renaissance Italy

Italians first transmuted these ritual customs into refined courtly pastimes. Petrarch's *Trionfi (The Triomphs,* allegorical poem, 1353–1374) inspired not merely poetic imitations but full-scale triumphal processions.

Lorenzo de Medici was the first to allegorize Roman triumphal cars for St. John's Day pageants. Using Caesar's triumph to signify Mercy and Octavian's car to denote Peace, Lorenzo secularized the religious *edifizi* and *spiritelli.* With Lorenzo's patronage Politian's *Orfeo* (1480), a forerunner of the opera, similarly transformed the more literary sort of religious drama, the *sacre rappresentazioni.* In Ferrara, Correggio's *Favola di Cefalo* (1487) followed much the same lines, interspersing drama with song, *balletti,* and light entertainment. Informal masquerades changed in this fashion from social amusements linked to *calcio* (a variety of football) and the *bufolata* (a buffalo race) into unified entertainments with classical subjects and coherent costumes and symbols.

French Renaissance

Catherine de Medici took with her to France the latest developments of the *masquerade, intermedio,* and *balleto.* New great open-air shows—the *mascarades à grand spectacle* and *mascarades de palais* adorned the French court.

In France the masque became a literary theme. Discovering opera and recitative (lately invented by Rinucci, Bardi, and the Florentine Camerata) Ronsard and other poets of the Pleïade in France devised rules for wedding music to classical prosody. The Académie de Musique et de Poésie, directed by the poet Antoine de Baïf and the musician Thibault de Courville, used royal patronage to develop a ballet in which dance rhythms corresponded to Greek metrical patterns. Although this project failed, other less pedantic efforts successfully harmonized the arts. Beaujoyeulx's *Circe,* or *Ballet comique de la Reine* (1581) and the *Notte d' amore* by Francesco Cini remain the most famous among these early ballet-operas.

English Renaissance

Legal statutes against masking and the prevalence of Burgundian ceremonial traditions kept English courtly fêtes well behind those that the Medicis sponsored in France and Italy. Edicts of 1418 forbade "mumming" and "eny other disgisyngs with eny feynyd berdis, peynted visers, diffourmyd or coloured visages in eny wise," and Henry VIII renews the "Act against disguysed persons and wearing of Visours." From the court at Burgundy English knights adopted personae (usually those of popular romances) for Henry VIII's tournaments, where they tilted and fought at barriers.

A more intimate masquerade on the Italian model, involving risqué conversation, buffoonery, and dancing, appeared as early as 1512. In that year, a dramatic performance described by the chronicler Hall as a "maske" scandalized the English court. To see the king "disguised after the maner of Italie, called a maske," so astonished the courtiers that "when these Maskers desired the Ladies to daunce, some that knew the fashion of it refused." Henry VIII had in effect imported the masquerie of Italy to serve as a prelude to dalliance and dancing.

These early masques reflected Henry's taste for the exotic. Dressed as Turks, Robin Hood's men (1515), Italians (1519), or Hercules and other heroes (1530), Henry VIII and his courtiers defeated wodwoses (wild or "green" men), savages, and others in "straung attier." But other works foretell the more complex literary masque. William Crane's *Riches and Love* (1528) proceeds from Fame's monologue, to a *débat* in song, to an old man's philosophical oration, all testing two contradictory bases of sovereignty.

Queen Elizabeth I rarely sponsored masques so elaborate, preferring that her nobles bear the expense. Gascoigne's *Princely Pleasures at Kenelworth Castle* (1575) coordinated the musical talents of William Hunnis and the poetry of George Gascoigne in a nineteen-day pageant mythologizing all Tudor history. At Leicester's behest Sir Philip Sidney wrote the most widely known of these Elizabethan pastoral dramas, *The Lady of May* (1578).

Elizabethan entertainments developed literary themes at the expense of the "commoning" or dancing that involved spectators with performers, the hallmark of earlier Tudor masques. Whereas Sidney's *Lady of May* uses the *débat* to allude to religious struggles, his *Fortress of Perfect Beautie* (1582) uses the tournament to allegorize and deplore the French Catholic duke of Anjou's suit to marry Queen Elizabeth. Among John Lyly's many pastorals of the 1580s and 1590s, several are designed to defend the interests of local magnates. Of all the Elizabethan courtly entertainments, only Francis Davison's *Masque of Proteus*

(1595) with its comic drama, stage machinery, and sudden entry of dancing masquers, truly prefigures the fully formed Jacobean masque.

Jacobean Masques

When the Early Stuarts once again gave masques royal support, the latent political dimension of the form emerged far more sharply. Paradoxically, the patron who most strongly encouraged the masque, King James's wife, Anne of Denmark, preferred light entertainment. The first masque that she commissioned, Samuel Daniel's *Vision of the Twelve Goddesses* (1604), offers two pretty transformation scenes but little drama and no political allegory. A courtly fashion show, in which a Sibyl gazing through a telescope introduced in turn each lady masquer, his program was, insisted Daniel, a "hieroglyphic of empire."

But that rubric applies more exactly to *The Masque of Blackness* (1605), the first collaborative effort of poet Ben Jonson and architect Inigo Jones. More in the style of Sidney than of Daniel, this masque transforms Queen Anne's order for a simple masquerade in blackface into a haunting allegory about Britain's quest for international fame. Much the same national perspective informs the next year's masque, *Hymenaei* (1606), which, though written by Jonson for the Essex-Howard wedding, focuses on another much-debated union, that of England and Scotland.

Other writers chose to exclude political controversy from their masques. Campion's musically superb *Masque of Flowers* (1607) turns on the dispute between the goddesses Flora and Cynthia, who has turned the masquers into trees; *Masque for Lord Hay's Wedding* (1607), also by Campion, is little more than a spectacular aerial dance of masquers disguised as stars. Some writers, including Samuel Daniel and T. Dekker, went so far as to score Jonson for loading his masques with weighty issues and allegories.

Yet the court's persistent recourse to Jonson ultimately gave his methods unchallenged authority. His lofty *Masque of Beautie* (1608) returns to his dominant key, national chauvinism, by illustrating that beauty "is peculiar to Britain alone." Breaking new ground, *The Masque of Queens* (1609) introduces a tightly unified antimasque of witches as "a foyle, or false masque," implying that any resistance to the Jacobean regime has infernal sources.

By making the antimasque integral to "the current and whole fall of the device," Jonson polarized the masque as sharply as James 1 polarized the kingdom. A wire-tight dialectic balances the courtierlike Satyrs of *Oberon* (1611) against Prince Henry, leading his nation of English Fairies. Every subsequent masque written by Jonson includes and defeats such topical menaces: Puritan pretenders in *Love Freed from Ignorance and Folly* (1611), pseudo-scientists in *Mercury Vindicated from the Alchemists at Court* (1616), arrogant wastrels in *Pleasure Reconcil'd to Vertue* (1618), and journalists in *Neptune's Triumph for the Return of Albion* (1623) and *Newes from the New World* (1620). Professional players acted these roles whereas the victorious masquers were the court's leading peers.

Rival poets belatedly introduced the dialectical tension that Jonson gave to each of his masques. Campion's *Lords' Masque* (1613) strikes an interesting discord when Poetic Frenzy saves the masquers from Mania, who has transformed them to trees. Beaumont's *Masque of the Inner Temple* (1613) includes so strange a panoply of antimasquers, among them a Pedant, a May Lady, and a She-baboon, that no cogent whole takes shape. Bacon's *Masque of Flowers* (1613) pits winter against spring. Daniel alone resolutely avoided conflicts, making his *Tethys' Festival* (1610) a "pleasant and artificial" vehicle designed to show off his ladies' costumes.

Only George Chapman succeeded, as Jonson acknowledged, in matching exotic sights with unified allegory. His Virginian sunworshippers, in *The Memorable Masque* (1613), convert their faith and adore the imperial head of Britain, its *roi soleil*. Chapman's allegory fits both King James's favorite symbology and the interests of the nobility, who in that year invested in Virginian joint stock ventures more heavily than ever before.

Caroline Masques

Since the formal properties of masques were now fixed, it remained for the Caroline writers to expand the scope of performances. Although the great spectacles performed during the 1630s grew even more pointedly contentious, Charles I, now king, himself selected the themes and even directed rehearsals. Throughout these masques one finds a Neoplatonic religion of love, a conviction that the political realm merely shadows an eternal world of forms, and a growing ominous sense that unworthy men, envying the king's superior wisdom, will make Charles I a martyr to their lusts.

Although Jonson returned from an enforced retirement to write *Chloridia* (1630) and *Love's Triumph Through Callipolis* (1631), his collaborator and now antagonist, Jones, had gained the upper hand. Even in these first great Caroline productions, dropping a god on a wire no longer served to astonish the spectator; Jones had already begun to organize his stage into a unified moving picture. Fond of night pieces, Jones had used candles by the thousands to transform gloom suddenly into brilliant gardens (in *The Vision of Delight,* 1617), and he had already arranged aerial ballets *(Tethys' Festival),* elaborate underscenes *(The Lords' Masque),* and vertically divided stages (W. Browne's *Ulysses and Circe* of 1614). Sliding shutters gave his stage depth and, most important, the capacity for innumerable scene changes.

The Caroline masques belong so completely to the designer that Inigo Jones rightly calls them, in his preface to A. Townshend's *Tempe Restored* (1632), "nothing else but pictures with light and motion." Swifter, more elaborate changes in *Chloridia* and *Love's Triumph* suggest a whole universe brought under royal control, for the courtly masquers suddenly revealed in heaven triumph visibly over baser earth and its common people.

Less reassuring premises inform James Shirley's *Triumph of Peace* (1634), a masque commissioned by the Inns of Court to heal their breach with the Crown.

"The world shall give prerogative to neither" party, runs one refrain, "They can flourish but together." Along with its criticism of royal monopolies, the masque fashions the king's myth of Platonic union into a case against his prerogative rule.

Thomas Carew's *Coelum Britannicum* (1634) constitutes the king's reply, imaging the new morality that Charles I felt he had brought to court. "Ganymede is forbidden the bedchamber," for example. Rather than end with the usual pastoral bower, this masque offers Windsor Castle, with Concord, Wisdom, and Government hovering in the clouds. Once more, the center of royal power emanates divine ideas.

Later masques exclude everything outside this Platonic and idealized world. In Davenant's exotic *Temple of Love* (1635), Asian magicians succumb to Divine Poesy's expressly Caroline Platonism, and the same author's *Britannia triumphans* (1638) connects the figures of Sea Power and Good Government. Thus it justifies the Crown's notorious Ship-Money lawsuit, which was in fact a desperate ploy to extend royal powers of taxation. The queen's companion piece, Davenant's *Luminalia* (1638), expounds the Platonic faith that the human mind might perfect the visible world.

Only the last Caroline masque, *Salmacida spolia* (1640), admits any awareness that the Crown's power was disintegrating. Presenting spirits from hell who destroy this "over-lucky, too much happy isle," Davenant presents a beleaguered king suffering the "fate to rule in adverse times, / When wisdom must awhile give place to crimes." Finally overwhelmed by "these storms the people's giddy fury raise," King Charles assumes the posture, which he has not lost, of a virtuous and patient monarch. The days of the great court masque had ended.

Theme and Motif

The masque assumed its definitive form in 1595. It came almost at once to symbolize for English writers the extravagance, arrogance, and aesthetic style of the Early Stuarts.

With the masque beginning to flourish as a genre, poets inevitably made this unique literary hybrid their theme. Although references to masques occur in the lyrics of Wyatt, Gascoigne, and Surrey, it is in Spenser that the masque attains the status of a major motif. In his *The Ruins of Time* (poem, 1591), where "strange sights presented were . . . like tragic Pageants seeming to appear," history takes on the form of a masque. Even more masquelike are the processional entries of allegorical figures in *The Faerie Queene* (epic poem, 1590–1596), which also includes a fully blown masque enacted by the Thames and the Medway when they celebrate their union in Proteus' banqueting hall (book 3, canto 12).

As Spenser's self-appointed heir, Milton quite naturally turned to the masqueing theme. He not only composed the most famous literary masque, *A Masque at Ludlow* (1634, miscalled *Comus*), but also alluded to masques in works as different as *On the Morning of Christ's Nativity* (poem, 1629) and the prose tract *Eikonoklastes* (1649), which was written to defend regicide. *Paradise Lost* is filled with passages that may have been suggested by Milton's memory of masques, and in one (the building of Pandemonium in book 1, 670 ff.) Inigo Jones, the greatest of masque architects, has been generally recognized in the figure of Mulciber.

The drama proved even more hospitable than poetry to the masque as theme and motif. Dramatists were eager to feed the popular craving for a glimpse of elite activities, including masques, going on at Court. But beyond good salesmanship dramatists found in masques the convenient means to present surprise entries, political and romantic intrigue, confusions of identity, moral allegory, escapes and kidnappings, dancing, music, and harmonious endings.

Shakespeare includes masques in an astonishing variety of plays. *Love's Labors Lost* (c. 1594) is the earliest example and *The Tempest* (1611) the latest, but in between come *A Midsummer Night's Dream* (c. 1595), *Merchant of Venice* (c. 1595), *Romeo and Juliet* (c. 1596), *Merry Wives of Windsor* (c. 1600), *Timon of Athens* (c. 1605–1608), *As You Like It* (c. 1599), and *Cymbeline* (1610). Jonson proved less willing, with his rigid sense of decorum, to mix his plays with masques, although *Cynthia's Revels* (1600) culminates in three masques exposing hypocritical courtiers and *A Tale of a Tub* (1633) includes a travestied masque arranged by a thinly veiled caricature of Jonson's rival, Inigo Jones.

Stuart playwrights used the masque motif for every sort of drama. Masques have central importance in Beaumont and Fletcher's *The Maid's Tragedy* (1610–1611), *Cupid's Revenge* (1612), and *Philaster* (1610); in Fletcher's *Women Pleas'd* (1620), *The Queen of Corinth* (1616), and *Custom of the Country* (1620); in Marston's *The Malcontent* (1604), *Sophonisba* (1606), *The Insatiate Countess* (1610), and *Antonio and Mellida* (1599); in Webster's *The Duchess of Malfi* (1613); in Chapman's *May Day* (1609), and *The Widow's Tears* (1605); and in Middleton's *Blurt, Master Constable* (1601), *A Mad World, My Masters* (c. 1606), and *Your Five Gallants* (1607). After his *Old Fortunatus* (1599) had established the drawing power of plays with masques, Dekker continued to exploit the theme in *Satiromastix* (1601), *The Welsh Ambassador* (1605), and *The Whore of Babylon* (1606).

The later Caroline dramatists also found masques to be a useful motif. Among them were John Ford with *The Sun's Darling* (1624) and *Love's Sacrifice* (1630); James Shirley with *The Maid's Revenge* (1626), *Love Tricks* (1626), *Changes, or Love in a Maze* (1632), and *The Duke's Mistress* (1636); William Cartwright with *The Siege* (1634) and *The Royal Slave* (1636); and Thomas Nabbes' *Hannibal and Scipio* (1635) and *Microcosmus* (1637). The list of minor plays following suit is a long one, including Glapthorne's *The Lady Mother* (1635), and Brome's *The Love-Sick Court* (1638). It was a rare play that overlooked the masqueing theme.

As the masque genre attained its spectacular zenith in Charles I's banqueting house, the masque theme achieved equal heights on the public stage. Theme and genre also had a parallel decline, one brought about by the Interregnum. A few masques were performed in private houses, including Shirley's *Cupid and*

Death (1653) and Crowne's *Calisto* (1675), but the days of the court masque were over. The theatrical public lost interest in the masque as a theme even though occasionally a playwright might try to revive the motif. Congreve did so in *The Judgment of Paris* (1701).

But by and large the masque and prerogative rule ended together. Even the attempted revivals failed to remain distinctively masques. The eighteenth-century productions of Milton's *Masque at Ludlow (Comus)* were regarded as a special kind of opera, not as masques at all. In foresaking the masque as genre and literary theme, English audiences were merely catching up with the fashion for opera that had now long ruled the Continent.

Yet, during its efflorescence, the masque had enormous impact not only upon courtly entertainment but also upon drama and poetry. The masque endures as a theme in plays as diverse as Kyd's *Spanish Tragedy* (c. 1585) and Peele's *Arraignment of Paris* (1584), as unlike as Shakespeare's romances and Webster's *White Devil* (1612). Spenser, Milton, and their lesser contemporaries all chose the masque as poetic motif. It gave England the proscenium stage and the opera. It inscribed itself so indelibly in English literary history that the masque theme emerges in novels by Sir Walter Scott and James Joyce. Although long defunct as a genre, the masque remains in English literature a vital theme and motif.

See also: Dance, Dance of Death, Dwarf, Emblem, Grotesque.

Selected Bibliography

Chambers, E.K. *The Elizabethan Stage.* 4 vols. Oxford: Clarendon, 1923.
Gordon, D.J. *The Renaissance Imagination. Essays and Lectures by D.J. Gordon.* Ed. Stephen Orgel. Berkeley: University of California Press, 1975.
Orgel, Stephen, and Roy Strong. *Inigo Jones: The Theatre of the Stuart Court.* 2 vols. Berkeley: University of California Press, 1973.
Welsford, Enid. *The Court Masque. A Study in the Relationship between Poetry and Revels.* Cambridge: Cambridge University Press, 1927.

HAROLD A. VEESER

MELANCHOLY

Melancholy as a pattern of human behavior has been the subject of inquiry for two and a half millennia. Since the term once included most varieties of madness and even of mania, study of the essence and cause of melancholy lead ancient doctors to the most fundamental questions of psychopathology. With the ancients, in the Middle Ages, and through the Renaissance the *morbus melancholicus* is anchored in physiological theories and from the Middle Ages important not only in medical but also philosophical and theological thought. Theories about melancholy as one of the four humors underlie the categorization of human traits and behavior (the temperaments) in these periods and thus become unconscious or conscious elements of characterization in literary works. For the Renaissance the potency of the notion of melancholy can be partly explained as the result of Ficino's successful blending of Hippocratic views with the (pseudo-) Aristotelian tradition (according to which melancholy is the necessary condition for genius) and Platonic notions of the enraptured *vates*. Called the "English malady" in the eighteenth century in England, melancholy and the fascination with it survived the demise of the notion's physiological base, that is, of the humoral theory; romantic and postromantic meanings of melancholy are allied to the notions of Weltschmerz, spleen, ennui, and fin de siècle sentiment.

Antiquity

Although there is in Homer a special link between choler and emotions, the color black is not used in this context. In nonmedical literature before Hippocrates, the only occurrence of "melancholic" is in Sophocles' *Trachiniai (Trachinian Women*, play, c. 430 B.C.); the word, however, should be glossed as "poisonous" and does not presuppose a theory of melancholy in a system of the four humors. The notion of melancholy to denote both one of the humors regularly constituting our body and an imbalance due to the predominance of that humor first appears in the works attributed to Hippocrates (5th century B.C.). The imbalanced state of mind characterized by an excess of melancholy is here understood to include both the depressive and the manic phase of radical mood changes. Drawing on Hippocrates, Galen of Pergamum (A.D. 129–?199) developed the notion that the noxious humor can predominate and be localized in different parts of the body. Should the brain be affected, melancholic fears may result in a variety of melancholic delusions (his catalogue of cases has served as a quarry for later medical and imaginative writers). One person believes his body is made of clay and avoids any physical contact for fear of being shattered; another thinks he is a cock and goes about crowing; a third thinks he is Atlas carrying the world on his shoulders. In his commentary on Hippocrates, Galen systematically includes the four elements in his presentation of the four temperaments, which he was also the first to link with characteristic mental tendencies as traits. (Klibansky, Panofsky, Saxl, *Saturn and Melancholy,* has a schematic table listing the characteristics for each temperament given by some major ancient and medieval writers.) Possibly in analogy to Plato's distinction of a good and a bad madness (*Phaidros* 244A [*Phaedrus*, dialogue, 4th century B.C.]) and subsuming madness under melancholy, Aristotle's *Problēmata* 30.1 (*Problems*), now usually attributed to Theophrastus (c. 370–285 B.C.), presents the distinction between a harmful melancholy and a melancholy leading to extraordinary achievement in answer to the question: "Why is it that all men who have become outstanding in philosophy, statesmanship, poetry or the arts are melancholic, and some to such an extent that they are infected by the diseases arising from black bile, as the story of Heracles among the heroes tells?" This work of only a few pages had a tremendous influence on later thinking—less perhaps by the attempted reasoning of the answer (which in somewhat Aristotelian fashion defines as propitious a moderately warm black bile that is neither all cold nor overheated) than by the presupposition that people of genius (in Latin they will be called *ingeniosi*) are melancholics. To Heracles, whose madness was to be a subject of Greek and Latin tragedy, the author of the *Problems* then adds Ajax and Bellerophon, "the former went completely insane, and the latter craved for desert places"; further the politician Lysander, and finally the philosophers Empedocles (who jumped into the Aetna), Plato, and Socrates. Most poets are claimed to have been melancholics, although only one is mentioned, the Syracusan Maracus, who "was even a better poet when he was mad," and whose work has not come down to us. In this quotation and throughout this essay, madness is subsumed under melancholy.

The other ancient Greeks most often considered melancholics are the misanthropist Timon of Athens, Heraclitus, and Democritus. As the weeping and the laughing philosophers the latter represent to later ages extreme varieties of the melancholic experience. By the seventeenth century their opposition is such a commonplace that their images appear even on theater columns to suggest the spectrum of human emotions. This view of Democritus as a melancholic of genius, intimately related to the ideas presented in *Problems* 30.1, derives for the most part from letters of now discredited authenticity that were included in editions of Hippocrates' works. Flashar has called these collections of letters "epistolary novels," although it may be doubtful whether in the periods when these letters had their major impact they were read as fiction rather than as historical documents. One group of letters purports to show how Democritus' fellow citizens of Abdera sent to Hippocrates for help because the philosopher was incessantly laughing, spurning public life, and living as a recluse; further, how Hippocrates went to Abdera and met Democritus (whom he found anatomizing animals and writing a work on the cause of melancholic madness and how Democritus explains his laughter as an appropriate reaction to the ridiculous concerns of his fellow Abderites: bearing children, digging for precious metals, acquiring possessions, and so on. In Democritus' spirited indictment of the Abderites, the stance of the melancholic anatomist blends with the stance of the satirist and sarcastic social critic, a blend that was to have considerable fortune. Although according to these letters Democritus persuades Hippocrates that he is not mad or melancholic, but that he is a man of extraordinary genius, in the later history of Western civilization and unquestionably through the persuasive force of *Problems* 30.1, Democritus emerges as a melancholic of genius.

Although Cicero reports the principal thesis of *Problems* 30.1, he is reluctant in subscribing to it and denies another claim made there, namely the interpretation of enthusiastic prophecy as melancholy. In agreement with Cicero's skepticism, the later medical writers of antiquity entirely omit the pseudo-Aristotelian or Theophrastian idea that people of extraordinary intellect are particularly susceptible to the dangers of melancholy.

The Middle Ages and Renaissance

According to *Saturn and Melancholy* the idea of melancholic genius was even less acceptable in the Middle Ages than it had been to the ancient doctors. In some literatures, as for instance in Old English there is of course a dominant elegiac mood, a mood of fated doom, but the term "melancholy" was not available to describe it. Nor was the word used in the Vulgate, although certain episodes (as for example David soothing King Saul's melancholic fit through his music) were soon to be topically associated with the melancholic's therapy. As the medical authorities reported, melancholics have a tendency to have a variety of dreams, and one can argue that the genre of the dream vision, so popular from Boethius to Chaucer (and beyond), owes something to the conception of the melancholic. Unquestionably, however, the basis of character typology in the High Middle Ages and the Renaissance were humoral medicine and the theory of the temperaments, and it is well known that most literary characters, as for instance Chaucer's Canterbury pilgrims, are conceived with this theory in mind.

This is the period in which the meaning of melancholy begins to change from denoting primarily someone who is crafty, avaricious, despondent, misanthropic, and timid to describing someone who is sad without cause. In deliminating melancholy from acedia (the "monk's disease"), theologians take an interest in the question whether melancholy is a sin or a sickness. The notion that melancholy is *balneus diaboli,* the devil's bath, is proverbial in the Middle Ages and will still form an important thread in Luther's discussions of melancholy (recorded in his *Tischreden [Table-Talk],* first printed 1566) and tribulation (i.e., *Anfechtung*).

Until the major break (by Paracelsus) with the tradition, the medical discussion of melancholy essentially continues along Hippocratic-Galenic lines, while at the same time by introduction of a number of "adust" varieties of the humors doctors try to account systematically for a larger number of phenomena. But within this tradition, important new elements are infused in the early Renaissance without which the thought of Paracelsus could not have emerged. The definition and estimation of melancholy takes a new turn with Renaissance humanists through their recourse to Neoplatonic, Hermetic, Arabic, and astrological speculation in which the heroic conception of melancholy as presented in *Problems* 30.1 received a new justification. In the speculation of such thinkers as Ficino and Cornelius Agrippa, melancholy emerges more clearly than ever before as the temperament under the influence of Saturn with all the potential curses but also all the gifts and blessings of that uncanny god or planet. Thus one can for instance trace the concept of the gifted melancholic from Agrippa von Nettesheim (1486–1535) through Belleforest (1530–1583) (who inserts into his Hamlet story a disquisition on melancholy) to Shakespeare's tragedy, *Hamlet* (c. 1600).

The ambiguity of the melancholic humor is reflected in a number of specific beliefs voiced in Renaissance works. (1) Since there was also the notion that the devil takes advantage of the black humor by possessing and misleading a person, a melancholic (like Shakespeare's Hamlet) may have gnawing doubts whether he is capable of divination or is being misled by the devil. (2) Since most behavior now called "psychopathologic" was associated with melancholy, it was important that some writers (Jan Wier, Reginald Scot) tended to consider reputed witches just melancholics. In some cases this saved the accused from the stake or the gallows. (3) While the melancholic is often presented as a person of imagination, this faculty was most usually conceived of as a faculty of lower rank than in the romantic or postromantic era (see e.g., Montaigne's essay on imagination [*Essais* 1.21, 1580–1588], or Spenser's spatial description of the imagination inhabited by melancholy Phantastes in the House of Alma, *Faerie Queene* 2.9 [epic poem, 1590–1596]). The melancholic was always in danger of being misled through it. (4) Not only in Petrarchan poetry but also in the romance genre, there is a long tradition of presenting the lover as a melancholic and as subject to sudden fits. In a fit of ecstacy or in his enthusiasm the lover can even lose consciousness and fall to the ground (as happens to many romance characters in such works as *Amadís de Gaula* [*Amadis of Gaul*, compiled by Montalvo in 1508] or Sidney's *Arcadia* [1590]). The negative elements of this sense of enthusiasm as associated with melancholy are emphasized in the religious controversy of the time in which the religious establishment (whether Zwinglian, Calvinist, Lutheran, or Elizabethan-Jacobean) calls the (often Anabaptist) opponents melancholic enthusiasts (eventually to be called Enthusiasts in England).

Not only were there more books written on melancholy than on all three other humors together, on the stage the melancholic revenger, malcontent, misanthrope, melancholic traveller and lover attest to the fact that the type (sometimes merely by crossing his arms) was easily recognized by the popular audience. In prose the greatest explorations of ambiguities of the black humor as a gift and as a liability are by Cervantes.

As to his physique, habits (e.g., occasional sleeplessness), his illusions and delusions, "el ingenioso hidalgo Don Quixote" is conceived as a melancholic of genius; from a certain perspective the novel consists of attempts at curing his imagination through artifice of the imagination—quite in agreement with the dominant therapeutic theory of the time—but in the course of therapeutic attempts the therapists begin to look more deranged than their patient. When, to the sense of loss of some of the characters in the novel (and also of some readers) Don Quixote finally regains sanity, Cervantes has him die. Cervantes explored a similar theme in *El licenciado Vidriera* (*The Licenciate of Glass*, part of the *Novelas ejemplares* [*Exemplary Novels*, 1613]), which has been said to derive from the medical case of a "melancholic" (whether in Huarte or Santa Cruz). Here a former ingenious melancholic is not allowed to live in peace after regaining sanity. He is hounded by his townspeople until he leaves Salamanca and dies in foreign lands. It has been said that by his parody of the romance tradition in *Don Quijote* (*Don Quixote*, 1605, 1615), Cervantes wrote a romance to end all romances. In his ingenious melancholic from La Mancha he may also have created the *non plus ultra* of that type in Renaissance literature. What Cervantes did through parody to both chivalric romance and the notion of the imaginative melancholic, Robert Burton did, possibly unwittingly, to the genre of books on melancholy that purport to compile, classify, and harmonize medical opinion.

Ostensibly written by the librarian of Christ Church, Oxford, to rid him of his own melancholy, the *Anatomy of Melancholy* (1st ed. 1621) was in several editions expanded to the largest monument to the topic. While Burton is above all a recorder of opinion, he has on the whole little sympathy for exalted notions of melancholy, particularly since he regards with suspicion the radical Protestants of his time (Puritans, Anabaptists, Enthusiasts, etc.), many of whom claim to be inspired to prophesy.

If members of established church hierarchies (Anglicans, Lutherans, or Roman Catholics) tended to be suspicious of melancholic enthusiasm, it may not be accidental that the last major humanist statement on noble melancholy in English comes from a poet with considerable sympathy for radical religious groups: John Milton. His poems "L'Allegro" (banning an unpleasant melancholy) and "Il Penseroso" (ushering in a goddess melancholy and climaxing in ecstatic poetic prophesy), both composed in 1632, are not contradictory or antithetical, since not the same kind of melancholy is banned and praised, but complementary. While Ficino, Agrippa von Nettesheim, and Melanchthon expressed their hate-love for the ambiguous humor in prose, Milton marshalled for his statement on noble melancholy the richest resources of poetic language.

From the Enlightenment to the Nineteenth Century

In the famous article on *Mélancolie* in the *Encyclopédie* (1751–1772, discussed in detail by F. Schalk, *Studien zur französischen Aufklärung* [1964], and H.-J. Schings, *Melancholie und Aufklärung* [1977]), the second section, written by Diderot, defines melancholy as "le sentiment habituel de notre imperfection [the customary feeling of our imperfection]." Curiously this definition is mitigated by a number of subtly attractive traits: "Elle se plaît dans la méditation qui exerce assez les facultés de l'âme pour lui donner un sentiment doux de son existence. . . . La *mélancolie* n'est point l'ennemie de la volupté, elle se prête aux illusions de l'amour, et laisse savourer les plaisirs délicats de l'âme et des sens. L'amitié lui est nécessaire. . . . [It enjoys meditation which gives sufficient scope to the soul's aptitudes to give itself a calm feeling of its existence . . . Melancholy is not the enemy of sensual delight; it is open to love's illusions and lets one savor the delicate pleasures of the soul and the senses. Friendship is necessary for it . . .]." The other sections (mainly on religious melancholy and uses of the word in psychopathology) collect only negative meanings. Religious melancholy is the result of a false idea of religion and fanaticism, and "pretended possessions by the devil" are seen as general symptoms of a pathological condition that only begins to lose its traditional humoral underpinnings. The *Encyclopédie*'s use of the word "melancholy" in a philosophical-moral content to describe what is possibly a new kind of sentimentality, and in a religious polemical contex to describe opponents ("Enthusiasts," "Schwärmer") can be documented from works of imaginative literature of the period.

At a time when rational philosophers criticized melancholy as an irresponsible and irrational condition (see Locke, *Essay Concerning Human Understanding* [1690], bk. 4, chap. 19, par. 5), Western Europe began to experience a wave of it; in fact in England the condition was felt to be so general and proper to the particular English geography and character that melancholy came to be called the "English malady" (see George Cheyne's book of that title [1733]). As a novel like Smollett's *Expedition of Humphry Clinker* (1771) indicates, it became fashionable at certain levels of English society to be restless and sad without cause, a condition now called "melancholy." That the English word "spleen" (originally denoting the organ filtering out noxious melancholy but then also "captious anger or low spirits" [E. M. Sickels, *The Gloomy Egoist* (1932)]) has entered other European languages may indicate the importance of English thought in this area. Even Samuel Johnson, often considered legislator of Augustan taste, while being driven by a desire for order and reasonableness, had a life-long interest in the subject. His philosophical tale *Rasselas* (1759) can be seen as a string of examples of how various kinds of melancholy can or cannot be overcome. (E.g., the story of the astronomer [chaps. 40–46], who lives under the affliction of believing that he regulates the seasons, has its antecedents in traditional medical case histories of melancholics in the sense of persons diseased in the imagination.) In poetry imitation of Milton's "Il Penseroso" combined with other elements, particularly the "picturesquely romantic and 'horrifically' Gothic" (Sickels, *The Gloomy Egoist*) brought forth a string of invocations to melancholy (from Thomas Warton's *The Pleasures of Melancholy* [poetry, 1747] to James Beattie's poem, *The Minstrel* (1771–1774), which profoundly influenced Wordsworth.

For an understanding of enthusiasm as melancholic and pejorative Meric Casaubon's *Treatise Concerning Enthusiasm* (1655) and Henry More's *Enthusiasmus triumphatus* (1656) mark an important stage. Translated into Latin these brief prose treatises had an extraordinary influence on German life and letters. Henry More expressly used elements of physiological explanation of genius in the pseudo-Aristotelian *Problems* 30.1 to reduce his religious opponents, the "fanatics" (by whom he means primarily the Quakers) to the pathological level. Although with some German orthodox thinkers the Platonist More was himself tainted by touches of melancholic fanaticism, his work contributed to a tendency in the period to screen the work and the biography of the religious opponent (usually of Pietist, Quaker, or "Enthusiast" persuasion) for signals indicating melancholy.

A century after More and Casaubon, it was primarily William Duff's thought about a sublime melancholy characterizing original genius (*Critical Observations on the Writings of the Most Celebrated Original Geniuses in Poetry* [1770]) that stimulated J. C. Lavater and through him German speculation about genius from Kant to Schiller. Melancholy, which here becomes almost exchangeable with sentimentality, appears as the poetic sentiment par excellence, a thought that will be almost axiomatic in E. A. Poe's essay "Philosophy of Composition" (1846). Goethe presented the reinvented poet of melancholic genius in his tragedy

Torquato Tasso (1790). The poet is blessed with certain talents but cursed with extreme sensitivity *(Empfindlichkeit)* and darkness of mind. "Goethe's Tasso transforms the topical madness of the poet found in tradition into the melancholy of the poet in the modern age" (Schings). Like Rousseau's *promeneur* or the characters in *La nouvelle Héloïse* (*The New Heloise*, novel, 1761), the poet is a stranger in his society who derives both pleasure and pain from being different from ordinary people. In *Über naïve und sentimentalische Dichtung* (*On Naïve and Sentimental Poetry*, 1795), Schiller reasoned that modern sentimental elegiac poetry is born out of a sense of loss of past ideals. His reasoning had the effect of dignifying this particular and, as he thought uniquely poetic, melancholy and of differentiating it from other pathological and hypochondriacal varieties.

Rousseau's programmatic revaluation of solitude in *Rousseau juge de Jean-Jacques* (dialogue, 1776) and his implied consciousness of uncomprehending others at some distance (*Rêveries du promeneur solitaire* [*Daydreams of a Solitary Stroller*], 1782) became blended and pitched to fitful extremes in Byron, for whom Rousseau was the eloquent apostle of affliction: "Yet he knew how to make madness beautiful" (*Childe Harold's Pilgrimage* [narrative poem, 1812–1818] canto 3). Harold, who calls himself "son of Saturn," finds an attractive melancholic solitude even in a crowd of people, while, in a famous phrase he is "among them, but not of them." Through Byron's intent to make madness beautiful and to be "proud though in desolation," the melancholy he describes takes on the contradictory elements characteristic of the mood so bitter-sweet in the romantic period, when the bitter part is often represented by a dose of the morbid, perverse, of masochism, sadism, or Gothic horror. When Keats's Isabella takes in the perfume of the flowers nourished by the head of her murdered lover, which she has buried in a flower pot, the speaker exclaims: "O Melancholy, linger here awhile!" (*Isabella*, stanza 55 [poem, 1820]).

In Leopardi and Baudelaire, oppressive images traditionally linked with melancholy (heavy, massive objects like columns, pyramids, Baudelaire's *couvercle,* etc.) are associated with boredom, ennui. As R. Kuhn has shown, Leopardi's ennui of the void is not, as it had been for Rousseau, a source of ecstasy and therefore of poetry. This pervasive mood, which for Leopardi takes on existential proportions, is always negative (R. Kuhn, *The Demon of Noontide* [1976]). Baudelaire's "Spleen et idéal," the first section of his collection of poems *Les fleurs du mal* (*The Flowers of Evil,* 1857), is about the somberness of melancholic boredom and about means of combatting it. Verlaine, who also claims to be born under Saturn, reduces the sense of despair that is the result of Baudelairian melancholic spleen to wistful nostalgia or sorrowful longing. In his *A rebours* (*Against the Grain,* 1884), J.-K. Huysmans may be said to have encoded Baudelaire's lyric moods as well as his famous theory of correspondence between different sense impressions in a novelistic form. His main character Des Esseintes, oppressed by "an immense ennui," is close to parodying in some perverse way traditional melancholics as he attempts to overcome his fits of spleen. Thus he has some black serving girls serve a banquet consisting of all black dishes: rye bread, olives, caviar, black sausages, and so on, and his invitations look like letters of condolence. In the Renaissance, while the basis of physiology was still humoral, physicians made patients suffering from excess black bile abstain from dark foods. Des Esseaintes, in a mood typical for the late nineteenth century, tries to overcome melancholy by sadomasochistic thrills derived from a cult of the black humor.

The Twentieth Century

Modern melancholy, sometimes taking intellectual support from Spengler and more often from Marx and Freud or Kierkegaard and Heidegger, enters into a variety of forms: from the indifferentism in the early works of Max Brod, the melancholy of the Left (see, e.g., the final entry in Günter Grass's imaginary diary *Aus dem Tagebuch einer Schnecke* [*From the Diary of a Snail*, 1972]), the existentialist dramatizations by Sartre (e.g., *Huis clos* [*No Exit*, 1944]) to the novelistic expressions of the Beat Generation (e.g., Jack Kerouac, *On the Road*, 1957). While a list of modern works of imaginative literature that focus in some way on melancholy would be too long to be helpful, there are at least two works in which the history of melancholy and reference to fictional or historical characters associated in some way with melancholy (e.g., Luther, Melanchthon, Dürer, Hamlet) become a central topic: Thomas Mann's *Doktor Faustus* (novel, 1947) and Walter Jens's *Herr Meister: Dialog über einen Roman* (1963). One might call them works of self-reflective melancholy or "meta-melancholy." Both associate melancholy on the one hand with genius but on the other with the demonic; more specifically, both present witchhunts and burning stakes as parables for fascist rule. *Herr Meister* may have remained a fragment because Mann's model was too compelling.

Selected Bibliography

Hellmuth, Flashar. *Melancholie und Melancholiker in den medizinischen Theorien der Antike*. Berlin: De Gruyter, 1966.
Klibansky, R., et al. *Saturn and Melancholy: Studies in the History of Natural Philosophy, Religion, and Art*. New York: Basic Books, 1964.
Lepenies, W. *Melancholie und Gesellschaft*. Frankfurt: Suhrkamp, 1969.
Lyons, B. G. *Voices of Melancholy: Studies in Literary Treatments of Melancholy in Renaissance England*. London: Routledge and K. Paul, 1971.

WINFRIED SCHLEINER

METAMORPHOSIS

"Metamorphosis" means basically the sudden change of a human into an animal or plant or object, the change being caused by a divine agent as a punishment or reward. But this basic pattern has many variations. Divinities, for example, are able to transform themselves into animals and then reverse the metamorphosis as required. Or humans can transform themselves by using a magic drink or spell. Throughout mythologies and folklore there occur figures like magicians, witches, wizards, devils, or djinns, who, although they are not divine, can impose shape-changes on themselves or others. The prestige of metamorphosis as a literary motif in Western literature derives to a great extent from the Roman poet Ovid's *Metamorphoses* (c. A.D. 2–17), although this epic-length work is only the culmination of a rich classical tradition. To the direct influence of Ovid can be added, especially in modern literature, the elaboration of the basic motif by associating with it other ideas, such as disguise, conversion, and evolution. Almost any long or complex work of literature deals with time and change, which are themes strongly associated with metamorphosis.

Homer's epic, *Ilias (Iliad,* c. 8th century B.C.) and *Odysseia (Odyssey,* c. 8th century B.C.) laid the foundations of literary interest in metamorphosis. The gods of Greek religion, which play a large role in these epics, have the power in principle to change their own form and also to cause changes of shape in humans. In the *Iliad,* for example, the gods Athene and Apollo take the shape of vultures (7.58 ff.) and perch in an oak tree to observe the progress of a duel that they have inspired. Their transformation is temporary, adopted so that they can watch without being noticed by humans. Near the end of the *Iliad* (24.602–617) Achilles refers to the story of Niobe, whom the gods Apollo and Artemis punished for boasting that she had more children than their own mother, Leto. The twin deities killed the human children and Niobe's grief caused her to change into a rock or cliff down which water runs, an image of her perpetual sorrow. This transformation is permanent; the rock can "still be seen."

The *Odyssey* shows a great interest in metamorphosis, which in fact forms an important theme of the poem. In the Proteus-episode (4.435 ff.), Menelaos, attempting to get home to Greece from Troy, has wandered to Egypt and is told that he must seek sailing directions from Proteus, a minor sea deity. Since Proteus lives in sea-water, Menelaos must go to a beach and there disguise himself as a seal, a kind of voluntary and temporary metamorphosis. Menelaos has to catch and hold Proteus while the god, reluctant to cooperate, rapidly changes himself into a lion, a serpent, a leopard, a boar, water, and a tree. This remarkable and frightening series of metamorphoses tests the courage and tenacity of Menelaos, illustrating the difficulty that humans often have in approaching gods. Circe, whom Odysseus and his men encounter on their wanderings (10.133 ff.), resembles in some respects a witch or enchantress, causing transformations in humans with magic drugs. She transforms part of Odysseus' crew into pigs (although their human intelligence remains in them) and curiously tame wolves and lions are present near her house, other humans whom she has transformed earlier. But the god Hermes, self-transformed into a youthful human prince, intervenes to provide Odysseus with a drug (moly) that counteracts Circe's magic, and he thus escapes metamorphosis himself and also rescues his crew from their metamorphoses.

Homer's *Odyssey* demonstrates in other ways the great flexibility of the theme of metamorphosis, for it deals with kinds of change that are not strictly sudden, complete, or permanent. On several occasions Odysseus is transformed in appearance by the goddess who constantly helps him, Athene. She intervenes to increase the impressiveness and youthfulness of his figure when he must meet strangers, or, conversely, she can age and disfigure his appearance when such a change is appropriate. The temporary, disfiguring metamorphosis is crucial to the plot, for it allows Odysseus to sustain the disguise (an itinerant beggar) under which he works out his revenge on the suitors of his wife. A more elaborate use of such themes is the contrast in his wanderings between the human Odysseus and the succession of creatures who are more or less grotesque distortions of human appearance and conduct. Among these are the giant, one-eyed Cyclops, Polyphemus; and Scylla, the complex sea-monster; or the Sirens, the deadly bird-women. The dangers to Odysseus' life and to his safe return often appear to be threats of assimilation to a metamorphosis, a distortion of his personality from which he must protect himself resourcefully.

Among major Greek deities two are especially associated with metamorphosis, Zeus and Dionysus. Zeus, king of the gods, marries his sister Hera, but they have only a few children. The complimentary epithet "Son of Zeus" was nevertheless attached to many lesser deities and heroes and consequently Greek mythology teems with stories that explain the origin of these offspring of Zeus. The tales of the "loves" of Zeus frequently show him using his power to transform himself temporarily into whatever creature might help him to carry out the seduction of lesser female deities and sometimes mortal heroines. Many such tales received their best-known form in Ovid's *Metamorphoses,* but they usually can be found in earlier Greek literature, narrated fully or referred to allusively. The shape Zeus assumes is determined by the particular situation in which he finds the object of his desire. To seduce Alcmene, for example, he changes himself into an identical twin of her husband, Amphitryon. To approach Callisto, a devotee of the goddess Artemis, he takes the form of Artemis herself. These temporary metamorphoses are essentially disguises, required because no respectable Greek female would allow herself to be accosted by a strange male. Zeus therefore sometimes uses self-metamorphosis to circumvent the rules of society in order to carry out an adulterous relationship. Another reason for his metamorphosis is to evade the jealous anger of Hera, who naturally resented her husband's extramarital sexual activity. Occasionally the object of Zeus's desire suffers metamorphosis. A richly developed example of such a fate occurs in Aeschylus' *Promētheus desmōtēs (Prometheus Bound,* play, c. 450 B.C.). Zeus pursued Io, a human female, but owing to Hera's jealousy, he changed Io into a heifer. The fates of Prometheus, punished for stealing fire from the gods, and of Io are complexly intertwined and counterpointed in the drama. Io is unique in surviving Greek tragedy in that she is brought onto the stage with evidence of her metamorphosis in progress, the horns of a heifer growing from her head.

Dionysus is another Greek deity closely associated with metamorphosis. As the god of wine he fosters the growth of the grape vine, the ripening of the grape clusters, and their conversion to wine. This process gives a natural model of slow metamorphosis, and wine itself is a strong psychotropic agent, the most commonly known one in antiquity, changing the nature of humans temporarily for good or bad when they consume it. Two remarkable poems testify to the power of Dionysus and the metamorphoses he can impose. In "Eis Dionyson" "To Dionysus," Homeric hymn, c. 7th century B.C.), the youthful god is abducted by pirates whom he punishes by transforming their ship into a kind of floating vineyard and the sailors themselves into dolphins. In Euripides' *Bakchai* (*The Bacchants,* play, c. 405. B.C.) the psychotropic power of Dionysus is shown when he meets the challenge of Pentheus, who denies that Dionysus is a god. Casting a spell over Pentheus, Dionysus clouds his mind and lures him to his violent death at the hands of his mother. She herself had become a maenad, one of the female followers of Dionysus who surrender their minds to religious ecstasy. Such transformations, while they are not physical metamorphoses, nevertheless present disturbing examples of psychic possession that are sophisticated variations of the theme.

The idea of metamorphosis as a distorting irruption of divine power into the minds of defenseless humans is also illustrated in many myths involving the goddess Aphrodite, whose sphere is sexuality. Just as the wine of Dionysus masters mortal intelligence, so the sexual power of Aphrodite can enrapture an individual's mind so strongly that a temporary transformation of personality takes place. Hera, in order to distract Zeus from the Trojan War, borrows the enchantments of Aphrodite and seduces him (*Iliad,* 14.153 ff.), an episode that furnished a staple of erotic rhetoric in ancient poetry. Even Zeus was overcome by love. The Homeric hymn *Eis Aphroditēn (To Aphrodite,* c. 7th century B.C.) shows the goddess disguising herself as a human princess in order to seduce the hero Anchises. In Ovid's *Metamorphoses* Aphrodite appears under her Roman name Venus and many of the stories there associate love and the power of transformation. Adonis, for example, beloved by Venus, is killed while hunting and she commemorates him by turning his blood into the flower anemone (*Metamorphoses,* 10.529 ff.; Shakespeare, *Venus and Adonis* [narrative poem, 1593]).

The spur to the imagination provided by many other major and minor Greek tales of metamorphoses is an important part of the past and present power of the theme. A simple narrative fact in Greek mythology is that Zeus in the form of a swan seduced the mortal Leda, who then gave birth to Helen, the most beautiful woman in the world and the cause of the Trojan War, and Clytemnestra, as well as Castor and Polydeuces (Pollux). This segment of the myth of Helen may be elaborated in many different ways. Mythographers, who are often concerned to tidy up and rationalize mythical material, will try to find or supply answers to questions about the place of Leda's seduction, the reason for Zeus's metamorphosis, the number of eggs from which the children were born, or the relative authenticity of competing local variations in detail. While the basic facts of this myth and many others involving metamorphosis cannot be altered without destroying the myth itself, many elaborations, versions, and rationalizations of the basic facts are possible. In particular the impulse to visualize the encounter of the swan-Zeus and Leda seems to be irresistible; it is the subject of numerous paintings, Leonardo da Vinci's lost *Leda* being perhaps the most influential. W. B. Yeats's poem "Leda and the Swan" (1923), a meditation on history, was apparently inspired by a painting of this subject; such close associations between myths of metamorphosis and the visual arts reach back to antiquity and have always been lively.

The poem *Eurōpē* by Moschus (*Europa*, c. 150 B.C.) is a good example of a writer's imaginative response to a myth of metamorphosis that is not, in itself, very elaborate. Zeus is attracted to the beauty of Europa, a Near Eastern princess, and seduces her in the form of a bull. In Moschus' version, Europa, an innocent young woman, comes to a meadow near the seashore to play with her girlfriends. The presence of a bull in such a setting is not implausible, whereas a male stranger would not be welcome. Zeus therefore takes the shape he does, but he must be sleek and exceptionally handsome even in a bull-disguise and so Moschus engagingly describes him. At the same time the bull-Zeus must be sufficiently gentle not to alarm a young princess. Europa, attracted to the animal, befriends it and becomes familiar enough with it to sit on its back. Once she does so the bull carries her out to sea and swims to the island of Crete, where, presumably restored to his normal appearance, Zeus seduces her. Moschus presents the episode as if it were a story of adolescent love, in spite of the underlying violence of the abduction.

Most important of all texts concerned with metamorphosis and one of the most influential books in any literature is Ovid's *Metamorphoses*. This epic-length poem contains within its framework more than two hundred stories of varying length narrated in an astonishing variety of styles and techniques. They all involve a metamorphosis of some kind. The poem opens with the creation of the world, a kind of universal transformation from chaos to order, and closes with the apotheosis of Julius Caesar, that is, with his transformation from human to divine status. The *Metamorphoses* has encyclopedic aspects, as is clear from the time-frame, but is not apparently intended to be an exhaustive compendium of classical mythology. The individual stories are arranged in several long cycles, with a highly inventive art of transition from one story or cycle to the next. These transitions are sometimes genealogical, sometimes geographical, sometimes amusingly arbitrary. One aim of Ovid's art is clearly to achieve entertaining variety in the length, focus, mood, and setting of his narratives. The question of the seriousness of the poem has been much debated, as well as the extent to which metamorphosis is the theme of the poem rather than just a literary device to achieve unity amid such variety of materials. Recent criticism tends to see the stories as studies in human emotions, by and large, especially love and fear, and to make that interest the central theme or the truly serious theme of the poem. The philosopher Pythagoras, nevertheless, is introduced toward the end of the epic and is given a long speech (15.60 ff.) whose main point is that change pervades the whole universe and that humans live in a world of constant metamorphosis.

A large proportion of the stories in Ovid's *Metamorphoses* involves the love of a male deity for a girl or woman of lower status. The tale of Apollo and Daphne, one of the first in the poem to be told in some detail, may serve as the type. The male god, a major Olympian in this case, is made to be completely obsessed with a girl, the obsession being inflicted by Cupid, the son of Venus. Since Apollo is normally a god of rationality, serenity, and self-control, an erotic infatuation that he cannot resist is like a temporary metamorphosis of personality. The girl, Daphne, a river-nymph, does not welcome the attentions of Apollo, being indifferent to love and marriage. In fact she has asked her father, a minor river-god, to allow her to enjoy perpetual virginity. Apollo's pursuit of Daphne turns into a footrace, and as she is about to lose she prays to her father to rescue her. He does so by turning her into a laurel tree just as Apollo is about to seize her. The change from girl to tree is narrated with a degree of graphic ingenuity that has inspired many painters, sculptors, and later poets; the pictorial imagination of Ovid, very suitable to tales of transformation, is one of his great strengths. Daphne's metamorphosis is irreversible and curiously disturbing in that she obtains her wish of perpetual virginity, but at the cost of her humanity. Apollo's lust for the girl is converted into an eternal respect for the laurel, which he adopts as his own symbol. Various ages have responded to various elements in the story, the charm of the youthful, amorous Apollo, the pathos of the frightened girl, the picturesque and witty transformation scene. Contemporary critics have explored the underlying violence of this and similar Ovidian stories. The cold, bleak finality of humans turned into objects, plants, or animals, treated as an entertaining and witty topic, will soon reveal dark tensions and Ovid does not avoid them.

Many stories of transformation from Ovid's *Metamorphoses* have taken on a life of their own and have developed a thematic tradition independent of their original setting. Such stories often involve figures who are emblematic in some way. Narcissus, for example, typifies the self-obsessed person; he drowns in the pool that he uses for a mirror, trying to touch his own image, his commemoration a flower. Pygmalion, a sculptor, cannot find an ordinary woman who pleases him and so creates a statue that represents his ideal. He falls in love with his own creation, an impasse from which he is rescued by Venus, who transforms the statue into a live woman so that Pygmalion can marry her. Such tales are essentially about love so intense yet so thwarted that an escape from the imprisonment of a particular shape seems to be the only possible outcome. Thus metamorphosis appears not only as a punishment, but it can be a relief, granted by a compassionate deity to whom a human turns when he is in an insoluble predicament. Other emblematic stories emphasize the arbitrary wrath of deities whose status is challenged. Marsyas challenges Apollo to a contest in musical performance; Apollo wins and flays Marsyas alive (a kind of metamorphosis) as a punishment. Similarly, when Arachne challenges Minerva to a contest in weaving, she comes very close to winning, but in anger Minerva changes her into a spider. Metamorphosis in these cases is a terrible punishment, demeaning the human and condemning him or her to an eternity of grotesqueness.

Ovid's almost inexhaustible material, drawn from stories of gods and heroes, is complemented in Roman literature by the novel of Apuleius also titled *Metamorphoses* (c. 150), but known in English as *The Golden Ass*. This story can stand as an extremely important type of non-Ovidian metamorphosis, in which the hero is temporarily transformed into an animal (or whatever), but retains human thoughts and feelings while in the changed shape and furthermore takes steps to try to reverse the change. Lucius, the protagonist of *The Golden Ass*, becomes curious about the ability of a witch to change herself into a bird. By an intrigue he gains access to the witch's potions, but unfortunately transforms himself not into a bird but into a donkey. A long, entertaining series of adventures follows in which the man-donkey goes from one owner to another, experiencing the world with human sensibilities yet from the low perspective of a common domestic animal. All the while he is intent on finding the means of reversing the transformation. Apuleius enriches the novel with many subordinate episodes and inset narratives, some of which mirror or vary the theme of metamorphosis. Lucius' long-delayed reverse transformation is finally achieved by the intervention of the goddess Isis, who appears to him when he is most desperate and tells him what to do to regain his human form. In gratitude he becomes one of her priests and undergoes an elaborate process of training and initiation that is perhaps intended to carry forward the theme of change from the ordinary world to that of religion.

The narrative device of the human transformed temporarily in such a way that he somehow stands outside a society that he can observe and comment on is a particularly rich one. Plutarch's brief dialogue "Peri tou ta aloga logō chrēsthai" ("Beasts Are Rational," c. A.D. 100) deals wittily with the situation in which one of the Greeks transformed into animals by Circe refuses to accept the offer of a reverse transformation because the life of animals is better and more virtuous than that of humans. His detailed explanation of the superior morality of the animal world becomes a general satire of human weaknesses. This man-pig who prefers to remain that way is named Gryllus, and the name is sometimes used as the title of the dialogue in translation. Swift's *Gulliver's Travels* (1726) is essentially in a similar form, despite manifest differences. The classical apparatus of divine or magical agents of metamorphosis has disappeared, but Gulliver arrives in societies in which he seems transformed because he is a man-mountain among the Lilliputians or a tiny figure among the giant Brobdingnagians. The theme of the desire to escape from the state of apparent transformation back to normal life is very strong in *Gulliver's Travels*, but Swift is more intent on the moral, social, and political satire that arises from the description of societies from the point of view of an intelligent outsider. Like Plutarch's Gryllus, who prefers his metamorphosis, Swift's Gulliver finally comes to prefer the company of horses to that of humans. The Alice books of Lewis Carroll (*Alice's Adventures in Wonderland*, 1865; *Through the Looking Glass, and What Alice Found There*, 1872) employ a variant of this narrative strategy. Alice goes down the rabbit hole and drinks a potion, which transforms her, although only in shape. In Wonderland or beyond the Looking Glass she retains her human consciousness but finds that she is in a realm of rapidly changing space and time, with unexpected flora and fauna that are transformed or anthropomorphized common objects, persons, or animals. She does not have much success in making her normal, untransformed intelligence function effectively. Alice does want to return to normal life, like Apuleius' Lucius or Swift's Gulliver, but her desire is oddly vacillating and her return seems almost to be a disappointment to her sense of curiosity and adventure.

Kafka's story "Die Verwandlung" ("The Metamorphosis", 1915) seems to share in several of the categories already outlined. The hero's transformation begins the story and the cause or agent is not made evident; in these two points the metamorphosis is not Ovidian. But it is Ovidian insofar as it is irreversible and demeaning. Gregor Samsa clearly retains human consciousness and reactions and would like to be able to escape back to normal life (at least in the early days of his transformation), and elements of satire appear in the narrator's description of the reactions of Gregor's family and associates. In these respects it shares features of the Apuleian reversible metamorphosis. To this mixture of narrative types, provocative psychological resonances have been added, which, together with the ambiguous tone of the ending, have given this text its unique prestige.

Ovid's presence as an influence in modern literature is characteristically allusive and oblique. Joyce's *A Portrait of the Artist as a Young Man* (1916) has an epigraph taken from the story of Daedalus and Icarus in Ovid's poem, while the hero's family name, Dedalus, identifies him with the "old artificer." Yet the novel is only remotely a retelling of the classic story, whose themes, creativity, transformation, flight, and escape have been fragmented and turned to symbolic and psychological purposes. Ovid's version of the myth of Teiresias is a major element in Eliot's *The Waste Land* (1922); the transformation of Teiresias into a woman and back again to a male makes him, according to Eliot's note, "the most important personage in the poem." If metamorphosis is a theme of the poem, it no longer appears as a narrative strategy but has been reformulated, so to speak, into themes of cultural decay, personal disintegration, and thwarted creativity. Daphne is an Ovidian figure that appears early in Pound's lyrics ("The Tree" in *Personae*, 1909). Her associations with Apollo, the laurel, and poetry make her one of Pound's many touchstones and emblems. In his *Cantos* (1925–1969) the mythical figure has dissolved into a constantly recurring series of images of trees, leaves, light, and sun, none of them any longer necessarily a direct allusion to her metamorphosis but all of them a proof of her continuing presence.

The attempt to present the world as constantly in change in a far more complex sense than claimed by Ovid's Pythagoras is best, perhaps uniquely, exemplified by Joyce's novel *Finnegans Wake* (1939). Here the metamorphoses are not the apparently simple reversible or irreversible change of a single person into animal or object, but metamorphoses of both kinds are constant, numerous, and normal. Space and time are no longer stable, but undergo continuous change. Two successive narrative moments may be dated to widely separated historical moments yet be transformed versions of each other and, this transformation may apply to persons and places as well as actions. Language is also unstable, allowing single sentences to change from one language to another or to incorporate several. As a dream-novel, *Finnegans Wake* exploits the typical effects of displacement, distortion, and symbolism that are the manifest content of dreams; the distance from classical physical metamorphoses is great. In Joyce's novel the narrative bite and shock of an individual transformation become diluted and the strategy perhaps begins to work against itself. Nevertheless, chapter 8 of book 1 of *Finnegans Wake,* with the metamorphosis of the two washerwomen into tree and stone, remains an unsurpassed realization of the theme.

See also: Androgyny; Bear; Rat, Mouse; Seduction; Werewolf.

Selected Bibliography

Galinsky, G. Karl. *Ovid's Metamorphoses. An Introduction to the Basic Aspects*. Oxford: Basil Blackwell, 1975.

Massey, Irving. *The Gaping Pig. Literature and Metamorphosis*. Berkeley, Los Angeles, London: University of California Press, 1976.

Skulsky, Harold. *Metamorphosis. The Mind in Exile*. Cambridge, Mass.: Harvard University Press, 1981.

Tomlinson, Charles. *Poetry and Metamorphosis*. Cambridge, New York: Cambridge University Press, 1983.

HARRY G. EDINGER

MIRROR

Prosaic objects that are an intrinsic part of everyday life, mirrors have been much used in literary works as a means of raising questions about the objects they reflect, conceal, or unmask, as well as about the universal theme of literature—the disparity between reality and appearance. To what extent is the mirror image, with its ubiquity and dumb eloquence, built into the structure of the universe, a piece of eternity in the bathroom? How much psychology, theology, philosophy, science and poetry is tied up with it?

The mirror is nonselective and therefore objective; "high fidelity" in its imitativeness; comprehensive, if one rotates it; instantaneous in operation. On the negative side, it is fragile, transitory, two dimensional, cold, silent, superficial, slavishly imitative. Being (unlike the tape recorder or the camera) preindustrial, the mirror is available to the most primitive of men, whether on the surface of an unruffled puddle or of another's eyes.

The mirror image stimulates thought; the propinquity of mirror and thinking is built into the language. The Latin word for mirror, *speculum*, is related to *speculari*, to watch, examine, observe; "reflection" (from Latin *reflectere*, to bend back) means to turn an eye or thought on something, to meditate, as well as to give back an image. In Dante's *Purgatorio (Purgatory*, a section of *La divina commedia* [*The Divine Comedy*, epic poem, c. 1320]), Rachel observing herself in a mirror is a type of contemplative.

The mirror has special importance because without it man is doomed not to see the most spiritual and expressive part of himself—his face—and this handicap in turn becomes a metaphor for the human inability to know oneself. As Shakespeare put it: "Nor doth the eye itself, / That most pure spirit of sense, behold itself"; "Since you know you cannot see yourself / So well as by reflection, I, your glass." For most people, peering into a mirror is a quick substitute for self-knowledge; a ready way of knowing how one looks, if not who one is; of making sure of one's best appearance, if not finding out how others truly see one.

The ready availability of such a duplicate of reality struck early man with awe and fear. He came to see it as a magical source of knowledge not to be had normally, a doorway to past and future or to present events unfolding far away. In many primitive cultures, the person's mirror image was thought to be the soul itself, not just a symbol of it. (In some languages, the word for soul even means optical reflection.) The mirror abstracted and retained the essential self; one had to beware of gazing into or breaking mirrors. Hence the widespread custom of covering mirrors during mourning periods, lest the departed take with him the soul of the person gazing into the mirror. The existence of mirror images with their insubstantiality and elusiveness, like that of dreams and shadows, generated (as Sir James Frazer, among others, surmised) beliefs in the existence of the soul, the ghost, the hereafter.

Antiquity

From the beginnings of literature and philosophy, two schools of thought existed on the question of whether mirrors are a blessing or a curse. Among the optimists is Socrates of Diogenes Laertius (3d century), who enjoined young men to use the mirror so that the handsome could conduct themselves correspondingly and the ugly could learn to conceal their defects through education. The same Socrates, speaking through Plato (middle 4th century B.C.), also articulated the pessimistic view. Postulating the existence of ideal forms ontologically superior to the objects of the senses, he sneered at the work of illusionist or "realist" painters, who achieved with great effort what a mere mirror provides in an instant: a duplication of the surface of things, a plausible but specious impression of the shadow, to the neglect of the real or whole. The mirror image, a two-dimensional version of a transitory three-dimensional world, is a semblance of the *un*real and therefore doubly removed from reality.

The Platonic view was boosted by Paul, who said, "Now we see only puzzling reflections in a mirror. . . . My knowledge now is partial.'' The mirror of this world, for Christian apostle as for Greek philosopher, by being slavishly imitative, gives only glimmers of the ultimate reality elsewhere; it nourishes sight, not insight. A classic imaginative expression of the pessimistic view that the mirror is a catalyst for the worst tendencies in people, or at least a danger to the unwary, is the Narcissus story in Greek mythology, given a definitive rendering in Ovid's epic poem *Metamorphoses* (c. A.D. 2–17). Here, self-contemplation turns into self-adoration rather than self-knowledge. The story bristles with ironic and psychological insights. Someone had prophesied that Narcissus could live to a ripe old age provided that he would never know himself; one of the nymphs he had spurned was Echo, who had a certain speech impediment, and his fate became an echo of hers, his watery image being a visual echo. His futile attempt to kiss his own reflection is a metaphor for the apparent futility of personal vanity, of love, and of the striving for self-knowledge.

The Middle Ages and Renaissance

The *Roman de la rose* (*Romance of the Rose,* didactic poem, c. 1230, 1275), in addition to retelling the Narcissus story, contains much lore about the role of mirrors in amatory matters and about the supernatural powers of mirrors, for example, to make ghosts appear. As in many other medieval works, the worldwide tradition that mirrors reflect a hidden, superior reality (Japanese Shinto temples, e.g., have only mirrors in the sanctuary) is Christianized, as mirrors are held to reflect divine abstractions or even be a symbol of God. Hence Dante often uses the mirror to explain theological complexity or express a religious experience in the *Divine Comedy*. Mirrors figure prominently also in sixteenth-century French and Italian poetry, notably that of Maurice Scève.

The optimistic view made a characteristic return in the early Renaissance. In Rabelais' blueprint for the Abbey of Thélème (*Gargantua et Pantagruel* [*Gargantua and Pantagruel,* novels, 1532–1564]), each retiring room would have a mirror ''large enough to give a true reflection of the whole figure.'' Amid the this-worldly interest in the self and in corporeal beauty, there is no alarm here over narcissism. (Contrast this with H. G. Wells's ascetic quasi-medieval attitude in *Men Like Gods* [novel, 1923]. The Utopians have no mirrors because they think it ''indecent to be reminded of themselves in that way.'') Such optimism appeared likewise in Leonardo da Vinci's notebooks (late 15th century), which urged the painter to use the mirror, with its receptivity, as a guide and touchstone; above all else, ''the mirror is our teacher.'' L. B. Alberti (fl. 15th century) even called Narcissus the inventor of painting.

One of the most poignant mirror scenes in literature, transcending questions of optimism and pessimism, takes place in Shakespeare's *Richard II* (play, c.1596). The king, forced to publicly renounce the crown and admit his ineptness, behaves in his usual exhibitionistic, procrastinating, self-pitying fashion. Finally, he asks for a mirror and, like an adolescent, indulges his vanity amid pressing affairs of state. The scene reminds us that he has been figuratively staring in the mirror throughout his reign. But now he is undergoing an identity crisis, having to discover what it is like to be "Richard" without being "King," if there even is such a person. Traumatized by events, he needs reassurance that he exists at all. The mirror image then becomes the occasion for an *ubi sunt* threnody and, lastly, a metaphor for fragility.

In seventeenth-century religious poetry, the Platonic-Pauline vein turns optimistic. George Herbert (*The Temple*, 1633) prays to see God's hand in everything: "A man that looks on glass / On it may stay his eye / Or, if he pleaseth, through it pass, / And then the heaven espy." How one goes from the mirror to heaven is made clearer by Traherne (fl. 1660s), who recalls in several poems that as a child playing near a puddle he had noticed another world "beneath" him and "within it." The mirror image of things above is an intimation of the other world and of the "unknown joys" prepared for him when he leaves this world. There is "Under our Feet there,/As o'er our Heads, a place of Bliss." To the Christian visionary, the other world is so close that glimmers of it are to be seen through the puddles, which are so many holes or windows in the fabric separating this world from the next.

The secular poets (e.g., Lovelace, Carew, fl. 1630s) took their cues from the Narcissus story rather than from Paul. They urged the beloved to "dress thy beauties in my eyes" rather than to contemplate her own image in the mirror, to see herself in the warm, animated eyes of the lover rather than in the cold, passive piece of glass. Mirrors, made for self-discovery and humility, can become the icons of self-love, the visible tokens of a spiritual imbalance. The greatest poet of the century took this platitude and brought it to poetic heights. In Milton's *Paradise Lost* (1667), the newly created Eve notices her reflection in a pool and likes it so much that, had not a voice sent her, with appropriate warnings, to meet him "whose image thou art," she would have "pined with vain desire." Indeed on meeting Adam she thought him less attractive than her own watery image. The incident represents Milton's incorporation of the Narcissus myth into scriptural story. It dramatizes woman's vanity and concern with appearances and mirrors. Her preference for a watery image over a living, vital husband adumbrates a weakness of judgment that Satan will exploit.

If Narcissus and Eve are at first too naïve to know that they gaze at themselves, Pope's Belinda (*Rape of the Lock,* poem, 1712) knows better and readily exhibits her sophistication and corruption. Waking up to another day of frivolities, she sits down at her morning toilet to perform the "sacred rites of pride" addressed to the "heavenly image in the glass," making, with the help of the "inferior priestess at her altar's side," the "various offerings of the world." Here is a religious service, as Pope's precise diction suggests, in which the lady is at once worshipper, goddess, high priestess. What was implicit in the love poets and Milton is here explicit. To the pagan concept of narcissism has been added the Hebraic proscription of idol worship, specifically the most heinous form of it, self-idolatry—the pride exhibited before the "vanity." Goethe's Gretchen (*Faust,* play, 1808) likewise, after putting on some jewels, is tempted to spend an hour before the mirror.

The Nineteenth Century

In the novel *Voĭna i mir* (*War and Peace,* 1865–1869) Tolstoy suggests a different principle at work in the case of some women. Princess Marya's gentle look is praised in a letter from a friend. The skeptical princess looks into the mirror and, seeing an unprepossessing image, thinks that she is being flattered. The narrator intervenes to remark that the princess never saw the beauty that flowed into her eyes when she was not thinking of herself: "As is the case with everyone, her face assumed an affected, unnatural, ugly expression as soon as she looked in the looking glass." Where for Ovid and Milton, the narcissism begot of mirrors leads the victim to see more than meets the eye, for Tolstoy it leads to less. (For somewhat different reasons, E. A. Poe, in the "Philosophy of Furniture" [1840], similarly reprehended mirrors.)

In the same novel, Tolstoy scientifically accounts for the survival of primitive superstitions about mirrors. Natashya, curious about her future love life with Andrey, gazes—in vain—into mirrors arranged in a special way. Her friend Sonya tries also but is unsure whether she actually sees something or is bamboozled by folklore into thinking she sees it. Much later, when Sonya comes upon Natashya nursing the wounded Andrey, she shrieks and says she had foreseen this scene. Tolstoy wryly remarks that Sonya, as a result apparently of a déjà vu feeling, actually believed what she was saying; even Natashya now thinks she recalls Sonya predicting the present details correctly.

Tolstoy is mocking people's credulity, but other major writers have exploited the folklore about the magic inherent in mirrors. Chaucer's Squire (*Canterbury Tales,* c.1380–1400) tells of a knight at the court of Genghiz Khan who bears, among other marvels, a mirror in which one can foresee many things; the witches in Shakespeare's play *Macbeth* (1605–1606) conjure up a king holding a mirror in which are pictured the many sons of Banquo destined to rule Scotland; in Hawthorne's tales, notably "Dr. Heidegger's Experiment" (1837), mirrors are tombs from which one summons shades of the past or prophesies the future; Tennyson's Lady of Shalott (1832) sees current events in seclusion through the medium of a magic mirror (presumably now called TV); and, even in our time, in Michel de Ghelderode's play *Sire Halewyn* (*Lord Halewyn,* 1934), the main character, upon seeing in a magic mirror glimmers of a far-off place and a lovely lady, begins a voyage (as does the hero of *Faust*).

But no one made use of the belief in magic mirrors as richly as did Lewis Carroll. The idea that what is reflected in the mirror constitutes another world offers two inferences. One, suggested by Traherne and Herbert, is that the mirror is but a window through which the passive observer glances. The other is that it is a doorway through which the beholder, no mere passive soul, can move. Following up the latter possibility, *Through the Looking Glass* (1872) is perhaps the only great work to deal centrally with the topography and peculiarity of the world in the mirror. Alice enters not the traditional hereafter, nor the moralist's inner world, nor the astronaut's world of outer space, but a world near ours, parallel to it in some hitherto undiscovered dimension. In that world, "things go the other way": A cake is first handed around and then sliced; to reach something one must "walk in the opposite direction." That such a world resembles ours is hardly surprising in a culture in which biologists speak of symmetries (e.g., of the human body), astronomers of twin stars, physicists of antimatter, literary men of doppelgänger, psychologists of repetition.

Besides being instruments of vanity or bearers of magic powers, mirrors pose important philosophical questions. Hawthorne was signally intrigued by this approach. On the one hand, the distorting mirror may reveal things about reality better than does the flat mirror that keeps all proportion; the scarlet letter—in the most mirror-haunted work of literature (1850)—is writ large in the reflection from nearby armor. (For Goethe, likewise, the mirror, by inverting things and altering reality, is a symbol of art.) On the other hand, the normal mirror offers metaphors of the human condition. In a little-known story, "Monsieur du Miroir" (1837), Hawthorne's narrator tells of a silent, well-studied but little-understood twin who mimics him but is never sullied by material things and is perhaps "the wiser" though his "whole business is REFLECTION."

In another work (*Old Manse*, tales, 1846), Hawthorne, with visionary zeal, treats the reflections in a river, which most people think inferior (because less colorful and more fragile), as quite the opposite: "Each tree and rock . . . however unsightly in reality, assumes ideal beauty in the reflection." To the philosopher's leading question, "Which was the most real?" Hawthorne offers something partly Platonic: "Surely the disembodied images stand in closer relation to the soul." Perhaps he meant that the reflection retains the beauty of, say, poison ivy but deletes the poison; the image of a handsome man or woman—in river, mirror, painting, or photo—appears as the Platonic idea of that person, without the moral defects and normal crotchets that make that person burdensome to others in the three-dimensional world. Moreover, "all the sky glows downward at our feet." That is, heaven is beneath us, dwells among us, lurks in the watery image of the poison ivy without the poison. These are glimmers of the only heaven available to us and the only one we need to know. Nature in repose, in other words, is the imagined afterworld in the here and now, and lakes reflect heaven not only because of the laws of physics and optics but because of the laws of psychology and because they tell us that only in nature can the imagined heaven be found. If for Plato the mirror image is a copy of a copy (e.g., a bed) of reality (the idea of a bed), Hawthorne, while agreeing on the imperfection of our world, locates Plato's ideal forms in the mirror itself.

The Twentieth Century

The modern writer is less conscious of the solace given by nature than of nature's disappearance. In one of the richest lyrics on the theme of mirrors,

Stanly Kunitz's "The War Against the Trees" (1958) describes a world in which beautiful trees and shrubs, the companions of children, are cut down to make way for suburbia, as land is given over to the oil interests, to the technology that they make possible, and to real estate developers. All this is seen for a moment in that peculiarly modern contrivance, "the rear-view mirrors of the passing cars," the very cars that run on products of oil, create the suburb, and cause the slaughter of vegetation. The irremediable social cost is seen only briefly in the small image of the rear-view mirror of a society hurtling forward into "progress." Modern man, intent on the technological utopia of the future, barely, belatedly, and dispassionately notices the carnage he leaves behind.

Some modern writers continue the Narcissus-Belinda theme, albeit with alterations. Thomas Hardy wryly notes of the sunken luxury boat, the *Titanic*, in "Convergence of the Twain" (1912), "Over the mirrors meant / To glass the opulent / The sea worm crawls—grotesque, slimed, dumb, indifferent." In I. B. Singer's story "The Mirror" (1957), the perpetrator of self-idolatry incurs adverse consequences that come directly from the instrument of self-contemplation. Zirel, a bored, beautiful wife, beholds her naked beauty for hours at a time. One day a demon emerges from the mirror and lures her into hell. A moral intimated by the *Rape of the Lock* is dramatized in this quasi-folktale.

Others continue the Pauline-Traherne theme but, in an age lacking faith, with a pessimistic emphasis. A. E. Housman notes in *A Shropshire Lad* (poems, 1896) that the trees and clouds in pools and rivers are more beautiful than any seen on earth. Then he articulates what had remained unspoken in Traherne and Hawthorne: "Oh that I were there!" The implied death wish is made explicit by the poet's revelation that he often wants "to strip and dive and drown." But as he looks directly overhead, he sees "A silly lad that longs and looks / And wishes he were I." Unlike Narcissus, he knows the image for what it is and proceeds to turn it into a symbol of the universe. If he wishes to be in a more ideal world, so does the face in the water wish to be in the poet's. The grass is literally greener elsewhere, all worlds are defective, and suicide is the pseudo solution of the naïve youth.

Pessimism of a related sort can be seen in the modern French Existentialist novel. The crisis of loss of identity confronted in the mirror by Richard II occurs in that genre to men of more modest means and rank, and not at historic junctures but in private moments of "quiet desperation." When nothing else seems real or certain, they turn to the mirror, only to find little psychic relief there. Camus, in *Le mythe de Sisyphe* (*The Myth of Sisyphus*, essay, 1942), typically speaks of moments of lucidity when one confronts absurdity, such as when "the stranger who at certain seconds comes to meet us in a mirror, the familiar and yet alarming brother we encounter in our own photographs." (Cf. Tolstoy's novel *Anna Karenina*, 1877, and Joyce's story "The Dead," 1914). At issue is not a deposed king's quandary, but everyman's metaphysical angst, in scenes that are pictorial renderings of the elusiveness of the ancient Greek prescription, "Know thyself."

In Malraux's *La condition humaine (Man's Fate*, novel, 1933), Clappique, a chronic liar, runs into a loneliness that not even alcohol or whores can assuage. In the mirror he meets for once the nothingness that he is, the absence of a character he can call his own. In panic, he begins to make faces at himself, each revealing "to him a part of himself hidden by life"—the self as gargoyle, monkey, idiot, apoplectic, terrified person. Needing as a result "to protect himself from the frightful mirror, . . . he withdrew with horror." In parallel fashion, Kyo, one of the protagonists, shocked at not being able to recognize his own voice on a phonograph record, reports to his father that it was like not recognizing himself in the mirror.

Roquentin, the main character of Sartre's influential novel, *La nausée* (*Nausea,* 1938), leads a shadowy existence working on a biography in a library and sensing himself cut off from people and even objects, from the future and even the present. Sometimes finding himself trapped in a mirror, he sees, as an aunt had once warned, a monkey. He brings his face to the glass until all features are flattened out and manipulates his features until he is overwhelmed by a sense of mortality. He concludes that it is impossible to understand one's face except through the mirror of human relations. (In Sartre's *Huis clos* [*No Exit,* play, 1944]), on the other hand, hell is repeatedly defined as, in part, a place without mirrors, and the dead are saddened by the thought that their mirrors on earth reflect only their furniture now.) In Genet's *Pompes funèbres* (*Funeral Rites,* novel, 1953), self-hatred is carried a step further when a drunken Nazi shoots at his own image in a mirror—an apt gesture, for what is the culture the presence of which prompts a Nazi to reach for his gun, if not man spiritually scrutinizing himself in a mirror?

Nazism (or nihilism) and the mirror are again germane in Ionesco's play, *Le rhinocéros* (*Rhinoceros,* 1960). The inhabitants of a town turn, first one by one, then in groups, into the thick-skinned, myopic, hostile, ugly beasts. Soon only the protagonist is left, and, insisting that men are not bad looking, he stares at a mirror. Doubts creep in; perhaps the others were right in thinking men to be strange looking and ridiculous. He envies the beasts their horns and wrinkled brows, their hard, dull-green skins. "I can't stand the sight of me. I'm too ashamed. I'm so ugly." Then he turns his back on the mirror and declares his resolve not to change.

The discovery in the mirror of the enigma or horror or absurdity of human identity is handled with greater philosophical detachment by Pirandello's Laudisi. The village skeptic and choral commentator in *Così è se vi pare!* (*It Is So, If You Think So,* play, 1917), he laughs at the futility of the other characters' efforts to establish which of two versions of events is the correct one. His reflection in the mirror becomes a metaphor for the self, for he can see himself clearly, but to others he is "just an image in the glass!" Carrying such a phantom in themselves, people vainly try to fathom the "phantoms in other people." Just as each faction in the play, by thinking the opposite one mad, is a mirror image of the other, so is "Who am I?" a question not easily answered, for each person is a collection of images reflected in others. The butler, entering and seeing

Laudisi gesticulating to himself in the mirror, thinks him insane, the more so as Laudisi says to him, "Are you really sure the Laudisi you are talking to is the Laudisi the ladies want to see?" The image in the mirror thus stands for the essential self, the inability to know that parallels one's inability to ascertain the truth about anyone else. Reality is a mirror in which each sees something different, something he brings to the mirror. What is actually out there is, like a mirror without reflections, beyond our grasp.

Hence the mirror is the central symbol for the pyrrhonism of the play—and the pessimism of modern literature. No longer does it arouse self-love or offer psychic security as it did for Narcissus or Belinda. To people seeking a foothold in the flux of reality, the mirror is more sphinx than icon. If women and youths have difficulty keeping vanity out of the mirror, mature modern men have difficulty finding identity or significance in that same dumb, ambiguous oracle. This despite the proliferation in the modern world of newspapers and magazines with titles like *Der Spiegel* or *The Mirror*.

A less alienated, more balanced view is achieved by Robert Graves. Shakespeare, in Sonnet 62 (1609), had felt humbled as a lover by the evidence of the ravages of time presented to him by the mirror, but Graves, about to shave in "The Face in the Mirror" (1961), after scowling at the same ravages, ends flamboyantly with the observation that the man behind that visibly decaying face "still stands ready, with a boy's presumption, / To court the queen in her high silk pavilion." The mirror has not conveyed the essence of the man, an essence he is sure of, unlike those dissolving Frenchmen in a state of crisis. A similar daily ritual in the life of a woman is the subject of Sylvia Plath's "Mirror" (c. 1950), which speaks of its own importance in a woman's life as she gazes into it every morning, pours into it her private agitation, and traces the erosions of daily life: "In me she has drowned a young girl, and in me an old woman / Rises toward her day after day, like a terrible fish." For Plath, as for Shakespeare and not for Graves, the mirror reflects quotidian reality all too faithfully.

The late nineteenth- and early twentieth-century French Symbolist poets— Baudelaire, Mallarmé, Valéry—were also drawn to the mirror, seeing the universe as a vast game of mirrors and the mirror as a symbol of symbolism. This tradition, together with the magical-Lewis Carroll approach, fed into the work of James Joyce and Jorge Luis Borges. In a surrealist scene rich with symbolism, Stephen and Bloom (*Ulysses,* novel, 1922) stare into a mirror, and a distorted image of Shakespeare stares back. Borges' writings, e.g., *El hacedor* (*Dreamtigers,* poems, 1960), are notably haunted by dreams and mirrors. In his *Ficciones* (*Fictions,* 1945, 1956), mirrors in a library hallway duplicate all appearances, and these to Borges "represent and promise the infinite." As is the case in a small restaurant with mirrored walls, mirrors bring a sense of spaciousness to the familiar world in which we are cabined, cribbed, and confined. The only infinity that we know from experience rather than from abstract theory is offered by them. No wonder that in some arcane book conjured up by Borges one reads that for the Gnostics, to whom the visible universe was an illusion, "mirrors and fatherhood are abominable, because they multiply and disseminate that universe.''

If the mirror is a doorway, need the traffic go all one way? The people in *Through the Looking Glass* do not threaten to enter our world—so far. Could not that change? Borges suggests that one day the creatures imprisoned in the mirrors will cease to imitate us, and (like Zirel arrested by the demon in her mirror) ''we will hear from the depth of mirrors the clatter of weapons.'' Here, via mirrors, is a doomsday not yet thought of by medieval divine or modern physicist.

See also: Dream, Shadow.

Selected Bibliography

Goldin, Frederick. *The Mirror of Narcissus in the Courtly Love Lyric.* Ithaca, N.Y.: Cornell University Press, 1967.

Grabes, Herbert. *The Mutable Glass: Mirror-Imagery in Titles and Texts of the Middle Ages and English Renaissance.* Trans. Gordon Collier. Cambridge: Cambridge University Press, 1982.

Prioleau, Elizabeth ''Humbert Humbert *Through the Looking Glass.*'' *Twentieth Century Literature* 21 (1975): 428–437.

Seligmann, Kurt. *The Mirror of Magic.* New York: Pantheon Books, 1948.

MANFRED WEIDHORN

MONEY

By ''money'' is meant, in the strict sense, currency—pieces of metal or paper that are used as a medium of exchange and a measure of value, that are accepted as substitutes for or as evaluators of labor or goods, as wages for labor performed or payment for objects received. In this narrow sense, money plays a limited role in literature until the nineteenth century. More broadly, ''money'' can mean wealth, possessions, lands, and, as such, always appears in literature.

Antiquity

In the Old Testament, money is unimportant, perhaps because it is not yet a widespread mode of exchange. The prosperity of the patriarchs is measured in cattle. In the Mosaic Law, the famous ''eye for an eye'' principle seems literal but later was construed by rabbinic commentators to refer only to financial equivalents.

While lacking references to money as we understand it, Homer's epic poem *Ilias (Iliad,* c. 8th century B.C.) contains many other tokens of wealth. The initial squabble between Agamemnon and Achilles is in part over possession of the girl Briseis. She has no amatory or sexual importance, and her forced removal to Agamemnon's tent is symbolic of what Achilles complains bitterly about, namely that he himself does all the fighting and Agamemnon gets the bulk of the spoils; in other words, that his wages are low. When Achilles then launches what is in effect the first recorded labor strike in history by withdrawing his services and that of his Myrmidons (his union local, as it were) from the war, the Greeks are routed by the Trojans. Agamemnon, regretting his folly and heeding the advice of Nestor (the "labor arbitrator"), attempts to lure the warrior back with huge outlays of property. Achilles insists however, that his own dignity—and his revenge—is beyond reckoning, beyond the reach of mere possessions and bribery. His eventual return is triggered by nonfinancial considerations—anger over the death of Patrocles—and when Agamemnon's gifts are offered again, he accepts them but says that they are a matter of indifference to him still. At the funeral games for Patrocles, he, as master of ceremonies, is generous in gift giving, even to his erstwhile enemy, Agamemnon.

Other warriors in the epic, on running into each other or breaking off a duel, exchange gifts; in one exchange Homer remarks that the Greek outwitted the Trojan, getting much more value than he gave. When in book 9 a despondent Agamemnon suggests returning home, the warhawk Diomedes indignantly tells him to leave and insists that others will fight on until Troy is sacked. This passage provides perhaps the only glimpse in the *Iliad* of the likely historical motives. Though the sons of Atreus may have come to wealthy Troy to bring back the pulchritudinous Helen, what prompted the rest of the Greek host to throw away ten years of their lives on the frontlines was probably booty, not beauty.

In Homer's epic poem *Odysseia* (*The Odyssey,* c. 8th century B.C.), the hero is intent mainly on getting home and resuming his role as lord of his manor and isle. Along the way, he will not, because of his many-sided character, ignore adventure or refuse gifts. As one "knowing profitable ways" and loving to collect possessions, he is careful to accept graciously, especially from Alkinoos, many rich offerings and to bring them home safely. (He also takes pride in the way Penelope beguiles gifts out of the suitors.) Such possessions freely given help him define his own sense of being the great Odysseus. Here is an early example of money (in the broad sense) as a signpost of importance. Such worldly judgments are precisely the ones that Socrates deliberately rejected; not only did he turn down his wealthy friend's proposal to free him from prison and execution by means of judicious payments, but he did so for the sake of a philosophy that explicitly favored self-examination in lieu of the "heaping up of the greatest amount of money" (Plato's *Apologia* [*Apology*] and *Kritōn* [*Crito*], dialogues, 4th century B.C.). And in the *Politeia* (*The Republic,* dialogue, c.380 B.C.), we are told that great wealth is no source of happiness to a man with a nagging conscience.

Money is notably absent from Greek tragedy but appears in the nonmythological milieu of Aristophanic comedy. One of the (unfair) charges levelled in the tendentious portraiture of Socrates (*Nephelai* [*The Clouds,* 423 B.C.]) is that he took money for his teaching. In the *Ornithes* (*The Birds,* 414 B.C.), the gods are thrown into panic by the disruption of what passes for currency in the relations of gods and men—the smoke from animal sacrifices. The rebellious women of the *Lysistratē* (*Lysistrata*, 411 B.C.) bring the Peloponnesian War to an end by withholding their bodies and capturing the state treasury on the Acropolis. Money and sex, implies the play, are what make men tick, and everything else is commentary. But the *Ploutos* (*Plutus*, 388 B.C.) is the first literary work to deal comprehensively with the impact of wealth on human relations. The god of wealth, wanting to consort only with the just, has been blinded by Zeus and therefore unwittingly favors the wicked. Despite a tirade from Poverty proving that she causes all the good in life, Plutus' sight is restored, and wealth now favors only the righteous. This line of thought is continued by Lucian (2d century) in some of his dialogues. The *Zeus tragōdos* (*Jupiter tragoedus*) presents the gods as highly dependent on animal sacrifices. In the *Kataplous (Cataplus)*, a poor man who while alive had envied the rich man living next door discovers to his delight that in the afterworld it is the turn of the rich man to suffer the lack of all the wealth he had had on earth and which he never had got around to enjoying while alive anyway. The poor man, having had nothing, misses nothing. In the *Timōn*, (*Timon*), a personification, Wealth, tells Zeus how Timon had ignored and mistreated him. Hermes also discovers that Wealth is lame, blind, and winged—blind because he serves individuals irrespective of their moral qualities, lame because it takes him a long time to reach a man expecting him, and winged because he quickly leaves a man. Zeus may think that Wealth visits people who merit him, but in fact Wealth simply goes with those he runs into by chance. Wealth is also ugly, yet many fall in love with him, the reason being their ignorance and self-deceit. Were someone to strip Wealth naked and show him as he is, people would kick themselves for their folly in loving something so hideous. Wealth brings in his wake, moreover, such characters as Arrogance and Sloth.

Less moralistic is Aristotle's scientific approach. In the *Rhētorikē technē* (*Rhetoric*, treatise, c. 360 B.C.), he asserts that activity or use of things (rather than owning them) constitutes wealth. Moreover, since the long established seems natural, we are much less critical of people possessing "old money" than of those newly coming into it; on the other hand, it is true that wealth, a fortiori new wealth, produces vanity, insolence, a tendency to judge everything by money, and, "in a word, . . . a prosperous fool." The *Ēthika Nikomacheia* (*Ethics*, treatise, 4th century B.C.) concedes riches to be necessary for happiness and desirable for the sake of honor, but making money is useful only for the sake of something else. In the *Politika* (*Politics*, essays), Aristotle briefly traces the origin of money (from the need for something portable in foreign trade); notes its use as an intermediary, a measurer, a medium of exchange by equating goods; and famously dismisses usury on the grounds that making a profit from money itself (and not from money's natural object as a means of exchange) is detestable, interest being the unnatural birth of money from money (and money itself existing by law, not nature). He finds it interesting to assemble stories of how men have grown rich, among them that of the pre-Socratic philosopher, Thales of Miletus, who, reproached for showing by his poverty that philosophy was useless, cornered the market on olive oil in order to prove that "philosophers can easily become rich if they care to do so, but that this is not their ambition."

A character in Terence (*Adelphi,* play, 160 B.C.) points out that if young people are reckless with money (as Aristotle also observed, adding that they do not know what it is to be without it), the aging process will more than take care of that problem, for one bad trait of older people is excessive anxiety over money. And fathers upset over their sons' sowing of wild oats merely forget that if they themselves lived with probity when young the reason was not virtue but lack of money to spend. Ovid *(Amores,* poem, c. 20 B.C.), in one of the first expressions of what will become a commonplace, attacks a world in which money governs all relations and wishes that love at least be uncontaminated by it. Money matters in Petronius' *Satyricon* (novel, A.D. 60) in two ways. The legacy hunters (also the object of Juvenal's scorn in *Satirae [Satires,* c. A.D. 100–127]) cluster around rich old men. And Trimalchio's dinner is the ultimate dramatization of nouveau riche behavior—the vulgarity and ignorance, the vanity, the unbelievable conspicuous consumption, the encouragement of shameless sycophancy in others, the belief that one owns the world because money and cheating can do anything, the garish ways of banqueting, entertaining, and even of attending one's own (mock) funeral. For the man who has everything except immortality, death becomes the central obsession, the one insuperable challenge.

The Middle Ages and the Renaissance

In the New Testament, money is more in evidence and more dubious than in the Old. While the patriarchs and men like David and Solomon were prosperous, Jesus is without possessions. His driving of the money changers from the Temple suggests that Judaism had become ensnared by vested interests, wealth, corruption, and literal-mindedness about financial reparation. One of his most curious parables is about the need to invest the money one is given; the point is the spiritual one about preparing for the hereafter, but the message is imparted in a way people will understand, through business terminology. And one of the most famous of all financial transactions is the thirty pieces of silver given Judas Iscariot for betraying Jesus. No wonder we are told in Timothy that the "love of money is the root of all evil."

In medieval religious and chivalric literature, money plays no major role. Beowulf (epic poem, c. 8th century) gathers gifts for his achievements and in turn doles some out to his followers in the spirit of comitatus, but he seems motivated rather more by achievement and fame than accumulation. Such rewarding takes place also in chivalric romances, as part of a gratuity (literally), a grace note, an added gesture; the knights are not presented as acting the way they do because of money. That is certainly true of the one knight to appear among the pilgrims in Chaucer's *Canterbury Tales* (c. 1380–1400). If Dante (*La divina commedia [The Divine Comedy,* epic poem, c. 1320]) has circles in Hell reserved for avaricious men, usurers, simonists, counterfeiters, Chaucer likewise portrays quite a few characters who are at the least shrewd in money matters—

the Sergeant at Law, the Physician, the Manciple, the Reeve, the Host—and some who are downright racketeers—the Shipman, the Summoner, the Pardoner. The latter in fact is a moral paradox. Preaching with a fearful eloquence that brings many people closer to God, he is motivated not by piety or fame but by the very avarice which is the subject of his fulminations. The tale he tells, moreover, is, appropriately enough, about a rat-race to the point of death among three thieves betraying each other in order to obtain complete possession of their plunder. Avarice, along with usury and cheating, is singled out in a parade of the Seven Deadly Sins (*Piers Plowman,* poem, c. 1362–1387), a typical medieval device at the juncture of literature and homilectics. If absent in chivalric works, money is often present in amatory ones. Jehan de Meung's continuation of the *Roman de la rose* (*Romance of the Rose,* didactic poem, c. 1275) notes the necessity of money if one is to thrive in love. Similarly Juan Ruiz, the Archpriest of Hita (*Libro de buen amor* [*The Book of Good Love,* poem, c. 1343]), although basically preoccupied with sex, includes a tirade in the style of Ovid and of the contemporary satirist-moralist-preacher on money ruling everything in society. Greediness with newly acquired wealth undoes the carthy and usually common-sensical bawd in *Tragicomedia de Calisto y Melibea* (*Celestina,* tradicomedy, 1499–1502), and, in the wake of the love death of his young daughter in that work, her rich but now desolate father finds his wealth to be of little help.

Erasmus (*Moriae encomium* [*Praise of Folly,* essay, 1511]) writes in the vein of Lucian, making Folly the offspring of Plutus, God of Wealth, who governs "all public and private affairs," even that of the gods. But vastly more searching and "modern" is the view expressed in More's *Utopia* (political romance, 1516). In a dialogue with More, Raphael declares that as long as there is private property and "everything is judged in terms of money," real justice and prosperity will remain elusive. In a market economy, a tiny minority—greedy, unscrupulous, and worthless—has most of the money but neither deserves nor enjoys it. Rich men have food surpluses while others starve. With money as the standard of value, dozens of unnecessary trades supplying luxury goods or entertainment are carried on, and money goes mainly to undeserving goldsmiths, aristocrats, and money lenders, not to the hard-working farmers and carpenters who produce the essentials for survival. Only an equal distribution of goods will beget a healthy society. When More responds that without the profit motive, no one would work and shortages would result, Raphael maintains that the Utopian system belies that. People in Utopia work only six hours a day because the goal is not capital accumulation but to free the body from drudgery in order to free the mind for cultivation. With the abolition of money and greed have gone the many social problems caused by money—crime, hunger, fear, anxiety, over-work, insomnia, and even poverty, which seemed to need money to be eradicated. For money, invented to make food more available, is the one thing making it unavailable to most.

Machiavelli (*Il principe* [*The Prince*, essay, 1532]) has not much to say on money other than the interesting observation that rulers should keep in mind that people more readily forget the slaying of a parent than the expropriation of their property. But in the *Discorsi* (*Discourses,* c. 1519), he insists that a fine army rather than, as is commonly thought, money constitutes "the sinews of war"; gold cannot procure good troops, but good troops can procure gold. Sir Guyon, the Knight of Temperance (Spenser's *Faerie Queene,* epic poem, 1590–1596) spends three days of temptation in Mammon's Delve; he beholds there huge treasures and, after listening to Mammon's by now commonplace declaration that money conquers everything, pronounces it to be rather a source of grief and evil. Marlowe's magician (*Dr. Faustus,* play, 1604) speaks in passing of obtaining wealth but greed is not a central motive of his.

Although the milieux and values in his plays are mainly aristocratic, Shakespeare sometimes deals with money. In *King Lear* (1606), the parcelling out of property and power is made to hinge on declarations of love. In *Othello* (c. 1604), Iago has many motives (and perhaps paradoxically none) for his malignity, a minor one of which is mulcting Rodrigo of his money. In *Timon of Athens* (c. 1605–1608), the rich hero naïvely spends prodigal sums on friends and entertainments only to discover, when in a bankruptcy from which no one would save him, how foolish he had been, how men flock only to wealth, not to people. Becoming an outcast and misanthrope and accidentally discovering gold in the ground, he now digs it out obsessively in order to bait and tease men with it. One of Falstaff's (*Henry IV,* 1597, 1600) activities is bilking others. Besides depending on Prince Hal, he makes a tidy sum as an officer by letting individuals buy their way out of military service. Later he turns up having, through careful exploitation of his exiguous connection with the royal court, borrowed a thousand pounds from Justice Shallow. He is not, however, an avaricious man; he spends his money prodigally on food and drink (and, in part 2, on women). In the *Merry Wives of Windsor* (c. 1600), Falstaff is mainly lecherous, but the play offers a rare early glimpse of middle-class people and values. Various individuals being eager to marry Anne Ford, her father suspects the young impoverished aristocrat Fenton to be only after her money. This is one of the first treatments in literature of a new phenomenon—the impoverished aristocrat marrying into the newly rising, prosperous middle class, in a blend of money and blood or of new money and old money.

Money is, above all, central in the *Merchant of Venice* (c. 1595), in which Shylock is one of the earliest examples in great literature of the Jew stereotyped not as a deicide or ritual slaughterer but as someone obsessed with money—making it, cheating for it, hoarding it, and using it to establish a niche for himself in a Christian society to which he is marginal. The play is in good part about business affairs. The "merchant" is Antonio, whose life, albeit it turns on making money through trade, is gracious because Christian and generous, while Shylock is ungracious because a Jew and a usurer; the who and how of money-making seem to matter more than the acquisition itself. Amid allusions to Jacob's and Laban's biblical commercial transactions, the central incident is a covenant about the lending of money. Shylock initially appears more interested in befriending

Christians than in trapping them (though that is a matter of interpreting ambiguous passages), but when his daughter elopes with a Christian and takes Shylock's hoard with her, he is obsessed as much by the loss of the money as by the departure of the daughter from the familial, communal, and religious fold. "My Christian ducats!" he exclaims, meaning perhaps (1) money he had had to earn in this unsavory money-lending way because the bigoted Christian society closed all other doors to him; (2) the terms of living in which money is central have been set by a mercenary Christian society and not by him; (3) the money is no longer his but, like his daughter, in the hands of the Christians; (4) money that is accursed—"Christian" having the meaning of "damned." And now his desire for revenge on a society that stole his dearest possessions replaces his lust for money as the matter of highest priority; hence, during the trial scene, when offered large sums if he relents, he, like Achilles, refuses to back down for any amount.

Ben Jonson is more "modern" than Shakespeare in showing man driven by the need to possess money. *Volpone* (play, 1606) and the *Alchemist* (play, 1610) are about intricate investment schemes for bilking people—the first by pretending to have the allegedly rich Volpone dying and thereby attracting, as in the *Satyricon,* the bequest hunters, and the second by pretending to have discovered the means of transmuting base metals into gold. The second ruse, of pretended alchemy, is itself successful alchemy indeed, judging from the financial harvest. George Herbert's sonnet "Avarice" (c. 1633) is about man falling into the very ditch that he has dug for the purpose of extracting precious metals, meaning that the avarice which motivates the rifling of the bowels of mother earth is counterproductive. Something of this is also adumbrated in Milton's portrayal of Mammon (*Paradise Lost,* poem, 1667). Even as an angel in heaven, he always walked with head downcast, adoring the gold that litters the heavenly pavement. Oblivious of God and higher things, he behaved like a beast with head near the ground, like a miser confusing means and end.

Neoclassical to Modern Periods

Making money sometimes proves to be an obstacle that, once overcome, creates new ones, and so the protagonist of Molière's *Le bourgeois gentilhomme* (*The Would-Be Gentleman,* play, 1670) turns his energies to obtaining a veneer of elegance and gaining an entry into high society by marrying his daughter to an aristocrat. Marriage and money. An increasing number of works begin to revolve around the need or desirability of obtaining an heiress as wife. In Etherege's *Man of Mode* (play, 1676) the erstwhile philandering citified hero, Dorimant, finally settles down with a woman who is not only beautiful, witty, and innocent but also rich, and in Congreve's *The Way of the World* (play, 1700), before Mirabell can marry the lady, he must foil the villain's attempt to take possession of her money. Money and beauty also are the joint rewards for the hero in such works as Fielding's *Tom Jones* (novel, 1749), Goldsmith's *She Stoops to Conquer* (play, 1773), Sheridan's *School for Scandal* (play, 1777).

Sometimes the race is on among women to catch a male heir, as in Austen's *Pride and Prejudice* (novel, 1813).

In such stories the money has been made, and the problem is merely the proper disposing of it, the wise passing on of it. How the money gets to be made in the first place is a topic that literature had so far mainly ignored and which, in the nineteenth century, with the rise of an industrialized form of capitalism, the consequent novel, quick, and easy forms of capital formation, and the coming to political power of a large and prosperous middle class, becomes a major theme. Thus where Molière shows (*L'avare*, [*The Miser*, play, 1668]) an avaricious man (the source of whose wealth is vague) busily preserving his money, Balzac in *Eugénie Grandet* (novel, 1833) exhibits the same type avidly increasing his hoard. For perhaps the first time in high literature, intricate financial arrangements, involving certificates, securities, interest rates, bequests, liquidation, creditors' bills, and government bonds, are discussed and analyzed with a relish usually reserved for matters chivalric, erotic, or divine. For the first time as well someone commits suicide over bankruptcy rather than honor, love, or health. If this novel is the *Miser* updated, Balzac's *Le père Goriot* (*Father Goriot*, (novel, 1834) is *King Lear* updated (and *Le bourgeois gentilhomme* extended). A story about a man victimized by two grasping, ungrateful daughters is transplanted into a capitalist context. Goriot is no king but a self-made man—a former spaghetti tycoon, no less—who, having made his bundle, is fulfilled in seeing his daughters marry into the aristocracy; no matter how indifferent in their elegance, selfishness, and hedonism they are to his suffering, he glories in them.

Wordsworth's "Getting and Spending" sonnet (1806) is a romantic version of Herbert's "Avarice" sonnet. Where the metaphysical religious poet sees money as causing a fall from grace, the romantic sees it rather as a cause (and effect) of the general drift of modern life to urban largeness, abstractness, atrophied emotions, and alienation from nature. Indeed if Adam Smith (*The Wealth of Nations*, essay, 1776) presented acquisitive and economic man as the basic component of a cohesive, healthy society, for Karl Marx (*Kommunistiches Manifest* [*The Communist Manifesto*, 1848]), the bourgeoisie has replaced all older (e.g., familial or feudal) ties between people with the nexus of "cash payment" and converted the toilers in even the loftiest occupations into "paid wage laborers"; all social forms and spiritual concepts could be traced back to a material and alienating basis—the power of money. Obsession with making money certainly seemed typical of Americans because, according to de Tocqueville (*De la démocratie en Amérique* [*Democracy in America*, 1835–1840]), in a society freed of rank and privilege, the poor dream of wealth and the rich dread losing it.

George Eliot's *Middlemarch* (novel, 1871–1872) is a powerful, lifelike rendering of middle-class struggles to make ends meet. Lydgate is a doctor more concerned with cures and medical reforms than with affluence; his wife Rosamund is interested in money and status. Theirs is a marriage torn apart by a clash of temperaments—the unworldly idealist and the shallow conformist—over financial problems. Money stolen, accumulated, lost, and found is the core of Eliot's novel *Silas Marner* (1861). In many Dickens novels, money and making money are central. *Great Expectations* (1860–1861), to cite only one, shows that money often is tainted or, as G. B. Shaw would have it, that all money, by its very nature under capitalism, is dirty. The beautiful Estella, whom Pip thinks of as far above the sordid world that surrounds them, turns out to be all too closely connected with it. Giovanni Verga's *Mastro Don Gesualdo* (1888) is a major novel about a self-made man who gauges everything, including human relations, by money, who compulsively accumulates wealth and the power attendant on it, and who finds the fruit of such greed and ambition to be isolation. If Gustav Freytag's *Soll und Haben* (*Debit and Credit*, novel, 1855) celebrates the replacing of a stagnant and parasitical aristocratic ethos by middle-class commercial dynamism, Thomas Mann's *Buddenbrooks* (novel, 1901) in turn diagnoses what would appear to be the next stage in a cycle, the eclipsing of bourgeois money-making values in a family by artistic and decadent ones.

Money is singularly important in Dostoevsky's *Brat'ia Karamazovy* (*The Brothers Karamazov*, novel, 1880). The old man, having accumulated it by unsavory means, is not about to hand it over to any of his sons, all of whom, varied as they are, he holds in contempt. The pious Alyosha and the intellectual Ivan have no need of it, and the sensual, worldly Dmitri lives for love. The latter, though, finds that (as the Roman elegists and others long ago noted) money is often necessary for thriving in wooing. A sum of 4,500 rubles, by means of which he hoped to obtain the haughty Katya's body, entangled Dmitri in her turbulent emotions instead. Just before the old man was murdered, Dmitri had been running around town trying desperately to raise 3,000 rubles, a sum spent on Grushenka and owed to Katya. It also happens to be the sum for which Dmitri had been willing to settle with his hated father and the sum that the father had promised to give to Grushenka—the very woman whom Dmitri loved—if she came for it. Right after the murder, Dmitri spends a large amount of money on an orgy in the company of Grushenka. Which 3,000 rubles Dmitri had had on him in the hours after the crime therefore becomes a matter of great importance during the inquest and trial. Money is thus seen not only as a magnet or source of power but, like sex, a way in which individuals establish their moral character or try to manipulate others. Hence Katya, knowing that Dmitri would not be able to resist the temptation to spend it frivolously, had lent him the 3,000 as a way of mortifying him and of thereby gaining ascendancy over him, which has been her goal throughout the novel. (Is the recurring number here—3,000—like the size of Shylock's loan and of several sums mentioned in Gogol's *Mërtvye dushi* (*Dead Souls*, novel, 1842)—itself a comic classic about swindling and about the social and psychological effects of money—perhaps an echo of Judas' tainted 30 pieces of silver?)

Ibsen's Nora (*Et dukkehjem* [*A Doll's House*, play, 1879]), needing to take care of a dying father and ill husband, resorts to forgery to obtain the necessary funds in a society where a woman cannot be a debtor on her own. Her husband

Torvald's rising career in a bank would be compromised by the revelation of the forgery; his distancing himself from her therefore precipitates her realization of how far the gap between their lives had always been. Thus money was the catalyst of revelation and, as in *Middlemarch*, the force that helped destroy a flawed marriage. "Genteel poverty" is a theme also of *Hedda Gabler* (play, 1890) and of *Vildanden* (*The Wild Duck,* play, 1884), where Hjalmar is more adept at self-pity than at making a living. And the tale of the disgraced tycoon in *John Gabriel Borkman* (play, 1896) seems to be a dramatization of Herbert's "Avarice" and Milton's Mammon: "The prisoned millions . . . deep in the bowels of the earth . . . shrieked to me to free them."

Money is important in Chekhov's *Diadia Vania* (*Uncle Vanya,* play, 1897); the pedantic professor, having lived off the hard work of Vanya and Sonia, would now sell the estate and leave them in the lurch, a decision that precipitates an explosion and a parting. In *Vishnëvyi sad* (*The Cherry Orchard,* play, 1904), an old landed family faces the prospect of having to sell its estate and property to someone who would parcel it out and turn it into that modern phenomenon, a real estate development. The play is one of the finest, most elegiac treatments of a common theme in modern literature: the replacement of the old, the landed, the leisured, the aristocratic, the humane, the nonrational, the esthetic, by the new, the pragmatic, the mobile, the mercenary, the frenetic, the functional, the corrosively, coldly, antiseptically rational—by, in short, what is now prosaically called "the bottom line." Lopakhin, the son of a serf, is a rich merchant who buys the estate of his father's former owners and who thereby knows the delights of having at once become a squire and the redeemer of his father's dignity.

The 300-year-old theme of the coming together of blood and money or old and new money is given a new twist in fiction by Henry James (notably in *The Golden Bowl,* novel, 1904) in terms of the transatlantic marriage (like the one that in actuality joined Winston Churchill's parents). The motif of the heiress continues also in his *Washington Square* (novel, 1881). The wary father, solicitous about his daughter's love life because his money is at stake, overrules her choice. Money may have brought happiness to the man who makes it but brings misery to the daughter he would pass it on to. It is even more important in *The Wings of the Dove* (novel, 1902), which contains a fine study of people moved by acquisitiveness. In London, Kate Croy, held down by poverty and a ne'er-do-well father, and Merton Densher, lacking both capital and the ambition to accumulate it, face a bleak moneyless marriage. She hatches the plot of having him pretend to love the dying American heiress, Milly Theale, a mutual acquaintance, in order to obtain her money—in a highly refined version of the bequest-hunter theme in the *Satyricon* in antiquity and *Volpone* in the Renaissance. Merton becomes conscience-stricken in the process; Milly, when she finds out the deception, loses her will to live yet leaves a large sum to Merton after all. Like the characters in Chaucer's *Franklin's Tale,* he is affected by her generosity and nobility. He offers Kate a choice of marriage without the morally tainted money or all the money without marriage to himself. Lacking his moral reserves, she does not rise to the occasion, and their love appears to have shattered on the rock of money.

Other writers produced works in which poverty, hunger, and inequities in the distribution of wealth were, as rarely in earlier literature (at least before Dickens), the main theme. Of such a sort are Zola's *Germinal* (novel, 1885) (about miserable coal miners on strike), Knut Hamsun's *Sult* (*Hunger,* novel, 1890) (about a suffering, penniless Bohemian and small-time writer), Gissing's *New Grub Street* (novel, 1891) (about artists), Stephen Crane's *Maggie* (novel, 1893) (about ugly, drunken, impoverished Irish-Americans in Lower Manhattan), Jack London's *People of the Abyss* (novel, 1903) (about London slums), Upton Sinclair's *The Jungle* (novel, 1906) (about Chicago meat-packers), and Michael Gold's *Jews without Money* (novel, 1930) (about New York's Lower East Side). Yet if D. H. Lawrence (*Lady Chatterley's Lover,* novel, 1928) sees money as grinding everyone down in modern society and especially denaturalizing workers, G. B. Shaw *(Major Barbara,* play, 1905) propounds the paradox that a well-run munitions factory provides prosperity for all concerned (and that charity props up the capitalist system and that the churches depend entirely on what they themselves consider "dirty money"). Challenging millennia-old pieties, Shaw iconoclastically asserts that poverty itself is a crime and that money can cure all the psychological, social, political, and spiritual ailments of individual and society.

The theme of the self-made man, the overnight millionaire (touched on in the *Bourgeois gentilhomme* and *Père Goriot*) is continued in Ibsen's *Borkman,* Dreiser's *The Financier* (novel, 1912) and *The Titan* (novel, 1914), and Fitzgerald's *Great Gatsby* (novel, 1925). In the latter, the finest of these works, money—mysteriously made and curiously not affecting the sweet nature of the hero—begets lavish party-throwing and futile dreams of possessing the girl of one's poverty-stricken youth.

Stephen Dedalus (Joyce's *Ulysses,* 1922) is so intent on initiating a career as a poet that he quits his job as teacher and gives his severance pay, with largesse, to his somewhat treacherous friend and housemate, Buck Mulligan. The other main character in the novel, Bloom, spends the day trying to sell advertising space, with little success—a rare portrayal in great literature of an average man's workday. A decent man, he has been none too successful in any of his varied ventures and appears to be living in part off some Canadian bonds left him by his father. The Jason section of Faulkner's *The Sound and the Fury* (novel, 1929) portrays a modern cynical scion of a declining old Southern aristocratic family whose being completely cut off from his familial and communal past is marked by his indifferent work as a clerk in a local hardware store, his playing of the stock market, and his fantasies of conspiracies by New York Jews. One of those New York Jews, Tommy Wilhelm (Bellow's *Seize the Day,* novella, 1956), is himself three decades later beset ironically by (besides personal and vocational failures) the vagaries of the stock market—that modern version of dreams and of money.

See also: Banker, Financier and Usurer; Capitalism.

Selected Bibliography

Dietrichson, J. W. *The Image of Money in the American Novel of the Gilded Age.* New York: Humanities Press, 1969.
Southall, R. *Literature and the Rise of Capitalism.* London: Lawrence and Wishart, 1973.
Templin, E. H. *Money in the Plays of Lope de Vega.* Berkeley: University of California Press, 1952.
Yunck, J. A. *The Lineage of Lady Meed.* Notre Dame, Ind.: University of Notre Dame Press, 1963.

MANFRED WEIDHORN

MONSTERS

Isidore of Seville in his seventh-century encyclopedia, the *Etymologiae,* claimed that the Latin noun *monstrum* derived from the verb *demonstrare* which means "to show" or "to demonstrate." Hence, in one specialized definition, the monster, like any omen or portent, showed or demonstrated things to come. Literature has used and abused the motif of monster from the very inception of language. In its broadest sense, the monster represents any anomalous creature or person and thus becomes "the other." As such, the motif occurs in nearly all works concerned with intrusions into a homogeneous perception of reality.

In a more manageable fashion, monsters can be categorized in literature as aberrations of the natural (human, animal, plant, or mineral) order or the artificial (machine) order. Certain notable monsters become aberrations by crossing these designated boundaries or combining attributes of different realms. As a result, the monster in literature almost always evokes aesthetic and ethical questions, because the different must invariably be judged as beautiful or ugly, good or evil. Similarly, such a total outsider lays special claim to the arena of true and untrue. Not surprisingly, then, every literature exploits the motif in one way or another, sometimes for mere sensationalism, sometimes for penetrating studies of the nature of the normal.

Mythology and Antiquity

The cosmogony of nearly every ancient culture involves monstrous creatures of some sort. Divinities who are not entirely anthropomorphic take attributes from the phenomenon with which they are associated. In this manner sun gods are endowed with flaming hair. Similarly, animal-shaped deities like the Egyptian falcon god Horus, or Thoth, shaped like an ibis, or Seth, like an unidentified mammal, occur in early stories along with demons depicted with many heads.

The Indian god Shiva is often represented with four arms, and his wife Kali, one aspect of the Great Mother Parvati, who rides upon a lion, has multiple arms to carry weapons. In Mithraic art, the Iranian deity Zurvān appears lion-headed.

If the divinity is not the personified earth and sky, as in the Greek story of Gaea and Uranus, oftentimes the cosmos is created from the parts of a gigantic deity. Akkadian mythological texts tell us that Marduk divided the dragoness Tiamat's corpse to create heaven and earth, just as the sacred book of the Hindus, the Rig Veda (compiled c. 1000 B.C.) records that parts of the body of Purusa correspond to parts of the cosmos. An Iranian account likewise has the sky derive from the head of a manlike body; the feet become the earth, the tears the water, the hair the plants, the right hand becomes the bull, and the mind produces fire. Chinese myth relates that after P'an-ku died, the wind and clouds arise from his breath, the thunder from his voice, the sun and moon from his left and right eyes, the four quarters of the world from his four limbs and so on down to human beings, who are created from the parasites on his body. In ancient Mexican lore, the goddess of the earth, composed of eyes and mouths, is split in two to produce the earth and sky. Out of the Indian god Vritra's belly emerge the cosmic waters.

A monstrous race of creatures, usually giants, is frequently the chief obstacle to the primary divinity. Zeus battles the Titans before establishing Olympia; Odin, in Norse mythology, contends with the giants of Jotunheim. Gods, and later, heroes, combat a variety of monstrous creatures in their legends. Often the less anthropomorphic the creature, the greater its animosity toward the ruling deity or the human race. The Sumerian god Ninshubur battles sea monsters, Canaanite Baal fights monsters in the wilderness, and China's Yü encounters winged people and expels dragons from the marshlands.

Mythography records many such gods and heroes insuring their fame by conquering monstrous beings. In Western literature, we find the earliest writers occupied with monsters. Homer's Odysseus survives the Cyclops, sirens and Scylla, and Charybdis. Monsters, both of the animal variety and of the human one (many of which came to be known as the marvelous races) were catalogued in very early travel accounts. Herodotus, in his fifth-century B.C. historical account, writes of the phoenix, winged snakes, giant ants, griffins, cynocephali (dog-headed people), and a race of men with eyes in their chests. The fragments of Ktesias, another Greek traveler (fourth century B.C.) discuss griffins, uni-cornlike animals, giant worms, mantichores (creatures with the body of a lion, the face of a man, a tail with the sting of a scorpion), giants, cynocephali, and other marvelous races. Later in the century, Megasthenes reports the existence of similar monsters, along with sea monsters and mermaids.

By A.D. 79 and with the Roman penchant for organization, Pliny's encyclo-pedia *Naturalis historia* (*Natural History* c. A.D. 77) firmly established the belief in, among others, unicorns, amphisbenae (two-headed snakes), dragons, basilisks (snakes that kill by their smell or look), griffins, the phoenix, werewolves, cynocephali, and the Antipodes (people with their feet on backward who live on the other side of the world). This work heavily influenced the subsequent encyclopedias of the third century by Gaius Solinus and Claudius Aelianus, who added such creatures as the satyr, chimera, gorgon, and onocentaur (with the upper half of a man and the lower half of an ass) to the common list.

Classical writers wove these creatures into their literature, with Virgil, of course, borrowing from Homer and cyclic epics as well to enrich the compendium of mythological knowledge found in his epic *Aeneis* (*Aenid*, 19 B.C.). Ovid, in his *Metamorphoses* (epic, c. A.D. 2–17), concentrates on the transformation of the ordinary into the extraordinary, and we see a definable interest in the process of becoming monstrous. He makes clear distinctions between being born a monster and being turned into one. Working with earlier myths, Ovid delineates how Morpheus specialized in imitating shapes of men; his brother Icelos (or Phobetor) specialized in beasts, birds, and serpents; and Phantasos changed himself into earth, rock, or anything inanimate. In his effort to link together artistically the body of myth handed down to him, Ovid draws attention to the nature of the monstrous by categorizing creatures, and, like his predecessors and the many medieval writers influenced by his work, he arrays more "literal" monsters alongside the sometimes monstrous allegorical gods like Sleep and Hunger.

The Early Middle Ages

In the centuries after the Roman Empire, the steady infusion of folklore elements from the diverse cultures of people who settled in Europe continued to expand the list of known monsters for people for whom confirmatory travel was virtually impossible. Monsters were corroborated not only by travel accounts and encyclopedias, but also by bestiaries (books describing animals and moralizing about them) and biblical exegesis itself.

The early Middle Ages gained its knowledge of the beasts of faraway lands at least partly from the loose collection of Latin works known as the *Mirabilia* (4th-9th century A.D.). Its English translation, the *Wonders of the East,* attests to gorgonlike creatures, two-headed serpents, giant ants, lertices (an animal with ass's ears, sheep's wool, and bird's feet), dragons, homodubii (onocentaurs), and varied marvelous races of men.

Isidore's highly influential seventh-century encyclopedia, *Etymologiae,* organizes monsters in a significant way. The word *monstrum* was reserved for humanlike beings, both members of marvelous races and individual mythological figures. Later, toward the end of the Middle Ages, the word "monster" seemed especially to signify "freak" or an individual suffering from a hideous birth defect as it will be used in Edward Topsell's seventeenth-century work, *The Historie of Fovre-Footed Beastes* (1607). Perhaps folklore and poor lines of communication make the Middle Ages more readily amenable to animal monsters (the elephant or giraffe as well as the dragon or hydra) rather than to the more theologically threatening notion of human monsters, which at one time included pygmies and black men in the same lists as races with ears like fans or eyes in their chests.

Isidore's animal monsters numbered the amphisbaena, basilisk, dragon, hydra (which he calls a fable), griffin, unicorn, and giant ants. A Latin collection of monsters called the *Liber monstrorum,* written in these centuries, signifies a marked interest in unusual creatures and races of men. Many monsters from classical myth are recalled and merged with a considerable list of monstrous races of the East.

The medieval bestiary has its origin in the Latin translation of the second-century Greek *Physiologos* (*Physiologus,* anecdotes). Early medieval versions listed the phoenix, siren, onocentaur, hydrus, and unicorn. The Christian morals attending the descriptions of animals along with the commentary of church fathers on the monsters found in the Bible (unicorn, basilisk, dragon, lamia, siren, onocentaur, griffin, and pilosus—which was probably a satyr or wild man) both contributed to the allegorization of such creatures that we see in the tales of the period. The Old English epic *Beowulf* (c. 8th century) has its hero battle evil creatures in the form of Norse trolls, sea monsters, and a fire-breathing, nearly apocalyptic, dragon.

The Late Middle Ages

By the later Middle Ages, a handful of monsters were commonplace in both the belief of the people and in written documents. The unicorn, phoenix, dragon, basilisk, and amphisbaena were usually included in catalogues of creatures of the wasteland.

Marco Polo's account of the east (1295) was disappointing to readers in its relative dearth of the monstrous. He mentions only the unicorn, giant clawed snakes, tailed and dog-headed men, and griffins. John Mandeville's fictitious report (1397) includes in his more popular text these creatures plus goat-men, dragons, the phoenix, centaurs, basilisks, and diverse marvelous races.

The great twelfth- and thirteenth-century encyclopedias by Honorius Augustodunensis, Alexander Neckam, Thomas de Cantimpré, Albertus Magnus, Bartholomaeus Anglicus, Vincent of Beauvais, and Brunetto Latini all describe monsters and marvelous races of men. The bestiary tradition flourished, providing beautiful illustrations of these creatures up until the fifteenth century, when the morals began to be omitted and the nature of the bestiary changes.

Saints' lives often pit the saint against a monstrous, usually dragonlike, form of the devil. St. Christopher is in some accounts called a cynocephalus or dog-headed man. Many knights in romances encounter dragons, giants, or trolls. King Arthur himself triumphs in a number of such combats. Fable collections tell pedantic stories not only of talking foxes and chickens, but also of talking unicorns, satyrs, basilisks, and dragons.

The Renaissance through the Eighteenth Century

Continued travel began to discredit the tales of monstrous races of men in distant lands, and the imaginative travel accounts with these creatures began to degenerate into lists of human freaks. These, in turn, gave way to early medical probings on the essential biological characteristics of humans and animals. Ambroise Paré, in the sixteenth century, wrote such a transitional work, which heralded the end of the marvelous race tradition. Similarly, Thomas Browne's *Vulgar Errors* (1646, treatise), as late as the seventeenth century, attempts to debunk the belief in the basilisk, griffin, phoenix, amphisbaena, and unicorn.

Meanwhile, the allegorical potential of the motif—especially with those monsters whose characteristics the writer himself designs—persisted in works such as Spenser's allegorical epic, *The Faerie Queene* (1590–1596), where theological error is a monster especially concocted for the poem. On the other hand, Marlowe, in his play *Doctor Faustus* (1604), shows that the traditional demons and devils of the Middle Ages continue in literature in the age of humanism but begin to follow the more limited path of the occult and magic.

Disbelief in one kind of monster could not suppress all varieties, and the older notions of the marvels of the East died hard. Othello wins Desdemona with his tales of men with their eyes in their chests. Shakespeare devises the creature Caliban in his play, *The Tempest* (1611), to explore the limits of the animal, human, and fairy. His witches in his play *Macbeth* (1605–1606) stem from an old tradition of creatures with such powers, and he characterizes Joan of Arc as one in *Henry VI* (1590–1592). John Milton, true to epic style, incorporates much material on monsters in his vast collection of allusions in his epic *Paradise Lost* (1667). Satan and his cohorts are alternately monstrously hideous or beautiful. Milton, like Spenser, creates his own allegorical monsters in the figures of Sin and Death.

Nearly a century later, in Pope's urbane world of wit, the parodic poem *The Rape of the Lock* (1712) sports monsters appropriately formed from inanimate parlor-society objects like tea cups in the Cave of Spleen. His "machinery," the fairylike sylphs, much akin to Puck and Ariel in Shakespeare, show that extraordinary beings—often from a magical or supernatural world—persist in literature after the Renaissance. Descendants in a way of the "good" monsters like the unicorn and phoenix, the elves and fairies of folklore become merged into stories of the now discredited but metaphorically powerful monstrous animals and men.

The Age of Reason perhaps more self-consciously than previous eras employed the monster as a literary device. Gulliver himself becomes a monster to the strange peoples he encounters until the ultimate theme of Swift's satirical travel book (1726) emerges—that all humans are monstrous.

Romanticism and the Nineteenth Century

At the very point when monsters might have been reduced to highly contrived literary conventions, the Romantics, enamored of the other-worldly, began to use strange creatures in new ways. Coleridge fashions his fiendish Nightmare Life-in-Death in the poem, "The Rime of the Ancient Mariner" (1798), and Keats borrows from ancient lore for the origin of his poetic *Lamia* (1820). Ghostly, mystical beings became a fundamental element of the neo-Gothic movement in novels. Edgar Allan Poe's stories (1830s and 1840s) revolve around creatures of this ilk, as does Washington Irving's tale of the headless horseman in "The Legend of Sleepy Hollow" (1819), and at the end of the century Oscar Wilde's novel *The Picture of Dorian Gray* (1891) explores the evil man's answer to mortality in a demonic world where for a time it seems that art is short and life is long.

Mary Shelley also concerns herself with a creature who is not restrained by the boundary between life and death, but her romance *Frankenstein, or the Modern Prometheus* (1818), involves a monster of man's making, the result of knowledge, not magic. Monsters became products of man's scientific progress and erring vision in the literature of the nineteenth century, the time when overwhelming discoveries in biology, geology, and astronomy revealed man's relative insignificance. In Stevenson's novel *The Strange Case of Dr. Jekyll and Mr. Hyde* (1886), a monster represents the basic evil in all men. H. G. Wells, in his story of *The Island of Dr. Moreau* (1896), has his misguided scientist create half-human, half-animal creatures who turn against him.

Monsters, however, endured as traditional allegorical figures. Christina Rossetti's poem of two young girls, *Goblin Market* (1862), represents one kind of male evil in the guise of goblin men who sell forbidden fruit. The poem has been taken for a children's tale, much like Lewis Carroll's Alice stories of the same century (1865). Wonderland's strange beings, including the half-human, half-inanimate playing-card society of the Queen of Hearts, help to relegate the work to juvenile audiences.

Unrealistic allegories, many populated with monstrous beings, became the literary fare for young readers. Early offerings in fantasy and science fiction, like Wells's *The Time Machine* (1895), invented monsters that elucidate the particular phenomenon of being human. Here the apelike Morlocks and the passive Eloi are the descendants of our blindly ambitious industrial society.

The Twentieth Century

In the second decade of this century, Franz Kafka's "Die Verwandlung" ("The Metamorphosis," story, 1915) combined the taste for the grotesque and monstrous with the modern literary fashion for realism. In his tale, the obsequious, buglike Gregor Samsa is rather mundanely transformed into a gigantic dung beetle. No one seems truly surprised, only embarrassed, and the hero withers away with neglect. Such toying with the bizarre by modern writers is not uncommon, but monsters themselves are usually relegated to a symbolic level, like the unicorn statue in the play *The Glass Menagerie* (1944), by Tennessee Williams. Often monsters appear in titles of novels: John Updike's *The Centaur* (1963), John Barth's *Chimera* (1972), and Robertson Davies' *The Manticore* (1972).

Monsters flourished and continue to do so, however, in all their variety in the genre of fantasy and science fiction. Horror movies and recent trends in romance have kept the monster before the public view. Tolkien's mid-century books

(1954–1956) about the little gnomelike hobbits encountering gigantic orcs, trolls, and even a dragon inspired many subsequent romances. The creatures of medieval Europe's folktales found themselves in twentieth-century fantasies. New monsters, created at times for symbolic purposes, were placed on new planets or in the future as man's technology spurred his imagination across space and time. Giant worms or Makers hold the secret of life in Frank Herbert's novel *Dune* (1965), and countless writers speculated on beings from outer space, some visibly monstrous, some invisibly so.

In the earlier part of the century, the robot, once again the product of man's knowledge, became the monster that joins man's intellect with an inanimate machine. Now, the robot's successor, an ultimately more universal and threatening foe, the computer, finds its place in literature as helpmate and often destroyer.

As always, the monster, the outsider or unknown, serves to delineate the known, and many writers illustrate their conjectures on human nature by such characters. Ursula Le Guin, with her androgynous beings in the novel *The Left Hand of Darkness* (1969), probes the distinctions between gender much the same as literature has for centuries probed the distinctions between human and animal or human and machine. The motif of the monster will perpetuate as long as the need exists to incarnate an aberration of the normal, and this need will exist as long as humans desire to know themselves. Thus, Isidore's etymology proves itself correct, it seems, since literature still uses the monster to show or demonstrate.

See also: Birth of Hero, Cave, Demonic Musician and the Soulbird, Dragons, Grotesque, Horror, Lion, Robots, Siren, Vampirism, Werewolf.

Selected Bibliography

Bernheimer, Richard. *Wild Men in the Middle Ages: A Study in Art, Sentiment and Demonology*. Cambridge, Mass: Harvard University Press, 1952.
Freidman, John Block. *The Monstrous Races in Medieval Art and Thought*. Cambridge, Mass.: Harvard University Press, 1981.
Lascault, Gilbert. *Le monstre dans l'art occidental, un problème esthétique*. Paris: Klincksieck, 1973.
Mode, Heinz. *Fabulous Beasts and Demons*. London: Phaidon, 1975.

LESLEY KORDECKI

MOUNTAINEERING

Mountaineering is the sport of climbing mountains and the techniques involved. As used in this entry, the term is understood to include hiking, trekking, and scrambling on hills as well as on the loftier heights. The climbing of mountains is one of the few outdoor sports to have sired a large body of serious, often excellent literature, fictional as well as factual.

Background from Ancient Times up to the Advent of Romanticism

For as long as man has ruled the earth, he has faced the presence of mountains. The great peaks often represent objects of worship: Biblical Mount Ararat or Mount Sinai; Grecian Mount Olympus; Navajo Mountain on the Arizona-Utah border, rising out of a welter of colorful, almost impenetrable canyons; Chomolungma, Tibet's sacred mountain, known to the Western world as Mount Everest; Alaska's Denali-McKinley—these among dozens of others. Mountain chains have sometimes been viewed as barriers against material progress and communication, as have the Andes in South America, or against invading hordes, as were the Pyrenees in keeping the Arabs from overrunning southwestern France in the Middle Ages. But the concept of mountains as a source of esthetic pleasure, untainted by fear, religion, or politics, was rare before 1750. Homer's passage in book 13 of his epic poem the *Ilias* (*Iliad,* c. 8th century B.C.) about the rock crashing down from some lofty crag and carrying all before it is both picturesque and accurate. It was dutifully copied and beautifully paraphrased by Virgil in book 12 of his epic poem the *Aeneis* (*Aeneid,* 19 B.C.). But ancient audiences did not picture Homer or Virgil re-creating appreciatively for them a sight he had actually seen in person, nor for that matter did anyone think Moses enjoyed his experience on Mount Sinai aside from the revelation he was vouchsafed. In the view of the ancients, and for most men through the Middle Ages, the Renaissance, and up to some two hundred years ago, mountains simply were not ascended for esthetic or recreational rewards.

To be sure, exceptions do exist. Philip V of Macedon is said to have ascended Mount Haemus in Thrace around 350 B.C. hoping to see both the Adriatic and the Aegean. Around the turn of the second century A.D. the Roman Emperor Hadrian climbed Mount Etna in Sicily, almost eleven thousand feet high, to witness the sunrise. Actually, Empedocles had reached its summit some six hundred years earlier, but Empedocles was a Greek philosopher, curious like all his kind, and Hadrian was in many ways a twentieth-century man born before his time. King Peter III of Aragon ascended Mount Canigou in the Pyrenees around 1280. How he felt we do not know, but the dragons he claimed to have seen on the mountain have rather troubled most modern skeptics. Petrarch, another figure ahead of his day, has left us a charming if somewhat allegorized account of his ascent, now almost six hundred and fifty years ago, of Mont Ventoux (elevation 6,271 feet) in southern France. It is only a hiker's mountain but the summit view is magnificent, and the Italian poet-humanist made the most of it. His description, given the predilection of those times for making philosophical hay out of even the most mundane activities, is more or less free from religious filler or slant. Antoine de Ville's scaling of Mont Aiguille in the French Dauphiné in 1492 was even more remarkable. It rises a mere seven thousand feet, scarcely higher than Ventoux, but its flanks are as steep as its name—the needle—implies. Montaigne's travel diary (1580–1581) of his journey through

Switzerland, Germany, and Austria on the way to Rome shows an unexpected feeling for mountain country, remarkable in a city man, Bordeaux judge, mayor, and philosopher. And a few other climbers or writers could be cited, among them the Swiss Konrad von Gesner (1516–1565) and his fellow countryman Josias Simler (1530–1576), native to the Alps and predictably partial to them. Many a Renaissance and neoclassical painting features a background of mountains, but somehow stylized and distant, hardly an open invitation to tread their slopes much less attempt their summits. Such landscapes were rarely rendered in situ, though Leonardo da Vinci actually climbed in the mountains, wrote appreciatively of his experiences, and even sketched a vivid "Storm Over the Mountains," revealing a sharp eye for natural grandeur. Again, however, Leonardo was scarcely of his age, but truly sui generis.

For the rest Du Bellay's judgment on the Swiss Grisons rendered during a trip from his beloved Loire Valley may be considered typical. Passing through them, noted the French poet, was punishment more than adequate for the most heinous of crimes (*Regrets,* 1558; sonnet 126). The neoclassicists who followed him in the seventeenth and well into the eighteenth century, whatever they may have written—nature descriptions well larded with classical clichés—tended to prefer the salons of Versailles and its many imitations, in the company of human, not outer, nature. If they no longer experienced the superstitious dread behind such legends as the one that professed that Pontius Pilate dwelt in a bottomless lake near the top of Mount Pilatus (elevation 6,995 feet) above Lucerne, whence he dragged down to Hell anyone rash enough to behold it, few travellers really enjoyed the wilderness, not to speak of the bleak mountain heights. They surely would not have appreciated the Pilatus view, today so famous, nor the railroad leading to it, nor the summit hotel. The charms of the seashore, Du Bellay's gentle Loire River landscape, or gardens, neoclassical in the seventeenth century, preromantic in the eighteenth (calculatedly rustic but not really wild), were far preferable to forbidding alpine fastnesses.

The preromantics started to view nature in a different light. It was, as Marjorie Hope Nicolson has written, more than mere enjoyment. To a greater or lesser degree, they experienced a sort of emotional ecstasy. As much as anyone, Jean-Jacques Rousseau led the way, albeit he stood upon foundations laid by his fellow Swiss contemporary, Albrecht von Haller whose descriptive poem *Die Alpen* (1732) had already glorified the mountain scene. Rousseau's epistolary novel *La nouvelle Héloïse* (*The New Heloise,* 1761) revealed the Citizen of Geneva, even if he made no pretense of scaling the higher peaks, as a sensitive, appreciative writer who not only described mountains but emotionally embraced the experience of being and walking in them. In his wake there followed the English Lake District group: Thomas Gray (journal entries dating from 1769 to 1770), also known for his Alpine experiences; William Gilpin (various books, 1770 and later); and best known of all, poet laureate William Wordsworth. His prose *Guide to the Lakes* (1810), and his poetic paeans to mountain beauty such as *The Prelude* (1799–1805; especially see books 6 and 14), did much to popularize both climbing as a sport and esthetic appreciation of the surroundings. Nor ought we to forget the agile Samuel Taylor Coleridge (1772–1834), scrambling up the rugged slopes of Helvellyn, Skiddaw, Scafell, and most of the other rocky Cumbrian summits early in the nineteenth century; Dorothy Wordsworth, who strode more like a man than a woman; John Keats, who composed a sonnet atop Ben Nevis in the Scotch Grampians, the highest point in all Great Britain; and others among the literati of the day.

Wordsworth had written not only of the relatively low Cumbrians, which caught the attention of so many others, but also (in *The Prelude,* book 6) of a climbing excursion to the high Alps in 1790. It was on Swiss terrain that the English were destined to make their mark, physically and literarily. It should be noted that the Romantics by now had developed a descriptive vocabulary adequate for the emotions they wished to convey. Older writers such as Montaigne or Gesner, whatever they wished to express, were hard put to find words for it. Now mountain lovers had the desire and the language. Mountaineering's golden age was soon to begin.

The Nineteenth Century

The Lake District retained its popularity with climbers and writers, but other areas as well began to exert a fascination. Henry David Thoreau describes climbing New Hampshire's Mount Agiocochook (i.e., Mount Washington) in *A Week on the Concord and Merrimack Rivers* (1849), though curiously leaves unsaid what he experienced on the summit. This much-discussed lacuna could have been the sort of epiphany he claims to have known on Mount Saddleback, where he tells of encountering God Himself. Less philosophical is Clarence King's *Mountaineering in the Sierra Nevada* (1872), in which the U.S. Geological Surveyor-author delightfully mixes veridical(?) accounts of his own perilous ascents with Bret Hartian sketches of various characters encountered in the mountains. John Muir (e.g., *The Mountains of California,* 1894) makes the Coast ranges that he climbs and chronicles and the wilderness that he fights to preserve part of the American heritage.

Meanwhile the British were just getting into full swing. The Alpine Club of London spawned a whole school of great climbers around the middle of the century, most of whom serendipitously wrote well. Their offerings, gathered together in *Peaks, Passes and Glaciers* (3 vols., 1859–1862, ed. by E.S. Kennedy), are a high water mark in the literature of Alpine mountaineering. Then disaster struck. A twenty-five-year-old wood engraver named Edward Whymper had tried, like others before him, again and again between 1861 and 1865 to scale the precipitous Matterhorn (elevation about 14,690 feet) on the Swiss-Italian border. Today considered only a grueling if occasionally dangerous climb, it was then thought by many to be unscalable. With a small party of fellow Englishmen, including Lord Francis Douglas and two guides, Whymper finally reached the summit on July 14, 1865. The ascent went rather smoothly. It was during the descent that disaster befell them. For his attempt he had joined forces with another party, one of whom was a youth of nineteen, soon to prove a very unsteady mountain climber. Coming down, the young man slipped and in his fall carried three of his companions, among them Lord Douglas, to their deaths. The whole incident became a cause célèbre, mountaineering accused by its detractors of being a sport that was reckless with lives. For an English lord to die on the icy slopes of some faraway peak seemed a bit much to his compatriots in that day. Some even demanded banishing the sport, though the novelist Anthony Trollope, no climbing man himself, actually made a case for taking risks to sweeten the enjoyment of life. As things turned out, defenders and opponents alike unwittingly conspired to legitimatize serious climbing. Then came Sir Leslie Stephen. Today he may be chiefly remembered as the learned editor of the English *Dictionary of National Biography* (1882–1891), but in his own time many read him for his immensely popular, literate, and able account of his climbs in the Alps, *The Playground of Europe* (1871). For a worthy sample, try his description of sunrise from the summit of Mont Blanc (elevation 15,782 feet), highest in all Europe.

In the years that followed, mountaineering, always particularly appealing to the literate, sired the greatest body of literature, both factual and fictional, both in quality and quantity, of any outdoor activity. Sailing, hunting, skiing and fishing, probably its closest rivals, have their devotees, but mountaineering would appear the most "compleat" of sports, perhaps because it embodies, besides all kinds of physical skills, the possible use and enjoyment of geology, zoology, biology, botany, photography, and other fields, all held together with a sense of the glories of outer nature.

Before leaving the century we should cite Edward Whymper's 1892 chronicle of his climbs in the Andes, A. F. Mummery's *My Climbs in the Alps and Caucasus* (1895), and Douglas W. Freshfield's *Round Kangchenjunga* (1903), which really finishes off the period. Soon there will be an embarrassment of choices.

The Twentieth Century

The current century has seen a rich selection of mountaineering literature. Consider Hillaire Belloc the historian and polemicist's recounting of a pilgrimage from his birthplace in the French town of La Celle St. Cloud to the Papal See, where he celebrated his return to the Faith. Poor and penitent he decided to walk, charting his course in a direct line over the Alps. The result was a charming little narrative, in no way freighted with philosophical complexities or spoiled by pangs of religious guilt, *The Path to Rome* (1902). Weak on aspects of technical climbing, Belloc compensates by his genuine love for the mountain heights and his professional writer's eye for their beauties. It is quite unlike Marco Pallis' *Peaks and Lamas* (1939), an early example of the influence of Eastern mysticism on Western minds. Also to be considered are Sir Martin Conway's *Mountain Memories* (1920) of his climbs over many parts of the world; H. W. Tilman's *Snow on the Equator* (1937), telling of his ascents of

Mount Kenya, Kilimanjaro, and other African peaks; and Dorothea Pilley's *Climbing Days* (1935) with her husband I. A. Richards, one of the finest of all mountaineering books. There are these and dozens more from literate, eminent British climbers. An Italian contribution is *Climbs on Alpine Peaks* (original Italian title *Scritti alpinistici . . . ,* 1923), by Achille Ratti, elected Pope Pius XI in 1922.

The British-American Archdeacon of the Yukon, Hudson Stuck, writes of his pioneer *Ascent of Denali* (1914), Tilman of his *Ascent of Nanda Devi* (1937), and his countryman Frank S. Smythe of *The Valley of Flowers* (1938), the latter judged by many the most beautiful of all the mountain-locked Himalayan vales. World War II caused a break in activities, but they soon picked up again, particularly in Asia. We note John Hunt's official account of the *Ascent of Everest* in 1953, and Peter Habeler's controversial *The Lonely Victory* (1979; trans. of his *Der einsame Sieg,* 1978) over Mount Everest achieved by the author and another Austrian, Reinhold Messner, without the use of oxygen, in the face of doubts before their attempt that it could be done and later assertions that it had not been carried out as described. This literature of exploration and achievement is characterized by generally good writing, occasionally fine writing, and at its best the excellence of a Pilley or a Belloc.

We have said nothing about mountaineering fiction. It comes almost exclusively from the present century, by and large closer to a good read, excellent yarn spinning, than true belles lettres. Pride of place, at least chronologically, must go to A.E.W. Mason's *Running Water* (1907), seemingly the first serious fictional treatment of mountain climbing, as opposed to fiction with a mountain locale (e,g., Maupassant's "L'auberge" ["The Inn," 1886], in his *Le Horla* [*The Horla*, stories]. Despite the stilted Victorian conventions that beset this novel, Mason does manage a heart-stopping climax on the knife-sharp Brenva Ridge route up Mont Blanc. At around the same time in the Alpine regions of Germany, Austria, and Switzerland, there existed a considerable popular literature of novels devoted to mountain life, some of them actually dealing with climbing. Worth noting are the Swiss Jakob Christoph Heer's *An heiligen Wassern: Roman aus dem schweizerischen Hochgebirge* (1898), the German Ludwig Albert Ganghofer's *Der laufende Berg* (*The Moving Mountain,* 1897), and others by them, Max Mohr, and Ernst Zahn. The Heer novel had sold over three hundred thousand copies in edition after edition by 1933 and was still in print as late as 1947; that by Ganghofer on the same date reached almost six hundred thousand.

The literate Glyn Carr (pseudonym of Frank Showell Styles) has turned out since the fifties a succession of mountaineering detective stories with Abercrombie Lewker, his equally literate protagonist, solving murders on mountain upon mountain, in the Alps, England and Scotland, and at other sites (for an example, *Death on Milestone Buttress,* 1951). Inasmuch as Carr under his real name is a well-known climbing writer, we are assured of accuracy in all pertinent details. Another excellent potboiler is Mary Stewart's *Wildfire at Midnight* (1956). Trevanian's *Eiger Sanction* (1972) has concocted a potent mixture of international intrigue, murder, and a climb up the treacherous north face of Switzerland's Eiger. If these novels are but an evening's entertainment, authors have occasionally aimed at bigger game. Jack Kerouac's *Dharma Bums* (1960) turns High Sierra climbing into an exercise in Zen Buddhism, and James Salter's *Solo Faces* (1979), whose plot is allegedly modeled on the tragic life and suicide of Gary Hemming, probes into the reasoning that drives a man to climb to the tune of constant, near-fatal danger. These are both American writers; francophone authors of at least equal importance, such as the Swiss Charles Gos (*La nuit des Drus,* 1929) or Henri Troyat (*La neige en deuil,* [*The Mountain,* 1952]), could swell our list. And an interesting if little-known novel by the Mexican writer Martín Gómez Palacio, *Entre riscos y entre ventisqueros* (1931), introduces an Indian guide who climbs to humiliate his white clients with his superior skill and stamina, thus regaining pride in his Aztec ancestry. Vladimir Nabokov's "Lance" has its hero climbing a peak during a lunar expedition (originally in *The New Yorker,* February 2, 1952). There are, as well, climbing poems both narrative and lyric, and the W. H. Auden-Christopher Isherwood play, *The Ascent of F6.* When it was first printed in 1936 and performed the following year in London, it received mixed reviews. More recently criticism is coming around to seeing in it some dramatic value and a feeling for mountaineering psychology. Finally, the spring of 1983 saw the rather successful Patrick Meyers drama *K2.* Powerfully acted if overly freighted with philosophical baggage, it boasted as well a remarkable fifty-foot-high set by Ming Cho Lee that was so realistic as to bring spontaneous applause from the Broadway audiences.

Like the Western, the detective story, or the romantic swashbuckler, the excesses of mountaineering have suggested satirical treatment. Alphonse Daudet's novel *Tartarin sur les Alpes* (*Tartarin on the Alps,* 1885), long ranked among his most popular successes, is still readable as a spoof on climbing heroics. Mark Twain's *A Tramp Abroad* (1880), though somewhat fictionalized travel sketches rather than true fiction, contains in chapters 30 ff. humorous accounts of his struggling up the Gemmi Pass and the Riffelberg, not to speak of ascending Mont Blanc by telescope. And H. G. Wells has left us the farcical short story "Little Mother up the Mörderberg" (1927); it scarcely needs saying that there is no Mörderberg (Murder Peak) on the world's maps.

Not unexpectedly, picturesque mountain locales cry out for cinematic treatment. Several novels have been metamorphosed into mountaineering pictures. Among others, James Hilton's *Lost Horizon* in 1937, not quite a true example of the genre; James Ramsey Ullman's *The White Tower* (1950); Troyat's *The Mountain* (1956); Trevanian's *The Eiger Sanction* (1975). All of them were large-budget productions with famous stars such as Ronald Colman, Spencer Tracy, and Clint Eastwood, and rated as box-office successes. *Solo* (1971), the exquisite short that won for its maker Mike Hoover several awards, depicts a climber setting off from a mountain meadow, through forest, over scree slope, snow, and ice, almost effortlessly surmounting every *mauvais pas,* until safe upon the summit, then rappeling, sliding, bounding, running down the endless alpine expanses back to his starting point, his rhythms choreographed like a ballet.

Mountaineering literature has enjoyed its share of factual classics but still awaits one transcendental fictional victory, one novel, play, poem, even cinema script, properly celebrating the inherent adventure, esthetic emotion, drama in climbing, some author to explain the incredible attraction for courting often fatal danger.

See also: Hunt, Psychic Landscape, Sublimity.

Selected Bibliography

Neate, W.R. *Mountaineering and Its Literature*. Seattle: The Mountaineers, 1980.

Spectorsky, A.C., ed. *The Book of the Mountains*. New York: Appleton-Century-Crofts, 1955.

Ullman, James Ramsey. *The Age of Mountaineering*. Philadelphia: Lippincott, 1954.

Unsworth, Walt. *Encyclopedia of Mountaineering*. London: Hale, 1975.

ARMAND E. SINGER

N
//

NAME AND NAMING

Mankind has attached a name to all the objects of the senses and to many invisible or theoretical entities. Most people, moreover, have a given name and a family name; many also have titles and nicknames. The relation of name to entity is, however, a subject of controversy and sometimes, in the case of personal names, of metaphysical anxiety. Aristotle (*Rhētorikē technē* [*Rhetoric*, treatise, c. 360 B.C.]) notes, for instance, that someone's forgetting of our own name is, however trifling, a legitimate cause of anger.

Antiquity and the Middle Ages

Primitive man stood in awe before the mystery of language and denomination. The word to him was in some crucial way related to the thing for which it stands. To say something was, therefore, to shape reality. For the Christian, this reverence was re-enforced by the Gospel sentence, "In the beginning was the Logos"—the word, language, thought, idea. This sentence means, first, that God, creating with words, said, "Let there be," and there was; and, second, that civilization begins, men come out of their caves to form communities, when language evolves.

The most mysterious part of language is the proper noun. Its importance is underlined by the story of God giving Adam the task of naming the animals. God creates the creatures by means of language, and then man names them, gives them thereby identity cards, and, locating them in a conceptual pyramid of created things, makes possible at first medieval cosmology and then modern science.

The fact that by naming something one obtains a grip on it is so important that the Bible ordains that man shall not take God's name in vain. To call on God without being in formal, humble, or pious relationship with Him is not only to blaspheme but also to tamper with the structure of the universe. Merely to curse God may conjure up the Devil and place supernatural powers at one's disposal.

The name is, furthermore, so reflective of reality that stages in the spiritual development of the patriarchs are marked by modifications, or even replacement, of the proper noun. Abram becomes Abraham after the Covenant with God, and Jacob becomes Israel after his own peculiar confrontation with Him. This procedure is even more appropriate under the new dispensation offered by the New Testament. Jesus renames (among others) Simon as Peter; the apostle to the Gentiles changes his own name from the Hebrew Saul to Paul. Pascal (*Pensées* [*Thoughts*, essay, 1670]) read into Isaiah the prophecy of the replacement of the name "Jews" by a new, better, and everlasting name. (In parallel fashion, Virgil's epic poem *Aeneis* [*Aeneid,* 19 B.C.] exhibits the gods easing the reconciliation of Trojan and Latin by the Trojan's dropping their language and culture, as symbolized by the newly amalgamated people's being called "Latins" instead of "Trojans" or "Teucrians.") To this day, those entering monastic orders or cults follow suit, for with conversion, that is, change in values, naturally goes change in identity and therefore of name.

In Homer's epic poem *Odysseia* (*The Odyssey,* c. 8th century B.C.), the hero, whose being named "distasteful" is described in detail, makes an important discovery: the paradox that sometimes in order to save one's identity one must (like men in the political or criminal underground) temporarily lose it. Trapped in the cave of the giant Polyphemus, Odysseus tells him that his name is "Nobody." When the giant's relatives ask Polyphemus who is bothering him, he answers, "Nobody," and they, misunderstanding, depart. Ironically, after having succeeded with this ploy, Odysseus nearly destroys himself by boastingly announcing his real name and address, incurring thereby the hostility of Poseidon and years of suffering. Ironically, as well, "Nobody" is what he in fact goes on to become when the perquisites of greatness are shorn from him by his misadventures and when he returns home disguised as a beggar and treated with contumely by suitors and fellow beggars alike. (In other circumstances—except when formally asked for his name by the genial King Alcinous—the circumspect Odysseus in a dangerous world gives himself assumed identities around which he weaves long fictions.)

A similar trick was resorted to by the Odysseus-like hero of Gottfried von Strassburg's *Tristan* (romance, c. 1210), who in Ireland went incognito under the name of Tantris and thereby for a while evaded the reprobation of Isolde for having slain her uncle in combat. In that work, moreover, (a work containing two Tristans and three Isoldes!) another role of the proper noun is suggested by the incident of Tristan, on the rebound from his love affair with Isolde, being attracted to Isolde of the White Hands, in good part because of her first name.

The question of the relation of name to thing was first broached in a methodical ratiocinative way by Plato (*Kratylos* [*Cratylus,* dialogue, c. 384 B.C.]). Is the name "natural," the same for "Hellenes and barbarians," permanent, and "true," or is it "conventional," detachable, a product of chance, artifice, locale, and habit? In the Middle Ages this problem metamorphosed into the philosophical disputation between the Realists and the Nominalists over the question of whether the general or abstract idea (e.g., "circularity") has a real existence apart from the thing (a circle) or is merely a name without an individual property or fact corresponding to it. That controversy sometimes spilled over into the realm of literature. More interesting, however, is the way in which Dante (*La divina commedia* [*The Divine Comedy,* epic poem, c. 1320]) dramatized the related idea that on earth some men have names and titles as part of their identity but in heaven they have only names; that is, only the moral self, established through relations with God, rather than the public self, established through relations with men and society. All of that is hammered home in just one grand line assigned to an inhabitant in the *Paradiso (Paradise):* "I was Caesar and am Justinian."

The Renaissance

The widening of horizons that characterized the Renaissance spilled over into language. The practice of writers in the vernacular broadening their vocabularies by incorporating words from the classical languages heightened everyone's sensitivity to words and names and made them vulnerable to the satire and parodies of a wit like Rabelais (*Gargantua et Pantagruel* [*Gargantua and Pantagruel,* novels, 1532–1564]). One of the things he does with relish is to have characters make speeches replete with obscure terms and phrases, or in the various European languages, or in nonsense words. Another is to have long lists—whether of games, library books, prominent souls in Hell, or foods and dishes—that express an almost God-like delight in the sheer sound and number of names no less than in the multiplicity and diversity of things. (Such sallies and lists were to be emulated in Shakespeare's *Love's Labour's Lost* [play, c. 1594], Sterne's *Tristram Shandy* [novel, 1759–1767], and, especially, Joyce's *Ulysses* [novel, 1922].) Rabelais also has a chapter on prophesying by means of proper nouns, a method which, he assures the reader by citing numerous ancient anecdotes, Pythagoras's practice, and Plato's *Cratylus,* is venerable and reputable. That is the secular, irreverent side of the Renaissance. The religious side on this matter is represented by the poetry of Richard Crashaw who wrote hymns to the "name" of St. Teresa and "To the Name Above Every Name, the Name of Jesus" (1648). Orthodox Jews to this day often refer to God as "The Name" in lieu of naming Him.)

In *Romeo and Juliet* (play, c. 1596), Shakespeare presents a condition in which the hero and heroine wrestle separately and jointly with the mystery of names. Juliet is attracted to Romeo before knowing his name and identity; and once these are revealed, the old prejudices against his family have been obviated because she has already fallen for him. Hence in the balcony scene she muses on the mysterious link between name and object, be it a rose or Romeo; are they consubstantial or only accidental? For his part, Romeo is willing to do away with the hateful name that separates them although he "know[s] not how to tell" who he is without it. The point is that though a name is a mere breath, though its location is uncertain and mysterious, though its assignment is arbitrary, it may still be lethal.

The power lurking in an appellation is nowhere enacted on so broad a scale as in *Julius Caesar* (play, c. 1599). Responsible for his death and for the spiritual dilemma of Brutus quite as Romeo's name caused the death of Tybalt and the dilemma of Juliet, the name "Caesar" also denotes a spirit and a historical force that bridges the epochs of Republican and Imperial Rome. Cassius confronted the spectre of future history. The name Caesar would become a title, a common noun signifying imperial power. Caesar spoke of himself in such haughty terms, as though he were already an institution, a principle, a spirit. The tragedy of the play is that one cannot get at the spirit or name without first killing the man, the body, any more than the mob can kill the hateful name of one assassin, Cinna, without also killing the innocent poet who happens to be his namesake.

Name is used differently in the other tragedies, where the heroes are rulers who have grown complacent about themselves and whom adversity forces to see through the fragility of title and name and of identity itself. Timon of Athens (c. 1605–1608) in his last hours identifies himself only as Misanthropos and in his epitaph urges men not to seek his name. Mark Antony (c. 1607), after declaring, "I am Antony yet!" is left with a name that, though once fearsome, now adds up to little. Othello describes himself as "He that was Othello." Thus also, at least at first, Cleopatra, grieving for Antony, ignores all the titles addressed to her by her servants—"Lady, Madam, Royal Egypt, Empress"—and, in a moment of spiritual incandescence amid profound sorrow, sees through the veil of titles and pretenses to her basic human attributes, which she shares with even the humblest milkmaid. The names were labels, not insulation against affliction. When she finally comes around to joining her lover in death, by committing suicide rather than negotiating for mere survival, she takes on as an ultimate title one that is more satisfying than the former regal ones and which Roman society had denied her, that of wife.

In the same way, Hamlet (c. 1600) is seen in most of the play with title and identity in uncertain state, swaddled in melancholy and in feigned madness, until near the end, after the aborted trip to England, which caused a "sea change" in him, he comes forward to assert his dignity and proper royalty, "This is I, Hamlet the Dane!" (Cf. "I am Antony yet!"). *King Lear* (1606) traces the ups and downs of its hero's name and sense of identity. Though he proposes to remain "King Lear" in retirement, he soon finds himself addressed as "My lady's father." He wonders if he is dreaming and asks who he is. He has discovered that by in effect ceasing to be king, he could not revert to mere citizen status; as if his name had been "King-Lear." If you remove the "King," no "Lear" is left. He insists he is king but, like Cleopatra, sees his human frailty as never before. So had Richard II (c. 1596) in the days of prosperity banked on his own name as worth twenty thousand names (men). But confronted by catastrophes, he wishes he could live up to his name, that is, the grandeur expected of a king, or be less than he was. Also seeing himself as frail and vulnerable, he would like to resign his kingship but discovers that he is unable psychologically to move from "King Richard" to "Richard." "I have no name, no title / . . . And know not now what name to call myself!" He would rather be nothing. He eventually dies with identity recaptured as simply Richard of Bordeaux, even as at the conclusion of Cervantes' novel *Don Quijote* (*Don Quixote,* 1605, 1615) the hero Don Quixote de la Mancha resumes his sanity and reverts to the quotidian name of Alonso Quijano the Good, the narrator reassuring us that under either name he was a kind man.

The play in which the theme appears most pervasively is *Coriolanus* (1607–1608). The hero, Caius Marcius, earns by his martial feats the agnomen of Coriolanus, as conqueror of Corioli. Later banished, he is unrecognizable to his former foes. His personal enemy and rival must ask no less than six times "What is thy name?" of a man sunk in self-doubts and undergoing—like Antony, Cleopatra, Hamlet, Lear, Othello, Richard II, Timon—loss of name and identity. The answer at long last given is "Caius Marcius," for he drops the "Coriolanus" as part of a past wasted fighting on behalf of an ungrateful Roman populace. When he concludes a peace treaty, he is turned on by Aufidius, who calls him three names—"traitor . . . Marcius . . . boy"—each of which he vehemently rejects. But these are exactly the names he earned by his recent actions.

The Eighteenth to Twentieth Centuries

Undertaking in the *Novum organum* (*The New Learning,* 1620) to reform the kingdom of knowledge by altering the very tools and building blocks of thought—language—Francis Bacon pointed to the "Idols of the Market Place," by which he meant imprecision in words and names, especially names of nonexistent entities like "Fortune" or the "Prime Mover." Locke began his *Essay Concerning Human Understanding* (1690) intending to deal with ideas and knowledge but soon found that words and names, acting as a medium between our understanding and the truths it would apprehend, had a central role; most disputes were therefore rather about confused definitions or meanings of words and names than over a "real difference in the conception of things"; language is also consequently a weak transmitter of divine revelation. In Baconian fashion, he then listed seven abuses of words and names, as well as the necessary remedies. (Hobbes, in *Leviathan* [essay, 1651], had listed four uses and abuses of names.) Such earnest efforts at clarification led, a generation later, to Swift's satire (*Gulliver's Travels,* 1726) of the scientific disciples of these philosophers (and descendants of the Nominalists), who tried to create a symbolic language that would replace the slipshod quotidian language. Since the aim was to prevent the disparity between object and name, the academicians of Lagoda did away with language and conversed by holding up the objects under discussion. This recourse clearly did away with the imprecision of names but created a new set of problems.

Laurence Sterne *(Tristram Shandy)* subjected names, along with many other prosaic details of everyday life, to the sort of scrutiny that the heroic and tragic literature of the West found beneath its dignity. The hero's father, Walter, believed that people were oblivious to the importance of the names they so casually assigned their children. Names had "a strange kind of magic bias," which they imposed on "our characters and conduct. . . . Had Luther been called by any other name but Martin, he would have been damned to all eternity." This is part humor, part primitive mysticism. A more telling and widespread romantic idea was expressed by Goethe (*Faust,* play, 1808)—the inability of mere words and names to grapple with reality. Gretchen, with the naïveté of untutored people, asks a commonplace question, "Do you believe in God?" and her lover, the philosopher who has exhausted all human inquiry and activity, has not her easy faith in language. All he can respond is that when one is filled with bliss, one can call the experience "heart," "love," or "God," or whatever: "I have no name for it / Feeling is all; / Name is but sound and fume." In other words, "God" is but a name meant to domesticate the mysteriousness of our strivings, anxieties, feelings. If under the Mosaic law "God" cannot be used because words and names are all too powerful and because of the fear of illicit exploitation of supernatural forces, the Romantics, on the other hand, avoided the word "God" because the concepts and categories of the mind, as expressed in language and names, are too weak, too remote from the richness of experience. Elsewhere as well Faust exhibits a reticence about naming, while people, including professors and experts, are shown to be unduly credulous about understanding every word (as Gretchen was critical of a woman everyone called "sinful" until she found herself in that predicament) and in believing every word to be backed by a concept or an entity. Faust has even the temerity to change the word in the opening line of the John Gospel from "Word" to "Deed."

Diffidence about the naming of God may also be associated with the naming of the self. Tennyson is cited in James's *Varieties of Religious Experience* (1902) as someone who fell into a trance when, through frequent repetition of his own name, individuality seemed to dissolve "into boundless being" and, in a mood of great clarity, "the loss of personality" seemed not "extinction, but the only true life." Not everyone has a "good trip," however; Lewis Carroll (*Through the Looking Glass,* novel, 1872) tells of "the wood where things have no names," that is, primal matter, pre-Adamic creation. Though the Fawn delights in its own name, Alice fears losing hers, despite the liberation such an event would effect—she fears in effect the undoing of the Logos. Carroll's works also revive the Platonic (and the Realist-Nominalist) question as to whether the name of a thing is arbitrary or is intrinsically connected to its nature. Humpty Dumpty entertains the latter—his name reflects his shape—but finally favors the former (the Nominalist) theory.

While Juliet—unlike Tybalt, her parents, and the world—realizes that name and object are not identical and that the latter rather than the former is important, Oscar Wilde's Gwendolen (*The Importance of Being Earnest,* 1895) thinks rather more along the lines of Walter Shandy's mysticism. She has always dreamed of loving someone called "Ernest," for that, "the only really safe name," somehow inspires confidence. She is full of pity for the woman married to a mere "John." Indeed, for both young men in that play, thriving in their court-ships depends more on acquiring the name "Ernest" than revealing their inner selves to the young ladies. Amid such mystiques and anxieties about the mystery of the relation of name to identity, it is helpful to recall the joshing but apt contribution, attributed to Mark Twain, to the authorship controversy—that it was not Shakespeare who wrote the plays but another man of the same name.

If G. B. Shaw (*St. Joan*, play, 1923) dramatizes the creation of certain names—Protestant, nationalism—in the crucible of events and disputes, García Márquez's *Cien años de soledad* (*One Hundred Years of Solitude*, novel, 1967) contains a Swiftian vision of the frail hold that men have on civilization because of the dependence on language and names. When a plague of insomnia hits the town, with the attendant problem of amnesia, one of the protagonists undertakes to mark every object and animal with its name and use. Living in a reality "momentarily captured by words"—and with signs everywhere that proclaim "God exists"—but lost irremediably once the meaning of the letters is forgotten, the people soon relax their vigilance and turn to an imaginary reality.

Until the twentieth century, literature concerned itself with the name as grappled with by mature men. But a whole new dimension for exploration was opened in modern times by the advent of the child and the childish point of view as a legitimate literary subject. For names mean a lot more to children, who are still exploring the meaning and limits of selfhood, than to adults anesthetized by habit, which makes the name only an attribute tying one's days together and a useful tag by which one can be referred to. Joyce's *Portrait of the Artist as a Young Man* (autobiography, 1916) recaptures the moment when the child becomes conscious of his appellation, looks at it from all sides, begins to fit it into the scheme of things. Stephen Dedalus, obtaining a sense of location and containment from his geography lesson, writes on the flyleaf of the geography book the names of concentric circles of identification that make up the individual's self-awareness. "Stephen Dedalus/Class of Elements/Conglowes Wood College/Sallin/County Kildare/Ireland/Europe/The World/The Universe." Inevitably he finds himself wondering what lies beyond the "universe"; even that all-encompassing name does not really cover everything. Then he mulls over other names in a way that makes Faust's erudite equivocation understandable. The relation of God's name to God's essence is just as mysterious as the significance of his own name; "God was God's name just as his name was Stephen. . . . God remained always the same God and God's real name was God." It is therefore understandable also that, as D. H. Lawrence remarks in the contemporary *Sons and Lovers* (novel, 1913), "children suffer so much at having to pronounce their own names" when asked by adults. "Those two words," as Robert Musil (*Der Mann ohne Eigenschaften* [*The man without Qualities*, novel, 1930–1943]) "are conceptually the poorest, but emotionally the richest in the language."

Perhaps the most subjective and protracted treatment of the impact of names on the sensibility of the child is in Proust's *Du côté de chez Swann* (*Swann's Way*, novel, 1913). The young Marcel weaves a mystique around the names of aristocratic old families, a mystique challenged but not undermined when the living bearers of the names turn out to lack the grandeur he had imagined. A similar process was at work in connection with place names, which set his imagination going just as did railroad timetables. (Winston Churchill had remarked [*My African Journey,* 1908] how a place name in bold print on the map may conjure up images of magnificence and then turn out to represent only a depressing village.)

The hero of another story, Mann's "Tonio Kröger" (1903), treats, besides every child's difficulties with his own name and identity, two other problems that affect only some children: a name that children in their wisdom think unattractive, and a sense of estrangement that the artistically inclined child feels from his "normal" peers. His name was as queer as everything else he felt about himself: his passivity, shyness, introspection. His only friend says, "Your first name is so crazy. . . . Though of course I know it's not your fault in the least." Tonio admits its silliness, wishes for "good, sound, familiar names, offensive to nobody"—"Heinrich," "Wilhelm," "Hans," or "Irwin."

One of the many ways in which the stylish, witty, nimble, amoral hero of Mann's *Felix Krull* (novel, 1954) is the polar opposite of the maudlin Tonio is in the matter of names. He treats that subject as cavalierly as he does everything else. When Felix contemplates his sister's impending marriage, he becomes preoccupied "with the fascinating subject" of her change of name and envies her (and all women) "the charm of novelty" provided by being able to change one's signature overnight. How nice it must be to have the "tonic and restorative" of giving "oneself a new name and to hear oneself addressed by it." Later, entering proudly a career free from the limitations of bourgeois good and evil, the rascal enjoys the "easy grace" with which for the first time he abandoned "like a soiled and worn-out garment the name to which I was born." Felix lacks the sullen idealism and conscientiousness of Gregers Werle, in Ibsen's *Vildanden* (*The Wild Duck,* play, 1884), who, burdened with self-hatred, expresses disgust with his own name as an irrevocable doom and who sees no way out.

The role of names in the American melting-pot process is dramatized in Bellow's *Seize the Day* (novella, 1956). Wilky, the son of the Jewish physician, Dr. Adler, feels himself eternally under the shadow of his father's success and of his aloof, self-satisfied personality. Always the loser, by contrast, and trying in vain to establish his own identity and career, Wilky betakes himself to the archetypal American dreamland, Hollywood, where a name change (to "Tommy Wilhelm") is as de rigueur as a "nose job" is for others. But neither in Hollywood nor in life does he ever become more than a bit player and, often admitting to himself that he is Dr. Adler's son, he has to hear his father's implicit contempt: "My son and I use different monickers. I uphold tradition. He's for the new." The narrator summarizes: "Wilhelm had always had a great longing to be Tommy. . . . But Wilky was his inescapable self."

The philosophical and historical upheavals of the century have had their impact on literature and on names. Insofar as names were thought to stand for identity, essence, philosophical certitude, they have undergone a battering in a modern world that has seen a dual loss of faith—first in a divinely created universe, then in worldly progress. The protagonists of Kafka's two classics are hardly heroes and have only fragmentary names, "K." and "Joseph K." The comic tradition of allegorical or self-descriptive names—often in Aristophanes, sometimes in Jonson, Shakespeare, and Dickens—reaches an extreme of grotesqueness in Joyce's novel *Finnegans Wake* (1939) and, with characters named Scheisskopf and Major Major Major Major, in Heller's *Catch-22* (novel, 1961).

Especially relevant to names and naming in the modern literature of silence are the plays of Eugène Ionesco. In *Le rhinocéros* (*Rhinoceros*, 1960), the logician obliviously sinks ever deeper into the morass of logic, syllogisms, words, and names while all about him earth-shaking changes are taking place. In *La cantatrice chauve* (*The Bald Soprano,* 1950), the anonymity of modern life and the interchangeability of people is suggested by the fact that nearly everyone turns out to have the same name, Bobby Watson, and seems to come from the same location. At the end of the play, moreover, all names and words degenerate into gibberish, as does the climactic speech by the putative savior in *Les chaises* (*The Chairs*, 1952) (and, implicitly, the teachings of the professor in *La leçon* [*The Lesson,* 1951]). This is the literary rendition of a bleak view of life that reached an unthinkable climax during the Holocaust, when millions lost all identity and, with an identification number branded into their arms, took their anonymous selves into the extermination chamber. In the end, there was no Logos or name, only a number and a darkness at the heart of things.

See also: Language.

Selected Bibliography

Garber, Marjorie. *Coming of Age in Shakespeare*. New York: Methuen, 1981.

Spitzer, Leo. "Linguistic Perspective in the *Don Quixote.*" *Linguistics and Literary History*. Princeton, N.J.: Princeton University Press, 1948.

Weidhorn, Manfred. "The Relation of Title and Name to Identity in Shakespearean Tragedy," *Studies in English Literature* 9 (1969): 303–320.

———. "The Rose and Its Name: On Denomination in *Romeo, Othello,* and *Julius Caesar.*" *Texas Studies in Language and Literature* 11 (1969): 671–686.

MANFRED WEIDHORN

NATURE: *NATURAE CURSUS* AND THE STATE OF NATURE

Two major notions concerning nature widely discussed in the eighteenth century had a significant influence upon the ideology of the American Revolution. One, the state of nature, involved the relations between governors and the governed; the other, *naturae cursus,* involved the question of change or permanence in the political system. These concepts seem to be mutually contradictory, *naturae cursus* suggesting a current or mobility, and the state of nature suggesting that which is static or immutable. This contradiction is only apparent, however, for both concepts admit change or transition as well as permanence. The main difference is that the course of nature may refer to both the human and the cosmic order, whereas state of nature concerns the human condition alone. When used in connection with the cosmos, the course of nature is assumed to be predetermined according to a pre-established order, but in connection with human affairs it may be either pre-established or free from control. From the theological perspective, God may have fixed the stream of events (determinism); he may have established a certain order, but interfere at will to change it (divine providence); or he may have left the physical world to operate by secondary causes and given man free will.

Hans Galinsky, the only scholar to have investigated the notion of *naturae cursus* in detail, has shown parallels between the phrases "course of nature's law," "course of necessity," "course of Providence," and "course of things," all of which are clearly deterministic. Benjamin Franklin interpreted the concept in both anti-deterministic and deterministic senses. In referring to the necessity of his own death, he wrote to Jonathan Shipley, February 24, 1786, "the Course of Nature must soon put a period to my present Mode of Existence," but in the persona of the astrologer Poor Richard in his *Almanac* for 1734, he remarked "'tis well known, that the Events which would otherwise certainly happen at certain Times in the Course of Nature are sometimes set aside or postpon'd."

John Keats in his poem *Hyperion* (1820) has the God of the Sea maintain "We fall by course of Nature's law, not force of Thunder, or of Jove." This joining of *naturae cursus* with the notion of the law of nature occurs also in the preamble to the Declaration of Independence, which refers to both "the Course of human Events" and "the Laws of Nature and of Nature's God." It has been suggested by Richard Ely Selden (*Criticism on the Declaration of Independence*, 1846, p. 6) that events are supra-human, the result of fate or divine Providence, and, therefore, should not be described as human—that it would be more accurate to speak of human affairs. Similarly, the laws of Nature seem to refer to order in the physical universe; whereas the laws of Nature's God seem to refer to the moral world. The same dichotomy exists in Franklin's speech of Polly Baker, in which his semicomical figure appeals to "the first and great command of nature and nature's God" to increase and multiply. She also asks rhetorically whether her giving birth to bastard children can be called a crime "in the nature of things," that is, in reference to what A. O. Lovejoy calls (p. 72) "the system of necessary and self-evident truths concerning the properties and relations of essences."

The dichotomy between laws of nature and those of nature's God also seems to suggest a separation between God and nature, comparable to the ancient Platonic notion of an ideal world imperfectly realized in empirical society. Plato, the Cambridge Platonists in the seventeenth century, and Shaftesbury in the eighteenth century, conceived of a fixed ideal order completely independent of God; whereas liberal theologians and Newtonians conceived of the empirical world as comprising the fixed order that was created by God. The former of these attitudes is reflected in the phrase "the eternal fitness of things" constantly on the lips of the deistical tutor in Henry Fielding's *Tom Jones* (novel, 1749). It is also suggested by Keats's line already quoted here.

In regard to the cosmic order, the poet Edward Young in his *Night Thoughts* (1742–1745) maintained, "The course of nature is the art of God" (book 9, line 1267). This is a novel reaffirmation of a commonplace antithesis between art and nature in which nature as empirical reality has not been transformed into something contrived by an exterior force (as it is ordinarily by the hand of man). Young's metaphor, moreover, buttresses the deterministic element in *naturae cursus*.

One of the passages of Jefferson's original draft of the Declaration of Independence supports the contrary concept of free will. This passage is the famous one embodying Jefferson's vehement protest against the slave trade, which Congress struck from the final version. Here Jefferson describes George III as waging "cruel war against human nature itself." In this phrase approbation is accorded to human nature, which is considered both to have liberty of action and to be good. Indeed, the fundamental notions of the Declaration of Independence, those of equality and of human rights, assume the rectitude of human nature. The assumption that human nature is good has both moral and sociological implications. It rests upon a hotly debated point of theology, whether a state of pure nature had ever existed in the world. The British monk Pelagius argued that men at birth, that is, in the state of nature, are neither virtuous nor vicious, but have freedom of choice to develop in either direction. St. Augustine, to the contrary, denied that any man can become perfect because of the corruption entailed by original sin. Pelagianism was officially condemned in 417, and the Augustinian doctrine became almost universally accepted. In the seventeenth century, the notion of a state of nature became involved in the Jansenist-Jesuit polemic over the conditions of grace, with all sides agreeing that Augustine was right in declaring "that the state of pure nature is impossible." The concept moved from the realm of theology to that of political science in 1690 when John Locke published his *Two Treatises on Government*. Before Locke, the state of nature concerned man's moral relations with God; after Locke, it concerned man's hypothetical moral and physical relations with his fellowmen. As the theologians spoke of man in a state of innocence, newly emerging from the hands of God, so Rousseau later described man as he emerged from the hands of nature.

Theology remained inextricably connected with the concept of state of nature throughout the Enlightenment and into the American Revolution. Locke in the first of his *Two Treatises* refutes the divine right theory of monarchy by reexamining the biblical texts that had traditionally been used to defend the doctrine, thereby assuming that forms of government had been established by God; in the second treatise, he explains the origin of government as a purely natural process.

In answer to those who denied that men ever existed in the state of nature, Locke not only called upon "the Authority of the Judicious Hooker," but also affirmed "That all Men are naturally in that State, and remain so, till by their own Consents they make themselves Members of some Politick Society." Richard Hooker did not use the actual expression "state of nature," although he clearly expressed the concept of a condition in which man existed prior to entering into mutual intercourse. His famous theoretical work *Of the Laws of Ecclesiastical Polity* (1593) depends upon the law of nature as an explanation for the origin of society, the result, according to his thinking, of man's inherent desire for companionship and of an orderly process in forming a life in common. In Hooker's words, "Two foundations there are which bear up public societies; the one, a natural inclination, whereby all men desire sociable life and fellowship; the other, an order expressly or secretly agreed upon touching the manner of their union in living together." The first notion of a natural inclination toward society derives from Aristotle's celebrated idea of man as a social creature (*Politika* [*Politics,* essays, 4th century B.C.] 1, 2, 9). The origins of the doctrine of political organization are less certain. The living arrangements that Hooker describes as "the Law of a Commonweal," came to be called in the eighteenth century the social contract. According to Hooker the motivation for communion and fellowship with others is to be found in the desire to supply the defects and imperfections of a solitary existence in order to obtain a way of life "fit for the dignity of man." At the same time, Hooker, in line with the Christian orthodoxy requisite to a clergyman in the Anglican church, asserts that all laws are improper "unless presuming the will of man to be inwardly obstinate, rebellious, and averse from all obedience unto the sacred laws of his nature; in a word, unless presuming man to be in regard of his depraved mind little better than a wild beast" (bk 1, chap. 10, sec. 2). This is just the opposite of Jefferson's assumptions concerning the goodness of human nature.

Contrary to popular belief, very few writers who accepted the notion of a state of nature considered it to be a happy or a desirable condition. Indeed if it were a condition in which man finds satisfaction and contentment, it would be logical to assume that he would wish to remain forever in that state instead of venturing into the unknown territory of society. Alexander Pope in *An Essay on Man* (poem, 1733–1734) gives one of the rare portrayals of the state of nature as a salutary condition: "The State of Nature was the reign of God; . . . / Pride then was not; nor Arts, that Pride to aid; / Man walked with beast, joint tenant of the shade." This is absolutely contrary to Hooker, who observes that beasts are not capable of speech, the chief instrument of human communion, and cites the verse from Genesis in which it is said of Adam that "amongst the beasts 'he found not for himself any meet companion' " (bk 1, chap. 10. sec. 13).

Locke considers the essence of the state of nature to consist in "a state of perfect freedom" by which men behave and dispose of their belongings as they think fit without asking the permission or depending on the will of any other man (bk 2, chap. 2, sec 4). This state of freedom coexists, according to Locke, with a condition of equality, that is, the absence of subjection or subordination of one to the other. Drawing upon Hooker, Locke considers this natural equality as the source of the obligation to mutual love among mankind. But despite this obligation there are bound to be conflicts, which should be settled by the law of nature, which represents for Locke as well as for Hooker the same thing as the exercise of reason. According to Locke's scheme, every person in the state of nature has the executive power of the law of nature. Locke does not interpret this situation as a state of anarchy or of war as Hobbes had done in *Leviathan* (essay, 1651), but he does consider the desire of avoiding war a motivating force for gathering into society. Locke makes a careful distinction between the state of war and the state of nature, a distinction that is somewhat tenuous. In his words, "Men living together according to reason without a common superior on earth, with authority to judge between them, is properly the state of Nature. But force, or a declared design of force upon the person of another, where there is no common superior on earth to appeal to for relief, is the state of war" (bk 2, chap. 3, sec. 19). The question that Locke completely ignores is whether the state of nature and any kind of living in society are mutually exclusive. In other words, he seems to be confounding a state of nature and society in his definition of the state of nature as "men living together according to reason." Strange to say the question of whether the state of nature may allow for any form of social relationship was not raised until nearly a century after the publication of Locke's treatise, when it emerged in the polemics inspired by the American Revolution.

Locke takes notice of conjugal society, the family, and political or civil society, and concludes that both conjugal society and the family group "came short of 'political society'" (bk 2, chap. 7, sec. 77).

Montesquieu in his *De l'esprit des lois* (*Spirit of the Laws*, essay, 1748; bk. 1, chap. 2) seems to consider the conjugal relationship as consistent with the state of nature, although his manner of treating it as one of the forces that impel men to associate together does not clarify the relationship. The natural inclination that the sexes feel for each other Montesquieu regards as one of four laws of nature, the others consisting of the desire for peace, the desire for nourishment, and the desire to live in society. The only author who unequivocally portrays the relationship between the conjugal condition and the state of nature is Giambattista Vico, whose *La scienza nuova* (*Principles of a New Science*, essay) appeared in 1725, but remained largely neglected until the twentieth century. According to Vico, man lived first in a bestial state, from which he graduated to a state of nature in which he was no longer bestial but monogamous and living in families. This is equivalent to the second of four stages into which Rousseau divided the state of nature. Indeed, Rousseau strongly suggests that in the bestial stage, that is, when man follows merely the impulse of nature, every woman is good enough for him.

The principal reason that Locke assigns for entering into society is the preservation and safeguarding of property. He includes liberty and security, however, as other advantages together with the acquiring of a method for the settling of disputes. Locke considered private property as the dominant cohesive force of society; whereas Rousseau rejected it as the root of many of the worst evils of civilization, the source of untold crimes, wars, miseries, and other horrors in his *Discours sur l'origine et les fondements de l'inégalité parmi les hommes* (*Discourse on the Origin and Bases of Inequality among Men,* essay, 1754). Rousseau's explanation of the manner in which private property became the catalyst for the transmission from the state of nature to society does not derive from Locke, however, but from another English predecessor, Bernard Mandeville. Mandeville, in his *Fable of the Bees* (poem, 1714), makes an important distinction between association and society. "A number of people that without rule or government should keep together out of natural affection to their species or love of company, as a herd of cows or a flock of sheep" is mere association. Society for Mandeville represents "a body politic, in which man either subdued by superior force, or by persuasion drawn from his savage state, is become a disciplined creature that can find his own ends in labouring for others" (Irwin Primer ed., 1962, p. 172). As Mandeville reconstructed the process by which savage man was broken—that is, persuaded to accept the curb of government, a crafty few recognized man's inherent pride and the power of flattery to control his behavior. The first rudiments of morality "were thus broached by skilful politicians" to render men useful and tractable "that the ambitious might reap the more benefit from and govern vast numbers of them with the greater ease and security."

This is essentially the process described by Rousseau in his *Discourse,* where he also breaks down the state of nature into various stages. In the first stage, Rousseau finds very few differences between man and beast except for the talent or the faculty to improve himself. It is this very quality that, according to Rousseau, has led to his downfall—that is, to social organization. As man acquired the ability to think, he felt for the first time the sensation of pride and also realized how he could use the universal motivation of self-love to his own advantage. Finally, after the recognition of private property, the crafty ones, in Rousseau's words, "easily invented specious reasonings" to lead others to their ends, that is, to the establishment of government. This is the stage that marked the end of the law of Nature. Like Mandeville, Rousseau proclaimed in effect that the whole human race was subjected to work, servitude, and misery for the profit of a few ambitious men.

Thomas Paine, in his famous tract *Common Sense* (1776), does not refer to the "state of nature," but he uses another expression for the same concept, the "state of natural liberty." He seems to follow Locke in asserting that man "finds it necessary to surrender up a part of his property to furnish means for the protection of the rest" and that security is "the true design and end of government." Paine affirms that "some writers have so confounded society with government, as to leave little or no distinction between them" even though the works of Locke, Mandeville, Montesquieu, and Rousseau imply such a distinction. Paine makes it explicit, however, by a series of contrasts. Society, a truly cohesive force, encourages intercourse and "promotes our happiness *positively* by uniting our affections; whereas government, a negative force, restrains our vices and creates distinctions." According to Paine, "society in every state is a blessing, but government even in its best state is but a necessary evil; in its worst state an intolerable one."

Paine's stress on the negative aspects of government seems to hark back to Hooker's orthodox Christian interpretation of man's depraved nature. "Government, like dress," Paine maintains, "is the badge of lost innocence; the palaces of kings are built on the ruins of the bowers of paradise." "Here then is the origin and rise of government; namely a mode rendered necessary by the inability of moral virtue to govern the world; here too is the design and end of government, viz. freedom and security."

The sociological aspect of the notion of the state of nature can be interpreted as another manifestation of the nature-art antithesis. Man, in passing from the state of nature to government, has moved from a natural to artificial society, part of the process known as the course of nature in human affairs.

See also: Reason, Universe.

Selected Bibliography

Aldridge, A. Owen. "The State of Nature: An Undiscovered Country in the History of Ideas." *Studies on Voltaire and the Eighteenth Century* 98 (1972): 7–26.

Galinsky, Hans. *Naturae Cursus. Der Weg einer antiken kosmologischen Metapher von der alten in die neue Welt*. Heidelberg: Carl Winter, 1968.

Lovejoy, A. O. *Essays in the History of Ideas*. Baltimore: Johns Hopkins, 1948.

A. OWEN ALDRIDGE

NIHILISM

Derived from the Latin word for "nothing," *nihil*, nihilism basically means a belief in a universe where nothing has any worth and, in Nietzsche's famous phrase from *Zur Genealogie der Moral (The Genealogy of Morals*, essay, 1887), "everything is permitted." The term is imprecise enough to slide off into meanings that include rejection of established religions, beliefs, or moral principles; radical discontinuity of cultural conventions; a perspective on life closely akin to boredom, emptiness, despair, self-destructiveness, and all-around negation; and philosophical skepticism that denies all existence and welcomes nothingness. In a specific historic sense nihilism refers to the extremist doctrines of Russian reformers and revolutionists prominent in the reign of Tsar Alexander II (1855–1881), who was assassinated by a bomb-throwing terrorist.

Political-Literary Nihilism

While Ivan Turgenev did not originate the word "nihilism" in its socio-political purport, his novel, *(Ottsy i deti, Fathers and Children,* 1862), gave it worldwide currency as a catchall description of a young generation rebelling against the authority and customs of its elders. Its protagonist, Yevgeny Bazarov, proudly calls himself a nihilist, parades his commitment to the denial of current values, and tells the tradition-minded Pavel Kirsanov, ''[Construction is] not our business now . . . the ground has to be cleared first.'' He practices the nihilist doctrines of his time by his positivism, scientism, utilitarianism, rejection of Russia's rigid class system, and strongly implied atheism. Yet Bazarov, despite his rudeness, coarseness, cynicism, and intense contempt for what he considers the older generation's ethical hollowness, is hardly a revolutionary. He has no coherent system, strategy, tactics; no opportunity or time for political action; no allies or friends, except for the timorous Arkady, who soon abandons him. He is defeated by his hopeless love for a frigid socialite; by his male pride, which pushes him into an outmoded duel that violates his emancipated theories; by a grim fate that infects him in his early twenties with fatal typhoid fever. Turgenev has been careful to deprive the man who wants to ''smash other people'' of weapons for smashing anything.

Russia's nihilists of the 1860s and 1870s were divided on many issues and therefore cannot be grouped under any coherent, comprehensive doctrines. Their most systematic and influential writer was Nikolai Chernyshevsky (1828–1889), who insisted in his essay *Esteticheskie otnosheniia iskusstva k deĭstvitel' nosti* (*Aesthetic Relations of Art and Reality,* 1855) that a good pair of boots was worth more than all of Pushkin's poetry. Bazarov echoes this ferocious anti-aestheticism when he encourages Arkady to replace his father's Pushkin volume with a text by the German materialist Ludwig Büchner, *Kraft und Stoff* (*Matter and Force,* 1855). Two other works by Chernyshevsky were to provoke a famous response from Fyodor Dostoevsky: The treatise, *Antropologicheskiĭ printsip v filosofii* (*The Anthropological Principle in Philosophy,* 1859), and a didactic novel that became wildly popular when first published, *Chto delat'?* (*What Is to Be Done?* 1863). Dostoevsky framed his novel *Zapiski iz podpol'ia* (*Notes from Underground,* 1864), the fictional foundation for his mature novels, as a satirical parody of Chernyshevsky's views.

Dostoevsky's strategy is to assimilate Chernyshevsky's major doctrines into the behavior of his first-personal protagonist, the underground man, only to expose the folly of these ideas by his anti-hero's hopeless conflicts. The interlocutor with whom the undergroundling argues in part 1 is a disciple of Chernyshevsky who considers all human life to be simply a mechanical product of the laws of nature, with no qualitative distinction between rocks, trees, and human beings. The underground man derisively welcomes this metaphysic of materialism, aware that it makes moral responses meaningless, with the notion of guilt eradicated from man's conscience. He proceeds to mock Chernyshevsky's ethics of ''rational egoism,'' which assume that man is basically good and reasonable and will seek his enlightened self-interest by establishing an earthly paradise based on scientific truths. Not so, he replies: Man's primary need is moral freedom. He will often deliberately seek the injurious, the stupid, the evil;

will insist on his autonomy to prefer the self-destructive to the sensible. In his novel Chernyshevsky had described a Fourierist, Utopian Crystal Palace where man, having discovered the essential laws governing society, would achieve astounding material prosperity. The undergroundling counters this vision with one of universal chaos and madness, with man preferring bloodthirsty but creative individualism to a deterministic "ant hill." Dostoevsky's final argument against the Crystal Palace is that it would eliminate suffering—which he regards as the sole source of man's moral consciousness.

In part 2 of *Notes from Underground* Dostoevsky shifts from a satire of the 1860s' nihilism to an attack on the 1840s' sentimental, Sandian romanticism— a liberal idealism in which he had himself participated as a member of the circle headed by Mikhail Petrashevsky. He parodies and reverses the cliché of the saved and saintly prostitute that pervades nineteenth-century fiction. In *What Is to Be Done?* a triangle involving the protagonist, his wife, and his friend, whom she loves, is easily resolved through rational agreement among the parties. To the contrary in *Notes,* where the underground man manipulates the prostitute Lisa's feelings by feigning compassion and love so as to humiliate her, only to be shamed by her forgiveness of his depravity. He is left with a burning sense of his viciousness, yet also with the satisfaction that his insults to her "will elevate and purify her" while asserting his moral responsibility for his self-willed actions.

Dostoevsky repeats the relationship between the liberal 1840's and the radical-nihilistic 1860s in his novel, *Besy (The Possessed,* 1871–1872). Here he totally dissolves any categorical distinction between politics, religion, and prophecy. He satirizes yet also loves the aimless sentimentalism of the older generation in Stepan Verkhovensky, dependent on the patronage of the conservative gentry. More significantly, by making Stepan the father of the appalling Peter Ver-khovensky, Dostoevsky suggests that dandified, apparently impotent buffoonery can nonetheless beget a demonic nihilism that will provoke murder, fire, and general chaos. *The Possessed* combines two dramas: a metaphysical conflict, centering on Nikolai Stavrogin (which will be analyzed later), and a political storm stirred up by Peter and based on the historic Nechaev conspiracy.

Sergei Nechaev (1847–1882) was a brilliant divinity student and teacher who organized student disturbances at Petersburg University, then went to Europe in the spring of 1869 to join Mikhail Bakunin (1814–1876) in establishing an émigré revolutionary movement. He returned to Russia in August 1869, established a "Society of National Retribution" in Moscow, and on November 21 had four members of his group murder the fifth, Ivanov, for allegedly having refused to obey Nechaev's orders. Dostoevsky followed the Nechaev circle's trial in the newspapers and modeled Peter's personality and conduct largely on Nechaev's. Both men are cold-bloodedly manipulative, ruthless, hypocritical, cynical, and vicious. Like Nechaev, Peter will use any means to achieve his end—but that goal is never clearly defined, with Dostoevsky drawing him as ideologically slippery though assuredly corrupt. He is often more the amoral adventurer than the revolutionary, with intrigue and betrayal his natural elements and destructiveness his delight. From a historical perspective Dostoevsky's portrait of Peter as a representative radical is spitefully distorted, since the followers of the fanatic Nechaev were a small minority compared to the admirers of such humanistic reformers as Alexandyr Herzen (1812–1870), Nikolai Dobroliubov (1836–1861), and Chernyshevsky. Psychologically, however, Peter Verkhovensky is a horrifyingly accurate forerunner of the Bolshevik-Stalinist type-to-come, a commissar who, beginning with a charade of absolute freedom, arrives at the necessity of absolute tyranny.

In the late 1870s and 1880s, terrorist crimes committed by Russian nihilists increased significantly. Provincial governors, police chiefs, and prefects were murdered; trains were blown up; several attempts were made to kill the Imperial family until Alexander II was mortally wounded. The myth of the nihilist as essentially a bomb-throwing anarchist swept not only Russia but Western Europe. In the early 1880s Turgenev planned a novel in which he would approve of the dialectical socialism advocated by Karl Marx (1818–1883) but reject the conspiratorial methods and violence urged by such "possessed" socialists as the anarchistic Bakunin. (In 1872, at a congress of the International, Marx had openly broken with Bakunin.) Turgenev's death in 1883 aborted his project, but its intent was largely executed by his friend Emile Zola in *Germinal* (1885), his novel about a miners' strike.

In *Germinal* Zola contrasts his protagonist, Etienne Lantier, the socialist workers' leader who has risen from a blue-collar background and admires Marx's and Darwin's ideas, with a Russian émigré intellectual of aristocratic birth, Souvarine. The latter, while personally delicate and gentle, is ideologically afire with Bakunin's religion of destruction. In one of several debates the two men have, Souvarine summarizes his aims: "To destroy everything. No more nations, no more governments, no more property, no more God or religion. . . . We must have a series of appalling cataclysms to horrify the rulers and awaken the people." The strike fails and Etienne's leadership is repudiated by the demoralized miners, but Souvarine sabotages the main shaft of the Moloch-like mine so that underground water floods the entire pit. His creator writes him a legendary exit. As Souvarine leaves the mine, "His shadow form dwindled and merged into the night. He was bound for the unknown, over yonder, calmly going to deal violent destruction wherever dynamite could be found to blow up cities and men. Doubtless, on that day when the last expiring bourgeois hear the very stones of the street exploding under their feet, he will be there."

Though socialistic, Zola was not radical enough to close his novel on such an apocalyptic note. Instead, he ends it with Etienne Lantier leaving the mining village to become a professional labor organizer in Paris, determined to vanquish the bourgeoisie through legal rather than terrorist methods. Yet Zola's portrait of Souvarine struck a deep response from both leftist and rightist readers. The poet Guillaume Apollinaire (1880–1918) wrote a school friend when he was 18: "I shall leave you with a prayer for the arrival of Souvarine, the man who must come, the fair-haired man who will destroy towns and men." From an opposite perspective the Polish-born Joseph Conrad (Jozef Korzeniowski) drew on Souvarine's character for his anarchistic dynamite manufacturer, the "Professor," in *The Secret Agent* (1907), one of his brace of political novels featuring Russian revolutionists; the other is *Under Western Eyes* (1911).

Conrad's father, Apollo Korzeniowski, was a romantic nationalist who sought to free Poland from Russia's domination, led a doomed rebellion in 1863, and was exiled with his wife and five-year-old Joseph to a Russian province. The son eventually escaped his father's world, became a naturalized British subject, and adopted the right-wing politics common among English gentry. Order, restraint, fortitude, and fidelity are the virtues he most values; anarchy, betrayal, and fanatic violence in behalf of any cause are his most feared enemies. In *The Secret Agent* Conrad derives his plot from a historic attempt to blow up the Greenwich Observatory and writes a psycho-political mystery of macabre satire that anticipates the thrillers of Graham Greene, Eric Ambler, and John Le Carré. While Conrad insists in his preface that he "had no idea to consider Anarchism politically, or to treat it seriously in its philosophical aspect," he does that and more. His protagonist, a Mr. Verloc, is a shopkeeper who provides a rendezvous for Russian and German anarchists whose secrets he sells to a foreign power; he is thus a secret agent among secret agents, inhabiting a political and psychological house of mirrors; a lost, squalid, and isolated person in an Edwardian London that Conrad draws morally as well as physically soiled. The author gloomily observes the "air of moral nihilism" that envelops him.

Virtually all the novel's persons, regardless of their ideologies, are described by Conrad with cold, mordant irony. Moral despair grips not only Verloc but the other two featured characters, his wife and her brother Stevie; and the police are as corrupt as the anarchists since, as the "professor" states, "the terrorist and the policeman both come from the same basket," buying and selling one another in a predatory world. Conrad subjects the anarchists to a corrosive scorn that turns them into caricatures, as foolish and infantile as they are sinister and obsessed. While Zola gave his Souvarine intellectual as well as physical audacity, Conrad grants his bomb-laden, bloodthirsty "professor" no more than a grotesque lunacy. In the novel's last paragraph Conrad apes Souvarine's departure by having the "professor" walk the streets, "terrible in the simplicity of his idea calling madness and despair to the regeneration of the world." Yet the dominant impression left by *The Secret Agent* is not that of political nihilism's horrifying menace, but rather of the author's profound sense of man's moral isolation and weakness, his nihilistic vision of the hollowness and vanity of human ideals.

The twentieth century's two central events, the Russian Revolution of 1917 and the Holocaust during World War II, have convinced many writers that modern history has become dominated by diseased dreams and moral barbarism. André Malraux, the most brilliant of contemporary political novelists, wrote in 1926 a dialogic essay, *La tentation de l'Occident* (*The Temptation of the West*), denouncing the West as a soulless, neurotic, masochistic, and disorderly community whose inhabitants are anguished by their disbelief in either God or man: "At the core of Western civilization there is a hopeless contradiction . . . between man and what he has created." In such novels as *Les conquérants* (*The Conquerors*, 1928), *La condition humaine* (*Man's Fate*, 1933) and *L'espoir* (*Man's Hope*, 1937), Malraux tries to transcend the demons of nihilism by resorting to the demons of a heroism wedded to a Herculean dream-vision of redeeming ideology. Thus, in *The Conquerors* his fictive surrogate is the tough-minded, courageous Commissar Garine, who heads Canton's Communists. In *Man's Fate*, his tragic protagonist is Kyo, idealistic head of Shanghai's revolutionists. Malraux's hope is that modern man, through active political commitment, can establish a "virile fraternity" that will dignify and ennoble his otherwise lonely and meaningless existence.

Yet Garine is more adventurer than ideologue, despising the "doctrinal trash" of both communism and fascism, interested primarily in leaving "his scar on the map" by gambling on violent action and historical momentum to overcome the weakness of his lack of belief, as Pascal and Kierkegaard gambled on God's existence to overcome the weakness of man's condition. *The Conquerors'* only committed revolutionary is the terrorist Hong, a brutal fanatic whose hatred of privilege turns into revolting sadism. Hong's type is more fully and sympathetically realized in Ch'en of *Man's Fate*, who finds that killing becomes his way of self-transcendence: "There was a world of murder and he was staying in it as if in a warm place." Ch'en soon finds himself intoxicated by the destructive element in which he immerses himself; like Zola's Souvarine, he assumes mythic status as the agent of implacable slaughter. For all their infatuation with force, however, Malraux's heroes are invariably defeated. Ch'en fails to kill Chiang Kai-Shek and dies an absurd suicide; both the Cantonese and Shanghai uprisings fail; Spain's Republicans succumb to Franco's Falangists. Malraux's characters find no lasting fulfillment in violence, sex, friendship, love, gambling, opium, political power, or ideological fervor. Malraux the novelist places his hope in political causes, but Malraux the existentialist has his characters unable to commit to them and therefore condemned to lives of tragic nihilism.

The end of ideology—indeed, end of human individuality—is prophesied in the desolate parable *1984* (1949) by George Orwell. Along with Evgenii Zamiatin's novel *My* (*We*, 1924) and Aldous Huxley's *Brave New World* (1932), it is an anti-utopian fable that can be classified under the rubric of what the critic Northrop Frye has called Menippean satire. It "presents us with a vision of the world in terms of a single intellectual pattern" (*The Anatomy of Criticism*, 1957). Its protagonist, Winston Smith, is a minor bureaucrat in the totalitarian state of Oceania, working at the Ministry of Truth to rewrite old newspaper articles so they will conform to the current Party line. He must use the official language, "Newspeak," which seeks to reduce the range of thought and expression to orthodox obedience, eliminating whatever words may make heterodox opinions communicable. Smith commits "Thoughtcrime" by denouncing "Big Brother" and having a sexual relationship with a coworker in violation of Party policy. He is arrested and relentlessly tortured by the Ministry of Love, until he betrays the woman he has loved and declares—indeed, feels—love for Big Brother.

Orwell has horrifyingly dramatized the anti-humanist dictum of Bakunin, "I do not want to be I, I want to be We" (*God and the State,* 1882, translated from the French *Dieu et l'état*) He poses one of mankind's most debated questions: Can human nature be totally changed by efficient conditioning? And he sadly answers it in the affirmative. Winston Smith's—and thereby every man's—desires and impulses can be denied and reshaped, so that he comes to believe that war is peace, slavery freedom, and personality a crime. In the legend of the Grand Inquisitor that electrifies Dostoevsky's novel *Brat' īa Karamazovy (The Brothers Karamazov,* 1880), the cardinal tells Jesus that the church does not seek power for its own sake, but for the welfare of the majority of men, who are too frail and base to use freedom responsibly. In *1984,* however, the Ingsoc Commissar, O'Brien, disdains even this rationalization for despotism. He reveals to Smith that the Party is "not interested in the good of others; we are interested solely in power. . . . Power is not a means; it is an end. . . . Power is in tearing human minds to pieces and putting them together again in new shapes of your own choosing." Beyond such total destruction of human values, even nihilism cannot venture.

Philosophic-Literary Nihilism

The philosopher whose ideas have most deeply influenced literary nihilism is doubtless Friedrich Nietzsche. In such essays as *Die Geburt der Tragödie (The Birth of Tragedy,* 1872), *Also sprach Zarathustra (Thus Spoke Zarathustra,* prose poem, 1883–1892), *The Genealogy of Morals* and *Der Wille zur Macht (The Will to Power,* 1906), he propounded aphorisms, ethical insights, psychological illuminations, and historical revaluations that constituted an intellectually dazzling though often paradoxical critique of Western culture.

Basic to Nietzsche's philosophy and psychology is his repudiation of Christianity and his consequent atheism. He refuses to believe in the existence of an incarnate God who, either directly or through His Son, created the world and controls human destiny, both in historic time and in any hereafter. Speaks Zarathustra: "I conjure you, my brethren, remain faithful to Earth, and do not believe those who speak unto you of superterrestrial hopes! Poisoners they are." To Nietzsche, Christianity is a religion false to man's innermost nature. It has sought to universalize the "slave morality" of its Hebrew origins, with its counsels of indiscriminate compassion, elevation of the last to be the first, and insistence on the equality of all humans before God. He holds it responsible for Western civilization's growing materialism, self-indulgence, feminization, and general loss of spontaneity and vitality. Man must learn to live without the false crutches of religious or metaphysical consolations—hence with nihilism, which Nietzsche equates with atheism.

In *The Will to Power* Nietzsche insists that the experience of nihilism as the malady of modernity is a necessary first step in the dialectic of its transcendence. He offers various definitions of it: *"That the highest values devaluate themselves"*; "the conviction of an absolute untenability of existence . . . plus the realization that we lack the least right to posit a beyond"; "the idea of valuelessness, meaninglessness." In its final form, "it includes disbelief in any metaphysical world and forbids itself any belief in a *true* world." So much for passive nihilism, which infects man with unregenerate weakness and despair and leads to the logical outcome of suicide.

Nietzsche, however, advocates an active, heroic nihilism. He believes in a rejuvenation of Western culture through the creation of works of art, particularly poetry and music. Whereas the scientist is bound by the limits and laws of nature, the artist is free to create his own world and establish his own laws. Nietzsche posits a free human spirit that imposes meaning on the world through the sheer strength of man's will—his "Will to Power." This will is at the core of all beings and at the bottom of every motive; it is vital everywhere in human history. The "superior man" will, like Caesar or Napoleon, rise from the herd of human mediocrity to bring about major changes in society, guided by magnanimity, candor, and courage. He will take his fate into his own hands, exhilarated by a "Dionysian affirmation of the world as it is," spurning pettiness, envy, and superstition, transmuting suffering into joy, mastering a Godless and indifferent universe. Nietzsche concludes, in *The Will to Power,* that "an ecstatic nihilism . . . can under certain conditions be indispensable . . . as a mighty pressure and hammer . . . to make way for a new order of life." He thus distinguishes between a base nihilism that succumbs to the world's weakness, decadence, and despair, and a noble nihilism that purifies and strengthens autonomous man as he rises from the ashes of a priest-ridden, obsolete civilization. The "death of God" is thus not only the death of Western, Judaic-Christian culture but also man's opportunity to destroy his enslaving past and renew his creative strength through the recognition of his inner Godhood. Paradoxically, Nietzsche regards man as a tight-rope walker who crosses the abyss of nihilism upon the rope that is his reborn self-confidence.

Without having directly confronted Nietzsche's writings, Dostoevsky dramatized his tension of man poised between nihilistic freedom and faith in God. We have seen that most of the undergroundling's attacks are in the socio-political arena, directed against both the Schillerian utopianism of the 1840s and the utilitarian rationalism of the 1860s. Morally and metaphysically, the underground man's premises are Nietzschean. Man is essentially irrational, capricious, and often vicious; he is inclined to follow the course of his free will—however foolish or self-destructive—against the laws of reason and nature. The "most advantageous of advantages" is the freedom to do only what one prefers: "What man wants is simply *independent* choice, whatever that independence may cost and wherever it may lead." Man is his own law, his own end. When the undergroundling humiliates Lisa, he does so to subject her will to his. He aspires to the condition of godhead by seeking to push man's capabilities to their utmost limits. Unlike Nietzsche, Dostoevsky regards such an aspiration as a psychic sickness. His undergroundling is morally depraved and impotent, unable to love anyone, obsessively egocentric, victimized by his chaotic self-conflicts. For Dostoevsky, whatever serves only the self, instead of surrendering the self to God's Providence, is evil. *Notes from Underground* undermines Nietzsche's notion of noble nihilism from within its protagonist's unresolved dilemmas.

Raskolnikov, protagonist of Dostoevsky's first major novel, *Prestuplenie i nakazanie* (*Crime and Punishment*, 1866), resembles the undergroundling in his pathological isolation and depression, mental brilliance, and subjection to powerful fantasies. Both men seek to assert the primacy of their self-wills; both are offered consolation and redemption by a saintly prostitute. However, whereas the undergroundling rejects rationalism and the concept of human beings as "organ stops," Raskolnikov advocates both and regards himself as a superman entitled to transgress the arbitrary rules of society. In his characterization of his complex hero Dostoevsky was influenced by two books: Napoleon III's *Histoire de Jules César* (*The History of Julius Caesar*, 1865), wherein the author justifies the right to absolute power of such great men as Napoleon I, and Ludwig Feuerbach's *Das Wesen des Christentums* (*The Essence of Christianity*, 1841), which argues for a religion of humanity as a substitute for Christianity.

Why does Raskolnikov kill? In his second visit to Sonya he tells her that altruism, hunger, or other social conditions were not the cause: "I longed to kill without casuistry, to kill for my own benefit . . . I needed to find out . . . whether I was a louse like everybody else or a man, whether I was capable of stepping over the barriers or not. . . . Was I a trembling creature or had I the *right*" Raskolnikov murders to test his nihilistic freedom to violate conventional laws and establish his own. Symbolically, his double slaying amounts to killing his two contending selves: his selfishness and ruthlessness, restated in the pawn-broker Polyana; and his kindness and compassion, restated in her meek sister Lizaveta. No wonder that Raskolnikov's name is rooted in *raskol*, the Russian word for "split" or "schism." Dostoevsky insists on purging Raskolnikov's tormented nihilism through a long course of penance, incomplete at the book's end, involving his contrition, suffering, and atonement through a newly found Christian faith dramatized in the story of Lazarus.

Dostoevsky's most mysterious and enigmatic character is also a self-willed nihilist: Nikolai Stavrogin of *The Possessed*. Stavrogin's literary ancestry is Byronic-Gothic: world-weary, aloof, melancholy, cynical, sexually magnetic, above all, diabolically charismatic. He drains men's souls so devils can enter them. Dostoevsky draws him as no less than a pretender to God's throne who controls the personalities of Peter Verkhovensky, Shatov, and Kirilov and bears the marks of a false Messiah. His behavior is often gratuitously scandalous. He pulls noses, kisses a married lady in public, bites the ear of a provincial governor—all this to signify his refusal of internal or external restraints. Dostoevsky emphasizes his masklike good looks, behind whose beauty fester evil, corruption, ennui, self-degradation. After a riotous young manhood he has become a cold rationalist, no longer able to respond to life spontaneously. He marries the crippled Marya Lebyadkin "through moral sensuality" to free himself from worship of beauty, then refuses to consummate the marriage. He represents the totally free, secular will, which in Dostoevsky's dialectic becomes despotic, divorced from not only God but love, friendship, pity, joy of life. Even his confession to the *Staretz* Tikhon of the violation of a young girl and her subsequent death leaves him unmoved. "I have neither the feeling nor the knowledge of good and evil," he states. Unwilling to submit his will to the discipline of a monastery, let alone surrender to an acceptance of Christ, Stavrogin instead hangs himself.

One critic has called Stavrogin "a dead sun about which the planets he has created continue to move with borrowed light and heat." One of these planets is Kirilov, one of Dostoevsky's most impressive creations, an unwilling nihilist who also ends a suicide. All his life he has been obsessed by his need to believe in God, yet inability to do so. Like a good Feuerbachian, he has come to consider that "the only God of man is man himself." By shooting himself he intends to inaugurate the era of the man-god, freeing humans from a God who is but man's token of his fear of pain and nothingness in a secular universe. His self-extinction will thus be what Albert Camus came to call "a pedagogical suicide" in his essay *Le mythe de Sisyphe* (*The Myth of Sisyphus,* 1942). Just as Christ's crucifixion testified to God's reality and man's sins, so Kirilov's martyrdom will testify to God's death and to the advent of the absolutely free human personality. Dostoevsky, however, shows Kirilov a grotesque fanatic rather than Promethean humanist, hysterically asserting himself as the man who would be God, yet going to his death like a howling animal after biting Peter Verkhovensky's finger to the bone.

Dostoevsky's last novel, *The Brothers Karamazov,* is dominated by what may be the most penetrating characterization of nihilism in fiction: the brilliant personality of Ivan Karamazov. Whereas his brothers Alyosha and Dmitri represent, respectively, man's spiritual and sensual nature, Ivan symbolizes not only man's pride of intellect but functions on a conceptual level far above his brothers' reach. He rebels against a universe whose nature fails to harmonize with his profound rationalism. He raises fundamental ethical and metaphysical questions that Dostoevsky finds himself unable to answer and thereby gives the lie to any simplistic theistic solution to modern man's predicament.

Unlike Stavrogin, Ivan is neither cold nor callow. Rather, he is a grievously puzzled and sensitive young man at hopeless war with himself. He passionately delights in the world's natural beauty, friendship, and great human achievements. Yet his mind and morality cannot reconcile the concept of God's omnipotence and omniscience with the presence of such senseless suffering as that endured by children subjected to atrocities. He is a humanist aghast at the beast active in human nature and unpunished by a Supreme Providence. Arguing from and against design, he refuses to accept his ticket of admission to such a cruel world.

Ivan's rebellion reaches its most dramatic peak in his legend of the Grand

Inquisitor. The Inquisitor is a 90-year-old Spanish cardinal who justifies the Inquisition to an imprisoned Jesus Christ. Essentially, he proclaims the historic failure of Christianity to illuminate and justify man's existence. The cardinal insists that Christ's tragic error was to overestimate man's ability to love his fellows and to bear the burden of free will. His fatal mistake was to reject Satan's triple temptation of miracle, mystery, and authority. The ecclesiastical hierarchy has corrected Jesus' mistake and has based its power on the devil's lures, pretending to speak in Jesus' behalf while enslaving the multitude with comforts of body, conformity of mind, tranquillity of soul. The Inquisitor's monologue is a coherent apology for totalitarianism as the most satisfactory organization of man's weak, vicious, and disorderly nature: "I tell you man has no more agonizing anxiety than to find someone to whom he can hand over with all speed the gift of freedom with which the unhappy creature is born." Christ, who has remained silent during the cardinal's harangue, chooses to respond not with words but with a kiss on the old man's "bloodless" lips. And Dostoevsky never refutes the Inquisitor's arguments, though he may have intended a response in the sequel to this novel, which he announced but did not live to write. Never before has he granted nihilism such formidable advocacy, ceding it the truth of human history.

Late in the novel the devil appears to Ivan in a nightmare and baits him with the authorship of not only "The Grand Inquisitor" but of the parallel essay, "The Geological Upheaval." This is a Feuerbachian tract in which Ivan announces that man, once he has renounced God, will find happiness in his mundane condition by becoming a man-god who will conquer nature, love his brothers, and serenely accept death as utter extinction. The devil then poses this problem to Ivan: Once man becomes his own God, then "he may lightheartedly jump over every barrier of the old moral code . . . 'everything is permitted' and that's all there is to it!" The Nietzschean phrase "everything is permitted" is a leitmotif in both Dostoevsky's anti-nihilistic dialectic and Ivan's writing, for the most significant thesis in Dostoevsky's mature fiction is that moral conduct must be anchored by a firm commitment to God and Christianity.

The devil, tormenting Ivan with the ethical consequences of his atheism, is, of course, his alter ego. Ivan, as an inverted theologian arguing the case of man against God, has based his revolt against divinity on the rights of children mistreated by their fathers or father-surrogates, and the rights of all human beings mistreated by God-the-father. Yet Dostoevsky organizes the novel so that the parricide that pervades it is intellectually sanctioned by Ivan's assertion that, in a Godless universe, man is guided by his self-interest, which may well include crime. After all, Fyodor Karamazov virtually invites his murder by his unloving neglect of his sons, his shameless hedonism, his greed, his degrading procreation of Smerdyakov with an idiot. Yet Ivan is nonetheless held accountable for his father's murder by having his half-brother act upon both their basest motives. Not only has Ivan inspired Smerdyakov to kill with his "everything is permitted" philosophy, he has also made his moral/immoral choice by leaving his father's side to transact a sale in "a dark wood," thereby signaling Smerdyakov to murder Fyodor. However, Dostoevsky's treatment of Ivan remains sympathetically double-edged. On his way to a crucial interview with Smerdyakov, Ivan pushes a peasant into the snow and leaves him to a freezing death. After Smerdyakov has confronted him with his responsibility for the parricide, however, Ivan recognizes his community with all human beings and rescues the fallen peasant. Nonetheless, he finds himself unable to undergo a course of spiritual penance. He ends the novel in a bitterly schizoid self-struggle, confessing his guilt for his father's death in such a demented fashion that the jury refuses to believe him.

Like the undergroundling, Ivan dramatizes harrowingly modern man's dilemma of individual abandonment and alienation. And both Dostoevsky and Nietzsche loom as the subtlest cultural diagnosticians of the nineteenth century. Both place freedom of choice regarding God and evil at the core of man's nature. However, whereas Nietzsche's superior being considers concern for his inferiors a waste of time and guiltlessly abandons the average person to his frailty, Dostoevsky wants the master to recognize the slave as his equal in conscience and love under the example of Christ. In his mature novels Dostoevsky demonstrates that authentic freedom is inseparable from the suffering of loneliness, terror, anxiety, and sometime despair. Yet he insists that the self can only reach fulfillment through continuous cycles of harrowing choices and defining decisions, even though man is strongly tempted to evade such meaningful actions. In this tragic awareness of freedom as mankind's truest rapture as well as keenest torture, Dostoevsky anticipates twentieth-century existentialism.

The contemporary heir of Nietzsche and Dostoevsky as a philosopher-dramatist of nihilism and freedom, as well as modern-day existentialism's most gifted littérateur, is Jean-Paul Sartre. He stresses the anxious, God-bereft individual's search for values and integrity in a world that provides no coherent explanation for the existence of anything or anyone. His intellectual roots are Cartesian. Descartes dreads above all the void of personal nonbeing; he therefore makes a fundamental axiom of his ego's absolute certainty of its—and his—existence: "I think, therefore I am" (*Discours de la méthode* [*Discourse on the Method*, essay, 1637]). While Descartes proceeds to posit God's presence as well as his own, Sartre stops with man and insists that no structure of essences precedes man's life, hence "*existence* comes before *essence*. . . . Man first of all exists, encounters himself, surges up in the world—and defines himself afterwards. . . . Man is nothing else but that which he makes of himself" (*L'existentialisme est un humanisme* [*Existentialism and Humanism*, essay, 1946]). Sartre thus bases both his philosophy and literary works on the conviction that man has neither a God nor a nature to provide him with a purpose or fate. His existence is therefore absurd in an irrational and indifferent universe. Nonetheless, Sartre's atheistic nihilism is far from hopeless. He considers life as a never-ending process of self-creation to which man can give meaning through exercising his freedom of choice and will to action. Hence, "man is condemned to be free."

Sartre thus transforms nihilism into a humanist doctrine stressing the central importance of every person's ethical responsibility. In his best novel, *La nausée* (*Nausea,* 1938), his protagonist is a thirty-year-old, depressed bachelor, Roquentin, who has no family ties, friends, home, or steady occupation. He is *dégagé,* or detached, hence he mocks his freedom by avoiding the connections that would root him in reality. He has no stability in a world whose laws are contingent and unpredictable. After he has experienced and worked through his nausea at such a meaningless cosmos, he learns that man's solitude endows him with the potential of gaining his genuine freedom. He passes from self-deception to self-knowledge, discovers that he can only be what he makes of himself, and decides to give validity to his life by writing a novel. In *Les mouches* (*The Flies,* drama, 1943) Orestes is Sartre's existential champion. Like Roquentin, he enters the stage a rootless, purposeless cosmopolitan. He converts to authentic freedom by killing, as in Aeschylus' *Choēphoroi* (*The Libation Bearers,* drama, 458 B.C.), his mother Clytemnestra and her lover Aegisthus. In Sartre's play Zeus is not a providential God but only a fiction—the belief of weak, fearful people in such a God. Orestes defies him: "Once freedom lights its beacon in a man's heart, the gods are powerless against him." Orestes therefore asserts his dreadful freedom through his matricide, assumes his guilt without shame or remorse, and thereby sets the people of his land an example of atheistic self-reliance that Sartre clearly applauds.

Sartre and Malraux are joined by Albert Camus in a brilliant triad of French writers who incarnate Western humanism at its most eloquent level as they confront the nihilistic crisis first addressed by Nietzsche and Dostoevsky. All three recognize the senselessness of the universe and finitude of man's journey in it. But whereas Malraux tries to have his characters dignify their lives through heroic political deeds, and Sartre denies the present world of contingency in behalf of a secular future often organized by a Marxist dialectic, Camus bases his ethic on a continuing revolt against the temptation of despairing nihilism,. celebrating a classic harmony between man and the earth. In his first important essay, *The Myth of Sisyphus,* he asks how the absurd hero, recognizing life as irrational in a random world, can avoid suicide. He answers that the very value of life is enhanced by man's lucid consciousness of its irreducibility to his understanding. Lacking transcendence, life offers man opportunities for stoic heroism that Camus illustrates by citing two myths: Don Juan's and Sisyphus'. Don Juan realizes an ethic of quantity through his many seductions, intensely enjoying the adventure of the passing moment while aware of the void to come. An even more congenial model is Sisyphus. The Greek gods had condemned him to roll a rock up a mountainside, only to have it fall back down to the valley as a tormenting example of man's hopelessly futile labors. Camus admires Sisyphus most when he follows his rock down the mountain, knowing he is condemned to ceaseless punishment. His lucidity is part of Sisyphus' grandeur. It makes him "superior to his fate . . . stronger than his rock." His greatness—indeed, happiness—comes from the absurdist protagonist's "struggle toward the heights.'' Once man has resolutely accepted an absurb existence, its meaning-lessness will lose the power to appall him.

Camus moderates his romantic exaltation of absurdism in a subsequent med-itation, *L'homme révolté* (*The Rebel*, 1951). Here he analyzes the failure of two kinds of revolt against man's condition: Vertical transcendence through religious faith, which he dismisses as an attempt to evade the meaning of man's suffering in historic time by promising him bliss in the hereafter; and horizontal tran-scendence through revolutionary ideologies such as fascism or Marxism. Camus divides ideological revolts into two forms of totalitarianism: A nihilistic structure such as Nazism, whose followers distort Nietzsche's doctrines of the superman and the will to power; and a rational structure such as the French or Russian Revolution, whose aim is to erect such false gods as Logic or History. Sooner or later, he concludes, revolts in the name of ''absolute freedom'' or ''absolute justice'' turn into murderous tyrannies warring on individual liberty and replacing democratic dialogues with authoritarian directives. Camus' solution is a return to the concepts of compromise and equilibrium practiced by the Greeks. Man should think in terms of ''a measure of freedom . . . a measure of justice.'' He should value decency, honesty, love, and friendship above fanatic commitment to sweeping systems of salvation.

The dramatization of this sense of modest human solidarity is best accom-plished in *La peste* (*The Plague*, novel, 1947). Camus here allegorizes the German occupation of France during most of World War II in the configuration of the North African port of Oran, afflicted by bubonic plague. More generally, he symbolizes mankind's response to the prospect of injustice, suffering, and sudden death. The pestilence is not only a physical but a moral and spiritual menace, threatening to paralyze people's conscience and will to act. Camus distributes his sympathy among three featured personages who represent three diverse responses to the plague and all it signifies. Father Paneloux stands for religious submission. The death of innocents passes human understanding, but ''all trials, however cruel, worked together for good to the Christian.'' Tarrou used to be a fervent Communist, only to discover that revolutionary actions often made him a party to murder in the name of building a better society. Disillusioned, he withdraws from all social causes and prefers meditation to commitment: ''I've learned modesty. All I maintain is that on this earth there are pestilences and there are victims, and it's up to us, so far as possible, not to join forces with the pestilences.'' Camus' preferred advocate is Dr. Rieux, a medical humanist who is calm, empiric, and humble before the mystery of evil. All he can do is work scrupulously at his calling, knowing that his victories are at best temporary in a Godless world shaped by death. A more diffident incarnation of Camus' Sisyphus, he wages a limited but persistent daily battle against sickness and pain in a cosmos closed to transcendence. Like Sisyphus, he knows man is doomed to ''a never ending defeat.'' More than Sisyphus, he nonetheless delights in his physical senses, the friendship of fellow beings, and the beauty of the sea, sun, and earth.

Nietzsche and Dostoevsky, Malraux, Sartre, and Camus are among many thinkers and artists of the past 100 to 150 years who have responded to a void-haunted, void-fascinated cultural crisis. It is by now a banal but nonetheless accurate diagnosis to state that the modern sensibility has largely lost faith in both God and nature. The roots of this sense of nullity and victimization can be found in an overwhelmingly complex set of circumstances impossible to address in this entry. All that is possible, is a summation of the leading causes and features of a revolution in sensibility that may be best defined in William Butler Yeats' poem, "The Second Coming" (1921), which dramatizes his sense of the dissolution of Christian civilization: "Things fall apart; the center cannot hold; / Mere anarchy is loosed upon the world, / The blood-dimmed tide is loosed, and everywhere / The ceremony of innocence is drowned; / The best lack all conviction, while the worst / Are full of passionate intensity."

The Renaissance notion that man occupied a God-favored place at the core of the cosmos has been displaced by modern astronomy, with its discoveries that not only the planet earth but the whole solar system is finite, with a near-vacuum of interstellar and absolute void of intergalactic space beyond it. Nineteenth-century geology and biology have taught man that, far from being unique, his nature is continuous with that of other beasts and his future liable to their extinction. Twentieth-century depth psychology insists that man must disobey Socrates' mandate to know himself, since his self is at the mercy of often uncontrollable, unconscious impulses. Modern physics has shown him that he is adrift in an uncertain, unstable, relative, and therefore absurd universe. The cynical and cruel power of the totalitarian state has demonstrated the fragility of individual freedom. The impact of brutally destructive world wars, culminating in the first nuclear explosions, has increased man's disillusionment with history to the point of despair. No wonder, then, that such a climate of thought and feeling has inspired an apocalyptic vision, a sense by many writers that life lacks authenticity and meaning, with the literary artist forced to labor in a world that no longer makes sense as it reaches the end of its destiny: "After us the Savage God" (Yeats, *Autobiographies,* 1955).

The author whose work most typically depicts the contemporary demons of nihilism is Franz Kafka. Kafka relates to Dostoevsky and Conrad in dramatizing a world of isolation and obsession, guilt, betrayal, and labyrinthine pursuit. Unlike Dostoevsky, however, he cannot accept saintliness on earth as a passage to transcendent love. Unlike Conrad, he cannot rest on such traditional virtues as honesty, courage, pity, and fidelity. Unlike Dante, Milton, or the later Eliot, he cannot walk across any comforting bridges of doctrine that would join man to God. Instead, ironically yet humbly, Kafka accepts life as essentially inscrutable for man, with the Court of Justice unavailable, the Castle of Grace unreachable. His writings reflect the spirit of the critic Cyril Connolly's statement: "It is closing time in the Gardens of the West. From now on an artist will be judged only by the resonance of his solitude or by the quality of his despair" *(Horizon* 20 [1949–1950] :362).

Kafka's protagonists are invariably victims, lost and often hunted in a nightmarish world governed by powers that are authoritarian, veiled, pitiless, and often unapproachable. They are condemned to face the trial of their lives in a fear-blanketed, enigmatic universe they can never hope to understand, let alone control. Thus "Das Urteil" ("The Judgment," short story, 1913) shows a father and son locked in a life-and-death struggle, with the son bending to his father's irrational tyranny to commit suicide because he regards his father as representing an incomprehensible Law of Life that the son has somehow violated. In "Die Verwandlung" ("The Metamorphosis," story, 1915) another son agrees with his parents and sister that he is unfit to live and dies when he has arrived at a full realization of the ingratitude and loathing with which his family rewards his love and devotion. In "Ein Hungerkünstler" ("A Hunger Artist," story, 1922) a performer starves himself to death because he has come to recognize that the modern age has no place for either the artist or the religious mystic, that a spiritual existence cannot compete with the cravings of materialism. In "Der Jäger Gracchus" ("The Hunter Gracchus," story, 1917) Kafka depicts a dead hunter who has followed the pattern of Christ's crucifixion but who fails to be received, either by his Father in the other world or by mankind in this one. In "Ein Landarzt" ("A Country Doctor," story, 1919) a physician is called out to heal the wound of man's mundane existence, to justify the meaning of man's life. He cannot do so and is condemned to wander astray, "naked, exposed to the frost of this most unhappy of ages."

In *Der Prozess* (*The Trial*, novel, 1925) Joseph K. is seized by the same truth as all of Kafka's other anti-heroes: by an awareness that he is accountable for his every act (and failure to act) before a summary court that will never adjourn and never acquit him, no matter how innocent he may be. In Kafka's world, not only Joseph K. but every human being is guilty. None of us has fully realized his possibilities, has lived a completely honest life, has failed to employ countless ruses to escape the tortures of self-awareness. Kafka's ultimate ethical rigor spares no one. He regards the tradition of Western individualism with hopelessness and dismay. He insists that loneliness and exclusion, anxiety and punishment are man's ineradicable stigmata. In one of his aphorisms he states, "There is a goal, but there is no way" (*Hochzeitsvorbereitungen auf dem Lande* [*Wedding Preparations in the Country*, posthumous collection, 1953]).

Nihilism is at least a shaping and perhaps the central theme of modern literature as it denies its classic heritage of rationalism, repose, harmony, order, confidence, and continuity. The most characteristic contemporary writing is marked by a preoccupation with cruelty, chaos, destruction, dissociation, impotence, impossibility and despair, by what the critic Lionel Trilling has called a "bitter line of hostility to civilization" (*Beyond Culture*, 1965). Thus Samuel Beckett (1906–   ) assumes the decline and often the death of Western culture's stock assumptions: parental and filial devotion, sexual attraction, love, honor, compassion, friendship, God's caring presence. Novelists such as Marcel Proust (1871–1922), André Gide (1869–1951), James Joyce (1882–1941), Virginia Woolf (1882–1941), and William Faulkner

(1897–1962) reject the traditional view of human nature as explorable, know-able, and definable, instead emphasizing flows of their characters' disorderly perceptions and sensations.

Taken to an irrational extreme, this atomism results in such assaults on es-tablished forms as dadaism and surrealism, warring against all conscious con-nections and controls, affirming the anarchy of the unconscious, of what André Breton termed "pure psychic automatism" (*Manifeste du surréalisme* [*What Is Surrealism?*, 1924]). In modern poetry symbolism is the dominant mode, seeking to remove poetic language as far as possible from its referential or representational contexts, instead stressing such nondiscursive elements as magic, the occult, the dream, the image. (See the works of such poets as Baudelaire (1821–1867), Verlaine (1844–1896), Mallarmé (1842–1898), Rimbaud (1854–1891), Pound (1885–1972), Eliot (1888–1965). Dominant in contemporary prose is randomness and fragmentation of both form and subject matter, with parodistic and self-consciously absurd fictiveness stressed by Vladimir Nabokov (1899–1977) and Jorge Luis Borges (1889–1986). The most programmatic school of contemporary novelists is that of the "chosistes," whose theories are best expressed in Alain Robbe-Grillet's *Pour un nouveau roman* (*For a New Novel*, 1963). Robbe-Grillet and such allied writers as Nathalie Sarraute (1902–   ) and Michel Butor (1926–   ), seek to exclude plot, characterization, social statements, even metaphors and symbols from their texts. They argue that no writer should attempt psychological analysis, that it is impossible to understand either individual human nature or man's cosmos. Hence the writer should content himself with *chosisme* ("thingishness"): the minute, precise, detached description of physical objects—period. "The world is neither significant nor absurd," says Robbe-Grillet, es-chewing even minimal interpretation. "It simply *Is*." Thus do the theorists and practitioners of the nouveau roman return to nihilism's first definition: they empty the world of meaning.

See also: Alienation, Anti-hero, Existentialism, Theatrical Absurdity, Un-derground Man, Universe.

Selected Bibliography

Barrett, William. *Irrational Man: A Study in Existential Philosophy*. Garden City, New York: Doubleday Anchor Books, 1958.

Glicksberg, Charles. *The Literature of Nihilism*. Lewisburg, Pennsylvania: Bucknell University Press, 1975.

Howe, Irving. *Politics and the Novel*. Cleveland and New York: The World Publishing Company, 1957.

Kurrik, Maire. *Literature and Negation*. New York: Columbia University Press, 1979.

GERHARD BRAND

NOBLE CRIMINAL

The noble criminal is a universal and enduring legendary figure, variously identified as romantic highwayman, social bandit, noble brigand, or robber-hero. Epitomized in the stereotypical character of Robin Hood, he has over the years often changed his dress, his habitat, and, superficially, the manner of performing his lawless deeds. The forest may be replaced by the city slum or the Western plains; the bow and arrow or musket, by the machine gun or six-shooter; but essentially the myth remains the same: the fearless, solitary outlaw (often accompanied by a band), dedicated more or less to the defense of the helpless, the righting of wrongs, the humbling of the rich and powerful, and the dauntless display of extraordinary courage, as well, at times, of superhuman powers deemed to be beyond the ken of the common run of men.

General Origin and Background

Often based on historical events and personages, the legendary type has, from earliest times, flaunted in bravura style the prevailing conventions. However, it is not until the eighteenth and nineteenth centuries that his real place in the historical or literary tradition is firmly and widely established, particularly as a popular figure in romanticism.

The appearance of the outlaw seems to occur when living conditions among the larger mass of a society are such that frustration, anger, fear, insecurity, poverty, discrimination, protest, and lack of hope are widespread among the people. Political corruption or ineffectualness, economic hardship, and discriminatory social justice most often create or accompany such conditions. It is then that the individual renegade, profiting from the breakdown of law and order or from the inability of government to administer efficiently and justly, takes to the hills or highways with a band of like-spirited companions. At first, to be sure, the dominant motive of the band is likely to be survival and personal gain. Soon, however, the bandit chief, being most often an astute strategist, recognizes the importance of popular support for his own protection and that of his band. It is then that he adopts the role of champion of the oppressed and that the mythologizing process begins. The poor and disenfranchised now discover a defender, an avenger, and one who can mete out justice ruthlessly and swiftly. The vanity of the outlaw feeds and grows on such adulation and is spurred to greater and greater feats of rebellious lawlessness that no longer challenge just the local gendarmerie but the national police and army as well. Except that no organized social or political group-protest is involved, the struggle takes on at times the character of guerrilla warfare. The fact that the odds against the bandit leader are now overwhelming only serves to increase the support and even the enthusiasm of the populace for the lonely "hero." When inevitably he is captured, in spite of his superior talents and superhuman powers, it is only, by the general popular belief, because of cowardly betrayal.

Early Examples

Since the topic of the brigand-hero is so common in almost every national literature, it is possible to give only a small sampling of its literary exploitation.

In Boccaccio's *Il decamerone* (*Decameron*, novellas, c.1350), the second tale of The Tenth Day, the story of Ghino di Tacco is told. Banished from Siena on account of his truculence, Ghino led a revolt against the Church of Rome. Head of an army, lord of a castle and notorious ruler of much land, he is a fearless bandit-plunderer who nonetheless manifests great courtesy and generosity toward the captured abbot of Cluny merely to prove to the latter (and through him to the world) his innate high qualities of mind and spirit.

In Shakespeare's *Two Gentlemen of Verona* (play, c. 1594), Valentine is invited to join a band of outlaws and become their leader. Like them, he is a victim of injustice and oppression; but, in addition, he is also noble, educated, handsome, and virtuous. In the end, he succeeds in gaining understanding and pardon from the authorities for his outlaw friends who deserve "great employment" on account of their "worthy qualities."

Cervantes' *Don Quijote* (*Don Quixote*, novel, 1605, 1615) contains a kind of prototype of the bandit-hero in the person of Rogue Guinart. He is an example of the high-minded highwaymen that abound in Spanish literature, particularly in the picaresque novel.

Examples in the Last Three Centuries

The Beggar's Opera (satire, 1728), by John Gay, through the figure of the handsome, well-mannered hero-outlaw Macheath, has enjoyed great popularity from its first presentation. He and his gang are indeed more virtuous and principled than the so-called legitimate gentlemen of authority who are given to corruption and hypocrisy as a way of life.

The case of Germany is of particular interest for two reasons. First, because the literature of the noble bandit is so popular a genre, special terms have been created to identify it; namely, *Räuberromantik* (bandit romanticism) and *Räuberromane* (bandit novels). Second, because two of the greatest German writers, Goethe and Schiller, each wrote a whole play on the theme.

Goethe's *Götz von Berlichingen* (play, 1773) is about a hero who is more knight than outlaw because he is a hero of the people in political rebellion. He is unlike the noblemen of his time, for he considers himself their superior in morals.

Eight years later, Schiller, in *Die Räuber* (play, *The Robbers*), was equally successful in making an impression upon the public with his highly dramatic treatment of the same theme. The outlaw-hero, Karl Moor, epitomizes all that the gallant, high-minded, intelligent, badly treated, and devil-may-care noble bandit-leader should be. *Sturm und Drang* is the romantic literary expression of the times, of which the play is an illustration.

Some other works that utilize the common romantic idea of the essentially good, moral man who is driven to violence or crime before the sight of cruel injustice are: Victor Hugo, *Hernani* (play, 1830); Walter Scott, *Rob Roy* (novel, 1817); Heinrich von Kleist, *Michael Kohlhaas* (novel, 1810); A. Pushkin, *Dubrovskiĭ* (*Dubrovsky*, published posthumously in 1841); Prosper Mérimée, *Carmen* (novella, 1845) and *Colomba* (novella, 1840); A. Dumas, *Le Comte de Monte-Cristo* (*The Count of Monte Cristo*, novel, 1844).

Where social banditry is endemic, the literature is replete with real or imaginary bandit-heroes. Bandits and bandit myths are important facts of life and impossible to overlook. Besides the Western European countries already mentioned, Hungary, Romania, Czechoslovakia, and Turkey are noted for many such literary types. Even in Chinese literature, as for example in *Wu Tse-t'ien ssu-ta ch'i-an* (*Dee Goong An: Three Murder Cases Solved by Judge Dee*), an anonymous nineteenth-century detective novel, we encounter "brothers of the green woods," who are highwaymen of the Robin Hood type. They too are compelled to turn to a life of crime following some injustice suffered.

In *A Criminal as Hero, Angelo Duca* (1979), besides recounting the story of a legendary eighteenth-century southern Italian noble criminal, Angelo Duca, I have tried to identify and describe the chief traits of this literary figure in various types of popular and classical writing.

It might be added, finally, that modern-day newspaper and magazine articles, as well as radio and television programs, offer continuous examples of scofflaws possessed, in varying degrees, of noble, unselfish compulsions to correct singly, when all other means are presumably denied, certain envisaged wrongs by society or persons in authority. When the forms of such individual unlawful action are carried to the unconscionable extreme of indiscriminate murder, assassination, kidnapping, or other violent mayhem, we then have terrorism and not, by definition, heroic criminality.

See also: Detective.

Selected Bibliography

Hobsawm, Eric. *Bandits*. New York: Delacorte Press, 1969.
————. *Primitive Rebels: Studies in Archaic Forms of Social Movement in the 19th and 20th Centuries*. New York: Norton, 1965 [originally published in 1959 under the title *Social Bandits and Primitive Rebels*].

PAUL F. ANGIOLILLO

NOBLE SAVAGE

A noble savage (n.s.) refers to a person possessing natural or primitive virtues (such as purity), candor, kindness, and bravery; someone who is free from the restraints and falsification of civilization. The notion of the n. s. is inseparable from that of Western European civilization which in its modern entente had only come into being as late as the eighteenth century, along with scientific rationalism, subjectivity, the making of the human being as object of its knowledge, democratization, and the ethnocentric universal comparativeness of *Kultur* soon afterwards to be stamped in Germany. This explains why the n. s. enjoyed his greatest literary vogue between approximately 1700 and 1850, without completely fading from Western artistic and ideological representations.

"Savage" traditionally meant untamed rather than cruel or fierce. An explicit or implied comparison between a more sophisticated European society and the n. s., seen as morally superior, has been a usual concomitant of the theme. Its typical representative was the native American. Otherwise the African, South Sea Islander, and (East) Indian were chosen as subjects as well. In the beginning, he was assumed to correspond to a Rousseauistic earlier stage of social development; he could also be mythologically identified with early Europeans or with a social class of farmers, the peasantry, thought to have remained at that stage. The latter are, however, somewhat marginal uses of the term. With recent socio-anthropological trends, such as structuralism and post-structuralism, the demystification of the n. s. does not preclude a protectionist idealization of cultures of the Third World that have not stepped into Western modern time.

Background in Antiquity and the Middle Ages

The belief that man at one time led a happier life in harmony with nature has been an abiding one. Various mythologies—indeed some contemporary Western but mostly non-Western religious denominations—treat intellectual knowledge and progress as a revolt against God or the gods and therefore sinful from at least the divine point of view. The Bible itself sets the blessed natural state in Eden before the Fall against the tainted and wretched condition of mankind subsequent to original sin. This fostered, until the Renaissance, a nature-culture polarity in Western thought. Simplicity and Ignorance were viewed as virtuous; knowledge and culture as wicked and corrupting.

The Greeks and Romans had a parallel with the Judeo-Christian concept of man before the Fall in their tradition about the Golden Age. Empedocles (c.493–c.433 B.C.) held that it was dominated by love; strife gradually took over in the course of history. Diodorus Siculus (1st century B.C.) transmits the belief that people untouched by civilization once lived on happy isles. The *Naturalis historia* (*Natural History*, c. A.D. 77) of Pliny the Elder assumes an earlier period in history when men were happy and innocent. Tacitus' *Germania* (A.D. 98) described the Germans as simpler and more virile and virtuous than the Romans. In much the same vein as Rousseau was to speak of his n. s., classical literature also developed the pastoral genre and convention to celebrate the primitive contentment of shepherds and shepherdesses in the lap of nature.

The idyllic note was carried on in the medieval *pastourelles*. More significantly, heathens of a noble turn of mind were occasionally introduced into literature. The most conspicuous example is Saladin, whose generosity and chivalry earned great praise; he appears among others in *Le cento novelle antiche* (stories, probably late 13th century but printed in 1525) and the famous ring parable (1.3) of Boccaccio's *Il decamerone* (*Decameron*, novellas, c.1350).

The Renaissance

In the Middle Ages ancient myths about the happy isles and the Golden Age tended to be confused with the earthly paradise. The discovery of America seemed to confirm these myths. In fact, Columbus had set out to find the terrestrial paradise, and his reports were designed to prove that he had done so. The natives were innocent, peaceful and open-hearted. Their nudity and propertyless state recalled Edenic images. The Caribbean especially came to be identified with the Garden of Eden.

On the other hand, the conviction that civilization is corrupt can be clearly discerned in sixteenth-century thought. Erasmus (*Moriae encomium* [*The Praise of Folly,* essay, 1511]) states that the simple people of the Golden Age needed no school knowledge; nature alone sufficed to guide them. Sir Thomas More, who set his ideal state (*Utopia,* political romance, 1516) on an island, was cognizant of accounts about South American natives.

A cry of protest soon rose against the inhuman conduct of the conquerors. Las Casas (*Brevissima relación de la destruyción de las Indias* [*A Brief Narration of the Destruction of the Indies,* 1552]) condemned the enslavement of Indians, emphasizing their modesty and loyalty. Ronsard, in "Complainte contre fortune" (poem, 1559), defended their rights. He portrayed the Indian as enviable and happy in his natural state and accused the white man of exporting an evil civilization to the New World.

Much of the literature of the age was favorable to the Indian's cause. Jean de Léry, who described American natives as friendly and happy in his book *Histoire d'un voyage faict en la terre du Brésil* (1578), brought back a group of indigenes who elicited a great deal of sympathy in France and were for centuries to serve as models for the n. s. Sir Walter Raleigh, in *The Discoverie of Guiana* (1596), delineates the proud, wise Indian chief, a Cacique by the name of Topiawari, ready to be adopted by Chateaubriand and Cooper.

Two of Montaigne's *Essais* (*Essays,* 1580–1588) extol the American Indian. "Des cannibales" ("Of Cannibals," 1.3) asserts that the European exceeds in barbarity the so-called savage, who is governed by the laws of nature. "Des coches" ("Of Coaches," 3.6) maintains the moral superiority of the savages over the unscrupulous whites.

The fictional treatment of the n. s. started in Spain, within the pastoral convention, which flourished during the Renaissance. Whereas Jorge de Montemayor's romance *Los siete libros de la Diana* (*Diana,* 1559) still pictures the Indian as more or less repugnant, Gil Polo, in *Diana enamorada* (pastoral romance, 1564), approximates the n. s. in his description of the Indian hero of a boat tournament. Alonso de Ercilla y Zúñiga's *La araucana* (*The Araucaniad,* epic, 1569–1590) relates the resistance of the Araucanian Indians in Chile; their chief, the brave Caupolicán, is tortured and put to death.

It is most certainly arguable that the Renaissance exploited the Christian notion of man's uniqueness on the planet and the universe and by doing so initiated an anthropocentric and ethnocentric perception of humanity in disparity with Nature. The discovery of America was to reinforce that anthropocentric notion and was to contribute to the shattering of a traditionally more stable concept of space and Nature. Within anthropocentricity lies the dissolution of a togetherness in Nature, and thus the nostalgia or idealization of a natural state, of the n. s.

The Seventeenth Century

While it put logic on a pedestal, seventeenth-century philosophy did not consider reason and nature to be necessarily contradictory. A case in point is Locke, for whom reason was a natural faculty possessed by all mankind. This requires, however, that we distinguish the notion of human nature with that of Nature. The first includes the separability of man from Nature, his reasoning uniqueness, and thus his power over Nature, which becomes idealized. In effect, Nature retained its appeal to many writers, and the tastes of the general public responded readily to the exotic and primitive.

Gomberville's *Polexandre* (*The History of Polexander,* heroic romance, 1629–1638), highly popular in its day, shows the first inroad of exoticism into French literature. It parades South American Indians side by side with chivalric Turks and Moors. Influenced by French adventure novels, the English drama of the restoration period reveled in the exotic. Incas, Persians, or Aztecs were used to satisfy the public's demand for outlandish costumes, bombastic speech, and violent action. Robert Howard's play *The Indian Queen* (1664) has Aztec characters shown without any true local color. John Dryden's *The Indian Emperor* (1665) pictures Montezuma committing suicide rather than converting to Christianity; his son chooses to live far from Mexico to remain free. The term "n. s." is thought to have been used in English literature for the first time in Dryden's heroic play, *The Conquest of Granada* (1670), where it is put in the mouth of Almanzor, a noble Moor who turns out to be the lost son of a Spanish grandee. "I am as free as nature first made man, / Ere the first laws or servitude began,/ When wild in woods the noble savage ran."

The same heroic-exotic tradition is responsible for Aphra Behn's seventeenth-century bestseller, *Oroonoko, Or the History of the Royal Slave* (1688). Though a novel, it was influenced mainly by contemporary drama. Oroonoko, an African sold into slavery in Surinam—Behn lived there as a child—is rather Europeanized both in manner and appearance, although his complexion is described as jet black. In Southerne's dramatization (1695), Oroonoko's beloved, Imoinda, actually became a white girl driven to Africa.

In sum, the seventeenth century might be viewed as casting the dice of rationalism that in turn will finalize in the West the disparity of man and Nature. Man will, from now on, belong to his world rather than Nature, whose idealization will remain, however, vivid. Instead of imitating Nature, man represents it, imagines it, and re-creates it and its n. s.

Eighteenth-Century Satire

Between roughly 1700 and 1750 the n. s. appears in literature chiefly as a weapon in the author's hands to castigate society's faults, in keeping with the spirit of the Enlightenment and presumably influenced by the critical attitude of the missionaries. The latter tended to set up natives as models for their own compatriots, even at the risk of attributing Christian virtues to unbaptized "savages." Thus du Tertre, a Dominican, stated in his *Histoire générale des isles . . .* (1654) that Indians possessed certain virtues *because* they were not civilized.

In 1710 four so-called Indian kings went to London, attracting much attention there. A year later Addison published papers in the *Spectator,* purporting to be by the pen of an Indian chief residing in London, in which he disapproved in particular of the Europeans' lack of religion. He could observe no devotion in St. Paul's; he ridiculed wigs, breeches and petticoats, calling them barbarous. The fourth volume of *Gulliver's Travels* (satire, 1726) describes the Houyhnhnms, stressing their simple mores. They have been cited as examples of the n. s. Yet Swift explicitly states that they do not merely obey the dictates of Nature. For Defoe's Robinson (*Robinson Crusoe,* novel, 1719) the servant Friday is not an ideal. Crusoe's primitive life is the result of necessity instead of choice. Yet Friday possesses a certain pleasing candidness not alien to the n. s. tradition; and the Englishman's embarrassments in trying to explain some Christian dogmas may be ironic on the author's part. Montesquieu's *Lettres persanes* (*Persian Letters,* 1721) only tangentially concerns the theme, since the Persians are not characterized as uncivilized or innocent; it inspired, however, a spate of works in the epistolary style attributed to fictitious savages. Of these, Françoise de Graffigny's *Lettres d'une Péruvienne* (*Letters of a Peruvian Princess,* epistolary romance, 1747), about an Indian girl residing in Paris and remaining faithful to her fiancé, may be mentioned as an example.

Although he preached tolerance, Voltaire did not have much sympathy for the natural state. Indeed, the French master of satire and reason, in opposition to the notion of the n. s. has written apologetically in favor of the epicurean way of city life and of the usefulness of commercial and industrial economics for the wealth of nations and the luxury of life, as illustrated in *Le mondain* (*The Man about Town,* poem, 1736). Nevertheless, he chose the fashionable exotic setting in three of his tragedies, *Alzire* (*Alzira,* 1736), where an Indian chief saves the life of the Spanish governor of Peru, *Zaïre* (*Zaira,* 1732), about a Christian girl brought up in a seraglio and *L'orphelin de la Chine* (*The Orphan of China,* 1755), on the Mongol conquest of China. The protagonist of *L'ingénu* (philosophical tale, 1767) is a young French Canadian raised among the Hurons (Iroquois) who travels to Europe and becomes a loyal soldier of the king ("Huron" was almost a synonym for n. s. in eighteenth-century France). As the title implies, Voltaire's hero resembles Candide, the naïve young man in search of truth, rather than the n. s. proper. Yet, as the embodiment of simplicity, frankness, and natural good sense coming into contact with the absurd conventions of French society, he is a related type.

Closer to the notion of the n. s., Diderot's dialogue *Supplément au voyage de Bougainville* (*A Supplement to Bougainville's Voyage,* 1796) expounded his belief that Western civilization had vitiated society and, in some respects, narrowly confined man's natural instincts. Although Diderot was not recommending a return to nature, in praising the lot of the n. s. of Tahiti he was suggesting, in the name of biological man, a modification of certain unnatural laws and artificial restraints in French society.

Like Lahontan's earlier (1704) *Dialogue de Monsieur le baron de Lahontan et d'un sauvage, dans l'Amérique . . .* , *Dialogues of the Dead* (1760) by George Lyttelton made use of the conversational form to drive home the point that the so-called savage is not inferior to the white man; scalping—taken by the author to be a custom of Indian origin—is seen as less abominable than dueling. In a similar spirit, the Danish bishop Erik Pontoppidan wrote *Menoza, en asiatisk prins* (epistolary novel, 1742) about Tandi, who travels around the world in a vain search for true Christians. Lenz's *Der neue Menoza* (*The New Menoza,* comedy, 1774) has the prince settle in Naumburg and fall in love with a German girl. This is a typical *Sturm und Drang* drama, where satire, although caustic, plays only a secondary role. *Die Indianer in England* (*The Indians in England*), a play by Kotzebue written in 1789, exploits the naïveté of Gurli, daughter of the "Nabob" of Mysore, for its comic potential.

Thus, on the wake of the Industrial Revolution, a new world is being structured, away from Nature, with which Western man has no more affinity with correspondences and reciprocities. From now on, he acts in a cultural, technician environment that will be vilified—and still is—by literature and the arts. It is the ideological guilty conscience. As stated by M. Foucault, it is the reign of subjectivity, the preeminence of finitude, and the will to power.

Sentimental and Romantic Treatment (1750–1850)

Just as romantic traits can be observed in earlier compositions, social criticism will not be absent from numerous works written after 1750. Nevertheless, the predominant mood becomes sentimental in the later eighteenth century. Rousseau's *Discours sur l'origine et les fondements de l'inégalité parmi les hommes* (*Discourse on the Origin and Bases of Inequality among Men,* 1754) taught that man, originally simple and natural, had been free and happy. It was the idea of personal property that led to exploitation and indigence. *Emile* (novel, 1762) sets forth the training of a natural man. Yet it may be noted that Rousseau denied wanting to sent Emile "back to the woods."

Interest in the child was a hallmark of English and German romanticism as well. The cult of the n. s. during the period may be seen as an aspect of this preoccupation. Montaigne had already called savages "children of nature." For the romantic temper the n. s. represented nature's innocent child as opposed to the corrupted and scheming man of the Old World. The story of Inkle and Yarico illustrates this contrast. Based on a story in Mocquet's *Voyages en Afrique, Asie, Indes . . .* (1617), it became the subject of countless adaptations in English, French, and German. On the island of Barbados, the Indian girl Yarico rescues a shipwrecked white, Inkle, from her savage tribe. She trusts his vows of fidelity and bears a child by him. But upon the arrival of a white ship he promptly abandons her and even sells her off into slavery. The story was taken up in Ligon's *History of Barbados* (1650), recounted in Marmontel's narrative *L'amitié à l'épreuve* (*Friendship Put to the Test*, 1761) and dramatized by George Colman's farcical comedy, *Inkle and Yarico* (1787).

The Romantic often perceived a parallel between his own childhood and that of humanity, whose extant specimen was the n. s. In *Prelude* (poem, 1799–1805) Wordsworth compares his early environment with that of an Indian child. Ruth, heroine of the short poem by the same title (1799), is an idealized child of nature growing up in an Indian village. Iddeah and Christina in Mary Mitford's *Christina, the Maid of the South Seas* (poem, 1811) are her spiritual sisters. So is Mooma in Southey's *A Tale of Paraguay* (poem, 1825). In this epic a couple, the last survivors of a tribe that had succumbed to barbarous rites, live alone in the jungle. Mooma is their daughter. Maturin's gothic novel *Melmoth the Wanderer* (1820) is about a Faustian figure, which makes the contrast all the more sharp with Immalee, reared on a deserted island in the estuary of the Ganges. She "lived like a flower" and could not distinguish herself from the plants surrounding her.

Byron, in canto 2 of *Childe Harold* (poem, 1812), attributes n. s. characteristics to the Albanians. The attraction of the country to him is that it reminds him of his native Highlands, where he once roamed as a "careless child." Finally, in his last poem he projected the nostalgic vision into the actual n. s. *The Island: or Christian and his comrades* (1823) relates the mutiny of the *Bounty*. A group of sailors settle on the island of Toobonai off Tahiti. Neuha, the native girl, enters into union with one of the sailors. A perfect n. s., she is faithful and innocent. Stories by two authors whose production falls already into the period of realism portray women belonging to a similar type: *Die Narrenburg* (*Crazy Castle*, 1841) by Stifter, and Gottfried Keller's "Pankraz der Schmoller" (1856).

The Romantics frequently perceived n. s. traits in European peasants, particularly in regions of scenic splendor such as Lapland, Norway, Scotland, Switzerland, and Wales. Europe's past (the Middle Ages and pre-Christian times; Celtic, Norse, and Teutonic mythology, both genuine and invented) was used to create analogous figures. In Southey's *Madoc* (poem, 1805) the medieval and exotic inspirations merge. A Welsh prince of the twelfth century, Madoc, who according to legend founded a colony in Florida, finds it easy to understand the simple religion of the Aztecs, who are portrayed as free, handsome, and happy.

Since preromanticism, there had been efforts to restore bardic poetry; owing to the supposed spiritual kinship of the primitive European with the aborigines of the colonies, bardic prosody was now utilized to apostrophize the Red Indian. The notion that the savage is a natural poet goes back at least as far as Montaigne's "Des cannibales"—where he is credited with extraordinary proficiency in the chanting of both war and love songs—and Sidney's *A Defense of Poetry* (prose essay, 1595). A talent for poetry and singing remained an intrinsic part of the n. s. as portrayed in literature.

The dying Indian stoically addressing his tribesmen or his executioners became a literary commonplace. "An American Love-Ode" (1747) by Thomas Warton is the oldest known example. His son, Joseph, wrote "The Dying Indian" (poem, 1748). Wordsworth's "The Complaint of a Forsaken Indian Woman" (1798) renders the lament of a sick squaw, left by her companions to die in the snow. Southey's "Songs of the American Indians" (1799) are short dramatic lyrics in blank verse, imitating Klopstock's revival of old German ballads. In Germany Christian Schubart wrote "Der sterbende Indianer an seinen Sohn" (1786) and Schiller composed "Nadowessische Todtenklage" ("Nadowessian Death-Lament," 1798 [both poems on the same theme]).

The black man too was credited with poetic gifts. In Thomas Day and John Bicknell's *The Dying Negro: A Poetical Epistle* (poem, 1773) the hero commits suicide to avoid separation from a white woman. Mungo Park's *Travels ... in ... Africa* (1796–1797) relates that blacks excel at extempore songs and love music.

The Red Indian was reputed to be a remarkable orator as well as singer. Examples of Indian eloquence go back to Columbus and Raleigh. Chief Logan's speech is perhaps the most famous of all. It was printed in Jefferson's *Notes on the State of Virginia* (1784–1785). Logan refused to participate in making a treaty. In Bowles' *The Missionary of the Andes* (poem, 1813), Attacapa's lament for his son is based on Logan's oration. Adalbert von Chamisso wrote several sentimental poems treating Indians, of which "Rede des alten Kriegers Bunte-Schlange" (1829) may be mentioned. Lenau published two melancholy poems after his return from a trip to America (1833). "Der Indianerzug" pictures a tribe, driven from their native land, being addressed by their chief. In "Die drei Indianer" a father speaks to his two sons before they commit suicide in the waves of the Niagara.

Another favorite motif was the courageous and morally superior Red Indian chieftain who saves the white man's life. This appears in *Manco-Capac, premier Inca du Pérou,* Le Blanc de Guillet's play of 1763 based on the life of the last Inca, treacherously murdered after giving refuge to Spaniards who had rebelled against Pizarro. In Henry Mackenzie's *The Man of Feeling* (novel, 1771), a soldier is found in the woods and is cared for by an Indian. Red men play rescuing roles in Marmontel's *Les Incas* (narrative, 1777), Seume's once highly popular poem "Der Wilde" (1800), and Campbell's *Gertrude of Wyoming* (poem, 1809).

By 1800, the extinction of the American Indian overshadowed many literary compositions. It was one of Chateaubriand's major concerns in the prose epic *Les Natchez* (*The Natchez*, 1793–1800, publ. 1826) as well as in the love stories *Atala* (1801) and *René* (1802). Chateaubriand does not show much familiarity with Indian ways; his idealized natives are mouthpieces for Rousseauesque ideas and men of sensibility like the autobiographical hero René himself. It was the author's rich emotionality and musical style that made Chief Chactas into a paragon of the n. s. *The Leatherstocking Tales* (novels, 1823–1841), on the other hand, display superb mastery of the native background. Cooper adopted the elegiac tone and drew a clear dividing line between good and bad Indians, which permitted the personage of Chingachgook to remain comfortably within the tradition of the n. s. In Longfellow's *The Song of Hiawatha* (narrative poem, 1855), a belated romantic work, the demigod Hiawatha symbolically withdraws to the heavenly hunting grounds at the appearance of the white man.

Latin American Writing

For Spanish America, France served as a particularly fecund source of inspiration. After the publication of *Atala,* literature became tinted with *indianismo.* The Ecuadorian Olmedo (1780–1847) adapted a passage of the work to poetry; his compatriot, Mera, inspired by Chateaubriand, told the tragic love affair of an Indian woman and a Spaniard in his novel *Cumandá, un drama entre salvajes* (1877). Echeverría, noted for introducing romanticism into the Argentine, wrote *La cautiva* (1837), a poem with an Indian setting, and the Columbian poet José Eusebio Caro wrote *En boca del ultimo Inca* (poem, 1855).

Indianismo was a prominent tendency in Brazilian romanticism as well. José Basilio da Gama is regarded as its greatest precursor; his *O Uruguay: poema epico* (1769) depicts the Spanish-Portuguese war against the revolt of 1750. Alencar's *O Guarany* (novel, 1857) extols the valor of the Brazilian Indian. In these works, whose motivation is very different from subsequent *indianista* literature, the native still figures as the embodiment of the n. s. as derived from traditional models.

Counterparts in Later Fiction

With the development of ethnography and comparative anthropology, the term "n. s." became gradually obsolete. Yet related and parallel concepts can be distinguished, and further references are confined to indicating the kinds of works in which these appear. In Russia, writers attracted by untamed vigor looked primarily to the indigenous peasant; for a more exotic inspiration they might turn though to the Siberian steppe, as did Leskov in *Na Kraiu sveta* (narrative, 1875–1876), whose heathen hero could teach a lesson to many a Christian. Nietzsche's blond beast of the Teutonic past, not altogether dissimilar to the n. s., haunts the twentieth century in a work like Gide's *L'immoraliste (The Immoralist,* novel, 1902).

In the United States, the post-frontier-era Western tended to see the Indian either as the bastardly enemy or the reformed but subservient native, and sympathetic treatments of rebellious Reds remaining faithful to their native gods, such as Iapi or Howling Wolf in Hamlin Garland's *The Book of the American Indian* (1923), were exceptional. By contrast, Westerns written by European authors, particularly for juvenile readers, left the n. s. idea almost intact. A case in point is Karl May's phenomenally successful *Winnetou* (1893–1910); novels in the same vein were published all over the Continent (e.g., *Sulle frontiere del Far-West,* 1908, by Emilio Salgari). Mowgli in Kipling's *Jungle Books* (1894–1895) and Burroughs' Tarzan (*Tarzan of the Apes,* 1914) may be considered distant cousins of the n. s.

Certain tendencies in the cultural climate since the 1960s have fostered the portrayal of characters similar to the traditional n. s., though in an altered context. One of these, man's reintegration into nature, stamps, for example, the last phase of Aldous Huxley's novelistic output: *Island* (1962) pictures a South Sea paradise. Arrabal's 1967 *L'architecte et l'empereur d'Assyrie* (*The Architect and the Emperor of Assyria)* reorchestrates Robinson Crusoe. The so-called Architect in the play, both innocent and immortal before coming into contact with civilization, becomes mortal when he loses his harmony with nature. Kopit's *Indians* (play, 1968) shows Sitting Bull in a positive light, alien to the stereotyped Western motion-picture image. So are also the movie series on Tarzan, or John Boorman's *The Emerald Forest Diary: A Filmmaker's Odyssey* (1985), which portrays the peaceful, culturally rich, lovable Brazilian Indians.

See also: Arcadia, Peasant in Novels.

Selected Bibliography

Bissell, Benjamin. *The American Indian in English Literature of the Eighteenth Century.* New Haven, Conn.: Yale University Press, 1925.

Chinard, Gilbert. *L'Amérique et le rêve exotique dans la littérature française au XVIIe et au XVIIIe siècles.* Paris: Hachette, 1913.

Fairchild, Hoxie Neale. *The Noble Savage: A Study in Romantic Naturalism.* New York: Columbia University Press, 1928.

Verdevoge, Paul, and Jorge Bogliano. "Littératures hispano-américaines." *Encyclopédie de la Pléiade, Histoire des littératures II: Littératures occidentales.* Paris: Gallimard, 1956.

JOSEPH LABAT

O

//

OEDIPUS COMPLEX

The Oedipus complex, a Freudian theory, connects two unconscious infantile impulses or wishes of universal import, incestuous love for the mother and jealous hostility toward the father. Since all feelings develop out of sexual desires modified by ancient taboos, the formation of the Oedipus complex in about the third year of life sets up in the unconscious essential countervailing mechanisms for its repression. These unconscious desires and restraints remain in psychic equilibrium throughout normal adult life.

The Fusion of Psychoanalysis with Greek Tragedy

In 1897 Sigmund Freud set forth the Oedipus complex, a theoretical cornerstone of psychoanalysis that he believed had clinical confirmation in the unconscious wishes animating adult dreams and aesthetic reinforcement in the universal validity and cathartic efficacy of the Oedipus myth and Hamlet's dilemma. He established the further interrelationship between psychoanalytic theory, ancient myth, and tragedy by allusion to the compelling power of fate in the *Oidipous tyrannos* (*Oedipus Rex,* play, c. 429 B.C.) of Sophocles. This classic had singularly stirred unconscious wishes in ancient and modern audiences in a way inaccessible to modern tragic literature. Both audiences recognize these normal primal wishes of childhood as still extant within themselves though repressed and they shiver and recoil from Oedipus, who has fulfilled them. Besides this cathartic effect of tragedy, Freud further qualified psychoanalysis as the heir of ancient myth and Greek tragedy by drawing on a clinical reference to dreams in the text of Sophocles' tragedy. Jocasta comforted Oedipus, her son and husband, that "men many times have dreamt they slept with their own mothers" (1.981). This recondite classical allusion supported Freud's position in *Die Traumdeutung* (*The Interpretation of Dreams,* 1900) that the Oedipus myth had its source in dream material of immemorial antiquity and that dreams and myths provide the royal road to the unconscious.

In this same seminal work, Freud contrasted the child's fantasy brought to consciousness and realized in *Oedipus Rex* with the repression of this fantasy in Shakespeare's tragedy *Hamlet* (c. 1600), a repression culturally determined after 2,000 years. In Freud's interpretation, Hamlet found the secret desires of his own childhood adumbrated in Claudius' murder of Hamlet's father and marriage to his mother. Freud contrasted Hamlet's princely dispatch of the court sycophants, Polonius, Rosencrantz, and Guildenstern, with his hesitations, self-reproach, and conscientious scruples brought on by the unconscious deterrent that he is no better than Claudius, the murderer he must punish.

Significance to Psychoanalysis and Literature

In 1923, Freud pronounced that the importance of sexuality and of the Oedipus complex constituted the foundations of psychoanalytic theory. In sum, the Oedipus complex, while it draws on and enhances understanding of tragic literature and ancient myth served also as the pivotal concept of psychoanalysis by illustrating and illuminating Freud's major interrelated theories of infantile sexuality, the unconscious, the pleasure-principle, repression, the role of dreams and myths, the castration complex, the genital stage of character development, determinism, the archaic heritage, the primal father, the origins of totemism, religion, morality, society, and the mass psyche. In addition, formulation of the Oedipus complex led to the yoking of the unconscious material of dreams, myth, religion, and aesthetics to new principles of symbolism and symbolic interpretation, instruments and perspectives as vital in literature as in psychoanalysis. In 1928, Freud again alluded to the literary masterpieces that undergird psychoanalytic theory. He now linked Dostoevsky's *Brat'īa Karamazovy (Brothers Karamazov,* novel, 1880) with *Oedipus Rex* and *Hamlet.* They dealt with one subject, parricide, and a single motivation, sexual rivalry for a woman.

Psychoanalytic Criticism

The Oedipus complex and psychoanalytic theory have drawn critical attention and influenced the fields of psychiatry, anthropology, sociology, mythology, the fine arts, philosophy, and education. On the other hand, they have been less influential in the fields of cultural history, political science, and world affairs. Anthropologists generally challenge Freud's notions of the archaic heritage. Overall, his primary theories have been further expanded, challenged, rejected, rectified, and refined by scores of eminent thinkers in psychoanalysis and literature during the twentieth century.

Among Freud's contemporaries, Carl Jung accepted the orthodox Freudian position and extended Oedipal fantasies to women in the Electra complex. He believed, however, that the infant's desire for food preceded a germinating eroticism and that emotional interplay between children and parents had a more pivotal influence than sexual attraction. He saw the danger of neurotic disturbance if emancipation from these complexes did not occur after puberty. Alfred Adler too moved away from Freud's purely phylogenetic account of the Oedipus complex to the environmental determinant. If it existed, the Oedipus complex represented simply a vicious, unnatural result of maternal overindulgence.

Otto Rank, like Sophocles and classical scholars, concentrated on the Oedipus myth and the mysterious questions of the origins and destiny of man and the birth trauma. While he acknowledged manifestations of the Oedipus complex at developmental stages, like Adler and Jung, Rank concentrated on parental influence or environment as pivotal in the development of individuality. Yet, like Freud, he remained deeply pessimistic about the human condition and the blindness of fate. Unlike Oedipus, who rooted out a bitter fatalistic truth, Rank argued for the efficacy of illusion.

Karen Horney and Erich Fromm reflect the important modulation from Freud's ontogenic and phylogenetic concentration on the Oedipus complex to the philosophical and social significance of the Oedipus myth. Horney argued that early social relationships mold character. Subsequent neurotic behavior reflects definable parental actions such as sexual stimulation of the child. Horney did not accept Freud's pessimistic view of man's biological nature, inimical environment, and fatal destiny. For Horney, cultural determinants influenced the interaction of biological and social conditions. As long as human destiny remained within human control, Horney affirmed the possibilities of individual and social goodness, decency, and growth.

Fromm, like Sophocles and Horney, considered the Oedipus myth within the larger context of the authoritarian patriarchal society. He agreed with Freud on the significance of sexual strivings in children, but placed sex within a spectrum of human imperatives and not centrally as Freud envisioned. He associated the Oedipus complex with neurosis and irrational fixation of children to their parents and not as a universal condition.

Fromm found repugnant the hierarchical order in the patriarchal society and state with its instruments for conformity, obedience, and repression. This social construct incites father-son conflict, neurosis, social disorder, and rebellion. In discussing the Oedipus myth as the conflict between the prevailing patriarchal principle and the more salutary matriarchal one, Fromm asserted that the Oedipus complex and myth would disappear as respect for the integrity of every individual gained ascendancy. His matriarchal principle, similar to Horney's social optimism and Fromm's perception of Sophocles' philosophic tendency, linked human equality, happiness, and dignity with willing acceptance of all natural phenomena.

While Freud's views on the primacy of sexual drives and the biologically determined archaic heritage have been seriously questioned and essentially modified by his followers and critics and while his mechanistic-materialistic orientation has determined his overdependence on scientific hypothesis and his bleak view of culture and environment, nonetheless, Freud's influence on modern thought beginning with his insights on the Oedipus complex transcend even his monumental achievement in the clinical treatment of neurosis.

Freud throughout dedicated his life and works to correct a European intellectual imbalance that neglected the role of the unconscious in human affairs. In retrospect, location of the origins of psychoanalytic theory and depth psychology in primal myth and Greek tragedy represents Freud's deliberate stance to affect a late Renaissance in this area repressed by modern society.

Poetic Fusion of Psychic and Philosophical Values in the Oedipus Myth

In 1979, the classicist John Hay assimilated the work of Richard Jebb, Bernard Knox, H.D.F. Kitto, Alister Cameron, and other major classical scholars with the dicta of Aristotle and the tenets of Freudian theory. Major criticism of Freud's analysis by classicists does not quarrel with his interpretation of the role of the unconscious in the Oedipus myth. Rather, classical critics concentrate on aesthetic, conscious, and rational values, which Freud's *Weltlehre,* scientific bias and theoretical-clinical constructs ignore. Classicists have generally recognized the surpassing poetic vision of the *Oedipus Rex* of Sophocles and its full realization of the myth.

Ironically, Freud's acute analysis of Sophocles' *Oedipus Rex* has contributed significantly to an understanding of the unconscious forces in the Oedipus myth, while ignoring Sophocles' poetic integration of the myth with the conscious, philosophical theme on the slim adequacy of human knowledge and, more particularly, self-knowledge. Freud's classic statement on the Sophoclean tragedy in *The Interpretation of Dreams* minimizes the tragic conflict between fate and human will and man's search for knowledge in order to focus exclusively on the unconscious in the myth. Freud's intense interest in the psychic mechanisms in the unconscious preserving dynamic equilibrium between irreconcilable primal impulses and ethical values sacrificed aesthetic elements to the cause of science. In Freud's cosmology of the unconscious, the dramatic presentation of the myth provides audiences with vicarious gratification of repressed instincts in a ritual setting that distances the Dionysian experience with a tempering Apollonian self-awareness.

As Freud contributed to the perceptions of the allied function of the unconscious in dreams, myth, and art, so his psychoanalytic theory on the Freudian nature of symbols vivifies Sophocles' use of sexual imagery throughout *Oedipus Rex* and especially its concentration in the messenger's report of Oedipus' self-blinding in Jocasta's chamber after the dénouement. Again, Freud's psychic concerns ignore the exquisite accretion of imagery that builds emotional intensity with an economy of affect to a breaking point and swift release. Hay has isolated the brush strokes of the sight-blindness inversion and of Oedipus as hunter and the animal hunted, and as helmsman steering fatally toward the womb-harbor.

Cumulatively, these clusters of patterned-images, brilliantly interwoven, serve simultaneously the psychic and philosophical purposes of the tragedy.

Hay has also analyzed the combined symbolism in the etymology of the name "Oedipus" and his staff. This imagery provides essential insights into Sophocles' supreme poetic vision and dual concerns with the unconscious and conscious: the legacy of fate and the questionable adequacy of human knowledge. Connotatively, Oedipus, the name frequently alluded to in the text, may mean "swollen-foot," with its phallic overtones, or lame, that is, limited knowledge. Oedipus' staff also accentuates the dual psychic and philosophical values; it serves as weapon for the parricide, pivotal clue to the riddle of the sphinx, sceptre of authority, and finally, sensor for the blinded Tiresias and Oedipus as they pursue esoteric knowledge denied to sight.

Classicists, as well as the latter-day psychoanalytic theorists Horney and Fromm, have been sensitive to the clash of the patriarchal-matriarchal principles in the Oedipus myth. In raising the psychic and philosophic issues, Sophocles' tragedy judged critically the patriarchal social order. Both Oedipus and his father, Laius, display a drive for dominance informed by egocentrism, anger, and preemptive strikes. In all their thoughts and acts, father and son intend to elude each other and ineluctable fate, manipulate inscrutable nature, and surmount human limitations with finite reason and acts of will. In this triangular classical tragedy, Jocasta acts the willing accomplice in the father-son conflict.

While it must be balanced with aesthetic analysis, Freud's psychoanalytic theory of the Oedipus complex has enlarged literary understanding of the force of Greek tragedy. On one hand, Freud has isolated and defined profoundly the role of the unconscious in myth. On the other, the subsequent twentieth-century treatment of the Oedipus myth by eminent psychoanalysts, classicists, and major authors provoked by his initial study has dramatically revealed new facets of the classical heritage that extend beyond Freud, yet nevertheless, within his logical system, mutually challenge most rational assumptions of modern thought and European society.

Literary History of the Oedipus Myth

The Oedipus myth has been alluded to in the eighth century B.C. in Homer's *Ilias* (*Iliad,* epic poem), 4.378; 23.679 f. and the *Odysseia* (*The Odyssey,* epic poem), 11.27 ff., and Hesiod's *Theogonia* (*Theogony,* poem), 326. Later the myth received full dramatic development in the fifth century B.C. in the plays of Aeschylus, Euripides, and Sophocles.

The myth was revived in the theater by Seneca (c. A.D. 50) and from the Renaissance to the present. Giovanni dell'Anguillara wrote his five-act tragedy in 1565. Pierre Corneille's mediocre work (1659) suffered from the stylistic gallantry of preciosity. In England, John Dryden and Nathaniel Lee gave it a weak rendering (1679). The eighteenth century brought the myth to opera. Antonio Sacchini's composition (1786) will be echoed by Sir Charles Stanford in England (1887) and, in the twentieth century, by three more compositors, Ruggero Leoncavallo (1920), Igor Stravinsky (1927), working from a text by Jean Cocteau, and the Romanian Georges Enesco (1936).

Voltaire launched his theatrical career with his neoclassical *Oedipe* (1718). In Italy (1823) Giovanni Battista Niccolini and in Spain (1829), Francisco Martínez de la Rosa offered romantic interpretations of the drama. In the twentieth century, Germany's contribution was Hugo von Hofmannsthal's drama, *Œdipus und die Sphynx* (1906). Jean Cocteau, while preparing his text for Stravinsky, wrote a French adaptation of *Oedipus Rex* (1928). Two years later, André Gide renewed the play by stressing predestination and man's inability to act freely. Synge's drama *The Playboy of the Western World* (1907) has dealt with the parricide theme; Joyce's novel, *Finnegans Wake* (1939), with the Oedipus myth; and Moravia's novel, *Agostino* (1945), with incest.

Lowell Edmunds, in *Oedipus—The Ancient Legend and Its Later Analogues* (1985), notes that

> It is odd that the Oedipus legend, perhaps the most famous story from classical antiquity, is almost never studied as a narrative. Classicists usually study it in the form of tragedy and thus from the point of view of literary history and literary criticism. . . . While these works of thought and art were being created in various cities of Europe, it was still possible . . . to collect the Oedipus folktale in the countryside. This folktale was, and may still be, a living inheritance from the Middle Ages and perhaps even from antiquity. This folktale preserves in rather pristine form the ambiguity of the protagonist that has been difficult to grasp in modern art and thought.

See also: Incest, Family, Parents and Children, Psychoanalysis of the Self.

Selected Bibliography

Hay, John. *Oedipus Tyrannus: Lame Knowledge and the Homosporic Womb*. Washington, D.C.: University Press of America, 1978.
Kallich, Martin, et al., eds. *Oedipus Myth and Drama*. New York: Odyssey, 1968.
Mullahy, Patrick. *Oedipus: Myth and Complex*. New York: Hermitage, 1948.

KENNETH CRAVEN

P
———— // ————

PACIFISM

Ancient and Classical Background

Pacifism is individual abstention from or collective resistance to war. Individualistic pacifism begins as a religious or philosophical theme. In India the *Bhagavad* (dialogue, c. 200 B.C.) argues pacifism in relation to a divine law of retribution for evil acts. A similar idea of divine judgment underlies the pacifism of Jeremiah in the Old Testament, where Isaiah presents an allegorical vision of a messianic age of peace. This vision becomes apocalyptic in Daniel, which is the basis of Christian imagery in some accounts of the life of Jesus, Matthew 24–25, and his messianic return, Revelation. The "Sermon on the Mount," Matthew 5–7, inspires early Christian sermons against military service; for example, Tertullian's "De corona militis" ("The Chaplet," treatise, c. 211).

In classical Greece pacifism is a comic theme implying fear and selfishness, from the figure of Theristes in Homer's *Ilias* (*Iliad*, epic, c. 8th century B.C.) and in *Batrachomyomachia* (*The Battle of Frogs and Mice*, mock-epic, c. 400 B.C.), through the comedies of Aristophanes, *Archanēs* (*Archanians*, 425 B.C.) and *Eirēnē* (*Peace*, 421 B.C.), to the *Nekrikoi dialogoi* (*Dialogues of the Dead*, satires, 2d century) of Lucian, whose "Hermes and Charon" complains of the inferior moral quality of death during peace. In Roman literature pacifism is either a despairing protest, as in the figure of Galaeseus in Virgil's epic *Aeneis* (*Aenid*, 19 B.C.), or a distant dream, as in Virgil (*Bucolica* [*Eclogues*, 42–39 B.C.]) or Horace (Carmina [*Odes*, c. 23 B.C.]).

Medieval and Early Modern Periods

The early medieval genre of hagiography, from Sulpicius Severus' *Vita Sancti Martini* (*Life of St. Martin of Tours*, c. 400) onward, includes many stories of Christian pacifism facing Roman and barbarian violence. Replaced by the Just

War theory even before the rise of feudalism, but maintained and isolated as a spiritual ideal for the monastic clergy, pacifism only appears in the minor characters, hermits, and monks, of the Chivalric Romances. In Renaissance continuations of Romances, such as Torquato Tasso's *Gerusalemme liberata* (1581), heroes are lured away from their quests by base illusions of peace and pleasure rather than principle. The sixteenth-century humanists appealed to the whole of Christendom for peace. Erasmus personifies his ideals in allegorical figures giving medieval sermons in his *Moriae encomium* (*Praise of Folly,* essay, 1511), and *Querela pacis* (*Complaint of Peace,* 1517), while Rabelais' Abbey of Thélème in *Gargantua* (novel, 1534) is a secularized version of monastic life for the well-bred, where they escape war. Mock-epic humor was adapted by the Lutheran Georg Rollenhagen in his fable *Froschmeuseler* (*Frogs and Mice,* 1595). Some anonymous protest poetry survives from the age of religious wars and the rise of absolutism, but pacifism for court poets means praising the ruler's policy as bringing true peace (Ronsard, *Ode de la paix* [*Ode to Peace,* 1550] and Góngora, *Panegírico* [*Panegyric,* 1617]) and counseling submission by his subjects (Pieter Hooft, *Geeraerdt van Velsen* [*Gerard von Velsen,* play, 1613]). Emeric Crucé's essay *Le nouveau Cynée* (*New Cyneas,* 1623) begins a new tradition of advice to princes, carried on by Guez de Balzac's *Le prince* (essay, 1631), the Duke de Sully's *Mémoires* (1638), and *Les caractères* (*The Characters,* essays, 1688) of Jean de La Bruyère, which all plead for peace. Pastoral poetry, revived by Jacopo Sannazaro's *Arcadia* (1504), laments war, criticizes imperial expansion—Francisco Sá de Miranda's *Basto* (1595) and Góngora's *Soledades* (*Solitudes,* 1612–1617)—and calls for the return of peace (Joost van den Vondel, *Leeuwendalers* [*Lion Merchants,* drama, 1647]). The antiheroic picaresque novel, after *Lazarillo de Tormes* (1554), contributes to the development of fantastic adventure stories by disillusioned veterans like Cyrano de Bergerac (*Histoire comique des états et empires de la lune . . . du soleil* [*The Comical History of the States and Empires of the Moon . . . the Sun,* 1657, 1662]) and Hans J.C. von Grimmelshausen, *Der abenteuerliche Simplicissimus* [*The Adventurous Simplicissimus,* 1669]).

The Eighteenth and Nineteenth Centuries

The Philosophes advocated the rational control of war, not pacifism, which appears only among the satirists and pietists. Jonathan Swift's novel *Gulliver's Travels* (1726) portrays the art of war as one of the puny, detestable traits of the human Yahoos in comparison to the strong, peaceful Houyhnhnms. The battle scenes in Voltaire's novels *Micromégas* (1752) and *Candide* (1759) satirize the idea of rational war, which owes something to his admiration for the Quakers in his earlier *Lettres philosophiques* (*Philosophical Letters,* 1734). The *Journal* (1774) of John Woolman, who preached in America against slavery and the French and Indian War, influenced Wordsworth, Coleridge, and Charles Lamb in the 1790s through their Quaker neighbor, the nature poet Thomas Wilkinson.

In the second generation of Romantics, Shelley's enthusiasm for revolution coexists in his dramatic poem *Hellas* (1821) with a vision derived from Isaiah and Virgil of a future age of peace, but the scorn of Byron's hero *Don Juan* (narrative poem, 1819–1824) for pacifism as the argument of slaves had more influence. Henry D. Thoreau's essays *Walden* (1854) and *Civil Disobedience* (1849) are the two most famous examples of pacifist withdrawal from the expansive, aggressive American society and of attempting to reform it by nonviolent resistance. But popular literature written by members of the peace movement—the novels of Lydia Maria Child *Hobomuk* (1824) and *The Rebels* (1825), Amasa Walker's essay *Le Monde* (1859), and the children's stories *A Kiss for A Blow* (1842) by Henry C. Wright—reveal that both aspects of Thoreau's thought were shared. Poets who turned from pacifism (John Greenleaf Whittier [*Poems*, 1838], William Lloyd Garrison [*Sonnets*, 1843], and James Russell Lowell [*The Biglow Papers*, 1848]) to the anti-slavery crusade are better known for their support of the North in the Civil War. Ralph Waldo Emerson read his address "War" (1838) to the founding convention of the American Peace Society in Boston, but his philosophically qualified statements affected them less than a zeal for reforming society.

The growth of a less optimistic, mystical pacifism in nineteenth-century Russia can be traced in the development of the character Pierre in Tolstoy's novel *Voĭna i mir (War and Peace*, 1865–1869) and the novels of historian Pavel Mel'nikov about the sect of the Old Believers, *V lesákh (In the Forests*, 1868–1874) and *Na gorákh (On the Mountains*, 1875–1881), as well as in book 6 of Dostoevsky's novel *Brat'ia Karamazovy (The Brothers Karamazov*, 1880) and Tolstoy's later stories. Under Tolstoy's influence A. Dobroliubov renounced writing, as a religious pacifist, by the time of his poems *Iz knigi nevidimoĭ (From the invisible book*, 1905), and the Danish novelist Henrik Pontoppidan, in *Det forjaettede Land (The Promised Land*, 1891–95), chronicled his attempt to live out Tolstoyan ideals. When Pontoppidan shared the 1917 Nobel Prize with his fellow Dane Karl Gjellerup, whose novel *Pilgrimmen Kamanita (The Pilgrim Kamanita*, 1911) combines Buddhist pacifism with European radicalism, it was a public tribute and epitaph to this movement, although Alfred Döblin's novel of a mystic forced to become a revolutionary *Die drei sprünge des Wang-Lun (The Three Leaps of Wang-lun*, 1915) is the final literary critique of its ideas.

Until the early twentieth century belief in peaceful human progress marked the novels of liberals like Benito Pérez Galdós (*La fontana de oro* [*The Golden Fountain*, 1870]), and the most popular socialists, as in the 10 volumes of Romain Rolland's *Jean-Christophe* (1904–1912). Pacifist novels were written in Japan by converts to Christianity and socialism: Kinoshita Naoe (*Hi no hashira* [*Pillar of Fire*, 1904]) and Kagawa Toyohiko (*Shisen wo koete* [*Before the Dawn*, 1920]). Such hopes were only partly shared by pacifists who were also anarchists, such as Pío Baroja (*Paradox, rey* [*Paradox the King*, novel, 1906]) and Ramón Sender (*Imán* [*Pro Patria*, novel, 1930]), and were not shared at all in Miguel de Unamuno's first novel, *Paz en la guerra* (*Peace in War*, 1897), Thomas Hardy's dramatic poem *The Dynasts* (1903–08), or Mark Twain's posthumous story *The Mysterious Stranger* (1916).

World War I

The outbreak of the war produced three kinds of pacifist literature. First, the reactions of writers whose hopes were destroyed may be seen in Rolland's essay *Au-dessus de la mêlée* (*Above the Battle*, 1915), the American poet Sarah Norcliffe Cleghorn's *Portraits and Protests* (1917), and the anguished novels of Leonhard Frank, *Der Mensch ist gut* (*Man Is Good*, 1917), and Elin Wägner's *Åsa-Hanna* (1918). The Dada group in Zurich after 1915, Hugo Ball, Hans Arp, and Tristan Tzara, is another example of this reaction. Second, combatants became pacifists in the lines of both the Allies (Henri Barbusse, *Le feu* [*Under Fire*, novel, 1916]) and the Central Powers; Fritz von Unruh's novel *Opfergang* (*The Way of Sacrifice*, 1916), and Stefan Zweig's play *Jeremias* (1917) marked the beginning of a series of pacifists works for each of them. Combat veterans who were pacifists briefly before becoming communists include the Hungarian poet Arpad Tóth (1886–1928) and the novelist Ludwig Renn (*Krieg* [*War*, 1928]), Erich Maria Remarque was not a pacifist, but his novels of combat (*Im Westen nicht Neues* [*All Quiet on the Western Front*, 1929]) and readjustment (*Der Weg zurück* [*The Way Back*, 1931]) were so received. Third, conscientious objectors (c.o.s) wrote of their own experiences and created a type used by other writers. Herman Hesse's novel *Demian* (1919) tells of two friends who want to object but cannot, while e.e. cummings' *The Enormous Room* (1922) novelizes his experience in military custody. In Britain J. Scott Duckers (*Handed Over*, 1917) and Walter Allen (*All In A Lifetime*, 1959) went to prison, as did New Zealander Archibald Baxter (*We Will Not Cease*, 1939), and their memoirs reflect their attitudes. American c.o.s chose titles reflecting their treatment: Ernest L. Meyer's *Hey! Yellowbacks!* (1930) and Harold S. Gray's *Character "Bad"* (1934).

Social Commitment and Disarmament

The use of c.o.s as characters by socialist novelists ranges from the sensationalized (*Jimmie Higgins* [1919] by Upton Sinclair) to the profound. (John Dos Passos' trilogy *U.S.A.* [1938] weaves fictional c.o.s and real pacifists [Carnegie, LaFollete, Randolph Bourne] into a story of war changing the character of American society.) Leftist playwrights George Sklar and Albert Maltz preach revolution in *Peace on Earth* (1934), while Irwin Shaw's *Bury the Dead* (1936) combines pacifism and revolt. Robert E. Sherwood's plays, from *The Road to Rome* (1927) to his Pulitzer Prize-winning *There Shall Be No Night* (1940), move from pacifism to antifascist resistance. Dalton Trumbo's novel *Johnny Got His Gun* (1939) attacks the romance of war, but Thornton Wilder's *Heaven's My Destination* (1935) satirizes a romantic pacifist.

In England George Bernard Shaw treated the war's disruption of society ironically in *Heartbreak House* (1919); the play aroused such hostility that it was not produced for two years, although his *Arms and the Man* (1894) enjoyed a revival as exservicemen applauded its deflation of heroism. The same themes appeared as tragedy in the novels of Vera Brittain (*Testament of Youth,* 1933) and D. H. Lawrence (*Kangaroo,* 1923), and in Siegfried Sassoon's fictional *Memoirs of George Sherston* (1928–1936). Once converted to the disarmament movement, Aldous Huxley included pacifist characters in his novels, beginning with *Eyeless in Gaza* (1936).

In France Jean Giono's novel *Que ma joie demeure* (*Joy of Man's Desiring,* 1935) made him the center of a back to nature pacifist movement, which became more radical when he published *Refus d'obéissance* (*Refusal to Obey,* 1937), four unpublished chapters of his autobiographical war novel *Le grand troupeau* (*To the Slaughterhouse,* 1931). But the characters of Jean Giraudoux' play *La guerre de Troie n'aura pas lieu* (*Tiger at the Gates,* 1935) seemed closer to the feeling of most French that pacifism was an illusion and another war inevitable. The novels of Jules Romains, *Les pouvoirs* (*The Powers,* 1935), *Prélude à Verdun* (*Prelude to Verdun,* 1938) and *Verdun* (1938), show pacifists swept into the confusion of individual and collective destinies that forms the theme of his multivolume chronicle *Les hommes de bonne volonté* (*Men of Good Will,* 1932–1947). In Greece Stratis Myrivilis followed his anti-war novel *Hē zōe ēn taphō* (*Life in the Tomb,* 1930) with one about civilians in the aftermath of war, *He daskala me ta chrysa matia* (*The Schoolmistress with the Golden Eyes,* 1933). In Japan the military banned Ishikawa Jun's novel *Marusu no uta* (*I Hear the War God Singing,* 1938), but the implications of Dino Buzzati's *Il deserto dei Tartari* (*The Tartar Steppe,* novel, 1940) eluded the Italian fascist censor.

World War II

Polemical pacifist literature was rare in World War II. Even the cynical war profiteer of Bertolt Brecht's play *Mutter Courage und ihre Kinder* (*Mother Courage,* 1939) was seen as a tragic figure by audiences. Women in England, including Elizabeth Goudge (*The Castle on the Hill,* 1942) and Vera Brittain (*Account Rendered,* 1944), wrote pacifist novels; American women wrote of draft dodgers (for example, Ann Chidester [*No Longer Fugitive,* 1943]) and conscientious objectors (for instance, Jessamyn West [*The Friendly Persuasion,* 1945] and Mary Borden [*You the Jury,* 1952]). Combat soldiers become pacifists in Jeb Stuart's *The Objector* (1950) and Heinrich Böll's *Wo warst du, Adam?* (*And Where Were You Adam?* 1951). Lowell Naeve's prison memoirs, *A Field of Broken Stones* (1950) and *Phantasies of a Prisoner* (1958), and Alfred Hassler's *Diary of a Self-Made Convict* (1954) make it clear that c.o. experiences laid the groundwork for a postwar movement of peace agitators, but a movement that only reached a wider public through grotesque satires of the war like the novels *Die Blechtrommel* (*The Tin Drum,* 1959) and *Hundejahre* (*Dog Years,* 1963) of Günter Grass, Joseph Heller's *Catch-22* (1961), and Kurt Vonnegut's *Mother Night* (1961) and *Slaughterhouse-Five* (1969), all written by veterans rather than c.o.s.

The Cold War and the Atomic Age

Related to this development of satire, allegorical pacifist literature began to appear. Walter Jens's novella *Das weisse Taschentuch* (*The White Handkerchief,* 1948) and parable *Das Testament des Odysseus* (*Testament of Odysseus,* 1957), and the novel triology *Fluss ohne Ufer* (*River without Banks,* 1949–1961) by Hans Henny Jahnn mark an increasingly stylized search for the roots of violence. On the same theme William Golding's novel *Lord of the Flies* (1954) shows the impotence of the pacifist boy Piggy. Sweden's Sivar Arnér wrote an allegory of the Cold War, *Fyra som var bröder* (*Four Who Were Brothers,* 1955), as did novelists Nikos Kazantzakis, *Hoi aderphophades* [*The Fratricides,* 1963]) of the Greek Civil War, and William Faulkner (*A Fable,* 1954) of war in general. More realistic treatments of the dilemmas of pacifism were Halldōr Laxness' novel describing Iceland as *Atómstöðín* (*The Atom Station,* 1948), Carl Zuckmayer's play *Das kalte Licht* (*Cold Light,* 1955) of a nuclear scientist betraying secrets, and Evan S. Connell's novel of a military cadet *The Patriot* (1960). During the ban the bomb movement in English-speaking countries Bertrand Russell (*Nightmares of Eminent Persons,* 1955) and Leo Szilard (*The Voice of the Dolphins,* 1961) propagandized in humorous short stories, while in Gaullist France the historical novels of Zoé Oldenbourg, *Les brûlés* [*Destiny of Fire,* 1960) and *Les cités charnelles* (*Cities of the Flesh,* 1961), retold the destruction of utopian pacifism among the Albigensian heretics.

Vietnam

The early form of literary pacifism in response to American involvement in Vietnam was the "performance event": a public reading, "Poets for Peace" (1967), in New York's Town Hall, and a pacifist musical by Gretchen Cryer and Nancy Ford, *Now Is The Time For All Good Men* (1967); then came a documentary literature by, and about, the members of the counterculture, (Raymond Mungo's *Famous Long Ago* [1970]), and the anti-draft movement (Daniel Berrigan's *The Trial of the Catonsville Nine* [drama, 1971]). The novels of William Eastlake (*The Bamboo Bed,* 1969) and Tim O'Brien (*Going After Cacciato,* 1978) portrayed the surreal quality of a war without fixed positions, while Marge Piercy's *Dance the Eagle to Sleep* (1970) criticized the protest's turn to violence at home. Alongside the writings of anti-war veterans such as Ron Kovic's *Born on the Fourth of July* (1976), novels linking Vietnam to previous wars began to appear from the perspective of the European peace movement. These included Ramón Hernández's *Eterna memoria* (*Eternal Memory,* 1975). Novels of the traditional American peace churches are represented by Solomon Stucky's *For Conscience' Sake* (1983).

Collective Pacifism

The theme of massive nonviolent resistance to war or injustice is rare, usually appearing in political satire, from Aristophanes' comedy *Lysistratē* (*Lysistratō,*

411 B.C.) to Warren Miller's novel *The Siege of Harlem* (1964), in poems of revolution such as Shelley's "The Mask of Anarchy" (1819) and Subramanya Bharathi's "To Mahatma Gandhi" (1920), and in novels about the Gandhian movement like R. K. Narayan's *Waiting for the Mahatma* (1955). In Fénelon's novel *Les aventures de Télémaque* (*The Adventures of Telemachus,* 1699) the prince visits a strange people who practice nonresistance to evil, and in Voltaire's tale *La Princesse de Babylone* (*The Princess of Babylon,* 1768) a peaceful nation cures an invader of his thirst for conquest. Aldous Huxley prepares his characters for the same test at the end of his utopian novel *Island* (1962).

See also: Escape.

Selected Bibliography

Dougall, Lucy, comp. *War and Peace in Literature.* Chicago: World without War Publications, 1982.
Hutton, James. *Themes of Peace in Renaissance Poetry.* Ithaca, N.Y: Cornell University Press, 1984.

MICHAEL L. PERNA

PACT WITH THE DEVIL

Originally formulated in the early Middle Ages, the pact with the devil later becomes a standard feature of the Faust myth. Represented as a formal and binding written document between the devil and a human, usually a professed magician who signs it with his blood, the pact offers a renunciation of Christianity in exchange for demonic services to be rendered at the price of the signer's soul. This theme recurs in modern literature either as a conventional literal pact with a diabolic tempter or as an equivalent psychological experience. Both the motive for signing the pact and the outcome of the agreement vary. In some versions the devil receives the soul as his due after the time specified in the pact, but in others the signer is saved from damnation, usually through intervention of a deus or dea ex machina on his behalf.

Early Medieval Background

The idea of the pact is prefigured in both the Old and the New Testament. In the book of Job the Lord wagers with Satan concerning the fidelity of his worshiper Job under conditions of extreme testing. Job's soul is at stake, but he is not aware of the danger as he undergoes severe suffering and loss. The Gospels of Matthew, Mark, and Luke also give an account of Jesus' temptation by Satan. The devil offers Jesus the world as his dominion if he will deny God and follow him, but Jesus refuses so that the pact is never made.

Jacobus de Voragine's *Legenda aurea* (*Golden Legend,* c. 1270) relates two early examples of the pact that predate Faust. In the fourth century it is associated with a certain Cyprian of Antioch who had a reputation for performing magical feats and who supposedly consecrated himself to the devil. When he was later converted to Christianity, he repudiated his alliance with Satan. He was subsequently martyred as a Christian and elevated to sainthood. In the sixth century the legendary pact is associated with Theophilus of Adana, who was not a magician at all but rather a disappointed steward of the church who turned to the devil through the instigation of a Jewish sorcerer. Once again the devil was cheated of his prey, for Theophilus repented and was released from the contract through the intervention of the Virgin Mary. He died in the odor of sanctity in circa 537.

The Faust Myth

The theme of the diabolic pact, part of the diffuse thought of medieval Christianity through a thousand years, becomes an established feature of the Faust legend with the 1587 publication of *Das Volksbuch von Doktor Faust*. This German account was based on the adventures of an actual sixteenth-century personage whose real name, according to some recent scholars, may not have been Faust at all. At any rate, the historical individual seems to have been an ambivalent figure, partly wandering conjuror and charlatan, partly scholar and philosopher, who was supposedly carried away by the devil in 1525. The German author, undoubtedly writing under the influence of Luther and Melanchthon, emphasized the negative side of the figure, making no distinction between white magic, traditionally regarded as permissible, and black magic, forbidden and based on direct dealings with the devil. Rather than admiring the genuine search for knowledge on the part of the roving conjuror-scholar, he condemns the use of magic as fully evil and accepts the justice of the dire punishment inflicted as a result. The Faust legend flourished during the 1560s, an era of unprecedented witch hunts on the Continent. In fact 1587 was the high point of witch burnings in Germany. At this time all magic practice implied a pact with the devil, as all magic was considered black and therefore damnable. Luther preached the prevalence of the devil's influence in the world, and he condemned the search for knowledge as a likely way to damnation.

The German chapbook was translated into English in 1592, when it became the major source of Christopher Marlowe's tragedy *Doctor Faustus* (1604). The English translator, clearly the intellectual superior of the original author, is both more knowledgeable about the reputed powers of the magic-working Faust and more sympathetic to his damnable fate in consequence of the pact. Working with the English rendering, Marlowe elevated this lively but episodic story into a genuinely moving tragedy. His tragic protagonist is a noble man, a renowned scholar who has mastered all the known disciplines of study and seeks yet higher knowledge. Law, medicine, theology, and logic no longer satisfy his thirst for learning. Only in magic does he see an opportunity for achieving God-like knowledge. He signs the pact in blood with Lucifer's agent, Mephistophilis, agreeing to surrender his soul to the devil after the stipulated twenty-four year period.

Although Marlowe follows the narrative framework of the *Volksbuch* translation, he expands the meaning of the pact intellectually and spiritually. His hero is no mere magician but a vital symbol of the Renaissance spirit of free thought and inquiry as opposed to medieval dogmatism. His characterization of the devil is also complex and convincing. The legendary tempter is portrayed as at once ruthless and desperate, scornful of Faustus' fate, yet bitterly aware of his own eternal state of damnation. He sees hell as a state of mind from which he can never escape. He is thus no mere folk demon with horns and tail, but a profound and troubled spirit. In his tragedy Marlowe gives us an image of the aspiring Renaissance mind, driven to transgress human limitations for the sake of learning. At the same time he adheres to the central surface features of the legendary material, including the signing in blood, the specified time span of the pact, and appearance of devils at the end to carry off their victim to hell. Faustus' damnation is depicted as not merely a justifiable punishment for sin but as a tragic loss of a noble human spirit. Marlowe was not the only Renaissance playwright to transfer the theme of the pact to the stage. Focusing on Cyprian rather than Faust, Pedro Calderón de la Barca's *El mágico prodigioso* (*The Wonderful Magician*, 1637) draws on the martyrdom of St. Cyprian and St. Justina. In Calderón's version Cyprian first angers the devil by winning an argument with him, as a result of which the tempter decides to ruin him through love. Cyprian then falls in love with Justina, whose mother was a Christian martyr and who has vowed never to marry. When the lovesick Cyprian admits in a soliloquy that he would give his soul in exchange for Justina, the devil promptly appears to take him up on the offer. The pact is duly signed in blood, but the devil admits that he may be unable to fulfill his part of the bargain because he cannot force Justina to comply. When Cyprian sees a mysterious cloaked figure approaching him, he at first believes it to be the desired object of his love, but it is revealed instead to be a skeleton. Shaken by this disillusionment and also by a grimly ominous warning spoken by the skeleton about the vanity of worldly desires, Cyprian seeks to undo the pact. Again powerless, the devil cannot stop him, and the repentant young man, now converted to Christianity, joins his beloved Justina, who has just been arrested for her Christian beliefs. The two are martyred together. In the late sixteenth and seventeenth centuries, there were also many imitations of Marlowe's *Doctor Faustus* on the Continent. The subject became especially popular on the puppet stage. In most of these versions the comic elements predominate over the tragic. Many make a point about a catch in the wording of the pact, and the devil in these cases usually plays a trickster role. In some the devil interprets the twenty-four-year period of service as actually meaning twelve years, counting days and nights separately.

In the eighteenth century there were further serious adaptations of the Faust myth as well, all including the central feature of the pact with the devil. Paul Weidmann's *Johann Faust* (play, 1775) is innovative in that for the first time literarily Faust is saved from damnation at the expiration of the pact. In Friedrich Maximilian von Klinger's novel *Fausts Leben, Thaten, und Höllenfahrt (Faust's Life, Deeds, and Journey to Hell,* 1791), Faust is portrayed as a moral idealist engaged with an antagonist named Leviathan. Somewhat in the Job tradition, Faust wagers with Leviathan on whether human beings are good or evil. As the scholar surveys the world about him, he is stunned by the appalling wickedness of mankind and eventually admits the loss of the wager. Klinger's theme emphasizes the spirit of rebelliousness against tyranny and arbitrary authority.

Goethe's Faust

The greatest version of the Faust myth with the demonic pact as its central motif is Goethe's immortal poem *Faust.* Divided into two parts, the first, cast in dramatic form, was published in 1808 and the second was published posthumously (1832). In a "Prologue in Heaven" suggested by the biblical narrative of Job, the pact presents the opposing forces of the Lord and the devil who make a wager concerning the scholar Faust. The cynical, derisive devil, the spirit of denial, scorns the nature of man and mocks the restless seeking of Faust. The Lord realizes, however, that the devil's prodding can only contribute to the ultimate victory of the good. He permits the devil to have a free hand with Faust because the skeptical, denying spirit is actually part of the divine purpose for the destiny of mankind. Unwittingly the devil will help to save Faust by stirring him to continual activity. Goethe sees man's mission in life in terms of endless striving rather than any particular achievement. Only when man ceases to act can he become a victim of the devil. In part 1 there are three scenes set in Faust's study. In the first Faust's cynical observations about the limitations of human knowledge already echo the spirit of Mephistophelian denial. Ever seeking enlightenment, Faust thinks of magic as a possible way. This thought becomes the devil's invitation, and in the second study scene, the devil appears, at first in the shape of a black poodle, then in the guise of a traveling scholar. The devil converses with Faust for a time, then leaves, charming the scholar into falling asleep. When Faust awakes the memory of the devil seems like a dream. In the third scene in Faust's study, the devil reappears to negotiate the pact. Despairing over his own contradictory nature, Faust agrees to accept Mephistopheles' offer of a life of pleasure in exchange for an eternity after death in bondage to him. Although willing, he remains skeptical and insists on specifying in the contract that the devil may possess his soul only when he is completely satisfied. Only when a moment offers him such complete contentment that he has no desire for greater fulfillment will he be willing to surrender his soul. Mephistopheles gladly accepts this condition in the wager. When a student then comes by to consult Faust, the devil assumes the scholar's role, hinting that he is a split-off part of Faust himself.

By the end of part 1, after a series of episodes concerning the experiences of the devil and the scholar, it is clear already that Mephistopheles is going to lose both his wager with the Lord and his compact with the scholar. Faust has not accepted any moment as entirely satisfactory, and his lapses into sensuality have been followed by greater spiritual awareness. His restless striving, prompted by the devil, is simply fulfilling the Lord's spiritual plan.

Throughout part 2 Mephistopheles continues to accompany Faust, but his diabolical negativism continues to aid the good. At the end of the poem, when Faust has reached an advanced age, the devil loses the pact and wager, and the soul of Faust is saved. Even in his old age, Faust has been busy planning and striving, ever dissatisfied. At the moment of death he is taken to heaven where his soul is received by an angelic chorus glorifying the power of love. Goethe's unique vision of the pact thus makes the role of the devil as tempter a positive, even necessary, feature of genuine human achievement.

The nineteenth century produced further instances of the literary pact with the devil, often with innovative variations on the traditional formula. Adelbert von Chamisso's novelle *Peter Schlemihls wundersame Geschichte* (*The Wonderful Story of Peter Schlemihl*, 1814) adds another legendary character to the growing history of the demonic pact. In this account the hero sells his shadow rather than his soul. He feels alienated from his fellow men after this and seeks the solitude offered by nature. Lord Byron's unfinished drama *The Deformed Transformed* (1824) introduces a new basis for the pact. Here the hunchbacked hero sells his soul for neither knowledge nor power but rather for a better physical body. The devil obligingly gives him a choice, and the cripple chooses the strong healthy body of the hero Achilles.

The pact with the devil also appears as a motif in the fairy tales published by the brothers Grimm in the early nineteenth century. In one tale the devil is outwitted by a peasant who offers him whatever he grows above the ground in return for favors over a two-year period. The peasant then plants turnips. When the devil renews the pact, requesting what grows under the ground, the wily peasant plants wheat. In another tale five soldiers outwit the devil with the aid of the devil's own grandmother. The soldiers agree to serve the devil for a period of seven years, after which they will be freed only if they can answer a riddle. Through eavesdropping, carefully arranged by the grandmother, they are able to give the right answer and escape the devil's mastery. In some of the nineteenth-century versions, the emphasis is on a catch in the precise wording of the pact. In a *Faust* fragment (1803) by Chamisso the devil cheats his victim by so wording the pact that he does not have to perform any service whatsoever in exchange for the soul of his victim. In E.A.F. Klingemann's tragedy, *Faust* (1815), the bargain is binding only if four mortal sins are committed before its expiration. The naïve signer commits three, forgetting that the pact itself already constitutes the fourth.

In general these nineteenth-century treatments of the pact after Goethe tend to be tragic rather than didactic. Romantic sympathy rather than Christian condemnation characterizes the attitude toward the unfortunate seeker who sells his soul to achieve some otherwise unattainable goal.

Modern Literature

Several versions of the pact with the devil have appeared in twentieth-century literature. Irish poet and playwright William Butler Yeats gives the theme a new spiritual and social meaning in his drama *The Countess Cathleen* (1891). Yeats depicts two demons disguised as merchants who offer to buy the souls of starving peasants in exchange for food. The wife of one of the peasants notices, however, that these supposed merchants have no shadows. In her simple faith she is able to see through their demonic ruse. Desperate for food nonetheless, several of the men are quite willing to sell their souls for even a small amount of sustenance. When the generous Countess Cathleen becomes aware of the situation, she offers to sell her obviously much more valuable soul for enough food to save the starving population. In a startlingly dramatic scene angels and devils clash in mid-air over possession of her soul while lightning and thunder strike. At the end of the conflict the countess dies, her offer accepted, leaving bags of money to provide the poor with the needed food. Although the countess has given her life, however, she has not given her soul. An angel appears explaining that the Light of Lights looks on the motive, not on the deed. The dead woman's sacrifice was not evil for it was intended to relieve suffering humanity. Her soul will not be forfeited; she will be saved. Stephen Vincent Benet's short story "The Devil and Daniel Webster" (1937) also gives the traditional theme a novel twist. Set in rural New Hampshire and related in the style of a simple folktale, the story concerns the farmer Jabez Stone, who sells his soul for ten years of prosperity. Jabez pricks his finger and signs the pact in blood, but when the devil comes to collect at the end of the specified period of time, the canny farmer begins to look for a way out. Jabez feels that as an American he should not have to submit to this sort of thing, although the discovery that the devil, called "Old Scratch," has the soul of a neighbor tied in his bandana gives him a fright. Nevertheless Jabez stubbornly persists and finally persuades Daniel Webster to plead his case before a jury of Americans selected by the devil. The devil's choice turns out to be a collection of renegades and traitors, infamous villains all. Webster warms to the cause and pleads with moving eloquence. His technique is to remind the jury of the meaning of freedom, the essence of being American. The hearts of the villains cannot help but respond to this appeal to their own deep love of their country, and they vote to free Jabez from the bond. "Old Scratch" leaves New Hampshire, never to return again. The story is thus an ingenious and wholly effective mixture of the traditional pact with the native American setting and historical personalities.

The pact with the devil returns to the stage again in Dorothy Sayers' 1939 play *The Devil To Pay*. Sayers combines Marlowe and Goethe but in a wholly modern idiom to make this a lively dramatic tour de force. As in Marlowe's play, there is a hell-mouth on stage awaiting its victim at the end, but as in Goethe's version, the hero is ultimately saved. Faust signs the pact with Mephistopheles in blood in spite of the warning "homo fuge," which appears written on the table in the flowing blood.

Mephistopheles delivers the signed bond to the devil, who takes it off to hell. At the end of the twenty-four-year period, the soul, which is delivered to the devil in fulfillment of the pact, is actually a small black dog. Mephistopheles complains of the illegality of this payment, demanding that the case be taken to court. As a result of the trial, the legality of the devil's claim is upheld and the real soul of Faust, held in a bag by the angel Azrael, is handed over to Mephistopheles. The devil gets his due only temporarily, for Faust is not actually damned but only sent to purgatory for a period of time after which he will be saved. The ideology in the Sayers play is close to that of Goethe. She sees evil as an offshoot of God, just as shadow is made by the light. The embodiment of evil, such as the diabolic tempter, can exist therefore only a brief time and then only as a test, an irritant, to spark active virtue. As he himself explains in the play, the devil is but the shadow on the world, thrown by the world standing in its own light, which is God. When Faust follows Mephistopheles into the mouth of hell, then, it is with the conviction that one day he will be released from suffering and be able to enter heaven.

The most ambitious rendering of the Faust myth and of the pact theme in the twentieth century is Thomas Mann's monumental novel, *Doktor Faustus* (1947). In Mann's view the devil may be a hallucination and the pact a creation of the imagination, but the experience of signing the pact with the devil is nonetheless a meaningful psychological reality. Mann's Faust is Adrian Leverkühn, a brilliant musician. A modern figure presented in contemporary surroundings, Leverkühn experiences the evil only in his mind. Haunted by a sense of evil since his youth, he thinks he sees the devil, Sammael, and enters into a pact with him. Even as a figment of a diseased mind, the devil is no less able to act as tempter, and the desperate musician agrees to deny himself human love in exchange for creative success as a composer.

When Leverkühn first encounters the demonic apparition, they discuss the traditional questions about the meaning of hell and the conditions of the pact, but the devil in this case changes his form and garments during the talks, moving from a seedy disreputable appearance to a more sophisticated one as the level of the discussion becomes more elevated in tone. Mann thus endows his devil with the medieval trait of demonic shape-shifter while maintaining the modern view of the devil as a projection of changing attitudes and states of mind.

Mann's Leverkühn, like the medieval and Renaissance Fausts, also undertakes remarkable voyages into space and under the ocean depths. The voyages are achieved through science rather than magic, but Mann suggests that science, as the heir of magic, carries a negative connotation. Whether scientific or artistic, the Faustian striving for something beyond the normal reach of the protagonist can lead to an infamous bargain with the demonic. In the case of Leverkühn, the major goal is a musical work of genius, for which he is willing to sell his soul. The pact denies him love, allowing only a loveless sensuality, but as a result of this denial he becomes infected with syphilis, a destructive disease but one that releases creative powers of composition. Driven to madness, he acquires the artistic power to create an extraordinary work of music.

Mann thus adheres to the traditional features of the demonic bargain yet at the same time confers modern meaning on the device. The surrender to the devil through the signing of the pact is a psychological encounter, but it produces both a real work of creative genius and the actual destruction of the creative mind through disease. The episode realizes the implication of the pact on both a symbolic and a literal level.

The pact with the devil remains one of the great themes in world literature. Even with its original medieval trappings of magic and trickery, it appeals to the modern writer in search of a meaningful subject, and it contains intimations of ultimate questions about the nature of evil and what it means to be human. In what sense can a person be said to sell his soul to the devil? What is the soul and what is the devil? What is the ultimate price a person will pay to achieve something beyond his reach? What kind of achievement is worth the ultimate price? Is the temptation an objective or a subjective reality? Is the devil a positive force or merely a negation? As consequences of the pact are damnation and salvation viable concepts? The medieval magician, the Renaissance seeker after knowledge, the romantic restless spirit ever striving, and the modern artist in search of rich creativity all testify to the universality of the theme, and doubtless future works of literature will add to the roster of blood signatures on the diabolic pact.

See also: Daemon, Evil.

Selected Bibliography

Butler, E. M. *The Fortunes of Faust*. Cambridge: Cambridge University Press, 1952.
————. *The Myth of the Magus*. Cambridge: Cambridge University Press, 1948.
Palmer, Philip Mason, and Robert Pattison More. *The Sources of the Faust Tradition*. New York: Oxford University Press, 1936.
Pfaff, Lucie. *The Devil in Thomas Mann's "Doktor Faust" and Paul Valéry's "Mon Faust."* Bern: Herbert Lang, 1976.

CHARLOTTE SPIVACK

PARENTS AND CHILDREN

Everyone is a child once, and most people become parents, often while their own parents are still alive. The average person, therefore, will have three important domestic relationships (besides the spousal one)—as a child with parents (or surrogates), as a parent with children, and as a child who is also a parent, with both parents and children. Because of dissimilar experiences and biological needs, parents and children are bound to see life differently, and literature treats of the ways tensions are resolved or become hardened into generational conflict. Love and self-sacrifice are often present in the relationship, but whether reciprocal or one-directional is another question. How values are transmitted or overthrown; how mistakes are repeated; how the dislocations of one generation affect the next; what constitutes true parenthood—all these are important parts of the theme.

Antiquity and the Middle Ages

Judging from the earliest extant stories—the legends of primitive and early historical man—the relations of parents and children have been stormy from the beginning. Greek mythology speaks of the rebellion of the Titan Kronos against his father, Ouranos, and in turn the rebellion of Kronos's son, Zeus, against his father. By the same token, various tales in folklore, based apparently on actual practices, depict the parental sacrifice of an eldest born son or a virgin girl to appease a deity. So the war of all against all, which some see as the basic condition of human society, spilled over even into the rivalry of parent and child, especially father and son.

Against this background one reads the famous story in the Old Testament of God ordering Abraham to sacrifice his only son, Isaac, and the patriarch dutifully obeying, as if this were a normal request for a deity to make. God turns out, however, to be testing Abraham's obedience, to be invoking a tradition merely to undermine it. The incident no doubt celebrates the replacement of human sacrifices by animal sacrifices, of polytheism by monotheism. Other scriptural stories touch on the parents and children theme—stories of sibling rivalry (Cain and Abel, Isaac and Ishmael, Jacob and Esau), of the fair-haired son (Joseph), of the rebellious son (Absolom)—but the next momentous, indeed unique, treatment is in the New Testament. For in the case of Jesus, at least according to one common way of understanding the references to the "son of man" or "son of God," the parents-children motif is translated to the divine sphere. Now the Father is God Himself, and Jesus is, depending on one's theology, a part of Himself or His Son. Instead of having man sacrifice a son to Himself, God sacrifices His own Son for the sake of man. What God at the last moment exempted Abraham from having to do, He proceeded to do Himself to Himself.

This story has an interesting counterpart in Greek mythology. For when Agamemnon was becalmed at Aulis, he had to sacrifice his virgin daughter Iphigenia. The parallel is curious. The sacrifice of the king's daughter enables the Greeks to proceed to their worldly goal of conquering Troy; the sacrifice of God's son enables mankind (or a portion of it) to proceed to its otherworldly goal of entering the Promised Land of salvation. Thus the tale of Jesus is an amalgam of Judaic and Greek traditions. Perhaps not so coincidentally, Jesus, as a future familial sacrifice, did not look kindly on family accord: "I have come to bring division. . . . Father against son and son against father."

Greek literature has numerous interesting portraits of family relations. The leading warriors of the opposing sides in Homer's *Ilias* epic poem (*Iliad,* c. 8th century B.C.) are defined in part through their family ties. Hector is seen tenderly in the context of his next of kin, while Achilles is a loner, with many of the eccentricities of a genius who lives detached from father, mother, wife, son. The climax of the work turns on the parents and children motif, as Priam can stir Achilles only by conjuring up the plight of Achilles' old, besieged father.

The *Odysseia* (*The Odyssey,* epic poem, c. 8th century B.C.) presents a more subtle portrait of parents and children relations. Achilles in Hades is proud to hear, amidst his unhappiness, of his son's martial exploits. The early books contain a realistic portrait of Odysseus' adolescent son entering manhood, with all the attendant insecurities of that phase aggravated by the absence of the father. Astonishing his mother by becoming self-assertive, Telemachus will fill his father's shoes sooner than he realizes and in conjunction with the very father he misses. Later, when father and son are reunited, they will plot together and jointly rout the suitors. And at the end of the work, Odysseus is reunited as well with his reclusive father, Laertes. He fights the last important battle in the book flanked by father and son. The role of the individual as a link in a family tradition and as concurrent son and father has rarely been more dramatically depicted.

Telemachus' initial plight is likened by the narrator to that of Orestes. In Aeschylus' *Oresteia* (trilogy of plays, 458 B.C.), the son, despite momentary hesitation, avenges the murder of his father, Agamemnon, by committing matricide. The greater allegiance that a man is expected to have to his male parent and role model has dictated (through Apollo) the outcome, but the ties to the mother exact their price. Sophocles and Euripides also dramatize the matricide, though with less archaic reasoning, but far more interesting treatments of the parents and children motif are found in Euripides' other major plays, in each of which, curiously, children are destroyed. *Hippolytos* (*Hippolytus,* 428 B.C.) adumbrates the Freudian triangle. A son is unwittingly killed by a father who mistakenly takes him to be in love with the father's latest wife. In the *Bakchai* (*The Bacchants,* c. 405 B.C.), a mother, carried away by the religious fervor of a new cult, unwittingly destroys her once strait-laced and now voyeuristic son. In *Mēdeia* (*Medea,* 431 B.C.), when a husband is about to marry a woman who is younger and socially well positioned, the abandoned wife reacts by, among other savage acts, destroying the children. As is true in many divorce cases, the hatred of a once loved spouse comes to be stronger than the love for the children. Amid this turbulence, the chorus catalogues all the miseries incurred by parenthood and nearly reaches the fashionable modern conclusion that childlessness is preferable.

In *Iphigeneia hē en Aulidi* (*Iphigenia in Aulis,* c. 405 B.C.), the virgin daughter is offered as a sacrifice to the gods, but again the realistic, universal dimensions of the tale are clear. Iphigenia represents all children, youth itself, and war is seen as a god or monster that devours the young. The Agamemnon of the play is a lifelike portrait of the ambitious father who, to succeed in his vocation, must finally sacrifice his personal life and the happiness of wife and daughter. After all, even for Aristotle (*Politika,* [*Politics,* essays, 4th century B.C.]), children are similar in status to subjects and slaves.

The comedies of Aristophanes often touch on the father-son rivalry. In the *Nephelai* (*The Clouds,* 423 B.C.), the father tries to de-program a son who has joined the latest cult, that of the pseudo-Socrates; in the *Sphēkes* (*The Wasps,* 422 B.C.), it is the son rather who needs to administer "cold Turkey" treatment to a father addicted to jury duty; in the *Ornithes* (*The Birds,* 414 B.C.), a son is eager to join the utopian Cloudcuckooland so that he can, under the liberal dispensation of the bird kingdom, legally do away with his father.

The tableau at the end of the *Odyssey* of the hero acting jointly with father and son is duplicated in time rather than space in Virgil's *Aeneis* epic poem (*Aeneid*, 19 B.C.). The hero flees burning Troy with his father on his shoulders and his little son at his side. The father soon dies, his place on the shoulders to be taken eventually by a shield on which is traced the glorious future of Rome. The cultural legacy of the past is thus to be turned into the triumphs of the future, a future founded by Aeneas and consolidated by the son now ready to take Aeneas' place as warrior-leader even as once Aeneas took Anchises'. The three generations of the Odysseus family acted in accord, in the here and now, on their own behalf; the three generations of the Aeneas family individually make their contributions to a continually unfolding Roman destiny.

But the most affecting, domestic, "modern," genially comic treatment of the parents and children relations in ancient literature is in Terence's *Adelphi* (play, 160 B.C.). Here each of a pair of contrasting brothers is bringing up a son. The result is paradoxical. The son of the permissive brother is the salt of the earth, while the son of the strict one is morally repugnant. Whether we have here moral wisdom or sentimental liberal preachment depends on the reader's taste.

St. Augustine's *Confessiones* (*Confessions*, c. 397–400) condemns the father but presents an interesting contrast (perhaps influenced by Paul's contention in Corinthians that Christianity does not require worldly wisdom) between the spiritually pushing, simple-minded mother, who has arrived early at the Truth, and the wayward intellectual son, who errs often before reaching the same goal.

The Renaissance

The masterpieces of medieval literature do not shed any important new light on the theme—the General Prologue to the *Canterbury Tales* (c. 1380–1400), for example, offers the ideal image of the father as proficient yet pious knight who seems on good terms with his lively, worldly son—but the case is altered with the Renaissance. Rabelais (*Gargantua et Pantagruel* [*Gargantua and Pantagruel*, novels, 1532–1564]) is in the Terentian tradition in his depiction of indulgent fathers. More important, his is one of the first major literary works to address the question of the child's education (which here proves to be Renaissance well-roundedness gone wild). Terentian optimism appears also in Montaigne (*Essais* [*Essays*, 1580–1588]), who was one of the first to attack corporal punishment of children and who reverently offered his own father as an example of a kind and thoughtful man with an ambitious plan for bringing up a son.

The writer in whom the parents and children motif is examined in great detail is, not unexpectedly, Shakespeare. Many of his major plays study a theme that was to become important in modern times and that only Aristophanes had broached: the generational conflict. Bacon had discussed some of the differences in his *Essays* (1597–1625), but Shakespeare proceeded to put dramatic flesh on these discursive bones. *Henry IV* (1597, 1600) contains, at first glance, the stock situation of the successful, workaholic father and the "drop-out" son. It turns out, however, that Prince Hal is cunningly putting his worst foot forward. Hal does not reveal his plan to his father—and this is Shakespeare's subtlest touch—because the latter, with the self-made man's assumption that what worked for him will work for everyone, would never comprehend it. The irony is therefore that Hal, despite his father's misgivings, is a Machiavellian indeed, a chip off the old block, but so good at it—at understanding that different problems require different solutions, not rigid formulas—that even his father does not see the continuity.

In *Hamlet* (c. 1600), which contains three pairs of slain fathers and avenging sons, the mother-son relationship is foremost. Young, pious, idealistic Hamlet, disillusioned by the hasty remarriage of the mother who has sworn undying love to his late father, finds it hard now to believe in anyone at all. He finds it necessary to tutor her in elementary morality and good taste.

The generational conflict explodes in *King Lear* (1606) into overt and total war. The authoritarian father and king disinherits or exiles children (and their defenders) who do not cater to his whims. In turn, two of his daughters, once they obtain power as a result of playing the game his way, think little of pushing him to the brink of nihilism now that he is too weak to do anything about it. He retaliates by wishing upon them the same troubles with their own children. As if this view of the family were not bleak enough, the subplot reenforces it. The duke of Gloucester is brought to similar straits as a result of a letter forged by his illegitimate son—a letter, purportedly from the legitimate son, railing against the tyranny of parents and urging rebellion by children.

In *Coriolanus* (1607–1608), Shakespeare reverts to the mother-son relationship of *Hamlet* but with roles reversed. Instead of a morally immature mother and an exacting, supersubtle son, we have a domineering matron and a childish son. The premier warrior of his age, Coriolanus is inept at human relations and responsive only to the periodic interventions of his mother. When, at the end, he yields to her and spares Rome, he speaks truer than he knows, "Oh mother, what have you done." For ultimately it was she who, by her warlike pride, had produced for herself a Frankenstein's monster.

In the last romances (1608–1611), Shakespeare moves on to yet another vision of parents and children. In the first half of these plays, the parents make the usual mess of things, with consequences like exile, enmity, usurpation, attempted murder. In the second half, after a decade or two, their children—free of the sins and malice of the parents, filled with hopefulness and innocence—are often attracted to each other without knowing of the wrenches that had separated the parents. Their love catalyzes the reconciliation of the parents. Children thus symbolize the hope that each new generation brings, the sense of a second chance in life, of a redemption of sorts, of vicarious fulfillment (all that is implied in the uneducated American immigrant's proud ejaculation, "My son, the doctor!").

The initial subjection and eventual triumph of children is more explicit in

Calderón de la Barca's *La vida es sueño* (*Life Is a Dream,* play, 1635), which deals with (as does the beginning of Wolfram's *Parzival* [epic poem, c. 1210]) nearly every parent's attempt to control the environment in order to shape one's child to one's liking. Heeding an ominous prophecy, King Basilio brings up his son in solitary confinement. An attempt, years later, to ascertain whether prophecy or upbringing has the upper hand issues in the prince's rebellion and entry on his own reign with maturity and self-control. The play suggests that the king meant well but assumed more power than it was given any human being, even a father, to have.

Children overcome odds as well in four of Molière's major plays: *Tartuffe* (1664), *L'avare* (*The Miser,* 1668), *Le bourgeois gentilhomme* (*The Would-Be Gentleman,* 1670), and *Le malade imaginaire* (*The Imaginary Invalid,* 1673). In each play, the neurotic father, whether obsessed with piety, money, courtly airs, or health, would force unhappiness on his daughter by making her marry a would-be pious man, a moneyed man, a nobleman, a physician. The daughter, in alliance with other family members, proves herself not only to possess reason, will, and independence, but to exercise them much better than the self-assured man with experience who happens to be the benighted father. (In Shakespeare's *Romeo and Juliet,* c. 1596, the same situation results in tragedy because of adverse fortune.)

The Nineteenth Century

In the major eighteenth-century works, as in those of the Middle Ages, few new insights are provided on this topic. Sheridan's *School for Scandal* (play, 1777) is simply an anglicized and updated version of Terence's *Adelphi,* while Richardson's *Clarissa Harlowe* (novel, 1748) and Fielding's *Tom Jones* (novel, 1749) owe something to *Romeo and Juliet.* Later versions of the amatorily frustrated daughter, Balzac's *Eugénie Grandet* (novel, 1833) and Henry James's *Washington Square* (novel, 1881), end poignantly, but James adds an original touch to the plot. Though the father's instinct about the wooing young man is, for once, correct, his manner of handling the situation transfers the reader's sympathy to the mistaken daughter.

The nineteenth century adds new ramifications to the parents and children theme. Balzac's *Le père Goriot* (*Father Goriot,* novel, 1834) brings the King Lear plot closer to modern capitalist society. Goriot is a self-made millionaire who dotes on the daughters for whom he has created an affluent environment. They thoroughly and ungratefully enjoy it, while he lives out his sick old days in penury without, unlike Lear, complaining. What Henry IV incorrectly feared would happen to Prince Hal has here in fact happened.

Capitalism brings with it new ideologies, and that is at the core of Turgenev's novel, *Otśy i deti* (*Fathers and Children,* 1862). The two older men, genial, decent, but hopelessly ineffective, dream of a gradual amelioration of life in Russia. The forceful, consistent, but dogmatic and intolerant sons, symbolized by Bazarov, preach dismantling of the social system and look to science and reason to replace superstition and even culture itself. The same contrast exists in Dostoevsky's *Besy* (*The Possessed,* novel, 1871–1872) between the lovable but ridiculous old liberal, Stepan, and the ruthless exploiter of the new radical ideology, his son Pyotr.

Such tensions, along with many others, mark the richest treatment of the parents and children motif, in one of the greatest novels, Dostoevsky's *Brat' ia Karamazovy* (*The Brothers Karamazov,* 1880). The Karamazov family represents a cross-section of basic human types. The father is man barely out of the cave, and the sons embody the three major forms of civilized life—sensual, intellectual, religious. The plot combines a murder mystery with a philosophical inquisition and the venerable parents and children tension. For Ivan holds that there is no God and therefore everything is permitted, yet, in the wake of the murder of the universally hated father, the mere thought of having desired the old man's death is enough to madden him. Thus the dilemma of modern man—intellectually liberated but emotionally subjected to traditional constraints—is brilliantly superimposed by Dostoevsky on the age-old rivalry of father and son. Indeed, the most archaic and savage of concepts—parricide—is returning to literature almost at the time that Freud was about to arrive at his theory of the Oedipus complex (in *Die Traumdeutung* [*Interpretation of Dreams,* 1900])—an idea adumbrated in passing in St. Augustine's *Confessions* and Diderot's *Le neveu de Rameau* [*Rameau's Nephew,* satire, 1762–1784]—and of the killing by the primal horde of its father (*Totem und Tabu* [*Totem and Taboo,* 1913]).

Yet more important ideas are churned up in the great trial scene at the end of Dostoevsky's novel. In the course of a brilliant oration on the theme of "What is a father?" the defense attorney articulates the modern notion—touched on briefly in Gottfried's *Tristan* (romance, c. 1210)—that paternity is not biological and automatic but psychological, existential, earned. And, in fact, the saintly Father Zossima functions as a surrogate father to Alyosha Karamazov.

Dostoevsky's contemporary, the playwright Ibsen, likewise dealt with the conflict between biological and existential fatherhood in *Vildanden* (*The Wild Duck,* 1884). Hjalmar, a vain, Micawberish man, lives in a ramshackle place with a ramshackle family, which includes a daughter who is not, though he does not know it, his own. Hjalmar's old friend, Gregers, the son of the local potentate, discovers and reveals the truth about the child's paternity. The resulting destruction of the humanly warm household suggests, as in the Dostoevsky novel, that biological paternity can mean nothing—Gregers and his father, after all, have long hated each other—and a makeshift psychological tie can mean everything.

Ibsen presents in *Bygmester Solness* (*The Master Builder,* 1892) an updated, naturalistic version of the theme clothed in mythology in *Iphigeneia hē en Aulidi*: the great man achieving his ascent at the cost of his private life. A fire that had led indirectly to the death of his children and the moral paralysis of his wife was paradoxically the start of the builder's successful career, and his successes are not capped with happiness in part because he is haunted by the awareness of the price paid—as is also the case in *Brand* (1866), *Samfundets støtter* (*The Pillars of Society*, 1877), *En folkefiende* (*An Enemy of the People*, 1882)—and in part because he fears being overtaken in turn by the younger generation. And in *John Gabriel Borkman* (1896) yet another twist is added, as the woman who has been victimized by the tycoon's success tries to manipulate the tycoon's son, even as do the wife and the tycoon himself. The new idea here is that everyone with a claim on a child attempts to imbue that child with his/her own philosophy and to use the child as a weapon in the family wars. Insights lurking in *Mēdeia* and Shakespeare's last romances have been clarified by Ibsen in the context of the modern family.

The Twentieth Century

In modern literature, the parents and children theme becomes the setting for the schism—exacerbated in good part by the findings of Darwin, Marx, Frazer, Freud, Einstein—between, on the one hand, religious faith and social traditionalism and, on the other, rationalism, skepticism, meliorism, hedonism, estheticism. A recurring pattern in late Victorian and early modern fiction is of the tyrannous, puritanic, tradition- or business-oriented father and the sensitive, rebellious, artistic, victimized son. This is the theme of Butler's *The Way of All Flesh* (novel, 1903), Gosse's *Father and Son* (novel, 1907), Bennett's *Clayhanger* (novel, 1910), Kafka's story "Das Urteil" ("The Judgment," 1913), as well as of such chronicles of the decline and fall of a patrician family as Mann's *Buddenbrooks* (novel, 1901) and Faulkner's *The Sound and the Fury* (novel, 1929). An attenuated working-class version (with mother-daughter) is Stephen Crane's *Maggie* (novel, 1893).

By contrast, too much of father-daughter or mother-son proximity is a source of difficulties in James's *Golden Bowl* (novel, 1904) and D. H. Lawrence's *Sons and Lovers* (novel, 1913). In the latter book, the domineering mother we know from *Coriolanus* appears in a working-class family and as a transmitter of refinement rather than pugnaciousness. Paul's mother, estranged from her coarse husband, lavishes her love and hopes instead on her son. He, when mature, is attracted to a woman, Miriam, who has some of the spiritual qualities of his mother, but he finds himself emotionally and sexually blocked in her company. To the Coriolanus situation have been added quasi-Freudian ideas about the sexual velleities between mother and son; to the Ibsen (and late nineteenth-century) theme, in *Gengangere* (*Ghosts,* play, 1881), of how parental discord physically cripples the child has been added the hypothesis that such discord also emotionally cripples the child. This novel also contains the first sympathetic portrayal since Sophocles of a crime—matricide—normally considered one of the most heinous, when Paul deliberately administers an overdose of morphia to end his mother's suffering from cancer.

An oedipal situation also appears in Virginia Woolf's *To the Lighthouse* (novel, 1927). That novel is a classic exploration of the nuclear family, with tender, protective, intuitive mother and aloof, blunt, cerebral father. The treatment of a boy's passage from father-hating, vulnerable childhood to late-adolescent achievement and earning of rare paternal praise has not been matched since the portrayal of Homer's Telemachus. The optimistic ending of this novel is unavailable in Kafka's "Die Verwandlung" ("Metamorphosis," story, 1915) because father and son never achieve reconciliation. Gregor, the young salesman on whom the aging parents depend for financial support, is turned into a roachlike insect. What follows is the gradual emotional withdrawal of Gregor and the family's loss of interest in him. The story dramatizes the insecurities of a young man whose relations with his parents have been tenuous at best and expresses the alienation an individual might, and perhaps many do, feel within the supposedly congenial family circle.

Alienation is presented more sympathetically in Joyce's *Portrait of the Artist as a Young Man* (1916), which celebrates the sensitive young man's need to— unlike the artists of the past—cut all ties with family, country, religion (mother, motherland, mother church). A much more powerful exploration of family ties is undertaken in *Ulysses* (novel, 1922). The hero of the earlier book, Stephen, is now adrift, ambivalent about his dead mother, out of touch with the father in whom ironically (as in Henry IV) are the seeds that flowered in the son. Stephen several times declares "amor matris" to be the central reality of existence, yet the phrase's syntactical ambiguity—it means "a mother's love" or "love of mother"—brings out the sense that the mother-son relationship is, as in *Sons and Lovers,* both necessary and harmful. Fatherhood, on the other hand, is an enigma. Stephen gives his personal quandary a metaphysical scope by ruminating on the theologians, Catholic and heretic, who wrestled with the mystery of the relationship of God the Father to the Son, as well as on Hamlet, who had a heavy burden placed on his shoulders by a ghostly, uncertain father.

The other main character, Leopold Bloom, a not very successful salesman and a Jew twice but unconvincingly converted to Christianity, is in some ways the opposite of Odysseus. Instead of having a faithful wife and, at the end, a father and a son fighting at his side, Bloom has an unfaithful wife and only disquieting thoughts about a father who long ago killed himself and a son who died as an infant. The two isolated protagonists drift about Dublin, come together for a few hours of animated conversation, and go their separate ways. The tedium of everyday life has been interrupted by a rare interlude rich with mutual intellectual and emotional satisfaction, as Bloom becomes to Stephen a surrogate father and Stephen serves as a vision of what Bloom would have wished his own son to have become. It is no accident that the definitive treatment of the idea of surrogate parents and children relations appears in the greatest modern novel, for, as a critic has pointed out, in an age of religious doubt, the search for the father becomes the central occupation of man.

Joyce's fellow Irishman, G. B. Shaw, produced a preface to his play *Misalliance* (1910) that is easily the best of all essays on parents and children. Typically Shavian, it questions all assumptions, pricks the commonplace foibles and sentimentalities, wryly suggests alternative arrangements and interpretations, propounds paradoxes, and good-naturedly advances ideas that must have shocked the contemporary reader as nihilistic and immoral. What is lighthearted and discursive in Shaw becomes grim and dramatic in O'Neill, whose play *Long Day's Journey Into Night* (1956) contains one of the most intense and depressing studies of parents and children. The dislocations of the parents are matched by those of the sons, and, in a work that has become the archetype of many modern plays, the members of the family quartet tear the veils of illusion and deception from each other and destroy their dignity as individuals. Another typically bleak, modern view of the relations of parents and children appears in Miller's play *Death of a Salesman* (1949), in which the father is as much a pathetic victim of false notions of success as the cause of his two sons' lack of bearings.

Two works written since World War II may serve as representative of some of the ideas in recent literature. In Bellow's *Seize the Day* (novella, 1956), the protagonist, Tommy Wilhelm, is a modern everyman facing failure as a son, brother, husband, lover, and father. Lodging in a hotel where his father lives, Wilhelm has futilely gone back to his roots, to what seems to him to have been the cause of his failure. His retired father, once a successful, admired physician who had had little time and less sympathy for his son, acts as if Wilhelm is still the uncouth fidgety boy with dirty fingers. Here is the family dynamic dramatized by Euripides and Ibsen—the father as great man who has sacrificed his family— but now seen from the vantage point of the victim.

The child's emotional victimization by the parents' rigidity and traditionalism is the theme of Roth's novel *Portnoy's Complaint* (1969), but in the author's earlier *Goodbye Columbus* (novella, 1959), about a love affair between a young librarian from a lower middle-class Jewish community in Newark and a Radcliffe girl from an upper middle-class suburban Jewish community, the focus of attention is on the relations between mother and daughter. Besides the implicit Freudian sexual rivalry, there is a sociological one; the mother, still haunted by the poverty she knew in Newark years before, is unable to get along with the spoiled daughter, whose affluent youth she envies. What seemed a typical summer romance is revealed in fact to be a battle between mother and daughter into which the young man happened to stumble and in which he is utilized as a weapon by the daughter. None of the characters is aware of this, for Roth, as a modern writer tutored by Freud, adds the dimension of unconscious motivation to the old theme of poverty and affluence intertwined with the even older theme of parents and children.

See also: Family, Incest, Oedipus Complex, Search for Father.

Selected Bibliography

Armens, Sven. *Archetypes of the Family in Literature*. Seattle: University of Washington Press, 1966.

Davidson, C. N., and E. M. Broner, eds. *The Lost Tradition: Mothers and Daughters in Literature*. New York: Ungar, 1980.

Schücking, Levin L. *The Puritan Family: A Social Study from the Literary Sources.* Trans. Brian Battershaw. London: Routledge and K. Paul, 1969.
Tobin, Patricia. *Time and the Novel: The Genealogical Imperative.* Princeton, N.J.: Princeton University Press, 1978.

MANFRED WEIDHORN

PEASANT IN NOVELS

The peasant is a member of the lowest class of society; he is defined more by his agrarian occupation than by his economic position. Unlike the industrial laborer, he is relatively independent of the economic structure that surrounds him because he can normally produce from the soil the minimum required for his sustenance. At the same time, however, he depends on the economy for whatever he might acquire beyond his minimum requirements. The result is that he finds himself suspended between his desire for security and his desire for more comfort. Although he would like more comfort, he is unwilling to let his security depend on an economy that he neither trusts nor understands. To preserve his status quo, he prevents the surrounding economy from penetrating too far into his culture by constructing barriers—usually traditions—to ward it off. Consequently his social and educational orientation is bounded for the most part by his village and is centered around the traditions and ceremonies peculiar to that village. His culture is thus self-perpetuating, subject to change-resisting traditions that may date back centuries.

The popularity of the peasant as a subject for literature undoubtedly has its roots in the concept of primitivism, which is basically an attempt to reflect the discontent of the civilized with civilization or some facet of it. From the perspective of a highly complex cultural condition, it asserts that a life that is simpler and less sophisticated is more desirable. This concept, which appears in the literature of antiquity as well as that of succeeding centuries, usually reflected in bucolic and pastoral poetry, is not new. However, from the Renaissance to the middle of the eighteenth century, undoubtedly because of the heightened interest in science and the new directions in philosophy, primitivism enjoyed little popularity. Yet it was destined to resurface in more modern times. Modern primitivistic literature can probably be traced back to Rousseau, who, in his *Discours sur l'origine et les fondements de l'inégalité parmi les hommes (Discourse on the Origin and Bases of Inequality among Men,* 1754) was the first relatively modern major figure to seriously extol the virtues of uncivilized man, a position that he reaffirmed in his novel *Emile* (1762). At about the same time Macpherson's Ossian poems (1760–1763) depicting the virtue of the primitive Celts began their rise to literary acclamation.

Around 1770 the German *Sturm und Drang* writers appeared on the literary scene, and weariness with civilization's hectic artificiality in contrast to the fundamental simplicity of rustic life was a major preoccupation of this influential group. Primitivism then becomes a primary theme of the romantic period, and in one or another form it can be detected in the works of nearly every major figure of that time. In some instances it is revealed through a yearning for communication with a pristine nature, as in Chateaubriand's novel *Atala* (1801). In others the escape from civilization is into history, as in Sir Walter Scott's works. In still other cases it is the rustic who is admired for the simplicity and goodness of his life; Wordsworth praises the virtue of the shepherd in "Michael" (poem, 1800). As for novels of the period, for the most part primitivism was reflected through the nobility of the savage in his untrammeled wilderness, through that of the idealized medieval hero, and finally through that of the peasant.

Jeremias Gotthelf was probably the first to devote a novel to the peasantry in *Der Bauernspiegel* (*Peasant Reflection,* 1837), but because the narrator moves through different villages, the novel does not reveal the closed nature of peasant life. Further, this novel failed to gain international recognition. The first recognized major novelist to devote a novel entirely to peasants was George Sand, who produced *La mare au diable* (*The Devil's Pool*) in 1846. Of course peasants had appeared in novels before this time, the most notable of which is Don Quixote's faithful Sancho Panza. And Balzac had already produced *Les paysans* (*The Peasants,* 1844). Yet in these novels, unlike in Sand's, the peasant was not a motif that was the primary concern of the novel, and thus they would not be considered peasant novels. Even in *La mare au diable,* Sand's concern is not with the external conditions of the peasants but with their morality; they lead idyllic lives and are characterized by their simplicity and virtue. Tolstoy, in *Kazaki* (*The Cossacks,* 1863), also idealizes peasant life, yet more realistically, for his peasants have vices, as seen in Lukáshka's involvement with Dunáyka while her husband is absent. He further hints at naturalism, which is later so profoundly to affect the peasant novel, for he reveals peasants as poor and struggling for what they get, though they are nonetheless happy because they can win the struggle. Still more realistic is the next major novel, Bjørnstjerne Bjørnson's *Arne* (1858), which presents the illegitimate Arne's father, Nils, as thoroughly vice-ridden; nonetheless the novel ultimately develops into a lyric idyll.

The myth of the idyllic life of the peasant, however, is destroyed by Flaubert in his short story "Un cœur simple" ("A Simple Heart," 1877). Flaubert does not place his protagonist, Félicité, in an agrarian setting, but his focus is nonetheless on her distinctively peasant characteristics. Although Félicité is simple and virtuous, she suffers indignity upon indignity, and through his craft Flaubert convinces us that we are learning precisely what it is like to be a peasant. The conclusion that we come to is that the simplicity and virtue ascribed to the peasant is not the result of morality or preference but rather of stupidity. Yet Flaubert, unlike his predecessors, was not concerned with the peasant as a class or with the life style of the peasant; instead he was concerned with his protagonist as an individual and with the social problems current to his time. The same is true of Giovanni Verga in *I Malavoglia* (*The House by the Medlar Tree*, 1881). This novel can be seen as an avant garde model of the impending naturalism, which is reflected in the subordination of plot, the emphasis on coarser facets of society, the shockingly squalid scenes, and the final implications of despair. The village that 'Ntoni is forced to leave remains as it has always been, rooted in tradition and ruled by circumstances that preclude the individual's transcending his environment. Yet despite the squalor and despair, Verga elicits sympathy from his portrayal of the Malavoglia family as good people but too weak to cope with the circumstances that are eventually their undoing.

During the next decade Guy de Maupassant moved further toward naturalism in his depiction of Norman peasants in his short stories. These stories depict the squalor of peasant conditions but express less sympathy for the peasant than was seen in Flaubert or Verga in that it is not the conditions but the peasant himself who is responsible for his own ruin, although his circumstances may have prevented his foreseeing various circumstances. In *La terre* (*The Earth*, 1887), however, Zola allows no sympathy for the peasant and subjects him to the sordid fate implicit in naturalism. Lacking in moral character of any kind, his peasants have only two motivations—material gain and sex. Even the only two characters with which one might expect to be sympathetic are reduced to a subhuman level, for our sympathy for Jean is subverted when he tries to seduce Jacqueline in a corn bin, and for Françoise when she realizes that she loves Buteau after being raped by him while his wife held her legs. Although *La terre* may have many deficiencies as a novel, Zola nonetheless displays great power in it, and no peasant novel of the nineteenth century had a greater influence on those of the succeeding century than this one.

Although later naturalists evince little interest in the peasant, turning their attention more to the lower urban classes, the large proportion of Nobel awards, nearly 10 percent, indicates his popularity as a subject for fiction in the twentieth century. In 1909 Selma Lagerlöff received it for *Jerusalem* (1901–1902); in 1920 Knut Hamsun for *Markens grøde* (*The Growth of the Soil*, 1917); in 1924, W. S. Reymont for *Chłopi* (*The Peasants*, 1902–1909); in 1938, Pearl Buck for *The Good Earth* (1931); in 1939, Frans Eemil Sillanpää for *Hurskas kurjuus* (*Meek Heritage*, 1919); and in 1965, Mikhail Sholokhov for *Tikhiĭ Don* (*The Silent Don*, 1928–1940). The various novels about peasants form a distinct subgenre of modern fiction, for when the reader accustomed to them finishes one, he is left with an impression that he has visited that village or met those people before. Not that these novels are all alike, of course, for authors of good peasant novels, like those of good novels about any topic, are highly individual in the presentation of their material. Yet something about the peasant causes different authors from highly dissimilar cultures to project characters and conditions that are essentially the same.

There are primarily three categories of peasant novels: political (including social realism), realistic, and primitivistic. In the political novels basically the same techniques are used to render the peasant and his condition as are used in the realistic category; however, there are some significant differences. For one, the political novel contains numerous passages of denotative dialectic that espouse the particular position of the author. Second, the political novel is generally structurally divisible into two distinct parts, the first peasant and the second political. In the first section the tone reflects oppressive immutability and despair, as occurs in the realistic novel. This tone comes through the scenes depicting the peasants in a hopeless struggle against their oppressors and is intensified as the oppressors increase in strength and harshness. In Ralph Bates's *The Olive Field* (1936), for example, Don Fadrique persistently applies greater pressure on Mudarra and the other olive pickers to increase production with less recompense, forcing them into such a level of poverty that they are even reduced to stealing water from each other. However, in novels of this kind, when the peasant becomes involved in the political cause, the tone changes from one of despair to one of hope, for the cause offers him both allies and the hope of overcoming his conditions. Thus Mudarra and Joaquín, bitter enemies earlier in the novel, unite together as members of the party to fight the oppression. Another reason for the change is that, since most of the dialectic is encountered in the second part of the novel, the focus shifts from the protagonist to the cause. Involvement with the cause, of course, implies ultimate victory for the protagonist, whether it be material or only moral.

The peasant of the realistic novel does not fare as well, for his roots trace to the pessimism of Zola. The primary intent of such novels is to draw attention to the wretchedness of the conditions under which these people live. They are surrounded by poverty, brutality, animality, and ignorance. Thus in *Meek Heritage* Juha has to turn his son out because they have too little food; Maja witnesses a dying woman's clothing stolen before she is even dead; Hilda dies as the result of rape; and Juha revolts without really understanding why. The tragedy of their lives is further borne out by their inability to control their environment; they are buffetted about by the random will of whatever forces prevent their improving their lot. Still, the twentieth-century novelist, unlike Zola, displays the peasant in a sympathetic light and attempts to elicit from the reader a favorable rather than a negative response; he renders the peasant as a man, not as a creature from some subhuman culture. Though partially responsible for his condition, he is a victim of circumstance; we pity his inability to cope with life but respect his capacity to endure it.

The peasant of the primitivistic novel, which finds its roots in Sand, is endowed with simplicity and an affinity with nature. He is strong and courageous, and his life is a good one. Isak, in Hamsun's *The Growth of the Soil,* is uneducated but understands the land. Through sheer strength and perseverance he fashions a thriving farm in the bleak outlands of Norway. At the same time certain characteristics of these novels can also be traced to Zola, for there are scenes of horror, brutality, and a certain, though less specifically rendered, sexual promiscuity. Inger strangles and buries her hare-lipped first-born baby; Brede will not help Axel when he is pinned beneath a tree; and the promiscuous Barbro has committed two infanticides. Despite occasional scenes such as these, however, these novels deplore the encroachment of civilization, which is inimical to a pure and simple existence; the protagonist is strong enough to overcome its ravages and thus remains a man to be admired leading a life to be envied.

There are certain features that seem common to nearly all peasant novels. Most are presented in conventional, straightforward narrative, and the level of language is not elevated, with the exception of the dialectic in the political novels. There are also certain attributes common to the peasants in all of them: brutality, sexual promiscuity, and at least formal ignorance. This would perhaps not be noteworthy were it not that these novels spring from vastly different parts of the world. One conclusion that might be drawn is that the peasant, or at least the concept of the peasant, is essentially the same throughout the world. And sophisticated or experimental techniques such as stream-of-consciousness and the like are inappropriate to this kind of novel not only because direct presentation is in harmony with the simplicity of the characters, but also because such techniques imply some sort of psychological or philosophical insight. The peasant in these novels has neither psychology nor philosophy. He may labor, he may endure, and on occasion he may even have an idea. But he does not think. He may wander helplessly in his environment or may overcome its hostility, but he will not think about it. By combining the nonreflective characteristic of the peasant with the other attributes common to him in these novels, we probably come to an apprehension of the peasant as he is conceived of in this century. He becomes an ignorant, sometimes brutal, sexually promiscuous man who knows few pleasures and is unaware of those he does not know. He labors hard for very little and endures the ravages of both nature and man. And oddly enough, through these novels we can see that despite the linguistic, cultural, and political differences among such countries as Russia and Norway and China and France, the concept of the peasant is the same.

Perhaps throughout the world the conditions of his existence are the same. Yet it seems that his popularity as a subject for literature is fading. It may be that rapid advances in technology and heightened interest in international politics have distracted attention from him, much as was the case in the Renaissance and the eighteenth century. Furthermore, communications, such as television and the automobile, are now so advanced that the peasant in most cases no longer is as isolated as was the case heretofore and may therefore be gradually assimilating into the overriding culture of which his village is a part. If such is the case, if technology takes over the land and in search of greater comfort and an easier life the peasant migrates to the cities, we may well have seen the last of the great peasant novels.

See also: Arcadia, Noble Savage.

Selected Bibliography

Lovejoy, Arthur O., and George Boas. *Primitivism and Related Ideas of Antiquity.* 1935. New York: Octagon Books, 1973.

"Peasant Studies in French Fiction" (anonymous). *Edinburgh Review*. 205 (1907): 299–325.

Runge, Edith Amelia. *Primitivism and Related Ideas in Sturm und Drang Literature*. 1946. New York: Russell & Russell, 1972.

Wolf, Eric R. *Peasants*. Englewood Cliffs, N.J.: Prentice-Hall, 1966.

MICHAEL J. HOLLAND

PERSONALITY (Double-Split-Multiple)

"Few concepts and dreams have haunted the imagination as durably as those of the *double*," notes Albert J. Guérard in *Stories of the Double* (1967), "from primitive man's sense of a duplicated self as immortal soul to the complex mirror games and mental chess of Mann, Nabokov, Borges." Yet Guérard also concedes that the word "double" is "embarrassingly vague" as used in literary criticism, a judgment shared by C. F. Keppler in *The Literature of the Second Self* (1972). The myriad of interchangeable names attests to its literary popularity and vagueness: double, *Doppelgänger*, secret self, second self, opposing self, alter ego, shadow, mirror image, split personality, dual personality, multiple personality. What do these terms have in common? They suggest a complex vision of human personality, a duality or multiplicity of warring selves struggling toward integration. Implicit behind this struggle is the idea of psychic imbalance, often caused by the domination of one self by another self. The result is fragmentation, duplication, loss of identity, and inner strife.

As a literary motif, double personality suggests an essentially dualistic conception of human nature, with a socially "higher" self at war with a "lower" more primitive self—the contrast, that is, between the Apollonian and Dionysian elements of personality, or the Freudian superego and id. Since literature tends to dramatize conflict more convincingly than it offers resolution, the double motif usually ends with the defeat of one self by another self or, at best, an uneasy reconciliation between the warring selves.

Defined narrowly, double personality occurs when two autonomous selves cohabit the same body. Most cases of multiple personality are dual. Keppler classifies the second self into the twin brother, pursuer, tempter, vision of horror, saviour, and the beloved. The other self may be human or nonhuman: a shadow, monster, disembodied voice, or autoscopic hallucination. Defined broadly, the double includes both the duplicate and the antithetical complement. Complementary characters, for example, often dramatize the conflicts within a single personality—good/bad, mind/body, reason/passion. Masculine and feminine components of a single personality (the Jungian animus-anima) may be divided into two or more characters. Similarly, character foils portray two sides of the same personality, as do biological twins, physical duplicates, and figments of the imagination. Doris L. Eder distinguishes two basic types of doubles in "The

Idea of the Double" (*The Psychoanalytic Review* 65 [1978]): "Either the double is an exact replica, mirror image, or identical twin (as in Plautus' *Menaechmi* [*The Two Menaechmuses*, c. 200 B.C.] or Shakespeare's *Comedy of Errors* , c. 1594) or the double is one's other self, a self irrupting from the unconscious, that is antithetical yet complementary to one's conscious self." Whether defined narrowly or broadly, multiple personality affirms what Keppler calls the "mystery of a contradiction, of simultaneous distinction and identity, of an inescapable two that are at the same time an indisputable one."

Background of the Double in the German Romantic Movement

Although the image of the double dates back to Plato's discussion of androgyny in the *Symposion* (*Symposium*, dialogue, c. 384 B.C.), the motif became popular and assumed its distinctive features in the late eighteenth century. Its development coincided with the romantic movement and its emphasis upon the bizarre and uncanny. The German Romantics popularized the double in their romances, fairy tales, and Gothic horror stories. Jean Paul introduced the term *Doppelgänger* and many of his stories contain doubles. The title character in the novel *Siebenkäs* (1796–1797) exactly resembles another figure with whom he exchanges names. Twin characters compete with each other in the unfinished novel *Die Flegeljahre* (*Years of Indiscretion,* 1804–1805). The great master of the double was E.T.A. Hoffman, whose characters leave behind reflections that return later to haunt them. In "Die Geschichte vom verlornen Spiegelbilde" ("The Story of the Lost Reflection," 1815) Erasmus Spikher seeks to gain his reflection after leaving it with the amorous Giulietta. Hoffmann's first novel, *Die Elixiere des Teufels* (*The Devil's Elixirs,* 1815–1816), influenced Dostoevsky's *Dvoïnik* (*The Double,* novel, 1846). Adelbert von Chamisso employs the double in his Faustian novelle *Peter Schlemihls wundersame Geschichte* (*The Wonderful Story of Peter Schlemihl,* 1814). Here the protagonist sells his shadow (conscience, integrity, soul) to a mysterious stranger, Mephistopheles, in exchange for unlimited wealth. Shadowless, he is mocked by the world and thwarted in his efforts to marry a beautiful young woman. At the end of the fairytale he does penance for the foolish decision to sell his shadow. In all these stories a character is confronted by a reflection who shares or seizes an element of his personality.

The Double in Nineteenth-Century Literature

Nineteenth-century writers gradually came to see the rich possibilities of double personality. Goethe's highly influential *Faust* (play, 1808) was one of the first dramas to portray the second self as a tempter. Although Mephistopheles is not an exact duplicate of Faust, the devil's power over him may be explained by their complementary nature. Mephistopheles insists upon his kinship to man; in embracing evil, Faust yields to his worst nature. This theme also appears in James Hogg's novel *The Private Memoirs and Confessions of a Justified Sinner* (1824), in which the second self symbolizes the devil. The treacherous son of a fanatical minister succumbs to the temptation to kill his good-natured brother. After committing other heinous crimes, he finally destroys himself in the belief he is a "justified sinner."

The opposite theme appears in Victor Hugo's *Les misérables* (novel, 1862). Here the evil second self aids in the protagonist's moral redemption. The hero of the novel, the ex-convict Jean Valjean, is pursued relentlessly by police inspector Javert. Hugo's intricate plot continually brings together the two men, each of whom is the instrument of the other's oppression and liberation. Despite Javert's harassment of Valjean, the latter rescues his nemesis from execution during the 1832 revolution. At the end of the novel Javert returns the favor by befriending Valjean, but the inspector remains entrapped in self-hate and plunges to his death in the Seine.

One of the best-known stories of double personality is Poe's "William Wilson" (1839). The title character confronts a mirror image at school bearing the same name, mannerisms, even birthday. They seem to resemble identical twins. What most offends William Wilson is his counterpart's plebeian name, "venom in my ears." The double evokes dim visions of William Wilson's earliest infancy, perhaps suggesting sibling rivalry. Fleeing from the "imposter," Wilson runs away from school and gives himself up to debauchery. His evil actions, however, are effortlessly thwarted by the morally superior double. At the end of the story Wilson challenges his counterpart to a duel, stabs him to death, and then— gazing at his own blood-stained reflection in a mirror—similarly dies. Poe's moral echoes in the dying breath of William Wilson's double: *"You have conquered, and I yield. Yet, henceforward art thou also dead—dead to the World, to Heaven and to Hope! In me didst thou exist—and, in my death, see by this image, which is thine own, how utterly thou hast murdered thyself."*

Dostoevsky's classic novel *Dvoĭnik* (*The Double*, 1846) remains the foremost example of double personality. Awakening from troubled sleep, Golyadkin visits a physician, Dr. Rutenspitz, to reassure himself he is not ill. Yet despite or because of his violent protestations, he seems emotionally unstable. His insulting behavior alienates his colleagues and friends. At the nadir of his pain and disgrace he encounters his double. Several clues hint that he is hallucinating. He is in the midst of a black depression, he suspects the mysterious passer-by may be part of himself, and he fears madness. The sight of the double—who shares Golyadkin's name, appearance, and dress—horrifies him. The central ambiguity of the story is whether the mysterious stranger is a fantastic delusion, paranoia, or the product of a sinister plot fabricated by Golyadkin's enemies to drive him mad.

After introducing the double into the story, Dostoevsky cleverly reduplicates the plot. Golyadkin generously befriends the lonely and impoverished double, who narrates a story remarkably similar to the one Golyadkin himself had told in the beginning. Moved by his namesake's plight, Golyadkin bestows the patronage upon the younger man that he has also been seeking. Soon, however, the double usurps Golyadkin's position at work, ingratiates himself with his employers, and besmirches his reputation. The imposter seems at once virtuous and sinister, achieving the success Golyadkin has been pursuing vainly.

In putting forward the thesis that "people wearing masks have ceased to be a rarity . . . and that it is difficult nowadays to recognize the man under the mask," Golyadkin embodies Dostoevsky's theme that unconscious and irrational forces shape human personality. Human nature consists of irresolvable dualisms: benevolence/cruelty, nobility/ignominy, innocence/guilt. The "real" Golyadkin is both helpless victim and merciless victimizer, servile bureaucrat and arrogant usurper. There is also a conflict between the loving son who wishes to merge with the omnipotent father and the rebellious son who desires to slay the tyrannical father. Foreshadowing Dostoevsky's underground man, Golyadkin is plagued by tormenting moral, social, and psychological problems. A servant's observation that "Good people live honestly, good people live without faking, and they never come double" must be qualified by the fact that Dostoevsky dramatizes the good-in-evil and evil-in-good. The motif of double personality allows Dostoevsky to demonstrate one of his most archetypal themes, the self-tortured hero or anti-hero caught up in his own web of deceit, insecurity, and rage. Juxtaposing dream and reality, paranoia and persecution, Dostoevsky never allows his bewildered character to grasp the complexity of human personality. His identity stolen by an insider, Golyadkin endures misery and self-degradation until at the end of the story he is certified insane by the authorities and banished, either by Rutenspitz or the physician's evil double, to a hellish darkness.

Other Nineteenth Century Stories of the Double

Other nineteenth-century stories of the double should be mentioned, including Dostoevsky's masterpiece, *Brat'ia Karamazovy* (*The Brothers Karamazov*, novel, 1880), in which the morally scrupulous Ivan bears a terrible affinity to his diabolical half-brother Smerdyakov. In Emily Brontë's passionate novel *Wuthering Heights* (1847) Catherine Earnshaw and Heathcliff share the same wild, primitive nature and may be viewed as doubles. Cathy rejects her stormy lover to marry the tame Edgar Linton, but she can never be apart from Heathcliff. As she affirms to Nelly Dean, "He's more myself than I am. Whatever our souls are made of, his and mine are the same; and Linton's is as different as a moonbeam from lightning, or frost from fire." In Guy de Maupassant's short story "Le Horla" ("The Horla," 1887), the solitary character is pursued by a phantom double who preys upon his body and soul. Driven crazy, the narrator manages to slay the monstrous Horla but, still fearing its return, also kills himself. The myth of Narcissus appears in Oscar Wilde's novel *The Picture of Dorian Gray* (1891). The beautiful hero falls in love with his own portrait and, in a reversal of the art-life dichotomy, the portrait decays while the human subject remains impervious to the ravages of time. Stabbing the portrait, Dorian Gray dies. In Henry James's novella *The Turn of the Screw* (1898), Peter Quint may be seen not only as a ghost returning from the world of the dead to haunt the living but as a projection or sexual hallucination of the repressed Victorian governess. In *The Jolly Corner* (novella, 1909) the aging Spencer Bryden has failed to participate fully in life. Returning from abroad, he tries to imagine how he would have lived differently had he remained in New York and dwelled in a house "on the jolly corner." He becomes obsessed with the idea and searches for an alter ego whom he believes has lived deeply and passionately.

Double Personality in Hawthorne and Melville

Hawthorne and Melville make extensive use of the divided self in their short stories and novels. The sadistic Chillingworth and masochistic Dimmesdale are complementary characters in Hawthorne's novel *The Scarlet Letter* (1850). Apollonian-Dionysian dualism pervades "Young Goodman Brown" (1935), "The Birth-Mark" (1846), and "My Kinsman, Major Molineux" (1851), to name only a few of Hawthorne's stories in which we find warring antinomies: civilization/nature, mind/body, control/chaos. Melville uses the latent double in his novella *Bartleby the Scrivener* (1853), in which the lawyer-narrator involuntarily becomes the title character's secret sharer. After hiring the scrivener, the lawyer proceeds to wall him behind a screen; he cannot separate himself from the passively aggressive employee, however, and gradually loses his composure in the face of Bartleby's defiant "I would prefer not to." Melville's novella *Billy Budd* (1891) recalls Hawthorne's "The Birth-Mark" in that characters of near-perfection are destroyed by a single minor flaw suggestive of the imperfection of nature. Billy Budd's fatal stutter resembles the tiny blemish on Georgiana's cheek with which her perfectionist husband cannot live. Additionally, Billy Budd and Claggart function not only as allegorical opposites—good/bad, angel/devil, love/hate—but also, as Richard Chase has pointed out, as psychological sons to Captain Vere.

The Double in Twentieth-Century Literature

Many twentieth-century writers have explored double personality but none more successfully than Joseph Conrad. "The Secret Sharer" (story, 1912) is an apt title for many of his works. By neglecting to retrieve the rope ladder hanging over the ship, the inexperienced and self-conscious captain unconsciously summons the fishlike Leggatt, who symbolizes the primitive, instinctual element of life necessary for survival. Yet Conrad does not sentimentalize instinct, for he shows that it may also be deadly. Leggatt is a fugitive from justice because he killed a man who had disobeyed him during a violent storm. *Lord Jim* (novel, 1900) is filled with secret sharer relationships. Captain Brierly commits suicide in silent acknowledgment that he too, like Jim, might have jumped from the crippled *Patna*. Jim enters into a secret sharer relationship with the contemptible "Gentleman" Brown, who has repeatedly jumped out of moral cynicism and ruthlessness. The authorial Marlow recognizes in Lord Jim a portrait of himself; despite Jim's crime he remains "one of us." Axel Heyst and the Satanic "plain Mr. Jones" are doubles in *Victory* (novel, 1915), as are Marlow and Kurtz in

Heart of Darkness (novella, 1902). With the exception of Leggatt's salutary influence on the captain, the secret sharer relationship usually results in paralyzed overidentification and death for Conrad's characters.

Herman Hesse's *Demian* (novel, 1919) and *Steppenwolf* (novel, 1927) contain numerous doubles. Harry Haller has a dual nature, "a human and a wolfish one." He and Hermine are mirror images, the latter a "looking-glass" for the former. Saul Bellow uses the double in *The Victim* (novel, 1947). The complementary characters Asa Leventhal and Kirby Allbee symbolize the Jew and Gentile who take turns victimizing each other. In *Seize the Day* (novella, 1956), the wrathful Dr. Adler and psychological con-artist Dr. Tamkin represent competing father figures to the lost son, Tommy Wilhelm. Joe Morgan and Jake Horner are philosophical doubles in John Barth's *The End of the Road* (novel, 1958). The two adversaries dramatize the struggle between reason/unreason, being/not-being, with Joe's vulnerable wife Rennie caught in the middle.

The supreme parodist of the double motif is Vladimir Nabokov, whose novels reveal an obsession with mirrors, reflections, and deceptions. Hermann plots to destroy his physical double, Felix, in *Otchaïanie (Despair,* 1936); Humbert Humbert (whose name itself is a double joke) engages in a deadly tragicomic duel with his alter ego, Claire Quilty, in *Lolita* (1955); John Shade is pursued by darker shades in *Pale Fire* (1962); and Van and Ada are perfect lovers precisely because they are complementary parts of one self in *Ada* (1969). Jorge Luis Borges similarly plays with the double motif in two short parables in *El Hacedor* (*Dreamtigers,* 1960). In "Borges y yo" and "Everything and Nothing" (the title is in English) the writer contemplates the paradoxical void behind the seeming multiplicity of life. In the poem "Los espejos velados" ("Shrouded Mirrors," 1960) Borges voices his fear of mirrors, which "threaten a spectral duplication or multiplication of reality."

Psychoanalytic Meaning of the Double

From its beginning psychoanalysis has been fascinated with the concept of the double. In his pioneering essay "Der Doppelgänger" (1914) and subsequent book (1925) Otto Rank first demonstrated the equivalence of the mirror and shadow as images, both of which appear to the ego as its likeness. Rank viewed the double as a defense against castration and death, which threaten narcissistic self-love. The impulse to rid oneself of the double, the psychoanalyst claimed, is an essential feature of the motif. Yet the slaying of the double is often a suicidal act. Rank's essay prompted Freud to discuss Hoffmann's story "Der Sandmann" ("The Sandman," 1817) in "Das Unheimliche" ("The Uncanny," essay, 1919). Freud links the double motif to the repetition compulsion principle, later developed into the "death instinct" in *Jenseits des Lustprinzips (Beyond the Pleasure Principle,* 1920). R. D. Laing investigated the psychiatric and existential implications of the true self/false self split in *The Divided Self* (1959). Although many writers who use the double motif have led tragic or disturbed lives, including Hoffmann, Poe, Maupassant, Dostoevsky, and more recently

Sylvia Plath (who used the secret sharer relationship in her novel *The Bell Jar,* 1963), we may disagree with Rank's assertion that the double motif implies a pathological personality. In the twentieth century the double has become a standard literary convention.

Multiple Personality: Clinical Definition

Clinicians define multiple personality as *Grande hystérie,* a rare and mysterious illness in which two or more autonomous personalities cohabit the same body, with one self having little or no awareness of the others' existences. Contrary to popular belief, multiple personality (less precisely called "split personality") is a neurosis, not psychosis (schizophrenia). A person experiences blackouts and enters another level of consciousness called "fugue," a major state of personality dissociation characterized by amnesia and flight from the environment. The psychological mechanisms of multiple personality consist of projection, splitting, and merging. A developmental defect in the ego contributes to the formation of multiple personality. In Freud's words, "If we throw a crystal to the floor, it breaks; but not into haphazard pieces. It comes apart along its lines of cleavage into fragments whose boundaries, though they were invisible, were predetermined by the crystal's structure. Mental patients are split and broken structures of this same kind." Therapeutic treatment aims for the reintegration of the autonomous selves into a complete and whole personality.

Surprisingly little has been published in medical literature on the subject of multiple personality. Medical discussions first appeared at the end of the eighteenth century. Henri Ellenberger has speculated in *The Discovery of the Unconscious* (1970) that "the phenomenon of possession, so frequent for many centuries, could well be considered as one variety of multiple personality." The best known medical case studies include Morton Prince's celebrated story of Miss Beauchamp in *The Dissociation of a Personality* (1906); Thigpen and Cleckley's *The Three Faces of Eve* (1957) and the patient's accounts in *The Final Face of Eve* (1958) and *I'm Eve* (1977); and Flora Rheta Schreiber's *Sybil* (1973). Each of Sybil's sixteen autonomous selves was analyzed during the eleven-year psychoanalysis and traced back to a complicated "capture-control-imprisonment-torture theme" that pervaded her terrifying childhood.

Multiple Personality in Literature

Although strictly speaking Robert Louis Stevenson's classic novel *The Strange Case of Dr. Jekyll and Mr. Hyde* (1886) does not accurately describe the clinical dynamics of multiple personality, the work is closely identified with the phenomenon and remains its most famous literary treatment. The two selves—the tall civilized scientist, Dr. Jekyll, and the deformed savage, Mr. Hyde—actually have different body structures. Moreover, Jekyll's transformation depends upon a mysterious drug. In a Faustian attempt to pursue forbidden knowledge, Jekyll drinks a potion that changes him into the bestial Hyde. The physician loses control over his dark self and, in a reversal of the children's game, seeks out

Hyde only to discover there can be no sanctuary from the hidden adversary. Jekyll's audacious experiment with transcendental medicine culminates in the unleashing of Satanic evil, and Hyde finally commits suicide. There is no integration of the warring sides of human personality. Jekyll's self-degradation has a strikingly modern quality, foreshadowing Kurtz's "exalted and incredible degradation" in *Heart of Darkness*. In a copy of a pious book which the Apollonian Jekyll had once admired, Stevenson's narrator discovers "startling blasphemies," much like Kurtz's misanthropic footnote to the long humanitarian report he had written in Africa: "Exterminate all the brutes!" Stevenson's vision of multiple personality emphasizes the irresolvable duality of the self and the problematic warning (to cite the philosophical ambiguity in Robert Penn Warren's novel *All the King's Men,* 1946) that "the end of man is knowledge."

See also: Dream, Mirror, Psychoanalysis of the Self, Shadow.

Selected Bibliography

Hawthorn, Jeremy. *Multiple Personality and the Disintegration of Literary Character*. London: Edward Arnold, 1983.

Keppler, C. F. *The Literature of the Second Self*. Tucson, Arizona: University of Arizona Press, 1972.

Rank, Otto. *Der Doppelgänger: Eine Psychoanalytische Studie*. Leipzig: Internationaler psychoanalytischer Verlag, 1925.

Rogers, Robert. *A Psychoanalytic Study of the Double in Literature*. Detroit: Wayne State University Press, 1970.

JEFFREY BERMAN

PHILATELY

Philately is stamp collecting and the study of stamps; by extension, it includes an interest in all phases of postal systems.

Philately has held a considerable if not spectacular interest for writers over the past hundred and more years. Since the first postal adhesives date from 1840, the subject, as far as it pertains to stamp collecting, is of necessity relatively recent. Even the word *philatélie* was coined only in 1865 by the French collector M. G. Herpin, whence the concept entered English and other languages. However, in view of the importance of mail systems to civilization going back to pre-Greco-Roman times, philatelic themes might expect wide acceptance in literature. Egypt, for instance, had a postal organization by 2000 B.C., China by a thousand years later. Mail service has been known even in such isolated areas as Tibet and Nepal for hundreds of years. Ancient Babylonians sent messages on clay tablets; the Incas sent them with knots tied in rope strands carried by runners. Medieval European merchants relied heavily on the mails, then and later managed by private concerns or government entities. Consider as well the dramatic balloon post that sent messages out of Paris during the German siege in the Franco-Prussian War of 1870–1871, or the whole matter of disinfected mail from quarantined cities such as Venice, among many others, from the fourteenth up to the early nineteenth century. Remember famous collectors as different as King Farouk of Egypt (1920–1965), George V of England (1865–1936), the eccentric American millionaire E.H.R. Green (1868–1936), and Franklin D. Roosevelt (1882–1945), who not only acquired stamps but actually designed them during his tenure as president. "The hobby of kings, and king of hobbies," a saying has it.

Note the interest generated by letter writing, especially in the eighteenth and nineteenth centuries, when almost all literate men and women indulged in voluminous correspondence, as is reflected, for instance, in the letter format in writing novels. Or think of Edgar Allan Poe's well-known exercise in detection and psychology, "The Purloined Letter" (1845). Meld the basic importance of letters and the mail system with the phenomenon of collecting in general—that strange hold upon the human race exerted by the acquisition of material objects (even to the point of becoming pathological, as in John Fowles's *The Collector* [novel, 1963]). Add the romantic glow surrounding the public's opinion of mail carriers ("Neither snow, nor rain, . . . nor gloom of night stays these couriers . . . ," the motto adapted from the ancient Greek of Herodotus for the inscription on the head post office in New York City), for example the postal runners of Nepal and Peru, who sometimes actually died of exhaustion in the high, thin, mountain air, or the adventurous Pony Express riders in our own Far West. Bear in mind the post and relay houses, found even today in Europe and America, remnants of the coach transportation networks for both people and mail, and the symbolic post horn still commonly found on country inn signs, some European buses, stamps, and so on. In short, philatelic themes are a likely source of inspiration among writers.

The Nineteenth and Twentieth Centuries

At times philately has been employed simply to indicate some character trait, perhaps a mere incidental mention, quite often derisive. At times it is a plot device, something to advance the story. But at others it represents a work's very raison d'être.

Perhaps the best known of the great Russian writer Alexander Pushkin's five *Povesti Belkina* (*Tales of Belkin,* 1830) is "Stantsionnyĭ smotretel' " ("The Postmaster" or "Stationmaster"). In truth, its principal aim is not to describe the Russian mail system, but rather an old man's sorrow over his daughter's seduction by a cosmopolitan army officer and the outcome of this twice-told tale. Still, the first few pages draw a sharp portrait of a typical village postmaster, imperious host of a relay station in days of long ago. As such, though predating philately by some years, it nevertheless presents the sort of background that would turn one day into a more major interest.

Almost a hundred years later Thomas Mann depicts life in the Berghof sanatorium of *Der Zauberberg* (*The Magic Mountain,* novel, 1924). The last chapter, devoted to boredom, contains a superb page on the inmates' interest in stamp collecting, at all times considerable, but periodically rising to an obsession, on which astonishing sums are spent by patients barely able to afford treatment. The atmosphere almost reaches the intensity of one of Balzac's novels where the character is gripped by a master passion, but unlike the Balzacian victim, nothing will come of it. The patients will soon take up what Mann calls the next folly, trying all the possible brands of chocolate, or solving geometrical puzzles. A generation later Marcel Aymé did a short story, "Le passe-muraille" ("The Man Who Walks Through Walls," 1943), in which the protagonist Dutilleul is a lonely bachelor who spends his free time reading newspapers and collecting stamps. When he falls in love, he forthwith abandons his stamp collection. But at least his hobby marks him as a man of principle and reserve. Compare Fernando Arrabal's absurdist one-acter, *Pique-nique en campagne* (*Picnic on the Battlefield,* 1954), in which the hero Zapo's father is described as a bright man, former student at the École Normale, *and* (emphasis Arrabal's) stamp collector. In the Nigerian dramatist Wole Soyinka's *The Lion and the Jewel* (1963), the local ruler impresses the village belle with his press, which he promises will print her face on stamps carrying letters all over the world. Oddly enough, a recent production of the play depicted the machine as an obscene sex symbol.

The preceding uses of philately have been mainly incidental, but the theme can be basic to the plot. Early in the present century Konrad Bercovici mixes ethnicity with philately in his story "The Little Man of Twenty-eighth Street" (from his *Dust of New York,* 1919). Karel Čapek (see his story collection, *Povídky z druhé kapsy* [*Tales from Two Pockets,* 1929]) adds a touch of his customary Central European urbanity to an account of a stamp collection. Charles Criswell's "The Hobby" (in his *Nobody Knows What the Stork Will Bring,* 1958) essays an O. Henry ending. It transpires that the collection on which the story hinges was not philatelic but pornographic. In Teddy Keller's story "The Plague" (1963) the germs are carried on stamp gum. Peter Ustinov's "Dreams of Papua" (in his *The Frontiers of the Sea,* 1966) posits the whimsical notion that if rulers of the East and West collected stamps, the world might find a panacea for its political ills. "Postpaid to Paradise" (c. 1952), by Robert Arthur, tries another tack: fantasy and the supernatural.

The truly recurrent use of philately lies more in connecting it with various illegal machinations. Rare stamps being costly (the British Guiana 1856 one-cent red recently sold for over three-quarters of a million dollars; a Confederate U.S. cover brought a million—by weight, as the auctioneer boasted, the most valuable object in the world—a few collections have sold for several millions), the hobby has suggested to writers plots based on greed, killings, theft, and the like. Hugh Pentecost's (pseudonym of Judson Philips) novel *Cancelled in Red* (1939) gives us as murder victim a dishonest stamp dealer, the crime being solved with the help of another dealer-cum-detective. Ellery Queen, nom de plume for the writing team of Frederic Dannay and Manfred B. Lee, in "One

Penny Black,'' features the 1840 British stamp that introduced postal adhesives to the world (in *Sporting Blood: The Great Sports Detective Stories,* 1942). Georges Simenon has aimed higher in his novelette *Le petit homme d'Arkhangelsk* (*The Little Man from Archangel,* 1956). A mild-mannered bookshop owner's wife has left him, taking with her some valuable stamps from his collection. Too proud to tell the truth, he lies to the police with unfortunate results. Simenon's keen psychological insights are, as usual, in full evidence. In Edward Wellen's story ''Fair Exchange'' (1976) the twenty-four cent U.S. airmail invert is grounds for a homicide.

It is just such opportunity for dishonesty and violence that has endeared the theme to television and motion picture scenarists. Over the past twenty-five years half a dozen or more television scripts have involved philatelic details, none displaying much merit or even knowledge of its subject. The well-regarded *Charade* (1963), screenplay by Peter Stone, from a story by Stone and Marc Behm, with Cary Grant and Audrey Hepburn, had the protagonists hunting down a quarter of a million stolen dollars invested in three rare stamps to throw pursuers off the track. Murder and mayhem are the order of the day, of course. Cinema yields other examples.

These stories for the most part obviously represent rather ephemeral uses of philately, however polished the prose or distinguished the authors, but two novelists have managed a somewhat more permanent contribution to literature: Robert Graves's *The Antigua Stamp* (original, English title *Antigua, Penny, Puce,* 1936) and Thomas Pynchon's *The Crying of Lot 49* (1965). Graves, after all, was a major modern poet, a novelist of skill, and, if his one philatelic foray scarcely constitutes a literary landmark, it cannot be dismissed entirely. The plot involves the only surviving copy of a putative Antigua stamp (the origin of the conceit is doubtless the historical British Guiana one-cent red mentioned before). An auction scene, accurate even in esoteric details, reveals an author far better versed in philatelic matters than most who dare to put them on paper. As is Pynchon. His *Crying of Lot 49* shorter, less abstruse and complex than his later *Gravity's Rainbow* (1973), already shows the young American, not yet thirty, capable of handling unconventional material, clothing it in an aura of mystery, at the same time mocking his own seriousness with humor and outrageous puns (one important character is named Genghis Cohen), and displaying his vaunted omniscience on any subject he proposes to treat. The plot concerns the Tristero System, Pynchon's imagined private postal organization that once thrived in Europe and has now been transplanted to America, and is presently being utilized by members of a California alternative life-style group as a channel of communication for their deviate sex practices. The system has its own stamps, counterfeited from real U.S. issues, but recognizable to the initiated through certain small intentional inaccuracies. The secret society is attempting to recover some copies being ''cried'' at an auction (in lot No. 49) before the authorities realize what is going on. The Tristero System finally comes to symbolize a whole secret para-culture, evil and threatening to the mores of the middle class.

All the foregoing may not constitute evidence of a major interest in a major theme, but it does indicate a lively, sustained use of interesting material.

Selected Bibliography

The two items mentioned below will give the reader some sense of the hobby's scope and its serious side. Its general connections with literature have not been investigated before now, as far as can be ascertained.

Sutton, Richard John. *The Stamp Collector's Encyclopedia*. 1966. 6th ed., rev. by K. W. Anthony. New York: Arco, 1973.

Williams, Leon Norman and Maurice Williams. *Stamps of Fame*. London: Blandford, 1949.

ARMAND E. SINGER

PICARESQUE

The picaresque is a recurrent literary theme of homelessness and the tension between integration and disintegration, between inclusion and exclusion, embodied in the adventures of a *pícaro*. Though the picaresque theme may be incidental to many literary works (Zola's *Germinal* [novel, 1885], for example, or Cervantes' *Don Quijote* [*Don Quixote*, novel, 1605, 1615]), in its pure form it is most fully worked out in what has traditionally been called *la novela picaresca,* or "the picaresque novel." A picaresque novel is a form of episodic narrative in which an economic and social outsider relates, from birth to a point of moral/spiritual conversion (either overt or implied), the trick-or-be-tricked techniques necessary for physical, emotional, social, and moral survival in a world rendered violently hostile toward the integration of a socially undesirable person into traditional and thus established bounds. "Nothing jars the world's harmony more than men that break their ranks," says Meriton Latroon in the fictitious biography *The English Rogue* [1665–1671], authored by Richard Head and Francis Kirkman. The protagonist's first-person point of view is essential because it provides the vertical and horizontal perspectives characteristic of the picaresque world view: a cross-section of the social hierarchy and a panorama of the human landscape, often dissected with fierce Juvenalian satire. Spatially and temporally, ideologically, phraseologically, and psychologically, the protagonist's very act of narrating provides a complex unifying force in a narrative often called, pejoratively, "sequential" rather than "consequential." Moreover, the narrative "distances" and multiple self-portrayals inherent in the confessional first-person point of view (between the self re-creating and the self being created) makes us aware—and wary—of the discrepancy between the *re*-member*ing I* and the *re*-member*ed I,* between the narrating "I" and the experiencing "I," a subtle and often problematic narrative process that gives picaresque narrative a crafty, often ironic texture that it shares with its narrative relatives, the confession, the autobiography, and the memoir. When Guzmán says, "Vuelve a nacer mi vida con la historia [With this story, my life lives again]" (Mateo Alemán, *Primera parte de la vida de Guzmán de Alfarache, atalaya de la vida humana* [*The Rogue, or the Life of Guzman de Alfarache,* 1599]), he is alerting us to the picaresque narrative situation, which is rich in gradations, attitudes, tones, and treatments—not only toward the narrative itself and toward the reader, but toward the teller himself. The picaresque point of view is narratively artful (in all the senses of that word), as the controversial last chapter of *La vida de Lazarillo de Tormes: y de sus fortunas y adversidades* (*Lazarillo de Tormes,* 1554) will show. We have been duped, through slyly manipulative narration, to like a narrat*ed* self created primarily for the justification of the spiritually corrupt narrat*ing* self—but we have also, through the carefully controlled narrative tricks of voice and point of view, been allowed to see behind the mask. The narrator is now a verbal trickster, a refinement on the crude, slapstick tricks he had to use to survive in life. And the reader wants the tricks, both "actual" and verbal, as long as he knows they are tricks. "The foolish world wants to be fooled," says Simplicius in Grimmelshausen's *Der abenteuerliche Simplicissimus* (*The Adventurous Simplicissimus,* 1669). Picaresque narration is itself a trick, a lure, the fictional analogy of the tricks of which his life and the world are composed. The act of telling is itself a picaresque gesture of self-assertion by a lowly, insignificant outsider "confessing" himself (and thereby making himself significant) to the reader by luring him into his world through ostensibly moral designs. Picaresque narration is then a narrative version—between the *pícaro* and the reader-victim—of the tricks in the *pícaro*'s life experiences—between the *pícaro* and his landscape—as rendered in the fiction that emerges from the narrative act. First-person narrative trickery is thus essential to picaresque narration and distinguishes it from other first-person narrative forms.

In its fictional literary embodiment (there are and have been *pícaros* in real life), the picaresque theme is rendered most powerfully and effectively in this unique narrative structure. It is difficult to distinguish between the picaresque *theme* and the picaresque *genre,* so closely intertwined are form and function, subject matter and technique. Plot, character, incident, image, point of view, tone, attitude, and action function together in specific ways to form the picaresque narrative structure. Mark Schorer wrote that "technique is the only means [a writer] has of discovering, exploring, developing his subject, of conveying its meaning, and, finally, of evaluating it." And for Schorer technique is "the uses to which language, as language, is put to express the quality of the experience in question" and "the uses of point of view not only as a mode of dramatic delimitation, but more particularly, of thematic definition" ("Technique as Discovery," *Hudson Review* 1 (1948): 68–87). When we speak of the picaresque, we cannot separate genre from theme.

The term "picaresque" derives from the Spanish *pícaro,* which has been variously translated as or given the equivalent of "rogue," "knave," "swindler," "sharper," "anti-hero," "outsider," "confidence man," "wanderer," "exile," "delinquent," and "picaroon," among others. In French, some equivalents are *gueux* and *voleur* ("beggar," "thief"); in German, *Schelm* and *Abenteurer* ("rogue," "adventurer"); and in Italian, *pitocco* and *furbone* ("vagrant," "rogue"). *Pícaro*, now usually anglicized (though there's still objection to that), is etymologically troublesome. Much scholarship has been expended on tracing the word's origins, but no single theory is universally accepted. It may come from a form of the verb *picar* ("to prick, puncture"; "to nibble, bite") and thus be related to *piqueros secos*, the "pike-men" of the imperial Spanish armies who were used in vast numbers to defend Spain's territories during the first part of the sixteenth century but who, in the latter part of the century, begged and stole their way home. It may derive from Picardy, a region of Flanders occupied by Spain from 1587 to 1659 and synonymous to the average Spaniard with roguery. There is also the early sixteenth-century expression *pícaro de cozina* ("scullion"), which, however inappropriate it may be in other ways, suggests the menial tasks a *pícaro* is always engaged in. Yet another theory suggests a possible origin in the word *bigardo*, a religious sect. In any case, the words *picaresco* and *pícaro* become a fact of literary history with Mateo Alemán's use of the terms in *Guzmán de Alfarache*, though, as Sieber points out (*The Picaresque*, 1977), "the etymological, semantic, social, and historical references provide the contexts for an understanding and appreciation of the picaresque novel, but tell us virtually nothing about it as a genre of fiction." Defining this genre has been as troublesome as tracing the etymology of the word that gave it its name.

From the time it traveled out of the Spanish context, the term "picaresque" has metamorphosed itself to fit any Western literary tradition that seems to approximate the picaresque of *siglo de oro* Spain. Like the adaptable *pícaro* himself ("My Travels, and my studies found est-soone / More Formes, and Changes, then are in the Moone," says Guzman in Mabbe's [1623] translation), the concept of the picaresque has undergone considerable transformation of "formes" in Western literature. It therefore might be helpful to delineate the picaresque in its most important contexts: socio-cultural, literary, critical, and generic (obviously, there is unavoidable overlap among these categories).

The form of narrative aware of itself as picaresque (as distinguished from earlier and later works that have since been labeled "picaresque") developed in sixteenth-century Spain, a time and place of considerable social change; with feudalism crumbling in the transition from a medieval to a modern state, Spain was filled with class confusion. Royal employment alone was worth having, and the only gateways to advancement were the church, the government, or the army. According to Chandler, "even the ignorant and the boors disdained to stoop to the patient business of life." The exile of the Jews and the ultimate expulsion of the *Moriscos* by Philip III in 1609 severely damaged the labor force in Spain, for they were the only groups who had not succumbed to the contempt for work.

Exhaustion and drainage as a result of its reaches abroad, internal mismanagement, expanding ecclesiastical power, the gypsy problem—all combined to make Spain ripe for a landscape of vagabondage and beggary. Again, according to Chandler:

The rogue of literature was only what he claimed to be. His creator brought him forward expressly to expose in effigy the vices of the day. Taken from life, to be met with on the street at every turning, he was the best instrument for satire to be found. . . . Thus social conditions in Spain in the sixteenth and seventeenth centuries furnished an ample pretext for making the literary reaction expressive of a social one. The decadence presented all the material to inspire a corrective fiction; and the peculiar form of that fiction was determined both by the foregoing literary development from which it recoiled and by the social facts and failures which it emphasized.

Many years later, Bjornson also emphasizes the socio-cultural dimension of the picaresque:

European society was undergoing significant changes in social organization; as the feudal order declined in most countries, the increasingly important middle classes began to provide a dynamic but often frustrated impetus toward a redefinition of established aristocratic values and modes of perception. Picaresque novels written against the background of these conflicting ideologies manifest numerous different attitudes toward the rise of bourgeois individualism, but because the essential picaresque situation involves the paradigmatic confrontation between an isolated individual and a hostile society, these novels almost invariably reflect a world view defined in terms of the author's position on precisely this question.

Both Bjornson and Parker take pains to explain that this was not a purely Spanish situation; the German *Liber vagatorum (The Book of Vagabonds,* c.1520), for example, divided beggars into more than twenty classes according to their different ways of cheating and robbing; and there is evidence that in Italy and England as well such trickery abounded. And Sieber says: "The emphasis of the picaresque on poverty, delinquency, 'upward mobility' (self-improvement of the *pícaro),* travel as an escape from despair, social satire of a system unresponsive to the needs and desires of a growing active community of 'have-nots,' all reflect the socio-historical contexts." Parker argues well that "delinquent" best expresses in current usage the meaning of *pícaro* in sixteenth- and seventeenth-century Spanish society. And Américo Castro, in his *Hacia Cervantes* (1960), has suggested that the picaresque reflects the converted Jew's resentment against the society that rejected him (evidence is strong that Alemán, author of *Guzmán,* was a *converso,* and there is speculation that the unknown author of *Lazarillo* may have been one as well). Though there is no universal agreement about the specific social, cultural, and historical contexts that may have given rise to the picaresque—historians and sociologists being as opinionated as the pícaro himself—the socio-cultural perspective is important. The picaresque grew out of a certain milieu, whatever its characteristics.

There is no doubt, however, about the literary context. From the beginning, there was a self-conscious literary tradition; it knew what it was doing. Most obvious from Alemán's use of the terms *pícaro* and *picaresco* in *Guzmán de Alfarache* and Cervantes' allusion in the Ginés de Pasamonte episode in *Don Quixote* as well as his portrayal of picaresque life in "La ilustre fregona" ("The Illustrious Kitchenmaid"; in *Novelas ejemplares* [*Exemplary Novels*, 1613]), the genre was popular both for writers and readers. The picaresque was, in its day, the equivalent of a contemporary TV "soap" or situation comedy *(Guzmán,* if the number of editions is any indication, far outsold *Don Quixote* and was, perhaps, the first best-seller in recorded history, though *Don Quixote* continues to be a most-read work). As such, the picaresque had a brief but very influential role in the history of narrative. External evidence alone proves convincing. In his anthology *La novela picaresca española* (1968), Angel Valbuena Prat uses as frontispiece a famous illustration from the first edition of López de Ubeda's *La pícara Justina (The Spanish Jilt,* 1605) in which we see Lazarillo and the bull of Salamanca in a small boat that appears to be towing a larger one called *La nave de la vida picaresca,* whose passengers include Guzmán and Justina. In the Ginés de Pasamonte episode in *Don Quixote,* Cervantes makes two allusions to the picaresque—one direct (to *Lazarillo)* and one indirect (to Guzmán, who is a galley slave, a fate awaiting Ginés). Thirty-one editions of *Lazarillo* appeared between 1554 and 1664, thus demonstrating the popularity of the picaresque fiction and also the revival of interest in *Lazarillo* after the publication of *Guzmán de Alfarache.*

Internal evidence, too, provides a strong case for a self-conscious literary genre. The influence—through imitation, borrowing, or modeling—of the structure and pattern of a group of other works on the writer in the act of writing is sufficient evidence of a rudimentary and inherent generic awareness in the making. Guzmán moves to another work and becomes Justina's husband; Estebanillo González in *Vida y hechos de Estebanillo González, hombre de buen humor* (1646) claims to be writing a "true" story, not "la fingida [false one] de Guzmán de Alfarache, ni la fabulosa [invented one] de Lazarillo de Tormes." The famous criminal Jonathan Wild's favorite book was *The Spanish Rogue* (that is, *Guzmán*); Head and Kirkman's *The English Rogue* is a deliberate imitation; Lesage shaped the Spanish tradition his own way in *Histoire de Gil Blas de Santillane (The Adventures of Gil Blas of Santillane,* 1715–1735); Smollett acknowledged (and translated) Lesage—in *Ferdinand Count Fathom* (1753) there are explicit references to *Guzmán,* to Petronius, and to *Gil Blas*; Grimmelshausen's Courage in *Die Landstörzerin Courasche (The Runagate Courage,* 1670) is writing "trutz Simplex," to spite the portrayal of herself in *Der abenteuerliche Simplicissimus,* which was clearly influenced by *Guzmán* through Albertinus' translation. In 1822 we have Johann Sachse's *Der deutsche Gil Blas,* so titled and introduced by Goethe; there is a Russian Gil Blas by Vassilii Narezhnyi, *Rossiĭskiĭ Zhilblaz* 1814), and Parker mentions *The Dutch Rogue, or Gusman of Amsterdam* (1683) and *Teague O'Divelly, or The Irish Rogue* (1690). Pito Pérez, in *La vida inútil de Pito Pérez* (1938), by José Rubén Romero, sees himself as a Periquillo, alluding to *Periquillo, el de las gallineras* (1668) by Francisco Santos and to *Vida y hechos de periquillo sarniento* (*The Itching Parrot,* 1816) by José Joaquín Fernández de Lizardi; Hans Schmetterling, the picaresque clown in Kern's *Le clown* (*The Clown,* 1957), meets Thomas Mann's Felix Krull in Paris ("He's nothing but a crook!") and is referred to as "our Simplicissimus," while Mann himself wrote an essay describing *Felix Krull* (novel, 1954) as part of the picaresque tradition. Günter Grass's Oskar in *Die Blechtrommel* (*The Tin Drum,* 1959) has as his ancestor the drummer Simplicissumus (2.4). And so on.

While some of these are no doubt the work of hacks copying formulas— like the TV writers of our own day, who give us spin-offs of spin-offs—there is a literary genetics at work here from the sixteenth century to our own day, and however crude the course of influence may be, the awareness of writing within—or even against—a specific kind of narrative fiction is internally traceable, both inside and outside Spanish literature. These examples provide us with both external and internal evidence that a picaresque tradition, a normative sense of genre, however rudimentary, did—and continues to—exist. Whether this sense of genre was ever codified into a conscious poetics, whether it ever became a regulative or even prescriptive generic concept or remained "unwritten" is another question. But we know that picaresque fictions were generating, influencing, and parodying other picaresque fictions; parody has its origins in a Greek root meaning "beside the song" or poem— thus much picaresque literature relies on the reader's awareness of such a genre. Both writers and readers experienced these works in the context of other similar works, with generic awareness, however informal or unformulated. And every work in a genre redefines our concept of that genre as a whole. A specific work not only signals its generic identity to us, directly or indirectly, but it also reshapes our concept of that very genre. We can, therefore, be reasonably sure that there was a specific picaresque genre, identified with a specific literature and a specific set of socio-cultural conditions at a particular time in history (*siglo de oro* Spain).

Parker says that "the picaresque novel itself had only a relatively short life in Spain; the last one that can be properly so called was [E. González, *Vida y hechos de*] *Estebanillo González* of 1646. After that date, the *genre* had its vogue abroad." Like the *pícaro* traversing diverse geographical regions, the term "picaresque" has travelled across national boundaries and adapted its meanings to suit the social and literary circumstances. The literary criticism of the last century is fittingly picaresque, reflecting the diversity (and perversity) of many points of view.

At one extreme are those who deny that the picaresque ever existed. At the other extreme are those who use the term so loosely that the latest book or film is tagged "picaresque," with no sense of the historical meanings of the term. In between there is a solid body of scholarship, with arguments that the picaresque ought to be restricted to a certain group of works—*Lazarillo* (sometimes called a "precursor"), *Guzmán,* Quevedo's *La vida del Buscón (The Swindler,* 1626), and *Simplicissimus,* with perhaps a passing glance at Lesage, Defoe, Smollett, and others. It's been suggested that we abandon the term altogether because it has lost all meaning. Nevertheless, the term, like the indomitable *pícaro,* persists in Western literature and requests attention, as others have argued. Perhaps the sanest approach to this dilemma is to adopt the perspective of Robert E. Scholes and Robert Kellogg in their *The Nature of Narrative* (1966), which relieves us of the burden of having to define "novel" (a peculiar literary critter, originating in Spain and Italy as *novela* [meaning "new"], and receiving its normative and still regulative concept by Erich Auerbach in *Mimesis* [1946]). Scholes and Kellogg point out that there are many forms of narrative, the novel being only one.

It has been, historically, the most various and changeable of literary disciplines, which means that it has been the most alive. For all its imperfections it has been—from the epic to the novel—the most popular and influential kind of literature, seeking the widest audience in its culture and being more responsive to extraliterary influences than any other kinds of literature.

Often called a "precursor" of the novel proper, the picaresque is actually a distinct type of narrative. Much of the difficulty in defining the picaresque can be circumvented if we think of it as a specific form of narrative rather than as a novel. As Scholes and Kellogg make clear, the novel should be put in its place and we should view "the nature of narrative and the Western narrative tradition whole, seeing the novel as only one of a number of narrative possibilities."

Nonetheless, picaresque and novel are inextricably bound in the literary scholarship on the picaresque tradition, partly because it seemed the first fictional mode to offer a realistic portrayal of society from a lower-class point of view, and partly because it was a deliberate antitype to the fabulous romances and pastorals of the time (it's been said that *Guzmán* did more to deflate books of chivalry than did *Don Quixote*). Chandler coined the term "anti-hero" to characterize the new kind of protagonist. And Parker suggests that the transition from idealism to realism in narrative fiction was heavily influenced by the Spanish churchmen of the Counter-Reformation: "Only in this sense did the Spanish picaresque novel arise as a reaction to the romances—not as satire or parody, but as a deliberate alternative, a 'truthful' literature in response to the explicit demands of the Counter-Reformation." In any case, the picaresque shattered traditional notions of the separation of styles and has served, in our own time, as a descriptive term for fictions as historically, thematically, geographically, and technically diverse as Apuleius' *Metamorphoses (The Golden Ass,* c. 150), Petronius' *Satyricon* (A.D. 60), Ellison's *Invisible Man* (1952), and Kosinski's *The Painted Bird* (1965), to mention only a few. Scholars exploring the picaresque, though they may have sharp differences about its social and literary origins, don't differ radically in their descriptions of this narrative type or in their delineations of which specific works are central to this narrative tradition. Literary history, however, has perpetuated (and distorted) a term that some scholars wish would go away (like the *pícaro* himself) and others wish to keep away from the general populace.

Given all these problems, the picaresque might best be conceived as an adaptable and thus metamorphosing narrative form expressing in any culture the devices of an outsider to be integrated into a social structure that he/she may ostensibly despise but nevertheless desires. The essential picaresque fictional situation—the world portrayed by the un- and dis-integrated protagonist—is thematically and technically the view and point of view of a character in circumstances worse than ours, rendering a chaotic world much worse than the one we think we live in. This character is on an eternal journey of encounters that allows him/her to be both victim of that world and its exploiter. The essential romance situation is that of a heroic protagonist in a world marvelously better than ours in which he is on a quest that confronts him with challenges, each of which is a moral challenge leading toward a final ordered and harmonious cosmos. If romance satisfies our impulse for vicarious participation in harmony, order, and beauty, then picaresque satisfies our impulse for a vicarious journey through chaos and depravity. Our journey into romance is a finite trip, ending in a goal unattainable in our actual world. Our journey into picaresque is an infinite foray into a world that is forever falling apart, disintegrating. Romance satisfies our craving for divine harmony, integration, beauty, order, goodness, and ultimate fulfillment. Picaresque satisfies our darker yearnings for daemonic disharmony, disintegration, ugliness, disorder, evil, and the lure of the abyss. The picaresque expresses such a view, and it has some specific narrative characteristics: (1) a panoramic structure; (2) an external rhythm that we might call (echoing Guzman's complaint) the "Sisyphus" rhythm; "Volver de nuevo," or "to beginne the world anew," is the *pícaro*'s condition; (3) an internal rhythm consisting of (a) a confrontation—self-willed or forced by "fortune" or adversity, the *pícaro*'s cosmic scapegoats; (b) some scheme to satisfy that need (if only for revenge); (c) a complication that endangers the *pícaro*'s safety; and (d) the extrication (or entanglement, if the *pícaro* is caught); Lazarillo's efforts to get the key from the priest illustrate such a rhythm, which is basic to the typical episode in picaresque fiction; (4) the first-person point of view; (5) the *pícaro* figure, a pragmatic, unprincipled, resilient, solitary character who just manages to survive in his chaotic landscape, but who, in the ups and downs, can also put that world very much on the defensive; the *pícaro* is a protean figure who can not only serve many masters but play different roles, and his essential characteristic is his inconstancy—of life roles, of self-identity—his own personality flux in an inconstant world; (6) the *pícaro*-landscape relationship, which focuses on the problems of exclusion and inclusion (Lazarillo says early on, "Solo soy"—"I am alone"); (7) a vast gallery of human types who appear as representatives of the landscape (e.g., the schoolmaster Cabra in *El Buscón,* and the blind man, squire, and priest in *Lazarillo);* (8) implied (if not overt) parody of other fictional types, even the picaresque itself; (9) specific themes and motifs: among the themes are "vanity," "freedom," and "hunger, or basic physical survival"; among the motifs are (a) the motif of unusual birth or childhood, (b) the trick motif, (c) the role-playing motif, (d) the grotesque or horrible incident, and (e) the ejection motif. Bjornson says that "the picaresque myth... corresponds to a complex situation outside the narrative, and when readers react ambiguously to a narrator whose life embodies the principal elements of that myth, they are indirectly responding to the difficulty of knowing the truth about a social reality in which traditional values no longer obtain." This myth was originally suggested by Guillén, who offered his own definition of the picaresque:

the picaresque *genre,* first of all; a group of novels, secondly, which ought to be called picaresque in the strict sense—usually in agreement with the original Spanish pattern; another group of novels, thirdly, which may be considered picaresque in a broader sense of the term only; and, finally, a picaresque myth: an essential situation or structure of meaning which has been derived from the novels themselves.

Literary history does not corroborate Guillén's fourth point (which is circular anyway), finding instead that the essential situation or structure of meaning expressed by the picaresque (though the articulation of this is a problem) is universal, timeless, and timely. Spain gave us the label for what has been happening—and continues to happen—in the literature of any culture that allows outsiders of any kind to express themselves. The essential picaresque myth has existed from the start, in mythology; a myth cannot be "derived from... novels." The picaresque does exist in the *experience* of readers, even if it has a troublesome history in the critical commentaries. Picaresque narratives satisfy a basic human need, resulting from the questioning of traditional (literary and social) structures; it *must* be essential, or the controversy would go away or be confined to scholars. Insofar as all perception of reality is a fiction, insofar as all the past exists only in the distortions of the present self that tries to re-create it, the picaresque narrative situation is exemplary of fiction-making itself. Ultimately, we are all distanced in our "I's." First-person narration, the most intimate form of storytelling, has most often been used in the service of alienation. Even the narrative act of communication does not integrate the *pícaro* into a stable order of things—and that is the essential picaresque theme.

See also: Anti-Hero, Fool, Grotesque, *Pícaro* in American Literature.

Selected Bibliography

Bjornson, Richard. *The Picaresque Hero in European Fiction.* Madison: The University of Wisconsin Press, 1977.

Chandler, Frank Wadleigh. *Romances of Roguery, An Episode in the History of the Novel. Part I, The Picaresque Novel in Spain.* 1899. New York: Burt Franklin, 1961.

Guillén, Claudio. "Toward a Definition of the Picaresque" and "Genre and Countergenre: The Discovery of the Picaresque." *Literature as System: Essays toward the Theory of Literary History*. Princeton, N.J.: Princeton University Press, 1971.

Parker, Alexander A. *Literature and the Delinquent: The Picaresque Novel in Spain and Europe 1599–1753*. Edinburgh: Edinburgh University Press, 1967.

ULRICH WICKS

THE *PÍCARO* IN AMERICAN LITERATURE

A *pícaro* is the protagonist of a picaresque novel, a tragicomic narrative form first fully achieved as art in a triad of Spanish works, the anonymous *Lazarillo de Tormes* (1554), Mateo Alemán's *Guzmán de Alfarache* (1559), and Francisco de Quevedo's *La vida del Buscón* (*The Swindler,* 1626). In these novels the *pícaro* is a lonely individual isolated within society, a society which also acts morally and psychologically within him. Loneliness becomes an evolving state, the outgrowth of the *pícaro*'s sense of failed identity, of the instability of an inferior social standing, and of the failure to find human solidarity. (One of the sure clues to the absence of a true *pícaro* in a novel is the representation of a fellowship, e.g., in Cervantes' *Don Quijote* [*Don Quixote,* 1605, 1615], Le Sage's *Gil Blas* [1715–1735], and Fielding's *Tom Jones* [1749]). Furthermore, the extent of the *pícaro*'s loneliness may be seen in the compulsive restlessness with which he goes forth in search of life. Increasingly those whom he encounters on the road tend to reflect his own lack of significant reality, and his jerky, episodic journey is thus precisely the form this experience takes. The more he seeks, the more disintegrated he becomes. Finally, in order to bring himself into precarious relation to society, the *pícaro* undertakes to create a deceptive identity out of social roles and appearances. Creating a self that his will supports but that he knows for an illusion, the *pícaro* evolves into a symbolic literary being, a confidence man, outwardly one who shares faith in existence, inwardly one reduced toward and to spiritual nothingness.

The hero of a genuine picaresque novel is thus always to a degree archetypal and has potential to be spontaneously reborn in literature outside Spain. Beginning as a kind of novel depicting the adventures of a trickster or delinquent in a chaotic, decadent world, the picaresque has developed, over four centuries, in new modes until, in recent times, the ethos of Western civilization can plausibly be described as "picarism": here the *pícaro* is in the largest sense modern man without a living faith, and the trickster hero of folklore is re-created as the lonely individual cut off from though yearning for community and love.

This recent development is especially evident in American literature from the 1830s to the present. Picaresque and part-picaresque novels have appeared in the United States, usually their *pícaros* symbolically represented as confidence men. And picarism—the way of life historically depicted in the fictional genre—

has found ubiquitous expressions (including nonliterary ones) as a cultural out-look of the American people.

The American *pícaro,* viewed against the nineteenth-century literary back-ground, is an expression of disillusionment with Adamic myth. For many writers of the period, appearances became impenetrable masks, the world a stage, and the existence of truth so dubious as to eliminate any difference between it and fiction. There followed a quest for higher or transcendental truth, but, with disillusionment, an artist might see all cultural enterprise as a great confidence trick. Hence the old idea of the *pícaro* reestablished itself in some writers' minds as an image or symbol of disintegration, as a state of being in some way non-human. The symbolic confidence man's character is accordingly unreal or at least opaque and impenetrable because reality has become endlessly contingent; and if ill-will enters into his con game, he is also grotesque. Indeed, as a creature of nihilism, the symbolic confidence man seems to be at times actively engaged in the destruction of whatever reality, goodness, and trust remain in the living world. If by contrast the Spanish *pícaro* is the victim of an atomizing process, the American *pícaro,* like as not, may be incarnate atomizer, destructiveness, devil, mankind corrupted, or civilization. In a sense, too, the American *pícaro* is simply "the" American. In various literary contexts one finds the figure of a lonely, rootless innocent, an Adam emancipated from history, from the Europe of the mind, and existing morally prior to the world, yet moving into the world that promises and provides experience. If at first the encounters between this radically self-reliant outsider and the alien world had seemed heroic, in time two Americans stride forth in Adam's guise, the one creative and Promethean, the other destructive and satanic, both wearing the masks of idealism. The archetypal Adam, protesting innocence and benevolence, might not be a radical new person emancipated from history but might, instead, be history personified—a dead soul, an invisible man with a self consisting of social roles taken on "faith." But the American *pícaro* is not the feudal outcast of Spanish picaresque novels. He is a representative figure who playfully brings to focus the whole paradoxical question of individualism in the American past.

The literary symbol of the American was Adam; the popular symbol was the Yankee, that sharp-witted Brother Jonathan who tricked Old John Bull. The bumptious certitude often scornfully attributed to Americans by foreigners was picked up by the fledgling culture as a nose-thumbing badge of identification. As the Yankee appeared on stage and in the literature and subliterature of the century—and he appears in cartoons to the present day as Uncle Sam—he in-creasingly reflected the deprecation of everything sophisticated and the exaltation of a shrewd, peasant common sense that was thought to be a native gift. He was a symbol, then, of triumph, of adaptability, of irrepressible life—of many qual-ities needed to induce confidence and self-possession among a new and una-malgamated people. But he was also paradoxically both innocent and cunning. The primary manifestation of the Yankee was the peddler, whose lonely, wan-dering lifestyle, true to the promptings of democratic patriotism, romanticism, and free enterprise, was the icon of self-confidence above all. This relatively harmless Yankee Peddler emerges into literature as Sam Slick of Slickville, Connecticut, in Thomas Chandler Haliburton's satirical *Clockmaker* series of 1836. Haliburton, a conservative Nova Scotian judge who wished to warn his countrymen about their base democratic neighbors, portrays in Slick, the clock peddler, a shrewd, garrulous parasite with an inherent love of barter. Like all marginal figures, however, the Yankee Peddler could also represent the dangerous side of cultural values and be viewed as a trickster exploiting confidence. The stage was set for the appearance of a native American *pícaro* when the Yankee Peddler, real and fictitious, traveled South, and in the frontier region between the southern Appalachians and the Mississippi River, then called the Southwest, underwent a literary transformation as the poor-white squatter.

Suddenly in the 1830s conservative lawyers, doctors, and journalists in the southwestern region began to write local-color sketches for the widely distributed New York sporting paper, the *Spirit of the Times*. These relatively cultured writers, aware of the older tradition of the East and seaboard South, were roused to fear and to laughter by the rampaging frontier environment. On the one side were the gentlemen (themselves) and on the other were the rogues (Jacksonian rabble variously depicted as loafers, pickpockets, cardsharps, actors, imposters, and confidence tricksters). One southwestern writer, Johnson J. Hooper, was to create an American rogue with a dimension as symbolic *pícaro*. In *Some Adventures of Captain Simon Suggs* (1845), Hooper all but removes himself from the narrative as a mediating influence between the confidence man and the reader; the author-gentleman having retired behind a curtain of irony, the world represented through the warped mind of Simon Suggs, forerunner of William Faulkner's Flem Snopes, is dark and degraded, and moral standards are dissolved in Simon's favorite motto, "It's good to be shifty in a new country." Indeed, *Simon Suggs* unfolds as the story of civilization running amuck. Son of an itinerant frontier preacher, Simon takes early to cards, tempts his father to "cut Jack," secures the family horse—which closely resembles Don Quixote's Rocinante—and hits the trail. When Simon next appears, he is married, the father of a large pinewoods family, and known all over Tallapoosa County as an unscrupulous speculator in Indian lands. Specializing in confidence tricks, Simon in successive episodes outwits greedy strangers by posing as a rich planter, a senator, and a wealthy Kentucky hog-drover. In later episodes Johnson broadens the social landscape to include the whole morally degraded frontier society. With his fellow citizens Simon joins in a cruel swindle of the Creek Indians; then, as rumor spreads that the Creeks plan revenge, Simon, privately informed of the rumor's falsity, fans the fears of the ignorant villagers into a drunken blaze, has himself named captain, declares martial law, and turns the hysteria to his own profit by fining those who stumble across the sentry lines. The hysterical—and significantly Jacksonian—mob is even more grotesquely revealed when Simon attends a revivalist meeting. Singled out by an ecstatic congregation as a well-known sinner, he pretends to undergo miraculous redemption, then passes a collection plate among the tear-stricken crowd and disappears into the swamps. It is not Simon's last, but it is his most memorable trick, and forty years later Mark Twain imitated this camp-meeting scene for similar reasons in *Huckleberry Finn* (novel, 1884).

The *Adventures of Captain Simon Suggs* combines several elements of the picaresque idea. It is concerned with the disintegration of reality, goodness, and trust. It represents evil on two planes, individual and social, for the confidence man fulfills the degraded desires of society, in this function appearing ironically as the people's true representative. Through the typical picaresque technique of unreliable first-person narration, Hooper is able to show a violent splitting apart of society from culture and of materialism and opportunism from the control of an older order of American democratic ideals. Although its episodes, originally sketches in the *Spirit of the Times,* are insufficiently integrated as novelistic art, *Simon Suggs* is the first lengthy picaresque fiction in American literature, its protagonist the prototype of later American *pícaros*.

By the 1850s, the American rogue was well entrenched in the popular consciousness, and a favorite stage for acting out his role had become the deck of a Mississippi steamboat. This was his stage in Herman Melville's *The Confidence-Man: His Masquerade* (1857), a complexly orchestrated fictional masterpiece that profoundly explores and exposes the picarism of modern life. The action of *The Confidence-Man* takes place from sunrise to midnight (and possibly beyond) on April Fool's Day aboard the steamer *Fidèle (Faith)*. The titular hero is a composite of all the various passengers, and their presentations of masked selves, in terms of costume, gesture, and role, constitute the bulk of a narrative with little progression save that between the appearance at sunrise of a Christlike deaf-mute and his exposure at midnight as a savage young peddler in collusion with a diabolic cosmopolitan who apocalyptically extinguishes a "solar lamp" in the gentlemen's cabin.

The ingenuity of *The Confidence-Man* is that Melville discovers a way to reexpress his familiar tragic themes in a picaresque schema. Whereas the protagonists of *Moby-Dick* (1851) and *Pierre* (1852) destroy themselves in efforts to make moral absolutes fit the practical conditions of everyday life, Melville himself in those novels speculates that life is a hoax, a comedy of thought, or a vast practical joke founded on man's confidence in gods that fail. In *The Confidence-Man* the supernatural jokers are no more than petty con men—as it were, Yankee Peddlers made as one cosmic *pícaro*—engaged in the symbolic action of picaresque myth in which the world heads blindly toward annihilation, all human beings unable to abandon eschatological hopes or the illusion that gods are made in man's image. Believing God and human nature to be past finding out, Melville exposes as fraudulent pretense all dogma, philosophy, and myth that present them in clear light, for the man who is tricked by rational explanations of the universe is soon apt to believe that God is Satan. Melville's *pícaro* has cosmic pretensions to credit he does not possess, and in the form of all the characters in the novel he appears as an imposter and usurper of identity.

The Ship of Faith has been man-created out of an inherent need for confidence in life, yet this very human aspiration of faith represents its greatest danger. What is created by man may be destroyed by man; a swindling faith may lead to the disintegration of reality, goodness, and trust; and such a disintegrating world is the *pícaro*'s, conceived in the image of the confidence man, loveless and unreal as a dream.

The Confidence-Man is a picaresque novel in a nonautobiographical symbolic form. Some of its characteristics relate it to central picaresque tradition. *The Confidence-Man*, like *Lazarillo de Tormes*, parodies heroic and epic literature, specifically the Bible from Genesis to apocalypse; presents life as a series of encounters between the *pícaro* and society; presents *pícaro* and society, as well as good and evil, as mutually reflective aspects of the same reality; shows reality functioning as an illusion; is structured to reveal disintegration into chaos and spiritual death; makes the world's lack of love desperately apparent; and has a *pícaro* for protagonist. Like the Spanish *pícaro*, Melville's confidence man is both a failed identity and a half-outsider. Behind his masks he is neither a true god nor an adequate human. Through the world's lack of Pauline charity, he has become deformed in a shifting, dehumanized nonself. He is another dead soul, another invisible man. Nevertheless, he has a kind of character as a stranger who seeks by means of imposture to enter in to the human community. In terms of his function vis-à-vis his victims, he yearns to be accepted by and necessary to them. An outsider with respect to humanity's need for confidence, he is doomed to the outside because, like the mature Lázaro of *Lazarillo de Tormes*, he hides a heart of stone.

Mark Twain's *Adventures of Huckleberry Finn* is both a conventionally Bad Boy or trickster story and a continuation, at the core, of picaresque myth. The thrust of the narrative is nonpicaresque in the sense that Twain apparently believes in a life of freedom, love, and moral choice. However, Twain is aggressively anti-historical, viewing culture as implacably determined by the corrupt past, and so in *Huckleberry Finn*, as in *Lazarillo de Tormes*, readers are deceived into approval of the protagonist and of his apparent (but empty) social success and moral regeneration. On the surface, it is a novel in which an apparent *pícaro* discovers right uses for his trickery and comes to oppose the symbolic confidence men, the King and Duke, with whom he becomes involved. But Huck's deceptive triumph over what Twain describes as "a deformed conscience" is negated by Tom Sawyer's evasion, those chapters in which Huck loses humanity and approximates the deformed identity of the confidence men. Therefore, because there is disparity between Twain's intention (a Bad Boy grows morally) and execution (the soul of the boy is deformed), it can be argued that *Huckleberry Finn* is truly picaresque, its hero a *pícaro*, not just another light-hearted roguish vagabond reminiscent of Gil Blas in Lesage's eighteenth-century novel of manners.

Beneath the surface of Twain's novel there is evident an interest in the *pícaro* as a lonely child confronted and trained by an unsympathetic, enslaving society.

Huck has some of the *pícaro*'s sensitivity about inferior social status. He is alienated from home and tends to become involved with persons existing precariously on social frontiers. For a while, he fosters charitable actions, finding in Jim the runaway slave a true father, but when the King and Duke take over their raft, Huck reacts passively: the con men symbolize a deformed part of Huck that is in conflict with his natural goodness, and hence Huck is reluctant to save himself. By the time of the Wilks fraud Huck has sickened of the imposters' fake sentimentality and decided to rescue Jim from their scheming. But it is a barren commitment. Precisely at this moment of what seems positive virtue, Huck surrenders to conscience, always for Twain the overlayer of prejudice and false valuation imposed upon all members of society in the name of religion, morality, law, and culture. Having resumed status in Tom Sawyer's complacent world of games-playing and moral sentiment, Huck soon joins forces with Tom to torment Jim as if the slave's humanity had never existed for him. No longer an outcast, Huck has entered into debased civilization as surely as Lázaro de Tormes finds social success—at the price of the soul. By the end of *Huckleberry Finn,* Huck's future course is a Guzmán-like extension of an ascetic's despair. He is going to "light out for the territory" so that Aunt Sally can't "sivilize" him, that is, have more Bad Boy adventures that, far from representing his freedom from bondage to civilization, must, according to Twain's logic, confirm his petrifaction at the heart of convention.

Because a *pícaro* takes his formal character from a hollow imitation of the corrupt society in which he struggles for existence, the *pícaro* may symbolize that society. Just so, the King and Duke symbolize society, conscience, civilization, and history. To reject such symbols is extreme, requiring absolute self-reliance, even escape from time—an impossibility according to Twain's own deterministic view of history whereby man's life is at best a long delaying action against corruption. So Huck cannot escape the confidence men; he reflects them, and his failed humanity can never be redeemed by freedom or by love. In *Huckleberry Finn,* as in the classic Spanish novels, there is no catharsis of roguery.

To the Spanish picaresque novelists, creation of self outside orthodox theological patterns is folly, the way of spiritual death; and though contemporary man, by contrast, sees his salvation in self-creation, there remains the possibility of frustration and failure, of escape from freedom, and of conditioning into spiritual death. Here, at the psychic root, is a continuity of picaresque myth, for what it comes down to is not just the way of life of vagabonds and juvenile delinquents but any way of life that seems to lead away and down from meaning and full humanity. Such a contingency shapes a great deal of twentieth-century American literature. Modern man struggles to find identity in a less than meaningful world. Outsidedness has become descriptive of the human condition, and the artist, like the *pícaro* both isolated from and imprisoned within society, has been elevated to the role of representative man, the trickster of eternity and master forger, through imagination, of reality. Because self-creation permits freedom from and transcendence of the destructive element in self, twentieth-century American literature offers an abundance of picarism but not of *pícaros*.

Ralph Ellison's *Invisible Man* (1952) seems often to conform closely to novels in the picaresque tradition. Mock-autobiographical in form, it is the episodic story of an innocent social outcast, who for most of his life has masqueraded in identities given him by others and whose own will to illusion has maintained these masks at the cost of achieved identity, reality, and humanity. The nameless narrator of the title is acutely conscious, at last, of the transparency of any selfhood superimposed by society, yet, because he is literally living underground in a state of total isolation from others, he seems to resemble the loveless *pícaro* reduced to a mechanical personification of the negative, rather than a person preparing to surface to a new life of responsibility. Distinctions between right and wrong are exposed as ambiguous, another picaresque motif. Even at the end, Invisible Man still embraces trickery, enjoying the joke of making society bear the expense of its failure to penetrate his confidence man's disguise.

But if Invisible Man enjoys his joke, he knows, unlike the *pícaro,* that his life is far from hollow. In fact, after all his violent experiences as a victim of racial stereotyping, he has achieved, not lost, his form and brought his soul boldly into the light. As he declares in the prologue, "Without light I am not only invisible, but formless as well; and to be unaware of one's form is to live a death. I myself, after existing some twenty years, did not become alive until I discovered my invisibility." Thus the actual form of Ellison's novel is an antipicaresque journey toward personal freedom and the eventual recovery of a soul left uncontaminated by society. Like Huckleberry Finn, with whom Invisible Man identifies himself, the archetypal American struggles against patterns of conformity, for these are inimical to democracy and personal passion. Identity is won when the individual self is freed from the definitions of others, and, thereafter, real life begins as a personal world "of infinite possibilities," as Ellison has his hero observe in the epilogue. Invisible Man's refusal to accept limits means he is no longer either an outcast or a tragic victim. His self-creation is salvation from disintegration. His role-playing, like the *pícaro*'s, enables him to survive by manipulating the illusions of society, but he himself has an un-compromising sense of who he is and where he has been. As soon as a *pícaro* is free to create his own reality, reconstituting out of experience a common and responsible humanity, he is no longer truly a *pícaro;* he is, rather, a rogue-survivor, one of the many permutations of the contemporary American confidence man.

The hero of Saul Bellow's novel *The Adventures of Augie March* (1953) is also a rogue-survivor. Like Invisible Man and like Yossarian in Joseph Heller's *Catch-22* (novel, 1961), Augie is playfully self-aware of the need for psychic survival in a world of heavy, overly serious people who cannot recognize the games they play. Like Huck Finn, he usually appears in a passive relation to others. They command him, punish him, dupe him, create roles for him. Con-stantly subject to outside influences, Augie tells more about them than about himself. Instead of trying to flee or to change the world around him, he accepts it as it is, risking little and disengaging easily, even from love. Nothing is a fate good enough, nothing deserves his full enthusiasm or commitment. His is a healthy pliancy, a force of opposition. So shape-shifting, adaptation, and impersonation are the styles with which Augie confronts the world, and the more or less aimless sequence of his adventures bears close resemblance to traditional picaresque narrative. But Augie is not fully a *pícaro*. He remains stubbornly himself, with exhilarating readiness to engage in the world, piece by piece. His adaptability, unlike the true *pícaro*'s, is a mode of being and essence of identity and discovery.

Nevertheless, Augie March, somewhat like Lázaro de Tormes, is to a degree an unreliable narrator and betrays a *pícaro*'s lack of belief in the reality of the human condition. "A man's character is his fate," he asserts at the outset of his story, conjuring up an image of a vast world of possibilities for making something of himself in life. But by the time he actually has come to writing his memoirs, he is still only a traveling man, tied to a less than fully devoted wife, and engaged in less than honest work on the Continent as the agent of the shady lawyer Mintouchian. The revelation of Augie's final position comes after a life of vicissitudes partly determined, in typically picaresque psychology, by low origins and early negative influences. As he is walking across a frozen Belgian field with the maid Jacqueline, his efforts to sing for warmth fail miserably. He can only retreat from her reality into a world of cold negation, not the world of bright prospects and genuine human feeling previously recounted. There is, in sum, a diminution, if not quite a disintegration, of Augie's sense of reality, goodness, and trust. A fatalistic despair links this American part-*pícaro* to Spanish precursors.

Elements of the picaresque idea can be found throughout American literature. Life presented as essentially a game is evinced in works from Benjamin Franklin's *Autobiography* (1868), Thoreau's *Walden* (essays, 1854), and Poe's tales of hoaxes and diddles to Jack Kerouac's novel *On the Road* (1957), John Barth's *The Sot-Weed Factor* (novel, 1960), and Ken Kesey's *One Flew Over the Cuckoo's Nest* (novel, 1962)—and in many other works past and present. If an artist adopts the quasi-picaresque strategy of acting, as a sort of confidence trickster, human life may be exposed as a set of tricks and defective rituals. For example, in Nathanael West's novel *Miss Lonelyhearts* (1933) a tormented, cheated mob forces a man to attempt to fashion an authentic self that will make his role effective in giving the mob authenticity in turn. Robert Coover, in *The Public Burning* (1977), also recalls the old picaresque pattern of relationship between a trickster and his world of trickery. In that novel the original Yankee trickster is recreated as a supernatural character called "Uncle Sam," advisor and instigator of another character named "Vice-President Richard Nixon." Obviously, with the growing relativism about moral codes in contemporary life and the widespread loss of deference to official public beliefs, authors are less tempted than in the past to disguise the fictional and actual shiftiness of the confidence man. The spread of official collective con games leads to a new imperative to be shifty in a new country. Where reality and appearances are inverted for the sake of self-performance, the people's primary duty can be seen as reinforcement of their mutual illusions. The outlook is playful rather than cynical, but it is clear that the *pícaro* remains a latently potent archetype in the national life.

See also: Anti-hero, Picaresque, Role Playing, Travel.

Selected Bibliography

Blackburn, Alexander. *The Myth of the Picaro.* Chapel Hill: The University of North Carolina Press, 1979.

Lindberg, Gary. *The Confidence Man in American Literature.* New York: Oxford University Press, 1982.

Lynn, Kenneth S. *Mark Twain and Southwestern Humor.* Boston: Little, Brown and Company, 1959.

Wadlington, Warwick. *The Confidence Game in American Literature.* Princeton, N.J.: Princeton University Press, 1975.

ALEXANDER BLACKBURN

PRIDE

The English noun *pride* and the adjective from which it is derived, *proud,* have a curious semantic history. The Latin verb *prodesse,* "to be advantageous to," seems to have given rise, through Low Latin, to the Old French adjective *prut,* in such expressions as *prus* (later *preux*) *chevalier* and *prud'homme.* It was apparently one of unqualified approval and might be translated "distinguished," "gallant," "noble." The *Grand Larousse* dictionary glosses *prud'homie* as "parfaite honnêteté et sagesse dans la conduite [perfect honesty and wise behavior]." In eleventh-century Old Icelandic texts *pruþr* also appears, perhaps taken over from the French, and is glossed in Cleasby, Vigfusson, and Craigie's dictionary as "fine, magnificent, stately." The umlauting of the vowel in Old English *prud* (proud) to form the abstract noun *pryd* (pride) is normal. No such abstract noun from this root is found in modern French and German, where such words as *orgueil* and *fierté, Stolz* and *Hochmut* take its place. It is hard to know whether their connotations are exactly equivalent to those of *pride,* and so this discussion will concern itself chiefly with the word in contexts of English literature—which is not to say that the *concept,* as defined here, may not be highly relevant to other literatures.

Unlike the favorable meaning of the Old French and Old Norse words having the same root, the sense of *proud* and *pride* in Old, Middle, and Early Modern English is almost invariably one of condemnation. To account for this strange discrepancy, the *Oxford English Dictionary* speculates, "The unfavorable sense, so early in English, may be due to the aspect in which a Norman *prud baron* or *prode chevalier* presented himself to an English peasant or townsman." (It is also interesting that the Modern English noun "prude," invariably derogatory, seems to be derived from *prud'femme.*) However that may be, the words are first encountered in medieval religious texts, such as the homilies of Aelfric and Wulfstan and the *Ancrene Riwle* (c. 1200), and it is clear that they are used there as the regular equivalent of Latin *superbus* and *superbia* (or occasionally *arrogans* and similar expressions), which occur so often in the Vulgate Bible used by their authors, in such familiar texts as the Magnificat: "Dispersit superbos mente cordis sui" [He hath scattered the proud in the imagination of their heart]. *Pride* occurs forty-four times and *proud* and *proudly* fifty-five times in the King James Bible, where, like *superbus* and *superbia,* they translate such New Testament Greek words as *hyperēphanos* ("being conspicuous above others") and, in the Old Testament, "at least six Hebrew roots" which "contain the idea of pride. . . . Almost all of them share the meaning 'to lift up' " (*Interpreters' Dictionary of the Bible, s.v.* "pride"). To be sure, in later English, *proud* and *pride* can have a neutral, or favorable, sense, implying a justifiable awareness of genuine excellence of some kind. But in much English literature the first signification of *pride* given by the *Oxford English Dictionary* applies: "A high or overweening opinion of one's own qualities, attainments, or estate, which gives rise to a feeling and attitude of superiority over and contempt for others: inordinate self-esteem." A shorter definition, using a facetious modern term, might be "one-upmanship, or the fancied need for it." *Pride* emphatically connotes the Greek *hyper* and its Latin cognate *super,* meaning "above" or "over" (both linguistically cognate with them), found in its biblical ancestors.

It might be thought that the Greek noun *hybris* (or *hubris),* so often used in discussions of classical Greek tragedy and epic, is etymologically related to *hyper,* but it seems not to be, but rather to Greek *barys* ("heavy, oppressive"). (For these relations, the appendix "Indo-European Roots" to the *American Heritage Dictionary* is useful.) It is best translated as "wanton insolence" or "unwarranted violence." Tempting as it is to interpret the wrath of Achilles or the haughtiness of Oedipus in terms of pride, the Judeo-Christian theology that lies behind the concept of pride differs too greatly from pagan Greek theology to make this profitable. On Sophocles' *Oidipous tyrannos* (*Oedipus Rex,* play, c. 429 B.C.), Samuel Johnson (probably) remarks that, to be sure, Oedipus is "in private life choleric, haughty, inquisitive; impatient of control and impetuous of resentment. . . . His obstinacy darkens the lustre of his other virtues; it aggravates his impiety, and almost justifies his sufferings." But "that his crimes and punishment still seem disproportionate is not to be imputed as a fault to Sophocles, who proceeded only on the ancient and popular notion of Destiny, which we know to have been the basis of Pagan theology" (*Samuel Johnson's Prefaces and Dedications,* ed. A. T. Hazen, 1937, p. 137). "Tragedy," writes George Steiner (*The Death of Tragedy,* 1961, pp. 4–5), "is alien to the Judaic sense of the world"—and to that of the Christian. "The Judaic spirit is vehement in its conviction that the order of the universe and of man's estate is accessible to reason. The ways of the Lord are neither wanton nor absurd. . . . Tragic drama arises out of precisely the contrary assertion: necessity is blind and man's encounter with it shall rob him of his eyes, whether it be in Thebes or Gaza." Thus in Milton's *Samson Agonistes* (dramatic poem, 1671), though avowedly an imitation of Greek tragedy, Necessity (or Fate or Destiny) has nothing to do with Samson's blinding in Gaza; pride has a great deal. "Thou art become, O worst imprisonment,/ The dungeon of thyself," the chorus tells Samson.

The Theological Context

Strictly, then, *pride* can properly be applied only to literature conceived in a matrix of Judeo-Christian theology and ethics, or (in the case of some modern writers) a matrix having basic ethical and theological values in common with it, whether those writers know it or not. In the biblical canon, man's need, as a precondition of his happiness, for humility—for the ability to see his own worth in proper perspective, as infinitely below that of his Creator, and so little different from that of his other creatures as to make comparisons between them pointless— is insisted on again and again, from the story of the Creation in Genesis, through the history of numerous backslidings of his chosen people, down to such parables of Jesus as those of the prodigal son, and the Pharisee and the publican. "Pride," writes St. Augustine in *De civitate Dei* (*The City of God*, treatise, 413–426 [14, 13]), "is the start of every sin" ("Initium enim omnis peccati superbia est"). He continues,

And what is pride except a longing for a perverse kind of exaltation? For it is a perverse kind of exaltation to abandon the basis on which the mind should be firmly fixed, and to become, as it were, based on oneself, and so remain. This happens when a man is too pleased with himself. and a man is self-complacent when he deserts that changeless Good in which, rather than in himself, he ought to have found his satisfaction.

The original sin of pride, of course, was that of Satan (formerly Lucifer, chief and brightest of the angels), who, as Milton recounts in *Paradise Lost* (poem, 1667), books 4 and 5, in spite of his exalted status and the gratitude he owes to God for it, cannot bear the thought of the Son of God—God himself—taking precedence over him. And then, in the Garden of Eden, Adam and Eve are tempted by him to disobey the one commandment laid on them, not to eat the fruit of one tree. It is, as St. Augustine says, a perverse kind of exaltation, for, having already all the happiness of life in paradise, the only additional pleasure to be gained by their disobedience is the thought that "Ye shall be as gods" yourselves; you will be "one-up" rather than, as they think, "one-down"—a poor exchange for having "brought Death into the world, and all our woe."

According to orthodox Christian teaching, we have all inherited that "original sin," and make ourselves and those around us miserable accordingly. A century or so after St. Augustine, Pope Gregory the Great and others expanded his affirmation that pride is the origin of every sin into the systematic doctrine of the "seven deadly sins," the six other sins, sloth, rage, gluttony, lechery, greed, and envy (acedia, ira, gula, luxuria, avaritia, invidia) being subordinate to, indeed emanations of, the prime sin, pride (superbia). They can be found, drawn up in order, in Chaucer's *Parson's Tale* (c. 1380–1400); Langland's *Piers Plowman* (poem, c. 1362–1387), (Passus 5); and Spenser's *Faerie Queene* (epic poem, 1590–1596), book 1, canto 4 (where pride is personified as the haughty Lucifera). To many readers, the seven sins may seem a quaint, archaic collection of little direct relevance to the modern world. Morton Bloomfield indeed suggests that by the time of Spenser they were already obsolescent. Of course, if, as Bloomfield points out, they were of use to the Roman Catholic confessor, who was thus helped to keep track, perhaps on his fingers, of the transgressions of his penitents, Protestant rejection of auricular confession, together with the insistence that there is merely "sin," whose wages is death, would help the tabulation to fall into disuse.

Some Modern Applications

But it is probable that human nature has changed so little since the time of St. Augustine that, whatever nomenclature we use, the behavior that the names of the sins designate is still with us. Modern psychiatry is far from rejecting the doctrine of pride as the original sin. Freud ([*Das Unbehagen in der Kultur Civilization and Its Discontents*, 1930, Chap. 8]) writes of "the constitutional tendency in men to aggression against one another"—the need to exalt oneself above another, by violence if necessary. Under "neurosis," *Webster's Third New International Dictionary* cites Gordon Allport, "The very nature of the neurotic disorder is tied to pride." Karen Horney, in her last book, *Neurosis and Human Growth* (1950)—though Horney, so far as we know, would not, any more than Freud, have considered herself an adherent of any formal religion—frequently uses the term "pride" to designate what seems to her the central ailment of the neurotic. A key chapter, entitled "Neurotic Pride," begins, "With all his strenuous efforts toward perfection and with all his belief in perfection attained, the neurotic does not gain what he most desperately needs: self-confidence and self-respect. . . . The great positions to which he may rise, the fame he may acquire, will render him arrogant but will not bring him inner security." T. S. Eliot's psychiatrist in *The Cocktail Party* (play, 1949) says much the same thing:

> Half the harm that is done in this world
> Is due to people who want to feel important.
> They don't mean to do harm—but the harm does not interest them,
> Or they do not see it, or they justify it
> Because they are absorbed in the endless struggle
> To think well of themselves.

A significant change in thinking (or perhaps only expression) from Augustine's "when a man is too well pleased with himself" and the *Oxford English Dictionary*'s "inordinate self-esteem" is that these modern students of the problem see that its roots lie not in *too much* but *too little* genuine self-esteem. Why do so many of us—perhaps all of us, in some degree or at some time or other—feel a need to bolster our "self-image" in these finally self-defeating ways? No doubt because, by some means, often in childhood, our legitimate claims to self-esteem have been overthrown—probably by some other individual who sought to bolster his own inadequate self-esteem by doing so. The converse of pride, and the antidote to it, is love—in New Testament vocabulary, *agapē,* the word badly translated as *charity* in 1 Corinthians 13 in the King James Bible (on the significance of the various Greek words lumped together in English translation, see Anders Nygren, *Agape and Eros,* tr. Philip S. Stanton, 1953). The remedy for the original sin of pride is the "great commandment" of the New Testament (though derived from the Old), which superseded all the law and the prophets, "Thou shalt love the Lord thy God with all thy heart, and with all thy soul, and with all thy mind, and thy neighbour as thyself" (Matt. 22: 37–39). But, Erich Fromm shrewdly points out *(The Art of Loving,* 1956), if one does not love oneself—if one is the victim of self-hate, self-distrust, however the disguises of pride may try to conceal the fact—clearly one is incapable of loving one's neighbor. One's universe continues to be eternally centered on the demands for attention of one's own battered ego and has no time for the needs of others.

If pride is thus understood, the six subordinate sins easily come into perspective as natural, God-given, human propensities invaded and made perverse by the prideful imagined need to assuage one's *amour propre.* It is now generally agreed that gross obesity from habitual overeating ("the sin of gluttony") is not usually the result of glandular imbalance but of the reassurance that eating gives to a neurotic insecurity. "Don Juanism"—sexual promiscuity—is now recognized as the result, not of hyperactive sexual glands (indeed, the Don Juan, the rapist, many prostitutes may well be undersexed rather than the opposite), but of the desire to tot up figures of "conquest" ("In Spain, one thousand and three," as Mozart's Don Giovanni's carefully kept account-book records). The figures bolster his neurotic pride—his innate sense of inferiority. Avarice is the perversion by pride—insecurity—of a healthy desire to enjoy the good things of the world. One often reads of seemingly poverty-stricken old men and women after whose death their shabby quarters are found to contain wealth that has been hoarded for decades. Envy: the average-featured girl or the average-muscled boy who suffers agonies at not becoming the "home-coming queen" or the outstanding linebacker, ignoring the potential talents each may have for excellence in other undertakings. Wrath: the pointless anger each of these may feel toward those more successful in a competition where they cannot succeed (and have no need to enter), ignoring the real injustices in the world at which anger might more properly be directed. On sloth, or acedia, see my "From Accidie to Neurosis," in *English Literature in the Age of Disguise,* ed. M. Novak, 1977.

Medieval writers such as Chaucer and Langland preached directly against pride and its six offshoots by name. In later imaginative literature, the warning against pride—if we prefer, we may call it egocentricity—occurs so often that it would be hopeless to do anything but give a small sampling.

In Christopher Marlowe's *Doctor Faustus* (play, *1604*), we have a medieval relic, a ballet of the (personified) seven sins. But the protagonist, Faustus, is a fully developed portrait of the self-deluded egocentric. His discontent, we are told in the Prologue, stems from his "self-conceit." In his opening soliloquy, Faustus lists the arts he has mastered and rejects them. They have brought him as much fame as it is possible for a human being to have. But this is not enough— he wishes to be "eternized": "Yet art thou still but Faustus and a man"—only Deity will do. A trained theologian, who knows that "The wages of sin is death," he also knows the way to salvation—to repent and accept the love of God. This Faustus can never bring himself to do: to accept love, as to give it, some abandonment of one's egoism is necessary. But Faustus is thoroughly hooked on his ego-assuaging dope. To the last stroke of the clock, he can save himself if he wishes, but he will never part with his precious pride and goes to his doom, alternately boasting, "I'm *really* bad"—"The serpent that tempted Eve may be sav'd but not Faustus"—and whining, and, at the end, blaming it all on something else: "I'll burn my books!" (Goethe's *Faust,* who *is* saved, is a very different person, who eventually does acquire some insight into himself.) It is interesting that these two types of the egocentric, Faustus and Don Juan, who later fascinated so many other writers and readers (Molière, Byron, Bernard Shaw, Thomas Mann, for instance) originated around the time of the Renaissance and perhaps represent a secularization of patristic and medieval teachings about the sin of pride.

Satan has sometimes been termed the "hero" of Milton's *Paradise Lost,* but this is nonsense. His rambling boastings, his maudlin outbursts of self-pity— they might be tape-recordings of a neurotic's self-justification at the beginning of a psychoanalysis—make him closer to comedy than to heroism. So is Eve as she debates whether or not to offer the apple to Adam. Should I thus allow him, she asks,

>   to partake
> Full happiness with me—or rather not,
> But keep the odds of knowledge in my power
> . . . so to add what wants
> In female sex . . .
> Or render me more equal, and perhaps,
> A thing not undesirable—sometime
> Superior, for, inferior, who is free?

"More equal," indeed! The Greek concepts of "heroism" and "tragedy" have often been applied to Shakespeare's later plays, "tragic heroes," from the time of Aristotle, being regarded as fundamentally admirable and pitiable. But we may begin to wonder when we find T. S. Eliot saying of Othello's final speech, "What Othello seems to me to be doing is cheering himself up. . . . He has ceased to think about Desdemona and is thinking about himself. . . . Humility is the most difficult of all virtues to achieve; nothing dies harder than the desire to think well of oneself,'' and we may conclude that Othello and Macbeth (and perhaps Antony and Cleopatra) are, like Faustus (and unlike Lear and Milton's Samson), egocentrics who never do find their way out of ''the dungeon of themselves.''

The great writers of eighteenth-century England had not lost touch with the traditional teaching concerning pride. Swift's devastating satire on the self-deceived and other-deceiving Hack, *A Tale of a Tub* (1704), opens by giving him the words, ''Whoever hath an ambition to be heard in a crowd must press, and squeeze, and thrust, and climb with indefatigable pains till he has exalted himself to a certain degree of altitude above them.'' Pope characterizes the dunces whom he pilloried as ''The dull, the proud, the wicked, and the mad,'' as having ''A trifling head, and a contracted heart''—egocentricity stultifies both the intellectual and the emotional responsiveness of its victim. In Jane Austen the most self-centered characters are also the stupidest and the most absurd—Lady Catherine de Bourgh, Mr. Collins, Mrs. Elton, the John Dashwoods. In her significantly titled *Pride and Prejudice* (1813) and in *Emma* (1816), the heroines are enabled to break through their egocentric limitations by experiencing a period of bitter humiliation, which opens their eyes to their own egoistic folly. ''I could not have been more wretchedly blind,'' cries Elizabeth Bennet. ''Till this moment I never knew myself.''

Much literature of the nineteenth and twentieth centuries could profit from analysis of the workings of egocentric pride in its characters. Emma Bovary, Hedda Gabler, and Anna Karenina have sometimes been wept over as tragic heroines, undeserving victims of a hostile Fate. But the chief trait of both Emma and Hedda is surely their overwhelming feeling of superiority to most of those around them. Anna Karenina has often been interpreted as the target of Tolstoy's Puritanical hatred of sensual pleasure. Anna, it is argued, is physically attracted to Vronsky, gives in to the sexual impulse, and so is duly punished. But nothing is made clearer in the novel than that Anna hates sex. After their first intercourse, Vronsky makes a conventional remark about the happiness it has brought them. '' 'Happiness?' cried Anna, with horror and loathing,'' and later, ''With loathing she thought of what was meant by that love.'' She endures sex only to try to keep possession of Vronsky. Her ownership of him bolsters her shaky ego, as Don Giovanni's sexual triumphs bolster his.

One could select from more recent literature much to illustrate (whether or not they were aware of it) how various authors have sought to demonstrate in their writings St. Augustine's teaching, ''Pride is a longing for a perverse kind of exaltation . . . to abandon the basis on which the mind should be firmly fixed, and to become, as it were, based on itself, and so remain.'' ''To know and love one other human being,'' Evelyn Waugh wrote in *Brideshead Revisited* (novel, 1945), ''is the beginning of wisdom.'' ''You shall love your crooked neighbor / With your crooked heart,'' proclaimed W. H. Auden. To take a modern novel almost at random, James Baldwin's *Giovanni's Room* (1956) gives an expert analysis of the mechanism whereby ego-generated emotional inhibition is transmitted from an American father to his son, and of the appalling cruelty the egocentric is capable of when his supply of ego-bolstering dope is threatened. Much work is waiting to be done on the role of the sin of pride in modern literature, as well as in that of past centuries.

Selected Bibliography

Bloomfield, Morton. *The Seven Deadly Sins*. East Lansing: Michigan State University Press, 1952.
Greene, Donald. "The Sin of Pride: A Sketch for a Literary Exploration." *New Mexico Quarterly* 34 (1964): 8–30.
Horney, Karen. *Neurosis and Human Growth*. New York: Norton, 1950.
Kuhn, Reinhard. *The Demon of Noontide: Ennui in Western Literature*. Princeton, N.J.: Princeton University Press, 1976.

DONALD GREENE

THE PROSTITUTE WITH A GOOD HEART

With few exceptions (possibly the temple harlot of the *Epic of Gilgamesh* [c.2000 B.C.] is one) articulations of the theme of the good-hearted prostitute are in the nature of a paradox, expressed memorably in the title of the Renaissance play *The Honest Whore* (Dekker and Middleton, 1604, 1630). The goodness perceived in a particular prostitute is in some way felt to be at odds with implied or expressed assumptions that prostitutes are low in rank and morals. This literary theme is thus closely connected with societal values according to which prostitutes have at times been subjected to special regulations, at others have been considered outside of society or altogether banned.

The *Epic of Gilgamesh* reports how a harlot, "a wanton from the temple of love" (i.e., a cult priestess of Ishtar), is used not only to entice and seduce the beastlike Enkidu but also thus to wean him away from the wild herds with which he has been roaming; the prostitute civilizes him. The poem says nothing about her status and little about her emotions as she carries out the trapper's plan. We know almost as little about the Canaanite prostitute Rahab, who first hides the two Israelite spies from their pursuers and then helps them escape by lifting a cord down from her window. Her distinctive characteristic is her kindness, although she expects the Israelites to display in return as much kindness to her and her father's home (Josh. 3:12).

While in Greek society and Greek literature prostitutes were notoriously mercenary, there are reports of generous *hetairai*, although their generosity often borders on or becomes lavish display. (The *hetairai*, literally "companions," who in addition to physical beauty often had artistic talents and some intellectual training, were a class distinct from and far above the slave girls.) The first of such Greek stories is of the Egyptian courtesan Rhodopis, reputed to have funded the building of a pyramid (although the report is discounted by Herodotus, 5th century B.C.). Equally morally ambiguous is the report that in Greece prostitutes collected the female newborns exposed by others, since their design would of course have been to raise them to be prostitutes. If faithfulness represents goodness, the courtesan Timandra (who briefly appears in Shakespeare's play *Timon of Athens* [1605–1608]) deserves mention. When her lover Alcibiades died in exile and dishonor, Timandra took care of his funeral.

New Comedy, which succeeded tragedy and Old Comedy as the national drama of Athens, was peopled with prostitutes (partly because slaves and courtesans were the only females that could be shown in scenes out-of-doors). Of all the plots in this genre, one was the most popular and influenced the articulation of the theme under discussion in Roman and Renaissance literature. A free young man falls in love with a young slave woman. He spins some intrigues to buy or steal her from the pimp who owns her and to keep her as a concubine. Her father appears and identifies her as a long-lost daughter by means of some piece of jewelry she was wearing when lost in infancy. With the revelation of her parentage, she is recognized as free-born, with no taint attaching from her former employment. Plautus' comedies *Cistellaria (The Casket Comedy*, before 202 B.C.) and *Curculio* represent Latin examples derived from such plots, although Plautus insists in both plays that the girl is young and innocent, apparently just setting out on a career as a courtesan. The young *meretrix* Selenium of *Cistellaria* prevents her lover, whom his father is ordering to marry another girl, from committing suicide. She is a courtesan *in love,* and thus a walking paradox attractive to later (and particularly romantic) writers. When it is revealed that Selenium is not the daughter of a prostitute but that she had been abandoned by her real mother (a free woman) who later and without success had tried to find her, she becomes socially legitimate. In *Curculio* the innocent girl Planesium has been bought and incarcerated by the pandar Cappadox. She is in love with a young man who is too poor to afford her. When she is about to be sold to a captain, she recognizes in that officer her brother, who has been considered lost—the young man's rival is thus eliminated and her free birth demonstrated.

It agrees with such periodizations as Erich Auerbach's (author of *Mimesis,* 1946) with his characterization of medieval Christianity as a fusion of sublimity and humility, that conversion accounts like that of the penitent public sinner (traditionally identified with Mary Magdalene) of Luke 7:35–40, would take on a central importance in that period. Mary Magdalene's conversion, which bridges the gap from the lowest of the low to the highest, and the related medieval versions of the Thais legend (which report how the Abbot Paphnutius converted the prostitute Thais) are in this sense some of the most Christian of motifs. Both in the play *Pafnutius* by the German nun Hrotswitha of Gandersheim (10th century) and in the popular version in Jacobus de Voragine's *Legenda aurea (The Golden Legend,* c. 1270), Thais is an example of an inveterate sinner brought to recognize her guilt. That Thais probably belonged to the privileged rank of the highly educated *hetairai,* as distinct from a common prostitute, is insignificant in the medieval accounts. Interestingly, these versions of the story do not tell us anything about her family, rank, or the reasons why she turned to prostitution. (Nor does Luke tell us anything about the background of the sinful woman who washed Christ's feet with her tears and wiped them with her hair.) From the start Thais is just the "perfect" sinner, who will have to change her life radically in order to turn to God.

Thais changes from prostitute to recluse—not to a married woman as some literary prostitutes of the Renaissance do after their conversion. This difference is no doubt important in itself, although we do not know whether it was really common for Renaissance prostitutes to marry and go straight. Willard Thorp asserts, without supplying any evidence, that it was not unusual in Elizabethan life for a whore to marry a gentleman and become respectable. But the marriage of the converted prostitute in some versions of the "good prostitute" theme reveals its proper significance only when considered in connection with other elements that characterize literary treatments of prostitutes in the Renaissance.

The imaginative core of the Renaissance versions of this theme is most apparent in Giovanni Giraldi Cinthio's novella about the loyal syphilitic prostitute who refuses to risk infecting the man she really loves (*Hecatommithi* [*Hundred Tales*, 1565]. This story could be considered the prototype of all later versions of good and generous prostitutes. Its heroine, the beautiful Melina, is identified in the first sentence about her as *gentile*. Any doubts we might have about the precise meaning of the word are cleared up when we find her repeatedly stressing her high origins. She mentions her "noble blood" and the "quality" of her lineage and declares: "I am not born of the vile rabble of the people, but of a father and mother not only noble, but lordly." Could she be lying about her background? Of course not; her lover knows that he could not have better proof of her high descent than her generosity. While in some Greek and Roman comedies we have seen revelations of the girls' true parentage to be a mechanical necessity to untangle the intrigue, the prostitute's nobility of blood here becomes truly thematic. In a sense the entire story functions to validate the importance of such distinctions.

This emphasis is also apparent in two English versions of the motif that imaginatively depict conversions of prostitutes and thus relate to the Mary Magdalene and Thais stories mentioned: the supposedly autobiographical speaker of Robert Greene's brief novel *Conversion of an English Courtesan* (1592) and Bellafront, the central character of the two-part play *The Honest Whore* (1604 and 1630) by Thomas Dekker and Thomas Middleton. Greene's story is quite carefully told. Within the courtesan's report of her descent to prostitution and subsequent conversion is a framed story that parallels it entitled "A pleasant discourse, how a wise wanton by her husband's gentle warning, became to be a modest matron." It is told by a lover of the courtesan after he has discovered that this woman with whom he was living as with a wife has been unfaithful to him. The lover tells her about an inventive and patient husband who, when he learns of his wife's adulterous relationship with a friend of his, decides to put a piece of play-money on her window sill each time he has enjoyed her body—

the same device used in Gascoigne's brief 1573 novel *The Adventures of Master F.J.* This unsubtle way of showing the wife that she is a whore has the desired effect and brings about her "conversion." The parallel with the courtesan's life remains incomplete, since she does not immediately prove responsive to the hint of the story, but continues her down-hill course until she is a common strumpet in London. Her reform will be the work of a devout and handsome young "clothier," whom she comes to love and finally marries.

Like the other husband's token-money device, the stratagem by which the young clothier brings his beloved back to the path of virtue bespeaks its origin in the earlier novelistic tradition. Seeming to want to evade all witnesses, he asks her to take him to the darkest room, in order to bring home his point that no one can shut out God, the all-knowing witness. This device is best known through Jacobus de Voragine's version of the Thais legend in his *Legenda aurea* and Erasmus' in his dialogue "Adolescentis et scorti" (*Colloquia* [*The Collo-quies*, 1516]). In this context, the details of the courtesan's conversion are less important than the circumstance that initiated the young man's unusual interest in a prostitute. He "noted" her "personage" and found an incongruity between "so good a proportion" and "whoredomes base deformitie," then began to question her about her origin and background. The term "personage" links suggestions of physical beauty and high birth.

When in what he calls "a home-bred historie" (possibly referring to Greene's title) Thomas Heywood tells the story of a prostitute who after a conversion brought about by the familiar dark-room stratagem becomes a model of charity and gratitude, he makes the societal scale even more explicit (*Gynaikeion*, 1624).

Although Bellafront, the heroin of both parts of *The Honest Whore*, is early in the play called "a poor gentlewoman," this may be intended as a double entendre. She may be understood to be "gentle" in the sense of "accessible." Her background is revealed only gradually as she gains in stature, becoming the dominant character in the play. Comparing Dostoevsky's Lisa with Anatole France's Thaïs and Aphra Behn's Angelica, C. Hayward judges that "none who have written about courtesans have ever expressed their paradoxical character better than Mrs. Behn does when she makes Angelica exclaim, 'My Virgin Heart, Moretta! Oh, 'tis gone!' " (*The Courtesan*, 1926, 11–12). But actually *The Honest Whore* anticipates many of the themes that later became standard in the literary treatment of prostitutes. As will happen to Behn's Angelica, Bel-lafront is chastised to her face for her vile profession by the man she loves, and like Angelica she has difficulty persuading him of her "innocence," meaning that she exercises her trade without enjoyment. As Behn's Angelica will suspend her commercial interests, at least temporarily, for the love of Willmore (and as Greene's courtesan had been converted through the love of a clothier), so Bel-lafront reforms through her exclusive love for Hippolito. Not only is Bellafront's love rejected by Hippolito, but also the courtier Matheo, her first seducer, rejects the idea of marrying her with derision. That the seducer is finally forced to marry her because he has stolen her "fine iewell" serves to satisfy the audience's sense of retribution at the end of the play's first part, and at the same time leaves enough dynamite for the plot of the second part.

There Bellafront's true stature is fully revealed as Hippolito, now desperately in love with Bellafront, begins to test her fidelity to her abject husband. (A similar reversal occurs in Aphra Behn's play in two parts *Rover* [1677, 1680] where, after loathing Angelica's baseness, Willmore will sue for her love.) As the reformed prostitute's moral greatness is unfolded, the hints about her noble origin are confirmed. In act 1, scene 2, a certain Orlando Friscobaldo, a noble-man, appears at court and is greeted with great respect. From him we learn of Bellafront's noble birth, for she is his daughter. It takes all of Bellafront's ingenuity to resist the cunning of the "bawd Necessity": besides being subjected to derogatory comments about her past, she has to provide food for her husband (by begging from her neighbors), to counter Hippolito's rhetoric and financial temptation (she cleverly returns the purse with which he hoped to buy her favors to his wife Infelice), and to suffer the indignity of being accused (falsely) of instigating his crime. That she emerges from all these temptations not only spotless but shining would surely have challenged the assumptions of a Renais-sance audience. The title of the play is deliberately close to those paradoxes of which the Renaissance was so fond. Bellafront is meant to be a truly extraordinary phenomenon, unheard of, almost in violation of natural laws. As the duke puts it: "To turne a Harlot / Honest, it must be by strong Antidots, / 'Tis rare, as to see Panthers change their spots" (*2 Honest Whore* 4.2, 46–48). It would seem that by having Bellafront derive from noble stock the authors of *The Honest Whore* assumed they could make this striking metamorphosis more believable.

In the light of these assumptions it is not surprising that Luke's conversion account of the public sinner is reinterpreted, that is, that Lewis Wager presents this convert as a "gentlewoman." In his interlude *Life and Repentance of Marie Magdalene* (1566), the heroine derives from "stocke right honorably" is nurtured "in noble ornature" and also has in her possession "the whole castel of Mag-dalene." Similarly, Tomaso Garzoni, a distinguished and reliable compiler of Renaissance knowledge, affects to know when he writes *Le vite delle donne illustri della Scrittura Sacra* (1586) that Mary Magdalene, about whose back-ground the evangelists are silent, was nobly born. "How shall I begin?" he wonders. "With her physical beauty? Or with the nobility of her family? Or with the outstandingly pleasing and unique virtue of her soul?" His conflict is easily resolved: "I will first name nobility as being more manifest in her, and say that Mary Magdalen was of illustrious stock, lady of Magdalo Castle two miles from Genezareth, and that she had from her family as honored and noble a reputation as any other illustrious and glorious person of those times."

There is some indication in Cervantes' novel *Don Quijote* (*Don Quixote*, 1605, 1615) that the good-hearted prostitute of high birth was so much a literary convention by the beginning of the seventeenth century that it could be gently satirized. The satire is very gentle indeed, for "kind-hearted Maritornes" is genuinely good to Sancho. She rubs him down when he needs care badly after his arrival at the inn with his melancholy master; the following day, after Sancho has been cruelly tossed in a blanket, she brings him water and, when he asks for it, even wine, "and likewise paid for it with her own money, for indeed it is said of her that, although she followed that trade, she had some faint glimmerings in her of a Christian." In the context of the work this sentence probably has to be read as an understatement that can and should be turned to the highest praise for this woman of active charity. But the reader can doubt whether Maritornes is of gentle birth (as she claims) or whether she only pretends to be so, for the narrator carefully "distances" the report on her origin by giving it only from her perspective. Since her gentility is used to explain and support her honest whoring, that is, her keeping her assignations, there is also at least a hint that the convention of the high-born prostitute is not only recognized but satirized.

A few well-known modern, post-Renaissance versions of the theme may by contra-distinction illuminate the older versions. Leaving aside Manon Lescaut, (novel, 1731) l'abbé Prévost's famous heroine, since her "goodness" may be too questionable, there is for instance Mlle. d'Aisnon of Diderot's famous story in *Jacques le fataliste* (*Jacques the Fatalist*, written 1773), a prostitute hired by Mme. de la Pommeraye as a tool to punish her unfaithful lover, le marquis des Arcis. The revenge consists in having the prostitute pretend to be a girl of unsullied morals until the marquis has fallen in love and married her. Unexpectedly, the scheme results in the young woman's reform and the marquis's forgiveness for her past. Significantly the young lady is not of the nobility; her rank can best be described as petit bourgeois, for her real name is, as we are advised at the beginning of the story, Mlle Duquenoi. Yet in her tastes, sentiments, and character she ultimately feels herself to have been born worthy of her noble husband. No Renaissance character (except perhaps an obvious villain) would have reasoned thus. On the other hand Mlle Duquenoi is still socially a step above (in the next century) Mercy Merrick, the prostitute of Wilkie Collins' *The New Magdalen* (1873), who, like Diderot's heroine, goes through a phase of impersonation of a respectable lady. Mercy's "innate nobility" and "innate grandeur," both, of course, qualities of the mind, are asserted by the narrator in the very first chapter of the novel.

There is no doubt that Alexandre Dumas (fils) conceived his famous *La dame aux camélias* (*Camille,* novel, 1848; drama, 1852) in the tradition of sentimental prostitute literature. Both Marguerite, the heroine of the title, and her lover Armand are readers of *Manon Lescaut*. Marguerite is the closest parallel to Giraldi Cinthio's beautiful Melina in her willingness to sacrifice herself for love. Generations of fans of Verdi's opera *La Traviata* (1853) have wept over the generous sacrifice that her love for Armand enables her to make. After his father convinces her that his son's liaison with a *femme galante* is jeopardizing the marriage prospects of Armand's sister, and therefore also Armand's happiness, she pretends not to love him and the resulting emotional upheaval precipitates her death. But the differences between this story and the Renaissance novella are salient, for this "proof of love," as Armand's father calls it, is not a proof of gentility. Marguerite Gautier's background is similar to that of Mlle Duquenoi. She has "neither parents, nor family," as she says. In fact she was adopted for sentimental reasons by a duke at an age when her moral conduct was already dubious.

In versions of the theme by the realist Guy de Maupassant and the Marxist Bertolt Brecht, the societal implications become, as one would expect, more explicit. The travellers with whom we find Elizabeth Rousset, nick-named Boule de suif (in the story of that name [1880]), are chosen to represent various ideological and economic groups in the France of 1871. There is a wine merchant, an industrial entrepreneur and opportunist politician, a nobleman (deriving from the nobility of the Ancien Régime), all with their wives, also carefully placed on the social ladder; then there are two nuns and finally Carundet, nick-named "le démoc." It is primarily the representatives of the French *société rentée* (moneyed class) who demand of the prostitute Boule de suif that she suffer the indignity of sleeping with the Prussian officer as a condition for their release and who then reject her.

With such characters as Boule de suif, Ida Starr (of George Gissing's novel *The Unclassed,* 1884), and Brecht's good woman of Sezuan from his 1943 drama (the only person in town willing to put up with the tottering old gods who come to visit), we have come to a radically different conception of the good prostitute. Both the selfless Ida Starr, who is the daughter of a prostitute, and the good woman of Sezuan, clearly a proletarian, work actively to improve the deplorable condition of the poor. Modern treatments of prostitutes generally present them as women who are exploited and held in contempt by most segments of society, and by asserting their value assert the value of working-class people, or at least of those segments of society that have little power.

The diachronic view of the theme of the prostitute with a good heart reveals distinctions that are roughly parallel to Erich Auerbach's large periodization scheme in *Mimesis*. In the Middle Ages, when the story of Christ with its radical mixture of workaday reality and the most sublime had conquered classical literary distinctions between levels of style correlated with social rank, the versions of the Thais legend illustrate this fusion of the very low and the very high. In numerous Renaissance articulations of the theme, by contrast, the social hier-archies are reinstated and even made explicit, so that even Mary Magdalene appears as "nurtured in noble ornature": as if by secret agreement Renaissance authors show only well-born prostitutes as truly charitable or repentant. Romantic versions can tap certain emotional resources first in evidence in Renaissance sentimental prostitute literature (as, for instance, in the Giraldi Cinthio story of generous and self-denying Melina) but post-Renaissance authors wipe out the societal assumptions of the previous era, and far from returning to medieval "realism" (in Auerbach's sense), turn the theme to a socio-critical and sometimes revolutionary use. In stories from the American Frontier or the American logging or small town (for instance Bret Harte's "The Luck of Roaring Camp" [1868] and "The Outcasts of Poker Flat [1869], Hemingway's "The Light of the World"

[1925], Faulkner's *The Reivers* [1962] as well as popular movies in that vein, e.g., Robert Altman's *McCabe and Mrs. Miller* [1971]) prostitutes sometimes assume the civilizing role that the harlot played for Enkidu in the *Epic of Gilgamesh*.

See also: Sex, (Heterosexual, Erotic)

Selected Bibliography

Greenwald, Harold, and Aron Krich, ed. *The Prostitute in Literature*. New York: Ballantine, 1960.

Hayward, C. *The Courtesan*. London: Casanova Society, 1926.

Pomeroy, Sarah B. *Goddesses, Whores, Wives and Slaves: Women in Classical Antiquity*. New York: Schocken, 1975.

Seymour-Smith, Martin. *Fallen Women: A Sceptical Inquiry into the Treatment of Prostitutes . . . in Literature*. London: Nelson, 1969.

WINFRIED SCHLEINER

PSYCHIC LANDSCAPE

Psychic Landscape (p.l.) is a literary landscape particularly of various American wild regions possessing a psychic presence and hence affecting one's psychological and spiritual state. "Psychic" applies specifically to a quality within woodlands, prairies, mountain ranges, canyons, or deserts that elicits a strong inner response. In no way is this response preconceived or superimposed by the beholder. It is, rather, generated independently by the land itself. Such a phenomenon has been depicted in American literature since the latter part of the eighteenth century.

The notion of landscape providing esthetic stimulus to the artist is as old as art itself and by no means limited to a wild America. Goethe, for instance, remarked in his *Dichtung und Wahrheit* (*Poetry and Truth,* autobiography, 1811–1832) that uncultivated nations sublimely excite us. Though traces of psychic landscapes can be found in American literature as early as the writings of Thomas Paine (*Rights of Man,* essay, 1791–1792), Lewis and Clark (1815), and later in Walt Whitman's *Leaves of Grass* (poetry, 1855), the conceptualization of this unique quality or aspect of wild landscapes was rendered more succinct by the essayist and novelist Frank Waters. He wrote in his book *The Colorado* (1946) that landscapes of the American West are "purely mystical in tone" with a "great spirit of place." He further elucidates by describing the first white trappers possessing a "psychical fear" of an invisible force of the immense hinterland, which has an overwhelming power of place. American Indians had long since integrated this psychical power of the land with their cosmology and religion (see "The Great Vision" chapter of *Black Elk Speaks,* 1932). Much time and many adjustments were needed for Euro-American settlers to make the transition from psychic fear to psychic integration. The American West is, for Waters, a story of human adaptation, psychically as well as physically, to the awesome and vast space of prairies, mountains, and deserts.

Such thinking may well have had its origins in concepts of the sublime of the Scottish rhetoricians Hume, Kames, and Blair, which was transmitted to American thought through John Witherspoon and Thomas Jefferson. New England transcendentalism may have been another, at least indirect, source, particularly Henry David Thoreau in works like *The Maine Woods* (essay, 1864). Thoreau contended that the forests of Maine "waylaid" and "compelled" him to return again. He felt that some invisible glutton seemed to drop from the trees and gnaw at the heart of the solitary traveller who threaded those wilds. Thoreau conjectured that no doubt the dark and dense Maine woods would at length react on the inhabitants and "make them natives." P.l. also *parallels* the contemporary French writer Michel Butor's concept of "le génie du lieu" (see *Où* [*The Spirit of Mediterranean Places, 1971*]). That is, each geographic location of the Earth planet has a particular genius of its own that affects the inhabitants and more particularly the artists and writers who come within its presence. No doubt Butor's stay in New Mexico had much to do with strengthening and confirming his sense of "le génie du lieu." The overwhelming vastness of the American wilderness elicits a marked response that is clearly reflected in literary genres of journals, essays, novels, and poetry of all nationalities coming into contact including Euro-American, American Indian, and Mexican American. It is necessary at this point to make a clear distinction between romantic projectionism and p.l. Perry Miller defines romantic landscapes in his study *Nature's Nation* (1967) as those upon which the artist has projected his emotions and moods. P.l. involves the reverse—the projection of the *land's* spirit into the mind. Of course one must heed the admonition of Longfellow that mountains alone do not make great poets. However, it cannot be denied that sensitive poets *can* be stimulated by the spirit of place. Turning to journals growing out of experience in the American wilderness, those of Meriwether Lewis and William Clark express early traces of a kind of psychic reaction to land (only early traces because Lewis and Clark were relatively brief visitors to the wilderness). For them the country beyond the Mississippi was "beautiful in the extreme." Captain Lewis confesses that when he viewed the Great Falls of Montana, they robbed him of his capacity to describe, because their forceful sublimity evoked an inner sense of *fearful* joy. Lewis and Clark serve as examples of Thomas Paine's belief that great scenes will inspire great ideas. Seventy years later Walt Whitman visited the Colorado Rockies (1879) to experience "new senses, new joys." John Muir, protegé of Ralph Waldo Emerson and Henry David Thoreau, expressed a sense of psychic presense in the Sierra Nevada of California in several of his works. Perhaps *My First Summer in the Sierra* (published in 1911 but based on an 1869 journal) is representative in its portrayal of p.l. in which the "very rocks seemed talkative." For Muir rivers of the Sierra flowed not by him but *through* him. Another turn-of-the-century writer, Jack London, wrote of the Canadian Northwest in short fiction in which characters are victims of "psychic fear" of the North where the land is still, calm, and uncanny. Mary Austin, however, portrays a sense of psychic integration with the land particularly in her book *Land of Little Rain* (1910), which has as its focus the desert regions of California and the Southwest. She depicted a desert full of a "palpable sense of mystery" where brown land lays a strong "hold on the affections." The desert with its rainbow hills and luminous radiance possesses such a "lotus charm" that it is almost impossible to abandon it for some other place. A similar effect of western lands can be seen in Owen Wister's novel *The Virginian* (1902), in which the protagonist proclaims that he wishes to mingle with the ground, water, and trees in the Grand Tetons of Wyoming until he no longer can distinguish himself from the land. He wants never to "unmix again." A psychic landscape, then, fosters a keen sense of universal interrelatedness within the mind of the beholder.

One can most clearly discern the concept of p.l. in modern western American literature from O. E. Rølvaag's *I de dage* (*Giants in the Earth*, 1924–1925) to the current writings of Edward Abbey (*Desert Solitaire*, 1968, *Beyond the Wall*, 1984). Perhaps the American West of the mid and late twentieth century still has enough wild and sublime elements in it that literature of this region is particularly strong in p.l. British author D. H. Lawrence wrote of the New Mexico Pueblo Indians' feeling for the pulse of their continent in his travel sketches *Mornings in Mexico* (1927). Their ceremonial drums pound like heart beat, wrote Lawrence, sending the spirits of the Indians out on ether to the "germinating quick of maize" that lies underground until the seed "throws forth its rhythms of creative energy" as a blooming plant. Clearly for Lawrence Indian ceremony helped inculcate a sense of spirit of place. Scores of other writers have given similar expression to a sense of mystical interrelatedness of man and land that the American West forcefully evokes.

Frank Waters further clarifies the manner in which a mere physical land can evoke a psychical response. He explains that Indians believe in a subtle aliveness of the land, and that non-Indians soon become aware of it. He gives in *The Colorado* an example of a white telephone mechanic who worked in the Mohave desert and who became so intrigued with the elephant-skin mountains that he wished to quit his job and go off "to see what's what." Kiowa Indian author N. Scott Momaday addresses the need for psychic integration in his book *The Way to Rainy Mountain* (1968), in which he admonishes that once in his life a person ought "to give himself up to a particular landscape" of his choosing and "to look upon it from as many angles as he can." Giving one's self up to landscape is astutely reflected in much fiction and nonfiction of the trans-Mississippi West. Willa Cather's novel *Death Comes for the Archbishop* (1927), for instance, is a clear manifestation of a fictional protagonist (Jean Marie Latour) becoming so familiar with a particular landscape that the spirit of New Mexico (with its pinyons, mesas, and turquoise skies) becomes very much a part of his psyche.

O. E. Rølvaag vividly portrays in *Giants in the Earth* psychical qualities of the land that may even affect those who are insensitive to the wilderness and who are in the process of attempting to subdue the land. The Norwegian settlers of the early Dakota territory feel a living presence in the prairies; they sense an unseen force around them which is "intangible and mysterious." Along similar lines, protagonist Boone Caudill of A. B. Guthrie's novel *The Big Sky* (1947) experiences powerful sensations emanating from the dark Montana hills, where strong Indian medicines and spirit people abound. The spirit force of the land "flung itself on the traveler where the going was risky." One is reminded of Thoreau's Maine woods, which had invisible gluttons falling from the trees and gnawing at the heart of solitary travelers. The characters' reactions in Rølvaag's and Guthrie's novels are clear illustrations of p.l. on the human mind.

Edward Abbey, in *Desert Solitaire,* gives expression to a living presence within the canyons of Utah, where there are "enough cathedrals and temples and altars here for a Hindu pantheon of divinities." Abbey full well expects to encounter disembodied intelligence that will actually speak his name. P.l. in Abbey's writings curiously parallels the concept of sacred wilderness found in Exodus of the Old Testament. And Rudolpho Anaya, Mexican-American novelist from Albuquerque, colors his novel *Bless Me, Ultima* (1972) with powerful psychic landscapes. The river that divides pasture lands from the Ilano or Plains contains a mysterious but ever-drawing presence. John McPhee, in essays like *Encounters with the Archdruid* (1971), also evokes a sense of p.l. Modern poets of the American West have presented p.l. in some of their poems. American Indian poet James Welch's *Riding the Earthboy 40* (1975) contains the poem "Thanksgiving at Snake Butte," in which the psychic pull of ancestral spirits can be felt in present-day Montana grasslands.

Richard Hugo strikes a similar note in "Indian Graves at Jocko" (from *The Lady in Kicking Horse Reservoir,* poem, 1973), as does William Stafford in "A Sound from the Earth" from the collection *Allegiances* (1970), or Richard Fleck in "Captive of the Land" in *Cottonwood Moon* (1979). Perhaps the most striking p.l. is found in William Stafford's "Earth Dweller" *(Allegiances),* in which the very earth speaks to us and give us dreams.

P.l. pervades late eighteenth- and nineteenth-century American literature and even more forcefully twentieth-century western American literature, but it has traces of origins in New England transcendentalism and in European concepts of the sublime.

See also: Arcadia, Mountaineering, Sublimity, Travel.

Selected Bibliography

Aldridge, A. Owen. *Early American Literature: A Comparatist Approach.* Princeton, N.J.: Princeton University Press, 1982.

Clough, Wilson O. *The Necessary Earth.* Austin: University of Texas Press, 1964.

Haines, John Meade. *Living Off the Country: Essays on Poetry and Place.* Ann Arbor: University of Michigan Press, 1981.

Lorsch, Susan E. *Where Nature Ends: Literary Responses to the Designification of Landscape*. Rutherford, N.J.: Fairleigh Dickinson University Press, 1983.

RICHARD F. FLECK

PSYCHOANALYSIS OF THE SELF

The "psychoanalysis of the self" term refers to a restricted sphere of interest within psychoanalysis focusing on the self, a superordinate concept that may assume different meanings depending on the context; for example, 1) the total person; 2) a seat of consciousness and organizing point of reference for subjective experience; 3) a separate center of initiative and intentionality; 4) and, more narrowly within psychoanalysis, the subjective area of self-representations and internalized representations of key figures of early childhood. It is with the latter, rather than with the ego's defensive and mediating functions, that the psychoanalysis of the self is mainly concerned.

Historical Perspective

The first appearance of the concept coincides with the first psychoanalysis, that is, Freud's *self*-analysis *(Selbstanalyse)*. This radical probing of the unconscious mind, which was mainly through early memories, dreams, and their associations, resulted not so much in a newer self as in a psyche of repressed wishes and instinctual drives that cluster around a nuclear conflict named after the Sophoclean hero. Freud's emerging theory of instinctual drives and his emphasis on the Oedipus complex still remain the mainstream concerns of psychoanalytic practice. What developed in later decades as the English school of object-relations and what in the 1970s came to be known in America as the "psychoanalysis of the self" can in some instances be seen as an expansion of Freud's ideas, in others as their modification, revision, and partial replacement.

Freud himself, however, had opened up the area of the self in *Zur Einführung des Narzissmus (On Narcissism*, 1914), which he defined as the libidinal cathexis of (or attachment to) the self. This work continues to serve as the base for later diverging investigations into the self, and over the decades some of the pejorative onus associated with the word has dissipated. Thus one now hears of a developmental line in narcissism, of a healthy or mature narcissism in contrast to a defective narcissism signaled by low self-esteem, a poor self-concept, grandiosity, and other negative characteristics. In short, the discourse on narcissism launched by Freud has grown and required that proportionate attention be given to the place of the self in the new schema. Incidentally, French literary studies, which would shun American ego-psychology equally with the newer branch of self-psychology, do not hesitate to draw their impetus from Freud's seminal paper.

But rather than find a place for the self among the psychic agencies of id, ego, and superego, Freud settled for phrases such as "self-preservative drives" and "ego-instincts." While later psychoanalysts would consider that products such as delusions and fantasies are aimed at repairing damage, healing injuries, or restoring losses to the self, Freud relied on the more restrictive term of *Ich* (ego). For present purposes, his 1909 paper, "Der Familienroman der Neurotiker" ("Family Romances") points the way out of this confusion, for in a few brief pages he succeeded in opening up an entirely new way of thinking about artistic creativity from the perspective of the self. The child, Freud wrote, suffers an inevitable blow to his fragile self-esteem when he senses that the parents he highly reveres do not so perfectly reciprocate his affections. Rather than accept their imperfections and scale down his idealizations, he (also the neurotic and the artist) may give vent to his imperious wishes by creating in his imagination a new set of exalted figures to be his true parents, while the actual but disappointing pair are reduced to a temporary, adoptive role. The artist will manage to build his fantasies into mythic and cultural traditions, while the neurotic's fantasies will remain private and self-enclosed. Thus the profound and pervasive motif of orphan / foundlings running through literature can be construed as the creative artist's adaptation to the "slings and arrows of outrageous fortune," which have inflicted injuries on the self and generated images of rebirth through adoption. The narcissistic-injury theory of creativity has been most fully developed by William Niederland, while the family romance has served as the ground for the far-ranging theories of poetic origins propounded by Harold Bloom. Yeats's "Myself must I remake" from his late poem "An Acre of Grass" makes the process explicit. From these preliminaries, it may be concluded that the earlier pathways into the psychoanalysis of the self lay through the fantasy layers and subjective structures otherwise and too narrowly associated with the ego.

The Self and Illusion

Being a person's fundamental reference point and the subjective sense of who he is, the self encompasses his identity along with his various roles, his past relationships along with his current ones, that is, his feelings about himself and others; and finally his body along with how the body has been mentally represented from infancy on. More subjective than character, it is also more elusive than the id, ego, and superego. In literature, character traditionally bears the seeds of destiny and expresses moral purpose, while the self affirms the present and says how it feels to be alive in a special place and time. With modern writing becoming more self-regarding and autobiographical, the concept of character has been yielding to that of self. Yet the self is not an exclusively modern invention. The bewilderingly rich ambience of its subjectivity always affirms that "we are such stuff as dreams are made on" and concurs even more explicitly with the lines from Calderón's play *La vida es sueño* (*Life is a Dream,* 1635): "The king dreams he is king; believing this / Illusion, he lives ordering, ruling, / And governing, [for] all life, it seems, / Is just a dream, and even dreams are dreams."

In this Pirandello-sense that the self is an illusion that allows us to feel real, psychoanalysis, which is nothing less than a science of wishes, concurs; for the fantasies we have about ourselves become the very substance of that psychoanalytic process whose aim is to deliver us to ourselves.

Literary studies of the self, like Wylie Sypher's *Loss of the Self* (1962) and Charles Glicksberg's *The Self in Modern Literature* (1963), have taken these quandaries into account by referring to the anonymous and relativist self, respectively. As it is becoming an absence, the self is becoming a subject of increasing cultural interest, and one of the more interesting contributions to the subject is Robert Jay Lifton's notion of the *protean self* to be found in his *The Life of the Self* (1976) and his other works.

Despite this pessimistic and paradoxical state of affairs, a healthy skepticism within mainline psychoanalysis is preferable to the other simplistic approaches now enjoying cultural respectability. The clinical writings of the English psychoanalyst R. D. Laing, for example, were popularized in the 1960s and then used as the basis for much English and American literary research in the 1970s. Having gleaned his concepts in part from his colleagues, Laing is nonetheless credited with drawing the sharp distinction between a false self and another self, which must by logic and semantics be called the true self. Since the false self is depicted as the individual's jerry-built system of responses to the demands of his social environment, one infers that somewhere there must be his pristine true self—by implication immune from subjective distortions, illusions, and idiosyncratic fantasies. The inference is false, however, and while such concepts lend themselves to convenient categories, their stark dichotomizing undermines their value in literary studies as it already has in psychoanalysis. To reify the self into a state of ideal wholeness is to lose touch with its relative subjectivity. Yet such labels as the romantic or existential self, true self / false self, androgynous or authentic self are often mistaken for the whole, and the loss of an aspect of the self is then construed as in the title of Sypher's study to be *Loss of the Self*.

Less problematic for developing a psychoanalysis of the self is the so-called English school of object-relations (out of which Laing emerged), including Melanie Klein, R.W.D. Fairbairn, Michael Balint, D. W. Winnicott, Hannah Segal, and Masud Khan, among others. Both the impact of their own applied studies and their influence on other scholars in articulating the inner reality of the individual have been enormous. But strictly speaking they do not constitute a school, and in America the work of Edith Jacobson, Otto Kernberg, and Margaret Mahler, among many others, can readily be fitted into an object-relations approach. What the early object-relations analysts accomplished was to make possible new ways of speaking about the individual's very early world, his most primitive emotional states, and the ways in which bodily sensations and experiences with the (maternal) environment are represented and bound up together within the psyche. Consequently, the cavernous pre-oedipal world began to be illumined, and instead of a climactic advance toward the Oedipus complex, a more graduated slope of psychosexual progress began to materialize. The controversy within psychoanalysis between the traditional and the newer wings has been popularly portrayed in the archetypes of Oedipus and Narcissus. And it is intriguing to find that this distinction also closely approximates that between modern and post-modern literature as outlined in Ihab Hassan's *The Dismemberment of Orpheus* (1971, 1982). The modernist emphasized symbolism, hierarchy, purpose, centeredness, total dedication—all oedipal derivatives, one might infer; the post-modernist is anarchistic, dispersed, less involved and committed, more eclectic—clearly pre-oedipal and more suitably narcissistic. Thus the shift in the arts and in some psychoanalytic circles may be part of larger cultural changes.

The Experiencing Self in Play

Credited with greatly advancing psychoanalysis, D. W. Winnicott is especially important for discerning the developmental role of play. The child during weaning manages to relinquish his tight emotional hold on his mother by investing the pre-existing objects of his environment (dolls, blankets, toys, etc.) with some of the same affective intensity. These *transitional,* or *subjective-objects* then perform self-reaffirming and self-sustaining roles as the child develops a sense of himself through play with the mother, playing alone in her presence, and eventually carrying on in her absence. Play helps the child to tuck inside himself the image of the good mother. An early object-relation becomes part of the self. But Winnicott's major insight from play activities was to see that cultural objects—art, literature, philosophy, religion—inherit the same intermediate sphere of experiencing first opened up by the spaces of play between infant and mother. Here the self first comes into its own, while culture continues and sustains the shared illusions that make up the self. Literary tradition as a pre-existing entity allows the ongoing play of creativity to sustain both its artists and those who share in its products. According to Winnicott, the work of sorting out inner from outer reality is a lifelong process for everyone. If such were not the case, literary studies would have long since completed their task and peacefully expired. But the application of play theory to literary study has barely begun. In D. H. Lawrence's novel *Sons and Lovers* (1913) for example, his self-character Paul becomes active through a play episode in which he first smashes then burns his sister's doll; that this is a key episode not only in the work but in the author's life is borne out by the portrayal of characters in almost all of his fiction through the metaphoric medium of breaking and burning, with flame becoming the image of the inner self.

A few other prominent contributions from object-relations round out this segment. Michael Balint would prefer to replace the emotion-laden notion of primary narcissism with primary object-love and has coined the "basic fault" to get at the early damages to the self incurred in a defective child / mother dyad. The extensive writings of Otto Kernberg address the issue of how early *affective states* trigger needs, wishes, and instinctual drives. The influential work of

Margaret Mahler in tracing the *separation-individuation* process deals with the hatching-out of the human being from the shell of maternal symbiosis some eighteen months after his biological birth. This psychological emergence is also the birth of the self, and literary studies have wisely begun to draw on the fruits of Mahler's major insights. Around each of these figures and their theories has grown an extensive body of informed writing, and what might otherwise appear as an unwarranted digression into a scientific field is justified in the realization that there are many avenues leading to the psychoanalysis of the self.

The Bipolar Self

We now come to a figure who is most important and most problematic in the psychoanalysis of the self, Heinz Kohut; for his views may be seen as equally an advance over Freud's and an unfortunate reduction of them. Kohut's theories have grown out of the earlier matrices of psychoanalysis—narcissism and object-relations. He too plays down the preeminence of the Oedipus complex, and when he refers to drives he emphasizes them less in terms of instinctual gratification than as serving the needs of the self.

Rather than highlighting instinctual renunciation and repression as essential steps in becoming human, Kohut refers to the early formation of a cohesive self. Technically speaking, psychoanalysts refrain from referring to an ego until it has been demarcated from the superego at the close of the oedipal period; so the notion of an early self bridges a certain void already implicit in the theory. The self begins during what classical psychoanalysis has always bracketed as the oral period but has increasingly been expanded to encompass the mother's empathic responses to the child during various caretaking activities. In particular, the mother's capacity to enter the infant's world as a *selfobject*, to be emotionally available, and not distracted into her own daydreams or driven to impose her needs, but to interact vitally with the child, and to mirror its early sensations of pleasure so that they become self-representations to cohere around an emerging core of self-experience—these processes are now seen as essential to later mental and emotional well-being. This healthy core of reflected self-images, punctuated, say, by the child's specific smile as an early awareness of the mother, combine for a healthy state of narcissism. They comprise the cornerstone of development according to Kohut.

Deficits in this area may eventuate in later borderline conditions, addictions, and narcissistic disorders, which either are becoming more common in society or are being more discussed—the issue has not been decided. But they have been given a certain edge and urgency outside psychoanalysis by Christopher Lasch's apt phrase and book title, *The Culture of Narcissism* (1978); and it may be said that Ann Beattie's 1980 novel *Falling in Place* has drawn for us one of the maps of that culture. It is not surprising that modern authors have for some time represented these conditions for us in translucently clear terms. For borderline or schizoid states, one thinks of Kafka and Beckett; for narcissism, of Proust, Hesse, and Nabokov, among others. In addition, many elusive psychological or existential states, such as feelings of numbness, emptiness, meaning-lessness, boredom, nausea, nameless dreads, and so forth, can be elucidated by recourse to the new data to be gleaned from a psychoanalytic probing of the self.

Returning to Kohut and before further outlining his theories, we should note that to introduce the concept of a cohesive self implicitly diminishes the im-portance of the dynamic unconscious and minimizes psychoanalysis's classic dual instinct theory of sex and aggression. Thus the controversial status of Kohut turns on his tendency to revert to a more unitary, pre-Freudian psychology of consciousness. All the same, Kohut introduced a novel mode of addressing mental reality when he devised the "bipolar" structure of the self. By this term he refers to features of the self that come to light as they are filtered through the analytic process. Certain patients, he observed, develop either a mirroring or an idealizing transference to the analyst. From this he extrapolates the *gran-diose self,* which still hungers for basic narcissistic validation, and the *idealized objects,* those internalized but unassimilated images of the parents from early childhood that are continually displaced onto other relationships in expectation of similar self-enhancing gratifications. To reach these patients, Kohut prescribes an empathic-introspective approach (which some fear exceeds the ideal of an-alytic neutrality). The Kohutian analyst must deal with himself as the mirroring object (and correct rather than interpret) or as the idealized, all-perfect parent from whom the patient may desire to be reborn (shades of the *family romance).* The analyst's traditional, even-hovering attention will favor the primacy of self-cohesiveness over that of repressed motives. The Freudian nomenclature of neurotic conflicts will accordingly give way to disorders of the self.

Clearly, Kohut has contributed to a psychoanalysis of the self, and despite the ultimate disposition of his theories, they hold promise for those who are engaged in sorting out the connections between individuals and their culture vis-à-vis the arts, provided there are not similar lapses into another set of simple dichotomies similar to R. D. Laing's true / false self.

Since a comprehensive review of literary works concentrating on the self would end up either being coextensive with literature itself or looking altogether ar-bitrary, a few examples will have to highlight our conceptual discussion. While Ibsen would properly fit into Hassan's schema of the modern artist, it is para-doxical—as well as a tribute to the ability of genius to transcend categories—that he most fully realized the first really post-modern hero in the play *Peer Gynt* (1867). Like the circular path of Peer's life, the play is circular, with Peer leaving his mother's cottage to roam over the face of the earth and return years later to his native village where his abandoned wife Solveig awaits him (in lieu of his mother). The lack of progressive development in Peer's character is clearly attributable in Ibsen's text to narcissistic deficits due to a faulty mirroring-empathic tie to his mother, depriving him of a cohesive self-core. "You're lying," the opening line of the play (W. H. Auden's version), ironically delivered by Peer's mother sets the tone for the revelations to follow. Peer recounts an episode in which he wounds a buck and is then carried atop the animal over a cliff. Falling into the still lake below, Peer sees his image—half-human, half-bestial (or subhuman) rising up to meet him in a violent splash that is both destructive and orgastic. Before the scene with his mother is over, Peer will re-enact the episode with the buck in which he is the beast and his mother, carried on his shoulders, is her son. Clearly there are interesting inferences about the son's defective self-representation, the morbid symbiotic tie to mother, and the incomplete hatching-out into a separate individual self—as his sojourns with trolls and madness will amply demonstrate. Moreover, Peer's mother relates to her son in a contradictory or double-binding way, so that he can never be sure of where he stands with her and therefore ultimately of who he is. She tells him he could be a "splendid bridegroom" instead of a "filthy ragamuffin"; later she will call him a beast, and Peer laments that he can't win: she will "moan if I'd win and moan if I lose." Consequently, the boundaries of his self are not established; his grandiosity leads him to aspire to be a "king—an emperor"; later he will claim, "I can fly." (The mother's inconsistencies with her son are explainable by her husband's alcoholism and abandonment of her. Peer becomes the focus of her prospects but also a reminder of her betrayal.)

Because Peer has not been able to separate from his mother, he projects the conflictual mother-relation onto other women in his life and avoids intimacy, with its threat of incest, by taking flight; thus his travels are repetitions and his journey a vicious circle: his ringaround self the onion he unpeels in search of a center. The Boyg of the undiscovered self as well as the Sphinx of adult sexuality remain enigmas that he skirts instead of facing. Along the way he attempts—with some worldly success—to convert his deficiencies into strengths. Following the troll-motto of "to your own self—be enough," he foists himself off as a self-made man but, like the onion of his self, lacks a core; and the button-moulder at the crossroads (echoes of Oedipus here) informs him that having failed to achieve selfhood he will be returned to the mixing vat. Buying time, Peer returns to Solveig, and it is she who provides him, belatedly, with the missed mirroring and empathy of his childhood. "Where was I, as myself, as the whole man, the true man?" he asks desperately, and she answers, "In my faith, in my hope, and in my love." This image of cohesive wholeness, which the mother can bestow through empathic mirroring of the child's early feelings and desires, is what Peer has failed to receive from his original ambivalent mother. When Solveig provides it, she becomes mother, and the question arises whether Peer will again feel the urge to take flight. But under the shadow of his own mortality, he lingers and asks, "You are mother yourself, to the man that's there?" (Or in Rolf Fjelde's translation, "to the boy within?"). And with the realization that Solveig is mother, comes the awareness that she is also not mother, albeit a maternal woman. Thus Peer accomplishes a much overdue separation when he exclaims with a favorable light from the dawning skies falling over him, "My wife—my mother. You innocent woman!"

If Ibsen has presented us with substantial material for a psychoanalysis of the self, William Wordsworth, in his various versions of *The Prelude* (poem, 1799–1805), has uniquely portrayed the processes of self-creation, which can be most profoundly appreciated through a psychoanalysis-of-the-self perspective. Although Renaissance humanism had legitimized a certain healthy self-interest, as in Montaigne's declaration that he himself is the subject of his essays, Wordsworth was the first to enlist the poetic conventions, or the epic, once evoked to celebrate a colossal war, the founding of an empire, or justify the ways of God to man, and adapt them to trace the evolution of a self. Among romantic scholars, Robert Langbaum's series of articles on the Wordsworthian variation of the world as a "vale of Soul making" is most useful, though the semantic shift of *soul*-making to *self*-in-process in the course of Langbaum's evolving awareness of the poet is a telling sign of our time.

In demonstrating how Wordsworth blends the materialistic psychologies of his day, notably associationism, with the perennial philosophy of Platonism, Langbaum justifies the poem as a genuinely creative, personal epic. But Wordsworth also exploits these theories for psychological ends, because his purpose is to comprehend the elusive "bond of union between life and joy" (1.558) at the very outset of life that forms the basis for subsequent self-experience and sustains one through the vicissitudes of adulthood and the disillusionments of world engagement. Thus the poem searches for a way to articulate the "passions that build up the human soul" (1.407); and the poet locates them specifically in the empathic-mirroring interchanges of infancy: "blest the Babe, / nursed in his Mother's arms, who sinks to sleep / Rocked on his mother's breast; who with his soul / Drinks in the feelings of his mother's eye" (2.235–238). Like the others, this quote comes from the 1850 version; the 1805 version reads more excitedly: "Doth gather passion from his mother's eye!" (2.243). But drinking in feelings from the mother's eye more aptly captures the empathy within the mirroring transaction and better conveys the basis for the bond of joyful union at the outset of life. It is this kind of empathy that Kohut's approach emphasizes as crucial for a cohesive self and that Wordsworth refers to as "fair seed time had my soul" (1.301). It also provides early experience with a sense of quality, something beyond the materialism of associationism and hinted at by the innate ideas of Platonism when we were born, as Wordsworth has it in a celebrated passage from his Immortality Ode, "trailing clouds of glory." This vitalist intuition is captured by early memories in *The Prelude*, especially when the "fairest of all rivers, loved / To blend his murmers with my nurse's song / And . . . sent a voice / That flowed along my dreams" (1.270–274). It is as the river "makes ceaseless music that composed my thoughts" that the self of the poet is born. By blending nursing with the river's flow and the nurse's song, the poet is also taking the first step toward his lifelong sustaining creative romance with the world. When inevitable self-loss or narcissistic injury occurs through separation or more dramatically when the poet lost his mother at thirteen, his other mother, rooted in nature with whom he has formed an equally strong bond through the family romance, will not abandon him as long as he can find his way back to feel "within / A correspondent breeze" (1.35). Through the quality of such early experience as exemplified by the river Derwent imagery, we begin to appreciate how empathy can breathe life and meaning into early sensations that otherwise might be compiled from a dry theory of associations. Wordsworth shows how early sensations and their associations, "those first born affinities," become vital self-representations and object-representations. "The composite experience of rivers and towers—which might be understood as an experience of female and male principles—stands behind the experiences of beauty and fear described in the rest of book 1, which are composite experiences of natural and moral power," writes Langbaum in *The Poetry of Experience* (1957). In the course of the poem the ideal of Nature absorbs these primal female / male images into a unified life-principle to which the poet may return after the upsurge of oedipal conflicts has been represented in delayed action through the poet's engagement in the French Revolution, its cruel excesses, and aftermath of disillusionment. Nature is now the ambivalent mother who leads her unwitting son (according to Richard Onorato's analysis in *The Character of the Poet* [1971]) into History, seeking a continuation of sympathy and sustenance in the world of man. But History turns out to be a ruthless castrator as the Revolution invents the guillotine. Although an enormous amount of psychic as well as political territory has been telescoped by this precis, it will be sufficient if we can recognize the child's early images of beauty and fear as being reconstituted and expanded in the oedipal figures of Nature and History.

Among twentieth-century moderns, D. H. Lawrence may be cited for having most deeply explored the self-regenerative capacities within the human life cycle. His emblematic self-representation for the creative process is the dying-reviving Phoenix. His life was largely a quest for the healing and life-giving symbols that would restore an organic relatedness to the segmentations of the self inflicted by rationalistic culture and industrialism. Seen more intensively, his major symbols—Phoenix, Plumed Serpent, and Rainbow—are both self- and object-representations, binding the individual to the cosmos. Virginia Woolf comes to mind for exploring most interestingly, as she puts it in her novel *The Waves,* (1931) "a world without a self"—that is, without a personal, affective center of experience. But it is in her intensely personal novel *To the Lighthouse* (1927) that she explores the ambivalent maternal powers of mirroring, through Mrs. Ramsay, who like the lighthouse casts a beacon of light over her surroundings and lightens up the lives of others (who all, strangely, seem to be her devoted children) by her presence. She is both a window and a mirror for the others, and around her at the dinner table, "All the candles were lit up, and the faces on both sides of the table were brought nearer by the candle light" Her death, counterpointed by the Great War, brings on darkness—the extinguishing of lamps, the abandonment of the summer cottage. Here the mother's loss is felt as a self-loss—"a world without a self." "The mystic, the visionary," we read in the second section of the novel, "walking the beach on a fine night, stirring a puddle, looking at a stone, asking themselves, 'What am I,' 'What is this?' "

And then, still in our anonymous context, we read, "that dream, of sharing, completing, of finding in solitude on the beach an answer, was then but a reflection in a mirror, and the mirror was but the surface glassiness . . . to pace the beach was impossible; contemplation was unendurable; the mirror was broken." Such elusive passages as these may be read more fully from a vantage point of psychoanalysis of the self. The third section carries on the restorative and reconstitutive powers of the self in the creative process as Lily Briscoe draws on her memories and association to the Ramsays to complete the painting she had begun and put aside before the war. The symbol of the lighthouse represents both parents—Mrs. Ramsay as beacon, Mr. Ramsay as the one who reaches it. It is on land but also on water, it is oblong but cylindrical, a source and a beam; thus it can function as a composite object-representation, an ideal of wholeness we all might desire for ourselves.

If we conclude that the greatest fear for the cohesive self is fragmentation, we can discern the arts voicing this terrible possibility as they are aroused by cultural crises, whether it be the breaking of the circle of perfection announced in Donne's poetry or Yeats' familiar "the center cannot hold; / Mere anarchy is loosed upon the world." Historically, the self as a valid center of inner experience began replacing character in romantic literature, most visibly so in *The Prelude;* and as the self has subsequently undergone the fracturing of annihilative upheavals of the twentieth century, it has not had the traditional props of character, with its assertion of moral purpose, or of soul, with its transcendent beliefs, to fall back on. Thus our present and ongoing sense of crisis. Now we contemplate the end of the self, but really it is of a certain cultural construct of the self, and we witness the arrival of new versions of the self as existential strangers, as consumer robots, as clones of our technology, as cult faddists, and as ambiguous survivors of undeclared wars and nameless ordeals. Such alarming prospects need to be subjected to disciplined analysis, and we should not be dismayed to discover the self as any less problematic than the human condition, for at bottom they are one.

It is in this respect that the psychoanalysis of the self will be most positively felt; for new definitions and meanings have begun to emerge. The self can be seen as a certain human capacity. It may be variously stated as the capacity to form a separate center of initiative, the capacity for empathy and introspection, the capacity to reflect and symbolize, or the capacity to construe viable meanings out of the total welter of our internal and external experiences.

See also: Dream, Family, Personality (Double-Split-Multiple).

Selected Bibliography

Dervin, Daniel. " 'Myself Must I Remake': Psychoanalysis of the Self in Literature." *Psychocultural Review* 3 (1979): 267–288.

Kohut, Heinz. *The Search for the Self: Selected Writings.* New York: International University Press, 1978.

Mahler, Margaret. *The Psychological Birth of the Human Infant*. New York: Basic Books, 1975.

Wolf, Ernest. "Psychoanalytic Psychology of the Self and Literature." *New Literary History* 12 (1980): 41–60.

DANIEL DERVIN

R

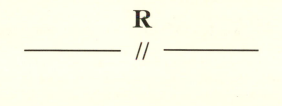

RAPE

Rape, according to the *Oxford English Dictionary,* is the act of carrying away a person, especially a woman, by force; the violation or ravishing of a woman. In this sense, the word ''rape'' implies the use of force against a woman's will. However, problems relating to whether abduction or seduction is a kind of rape, whether rape is a crime, and whether woman is responsible for rape remain the focus of scholarly discussion.

Some anthropological studies show that rape was not considered a crime in ancient times. Many incidents of gang rape, abduction of virgins, or theft of brides have been justified as necessary for the survival of certain tribes. Furthermore, rape has been sometimes used by primitive people as an expression of manhood, an indication of the concept of women as property, and a mechanism of social control to keep women in line.

While some theorists, like Freud, Jung, Marx, and Engels, subtly avoid the issue of rape, others like Helene Deutsch and Karen Horney interpret it as an ''innate masochism'' that is part of every woman's fantasy world. Feminist scholars, on the other hand, accept Susan Brownmiller's idea of ''penis as weapon'' and see rape as indicating man's supression of woman. For the feminists, rape is a crime, and woman is the victim. The theme of rape has been dealt with from the classical to the modern period; it gets serious scholarly attention in the twentieth century due to the rise of the feminist movement.

Classical Antiquity and the Middle Ages

In the classical era, rape is considered a crime in both Greek and Roman society. According to Athenian law, the rapist is legally guilty and the penalty is a monetary fine. The raped victim, on the other hand, is punished with varying degrees of social ostracism. Under Roman law, the rapist could be prosecuted by the man under whose authority the wronged woman falls. Yet, the raped virgin is to be punished too. If she is willing in the act of rape, she will be burned to death; if it is forceful rape, she still receives light punishment, since she could have screamed for help.

The theme of rape appears in two comedies by Terence, *Eunuchus* (*The Eunuch,* 161 B.C.), and *Hecyra* (*Mother-in-Law,* 165 B.C.). In the first play, a young Athenian impulsively rapes a slave girl whom he loves; in the second play, another Athenian marries his wife reluctantly without the least knowledge that the latter was once ravished by him. In both cases, punishment for the rape is avoided when the rapists marry the victims.

In Livy's *Ab urbe condita libri* (*History of Rome,* c. 27 B.C.–A.D. 14), the heroine, Lucretia, is threatened either to submit to the rapist's lust or to be killed and have the dead body of a slave put in her arms so that she would be falsely accused of commiting adultery. In order to avoid such a false accusation, Lucretia has to yield to Tarquin and thus be raped. In the end, she commits suicide. Though a rape victim, Lucretia is still technically an adulteress from the Romans' point of view.

The Roman legend of the rape of Lucretia became an important literary source for many works in different countries and periods. It appeared, for example, in Chaucer's poem *Legend of Good Women* (1386); in Juan Pastor's *Farsa de Lucrecia* (play, 1528); in Nathaniel Lee's *Lucius Junius Brutus* (play, 1680). The Italian Alfieri covers it in his *Bruto primo (The First Brutus,* play, 1787); and in France, François Ponsard wrote *Lucrèce* (play, 1843). In the twentieth century, the music drama *The Rape of Lucretia* (1946), with music by Benjamin Britten, is an operatic version of the legend.

The theme of rape appears often in Greek mythology, usually with a god as the rapist, and a goddess, or more often a mortal woman, the victim. The rape of female mortals by gods is one of the recurring subjects in Ovid's epic *Metamorphoses* (c. A.D. 2–17). There are about fifty stories on rape in *Metamorphoses,* which can be catagorized into "grand rape" and "petit rape."

"Grand rape" means forceful or violent rape, which often involves torture, wrestling, or killing. This is exemplified in the rape of Philomela by Tereus, in which Tereus cuts off the victim's tongue during the rape. In another story, the rape of Orithyia by Boreas is also described as an irresistible violent force. "Petit rape" involves less action and violence but more often seduction, abduction, or deception. For example, both Jupiter in his rape of Io and Apollo in that of Daphne begin with long flattering speeches to their victims. Sometimes the rapists deceive the victim by assuming different forms. Jupiter's rape of Leda in the form of a swan and his rape of Danae in the form of a shower are typical examples.

Whatever kind of rape it may be, the passive, vulnerable, and frightened status of the rape victims is clearly presented. Caenis, after being raped by Neptune, wants to be transformed into a man, Caeneus, to avoid being raped again. And the result of rape in Ovid is almost always the threatening of the victims' identity and their final transformation into non-human beings. Io is transformed into a cow; Callisto, a bear; Philomela, a nightingale; Arethras, a dove; and Daphne, a tree. The various metamorphoses of the rape victims indicate the dehumanizing reduction of a woman to the level of a hunted animal or even object.

The medieval knights, like the Greek gods, also have a notorious reputation for raping common women. Although, according to the Arthurian ethic, if a knight forced a girl against her will, he would be scorned or punished, we still find incidents of rape in the romances. Among them, the rape of a young girl by the knight in the "Wife of Bath's Tale" in Chaucer's *Canterbury Tales* (c. 1380–1400); the rape of Grande Lis by Sir Gawain, a knight of King Arthur's Round Table; and the rape of a woman by another knight in Sir Thomas Malory's *Morte d'Arthur* (c. 1469).

The Renaissance and Seventeenth Century

The catalogue of rape in classical myths and legends becomes the literary source for many writers in the Renaissance period. In Christopher Marlowe's poem *Hero and Leander* (1598), the myth of Jupiter's rapes helps to move the narrative and set the tone for the love epic. In Spenser's *Faerie Queene* (epic poem, 1590–1596), book 11, the tapestries that depict various stories of Zeus's rape serve a didactic function. In Shakespeare's works, the story of Philomel appears in his play, *Titus Andronicus* (c. 1594) and the legend of Lucrece in his poem, *The Rape of Lucrece* (1594).

In the Renaissance, the power of the man increases dramatically, and he is almost a "legalized petty tyrant" at home. The status of women, on the other hand, is reduced to mere sexual property ready to be sold or exchanged by and among men. A woman not only has to live according to the male standard but, in time of crisis, like rape, has to sacrifice her own life to fulfill man's sense of vanity. Once a woman is raped, she is seen as damaged property not to be accepted by her husband, family, and society.

In *Titus Andronicus,* Lavinia is violently raped and maimed by both Demetrius and Chiron. The mute Lavinia later reveals the story by drawing in the sand, much like Philomel uncovers her secret by weaving. Though the victim's father, Titus, kills the rapists, he eventually stabs Lavinia to death, for her loss of chastity is a shame to both herself and her family.

It is in Shakespeare's poem *The Rape of Lucrece,* that the old legend and the theme of rape are handled with ethical and psychological insight. Lucrece, the virtuous wife of Collatine, is first threatened and then raped by her husband's friend, Tarquin, after which Lucrece reveals the truth to her husband and then stabs herself. The author succeeds in depicting the conflict between desire and reason within the rapist before the act of rape as well as the struggle between life and death inside the victim's mind after being violated.

In Shakespeare's poem, the punishment for the rapist is dealt with only briefly at the end. In Thomas Heywood's play *The Rape of Lucrece* (1608), however, the bloody consequences of Tarquin's rape and Lucrece's suicide are the subject of almost all of the last act, in which Tarquin and Brutus fight to the death, and the order of Rome is eventually restored.

In the seventeenth century, three Spanish plays deal with the theme of rape. In Lope de Vega's *El alcalde de Zalamea* (play, 1600), Leonor and Ines, the two daughters of the mayor, are deceived and then deserted in the wood by Don Diego and Don Juan, two captains. Crespo, the mayor, later has the two captains taken prisoners and forces them to marry his daughters. After the marriage, Crespo orders the men to be hanged for their misdeeds and his daughters to be sent to the convent. Throughout the play, the two rapists are depicted as people with animal passion, who, given the chance, would violate all the women with whom they come in contact. While the two daughters, being silly, vain, and idle, are half-willing prey for their seducers.

While Francisco de Rojas Zorrilla's *Lucrecia y Tarquino* (1636) is a very skillful adaptation of the rape of Lucrece into a dramatic tragedy, Calderón de la Barca's *El alcade de Zalamea* (*The Mayor of Zalamea*, 1636) is a more successful version of Lope de Vega's treatment. In Calderón's play, the rapist is executed after refusing to marry the victim, who is subsequently sent to a convent. It is more dramatic than that of Lope de Vega in depicting the mayor as an affectionate father torn between love and justice and Isabel as a virtuous, innocent victim of rape.

The Eighteenth Century

In the early eighteenth century, Alexander Pope's *The Rape of the Lock* (1712) is a mock heroic epic satirizing social vanity. In the story, a lock of the heroine, Belinda, is cut by Lord Peter, one of her suitors, as a trophy of his victory over the proud nymph. Belinda's loss of her lock is compared to the loss of her chastity, and Lord Peter's forceful action is a kind of metaphorical rape, which he compares to the Greek triumph over the Trojans. The scissors, the Greek swords, and the male sexual organ can be related to aggressive arms, and the rape of the lock, the conquest of man over woman in the battle between the sexes.

The story of Helen, the cause of the Trojan War, was dealt with in John Breval's mock opera *The Rape of Helen* (1737). Following its classical predecessors—Colluthus' (fl. 491–518) poem *Harpagē Helenēs (The Rape of Helen)* and Euripides' play *Helenē* (*Helen*, 412 B.C.)—the word "rape" in Breval's opera means the transporting of Helen to Troy. In the opera, Meneleus is depicted as a jealous tyrant husband and Helen as willing prey, who is seduced and then runs away with Paris.

Samuel Richardson, in his novel *Clarissa Harlowe* (1748), shows how an upper-middle-class woman strives to preserve the decorum of a society through her strict sense of idealism and propriety. Clarissa runs away from a marriage arranged by her parents and escapes with Lovelace, who then drugs and rapes her. Refusing to forgive the repentant young man, who asks for her hand, Clarissa eventually dies in guilt and shame. The theme of rape in this novel provides an

index of the general plight of mid-eighteenth-century women, the conflict between individual will and social morality, as well as the gradual awareness of
the problem of equality between the sexes.

With the growth of individualism and the concept of freedom, there arose the
idea of libertinism in the late eighteenth century, particularly in France. In the
work of the Marquis de Sade, "libertinage" is "the cruel use of others for one's
own sexual pleasure." Sade believes that brutality is the essence of eroticism,
and that man has the absolute freedom and right to rape and brutalize any "object
of desire" at will. For Sade, women—wives, daughters, mothers, slaves, prostitutes—have no bodily rights; they are merely sex objects to be used for either
pleasing or exciting men. In his novel *Justine* (1791), the heroine is raped,
tortured, and violated throughout the story. Justine, the victim sacrificed, hates
her situation and struggles against it. The heroine in *Juliette* (1797), another
novel by Sade, on the other hand, eventually enjoys being raped and tortured;
she is depicted as a "female libertine" seemingly free from the bondage of the
same system.

In Sade's works, not only are women raped, but also male and female children,
even men themselves—servants or male prostitutes. The victims are not only
raped and tortured, but maimed, killed; and their bodies sliced up, burned, or
eaten alive. Such outrageous sadistic deeds have gone beyond the crime of rape
and vampirism toward cannibalism.

Near the end of the eighteenth century, Charles Lamb's *The Tale of Rosamund
Gray* (1798) dealt with the theme of rape and tragic love. In the tale, the young,
virtuous, pretty Rosamund is violated by the ugly and evil Matravis. She soon
dies and leaves her young love, Allan Clare, in misery until poetic justice prevails
in the end of the story. Clare by chance meets the rapist who is dying in pain
and remorse.

The Nineteenth Century

In Germany, the traditional idea of virtue was also questioned in the early
nineteenth century. In the novelle *Die Marquise von O.* (*The Marquise of O.*
1808) by Heinrich von Kleist, the theme of rape is treated with great subtlety,
and the conventional idea of chastity and love is reexamined. The heroine, the
Marquise, is first saved by a Russian count from being raped by his own soldiers
and then becomes mysteriously pregnant without having the slightest idea of
how it might have come about. Surprisingly, the rapist turns out to be Count F,
the man who has originally rescued the Marquise. Throughout the story, Count
F, the angel and devil, is depicted as a man who submits to his desire and then
tries everything he can to amend his transgression. Though the scene of rape is
not described in the story, it is, far from being a destructive and evil deed, a
symbolic act of tenderness, even of virtue from Kleist's humanistic point of
view.

In a French story "La petite Roque" ("Little Louise Roque," 1886) by
Maupassant, the theme of rape and murder is subtly dealt with. Little Louise,

a twelve-year-old girl, is found dead and naked under a tree, obviously having been raped, strangled, and then deserted in the wood. Renardet, the mayor of the village, turns out to be the rapist who is tormented by the sense of guilt after the impulsive violent deed. Throughout the story, Maupassant succeeds in describing the psychological turmoil of the rapist.

It is in Hardy's novel, *Tess of the D'Urbervilles* (1891) that the Victorian idea of chastity and purity is questioned. In the novel, the innocent Tess is deceived, seduced, and then possessed by Alex, whom she eventually kills to preserve her relationship with her true lover, Angel. As the subtitle of the novel—"A Pure Woman, Faithfully Presented"—suggests, Hardy presents Tess, the ruined maid or the fallen woman in the eyes of the Victorians, as the symbol of purity and innocence in the novel.

Throughout the Victorian period, underground or pornographic literature dealing mostly with the themes of incest, homosexuality, and rape provided the male readers endless material to titillate their sexual fantasies. In one popular novel, *The Lustful Turk* (1828), a series of violent rapes is described between the "Byronic" hero, the Day, and his harem girls, Emily and Silvia. By transforming the two girls into willing victims of the rapist, the author praises the penis as a "wonderful instrument" for voluptuous delight and lustful pleasure. Another typical example of the theme of rape is *Raped on the Railway* (1894), with the subtitle "A True Story of a Lady who was First ravished and then Chastised on the Scotch Express." It is a story about Robert Brandon's rape of a veiled lady on a train. Throughout the story, rape is described as a kind of game between man and woman, and the veiled lady, who first fights against Robert and then forgives him soon after the rape, seems to enjoy the experience herself.

Hughes Rebell's novel *Dolly Morton* (1899) deals with the theme of rape and flagellation. In the story, Dolly, an eighteen-year-old orphan, who helps slaves to escape, is raped by the plantation owner Randolph and eventually becomes a prostitute. Throughout the novel, women are compared to slaves bound to be exploited and used by men, who are symbolized by the plantation owners.

The Modern Period

In the modern period, with the rise of the sexual revolution and the feminist movement, traditional taboos on such topics as rape, incest, homosexuality, and adultery are gradually eliminated. Famous writers deal with subjects of sex and violence in their works, and the theme of rape in literature appears more often in the twentieth century than in any previous era.

The Greek myth of the rape of Leda by Zeus in the form of a swan is the source of W. B. Yeats' poem "Leda and the Swan" (1923). D. H. Lawrence, fascinated by the idea of primitivism, wrote a number of short stories dealing with rape fantasy—the rape of a white woman by savages. In three of these stories, "None of That" (1928), "The Princess" (1925), and "The Woman Who Rode Away" (1928), the victim of rape is an American woman, while the role of the savage rapists is played alternatively by a group of toreadors, a

Mexican mountain guide, and a group of primitive tribesmen. Influenced by Freud, Lawrence relates the idea of woman to passivity and masochism. In his novel, *Women in Love* (1920), a love scene between Gerald and Gudrun can be seen as a kind of metaphorical rape, in which Gudrun is described as possessed, tamed, and used. Within the primitive system of Lawrence's works, woman is to be sacrificed to the sun—the symbol of male power.

In American novels, William Faulkner's *Sanctuary* (1931) deals with the rape of a woman on a Southern farm. The heroine of the book, Temple, after leaving home in order to live independently, is raped with a corncob in the hand of the impotent Popeye. Although the rape scene of Temple is described as horrible, it seems to be justified as an ''appropriate punishment for a woman trying to be independent without paying the price.'' In Saul Bellow's *Herzog* (1964), the homosexual rape of Herzog himself as a young boy is seen as ugly and terrible for it threatens Herzog's sense of male identity.

Not only male writers but some female writers believe that women are responsible for rape. Their basic assumption is that women are masochistic; they like to be possessed, dominated, and even raped. The theme of rape as female fantasy is dealt with in Ayn Rand's novel *The Fountainhead* (1943). The title suggests that male sexual power is the origin of joy, and the heroine, Dominique Francon, is depicted as a woman who feels both terror and joy after being raped. Nancy Friday's *My Secret Garden* (1973) is composed of a series of female confessions about rape fantasies. It is in Gael Greene's novel *Blue Skies, No Candy* (1976) that the idea of rape fantasy is carried to its extreme. Kate, the fantasizer, after admitting that she enjoys being a sex object, declares that she likes to be possessed, controlled, and raped.

Do women really want to be raped? Are they responsible for it? Or are they merely victims? Similar questions concerning rape have been treated in many contemporary movies from different points of view. Peckinpah's *Straw Dogs* (1971), Herbert Leonard's *Going Home* (1971), and Hitchcock's *Frenzy* (1972) are notable for their glamorization of the rape scene, while John Boorman's film adaptation of James Dickey's novel *Deliverance* (1970) presents an ugly homosexual rape scene.

Tennessee Williams' two plays *Twenty-Seven Wagons Full of Cotton* (1946) and *A Streetcar Named Desire* (1947), which have been turned into movies, sensitively explore the theme of rape. In the first work, woman is compared to property and rape to the battle between men; in the second work, the heroine Blanche DuBois, symbol of vulnerability and fragility, is raped by Stanley Kowalski, symbol of the dark force of nihilism. Another symbol of the dark, natural savage is the young Alex in Stanley Kubrick's famous movie, *A Clockwork Orange* (1971). In the film, the sadistic Alex rapes and kills women without any sense of guilt. He is portrayed as the symbol of instinctive sexual desire and violence of everyman.

The multiple perspectives of rape are best summed up in Kurosawa's *Rashomon* (1950), a Japanese film based on Akutagawa's two short stories—''Rashōmon" ("Rashomon," 1915) and "Yabu no naka" ("In a Grove," 1921). The movie tells the story of the rape of a young nobleman's wife in four different versions, from the point of view of the rapist, the victim, her husband, and a peasant witness. As damaged property, the Japanese woman is deserted first by her husband and then by the rapist.

Because of different cultural backgrounds, the theme of rape appears rarely in Eastern literature. In classical Chinese literature, rape scenes appear sometimes in pornographic novels but are treated only as minor incidents. In modern Chinese literature, one opera by Ho Ching-chih *Baimao nü* (*The White-Haired Girl*, 1945), presents the theme of rape from the Communist point of view as a political accusation of the rich, middle-class landlord. In Japanese literature, there is an attempted rape in "Otomi no teiso" ("Otomi's Virginity," 1922), a short story by Akutagawa. But as soon as the heroine, Otomi, yields herself totally to the desire of the rapist for the sake of a cat's life, the rapist leaves out of shame. In Abe Kōbō's novel *Suna no onna* (*Women in the Dunes*, 1962), the heroine fights against a man's sexual assault, but the attempted rape is not actually carried out.

In the modern period, male writers, for example, Lawrence and Faulkner, seem to consider rape a justified punishment for the liberated woman, and female writers, Friday and Greene, believe that women are responsible for the act of rape. Even in Kurosawa's work, in which rape is presented in a seemingly objective perspective, women are viewed as property and the source of disaster. Although feminists assert that rape is the male exploitation of the female body, in literary works, such a voice is still lacking and women are depicted as as passive and silent as before, even by the hands of the sexually liberated modern writers.

See also: Incest, Libertine, Seduction.

Selected Bibliography

Brownmiller, Susan. *Against Our Will: Men, Women and Rape.* New York: Bantam, 1975.
Charney, Maurice. *Sexual Fiction.* New York: Methuen, 1981.
Dworkin, Andrea. *Pornography: Men Possessing Women.* New York: Perigee, 1981.
Hazen, Helen. *Endless Rapture: Rape, Romance, and the Female Imagination.* New York: Scribner, 1983.

YING-YING CHIEN

RAT, MOUSE

Any of several rodents with long, hairless tails of the family *Muridae*, rats and mice are distinguished solely by size. The most common generic names are *Rattus* and *Mus*. Especially in the Romance languages, and sometimes in English, the two terms are used almost interchangeably. From earliest times both are identified by historians as creatures of destruction and carriers of disease. At the same time, they have also been closely associated with humankind throughout the ages. Their invasion of dwellings, their adaptability, their hierarchical social structures, their shared diet, indeed, even their vulnerability to natural predators, have made them a common symbol both for human foibles and for human strengths.

Background in Myth and Folklore

In religious myth the rat or mouse frequently appears as a sacred animal associated with storms and lightning, as an attribute of the old Indian storm god Rudra, the Germanic storm god Wotan, and the Greek Apollo. In newer Indian mythology the rat, as a symbol of sagacity, is the vehicle for the Indian god Ganesha, and rats are honored at Ganesha's temple in Rajasthan much as they were once honored at Apollo's temple on Tenedos. By appropriate offerings to the storm gods, it was believed that plagues of rats and mice could be averted. Prophetic qualities were often ascribed to these animals. Pliny the Elder (*Naturalis historia* [*Natural History,* c. A.D. 77]) described their prophecy through selective gnawing of shoelaces and shield straps; he noted, too, their tendency to desert a house shortly before its fall. He referred to white mice as prophetic harbingers of good fortune. In China and Japan white mice were similarly honored as prophetic creatures of plenty and fortune, while black mice were viewed as creatures of godlessness and evil. In the Old Testament the mouse is named an unclean creature (Lev. 11:29; Isa. 66:17); in 1 Samuel 6 images of gold mice are constructed as an offering to avert the plague.

In the Germanic countries mice and rats became associated with human souls and could be white and pure or dark and godless. Swarms of rats and mice were frequently associated with punishment and with dark, demonic forces. They appear as avenging spirits in the legend of Germany's Bishop Hatto (cf. Robert Southey's poem of this title, 1799), Poland's Popiel II, and Denmark's Canute the Holy, whose murderer was devoured by rats. In medieval art rats and mice took on similar symbolic content. Saint Gertrude of Nivelles is pictured with a mouse. In her legend, the mouse is the devil come to plague her; in common folklore the mouse is the pure soul that enjoys Gertrude's hospitality on its three-day journey up to Heaven. St. Augustine, (354–430) in his *Sermones,* described the Cross as the devil's mousetrap; the Merode Altarpiece of the Master of Flemalle pictures Joseph busily constructing mousetraps in his workshop.

The plagues of rats and mice during the Middle Ages introduced the professional ratcatcher; the honors bestowed upon Dick Whittington and his cat in the legend of this historical figure (1358–1423) demonstrate the prestige accorded successful ratcatchers of this period. The legendary Pied Piper of Hamelin (cf. Robert Browning's verse of this title, 1842) can be viewed either as a real practitioner of this trade or as a folk reinterpretation of beliefs attached to the storm god Wotan and his clouds of rat followers. The old nursery rhyme "Three

Blind Mice'' makes reference to the medieval custom of collecting rat tails as proof of their destruction.

Over the centuries white, and, later, checkered mice were cultivated as house pets, first in the Orient, and, in the last two centuries, in Europe and America. The good luck symbolism of the white mouse and rat in the Orient played no small part in their popularity as house pets. These same white rodents are now cultivated as subjects for laboratory experiments, where their intelligence, adaptability, and fecundity make them fitting stand-ins for human subjects.

Fable and Satire

Rats and mice appear with some frequency in Eastern and European fable, but are strikingly rare in the animal folktales of Africa. In the *Panchatantra* of India (*Five Books,* tales, c. 300–500) a mouse proves a loyal friend to a number of animals and saves them from the hunter's net and thongs. This mouse is characterized by wisdom, generosity, and kindness. In another tale in this same collection a sage rescues a female mouse, transforms her into a maiden, and raises her as his daughter. When it is time for her to wed she renounces the sun, the cloud, the wind, and the mountain as possible mates in order to return to her own kind, with the recognition that the tiny mouse has the strength to weaken even mountains.

The Greek fables ascribed to Aesop (died c. 560 B.C.) demonstrate the wisdom of the country mouse over its pampered city cousin; and the grateful loyalty of a mouse that releases a captured lion from a net. In other fables of Aesop the mice are more foolish. One seeks to wed a lioness, which accidentally crushes him to death (as in the *Panchatantra,* he should have stuck to his own kind); another trusts and is devoured by a friendly looking cat. In yet another fable mice and frogs battle for sovereignty over the fens; a kite descends from the sky to capture and devour the leaders of both armies.

The common association of frogs and mice may reflect the old pre-Christian belief that both are created by storms (cf. Aelianus' *Peri zōōn idiotētos* [*De natura animalium,* anecdotes, c. 200]). The old English tale "A Frog He Would A-Wooing Go" has a similar pairing. The frog, with the assistance of a rat, woos a lady mouse; the mouse is devoured by kittens, the rat by a cat, and the frog by a duck in this tale of hapless love.

The satirical parody *Batrachomyomachia* (*Battle of the Frogs and Mice,* c. 400 B.C.) mocks the heroics of Homeric verse by parodying human battle and divine intervention. The mice believe themselves to be the frogs' superiors because their diet includes the best of man's food, not merely vegetables and greens. The entire course of battle, from its accidental cause, through its twists and turns, to the point of divine intervention on behalf of the frogs, is treated with broad humor by this unknown Greek writer.

These early fables and satires may be considered forerunners of a large body of children's literature in which the whole gamut of human strengths and weaknesses, virtues and vices are embodied in the figures of mice and rats. They appear as prominent figures in the tales of Hans Christian Andersen, Charles Perrault, E.T.A. Hoffmann, Clemens Brentano (his 1805 tale "Gockel, Hinkel, und Gackeleja" ["The Wondrous Tale of Cocky, Clucky, and Cackle"] contains a delightful prayer by pious mice), Lewis Carroll (the tail-shaped "Tale of a Mouse" is a highlight of *Alice's Adventures in Wonderland,* 1865), Beatrix Potter, Kenneth Grahame, E. B. White, and countless other authors of children's classics. Size and vulnerability appear to make them especially loved by child readers.

La Fontaine incorporated tales from Aesop and the *Panchatantra* in his own published fables written between 1668 and 1694, in which he often makes pointed reference to contemporary European politics. In "Conseil tenu par les rats" ("The Rats in Council") all rats agree that a bell must be tied around the cat's neck, but none is brave enough to put words into action. Asked to write a fable about "Le chat et la souris" ("The Cat and the Mouse"), La Fontaine puzzles as to whom the cat should represent—a cruel girl? fortune? the king?—then decides to make the mouse his muse, which his sponsor, the young prince, may toss about at his pleasure. In his "La ligue des rats" ("League of Rats"), a mouse (Holland) asks an aristocratic rat (the Austrian emperor) for protection. Louis XIV (the cat) crosses the Rhine in 1672 and the emperor's league (rats) turns tail and flees. Many of La Fontaine's rats and mice are victims of cats and weasels because of their own pride and lack of caution. But he also has a canny rat, a tailless veteran of battle, who will not be tricked by a wily cat; a rat who frees a cat (like Aesop's mouse freed the lion), while having the sense to keep his distance; and a rat who retires from the world to a Holland cheese and refuses aid to the beggar rats who approach him. In "Les deux rats, le renard, et l'oeuf" ("The Two Rats, the Fox, and the Egg"), he tells how rats transport an egg while at the same time eluding a fox, but notes that, despite this sign of ingenuity, these animals lack the conscious powers of man. Like Aesop and the *Panchatantra,* he draws parallels between men and rodents, but he never carries the lessons of the tale too far. Of the "La souris métamorphosée en fille" ("Mouse Metamorphosed into a Maid,") for example, he rejects the *Panchatantra* notion of the mouse's superior strength and says that the love match between mice is simply a matter of kind reverting to kind.

Giacomo Leopardi resurrected the Homeric war of mice and frogs in his poetic continuation of the tale, *Paralipomeni della Batracomiomachia* (1842), or war of mice and crabs. This poem begins where the Homeric satire ends, and the parallels drawn between animals and human armies take on much more specific reference to contemporary political events. Here the crabs represent Austrians, and the mice Italians.

Metamorphoses of Men to Mice

Metamorphoses of mice to humans and back again became a common theme of late medieval literature and continued through several centuries. Japanese literature has several seventeenth-century tales entitled *Nezumi no sōshi (The*

Tale of the Mouse) that deal with this theme. In one, a girl's lover is attacked by her mother's cat as he reverts to his original mouse form. In another, a mouse or rat seeks out a human connection in order to achieve rebirth as a human being. And, in a third, a meditating Zen priest is annoyed by the disturbances created by a mouse; he turns himself into this mouse and is humorously catechized by it. The mouse instructs the priest about the purity of mind in mice and about their awareness of ultimate truths. It defends its destructive ways as the result of a lost harmony between all living creatures.

In Western literature of the same period rats and mice are frequently viewed as chthonic forces, and the devil frequently assumes their shape. In Christopher Marlowe's drama *Tragical History of the Life and Death of Dr. Faustus* (1604), Wagner's conjuring tricks involve just such transformations. Johannes Praetorius, in his *Blocks-Berges Verrichtung* (treatise, 1668) describes a red mouse that springs from the mouth of a sleeping girl; such embodiments of the soul occur numerous times in the legends collected by the Grimm brothers, and Goethe incorporates them into the Walpurgisnacht scene of his drama *Faust I* (1808), by having mice swarm upon a witches' mountain and a red mouse leap from the mouth of an attractive young witch. Sigmund Freud's *Bemerkungen über einen Fall von Zwangsneurose (Notes Upon a Case of Obsessional Neurosis,* 1909) develops a vast treasury of associations with rats in folklore—with anal eroticism, money, gambling, syphilitic infection, souls, and children, all of which were tied up in his young patient's close identification of himself with a rat. This association of self with rat is triggered by conversation about Ibsen's play *Lille Eyolf (Little Eyolf,* 1894), in which a child is lured to his death by the Rat-woman; here, as in the pied piper legend, the ratcatcher leads both rats and children to a watery grave.

Representatives of Ideological Movements

Freud pointed out that in legends rats and mice are less disgusting than they are uncanny. Part of the uncanniness lies in their tendency to swarm and devour all within sight. Poem no. 113 of *Shih Ching (Book of Songs,* compiled around 600 B.C. by Confucius) reads:

> Big rat, big rat,
> Do not gobble our millet!
> Three years we have slaved for you,
> Yet you take no notice of us.
> At last we are going to leave you
> And go to that happy land,
> Happy land, happy land,
> Where we shall have our place.

The poem is the farmer's complaint against rapacious tax collectors.

Swarms of rats and mice often suggest armies or threatening ideological movements. Heinrich Heine's poem "Die Wanderratten" ("The Wandering Rats," c.1843) identifies "two sorts of rat: the hungry and the fat." The hungry, wandering rats are the Communists, who threaten the established bourgeoisie. Heine: "In hungry mouths enters alone / Logic of soup, grounded in bone, / Such arguments as chunks of beef / With sausages to seal belief."

Gerhart Hauptmann's play *Die Ratten* (*The Rats*, 1911) has a similar theme. It is set in a former Berlin cavalry barracks that is now full of poor, desperate people. Rat infested, the house becomes a symbol of the German empire and impending political catastrophe. The older generation regards the younger one as the "rats," who are undermining the new Germany by attacking German idealism and by eating away at the fabric of Germany from within. The German youth rejects German classicism for naturalism, seeing the falseness of the older ideals; the once splendid barracks, now completely rotten, threaten collapse. Spitta, the young hero of the future, is now mocked and leads a "subterranean" existence, but knows that eventually his time will come.

In Johannes Bobrowski's "Mäusefest" ("Mouse Festival," short story, 1961), the community of mice is identified with the community of Jews in German-occupied Poland; frightened momentarily by the German presence, they are foolish enough to think they can hide and survive. They are the too-trusting victims of an impending holocaust.

More recently Christoph Meckel has suggested that larger evils are made possible by the obliteration of small ones. In a poem "Mäusejagd" ("Mouse Hunt," 1962) he writes of the cleansing of a mouse-infested house, then closes with the exclamation: "Kill off the mouse! Kill off the mouse! / The rat's now entering the house!"

Rats and Mice as Victims

More often than not, rats and mice appear as victims in literature. In her cycle entitled "Our Little Kinsmen" (c. 1875) Emily Dickinson writes sympathetically of the rat's "brief career of cheer and fraud and fear," noting how temptation leads to its destruction. Robert Burns ("To a Mouse," 1785) calls the mouse a "wee, sleekit, cow'rin' tim'rous beastie," and makes it a victim of chance accident, noting ironically, that "the best-laid schemes o' mice an' men, Gang aft a-gley."

John Steinbeck took up this theme in *Of Mice and Men* (novel, 1937); here the deaths of mice and a dog presage the deaths of Curley's wife and Lennie Small. Marguerite Young's poem "The White Rat" (1944) contemplates the caged animal as imprisoned body-soul, something of a laboratory animal to the deity: "Here, in this case, Platonic double moons, / Here, in this cage, St. Augustine / Crying, O, my God, art Thou without or within?" and asks: "Does God with diamond eyes look down on these / For the purposes of what intrinsic studies?" Dostoevsky, who introduced a good deal of rat and mouse imagery into his *Zapiski iz podpol'ia* (*Notes from Underground*, novel, 1864), created a saintly fool in *Idiot* (*The Idiot*, novel, 1868) in Myshkin ("little mouse"), a childlike, innocent soul much like the white mouse-soul of Germanic folklore.

In "Josefine die Sängerin, oder das Volk der Mäuse" ("Josephine the Songstress or the Community of Mice," short story, 1924) Franz Kafka portrayed the conflict between the individual artist and a collective, worker society; here one member of the mouse collective tells of the weakness of the artist/muse as opposed to the strength of a threatened worker community. This work suggests several interpretations as to possible identifications with the society presented here. In Albert Camus' *La peste* (*The Plague,* 1947) the death agonies of rats are the precursors of human agonies in the novel, and the rats' return at the close of the work signals both the end of the plague and the possibility of its recurrence. The plague can be interpreted both politically and existentially.

In his novelle *Katz und Maus* (*Cat and Mouse,* 1961), the German author Günter Grass creates his own saintly hero, an adolescent who is the "mouse" victim of his teachers and society. The symbolic mouse is the hero's large Adam's apple, which he bares only before the Virgin Mary. As a boy he is both manlier and purer than his counterparts, and his brief life is a legend remembered by the society that victimized him. James Clavell's *King Rat* (novel, 1962) is in many ways a similar "hero"—an outsider whose actions enrage those imprisoned with him while also giving them the will and the means to survive captivity. At the close of the imprisonment, the other prisoners turn upon him and defeat him. Here, as so frequently in fiction, actual rats and mice are also depicted as companions of imprisoned and persecuted men, as lost souls or outcasts of society and victims of tyranny.

Good Luck Creatures

Mice and rats as lucky animals—and survivors—are most visible in children's cartoon shows, although one can argue that the rats in Clavell's novel are both victims and survivors. Mickey Mouse amulets are worn as good luck charms in some parts of Germany. Lucky white mice crop up, in name at least, in Stephen Crane's tale "The Five White Mice" (1898). Here the lucky white mice are a winning combination at dice; the hero's life is spared, and disaster averted, because they *do not* appear for him when he calls them up. Such irony is reflected in Poe's classic horror tale "The Pit and the Pendulum" (1842), where the evil and repugnant rats become the saviors of a threatened hero. Poe's tale reflects the ambivalence humans feel for rats and mice. These rodents are considered primarily to be creatures of destruction, but their vulnerability tends to evoke a certain degree of sympathy and identification. Over the centuries they have been carriers of dreaded diseases, but as laboratory animals they may provide clues to the conquest of human illnesses. As Hans Zinsser has pointed out, humans and rats share a good many of the same vices; perhaps this is why they play such a prominent—and ambivalent—role in world literature.

See also: Bear, Lion, Metamorphosis.

Selected Bibliography

Hagemann, Eberhard and Günter Schmidt, *Ratte und Maus*. Berlin: Walter de Gruyter, 1960.

Zinsser, Hans, *Rats, Lice and History*. Boston: Little, Brown, and Company, 1935.

BEVERLEY D. EDDY

REASON

Reason has appeared as a theme throughout the history of literature. In Western literature it appears as early as the works of Hesiod and Homer. Here it is an undifferentiated concept, as the reasoning power of men distinguishing them from other creatures. It is called sometimes *nous,* sometimes *logos*.

Reason is the ability to interact with the external world, to name the parts of the world and to direct one's actions and the actions of groups to control the environment through the use of the brain. In short, to think in general terms expressed in language. By so doing, people can preserve the results of their reasoning. Let us consider the development of reasoning power and its reflection in literature.

The Ancient World

The mythical representation of the role of Reason in the rise of civilization is to be found in the story of Prometheus. Prometheus, first presented in Hesiod's poem, *Theogonia* (*Theogony*, 8th century B.C.), created man and bestowed on him the gift of fire, stolen from the gods. This story is important because it recurs in the nineteenth and twentieth centuries. The key version is that of the tragedy by Aeschylus, *Promētheus desmōtēs* (*Prometheus Bound,* c. 450 B.C.). Aeschylus dramatizes Prometheus (forethought) being chained to a mountain by the servants of Zeus for the crime of giving mankind fire. George Thompson (*Aeschylus and Athens,* 1941) argues that the intent of Aeschylus is clear. Zeus must become less tyrannical, and Prometheus must become more cooperative. Thus with Prometheus' aid Zeus will continue to rule.

In his trilogy of tragedies the *Oresteia* (458 B.C.), Aeschylus becomes the champion of a reasoned, ordered life of humankind. As we shall see, later interpreters of the Prometheus story, for example, Shelley, adopted a different attitude.

A division between Intellect, Reason, and Knowledge began early in the history of philosophy. Reason meant the faculty of thinking correctly. Intellect meant the ability to find the essences of phenomena. Knowledge meant the accumulation of facts.

The pre-Socratics, from Thales (c. 636–c. 546 B.C.) through Heraclitus (fl. 500 B.C.), developed a confidence in the reasoning power that reflected the progressive development of Greek society. The trading society in the Ionian

Islands led to the use of Reason, based on action. But beginning with Socrates and continuing with Plato, a turn to a more abstract and negative approach reflected less confidence and the separation of the mental powers from practice. The Platonic Forms were ideals separated from sensuous activity.

The early optimistic approach to the power of Reason gave way to a negative approach, to a tendency to anti-intellectualism. To understand why reasoning power was first glorified, then denigrated, we must consider the development of society.

In Greek tribal society, as in all tribal society, thought and action were united. People followed the way of their tribes. Thought sprang from action and was dialectically related to new action. But with the rise of civilization and the development of class society, some people (the rulers) thought and did not work, and others, slaves, worked and had no leisure to develop theory. Among the rulers were, of course, the intellectuals, since those rulers had leisure to theorize. Concerned with thought separated from work, from action, the intellectuals developed a static view of the world and embodied thought in the "Forms."

Soon Socrates (c. 469–399 B.C.) was mocking Thales for having his eyes on the clouds and falling in a ditch, and soon Aristophanes (c. 448–c. 385 B.C.) was mocking Socrates in a similar vein. The accumulation of Knowledge as a product of Reason made another definition possible. So we must concern ourselves with Reason as a process, with Reason as a Platonic Form, and with Knowledge. Reason as a Form represented the thinking of a ruling class reluctant to change and devoted to timeless ideals. And the accumulation of knowledge heralded the appearance of the pedant who knew many facts but could not relate his theory to practice.

Thus, after the rise of class society, the split between reason and action occurred. Plato reflected this in his "myth of the cave" in the dialogue, *Politeia* (*The Republic*, c. 380 B.C.). Those who lived in the world of sense were trapped in a cave where they saw reflected on a wall the creatures and objects behind them. These actual images grasped from the cave were able to see the real world, the world of abstractions or Forms. Here Plato embodied two developments. He was clarifying the process by which the mind creates abstractions, and he was asserting that those abstractions were eternal forms. We may accept the one process without the other. The abstractions or Forms, ideals separated from practice, became the basis for ideal Reason, the Reason of the philosopher kings who were separated from the world of action, the world of those in the cave.

Heraclitus had combined a materialist explanation of the universe with a dialectical presentation of the role of the individual and society. All are ruled by the everliving divine wisdom, which no man or god ever created. The universe is ruled by reason and society and the individual must obey the same wisdom. Thus Heraclitus arrived at a unified view of man and the universe. He saw the universe, then, as an everliving flame, now flaring up, now dying down. He saw the conflict of opposites as resembling a bow in tension with its string.

Plato turned away from the materialism of the pre-Socratics to concern himself with how man should know himself and how he should live. He saw the soul of man as tripartite. The animating principle of the body, it consists of reason that ascertains the course and governs, enlisting the aid of the will (passion) to control the appetitive.

Aristotle (384–322 B.C.) follows Plato in making Reason the dominant part of the human soul and the element that distinguishes humans from other sentient beings. Aristotle's work has little literary value; he is of interest to us as a source of ideas important to literature in the succeeding centuries, especially the concept of right reason.

The Stoics, Zeno (335–263 B.C.) and Marcus Aurelius (A.D. 121–180), sought to synthesize the views of Plato and those of the pre-Socratic philosophers of the natural sciences. The early Stoics adhered to a world view that upheld divine reason and maintained that the society as well as the individual could be changed. Later Stoics under the domination of the Roman Empire sought change within the empire.

One of the major literary contributions of the Stoics is the hymn to Zeus of Cleanthes (331–232 B.C.) who unified Zeno's dualism of God and matter by his concept of tension, reflecting the "all is Flux" of Heraclitus. The tension between opposing forces is what rules in ethics and in the universe. The Stoic universe was precisely ordered. Materialists, they recognized spirit—they only insisted that it was corporeal.

Epicurus (341–270 B.C.) drew on the materialistic tendencies of the pre-Socratics. He denied the interference of the gods in the affairs of the world and recognized the eternity of matter. He developed that strand of Reason that was based on the experiential theory of knowledge. He maintained the truth of sensation and the importance of freeing men from fear of gods and of death. Epicurus sought to establish, then, that man could reason about the world and test his reasoning by experience. This amounted to rejection of the Platonic world of forms. Such an approach glorifies Reason as capable of dealing with man's problems.

Lucretius (c. 94–55 B.C.), an outstanding Roman poet and philosopher, carried on the work of Epicurus in his long philosophic poem *De rerum natura (On the Nature of Things)*. The individual was to seek happiness by accepting the philosophy of Epicurus. Since the soul, like the body, ceases to exist at death, one need not fear death nor the gods. Lucretius glorified Venus, the patron goddess of the Romans, as the birth giver of all things. *On the Nature of Things* is perhaps the supreme embodiment of the theme of Reason in literature. By pursuit of philosophy, man can free himself of all earthly evils. Lucretius glorifies understanding and rejects superstition and fear.

In *Biōn prasis (Philosophers Up for Sale,* A.D. 2d century), a dialogue, Lucian mocks Socrates and many other thinkers. Lucian's own views seem close to Pyrrhonist skepticism. He says: "For every laughing Democritus, there is a weeping Heraclitus." This amounts to a rejection of the idea that people can move forward or resolve their problems through the use of Reason.

Parallel to the Greeks, the Jewish people were developing their own attitudes toward Reason and Knowledge. Their approach was tainted with more anti-intellectualism than that of the Greeks. The warning to Adam and Eve of the equation of wisdom and grief (Gen. 2:90) is echoed in Ecclesiastes as the Preacher warns that "knowledge increases sorrow." The Jewish thinker, Maimonides (Moses ben Maimon), codified the *Mishne Torah* (the Jewish book of law, 1180) and wrote *Dalalat al-Ha' irin (The Guide of the Perplexed*, 1190), a prose work continuing the Jewish discussion of Reason.

Boethius carried on the traditions of Plato, Aristotle, and the Stoics. In a work of great literary value, *De consolatione philosophiae (The Consolation of Philosophy*, c. 524), a philosophic dialogue, he mingled poetry and prose. Here an embodiment of Reason, Lady Philosophy, appears to him and argues that the pursuit of material goods is of little value since these can be lost or stolen, but the pursuit of Reason and virtue gives rewards that cannot be lost. Boethius' work exerted great influence for centuries, linking the classical world to the work of Dante and Chaucer.

The Middle Ages

In a long allegorical poem *Le roman de la rose (The Romance of the Rose)* Guillaume de Lorris (part 1, c. 1230) and Jehan de Meung (part 2, c. 1275) personify Reason as one of the advisers of the Lover who woos the Rose. She seeks to free the lover from his folly by urging him to abandon his pursuit of the Lady and by advising him on many other subjects: youth and old age, the higher love of friendship, and the wheel of fortune. Reason also argues that had not the common lands been stolen by the rich, and if all society were more rationally organized, all mankind might live happily.

St. Thomas Aquinas argued in the *Summa theologica* c. 1266–1274) that the indivisible divine truth may be derived from two sources: revelation and human reason. Thus, he made Reason acceptable but limited it to areas other than faith.

The tradition of the *Consolation of Philosophy* and the world view of St. Thomas Aquinas are embodied in what is perhaps the greatest work of the medieval period, Dante's long poem *La divina commedia (The Divine Comedy*, c. 1320). The figure of Virgil, who guides Dante through Hell and Purgatory, is, by common agreement, the embodiment of Reason. After leading Dante out of the dark wood of error, Virgil withdraws, giving place to Beatrice, the embodiment of divine Reason. Virgil can go no farther, because he is a pagan, and because only divine Reason can light the way to paradise.

Strongly influenced by the *Romance of the Rose* and by the *Consolation of Philosophy* of Boethius, both of which he had translated, Geoffrey Chaucer was concerned with the rule of Reason over sensuality. In the *Franklin's Tale* (c. 1380–1400), he shows the effects of false reason, of a confidence man who calls himself a philosopher. But in another Canterbury tale, *Melibee,* he suggests a moral outcome. Melibee, whose daughter Sophia (Reason) was severely wounded by three foes (the world, the flesh, and the devil), learns through the advice of his wife, Prudence, that he must not react violently, must win over his enemies, and must rule his own world with Reason, seeking wise counsel. Throughout his works Chaucer seems to be expressing the point of view of Reason. Those characters who are not attuned to Reason turn out badly.

The Renaissance

In the Renaissance, Petrarch (1304–1374) and other humanists transferred their thoughts from divine to humane studies. They launched that glorification of Reason so characteristic of the time. Erasmus, in his prose work *Moriae encomium* (*The Praise of Folly*, 1511), glorified wisdom by making Folly praise herself. He denounced war, corruption, and greed from the viewpoint of Christian humanism. Raphael (1483–1520) painted a fresco of the School of Athens for Pope Julius II in his decoration of the Vatican, glorifying Reason. Such humanism also inspired Rabelais (c. 1494–1553). He mocked the metaphysical approach of medieval philosophy and valued wisdom.

In the Renaissance we see the triumph of humanism over the scholasticism of the Middle Ages. Especially in writer Giordano Bruno (1548–1600), we see the struggle for liberation from old ways of thought. Opposed to elements of Aristotelianism, Bruno was drawn to the pre-Socratic philosophers, especially Anaxagoras, Pythagoras, and Democritus, whose atomism he accepted, although he sought to purge it of mechanism.

Influenced by Copernicus, he rejected the Ptolemaic system and sought to give a scientific explanation of the universe. He eliminated the idea of the sun as motionless center and of fixed stars in the eighth sphere, which Copernicus had retained from the old system. Rejecting all transcendental hierarchies and battling against Aristotelianism, Bruno sought in his dialogues to demonstrate that reality is a process in which matter and spirit are different aspects of a unitary substance.

Form, a world intellect or soul, produces all actual forms. This spirit, or Reason, is one with matter. They are two aspects of a single substance. So Reason rules the universe, but, as with Heraclitus, all things move through a struggle of opposites.

Erasmus's friend, Sir Thomas More created a kingdom of ''Reason'' in his *Utopia* (political romance, 1516). He projected a society in which people worked but six hours a day and devoted the remainder of their waking hours to science and art.

In his *Essais* (*Essays*, 1580–1588), Montaigne revived the skepticism of Pyrrho, arguing that all knowledge, including the testimony of the sense, is uncertain. Thus Montaigne arrived at the position of fideism, arguing that since Reason is not reliable the only sensible thing to do is to turn to the Catholic church and rely on faith.

The second book of the allegorical poem *The Faerie Queene* (1590–1596) of Edmund Spenser expresses a world view based on neo-Platonism. The universe is seen as a unity woven around the story of Man's fall and his redemption through Jesus Christ. A hierarchical structure in which God rules all, the king (or queen) rules the state, and the soul rules the body is part of this world view.

Divine love manifests itself in human affairs as right Reason. Right Reason is analogous to natural law and sanctions the hierarchical structuring of society. This right Reason corresponds to the lady Philosophy of Boethius' *Consolation of Philosophy*.

In book 2 of the *Faerie Queene* the knight on a quest, Sir Guyon, travels with a palmer who represents right Reason. When Guyon follows the advice of right Reason, he succeeds in his search for Temperance. But when separated from right Reason, he nearly assaults the Red Cross Knight, misled by the lies of Archimago, the spirit of evil. At the last moment, however, his own Reason and the sight of the red cross on the knight's shield save him from an ultimate error.

In the tragedy *Hamlet,* (c. 1600) Shakespeare speaks of man as being "infinite in reason." And Hamlet, reproaching his mother, cries, "A beast that wants discourse of reason would have mourned longer." Here Shakespeare is drawing on the tradition of the great chain of being and of right Reason—the world view that developed from Greek philosophy, was elaborated by the neo-Platonists, and developed further in the Middle Ages. This was a unified view of the universe stretching from rocks up through animals and humans through angels to God. Another view links the cosmos, the state, and the individual. The whole was ruled by the "right Reason" of God, and it was the duty of fallen man to use his human Reason to seek to comprehend the laws of right Reason—God.

The Age of Reason

Sir Francis Bacon attacked the "Idols" of false learning. His *New Atlantis* (novel, 1627), a utopian sketch, is notable for its portrayal of "Solomon's House," a research institute for scientific workers.

In 1602, Tommaso Campanella wrote his *La città del sole* (*The City of the Sun,* utopia). It was a republic ruled by pure Reason, with no private property and equality for all. Citizens worked but four hours a day, with the remaining time free to pursue art and science. "Throughout the sixteenth century human Reason had, in different places and different subjects, asserted its independence of authority and challenged scholastic methods of thought" (Introduction, *The Age of Reason,* Stuart Hampshire, 1956). Descartes, the first great modern philosopher, invented a method for the "well guiding of reason" in his *Discours de la méthode* (*Discourse on the Method,* 1637), and Reason plays an important role in the plays of Corneille (1606–1684), whose heroes "reason out" their choice of duty over love. Baruch Spinoza (1632–1677) freed philosophy from scholastic chains by equating God with the universe and advocating a secular state free from religious persecution. Following Descartes, he sought to develop Reason with mathematical rigor. In his *Art poétique* (*The Art of Poetry,* didactic poem, 1674) Boileau introduced Reason into the field of literary theory, attempting to reduce all to a clear system.

The Age of the Enlightenment

In his satirical novel *Gulliver's Travels* (1726), Jonathan Swift portrays the virtuous Houyhnhnms (book 4), whose "grand maxim is to cultivate reason and be wholly governed by it." Swift's friend, Alexander Pope, portrayed man as a creature ruled by Reason in his poem *An Essay on Man* (1733–1734). He argued that belief in God could be justified by Reason, unaided by revelation. This work expressed the rationalism of the century, "The Age of Reason."

Thomas Paine titled one of his books the *Age of Reason* (1794–1795). A large part of this work is an analysis of the fallacies in the biblical texts that form the basis of Christianity. Although, like many other thinkers of this period, Paine was not an atheist, he was clearly a deist and used Reason as a weapon in his analysis of Christianity, which he saw as a tool of oppression.

In the Age of the Enlightenment, Reason was related to mechanistic development and philosophers sought to convert philosophy into a natural science. David Hume (1711–1776) had said: "As the science of man is the only solid foundation for the other sciences, so the only solid foundation we can give to this science itself must be laid on experience and observation" (*The Age of Enlightenment,* Introduction, Isaiah Berlin, 1956). His French disciple, Etienne Condillac (1715–1780), sought, in the words of Sir Isaiah Berlin, "to reconstruct every human experience—the most complex and sophisticated thoughts or 'movements of the soul,' the most elaborate play of the imagination, the most subtle scientific speculation—out of 'simple' ideas, that is sensation classifiable as being given to one or the other of our normal senses."

Voltaire, Denis Diderot (1713–1784), and others adhered to this "sensationalist" approach. So the priority of Reason was recognized by the Philosophes. And their attitudes held sway until the period of the primacy of Kant and Hegel. Voltaire struggled against the clericalism and religious fanaticism of this period, and in his philosophical novel *Candide* (1759), he mocked the erroneous philosophy of Leibnitz. Candide debates at length with his tutor Pangloss whether all is for the best in the best of all possible worlds. In chapters 17 and 18 Voltaire portrays a reasonable land of Eldorado, where precious stones are treated as pebbles and people are not overwhelmed by greed.

Immanuel Kant, German philosopher, wrote extensively on Reason, but denied the possibility of knowing the "Thing in Itself." However, his work laid the basis for the advances of Hegel, who showed how the divine ideal underlies the dialectical development of the mind of mankind. In the essay *Zum ewigen Frieden* (*Perpetual Peace,* 1795), Kant applied Reason to the solution of problems of international conflict. He devoted himself to the study of Reason in his *Kritik der reinen Vernunft* (*Critique of Pure Reason,* 1781) and other works. He made his devotion to reasoned analysis explicit in his essay *Idee einer Universalgeschichte . . .* (*Universal History,* 1784): "In man (as the only rational creature on earth) those natural faculties which aim at the use of reason shall be fully developed in the species, not in the individual. Reason in a creature is the capacity to enlarge the rules and purposes of the use of his resources far beyond the natural instinct.'' The implication here is that man, through the use of language, can advance the gains of Reason and pass on those gains to subsequent generations—hence this use is ''fully developed in the species.'' Kant felt that humans, differing from all other species in the use of Reason embodied in language, had the destiny of moving from the individual to the species, developing the achievements of the group according to Reason through generations.

Hegel went even further. In his *Vorlesungen über die Philosophie der Geschichte* (*Reason in History,* 1837) he stresses that the development of all human history is in accord with Reason. All moves toward culmination in the divine idea. In part 2 of *Reason in History,* Hegel writes: ''The sole thought which philosophy brings to the treatment of history is the simple concept of Reason: that Reason is the law of the world and that, therefore, in world history, things have come about rationally.''

During the French Revolution Reason was worshipped as a goddess and hymns were written in her honor.

The Nineteenth Century

But with the nineteenth century and the reaction after the French Revolution, the Age of Reason was at an end. The dreams of a reasonable world of More, of Campanella, of Pope and of the Philosophes ended when the ideal of liberty, equality, and fraternity gave way to the bourgeois ideal of property rights. At the end of the century, Anatole France was to write with savage irony: ''The Law in its majestic equality forbids the rich as well as the poor to sleep under bridges, to beg in the streets, and to steal bread'' (*Le lys rouge* [*The Red Lily,* novel, 1894]). George Eliot (Mary Ann Evans) depicts Reason or ''knowledge'' divorced from passion and love in her tale of the loveless marriage of the scholar Casaubon and Dorothea Brook in her novel, *Middlemarch* (1871–1872).

In his novel *The Adventures of Huckleberry Finn* (1884), Mark Twain portrays the debates between Huck and the slave, Jim. Jim argues that Solomon could not have been wise or he would not have had so many wives and children. He would have no more peace and quiet than in a ''biler factory.'' Huck concludes that it is hopeless to try to talk sense to Jim. In Twain's novel *Pudd'nhead Wilson* (1894) a ''white'' who has been found guilty of murder is found to be a black who should have been a slave. As such, he is a valuable piece of property, and who would lock him up? So his sentence of imprisonment is eliminated and the rediscovered slave is sold down the river.

Mark Twain gives reason a local habitation and a name. He reveals the ''reason'' of the slaveholding society and leads the reader to analyze it.

An amusing facet of the theme of Reason in literature is found in the genre of the detective novel. Edgar Allen Poe created Monsieur Dupin, who, like Poe himself, was a devotee of Reason. He solves the ''Murders in the Rue Morgue'' (story, 1841) and other cases through logical analysis. He was followed by Sir

Arthur Conan Doyle (1859–1930) with Sherlock Holmes, whose great mind was much admired by Doctor Watson.

The positivist movement of Auguste Comte (1798–1857), which limited Reason to the scientifically verifiable and eschewed all metaphysics, exerted considerable influence on literature. A number of writers, most notably the Pole Aleksander Głowacki, author of the novel *Lalka* (*The Doll,* 1890), became adherents of this movement.

Karl Marx (1818–1883) agreed with Hegel in finding Reason in the course of human history. However, he argued that Hegel had stood everything on its head by making history embody the ideal. Marx argued that the evolution of history reflected the evolution of society, that the reasoned development of human history resulted from the struggle of classes, the ideas reflecting the material development. Reason—or dialectical materialism—would become predominant and rule the rational development of society with the rise of the proletariat to power.

The Twentieth Century

Dialectical materialism is embodied in literature in the work of various Soviet writers like Mikhail Sholokhov (1905–1984) and Ilya Ehrenburg (1891–1967). In addition, it appears in the works of Henri Barbusse (1873–1935), Louis Aragon (1897–1982) and Martin A. Nexø (1869–1954).

In the United States this point of view has been adopted in part by Jack London (1876–1916), Upton Sinclair (1878–1968), Theodore Dreiser (1871–1945) and Richard Wright (1908–1960). Dreiser and Wright specifically adopted the dialectical materialist point of view upholding the idea that Reason as related to practice by the revolutionary proletariat would transform society.

Jack London adhered to the socialist movement and the ideas of Marx in his early years. These ideas are argued at some length in his novel *The Iron Heel* (1907). He presents a working-class hero who argues metaphysics with the members of an upper-class club and the problems of small business with a group of businessmen.

Theodore Dreiser played a major role as an advocate of various ideologies in his novels. A realist, his work can be compared with that of the painter, Edward Hopper. In 1925 Alfred Kazin describes the similarity in his introduction to Dreiser's novel *The Titan* (1914), as follows: "Dreiser sees the modern scene precisely as did the tender realists of the 'ash can' school of painters who discovered the beauty of the big city. . . . Dreiser's loving realism is directed toward an urban world that is always various and colorful."

Dreiser moved ever closer to that strand of reasoned predominance that is known as dialectical materialism. One of his last acts before his death in 1945 was to write a letter, expressing his desire to associate himself with the Communist movement of the United States.

Richard Wright specifically adopted the point of view of dialectical materialism and attempted to embody that point of view in his early writings, in the short stories in *Uncle Tom's Children* (1938) and in his novel *Native Son* (1940). In

Native Son the point of view is made explicit in the arguments and statements of the Communist lawyer, Max, who defends the accused black youth, Bigger Thomas. In later years Wright abandoned this point of view, and after moving to France adopted an ideological position closer to existentialism.

Existentialism, of course, played its major role as an influence in France. Jean-Paul Sartre (1905–1980) adhered to this school. It stresses the role of the individual and rejects analyses (like the Marxist), which hold that nature and society can be controlled.

Let us now return to Prometheus. Prometheus is associated in mythical form with man's earliest efforts at Reason and technology. But his story recurs. As we have seen, Aeschylus presented the story of Prometheus, leading to a reconciliation with Zeus. But in the nineteenth century Shelley wrote his drama *Prometheus Unbound* (1820), portraying the victory of Prometheus over Zeus. Robert Bridges wrote a long poem, *Prometheus the Fire-Giver* (1877). Bridges portrays Prometheus bringing fire, the source of all man's powers, to King Inachus in defiance of Zeus. Although Zeus does not appear, the work implies that he remains the enemy of mankind and that mankind and Prometheus eventually will triumph. This is the message also of John Lehmann in his description of Georgia, *Prometheus and the Bolsheviks* (1937), which has Prometheus come in a dream and spend several years studying the Soviet Revolution, concluding that his future is embodied in the Communist movement.

Prometheus has become a popular figure in the Soviet Union, where his contribution of fire to mankind is identified as foreshadowing the ultimate triumph of Reason in the form of proletarian revolution. The writers of the West are less unified and less optimistic in their portrayal of the role of Reason and the possible future solution of the problems of mankind.

In the late nineteenth and twentieth centuries, thought about Reason was increasingly divided into two channels. Karl Marx and his followers among intellectuals in the West, the Soviet Union, and eastern Europe stressed the power of Reason when allied with practice—"the unity of theory and practice"— to solve conflicts. In so doing, they carried forward the traditions of Democritus, Epicurus, and Lucretius.

On the other hand, many writers in the Western tradition rejected such an approach and continued the anti-intellectual and skeptical strands that developed from the writings of Aristophanes and Lucian. Other writers, like Kurt Vonnegut, played the roles of clowns and mockers within the dominant Western tradition. In his novel *God Bless You, Mr. Rosewater* (1965) Vonnegut creates a mad capitalist who writes a will in which he expounds on the evils of capitalism. Through irony and humor, Vonnegut exposes hypocrisy. In his science fiction novel *Slaughterhouse Five* (1969) he portrayed himself as waking in the middle of the night to say to his wife that all information about the bombing of Dresden is classified as top secret by the U.S. government. "Secret from whom?" he cried. The same mad humor appeared in Joseph Heller's novel *Catch 22* (1961), echoing Jaroslav Hašek's *Osudy dobrého vojáka Švejka za Světové valky* (*The

Good Soldier Schweik, 1920–1923). Yossarian continually struggled to find sanity in the world of military thinking. Langston Hughes recaptured the commonsense world of Lancelot Gobbo, Sancho Panza, and Huck Finn with his Harlem sketches of Simple (see, for example, *The Best of Simple,* 1961).

One writer who consciously developed the theme of Reason in a major novel was Pirsig who wrote *Zen and the Art of Motorcycle Maintenance* (1974). He had his hero, a college professor, deal with Reason in the Platonic sense and the problems it presents to the thinker who tries to deal in a commonsense way with the modern world.

In the foreseeable future, the dichotomy we have discussed here will continue. The writers of the Marxist world will stress the power of Reason allied with practice to solve the problems of humanity. The leading writers of the Western world will engage in anti-intellectualism or satire.

See also: Epistemology; Nature: *Naturae Cursus* and the State of Nature; Universe.

Selected Bibliography

Gras, Vernon W. *European Literary Theory and Practice: From Existential Phenomenology to Structuralism.* New York: Dell, 1973.

Hoopes, Robert. *Right Reason in the English Renaissance.* Cambridge, Mass.: Harvard University Press, 1962.

Lovejoy, Arthur P. *The Great Chain of Being: A Study of the History of an Idea.* Cambridge, Mass.: Harvard University Press, 1936.

Thompson, George Derwent. *Aeschylus and Athens: A Study in the Social Origins of Drama.* 2d ed. London: Lawrence and Wishart, 1950.

PAUL A. BATES

REBELLION

Man is a herd animal; he lives in groups and societies. In what the sociologist David Riesman calls "the tradition-directed society," the individual assimilates the received wisdom and takes his place unself-consciously within that tradition. He does not think about why he does something—he merely does it because it has always been done. When such a society is jarred by adversity, by contact with a different set of values, or when some of its principles are brought into open contradiction, custom comes under fire, and an individual may begin to question, to modify the tradition, or to find himself in open conflict with the society. He becomes what Riesman calls "inner directed," taking his bearings and values from some inner voice, daemon, intuition, or from something higher, which he sees as transcending the tradition. He tries to define himself within, without, or against his society. Literature is centrally about tension and conflict, and no tension is as fascinating as the one between the individual and society or between the individual and the universe as viewed by that society.

Antiquity

The first rebel was Adam who, though in an ideal situation, found that his own imperatives clashed with God's. This primal act of human rebellion estranged man from God, nature, and fellow man. Projecting him from a divinely sponsored idyllic Garden of Eden, it landed him in an alien, strife-ridden society in which many individuals, as if by neurotic compulsion, repeat the original rebellion; for example, Adam's son Cain, resenting the favor shown his sibling rival, repeated with the murder of Abel the rebellion against God. So did, much later, Saul and the other errant kings of Israel. One important act of rebellion, however, was that of Abraham, who, under the tutelage of God, nobly turned away from idolatrous father and tribe and undertook his solitary journey to fashion an individual destiny for himself and his descendants. He is the first of those creative rebels called by Emerson "rugged individualists," by Nietzsche "free spirits" or "overmen."

Founding a new society does not mean an end to rebellion. On the contrary, even the early generations of the "chosen people" lapsed into lethargy and required renewal. Thus Joseph, as a fair-haired son, was at odds with his brothers and sold into slavery. Thus Moses, after dissenting from Egyptian society, needed to bestir and then keep in line the Israelites. Above all, the prophets, especially Jeremiah, were at odds with an Israelite society they saw as backsliding, materialistic, idol-worshipping, benighted. Out of this prophetic tradition came a man who either by his own momentum or that of his followers ceased to be a critic and rebel within that society but started (or had started in his name) a new one—Jesus, the most fateful and charismatic rebel since Abraham. Inner directed, he promulgated an intuitive, ad hoc ethic to be set against rigid official Judaism. But then a paradoxical thing happened (which was to be repeated in inverse form in Milton's *Paradise Lost* [poem, 1667]). The rebel found himself in turn betrayed by a rebel, Judas Iscariot, who, apparently expecting a rising against Rome and an independent Israel, was confused and embittered by the talk about a kingdom not of this world. If Judas went in one direction, however, Paul went in exactly the other; having begun as a Jewish zealot persecuting the Christians, he rebelled against his Judaic origins and became, like Abraham, one of the founders of a new religion.

Homer's epic poem *Ilias* (*Iliad,* c. 8th century B.C.) is centrally about the individual against society. The Greeks, as against the more cohesive, disciplined Trojans, are a collection of individualists tenuously held together by a first among equals, Agamemnon. In going on strike because of what he considers inadequate wages and slighted dignity, Achilles has the implicit approval of his fellow Greeks. He finds it difficult to accept any limitations on his selfhood; his is the uncompromising absolutism of the idealist, but his sole ideal is his own self. Only through experience, mainly adverse, does he learn that even he cannot rebel against the human condition. He makes up with Agamemnon, accepts his fated short lifespan and the fact that—because of the will of Zeus, because of compassion for his own father and, through him, Priam, because his anger with Hector and his grief over Patroclus will end and life will continue—he must return Hector's body.

The next important rebel is Prometheus (Aeschylus' *Promētheus desmōtēs*, [*Prometheus Bound*, play, mid-5th century B.C.]), who is punished by an angry ruthless Zeus for the rebellious act of helping frail man. The story of a god who incurred suffering through pity for man was not to end here. A classic drama-tization of the clash of individual will and societal imperative is Sophocles' *Antigonē* (play, c. 44 B.C.). This confrontation is rather like that of Achilles and Agamemnon, except that the two characters in the epic are more self-centered than principled, while with the two in the play, the values are nearly reversed. In the *Oidipous epi Kolōnō (Oedipus at Colonus*, play, c. 406 B.C.) and the *Philoktētēs (Philoctetes, play*, 406, B.C.), a man who has been ejected from the community (one for a heinous deed, the other for a noisome incurable wound) has taken on, through the mysterious will of the gods and perhaps some individual maturation produced by adversity, a special value, even a holiness. Now the communities that ejected them resort to war or to deception to get them back, while the exiles, seeing no value in the others' change of mind, sulk.

Euripides' *Mēdeia (Medea*, play, 431 B.C.) is perhaps the extreme case of an outsider: a woman, with all the attendant disabilities; a foreigner, especially from a remote savage country; a clever person, with magical powers that are regarded with suspicion; a jilted person, highly conscious of being mocked at, of having lost face; a tempestuous individual known to have done violence to her kin. In her war with a society that never fully accepted her, she is one person—and what is even rarer, one woman—who takes her destiny into her own hands and retaliates in kind. What is also rare in literature, she escapes without punishment for having done something as shocking as destroy her children. A similar rhythm runs through the *Bakchai (The Bacchants*, play, c. 405 B.C.), in which the god Dionysus is an outsider who injects himself into an established social and religious order, in the face of strong resistance from the power structure. As he implicitly becomes part of the new power structure, he deals ruthlessly with the old order and even with innocent bystanders. The heroine in *Iphigeneia hē en Aulidi (Iphigenia in Aulis*, play, c. 405 B.C.) at first makes a plea for life and self in the face of the demands of the ambitions of her father, the sullied honor of her uncle, the momentum of an army bent on booty, the common cause of the Greeks, and even presumably the will of a goddess; then she changes her mind and, for sake of duty and glory, accepts the martyrdom desired by her society.

In Aristophanes' plays, individuals set themselves against a society that is bogged down in endless war (*Acharnēs* [*The Acharnians*, 425 B.C.]; *Eirēnē* [*Peace*, 421 B.C.]; *Lysistratē* [*Lysistrata*, 411 B.C.]), litigation (*Sphēkes* [*The Wasps*, 422 B.C.]), or turbulence and decline (*Ornithes*, [*The Birds*, 414 B.C.]; *Ekklēsiazousai* [*Women in Parliament*, 392 B.C.]). The means they resort to are, as befits comedy, fantastical—a separate peace, a sex strike, or a utopia in the air. But the feats work, and, in fantasy at least, the society is bested by an ingenious and persistent individual. In the *Lysistrata,* as in *Women in Parliament,* the rebellious individuals are women tinkering with a society badly constructed by men. In their rebellion and sense of sisterhood, they are kin to Medea, but where she is destructive and vindictive, they are constructive and reformist. Women are also given respect in Plato's *Politeia* (*The Republic,* dialogue, c. 380 B.C.), but the conflict of individual and society takes a different turn here. According to Socrates' parable of the cave, men bogged down in their corporeal lives are like people riveted by illusions in what we would now call movie houses. Here is a paradigm of the visionary challenging the bland and specious certitudes of a society and being martyred by those fond of taking the cave-movie for reality itself. Such a person was ironically Socrates himself and the *Apologia* (*Apology*), *Kritōn* (*Crito*), and *Phaidōn* (*Phaedo*) dialogues (4th century B.C.) trace the trial, self-defense, and execution of the individual. Aristotle (*Politika* [*Politics,* essays, 4th century B.C.]); might have had his eye on Socrates in his dictum on the exceptional individual, "There is no law for men of transcendent superiority, for they are themselves a law," which was adapted by Cicero, quoted by Emerson, developed by Nietzsche (who would take it to heart) and by Dostoevsky (who would malign it by offering pathetic claimants to that dispensation: the Underground Man, Raskolnikov, and Ivan).

The Middle Ages and the Renaissance

With the advent of Christianity, the encounter of individual and society was given new dimensions. The Judaic shrinking from social intercourse with Gentile culture, like the Platonic shrinking from the material realm, reappears in altered form (even though overcome by Paul, who would be all things to all men so that he might bring them to Christ) in a work like St. Augustine's *Confessiones* (*Confessions,* c. 397–400). The narrative shows that to be a Christian is to continually rebel—to withdraw from the coarse pagan world around him, whether from the vulgar pleasures of the gladiatorial shows that undid someone as self-confident of his powers of resistance as Alypius, or from the subtle esthetic ones, such as even church music; or from worldly ambitions and from the occupations of the adult world that are, under the aspect of eternity, no different from the toys we so readily take from children in the name of those more serious things.

In the medieval drama *Everyman* (c. 1500), the hero, immersed in a quasi-pagan society devoted to worldly matters, is unconscious of his Christianity. Only the advent of death provides him with enough selfishness to separate him from the society and to prepare him for a hereafter where he could lose his self in a more permanent and valid fashion. Something of the same experience is undergone by the pilgrim in Dante's epic poem *La divina commedia* (*The Divine Comedy,* c. 1320). The catalyst of regeneration here is not death but being lost and being granted a special vision through intervention from on high. Everyman's sundering from society is fairly simple and direct; Dante's is not, partly because he is an intellectual, writer, visionary, and prophet who, despite exile, presumes to hold the mirror to society and to lash its secular and religious leaders. The

Inferno (Hell) also contains images of men that, like Cain, rebelled against God and remain frozen in this posture forever. The rebellious hero of Wolfram's *Parzival* (epic poem, c. 1210), on the other hand, is brought by time and experience back to God.

Yet another twist is given to the theme under the auspices of the Courtly Love Tradition. As delineated in such works as Andreas Capellanus' discursive *De arte honeste amandi* (*The Art of Courtly Love*, late 12th century) and more lyrically in troubadour poetry, love is available only to special people, and it in turn ennobles them. These traits, in combination with virtues like secrecy and constancy, distinguish them from the rest of coarse humanity. The shrinking of Jew, Platonist, Christian is now redefined once more. In Gottfried von Strassburg's *Tristan* (romance, c.1210), the distinctiveness of the lovers and their being out of place in society, which cannot understand or tolerate them, is underlined by their being spied on and made the subject of continual backbiting. They finally must leave the court and civilization itself to find fulfillment in an idyll in a cave. In *Sir Gawain and the Green Knight* (romance, c. 1370), the hero is a rare, pious individual having the resources to resist the new cult of adultery. That is, when courtly love becomes widespread and inevitably coarsened, it is the turn of the chaste man to be the rebel against the fashionable rebellious subculture.

That pleasure-loving upper crust is looked at much more sympathetically in Boccaccio's *Il decamerone* (*Decameron,* novellas, c. 1350). The hedonist portrayal of sexual activism suggests that this is the norm, yet the narrator who portrays that world is, judging from the many passages of apologia, the one who feels himself to be at bay, a rebel against the solemn views of society. In other words, his stories and vision conform to the way morally untidy people behave but are dissentient from the way the Christian establishment wants it to be known that they behave or wants them to behave. In Chaucer's *Canterbury Tales* (c. 1380–1400), the rebels are the Wife of Bath, with her unfettered view of woman and sexuality (somewhat paralleling those of Dame Nature in Jehan de Meung's *Roman de la rose* [*Romance of the Rose,* didactic poem, c. 1275]); the Pardoner, with his manipulation of the piety of the mass of people for selfish purposes; and the Nun, with her curious mixture of worldliness and otherworldliness.

Machiavelli's successful ruler (*Il principe* [*The Prince,* treatise, 1532]) is, like the Pardoner, an individual who sets himself against the official religion and the moral norms, but his purpose is the preservation and stability of the state, not avarice. In his celebration of wine, women, and song and his satire of warmaking rulers, Rabelais (*Gargantua et Pantagruel* [*Gargantua and Pantagruel,* novels, 1532–1564]) offers a rebellious individualism that is, like those of the Wife of Bath and Dame Nature, directed against official morality. Perhaps the greatest of all individualists is Montaigne (*Essais* [*Essays,* 1580–1588]), with his sense of the inviolability of the self in the face of the claims made on it by all the philosophies, political parties, and zealots of the world. Perhaps no one has ever been so determined to be his own man, been so conscious of the ultimate aloneness of each individual and of the speciousness of the demands on him that the world makes. If Montaigne is bemused and passive, Marlowe's magician (*Dr. Faustus,* play, 1604) is active and restless. Having plumbed all fields of knowledge and come up with nothing substantive, he makes a pact with the Devil in order to carry on his quest under supernatural auspices, to know unbridled freedom, and to master the world. This rebellion against God, like Adam's, Cain's, and Judas', must be paid for, and at the end of the allotted twenty-four years, his regrets notwithstanding, he is carried off by Satan to hell. The rebellious attempt to define individualism not through but against God's will has failed.

Such rebels, who set themselves illicitly against God, albeit without Faustus' erudition and his noble quest for answers and experiences, are the villains in Shakespeare's plays (c. 1590–1610), most memorably Richard III, Iago, and Macbeth. By contrast, in the noble characters rebelliousness is directed rather at society. Hamlet is a social critic addressing to those at the court his awareness of their failings (as well as a philosopher pondering the anomalies and enigmas of existence). Like Montaigne, he is his own man (though a pious Christian), someone for whom, as a result of disillusionment with his mother, the world is mainly a construct of façades. Prince Hal acts out the role of "drop out" in order to, by means of surprise, heighten his charisma and effectiveness as future king. Assuming the stupidity and credulity of people, he is intent on bringing the world to heel and shaping it to his satisfaction. Where Hamlet would educate it, Hal wants to master it (while Montaigne would educate only himself—and the choice few who read his essays).

Hal's needing to go underground is literally the case with Edgar, who, when the evil ones take over society, must become a "nobody" to preserve himself, like Odysseus in an Ithaca controlled by the usurping suitors or Hamlet at a court controlled by Claudius. Cleopatra's sensual languor is by implication no more than representative behavior in the indolent Egyptian society, but Antony's gravitation to her represents a resignation from his Roman upbringing, Roman wife, and, above all, his forte as soldier and statesman. The dropping out into pleasure, which Hal feigned, Antony really does; Edgar flees from the evil in society, but Antony seeks out a new good elsewhere. His rebellion consists in nothing less than in a conversion, from Roman politics and duty to Middle Eastern love, whimsical humor, and languorous detachment. Under the aegis of Cleopatra, he discovers that the individual he had been is not the individual he really is or wants to be.

Coriolanus is a martial man at war with the very Roman citizens he led and fought on behalf of. This is partly due to their cowardice and mediocrity, partly to his own insensitivity to their basic needs—in bread and in dignity. If we sympathize with the individualism of Hal and Hamlet and perhaps find meaning in Antony's martyrdom for love, few would defend a rebellious Coriolanus marked by hotheadedness, obtuseness, arrogance, lack of self-awareness, inflexibility, and, finally, pathetic vulnerability. He is an Achilles without the nobility and the capacity to grow, an idealist without a set of ideals that differ from a child's or a bully's. Timon and Lear are men too trusting and naïve before, too bitter and vindictive after having (like Hamlet) discovered the hollowness of society. But Timon, more even than Coriolanus, sinks into narcissistic cynicism and rant, while Lear learns and grows. Beatrice and Benedict, as well as Rosalind and the King and courtiers in *Love's Labour's Lost* (c. 1594), rebel against customary love and marriage; their rebellion lasts long enough to ventilate the absurdities of love, but the tradition proves strong enough to swallow them, with demurrals still on their lips. Romeo and Juliet alone find love in a society that knows only hate, fighting, factionalism, and cynical mockery; their love is a fragile flower that cannot survive the frigid climate.

Among the plays of Shakespeare's contemporaries, Webster's *Duchess of Malfi* (1613) is noteworthy for its poignant portrait of a rebellious woman who goes against the mores of her society and the will of her two powerful brothers by remarrying, and doing so below her class, with tragic consequences. Cervantes' novel *Don Quixote* (*Don Quijote,* 1605, 1615) is one of the greatest portrayals of the rebellious individual. Reacting against an unromantic, stale, compromising society in a unique way, he tries to fashion his life by the light of his chivalric dream, regardless of the cost in delusion within and cudgels from without. He persists in imposing his personal vision on the recalcitrant society, and after numerous resulting incongruities, society responds by entering into his vision and at the end even seeing a beauty in his delusion.

Milton's *Paradise Lost* (poem, 1667) is another profound treatment of individualism and rebellion. Like Abel, Cain, and Judas, and unlike the somewhat cynical, cooperative Satan in the Book of Job, Satan is, in Milton's Christian perspective, a deluded pseudo-individual. As out of contact with reality as Narcissus, he sets himself against God and His moral order. Though eventually degenerating into something flimsy and absurd, he wreaks damage on a few innocent human bystanders caught up in the crossfire with God. Satan's rebellion against God, however, crosses paths with Abdiel's against Satan, even as Judas' rebellion against the rebel Jesus is balanced by Paul's against Judaism and for Jesus (or Adam's against God and Abraham's for God). To rebel against the rebels, as Milton saw himself doing against a derelict king and society, and to be for a while an alien in one's own land is in fact to side with God and not to be, as the shallow or reactionary maintain, a rebel at all. The theme of rebellion is intimately tied up with that of freedom (both examined in depth in this epic), for individuality and freedom are seen as conformity to God's will, which often requires rebellion against society, while individuality and freedom as ordinarily understood are really conformity to Satan, sin, and society at the cost of estrangement from reality and rebellion against God.

The Neoclassical to Modern Periods

Molière shows two modes of rebellion against society. The hero of *Dom Juan* (*Don Juan,* play, 1665) dissents from the sexual norm and is, with Shakespeare's

Edmund, one of the few avowed atheists yet to appear in literature. He undergoes an ironic metamorphosis when, near the end, he decides (as Tartuffe must have) to adopt the latest fashion, hypocrisy, and so appear to conform to society after all. And *Le misanthrope* (*The Misanthropist,* play, 1666) is one of the clearest confrontations between the idealistic, sincere (if somewhat obtuse) individual and a society that muddles through on mediocrity, hypocrisy, sentimentality, and compromises.

Diderot's *Le neveu de Rameau* (*Rameau's Nephew,* satire, 1762–1784) is a landmark work, the first expression of the rebellious individual in modern counter-cultural or sociological terms rather than the older moral terms of Quixote or Alceste. The hero is someone who would formerly have been called a "philosopher" but would now be called an "intellectual" or "Bohemian" or "Hippie." With talent and perhaps some artistic resources, he is alienated from the fashionable society he sees through yet needs to hang on to for his survival. Quixote's and Alceste's wars were with society; Rameau's is sometimes with the upper middle class and often with the human race itself. They warred upon insincerity, he upon vulgarity, Philistinism, and self-delusion. They would improve the world, he, giving it up as intractable, would live off it. They are outsiders, he is a parasite. They crusade, he rants—and confesses. Confession is indeed in the air; Rousseau's contemporary *Confessions* (1781–1788) is another landmark statement of modern individualism. For one thing, it ushers in the modern genre of the autobiography (St. Augustine's dealt only with his gravitation to God, and Montaigne's is whimsical and sui generis). Here is a person who self-consciously dissents from polite society by making a point of analyzing at length in print things hitherto left out. He does it in the name of the new sacredness of the self; what happened to him, no matter how unsavory, is important simply because it happened to him. The picture of himself that he projects is nearly paranoiac. He alone is sincere, loyal, emotional; he is a solitary rebel against a cold urban civilization with its cliques and rat race. What had been the comic climax of the *Misanthrope*—the retreat to the wilderness—is now turned upside down and tragic. One can be fully human only in the lap of nature and solitude, not in the corrosive city. Much of this outlook pervades also Wordsworth's *The Prelude* (poem, 1799–1805), in which a brief stay in London and Paris confirms the poet's sense that the city is the death of instinct, feeling, nature. Here and in the Preface to the *Lyrical Ballads* (1800), Wordsworth dissents from a society that is becoming "modern"—impersonal, sensationalist, overcrowded, exploitative.

In Goethe's *Werther* (novel, 1774), the individual, suffused with introspection, imagination, emotion, and love, feels superfluous in a society devoted to reason, order, work, routine. Werther is perhaps the first protagonist since Sophocles' *Aias* whose suicide is treated at least half sympathetically. The hero of *Faust* (play, 1808) rebels against a religion he cannot believe in and a rationalistic body of academic knowledge he finds otiose. He turns rather to nature, feeling, and, above all, experience. The ego's quest for fulfillment through living rather than contemplation has its tragic component—the victimization of Gretchen and her family and Faust's own guilt feelings. Even in part 2 (1832), old Faust, still intemperate and demanding, is working away on reclamation projects and victimizes an old couple who are not compliant with his grandiose visions. The work dramatizes the perception, implicit in Rousseau and absent from the optimism of Wordsworth, that the full development of the individual exacts a heavy price from the society. It is a romantic version of the theme in the *Iliad*. Faust's rebellion is, moreover, helped along by a Satan whose own rebellion against God no longer takes the ominous form it took in Dante and Milton. Witty, cynical, urbane, the modern Satan has become a boon companion—and will remain so in the writings of Burns, Dostoevsky, Shaw, and Mann.

Another central parable of the clash of individual and unjust society is Heinrich von Kleist's *Michael Kohlaas* (novel, 1810). Privilege, ignorance, indifference, face-saving actions and cover-ups rule out any righting of wrongs by conventional means through "channels," which are given only lip service. The individual who takes his dignity seriously must be prepared to resort to arms, turn the permanently corrupt society upside down, and face martyrdom. This is the age of the Byronic man. Adventurous, accursed, brooding, yet also poetic, above all rebellious—explicitly against society, implicitly against God—he is a doomed wanderer: Byron's Harold, Cain, Manfred; Maturin's Melmoth; Lewis's Monk. In Brontë's *Wuthering Heights* (novel, 1847), the almost satanic, vindictive, domineering Heathcliff, who would by older standards be a villain, is now seen to embody rather vital energy. Less melodramatic versions are in French fiction. Stendahl's Julien Sorel and Fabrice del Dongo and Balzac's Eugène de Rastignac are young men trying to make their way in a society that is stultifying. They need cunning; they are often defeated; but whatever the outcome, they retain a sense of self and dignity. The gentle Pickwick is a Christ-like figure, like Dostoevsky's Prince Myshkin, out of place in a society ostensibly Christian but actually coarse. Hester Prynne (Hawthorne's *Scarlet Letter*, novel, 1850) is victimized by a repressive society that is ruthless over a sexual sin in which the society itself is implicated. Her life in exile and solitude enhances her dignity and assigns her a role as individual and rebel she did not at first possess when she had an affair with the local minister. In the same way, Huck (Twain's *Huckleberry Finn*, novel, 1884) finds himself at odds with society—oversimplifying, racist, slave-holding—by his encounter with Nigger Jim. The sensitive individual drops out morally when, by opening himself to experience, especially to one other human being, he sees the contradiction between what his sensibility tells him and the vapid generalizations the society lives by.

In Melville's novel *Moby-Dick* (1851), the individual sets himself against the universe rather than society, Ahab's quest for the whale being as imperialist and hopeless (even if heroic) as man's quest for the absolute, or as Faust's and Peer Gynt's typically romantic desire for comprehensiveness of experience. By contrast, the hero of *Bartleby the Scrivener* (novella, 1853) is an individual of mysterious origins who simply says "no," first to society and eventually to the universe. His rebellion, unlike that of the romantics, takes the modern form of passivity. Rather than expanding by means of experience and adventure, his ego shrinks to nothingness. It is as if in response to optimistic visions of rugged individualism, Melville showed just how difficult it is for a sensitive person in a modern bureaucratic job to heed Emersonian advice and forge his own destiny. And commonplace that advice was indeed becoming, for the nineteenth century produced a series of thinkers who are the philosophers of absolute individualism in a more forceful, assertive, iconoclastic way than was the gentle Montaigne. Emerson and Thoreau in America, Mill in England, Nietzsche in Germany, Kierkegaard in Denmark, Herzen in Russia posit a self that rejects all received pieties, questions or ignores the institutional Jesus and church, dismisses society as flabby or unreal, and derives values from within. They leave themselves open to the charge that the Hitlers of the world may be the result of an individualism that takes so little heed of the claims of society and the reality of other people. Certainly Raskolnikov (Dostoevsky's *Prestuplenie i nakazanie* [*Crime and Punishment*, novel, 1866]) is an example of Emersonian, Nietzschean individualism gone sour. Though an impoverished and uneven college student, he dreams of being a Napoleon figure. As a would-be "free spirit," he demands to be judged by a unique standard, but all he has to show is the brutal slaying of a pathetic old woman.

In George Eliot's *Middlemarch* (novel, 1871–1872), Dorothea, first a well-off young woman and then a wealthy wife, tries to find a creative way of helping people, even as Mr. Lydgate the doctor tries to do the same through medicine. Each is undone, however, partly through personal ineffectiveness, partly through a bad marriage, and partly through the sheer recalcitrance of a society sunken in its lethargy and indifference. In fact the nineteenth-century theme of the individual asphyxiated by society is now more often given from the feminine perspective, for the status of woman is becoming a question as it had not been since the days of Euripides, Aristophanes, and Plato. Works with Jane Austen-like marriageable young heroines are replaced by marriage tragedies. Flaubert's Emma Bovary, Tolstoy's Anna Karenina, and Ibsen's Hedda Gabler are three classic nineteenth-century women married to boring, pedantic husbands, living in stuffy societies, and seeking relief in adultery or coquetry and finally in suicide. Lawrence's Constance (*Lady Chatterley's Lover*, novel, 1928) is a modern and optimistic version of the theme.

The individual's rebellion takes ideological form in Turgenev's *Otṡy i deti* (*Fathers and Children*, novel, 1862). The target is not this or that injustice but the very structure of society itself and the values and thinking processes that make it possible. Bazarov derives a sense of justification from communion with like-minded souls springing up everywhere as the wave of the future. Concurrently Marx took the old religious concept of alienation from God and gave it a secular, sociological meaning by applying it to the proletarian's impaired relations with the products of his labor, with his colleagues, and with his society. The fulfillment Bazarov seeks in ideology and Anna in adultery, Levin (Tolstoy's *Anna Karenina,* novel, 1877) seeks by dropping out of urban culture and turning to a farming community on his estate, while Thoreau *(Walden,* essays, 1854) exchanges society for solitude and nature. Even so had André and Pierre (Tolstoy's *Voïna i mir* [*War and Peace,* novel, 1865–1869]) rejected the platitudes of men in high society and rethought the meaning of life from the ground up. The latter especially went through many phases of embracing an answer that sufficed some people and then becoming disillusioned with it. And Ivan (Dostoevsky's *Brat'ïa Karamazovy* [*The Brothers Karamazov,* novel, 1880]), facing a universe in which pain is widespread, rebelliously returns his entrance ticket to God. (''A world I never made'' is how A. E. Housman, in *Last Poems,* 1922, articulates modern man's rebellion.) The individual has, however, never been so isolated and so hostile to society and universe as in Dostoevsky's *Dvoïnik* (*The Double,* novel, 1846) and, signally, his *Zapiski iz podpol'ïa* (*Notes from Underground,* novel, 1864). The incipient paranoia of a Rousseau, the implicit contempt (for society and its idols of rationality and progress) harbored by some of the other romantic heroes here reaches a dead end of solipsism, perversity, and insanity.

The shallowness of society is the target of Ibsen's rebels, whether they see things in his plays from a Christian standpoint (*Brand,* 1866) or a profane one (*Samfundets støtter* [*Pillars of Society,* 1877]; *Et dukkehjem* [*A Doll's House,* 1879]; *En Folkefiende* [*An Enemy of the People,* 1882]). As Nora puts it about herself and society: ''I can no longer content myself with what most people say, or with what is found in books.'' Solness *(Bygmester Solness* [*The Master Builder,* 1892]) likewise finds books irrelevant and no longer feels fulfilled by building either churches (as at first) or beautiful homes for people (as later). Henry James gives the theme a trans-atlantic variation. His young and beautiful heroine (*Daisy Miller,* story, 1878) is American, that is, naïve, uninhibited, with large demands on life. She insists on autonomy in the face of a European society bowed down by age, customs, pessimism, constraints. She is defeated, as is Christopher Newman (*The American,* novel, 1877). The values are reversed in *The Ambassadors* (novel, 1903), in which the hero, Strethers, converts from allegiance to a Puritanic society now seen as sterile to an esthetically and morally far more attractive life style in corrupt, old, Babylon-like Paris.

Conrad's novels deal with individuals who find themselves, after an attempt to revive a life marred early by disaster, alienated and alone at a critical juncture. Joyce's Dedalus is a young man who, because of his intellectual proclivities, is set apart from society and even friends and family. The only contact he makes (in *Ulysses,* novel, 1922) is with Bloom, an outsider who is a passive rebel, with his socialist velleities and his peculiar observations on the Christian society around him. In Kafka, the individual is at the mercy of society and cosmos, both of which are inscrutable. Joseph K. and Gregor

Samsa are victims (the latter passive) who are quickly dehumanized and, for mysterious reasons, destroyed. The protagonist of *Das Schloss* (*The Castle,* novel, 1926), K., by contrast, brashly takes on the authorities and does everything he can to gain entry or at least fathom his destiny. D. H. Lawrence's protagonists rebel against hitherto sacred institutions; they make sexual experience precede rather than follow love and marriage. Ursula Brangwen (*The Rainbow,* novel, 1915) comes to see that mere love and marriage, which had at first seemed sufficient for her parents and grandparents and then had dubious results, cannot be the be-all of existence. Such questioning, together with critiques of the sterility of modern society, is carried on by Rupert Birkin (*Women in Love,* novel, 1920) and Lady Constance Chatterley.

In *Das Unbehagen in der Kultur* (*Civilization and Its Discontents,* 1930), Freud used a new terminology for the old tension between individual and society (as dramatized in the *Iliad* and the *Antigone*). For civilization to be possible, man must curtail his instinctive drives and needs; that constraint causes frustration and neurosis, but without it man is still a brute. Modern society is bent on getting out of the dilemma by means of technology and progress. Huxley's *Brave New World* (novel, 1932) sees the fulfillment of the dreams of individualists of earlier eras who had celebrated the body. The result is a society in which the spiritual, emotional dimensions have been snuffed out, and the individual is as atrophied as he had been in societies in which religion had oppressed the body and desire. The ominous overtones in Bazarov's rationalist rhetoric and in the rationalism sneered at by the Underground Man have come true. Now the individual, the savage John, manifests himself by making a stand on behalf of, of all things, sorrow, tragedy, adversity, and suffering. In Orwell's novel *1984* (1949), the individual's rebellion against feudalism, church, theocracy, monarchy, and privilege has resulted in an egalitarian secular state in which the individual is paradoxically weaker than ever.

Man's being a herd animal is dramatized by Ionesco's *Le rhinocéros* (*Rhinoceros,* play, 1960). Metamorphosis into rhinoceri—a metaphor for any cult or movement, like Christianity, communism, fascism—rapidly becomes contagious, and at the end only one individual makes a stand, however shakily, for mankind and individuality over bestiality. In Márquez's *Cien años de soledad* (*One Hundred Years of Solitude,* novel, 1967) rebellion against political and economic oppression is an endless and ultimately futile act and yet a precondition of dignity and manliness. Something of the same conclusion is drawn by Camus about metaphysical rebellion, in *Le mythe de Sisyphe* (*The Myth of Sisyphus,* essay, 1942) and *L'homme révolté* (*The Rebel,* essay, 1951): "There is no fate that cannot be surmounted by scorn."

See also: Alienation, Beat Generation, Nihilism.

Selected Bibliography

Glicksberg, Charles Irving. *Literature and Society.* The Hague: Nijhoff, 1972.

———— *The Self in Modern Literature*. University Park: Pennsylvania State University Press, 1963.

Underwood, J. C. *Literature and Insurgency*. New York: Biblo and Tannen, 1974.

MANFRED WEIDHORN

RELIGION IN SCIENCE FICTION

Within science fiction, religious themes have often been employed in connection with familiar literary motifs. Thus the utopia may become an Eden, the Faust figure a diabolical "mad scientist," the imaginary voyage a space pilgrimage, or the creation of robots an analogue of the creation of the human species. The scientific explanations and predictions used to give plausibility to the stories transform the meaning of the religious themes, sometimes in surprising ways.

What sets a distinctive function for these motifs within science fiction, however, is often not so much their scientific or pseudo-scientific explanations as the ideology within which they are written. When science fiction was first named and defined as a genre, in the United States in the early twentieth century, a certain conviction about the power of science and technology to bring about a perfect society, coupled with a suspicion of traditional religions as enemies of scientific progress, was prescribed for writers. While there have always been some, chiefly among the novelists rather than among the contributors to popular magazines, who did not conform to the dominant view, it has only been in the last few decades that the genre has burst some of its earlier ideological conventions.

Precursors to Science Fiction

The roots of science fiction have been traced in writings of many periods, including ancient times. Plato's *Kritias* (*Critias*, dialogue, 4th century B.C.), for example, presented Atlantis as a cultural and scientific utopia, while Voltaire's *Micromégas* (tale, 1752) described an imaginary voyage of two gigantic aliens to the planet earth. Such literary discussion of the possibilities and dangers of science became common during the nineteenth century. Mary Shelley's Gothic romance *Frankenstein* (1818) is often identified as a direct ancestor to the science fiction story, and many other writers, especially in Britain and the United States, develop similar themes. Even Nathaniel Hawthorne's short story "Rappacini's Daughter" (1844) contributed to the tradition by pointing to the danger of a single-minded dedication to botanical research at the expense of human values.

The examples given here, however, do not as a group display the degree of unity that would identify them as members of a common genre. Nor do they show any unified treatment of religious motifs. The difference is great between Plato's polytheistic coloring of an ancient myth, Voltaire's use of an imaginary encounter to illustrate his deism, Shelley's Faustian warning against careless science, and Hawthorne's Puritan parable.

The novelist H. G. Wells provided a bridge from nineteenth-century literature to the emerging genre of science fiction in the twentieth. In his novels and short stories, as well as in his essays, Wells promoted a religious version of scientific humanism; for example, in *The Time Machine* (novel, 1895), in which science provided the way of salvation for a species threatened by the extinction of the planet. Wells' confidence in the ability of the masses to accept such a religion sometimes wavered, and his picture of the limited, Promethean god who is man's ally is not always clear, but his conviction that men of science could and would bring in the "kingdom of God" did not falter, and his writings both reflected his era's optimism about technology and also influenced the intellectual currents that were developing.

The Emergence of Science Fiction as a Genre

The distinctive treatment of religious motifs within the genre of science fiction was determined by the way in which it was introduced. In 1926 Hugo Gernsbach began a new adventure magazine to be devoted to "scientification." In his first editorial Gernsbach wrote "By 'scientification' I mean the Jules Verne, H. G. Wells, and Edgar Allan Poe type of story—a charming romance intermingled with scientific fact and prophetic vision." The name of the new form quickly became "science fiction," and in the hands of other editors, notably John W. Campbell, Jr., limits of the magazine genre were set.

The "prophetic vision" for which Gernsbach called, and which science fiction set out to provide, was a vision of a world governed by scientists and engineers. Technology would offer the happiness that traditional religion and morality have failed to give. Wells' peculiar theology did not find a wide following, but his religious belief that the world's hope lay in a society ruled by science became a formative idea for science fiction writers during the depression era. The magazine editors encouraged speculation in every other direction, but this central idea was sacrosanct.

Outside magazine science fiction, futuristic novels were written during this period that discussed the position of religion and a technological society. André Maurois' "Le peseur d'âmes" ("The Weigher of Souls," story, 1931), Aldous Huxley's dystopian *Brave New World* (novel, 1932), and Franz Werfel's *Stern der Ungeborenen* (*Star of the Unborn,* novel, 1946) all treat religious themes in a way that would have found little acceptance by science fiction editors, and for that reason would at that time not have been considered to be primarily science fiction. Even novels written explicitly within the science fiction tradition, such as C. S. Lewis' trilogy *Out of the Silent Planet* (1938), *Perelandra* (1943), and *That Hideous Strength* (1945), could find only limited acceptance. The characteristic motifs are all there—for example, space voyages to Mars and Venus, a new Eden, the mad scientist Weston, among others—but the novels' casual treatment of scientific explanations and, even more, the point-by-point attack on science fiction ideology, disqualify them as science fiction in the magazine genre sense.

Science Fiction since World War II

The period following the Second World War saw a weakening of the authority of the science fiction magazine and a consequent broadening of the scope of science fiction that encouraged the treatment of religious themes.

Part of the change was brought about by a disillusionment with the ideal of scientific progress. While many fans hailed the events of that world war, and even the first explosion of an atomic bomb, as a vindication of science fiction prophecy, others became discouraged about the prospects of a religion of science. Ray Bradbury, for example, who had been a member of Technocracy, Inc., during the 1930s and had accepted that group's combination of scientific humanism and authoritarian politics, was turned away from it by the rise of Hitler and later rejected technocracy through writing his novel *Fahrenheit 451* (1954).

The widening of science fiction's scope encouraged an increase of novels and short stories on religious themes. Some of these novels were deeply skeptical of scientific progress, such as James Blish's *A Case of Conscience* (1958), in which a priest-botanist tries to isolate an innocent planet from exploitation (and the destruction of earth morality that contact with an innocent planet would bring), and Walter M. Miller, Jr.'s *A Canticle for Leibowitz* (1959), in which the earth has been thrown into a new "Middle Ages" by the nuclear war at the end of the twentieth century. In general, the explosion of postwar novels and short stories on religious themes has declined to follow earlier paths and has felt much freer than before to explore traditional religious traditions, including Eastern religions.

One motif that has become especially prominent is the destruction of the world. As has been pointed out by several recent critics, such as David Ketterer, this apocalyptic theme is an old one and has been constantly present, especially in American literature. During the past decades, however, the constant threat of nuclear destruction has lent new strength to dystopian fears. Whereas H. G. Wells could write *The War of the Worlds* (novel, 1898) and yet retain full confidence in human history, recent events have seemed to many writers to point to an imminent Armageddon, though one for which man and not God is responsible.

The recent apocalyptic emphasis has caused one critic, Frederick Kreuziger, to conclude that apocalyptic literature and science fiction are allied genres, which arise in analogous sociological circumstances. He has argued that the genesis of such apocalyptic writings as the biblical "Revelation of John" is not unlike that of science fiction. In both cases a study of the historical origins points to a beleaguered cult producing a symbolic popular literature predicting by an arcane method events in the immediate future that would vindicate the group's existence. Although there are obvious dissimilarities between the two movements, this approach offers promising insights not only into the origins of science fiction,

but also into deeply problematic questions about the beginnings of biblical apocalyptic literature.

See also: Apocalypse, Science, Utopia.

Selected Bibliography

Ketterer, David. *New Worlds for Old: The Apocalyptic Imagination, Science Fiction,
and American Literature*. Garden City, N.Y.: Anchor Press, 1974.
Kreuziger, Frederick A. *Apocalypse and Science Fiction: A Dialectic of Religious and
Secular Soteriologies*. American Academy of Religion Academy Series 40. Chico,
Calif.: Scholars Press, 1982.

ANDREW J. BURGESS

RESPONSIBILITY

The term "responsibility" is derived from the Latin *respondere* meaning "to
respond," "to answer." Responsibility is the "state or fact of being responsible," that is, answerable, accountable *(to* someone, *for* something). The *Oxford
English Dictionary* cites the earliest use of the adjective "responsible" in 1643
in a passage referring to the king as being "responsible" to Parliament. Its
original usages, by and large, referred to the operation of political institutions.
It is principally in the nineteenth and twentieth centuries that its present usage
as an ethical phenomenon indicating duty, morality, and virtue has come into
currency. Responsibility in modern times is a multi-faceted term that is usually
qualified, for example, individual/personal, social, moral, and so on, as well as
being applied to such general areas as law, politics, ideology, and ethics. As a
literary theme it will be defined as (1) the awareness, recognition, interpretation,
and acceptance of a situation to which the individual or a group is antecedently
committed to respond or answer; (2) the response itself; and (3) the subsequent
acceptance of accountability for the answer or response rendered. In its more
restrictive usage it is often synonymous with duty or obligation in so far as it
functions within an accepted social structure, moral order, and system of values
and norms by which the response itself can be judged. As such, its nature is
more authoritative and fixed in definition. In its least restrictive and more recent
usage, it indicates a moral choice (often without the presence of a clearly defined
system of values) between or among alternatives that, more often than not, cause
a serious dilemma within the individual. Whatever qualification, that is, moral,
social, and so on, may be applied to the term, it is through one's responses that
the individual arrives at self-definition and is judged by others. While the idea
of responsibility with its multiple renderings, both by way of its presence and
absence, its affirmation and negation, might be observed in a sizable number of
literary works, the following survey will give illustrative background references
to the multiplicity of its meanings and will focus on those works where respon-

sibility as a theme is an essential element in the understanding of a central character or the work as a whole. Generally speaking, it is only in the twentieth century that responsibility becomes the central theme of a literary work.

Background in Antiquity and the Middle Ages

The beginnings of what will become the multiple definitions and perceptions of responsibility are present in early literature. Classical mythology often depicts man as subject to the whims of the gods, without free will, and therefore without responsibility. In the Greek concept of *moira* (Fate) man is destined before birth to certain actions in which any responsible choice on his part is purely negated. This is most evident in Sophocles' *Oidipous tyrannos* (*Oedipus Rex*, drama, c. 429 B.C.), since Oedipus is fated to kill his father and marry his mother.

On the other hand, the affirmation of choice is presented in Aeschylus' *Oresteia* trilogy (drama, 458 B.C.) when Orestes freely vows to Apollo to accept the responsibilities of his role as son and heir and to kill his mother Clytemnestra, a type of destiny that is ultimately purified and judged by Athena to be a responsible action. In Sophocles' *Antigonē* (drama, c. 441 B.C.) the protagonist, motivated by a sense of responsibility to her family and to her own concept of morality, desires to bury her brother Polynices and thus violate the custom of denying burial to traitors. Out of such action arises the conflict between responsibility in obedience to civil authority and to one's own moral responsibility. Euripides' *Alkēstis* (*Alcestis*, drama, 438 B.C.) shows the personal self-sacrifice of Alcestis to be a responsible decision when she chooses to die in place of her husband for personal and political reasons. In Aristophanes' *Lysistratē* (*Lysistrata*, drama, 411 B.C.), the women of Greece unite in the determination to abstain from sexual relations with their husbands until the latter bring the war to an end, a decision that transfers through free will social responsibility to a new controlling group.

Plato, in his *Apologia* (*Apology*, dialogue, 4th century B.C.), examines the problem of civil and criminal responsibility in his version of Socrates' defense when the latter is charged with not believing in God and with corrupting the youth of Athens. Aristotle examines the idea of accountability in *Ēthika Nikomacheia* (*Ethics*, 4th century B.C.) when he identifies voluntary actions as the only ones for which a person can be praised or blamed. They are actions which encompass circumstances that the individual is aware of and in which a choice is made.

With regard to social responsibility, there is normally the assumption of a community that poses the general bounds of responsibility underlying and justifying obligations spelled out in law, custom, moral, and religious contexts. The Bible expands on this idea in the commandment to love one's neighbor as exemplified in Cain's asking if he is his brother's keeper, Jesus' statement suggesting that the supreme demonstration of love is to lay down one's life for another, the parable of the Good Samaritan, among numerous others. The mythic parallel to the biblical account of the Samaritan's humane behavior is the Greek myth of the archer Philoctetes, banished because of a septic wound, who is nursed back to health by Neoptolemus (or Machaon).

In the medieval period responsibility in feudal society was perceived to be a mutual relationship with obligations placed on both the lord and his vassals. The medieval mind, for the most part, was primarily oriented toward a religious context wherein man responds to fulfilling his duties in this world since his worldly actions will determine his meriting immortality in the life hereafter. In epic poetry the hero is viewed as responsible for realizing his task and this idea is expanded in the *Poema de mío Cid* (*Poem of the Cid,* epic, c. 1140) when the Cid (Rodrigo Díaz de Vivar), exiled by the king, still remains the loyal vassal and complies with his obligations to his lord. This feudal responsibility is also seen in the *Chanson de Roland* (*Song of Roland,* epic, c. 1100). Roland also learns a lesson from his vain behavior and emerges with humility and a new sense of responsibility for the dead, which in the end makes him worthy of heaven.

The Renaissance

With the advent of the Renaissance, man becomes more aware of his role in this world and of himself as a designer and creator. The Protestant Reformation made him responsible for his own interpretation of the Bible. There is a growing consciousness of his finiteness and an interest in his control of the social order. The codes and norms of conduct are now determined more by a social rather than a spiritual orientation. Reflective of the spirit of the age, Pico della Mirandola in his *Oratio de hominis dignitate* (*Oration on the Dignity of Man,* essay, 1486) declares that man is free, self-reliant, and has the power of choice depending on his will to exercise it responsibly.

Perhaps the most telling example of this concept of responsible man is found in the Spanish Golden Age comedia wherein man's concept of honor is the governing principle of human conduct. While it is generally applied to nobility, all men participate in this phenomenon. In Lope de Vega's *Fuenteovejuna* (*The Sheep Well,* drama, 1619) the townspeople, sensitive to their own code of honor (in spite of their not belonging to the nobility), rise up in unison against the Comendador and slay him. They view their action as justifiable since the lord's reprehensible behavior was in direct conflict with his duties to the crown. When asked who killed the Comendador, the answer is "Fuenteovejuna." Their action thus converts into a case of the collective assumption of responsibility for the actions of a few and thus transforms personal responsibility into the moral responsibility of an entire community. The king judges the murder to be fitting and proper and, while the people are responsible for a crime, he pardons them since they were also responsible in defending their honor. Calderón de la Barca in *La vida es sueño* (*Life is a Dream,* drama, 1635), while examining the basic concept of life as a dream, poses the age-old conflict of free will versus predestination and shows how an individual (in the drama, the prince Segismundo) has free will and must act in a responsible manner, even if it is only in a dream.

Calderón viewed man as the maker of his own destiny (unlike Oedipus) who must act as a responsible individual. Shakespeare echoes this same idea in *Hamlet* (drama, c. 1600) and *King Lear* (drama, 1606). Hamlet feels responsibility for the "safety and health" of his kingdom and accepts his role. In contrast, one of King Lear's flaws lies in his belief that he can retain the privileges of kingship without the responsibilities; the drama shows that he must be held accountable.

The Age of Reason

The seventeenth- and eighteenth-century mind conceived of the world as based on a rational order and believed in the progress and perfectability of man so long as he worked within that given order. As a result, man was expected to behave in a reasonable way and to assume the responsibility of his role. The neoclassical literature of this age, which found its inspiration in the original classics, reflects well these views and values.

Pierre Corneille's dramas embody the concept of a life governed by a knowledge of what is right and a faith in free will. His heroes are aware of their responsibility to self and the matter of choice in confronting a hostile destiny. *Le Cid* (1637) and *Horace* (1640) examine the theme of contrary obligations, *Nicomède* (1651) is in essence a statement on the triumph of will, while *Œdipe* (1659) is an anti-Jansenist treatment of the question of free choice and responsibility. Jean Racine's dramatic works, on the other hand, reflect the influence of Jansenism. In *Phèdre* (*Phaedra*, 1677) the fated and flawed victim of her own passion (much like the protagonist of Euripides) is driven to ruin. Even though she is fully aware of her sins, she lacks nonetheless the will for responsible action and is unable to overcome them. On the other hand, *Andromaque* (1667) demonstrates that when reason governs the individual's behavior, one's force of will and sense of responsibility are superior to the extremes of one's passions.

Vicente García de la Huerta poses the conflict of love versus responsibility in *Raquel* (drama, 1778). When the king allows his heart to rule and thus fails to sustain the responsibilities invested in his position, he unwittingly causes a disruption in the social-moral order. Order is reestablished only when he recognizes that his first responsibility is to his people. *Lucrecia* (drama, 1763) by Nicolás Fernández de Moratín illustrates the idea that the mere status of one's nobility grants no immunity to responsible conduct, and once again the lesson to be learned derives from the belief that the individual must behave in a responsible manner that is in keeping with the standards of conduct promulgated by society.

The Nineteenth Century

In romantic literature the idea of responsibility as a characteristic of human behavior emanates out of a conscious self-reflection of man as an individual unfettered by social constraints. The subjectivity of the romantic spirit, which puts the individual first, shows an attitude that is based on emotion, not reason, and as such the norms of conduct are relegated to secondary importance. The idea that man is not in control of his destiny but is a victim of fate surfaces in many romantic works.

In this regard Friedrich Schiller's *Die Braut von Messina* (*The Bride from Messina,* drama, 1803) resembles a Greek tragedy in so far as the future destruction of a family is based on a prophecy. While the prophecy is fulfilled, Schiller makes it clear that it is not the gods or divine will that causes the tragedy, but rather it is man himself who is responsible for his doom. His very impulsiveness, passion, and human errors bring on his tragic end. *Prinz Friedrich von Homburg* (*Prince Frederick of Homburg,* drama, 1810) by Heinrich von Kleist adroitly explores the interplay between two conflicting value systems of responsible social behavior as represented by the prince and the elector. The ambivalence of interpretation as to what should be deemed responsible behavior is articulated through the duality of the individual (romantic) versus the public (Enlightenment) perceptions. The drama captures well the inherent problem of the exclusive assignment of responsibility and irresponsibility, since the conflict does not arise from a simple either-or situation.

The dramatist Georg Büchner, in *Dantons Tod* (*Danton's Death,* 1835), *Leonce und Lena* (1836), and *Woyzeck* (c. 1837), assumes the role of precursor of the literary school of naturalism as he focuses on man's predetermined destiny, his lack of free will, and the futility of his individual action. The drama *Woyzeck* is based on an actual murder case that examined the legal accountability and guilt of an accused who may be innocent by reason of insanity. The drama shows how the concept of accountability before the law is potentially absurd since it is based on the belief that rationality and normalcy can be sustained. In *El gran Galeoto* (drama, 1881) José Echegaray studies the problem of the assignment of responsibility (i.e., the individual versus society) when he explores how a false accusation of an adulterous love repeated as truth by society can result in its very realization. Tamayo y Baus in *Un drama nuevo* (*A New Drama,* 1867) asks who is ultimately responsible for the murder committed by an actor who portrays the stage role of a cuckold only to later discover that he is in effect portraying his own personal circumstances. Ibsen in *Et dukkehjem* (*A Doll's House,* drama, 1879) focuses on the individual's responsibility to himself, when Nora throws off the yoke of subjugation imposed by her selfish and egotistical husband. Her actions are a plea to society to accept those who, while not conforming to societal demands and expectations, are nonetheless socially responsible individuals with independent ideas. The title of Ibsen's *En folkfiende* (*An Enemy of the People,* drama, 1882) refers to the villagers' condemnation of the doctor whose reforms and responsible behavior conflict with their selfish interests. August Strindberg in *Brott och brott* (*There are Crimes and Crimes,* drama, 1899) shows that guilt and responsibility cannot be eradicated by the fact that a man is cleared of a crime by a court of law; there remains a higher judgment, man's own conscience.

Huck in Mark Twain's *The Adventures of Huckleberry Finn* (novel, 1884) grapples with the question of one's conscience, given his involvement in the escape of the slave Jim. His dilemma grows out of his responsibility to tell the truth and obey the dictates of society versus his loyalty to his friend. Dostoevsky's *Prestuplenie i nakazanie* (*Crime and Punishment,* novel, 1866) probes the inner psyche of a student who—believing himself above any standard of law or morality—first imagines and then executes a crime. His subsequent ordeal evolves from his attempt to escape, his confused state of mind, his expiation, and his final redemption. In *Brat'ia Karamazovy* (*The Brothers Karamazov,* novel, 1880), Dostoevsky pursues further the implication of defining and accepting responsibility. Through his portrayal of Dmitri and Ivan, although innocent of the actual crime, the novelist studies the broader application of responsibility in its all-encompassing role in the life of the individual. We are all responsible for what happens in the world.

Giuseppe Mazzini, in his essay *Dei doveri dell'uomo* (*On the Duties of Man,* 1858), indicates that the basic rights of man can mean nothing to humanity unless humanity becomes aware of the duties and responsibilities that those rights entail. John Stuart Mill, in his essay *On Liberty* (1859), deals with the nature, limits, and responsibilities of freedom, blending idealism with practicality.

In the second half of the nineteenth century consciousness of society emerges and there is an attempt to present it with objectivity and in detail. This realism is most abundantly present in fiction, specifically in the works of Dickens, Balzac, Pérez Galdós, Tolstoy, Maupassant, Hardy, Zola, to name but a few. With the increasing emphasis on scientific methods, the end of the century saw the development of the literary school of naturalism. Based on scientific theory as applied to literature, it proposes that man is a product of his heredity and environment and thus negates, in effect, the idea of free will and responsibility This movement is most apparent in the works of the French novelist Emile Zola in his Rougon-Macquart series of novels, among which stand out *L'assommoir* (*The Dram-Shop,* 1877), *Nana* (1880), and *Germinal* (1885). Thomas Hardy, in *Jude the Obscure* (novel, 1896), as well as in *Tess of the D'Urbervilles* (novel, 1891), depicts in the naturalist view the losing struggle on the part of man against the pressures of natural and social forces.

The Twentieth Century

In many ways, the currents seen in the previous century continue to be prominent in the twentieth, that is, naturalism, responsibility to social norms, and so on. An example of American naturalism is Theodore Dreiser's *An American Tragedy* (novel, 1925). Based on an actual case, the novel traces the life of a murderer from boyhood to the electric chair and shows how an unfortunate early environment was responsible for his weak character.

Personal responsibility, that is, commitment to self-imposed goals and the realization of psychic growth, weaves itself into a great quantity of twentieth-century literature. Franz Kafka uses the context of legal responsibility in *Der Prozess* (*The Trial,* novel, 1925) as a metaphor for the inner trial of conscience. K. is guilty of an unauthentic existence, of the failure to realize self and his potentiality. The novel demonstrates that moral responsibility is a continual challenge; no one is ever completely innocent—to plead "innocence" is an evasion and a self-righteous denial of one's moral nature. Bernard Malamud's *The Assistant* (novel, 1957) treats the idea of personal commitment wherein a thief is driven by guilt to aid an impoverished grocer. When the latter dies, the assistant assumes the role of the grocer, takes on the responsibility for the family, and thereby tries to find his own sense of being through the image of another. Brian Moore in *The Emperor of Ice-Cream* (novel, 1965) presents the maturing of the protagonist's conscience when he discovers that he has to assume responsibility to himself and others and to subordinate the internal "voices" that had previously influenced his life.

Closely related and another common denominator in twentieth-century literature is the idea of collective responsibility, in which man acknowledges his relation to others. The isolation, dehumanization, and narcissism of contemporary man cause him to reflect upon his interrelatedness with others. In Alfred Döblin's *Hamlet oder die lange Nacht nimmt ein Ende (Hamlet or the Long Night Comes to an End,* novel, 1956) a young man, much like Hamlet, returns from the war in search of truth. The central issue of whether man is a free agent responsible for his actions or a puppet manipulated by supra-individual powers is expressly debated throughout the novel. The protagonist, in achieving his own positive psychic growth, discovers that men can reciprocally save each other. The protagonist of Döblin's *Berlin Alexanderplatz* (novel, 1929), after a life of egocentric behavior in which he attempts to survive alone in the world, discovers the need for solidarity with others. In Albert Camus' *La peste (The Plague,* novel, 1947) man becomes aware that he shares a basic oneness with his fellow men as a part of a collective destiny. *La hoja roja (The Red Sheet of Paper,* novel, 1959) by Miguel Delibes notes the need for responsibility and concern for humanity by focusing on society's rejection of the aged.

The existential dilemma of contemporary man forms a major literary focus that is present in numerous works of this century. For the most part, its central thesis relies upon the idea that man is what he makes of himself; he is neither predestined nor predetermined by God, biology, or society. Rather he has a free will and the responsibility to use that will to make choices. This matter of choice and the difficulties in making them are apparent in Graham Greene's *The Quiet American* (novel, 1955). An ethical dilemma of responsibility is presented when Fowler comes to realize that he must become involved and assume moral responsibility. His choice involves the betrayal and murder of the idealist Pyle in order to prevent further violence and suffering. While Fowler is destined to carry the burden of guilt because of his choice, the essential lesson learned is that man must make choices, however difficult or onerous they may be, if he is to remain human. Miguel de Unamuno's *San Manuel Bueno, Mártir (St. Manuel Bueno, Martyr,* novel, 1933) displays the committed responsibility of a disbelieving priest who chooses to fulfill his role as the spiritual caretaker of his parishioners. Greene's *The Power and the Glory* (novel, 1940) echoes a similar aspect of responsibility when his whiskey priest cowardly flees from his sacerdotal responsibility in the face of the government's anti-clerical persecution during the Mexican Revolution. However, confronted ultimately by an overwhelming sense of humanity, he returns to his religious responsibilities, even though he knows it will mean his eventual execution. In Albert Camus's *La chute* (*The Fall*, novel, 1956), a lawyer's failure to come to a stranger's aid turns out to be only the objective symbol of a life that is an inward mockery of itself. The protagonist's denial of his responsibility to others becomes an internal self-betrayal and his symbolic "fall" represents an understanding and awareness of truth and man's freedom founded in an acknowledgment of one's responsibility. *L'étranger* (*The Stranger*, novel, 1942), also by Camus, presents the trial of the forlorn and existential outsider Meursault from whose actions we discover that in order to have a measure of happiness, man must be aware of his freedom and must accept total responsibility for all his actions.

While responsibility surfaces as an ancilliary theme and/or as an underlying issue throughout the twentieth century, there are numerous works in which we can perceive it as a central theme encompassing its multiple ramifications (legal, moral, social, etc.) with an in-depth examination of the dilemmas involved. This is especially apparent in recent literature, which reflects a society of fragmented value systems, changing norms, multiple and conflicting authorities, and at times an absurdist world view. Alvin Toffler's works *Future Shock* (1970) and *The Third Wave* (1980) identify such issues that face contemporary man. This is even apparent in such popular genres as the detective novel. For example, Georges Simenon in *Maigret hésite* (*Maigret Hesitates,* novel, 1969) reexamines legal accountability in determining one's responsibility for a crime. The central axis of the novel is the legal statute: "If the person charged with the commission of a felony or misdemeanor was then insane or acted by absolute necessity, no offense has been committed."

Peter Weiss's *Die Ermittlung* (*The Investigation,* drama, 1965) is a documentary drama that inquires into the war crimes committed in the Nazi concentration camps. The audience sits in judgment and must determine to what extent moral responsibility played in the guilt or innocence of the accused, who vigorously contend that they were simply obeying orders or knew nothing about the perpetrated atrocities. The work investigates collective guilt-responsibility and reports on the bestial inhumanity of man toward man that belies his sense of responsible action in response to the needs of others. Rolf Hochhuth's drama *Der Stellvertreter* (*The Deputy,* 1963) questions the lack of action on the part of the Papacy during the Nazi persecution of the Jews, and echoes the same concerns advanced by Weiss. The work demonstrates the surrender of man's humanity when he chooses not to respond to the basic human needs of his fellowman.

Heinar Kipphardt's *In der Sache J. Robert Oppenheimer* (*In the Matter of J. Robert Oppenheimer,* 1964) is a documentary drama based on the 1954 proceedings instituted against the nuclear physicist and father of the atomic bomb by the U.S. Atomic Energy Commission. At the heart of the inquiry stood the question of his role, motives, and loyalties in the delay of the development of the hydrogen bomb. The work explores the conflicts inherent in the scientist's responsibility to his profession and to his country as well as his responsibility to himself as an individual in respect to his own moral principles. *Die Physiker* (*The Physicists*, drama, 1962), by Friedrich Dürrenmatt, postulates that nothing in the twentieth century can depend on the responsibility of one individual; it has to be a collective responsibility. The issue put forth is that man must be aware of his responsibility (personal, professional, and moral) for the potential destruction of the world through the use of scientific knowledge in the creation of the bomb. The physicist Möbius feigns madness and even goes so far as to murder in order to preserve the scientific secrets and thereby save the world from total destruction. He inevitably fails in the end since he, along with his companions, has been manipulated by the Fräulein Doktor who steals and sells the secrets.

In "Slucha ̆ na stantŝii Krechetovka" ("An Incident at Krechetovka Station," short story, 1963), by Alexander Solzhenitsyn, a devoted soldier during the war suspects another soldier of being a potential spy and turns him over to the KGB. In spite of having properly performed his duty, he is troubled by his moral responsibility for the certain death of an innocent man, should his suspicions prove to be false. Vladimir Tendryakov's short story "Sud" ("The Trial," 1961) examines the burden of responsibility and the trial of conscience that the protagonist inflicts upon himself as he seeks to determine what choices can be made in ascribing guilt for the accidental shooting of a young man during a nighttime bear hunt. The assignment and shirking of responsibility, the lies, and the erroneous assumptions about the nature of man make this work probably the most complete examination of the theme in its multiple definitions.

Selected Bibliography

Gallaway, Francis. *Reason, Rule and Revolt in English Classicism*. 1940. Lexington: University Press of Kentucky, 1966.

Goldman, Lucien. *Toward a Sociology of the Novel*. London: Tavistock, 1975.

La France, Marston, ed. *Patterns of Commitment in American Literature*. Toronto: University. of Toronto Press, 1967.

Reck, Rima Drell. *Literature and Responsibility: The French Novelist in the Twentieth Century*. Baton Rouge: Louisiana State University Press, 1969.

ELIZABETH S. ROGERS

RETREAT

The world being a hardy place, the temptation is strong in some persons to isolate or insulate themselves. Such a retreat is envisioned in terms either of life style—as a shift from activism and deeds to passivity and contemplation—or of locale—as a move from the activism, temptations, distractions, and dangers of the town to the quiescence, simplicity, and security of the country. Whether the change constitutes a "retreat" *to* an ultimate timeless reality from worldly illusion or an "escape" *from* harsh reality is, of course, a matter of assumptions, perspective, values. Literary works dramatize not only the temptation to "drop out" but also the consequent price to be paid by, or the impossibility of, suppressing one side of the multifarious human personality.

Antiquity

In the Bible, life begins in an ideal place. As a result of the Fall, man is ejected from it into turmoil. The messianic dream, notably the explicit language on a new earth and new heaven in the closing pages of Revelation, offers a return to what has now become a permanent retreat from the vanity and flux of this life, of history. But the intervening years—which constitute history—require activism, according to Judaic and Christian traditions deriving from the Bible. Man must worship God and aid his fellow man. Mere reflection is not enough. For when the Israelites were given the Law, they responded, "We will do and obey," which rabbinic lore interprets as meaning that first in priority and chronology is action and only then comes reflection and understanding. Yet both traditions also developed a limited contemplative ideal; one studies God's works and words for the sake of a better appreciation of the marvels He has wrought, for the sake of a better activism, a more informed worship. Does not the Scripture present a retreat as a temporary phase necessary for the harnessing of resources, for stock-taking, for finding one's spiritual depths? Hence Moses spent forty days atop Mt. Sinai (receiving the Ten Commandments) and Jesus spent forty days in the wilderness (being tempted by Satan). For some, especially in Catholicism, the means came close to becoming the end; hence the monastic orders, the vows of silence, the emphasis on contemplation.

In Homer's epic poem *Ilias* (*Iliad,* c. 8th century B.C.), Achilles, when young, was offered the choice of dying after a short life of achievement and glory or living long in obscurity. In this, the earliest version of the active versus contemplative motif, he chose the former. (In the *Odysseia* [*Odyssey,* epic poem, 8th century B.C.] he came to regret it—too late.) Yet as he approached the climax of his career, a retreat of sorts was forced on him. Feeling himself slighted by Agamemnon, he painfully withdrew himself from the one thing he enjoyed above all others, making war. He now watched the battle from afar with envious eyes or he sang songs "of men's fame." Unable to do the daring deeds that established his fame, he could but sing of others doing them, and poetry and song were a form of contemplation, of vicarious activism. This retreat is, to be sure, undertaken not for its own sake but in order to exact revenge; somewhere down the line he would be returning to his vocation, albeit on his terms, not anyone else's. And when he did so, he was carried by events into the first example in the West of philosophic reflections. Priam, trying to ransom Hector's body by shrewdly and poignantly referring to Achilles' own besieged father, precipitated in Achilles a transcendent moment, in which the distinction between Greek and Trojan fell away and in which he shared with his enemy the realization of the common human heritage of suffering and mortality. This was a mere interlude in an activist life, and the momentary insight had no practical consequences other than the return of Hector's body; the war would resume, and Achilles would rampage again. This rare moment of nonfunctional contemplation of the human condition and of the reality of death—by one normally given to the active life, to the nearly mindless infliction of suffering and death—is close to what Joyce was to call an epiphany.

In Homer's *Odyssey,* images of retreat recur with great frequency, understandably so in the context of a story of the wanderings and sufferings of the hero. The Lotus Eaters are drug addicts who have permanently retired from the rat race to a life of ease. Circe offers a similar escape to men who are willing to undergo the humiliation of metamorphosis into swine. The Sirens make available a retreat to esthetic beauty (in aural form); here the price is not passivity or bestiality but outright destruction. Most lifelike, Helen and Menelaus live now in a godlike serenity, one helped along by a potion, an upper-class form of drug taking or lotus eating. With their ease and elegance, they embody the goal of most people's aspirations. Yet theirs is a retreat that, if obtained, dehumanizes us, as is seen by the way it contrasts with the heroic endeavors of Odysseus and of his son Telemachus, who visits the couple. Put another way, Helen and Menelaus, having been to the big city—Troy—and having experienced all the conflict which that journey involved (nothing less than a ten-year world war), have retired to their rural homestead. Lastly, Calypso offers—and for a year Odysseus accepts—the sexuality of Circe as well as the immortality of the Spartan couple but at the cost of one's being cut off from struggle and achievement, family and home, world and reputation, status and identity.

Furthermore, if Achilles has his pause for reflection amid activism, so does Odysseus. In retelling his adventures, he acknowledges the errors he committed with Polyphemus. And the analogy Homer uses to describe Odysseus' weeping over the story of the fall of Troy (i.e., the tears of the wife of a slain warrior) suggests that, like Achilles, Odysseus (though hardly able to articulate it) is temporarily seeing through the enmities and tribalisms of the moment to the lot of grief and death for all combatants.

In Aeschylus' *Oresteia* (trilogy of plays, 458 B.C.), there is the sense that violence must have an end. Hence at the close of the *Agamemnōn* (458 B.C.), Clytemnestra, breaking up the contention between Aegisthus and the chorus of townspeople, thinks that after all the dislocations of the past decade the good times are at long last here. It is a delusion, and Orestes, who by killing her proves it to be that, does not even have that delusion. In the same way, in Sophocles' *Oidipous tyrannos (Oedipus Rex,* c. 429 B.C.), young Oedipus' flight from Corinth is a futile attempt to retreat from his destiny. (That the very attempt to evade the oracle by withdrawal only leads to its fulfillment is the theme also of the story of Croesus in Herodotus' *Historia* [*History,* 5th century B.C.]). When he then solved the riddle, destroyed the Sphinx, and entered into a glorious reign at Thebes, he little realized that this also constituted an interlude between storms and that a bigger riddle would have to be solved. In the *Oidipous epi Kolōnō* (*Oedipus at Colonus,* play, c. 406 B.C.), he is in a phase of contemplation and passivity as a blinded old exile, before coming upon, as a result of a mysterious access of holiness, one last spurt of activism prior to his death. The hero of the *Philoktētēs* (*Philoctetes,* play, 409 B.C.), because of his festering incurable wound and the consequent rejection of him by the Greek army, cleaves to the isolation of a permanent hospital stay on an uninhabited isle in the face of attempts to draw him back into the world of treachery, ruthlessness, and selfishness. Sophocles' *Aias* (*Ajax,* play, c. 441 B.C.) has as hero someone who, losing the contest with Odysseus for the right to Achilles' armor, takes the permanent form of retreat known as suicide.

The protagonist of Euripides' *Hippolytos* (*Hippolytus,* play, 428 B.C.) chooses Artemis and the life of hunting over Aphrodite and the life of love. His retreat from one part of the psyche and one of the human imperatives costs him his life at the hand of a vindictive Aphrodite. In *Mēdeia* (*Medea,* play, 431 B.C.) Jason's new marriage is a would-be retreat from exotic adventures into a life of power and ease, into something like the social security of Helen and Menelaus, but the exotic past, represented by the first wife, has its demands to make. In short, Hippolytus turned his back on a side of himself, Jason on his own past. Yet a third version of the theme appears in Euripides' *Bakchai* (*The Bacchants,* play, c. 405 B.C.), in which Pentheus' escape into tradition, law, and order is shattered by an upsurge of instinctive, nonrational, nontraditional, contagious currents.

The first nonmythic presentation of a retreat from the turbulence and litigiousness of the metropolis (Athens) to a quiet place in the country is in Aristophanes' *Ornithes* (*The Birds,* play, 414 B.C.). The escape is led significantly enough by those denizens of the pastoral world, the birds. The utopia established in their realm in the sky, however, soon attracts all the parasites and troublemakers one thought to have left behind; no retreat is possible for long. The fantasy of an intellectual retreat from the rambunctious Athenian democracy into an orderly rational society built on the principle of Justice is also offered by Plato's *Politeia* (*The Republic,* dialogue, c. 380 B.C.). This republic is avowedly unattainable but, like the North Star, can serve as a beacon for existing ones to navigate by. Eradicating many familiar problems, it, like the comic cloudcuckooland and the *Odyssey*'s Sparta, is a fantasy of how life could be and, given human nature, perhaps fortunately isn't. In that work, Plato anticipated the Christian transvaluation of the natural and supernatural when he tells the parable of the Cave, the gist of which is the paradox that the cinemalike Cave in which most of mankind dwells turns out to be a false retreat into the material and ephemeral. Plato also is the first to overtly confront the issue of the active versus the contemplative life. His notion of the necessity of a philosopher-king for an ideal republic suggests that contemplation ultimately must serve activism. The reverse conclusion appears to be drawn in his theory of knowledge (involving the ladder of love) as well as by Aristotle in the *Ēthika Nikomacheia* (*Ethics,* 4th century B.C.) and, more conclusively, by Lucretius (*De rerum natura* [*On the Nature of Things,* 1st century B.C.]) who finds an inner, intellectual retreat from the superstition and stupidity all around him by contemplating the ultimate reality, which is not interfering gods but atoms in motion.

In what has been called a "failure of nerve," many thinkers of later antiquity— Epicurus, Plotinus and the Neoplatonists—opted for the contemplative. Epicurus made it the center of his philosophy. Though committed in principle to pleasure, he, because of a dour view as to its availability and of what might be called the hangover principle—that every pleasure is surrounded by a host of woes— counseled a life of retreat (like his own) to one's garden, to a spare diet, shrunken ambitions, and simple life style. The Stoics, by contrast, counseled an outer activism and an inner withdrawal of the emotions. Not where one is or what one does but the state of mind one does it with determines whether one is in a contemplative retreat or an activist involvement. Horace (65–8 B.C.) likewise suggests that retreat is not achievable by physical means, for whatever place one flees to one is under the same sky. In other poems he subscribes rather more to the Epicurean ideal, to the contraction of expectation, the cultivation of one's garden and moderately sized manor. He also retells the old fable of the country mouse visiting the town mouse, a classic dramatization of the town versus country debate. The visitor, at first impressed by the town mouse's lavish diet, has second thoughts on seeing its cousin's anxieties. That debate is at the heart of Terence's *Adelphi* (play, 160 B.C.), in which each of a pair of brothers raises a son, the city one doing so permissively, the country one rigidly; judging from the results, the urban life style is superior.

The country life is idealized in the pastoral tradition, a genre of poems written by refined, urbane court poets, beginning with Theocritus (*Eidylla* [*The Idylls,* c. 270 B.C]) and continued by Virgil, among others. The temptation to retreat from an arduous destiny overtakes the hero of Virgil's *Aeneis* (*Aeneid,* epic poem, 19 B.C.) twice. First, when Troy is falling, he would prefer to go down fighting, like one of those Homeric individualists overcome by *amor fati* or by self-glorification. Then, when he is apparently overcome by a different *amor* (or by lethargy) at the hands of a Calypso-like Dido, the gods themselves (not just the sailors, as in the case of Odysseus) must return the hero to activism. The cave in which the love affair with Dido is first consummated now turns out to be not an idyllic place but rather something resembling the cave that in Plato's parable stood for illusion.

The Middle Ages and the Renaissance

The remark in St. Augustine's *Confessiones* (*Confessions,* c. 397–400) that it is more important to find God and leave questions unanswered than vice versa is, like "we will do and obey," a philosophically important gesture in the direction of the active life. The saint's description of the years of errancy in the toils of Platonism and heretical Christian sects implies, with the wisdom of hindsight, that he had sought in folly and illusion a retreat from confrontation with the Truth. Early medieval epics like *Beowulf* (c. 8th century) and *La Chanson de Roland* (*The Song of Roland*, c. 1100) are staunchly activist, containing no temptations by images of ease nor contemplation, even on the part of Bishop Turpin. Wolfram von Eschenbach's *Parzival* (epic poem, c. 1210) begins as the young father of the hero is killed in combat (as is the case also with Tristan's father). The wife is so intent on preventing history from repeating itself that she brings up the lad in isolation in the forest, ignorant of the knightly vocation. The attempt to shelter him breaks down, however, when some knights ride by on a hunt and captivate the lad's imagination.

With the rise of the Courtly Love Tradition, a new sense of retreat emerges, that from the responsibilities of religion and chivalry into love. In *Sir Gawain and the Green Knight* (romance, c. 1370), the hero, on the way to keeping his compact and fulfilling his chivalric duty, rests up for his ordeal. Perhaps because even that brief respite, that abstention from the ardors of aristocratic hunting, is dangerous, he, like the biblical Joseph or the mythical Hippolytus, must put aside an offer of adultery. In Gottfried von Strassburg's *Tristan* (romance, c. 1210), the lovers in fact leave society for a retreat in a cave in the midst of nature. Only there can their love flourish, without the luxuries but also without the back-biting and tensions that civilization so well provides. There, they are propelled—she out of her wifely, queenly responsibilities, he out of his chivalric ones—into a contemplative life that is physical rather than cerebral, emotional rather than intellectual, under the aspect of Venus rather than of Saturn. The idyll cannot last, however, and the cave seems to be like Plato's and Aeneas'— except that Gottfried, undermining Plato's and Virgil's metaphysical certitudes, implicitly asks, which is real, the cave of love or the turbulence of society? Modeled on this tale is the Lancelot-Guinevere retreat in Malory's *Morte d'Arthur* (prose romance, c. 1469) and the many Continental works it is based on.

In Dante's epic poem *La divina commedia* (*The Divine Comedy*, c. 1320), a moral retreat into apathy or neutrality is called ''il gran rifiuto'' (''the great refusal'') and earns consignment to hell. Dante himself is rebuked by Beatrice for having turned aside from her to other things—other loves? promiscuous sex? secular philosophy? all three?—before being, like Aeneas, jolted out of his escapism by intervention from on high. Yet a balance is achieved near the end of the *Purgatorio* (*Purgatory*), in the pilgrim's dream of Leah and Rachel, the one standing (along with Matilda) for the active life and the other, eyes always on a mirror, standing (along with Beatrice) for the contemplative life. The latter appears to be superior, as the *Paradiso* (*Paradise*) contains various contemplative saints who had on earth made their retreat from worldly matters. If the *Inferno* (*Hell*) and the *Purgatorio* are mirrors of the world as a place of frenzied activity, the *Paradiso* is the grandest literary vision of the ideal of the reflective life, the goal of all devout people, the locale where they contemplate God for eternity. The moments of contemplation achieved on earth are but microcosms or ''coming attractions'' of that finality.

In Boccaccio's *Il decamerone* (*Decameron,* novellas, c. 1350), a group of aristocratic young men and women retreat from Florence during the Black Plague and, in a countryside manor, pass the time telling pleasant stories that often constitute a parallel retreat or escape from Christian morality. Many of the clerics in the *Canterbury Tales* (c. 1380–1400) have retreated from their religious vocation, not into contemplation but into an active life of misbehavior. The monk, for instance, exchanges monastic responsibilities for a life of venery, finery, and sloth. More's *Utopia* (political romance, 1516) is, like Plato's *Republic,* an intellectual retreat into society as it might be, were man rational. The character Raphael, seeing present society as hopelessly corrupt, opts for a "dropping out" into reflection, while More favors doing one's little to improve conditions. The latter's optimism or activism also inspires Rabelais (*Gargantua et Pantagruel* [*Gargantua and Pantagruel,* novels, 1532–1564), who, in setting forth his all-inclusive educational plan, proclaims its goal to be readying for action and leadership "against the attacks of evil doers." Yet the Abbey of Thélème is a retreat to a coeducational communal life of beauty and pleasure (modeled on the tableau at the beginning of the *Decameron* of young Florentine men and women together), the antithesis of monastic sequestration, segregation, austerity, and other-worldliness. If Castiglione's *Il cortegiano* (*The Courtier,* treatise, 1528) is clearly oriented toward action and service rather than contemplation, Montaigne (*Essais* [*Essays,* 1580–1588]) just as clearly chose the reflective life. At a relatively early age, he withdrew from politics and retreated to his library in a tower. He saw little to choose from between the Catholic and Protestant sides in the contemporary civil war. Everything about his essays conveys the sense of a man savoring his leisure and insulation (even from wife and child), loving to contemplate from a distance the wisdom of thinkers and the actions of men. The religious and methodical version of retreat, for the sake of a willed attachment to God rather than a temperamental detachment from the world, finds its *locus classicus* in Ignatius of Loyola's *Ejercicios espirituales* (*Spiritual Exercises,* 1548).

The theme (in its secular form) is prominent in Shakespeare's plays. The attempt of Beatrice and Benedict to insulate themselves from love is soon undermined. The king and his courtiers in *Love's Labour's Lost* (c. 1594) take monastic vows with the intent of devoting themselves to three years of study in a quasi-Platonic academy. The hero Berowne predicts the futility of the step, and his wisdom quickly becomes apparent. The mere appearance of some young ladies propels the initiates back into the world. Love, instead of being the retreat it is in *Tristan,* is here presented as an active part—thanks, paradoxically, to the Courtly Love Tradition itself—of what one must do to be human and fulfilled. On the other hand, in *Antony and Cleopatra* (c. 1607), politics represents the active life and love the contemplative; Alexandria, a realm of timeless, lotus-eating pleasure, contrasts with busy, mutable imperial Rome. Antony's periodic amatory retreats with Cleopatra come at the expense of his participation in the running of the vast empire, and the flouted active life takes its revenge.

In *As You Like It* (c. 1599), the deposed good duke and the other decent people exiled by the bad duke and the predatory brother find their peace in nature and in contemplation, "books in running brooks ... and good in everything." When the new regime collapses, however, all concerned make an indecently hasty return to society. King Lear's choosing the wilderness rather than submission to the two malign daughters parallels the choices of Parzival's mother, of Tristan and Iseult, of the good duke. Nature, even with storm or cold, cannot match in severity human ingratitude and treachery. One ruler's (Richard II) evasion of responsibility during his reign results in a forced retreat and contemplation of his errors. Such an unhappy outcome is prevented by another ruler, who wittingly chooses his retreat *before* he comes to power. Prince Hal's (*Henry IV*, 1597, 1600) time spent in the Boar's Head tavern is an immersion in levity, bonhomie, and irresponsibility. It must end with an acceptance of his destiny, even a turning against his boon companions, whom he has avowedly in the past made politic use of. But without this retreat—the play suggests—he would be the poorer as king, the lesser as man, rather more like his frigid brother John and his unimaginative father Henry IV. Reality must be reached circuitously. So too, if Hamlet in mourning performs the gestures of retreat, his "madness" after the ghost's revelations is a serious retreat from the norms of the court, undertaken in the service of detection and action. And in *Measure for Measure* (1603–1604) the duke ostensibly goes into a retreat but in fact remains on the scene in order to get a better look at the workings of his duchy. His assuming the guise of a monk is symbolical, contemplation being ultimately in the service of activism.

Brutus, in *Julius Caesar* (c. 1599), is an intellectual and contemplative man undone by his lack of the activist's decisiveness and intuitions about others. More fortunate or effective is Prospero in the *Tempest* (1611). Also an ineffectual contemplative at first, he, like the duke in *As You Like It,* is deposed and exiled. But his fifteen-year-long stay on an uninhabited magic island enables him to put reflection to practical uses. Together with the books he brought with him, it proffers mastery over nature, which in turn facilitates the eventual taking (and renunciation) of revenge. As in many works, the retreat is presented as a necessary stage in the marshalling of new powers, not as a permanent point of stasis. In *Pericles* (1609), *Cymbeline* (1610), and the *Winter's Tale* (1611), young children of the royal blood find themselves in humble surroundings. It is a form of retreat that is forced on them by the errors of their elders, in which their innocence is maintained, and from which they return to the realm of activism proper to them and to their parents.

An ominous prophecy in Calderon's play *La vida es sueño* (*Life Is a Dream,* 1635) makes a king place his newborn son in a tower to be brought up in isolation. Attempts years later to test the prince via a simulated dream experience first validates the prophecy and then brings him finally to his rightful throne. Did the enforced retreat—the attempt to evade the prophecy—make the prince as beastly as was prophesied (so the prince asserts), or did it paradoxically help make him a true prince? The story makes contact here not only with that of Parzival but also with Oedipus and Croesus.

The Neoclassical to the Modern Era

Molière's *L'école des femmes* (*The School for Wives*, play, 1662) is a variant of the *Parzival* and *Sueño* motif. Having seen too many misbehaving wives, Arnolphe proposes to raise his future wife himself from a tender age and to keep her locked up in his attic. But, as in *Love's Labour's Lost*, nature takes its revenge; refused entry through the front door, it comes in through the rear door, for the girl falls in love with a young man she sees by chance. Similarly Orgon (*Tartuffe*, play, 1664) takes refuge in piety but finds that in bringing a pious man into his family he has nursed a serpent in his bosom. There is no retreat or insulation from the corrosive forces of life, at least not in society, and so Alceste (*Le misanthrope* [*The Misanthropist*, play, 1666]), having failed to affect the imperfect world with his noble principles, retreats to the wilderness where he at least can be himself.

The newly created first couple in Milton's epic poem *Paradise Lost* (1667) settles into a prehistorical retreat, a countrified place made for reflection, admiration, and worship. Their misstep means ejection from all this into history, into the city, into the ambiguous benefits of the postlapsarian active life. The Jesus of the epic poem *Paradise Regained* (1671) goes into a retreat in the wilderness for forty days in order to meditate and find himself. He finds instead Satan and temptation, but from this encounter in the midst of a retreat emerges a sense of his identity and destiny. In *Samson Agonistes* (dramatic poem, 1671), the retreat is near the end of the tale rather than at the beginning. After a lifetime of beating Philistines, the hero is plunged, because of uxoriousness, into a retreat quite different from Adam and Eve's: imprisoned, blinded, beaten, dejected, self-hating, alienated from God and his own people, ready to give up God's fight (as, judging from Sonnet 19, was Milton himself, blinded and isolated during the hostile Restoration). He soon intuits that the introspective retreat is a mere halting place, a step back before two large ones forward, a period of stock taking (which constitutes the body of the play) before the climax to the life of activism.

The Epicurean retreat into the garden is a current in the seventeenth-century lyric. If Donne in a poem like "The Canonization" (1635) had suggested that lovers are a world unto themselves, far from the quotidian concerns of others, and if the citified philanderer Dorimant (Etherege's *Man of Mode*, play, 1676) is redeemed by his love for a witty young heiress with the innocence of the country on her, Cowley's and Marvell's poems on gardens deal with escape from eros as well as from activism and seek pure contemplation as an end in itself or as an initiator (in Marvell) of platonic flight to the empyrean.

Addison begins the *Spectator* (essays, 1711–1712) series by presenting himself as a silent wanderer and observer in London: "Thus I live in the World, rather as a Spectator of Mankind, than as one of the species." He is a speculative "looker on," "without ever medling with any practical part." Not at all reflective is Pope's Belinda (*The Rape of the Lock,* poem, 1712), blithely immersed in the specious social whirl of her leisured class until the day when fun and games turn, as often happens, serious. Now lacking one lock of hair—symbolic of her innocence and perhaps her virginity—she articulates the great dilemma of town versus country: "Oh, had I rather unadmired remained / In some lone isle, or distant northern land." She thinks, no doubt erroneously, that the alternative in this social version of the Achillean choice would have contented her more.

In Fielding's *Tom Jones* (novel, 1749), Voltaire's *Candide* (novel, 1759), and Johnson's *Rasselas* (novel, 1759), the hero, like Adam or Parzival, grows up in an ideal environment, and the story is of his making his way through the tortuous world once he finds himself ejected from this womb- or nurserylike retreat. Candide's thorough immersion in life results in a conscious choice of the Epicurean credo, "one must cultivate one's garden," leaving politics and the meaning of life—those two key foci of energetic response—to others not yet disenchanted. For Rousseau (*Confessions,* 1781–1788) retreat to an island and walks in the countryside or near a lake are the summit of experience. In this romantic version of the town versus country debate, Paris is a den of iniquity and intrigue, but outside it one can live in accord with nature. Burns ("The Cotter's Saturday Night," poem, 1795) finds authentic piety in the peasant hut rather than in the lavish city church filled with elegant worshippers. Even more outspoken is the poet Wordsworth ("Tintern Abbey," 1798 and *The Prelude,* 1799–1805). Raised in the bosom of nature, he feels it to have nurtured in him everything humane and worth living for. The time in the city is not without its attractions (the "Westminster Bridge" sonnet, 1802), but the urban life's obsessive money making (the "Getting and spending" sonnet, 1806) and jaded tastes (Preface to the *Lyrical Ballads,* 1800) make a return to nature necessary if one is to retain one's humanity. Alceste's flight (in Molière) to the wilderness was a retreat from civilization to brutishness, a laughable surrender of humanity, but for Rousseau and Wordsworth, as for Pushkin (*Evgeniĭ Onegin* [*Eugene Onegin,* novel, 1823–1831]), Thoreau (*Walden,* essays, 1854) and Twain (*Huckleberry Finn,* novel, 1884), such a retreat is from artificiality to self-discovery and human fulfillment. Goethe's Faust (play, 1808), on the other hand, while responsive to the beauties of nature, opts for a life of striving, experience, and creation rather than of content, inertia, and ease—for activism rather than contemplation.

Mme Bovary's (novel, 1856) escape from provincial boredom, bourgeois conventionality, and a dull marriage is into adultery and promiscuity, an internal, emotional retreat rather than a movement to another locale. Tolstoy's Anna Karenina (novel, 1877) makes a similar retreat into a protracted adulterous love affair. Though Bazarov (Turgenev's *Otĭsy i deti* [*Fathers and Children,* novel, 1862]), by contrast, believes, like the ancient Greeks, that love is a madness or something nonsensical, he finds that even he, like such abjurers of love as Hippolytus, the King of Navarre, Beatrice and Benedick, is overtaken by it. A more successful escape from modern life is worked out by the lawyer's clerk Wemmick (Dickens' *Great Expectations,* novel, 1860–1861), who lives in a castlelike home with a moat and a drawbridge. He has been able to make a retreat within the city, within the confines of an oppressive job, in a nineteenth-century version of what is now called "inner exile." A period of misanthropic retreat and solitude is gone through by the hero of George Eliot's *Silas Marner* (novel, 1861). In Dostoevsky's novels, *Dvoĭnik (The Double,* 1846) and even more in *Zapiski iz podpol'ĭa (Notes from Underground,* 1864), the hero is repeatedly foiled in his brief misanthropic forays into the world of men. Retreating to his lodging for good, he broods there, lording it over the world and, in the later work, over the reader. So does Raskolnikov (Dostoevsky's *Prestuplenie i nakazanie [Crime and Punishment,* 1866]), but he emerges long enough to murder the pawnbroker and thereby unwittingly start on a spiritual journey that reverses his earlier retreat away from the moral and metaphysical norms of Christianity.

Tolstoy's Levin in *Anna Karenina* sees enough of Moscow to know that, as others knew of Paris and London, it is a moral cesspool. While Anna finds temporary refuge in the pleasures of adultery, he finds redemption rather in the countryside, working on his manor, living in proximity to the soil, to nature, to authentic people and emotions, to peasant wisdom. Only there do the commonest experiences, like those of marriage and childbirth, become saturated with meaning. Pierre (*Voĭna i mir [War and Peace,* novel, 1865–1869]), after similar disillusionment with the urban frivolities and corruptions, tried various kinds of retreat (including administering his country estates) but really found his epiphany (during the long winter march from Moscow) in the company of a child of the soil, the peasant Platonov, with his simple wisdom and ability to survive.

The heroes of Flaubert's *Bouvard et Pécuchet (Bouvard and Pécuchet,* novel, 1881) retire to the country from the wretched workaday world of Paris and initiate a series of explorations of Western man's intellectual heritage in quest of something definitive. The results of this long study only leave them confused and beleaguered. Where Levin—like Rousseau, Wordsworth, Thoreau—found fulfillment in the natural and the affective, Flaubert's pair opt for cerebration—albeit in a rustic setting—and find only frustration. Another frustrating flight from life to barren contemplation, from emotion to intellection, is made by Mr. Casaubon the pedant (Eliot's *Middlemarch,* novel, 1871–1872).

In Henry James's *The Bostonians* (novel, 1886) and D. H. Lawrence's "The Fox" (story, 1921), a pair of women attempt to sequester themselves from society but are defeated by a man bearing love and tearing one from the clutches of the other. Their retreat, which has ideological overtones, is into sisterhood, into an Amazon-like or lesbian casting off of dependence on men. It is the female version of what the men propose at the beginning of *Love's Labour's Lost.* A parallel bonding that is too intense to be healthy is the joint retreat of father and daughter in James's *Golden Bowl* (novel, 1904). In *The Wings of the Dove* (novel, 1902) retreat is catalyzed by terminal illness, and in *The Beast in the Jungle* (novel, 1903) it is a waiting for something dramatic that in fact never happens.

The rebellious Lona (Ibsen's *Samfundets støtter* [*Pillars of Society*, play, 1877]) emigrates from a puritanical Norwegian society to a turbulent America, which paradoxically functions as a sort of spiritual retreat, for she returns years later, like a Moses or Jesus from quasi-exile, as a bringer of the light of truth and moral liberation. In *Et dukkehjem* (*A Doll's House*, play, 1879) the traditional status of wife and homemaker comes to seem an asphyxiating retreat or escape from which a woman must free herself if she is to establish her humanity by accepting the challenges of independence and uncertainty. Hedda Gabler (play, 1890), by contrast, can never adjust to that retreat—from marriage, home, bourgeois life—and needs to flirt with the daring possibilities of adultery, of creativity, and of destructiveness before taking Ajax's form of retreat, suicide. Central to *Vildanden* (*The Wild Duck*, play, 1884) is Hjalmar's self-pitying, ineffectual existence, even as in O'Neill's *The Iceman Cometh* (play, 1946) everyone wallows in the escape of drink and pipe dreams. For Chekhov (*Diā diā Vaniā*, [*Uncle Vanya*, play, 1897] and *Tri sestry* [*Three Sisters*, play, 1901]) unremitting drudgery work is paradoxically a retreat (for Vanya, Sonya, Olga, Andrey) from one's vocational and amatory failures, and in *Vishnëvyĭ sad* (*The Cherry Orchard*, play, 1904) being a spendthrift—whether with money, emotions, or fantasy—is the response of Mme Ranevskaya and her brother Gaev to a similar inability to cope with the changing world around them.

Conrad's *Victory* (novel, 1915) is one of the most overt modern treatments of the impulse to retreat in pessimism from society itself to a South Pacific island (in the tradition of Gauguin and Stevenson) and of the subsequent breakdown of isolation through human vulnerability—first to love (i.e., the part within oneself that, as with Hippolytus, Molière's Alceste, and Bazarov, will not cooperate) and then to evil (i.e., the external world that, as in the *Birds*, insists on pursuing one). Similarly Razumov (*Under Western Eyes*, novel, 1911) seeks only a safe career and is overtaken by politics and feelings. Close to *Victory* in spirit or theme, though hardly in treatment or plot, is Kafka's bizarre "Der Bau" ("The Burrow," story, c. 1924), one of the most intense portrayals of free-floating anxiety and of man's consequent obsession with shelter and security. The nameless animal's ruminations on building a private place, as well as its recurring fears that an intruder is coming, is a harrowing parable of the futility of the attempt to escape. Kafka's "Die Verwandlung" ("Metamorphosis," story, 1915) is about one young man who has undergone an inner exile from the very family he lives with and supports financially, an exile symbolized not only by his change into an insect but also by the fact that the doors to his bedroom, which is in the center of their apartment, always are locked.

Active versus contemplative takes a modern form under the rubric of acquisitive or bourgeois versus artistic or bohemian. This is the tension in James's *The Ambassadors* (novel, 1903) and in Joyce's *A Portrait of the Artist* (1916) and

Ulysses (novel, 1922); in the latter, Dedalus orbits in the empyrean regions of intellect and art but, until his encounter with the earthy Bloom, lacks that humane contact with his own emotions and with other people that would give a firm grounding to his art. If the *Iliad* celebrates a moment of reflection in the middle of the active life, *Ulysses* celebrates a moment of communion between two atomized, solitary individuals, a moment of reflection in the middle of lives superficially active and apparently somewhat barren. The theme is more explicitly treated in Mann's work—"Tonio Kröger" (story, 1903), *Der Tod in Venedig* (*Death in Venice,* novelle, 1912), *Doktor Faustus* (novel, 1947)—in each of which the detached artist, however great, lacks a fulfillment through normal love so readily available to those less gifted (the theme also of Ibsen's *Bygmester Solness* [*The Master Builder,* play, 1892] and *Naar vi døde vaagner* [*When We Dead Awaken,* play, 1899]). In *Der Zauberberg* (*The Magic Mountain,* novel, 1924), the bourgeois Hans Castorp is plunged by tuberculosis into a stay at a sanatorium. There, in a mountain-top setting traditionally associated with contemplation, he undergoes in seven years a post-graduate course in Western civilization. As in *Bouvard et Pécuchet,* nothing definitive is arrived at, and World War I curtails, does not answer, the reflections; as in *Gargantua,* contemplation is not an end in itself. The reader last sees the hero disappearing in the smoke of war honorably doing his part as a soldier for the fatherland.

Proust (*A la recherche du temps perdu* [*Remembrance of Things Past,* novels, 1913–27]) spent the last years of his life in a by-now legendary cork-lined room—a hermit's cave in the heart of Paris. There, isolated from normal intercourse, he devoted himself to writing his great book, which would, as he said on the closing pages, be the one thing salvaged from a wasted life, and would be the goal the elusiveness of which had long plagued the sensitive man in search of a vocation. What he periodically celebrates in his work, the involuntary memory—the recapture of the past via present sensuous experience—are moments of noncerebral contemplation in the midst of life, moments that are analogous to the brief reflective insights gained by Achilles and Odysseus, to Wordsworth's "spots in time," and to Joyce's "epiphanies."

In Huxley's novel *Brave New World* (1932), an entire society makes a lotus-eating retreat from human complexity by means of eugenics, drug-taking, stratification in class and vocation, elitism, and other forms of manipulation. The results seem satisfactory except for a few isolated malcontents who betray a fondness for such quaint archaisms as soul-forging through adversity. If Hemingway's *A Farewell to Arms* (novel, 1929) is a classic statement of withdrawal from a World War I fought over concepts like "honor," which are suddenly seen to be hollow, Heller's *Catch-22* (novel, 1961) is a parallel classic statement about World War II, though the grounds of dissent differ. Yossarian retreats from adherence to the dictates of an irrational institution like the wartime U.S. Air Force into periodic nudity and increasing eccentricity; he has opened up his own second front against the Air Force. In Beckett's *En attendant Godot* (*Waiting for Godot,* play, 1952), as in the *Beast in the Jungle,* all of life itself is a retreat, a reflective waiting for something, anything, to happen. Blanche Du Bois (Williams' *Streetcar Named Desire,* play, 1947) has neurotically retreated into gentility and vulnerability as a way of disabling the world by making it awed and deferential; it is not. She is the latest in a line of people psychologically arrested because of some personal trauma, people who retreat by standing still while time surges on all around them: Sir Roger de Coverley (Addison's *Spectator*), Balzac's Eugénie Grandet (novel, 1833), Miss Havisham (Dickens' *Great Expectations),* old Ekdal (Ibsen's *Wild Duck*), Faulkner's Benjy and Quentin (*The Sound and the Fury,* novel, 1929), Rev. Hightower (*Light in August,* novel, 1932), and Emily ("A Rose for Emily," story, 1930). Retreat in time is treated in a novel fashion by H. G. Wells in *The Time Machine* (novel, 1895). This story grows out of an old tradition. In the legend of the Seven Sleepers, God organized a retreat from time in order to protect the faithful few until Christianity would triumph; in Washington Irving's "Rip Van Winkle" (story, 1820), the author organizes the retreat, and Rip discovers, on awaking from a protracted sleep, that life is flux, not spiritual progress; in Wells's tale, modern technology organizes the retreat from time, and the findings are ambiguous.

The old insight that retreat need not mean escape, that contemplation may be at the service of, or in symbiosis with, activism, is iterated in unusual fashion by Frost ("Birches," poem, c. 1916). The boy loves to climb the birch tree "toward heaven," to ride the branches, and to be set down gently by them. "I'd like to get away from earth awhile / And then come back to it and begin over."

See also: Arcadia, City and Literature, Escape, Hermit.

Selected Bibliography

Festugière, André Jean. *Contemplation et vie contemplative selon Platon*. 3d ed. Paris: Vrin, 1967.

McClung, W. A. *The Architecture of Paradise*. Berkeley: University of California Press, 1983.

Redner, Harry. *In the Beginning Was the Deed*. Berkeley: University of California Press, 1982.

MANFRED WEIDHORN

ROBOTS AND COMPUTERS

Robots and computers are twentieth-century inventions, but tales of machines that perform with apparent intelligence exist in the earliest literature of Egypt, Persia, and Greece. Over the centuries a variety of names have been given to these artificial constructs. The definition of robots and computers in the technological world today is made easily enough. An engineer would describe a robot as "a program-controlled, automatic manipulator capable of doing operations without human attendance.'' A computer is an electronic machine that processes data. The definitions suggest a tidiness that was lacking from discussions of machine intelligence until after World War II. Mechanical devices over the centuries have been variously known as talking statues, automata, simulacra, and machines. Not until the twentieth century does literature regularly refer to them as robots and computers.

The name ''robot'' was first used by Karel Čapek in his play *R.U.R.* (1921). *Robot* is the Czechoslovakian word for servant. Today literary robots and computers most often appear in science fiction, and in this literature a set of terms has evolved to describe the various man-made devices that perform with intelligence comparable to natural forms. Robots are anthropomorphic mechanical devices made from inorganic material, and they are differentiated from androids, devices of organic materials. Computers, which did not appear in fiction until much later than robots, are complex machines able to engage in intellectual activities that if performed by natural forms, would be called intelligent. The term ''cyborg'' is a contraction of cybernetic organism, and it refers to the product of a man/machine hybridization. ''Cybernetics'' is another term often associated with machine intelligence. It was coined by mathematician Norbert Wiener in 1947 to describe a new science in which he and his colleagues were attempting to develop a theory of control and communication both in machines and in living organisms.

Robots in Antiquity and the Middle Ages

Myth and legend tell of man-made creations that functioned as though they were alive. John Cohen's *Human Robots in Myth and Science* (1966) is the most thorough study available of early automata. According to Greek myth, Hephaestus, god of fire, built a giant figure called ''Talos,'' which was used to defend the island of Crete. He also forged mechanical females from gold and used them in his smithy. Daedalus, a legendary descendant of Hephaestus, is said to have built statues that could move by themselves.

According to another legend, a statute of Memnon built at Thebes in the fifteenth century B.C. was able to speak. It emitted sounds when touched by the first rays of the sun. Other prophetic statues, able to answer questions with a nod of the head or by a movement of the arm in an articulated statue, were attributed to Thoth, the Egyptian god of wisdom (the Hermes Trismegistus of the Greeks). Frances Yates writes about the place occupied by prophetic statues in hermetic tradition and cabbalist thought in her *Giordano Bruno and the Hermetic Tradition* (1964).

Legends from the Middle Ages continued to report mechanical devices that simulated living forms. The Bavarian Scholastic philosopher Albertus Magnus (1204–1282) worked on a robot for thirty years. When completed, it could answer questions and solve problems. Medieval writings referred to a man-made creature either as a ''homunculus'' or a ''golem.'' The alchemist Paracelsus (1493–1541) in his writings actually provided a recipe for a homunculus to be made from semen and human blood incubated for eighty days in a medium of horse dung. The golem legend is associated with the Jewish folklore of the city of Prague. Jewish literature contains various references to a golem, but the most famous is the one attributed to Rabbi Judah Loew, who was chief rabbi of Prague in the sixteenth century. Tradition has it that the golem first did housework but then became unmanageable. It was feared that he would annihilate Prague, and so he was dismantled.

The Renaissance and Seventeenth Century

Clocks built during the Middle Ages often had automata that moved as the gears of the clockwork circled. The skill of the technologists increased and by the time of the Renaissance, a variety of increasingly complex automata began to appear. For instance, Leonardo da Vinci built an automatic lion in about the year 1500 in honor of Louis XII. The literature of the time makes reference to these mechanical devices, although often the imagination of the writer seems to have embellished considerably the actual constructs. Rabelais tells how Gargantua spent his time in rainy weather ''building little automatory engines, that is to say, moving of themselves.'' Ariosto, in *Orlando furioso* (epic poem, 1516), describes a flying charger carrying a knight in shining armor, and Cervantes, in *Don Quijote* (*Don Quixote,* novel, 1605, 1615), also describes a horse that can fly. Descartes reportedly constructed an automaton that he called Francine.

Descartes raised an interesting question. What is the boundary between the living and the mechanical? His immediate purpose was to differentiate between man and beast, to propose that man was different because he possessed a soul, something animals lacked. The body is purely mechanical, a machine, he argued. An animal possessed a body but nothing more; he was the *bête* (beast) machine. True, man had a body, but he also had a mind that housed the soul. With his mind man can not only think but has knowledge that he does. He is self-conscious. Descartes' analysis established a mind-body dualism that would flare into the arguments between the vitalists and the mechanists in the nineteenth century.

In 1645 Blaise Pascal created a calculating machine that could add and subtract. Twenty years later Gottfried Leibnitz studied Pascal's machine and dreamed of building a more complex one that would not only do arithmetical operations but reason as well. The calculating machine, however, attracted much less attention than the more interesting mechanical devices that simulated living forms.

The Eighteenth and Nineteenth Centuries

The making of intricate and marvelous mechanisms flowered in the eighteenth century. A menagerie of mechanical animals—tigers, horses, dogs, cocks, songbirds—entertained and amazed the aristocracy with their ingenuity in simulating life and motion. That most of these devices were toys for entertainment indicates that the experimentation was more imaginative play than purposeful research.

E.T.A. Hoffmann is the first writer to give automata serious fictional consideration in his stories with his Talking Turk, "Automata" (1814) and Olympia in "Der Sandmann" ("The Sandman," 1817). Other mechanical men are rare in nineteenth-century literature. Edgar Allen Poe's "Maelzel's Chess Player" (1836) pictures an automaton that turns out to be a hoax. An automaton appears in Herman Melville's "The Bell-Tower" (1855), and a chess playing automaton kills his inventor in "Moxon's Master" (1894), written by Ambrose Bierce.

The best-known nineteenth-century fiction about an artificial man is Mary Shelley's *Frankenstein, or the Modern Prometheus* (1818), although the creature is more properly called an android, since it was made from organic materials. *Frankenstein* is regarded as the first science fiction novel, the literary form where most twentieth-century robots and computers appear. Mary's to-be husband, Percy Bysshe Shelley, who was interested in chemistry as well as poetry, served as a model for Victor Frankenstein and for Frankenstein's friend Clerval. The novel was written while Mary, Shelley, Lord Byron, and Byron's physician, Dr. Polidori, were summering in Switzerland. Shelley was working on *Prometheus Unbound* (play, 1820) at the time. Shelley's interest in the Prometheus myth (according to which the Greek god created man from clay), his reading of Erasmus, Darwin, and Galvani, and his study of the chemical and electrical properties of matter—all these were influences as Mary wrote her first novel. Evidence is good that she had also read Hoffmann's tales about automatons while in Germany the previous summer. Byron's only daughter, Augusta Ada, Countess of Lovelace, would later in the century become a close friend of Charles Babbage, whose difference machine is the precursor to the modern computer. The Countess' essay on his mechanical calculator is the best record we have today of Babbage's work.

In Samuel Butler's *Erowhon* (novel, 1872), chapters 21–23, entitled "The Book of the Machine," he considers the possibility of machines evolving to higher levels of intelligence. Herbert L. Sussman in *Victorians and the Machine* (1968) suggests that Butler was probably satirizing Darwin's theory of evolution by imagining machines, rather than animals, that have become as intelligent as humans. Generally the nineteenth century had faith in the power of an industrial society to produce material abundance for all, and strong hostility toward the machine did not develop until the following century. H. G. Wells, considered the father of science fiction, published his first scientific romance, *The Time Machine,* in 1895. In the novels that followed he speculated about a variety of futures possible through science and technology, but none contains an automaton. His *A Modern Utopia* (1905) praises machines and assumes that technology will be an important means of achieving social progress.

The Twentieth Century to World War II

Writers in the European literary tradition began to react against science and technology early in the twentieth century. A rare critic had existed earlier; for example, Jonathan Swift satirized the scientist in book 3 of *Gulliver's Travels*

(1726), and Dostoevsky rejected the mechanistic model of man as a creature of reason in *Zapiski iz podpol'īa (Notes from the Underground,* novel, 1864).

The dystopian reaction against machines in the early twentieth century appeared primarily in European literature. One of the earliest and still one of the most powerful condemnations of a mechanized society was E. M. Forster's "When the Machine Stops" (story, 1909). Although he does not use the word "computer," he imagines a future society where people live in an artificial environment totally controlled by a giant machine. Mark R. Hillegas, in *H. G. Wells and the Anti-Utopians* (1967), provides extensive documentation for Forster's use of imagery from Wells's fiction while attacking Wells's optimism. Forster's future city is much like the one Wells outlined in *A Modern Utopia,* but Wells hailed machines and the products of engineering, while Forster attacked them.

World War I was a mechanized war that devastated Europe. In the following decades a number of works began to appear that attacked industrial society. Evgenii Zamiatin in *My (We,* novel, 1924) makes a powerful, ironical statement about a society where machine regularity and conformity become more important than creativity and individuality. With Čapek's *R. U. R.* the term "robot" finally came into use to describe the dull creatures that are manufactured by the engineer Rossum to do only one thing—work. Čapek's play is essentially a satire attacking capitalism and the alienation of the masses by industrialism, not an exploration of machine intelligence. In fact, his robots are built of organic material, and according to present-day terminology would be considered androids. Aldous Huxley's *Brave New World* (novel, 1932) also attacked industrialism with its production line efficiency and its dehumanizing effects on man. His attack was particularly aimed at Henry Ford's automobile plants. Zamiatin, too, aimed his criticism at industry and especially the American efficiency expert, Frederick W. Taylor. Elmer Rice's drama *The Adding Machine* (1923) also satirized man and his machines.

The phenomenon of the pulp magazines in the United States in the first decades of the twentieth century had a powerful effect on fiction—dividing it into two camps, main stream and science fiction. (This split did not occur in European fiction.) Thus, to trace the history of robots and computers in American literature in the twentieth century, we must look primarily at science fiction. Many of the titles that appear in the following discussion will not be familiar unless one has read extensively in the short stories appearing in pulp magazines. Hugo Gernsback, American writer and editor, began publishing tales that he called "scientifiction" in *Amazing* in 1926. The name was soon shortened to science fiction. Other pulp magazines followed, publishing both fiction and nonfiction about new developments in science and technology. Almost all the stories about robots and computers were published in the pulps until after World War II, when science fiction also began to appear in paperback form.

In the earliest story about a mechanical brain (*The Metal Monster,* 1920), A. Merritt describes a huge metal brain hostile to man. Edmond Hamilton's "The

Metal Giants'' (story, 1926) also describes a giant brain of metal, this one able to solve scientific problems. The brain constructs metal giants that destroy a town and set out for the conquest of the world.

An early robot story, David H. Keller's "The Psychophonic Nurse" (1928), presents a mechanical woman who efficiently cares for a baby, although she is unable to give it mother's love. Another interesting story is "Automata" (1929), by S. Fowler Wright. He imagines a future where mechanical devices first work as servants and then eventually become the surviving form of intelligence as mankind dies out. The term "robot" was not yet in common usage in science fiction, and these constructs are called "automata."

Stories about robots began to appear regularly in the pulps during the 1930s. Among the best is Harl Vincent's "Rex" (1934), where an electronically operated robot dreams of developing emotions like humans and commits suicide when he thinks he has failed. Other excellent stories were Lester del Rey's "Helen O'Loy" (1938), where a man falls in love with his servo-robot, and "I, Robot" (1939), by Eando Binder, the first in a series of robot stories (1939–1942) that would eventually be published as *Adam Link, Robot* (1965).

The fictional treatment of intelligent machines that operate like computers occurred much later than stories about robots. Only John W. Campbell, Jr., wrote about them in the 1930s. His first story, "When the Atoms Failed" (1930), describes an engineer who uses an electric calculator in discovering the secrets of atomic energy. Campbell followed with several other stories about intelligent machines, including his memorable "Twilight" (1934). In 1938 he became editor of *Astounding* and stopped writing science fiction. But as an editor, he would encourage and tutor several young men who were destined to write some of the finest stories about robots and computers: Isaac Asimov, Lester del Rey, and Robert Heinlein.

From World War II to the Present

In 1940 a young man named Isaac Asimov published his first story about a robot. Titled "Robbie," it was about a friendly robot who was the playmate and guardian of a little girl. During the next two decades, Asimov wrote three dozen stories about robots and computers, all of them picturing machine intelligence as a friend to man. Asimov was impatient with persons hostile to innovation. He called this attitude "the Frankenstein complex." To assure his readers that robots need not be the threatening monsters pictured in early science fiction, he developed the Three Laws of Robotics and programmed all his robots with three ethical requirements: (1) A robot may not injure a human being nor, through inaction, allow a human being to come to harm; (2) A robot must obey the orders given it by human beings except where such orders would conflict with the first law; (3) A robot must protect its own existence as long as such protection does not conflict with the first or second law.

Asimov's robots explored space, mined ore on an asteroid, maintained space stations. Then they returned to Earth where they served in public office with great efficiency and honesty. His later robots developed intuition and creativity, and finally, in "The Bicentennial Man" (1976), probably Asimov's finest story, the robot Andrew Martin evolves into a man. Asimov also wrote a number of excellent stories about computers. The best of the early stories were collected and published as *I, Robot* (1950). In 1982 all the robot stories were published under the title *The Complete Book of Robots*. Asimov's large body of imaginative, intelligent stories about machines that think has earned him the title of the father of robots in science fiction. He also contributed the term "robotics" to the language.

The first mechanical computer (a machine more complex than a calculator) was developed in 1937. Each decade since has produced a new generation of computers: the vacuum tube, the transistor, the integrated circuit, and finally, in the 1970s, the silicon chip and miniaturized circuitry. The advance and utilization of computers is an unparalleled event in the history of technological innovation. It occurred so rapidly that science fiction generally did not stay abreast of new developments. In the 1940s and 1950s, fiction about robots was common enough, but not until the 1960s and 1970s did writers concern themselves with computers. This phenomenon is an interesting reversal of fiction and reality. Over the history of the development of machine intelligence up until the modern period, the fiction typically has appeared before the actual technology. In the twentieth century, the same pattern was true for robots. Fictional robots tended to precede real ones. The first industrial robot, called "Unimate," was built by Joseph Engelberger in 1958. (Engelberger had read Asimov's robot stories when he was young.) Industrial robots did not become common until the 1980s, long after they had appeared in fiction, and none resembles the anthropomorphic robots of literature. In contrast, the actual computer technology that developed in the 1950s was rarely pictured in fiction until a decade later.

In the robot stories written from World War II to the present, robots befriend men, attack them, replace them—endless possibilities are explored by the literary imagination. Robots are often portrayed as faithful servants to men, as the gentlemanly robot in Clifford Simak's *City* (1952). They may serve man so well, as in Jack Williamson's "With Folded Hands" (story, 1947), that man finds he has nothing left to do.

Robots are utilized by the military, masquerading as humans. In Philip K. Dick's "Impostor" (1953), attacking aliens smuggle a humanoid robot into a military research project on Earth. The robot is a bomb, programmed to explode. In Dick's "Second Variety" (1953), the Russians build robots programmed to kill mechanically and then direct them against the enemy. The robots can not easily be detected since they masquerade in the form of women and children. In Harry Harrison's "The War with the Robots" (1962), warfare moves underground after Earth's surface is destroyed. The war machines are fully automated and tended by robots.

In many stories robots perform roles as competently as humans. A priest who after his death was declared a saint turns out to have been a robot in Anthony Boucher's "The Quest for Saint Aquin" (1951). Idris Seabright's "Short in the Chest" (1954) portrays a robot psychiatrist who does counseling in the military service.

The robot as a metaphor for mechanized, dehumanized man provides the structure for Philip K. Dick's *Do Androids Dream of Electric Sheep?* (1968). Dick uses the terms "android" and "robot" interchangeably when he writes about mechanical constructs. In his extensive fiction about machine intelligence and simulacra, Dick continually asks: How can we tell a human from a machine? His answer: A man can feel empathy for his fellowmen, a machine cannot. If a man acts in an unfeeling, mechanical manner, then he is as much a robot as if he had been constructed artificially. Dick also explores this theme in *The Simulacra* (1964), *We Can Build You* (1972), and numerous short stories.

Fiction about computers written in the modern period tends very often to be hostile in its view. These stories are written primarily by science fiction writers. Main stream writers have rarely concerned themselves with machine intelligence. Kurt Vonnegut is an exception to that rule with his early novel *Player Piano* (1952), a dystopian novel picturing a future automated society so dismal that the workers finally rebel and smash the computers. Actually, early in his career when this novel was written, Vonnegut was considered a science fiction writer.

By the 1960s, many other writers had joined Vonnegut in his pessimistic view of a cybernetic future. D. F. Jones's *Colossus* (1967) describes two computers, one built by the United States and one by Russia. The two computers mysteriously join forces and make plans to take over the world. In Martin Caidin's *The God Machine* (1968), the computer's attempts to control the world are thwarted only when it is destroyed. Dystopian fiction about computers continued through the 1970s, a trend reflective both of the fear of machines common to many people, and of the negative attitude toward technology and science that was widespread after World War II.

Computers frustrate, as in Gordon Dickson's "Computers Don't Argue" (1965), where a computer used by a book club for its billing compounds rather than corrects a mistake reported by a club member. Computer data banks terrorize as in Poul Anderson's "Sam Hall" (1953) and D. G. Compton's *The Steel Crocodile* (1970), where they are used repressively by a politico-technocratic elite.

The development of high-level artificial intelligence that exceeds human intelligence is an often explored theme, and without question the most profound treatment is Frank Herbert's *Destination: Void* (1966). Perhaps machine intelligence is the next evolutionary step and computers are the species that will follow after man. Olof Johannesson's *Sagan om den stora datamaskine* (*The Tale of the Big Computer*, 1966) imagines this development. If the intelligence of the computer keeps growing, might it someday become like an all-knowing god, or in fact become God? This is a possibility suggested by many stories, the first of which was Fredric Brown's "Answer" (1954).

Sometimes the computer is treated anthropomorphically and given a personality, as Mike in Robert Heinlein's *The Moon Is A Harsh Mistress* (1966), and Hal in Arthur Clarke's *2001: A Space Odyssey* (1968). Clarke uses the computer in *The City and the Stars* (1956) to maintain a totally artificial environment in the city of Diaspar. His computer also provides immortality by allowing a man to periodically store his memories in the computer for perhaps a hundred thousand years that pass as a dream. Then he returns to a new body.

A few novels suggest a true man-machine symbiosis. Man becomes a cyborg working cooperatively with the computer to become a superman whose accomplishments far exceed those possible for man alone, as in Samuel Delany's *Nova* (1968) and Frederik Pohl's *Man Plus* (1976). What kind of consideration should we give a mechanical construct mentally similar to a human being? Stanisław Lem, Polish writer of cybernetic fiction, suggests that ethically such a robot must be regarded as a human. He has written *Cyberiada* (*The Cyberiad*, 1965) and also *Bajki robot'ow* (*The Robot Fables*, 1964). The stories in these two collections, told from the point of view of robots, remind the reader of Aesop's animal fables. But as the titles suggest, these are tales for our modern cybernetic age, and so the actors are robots, not animals. Lem writes with a capricious wit often edged with irony. Because the zany adventures of his constructs, Trurl and Klapaucious, in *The Cyberiad* usually end with a moral observation, many readers are reminded of Voltaire and Swift's satire.

By the end of the 1970s, computer usage had become so widespread that fiction writers generally ceased writing anti-computer stories. They either ignored robots and computers, as did mainstream writers, or began to deal knowledgeably and intelligently with machine intelligence. In A. J. Budrys' *Michaelmas* (1977), a newspaper reporter develops his own data base to fight political repression. *The Genesis Machine* (1978), by James Hogan, describes a future world where the computer is used to prevent rather than make war. His *The Two Faces of Tomorrow* (1979) explores in depth the possibilities of creating artificial intelligence.

See also: Monsters, Science.

Selected Bibliography

Dunn, Thomas and Richard D. Erlich, eds. *The Mechanical God: The Machine in Science Fiction*. Westport, Conn.: Greenwood Press. 1982.

Geduld, Harry M. and Ronald Gottesman, eds. *Robots, Robots, Robots*. Boston. New York Graphic Society, 1978.

Mowshowitz, Abbe, ed. *Inside Information: Computers in Fiction*. Reading, Mass.: Addison-Wesley, 1977.

Warrick, Patricia S. *The Cybernetic Imagination in Science Fiction*. Cambridge, Mass.: MIT Press, 1980.

PATRICIA S. WARRICK

ROLE PLAYING

The interdisciplinary concept of humans as role-taking and role-playing animals has been an influential concern in anthropology, sociology, and psychology since the early 1930s. George H. Mead (1934) saw role taking as a process essential to socialization and the development of the self. Ralph Linton (1936) defined "role" in the double sense of both being a series of rights and duties enacted by the individual and as the sum total of these discrete roles, which then determines his social status. J. L. Moreno (1934) pioneered the technique of psychodrama, in which the therapeutic patient seeks to understand the drama of his life by performing the roles of persons significant in it. Erving Goffman (1959) stresses the histrionic aspects of the self, comparing the presentation of personality to others with the presentation of a character by an actor.

Literature and literary criticism have long been fascinated by role concepts but have shied away from precise definitions, probably because of a persistent awareness of the plasticity and variability endemic in human nature. Friedrich Schiller wrote vaguely but grandly in *Briefe über die ästhetische Erziehung des Menschen* (*On the Aesthetic Education of Man,* essay, 1795): "Man plays only when he is in the full sense of the word a man, and *he is only wholly Man when he is playing.*" Perhaps the most famous formulation in drama of the role-playing motif is Jacques's monologue on the seven ages of man: "All the world's a stage, / And all the men and women merely players; / They have their exits and their entrances; / And one man in his time plays many parts, / His acts being seven ages" (*As You Like It,* c. 1599; 2.7.139–143).

Four types of role playing can be distinguished in literature. The first is the literal performance of a part in which the character imitates a person from an earlier literary work or historic event, as when Dante's Paolo and Francesca re-enact the romantic adventures of Sir Launcelot (*La divina commedia* [*The Divine Comedy*, epic poem, c. 1320]) or inmates of the asylum of Charenton act out the assassination of Jean-Paul Marat in Peter Weiss's play (*Marat/Sade,* 1964). The second is an alien role that a personage assumes for an immediate and temporary occasion as a way of adapting to the demands of his total situation— for example, Sancho Panza presents a passing peasant girl as the peerless Lady Dulcinea to his master, Don Quixote (novel, 1605, 1615). The third is a dramatically established part that sets up traditional gestures and actions within whose parameter the character is expected to perform, as when Hamlet swears to avenge his father's murder (play, c. 1609), Shakespeare's Richard III insists on being a melodramatic villain (play, 1591–1594), and Don Quixote enacts the ritualized agony of a courtly lover. The fourth type of role playing links literature with the social sciences: the character enacts a core role by virtue of his place in the social structure of his community. This role is central to his identity. Thus Agamemnon, Oedipus, and Lear are heads of state, Faust is a scholar, Anna Karenina a society matron, Willy Loman a salesman. Each of these—and countless other literary personages—performs his core role before an audience of what may be relatives, friends, foes, lovers, masters, servants, and acquaintances in cycles of face-to-face encounters. Great literature usually stresses the multiplicity of roles—or selves—devolving upon or issuing from a protagonist.

The Ancient World and Middle Ages

Western drama stems from the tragedies written by Athenian playwrights in the fifth century B.C. Tragedy in turn derives from primitive Greek religious dances and songs, to which first one and later several actors added speeches, thereby creating dramatic situations and plots.

In *Oedipus tyrannos* (*Oedipus Rex*, play c. 429 B.C.), the hero clarifies his social role in his opening speeches, when he responds to the supplication of petitioners in benevolent, grand, compassionate fashion. He is not only the absolute ruler of his land, but "the first of men" who saved Thebes from the Sphinx's terror and now vows to save the city-state again by driving from it the pollution that blights it. Sophocles (and the myth from which he derived his plot) thus present Oedipus with what turn out to be tragic alternatives. Should he refuse to rescue his people, he would forfeit their respect and his authority, would abdicate his role as shepherd of his community, helmsman of the ship of state. He would, above all, violate his basic nature as a vigilant, vigorous, responsible, courageous ruler. However, obedience to Apollo's oracle means to search for and banish the pollution's source, the killer of his country's previous king. The ironic issue of the plot is universally known. Oedipus the hunter becomes Oedipus the hunted; the detective discovers himself to be the criminal; the ruler becomes the outcast; the savior becomes the damned. In assuming the consequences of his self-recognition, Oedipus enacts the archetypal role of man insisting upon pursuing knowledge of himself, no matter how bitter the fruit of such understanding.

Euripides' *Bakchai* (*The Bacchants,* play, c. 405 B.C.) is a problematic play that has incited many interpretive disputes among critics. It features a Dionysus who plays a central role as both actor and personalized fate in the drama. He is described in the opening scene as "of soft, even effeminate appearance . . . his long blond curls ripple down over his shoulders. Throughout the play he wears a smiling mask." His identity remains elusive as well as daemonic as he mingles gentleness with cruelty, flirtation with terror, coldness with passion. He presents himself as universal humanity, protean, both female-in-male and male-in-female. Euripides symbolizes in him the primitive, amoral constituent of the psyche, free from ego-restraint.

Dionysus' chief victim is the young ruler Pentheus, intemperate, self-willed, hubristically arrogant. Pentheus masks his primitive instincts in authority and orderliness, only to have Dionysus crack his wall of artificial self-control, maddening him into frenzies of voyeurism and sadism. The civilized, rational general is transformed into a bisexual Peeping Tom who costumes himself in women's clothes so he can spy upon the Bacchants' supposed orgies. His mother Agave takes her son for a wild beast and, in the grip of Dionysian delusion, slaughters him. Pentheus dies as both a convert to and scapegoat for the ecstasy of the instinctual life. By his hermaphroditic role playing Dionysus has demeaned and destroyed the self that is ignorant of its nature. Euripides has thus dramatized a disturbing tribute to the pitiless drive of the unconscious.

The Middle Ages span approximately a thousand years, beginning with the collapse of the Roman Empire in the fifth century A.D. and ending with the invention of the printing press and the Protestant Reformation of the fifteenth and early sixteenth centuries. The *Nibelungenlied* (c. 1200) is a heroic epic that culminates a martial tradition reaching back to the tribal societies of the fifth and sixth centuries A.D., when courage, prowess, and loyalty were prized above all other virtues. The poem's unknown author has successfully assimilated this primitive pattern with the fashionable refinement in conduct, clothing, and ceremony dominant in the medieval courts of the twelfth and thirteenth centuries. Geoffrey Chaucer (c. 1342–1400) was an accomplished poet who read prodigiously in Latin, French, and Italian literature and chose a religious pilgrimage as the framework for the most panoramic portraits of men and women in medieval letters.

The *Nibelungenlied* is the greatest achievement in medieval German letters. Its crucial action is the murder of Prince Siegfried of Worms by his hosts, the royalty of Burgundy, with King Gunther conniving at the slaying done by his kinsman Hagen. Gunther is vain, deceitful, weak in every sense. He aspires to the hand of the powerful Princess Brunhild of Iceland, though unable to woo and tame her on his own. He therefore prevails upon Siegfried, endowed with mythical strength and magical skills, to foist three crucial deceptions, all involving role playing, upon Brunhild. First Siegfried pretends to be Gunther's vassal. Then he uses his cloak of invisibility to replace Gunther as Brunhild's competitor in athletic contests, besting her while Gunther goes through the motions of doing so. Brunhild is nonetheless fascinated by Siegfried, perhaps sensing that they are natural mates. When Gunther seeks to consummate their marriage, she rejects him: "I intend to stay a maiden till I have learned the truth about Siegfried." Brunhild then binds Gunther and hangs him on a wall hook throughout their wedding night. Siegfried to the rescue! The following night he again uses invisibility to impersonate Gunther, mastering Brunhild, and taking her ring and girdle as trophies of his triumph. The poem evades the question as to whether Siegfried actually deflowers Brunhild, though ring and girdle signified as much in ancient poetry. What matters more is that he should give them to his wife Kriemhild, who flaunts them before Brunhild, whose humiliation and resentment prompt Hagen and Gunther to plot Siegfried's death.

In Chaucer's *Canterbury Tales* (c. 1380–1400), perhaps the most brilliantly conceived character is also their most accomplished role player—the pardoner. He is a complete scoundrel, cynical, vicious, cunning, profoundly contemptuous of his dupes: "For myn entente is nat but for to wynne, / And nothyng for correccioun of synne. / I rekke nevere, whan that they been beryed, / Though that hir soules goon a-blakeberyed."

In the "Prologue" he confesses his tricks candidly, inviting his fellow-pilgrims to admire his craftsmanship in gulling believers into buying ecclesiastical "indulgences" and "relics" that will "benefit" their sinful souls. He glories in his rascality and would rather be taken for a clever criminal than for a fool. The "Tale" itself is an ironic sample of his sermons, preaching against the very vice of which he is guiltiest—avarice. In an excess of exhibitionism he concludes by calling on his auditors to buy the goods whose fraudulence he has just finished revealing. For once, the hypocrite has overreached himself. Does the trickster tire of his shamming pose and revel in the opportunity for honesty, however crass? Or does the momentum of his role as preacher obsess him beyond bounds that he can control? The text raises role playing to the level of profound social satire.

The Renaissance

The meaning of "Renaissance" is both "rebirth" and "renewal"—a revival of Greco-Roman culture and a renewal of cultural vigor, innovation, and exploration. The period is generally considered to have begun with the humanists' renewed interest in classical learning in the early fifteenth century and to have ended with the Counter-Reformation of the middle and late sixteenth centuries.

Shakespeare's plays abound in role playing of all four categories, with Jacques and Richard III prominently joined by Iago, Macbeth, Prospero, Lear, Edmund, Rosalind, Viola, Petruchio, Beatrice, Benedick, Falstaff, and others. Only one Shakespearean work, *Hamlet,* the most representative choice, will be analyzed.

The play has hardly a scene where at least one character is not role playing; hardly a character who does not act like a would-be dramatist or director, seeking to impose postures, attitudes, or actions upon another person. Claudius has violated the moral and social standards of his role as brother by having murdered the senior Hamlet, usurped the throne, and incestuously married Gertrude. When he addresses Hamlet as "my cousin . . . and my son," the latter immediately responds, "A little more than kin and less than kind!" (1.2.64–65). Cousins are of course more distant than sons—Hamlet's analytic wit pounces on the role discrepancy that Claudius seeks to perpetrate, punning on Claudius' lack of kindliness in attempting to combine the roles of uncle and father. Undaunted, Claudius urges Hamlet to "think of us / As of a father." Sardonically, Hamlet later bids farewell to the king with the salutation "dear mother." Claudius replies, "Thy loving father, Hamlet," only to be countered with, "My mother—father and mother is man and wife, man and wife is one flesh, and so, my mother" (4.3.48–51). Claudius is continually corrupting his role as would-be surrogate father to Hamlet by dramatizing and directing scripts against him. He sends Polonius to spy on him, authorizes Ophelia's entrapment, calls upon Rosenkrantz and Guildenstern to violate their friendship with Hamlet by playing on his trust, orders Hamlet's execution by the English, and plots with Laertes the duel that will kill the prince.

Hamlet is sometimes advised and more frequently advises others concerning his and their proper roles. His mother joins her husband in urging him to abandon his mourning for his father; Horatio urges him not to follow the ghost or fence with Laertes; crucially, his father's ghost enjoins him to "Revenge his foul and most unnatural murder" (1.5.24). However, the ghost also warns him not to taint his mind or soul against his mother. Hamlet at first enthusiastically welcomes the ghost's commands and decides to pretend madness as a protective ruse while he organizes his vengeance against Claudius—a plot device Shakespeare derived from Saxo Grammaticus' *Historia danica* (*Danish History*, c. 1200). In welcoming the travelling players and orchestrating their performance of "The Murder of Gonzago" as a mousetrap play with which he will expose Claudius' guilt, Hamlet relishes his open opportunity as dramatist-director, giving the actors specific instruction on their art as well as parts. Later, in the heated bedroom scene with Gertrude, he tells her to avoid sex with Claudius by absenting herself from his bed until the role of celibate will, by habit, become ingrained in her character. Even in his last moments of life, Hamlet addresses the members of the Danish court, who have watched the violent deaths of Claudius and Laertes as well as his impending doom, as "mutes or audience to this act," apologizes for his lack of time in which to explain the drama enacted before them, and urges Horatio to refrain from a Roman suicide but instead, "in this harsh world draw thy breath in pain, / To tell my story" (5.2.335–336). This story may well be the tragic tension between Hamlet's conflicting roles: revenger/non-revenger; good son/bad son; playmaker/passive victim; idealist/cynic; soldier/philosopher; lover/reviler of women; actor/meditator.

Like Hamlet, Don Quixote is lonely, imaginative, and fond of the theater, pretends madness, and performs as the best actor in his fictive world. A bored bachelor of 50, he invents a chivalric occupation for himself, achieving total identification with the knights-errant of such romances as *Amadís de Gaula* (*Amadis of Gaul*, 1508) and Ariosto's *Orlando furioso* (1516). He changes his name from Quixada or Quesada or Quexana—Cervantes playfully refuses to provide his precise identity—to Quixote; assembles the romantic supporting cast of squire, horse, imaginary if not real mistress; subscribes to the courtly love attributes of humility, courtesy, and adoration of the beloved; and makes the towns and highways of Spain the stage for his gallant adventures. How "mad" is the Don? From a clinical point of view, his is a personality disorder marked by obsessional transferences, weakness of object-love, distortions of external reality, and grandiosity. From a literary perspective, however, the Don becomes a completely realized archetypal personage who creates a new life for himself by pitting sublime ideals of courage, compassion, and fairness against an uncomprehending, fallen world of shallow pragmatism. Don Quixote is the play-wright-director-player of his deeply contrived role, acting it so well that it becomes his self. In one brilliant episode Cervantes has him play-act the woes of a victim of unfulfilled love, self-consciously fulfilling a precise ritualistic program that includes tearing his clothes, knocking his head against rocks, and praying to his peerless "Dulcinea." When Sancho asks the Don, "what reason has your worship for going mad?" His master replies, "The thing is to do it without cause,"—as a dry run for the day when he will have cause. The only conclusion Cervantes provides is to dramatize both Shakespeare's metaphor that the world is a stage and Calderón's that life is but a dream.

Neoclassicism

This period, alternatively termed "the Enlightenment" or "The Age of Reason," spans approximately one hundred years from the mid-seventeenth to the mid-eighteenth centuries, from Molière's earliest plays to Voltaire's and Samuel Johnson's last texts. It was an era of consolidation and relative order after the vital turbulence of the Renaissance. Its ideals were those of logic and restraint, correctness and reason, wit and decorum, wordly common sense and sophisticated moderation. It preferred the control of the mind to the urgency of the feelings.

Molière's *Tartuffe* (play, 1664) is subtitled "or the Impostor," with the title character's name derived from the verb *truffer,* meaning "to deceive" or "to cheat." He is a monster of lust, greed, and ingratitude, who has become the religious director of Orgon's wealthy household and shams piety while plotting to seduce his benefactor's wife, marry his daughter, defame his son, and dispossess the family. What is perhaps most appalling is the thinness of Tartuffe's mask of devoutness, the brazen carelessness with which he alternately wears and discards it. He is a sinister outsider who disrupts the vital unit of the family, dividing it into skeptics who have the good sense to penetrate his pretensions and constitute most of the cast, and the bourgeois establishment's husband/father, Orgon, whose bad sense borders on imbecility, but whose power as head of the house overmatches that of the party of moderation. Molière has here written a dark fable that stresses Tartuffe's capacity for yet frequent indifference to polished role playing, since Orgon's religious fanaticism blinds him, in any case, to reason, love, or the truth of empiric evidence.

In *Le misanthrope* (*The Misanthropist,* 1666) Molière fashions a profound satiric comedy that rejects romantic comedy's usual movement toward private and public harmony and reconciliation. Instead, he creates a protagonist, Alceste, whose first words are, "leave me alone." Alceste prefers to sit apart from others, cherishing his solitude, engaging in egoistic, tactless, often petulant outbursts, brooding over his grievances against the world. Instead of advancing the play's action he criticizes it, passing a moralist's judgment on what he regards as a depraved human race. In sum, he refuses to play any role but that of alienated outcast. When his only friend Philinte suggests that social hypocrisy is not always "a hanging matter," Alceste insists on absolutely plain dealing: "I'd have [men] be sincere and never part / From any word that isn't from the heart."

Such bristling insistence on moral perfection is of course ridiculous, and Alceste can validly be called cranky and splenetic, eager to lose his litigation— his only public activity—so as to justify his misanthropic view of mankind. In answer to Philinte's genial tolerance of defective human nature he can only envision "Some desert land unfouled by humankind." Yet Alceste is also a romance hero who would join the inward with the outward heart. He is justifiably offended by an inauthentic, irresponsible, unjust society marked by pretentious foppery, frivolous coquetry, malicious gossip, vanity, smugness, envy, and cruelty. He rejects its fraudulent terms and hypocritical roles. But neither he nor Molière can envision any alternative.

Diderot's *Le neveu de Rameau* (*Rameau's Nephew*, satirical dialogue, 1762– 1784) is one of the Enlightenment's masterpieces, with its title character one of the most disconcerting yet appealing personages in fiction. "He," as Diderot names him in this dialogue-novel, cheerfully proclaims his buffoonery, power-mongering, addiction to flattery, and outright lying, scornful hatred of social-ethical norms, even his occasional services as procurer. "He has no greater opposite than himself" judges the moderate, stable "Myself"—narrator who is continually perplexed by the nephew's mercurial behavior. The nephew admits his envy of his distinguished musician-uncle's achievements yet compensates for his own inadequacies by unfailing liveliness, sincerity, wit, and above all, unsparing candor in exposing his most shameful qualities. He parades many of his roles, the principal ones being incessant parasitism and dazzling mimetic skills, which culminate in his imitation of all the instrumental sounds in an orchestra. By disclosing his desires, no matter how base, he symbolizes what Freud was to call the id or pleasure-principle. Yet his reality-conscious ego is strong enough to drive for his self-preservation and self-promotion in an amusing but also pathetic dance of survival.

The eighteenth century's worldliest literary text is Choderlos de Laclos' *Les liaisons dangereuses* (*Dangerous Acquaintances*, novel, 1782). Both of its letter-writing protagonists are elegant, frozen-blooded role players, ostensibly friends, who pride themselves on practicing a sophisticated science of seduction that disparages love as weakness. As they cavalierly sacrifice the affection and trust of mere human beings to their jaded intrigues, they behave as serpents who carry their venom in their loins. The Don Juan, Vicomte de Valmont, has the easier part since society tolerates the male libertine. His only difficult conquest is a pious married woman whom he disarms by presenting himself as a reformed rake requiring moral rehabilitation. The novel's most shocking character is Madame de Merteuil, a femme fatale who relies on a brilliantly ingenious mind and unfailing capacity for dissimulation to debauch a large population of innocents while playing the role of prude before society at large. In her most confessional letter she glories in displaying "on the great stage the talents I had procured myself." She invokes as her chosen fate the myth of Delilah, delighted to not only conquer but humiliate unsuspecting Samsons, relishing her role as crusader for female superiority.

Romanticism and Realism

Just as Neoclassicism is a reaction to the Renaissance, so romanticism is a counterswing to the rationalism and formalism of Neoclassicism. Jean-Jacques Rousseau (1712–1778) is generally considered the movement's germinal philosopher, with his stress on the uniqueness of each individual and the primacy of egoistic impulses over the constraints of society, his insistence on the innate goodness of man, and his lyrical worship of external nature.

By the fourth decade of the nineteenth century the romantic wave had pretty well crested, and Western literature became dominantly influenced by realism, which was centered in the novel and most prominent in France, England, Russia, and the United States. While realism is difficult to define, its program is easy to recognize: A truthful, verisimilar representation of contemporary society's norms and manners. Where the romanticist is drawn to the sublime and ideal, the realist prefers the pragmatic and the immediate. He is particularly attracted to the specific, verifiable consequences of scientific materialism and the enormous social changes achieved in nineteenth-century cultures by the triumph of the middle classes.

The hero of Stendhal's *Le rouge et le noir* (*The Red and the Black*, novel, 1830), Julien Sorel, asks himself throughout the novel how he, talented, energetic, romantic, brilliant, can protect his precious individuality in a world of hypocrisy and shame organized to keep its prizes for the well-born and to keep persons of the lower class, like himself, inferior. He goes to war against society by camouflaging his virtues of spontaneity, sincerity, generosity, and warmth. As he learns to assert mastery through a battery of calculated subterfuges and disguises, he rises from peasant, to tutor, to confidential secretary, to officer, and cleric. Stendhal's strategy of subversion and duplicity extends everywhere in the novel, with the reader learning that "no" and "yes" often mean their opposites, that lip service to a reactionary aristocracy and clergy is Julien's calculated defense of his inner integrity. Dissimulation becomes second nature to him, submerging and blunting his natural sensibility; he learns by heart the part of "his master Tartuffe." Only when his career crashes and he is imprisoned does Julien strip off his costume of calculated hypocrisy and come into refreshed possession of his natural self. Rather than resume his tense role playing, he provokes his jury to pass the death sentence on him, so he can in turn pass a martyr's judgment on a class-ridden, evil era.

Nikolai Gogol's *Revizor* (*The Inspector General*, play, 1836) gives the traditional comic motif of mistaken identity an ingenious twist. The plot could hardly be simpler. The knavish and incompetent officials of a small provincial town hear rumors of the impending arrival of an inspector general from the capital to investigate their shoddy, venal administration. They mistake a destitute gambler for the high dignitary and fall over him—and themselves—to fawn on him, wine, dine, and bribe him so as to avoid his exposure of their frauds. The young man barely manages to skip town, much enriched, before his true identity is made known—and the "real" inspector general's arrival is announced to the stupefied and embarrassed bureaucrats. What distinguishes the protagonist, Ivan Khlestakov, from the ordinary run of literary scoundrels is that his role, rather than schemed, is foisted on him by a windfall of false perceptions on the town's part. He is a phony rather than a swindler, a flimsily sketched nonentity who drifts into his good fortune rather than contriving it, coming from nowhere, hollow to the core, convinced of nothing or everything depending on who offers him what or whom, and vanishing no one knows where. He improvises his part in tune to the temptations tendered him, with his hosts inflating his weightlessness to balloons of grandiose daydreaming, of ardently uttered nonsense. Thus does Gogol's stinging laughter skewer a world of irredeemable pettiness, panic, drabness, and inanity.

Honoré de Balzac's announced intention, when he wrote *La cousine Bette* (*Cousin Bette,* novel, 1846), was to make the title character his protagonist as the female half of a brace of "poor relations," with Cousin Pons (1847) her male counterpart. And Bette does occupy a prominent place in the novel. She is the ugly, brooding relative of the beautiful, gentle Adeline, who makes a dazzling match with Baron Hector Hulot, while Bette is deprived of love, spends her life in the homes of others, and becomes a rancorous, wronged soul who counts and hoards her frustrations and humiliations. She chooses the vivacious, sexually magnetic Mme Valérie Marneffe as both her bosom friend and the instrument of her revenge upon the Hulot household. And Valérie proceeds to sweep not only the Baron but Balzac off their feet. Both fall in love with her, and the writer pushes Bette into the background to make room for Valérie as his central character. Valérie is a bourgeois version of Mme de Merteuil, a female usurer who hires out her body instead of—but for—money. Balzac calls her "Machiavelli in petticoats." No man can resist her sexual lure or refuse her avaricious demands; as a result she spends fortunes, ruins families, and wastes artists' talents. Disregarding her presumably impotent husband, she takes on no less than four lovers in the same period, playing her role of devoted mistress with such skill that each of them is persuaded that he is the father of her expected child—and must provide handsomely for the mother-to-be's expenses.

Like *Cousin Bette* Henrik Ibsen's play *Peer Gynt* (1867) is a countertext to another work, in this case the tragedy *Brand* (1866). Whereas the idealistic Pastor Brand, fanatically uncompromising, is locked into Kierkegaard's ethical category of spiritual zeal, the irresponsible Gynt belongs to the aesthetic stage, charming but irresolute, incapable of keeping a promise or attaining a goal, unwilling to think through the purpose of his life. His mottoes are selfishly egoistic: the troll's "to thyself be—*enough,*" and the Boyg's "Go round about." Both prompt him to replace caring concern with crass indifference, emotional openness with calculated opportunism. Peer wastes his potential in many roles— seducer and forsaker of women, idol seller, slave trader, pseudo-prophet, and speculator—driven by momentary desires and self-delusions, refusing to commit himself to any person or principle. In his old age, home from his wandering and seeking a point of rest, Peer peels a wild onion only to discover no center as he strips layer after layer. The analogy is clear enough: Peer's many roles have been so many personae hiding an essential emptiness. His blindness to his authentic needs has made him waste his life.

The Modern Era

The term "modern" is usually applied to a complex, loosely defined pattern of characteristics. It often rejects the traditional values and assumptions, regarding any cultural certainty as dangerously false. It is skeptical of any claim to systematic knowledge. It discounts stable perceptions regarding human nature, preferring the unconscious to the self-conscious and stressing the psychological ambiguities of the inner self over the imperatives of the social self. Its governing temper is one of alienation and anxiety, dread, loss, and despair.

Luigi Pirandello is probably not the greatest modern playwright, but he is most likely the most influential. In his addiction to the drama of philosophic speculation, he parallels Shaw and anticipates Sartre, Beckett, and Camus; in his view of the tension between public mask and private face he paves the ground for Brecht, Giraudoux, and Ionesco; and in his concept of man as a role-playing animal, especially his use of the interplay between actors and characters, he is the forerunner of Anouilh, Genet, Weiss, Pinter, and Stoppard—to name a few among a host. Pirandello's basic premise is that life is fluid, indeterminate, and instinctual, yet man needs to attempt to categorize and order it through rational definitions that give him an illusory sense of form. Hence the insoluble but inevitable conflict, with each Pirandellian character laboring to find his place in the shapeless, purposeless dance of existence. In the preface to *Sei personaggi in cerca d'autore* (*Six Characters in Search of an Author,* 1921) Pirandello writes, "Conflict between life-in-movement and form is the inexorable condition not only of the mental, but also of the physical order." In all his plays Pirandello dramatizes this perception as an irreconcilable battle between the "face," representing man's suffering as a complex individual, and the "mask," symbolizing social laws and customs.

In the first of his two masterpieces, *Enrico IV* (1922) the title character is an unnamed, forty-six-year-old Italian aristocrat who, twenty years earlier, had ridden in a pageant costumed as the medieval Holy Roman Emperor Henry IV. His horse, pricked by his romantic rival, had stumbled; he had fallen, hurt his head, and subsequently awakened with the delusion that he was in fact the emperor—a delusion he believed for twelve years, but not during the last eight. He therefore enacts a masquerade within a masquerade, complete with a set of "retainers," each of whom plays a historic personage in the life of the historic Henry. A doctor seeks to "restore" the protagonist to his prepageant "sanity" by dressing up his former mistress's daughter in her mother's costume and having her speak to him from within a portrait's frame. The shock almost maddens the already-sane Henry, who informs the company that he prefers enacting his royal "madness" so as to renounce a previous existence where love and trust had been betrayed. When his former rival seeks to destroy this mask, Henry kills him with his sword and thereby locks himself into his role of madman to escape legal punishment for the murder. He has emerged as actor and author of his part, has imposed artistic form on haphazard life.

In *Six Characters in Search of an Author*, the drama is constructed on stage by the players. Six "characters" belonging to one family appear before the "director," who is rehearsing another Pirandello play. Abandoned by their author, they offer their melodramatic life story to the artists on stage and persuade the director to improvise a play that will highlight the two lurid scenes they relate: the father's incest—or near-incest—with his daughter, and the violent deaths of the two youngest children. The interaction between the "characters" and "actors" becomes complex and confusing. The characters' intense feelings about their broken lives collide with the casual distance of the actors. The tragic "faces" of the characters, bound together by guilt and hatred, are unable to perform their roles on stage because they lack professional training and disagree about the meaning of their story. The "masks" of the actors, on the other hand, lack empathy for the characters' experiences and stress the primacy of theatrical values. "Acting is our business here," states the director. "Truth up to a certain point, but no further." The "play" fails, with the director throwing his hands up in frustration and the characters leaving the stage. Pirandello has made drama self-aware to the point of its undoing, has dramatized a debate of the theater with itself on the subject of art versus life that continues to our day.

F. Scott Fitzgerald's *The Great Gatsby* (novel, 1925) has a title character whose role-playing nature embodies a mythic critique of the American Dream. James Gatz, a poor farm boy from the Middle West, changes his name to Jay Gatsby and drives his romantic dream of wealth and privilege by underworld means that the author keeps nebulous, but which apparently involve bootlegging and dealing in dubious stocks. Gatsby never succeeds, however, in being socially accepted by the Long Island set he lavishly entertains. Nor is his love for Daisy, married to a fabulously rich philanderer, returned anywhere near the order he feels. He is ready to take the legal blame for her hit-and-run murder of her husband's mistress; she is unready even to leave her husband. Gatsby's dream is shown as sleazy and shallow: To be accepted into corrupt realms of materialism and self-indulgence, where people drift from one empty and shallow gesture to another. Yet the poetic, Platonic resonance of Gatsby's illusions is sympathetically portrayed by Fitzgerald: Like Benjamin Franklin, he disciplines himself with a rigorous schedule; like a medieval knight he passes through a series of tests; like Julien Sorel he campaigns to conquer the established society that disdains him as an outsider of mean origins. In the novel's concluding paragraphs the author ironically exposes the futility of Gatsby's dream of landing his boat at "the green light at the end of Daisy's dock"—it is headed against the current of America's modern nature, hence doomed to be "borne back ceaselessly into the past."

Eugene O'Neill's *Long Day's Journey Into Night* (1956) is by common judgment his greatest play. In it he confronts the harrowing history of his unfortunate family, compressing into a single day the love-hate relationships of "the four haunted Tyrones": the overbearing actor-father, drug-addicted mother, alcoholic older son, and tubercular younger one—all based faithfully on the O'Neills of 1912. The quartet takes turns playing predator and pawn in a circle of resentment yet forgiveness, recrimination yet compassion. Mary Tyrone is the most accomplished of the four in enacting the role of victim-turned-persecutor. She was a shy convent girl when she met and married the famous James Tyrone, who took her touring for many years and never made a proper home for her; as she repeatedly points out, "I've never felt at home in the theater." Moreover, Tyrone's miserliness made him hire a cheap quack physician who prescribed morphine for her delivery pains and instigated what became her addiction to it. During the course of the play Mary removes herself increasingly from her family, denying the reality of Edmund's just-diagnosed tuberculosis, playing the role of a fastidious girl-woman mourning her forsaken vocation for the convent, while her family turns to her in vain for stability and emotional nourishment. Drugs become the only surcease from sorrow for her as she shrouds herself with a fog-bound veil of unworldly innocence and purity. In the drama's last scene she enters trailing her wedding gown and re-enacts her selective girlhood memories of preparing for a nun's life and adoring the Virgin Mary—until "I fell in love with James Tyrone and was so happy for a time."

Bertolt Brecht's theories and practice of dramaturgy both stress role playing. His concept of the theater, *Verfremdung,* "alienates" or "distances" both plot and character. Whereas in the illusionist theater of Stanislavski and Reinhardt the actor tries to identify completely with the character, so as to enable the audience to identify completely with him and empathize with the lives dramatized on stage, Brecht's dramaturgy seeks to have the actor demonstrate his role from outside the plot, maintaining a deliberate distance from his part as though he were relating rather than absorbing it. By not losing himself in the character, the actor, Brecht maintains, will remind the audience that it is witnessing a stage performance, not life itself, and should apply the lesson of the performance to the meaningful stage of the world at large instead of dispersing its feelings in a darkened theater. In practice the difference between cathartic and Brechtian theater has proved one of degree rather than kind. No audience could completely detach itself from a performance, since that would mean walking out of the theater. Nor could an audience completely identify with the events and characters on stage, or it would blind itself with Oedipus and rage with Lear. Yet by having his actors often step into and break out of a scene Brecht does remind spectators that they are taking roles rather than feeling them, and that the reality of his plays is artificial and didactic, designed to constrain audiences into thought and action rather than pity and terror.

A representative example of Brechtian drama is *Der gute Mensch von Sezuan* (*The Good Person of Szechwan,* 1943). The heroine, Shen Teh, is naturally loving, open, and motherly; she fulfills herself by sharing her goods and feelings.

Alas for her, the world repays her generosity with greed, betrayal, envy, and ruthless exploitation. To survive—and protect her expected child—she needs to call with increasing frequency on the services of her calculating, harsh male "cousin," Shui Ta, who meets the world on its base level. Shui Ta turns out to be Shen Teh masked, with one actress taking both roles to enact Brecht's parable of the divided self. The playwright concludes the play proper with Shen Teh in despair, unable to achieve a reconciliation between her conflicting needs for self-fulfillment and self-preservation. In an epilogue one of the players beseeches the audience for a satisfactory conclusion: "Ladies and gentlemen, in you we trust: / The ending must be happy, must, must, must!"

Tennessee Williams' most complex character is Blanche Du Bois in *A Streetcar Named Desire* (play, 1947) She is a romantic product of the Old South's plantation society, imbued with the rituals and style of a culture that encouraged white ladies to indulge in coquetry and polite courtship, courtesy, passivity, and refinement. When Blanche's genteel upbringing is debilitated by economic ruin and a catastrophic marriage, she is unable to cast off her role of antebellum Southern heroine. Even though forced into flight to the bohemian slums of New Orleans, she insists on playing Scarlett O'Hara in a proletarian melting pot lacking either gentlemen or gentleness. She shades her faded looks with paper lanterns, lies about her alcoholism, holds on to dreams of rescue by a gallant but nonexisting Shep Huntleigh, and tries to train a lower-class suitor to become her "Rosenkavalier." The schizoid tension of Blanche's frantic attempts to play a role bizarrely unsuited to her seedy circumstances provokes an aggressive response from her loutish brother-in-law, which climaxes in his raping her. Thereafter she withdraws wholly into her role of a magnolia-scented belle whose inevitable resting place becomes a mental institution. She is hopelessly caught between two worlds, one gone with the wind and the other marked by a brutishness unbearable for her.

Samuel Beckett's plays are dramatic nightmares that mingle horror with farce and work for ambivalence through grotesque buffoonery. In *En attendant Godot* (*Waiting for Godot*, 1952) the two tramps, Vladimir and Estragon, are united by a friendship that flickers in an existential void, as the former waits for Godot's redemption while the latter waits for companionship's sake. They organize fruitless scenes to pass their time: horseplay, burlesque routines, periodic separations and reunions, badinage about each other's bodies—all trivial rites that, they admit, are substitutions for significant action. Their behavior parodies the death of vaudeville: they refuse to get off the stage of life. As for the man of property, Pozzo, he exhibits pathetic insecurity beneath the complacent ceremonies of his pose as capitalist-consumer. He plays impresario to his slave Lucky's beasthood, prize pupil to Lucky's former tutelage. Yet his sinister arrogance soon dwindles into pathetic dependence on audience approval and frantic worry over the loss of his possessions.

Fin de partie (*Endgame*, 1957) is an apocalyptic coda to *Godot*, reversing the myth of Genesis to indicate the disintegration of the world and a return to darkness and nullity. Beckett maintains the metaphor of life as a game throughout the drama, as a blind, paralyzed Hamm confronts his shuffling servant Clov, also going blind; his parents, legless, toothless, and dying in a dust bin; and an otherwise uninhabited universe. He is a ham-actor with fulsome soliloquies reminiscent of Shakespeare's royal hero-villains, continually aware of his role as a cruel, capricious master: "Since that's the way we're playing it . . . let's play it that way." Beckett has also plotted the text as a chess game, with the parents as pawns while Clov as knight is controlled by Hamm as king. Throughout the action Hamm wants to die, Clov wants to leave him, and Hamm's parents, hating and hated by their son, do perish in their bins. Hamm and Clov play their respective parts of sadist and sufferer, agreeing only in their desire to be done with everything. Hamm tries cunningly to stage-manage Clov's farewell, but when the curtain falls Clov remains ambiguously at his side, though dressed for departure. Hamm, however, knows his game is up: "Old endgame lost of old, play and lose and have done with losing."

Thomas Mann, intrigued by role playing throughout his career, used it with consummate skill in his last work, *Felix Krull* (1954), the longest interrupted novel in literature. Felix is a charming rogue whose fictional experiences both parallel and parody the traditional adventures of a *pícaro,* such as theft, card-sharping, confidence tricks, and a wide range of other deceptions. He also belongs to the gallery of artist-figures portrayed by Mann for two generations, with the author both ironically indicating that the artist is only a scamp and playfully admiring the scamp's artistry. Indeed, the nature and role of the artist is Mann's central concern in this tale as in most of his others. Felix loves all the guises of disguise: Costuming, make-up, mimicry, masquerading, and of course acting. From early childhood his sense of needing—and success in pleasing—an audience is constant. He likes "with a thoughtful fellow-feeling" to watch circus performers and matadors. He assumes unlearned roles with amazing ease, including violin-playing; spouting many languages, changing identities with a marquis, and triumphing at tennis although he does not know the game. He even fakes epileptic symptoms convincingly before a board of medical examiners. Felix's identification is with Hermes, God of not only travel but thieves, patron of literature, master of masks, lover of eloquence and beautiful women. Moreover, Mann symbolizes the artist's role as cultural unifier in his protagonist. Felix attracts both sexes and frequently experiences a "double vision" that merges brother and sister, mother and daughter. He is the artist-as-hero and artist-as-shaper, but also—Mann whimsically reminds us—the artist-as-larcenist and artist-as-exploiter.

The most Pirandellian playwright of the mid-twentieth century is Jean Genet, who regards life as a ceremonious masquerade to be illumined with elaborate mirror-images. In *Les bonnes* (*The Maids,* 1946) one sister, the maid Solange, plays the other maid, her sister Claire. Claire, meanwhile, plays "Madame" in Madame's clothes, while the real mistress is away. The two sister-maids enact charades of debaser and debased, lover and hater, taking turns playing lady and servant. When Madame's lover—arrested on information furnished by the sisters—is released from jail, they prepare a poisoned cup of tea for their mistress to drink upon her return, so as to protect themselves. However, the mistress rushes off instead to meet her liberated lover. Thereupon Claire-Madame drinks the deadly tea to die like a lady, while Solange-Claire declares, in a final speech, that they are now "beautiful, joyous, drunk, and free!" At the play's original production, Genet insisted that the three female parts be played by males, indicating that he was not only a homosexual author but an author of homosexuality.

Genet's most dazzling mirror-play is *Le balcon* (*The Balcony,* 1956), set in a brothel that turns out to be a house of illusions where ordinary men can indulge in extraordinary fantasies. The customers provide the scenarios, while Madame Irma and her whores supply costumes, props, and sado-masochistic services. Thus a gas man becomes a "Bishop" who "confesses" his "penitent" prostitute; another customer a "Judge" who licks the feet of a "thief"; a third a "General" who tours his "battlefield" astride a "whorse." The play soon opens its vistas, moving from pornography, to a parody of a Black Mass, to a theatricalized vision of society at large. As a revolution outside the brothel threatens to destroy the regime's—and Madame Irma's—central institutions, she and her clients decide that the make-believe of their role playing is identical with the make-believe of the world, that whorehouse and world-at-large are reflections of one another. Irma thereupon assumes the robes and role of the queen who has been killed in the uprising, and the would-be bishop, judge, and general also assume their posture-roles in earnest to replace the "real" dignitaries who have been shot, aware that the people require illusion and authority, even if it be the illusion of authority. In their turn the rebels canonize Chantal, a whore rescued from the brothel who becomes their Joan of Arc "and is virginified." The revolution is defeated, and the victorious regime's Chief of Police—also Irma's lover—is saluted as a "Hero of the Republic." However, his ambitions loom larger. The chief wants to join the Great Nomenclature of Government, Clergy, Magistracy, and Army enshrined in the Grand Balcony of Madame Irma's establishment. The leader of the vanquished rebels, Roger, obliges him. He enters the brothel dressed as the Chief, castrates himself, and thereby proves the sacredness of his model. The Chief, through the self-mutilation of his surrogate, has assumed the MAN-GOD divinity of an Osiris or Christ, and Genet has dramatized his outlaw concept of life as a sacrilegious, erotic, violent façade.

Harold Pinter's *The Homecoming* (1965) may be his most puzzling and shocking play. Why should Ruth, wife of a philosophy professor and mother of three young children, coolly accept an offer by her husband's family to set her up as a fancy prostitute, providing she serve their sexual needs at home? Why should her husband Teddy encourage her to accept the proposition, then bid her a casual farewell, to be met by her equally casual, "Don't become a stranger"? Pinter's plot has the London-born but U.S.-living Teddy-Ruth couple return to the house of Teddy's relatives for a visit, encountering a womanless, working-class household consisting of Teddy's widowed father Max, Uncle Sam, and two younger brothers, Lenny and Joey. The all-male ménage of Max-Sam-Lenny-Joey snarls with brutal backbiting, temper tantrums, vicious gamesmanship, and foul-mouthed name-calling. Yet the Teddy-Ruth marriage, while superficially attractive, is soon seen as a broken-down mismatch. He is an arid, smug intellectual; she is an earthy sensualist who prefers elemental action to tedious words. "We live a closer life here," Lenny states, and Ruth's premarital past as a nude model (and possibly call girl) indicates a temperament more congenial to Teddy's carnivorous clan than to her husband.

So Ruth has her homecoming, which is a matriarchal one. She will replace Max's dead wife as nourisher for Lenny and Joey. These sons will have a sexual partner, a whore as well as mother, while their humbled father ends the play whimpering and crawling near Ruth's chair, begging in infantilized fashion for her favor. From the sons' perspectives, Ruth's presence will gratify their Oedipal wish: to possess the mother and displace the father; from the father's perspective, this ending constitutes his progeny's revenge upon him for his abusive tyranny; from Ruth's perspective, she will rule this roost with easy superiority, alternating her mythic roles of wife/mother/whore while expressing her essential erotic inclinations; from Sam's prudish, asexual perspective, this newly formed community overwhelms his role as the family's superego—he collapses at the drama's culmination.

Tom Stoppard, wittiest and most intellectual of contemporary dramatists, has taken the category of role playing where a literary personage is modeled on a literary personage from a previous text to ingenious dimensions of parody and travesty. In *Rosencrantz and Guildenstern Are Dead* (1967), he constructs the entire play within the embrace of *Hamlet,* with the title characters' every entry and exit circumscribed by the plot and decor of Shakespeare's tragedy. Rosencrantz and Guildenstern are, in Pirandellian fashion, two characters in search of their parts, which have been ineluctably established by their Elizabethan author but are unknown to them. Like Beckett's Vladimir and Estragon, they are caught in a world of uncertainty and anxiety, confusion and mistrust, ignorant of their purpose or fate. "We only know what we're told," says Guildenstern, "and that's little enough. And for all we know it isn't even true." When Stoppard revises Hamlet's mousetrap play to include enactment of Rosencrantz and Guildenstern's death, he offers a Byzantine maze of an existential drama enclosing a play-within-the-play in turn enclosing a play-within-the-play. As the coprotagonists await their orders to wander into and out of Shakespeare's scenes, they can only resign themselves to the meaninglessness of the roles they are condemned to execute. Sighs Rosencrantz: "We don't question, we don't doubt. We perform."

Stoppard's *Travesties* (1974) echoes and distorts Beckett, Shaw, limericks, and "Mr. Gallagher and Mr. Shean" vaudeville routines, but the dominant models are furnished by Wilde and Joyce. Stoppard discovered that Lenin, James Joyce, and Tristan Tzara all happened to reside in Zurich during the First World War, and that Joyce, managing an English troupe, cast a minor British consular official, Henry Carr, as Algernon Moncrieff in a production of Oscar Wilde's drawing-room farce, *The Importance of Being Earnest* (1895). With brilliant fancy, Stoppard dramatizes the verbal, philosophic, and aesthetic fireworks that explode when the political revolutionist, revolutionary artist, and revolutionary anti-artist collide. Moreover, he converts Carr into the play's protagonist, whose bourgeois philistinism challenges Joyce's and Tzara's notions of art, while his dandyism travesties Wilde's.

All but one of *Travesties'* featured roles parody parts in *The Importance of Being Earnest,* which is itself an elegantly controlled travesty of British upper-class customs. Not only does Carr often reproduce the lines of Wilde's Algie, but Tzara corresponds to John Worthing (who in Wilde's comedy takes the double role of "Earnest" when in town); both Carr's sister, Gwendolen, and Tzara's friend, Cecily, share names, beauty, and plot predicaments with the two young ladies in *Earnest*; as in Wilde, a crucial mixup of possessions perplexes the players, with the traveling bag in which Jack Worthing was misplaced as a baby replaced by folders in which Joyce's and Lenin's manuscripts are misplaced; and then there is Joyce the character, who intermittently assumes the lines of the imperious Lady Bracknell, with the result that a question-and-answer scene between him and Tzara functions on three levels. It corresponds to Wilde's famous interview scene in which the lady investigates Worthing's worth as suitor for her niece's hand; it is fashioned akin to the "catechism" episode in Joyce's novel *Ulysses* (1922); and it gives Tzara the oportunity to profess his doctrine of dadaism, which he defines as "The right to urinate in different colors." Only Lenin's role confounds Stoppard's Wildean choreography. He considered matching the part with Miss Prism's, Wilde's governess, but concluded that to do so would trivialize it. Whether Stoppard's marriage of parodistic role playing with a Shavian comedy of ideas is a happy dramatic match is subject to critical controversy; that his collage of role-taking and style-slanting is fiendishly clever cannot be doubted.

Clearly, the texts discussed in this entry are only a sample of the literary works in which role playing assumes significance. After all, role is the basic unit of socialization, with each person performing a variety of roles as he functions in a variety of situations. And literature, as a symbolic presentation of human experiences, portrays man as a self who offers his manifold actions to others as witnesses and respondents and in turn witnesses and responds to the actions of others—thus assuming interchangeably the parts of actor and audience.

What is noteworthy in modern literature is its increasing self-consciousness of theme and sophistication of form. Beginning with Pirandello (or Kafka, Proust, Joyce, Lawrence, Mann, and others), modernism abandons faith in progress and belief in a universal, stable, purposive human condition. It experiments instead with open-ended, improvisatory literary devices to mirror a haphazard existence, at war with itself, which warrants no solutions yet persists in posing problematic questions. Thus Genet is more explicit and subversive than Euripides in casting off the coating of social restraint and the taboos of civilized norms. Whereas

Sophocles dramatizes the individual necessity to obey the oracles of a divinely designed world order, Fitzgerald scorns the values of his society, regarding them as injurious to individual development. And Beckett goes so far as to jettison Western civilization's stock standards of happiness and merit: individual dignity, marital affection, parental and filial devotion, sexual attraction, empirical knowledge, fulfillment in one's work. The modern temper can no longer accept an outer world of Goethean harmony, serenity, rationalism, and wholeness. Modern artists tend to value a truth-telling soul, no matter how narcissistic or depraved—for example, Rameau's nephew—above conformity to an inauthentic, insincere, impersonal society. They attempt to capture that honest inner life in faithful language—no matter how harsh—and complex role playing—no matter how perverse. They regard human nature as a psychic battlefield in which a person can only survive by exploring that inner life while playing a self-protective role in a culture indifferent or hostile to the rich unfolding of his faculties. "Give us this day our daily mask," implores Guildenstern in Stoppard's play.

See also: Masque or Mask.

Selected Bibliography

Goffman, Erving. *The Presentation of Self in Everyday Life*. 1956. Garden City, N.Y.: Doubleday, 1959.

Mead, George H. *Mind, Self and Society*. Chicago: University of Chicago Press, 1934

Van Laan, Thomas F. *Role-Playing in Shakespeare*. Toronto: University of Toronto Press, 1978.

Wilshire, Bruce. *Role Playing and Identity*. Bloomington: University of Indiana Press, 1982.

GERHARD BRAND

S

//

SCAPEGOAT

In the Old Testament, God orders Aaron to take a goat, consign to it all the sins of the Israelites, and send it into the wilderness. This simple religious ritual touches deeply on human psychological needs; it becomes, in metaphorical form, a central theme in literature. There are several aspects to the scapegoat principle: first, the idea that sinfulness is transferable and, in compact form, can be taken on by one individual on behalf of many others; further, that that individual is often unwillingly assigned the role of scapegoat or victim, the cause or result being moral isolation; third, the bearer of bad tidings is in some irrational, primitive way associated with the evil events he tells about and is punished (literally in primitive societies, figuratively or indirectly in advanced societies) as if he has become the scapegoat and as if "killing the messenger" will somehow make the adverse events vanish as well.

Antiquity

In the Old Testament, the omnipotent God creates everything according to a master design, yet evil crops up repeatedly. Hence the ubiquity of the scapegoat principle, as God blames and severely punishes Cain, Sodom, Pharaoh (whose heart he himself had hardened), Canaanites, Amalekites, Philistines, or backsliding Israelites for imperfections ultimately of His own creation. This is logically inconsistent, and the New Testament (and, even more, later Christian theologians) tried to get around the solecism by developing an explanation latent in the Old Testament—Satan. He (the Adversary, the Devil) is the cause of man's failings and ills, from original sin on. In his *De civitate Dei* (*The City of God*, treatise, 413–426), St. Augustine renders a detailed account of the diabolical machinations; not Pharaoh or Haman but Satan has become the scapegoat for evil. In ages and periods too sophisticated to believe in a literal Satan, some vulnerable individual or group takes his place, in what is known as the "Devil [or "Conspiracy" or "Paranoiac"] Theory of History." The popularity of this theory is due to its elegance. It absolves oneself or one's group of any blame; it provides a simplistic answer to complex problems; it makes the world intelligible and orderly.

The scapegoat principle antedates the Bible. Attis and Adonis, Tammuz and Osiris, Dionysus and Orpheus are superhuman beings whose castration and dismemberment (and sometimes resurrection) were commemorated by primitive peoples, often in the spring. The New Testament draws on these various pagan myths while concurrently dealing with Old Testament ritual in internalized, spiritualized form. Thus the literal sacrifice of an actual goat as prescribed in the earlier work becomes the self-sacrifice of the man-god, Jesus, who takes upon himself not just the sins of the community for that year but the sins of all mankind for eternity. He has become a cosmic, divine scapegoat, and in a curious way, his role is parallel though antithetic to that of Satan. Hence Adam, who had been the recipient of much blame as a result of his fiasco, is relieved in Christianity of part of his scapegoat role by the fact that he, in a *felix culpa,* prepared the way for Jesus, the second Adam, the real and redemptive scapegoat, even as Satan, the other scapegoat, turns out to be only doing God's work.

In psychological terms, Jesus is a special version of the scapegoat principle: the rebel-teacher-reformer who, bringing both good and bad tidings and being morally isolated, must die. Many of the great improvers of mankind have been martyred first and venerated later, because in their time they questioned basic assumptions, confronted people with the fearful unknown, and seemed to undermine those with power and vested interests. Thus Socrates functions in four Platonic dialogues as a scapegoat, a bringer of the news that the assumptions men live by are worthless; he must be killed if the Athenians are to feel cleansed and once more secure.

Fiction often illustrates the scapegoat principle. At the beginning of Homer's epic poem *Ilias (Iliad,* c. 8th century B.C.), the Greek camp is afflicted by a plague and when a prophet reveals that the cause is an offense against the gods perpetrated by Agamemnon, the king, instead of trying to appease the offended ones, turns his ire on the prophet; the truth-telling messenger is made a scapegoat for Agamemnon's guilt. Similarly in Homer's epic poem *Odysseia (Odyssey,* c. 8th century B.C.), an old man of Ithaca reproves the suitors and is scolded by them for telling what the reader knows to be the truth. In Sophocles' *Oidipous tyrannos (Oedipus Rex,* play, c. 429 B.C.), the blind prophet Tiresias, sent for against his will, reluctantly hints at the horrid truth and, for his pains, is accused by Oedipus (as is, later, Creon) of conspiracy and treachery. In the *Antigonē* (play, c. 441 B.C.), when it is his turn to govern in the wake of Oedipus' fall, Creon repeats the error, accusing both Tiresias and his own son of ulterior motives. These are all examples of "killing the messenger" as a scapegoat.

A classic example of something common in everyday life—making a scapegoat of someone who is prostrate or who cannot respond—occurs in the *Odyssey.* When the hero returns home, kills the leading suitor, Antinous, and rebukes the others, the second leading suitor, conceding the justness of the charges, lays all the blame on Antinous and even reveals evil actions not mentioned by the hero, ending with the gleeful, mischievous words, "Now he has perished by his own fate." Euripides' *Hippolytos* (*Hyppolytus,* play, 428 B.C.) contains a variant of the theme. Phaedra makes advances to her stepson, who rebuffs her, whereupon she clears her reputation, if not her conscience, by accusing him of having made advances to her. Very much like the case in the *Odyssey* is Caesar's telling in his *De bello gallico* (*On the Gallic War,* c. 50 B.C.) of his conquest of the Bellovaci. The defeated ones said that one great benefit from their loss was the death of "Correus, a demagogue and the only begetter of this war." But Caesar, seeing, like Odysseus, through this maneuver, remarks on how easy it was to "lay the blame for one's own misdeeds on the shoulders of a dead man" and that no such revolt could have taken place did not the leader have the cooperation of the tribal authorities and the mass of the people. Centuries later, the satirist Lucian, accused of besmirching philosophy, responds in his *Halieus e anabiountes* (*Fisherman,* dialogue, 2d century) that the blame should fall on those hypocritical avaricious pseudo-philosophers whose misbehavior justifies the criticism, not on the satirist who simply submits the evidence.

The Renaissance

What is shown as reprehensible in classical epic and war memoir is actually prescribed by Machiavelli in *Il principe* (*The Prince,* treatise, 1532). The carrying out of violent deeds is to be assigned to a surrogate ruler who, when popular revulsion gathers, is to be blamed and removed. The Machiavellian mode is seen in its most common and least palatable form in a discussion, in Montaigne's "De l'experience" ("On Experience," *Essais* [*Essays*], 3.13, 1580–1588), of a case of men incorrectly found guilty of a murder; when the real murderers were discovered, the innocent ones were still executed for fear that releasing them would "set up a precedent for the reversal of judgments." How many others, Montaigne wonders, are victims of such "judicial formality," made scapegoats by the need of professionals and experts to maintain the luster of their discipline by burying their errors.

In Shakespeare's plays, the scapegoat principle is often at work. Richard III and Cleopatra whip the bearers of ill tidings. In *Macbeth* (1605–1606) the murderous couple contrive circumstantial evidence to pin the murder of Duncan onto two "sleepy grooms," that is, servants whom Macbeth peremptorily executes; at a trial, as Lennox remarks later, the grooms might inconveniently have proclaimed their innocence. In *Othello* (c. 1604) Iago kills Rodrigo and then blames him for the assault on Cassio. But the really powerful treatment of a tragic scapegoat is in *Coriolanus* (1607–1608). The banishment of Coriolanus from Rome is partly due to the political intrigues of the tribunes who want to benefit from the routing of the patrician party, which he represents, and partly the expression of the populace's return of the contempt the hero has showered on it. It is as if his forfeiture of citizenship or life is the price to be paid for stability and peace in Rome, not unlike the situation in the Jerusalem of Jesus' time. But there is a further twist in the story as, after later being deterred at long last from making the whole city of Rome the scapegoat for his humiliation, he is treated as a sort of scapegoat by his new ally, Tullus Aufidius. Jealous of Coriolanus' ascendancy among the Volscians he himself had led, Tullus wants to be rid of a competitor, but, instead of acknowledging this openly, he makes much ado about Coriolanus' peace with a prostrate Rome. Hence the slaying of Coriolanus, which the mob thinks of as revenge for the many Volscians he had killed, is really like the ritual killing of that member of the community who is an outsider.

It is an open question, of course, as to whether, in one modern reading of the *Merchant of Venice* (c. 1595), Shylock is not a scapegoat for a Christian society that is shown to be prodigal, prejudiced, harassing, mercenary, authoritarian, slaveholding, and hypocritical. Without turning him into an angel, does not the play, according to this interpretation, suggest that he has become in good part what the Christian society made him? If so, the society is guilty of the self-fulfilling prophecy, a phenomenon closely linked to the scapegoat principle, for the putatively self-evident guilt of the scapegoat enables one's theories and prophecies to look good.

The linkage is even stronger in Cervantes' novel *Don Quijote* (*Don Quixote*, 1605, 1615). The Don maintains his bizarre theory by speaking of the wicked enchanters (the devil theory of history) whose machinations account for all adverse events and embarrassing facts. When at an inn he and his fantasies turn the place upside down, he feels vindicated and even half converts Sancho Panza to belief in the enchanters, who are his personal scapegoats.

Milton is in the Augustinian tradition of making Satan the cosmic scapegoat of *Paradise Lost* (poem, 1667). However, closer to home, a good part of the blame for the Fall is also shared by a uxorious Adam and, even more, a narcissistic Eve. An unkind cut is that she, after the debacle, blames Adam for having granted her the very freedom to work separately she had so insistently demanded; to make a scapegoat of someone is often merely a form of "passing the buck."

The protagonist of Molière's *Le misanthrope* (*The Misanthropist*, play, 1666) persists in irritating everyone by holding up the mirror of fallibility to the many imperfect individuals that swarm in society. When at the end he retires with bitterness to the wilderness, he undergoes willingly, as does Socrates, the punishment for having been a witness to the truth rather than lubricating human relations. In *Tartuffe* (play, 1664), when his son informs Orgon that Tartuffe is a fraud and cites the evidence, Orgon turns on the son (as did Agamemnon, Oedipus, Creon), impugning his motives and suspecting conspiracy. Later, Orgon learns his lesson and, trying to impart it to *his* mother, finds out for himself what it feels like to be the carrier of painful truths.

The Nineteenth Century

The hero of Goethe's *Faust* (play, 1808) makes a pact with Mephistopheles, but when the love affair with Margaret sours, he, in a traditional vein, blames the satanic being for troubles of his own creation. In Hawthorne's *Scarlet Letter* (novel, 1850), Hester Prynne is forced to wear a scarlet "A" on her forehead and to live in exile on the outskirts of the community because she has been found guilty of adultery. This is one of the greatest fictional portrayals of the sophisticated or psychological workings of the scapegoat principle, for the society that condemns this young, dignified, and beautiful woman is not shown to be morally superior to her. She must be made to pay, as if her doing openly what they do secretly, or what they would like to do if they had the chance, is an embarrassment to them for revealing their depravity or their cowardice. By punishing her, furthermore, they reassure themselves of their own probity. Thus a Puritan society is re-enforced in its self-suppression by its periodic turning on someone who chooses experience and life rather than denial and passivity.

That the guilty partner was not just any passing vagabond but the highly esteemed local minister underlines the severity of the judgment implicitly passed on the community, as does the irony that his ritual acknowledgment of general guilt from the pulpit merely enhances his standing in the community as a noble Christian. That he for long has not the courage to either defend her or accept his specific guilt by joining her on the block undermines the value of this Christianity even more. What this story adds to the scapegoat theme is the suggestion that, if the scapegoat takes on the sins of the community, the community has a lot of sinfulness to pass on. Further, as feminists would be quick to point out, women are the scapegoat-victims of both biology and society. It takes two to create a child, but nature makes only the woman's body reveal the sin, so that her guilt grows daily while the man can disappear. Then a patriarchal society, instead of taking account of that unfair difference, merely exploits it to punish the woman all the more (though, to be sure, the women in the community are as punitive as the men).

There is a sense also in which Melville's *Bartleby the Scrivener* (novella, 1853) is about a scapegoat. Bartleby says what people would like to say to their superiors but keep to themselves: "I would prefer not to." He even proceeds to act on his preference. As in the case of the *Scarlet Letter,* this is offensive to the average person. Not only does he disrupt routine, but by revealing that the option to say "no" exists, he shows up everyone else as cowardly or lazy. They get their revenge by ostracizing him. Neither the Wall St. office nor the society at large appears to have room for someone who will not play the game of life according to the venerable oppressive rules. He is a scapegoat for bringing preferences into play in a universe that recognizes no such rights. Perhaps also the universe cannot offer any positive preferences, only negative ones, and so, like Ivan Karamazov, he returns the entrances ticket to God, an act that outrages even the most victimized conformists.

In Melville's *Billy Budd* (novella, 1891), the hero has a daily beauty about him that offends the gratuitous villain Claggart. Claggart is one of life's losers, the type that must get his revenge by undoing someone who seems to have luck on his side. Billy is the individual that the universe must expel if Claggart is to feel relieved. When Billy, because of inarticulateness, strikes Claggart dead, it is society's turn to victimize Billy. No matter how right Billy may have been, or how noble vis-à-vis Claggart, society, as embodied in the laws and in the captain who applies them, is bound to exact capital punishment; men cannot be allowed to take the law into their own hands. Thus Billy, from having been the private scapegoat of Claggart, becomes the scapegoat for a society—any society—that demands above all adherence to laws and codes.

Insofar as picking on a scapegoat springs from a sense of insecurity—because of cowardice, conformity, jealousy, or vindictiveness—it is ripe material for Dostoevsky, who specialized in writing about such anti-heroes. Thus in the *Dvoĭnik* (*The Double,* novel, 1846), the protagonist is a man ostracized from society because of his ineptness and moral squalor. He hallucinates about another self, who embodies all the things that the protagonist would like to be. Because of ambivalence, this alter ego soon becomes the repository of all that the protagonist hates, as the scapegoat of society conjures up a personal scapegoat made up of his own aspirations. But because he is losing control of his mind, his fantasy takes the form of seeing the alter ego make a scapegoat-victim of him and pushing him into even more isolation and, in the end, into madness.

The protagonist of *Zapiski iz podpol'ia* (*Notes from Underground,* novel, 1864) is like the man in the *Double,* but he no longer even has a job. Blaming those who are worldly and successful, this self-destructive, self-appointed scapegoat gets even with life by presuming to make others his scapegoats (even as Shakespeare's Coriolanus, banished, turns the judgment on his judges with "I banish you!"). Later, in his encounter with the sympathetic, vulnerable prostitute, he treats her brutally, making yet another scapegoat out of her. When he comes to his senses, she has gone out of his life forever, and he realizes that in the end he is his own main victim and scapegoat.

In *Prestuplenie i nakazanie* (*Crime and Punishment,* novel, 1866), Sonya, the saintly prostitute, is *déclasse,* while Raskolnikov's sister, marrying in order to send her brother to college, practices a covert middle-class form of prostitution. Yet the respectable sister refuses even to meet Sonya; is she not, Dostoevsky implies, using the whore as a scapegoat for her own bad conscience? Dmitri of the *Brat'ia Karamazovy* (*The Brothers Karamazov,* novel, 1880) is incorrectly found guilty of the murder of his father. The suggestion is strong that when a heinous crime is committed, society needs a culprit, and whether the victim is the guilty one is (as in lynch justice) incidental to the case. If, as here, he is innocent, he has been made a scapegoat for society's imperatives, that is, a sense—or myth—of design, of crime being punished. Something similar operates in his brother Ivan's parable of the Grand Inquisitor. Jesus returns to earth only to be rebuked by the inquisitor for having been a negative force, for bringing truth and idealism to a mankind that wants only bread and illusions. Even though this is a Christian society, Jesus is a scapegoat all over again, albeit this time through ostracism, not execution, and as a result of the moral cowardice and weakness, not the sins, of man. If such incongruities suggest that the world is mad, that precisely is the theme of Chekhov's *Palata No. 6* (*Ward Number Six*, story, 1892). A doctor ministering to a lunatic asylum and gradually perceiving the anomalies and inequities of life, ends up as an inmate. Society gladly sends him there because his sensitivity raises questions that people do not want to hear. He is, in the Socratean tradition, another messenger killed.

One writer who specialized in the scapegoat theme was Ibsen. In the early realistic play *Samfundets støtter* (*The Pillars of Society*, 1877), Lona, a rebellious woman, is forced by an intolerant Norwegian society to emigrate to America. Her situation is similar to that of Hester in the *Scarlet Letter*: a repressive puritanical society; a young woman full of joie de vivre; an affair with a prominent member of the community; the woman forced into exile while the man thrives in his vocation. But in this more modern and secular version, the woman returns and triumphantly brings the light of truth to bear on everything; here is a rare case in which the scapegoat is victorious. The feminist theme implicit in the *Scarlet Letter* and in *Pillars* becomes central in *Et dukkehjem* (*A Doll's House*, play, 1879). Torvald, with his reputation and career on the line, is willing to sacrifice his wife's reputation and independence; he would be, in short, an accomplice of a society that, more interested in legal technicalities than in mitigating human factors (as in *Billy Budd),* is ready to make a scapegoat of Nora. But one of the strongest treatments of the theme is surely in *En folkefiende* (*An Enemy of the People,* 1882). Dr. Stockman is one of those Socratean re-former-teachers who, in trying to bring the truth to his fellow man, finds himself the target of everyone's ire, and anyone who aids him is himself the victim of ostracism. What Ibsen adds here to the theme is an even-handedness and irony. Stockman, with his naïveté and self-righteousness, surely has his deficiencies. The play ends as society wins, polluted wells and all, and the defeated, isolated Stockman dreams of his eventual vindication.

In Tolstoy's *Khadzhi-Murat* (novel, 1900), the hero leaves the Mohammedan side in a frontier war and joins the Russian side. The tsarist government is, like all governments, highly fragmented, as each prominent individual tries to turn this good fortune to his own personal advantage. Hence, neither the noble char-acter of the hero nor the merits of the case come into consideration—only cunning and expediency. His life is finally sacrificed by the Russians, who have bigger fish to fry and cannot be concerned with one who, falling by the wayside, has ceased to be important; he is a scapegoat for power politics.

The Twentieth Century

In Conrad's *Nigger of the Narcissus* (novel, 1847), the black man on the ship is the scapegoat because of his color and his terminal illness. Yet this hated man is mysteriously revered by the crew because he faces a fate they know must be theirs as well. He is a cosmic scapegoat in being the first to die in their little community. In Kafka's "Die Verwandlung" ("Metamorphosis," story, 1915), young Gregor has been supporting his parents and sister, but when he turns into an insect, the family soon detaches itself from him, the kind sister being the last to do so. When even she does, he curls up and dies. It is as if he lived only to support others and when he finds himself no longer needed or wanted, he loses the will to live. In a way, he is like Bartleby, withdrawing himself from the universe. The American does it as an act of will; the Austrian/Czech first suffers transformation and loneliness, then withdrawal of will. The transformation into an insect might, of course, have come about because he already sensed himself to be insectlike. Emotionally ostracized, isolated in a universe that entrapped him and sapped his will, he was a scapegoat who had to work for a family with failing resources. The metamorphosis is thus a metaphor.

Often the operating principle is social and political rather than cosmic. In Joyce's *Ulysses* (novel, 1922), Bloom is the scapegoat for some of the Dubliners leading empty, frustrated lives, because he is an outsider, a Jew (like Jesus and God, he says), and an eccentric (like the other loner, Stephen, he has "a bit of the artist"). In Faulkner's *Old Man* (novel, 1939) a criminal escapes from prison and saves a pregnant woman's life, but his kindly gesture is not taken account of by a governor's staff that needs upbeat statistics on crime, and he is thrown back into prison for the rest of his life. Being made a scapegoat for apparent affectlessness is the theme of Camus' *L'étranger* (*The Stranger,* novel, 1942). The hero's mother dies, and he is unable to weep for her at the funeral. A little later he kills an Arab and is put on trial; the jury finds him guilty not for the killing but because he had not wept for his mother. He is thus punished for violating one of the norms of behavior, not in lacking feelings but in appearing to lack them. Orwell's *1984* (novel, 1949) presents the classic way modern dictatorships use to make scapegoats of individuals and groups, and Heller's *Catch-22* (novel, 1961) shows the same principle at work in the mindless bureaucratic dictatorship within the U.S. Air Force during World War II, as individuals are victimized simply because there are requisitions to be met, forms to be filled out.

The most succinct, incisive, haunting, poetic treatment of the scapegoat theme is in Shirley Jackson's short story "The Lottery" (1948). Every year in a town the people gather to draw lots to see who will be stoned to death that day. The story reverberates on various levels. It depicts the irrationality and unfairness of life; the reign of chance; the role of violence in civilization; the rule of custom and the inherent conservatism of any group; the atrophy that overtakes a community or a set of rituals. But always at the juncture of all these intersecting themes is the inexorable fact that the community is constituted, or at least held together, by the elimination of one of its own, for no reason other than that it is done and that it is therefore right.

The story looks (with a glance at the Holocaust) all the way back to the biblical goat—a ritual ordered there by God, here by the god Custom. This is a secular vision; no sin or redemption is in question, no divine mandates. What the story says, at one level, is that the biblical injunction on the scapegoat is itself merely one manifestation of a principle that goes deeper than any religion. Society needs to isolate an individual, without questions of reason or merit, and do away with him or her, as if it could not survive without shedding blood. Religion merely tried to uplift the observance by substituting a goat or god for the virgin, youth, or prince used in primitive spring rituals; by devoting the ceremony to God; and by giving the rationale of transference of sin and redemption. Whether the impulse springs from sadism, self-hatred, guilt, or the sense of a cosmic price or tax to be paid, most people feel that someone must die for the health of the community.

See also: Anti-Hero, Christian Hero, Hermit.

Selected Bibliography

Frazer, James, Sir. *The Scapegoat*. London: Macmillan, 1913.
Thomas, N. W. "The Scapegoat in European Folklore." *Folklore* 17 (1906): 258–287.
Vickery, John, and J. M. Sellery eds., *The Scapegoat: Ritual and Literature*. Boston: Houghton Mifflin, 1972.

MANFRED WEIDHORN

SCATOLOGY

In literature, scatology is the study of the use of references to the body's waste products; also, allusions to intestinal gas or to those parts of the body involved in the processes of elimination, as well as to toilet fixtures and equipment and lavatories.

Generally speaking, civilized people have been taught to be ashamed of their waste matter and not to discuss it in public. Even in the midst of today's relaxed moral standards and explicit language, the waste products and secretions of our bodies—urine and feces, perspiration and mucous—represent the last real taboo. The basic fact that excrement is part of all human beings and the world that they inhabit has generally been ignored or suppressed by those writers with a tendency to idealize, while many realistically inclined artists have acknowledged the existence of excrement and have incorporated it into their works.

The use of scatological elements in literature serves a surprisingly large range of artistic intentions. Due to the disgust with which most people view fecal matter, scatology possesses a most powerful shock value in the hands of the satirist who wishes to debunk all human claims to greatness and who wants to stress the basic earthiness of all persons. Sometimes, however, scatology provides light humor, very often it is part of the author's gentle satire, and at times excremental references signal the reversal of standard societal values. In the latter case, the writer clearly demonstrates that those elements that society condemns as excremental really represent the nobility of life, while those parts of human life that society considers valuable often should be discarded and despised. Then there are some writers who have an ambiguous view of excrement. They acknowledge it as part of nature and the life cycle and see some good in it, but they never manage to free themselves totally from feeling a certain repulsion toward it. Finally there are also those extreme pessimists who see this world as nothing more than a mountain of excrement.

In addition to the occasional use of scatological elements by renowned authors, one also finds excremental outbursts and accusations among the anti-establishment artistic underground. The increase in recent years in the use of scatological terms and actions by members of underground artistic and literary circles in German-speaking countries was sharply reflected in a performance in 1969 by one Günter Brus. Stripping off his clothes on the stage of a University of Vienna auditorium, Brus urinated, drank the urine from his cupped hand, and promptly vomited. For his finale, the artist turned his back to the audience and defecated; he then smeared the excrement on his nude body while singing a rousing rendition of the Austrian national anthem. By reducing artistic expression to the mere acts of defecating or urinating, the artistic underground attempts to shock and aggravate the establishment, hence giving the artists temporary feelings of freedom. In addition, this emphasis on the primitive excremental act also conveys intense feelings of helplessness on the part of the artists (assuming, of course, they had serious intentions to begin with), since their scatological outpourings serve in a way as primal, expressionistic screams, their last hope of being heard. Convinced that centuries of serious attempts to improve the world by more traditional artistic means have produced no noticeable change for the better, these pessimistic artists, who feel themselves imprisoned in a meaningless world, finally express their independence in a most primitive infantile fashion: by defecating upon the world. Real literary concerns are in fact secondary to these writers and their work will therefore not be included in this overview of scatology in literature.

Antiquity

Neither the Greeks nor the Romans shied away from including scatological elements in their works. Aristophanes certainly utilized a number of excremental motifs in his comedy *Nephelai* (*The Clouds,* 423 B.C.), most notably that of flatulence. The absurdity of sophistic thinking is illustrated when a student of Socrates describes in great detail Socrates' theory that gnats "tootle" through their tails rather than their mouths as a result of the fact that their intestinal gas has to pass through a very narrow tube until it is finally released with a great rush. Later in the play Socrates himself compares the creation of a thunderstorm to the explosive passing of gas that occurs after one has eaten too much. Since Socrates displays such a keen interest in scatological explanations, it is, of course, not at all inappropriate that a lizard defecates upon him one night as he is contemplating the orbit of the moon. The befouling of an esteemed person is a relatively common scatological technique and such ridicule is obviously quite destructive.

Probably the earliest scatological depiction of war and its perpetrators also comes from Aristophanes. In his play *Eirēnē* (*The Peace,* 421 B.C.), a huge, stinking dung beetle that voraciously devours filth becomes associated with Cleon and other warmongers. When peace finally is restored, Trygaeus, the hero of the play, tells the broken warriors in a mocking tone that he intends to use part of their magnificent armor as a chamber pot. The dirt and destruction that are an inevitable part of every war have led not only to such satirical scatological depictions of war but also to more serious writings on war that use scatological references to convey a gruesome sense of realism. Such techniques are especially common in the war literature of the twentieth century.

The Roman satirists were particularly adept at employing a large variety of scatological allusions as tools of ridicule. No image was too repulsive to be used. This acceptance of the excremental was at least partially due to the fact that the Romans had developed a very sophisticated sanitary system and were accustomed to public latrines. Furthermore, the Roman deities included the gods of ordure, Stercutius and Crepitus, as well as a goddess of the sewers, Cloacina. In one of Horace's satires (1.8) (c. 35 B.C.) Priapus defeats the witches and chases them away by having his wooden statue crack "like a bursting bladder." Earlier in the work Priapus swears that he is telling the truth when he is describing the horrible doings of the witches. If it is not so, he says, may he be showered with the "white droppings" of the ravens.

Martial also makes occasional use of scatology in his epigrams (A.D 84–103). To be sure the number of his scatological epigrams is small, but their impact is nevertheless very strong. On one occasion (1.37) Martial takes a man to task for depositing his excrement in a container of gold, while the vessel from which he drinks is merely made of glass; thus this man has invested more money in the process of elimination than in gaining nourishment. In another epigram (1.83) a woman is insulted by means of Martial's statement that he is no longer surprised to hear that dogs eat dung now that he knows that her lap dog licks her mouth and lips. Similarly pungent is the attack against a certain Zoilus (2.42), who is asked why he bothers to soil the bath with his buttocks; insult is added to injury when Martial continues by suggesting that the water would be even more befouled if Zoilus were to stick his head into it. A final example of Martial's very personal scatological attacks is directed at another man, Aethon (12.72). This poor soul once had to break wind while praying to Jupiter. Not only did others laugh at him, but Jupiter also punished him by making him dine at home for three days. The embarrassed Aethon can never get over his terrible deed. Even though he develops the precautionary habit of entering a privy and passing gas up to twenty times before entering the Capitol, he can never again face the king of the gods without squeezing his buttocks tightly together. Martial presents here a most effective scatological metaphor for the fact that human beings are eternally impeded by their physiological shortcomings.

Juvenal was a Roman author who employed scatology in order to uncover the most heinous personal and societal immoralities. This satirist finds no pleasure in wallowing in excremental verbal attacks; nevertheless, when he deems it appropriate he sallies forth with striking scatologically invective language. On several occasions in Juvenal's satires (A.D. c. 98–140) chamber pots appear as a means of defusing any human claims to greatness. In the Third Satire the speaker expresses the desire to leave Rome, since the city has been overrun by unprincipled parvenus who are willing to do anything for material gain, including the building of cesspools. A little later he mocks the Greek parvenus in Rome who are always ready to flatter "if you but belch, piss, shit, or just guffaw or your tipped chamber pot begins to gurgle." Juvenal's attacks at times get even more distasteful. In order to unmask the incredible immorality of some Roman ladies, the Sixth Satire creates a sharp contrast. On the surface these women display a chaste and devout behavior. However, once they are protected by the darkness of night they engage in the most obscene and sacrilegious behavior. Among other misdeeds, they urinate on the altar of Chastity and the next day their husbands step into this offal as they go off to visit respectable friends.

From the Middle Ages through the Seventeenth Century

During the Middle Ages a highly ambivalent attitude toward fecal matter developed. On the one hand the church resorted to excrement to provide a hard-hitting and easily recognizable metaphor for the devil and the sins that he instigates. One encounters, for example, numerous visual depictions of the devil as a creature with a mouth in the anal region. At the same time the middle class also derived quite a bit of enjoyment from rather vulgar scatological humor. Such attraction toward ordure expressed itself particularly well in jests, fabliaux, facetiae, or *Schwänke*.

One of the best examples of the didactic and moral use of scatology occurs in Dante's epic poem *La divina commedia* (*The Divine Comedy,* c. 1320), where a considerable amount of scatological imagery can be found in the *Inferno* (*Hell*). Feces and their accompanying stench clearly constitute a shocking metaphor for evil in this world. According to Dante, the world's sinners are cast into hell, depicted as an immense scatological dungeon where they are forced to endure gross smells, sights, and sounds. Everything is crusted by excrement or filth here and some people are even stuck directly in the dung.

Martin Luther's *Tischreden* (*Table-Talk,* 1566) is even more pessimistic in its use of scatology. While Dante condemns only sinners as excremental, Luther automatically sees every human body as nothing more than a combination of excrement, urine, mucous, and sweat. The fact that water gets dirty when we bathe is again seen by Luther as proof that the human body is constituted of nothing but filth or excrement and is therefore worthless. He speaks of his own dysentery as proof that the world is in actuality ruled by the intestinal tract and not the brain and that life will always be nothing but suffering, a constant fluctuation between constipation and diarrhea. The fact that the physical aspect of humanity is to be seen entirely in excremental terms also means for Luther that the world is ruled by the devil. The only way to escape from the grasp of this evil demon is to believe in God. God will eventually resurrect the souls of the believers and at that moment the excremental part of humanity will drop away.

Luther directed his scatological anger not only at the devil (he frequently recommends breaking wind or defecating as a defense against Lucifer) but also against the pope and other opponents of the Reformation. *Abbildung des Papstes* (*Depiction of the Pope*, 1545) constitutes one of the coarsest diatribes of this period; it includes as an illustration a woodcut in which the origin of the pope is depicted. A disgusting devil excretes the pope and five cardinals. The Catholics, however, attacked the Protestants in equally vulgar fashion. Johannes Cochlaeus, who published many satirical leaflets of his own between 1521 and 1550, once depicted the reformer in the following way: Luther is excreting some of his writings while ugly devils dance around him and the people watching the whole scene have to hold their noses to shut out the stench.

One of the all-time masters of scatology was François Rabelais, who presents his readers with a great variety of scatological material in his novels on Gargantua and Pantagruel (1532–1564). Although Rabelais employed excrement as a satirical weapon, he is not as negative as either Dante or Luther. In fact, he tends toward the hearty scatological joke that also characterizes the fabliaux. Rabelais delights in describing how the three- to five-year-old Gargantua maintains his individuality by being totally slovenly. Among other things, he urinates into his shoes, defecates into his shirt, and expels gas loudly (1, chap. 11). The reader is told in great detail how the five-year-old tried out many items in order to find the best possible ass wiper; Gargantua finally decides that nothing can compare to the neck of a downy goose (1, chap. 13). An additional benefit of his scatological research is the fact that Gargantua has also learned how to rhyme. Later the gigantic protagonist travels to Paris and urinates on the stupidly gawking citizens; over 260,000 Parisians are drowned in this scene (1, chap. 17). No segment of society escapes Rabelais' scatological ridicule. Monks are described as eaters of ordure and their convents are thus the privies of the world (1, chap. 40). Philosophers are shown extracting farts from a dead ass and selling them (5, chap. 22). Although Rabelais certainly besmirches every strata of society, one must not overlook the positive note of Gargantua's proud acceptance of his own excrementality.

The fun that many medieval as well as sixteenth-century writers derived from telling excrementally vulgar stories is quite apparent in an example from Jörg Wickram's *Rollwagenbüchlein* (*Stories for Travellers,* 1555). One of the *Schwänke* in this popular book tells the story of a simpleminded man who dreams of meeting the devil in a forest. Satan tells the man that a treasure is buried under a tree. All he has to do is to run home and return with a shovel and the treasure is his. In order not to miss the location of the treasure the devil convinces the man to shit. Instead of finding the treasure the man defecates in his bed and befouls himself. In the morning he is scolded by his wife and has learned never to trust the devil again.

The seventeenth century was characterized by the destruction of the Thirty Years' War in central Europe. Furthermore there still were no decent sanitary sewer systems, and European cities continued to engage in such medieval practices as the dumping of chamber pots onto the street. Since most people were still living in a rather unsanitary environment, it is not surprising that the tradition of scatology in literature also lived on. Jests and facetiae were still popular, and new ones continued to be written. Most of these collections of jests, such as William Hickes' *Coffee-House Jests* (1677), included a few stories with scatological references. Especially prevalent was the tendency to befoul or ridicule characters in the tales by showering them with urine, having them lie in excrement, or directing a flatus at them. Just as is true in these jests, scatology tends to be scattered here and there throughout literature of the seventeenth century. In Andreas Gryphius' comedy *Horribilicribrifax oder wählende Liebhaber (Horribilicribrifax or Choosing Lovers,* 1663) a page relates how his frustrated nobleman threw his hunting horn at a stag during a hunt in Persia. The horn lodged in the stag's anus and the animal's breaking wind now sounded so strange that all the hunting dogs came running and cornered the stag. Another example of the usefulness of the scatological appears in Hans Jakob Christoffel von Grimmelshausen's *Der abenteuerliche Simplicissimus (The Adventurous Simplicissimus,* 1669); in this novel dung plays an important part in the peasant life into which the main character, Simplicissimus is born. In Molière's comedy *Le malade imaginaire (The Imaginary Invalid,* 1673), the hypochondriac spends an entire scene grumbling about the use and effect of enemas. A final example might be John Dryden's poem "Mac Flecknoe. Or a Satyr upon the True-Blew Protestant Poet, T.S." (1682), in which Tom Shadwell, the victim of Dryden's satire, is gradually reduced to a load of manure.

The Eighteenth Century

Since the eighteenth century and part of the nineteenth tended toward idealism, the number of writers to employ scatology in their works dropped sharply compared to the previous two centuries. Yet, even these highminded times exhibited their share of scatology. Certainly one of the most important practitioners of the justified literary use of excremental matter was Jonathan Swift. Swift employed scatological humor in such poems as "The Gulph of All Human Possessions" (1724), but he also made repeated use of scatology as a satirical weapon, especially in such prose works as *The Wonderful Wonder of Wonders* (1720) or *An Examination of Certain Abuses, Corruptions, and Enormities in the City of Dublin* (1732). Most striking, however, are the scatological motifs in *Gulliver's Travels* (satire, 1726). For example, Swift utilizes the process of urination to underline the size differences between Gulliver and those he encounters. In the land of the Lilliputians, Gulliver's urination strikes down these minute creatures as if a dam had burst (1, chap. 1); later, in a humorous reversal, Gulliver insists on withdrawing a considerable distance from the giants in order to relieve himself between some leaves (2, chap. 1). In book 4 Swift employs scatology to satirize the depravity of human beings who resemble the nefarious Yahoos, as he depicts the Yahoos' habit of emptying their bowels from trees upon those who pass below.

Another significant work in the area of scatology is Alexander Pope's *The*

Dunciad (poem, 1728–1743). In book 2 Pope associates a great deal of scatological behavior (a urination contest, prayers to Cloacina, diving into mud and
excrement) with the dunces who have triumphed and abolished all social order.
The excremental imagery intensifies the immorality of these contemptible characters.

Even the idealistic Johann Wolfgang von Goethe did not always avoid scatological language. In his *Götz von Berlichingen* (play, 1773), Götz retorts at
one stage with "Leck mich im Arsch" [kiss my ass], a classic rejoinder that
practically every German can still quote today. When Christoph Friedrich Nicolai
wrote a parody of Goethe's *Leiden des jungen Werthers (The Sorrows of Young
Werther,* novel, 1774) called *Die Freuden des jungen Werthers (The Joys of
Young Werther,* 1775), Goethe replied with a mocking poem "Nicolai auf Werthers Grab" ("Nicolai on Werther's Grave," 1775), in which Nicolai is depicted
as moving his bowels on Werther's grave, claiming it is more noble to "shit"
than to commit suicide.

The Nineteenth and Twentieth Centuries

As literature moved away from idealism to realism in the nineteenth century,
scatological metaphors also began to reappear, with a major eruption occurring
in the twentieth century; during this period German writers have undoubtedly
become the primary champions of scatology. Modern German literature contains
not only a large amount of scatology but also a variety of uses of excremental
motifs that has been unmatched anywhere else. The desire of these German
writers to be honest and in touch with the basic realities of life, to create a
menschliche Kunst [human art], has caused them to cast aside straitlaced aesthetic
standards and to express their ideas in most down-to-earth terms.

Scatological satire was an important part of the artistic and literary revolt that
took place in the early part of the twentieth century. Far from light humor,
however, the satire prevalent at this time was more of a dismal railing against
current aesthetic ideals and bourgeois society; basically deeply serious in its
intentions, it questioned current views of human nature and the external world.
This type of black humor is present in Bertolt Brecht's play *Baal* (1922), which
depicts a Darwinian universe in which everyone devours everyone else, leaving
only waste products behind; such satire also plays a part in the drama's nineteenth-
century forerunner, Georg Büchner's *Woyzeck* (c. 1837). Like Brecht, Büchner
uses extremely explicit, crude language to convey the image of human beings
as slaves of their instincts, as prisoners of what he terms *unideale Natur* [im-
perfect nature]. Even more extreme than Büchner and Brecht are the Dadaists,
anti-artists of the early twentieth century whose slogan "Art is shit" is typical
of their outrage not only against the art of their day but also against bourgeois
ideals in general.

Transmute the dadaists' motto to "War is shit," and one has the epitome of
the attitude expressed in a number of works by modern German authors who
have found scatological imagery highly appropriate for conveying their views

of the two world wars. Not only do these writers find excremental allusions suitable for depicting the horrors of war, but they have seized upon a Freudian prototype—the anal personality—as the incarnation of the Nazi sickness. For Erich Maria Remarque in *Im Westen nichts Neues* (*All Quiet on the Western Front,* novel, 1929), the relaxation of normal attitudes toward the excremental during wartime has both positive and negative connotations. On the one hand the need to move one's bowels becomes pleasurable because it frees the soldier temporarily from his duty to kill or be killed. At the same time, however, Remarque shows how in the final analysis war renders human beings no more than grotesquely twisted bodies that continually dribble excrement as a result of dysentery. Heinrich Böll in the novel *Wo warst du, Adam?* (*And Where Were You, Adam?,* 1951) and Peter Weiss in his documentary drama *Die Ermittlung* (*The Investigation,* 1965), however, are more one-sided in their use of excremental elements to convey the pathological nature of war and those who conduct it. Both Böll and Weiss have made a distinctly German contribution to literary wartime characterization: the anally preoccupied Nazi. Combining a keen national self-knowledge with the insights of such psychologists as Sigmund Freud and Erich Fromm, perceptive German writers (and artists such as George Grosz) have developed an unforgettable character type. Lieutenant Greck's death scene in *Wo warst du, Adam?* is particularly memorable. This character has an attack of diarrhea while grenades are landing in an adjacent cesspool, causing the sick man to be showered with liquid manure. Considering Böll's depiction of Greck as a sick anal personality, the excremental nature of his demise is strikingly fitting and undeniably sad.

It is a natural step from Böll's view of war as a sickness to his depiction of the openly scatological, uninhibited Leni Pfeiffer and her mentor, Sister Rahel, in the novel *Gruppenbild mit Dame* (*Group Portrait with Lady,* 1971) as individuals possessing healthy, admirable traits. In their frank acceptance of excrement as a natural part of human life, Leni and Rahel contrast sharply with hypocritical, excessively fastidious persons such as those who perpetrated World War II. Böll learned from personally experiencing the results of twelve years of rule by the Nazis that the real moral filth of this world was to be found precisely in obsessively clean Nazis who would wear white gloves and listen to the music of Mozart and Beethoven while murdering some twelve million people and not in the harmless and often beneficial human or animal wastes. If there is one particular German contribution to the realm of scatological literary imagery that is most unusual, it is precisely Böll's meticulous development of the theory that an open acceptance of the excremental is beneficial to both individuals and society. This view presents a revolutionary challenge to the negative values that civilized society has attached to excrement.

German writers and artists had, of course, demonstrated an awareness of excrement's useful qualities prior to the publication of Böll's works. One of the most important precursors of this theory was the nineteenth-century humorist Wilhelm Busch. Throughout his works Busch (1832–1908) underlines the animalism and depravity of all of humanity by way of numerous scatological allusions. However, he also indicates at times that a comfortable acceptance of bodily functions is an indication of a person's naturalness. Furthermore, Busch impishly observed in *Der Geburtstag oder die Partikularisten* (*The Birthday,* farce, 1873) that a well-filled chamber pot could serve as a handy, life-saving fire extinguisher. In Ernst Barlach's drama *Der tote Tag* (*The Dead Day,* 1912), a frankly scatological gnome proves his superiority over supposedly more highly developed and more intelligent human beings; the clever gnome has two excremental victories over the grasping mother. Once he frees himself from her by urinating on her, and later he asserts himself by ascending in the air after breaking wind.

Another very different use of scatology occurs in Thomas Mann's urbane novelle *Herr und Hund* (*A Man and His Dog,* 1919). In order to depict the contrast between the refined, civilized narrator and his earthy dog Bauschan, Mann turns repeatedly to scatological actions and attitudes, conveying in a strikingly effective way the narrator's fascination with the untamable nature of his dog. The narrator grapples to discover his own identity through an examination of Bauschan's and his own attitudes toward the excremental.

Neither Böll's hopeful view that men and women will become more humane by accepting their own bodily functions nor Thomas Mann's ambivalent attitude are acceptable to the most pessimistic German writers. Such writers as Gottfried Benn in poems like "Der Arzt" ("The Doctor," 1913) or Erich Kästner in "Die Welt ist rund" ("The World Is Round," 1928) as well as Günter Grass in his novelle *Katz und Maus* (*Cat and Mouse,* 1961) or the novel *Der Butt (The Flounder,* 1977) depict human beings as forever trapped in an excremental life cycle of eating, digesting, and defecating. For these writers, that is all there is to life. One's experiences are persistently linked to excrement and thus to death; there is no escape. The viewpoints of these authors might best be encapsulated in still another variation of the dadaists' slogan: Life is shit.

Although German literature of the twentieth century places an unusually great emphasis on scatology, modern writers in general have exhibited a growing interest in excremental motifs. However, in non-German literature scatology is almost invariably a literary device rather than a source of subject matter, as it is for such writers as Böll and Weiss. Excremental references in the literature of non-Germanic countries usually have the limited role of aiding in coarse ridicule, just as they did in the medieval jests or facetiae. In Eugène Ionesco's *La cantatrice chauve* (*The Bald Soprano,* play, 1950) the old reliable chamber pot is the agent of humor again. Samuel Beckett interrupts the dramatic flow of *En attendant Godot* (*Waiting for Godot,* 1952) by having Vladimir suddenly dash from the stage in order to relieve himself. The boys in William Golding's novel *Lord of the Flies* (1954) get diarrhea as a result of eating tropical fruits and eventually their whole orderly way of life collapses. Similarly, in John Barth's *The Sot-Weed Factor* (novel, 1960) John Cook and his men suffer from dysentery as a result of having drunk some polluted water. They not only befoul themselves but end up being captured by a group of Indians. Philip Roth in *Portnoy's Complaint* (novel, 1969) portrays Alexander Portnoy's father as suffering from a chronic case of severe constipation, a metaphor for the father's impotence in regard to life.

John Updike, in his novel *Couples* (1968), uses the bathroom as the setting for a serio-comic romantic scene. At a party, the protagonist, Piet Haneman, surprises his lover, Foxy Whitman, while she is sitting on the toilet; when she is done, Piet urinates and then attempts to resume their affair until they are interrupted by his wife's knocking on the door. By the juxtaposition of romance and scatology, of both pretentious and concrete words to describe the act of urination (i.e., "golden arc" and "splashing"), and of the sensuous excitement of the encounter with the ludicrousness of Piet's clumsy exit from the window, Updike conveys to the reader the intertwining of love and lechery that he finds in modern suburbia.

Scenes that unabashedly link scatology and sex are not uncommon in modern literature. There is no question that contemporary readers have to some extent become desensitized to the prevalence of sexual motifs in literature, and scatological references may soon lose their shock value also. Just as Updike's couples lived in "the post-pill paradise," modern readers of all nationalities are witnessing the demise of literary taboos and inhibitions. Future generations are likely to witness the increasing use of scatological references for a wide variety of purposes beyond the traditional one of satire.

Selected Bibliography

Englisch, Paul. *Das skatologische Element in Literatur, Kunst und Volksleben*. Stuttgart: Julius Püttmann, 1928.

Hermand, Jost. *Stänker und Weismacher: Zur Dialektik eines Affekts*. Texte Metzler, No. 18. Stuttgart: Metzler, 1971.

Lee, Jae Num. *Swift and Scatological Satire*. Albuquerque: University of New Mexico Press, 1971.

Rollfinke, Dieter and Jacqueline Rollfinke. *The Call of Human Nature: The Role of Scatology in Modern German Literature*. Amherst: The University of Massachusetts Press, 1986.

DIETER J. ROLLFINKE

SCIENCE

Although the word came into English in the fourteenth century, "science" did not acquire its modern association with the natural sciences until the nineteenth century, and "scientist," used originally to describe "a cultivator of science in general," did not appear until 1840. In the medieval world, "science" meant simply knowledge as such; the term was interchangeable with "art" and described a particular area of knowledge or skill. By the seventeenth century, science was being distinguished from art, the former requiring theoretical knowledge and the latter practical experience. From the beginning of the eighteenth century, science was increasingly thought of as a particular type of knowledge (derived from experiment rather than experience) and methodological argument. Various changes in the concept of Nature resulted in additional emphasis on method and demonstration directed at the external world, and by the end of the eighteenth century the definition of science as the theoretical and methodological exploration of objective external nature was pretty much complete. During the nineteenth century, such terms as "scientific," "scientific method," and "scientific truth" became associated with the specialized methods of the physical and biological sciences.

Background in Antiquity and the Middle Ages

From the very earliest times, literature has been used as a *vehicle* to transmit the science (knowledge) of a particular culture. Essays such as Aristotle's fourth-century *Physikē akroasis* (*Physics*), *Peri ouranou* (*Skies*) and *Peri ta zōa historiai* (*The History of Animals*) can be examined for their literary quality as well as their ideas. Narrowing the definition of literature to emphasize the formal properties of writing as well as ideas, one might point to Lucretius' *De rerum natura* (*On the Nature of Things*, 1st century B.C.) as the most significant poetic treatment of natural philosophy in classical times. Lucretius posits an atomic theory of nature in what some consider to be one of the greatest didactic poems in any language.

The emergence of science as a theme in literature and the scientist as hero or villain is lost in the past. Where one begins to see this theme emerge depends upon one's definitions. The central issue is the relationship of science to knowledge. The etymology of science suggests that the first texts celebrating science were advocating the search for knowledge as such, and the scientist was the hero or villain seeking knowledge. Significantly, the context in which this search takes place, the role of the man of knowledge, the structure of the search itself, the means used to achieve knowledge and, finally, the ultimate ends or purposes of knowledge have always been treated equivocally by every culture. That is to say, some scenes are more appropriate than others for the pursuit of knowledge; some people are more fit than others to conduct this search; some methods are more appropriate than others; and some ends, which motivate the search, are more legitimate than others.

For the ancients, to pursue knowledge, to seek the Truth, to wrest from Nature her secrets was a dangerous enterprise. If not done with the proper humility and caution, this search was tantamount to challenging the authors of those secrets— the gods themselves. Thus, the early "scientists" were often guilty of pride. Satan tempts Eve to eat of the Tree of Knowledge by saying, "your eyes shall be opened, and ye shall be as gods, knowing good and evil" (Gen. 3.10). Only one figure from biblical literature, Solomon, the greatest king of the Hebrew monarchy, seems to be treated without ambiguity. Solomon introduced horses, chariots, and other military innovations. He constructed a copper refinery on the Gulf of Akabah. A poet, musician, and naturalist, he becomes the model of the learned man. Francis Bacon's Savants, described in the *New Atlantis* (novel, 1627), live in the "House of Solomon." The mysterious figure from Greek mythology, Prometheus (Forethought), is severely punished by Zeus for bringing the rudiments of civilization, especially fire, to man, and as Aeschylus shows in his tragedy, *Promētheus desmōtēs* (*Prometheus Bound*, c. 450 B.C.) Prometheus was rebellious and arrogant toward the gods. Another mythical figure, the Athenian master craftsman and inventor, Daedalus, was given a commission by King Minos of Crete to build a labyrinth, a prison for the man-bull monster, the Minotaur. Later, Minos imprisoned Daedalus and his son, Icarus, in the labyrinth. The two escaped on wings made by Daedalus of wax and feathers, but Icarus flies too close to the sun, his wings melt, and he falls into the sea. Daedalus' career was associated with the spread of Minoan culture. He is mentioned in *Bibliothēkē* (*The Library*), the work of the Greek mythographer, Apollodorus of Athens (2d century B.C.) and in Ovid's *Metamorphoses* (epic poem, c. A.D. 2–17).

The scientist, who because of his knowledge has the power to transform the world, for good or evil, is foreshadowed in the narratives and poems concerned with the activities of sorcerers and magicians, such as Merlin, the magician and prophet serving as counselor to King Arthur. Fragments and allusions to the Arthurian legend appeared as early as the *Historia Brittonum* (c. 800) of Nennius. Geoffrey of Monmouth's *Historia regum Britanniae* (*History of the Kings of Britain*, c. 1137) makes Arthur a historical person. During the twelfth century, Geoffrey's narrative appears in the poetic romances of Chrétien de Troyes (last quarter of the twelfth century) and in the German romances of Hartmann von Aue.

Society's ambiguous attitude toward man's search for knowledge is nowhere more clearly depicted than in the legends of Faust. Its origins in the legends and chapbooks of the late fifteenth and sixteenth centuries, the story dramatized the life of a real person, Doctor Johann or Georg Faust, known as a magician and practitioner of black magic and rumored to have sold his soul to the Devil in exchange for knowledge. Attempting to pry into nature's secrets, to see and experience what no man has seen or experienced, Faust surrenders a portion of his humanity. The price for knowledge can be too high; there are things that man is not meant to know, and the penalty for attempting to transcend those limits is very severe indeed. From the late Middle Ages until the present, the Faust legend has been individuated in countless literary works. The legend formed the basis for Christopher Marlowe's play *Doctor Faustus* (1604) and Goethe's poetic drama, *Faust* (1808; part 2, 1832). Marlowe's Faust is a tragic hero, torn between human responsiveness and human limitation, whose desire for knowledge is distorted and corrupted by his desire for infinite knowledge-for-power. Faust lusts for power obtained through special learning. His latter-day counterpart is the technocrat who gains power because of his scientific and technical knowledge and who undermines democratic institutions by engendering the cult of the expert.

The Renaissance

The early literature of the seventeenth century did not take science as a theme per se or create a role for the scientist as a major character as much as it imaginatively reflected man's new consciousness of the new scientific break-throughs and of the vaster universe that they suggested. Until the end of the sixteenth century, the writer, like the great majority of the people, saw himself at the center of a visible cosmos. The moon and sun circled the earth to provide it with light. The stars, placed by God, were fixed and unchanging and visible to the naked eye. Each planet and star was part of the divine plan and influenced man's life. The regions below the moon, composed of fire, air, water, and solid earth, were imperfect and subject to decay; man's body was made of these same elements and was regulated by the stars. Like man, the world had a soul, and man's form and structure were model for the entire cosmos. Two new stars— Tyco's nova in 1572 and Kepler's nova in 1604—and the sudden appearance of a huge comet in 1577 as well as the publication in 1543 of Copernicus' *De revolutionibus orbium coelestium* (*On the Revolution of Heavenly Bodies*) and Galileo's *Dialogo sopra i due massimi sistemi del mondo* (*Dialogue Concerning the Two Chief World Systems,* 1632) doomed the old earth-centered cosmology.

The metaphors and images of the "new philosophy" entered into the imaginative literature of the day. In "The First Anniversarie" (1611), the English poet, John Donne, writes: "And new Philosophy calls all in doubt, / The element of fire is quite put out: / The sun is lost, and th'earth, and no man's wit / Can well direct him, where to looke for it." While Donne laments the "breaking of the circle" (i.e., the perfect unity of the cosmos), his younger contemporary, George Herbert, both laments and celebrates this new vision and acknowledges the power of the scientist: "Philosophers have measur'd mountains, / Fathom'd the depths of seas, of states, and kings, / Walk'd with a staffe to heav'n, and traced fountains." Richard Crashaw, Henry Moore, Henry Vaughn, Thomas Traherne, and John Milton were all affected by this new vision. Some authors, such as Ben Jonson, were less impressed with the new science and its practitioners. In *The Alchemist* (play, 1610), Subtle, the Alchemist, cheats gullible people by promising them the Philosophers' Stone. But the Italian, Tammaso Campanella, in his *La città del sole (The City of the Sun,* 1602) describes utopian communities where the inhabitants live according to Power, Wisdom, and Love and celebrate science by practicing eugenics and painting murals on the walls of their city describing the activities of science.

In 1634, the German astronomer, Johannes Kepler, published the story *Somnium,* which for the first time depicts a student of science, Duracotus, as a major character. In Kepler's dream, a daemon of Levania (the Moon) tells Duracotus, a young man who becomes a student of Tycho Brahe's, about the nature of the moon. However, Domingo Gonsales, the main character in Frances Godwin's story *The Man in the Moone* (1638), is the first real scientist who figures as a hero in imaginative literature. Gonsales goes to the moon in a flying machine pulled by wild geese. Along the way, Gonsales makes scientific observations verifying the truth of the "new science" of Kepler and Galileo. Living in a lunar utopian community, he discovers that the inhabitants have perfected their scientific research and have discovered the Philosophers' Stone. Gonsales returns to earth and tells of his adventures, thus creating a whole genre of narratives of moon voyages from Cyrano de Bergerac's *Histoire comique des états et empires de la lune . . . du soleil* (*The Comical History of the States and Empires of the Moon . . . the Sun*, 1657, 1662) to H. G. Wells' novel *The First Men in the Moon* (1901). Godwin's hero is important because he rejects the older Aristotelian tradition of science proceeding from logical deduction in favor of experimentation and empirical evidence. He is an inventor; he experiments with gravity. He does not trust the mind or the senses, and he uses orderly experiments to overcome their limitations.

Some scholars suggest that Domingo Gonsales was patterned after Sir Francis Bacon's model of the new experimental scientist. In the early part of the seventeenth century, in his essays *Advancement of Learning* (1605), *Novum organum* (*The New Learning,* 1620), and *Sylva sylvarum* (1627; containing *The New Atlantis),* Bacon called for a new science to produce new knowledge. While the traditional Aristotelian scientist was useful in distributing information and inspiring logical thought, an additional type of scientist was needed, one who created new knowledge through experimentation. Bacon argued that science would be a collective effort, each scientist building on the work of others, past and present. In *The New Atlantis* Bacon describes an imaginary society that contains a "Solomon's House." This is a college of natural philosophy "dedicated to the study of the works and creatures of God." Bacon gives an account of the mechanical wonders to be achieved by the pursuit of science. (The work was probably written as an advertisement for a Royal College of Science that Bacon hoped to persuade James I to endow.) Though it is not much more than a catalogue, it remains an extraordinarily accurate evaluation of the potential of the scientific renaissance.

From the early seventeenth century until the founding of the Royal Society in 1662, the implications of the new science echoed in the imaginative literature of the period. While the Latin works of Kepler and Galileo were addressed to other scholars, writers sought a larger audience to communicate their increased consciousness of a larger universe and their awareness of the possibilities of the new science. However, the relationships between imaginative literature and science were beginning to change. The Royal Society began to function as an arbiter of science *and* literature and with this, there was a change in attitude toward poets, poetry, and science. They were not supposed to mix. The historian of the Royal Society, Thomas Sprat, declared that any writing that depended on metaphorical language—words associated with "fancy" and imagination—might obscure the truth. He advocated a "plain style" for science and attacked the poets. Spratt seemed to reinforce Bacon's separation of imagination, the province of poetry from reason, the basis of philosophy, including science. For some, poets and scientists belonged to two incompatible worlds, and they should go their separate ways. Moreover, as the seventeenth century came to a close, there was a feeling among some members of society that the Royal Society had promised more than it could deliver in terms of its pledges to create new knowledge for the benefit of all mankind. The Society had difficulties organizing itself and obtaining funds and had fallen victim to a number of well-publicized hoaxes. It is not surprising, given this situation, that English writers took their revenge and during much of the Restoration and eighteenth century satirized science and its practitioners.

The Restoration and Eighteenth Century

By the 1680s there had appeared in English literature the stock figure of the "virtuoso," a dabbler in science who understood practically nothing and accomplished even less. In a parody of Bacon's *New Atlantis* and a foreshadowing of Swift's satire *Gulliver's Travels* (1726), Margaret Cavendish, duchess of Newcastle, writes *The Description of the New World Called the Blazing World* (1666). The Blazing World is a utopia inhabited by the intelligent animals. The heroine of the story assigns the animals to study science according to their kind (e.g., bird men are astronomers; spiders are mathematicians; flies, worms, and fishes are natural philosophers). Their studies lead them to no new knowledge whatsoever but only to stupid quarrels. The upshot of the story is that the scientist is powerless to discover truth or to produce practical applications; he produces only discord. The virtuoso is also a character in Samuel Butler's *Hudibras* (verse satire, 1663–1678) in the character of Sidrophel, who represents the new scientist seeking wonderful new truths. Sidrophel mistakes a lantern suspended in the air by a kite for the planet Saturn. Butler enlarges upon this theme in his satiric poem, "The Elephant in the Moon" (written c. last quarter of 17th century; published posthumously, 1759). A group of virtuosi gather with a telescope to witness a monumental battle on the moon, which is interrupted by the entrance of an elephant. After opening the far end of the telescope, the astronomers discover that they were watching a swarm of flies and gnats—and a mouse. The virtuosi's vision was merely a magnified sense of their own worth. They lost their desire to recognize truth because of their need to display their intellectual power. In Thomas Shadwell's *The Virtuoso* (1676), the "scientist," Sir Nicholas Gimcrack, is ruined financially because of his desire to do the impossible and his willingness to believe anything. Gimcrack laments at the end of the play: "I would that I had studied mankind instead of spiders and insects." By the late 1680s interest in the Royal Society was at an all-time low. Aphra Behn wrote *The Emperor of the Moon* (play, 1687) in which a totally gullible virtuoso, Dr. Baliardo, leaves science to associate with the Rosicrucian Order. He is so affected by his passion for the moon that two young gentlemen steal his daughter by claiming to be moon men. Satires on the virtuoso as an insatiable collector of useless objects, as one who confuses collection with science, can be seen in issues of the *Tatler* (August and September, 1710), in No. 82 of Samuel Johnson's *Rambler* (1750–1752) and in Alexander Pope's "The New Dunciad" (book 4 of the poem *The Dunciad,* 1728–1743). The new scientist is still powerless. In the Restoration his dreams were too ambitious; in the early eighteenth century his vision was too narrow.

During the Restoration, another stereotype of the scientist emerges—the "projector." The projector is a scientist, who, by use of his knowledge, obtains political power and threatens society. Jonathan Swift's character, Peter, in the allegorical satire *A Tale of a Tub* (1704), makes several scientific studies that he tries to sell to the public. Swift's projectors in Balnibari and Laputa in *Gulliver's Travels* are scientists whose work does not improve human life. Their feet are not on the ground but in abstract science; they are ridiculous but potentially dangerous. Swift argues that abstract science mixed with politics will produce an unreasonable world. (There is good evidence that Swift used Isaac Newton as a model for the Laputans. Both Newton and Edmund Halley were caught up in the politics of their time.)

Many writers, such as Murtagh McDermot (pseud.) in *A Trip to the Moon* (1728), followed Swift in satirizing some of the absurd schemes of natural philosophers, for example, attempting to build a house out of light. One year after the publication of *Gulliver's Travels,* there appeared *A Voyage to Cacklogallinia* (1727; anonymous author), which depicted a scientist, Volatilo, who discovers new knowledge. This knowledge is not put to practical use, and Volatilo is an easy pawn for politicians. The moral of the story is that science must be moral. Woe to the individual who misuses science to gain money, fame, or power.

Many of these early pictures of scientists show them as men whose interest in science obscures their vision of reality and whose work interferes with the study of man himself. As Alexander Pope's *Essay on Man* (poem, 1733–1734) argues: "The proper study of mankind is Man." By 1750, Jean-Jacques Rousseau could argue in his *Discours sur les sciences et les arts* (*Discourses on the Sciences and the Arts*) that the study of science was dangerous, that it did not produce true knowledge, and that it was a waste of time.

Despite this injunction, the science of the late seventeenth century and early eighteenth century was opening up whole new worlds to man. A very selective list of important scientific publications between 1680 and 1740 would include Anton von Leeuwenhoek's *Arcana naturae detecta* (1695); Carl von Linné's *Systema naturae* (*A General System of Nature,* 1735); Robert Boyle's *De ipsa natura* (1687); Isaac Newton's discovery of the law of gravitation (1682), *Philosophiae naturalis principia mathematica* (*The Mathematics of Natural Philosophy,* 1687); Gottfried Leibniz, *Hypothesis physica nova* (*New Philosophical Hypothesis,* 1671); and Gabriel Fahrenheit's discovery of the thermometer scale (1730). The combined effect of these discoveries and publications was inevitable; society was forced to take science more seriously and to look more closely at the social role of the scientist and how science related to the other principles, especially the religious doctrines, upon which the social order rested.

Hence, during the eighteenth century, there were some attempts to depict nonsatirical roles for scientists and to view the activities of science as a means for glorifying God and his creation. In his poem, *Creation* (1712), Richard Blackmore argues that through science one can discover the awesome work of the Creator. The more one studies nature, the more one learns about the First Cause—God. Oliver Goldsmith makes much the same point in his *Survey of Experimental Philosophy* (1776). There was a sense that the scientist could function as a prophet to give man a vision of the Divine. The model for this kind of scientist was Isaac Newton, who became in the poetry of such writers as Alexander Pope, William Cowper, Richard Glover, and James Thomson almost a saint. Pope writes: "Nature and Nature's laws lay hid in night; / God said, 'Let Newton be!' and all was light." Even the great Voltaire paid tribute to Newton's discoveries concerning the nature of light and wrote a poem praising Newton's *Opticks* (1704). Yet even with the figure of Newton as the example of a man who was both a scientist and a deeply religious figure, some writers had their doubts as to whether science could be morally uplifting or whether it had the power to make men happy. Matthew Prior's poem *Solomon on the Vanity of the World* (1718), Pope's *Essay on Man,* William Cowper's poem *The Task* (1785), Samuel Johnson's poem *The Vanity of Human Wishes* (1749), and *Rasselas* (novel, 1759)—all of these works made the points that science itself is not a moral power and that it is not capable in itself of making man happy.

All the same, there were intellectuals and writers who believed that science could provide *practical* knowledge and benefits for mankind. Stephen Hales's *Vegetable Staticks* (1727) celebrates the practical advantages of studying nature as does Erasmus Darwin's *Zoönomia* (1794–1796) near the end of the eighteenth century. In addition, the intellectual forces of secularism and rationalism seemed to be irresistible. By the middle of the eighteenth century, the intellectual climate of the Enlightenment, reinforced by the scientific bias of Puritanism, the Protestant ethic, and the demands of a developing capitalism, with its need for technology, worked together to increase science's status. As editor and coeditor of the *Encyclopédie* (1751–1772), Denis Diderot and Jean d'Alembert enlisted such writers as Quesnay, Montesquieu, Voltaire, Rousseau, Turgot, and others to provide a compendium of knowledge in the arts and sciences from a rational, secular perspective. The encyclopedia was a celebration of the spirit of the Enlightenment. It was immediately successful and its influence incalculable. It emphasized the concept of scientific determinism and philosophic materialism. It attacked legal and political abuses and provided the intellectual legitimations for the French Revolution.

During the middle half of the eighteenth century, science began to catch the eye of writers who were beginning to write for the growing middle class. Among this class there was an increasing interest in science and its application. (Between 1748–1757, there appeared in *Gentleman's Magazine* alone over 1,227 scientific and technical articles.) In such narratives as Ralph Morris' (pseud.) *A Narrative of the Life and Astonishing Adventures of John Daniel* (1751) and Robert Paltock's *The Life and Adventures of Peter Wilkins* (1751), the scientist-heroes use their scientific knowledge to change the world through new machines. In the latter story there is the suggestion that God uses science and technology to promote human happiness. In these stories the scientist is a true hero. There is a growing sense that science is becoming a formidable force in society.

This is the case even in such science fantasies as *Nicolai Klimii iter subterraneum* (*A Journey to the World Underground,* 1741), written by the Danish writer Ludvig Holberg. Klim, a science student at the University of Copenhagen, falls through a cave to the center of the earth. He verifies the theories of the motion of bodies and lands on a planet, Nazar. He encounters many wonders, including intelligent trees. By using his knowledge to invent weapons of destruction, he subdues the nations of Nazar and becomes king. Here again, science is seen as a power that can change the world. In Nicolas Edme Restif de la Bretonne's *La découverte australe par un homme-volant, ou Le Dédale français* (*The Southern Discovery of a Flying Man, or the New French Daedalus,* 1781) a scientist flies using wings and a small parachute device. With his girl friend, Victorin founds a utopian society, and later, with his son, goes to live with the Metapatagonians, a utopian society based on natural and rational principles and advanced scientific knowledge. In this narrative, the principles of science can be used to reorganize an entire society. This idea was to become in the nineteenth century the guiding assumption behind the majority of blueprints for actual utopian societies.

The Nineteenth Century

By the beginning of the nineteenth century, the importance of and power of science and its application as technology was no longer in question. Moreover, eighteenth-century writers had prepared the public for literary works depicting science as a theme and the scientist as a major character.

The Romantics absorbed the scientist into their concept of the Romantic Hero, a promethean-like figure who, in splendid isolation, challenges all authority and seeks the limits of experience. Like the romantic poet, the romantic scientist is a creator. He does not simply copy nature but like God attempts to create something new. He is intelligent, arrogant, power-hungry, and a bit mad. He is epitomized in Goethe's *Faust*. Faust represents every individual who is inspired to action by visions of power—physical and intellectual—to attempt to transcend his or her limitations. Faust uses his knowledge to gain power, lands, and people. He works on a huge land reclamation project to provide homes and jobs for millions of people. He embodies the age-old concept that knowledge is power, but unlike Marlowe's Faust, Goethe's hero is saved because of his striving to be more than he is—the essence of the Romantic Hero.

That man should seek the limits of experience, even if it entailed challenging the gods, was an assumption of the Romantics. It was also assumed that like

Prometheus, he must face the consequences of his actions. And herein lies the theme of Mary Shelley's novel *Frankenstein, or the Modern Prometheus* (1818). Doctor Frankenstein, one of the first modern scientists, assembles an inanimate human form and by some mysterious force (associated with electricity and magnetism) brings it to life. Frankenstein attempts to repudiate his creation, and his neglect provokes the monster on a course of murder and vengeance.

The figure of the scientist pursuing the limits of experience, obsessed by the Absolute, was a common figure in eighteenth-century fiction. Mary Shelley's novel was probably inspired by her father, William Godwin, and his novel *St. Leon* (1799), which deals with the hero's obsession with the two absolutes of the alchemist, the Philosophers' Stone and the elixir of life. The same theme is treated in Robert Browning's dramatic poem, *Paracelsus* (1835). In France, there was Honoré de Balzac's *La recherche de l'absolu* (*The Quest of the Absolute*, 1834) in which the hero, Balthazar Claes, sacrifices all his earthly happiness—including that of his wife and children—to search for the Absolute, the "single element" to which "all natural productions might be reduced." Similar to Balzac's story is Edward Bulwer-Lytton's *A Strange Story* (1861), dealing with a philosopher-scientist-alchemist who attempts to cheat death by discovering the elixir of life. And in America, stories such as Hawthorne's "Artist of the Beautiful" (1844) and "Rappacini's Daughter" (1844) dealt with the problem of science leading one beyond moral and humane considerations. The danger of scientific obsession is epitomized in Fitz-James O'Brien's, "The Diamond Lens" (1858), in which the hero, Linley, uses a medium to get advice from Leeuwenhoek on how to make a super microscope. He gets the diamond he needs for his lens by murder. Through the lens, he sees and falls in love with a microscopic nymph, Animula. As the droplet containing Animula dries up, causing her death, Linley goes insane.

The power of science as exemplified in its method of data collection, induction, hypotheses testing, and generalization was coming to be recognized. Edgar Allan Poe's C. Auguste Dupin, hero of "The Murders in the Rue Morgue" (story, 1841) prefigures Arthur Conan Doyle's hero, Sherlock Holmes. Dupin and Holmes use the scientific method to discover truth with spectacular results. H. G. Wells, in his essay, "Popularizing Science" (1894) pointed to Poe and Doyle as models for the construction of science fiction.

The Development of the Scientific Romance: 1860–1930

By the mid-nineteenth century, with the Industrial Revolution in full stride, science had gained a prestige that was to continue undiminished until the 1930s. Along with the discoveries in the physical sciences came Charles Darwin's *Origin of Species* (1859), which focused new light on the biological world, and Charles Lyle's *Principles of Geology* (1830), which opened up enormous vistas in time and implicated the whole cosmos in the concept of evolution. To the theory of evolution was linked the growing belief in progress, so that for much of the literate, prosperous, middle class living in the 1870s, everything seemed possible. And this optimism was to a large degree based on faith in science and technology.

From 1860 onward, an increasing number of scientists, engineers, inventors, medical men, archeologists, and even students of such exotic topics as Egyptology and the occult became central characters in popular literature. For example, in the new science of psychology, Oliver Wendell Holmes anticipated the phenomenon of multiple personality in *Elsie Venner* (novel, 1861), and Thomas Bailey Aldrich's novel *The Queen of Sheba* (1877) focused on the issues of amnesia. Edward Bellamy's early novel *Dr. Heidenhoff's Process* (1880) featured a scientist who could erase harmful memories. The interest in psychology culminated in Robert Louis Stevenson's *The Strange Case of Dr. Jekyll and Mr. Hyde* (1886), the classic study of multiple personality. In Stevenson's narrative, a scientist deliberately sets out to purify his moral nature but ends up freeing the dark monster of the id, which finally conquers him.

In France, Jules Verne combined the public's interest in evolution, progress, and the future with an adaptation of the traditional, fantastic voyage and an increasing curiosity about new technology—especially the technology of transportation—to produce a number of extremely popular novels, which included scientists, engineers, and inventors as main characters: *Voyage au centre de la terre* (*A Voyage to the Center of the Earth*, 1864); *De la terre à la lune* (*From the Earth to the Moon*, 1865); *Vingt mille lieues sous les mers* (*Twenty Thousand Leagues Under the Sea*, 1870); and *L'île à hélice* (*Propeller Island*, 1895). Verne's novels were designed as much to teach science as to celebrate it. His travelers usually included a man of reason, who invented the needed technology, and a man of action, an adventurer, daring enough to use it. Verne's stories were optimistic celebrations of technology. In contrast to his British contemporaries, many of whom viewed their technology as a mixed blessing, Verne captured the imagination of millions, especially Americans, with his faith in the machine.

Like Samuel Butler's satire on machines in *Erewhon* (novel, 1872) and W. H. Hudson's novel *A Crystal Age* (1877), most of H. G. Wells's scientific romances are ambiguous concerning the value of science and the role of the scientist. Wells was not entirely comfortable with the complacent assumption of inevitable progress; his constant theme is the uncertainty of man's existence and the possibilities for the abuse of knowledge and power. For Wells, science was a vehicle of a moral vision and social criticism. In some of his novels, for example, *The Island of Dr. Moreau* (1896) and *The Invisible Man* (1897), one sees the almost typical image of the scientist as an obsessive neurotic. Other novels such as *The Time Machine* (1895), *The War of the Worlds* (1898), *The Food of the Gods* (1904), *In the Days of the Comet* (1906), *The War in the Air* (1908), and *Men Like Gods* (1923), are generally pessimistic and do not show science and technology as able to bring man happiness. Man's science is either impotent in the face of superior forces or it is used to oppress others.

Along with *Dr. Jekyll and Mr. Hyde* and Wells's Dr. Moreau, an interesting depiction of scientific creativity as a kind of insanity is given in novels such as J. S. Fletcher's *Morrison's Machine* (1900), Professor Lerne in Maurice Renard's *Le docteur Lerne, sous-dieu* (*New Bodies for Old,* 1908), E. Charles Vivian's *Star Dust* (1925), and Philip Wylie's *The Murderer Invisible* (1931). The idea that the secular, "unholy" pursuit of science could lead to madness is an extraordinarily persistent theme that continues to this day. It is most probably linked to society's ambiguous treatment of knowledge, the "profane" nature of science, and the scientist's links with alchemy, astrology, and sorcery. But it is also related to the writer's uneasiness with the implications of modern science. This anxiety is seen clearly in such works as Henry Adams' *The Education of Henry Adams* (1907). Adams visited the Paris Exposition (1900), where he viewed the huge dynamo that became for him a symbol of the power, energy, and complexity of the twentieth century. He contrasts the dynamo with the image of the Virgin, "the ideal of human perfection," representing the unity of the medieval period. At one point he says, "If Karl Pearson's notions of the universe were sound, men like Galileo, Descartes, Leibnitz, and Newton should have stopped the progress of science before 1700."

Henry Adams' uneasiness was not reflected in the popular literature of the day, especially in America. From the beginning of the twentieth century until the present, one can observe a rather distinct difference in attitudes toward science and the role of the scientist in society. On the one hand, the more elite writers implicate science, with its cold objectivity, its materialism and determinism, its *dis*-enchantment of the world, with its application as technology, with all of the problems of the modern world, especially man's domination by technology. On the other hand, popular writers, especially those writing for the mass market in popular magazines, exploit society's ambiguous attitude toward science by treating science as melodrama, with larger-than-life heroes and villains and their impossible inventions and theories as man's salvation or his doom.

By the end of the eighteenth century, positive images of the scientist began to appear, particularly in American popular fiction. In the United States, Thomas Edison was a national hero and appeared in Garrett P. Serviss's *Edison's Conquest of Mars* (1898) and in dozens of dime novels relating the adventures of Tom Edison, Jr. Similar stories were built around Louis Pasteur and Albert Einstein. In these dime novels, the scientist was sometimes treated as a stock villain who, like Victor Frankenstein, oversteps the limits, even if it is for a good cause. In Stewart Edward White's *The Sign at Six* (1912), the scientist threatens the destruction of New York, by lowering the temperature to absolute zero, in order to correct the evils of society. In Arthur Train and Robert Wood's *The Man Who Rocked the Earth* (1915), a mad scientist uses atomic power to end the stalemated European war. Geoffrey Hollis' *The Man Who Ended War* (1908) depicts a scientist who develops the ultimate weapon to disintegrate warships. The novel ends with a world peace conference. In the popular fiction, with the exception of astronomy, there were few "pure" scientists (i.e., those doing pure research); writers must have discovered that they did not excite the public's imagination. Instead, the main character was usually an inventor or scientist-engineer; indeed, between 1880 and 1920, there was practically no distinction between the scientist and inventor/engineer.

In such popular novels as *The Mystery* (1907) by Stewart Edward White and Samuel Hopkins Adams, the scientist looked for the ultimate energy source—celestium. In Arthur B. Reeve's novels, such as *The Dream Doctor* (1914), the scientist became a detective and fought crime using his scientific training. In Garrett P. Serviss' *The Moon Metal* (1900) and Ray Norton's *The Vanishing Fleets* (1908) scientists were heroes, opposing right to wrong and saving mankind. In Stanley Waterloo's *Armageddon* (1898), Simon Newcomb's *His Wisdom, The Defender* (1900) and J. Steward Barney's *L.P.M.: The End of the Great War* (1915), scientists were heroes in predicting wars, saving civilization from destruction, and creating a peaceful world order dominated by science. This wholehearted worship of the scientist and the benefits of science reached a high point in Hugo Gernsback's *Ralph 124C 41+: A Romance of the Year 2660* (1911–1912).

Outside the popular fiction and the science fiction magazine there were attempts to provide a more realistic conception of science and the social role of the scientist. In contrast to the optimistic view of science produced in popular literature, the more elite writers were less sanguine over science's long-term benefits. The Czech writer, Karel Čapek's drama *R.U.R.* (1921) introduced the modern concept of robots to the world. In Czech, robot means something close to slave labor, and in the play the robots-proletarians revolt against their creator. In *Krakatit* (*An Atomic Phantasy: Krakatit,* novel, 1924) Čapek writes of man's inability to control his weapons, in this case a proto-atomic bomb. In the novel *Továrna na absolutno* (*The Absolute at Large*, 1922) Čapek treats the same theme. E. C. Large's novel *Sugar in the Air* (1937) explores the social maladjustment as a consequence of the scientist's work. The hero-scientist, Charles Pry, is a visionary and idealist working within a stupid and irrational system. A series of novels by George Duhamel, *La chronique des Pasquier* (*The Pasquier Chronicles*, 1933–1945), especially *La nuit de la Saint-Jean* (*Saint John's Eve*, 1935), *Les maîtres* (*The Masters*, 1937), and *Le combat contre les ombres* (*The Struggle Against the Shadows*, 1939) follows the life of a medical research scientist, Laurent Pasquier, as he tries to steer a middle way between the cold, rational, and objective scientist and the enthusiast, as he exposes the political manipulations going on in the laboratories. In 1925, Sinclair Lewis published *Arrowsmith*, acclaimed as one of the best novels of science. Martin Arrowsmith, a bacteriologist, fights against the ''shame and compromises, the temptations and false values, and finally the commercialized idealism of the vested interests of the medical professions,'' and learns the price one pays in the search for truth. A number of writers involved in the modernist movement had scientists as their heroes. Some of these narratives are purely fanciful, such as Alfred Jarry's *Gestes et opinions du Docteur Faustroll* (*The Exploits and Opinions of Doctor Faustroll Pataphysician: A Neo-Scientific Novel,* published posthumously, 1911), whose hero, Faustroll, invents "pataphysics," the science of imaginary solutions, which "symbolically attributes to the properties of objects, described by their virtuality, to their lineaments." In what seems to be almost a parody of Bacon's "Solomon's House," (*The New Atlantis,* novel, 1627), the hero of Raymond Roussel's novel *Locus solus* (*Solitary Place,* 1914), Canterel, leads a group of visitors around his estate showing them the discoveries and inventions of his fertile mind, including a road-mending tool activated by the weather. Mikhail Bulgakov's play *Sobach'e serdtse* (*The Heart of a Dog,* 1925) is a light-hearted parody of Mary Shelley's *Frankenstein.* A surgeon turns a dog into a human being who proceeds to make the doctor's life miserable. Finally, the scientist operates and turns his creation back into a dog. Sometime later and in a more serious vein, Olaf Stapledon wrote *Sirius; A Fantasy of Love and Discord* (novel, 1944), which tells the story of a scientist who creates a super intelligent dog, Sirius. The mutated dog is a believable human being and is more interesting than the usual stereotype of animals used by authors to allegorize the human condition.

In the political turmoil of the 1930s, writers turned to the relationships between science and socio-political questions. In Aldous Huxley's *Brave New World* (1932) science and technology are used to condition people, from the time they are fetuses in the test tube to the time they submit to euthanasia, to happily submit to the existing social order. Pure scientific research is subordinated to social stability. Huxley's novel was influenced by the Russian novelist Evgenïi Zamiatin, whose *My* (*We,* 1924) satirizes a utopia based on science that has gone insane. The twenty-sixth-century society is regimented like a machine. Committed to the scientific method, so that his narrative imitates laboratory notes, the hero makes the mistake of falling in love. He finally lets the state operate on his brain so he can never again deviate from the norm. Influenced by both *Brave New World* and *We,* George Orwell's novel *1984* (1949) describes a totalitarian society in which technology (e.g., two-way television sets) is used to control the population and in which the very concept of the existence of scientific truth is destroyed through total brainwashing. The scientist as Nazi is seen in Edmund Snell's novel *Kontrol* (1928), in which a slightly mad doctor transplants the minds of a potential power elite into young, healthy bodies. The concept of the Übermann is continued in the Doc Savage novels, beginning with Kenneth Robeson's *The Man of Bronze* (1933). Doc Savage is a scientifically trained superman who is the judge, jury, and executioner of the countless criminals. In C. S. Forester's novel *The Peacemaker* (1934), a mathematician is also a pacifist. He plans to force England to disarm by building a machine to disrupt all magnetic forces and stop all machines; he is killed by a mob.

The Modern Period

Following World War II and the utter devastation of Hiroshima and Nagasaki by the atomic bomb, few people could doubt the awesome power of science and its application in technology. For many writers the most important date in recent human history was June 16, 1945; on that day, near Alamogordo, New Mexico, the first atomic bomb was successfully tested. For many, it was the day science lost its innocence, and for many it symbolized the day on which modern man had finally to acknowledge that science had become the most important institution in the world for shaping man's destiny.

With this awareness, there is a growing concern over the role of the scientist in society and a special urgency in dealing with the moral responsibility of the scientist for his creations. The German dramatist, Bertolt Brecht, in his *Leben des Galilei* (*The Life of Galileo*, play, 1938), uses Galileo's recantation and submission to the church to argue that a scientist is a criminal if he makes his science a servant of authority rather than asserting its right to transform the world to the benefit of mankind. C. P. Snow wrote *New Lines for Old* (novel, 1933) dealing with the discovery of a hormone that eventually causes the moral break-down of the West. In *The Search* (1934) and his *Strangers and Brothers* novels (1940–1964) Snow deals with the education of the scientist and contemporary life as seen from an academic, political, and scientific perspective. In his lecture *The Two Cultures and the Scientific Revolution* (1959), Snow deplores the failure of the arts to adjust to the requirements of an age in which science and technology are transforming civilization. How can a society that is, with the exception of a few, totally ignorant of science provide informed criticism and moral guidelines for scientists? The scientist must be responsible for his creation. One of the main characters in Friedrich Dürrenmatt's play *Die Physiker (The Physicists,* 1962), the physicist Johann Möbius, becomes aware that his discoveries could destroy the world. He confines himself to a sanatorium saying, "Today it's the duty of a genius to remain unrecognized. . . . Either we wipe ourselves out of the memory of mankind or mankind wipes itself out." The moral responsibility of the scientist and the relationship between science and the state is examined in the literature chronicling the rise and fall of J. Robert Oppenheimer, the American physicist, father of the atomic bomb, who had his security clearance revoked because of his campaign against the hydrogen bomb. Oppenheimer's trial and disgrace are the subject of Heinar Kipphardt's documentary play *In der Sache J. Robert Oppenheimer (In the Matter of J. Robert Oppenheimer,* 1964).

The consequences of the irresponsible use of atomic power, the mistakes that lead to and the consequences of nuclear war are explored in several contemporary novels. Some of the best are the Australian writer, Nevil Shute's *On the Beach* (1957), Walter Miller, Jr.'s *A Canticle for Leibowitz* (1959), and Eugene Burdick and Harvey Wheeler's *Fail-Safe* (1962). The possibility that society will—through ignorance or as a reaction to the irresponsible use of science—revolt against science and the scientist is explored in such novels as Leigh Brackett's *The Long Tomorrow* (1955), where the scientist hero lives in an anti-scientific age, and James Gunn's *The Burning* (1972), in which the masses revolt against science and persecute the scientist-hero, John Wilson.

The contemporary scientist as a hero working for the good of humanity is seen less and less in fiction. However some do stand out. The Japanese novelist,

Abe Kōbō, in his *Daiyon kampyōki* (*Inter Ice Age 4*, 1970) shows Japanese scientists who foresee worldwide flooding and force adaptive changes on human fetuses in the name of survival. Robert Merle's novel *Un animal doué de raison* (*The Day of the Dolphin*, 1967) has Professor Sevilla establishing full communication with dolphins. Michael Crichton's *The Andromeda Strain* (1969) tells the story of a group of virologists who save the earth from a deadly super virus brought back to earth by a space capsule. The great physicist, Sevek, in Ursula Le Guin's novel *The Dispossessed* (1974) fights to overcome prejudice, oppression, and secrecy by giving his great discovery of instantaneous communications to all mankind. However, in all of these novels, one still has the feeling that society does not really understand the real nature of science; by virtue of his knowledge and commitment, the scientist is still a social misfit.

In modern literature there is a clear separation between the theoretical scientist (the absent-minded, naïve genius) and the scientific worker; to a large extent the latter are seen less. More importantly, scientists in general are less frequent as major characters than in the early part of the twentieth century. Perhaps it is the collective nature of modern "big science," that makes it difficult to dramatize the drama of science. In any case, there seems relatively little understanding—given the importance of the scientific enterprise—of how science advances.

See also: Reason, Travel, Universe, Utopia.

Selected Bibliography

Barron, Neil. *Anatomy of Wonder: Science Fiction*. New York: R. R. Bowker, Co., 1976.

Crouch, Laura E. "The Scientist in English Literature. Domingo Gonsales (1638) to Victor Frankenstein (1817)." Ph.D. diss., University of Oklahoma, 1975.

Nicolson, Margorie Hope. *The Breaking of the Circle: Studies in the Effect of the "New Science" upon Seventeenth-Century English Poetry*. Rev. Ed. New York: Columbia University Press, 1960.

————. *Voyages to the Moon*. New York: Macmillan, 1948.

CHARLES ELKINS

SEARCH FOR FATHER

The search for father theme seems to occur in the folk tradition of most peoples and has been prominent in literature down to the present time. Although it frequently overlaps with such concepts of fatherhood as the relationship between father and son, father and daughter, parents and children, it has a distinctive feature—a son or, occasionally a daughter, sets out to find his or her father.

Among the different versions of the theme, three basic groups of motifs prevail, with considerable overlapping:

1. The child is either not raised by his parents, or only by his mother, whom the father left before or soon after the birth took place. Frequently, the son does not know the father but has a token that makes him recognizable to him.

2. The child and the father engage in a fight, the outcome of which may be tragic. But, importantly, they do not know or do not recognize each other when they begin the fight, which, therefore, is not the result of familial hatred.

3. The child is raised away from his father, but is drawn to him, often because he is rejected or mocked by those around him.

In the diverse literary forms in which it has occurred, different potentials of the theme have been utilized. In ancient times it served as a powerful myth, later it became an adventure story, and in more recent times it has served as a plot for didactic, psychological, and symbolical literature.

Antiquity

In early, mythic versions of the theme, the urge to learn about origins is dominant. In the Tongan legend, *Sisimatailaa* (first published in 1925), a young man wants to find out about his ancestry before getting married. After several adventures, he comes to an island to discover that his father is the Sun.

To be fatherless means to be without origins, and it results in being an outcast from the community. The fatherless son, therefore, is often prepared to sacrifice even his life to find out about his father. In the legend of Laka, in the Hawaiian Wahieloa-Laka cycle (first published in 1907), Laka's father disappeared before the boy's birth. The other children jeer at him because he is fatherless, so Laka sets out on a perilous voyage to look for his father's bones.

The theme is significant in the ancient Greek epic cycle. The main motivating factor in Homer's *Odysseia* (*Odyssey,* epic, c. 8th century B.C.) in the search for the father, Odysseus, is the mockery to which the son, Telemachus, is subjected. Thanks to the broad epic potential and universal appeal of Homer's work, the theme of the Greek hero's wanderings, his son's search for him, and their final reunion inspired writers from early times down to the twentieth century.

In Homer's epic, Odysseus, lord of Ithaca, having provoked Poseidon, god of the sea, is prevented from returning home to his family after helping the Greeks to take Troy. His wife is surrounded by suitors, who, claiming that Odysseus is dead, use up the resources of his household and make fun of his heir, Telemachus. The young man then goes off in search of his father. Of course, here the emphasis is on the wanderings of the father, not those of the son. The central figure is Odysseus and not Telemachus. The most crucial point in the epic is the father's homecoming, which brings about the restoration of order in the home and the reassertion of the authority of Odysseus and Telemachus. The son's search for his father is not successful; it is through the aid of the gods that Odysseus finds his way home. Nevertheless, Telemachus' determination to undertake the voyage in search of his father is a very important element in the story, not least because it emphasizes the atmosphere of order and harmony prevailing in Homer's world.

In later Greek literature, where the stature of Odysseus is downgraded, and he is involved with mistresses who bear him illegitimate children, the motif of fighting and accidental murder between father and son gains prominence. This adds to the adventurous nature of the theme. The story of Telegonus, son of Odysseus and Circe, was treated in the *Niptra* of Sophocles (tragedy, late 5th century B.C.), from which only fragments survive. In the now almost entirely lost epic, *Tēlegonia*, by Eugammon of Cyrene (6th century B.C.), Telegonus comes to Ithaca searching for his father, whom he kills in self-defense with his spear when he fails to recognize him. After the death of the father, the two half-brothers, Telemachus and Telegonus, meet and marry each other's mothers, Penelope and Circe.

The story of Euryalos, Odysseus' illegitimate son from the Thesprotian Euippe, appears in another of Sophocles' lost dramas, the *Euryalos* (late 5th century B.C.) and also in the third chapter of *Erōtika Pathēmata* (*The Sorrowful Love Stories*, 1st century B.C.) by Parthenius of Nicaea. Euryalos is sent off to Ithaca by his mother to look for his father. He brings several tokens to identify him to Odysseus. Penelope, however, is first to realize who the young man is, and she contrives his death at the hands of his unknowing father.

The Middle Ages

The element of a fight between father and son remained an important part of the theme. The story of combat appears in Middle Eastern and European tales, legends, and sagas. This adventurous turn suited the ideals of medieval epic poetry. The Old High German alliterative heroic poem, the *Hildebrandslied* (*The Lay of Hildebrand*, c. 810) gives an account of the encounter between Hildebrand and his son Hadubrand in a joust. Before the murder of the son, the narration of which is missing in the manuscript, Hildebrand recognizes his own child, but the young warrior looks upon his attempts at reconciliation as cowardice; the heroic code of behavior does not make any other conduct possible for Hildebrand than to go ahead with the fight.

The theme is significant in numerous versions of the Russian *Il'ia Muromeţs i soloveĭ razboĭnik* (*Ilia Muromets and the Falcon*, folk epic, 13th century). Only Ilia Muromets, the old Cossack, is strong enough to fight against the powerful intruder. When Ilia conquers the falcon, he forces him to reveal his origin and learns that he has fought his own son.

In one of the Onega ballads, Ilia Muromets encounters his daughter in combat. After she had grown "mighty in strength," her mother sent her to Russia to find her father. Hearing that Onega is the daughter of the widow who is a "calatch baker," Ilia recognizes the girl to be his own child and narrates how he stayed and slept with the widow. The girl is furious, however, to have her mother revealed as a harlot and herself, by extension, as illegitimate, and decides to kill Ilia Muromets.

In many late medieval versions of the theme, the outcome of the fight between father and son is peaceful, because the recognition and reconciliation take place in time, often leading to the reunion of the family. In Marie de France's lay, *Milun* (c.1170), an illegitimate son is born following the amorous encounter of two lovers kept apart by unfavorable circumstances. The son is raised by an aunt, and when he hears about the fame of his father, who is a knight, he too sets out to try his fortune and find his parents. He, in turn, earns such a reputation as a valorous knight, that his father's envy leads him to fight against the young man. But the two quickly recognize each other, stop fighting, and depart together to find the mother. The lay concludes with the marriage of the parents.

Similarly happy is the outcome of the German *Biterolf und Dietlieb* (*Biterolf and Dietlieb,* epic poem of unknown author, 13th century). Biterolf sets out and leaves his wife and two-year-old son behind. The vicissitudes of fortune keep him away for so long that his wife assumes that he is dead. Their son, Dietlieb, however, is reluctant to believe this and, as a doughty young man, leaves home to search for his father. The two meet, challenge each other to a fight, but they recognize each other before long and return home together.

The theme appears in the sixteenth and seventeenth centuries in vendetta plays or to illustrate the spelling of parricide committed in the name of the Machiavellian thirst for power, as a result of which unknowing sons murder their fathers or the other way round, as is the case in act 2, scene 5, of Shakespeare's *Henry VI, Part Three* (chronicle play, 1590–1592).

The Seventeenth and Eighteenth Centuries

The end of the age of chivalry, the growth of towns, and the appearance of middle-class manners and values brought about a relative lull in the popularity of the theme. In the age of Neoclassicism, however, there was renewed interest in the classical epic cycle and, consequently, this led to the increased application of the theme of the search for father in serious and satirical literary pieces alike.

In Fénelon's novel, *Les aventures de Télémaque* (*The Adventures of Telemachus,* 1699), Odysseus does not even appear until the very end; the son and his adventures during the voyage undertaken in the search for his father are at the center of attention.

The novel starts in medias res on Calypso's island. Telemachus is guided by the goddess Minerva, who assumes the shape of Mentor. They embark upon their own "odyssey," suffering shipwrecks and encountering various kings and heroes. Wherever they go, they try to obtain information on the whereabouts of Ulysses. At last, they see him on an island, which is the last stage of his voyage before reaching Ithaca. At the end of Fénelon's novel, we see Telemachus go to Ithaca to be reunited with his father in Eumaeus' house. The plot of *The Adventures of Telemachus* is a colorful framework for moralizing, suited to the purpose of the educational novel. Ulysses and his son appear as models of finesse, nobility, and heroism. A great part of the dialogue consists of discourses about taste and morals.

Also didactic in nature is Lillo's sentimental, middle-class tragedy, the rather pompously written *Fatal Curiosity* (1736). Based on a true story, it is about a young man who, having acquired great wealth in India, returns to his hometown amidst several misfortunes in order to find his aging parents. Upon his return even his closest childhood friends fail to recognize him because of his altered looks. This gives him the idea of pretending to his parents that he is a stranger for the first few hours, to lessen their shock at seeing their only son, whom they have long believed dead. As he withdraws for a short sleep in the parental home, his mother, overcome with greed upon seeing the riches of the youth, persuades the father to murder and rob their guest. The recognition comes too late, when the son is almost dead. In the last scene most of the remaining characters also die, some of grief and others by their own hands, thus making the point that both greed and murdering one's guest are evil.

The Nineteenth Century

Romanticism brought with it a thirst for the exotic amid the growing insensitivity of nineteenth-century capitalism. The general interest in times past, the Middle Ages in particular, is reflected in the literary treatment of the theme. In Clemens Brentano's novel fragment, *Aus der Chronika eines fahrenden Schülers* (*From the Chronicle of a Travelling Student*, 1818), the reader is taken back to the fourteenth century. Johannes, a young man who set out on a journey to find his missing father at the request of his dying mother, arrives in the city of Strassburg. It is to a sensitive knight, who employs Johannes as a scribe, that the young man narrates the history of his fatherless childhood.

Victorian morality and historical costumery go hand-in-hand in Matthew Arnold's *Sohrab and Rustum* (epic poem, 1853). The origin of Arnold's work is the episode "Sohrab and Rustem" in the Persian epic by Firdausī, *Shāhnāmah* (*Book of Kings*, 100). The story concerns a battle between a father and a son, who, in Arnold's version, is not illegitimate; his mother is not the former mistress but the wife of the father, Rustum. Rustum has always thought, however, that they had a daughter, as the wife misleads him about the sex of the child, lest Rustum should take away their son and raise him to be a soldier. Sohrab was educated away from his father, whom he wants to find more than anything when he becomes a brave warrior. He happens to be fighting for the Tartars against the Persians in whose army his father is serving. In order to attract his father's attention, he challenges a Persian to a fight. Sohrab feels sure that the man who comes forward is his father, but Rustum, assuming that he has a daughter, dismisses Sohrab's queries about his name as trickery. Only when he has slain him does he discover that he has fought his own son, as Sohrab reveals the seal his mother had put on his arm when he was born.

In spite of the romantic exoticism of the Oriental tale, the detailed epic description of tents, soldiers, weapons, and clothes, and the carefully emphasized features of heroism, Arnold's poem cannot avoid becoming unrealistic in parts.

Modern Literature

From the end of the nineteenth century, the theme was approached increasingly for its psychological potential. The search for father is often the way to self-realization for modern man. Dostoevsky's *Podrostok* (*A Raw Youth,* novel, 1875), captures a young man's process of maturation, which is strongly connected with the development of his relationship to his father.

Born an illegitimate child, Arkady does not meet his father, Versilov, properly until the age of twenty. He always resented his father's lack of interest in him and yearned for him as a school-boy, as he was being raised in a boarding school in Moscow, where the other pupils mocked and despised him. His attachment to his father, when they finally became acquainted, was based on a strong attraction to Versilov's personality. The better the young man understood his father, the better he came to know himself. Through Arkady, the author reveals memories and secret desires of his own childhood, heralding a biographical tendency to come in modern novels.

In Thomas Wolfe's *The Web and the Rock* (novel, 1939), George Webber's father leaves his wife and son because of another woman. The boy is raised by an uncle and an aunt, who constantly denigrate George's father. The far-away father, whom the boy seeks constantly in his dreams, becomes the symbol of a happy, healthy, and full life.

The use of the grotesque provides the means for the expressionist Ernst Barlach to evaluate modern life without offering direct commentary in his play, *Der tote Tag* (*The Dead Day,* 1912). The origin of the theme in his play is in an Old Norse myth; a young Everyman is raised by his mother, who symbolizes earthiness in life, while the mysterious distant father stands for divinity. In spite of his wish to do so, the hero, representing humanity, fails to go to his father (divinity) because his mother (earthiness) prevents him.

Gerhart Hauptmann's play, *Der Bogen des Odysseus* (*The Bow of Odysseus,* 1914) has an expressedly psychological interest. In the second act of the play, Telemachus returns home from a journey, undertaken to find his father, with the conviction that Odysseus is dead. The Telemachus of this twentieth-century play lacks the backing of a stable family; his grandfather is reduced to a senile tramp and his mother, Penelope, is not the faithful woman of the Homeric tradition. Whereas in Homer the question why Penelope tolerates the presence of the suitors never arises, in Hauptmann's play the son's and the father's confusion about the personality of the mother constantly lurks behind the plot. Word has it that Penelope has betrayed her long-absent husband with the suitors. Telemachus is uncertain and weak; he looks upon his father as a god, and to him their reunion means the affirmation of his manhood. By using the bow, Odysseus can destroy the suitors and restore order. But the last words spoken in the play suggest that the union of father and son cannot solve the crisis of the family: "What will thy mother say, O Telemach, / That I her favourite playthings broke so soon?"

The family is in ruins in Jean Giono's novel *Naissance de l'Odyssée*, (*The Birth of the Odyssey*, 1930). This marks a return to the classical anti-Odyssean tradition and seventeenth-century burlesques on the theme. Giono's Ulysses is an overweight and cowardly anti-hero, who fabricates a whole series of false adventures. Penelope is an unfaithful wife, who keeps her favorite lover, the handsome Antinous, even after her husband has returned. Telemachus had been unsuccessfully searching for his father. When the two meet, the son is disappointed to see that his father is a worthless coward, not prepared to fight with Antinous. Trivial concerns, empty bragging, and gossip are prevalent in Ithaca. The mendacious father tries to oust his son, and the last event in the plot is a frighteningly resentful Telemachus sharpening the point of a boar-spear—to stick Odysseus like a pig.

James Joyce's novel, *Ulysses* (1922), which is as great a masterpiece of its kind as the Homeric prototype, contains some similarities with Hauptmann's play and Giono's novel. The stable family seems to have disappeared altogether, heroes are replaced by everyday people, the heroic yields its place to the trivial. Yet, importantly, Homer's and the author's worlds are not contrasted as they are in Giono's *Birth of the Odyssey*. Like Homer's epic, Joyce's novel emphasizes the universal. As Richard Ellmann puts it, "Joyce looked into the events of the *Odyssey* for that core of humanistic significance which would awaken his imagination and impart an epic loftiness to his modern material." ("*Ulysses* and *The Odyssey*," *English Studies* 43 [1962]: 423). The chapters of *Ulysses* correspond to the episodes of the *Odyssey*, although the perspective is different: in Homer's work, the third part, "Homecoming" ("Nostos"), is of primary importance, while in *Ulysses* the adventures of Bloom, the twentieth-century Odysseus, form the bulk of the novel. In Homer, finding the father and returning home is the purpose of all the wanderings; whereas in Joyce, since both Stephen, the symbolical son, and Bloom, the symbolical father, are homeless (Bloom figuratively, Stephen literally) the wandering is an end in itself.

Joyce's novel takes place in Dublin, on June 16, 1904. It is the history of a day in the lives of Leopold Bloom, a middle-aged Dubliner, his wife Molly, and Stephen Dedalus, an unacknowledged young artist. The characters know nothing about the Homeric parallels in their lives. Stephen's search for a father figure and Bloom's search for a son remain completely outside of their consciousness. Both Stephen and Bloom spend the day wandering around in Dublin. Several times they are close to each other but their paths do not cross until late in the evening. Bloom meets Stephen in the red-light district of Dublin—a twentieth-century Circe's den—where, abandoned by his friends, Stephen is about to get into trouble. Bloom helps him out, walks home with him, and offers his hospitality to the young man. They have a talk over a cup of hot chocolate in Bloom's kitchen, and against his will, Bloom sees Stephen leave. The appearance of Bloom is unheroic; he is a petty bourgeois with mundane thoughts, but his experience, wisdom, and endurance place him on a par with Odysseus. These qualities make him stand out against the events of the book: the usurping of one's friend, blind and vicious chauvinism, lack of compassion, and the loss of family ties. Even though Bloom is not Stephen's real father, the young man, during their temporary encounter, finds in him important paternal virtues that he cannot acquire elsewhere.

In contrast to what happens in Homer's epic, in *Ulysses* it is Stephen, the son figure, who abandons home and rejects society, while Bloom resigns himself to accepting his situation as a rejected foreigner, a Jew and a cuckolded husband, and to trying, with unceasing perseverance, to improve it. As Stanford remarks in his book, *The Ulysses Theme,* Bloom and Stephen encompass the entire Ulyssean tradition. Stephen Dedalus embodies the "centrifugal" or "negative," Bloom the "centripetal" or "positive" poles of the Ulyssean character.

The home does not exist any more in Otto Walter's *Der Stumme* (*The Dumb Man,* novel, 1959). The dumb son comes to work to a camp of builders where he knows his father is. The father does not recognize the son until the end of the novel, in spite of his token of recognition, his dumbness. The sensible and warm-hearted youth hates his father, who—as we learn through the flashbacks in the novel—is responsible for his dumbness. He lost his voice as a result of shock when he witnessed as a child how his father physically abused his mother, who died. Yet Lothar, the dumb young man, cannot help being drawn to his now aging but once energetic and strong father. This dichotomy is symbolically reflected in the father's death in an accident, for which the son is not responsible yet feels implicated in its cause.

See also: Family, Parents and Children.

Selected Bibliography

Lee, Anthony van der. *Zum literarischen Motiv der Vatersuche*. Amsterdam: Noord-Hollandsche Vitg. Mij., 1957.

Potter, Murray Anthony. *Sohrab and Rustem: The Epic Theme of a Combat between Father and Son*. London: David Knutt, 1902.

Stanford, W.B. *The Ulysses Theme: A Study in the Adaptability of a Traditional Hero*. 2d ed. New York: Barnes and Noble, 1968.

PETER I. BARTA

SECRET LOVE

The term *"secret love"* requires no highly specialized definition; for the most part, its meaning is self-evident. Here it includes any romantic or sentimental passion kept hidden, for an unspecified period of time, from one or more persons. As a literary theme or motif, secret love can and does appear in many forms. Sometimes, the love is presented as one-sided; the beloved does not know that he or she is loved. More often, the love is shared, and the secret is being kept from outsiders. Occasionally, the lovers are married to each other, and their marriage, for some reason, must be kept a secret.

Possible motives for the secrecy vary a great deal. Quite often, the love is adulterous, and secrecy is necessary. Sometimes the love appears shameful either to the lover or to the society at large, and revelation of the love would bring disgrace. In many literary works, the lover does not reveal him or herself for fear of rejection; the beloved is perceived as too far above the lover, socially or personally, and the lover lacks the courage to reveal him or herself. Motives for secrecy are often mixed; they can be a combination of some of the reasons suggested here and other reasons unique to a particular literary work. In almost every case, secrecy intensifies the love, keeps it flaming and obsessive; in some instances, when the secrecy ends, mystery and passion end with it.

As a literary theme, secret love cuts across genres. It seems equally appropriate to drama, both comedy and tragedy, lyrical poetry or fiction. We find it often as the primary theme of a work and, more frequently, as a minor motif in service of a larger or more pressing theme.

Secret love is common, too, to most periods of literary history and to the literature of many nations and cultures. Naturally, there are moments in literary history during which romantic love dominates the literature, and in these moments, the theme of secret love flourishes.

Background in Antiquity and the Middle Ages

The literature of antiquity contains few if any important examples of detailed treatment of secret love. This theme has little role to play in epic poetry with its warrior values of courage and endurance on the battlefield; it has little part to play as well in religious drama or even in the tales of the playful or malicious lusts of the gods of pagan antiquity.

If this is true, the reverse is equally true for the medieval period. The Middle Ages constitute the literary period during which we find the most frequent occurrence of the theme, the greatest number of secret lovers, and the most emphasis in literature on individual love affairs. It is not too much of an exaggeration to say that individual personal love is a primary subject for medieval literature. Scholars and students of this period have found, and still argue over the meaning of, the concept of "courtly love." Although there is much dispute over the various individual aspects and manifestations of this phenomenon, generally speaking, courtly love involves secrecy, whether mandated by adultery or unattainability or by a need for intensity in love. For the lovers, their love becomes all to them. It is an obsession, and the lovers (usually men, more often, knights or lords) become servants of love. In many writers, love takes on religious implications; in others, the social aspects are foregrounded. In almost every case, secrecy is paramount.

In many poems of love, the lovers themselves become subordinated to the love, its characteristics, and its implict or explicit contingent "code" of behavior (how codified the rules of love actually were is another subject under debate, but certainly there is a clear interest even emphasis on the appropriate way for a lover and a beloved to behave). A good example of this occurs with one of the most famous of medieval love poems, *Le roman de la rose* (*The Romance of the Rose*), a 13th-century French poem of 22,000 lines. The first 4,000 or so lines were written by Guillaume de Lorris (c. 1230). The poem was finished by Jehan de Meung (c.1275). This work, particularly in the longer part composed by de Meung, presents highly allegorized lovers and demonstrates a concern with social situations and "correct" behavior on the part of the lovers. This is a pattern that recurs throughout these courtly works: an emphasis on manners, at times even overshadowing the apparent subject of the poem, the lovers themselves.

However, some very important and highly individualized lovers appear and play important recurring roles in medieval literature: Tristan and Iseult, Lancelot and Guinevere, and Troilus and Criseyde.

Tristan and Iseult (there are many variations on the spellings of their names—Tristran, Tristram, Tristrem, Isolde, Yseult, Isolt) are favorites in twelfth- and thirteenth-century lyrics and romances, appearing apparently for the first time in a romance in Anglo-Norman French verse written by Thomas of Britain (c.1170). In its various versions, the story changes in minor ways, but consistently at the center is Tristan's falling in love with Iseult, a young bride of his uncle, King Mark, whom he has been sent to escort to her husband. Tristan appears in Dante's *Inferno (Hell)* of *La divina commedia (The Divine Comedy,* epic, c. 1320) in the Second Circle, and the lovers appear in Thomas Malory's *Morte d'Arthur* (prose romance, c. 1469).

Morte d'Arthur is the superlative medieval bringing together of the existing Arthurian legends. The spread of the popularity of the Arthur story seems to begin with *Historia regum Britanniae* (1137) by Geoffrey of Monmouth; in this blend of fact and legend, Arthur appears, and he and his followers catch the interest of European readers. But in this work, Arthur is much more important than any of his followers; gradually other members of his court take on more importance, particularly Lancelot whose illicit and secret love for Arthur's Queen Guinevere soon dominates the stories of the Round Table, the court which this love helps to destroy. Chief among the works that deal with this love is Chrétien de Troyes' *Lancelot* (c.1180); in this romance in French verse, the love of Lancelot for the queen is almost religious in its devotion and constancy (Chrétien de Troyes is believed to have written also a no longer existent romance dealing with the Mark-Iseult-Tristan story). Lancelot's story has proved enduring; it and other Arthurian romances reappear through literary history, in the nineteenth century in Alfred Lord Tennyson's *Idylls of the King* (poetry, 1859–1885), in the twentieth century in T. H. White's *The Once and Future King* (prose stories, 1958) and in any number of other versions. It is perhaps the definitive story of secret lovers, illicit passions, and eventual destruction.

The third pair of medieval secret lovers, Troilus and Criseyde, also have an interesting literary history. Their story appears, apparently for the first time in *Roman de Troie* (poetry, c.1160–1170) verses by a Norman French poet, Benoît de Sainte-Maure; their story is not central to this work, and Benoît does not put much emphasis on the character of Criseyde, here spelled Briseida. We find the same story retold in Latin prose in *Historia destructionis Troiae* by Guido delle Colonne (c.1285). The story of these lovers is fleshed out in Giovanni Boccaccio's romance *Filostrato* (c.1338), in which the heroine becomes Criseida, and her role grows, although Troilus is still the more important character.

This story has its best and most important telling in Chaucer's masterpiece, *Troilus and Criseyde* (c.1385), 8,000 lines of poetry written in stanzas of rime royal. Chaucer's work is, in part, an adaptation of Boccaccio's. It tells the story of Troilus, a Trojan prince who falls in love with a young widow, Criseyde. With the help of her uncle, Pandarus, Troilus' suit is made to Criseyde. Criseyde worries about her reputation and resists his suit. Eventually, she yields. Her father is a traitor, and she is sent in an exchange for prisoners to the Greeks. Although she has sworn her fidelity, she betrays Troilus with Diomede. Troilus, broken-hearted, is killed in battle.

Although Chaucer's work is built on the work of Boccaccio and his sources, *Troilus and Criseyde* is far superior in its treatment of the lovers and especially of the faithless Criseyde. Chaucer manages to make her into a sympathetic and complex character. The element of secrecy is crucial to the passion developed in the poem; initially, Troilus' love for Criseyde is kept to himself, because, as a courtly lover, he sees himself as inferior to her and fears to reveal himself; he requires a confidant and go-between. At no time does Troilus lose this deference to her, even after he has won her, and he keeps the secret in order to protect her reputation. He is the perfect courtly lover; she, however, is unable to remain faithful in spite of her love for him. Chaucer tries as no one else before or after (including Shakespeare, who treats her as a strumpet) to see her with sympathy, as weak and "slydynge of corage" (book 5, 1.825). The strength of the poem is in Chaucer's ability to integrate the psychology of lovers within the conventions of courtly love.

Secret love blossoms as a theme in this period of literary history because it is a crucial component of love between men and women as creatively conceived at this time. Within the literary convention at work here, love can be both illicit and ennobling; fidelity to the lover, and not necessarily the spouse, is of primary importance, hence the need for secrecy. Moreover, secrecy inflames the lovers and allows no complacency; the intensity of passion that we associate with these sets of enduring literary lovers is often a product of the special circumstances that prevent the public acknowledgment of their love.

The Sixteenth and Seventeenth Centuries

One of the best places to look for secret lovers in the sixteenth century is in the plays of William Shakespeare. The theater in general is a place to find lovers during this period, and Shakespeare offers a wealth to choose among. The environment most conducive at this time is the comedies. There exist many comedies from this period, written by Shakespeare and others, in which secret lovers play a part in an overall pattern of intrigue, complicated plot developments, disguises, and go-betweens. *Love's Labours Lost* (c. 1594) provides an apt example.

In this play, King Ferdinand and three young lords vow to live as monks: fasting, studying, and avoiding women. This vows lasts until they meet and fall in love with the princess of France and three of her ladies in waiting. Each must then hide his love from his fellows. The play centers on wit, costume and disguise, and clowning; the love is the occasion for the antics, and there is never any doubt that all will end well, as is the rule in Shakespeare's comedies.

One of Shakespeare's pre-1600 plays, *Romeo and Juliet* (c. 1596 offers a much more serious, even tragic, look at secret love. As everyone knows, Romeo and Juliet are the children of feuding families; consequently, their love is impossible and must be kept secret from their parents. Juliet's father, in addition, is forcing her to marry another man, the wealthy Paris. To avenge his friend Mercutio's death, Romeo has killed Juliet's cousin, Tybalt, and the union of the lovers becomes even more difficult. Messages fail to reach Romeo, plans are thwarted, and the two lovers die. At their deaths, their families learn of their secret love, and the feud belatedly ends. This play contains many elements involving secret love that are common to the comedies: disguises, go-betweens, unreceived letters. Nevertheless, the play also contains a blood feud, fatal duels, and tragic deaths. The love, rather than a plot device as it is in *Love's Labours Lost,* is central to the play, all-consuming, and as ennobling as (though less stylized than) that of the medieval lovers. The beauty and tragic quality of the play make Romeo and Juliet, like Lancelot and Guinevere, enduring names for transcendent lovers.

Romeo and Juliet is Shakespeare's only real treatment of secret love in the tragic mode, but we find secret lovers populating the later, more mature comedies as well as the early ones. Once again, in *As You Like It* (c. 1599) and *Twelfth Night* (c.1600), we find the intrigues and disguises and the sorting out of everything at the end.

In *Twelfth Night,* the heroine, Viola, is unable to reveal her love for the duke, Orsino, because she is disguised as a boy and employed in his service. This disguise frees her from some conventions and binds her to others. As in the earlier comedies, Shakespeare uses conventions of disguise and complicated plotting to provide a testing period for lovers, a period in which they can unknowingly demonstrate that they are worthy of love and are appropriate mates for other characters. Individual loves seem less important than social harmony; in many of these comedies, the final matchings strike us as not always completely desirable, but again the individual is often sacrificed to the general good. The marriage, not the individual lovers, is what matters. Secret love is often little more than a plot device that leads to this end.

Shakespeare is not the only playwright working with these conventions. In the seventeenth century, we find the romantic dramas of Beaumont and Fletcher dealing with many of the same concerns and using many of the same techniques. A case in point is *Philaster, or Love Lies a Bleeding* (1610). In this play, the king of Calabria promises his daughter to the prince of Spain. She loves another, however (Philaster), and promises herself to him. Philaster is then deceived into believing her unfaithful. After various confusions and acts of violence, the rightful lovers are together as the play ends. The secret love is a part of the general intrigue, and the play seems to be about honesty and loyalty and the eventual recognition and rewarding of the faithful, rather than about love itself.

The general point can be made with respect to many seventeenth-century dramas that involve secret love; plays such as Corneille's *Don Sanche d'Aragon* (1650) are only incidentally about love and lovers; the secrecy does not have the heightening effect we have seen in earlier periods, and the love is only one of many deceptions within the work. In John Webster's *The Duchess of Malfi* (1613), the Duchess' "unsuitable" marriage is kept a secret from her wicked brothers, but no one would call this a play about secret love.

One final example will suffice to demonstrate one more direction possible for this theme. William Wycherley's *The Country Wife* (1673) is a play about adultery and cuckoldry, and so secrecy plays a part, but again "love" (really lust) is a contrivance of plot and serves to further the jokes aimed at the impotence of the well-deceived husband.

In general, in the plays of the sixteenth and seventeenth centuries, we find a fondness for complicated plots, intrigues, and deceptions. The theme or motif of *secret love* fits in nicely but with few exceptions never dominates and defines the play. The obvious exception, of course, is *Romeo and Juliet,* but it is worth noting that even this play contains all the trappings of deception and disguise; Shakespeare, like Chaucer in *Troilus and Criseyde,* transcends while working clearly within the conventions of the day.

The Eighteenth Century

The eighteenth century, a literary age generally of satire and comedies of manners, provides no very fertile ground for the development of the theme of secret love. An interesting exception is *The Conscious Lovers* (1722) by Sir Richard Steele. Generally classified as a "sentimental comedy," this play presents two pairs of lovers, Bevil and Indiana, and Myrtle and Lucinda, who keep their affections secret from each other and from the outside world for much of the duration of the comedy. The primary reason for secrecy in this play is propriety. Lucinda and Bevil are engaged as the play opens. This is to be an arranged marriage; neither is in love with the other. However, as long as this engagement lasts, no one of the four characters will consider declaring his or her true affections. The matter is further complicated by the fact that Bevil and Myrtle are best friends.

As might be expected in a "sentimental comedy," all of this is sorted out by the end of the play, and it is all managed without anyone behaving with impropriety.

What makes this play especially interesting in the development of the secret love motif, is the social standing of the main characters. They are situated firmly in the middle class; their values are middle class, and yet they are capable of ennobling love. Any impropriety, let alone adultery, is out of the question when talking of love. The social values are paramount. Also in keeping with the social values of the play, Steele shows himself a reformer. The play certainly argues for an end to contractual, loveless marriages, showing how such practices encourage fortune hunters and discourage real gentlemen. The firm placement of this and similar sentimental comedies within the everyday world, the middle class, the urban contemporary world, sets the scene for the strong social concerns that frame the secret love motif in the nineteenth century.

The Nineteenth Century

The motif of secret love is quite common through the literature of the nineteenth century. It appears in a variety of guises, in various genres, and receives varying degrees of emphasis.

One obvious working of the motif in the early part of the century appears in Keats' "The Eve of Saint Agnes" (1820). Here we find echoes of the Romeo and Juliet story. The young lovers, Madeline and Porphyro, have, at the end of the poem, "fled away into the storm" (1.371) to escape the hostilities of family, the external obstacles to their love. The action of the poem is set "ages long ago" (1.370), and the story with Keats' addition of folk superstitions and hints of magic, has a fairy-tale quality; the lovers take on mythic qualities and exist outside time. The poem is pure sensual romance.

At approximately the same time, the motif of secret love is undergoing a different sort of treatment by Sir Walter Scott in his historical romances. One good example is found in the novel, *Kenilworth* (1821). In this work, the secret love is in fact a secret marriage. Amy Robsart and the earl of Leicester are married, but Leicester fears the displeasure of the queen, Elizabeth I, if she learns he is married. The queen is deceived into believing that Amy is actually married to Richard Varney, an accomplice of Leicester's in this scheme. Varney is, however, dishonorable and eventually convinces Leicester that Amy has been unfaithful to him. Leicester eventually learns the truth (as does the queen) but not in time to save Amy. The story is one of political intrigue, scheming, and struggles for power. The focus of interest, as with most of Scott's novels, is on historical background and detail; the secret love is important to the extent that it demonstrates the perils of court life.

There are also examples of uses of a secret love motif that seem to have little plot function at all. For example, in American literature, Nathaniel Hawthorne often includes this secrecy in works that probe larger themes. In its most functional appearance, secret love plays a part in *The Scarlet Letter* (novel, 1850); Hester Prynne's lover and the father of her child Pearl is kept a secret from the upstanding community. However, in Hawthorne's novel *The Blithedale Romance* (1852), Miles Coverdale's secret love for Priscilla Moodie is arguably irrelevant to the issues of the prose romance, issues of social and satiric import.

There are many literary works in this period that move the secret love back to center stage. The medieval and Arthurian legends return in a form shaped by contemporary values. We have, among other versions, Matthew Arnold's poem *Tristram and Iseult* (1852) and Alfred Lord Tennyson's *Idylls of the King*. In Tennyson's poem, much of the earlier ennobling through passionate love is lost, and Guinevere becomes primarily the fallen wife of a Victorian husband.

Adultery is also the motive for secrecy in one of the best known of nineteenth-century novels, Gustave Flaubert's *Madame Bovary* (1856). In this novel, Emma Bovary has more than one secret love; after her unhappiness has led her to a gruesome and lingering suicide, her previously unsuspecting husband finds letters that provide the evidence of her affairs. Again, as is common and consistent with the values of the period, there is little suggestion of adulterous lovers being transported or ennobled by their loves. Emma Bovary's loves are the external manifestations of her unhappiness and boredom, her dissatisfactions with her ordinary life. They provide distractions at best, added misery at worst.

However, not all nineteenth-century lovers are as weak spirited or as morally unimaginative as Madame Bovary. And not all secret lovers are adulterers.

The quiet rural life so offensive to Emma Bovary is the same life that is celebrated in other novels of the period. One of these, which is often classified as a "sentimental romance," is *L'abbé Constantin* (*The Abbé Constantin*, 1882) by Ludovic Halévy. The main female character in this novel is a young lady, Miss Percival, a French Canadian who has been staying in Paris and longs for a simpler, quieter life. She is loved by Jean Reynaud, the godson of the title character. This love remains a secret for much of the novel because Jean sees her beauty and elegant manners and believes that she could never love him. She does, of course, and is finally obliged to declare her love in order to elicit a similar declaration from him.

Finally, the nineteenth century saw some examples of the use of the secret love motif in works that celebrated a truly selfless sort of love, a genuinely noble love that will not allow the lover to put him or herself first. The beloved's happiness is of primary importance, even if this means keeping silent or serving the cause of another suitor.

In Henry Wadsworth Longfellow's American narrative, *The Courtship of Miles Standish* (verse, 1858), John Alden is sent to propose marriage on behalf of Captain Standish to a young lady whom Alden himself loves. This story ends happily with the union of the appropriate lovers and the blessings of Standish himself on the union.

Not all such stories end so patly, particularly not the best known of the type, Edmond Rostand's drama *Cyrano de Bergerac* (1897). In this French play, the hero, Cyrano, a man whose lack of physical beauty is more than compensated for by spiritual beauty, loves a young woman, Roxanne. Roxanne loves, or believes she loves, Christian, a somewhat shallow but physically beautiful young man. For Roxanne's sake, Cyrano helps Christian to court her, writing beautiful love letters in his name. By the play's end, Roxanne has realized that Cyrano is the author of the letters and also that it is Cyrano whom she loves. But Cyrano dies as she comes to this realization, and the character of Cyrano de Bergerac becomes a symbol, along with Sidney Carton from Charles Dickens' *A Tale of Two Cities* (novel, 1859), of self-sacrificing perfect human love as represented in the literature of the nineteenth century.

The Twentieth Century

If there is a common thread that runs through the highly diverse treatments of this theme in the literature of the twentieth century, it is the growing impossibility of the love in question. The love is impossible not because it is unattainable but because it does not provide what the characters need. More and more frequently in this literature, no happy resolution is in store for the lovers; more and more, the love represents a desire for escape from an increasingly bleak life.

The idea of a selfless and self-sacrificing secret love that emerged so strongly at the end of the nineteenth century is still flourishing at the beginning of the twentieth. An excellent example of this is Henry James' late novel, *The Wings of the Dove* (1902). In this work, Milly Theale, a woman with beauty, wealth, and charm, is tragically ill. She falls in love with Merton Densher, unaware that Densher is secretly in love with Kate Croy. Kate and Densher have plotted together to marry Densher to Milly and gain her fortune on her death. The plan fails when Milly learns about their relationship; however, her selfless love continues and encourages her to provide the money for them. In a Jamesian twist, the secret lovers have been influenced for the better by Milly and are, in conscience, unable to take advantage of their "good fortune."

Selflessness is not always the order of the day, of course. In many early twentieth-century works, the secret lover is concerned very much with himself and with an attempt to find a way out of the dreariness of his life. In Edith Wharton's novel *Ethan Frome* (1911), we have such a case. The title character is trapped in a loveless marriage. He falls in love with his wife's cousin, Mattie Silver, who has come to live as a companion and helper to Frome's sickly wife, Zeena. Zeena eventually decides to send Mattie away, bringing Frome's misery to a head. In a botched attempt at a double suicide, both he and Mattie are injured, Mattie quite seriously, and both must live under Zeena's care. The emphasis in the story is on wasted lives and hopelessness.

Similar concerns dominate the early work of James Joyce. In his collection of related short stories, *Dubliners* (1914), the characters find themselves trapped in dreary lives defined for them by the colorless provincialism of Dublin society. In several of the stories, a secret love becomes the symbol of a longing for escape, adventure, beauty. The most obvious example is "Araby." In this story, a young boy believes himself in love with the older sister of one of his companions. He tells no one, of course; his love for her is highly idealized; he thinks of himself as a bearer of the Holy Grail, carrying his love for her through the ugly Dublin streets. He plans to visit a bazaar (the Araby of the title) and to bring home a gift for her. When he arrives at Araby, he finds it as shabby and commercial as everything else, not a magical place at all. The story ends with his despairing perception of himself as a deluded fool.

A third variation on this idea of a secret love as an expression of a desire for escape from ugliness comes much later in the century with *The Heart of the Matter* (novel, 1948) by Graham Greene. In this novel, Major Scobie, a policeman in British West Africa during World War II, is living through one of the worst times of his life. His career is going badly (he has been passed over for promotion), and this damages his already fragile marriage. He pities his wife for her unhappiness and involves himself in a morally dangerous situation in order to pay for her passage on a holiday trip. He begins, while his wife is away, an affair with a very young woman who was rescued from a torpedoed British ship. Scobie's problems become compounded, and he turns to suicide. In this novel, the love affair is not central to Scobie's predicament. Rather it is a manifestation of his predicament and a small attempt to escape the tightening net of circumstance; instead of escape, it brings final catastrophe. As in the works of Wharton and Joyce, the darkness wins.

One other trend in twentieth-century literature is worth mentioning. There is in the literature, particularly in fiction, a continuing absorption in the aesthetic and narrative questions of fiction writing; a large number of works exist that show the author himself questioning the conventions of the form and playing with these conventions. Occasionally the motif of secret love has a role to play here. An example from early in the twentieth century is a story by the French writer, André Gide, "Isabelle" (1911). In this story, Gide is experimenting with the role of the narrator and its relation to the tone of the story. The story is told within the framework of another, larger story, and the narrator makes claims for its "truth." The narrator falls in love with the title character, secretly, without having met her, in other words with an idea of her. The real Isabelle appears and, not unexpectedly, problems ensue. In this work, Gide makes much satirical use of the conventions: mysterious events, hidden documents, and letters.

A much more contemporary experimental treatment of these conventions is British novelist John Fowles' *The French Lieutenant's Woman* (1969). The woman of the title is enigmatic, not exactly what she seems to be, exotic, and secretly loved by Charles Smithson, the hero of the novel. Again all the conventions are present including outside hostility and the use of the servants as go-betweens. The love must be kept secret because the woman, Sarah, is a scandalous figure and because Charles is engaged to someone else. In keeping with the experimental nature of the novel (and the fun), Fowles provides the reader with a choice of endings.

Fowles keeps the reader's attention on the lovers, and at the same time, emphasizes rather than attempts to camoflage the machinery of secret love conventions, the same conventions that have accompanied the use of this theme through centuries of literary history.

See also: Escape, *Liebestod*, Love in Greek and Roman Literature, Love Triangle, Marriage.

Selected Bibliography

Lewis, C.S. *Allegory of Love*. 1936. London: Oxford University Press, 1971.
Owen, D.D.R. *Noble Lovers*. New York: New York University Press, 1975.
Rougemont, Denis de. *Love in the Western World*. Trans. Montgomery Belgion. 1956, Princeton, N.J.: Princeton University Press, 1983.

MARY J. ELKINS

SEDUCTION

The prevailing sense of the word "seduction," and especially as it relates to literature, involves inducing a woman to surrender her chastity. There are, of course, collateral and more general uses of the term that are usually associated with sacred or moral literature. These uses refer to leading a person astray in conduct or belief, temptation, enticement, and beguiling in order to do something immoral. These senses of the term are used frequently in the Old Testament. For example, the apostatizing seductions of King Manasseh (667–642 B.C.) were thought to be so evil that Yahweh withdrew his Davidic covenant, thereby permitting the exile of 586 B.C.: "But they hearkened not; and Manasseh seduced them to do more evil than the nations whom the Lord destined before the children of Israel" (2 Kings 21:9). Spenser, in *The Faerie Queene* (epic poem, 1590–1596 4.5.11), uses the term in the sense of beguiling: "Duessa . . . who with her forged beauty did seduce / The hearts of some that fairest her did weene." A rarer use of the term implies winning by charm. An example of this usage is found in Thomas Hardy's *Tess of the D'Urbervilles* (1891), a major novel dealing with every aspect of seduction: "Perhaps one reason why she seduces casual attention is that she never courts it" (chap. 14). Perhaps Scheherazade, the narrator of *Alf Layla wa-layla* (*The Arabian Nights*, 8th to 17th centuries), is the supreme example of the most general sense of seduction, since she must beguile her husband, the sultan Schahriah, by telling such enchanting stories that he is willing to postpone having her killed. She is so successful that he gives her his affection, calling her the liberator of her sex.

Used in its more specialized and commonly accepted sense, seduction is, nevertheless, a superordinant theme to which many other major themes are hyponymous. These include those of abduction, rape, libertinism, lechery, the rake, and the philanderer. Still other related themes are based on specific characters whose significance serves as the basis for an identifiably separate theme. Among these are Faust, Casanova, Lothario, Lovelace, Romeo, Tristan, and Don Juan, each representing a particular aspect of the theme of seduction. In addition, many prominent characters throughout the history of world literature, from Satan in the Old Testament or Zeus in the *Ilias* (*Iliad,* epic poem, c. 8th century B.C.) to Hans Castorp in Thomas Mann's *Der Zauberberg* (*The Magic Mountain,* novel, 1924) and Aureliano Buendía in García Márquez's *Cien años de soledad* (*One Hundred Years of Solitude*, novel, 1967) are famous for their seductions of women, although, unlike those characters mentioned earlier, these latter ones are not known primarily as seducers.

Antiquity

The moral and theological or religious aspects seen in the theme of seduction in antiquity give a strong negative connotation to the etymological denotation of "leading away" or "drawing aside from" that has remained in force throughout the history of Western literature. Like the Latin-based term used in English and the Romance languages, the equivalent Greek and Germans terms also mean to lead astray or into error. Thus, one of the epithets associated with Dionysus, a notable arch seducer from classical antiquity, is "beguiler" or "wanderer" (*plagktēr*). (Homer uses the passive form of the same epithet to characterize Odysseus, a literal wanderer who oxymoronically incarnates fidelity.) In antiquity, then, the terms for seduction reflect the close relationship seen between apostasy and illicit sexual relationships. King David's conquest of Bathsheba (2 Sam. 11–12), a model of primitive seduction, exemplifies the powerful forces of physical attraction, moral error, and divine punishment. David is drawn to her on sight: "From the roof he saw a woman bathing. The woman was very beautiful." He uses his royal prerogative (*ius regis*) to procure her: "David sent messengers to get her. She came to him, and he slept with her." He has her husband Uriah killed in battle, and God punishes him by having David and Bathsheba's child die in infancy. As is true regarding the theme in general, so is it true in this particular case—while the seduction ends with a moral and physical defeat for the seducer and his victim, there nevertheless, follows a subsequent victory for the couple or the community at large. In the case of David and Bathsheba, they then beget Solomon, Israel's greatest king.

In the earliest narrative literature of the Western world, seduction is a complex force that sets those works in motion. In the *Epic of Gilgamesh* (c. 2000 B.C.) the hero is portrayed as an archetypal seducer who "leaves no virgin to her lover, / The daughter of a warrior, the chosen of a noble." Moreover, the goddess Aruru, in order to save Gilgamesh's subjects from his tyranny, molds a wild, monstrous man named Enkidu out of clay in order to seduce Gilgamesh. Before this occurs—the two heroes eventually become inseparable friends—Gilgamesh sends a courtesan to seduce Enkidu in order to destroy his great strength. This episode is reminiscent of the more familiar biblical account of Samson, a notoriously strong and attractive womanizer, and Delilah (Judg. 13–16), which pair constitute the subject of many later works such as *Samson Agonistes* (dramatic poem, 1671) by John Milton.

In the Bible itself, immediately after the account of creation, the entire sacred narrative is motivated by a double seduction. First, the serpent deceives Eve into eating from the tree of the knowledge of good and evil (Gen. 3:13: "The serpent deceived me and I ate"), and then she gets Adam also to eat the fruit. In Milton's reworking of this scene in *Paradise Lost* (poem, 1667, bk. 9), psychology and rhetoric change the Bible's cryptic determinism into plausibility and verisimilitude. Another attractive male from the early history of the Hebrew nation who repeats this pattern of being the object of a woman's seductive advance is Joseph. He is "well-built and hansome" (Gen. 39:6) and so talented and moral that his master Potiphar's wife cannot resist entreating him to go to bed with her, but when he continues rejecting her advances, she has her husband punish him by throwing him in prison. Two other characters from the Bible, whose seductions are more successful in causing apostasy and the sin of fornication, are Jezebel (I King 16–21), the cunning wife of King Ahab, and her New Testament namesake in St. John's apocalyptic condemnation of the church of Thyatira (Rev. 21:20).

Like other works from antiquity, the action of Homer's *Iliad* arises from a hero (Paris) being seduced by a woman of goddesslike beauty (Helen) and by his subsequent abduction of her (to Troy). In this epic world of love and war waged among gods and mortals, seduction works on many levels and in the double sense of a man beguiling a woman to enjoy her sexual favors and of leading one astray in order to change the course of events. In the first sense, in book 3, we see Helen, favored by Aphrodite, lured to bed by Paris' handsomeness and by his hero's desire to possess her despite the fact that he has just fled like a coward from battle with Helen's husband Menelaus. In the second sense, in book 14, the goddess Hera, with the help of Sleep, turns the battle in favor of the Achaeans by using her husband Zeus's own "desire to lie with her / and make love to her nakedness." In this way Hera is able to distract Zeus from his vigilant defense of the Trojans. The Greeks' ultimate victory turns on this divine seduction on Mount Ida. Not incidentally, during this seduction, Zeus recites his catalog of amorous conquests who include Danaë, Europa, Semele, Alcmene, Demeter, and Leto. The modern counterpart to Zeus's catalog is the seducer's famous list read by Leporello in Mozart's opera, *Don Giovanni* (1787).

Seduction in classical literature is a complex interweaving of mythical, literary, and psychological levels of narration. Often the passion experienced by the characters is a result of direct divine intervention in their mortal lives. The stories of Hippolytus and Phaedra in Euripides' play *Hippolytos* (*Hippolytus,* 428 B.C.) and of Aeneas and Dido in Virgil's epic poem *Aeneis* (*Aeneid,*, 19 B.C.), among others, illustrate how the desires of the gods motivate and explain human actions and how both mortal and supernatural levels combine in a third, perfectly structured level of art. For example, while Aeneas ostensibly "seduces" Dido in book 4 by his physical presence, his fame, his lonely vulnerability, and his eloquent recitation of heroic deeds, in fact, the seduction is carried out beforehand by Venus and her son Cupid in order to bind Dido to them and to the Trojans sponsored by them, thereby defeating Juno, Dido's protectress and the Trojans' principal divine enemy. The human lovers are locked in the psychological plight of unequal bondage ending in Aeneas' god-ordained flight to Italy and Dido's passionate derangement and suicide. In this epic poem, in other classical tragedies, and in neoclassical and modern recreations of the same stories (e.g.,

Racine's tragedy *Phèdre* [*Phaedra*, 1677] and Mary Renault's novel, *The Bull from the Sea,* 1962) seduction is predicated on fate controlled by an anthropomorphic pantheon. Paris, Aeneas, Hippolytus, and other lovers often are passive or even innocent seducers, and their female victims and the gods and goddesses who direct them frequently display the seductive traits of energy, strategy, and cunning usually associated with the male.

Not all seduction in antiquity, of course, is a product of divinely controlled fate. A significant body of Greek and Roman literature is dedicated to hetero- and homosexual eroticism wherein mortals seduce each other with no direct divine aid or instigation. In these works the affairs of gods and goddesses are alluded to solely as authoritative analogies in order to give credence and perspective to human actions. An example of seduction without divine aid is found in Plato's *Symposion (Symposium,* dialogue, c. 384 B.C.), in which Alcibiades says that his own seduction by Socrates is due to the attraction of the philosopher's intellect, which is so subtle that Socrates the seducer makes himself into the "beloved rather than the lover." Following this first step in the descent of seduction from the level of the gods to that of mortals, in the Augustan age the love elegy idealizes the desired woman at the same time that it serves the persuasive, practical purpose of seducing the woman to whom the poem is directed. Ovid's poem *Amores* (c.20 B.C.) and *Ars amatoria (The Art of Love,* didactic poem, c.1 B.C.) are perhaps the most outstanding examples of both the idealizing and practical approaches to love and seduction. A last step is taken in the descent to realistic lechery by Petronius' novel *Satyricon* (A.D. 60). In this last work, Trimalchio's slave Massa is a typical example of a degraded seducer even though Scintilla calls him a Don Juan (*Agaga est*). He is described as a cross-eyed snorer who was educated by the hawkers in the market. Like exalted seducers, this slave of all the talents (*omnis musae mancipium*) is very clever. In addition to his talent for seducing women, he has other, totally plebeian talents such as those of shoemaker, cook, baker, mule-driver, and hawker.

Lyric poets from Sappho (fl. c. 600 B.C.) to the present have sung the praise of their beloveds in such a way as to immortalize or even deify them. However, there is in this type of poetry a secondary effect and object; namely, the poems themselves can function as aphrodisiacs or erotic philters and are central elements in a strategy of seduction. Ovid, for example, sings the praise of Corinna, his mistress, with the object of flattering and beguiling her while at the same time he instructs his readers in proven techniques: the use of rivals to heighten jealousy, the employment of a confidant for communication, and such mundane matters as poetry, make-up, wine, and so on. While many poets who single out one woman for their love elegies, such as Catullus (87–?54 B.C.), Dante (1265–1321), and Petrarch (1304–1374), celebrate or worship the woman, other poets—especially romantic poets of the nineteenth century—both celebrate the woman and use poetry as an aid in seduction. In fact, one of the major requirements of actual and fictional seducers is that they be talented poets. Among those who exemplify such seducer-poets or poet-seducers are Ovid, Tristan, Casanova

(1725–1798), Byron (1788–1824), Baudelaire (1821–1867), Lovelace, and Dr. Zhivago. The last two are, respectively, the protagonists of the novels *Clarissa Harlowe* (1748) by Samuel Richardson and *Doktor Zhivago* (*Doctor Zhivago,* first published in Italian in 1957) by Boris Pasternak.

The Middle Ages

In the Christian Middle Ages the theme of seduction tends toward either the moralizing condemnation or irreverent celebration of common lechery and adultery. At the same time, in the literature arising from pagan Europe a supernatural element, with its attendant mythicizing seriousness, continues to pervade the stories of seduction. On the one hand, seduction involves both an Ovidian sense of art or cunning strategy and an immediate need for sexual fulfillment and possession. The characters in the Latin plays of Hroswitha of Gandersheim, a 10th century Benedictine nun from Saxony (see especially her *Dulcitius* and *Callimachus),* the frankly erotic exploits of don Melón, the author's allegorical alter ego in Juan Ruíz, the 14th century Spanish archpriest of Hita's *El libro de buen amor (The Book of Good Love,* poem, 1343), the first and tenth stories for the third day from Boccaccio's *Il decamerone (Decameron,* novellas, c. 1350), and the exploits in *The Wife of Bath's Prologue and Tale* in Chaucer's *Canterbury Tales* (c. 1380–1400), are examples of this kind of post-pagan medieval seduction. These works and others are full of lechery and seduction originated and carried out by very human characters. In this body of literature, written for the most part within the Christian domain, there is, to be sure, a secondary, rhetorical identification of excessive desire as motivated by the supernatural intervention of the devil. Boccaccio's ribald treatment of this motif in the story in which the monk Rustico teaches a beautiful young virgin named Alibech to "put the Devil back into hell" by means of fornication exemplifies the degree to which true daemonic forces had ceased to be regarded as the real motivators of seduction.

On the other hand, seductions by medieval heroes such as Cú Chulainn, Siegfried, and Tristan, who arise from non-Christian and quasi-Christian backgrounds, retain a supernatural power similar to that possessed by pre-Christian seducers from Gilgamesh to Aeneas. Although seduction is not the foremost theme in the works dealing with these heroes, it is, nevertheless, an important element in terms of plot and characterization. Moreover, it must be remembered that because of the nature of medieval symbolism, and because these heroes possess superhuman power, the semantic and social distinctions that separate seduction and rape were less significant in the Middle Ages than they are in the twentieth century. Cú Chulainn is the most famous of the heroes of ancient Irish sagas. His exploits are recounted in the Ulster cycle, which dates from the eight century, and his historical background predates the destruction of Emain Macha, the chief stronghold of ancient Ulster in 332. Represented as the son of the sun god Lugh, Cú Chulainn is feared by the men of Ulster as a threat to their daughters. In the process of learning the "soldierly arts" from Scathach, the Amazonian warrior-queen of Alba, in order to prove himself worthy of marrying

Emer, the most beautiful and talented maiden of Erin, Cú Chulainn alone conquers the army of Aife, "the hardest woman-warrior in the world," and, at sword point ravishes her with the purpose of begetting a son as heroic as he. Then, using the "hero's salmon-leap" to enter the stronghold in which Emer is guarded by her noble father Forgall, he kills Forgall and her three brothers and carries his beautiful trophy to Ulster where they are married. For other epic heroes the seduction of a central woman—Brunhild for Siegfried, Iseult for Tristan, and even Guinevere for Lancelot—is achieved by superhuman or magical power and involves the couple in fatal consequences that lead ineluctably to the death of one or both of them.

By the twelfth century, with the re-emergence of classical motifs and the entrance of Arabic themes into European literature, and with the development of courtly love, what Denis de Rougemont calls *askēsis* in *L'amour et l'occident* (*Love in the Western World*, 1939 and 1956) replaces both the violence and the daemonic element in the theme of seduction in the Middle Ages. According to Rougemont, the Tristan myth is the supreme expression of a late Medieval eroticism in which it is impossible for the lover to conquer the female object of his desire in this world because this woman and the union with her are elevated to an ideal, sublime level. While the ideal in courtly love is a seduction eternally unfulfilled for the sake of chastity, the most prominent courtly or Neoplatonic seductions, including the actual case of Abélard and Héloïse in the early twelfth century, Tristan and Iseult, and Calisto and Melibea in the medieval Spanish dramatic masterpiece partially attributed to Fernando de Rojas, *Tragicomedia de Calisto y Melibea* (*Celestina or the Spanish Bawd*, 1499–1502), involve a physical conquest that leads to remorse, jealousy, castration, suicide, and other tragic ends. The failure of the seduction to bring joy to the lovers is due to the preconception that this type of love is necessarily impossible to achieve within the institutional bounds of concrete human affairs.

The Renaissance

From the Renaissance until the present, that is, for example, from Shakespeare's tragedy *Romeo and Juliet* (c. 1596) until Boris Pasternak's *Doctor Zhivago,* the type of seducer who focuses on one woman, but whose desire is doomed to failure, never ceases to exist. Despite this uninterrupted succession of Tristan-like lovers, however, in the Renaissance, there arises a new type of seducer who combines the amorality, lechery, and wantonness of one medieval type with the lawlessness, passion, and heroic or quasi-godlike stature of the other. This new character is the libertine or rake, and rather than focus on one object of desire in the form of an idealized woman, his desires are so universal that he seeks to conquer much more than one woman. The Faust legend, beginning with *Das Faustbuch* (*The Faust Book,* 1587), embodies such a character in the context of orthodox German Protestantism. Although the early versions of this theme, including Christopher Marlowe's play *Doctor Faustus* (1604), do not characterize Faust as a womanizer, the legend's basic concept of making a pact with the devil in order to achieve absolute knowledge and to experience pleasure to the fullest degree possible allows for the later and definitive development wherein one of Faust's rewards is aid in the seduction of a beautiful young woman. *Faust,* Goethe's dramatic masterpiece in two parts (1808 and 1832), centers the hero's ability to seduce Gretchen on his pact with Mephistopheles, the great negating spirit of hell.

John Milton, in *Paradise Lost,* combines biblical sources, contemporary history, and the form of the Renaissance epic poem to make Satan himself one of the greatest seducers in the history of literature. The Evil One not only seduces Eve into eating the forbidden fruit, but also thereby causes the Fall of mankind from the state of Edenic grace, a feat unmatched by any other seducer. In Milton's Satan are combined all of the traits that characterize most of the seducers of the Renaissance. These traits include deceitfulness, rebelliousness, daring, independence, and seemingly universal knowledge. Furthermore, they are generally thought to be in league with the devil or to be evil personified.

Despite the universality of these epithets, the theme of seduction in the Renaissance begins to display distinctive national features. The theme localizes itself in particular, specialized characters only when, in the postmedieval world, seduction ceases to be treated as a universal phenomenon and, instead, is seen as culturally bound. For this reason, Don Juan Tenorio, first created by Tirso de Molina in *El burlador de Sevilla y el convidado de piedra* (*The Libertine of Seville,* play, 1630) is on the one hand the archseducer virtually antonomastically, and on the other he is specifically Spanish. Likewise, Faust exemplifies Germanic thirst for knowledge. Shakespeare's comic seducer, Sir John Falstaff, as seen especially in *The Merry Wives of Windsor* (play, 1600), though having a reputation as a seducer, nevertheless fits the image of the peculiarly English type of the lecher. He is fat, pompous, no longer young, and unsuccessful in his attempt to seduce Mrs. Ford and Mrs. Page. Whether or not a lecher actually satisfies his desire is secondary to the fact that his main goal is to experience lust, licentiousness, and sexual indulgence. In national literatures in which lechery is a prominent separate theme (e.g., England), it covers a large area ranging from frivolity to the evil inherent in hypersexuality. On the other hand, in national literatures where lechery is seldom distinguished from libertinism (e.g., Spain and Portugal), sexuality is often less important than the issues of good and evil vis-à-vis the spirit and the will. In contrast to a lecher, therefore, a seducer must at least be able to instill the fear of a successful conquest in his potential victims and, in addition, they must fear that the seduction, despite a promise of bliss, may result in or be the product of evil. Shakespeare's two wives of Windsor, fearing neither evil nor sexual threat from Falstaff, know they are dealing with a lecher whose power as a seducer has long since disappeared in excessive dissipation.

The paramount purveyor of promised bliss and resultant evil is Don Juan. So monumentally significant is the creation in the early seventeenth century of this rake, libertine, and seducer that his name is synonymous with seduction; indeed, hundreds of writers in all countries of the Western world, in all periods, and in every literary genre have dealt with him. The myth of this Spanish character is so pervasive that it is as if he is as important to postmedieval culture as Eros was to classical culture. While each version of Don Juan varies superficially, the myth has, nevertheless, a basic identity that varies little from author to author, nation to nation, and century to century. Once Tirso de Molina unites the two separate medieval legends of, first, a profligate young libertine who seeks women on his way to church, and second, of a double invitation to last suppers, a major myth for the modern world is launched.

There are three constituent elements on which all versions are based: 1) a dynamic seducer; 2) a group of replaceable female victims, one of whom is prominent; and 3) death personified or present. In the older versions, from Tirso and Molière (*Dom Juan* [*Don Juan*, play, 1665]) to Antonio de Zamora (*No hay plazo que no se cumpla ni deuda que no se pague* [*All Accounts Must Be Settled, All Debts Paid,* play, 1744]) and Mozart, the figure of death is usually represented as the animated stone statue of the commander, the most prominent victim's father, whom the hero kills. In later versions, death is represented by less fantastic forces such as old age (e.g., the Marqués de Bradomín in Ramón del Valle-Inclán's novel *Sonata de invierno,* 1905) and cancer in Gilbert Cesbron's novel *Don Juan en automne* (1975). But in all versions, death intervenes to block the archseducer's career of challenging everything that would limit his personal independence. In this way, death enforces the value structure of society. Consequently, the seducer is always seen to operate outside the norms of the law and morality.

Occasionally throughout the history of literature there have been female lechers and seducers: the goddess Hera, Delilah, the Wife of Bath, Fanny Hill, Lamiel (Stendhal's female Don Juan), and several others. Usually, however, these women merely play a male role. It is far more common for women to be the victims of a male seducer, and the Don Juan myth expresses this fact with great paradoxical force. This seducer engages in seduction for its own sake, but in doing so, on the one hand, he exalts himself as masculine individuality incarnate while individuating each woman as a worthy source of passions; but, on the other hand, he leaves the woman dishonored and himself abhorred as an evil prevaricator. In fact, Don Juan exemplifies the very anatomy of a seduction. First, a man focuses on a woman with the object of drawing her toward him and away from her self and from all other allegiances, including father, husband, brother, religion, social duty, morality, and God. Then she yields to him through genuine attraction or through deception. He possesses her and then abandons her quickly, thereby preparing to begin the process anew. Don Juan is known as the archseducer because he has the almost supernatural energy to engage in seduction as frequently as he wishes. From this protean, Zeus-like profligacy comes the comic list of names of victims, the most famous example of which is Leporello's catalogue on *Don Giovanni* including reference to 1,003 in Spain alone.

The Enlightenment

The typing of seducers by nationality, a process begun in the Renaissance, continues in the eighteenth century. Furthermore, in this period the mythical figures of Tristan and Don Juan, while still present, give way to portraits of highly individualized characters who seldom recur outside the works for which they are famous: the Chevalier des Grieux from the Abbé Prévost's novel *Manon Lescaut* (1731), Lovelace from *Clarissa* by Richardson, Valmont and the Marquise de Merteuil in Laclos's novel *Les liaisons dangereuses* (*Dangerous Acquaintances,* 1782), and Casanova (1725–1798) in his memoirs. In contrast to the tripartite structure of Don Juanism, these seducers tend to focus on a single woman—Manon, Clarissa, the Présidente de Tourvel, and so on—although, of course, in the case of the two most famous quasi-autobiographical seducers during the century—the Marquis de Sade and Casanova—there are many victims. Also, while the most prominent seducers die at the end of their stories, the immediate link between seduction and death that is so strong in the Don Juan myth is weakened. When the seducer replaces plural objects of desire with a single one, he exchanges the attributes of surprise and courage for planning and perseverance. In short, he loses his dynamism. Rather than relying on supernatural powers, the threat of evil or an innate, natural sense of superiority, he relies on reason. Gamesmanship and strategy are constants in the theme of seduction from Zeus, Aphrodite, and Ovid to Siegfried, Falstaff, and Don Juan; nevertheless, during the Enlightenment, they became the dominant forces in seduction. Lovelace, Valmont, and Casanova are particularly outstanding examples of the new emphasis on reason.

In the eighteenth century, seduction becomes such an important theme that one can identify a new art and discourse dedicated to it. Weighty epistolary novels such as *Clarissa* and Rousseau's *La nouvelle Héloïse* (*The New Heloise,* 1761) are dedicated to the conquest and surrender of one woman. In fact, in the absence of the supernatural, once the woman is the object of an elaborate strategy, she herself becomes at the same time the seducer's egotistical equal and the repository of justice and morality. The woman now acts as the judge in the libertine's plot against her, and she is seen as so dangerous an adversary that she rivals the stone guest in the Don Juan myth. Therefore, whereas the conquest previously is accomplished with divine aid (Aeneas), rape (Cú Chulainn), a magic potion (Tristan), or erotic spontaneity (Don Juan), the Enlightenment seducer is forced to refine his art by developing a highly complex aesthetic discourse, the object of which is to trap the victim by the aphrodisiacal power of language. The male-dominated discourse of seduction is then used as the only potentially successful arm in the battle against a female victim who, in this period, begins to regain the Venus-like quality of inspiring love without herself being affected by it. For example, Clarissa admits to only "a conditional kind of liking" for Lovelace, yet for him she is a goddess and an "angel of a woman."

From the first moment seduction appears as a literary theme, all of society's moral, legal, and sacred values are invested in women; the seducer's object is to draw women away from these values in such a way that he becomes a substitute for them. In the Enlightenment, these values are so strong that a bold heroic assault on the victim is nearly impossible. Even Casanova, whose literary persona seems the most frivolous of these famous seducers, must pay attention to the details of his strategy. Between the seducer and the seduced there are always large obstacles. Witness Venus between Cupid and Psyche, tests of strength between Siegfried and Brunhild, and family enmity between Romeo and Juliet. In the eighteenth century the whole fabric of society constitutes the obstacle. Because overcoming this obstacle involves more strategy than Theseus finding his way out of the labyrinth, the center of attention in stories of seduction passes from masculine heroism and aggression to the female will. This new configuration results in the supremacy of many female characters such as Manon, Pamela, Clarissa, Fanny Hill, Julie, and Madame de Merteuil, and at the same time serves as a link to the ensuing period.

Romanticism—The Nineteenth Century

In this period sentiment replaces reason as the fuel for the fires of seduction, and the role of the female victim becomes so strengthened that the woman on occasion becomes the aggressor. Lamiel, the heroine of Stendhal's last unfinished novel (*Lamiel*, 1842), and Flaubert's Madame Bovary (novel, 1856) are both seducers in the former, male sense of the term, but even those who are not, such as Gina Pietranera from Stendhal's novel *La chartreuse de Parme* (*The Chart-erhouse of Parma*, 1839), Tolstoy's *Anna Karenina* (novel, 1877), and Fortunata from Pérez Galdós' novel *Fortunata y Jacinta* (1886–1887), are stronger characters than their male antagonists. This is not to say, however, that this century lacks male seducers. On the contrary, so pervasive is the theme that there is scarcely a writer who does not deal with seduction in a significant way. Some give new vitality to the Don Juan myth (e.g., Byron, *Don Juan,* epic satire, 1819–1824; Grabbe, *Don Juan und Faust,* play, 1829; Pushkin, *Kamennyĭ gost'* [*The Stone Guest*] play, 1830; Dumas (père), *Don Juan de Maraña,* play, 1836; Zorrilla, *Don Juan Tenorio,* play, 1844). Others deal with psychological (Hawthorne), social (Balzac), aesthetic (Baudelaire), philosophical (Nietzsche) and moral (Tolstoy) problems. Moreover, the theme is dealt with in all genres and by writers major and minor.

The most outstanding work on seduction in the nineteenth century is arguably Kierkegaard's essay, "Diary of the Seducer," in the first part of *Enten-eller* (*Either/Or,* 1843). The "Diary" is the centerpiece in Kierkegaard's exposition of the aesthetic mode of existence. The subject of this essay, Johannes, plans an erotic siege of Cordelia, a beautiful young woman chosen because he sees her as a paradox, and therefore as a paragon of femininity. She is, for him, both a witch and a fairy. Johannes approaches this conquest as consciously and with as much relish as do Valmont and Lovelace theirs. Furthermore, the rhetoric he uses in listing the three requirements for an affair with Cordelia reflects the rationalism of the Enlightenment. First, he will attract her with "the repulsion of misunderstanding"; second, he insists her love can grow only in freedom; and third, he maintains that contradiction is the key strategem in seduction. Kierkegaard's philosophical persona in this essay belongs, however, more to romanticism than to the Enlightenment inasmuch as he says he wants to possess his victim artistically, not just physically or even psychologically. "To be loved," he says, "is higher than anything in the world. To poetize oneself into a young girl is art, to poetize oneself out of her, is a masterpiece."

Seduction in the nineteenth century is predicated on the search for the ideal other, the *idéal féminin*. As in other ages, the result is still the inability of the subject to possess eternally the object of desire. This is so because the process takes place in perfect freedom outside the norms of laws and society. The seducer, by attempting to draw the objective woman away from her ideal self to his subjective, real self destroys both himself and her. Despite the rhetorical idealization, romantic seduction is as doomed to failure as any other type. This is because, like Johannes, romantic seducers are narcissistic and engaged in self-annihilation. Witness, for example, Félix de Montemar, the hero-rake of José de Espronceda's long poem, *El estudiante de Salamanca* (*The Student of Salamanca,* 1839–1840), who pursues a mysterious woman only to find that she, his bride-to-be, is death personified. With the reintroduction in this century of the supernatural into eroticism, the three separate aspects of the romantic seducer—those of poet, lover, and libertine—fuse into a single complex structure. The poet seeks an artistic muse, the lover desires an ideal woman, and the libertine courts the attraction of novelty but finds the escape of death.

In the second half of the century, seduction is an especially prominent theme of realist and postrealist fiction. Although the male protagonists of novels such as *Besy* (*The Possessed,* 1871–1872) by Dostoevsky, *Anna Karenina, La regenta* (1884–1885) by the Spanish novelist Clarín, *Fortunata y Jacinta,* and *Tess of the d'Urbervilles* are identified as Don Juanesque seducers, the female characters for which the works are titled are seen as much as victims of social typing and moral pressures as they are of their respective seducers—Stavrogin, Vronsky, Alvaro Mesía, Juanito Santa Cruz, and Alex d'Urberville. These works generally begin with the seduction of an attractive and intelligent woman with tendencies to independence, and then, in great didactic detail, they develop the disastrous consequences for the female victims. In these novels the men are characterized as handsome, proud, energetic, and capable of evil, the women are seen as fated for special treatment due to their beauty and character, and the plots often end in death. Despite what appears here to be the outline of a mythical orientation similar to Don Juanism, the theme of seduction in these novels is firmly planted in the ground of biological, psychological, and social reality. By the end of the nineteenth century, seduction is no longer a matter for gods, devils, legendary heroes and enlightened gentlemen and their ladies. On the contrary, seduction returns to the material level addressed by Ovid nearly two millennia before.

The Twentieth Century

In *Man and Superman* (play, 1903) George Bernard Shaw predicts, not altogether without reason, that the age of Don Juan has ended, but that the age of Doña Juana has begun. While twentieth-century letters only exceptionally deal with women seducing men, it is nevertheless true that the myth of the great male artists of seduction gives way to the myth of the seduction of art. From the earliest stories of seduction in world literature to the present, this theme is always predicated on the dangerous conjunction of the attraction of physical beauty with the deceiving power of language. The affairs of Satan and Eve, Asmodeus (the Talmud's "king of the devils") and Raguel's daughter Sara, Zeus and his ladies, Abélard and Héloïse, Faust and Gretchen, and Humbert Humbert and Lolita are all made possible by the special conjunction of beauty and language. From the Renaissance to the end of the nineteenth century, writers explore the historical, social, theological, philosophical, moral, and psychological causes and ramifications of seduction. But in the present century, what remains to explore are the two principal vehicles by which seduction takes place: sex and language. What results is an understanding that the sense of seduction is derived less from the reporting of acts than from the erotic exercise of language itself. For example, the lesbian narrator in the title story of the Argentinian writer Pacho O'Donnell's book *La seducción de la hija del partero* (1975) refers self-consciously to the role language plays in her report about the seduction of a Lolita-like girl of fourteen: "Everything I'm writing here has a frankly vulgar smell, but words are to blame. Those same words act in a distinct way and with certain additions or subtractions to file a complaint with city hall because the street sweepers are making too much noise in the morning or to present a common sense proof for squaring a circle. There is no way to escape that botch of the alphabet."

Ramón del Valle-Inclán signals this new approach to the theme in his *Sonatas* (novels, 1902–1905), in which, in exceedingly ornate and sensorial language, he chronicles life's four erotic seasons as exemplified by the fictional experience of the Marqués de Bradomín. In the "Sonata" dedicated to autumn, Bradomín, who, like many of the seducers in this century, is old and ugly, is more a decadent lecher than a seducer. Devoid of heroic energy and glamor, nevertheless, with consummate artistry, he manipulates the delicate balance between pain and pleasure and between depravity and sublimity in order to seduce Concha, a dying, middle-aged woman. Other prominent lover-seducers, such as Hans Castorp in *The Magic Mountain* by Thomas Mann and Humbert Humbert in *Lolita* (novel, 1955) by Vladimir Nabokov, turn the objects of their morbid or perverted desire into quasi-fetishistic objects of art.

Twentieth-century writers attempt simultaneously to harmonize Freud's discovery of the libido with the ancient mythical motifs and to raise the tradition of underground erotica (including such diverse works as Cephalas' *Anthologia*

[*The Greek Anthology,* 10th century], Goliardic verse, the *Panchatantra* [tales, c. 300–500], the sonnets of Pietro Aretino and the Marquis de Sade) to the level of major art. André Breton, the founder of surrealism, uses free association, automatic writing, and many other devices to free language for its prophetic role in communicating a new, full understanding of eroticism (see especially Breton's books *Nadja,* novel, 1928; *L'amour fou,* poem, 1937; and *Arcane 17,* poem, 1945). In other words, in twentieth-century literature the sexual substratum in the theme of seduction is no longer hidden by linguistic taboo. Henry Miller's autobiographical *Tropic of Cancer* (1934) and even Ian Fleming's popular spy-seducer series about James Bond (from *Casino Royale,* 1953, to the *Man with the Golden Gun,* 1965) are prominent examples of the age's parallel freedoms of languages and morals. In fact, the theme is so pervasive that popular fiction is almost unmarketable without one or more seductions.

Possibly the author most renowned for elevating language, sex, the unconscious, and nature into a philosophy dealing with the liberation of modern individuals from the oppressions of industrial society is D. H. Lawrence. In his novel, *Lady Chatterley's Lover* (1928), many of the aspects of the theme of seduction, from the myths of antiquity to present preoccupations, are encapsulated. As in the traditional Don Juan myth, there is a triangular distribution of characters, with the game-keeper Oliver Mellors as the seducer, Lady Constance Chatterley as the central woman, and the invalid Lord Clifford Chatterley as the representative of the law, morality, and society. As is the case with most seducers, Mellors is endowed with the archetypically male attributes of strength, independence, pride, aristocracy of spirit, military bearing, and an aura of mystery. In addition, he is identified with supernatural forces such as the devil and the Greek gods Vulcan and Priapus. Indeed, like many other seducers in contemporary literature (see especially, *The Adventures of Don Juan* by Richard Gardner, 1974), Mellors' sexuality is so explicit that the words that express it are said to have fully as much natural physical reality as do the bodies of the lovers or the flora and fauna in Lord Chatterley's woods. Indeed, the language with which sexuality is described in this novel has the effect of finely wrought lyricism.

In D. H. Lawrence, as in so many other twentieth-century writers so diverse as Carlos Fuentes *(Terra nostra,* novel, 1975), Roland Barthes *(Fragments d'un discours amoureux* [*A Love's Discourse: Fragments,* essays, 1977)], and Norman Mailer *(The Executioner's Song,* novel, 1979), the language of seduction rises to the level of, and fuses with, the acts of seduction. Furthermore, having been freed from the linguistic taboo associated with sex, the theme of seduction has undergone a shift in emphasis. It has returned to share ground with the ancient topos of betrayal. As seduction and betrayal are inextricably linked in Satan and Don Juan, so are they linked in works of contemporary literature so seemingly diverse as Bernard Malamud's *God's Grace* (novel, 1982) and John Le Carré's anti-heroic spy trilogy about George Smiley, *The Quest for Karla* (1982) and his erotic spy novel, *The Little Drummer Girl* (1983). In this way seduction in contemporary literature recapitulates the theme's origins in mythical and sacred texts, thereby allowing modern readers to re-experience the awe and mystery of one of the world's most powerful, diverse, attractive, and threatening themes.

See also: Libertine, *Senex Amator*, Sex (Heterosexual, Erotic)

Selected Bibliography

Chandos, John. *A Guide to Seduction: Notes Towards the Study of Eros in the Western Tradition*. London: Muller, 1953.

Fowlie, Wallace. *Love in Literature: Studies in Symbolic Expression*. Bloomington: Indiana University Press, 1965.

Gendarme de Bévotte, Georges. *La légende de Don Juan*. Paris: Hachette, 1911.

Singer, Armand. *The Don Juan Theme, Versions, and Criticism: A Bibliography*. Morgantown: West Virginia University, 1965. [Supplements: West Virginia University Philological Papers 15 (1966), 17 (1970), 20 (1973), 22 (1975), 26 (1980).]

WILLIAM T. LITTLE

SENEX AMATOR

Senex amator, the lecherous old lover, descends from Greek New Comedy of the fourth and third centuries B.C. and the popular Roman comedies of Plautus (c. 251–184 B.C.). Since then, this oversexed laughing stock, *ludibrium,* busy as a bigamist, has tickled urban and urbane audiences in the plays of the Renaissance formal *commedia erudita* and improvisational *commedia dell'arte,* Shakespeare, Ben Jonson, and Molière. In the eighteenth century, the old lover returned to Italy in the plays of Goldoni and Gozzi and in opera buffa. He reappeared as the count, victim of feminine disguises, in Mozart's opera, *Le nozze di Figaro* (*The Marriage of Figaro,* 1784), Da Ponte's adaptation from Beaumarchais.

The Standard Plot

Senex is the nominal ruler of a little household kingdom composed mostly of conspirators against him. The old man's lusty obsession and illicit intrigues in sexual pursuit of a desirable young woman belie his normal respectability as husband, father, and master. His outrageous and transparent amorous plot sets in motion a blistering, farcical counterplot instigated by his shrewish wife and clever servants that ultimately dupes and humiliates him. All the household reponds to the perversity of the old man in this comic *agōn* or contest. He, in turn, incongruously combines the most tortured avowals of young love with the seasoned sentiments of a roué. Solemnity and dignity give way to the role reversal of *servus*. At the play's end, victim of his own indiscretions, his wife and the audience offer *senex* forgiveness and reconciliation.

Classical Comedy

Tracing the 2,400–year descent of the silly, old lover reveals his dramatic durability, humorous universality, and special adaptations to time and place. The old lover represents but one aberration of the stock character *senex, paterfamilias, Pappus,* master, or householder. In the Greek New Comedy of Menander and in all but six of the twenty-six extant plays of Plautus and Terence, which constitute Roman Comedy, *senex* commands a prominent and powerful role as either the barrier or the assistant to the socially approved consummation of young love in marriage. In this business, the B.C. *senex* meddles as harsh or indulgent father. Yet while *senes* fussily admonish their children on many subjects in B.C. comedy, they never warn offspring about the perils of the marital state. Meanwhile these old men invent their own imaginative flights from household obligations, social respectability, and *matrona*.

In transforming Aristophanes, Menander, and the popular Atellan farces to the Roman stage, Plautus moved from earlier social interest in the parental obstacles that delay young lovers to the obsessions and frustrations of old men. Attuned to the fine distinctions between the humorous, the pathetic, the despicable, and the tragic in old age, Plautus rebelled against the tone of Greek New Comedy, whose fragments recommended sober resignation, restraint, and limitation. In the Plautine innovation, slaves played enhanced roles at the expense of *senes* who in their silliness reversed the master-slave relationship.

Plautus fashioned his comedies to the festival days on which they were performed. On these ritual occasions of saturnalian unrestraint and revelry, audiences, having escaped usual routines and taboos, would have been primed to witness the pillars of respectability in senate and forum hilariously caught up in the full fire of some uncontrollable passion, only to be ultimately chastened and restored to social conformity. Ringed about with a house, money, a contentious wife, an incorrigible son, clever slaves, and a sympathetic, but equally inept old crony, *senex* battles flailingly with society and existentially with the transcience of life itself. Thus four plays of Plautus and none of Terence gave the stage to the sexual passion of *senex amator, Asinaria* (*The Comedy of Asses,* c. 214 B.C.), *Bacchides* (*The Two Bacchises,* c. 214 B.C.), *Mercator* (*The Merchant,* c. 192–184 B.C.), and *Casina* (c. 185 B.C.).

Old Lysidamus, the lewd *senex amator* of Plautus' *Casina,* stereotypically fits this self-victimized role. Reworked from the Greek Diphilus' *Klēroumenoi* (c. 332 B.C.), of which only the title survives, *Casina* itself was adapted by Machiavelli in 1520 as *Clizia.* The lust-driven Lysidamus pursues his son's sweetheart, the chaste and free-born Casina, through a dizzying maze of schemes and counterschemes, marital recrimination, war between the sexes, slave legates, role reversals, eavesdropping, discoveries, deceptions, elaborate and vulgar sensory images, mistaken sexual identities, obscene innuendoes, transvestism, homosexual suggestiveness, asides to the audience, all culminating in a burlesque wedding, hilarious unmasking, feminine triumph, masculine shame and capitulation. Yet ironically, his excessive passion has made this cuckoo most endearing in the end.

The Revival of Roman Comedy in the Italian Renaissance

Derived from Plautus and Terence and revived at Rome and Ferrara, Renaissance drama began with late cinquento comedy. Just as Plautine comedy had 1700 years earlier reflected the felicitous marriage of more formal Greek New Comedy and Atellan popular farces so this Roman comedy revival split just as neatly into its original components. The revered classical sources provided character types and comic formulas equitably to both the learned comedies or commedia erudita and the popular commedia dell'arte. *Senex amator* turned up in the translations, imitations, and adaptations from the Latin originals in the academic comedies of Machiavelli and Ariosto as the Old Signior.

Pantalone in Commedia Dell'Arte

More pivotal for European drama, the old lover was further adapted from the classical plays into the popular theater, commedia dell'arte, through a shock of recognition with a contemporary figure, Pantalone, the Venetian merchant. In *As You Like It* (c. 1599) Shakespeare referred to "the lean and slipper'd pantaloon" as the sixth age of man. He possesses the merchants' smugness and social respectability. Like *senex,* he peddles his conceits, worn arguments, wise saws, and unattainable fantasies. Pantalone's ridiculous seizure by love for a courtesan belies his decrepit mien and pose of authority. Pantalone is an actor's part richly dependent on improvisation, buffoonery, masks, and costumes. In commedia dell'arte, Pantalone and Zanni, the clown, dominate the stage with standard plots, *lazzi,* improvised harangues, comic formulas, vulgarities, devices, witty shenanigans, and pantomine.

Commedia dell'arte arose in the first half of the sixteenth century. In the Italian popular theater, as in the early Elizabethan, the Roman comedy characters became still further fused with the popular buffoons and clowns that relieved the sacred dramas and heightened the carnivals and festivals in the Middle Ages. Still the father, husband or widower, master and lover, but also a blend of these contemporary and medieval influences, Pantalone acted more grossly amorous and venal than his ancestor. What Pantalone gained in modishness and dexterity, however, he lost in vestiges of decency over his more homely *senex* ancestor. His uglier traits thus stalked him and brought on his modern demise by the nineteenth century.

Reformation of *Senex*

Due to the unceasing cross-fertilization between the ancient and Renaissance worlds, between learned and popular dramatic traditions, and between the theater and life, isolation of the multiple sources of the old one, this most universal of comic characters, remains extremely difficult. *Pappus* on the farm, *senex* at home, and Pantalone in Venice have lived next door for centuries. Audiences have universally laughed at their antics in blind pursuit of love and money and over their tentative vacillations between caution and boldness.

Commedia dell'arte, with its predominant old lover, thrived in Italy and spread to all corners of Europe until the middle of the eighteenth century and then declined. The comic influence of the old lover can be traced in the later formal drama of Italy, England, France, and Spain over these two centuries.

But as Roman comedy and commedia dell'arte spread from the Italian states, the pagan hilarity of *senex amator* and Pantalone encountered Christian ascetic views of old age. Medieval *contemptus mundi* equated aging with physical decay, the ugly, self-mortification, and Christian repentance. Thus new possibilities opened for the classical sources and their derivatives. In comedy and even in tragedy, the pagan moral blindness, venality, and worldliness of *senex* set off the larger struggle between Christian good and satanic evil; at the same time, the old lover's passionate extremes afforded the comic relief and delight in the North European dramas of moral instruction.

Senex in Elizabethan Drama

From 1517 forward, this moral diet nurtured English school boys. Compulsory access to Plautus in Latin helps explain Shakespeare's extensive borrowing of *senes*. No modern dramatist had more affinities with Plautus than Shakespeare. Both made their livings in the theater as playwrights, actors, and company managers. Both were thus uniquely sensitive to the taste of popular audiences and the comic possibilities of their actors. In concentrating on universal themes and universal characters, both borrowed liberally from the past, yet imaginatively transformed the older material. Like Plautus, who set his comedies and characters in some Greek city like Athens rather than his native Rome, so Shakespeare chose Italy over England for many of his settings and characters. Shakespeare used *senex* in tragedy and comedy. Polonius in *Hamlet* (c. 1600) and Old Capulet in *Romeo and Juliet* (c. 1596) betray all the *senex* traits. They are bent on fostering an advantageous marriage, proffering worldly advice to children, eavesdropping and intrigue, fussy housekeeping, and rash and foolish intrusions that turn tragic as they come between fell opposites.

Senes as fathers also appear beguiled in the early *Comedy of Errors* (c. 1594), *Two Gentlemen of Verona* (c. 1594), and *The Taming of the Shrew* (c. 1594). But Shakespeare's old lovers, stripped of the conventions and rich inventions of the classical and Italianate sources, suffered dramatic indignities at the hands of the Elizabethans. Old Gremio, the squeamish pantaloon in *The Taming of the Shrew*, woos the young Bianca by proxy only. Lost in the crowd of young lovers, the unobtrusive Gremio acknowledges early and late, "my cake is all dough." Shakespeare has set down one other old lover, the Falstaff of *The Merry Wives of Windsor* (c. 1600), among English rustics who shame and ridicule him mercilessly.

Like Shakespeare, Ben Jonson and Molière also literally were schooled in Roman comedy; but they have exploited the old lover within two other classical traditions: the Aristotelian golden mean and the combined Hippocratic and Galenic humors. They too have heaped more contemporaneous opprobrium on these symbols of authority even as they exploited more of the comic potential of the originals. Pantalone or Il Magnifico resembled both the Roman comedy *senex* and the contemporary merchant of Venice. But to the Elizabethans and the French, he became a symbol of the carnal, the greedy, and the depraved combined. Plautus had never joined physical lust with avarice, and the penalty in either case was shame, not ignominy and base cruelty. While Plautus welcomed the old man back to home and society such as they and he were, Jonson increased the old man's crime and his punishment. In *The Devil is an Ass* (1616), Jonson's Fittzdottrel acted the vain old lecher, money-grabber, cruel husband, and wittol cuckold. Utterly depraved and conclusively shamed, this outstripper of the devil proved fatally symbolic to Jonson of the commercial awakening of England. The coarse and seamy Italian merchant served as Jonson's epitome of greed. Like Fittzdottrel, *Volpone* (1606), another creature compact of fraud, gluttony, lust, and avarice, turned *senex* odious.

Senex amator in Molière

In both Jonson and Molière, *senex amator,* like other comic butts, suffers against the standard of the golden mean. For both dramatists, lovers are a mad, impulsive breed, socially redeemed through marriage. In the comedies of these classically inspired men of humor, a *raisonneur* weighs the obsessions of the humorous characters in the balance of social harmony. He contributes sanity, good humor, and stability.

In *L'avare (The Miser,* 1668), Molière confronts the repulsive old lover Harpagon with a dilemma. The plot ultimately forces him to choose between his seamy love for a poor young girl or his money. As he fades, money becomes his substitute for love and life; at the end, he clutches his only true love, the cashbox. Molière's other *senex amator,* the pedant Arnolphe, in *L'école des femmes, (The School for Wives,* 1662) imprisons his young ward in a cottage to preserve her innocence until he may possess her as his wife. Love finally conquers all. She and her true love outwit Arnolphe. Arnolphe remains isolated, agonizing, hand-wringing, sputtering, and aging. Scholars have suggested Molière's use of this stock comic character to reflect on a deeper social issue. Both Harpagon and Arnolphe, figures of disgust, usurp nature's and society's laws even as they should be gracefully retiring from the human scene. This unregenerate use of their authority and wealth to serve an unchecked passion, placed them beyond hope and redemption.

Pantalone in Eighteenth Century Venice

As Shakespeare, Jonson, and Molière exhibited deep familiarity with Roman comedy and commedia dell'arte, so Carlo Goldoni (1707–1793) and Carlo Gozzi (1720–1806), two Venetians, delved as fully into these two comic traditions and into the subsequent English, Spanish and French comedies, especially Molière.

In the spirit of contemporary social and structural reform of the Italian theater, Goldoni moved away from the loose sketches of the commedia dell'arte toward verisimilitude and greater austerity. While he retained the characters, dialogues, and plots of the commedia dell'arte, he returned modern Italian theater to the greater formality and literary structure of the commedia erudita. As in Jonson and Molière, and as in Menander and Terence before them, so Goldoni introduced social commentary. The Venetian bourgeoisie became the audience he wished to influence with social value rather than the native source he wished to exploit for its comic potential. Already the reformist ideas of the Enlightenment blend with Roman and Italianate comic traditions in his prodigous production of over a hundred plays. The rise of his influence accompanied the decline of commedia dell'arte after 1750.

Contrarily, his contemporary Gozzi vigorously opposed Goldoni's reforms in Italian theater. Gozzi dedicated himself to preserve the fantasy and imagination of the popular comedies and the original Pantalone, Brighella, and other stock characters. Yet the reviving of this popular tradition from 1761 until 1765 proved short-lived. As Goldoni had blended the earlier commedia dell'arte with social commentary, so Gozzi diluted the Italian popular comedy with dramatized fairy tales.

Senex amator in Opera Buffa

The blending of social reform and moral instruction by the caricature of the stock characters of commedia dell'arte in Italy had a cumulative effect on the rise of opera buffa, comic opera, throughout Europe over the course of the eighteenth century. Pantalone as miser and lover proved to be at once the butt of the laughter and the example of social tyranny. Mainly in Italy with dramatists like Goldoni, but throughout Europe from 1720 on, the thrust was toward tempering the burlesque and caricature, the mockery and clowning, in favor of a gentler representation of human foibles generally, but toward a more serious indictment of the tyranny of rich old age.

In 1772, Beaumarchais, like his Italian contemporary Gozzi, realized the comic potential of reviving the archival plots of Menander and Plautus with an admixture of the urbanity, wit, and colloquial vigor of Molière. *Le barbier de Séville (The Barber of Seville),* staged as a comic opera by the Comédie Française in 1775, concentrated on the four stock characters of Roman comedy, the young lovers, the wily slave, Figaro, and *senex amator,* Bartholo. Beaumarchais identified his own life with Figaro and cast himself autobiographically as this stock character. In the play as in life, Beaumarchais, much like his contemporary Mozart, served at the behest of the rich and powerful. Reminiscent of Molière's Arnolphe, Old Bartholo loses his beautiful young ward Rosine to Count Almaviva through the machinations of Figaro.

In 1784, within the shadows of the impending French Revolution and the Bastille, Beaumarchais produced the play, *Le mariage de Figaro ou la folle journée (The Follies of a Day or The Marriage of Figaro).* It proved the incendiary sequel to his earlier comic opera. While the play became another vehicle for Beaumarchais' picaresque life story and a political populist message, the married Count Almaviva now appeared as the new *senex amator*. Count Almaviva, another Bartholo and no longer just a comic *senex,* but a tyrant that could provoke revolutions, claims his unofficial droit du seigneur, the lord's traditional right to deflower the local bride. The old *senex amator* has turned introspective, libertine, irascible, tyrannical, and dangerous. Like Jonson and Molière before him, Beaumarchais explored this darker side of *senex.* At the same time, Beaumarchais' brilliant and witty treatment of all the conventions of the classic plot even to the final joke preserved the buoyancy of this comedy of manners.

When the librettist Lorenzo da Ponte adapted this play for Mozart's *The Marriage of Figaro,* he pruned Beaumarchais' political message and personal resentments, added comic detail and action, but kept the social tension. The power and menace of the count and Bartolo remain in the vengeance arias. While the traditional plot, characters, conventions, and swift actions remain from commedia dell'arte, complexity of character, motive, emotion, and moral force has replaced pure farce. Mozart's musical genius has invested the comic opera with playfulness, vitality, lyrical passages, and symphonic force in its final ensembles, which recapture the servants' mischief, the household's exuberance, the lovers' quests and the old lover's reconciliation in fidelity to the classic tradition. Mozart's comic opera represents *senex amator's* final stage bow to the late eighteenth century tide of social reform, sentimentalism, and romanticism. In his stead, modern fiction has cast an uncomic aged lover as tyrant, egoist, or authorial image.

See also: Love in Greek and Roman Literature, Seduction.

Selected Bibliography

Duckworth, George E. *The Nature of Roman Comedy: A Study in Popular Entertainment.* Princeton: Princeton University Press, 1952.

Lea, Kathleen M. *Italian Popular Comedy: A Study in the Commedia dell'arte, 1560– 1620 with Special Reference to the English Stage.* Oxford: Clarendon Press, 1934.

Nicoll, Allardyce. *World Drama from Aeschylus to Anouilh.* London: Harrap, 1949.

Stade, George, ed. *European Writers: The Age of Reason and the Enlightenment. Voltaire to André Chénier.* European Writers Series 4. New York: Scribner, 1984.

KENNETH CRAVEN

SEX (HETEROSEXUAL, EROTIC)

In literature, sexuality takes at least five major forms: (1) Abstract or cerebral ("sex on the brain")—generalized references or allusions to sexual matters, unrelated to specific incidents or graphic details, often accompanied by the levity and smirking common to, for example, adolescents or Broadway musicals; (2)

Decorous—references to specific incidents of sexual activity that are subsidiary parts of plot or theme, for example, the woman taken in adultery (in the New Testament); (3) Dramatized—the portrayal of sexual intercourse as a central event in a story but without biological details or "obscene" terms; (4) Graphic—descriptions of the sexual act or of genitalia (rare in high literature until modern times); (5) Philosophical—celebration of sexual intercourse as a supreme pleasure or value and a part of a hedonist or quasi-religious outlook, as an important component of love and mutual tenderness, or as the key to a monocausal explanation of reality.

Class 1 passages—bawdy, ribald, risqué—laugh at sex, whether out of embarrassment, sadism, or philosophic hauteur. Class 2 and 3 passages may be written in a spirit of scientific detachment and fidelity to human behavior and misbehavior or in a moralistic, judgmental fashion that presents sex as shocking, disgusting, lewd, obscene. Class 4 and 5 passages usually aim at empathy, arousal, and activism. About sex in literature a great debate rages between what might be called the "literalists," the many (like Norman Mailer) who maintain that D. H. Lawrence and Henry Miller achieved a breakthrough by discussing openly what, say, Jane Austen and Henry James, notwithstanding their numerous merits, dared not confront; and, on the other hand, the "hierophants," the few (Jorge Luis Borges, Pamela Johnson Snow, George Steiner) who hold that Austen and James write richly about sex and that Lawrence and Miller coarsened the terms of discourse and contracted the imagination by rendering overt what is best dealt with by suggestion. What is clear, though, is that sex (like politics) is touched on by nearly all works of literature—especially if the reader heeds his Freud (or Marx). Cited here therefore will be only those works where it is notable or overt.

Antiquity

Though a holy book to many, the Old Testament contains enough material on sex to have prompted some to expurgate it. The material is mainly Class 2 ("decorous") in handling, albeit often bizarre or "kinky" in subject. Lot has incest with his daughters; Sodom and Gomorrah are hotbeds of all sorts of sexuality; the patriarchs practice polygamy; Tamar has a complicated erotic life with the sons of Judah and with her father-in-law as well; Joseph must avert the amatory advances of Potiphar's wife; another Tamar, a daughter of David, is raped by a brother; David himself commits adultery with Bathsheba and in old age is "warmed" by a young girl; Solomon "knows" a thousand wives. With such a paradigm of "normal" behavior, it is no wonder that the legalistic part of the Bible has stringent rules on sexual conduct in order to keep people under some sort of control. But quite unexpected and therefore freely allegorized is the Class 4 ("graphic") and 5 ("hedonist") quality of the Song of Songs.

Homer's epic poem *Ilias* (*Iliad*, c. 8th century B.C.) is about a nonerotic incident during a war caused by the seduction and adulterous elopement of Helen (Class 2); her lover, Paris, is shown to be better at lovemaking than at combat.

With the men busy fighting or arguing and the women lamenting, the only Class 3 ("dramatic") incident involves the gods. In order to let the Greeks thrive, Hera plots to distract Zeus; dressing herself in her very best with the significant help of Aphrodite, she arouses Zeus, whose artful expression of love is as good a male seduction "line" as can be found in literature. The divine husband and wife, wrapped in a concealing cloud, proceed to copulate. While lacking in graphic details, the incident is erotically charged. In a parallel scene in the epic poem *Odysseia* (*Odyssey*, 8th century B.C.), in which details are again omitted and which trembles even more precariously between the erotic and the ironic or comic, Ares and Aphrodite have an assignation only to find themselves trapped in a net woven by the cuckolded Hephaistos. Meanwhile, Odysseus, though mainly desirous of returning home, is never one to turn aside from any adventure or experience that comes his way; hence a brief sexual affair with Circe and a longer one with Calypso (though he is so modest in approaching young Nausicaa as to cover his genitals). On returning home, cleansing his house of the suitors, and being reunited with Penelope, he promptly has connubial relations with her, the first in two decades. While Odysseus' own sexual escapades in no way diminish his heroic stature, he himself exercises no such liberality. He executes those of his maidservants who slept with the suitors.

Greek tragedy contains mainly Class 2 ("decorous") sex: Thyestes' adultery with Atreus' wife; Helen's with Paris; Agamemnon's bringing back of Cassandra as his mistress; Clytemnestra's affair with Aegisthus (Aeschylus' *Agamemnōn*, 458 B.C.); the mother-son incest of Oedipus and Jocasta (Sophocles' *Oidipous tyrannos* [*Oedipus Rex*, c. 429 B.C.]); Medea's original passion for Jason and Phaedra's for Hippolytus, as well as Jason's harping later on Medea's alleged feminine sexual jealousy (Euripides' *Mēdeia* [*Medea*, 431 B.C.], and *Hippolytos* [*Hippolytus*, 428 B.C.]); Electra's obsession with the physical aspect of the Aegisthus-Clytemnestra affair (Euripides' *Ēlektra* [*Electra*, 414 B.C.]). Hippolytus in particular is punished for priggish purity, his refusal to worship Aphrodite and all that she stands for. Aristophanes' comedies contain many references to sexuality (Class 1, "abstract"), but the one play in which it is dramatized and graphic is *Lysistratē* [*Lysistrata*, 411 B.C.). The centrality of sex is as much its main theme as is exasperation with the endless war. The women's plot—to withhold their bodies until their husbands make peace with the enemy—works, despite a weakening of their resolve because they need sex as much as do men.

Among philosophers, sex does not fare well, at least at first. Plato dismisses heterosexual relations as biologically necessary but intrinsically uninteresting. To the clownish Aristophanes he assigns (*Symposion* [*Symposium*, dialogue, c. 384 B.C.]) the fanciful explanation of the origins of copulation in the vain attempt of the two sundered halves of the human body to reunite. While Aristotle (*Ēthika Nikomacheia* [*Ethics*, treatise, 4th century B.C.]) stolidly accepts bodily pleasure as one of the goods of life and a component of happiness, it remained for the intellectually unimpressive Aristippus, one of the first avowed hedonists, to hold that pleasure is the goal of life and that bodily pleasure is far better than the mental sort. Diogenes the Cynic copulated in public on the grounds that the act is legitimate and natural. Lucretius (*De rerum natura* [*On the Nature of Things,* 1st century B.C.]) is the first to give some graphic details of erotic dreams and of sexual intercourse. His indulgent description of the place of sex in human affairs includes such observations as that the female is as delighted as the male by the experience (a subject of contention even in Greek mythology); that the act is perhaps best enjoyed when detached from the deep and futile yearnings associated with love; and that it is a striving for a union or fulfillment that often eludes the participants and the desire for which quickly returns in the wake of satiety.

Sexual intrigue and venial misbehavior (Class 2 and 3) is in the plot of many a Latin comedy by Terence and especially Plautus. The late Greek Anthology contains some graphic material, but it is partly pederastic. More explicitly heterosexual matter may be found in the Roman love elegists, Catullus especially, and in the waspish Martial. Horace (*Satirae* [*Satires,* c. 30–37 B.C.]) avows his preference for sex with easy-to-obtain freedwomen (he even provides quite a few names) in lieu of others' snobbish compulsion to seduce high-born wives, with all the attendant risks—implying thereby that physical gratification counts more than ego tripping. The first writer to discourse on sexual relations extensively was Ovid. Besides narrating amusingly his own erotic escapades (*Amores,* poem, c. 20 B.C.) and those of the gods (*Metamorphoses,* epic poem, c. A.D. 2–17), he wrote the *Ars amatoria* (*The Art of Love,* didactic poem, c. 1 B.C.), the earliest extant Western manual of seduction. It treats sex as a supreme value and as an area worthy of intense if lighthearted study rather than as only matter for Homeric laughter, philosophic deprecation, or, conjoined with love, tragic revulsion. It deals with the psychology of sex and not, as does the clinically inclined Hindu manual, Vātsyāyana's *Kama Sutra* (c. 300), with the physiology and (sometimes dubious) acrobatics of sex.

The love springing up in Dido (Virgil's *Aeneis* [*Aeneid,* epic poem, 19 B.C.])—based as much on the *Argonautika* (*Argonauts,* epic poem, 3d century B.C.) of Apollonius of Rhodes as on the *Odyssey*—finds fulfillment between two experienced, mature exiles in a cave; while the physical details are withheld, the sexual act affects the universe. The two proceed to have a protracted "affair," rumored to be full of lust and squalid pleasure, until the gods blow the whistle on them. As it was for Odysseus, sex is a pleasant interlude, but, much more than was the case with the Greek, it must yield to duty to higher things. Nobler values are also apparent in Apuleius' *Metamorphoses* (*The Golden Ass,* novel, c. 150). The hero has a rich dalliance with the maidservant of a witch and, in the event, is accidentally turned into a donkey. The quasi-platonic hostility to sex implicit in that incident is reenforced when the hero-donkey's refusal to copulate with a woman as part of a spectacle in an arena initiates his return to human form and his assumption of a chaste holiness.

Petronius (*Satyricon,* novel, A.D. 60) tells the famous story of the widow of Ephesus, that model of fidelity who is yet seduced by a soldier before her husband's corpse has turned cold. The tale is less a celebration of sex than a broadcasting of the idea that "frailty thy name is woman." The *Satyricon* is filled with the falling in and out of bed of the main characters, with jealousy and eroticism that cut across relationships, sexes, social classes; some women, for example, are aroused only by lower-class men. In this, the first realistic novel and sexual odyssey, with not a few graphic details, the narrator prays to the reigning god Priapus. At one point impotent, he in a self-destructive rage would slash off his own genitals but, his penis shrinking, he satisfies himself with berating it and then with berating himself for stooping to argue with a part of the self that no man thinks worthy of any thoughts. The point is well taken, for no writer had till now dramatized the incongruity of male sexuality: the paradox of a thinking human being attached to an animal body with a curious appendage; the mystery of great joy and misery springing from an organ that by turns swells and hangs limp, that, with a will of its own, does not always respond to opportunities and wishes, and that seeks from soft enclosure, moist warmth, movement, and friction—best provided by somewhat different human beings whose bodies possess an accommodating pouch or receptacle for that purpose— satisfaction through spasmodic contraction and emission. That great pride or humiliation depends on such an extremity is an anomaly of being human.

The Middle Ages and the Renaissance

Under the Christian dispensation, sex falls into further disrepute. At the heart of the Christ story is a concept—the Virgin Birth—which, unlike the seminal or parallel Greek myths of the intercourse of gods and women, forcefully separates sex from anything divine or sacred. Christian theologians made much of the fact that Adam and Eve, right after disobeying God's order, knew nakedness as shameful and covered their genitals. Paul only grudgingly accepted marriage on the basis that it is better to marry than to lust, and in Revelations pride of place is held out for men who have abstained from sex. A puritanism latent in Judaism and some Greek cults now comes into its own. St. Augustine, in his philosophical writings, makes much of the propinquity of the organs of procreation and excretion. Consolidating the concept of original sin, he sees it as being transmitted through the sexual act, a most damning burden to place on human desire. One of the things he reprehends in his *Confessiones* (*Confessions,* c. 397–400) is his having had an occasional mistress and his subjection to his sexual needs. Even the love of a wife and the institution of marriage are implicitly dismissed as distracting from the love of God. In *De civitate Dei* (*The City of God,* treatise, 413–426), he correlates the shame that Adam and Eve felt after the Fall with the shame attendant on even "such fornication as the earthly city has legalized," for all sex (even among pagans and barbarians) is accompanied with "a shame-begetting penalty of sin." He deeply regrets therefore (as did Euripides' Jason and as would, among others, Sir Thomas Browne and George Herbert in seventeenth-century England) that procreation is by means of "the greatest of all bodily pleasures." At the resurrection, the body with its beauty shall return, but sex shall be withdrawn and the genitalia put to new uses in praise of God.

In the writings of medieval hagiography, Satan is often depicted as tempting the saints and hermits with spectacles (or dreams) of large banquets and lovely women. This fanciful or unconscious way of articulating the fact that, when one is deprived of physical needs, the imagination becomes obsessed with fantasies of fulfillment is a backhanded tribute to the centrality of sex. The power of Eros to snarl up human order and design has perhaps never been so clearly demonstrated as in Peter Abélard's *Historia calamitatum* (c. 1134). A man devoted to a life of scholarship and philosophical debate—an exponent of rationalism, at that—has his career, soul, and even body mutilated as a result of a single love affair with a beautiful young pupil. Here is perhaps the earliest version of the teacher-student love affair syndrome or of the intellectual humbled by erotic attraction to a woman or girl who is not on his mental level (e.g., Milton, Hazlitt, Joyce, and, in fiction, Goethe's Faust, Hesse's Harry Haller, Proust's Swann, Nabokov's Humbert).

The consequence in this case was a turn (or return) to piety, but the advent of the Courtly Love tradition in the literature of the later Middle Ages gave sexuality a new lease on life in the very midst of the so-called Age of Faith. Manliness, which had been defined in terms of martial and chivalric prowess, now had to include the leavening and mellowing that only intense love for a woman can bring about. While such new amatory lawgivers or codifiers as Andreas Capellanus (*De arte honeste amandi* [*The Art of Courtly Love*, late 12th century]) might distinguish between pure (nonphysical) and mixed (physical) love, the focus in the tales of the new religion of adultery was on the love fulfilled by sexual intercourse. We deal here with Class 3 ("dramatized"), little with Class 4 ("graphic"), sex. Of such a nature are works by romancers like Chrétien de Troyes and Wolfram von Eschenbach. Above all, in Gottfried von Strassburg (*Tristan*, romance, c. 1210) is the focus on the sexual consummation of love. Surrounded by backbiting, suspicion, and subterfuge, the lovers flee to the heart of nature, to an idyl in a *locus amoenus* (a delightful place) in the forest and in a cave of love (which harks back to the cave in the *Aeneid*).

The fashionable adultery is seen from an entirely different perspective in Dante's *Inferno* (*Hell*, *La divina commedia* [*The Divine Comedy*, epic poem, c. 1320]). Paolo and Francesca are swept by infernal winds as a punishment for the sexual intercourse catalyzed by their reading of courtly love romances about adultery. The punishment fits the crime. The lovers who in the sexual act (as Plato's Aristophanes and as Lucretius had remarked) wished to be united forever now obtain their wish, but it proves to be—because of satiety, the unpleasant environment, and the nature of all human expectations—a torture rather than a joy. What happened to Ares and Aphrodite for a spell through the trap of angry Hephaistos—the lovers held together too long and in public—is happening to the two lovers here forever through the grace of an angry God. Moreover, this couple, though sinning apparently only once, pays the supreme penalty, while the promiscuous Cunizza is in heaven, the difference being that she repented and they did not. (Dante himself is accused by Beatrice of having lapsed, but whether she means sex is unclear.)

Jehan de Meung's continuation of the *Roman de la rose* (*Romance of the Rose*, didactic poem, c. 1275) has many passages that, taken together, constitute the longest discussion yet of sexuality. Passages of Ovidian advice—addressed sometimes to predatory men, sometimes to amorous women—mingle with evocations of free love in the Age of Gold, apologies for candor on the subject, and urgings to seize the day. The Duenna is a go-between who anticipates in her rhetoric the Convent Trotter, the Wife of Bath, and Celestina. Dame Nature favors fecundity, and Jupiter favors delight. Nature made woman inclined to promiscuity, and only society, necessity, law, and orderliness impose such constraints as monogamy on us. After advice for achieving joint orgasm comes the first protracted, graphic description—albeit in a transparent veil of allegory—of entry, deflowering, climax, and what one critic has called the first important pregnant heroine in European literature. Somewhat different is the poem *El libro de buen amor* (*The Book of Good Love,* c. 1343) of Juan Ruiz, the archpriest of Hita. It is partly a Hispanic version of Ovidian instructions for seduction, and partly the rhetorical tale of the priest's attempts, through an intermediary—the crone known as the Convent Trotter—to conquer in turn a lady, a nun, and a Moorish damsel. The results are nebulous, and the suggestion is strong that the narrator is a frustrated lover with sex on the brain, a man who has sex only when he is, or fantasizes of being, raped by coarse mountain girls.

Sexuality in conjunction with joy comes into its own in Boccaccio's *Il decamerone* (*Decameron*, novellas, c. 1350), which portrays it as consonant with religion and nature (Class 5). Here is tale after tale of sexual behavior and misbehavior (Class 3), often involving monks and nuns. With hardly a trace of the consequences familiar to everyone—pregnancy, venereal disease, emotional stress—this is a sexual utopia and perhaps the first unabashed celebration in story form in high literature of the West of sex and hedonism. (Even in the *Satyricon* sexuality was dogged by strife and melancholy.) The only requirements for bliss are secrecy, in order to keep society content, and rationalizations, in order to keep one's partner (or one's conscience) content. Some of this joie de vivre spills over into Chaucer's *Canterbury Tales* (c. 1380–1400), as in the *Miller's Tale*, which contains a few graphic details in telling of the merry cuckolding of a carpenter by a college student. The Wife of Bath reveals herself in her Prologue to be an adept at sexual intercourse and a keen debater who justifies her values with some shrewd gibes at Christian doctrine, gibes that echo Jehan de Meung and look ahead to Renaissance iconoclasm. (A brief sexual affair is at the heart of Chaucer's *Troilus and Criseyde,* poem, c. 1385, based on Boccaccio's romance *Filostrato,* 1338.) Sharing the Convent Trotter's vocation with the Wife of Bath's earthiness and hedonism is the main character of the *Tragicomedia de Calisto y Melibea* (*Celestina*, 1499–1502), a tale about a star-crossed Romeo and Juliet-like pair who, in the modern fashion, carry on a prolonged and intense physical affair (no graphic details are given) in lieu of any nuptial interests. Somewhat more melancholy glimpses of sex are offered in passages in the poetry of Villon (mid-15th century). The influence of Boccaccio in France can be seen in *Les cent nouvelles nouvelles* (*The Hundred Tales*, c. 1460) and Marguerite de Navarre's *Heptaméron* (tales, 1559), while the Italian Aretino wrote immensely influential overt pornography with his *Sonetti lussuriosi* (1524) and *Ragionamenti* (dialogues, 1534–1536). By contrast, the *Alf Layla wa-layla* (*Arabian Nights*, tales, 8th-17th centuries), which contains risqué tales and lush descriptions, and the *Er roud el aater* (*The Perfumed Garden*, 16th century) by the Shaykh Nefzawi, an Arab work that blends advice, highly graphic details, hedonist philosophy, and lubricious short stories, were not made available to the West until, respectively, the early eighteenth and the late nineteenth centuries. Confined to the Jewish community were the detailed and authoritative prescriptions and proscriptions on sexual behavior (e.g., what positions, what frequency, and what times of the month are permissible) compiled in Rabbi Joseph Karo's *Shulhan 'Arukh* (*Arranged Table*, 1555) and based on scattered Talmudic inferences from Mosaic dicta.

Boccaccio's vision of sex informs Machiavelli's comedies, the *Clizia* (1520) and especially *La Mandragola* (*The Mandrake*, c. 1512–1520). More philosophic and detached is Erasmus (*Moriae encomion* [*The Praise of Folly*, essay, 1511]). There Folly boasts that even the wisest or most Stoic man must, if he wants to be a father, act the fool at least for a few minutes. For procreation is made possible by the ridiculous part of the human body, a part that cannot even be named without accompanying laughter. Furthermore, the desire to put that part to proper use requires a man to tell a woman absurdities. So much for the glories of sex; Erasmus looks back to Petronius and ahead to G. B. Shaw's (or is it Lord Chesterfield's?) coldly philosophic observation of sex—that the posture is ridiculous and the pleasure transitory. The people in More's ideal republic (*Utopia*, political romance, 1516) make pleasure a supreme value, equating it with reason, virtue, and religion. Before marriage, moreover, couples are to view each other naked in order to know what kind of sexual goods they are getting. Yet premarital sexual intercourse is condemned for fear that no one would put up with the inconvenience of spending one's life with only one other person if sexual experience were otherwise available.

Rabelais (*Gargantua et Pantagruel* [*Gargantua and Pantagruel*, novels, 1532–1564) is another writer devoted to hedonism on principle. But sexual activity à la Boccaccio and sexual love à la D. H. Lawrence are strangely absent from his work. What is present is a plethora of Class 1 material: levity about animal functions, smirking jokes, nimble wordplay, verbal virtuosity, exaggerated catalogues, occasionally sadistic "sex on the brain" witticisms. In Tasso's *Gerusalemme liberata* (*Jerusalem Delivered*, epic poem, 1581), the heroic crusader Rinaldo is distracted from fighting the Moslems by a bewitching beauty working for Satan, Armida, who immerses him in sexual dalliance in her bower. This is a Christianized version of Odysseus with Circe and Calypso and of Aeneas with

Dido. Such a locus amoenus, with lush but not necessarily graphic details, recurs in Spenser's *Faerie Queene* (epic poem, 1590–1596), in the adventure of Sir Guyon in Acrasia's Bower of Bliss, a place of lewdness and excess, the charms of which he, unlike Rinaldo, resists. The various virtuous knights in fact encounter numerous enticing sexual temptations throughout this huge moral-allegorical work. Christian morality is suspended, on the other hand, when Vasco da Gama and his sailors are rewarded for their toils with an encounter with naked sea nymphs (Camões, *Os Lusíadas* [*The Lusiads,* epic poem, 1572]). Montaigne (*Essais* [*Essays,* 1580–1588]) exhibits, in his later writings, great respect for pleasure; he tends to be secretive about sex, except for the remarkable passage in which he describes how he cured himself of impotence. In Cervantes' novel *Don Quijote* (*Don Quixote,* 1605, 1615) sex becomes central only in the story within the story, "The Too Curious One," in which anxiety over a wife's established fidelity leads a husband to unwittingly bring about an affair between his best friend and his wife. Marlowe's *Dr. Faustus* (play, 1604) has Helen of Troy made available to him as part of the treasures of this world, which Mephistophilis is bound to give him.

Shakespeare (fl. 1590–1610) offers no graphic sex and little philosophic matter (Class 4 and 5) in his plays. Risqué jokes and puns appear in *Romeo and Juliet* (c. 1596), *The Taming of the Shrew* (c. 1594), *Much Ado about Nothing* (c. 1598), *All's Well That Ends Well* (1601–1604), *Troilus and Cressida* (1601–1602). Scenes of lovemaking, with sexual activity either impending or just experienced, appear in *Romeo, Antony and Cleopatra* (c. 1607), *Troilus.* Decorous sex, which is part of the plot but not dramatized, is central to *Hamlet* (c. 1600), *Measure for Measure* (1603–1604), *Antony,* and is alleged falsely, with serious consequences, in *Much Ado, Othello* (c. 1604), *Winter's Tale* (1611), *Cymbeline* (1610) (and peripherally in *King Lear,* 1606). The early narrative poems, *Venus and Adonis* (1593) and *The Rape of Lucrece* (1594), dwell at length (but without graphic details) on, respectively, the beauty and ugliness of sexual behavior. Perhaps Shakespeare's greatest contribution to the theme is Sonnet 129 (1609), a searing brief presentation of man as a prisoner of the erotic drive, which lures one on with the promise of delight and causes almost every sin beforehand and revulsion quickly thereafter. (The problem of the brevity of sexual climax is addressed memorably in Donne's poem "Farewell to Love," 1635). The plays of Shakespeare's contemporaries and successors (e.g., Tourneur's *The Revenger's Tragedy,* 1607; Webster's *The Duchess of Malfi,* 1613; Middleton's *Changeling,* 1622; Ford's *'Tis Pity She's a Whore,* 1633) are laden with an atmosphere of pervasive, brooding, obsessive sexuality. In Jonson's *Volpone* (1606) the hero's attempt to seduce Celia is enacted first with a pithy translation from Catullus and then with a lush but curiously cold rhetorical invitation to dalliance. The Don Juan story, celebratory of incredible sexual prowess that most men dream of and some men actually exhibit, begins a rich adventure in the imagination of the West with Tirso de Molina's *El burlador de Sevilla* (*The Libertine of Seville,* 1630) and is soon adapted by Molière (1665).

An important writer on this subject was John Donne (fl. 1590–1610), who, in his early poetry, put together an impressive group of lyrics dramatizing the attempt of the persona to seduce a woman. In these ingenious poems, the renowned metaphysical conceits take the place of either suggestive details or of Elizabethan evocation of sensuous beauty. They constitute a view of sex as filtered through the sensibility of an intellectual. (In his Elegies 18 and especially 19, however, the sensual presence of the woman's body for once replaces intellection.) Far more relaxed are the sometimes graphic Cavalier lyrics of Carew, Lovelace, Suckling, and Marvell. Outright pornography was becoming now a growth industry, led in Italy by Ferrante Pallavicino (*La retorica delle puttane* [*The Whore's Rhetorick*, dialogues, 1642]) and in England by the anonymous *School of Venus* (1655, 1680).

Even the Puritan John Milton (*Paradise Lost,* poem, 1667) betrays a marked eroticism. Celebrating prelapsarian nakedness and bemoaning clothing and hypocrisy, he lavishes great poetry on the physical charms of Adam and Eve and on their lovemaking. The first thing they do after the Fall is to fornicate. The point (an elaboration of St. Augustine) is that prelapsarian sex had been a mutual experience, sex melded with love, body with soul, but now it is, as is often the case, each partner making use of the other's body, each imprisoned in the ego, trapped in the vanity of flirtation and seduction, haunted by guilt and shame. The battle of the sexes and the man's special sexual vulnerability is also central in *Samson Agonistes* (dramatic poem, 1671).

The Neoclassical and Preromantic Eras

Some of the poems of Lord Rochester continue in the vein of the Cavaliers, albeit with greater cynicism and coarseness, while the Restoration drama turns the sexual obsessions of Jacobean tragedy into material for comedy. Dorimant (Etherege's *Man of Mode,* play, 1676) handles mistresses as a juggler does balls; sexual intercourse is never, of course, onstage but always in the vicinity. In an updating of a Latin comedy, Horner (Wycherley's *Country Wife,* 1675) pretends to be a eunuch in order to gain access to men's wives, and in one famous scene, in which he has more women available than his penis can handle, the language of porcelain china is used wittily as a code for sexual intercourse—a triumph of innuendo. That famous metaphor influenced Pope in *The Rape of the Lock* (poem, 1712), in which breaking a china jar or losing virginity are casually equated. This work is an outstanding figurative treatment of sex. The rhetoric (even in the ambiguous title) makes it clear that the subject, ostensibly about a skirmish in a salon over the cutting of a girl's lock of hair, is really a man's seduction of a woman, the deflowering of a society belle.

Richardson's novels *Pamela* (1740) and *Clarissa Harlowe* (1748) are about the sexual designs of a young man on a young woman. Pamela holds out for the better terms of marriage and gets them; Clarissa is raped. The latter novel is probably the longest, most elaborate work devoted to the eventual sexual intercourse of one man and one woman (Class 3, "dramatized sex"), yet it is free of graphic details. In Fielding's briskly moving *Tom Jones* (novel, 1749), by contrast, is an extroverted hero who experiences more than a few sexual encounters in the course of his varied adventures in town and country. Where Richardson has a somewhat peculiar attitude to sex—partly bourgeois, partly puritanical, partly obsessive—Fielding presents it as something as normal, bracing, and enjoyable as eating, something that is necessary in a respectable young man's (but not respectable young woman's) quotidian life. Laurence Sterne (*Tristram Shandy*, novel, 1759–1767) exhibits yet a third approach. Without the moralistic ambivalence of Richardson or the brisk, extroverted acceptance of Fielding, he, like Rabelais (whom he sometimes resembles, sometimes adverts to), delights in allusiveness rather than in dramatized sex; hence the stories about winding up the clock, about the nose, and about sausages. Rabelais' brashness, iconoclasm, and sadism is, however, replaced by a coy slyness and mock gentility. The book ends with plaintive, "modern" words on the absurdity that we conceal sexual intercourse and the creation of life while we openly parade cannons and the taking of life.

A variant of such a dissonant chord was soon to be sounded by William Blake (late 18th century), one of the first to rebel against the traditional interpretation of Christianity. He saw it as a religion substituting "thou shalt not" and exploitation for energy and desire. The cryptic last two stanzas of "London" (poem, 1794) paint a picture (of a street harlot blighting the "marriage hearse") of a society that is deeply flawed in its channeling of the sexual instinct. Various poems suggest that chastity is a form of self-centeredness, while sexuality is a form of giving and communion. In him one hears early the modern theme of sexuality (irrespective of marital status) as precious not merely because it is pleasurable but because it is something holy, in harmony with nature, almost a matter of duty (though not for procreation) and of nondoctrinal piety. A similar and contemporaneous attack is carried out by Diderot (*Supplément au voyage de Bougainville* [*A Supplement to Bougainville's Voyage*, dialogue, 1772; printed 1796]) who suggests that the channeling of sex into the institution of monogamy, the taboos on numerous forms of sexual intercourse, and especially the Catholic value of abstinence appear ridiculous to the Tahitians, those sensible "noble savages" living close to nature, acceding gracefully to the biological urges and rhythms, and rejoicing in a sexual life nearly uncontaminated by rules.

Blake and Diderot are part of a change in intellectual climate brought about by the decline of the Christian consensus, a decline made manifest by the contrast between Defoe's novel *Moll Flanders* (1722) and John Cleland's novel *Fanny Hill* (1749). Both books contain heroines who are highly experienced in the ways of the flesh. But the former work—despite much fornication, adultery, bigamy, incest, and whoring—contains no graphic details; aspiring to literature, paying at least lip service to traditional values, and claiming a didactic, moral purpose, it concentrates on the psychological and sociological aspects of the story; guilt feelings are never far from the sexual (or criminal) activities of Moll. On the other hand, the latter work—while free of bigamy and incest—is frankly devoted to a graphic, delighted description of numerous sexual acts. Pornography and erotica have been written in many ages and countries, but here is a work whose sexual lyricism, brisk narrative, atmosphere of pagan joie de vivre, and freedom from abnormalities, sadism, offensive words, or guilt feelings brings it to, and perhaps across, the threshold of literature. As such, it is the first and still one of the finest examples of extended Class 4 (''graphic'') and, implicitly, Class 5 (''hedonist'') writing.

Also at the juncture of literature and pornography (and, in this case, of ''philosophy'') are the works of the Marquis de Sade, which constitute a landmark and a dead end in erotic writing. A child of Enlightenment rationalism and atheism, Sade is the embodiment of Ivan Karamazov's principle (to be enunciated a century later) that if God is dead, all is permitted. In his writings, ideological attacks on God, religion, morality, optimism, and sentiment punctuate scenes of varied, sometimes fantastical, sex and violence. His *Les 120 journées de Sodome* (*The 120 Days of Sodom,* 1785) dwells graphically on genitalia and on almost every imaginable sexual act by individual or group, often accompanied by cruelty (such as strangling the woman at the moment of ejaculation). The natural complement to his writings are those of Leopold von Sacher-Masoche a century later, in whose tales, notably *Venus im Pelz* (*Venus in Furs,* novel, 1870), the erotic in man is catalyzed, accompanied, or heightened by pain, which the woman inflicts on him. Both writers operate at a low level of literature and a high degree of abnormality, but their names have become proverbial because, psychologists suggest, they give a magnified version of sexual tendencies latent in all human beings.

A classic of erotica that happens also to be a literary classic is Choderlos de Laclos' epistolary novel *Les liaisons dangereuses* (*Dangerous Acquaintances,* 1782). Albeit bereft of graphic details, it presents a dramatic picture of a pair of ruthless aristocrats bringing members of the young generation of innocents into its corrupt, jaded life style. In a blend of the principles of Ovid, Machiavelli, and von Clausewitz (by anticipation), sexual intercourse as practiced by Valmont and Mme de Merteuil has less to do with physical gratification, let alone love or procreation, than with vanity, conquest, jealousy, and revenge. Like a chess player who, enroute to capturing his opponent's queen, takes a pawn in passing, Valmont, on the way to seducing the religious Mme de Tourvel, casually deflowers the innocent young Cécile. He is not as famous as some of the other lovers in literature or life, but he embodies one of the most penetrating portraits of the libertine. The book suggests that, highly civilized though people may appear in their dress, manners, and, above all, words and sentiments, underneath it all, men and women are still only animals by turns randomly coupling and fighting over territory. It is a unique dramatization of the psychology, politics, strategy, and metaphysics of sex.

Certain memoirists, diarists, and autobiographers dwelled on their sexual conquests. Samuel Pepys (*Diary,* 1660–1669) offers an amusing portrait of *l'homme moyen sensuel* periodically cheating on his wife (in passages written in a mixture of foreign tongues to forestall discovery) with her housemaids, with wives of sailors whose careers he could affect, and with other choice morsels of femininity who happened to cross his path; and all the while he holds his wife to a rigid standard, the merest suggestion of a mild flirtation on her part generating great jealousy in him. The double standard in sex has never been depicted so richly, amusingly—and unintentionally. Boswell's *Journals* (1762–1773) record the sexual wanderings of a young laird who is concurrently in quest of career, fame, identity. These were private records, perhaps never meant to be published. But late in the eighteenth century, the autobiographical impulse is nascent, and with it a certain compulsion to parade one's amatory conquests. One of the most famous of these memoirists is Giacomo Casanova (*Histoire de ma vie* [*History of My Life,* 1798, published 1826–1838]), whose name has become proverbial because, as he said, he was "a bachelor whose chief business in life was to cultivate the pleasures of the senses." His wandering from country to country is paralleled by his wandering from love affair to affair; more an effusive and accomplished lover than, like Don Juan or Valmont, a cold-hearted seducer, he appears to have been unable, by dint of character or fate, to settle down with any one woman. He lacks reflective powers, and his amatory experiences, casually recounted, interweave with his incarcerations, his adventures in high society, his meetings with great men. Different in atmosphere is the autobiography of his sedentary contemporary, Restif de la Bretonne (*Monsieur Nicolas,* 1794–1797), who offers a somewhat more graphic and reflective version of his own numerous affairs, but then he was a littérateur who wrote about sex in many other books as well. The erotic impulse preoccupies him, and he is struggling toward some vision of it not too different from Blake's contemporary one.

The greatest of the memoirists of this period, Rousseau, also produces (*Confessions,* 1781–1788) a milestone in the treatment of sex. Novel here is the way in which his erotic life is a subject worthy of serious thought and not something ludicrous (Petronius, Erasmus, Rabelais), rhapsodic (Cleland) or, like eating and elimination, trivial. Novel also is the way in which his affairs, comparatively few, are not presented as so many achievements, like those in Tom Jones's, Casanova's, or Restif's triumphal march on the road of life, but rather as almost crises of the soul. And novel, lastly, is the minute psychological analysis brought to bear on his sexual experiences. Thus his copulating with Mme de Waren is unique because erotic feelings are hopelessly entangled with those aroused by their mother-son relationship; Rousseau is here on the threshold of Freudian insights (cf. Diderot's contemporary anticipation of Freud with the remark that the infant in the cradle would like to sleep with its mother). Rousseau sounds modern also when he remarks that his affair with Mme de Larnage involves the best sex he ever had and then tries to account for that judgment. He sounds almost Proustian or Lawrentian in relating how his sexual tastes were formed and malformed by the punishment administered to him at age eight by a woman of thirty or how his observation that one woman's nipple was misshapen led him into an emotional quagmire. This is the first work (at least since the *Satyricon*) in which sexuality is shown to be problematic—not simply a matter of "chercher la femme" and ejaculating inside her—and is made a major theme, alongside such traditional ones as one's intellectual, emotional, vocational, and political maturation. Even masochism and masturbation make here a virtually unprecedented appearance in literature. The late eighteenth century was indeed a period of great ferment in musings on sex, mainly in Enlightenment and Revolutionary France.

The Romantic and Modern Periods

The nineteenth century is recessive. Goethe's *Faust* (play, 1808) ends rather anticlimatically with the affair, impregnation, and execution of Gretchen. More compelling is the lush depiction of erotic fulfillment in Keats's "Eve of St. Agnes" (poem, 1820) as, in the spirit of *Romeo and Juliet,* a brief moment of supreme beauty and the climax of life for those who are young, handsome, and daring in a world of darkness, cold, hostility. Considering the achievements of Rousseau and others and considering the complicated private life of the poet, one is surprised that Byron's epic *Don Juan* (1819–1824) should seem an old-fashioned work on this theme, an updating of Petronius, Boccaccio, and Fielding. The somewhat passive hero has various sexual affairs thrown his way, and they are presented light-heartedly, without graphic details, and with not too seriously meant apologies for treating forbidden matter. The psychological rather than physiological aspects of sex are central in two famous works. Sex may be entangled with ambition and intrigue (Stendahl's *Le rouge et le noir* [*The Red and the Black,* novel, 1830]) or with egoism and a savoring of life (Kierkegaard's "Diary of a Seducer" in *Enten-eller* [*Either/Or,* 1843]).

In Flaubert's *Madame Bovary* (1856), a woman bored by her pedestrian husband and by their provincial milieu tries to make her life approximate the heightened version that she finds in cheap romances. And that involves sexual affairs, which however turn out to be increasingly sordid. Sex being her would-be avenue of escape and actual form of self-destruction, her amatory encounters are, as in few novels till now, at the heart of the plot. They are carefully dramatized, yet without many graphic details. Similar is the predicament and reaction of the heroine of Tolstoy's novel *Anna Karenina* (1877), who, by contrast, lives in a sophisticated milieu and tries to make her escape by means of a love affair with one man. This proves to be as bad for her as does the series of encounters for Emma. (The penalty for sexual jealousy is also preachily dramatized in Tolstoy's novel *Kreitserova sonata* [*Kreutzer Sonata,* 1889].) Yet a third variant of this theme is Hawthorne's *Scarlet Letter* (novel, 1850). Hester, separated from her scholarly husband, has an affair with a minister. Her pregnancy invites an ostracism that reveals her dignity in adversity and unmasks the pettiness of the apparently envious society that ejects her. Some other famous female victims of a sexual double standard are Maggie Tulliver (George Eliot's *The Mill on the Floss,* novel, 1860), Tess (Hardy's *Tess of the D'Urbervilles,* novel, 1891), and Maggie (Crane's novel, *Maggie,* 1893).

In Dostoevsky's *Brat'īaKaramazovy* (*The Brothers Karamazov,* novel, 1880), the father is a bestial man who is not above raping the village idiot girl. His oldest son, Dmitri, a worldly officer and philanderer, is in love with Grushenka, a woman whose favors his own father is trying to buy. This Oedipal rivalry— underscored by Dostoevsky—again brings us to the threshold of the Freudian vision. Abnormal also is Stavrogin's seduction of a twelve-year-old girl, who then hangs herself while he punishes himself by marrying a lame woman (*Besy* [*The Possessed,* novel, 1871–1872]). Less lurid sexual affairs are at the heart of Henry James's novels, *Portrait of a Lady* (1881), *The Ambassadors* (1903), *The Wings of the Dove* (1902), and *The Golden Bowl* (1904). Powerfully dramatized are the assignations of Kate and Merton and of Charlotte and Amerigo in the latter two novels, but there is hardly a graphic detail. The sexual affair leads to disillusionment and tragic endings in the *Portrait* and the *Wings,* to liberation or reconciliation in the *Ambassadors* and the *Bowl.*

In the playwright Ibsen's *Samfundets støtter* (*The Pillars of Society,* 1877), the sexual affair is an event in the past that leads to exposure and enlightenment in the present. In *Rosmersholm* (1886) and *Naar vi døde vaagner* (*When We Dead Awaken,* 1899), the woman with whom the hero slept in the past now pushes him out of conventional existence into the mystical heights of suicide. In *Et dukkehjem* (*A Doll's House,* 1879) and *Gengangere* (*Ghosts,* 1881), a man's libertinism leads to premature illness and death for his son, as the sins of the father are visited on the next generation (congenital syphillis, in less biblical terms). Sexual affairs constitute merely a series of incidents in the dense social and psychological network of Chekhov's plays. Thus, Trigorin (*Chaĭka* [*The Sea Gull,* 1895]), in the midst of a protracted relationship with the popular actress, Irina, takes advantage of the callow aspiring actress, Nina, who throws herself at him. After a while, he returns to his earlier love, while Nina embarks on her career with heightened determination and maturity. In the *Tri sestry* (*The Three Sisters,* 1901), Masha has a brief affair with Vershinin and then must resume her frustrating married life. In the *Vishnëvyĭ sad* (*The Cherry Orchard,* 1904), Mme Ranevskaya, her family wealth dissolving before her eyes, stills holds on to a love affair she had with a selfish man. In *Dīadīa Vanīa (Uncle Vanya,* 1897), sexual longings—Vanya's for Yelena, Sonya's for Dr. Astrov— remain frustrated, as part of the atmosphere of futility in the play.

At the turn of the century occurred another revolution in thinking about sex. No part of the reaction against Victorian repressiveness on the subject was more stimulating than the theories of Freud. Doing for sex what Marx did for money, he suggested, in *Die Traumdeutung* (*The Interpretation of Dreams,* 1900) and after, that most phenomena could be explained as sublimated or distorted forms of sexuality. Hence his notions of a sexual rivalry between father and infant son for possession of the mother; of sexual overtones in slips of the tongues and in components of dreams; of sexuality in infants and in people thought to be saintly. Anticipated in some of these insights by Sade, Diderot, Rousseau, Dostoevsky, and Nietzsche, Freud alone put together a vast system. He did not create the modern openness, even obsessiveness, with sexuality; he merely gave it a tongue. Concurrent with this change in thinking about the psyche (and perhaps as a result of it), love, which had been a dominant theme in literature from the twelfth century on, died a natural death and left a large residue of sex. The modern novel or play is about coupling, rarely about love. The traditional view—that first comes love, then marriage, and lastly, implicitly, automatically, a happy sexual consummation—had been subscribed to by most writers, so that pre- or extra-marital sex invariably had a tragic *(Tess)* or punitive *(Les liaisons dangereuses)* ending, and those who celebrated sex as prior to or separate from marriage were comic writers whose heterodox attitude could be tolerated as merely clowning. But now serious writers are tinkering with the sequence. If Proust sees none of the three as related to each other—Swann first has sexual relations with Odette, then falls in love with her, and marries her only when the love ceases—Lawrence sympathetically (and noncomically) presents his major characters (in early literary examples of what has come to be known as the Sexual Revolution or the New Morality) experimenting with sex prior to or together with love, but before marriage; they will not marry anyone they have found no sexual communion with, and that means erotic exploration, trial and error, and what looks to traditionalists dangerously like promiscuity.

In Joyce's *Ulysses* (novel, 1922), the only act of sexual intercourse (adulterous) takes place offstage, and the book, like those of Rabelais and Sterne, has many Class 1 ("abstract") allusions and references. Yet the language used to depict the inner landscape of people, notably Bloom (who even masturbates), is so imitative of the way most individuals think and speak that the book was banned as smutty. (Molly's closing reverie is, to be sure, graphic.) Different yet parallel is the nearly contemporaneous *A la recherche du temps perdu* (*Remembrance of Things Past,* novels, 1913–1927) by Proust. Here the sexual interests of Swann, Marcel, Albertine—riddled though these are with what for Proust is the major component of love, jealousy—are gone into at great length. Marcel in particular often thinks about sex. Yet no coupling takes place onstage, and when it comes to dramatic incident or graphic details, Proust is as reticent as any Victorian. The work offers a peculiar blend of hothouse atmosphere and reserve, and the strongest term for making love, the closest one comes to naming the act, is "Do a cattleya." But much other modern fiction suggests a universal indulgence in pre- or extra-marital sex, and that post-post-Victorian vision was adumbrated early in the century by Schnitzler's *Reigen* (*Merry-Go-Round,* 1900). The play depicts sex as being like musical chairs or a daisy-chain pattern; coming from various social classes and family situations, individuals seek, from the variety of experience and the erosion of class stratification that only sex offers, a fulfillment they never find. What is suggested is that, as in Shakespeare's sonnet 129, people are prisoners of sex, trapped in its rounds, never sated, never learning, and spreading its lovelessness the way they spread venereal disease, from partner to partner. Sex as a means of cutting across class barriers is also central to Strindberg's play *Fröken Julie* (*Miss Julie*, 1888) and, in a way, Williams' play *A Streetcar Named Desire* (1947).

Another major figure in the literary history of sex is D. H. Lawrence. In *Sons and Lovers* (novel, 1913), he shows how the amatory dislocations of one generation distorts the erotic lives of the next. Her love for her coarse husband soon dead, the sensitive Gertrude lavished it rather on her son Paul, who found himself falling in love with a young woman who resembled somewhat his mother and with whom he could not have a satisfactory physical relationship. That one's sexual—not merely one's emotional—life is an important component of one's happiness and is shaped by one's parents is an idea few earlier writers dealt with so explicitly. In Lawrence's later novels, the main characters, dissatisfied by conventional life styles, seek in the sexual experience a doorway to a more authentic, fuller life. (Sex is also redemptive in Hesse's novel *Steppenwolf*, 1927.) The wisdom of the body is contrasted with the hollow wisdom of the intellect. Sex is a natural force that must not be denied; it is for Lawrence (as in Euripides' *Hippolytus* and Blake's poetry) a quasi-religious experience putting one in touch with something cosmic rather than, as for hedonists (Boccaccio, Cleland), a supreme delight, or for comic writers (Petronius, Erasmus), something ludicrous, or for memoirists (Pepys, Casanova), a track record. Lawrence's *Lady Chatterly's Lover* (1928), in particular, broke new ground (despite literary flaws) in its lengthy exposition of the sexual act and of the states of mind accompanying it, and in its repeated use of the forbidden four-letter words.

Not all modern works are liberated and celebratory. In some, sex is shown to be trivial and casual. The hero of Kafka's *Das Schloss* (*The Castle*, novel, 1926) has a brief affair with Frieda, partly in the hope of gaining access thereby to the higher powers at the castle and partly because she just happens to be there. The sexual act takes place amid garbage. Later, one also learns about the sexual advances made by one of the higher officials to Amalia and the adversity that her refusal brings upon the family. The brief, casual affairs of K. and of Joseph K. also illustrate the principle that (some? many?) women are erotically attracted to men in trouble. T. S. Eliot's dour view of sex is sketched in brief meaningless encounters (*The Waste Land*, poem, 1922), which are offered as symptomatic of the emptiness of modern secular life. When it is not trivial, sex may be a device of public policy. In Huxley's *Brave New World* (novel, 1932), it becomes an instrumentality of the well-organized society, a means—like the drug soma, like eugenics and social conditioning—of keeping everyone distracted and content. In the puritanical totalitarian society of Orwell's *1984* (novel, 1949), by contrast, sex, like other forms of individual fulfillment and expression, is severely circumscribed for the good of the state. In Mann's novel *Doktor Faustus* (1947), the composer-hero is an aloof individual, virtually asexual. In a chance encounter with a young lady at a brothel, he seems bestirred, follows her to another city, and, in the face of warnings about ill health, deliberately copulates with her and contracts syphilis. This sexual encounter (allegedly based on an incident in

Nietzsche's life), which leads paradoxically to musical creativity and to eventual madness, constitutes the modern version of the pact with the Devil and dramatizes the moral ambiguity both of art and of sex.

If nineteenth-century novelists, no matter how much eroticism they dealt with, eschewed graphic details, a reaction set in, especially after World War II, with the result that hardly a serious novel could be written that did not have the obligatory description in clinical detail of some form of sexuality. The trailblazers in many respects were *Lady Chatterly's Lover* and Henry Miller's autobiographical *Tropic of Cancer* (1934), as well as, in the field of memoirs, Frank Harris' *My Life and Loves* (1922–1927). Lawrence and Miller make an interesting contrast. Lawrence dramatizes sex (1) in connection with some form of tenderness or attraction; (2) among aristocratic or at least cultivated people; (3) in a lyrical manner, the physiological description being accompanied by an attempt to convey the attendant feelings; (4) in limited doses that punctuate the vocational and philosophical concerns of people. Miller, on the other hand, presents sex often; without love; among not quite reputable people; in an earthy manner, without gushes of emotion; and, throughout his major works, the philosophical and vocational concerns of his characters are almost invisible. Lawrence sees sex as an important repressed element in human psychology; Miller sees sex as virtually the only thing that matters. Lawrence tries to convey both the man's and the woman's sensibility in sex; Miller is interested in and persuasive about only the man, mainly himself, mainly his own penis. Lawrence is not afraid to hazard purple passages, mysticism, and quasi-religious sentiments; Miller is never afraid of being thought coarse, vulgar, indecorous, crude.

It is futile to try to list all the serious postwar writers who have wallowed in graphic details. It sometimes seems as if, from having not been considered a proper subject for literature, sex has become the only proper subject. Certainly one work remarkable for originality amid the new conformity to explicitness is Nabokov's novel *Lolita* (1955), which turns on the taboo subject of sexual encounters between a mature man and a pre-adolescent girl. The latest variant of the Heloïse and Abélard story or, according to one critic, the last decadent gasp of the Courtly Love tradition, its theme could easily become pornographic, sleazy, sadistic, or sensationalist. It results instead in a classic of the modern American novel because, while the story and the scenes are erotically charged, graphic details are sparingly and subtly used in conjunction with deft psychological observations, a masterful style, and a delicious comic perspective based on a running satire of contemporary American folkways.

Then, in the 1970s, the rise of the Woman's Liberation Movement in an age of total candor has opened a new approach to the subject: sex as women experience it rather than as men (even sympathetic and outspoken ones like Joyce and Lawrence) think they do or should. Erica Jong's *Fear of Flying* (novel, 1973) may be taken as a representative amusing and, because so different from the restraint of a Jane Austen or George Eliot, initially shocking work. If some would say that now, after *Lolita* and *Fear of Flying,* all parties to ''sexperience'' have been heard from, except possibly the humble subhuman semen, they have overlooked "Night-Sea Journey" (story, 1968), a monologue by a sperm cell (as overheard and faithfully translated by John Barth).

See also: Homosexuality, Lesbianism, Libertine, Love in Greek and Roman Literature, Seduction.

Selected Bibliography

Atkins, John. *Sex in Literature*. 4 vols. London: Calder and Boyars, 1970–1982.
Larue, Gerald. *Sex and the Bible*. Buffalo, N.Y.: Prometheus Books, 1983.
Partridge, Eric. *Shakespeare's Bawdy*. New York: E.P. Dutton, 1948.
Thompson, Roger. *Unfit for Modest Ears*. London: Macmillan, 1979.

MANFRED WEIDHORN

SHADOW

In English and other Indo-European languages, the word "shadow" covers a field of meaning usually articulated into three families of connotations: (1) comparative darkness and, figuratively, gloom, that is, shade; (2) image (dark figure) cast by a body intercepting light and, figuratively, an unreal appearance, a phantom (and in many languages, although rarely in English, the shade or ghost of a dead person); (3) shelter, especially from light and heat. In heraldry, the terms *umbra* (Latin), *ombre* (French), shadow and umbrage all mean ghost. This entry will concentrate on folkloric assumptions about the shadow as the dark image cast by a body and the literary themes and motifs developed on the basis of these beliefs: for example, the shadow as the measure of a person's vitality, the shadow lost or sold to the devil, the shadow in the form of a person's double. Some of the related connotations of the word "shadow" as used in language and literature will also be indicated briefly.

Folklore

It is one of the universal postulates of folklore that a person's attributes, such as his name and image, whether reflected naturally (in water, on a polished surface, in a mirror or as his shadow) or artificially (in a two- or three-dimensional shape, as a picture, sculpture, doll, or puppet), partake of that person's "essence" share his/her destiny and may, therefore, be subjected to danger and injury, natural or, in particular, magical. Such beliefs are attested to historically for all periods (from the ancient civilizations of the East and Graeco-Roman times to the twentieth century) and are found geographically in most, if not all parts of the world; they are abundantly documented, particularly for the so-called primitive tribes, and, in more developed nations and societies, for populations in relatively backward regions and among the less-educated strata. The types of beliefs and examples selected in this entry must, therefore, do duty for a multitude of others.

Basically, a person's shadow or reflected image is not just an optical phenomenon or, when separated from its source, a psychologically explainable hallucination, but an entity intimately linked with that person and often equated with his life-essence, strength, or soul. Among the many indigenous peoples of north-eastern Europe, northern Asia, the two Americas, sub-Saharan Africa, Tasmania, and the Pacific islands, linguistic designations for shadow and soul are related or identical. In certain tribal religions, but also in ancient Egypt, the shadow is one of the souls or the double of the soul that is in the living body. The shadow possesses the qualities of the person or object casting it and, in principle, is exposed to those same perils that attend the soul.

Consequently, the shadows of nefarious objects, animals and people are to be avoided: for example, the shadows of gallows, tombs, and certain stones (the rocky summit of Raggedstone in the Malvern Hills in England), or of women, particularly those menstruating or in mourning, or of the mother-in-law. In contrast, trees, saints, and gods have shadows that may heal or give life. Thus, the shadow of the breadfruit tree impregnates the Tahitian goddess Hina, the apostle Peter's *skia* in the Greek Acts of the Apostles (5:15), his *umbra* in the Latin Vulgate, cures the sick; in medieval legends and later sermons, the shadows of Christ and the Virgin perform miracles; there is a Christian tale in which the shadow of one corpse recalls another to life. (This is the origin of the expression "to overshadow," Gr. *episkiazein*, L. *obumbrare*, Ger. *überschatten*, used also in Luke when the angel salutes Mary as the future mother of Christ: "the power of the Highest shall overshadow thee" [1:35, King James's version].) For analogous reasons, in very many parts of the world, including North America and Europe, it was, and sometimes still is, improper or prohibited to step on somebody's shadow; generally, the shadow was accorded the same protection as a person.

Certain objects (e.g., stones, graves), animals (e.g., the hyena and crocodile, certain snakes), and most shamans and sorcerers could injure and capture the shadow; the rainbow is at times imagined to be a giant net cast to catch shadows. In the Balkans, masons are traditionally suspected of attempting to immure shadows (or their measurements) as a substitute for human sacrifice; in these regions, and especially in Romania, there are merchants who measure shadows and sell them to builders. A weak shadow (e.g., at noon) is a sign of diminished vitality and may provide an adversary with an opportunity for slaughter. The strength of Tukaitawa, the mighty hero of the Mangaians in South America, resided in his shadow; another warrior discovered his secret and slew him at noon. A shadow that grows, however, is a promise of good fortune, as in the Indian tale "The Carpenter's Daughter" in Somadeva's *Kathāsaritsāgara* (*Ocean of the Rivers of Tales*, c. 1070).

A disfigured or missing shadow may be an omen of death. In Ireland, the shadow can be bewitched and stabbed, thus prefiguring its owner's death. Fionn at last killed Cuirrech by thrusting a spear through his enemy's shadow. Similar legends are reported from the island of Wetar and from Nepal. Thus, the hero

Sankara was slain by the Grand Lama. A person whose shadow has been "snatched away" is expected to die within a year. In Wales it is said that anyone seated round the fire on Christmas Day and casting a headless shadow will die during the coming year. Similar beliefs about Christmas or New Year exist among the Germans and the Slavs; the old Germanic peoples linked such portents with the yule feast, which took place at approximately the same time of year as Christmastide. The loss of the shadow as punishment is part of Greek (and later of Christian) lore. Unwanted visitors to Zeus's sanctuary in Lycaeos were punished by losing their shadows and within a year their lives (mentioned as a fact by Polybius [c. 200–120 B.C.], Plutarch [c. A.D. 46–120], Pausanias [A.D. second cent.] and other sources). In the *Zohar* (an anonymous Jewish mystical text belonging to the Cabbala, written before the end of the thirteenth century), the shadow is the messenger who leaves shortly before death to proclaim to the four quarters of the earth that the body will follow.

It is possible to be without a shadow altogether, but this usually signifies impending doom or it is the consequence and external sign of illicit dealings with supernatural powers (Germanic countries, Spain). Those going to the devil's school of black magic (Iceland, Scandinavia, Scotland, Germany, Transylvania, Spain) or who seek his help in their work or in a competition (Ireland, Scotland, Lithuania, French Missouri) may have to pay with their shadow—the demon literally gets "the hindmost." Although the evil one is usually depicted as duped, because he really wanted the whole person, the shadowless man suffers, because he becomes an outcast. A woman refusing to bear children, especially if she uses magical means, may also forfeit her shadow (Finland, Sweden).

The particular idea that the shadow is both linked with the body casting it and is of lesser value or of no value at all is used in tales about imaginary offences and fraudulent bargains. For intercourse in a dream or the kissing of an image in a mirror, restitution is asked from the shadow; in Plutarch, for example, and in the Indian story "Bahur Danus," preserved in the collection of Sanskrit fables entitled *Panchatantra* (*Five Books*, c. 300–500). In an altogether serious context, this idea, well documented in law and custom, is also the basis of a range of medieval punishments inflicted on the shadow instead of the person himself (Germanic countries).

As they are already shades, the departed do not cast shadows. Similarly shadowless are ghosts, demons, ogres, gods, and even prophets (Muhammed, according to some Arabic legends), holy men (in Persian legends), and immortals (in Chinese lore). In a famous episode in the Indian epic *Mahabharata* (c. 5th century B.C.-A.D. 4th century), Nala's faithful spouse Damayanti recognizes the four gods (or the four-fold Indra) transformed into the shape of her husband, because their feet do not touch the ground, their flower garlands do not wilt, and they cast no shadows.

There are mythological and folkloric suggestions that the shadow may exist independently, or as a kind of double, or at least as a personal protective spirit, such as the Egyptian *ka,* the Germanic *fylgja,* the Christian guardian angel, and the modern Greek *iskios*. The shadow may, therefore, perform the role of helper or warning agent as, for instance, in the Irish folktale about a wife whose husband is a vampire. In Bulgarian and Serbian lore, probably inspired by the Bogomil creed, God felt so lonely that He created a companion, Lucifer, out of His own shadow. In other Gnostic legends, both Leviathan and Behemoth are created from God's shadow; Christ cuts off His shadow when He withstands Satan's blandishments. In Christian tradition, the term "shadow" is also used to designate the Holy Ghost.

It should be noted that most of these beliefs and customs are to be found not only in tales and legends, but having been used as literary motifs, they have left traces in popular sayings, which are in turn quoted and adapted by writers and philosophers. These range from the sombre to the light-hearted. The English proverb "No man can escape his shadow" is a faint echo of archaic beliefs about the shadow as an observer and judge of a person's deeds (central Africa, Chinese Taoist texts) and, after death, as an accusing witness of his actions (Lucian, *Menippos,* 11 [*Menippus,* dialogue, second cent.]). "To follow like a shadow" already used as a proverbial expression by Plautus (c. 254–184 B.C.) and Erasmus (1466–1536), becomes the modern "to shadow somebody." Because the shadow seems to flee when one attempts to approach it and to follow when one walks away, it has been compared to worldly honor (Spain), care (Elizabeth I, 1533–1603), and a mistress (Ben Jonson, 1572–1637). The fainthearted are "even afraid of their shadow" (Aristophanes, c. 448–380 B.C., Plato c. 427–347 B.C., Cicero, 106–43 B.C., and a familiar saying in French and German). "Beware lest you lose the substance by grasping at the shadow" is proverbial in many languages and the moral of the fable "The Dog and the Shadow," attributed to the semi-legendary Greek fabulist Aesop (c. 550 B.C.); it appears again in Jean de La Fontaine's *Fables* (1668–1694, in bk. 6, no. 17) and in similar collections by Lessing (1759), Krylov (1809–1844), and others.

Antiquity to the Enlightenment

Greek and Roman authors refer to beliefs about the shadow but do not develop any of the related motifs, with the exception of that describing the shadow's lack of substance. The "nothingness" of the shadow is in itself an age-old characteristic. It is popularized by proverbial expressions such as "to fight with shadows" by the Bible in expressions such as "our days on earth are as a shadow" (1 Chron. 29:15; cf. Job 14:2; Eccles. 6:12; The Apocrypha's Wisdom of Solomon 2:5), and by the classics in lines such as "like a shadow, like a dream" (Homer, *Odysseia,* [*Odyssey,* epic poem, bk. 11, ll. 204f.; c. 8th century B.C.]; Aesop and other fabulists; Democritus, Fragment 145, [c. 460 B.C.]; Aristophanes, *Ornithes* [*Birds,* 1.685, play, 414 B.C.]; Horace, *Carmina* [*Odes,* bk. 4, Ode 7.1.16, c. 23 B.C.]). There are many similar passages in Buddhist, Taoist, and Islamic (especially Sufic) writings. This idea appears later in such works as the medieval exemplum about a fool who cracks his skull while attacking his shadow with a cane (reproduced in nineteenth-century Italian and French collections—cf. *Index exemplorum,* ed. F. Tubach [1969], No. 2123), as well as in passing references in Sebastian Brant's satire *Das Narrenschiff* (*The Ship of Fools,* 1494), William Shakespeare's play *A Midsummer Night's Dream* (5. 1. 1.215; c. 1595), James Shirley's play *Contention of Ajax and Ulysses* (sc. 3; 1659), Daniel Defoe's political pamphlet *The True-Born Englishman* (pt. 2, 1.315; 1701), and in other works. The paradox of appearing as "something" and being almost "nothing," usually implied in the family of expressions mentioned so far, is exploited in popular riddles in many languages, including English. It is developed by Plato in the famous parable of the cave, which equates all phenomena of the world to shadows and images reflected in water and attributes essence only to Ideas (*Politeia* [*The Republic,* dialogue, c. 380 B.C.]). The idea that the shadow is more appearance than substance is used also by playwrights such as Shakespeare: "Life's but a walking shadow" (*Macbeth,* 5.5. 1.24, 1605–1606). This same idea is developed later by such authors as Johann Gottfried Herder (in the epigrammatic poem "Der Mensch und sein Schatte" ["Man and His Shadow"], 1787), Robert Louis Stevenson (in the humorous poem "My Shadow" in *A Child's Garden of Verses,* 1885, which also playfully employs some of the folkloric connotations), Robert Hamerling (in the philosophical poem *Homunkulus,* song 9, 1888), Richard Dehmel (in *Deutsche Chansons (Brettl-Lieder),* ed. O. J. Bierbaum [1900]), and, more importantly, by Friedrich Nietzsche (in "Der Wanderer und sein Schatten" in *Menschliches, Allzumenschliches,* bk. 2, pt. 2 ["The Wanderer and His Shadow" in *Human, All Too Human,* 1878]). The shadow as "not the real thing" is also used by T. S. Eliot in "The Hollow Men" (poem, 1925); Dylan Thomas's "shadowless man" is a vampire, living off the lives of others, a metaphor for the sterile self ("I, in my intricate image," pt. 1, 1935).

As a literary motif, the idea of the shadow's insubstantiality takes shape in an old Greek anecdote about the quarrel prompted by the shadow of a hired donkey. Does the shadow belong with the ass or not? As a proverbial saying, this is alluded to by Plato, Aristophanes, Plutarch, Lucian, and others; as an anecdote, it provided the basis of a comedy by Archippus (toward the end of the fifth century B.C.), of which only the title and fragments are extant. The German poet and novelist Christoph Martin Wieland turned this futile altercation about a donkey's shadow into an important litigation, utilizing it as a plot element in his satirical *Die Abderiten* (*The Abderites,* 1774), a novel that combines ideas of the Enlightenment with the rococo style in literature. The fourth book of this work, published in 1779 with the telling title *Onoskiamachia oder der Process um des Esels Schatten,* is imitated in a series of works: the burlesque comedy by August von Kotzebue (1810), the satirical comedy by Ludwig Fulda (1922), Friedrich Dürrenmatt's radio play (1951/1958), and a number of works by German writers of local renown. The main point is always that considerable consequences arise out of a fight about "nothing."

Passing references to the full range of folkloric beliefs and customs linked with the shadow are frequent during the pagan and Christian Middle Ages, as well as during the Renaissance and baroque; these beliefs are also often exemplified in short tales and legends. The healing shadow is depicted by artists; for instance, by Masaccio (1401–1428) in a fresco in the Brancacci Chapel of Santa Maria del Carmine (Florence); it is mentioned not only in pious legends, exempla, and sermons, but also by skeptical authors, albeit ironically, for example, the curative shadow of a monastery in Rabelais' novel *Gargantua* (1534).

Among the motifs, which usually gain popularity only with romanticism and the nineteenth century, the first to obtain literary status is that of the man who attends the devil's school to learn witchcraft and has no shadow afterwards. The demon is to have the last one who leaves the black school, but the apprentice steps aside, so that his shadow is caught—in S. Thompson's standard *Motif-Index of Folk-Literature* (1955–1958), these plot elements are classified as F 1038.1, S 241.2 and K 525.2. The devil is duped, for the moment at least, but the disciple is a marked man. These events are told in almost all parts of Europe about many legendary and historical figures, including priests and prelates, but the literary treatments crystallize around Salamanca in Spain and the notorious Don Enrique de Villena (1384–1433). In fact, it is only in the seventeenth century that Villena becomes linked with tales about magic rejuvenation, an attempted rebirth in a bottle, and the loss of his shadow. Comic and serious treatments of the nobleman's legendary life, including references to the shadow, are found in Ruiz de Alarcón (the comedy *La cueva de Salamanca* [*The Cave of Salamanca*, 1628]), Cervantes (the humorous interlude with the same title, 1615), and Francisco de Rojas Zorilla (the play *Lo que quería ver el marqués de Villena* [*What the Marquis de Villena Wished to See*, 1645]). There are a number of other Spanish and German texts that mention the same shadow motif, of which the best known are J.K.A. Musäus' free adaptation *Elias Walther* (in the collection of stories *Straussfedern*, 1787), Theodor Körner's ballad "Der Teufel in Salamanka" (1815), and especially José de Espronceda's romantic verse epic *El estudiante de Salamanca* (*The Student of Salamanca*, 1839–1840). An analogous experience, attributed to Michael Scott, is mentioned by Sir Walter Scott in the poem *The Lay of the Last Ministrel* (canto 2, stanza 13; 1805).

Romanticism and Beyond

The heydays of the different motifs associated with the shadow begin with the romantic period. One of the folkloric ideas, that of the shadow as strength and life-force, is first taken up by Goethe, who strongly contributes to the new interest in popular traditions. In an episode of his *Märchen* (*The Fairy Tale*, 1795), conceived as part of his *Unterhaltungen deutscher Ausgewanderten* (*The Recreations of the German Emigrants*, 1795), a giant's strength is in his shadow. Much later, in a historical romance set in China, *Le dragon impérial* (*The Imperial Dragon*, 1869) by Théophile Gautier's daughter Judith, the destiny of the peasant Ta-kiang, who leads the peasants in a civil war, is defined by the legend that "if the shadow of a man takes the form of a Dragon humbly following in his master's footsteps, he will one day hold in his hand the jade hilt of the

Imperial Sceptre," provided that the man remains totally unaware of this shadow. Ta-kiang has such a shadow, but in the decisive combat the young heir to the throne makes him confront the shadow and he is duly captured and executed. In folkloric terms the shadow is Ta-kiang's strength; psychologically, it is that self-knowledge that paralyzes.

The taboo of touching or being touched by the shadow, which is related to the idea that somebody's vital life-force rests in it, is mentioned repeatedly by Rudyard Kipling (e.g., in the novel *Kim,* chap. 10; 1901; and in the story "The Knife and the Naked Chalk," 1909). His ghosts (e.g., "The Phantom Rickshaw," 1888) and the double ("At the End of the Passage," 1890), are, true to form, shadowless. (With the same belief in mind, in Dante's epic *La divina commedia* [*Divine Comedy,* c. 1320] the dead recognize the poet as a living being, because he casts a shadow.) The best-known modern treatment of the shadow that disappears as the life-force ebbs away is Guillaume Apollinaire's tale "Le départ de l'ombre" ("The Departure of the Shadow," 1911). In the story by this avant-garde French author, who is associated with futurism and cubism and is considered a forerunner of surrealism, a man committing suicide in Rome is shadowless and the shadow of the narrator's mistress, Louise Ancette, leaves the girl after a bizarre encounter in the Marais quarter of Paris with a Jewish dealer in pawned goods. This happens on a Sabbath, exactly thirty days before her death, in keeping with Jewish lore, which is evoked by the merchant David Bakar. The psychological meaning of the events is in part linked with the narrator's unconscious wish to rid himself of his lover. Apollinaire displays interest in the supernatural and in shadow symbolism in other works, too. *L'ombre,* in dialectic tension with its opposites *lumière* ("light"), *soleil* ("sun"), and so on, is one of the key words and images of the poems in *Alcools* (1913), and the poetic voice addresses itself repeatedly to his own shadow. In the poem "L'ignorance" in *Il y a* (1925), Icarus, with the Faustian desire to become more than human, relinquishes his shadow and crashes to death, while the poet refuses to give up his own: "I gave everything to the sun / Everything but my shadow" (in the poem "Les fiançailles" ["The Betrothal"] in *Alcools),* because to "sell one's shadow" means to "sell one's soul," and therefore to die ("La chanson du mal-aimé" ["The Ballad of the Unloved One"] in the same collection). About his future the poet is ready to consult ordinary prophetesses, but not his shadow—"I know a sciomantic but I didn't want him to interview my shadow" (in the poem "Sur les prophéties" ["On Prophecies"], first published in 1914 and again in *Calligrammes* [*Calligrams,* 1918]). And in the poem "L'ombre" ("Shadow," in the same collection), the shades of his dead comrades-in-arms blend with the poet's own shadow as a symbol of his continuing unity, through memory, with those who have been close to him.

A whole variety of motifs about the shadow is used in the historical novel of the German expressionist Alfred Döblin, *Die drei Sprünge des Wang-lun* (*The Three Leaps of Wang-lun,* 1915), and among them those of the separated shadow and of subsequent inevitable death. Like Apollinaire, the contemporary German poet Hans Magnus Enzensberger'' refuses to put his shadow up for sale (''Schattenreich'' [''The Realm of Shadows''] in the collection *Blindenschrift* [*Braille,* 1964) while the novelist Günter Grass is proud that his ''body casts a shadow'' (in the poem ''Diana—oder die Gegenstände'' [''Diana—or the Objects,'' 1960]).

One of the forms taken by the motif about the shadow forfeited to the devil, that of the payment for forbidden knowledge, is used in baroque literature and revived by the romantics (Körner, Scott, Espronceda). Another variant, also linked with legends about satanic pacts and other folkloric materials, is created by an aristocratic refugee from the French Revolution who, as Adelbert von Chamisso, became an important lyric poet of German romanticism, a famous world traveller, and a respected botanist. In his novelle *Peter Schlemihls wundersame Geschichte* (*The Wonderful Story of Peter Schlemihl,* 1814), the protagonist, a poor young man without much experience, talent, and will-power (the Yiddish *shlumiel,* English ''schlemiel'' is a foolish or unlucky person), sells his shadow to the devil who, dressed in grey at a party, pulls out of his pocket everything rich people might desire—from a wallet and bandages to a tent and three black horses. For his shadow, which the man in grey picks up, folds, and puts away as though it were a piece of cloth, Schlemihl obtains an inexhaustible bag of gold (the purse of Fortunatus, another figure of German lore), but he soon rues the bargain. Everybody shuns a man without a healthy shadow, so that he has to avoid both sun and moon and arrange a home with special lighting to abolish all shadows; rich as he is, he loses his beloved Mina to his former servant, the false Rascal. While the fate of the girl is still in the balance, the man in grey appears mockingly before Schlemihl and proposes to return the shadow in exchange for his soul. The young man faints at the crucial moment and is thus saved ''not by a decision, but an event.'' At a subsequent meeting with the devil, he throws away the magic purse, and having inadvertently bought a pair of seven-league boots at a parish fair, he decides to find his peace of mind in travels and in the study of nature.

Narrated with mild irony vis-à-vis middle-class values, the story is partly autobiographical, concerning the author's alienation in Prussia during the Napoleonic Wars; in spite of or perhaps because of its didactic flavor, it enjoyed world-wide success in the nineteenth century and elicited a very considerable body of interpretative criticism. Besides exploring Chamisso's probable folkloric and literary sources (although a convincing older example of the particular bargain in question has yet to be established), critics have concentrated on the meaning of the shadow and its loss. Thus, the shadow has been equated with a person's country, with the totality of a man's social external position, or with certain aspects of middle-class existence (external honor, reputation, respectability, sociability), with alienation in capitalism, and with sexuality and impotence. In any case, the shadow is not the soul, because the devil is trying to arrange a second deal amounting to the bartering of the one for the other. It is also possible to analyze this modern fairytale *(Kunstmärchen)* as an artistic experiment exploring logically the natural, legal, financial, and social results of a fantastic and fanciful premise—something in the nature of Franz Kafka's "Die Verwandlung" ("Metamorphosis," story, 1915). Be that as it may, the shadow is here a symbol and, since significant indefiniteness is characteristic of symbols, several meaning may apply simultaneously. There is no doubt that the author, who has a role in the narrative and who later hints at contradictory interpretations, is also playing a game that abounds in humor, satire, irony, and paradox.

There have been many adaptations and continuations of Peter Schlemihl's marvellous adventures, some as narrative fiction, others in dramatic form; as a rule, they include the problem of the shadow. Chamisso's novelle inspired episodes in otherwise unrelated plots, too, as for example in Théophile Gautier's fanciful story "Onuphrius" (1832), in which the protagonist is obsessed with the idea that, because of his dabbling in magic, he has lost both his mirror-reflection and his shadow. Better known is J(ames) M(atthew) Barrie's play *Peter Pan,* or *The Boy Who Would Not Grow Up* (1904), which was transformed much later into a popular full-length animated cartoon by the Walt Disney Studio (1952). The sash-window in the children's room cuts off Peter Pan's shadow like a guillotine, and Mrs. Darling, like the man in grey, rolls it up, commenting: "There is money in this, my love." Peter Pan, the flying boy from Never Never Land, has to return, looking for his lost companion. Once the shadow is found, he tries to attach it to his body through contact, then with soap, and, at last, the girl Wendy has to stitch it on. The question of the shadow as symptomatic of the "incomplete," "arrested" human (and sexual) development of the youngster is not explored further.

In a more serious and sometimes sombre fashion, Chamisso's novelle contributed features to works about doubles *(Doppelgänger)* and mirror-images *(Spiegelbild)*. Of the lost mirror-images indebted to Chamisso, the best known are those in E.T.A. Hoffmann's story "Geschichte vom verlornen Spiegelbilde" ("The Story of the Lost Reflection," 1815), in which Schlemihl appears also as one of the characters, a yarn adapted in Jacques Offenbach's best-known opera *Les contes d'Hoffmann* (*The Tales of Hoffmann,* 1881) and revived in 1951 in Powell and Pressburger's British film combining dancing and singing; in Nathaniel Hawthorne's story "Monsieur du Miroir," 1837; probably also in Guy de Maupassant's short story "Le Horla" ("The Horla," 1887); an episode in R. M. Rilke's novel *Aufzeichnungen des Malte Laurids Brigge* (*The Notebook of Malte Laurids Brigge,* 1910); and Franz Werfel's drama *Der Spiegelmensch* (*The Man in the Mirror,* 1920).

Another folkloric loss of the shadow, this time because of a woman's refusal to bear children out of concern for her beauty and life, is the central motif of the cycle of ballads *Anna* (1838), written by the Austrian romantic poet Nikolaus Lenau. The same basic story is told in innumerable Scandinavian and in some Lettish, West Slavic, and Romance oral variations; Lenau knew a Swedish oral source and the ballad of his friend L. A. Frankl, "Die Kinderlose" (1836), but he goes beyond a simple exploitation of a traditional theme and form. In his work, the lost shadow becomes the gripping symbol of diminished humanity. A similar motif about an unfaithful man who loses his shadow, known in Scottish and German legends, yields the weft for another Lenau ballad, "Der einsame Trinker" (1840).

The theme of the barren and shadowless woman finds other German and Scandinavian treatments in the nineteenth century. Nevertheless, the best known and artistically most important works using this theme are firstly, the opera *Die Frau ohne Schatten* (*The Woman without a Shadow,* libretto by the Austrian modernist poet and writer Hugo von Hofmannsthal and music by Richard Strauss (written in 1913–1915, published in 1916, performed in Vienna in 1919) and then, Hofmannsthal's story under the same title (written in 1913–1919, published in 1919). The plots of the two texts are similar, but the author, and most critics, preferred the more complex "artistic fairy-tale." The use of the shadow motif is twofold: the Empress, daughter of the King of Spirits, is shadowless because of her origin and her secluded life style. Through prophecies, she learns that if she fails to acquire a shadow, as punishment for her desertion of her father's realm, she will remain childless and her beloved husband will be turned into stone. At first, the Empress accepts her evil nurse's advice to buy the shadow of a poor, pretty, and discontented woman in exchange for magic prosperity and love, but also for the curse of infertility. After many temptations and vicissitudes, the Empress undertakes human suffering and renounces magic solutions; she then obtains her shadow and her husband comes back to life. It is only in this way that she becomes part of humanity and achieves existential reality. The fairy-tale elements and Oriental traits are reminiscent of *Alf Layla wa-layla* (*The Arabian Nights,* 8th to 17th centuries) and of Goethe's, Novalis's, Chamisso's and Andersen's experiments with *Märchen*; the folkloric motifs are authentic, while the loss of the shadow is indebted to Lenau. Still, the artistic maturity and ethical and religious meanings are Hofmannsthal's alone.

A very different link between shadow and maternity is established in a short story by the contemporary Australian author Gwen Kelly. In "The Shadow" (1973), in a family obsessed with progeny, a woman gives birth to three children; she is first reduced to her shadow and then swept away with the dust. In itself, the shadow that remains after a person passes away is also a motif with folkloric connotations. The two best known literary transpositions are probably the ballad "Der Schatten" (1855), by the late romantic poet Eduard Mörike, and the sonnet under the same title, published in 1963, by the contemporary German poet Günter Kunert. In the ballad, the unfaithful Frau Hilde poisons her husband, who takes revenge as a phantom; after the woman's death, her shadow remains on the wall exactly in the position she had occupied while falsely pledging to remain constant. The shadow is also a warning sign in Kunert's sonnet, but there it announces the guilt of somebody else. In Hiroshima visitors are shown the arch of a bridge on which is imprinted the shadow of a human being who disappeared in the explosion of the atomic bomb.

From the folkloric and psychological perspectives, the ultimate development of the shadow motif is its blending with that of the double (examples are restricted here to those employing the shadow itself). The oldest and most significant literary work of this kind is Hans Christian Andersen's short novella *Skyggen* (*The Shadow,* 1847). The Danish poet and writer of world-famous artistic fairy tales, who was a personal friend of Chamisso and who knew E.T.A. Hoffmann's works very well, depicts the destiny of a scholar who inadvertently loses his shadow through curiosity when he sends him to explore a mysterious house across the street. At first, the narrative proceeds in a light-hearted ironic tone. The scholar grows another shadow, as if it were his hair or nails, and is more concerned about his adventure's lack of originality than about other adverse consequences. But the tale becomes increasingly dark and the events tragic. The shadow reappears and while the learned man pursues, without social success, "what is true, good and beautiful," the shadow finds public acclaim and wins a princess's heart. As the shadow is without a proper shadow, he hires his former "master" to play the shadow's role and so offers himself the luxury of being a shadow with a shadow. In the end, the scholar rebels and is beheaded. In many aspects, the shadow is here the individual's dark brother, but his function is essentially that of unmasking society's preference for appearance over substance and for a knave over an idealist.

Translated into most languages, this novella has been adapted into a television film (West Germany, 1963) and freely dramatized by Hans Reinhart (1921) and Evgenii Shvarts (*Ten'* [*Shadow,* 1940]). A specialist of dramatizations of fairy tales by the brothers Grimm and by Andersen, Shvarts retains the original plot but uses one of the aspects of the motif of the double so as to attenuate the outcome. In genuine stories about the double, there is usually a vital link between the "original" and the "copy" or between the two elements of the pair. In the play, when the head of the scholar rolls, the enthroned shadow suddenly becomes headless also. Both are revived by "the water of life," familiar through many folktales, and the scholar is rehabilitated, but the shadow escapes and remains an ever-threatening adversary. (Allusions to the historical moment and ideological emendations are designed to make the play suitable for the Soviet public.)

In a very limited way, Nietzsche in "Der Wanderer und sein Schatten" ("The Wanderer and His Shadow") is also using the shadow as a double. Added in 1880 to a collection of aphorisms written in 1878 and 1879, it is a framing text, respectively two and three pages long, explaining that in his solitude, the Wanderer (identified with the author) reverted to dialogue with his shadow and that the aphorisms are the result of their conversations. The shadow is "natural," but able to speak and symbolically linked with that insight which is the product of "the sunshine of understanding" and of reflection, but he is not an antagonist or antipode: "It seems almost as if I were talking aloud to myself." The shadow dissipates with the sunset, begging to take leave, because "the grass is damp and I am cold." Later, the even lonelier wanderer Zarathustra (*Also sprach*

Zarathustra [*Thus Spoke Zarathustra,* prose poem, 1883–1892]) addresses his monologues to his shadow and in the chapter entitled "The Shadow," unsuccessfully attempts to flee from him.

In Oscar Wilde's novella *The Fisherman and His Soul* (1891), a fisherman falls in love with a mermaid and follows her into her idyllic realm. To be able to do so, he sends his shadow-soul into the world and refuses to give him the heart that belongs to the little siren. The shadow returns and tempts the fisherman with wisdom, then wealth, and when this is of no avail, with stories about unknown pleasures and a young girl who has feet and can dance. The fisherman leaves the sea and can never return; it is only in death that the repentant lover is reunited with both his shadow-soul and the beloved siren. Although the story is anchored in folklore (there is, for instance, a flat statement that "What men call the shadow of the body is not the shadow of the body, but is the body of the soul"), the meaning depends more on the psychological split of the personality into its loving, emotional, irrational, trusting, introverted part and its materialistic, rational, deceitful, egotistic, even evil, extroverted component.

Another detached and aggressive shadow, hated and feared by the person who had once projected it, is staged by Stanisław Przybyszewski, a Polish fin-de-siècle Satanist. In his short play *Goście* (*The Visitors,* 1901), the shadow returns to hound the protagonist, with the characteristic name of Adam, threatening never to leave him again; the shadow claims that it may grow vampiric wings and claws and may strangle his former master (sc. 5). Not altogether different is Franz Theodor Csokor's expressionist drama *Der Baum der Erkenntnis: Ein Mythos* (1919). The shadow embodies the Man's sexuality and leaves him during the day; the Woman prefers the shadow, but returns to the Man in her need for protection and help.

It is fitting to close this overview of literary works dealing with the shadow with a curious short narrative by the German writer and graphic artist Christoph Meckel, "Die Schatten" (1962), which combines folkloric elements with metatextual surrealism and with the postmodern technique of "a text which is writing itself." On the level of the plot, instead of concentrating on the victim, Meckel's narrative voice is that of a dealer in shadows, who, with his agents, openly collects shadows of objects, plants, animals, and people, selling them for money or bartering them for other shadows. In the great Oriental city on the two sides of a mighty river, in which his trade is flourishing, it becomes fashionable to exchange shadows or to acquire a more imposing one, until rebellious shadows start taking over and influencing their carriers in nefarious, even lethal ways. A second level of the grotesque narrative is established by intertextual references to previous treatments of the shadow motif, especially Chamisso's and Hofmannsthal's, and a third one is created by steadily positioning the writing process itself in the foreground, so that the catastrophe in the action coincides with the author's inability to manipulate the story any further.

Marginal and Allusive Uses of the Shadow

A number of literary works, some of them fairly well known, employ "shadow" in their title. This is already the case with Jean Renart's famous romance *Le lai de l'ombre* (*The Lay of the Shadow*, thirteenth century), which does not concern the shadow, but the shadowlike image of a lady in a fountain. Edgar Allan Poe's renowned tale "Shadow" (1835) and Franz Theodor Csokor's short story "Schattenstadt" (1931) are about the dead. The Argentine modernist and postmodernist Jorge Luis Borges published in 1969 a poem and a collection of poetry both with the same title *Elogio de la sombra* (literally, In Praise of the Shadow, 1969), but *sombra* here signifies "darkness," so that the two titles are correctly translated as *In Praise of Darkness* (1974).

Other titles either rely on existing connotations or create new connotations of the word itself, without reference to the usual folkloric or literary motifs. In Wilhelm von Scholz's drama *Der Wettlauf mit dem Schatten* (*The Race with the Shadow*, 1921) and in Edzard Schaper's tale *Schattengericht* (*The Shadow Trial*, 1967), the shadow points to an author's fictional characters; in Siegfried Lenz's novel *Duell mit dem Schatten* (*Duel with the Shadow*, 1953), and in Fried Noxius' novel *Der verlorene Schatten* (1959), the shadow stands for the past. In Colin Wilson's novel *Man without a Shadow: The Diary of an Existentialist* (1963) and in Fathī Ghānim's novel *Al-Rajul alladhī fagada zillahu* (*The Man Who Lost His Shadow*, c. 1960), the shadow is a symbol of lost freedom and integrity; it is a positive sign of the dissolution of the individual self in Barbara Frischmuth's novel *Das Verschwinden des Schattens in der Sonne* (*The Disappearance of the Shadow in the Sun*, 1973). Peter Weiss's experimental prose *Der Schatten des Körpers des Kutschers* (*The Shadow of the Coachman's Body*, 1960) concentrates in some passages on the precise description of the shadow, employed as synecdoche. And in the chapter "Die Heimat der Schatten" ("The Homeland of Shadows") in Joseph Roth's meditation about contemporary society, *Der Antichrist* (*The Antichrist*, 1934), the home of shadows is Hollywood, since films are flickering shadows, a topic that is linked with shadow-plays, the Chinese and Javanese shadow-theater, the eighteenth-century infatuation with drawing, cutting, and projecting silhouettes, and so on.

A more complex case is the novel *Don Segundo Sombra* (translated as *Don Segundo Sombra: Shadows on the Pampas*, although there is no subtitle in the 1926 original) by the Argentine modernist Ricardo Güiraldes. The narrator, Fabio Cáceres, matures and becomes a gaucho under the mentorship of Segundo Sombra, who enters and leaves his life like a shadow: "Without moving, I observed that silhouette which was cut against the lighted horizon by the rider and his horse; it seemed to me that I had seen a phantom, a shadow, something which passes and is more like an idea than a being." The name of the old gaucho is highly symbolic. He is "the second one," because the first is the national hero, the exemplary gaucho Martín Fierro in José Hernández's epic by the same name (1872–1879); he is a "shadow," because he is an embodiment of the legendary past and, in some ways, is also the narrator's guardian spirit. Despite the realism of the novel and the convincing flesh and blood plasticity of Segundo Sombra's character, the presence of the mythic dimension in the work is alluded to clearly in two passages (one quoted here) and in the symbolism of his name.

Interpretation

The shadow as motif, symbol, and literary theme is subject to folkloric, psychological, philosophical, and literary interpretations. Although intimately interrelated, these explanations have distinctive features.

Manifestations of folklore, that is, the body of customs, legends, beliefs, and superstitions passed on by oral tradition, are studied today as a people's imaginative expressions of its desires, attitudes, and cultural values at a prerational, prescientific stage of development. Whether in custom and ritual or in folkliterature, the shadow has both positive and negative potential, but with the exception of certain riddles, it is normally treated seriously. Frequently, it is associated with danger and premonitions of death; the realm of the departed is at a secondary stage of beliefs in immortality (the primary one being apparently very material), presented as the world of shades, in which shadows live out a shadowy existence, feeding on shadows of things.

The psychological significance of the shadow is established mainly in two ways. It is taken to be instrumental in a child's development of a personal body image, and it is defined as one of the major human archetypes. The French psychoanalyst Jacques Lacan argues in his article "Le stade du miroir" ("The Stage of the Mirror," 1936) that the awareness of the "I" *(je)* and of its alienating separateness is formed by mirror images of the self, primarily those in the looking-glass, but also by the shadow. (Children's games with the shadow could be quoted in support of such a theory.) For Sigmund Freud, the shadow is part of the potent and often mythical dream symbols of the individual unconscious. When Carl Gustav Jung postulated two dimensions of the unconscious—the personal and the collective—he defined the shadow as one of the essential archetypes, that is, images, patterns, and symbols that are seen in dreams or fantasies and that appear as themes in mythology, religion, and fairy tales. In contrast to the light of consciousness, the shadow is the darkness of the personal unconscious, the other, unfathomed side of the personality, its secret sharer. The shadow includes those sombre traits belonging to the same sex and is representative of the least-developed, inferior function of Jung's four types of consciousness (thinking, feeling, perceiving, and intuiting); the shadow is everything that the individual refuses to accept or understand in himself, in spite of the fact that these tendencies or character traits present themselves with persistence, directly or indirectly, in dreams, unguarded words, and impulsive actions. If not assumed and integrated, the shadow may become evil and destructive. In the collective unconscious, the shadow represents archetypal evil; referring to gnostic and alchemic lore, Jung extends this analysis to God or Christ and Satan. For him, in myth, one of the antagonistic brothers or twins is a shadow symbol; in folktales this is, among others, the function of serpents and dragons (cf. Marie Luise von Franz, *Shadow and Evil in Fairy Tales,* 1974).

In a broader anthropological, even philosophical perspective, the shadow is one of the polarities in the binary set of light and darkness; it is also a symbol of appearance and transience and therefore opposed to substance and stability. While the latter idea is developed, for example, by Plato and Neoplatonism, including that of Christian thinkers and Islamic mystics, the former stands, for instance, at the very heart of the Chinese philosophy of *yin* and *yang.* Etymologically and according to the ideographic signs for these two principles, they have been developed from the concepts ''the side of the valley which is covered by clouds and in the shade'' and ''the side of the valley which is exposed to sunshine,'' and they were later expanded to include all the major polarities of life and the universe. In a broad symbolic sense, as the sun is the light of the spirit, so the shadow is the negative double of the body, the image of its wicked and base side.

Interpretations of particular literary works depend upon all these possible meanings and their interaction. Nevertheless, as a rule two considerations go beyond the particular: firstly, the author's position within or outside specific beliefs and significations attached to the shadow; secondly, the text as it pertains to a particular genre and mode of literature. The first consideration is usually determined by the time and place of an author's activity; within the Western tradition, beliefs of this kind cease to be accepted by the official culture in the Age of Enlightenment, but are revived for artistic purposes by romanticists and for personal reasons by individual authors. Compared to other motifs belonging to this type, such as the double, enchanted images, phantoms, and so on, the shadow is rarely used as a vehicle for the supernatural and fantastic. In nineteenth- and twentieth-century fiction, these are often presented as disquieting irruptions of the inexplicable into a world which is otherwise realistically depicted and that is in conformity with the laws of causality and nature as defined by science. This motif usually shifts more radically from folkloric attitudes to symbolic and psychologic interpretations.

The second consideration is that of genre and mode. The shadow is used in all three basic kinds of literature, that is, poetry, drama, and narrative fiction, and within each kind in a variety of genres and subgenres, as well as modes (tragic, comic, ironic, parodic, etc.). The most important differentiation in this respect is still that inherited from the stances embedded in two of the basic forms of oral narrative: the legend and the folktale. Whether presented as personal experience, as a story about particular figures, or as a general explanation of certain phenomena, legends lie somewhere between myth and fact and always maintain a claim to truthfulness. The folktale, especially when embodying marvellous elements (therefore often called fairy tale or tale of magic, *conte de fées, Zaubermärchen),* gingerly oversteps most boundaries of reality and freely admits its fictional, fantastic, and playful status. While this division is essential to folklore, it has left its traces in romantic and later treatments of the shadow.

Many of the best-known texts, from Goethe to Hofmannsthal, by way of Chamisso, Andersen, and Wilde, belong to the genre of the artistic fairy tale *(Kunstmärchen)*; in addition and to different degrees, they incorporate elements of legends and of modern psychology, but also features characteristic of didactic literary forms such as the parable, fable, and allegory. Other texts (by Lenau, Mörike, Kipling, and Apollinaire, e.g.) are closer to the position adopted by legends.

Empirical reader reaction will depend on the work in question and on the individual's world view and literary sophistication. What is important is not only the reader's belief or disbelief in shadow lore and his ability to exercise a willing suspension of disbelief, but also his capacity to perceive and accept the conventions governing the different genres and modes.

See also: Evil, Mirror, Personality (Double-Split-Multiple).

Selected Bibliography

Bieler, [Ludwig]. "Schatten." *Handwörterbuch des deutschen Aberglaubens*. Ed. Hanns Bächtold-Stäubli. Berlin-Leipzig: de Gruyter, 1927–1942. 9: Nachtrag 126–146.

Jameson, Raymond Deloy. "Shadow." *The Funk and Wagnalls Standard Dictionary of Folklore, Mythology and Legend*. New York: Funk and Wagnalls, 1949–1950. 2:1000–1001.

Peterkiewicz, Jerzy. "Cast in Glass and Shadow." *New Literary History* 5 (1974):353–361.

Wilpert, Gero von. *Der verlorene Schatten: Varianten eines literarischen Motivs*. Stuttgart: Kröner, 1978.

MILAN V. DIMIĆ

SIREN

The ancestor of the mermaids can be traced to the Babylonian fish god Oannes, represented as a benevolent deity in human form, but decked in a fish headgear and scaly mantle. His female counterpart was Phoenician Derceto, also known as Atargatis, a goddess whose upper half was female but lower body ended in a fish tail. She was a Moon goddess associated with sexual attraction, fickleness, and cruelty, characteristics that can be found in mermaids up to modern times.

On archaic Greek vases sirens might be depicted in either male or female guise, half bird and half human. They soon, however, became exclusively half woman and half bird. In later mythologies and in different parts of the world, they became half woman and half snake, as is the case for Mélusine, or half woman and half fish, as is the case for nixies, nereids, water sprites, or undines. In the case of the Rhine maidens, they are often pictured with extremities that end in one fin, while such monsters as the Mediterranean Scylla would have octopus or hydralike lower bodies. Already in his *Romaunt of the Rose*, 5.1.684

(c. 1366), Chaucer noted that the French had confused sirens with mermaids at an early period.

By definition, sirens are seductive women whose song is superlatively sweet and who lure unwary males, especially sailors, to a watery grave. There are, however, exceptions to that sweeping statement, as sphinxes are half feline and half female, and evil spirits such as lamias, empuses, and vampires may be included in the group of temptresses. In any case, most sirens are associated with water, whence they issue, and their undulating hair is flowing like seaweed. In more general terms, they are dual creatures, human or even angelic on top, and animal in their lower parts.

Background in Pagan Antiquity

In book 12 of the epic poem *Odysseia* (*Odyssey,* 8th century B.C.), Homer's Odysseus is warned by the enchantress Circe to outwit the lures of the sirens' song by filling his crew's ears with wax and by attaching himself to the ship's mast. Yet Circe herself bears all the attributes of a siren. She too sings sweetly, lures, and detains men, whom she magically transforms into beasts by a reverse process. She also can be outwitted by the more potent magic of the initiated. Just after Odysseus escapes from the song of the sirens, he encounters Scylla, a sea-monster who is half female and fair of face and torso, yet a tangled mass of fearful serpents from the waist down. It is significant that Homer mentions but two sirens whereas the poet Apollonius of Rhodes, in his *Argonautika* (*Argonauts,* epic poem, 3d century B.C.), mentions three who live on the Island Anthinoussa off the Italian coast and who constitute a regular musical trio. One sings while the second plays the flute and the third provides the lyre accompaniment. According to other later classical authors, such as Ovid in his epic poem *Metamorphoses* (c. A.D. 2–17, bk. 5, 552–653), Hyginus in his *Liber fabularum* (mythology, dates unknown, bk. 14, 125–141), and Pausanias in his *Periēgēsis tēs Hellados* (*Description of Greece,* 2d century A.D., bk. 9, 343), the sirens are shown in a rather favorable light. They sing mournfully while lamenting the demise of their companion Proserpina. They had once been princesses, daughters of King Archelaus and Queen Calliope, and voluntarily transformed themselves into birds in order to search for their departed friend Persephone. They live off Sicily on an island close to Scylla and have retained the glorious beauty of their voices. In Hellenistic tradition, they are said to represent music as much as the Muses. According to Apollonius, Orpheus saved the Argonauts from the lure of the sirens' song. In this case they were reputed to live in Hades and to be the daughters of Gaia. Some authorities think they were birds inhabited by the souls of the dead.

In his Latin epic poem *Aeneis* (*Aeneid,* 19 B.C.), Virgil transposes the themes offered by his mentor, Homer. He again paints Scylla as a maid transformed into a sea monster by a marine god she spurned. Thus her upper half remains that of a pretty maiden, while her lower extremities end in dolphins' tails and other snakelike appendages (bk. 3, 425). As far as his version of the sirens is concerned, he infuses characteristics borrowed from the Harpies as depicted in Homer's *Odyssey*. Celaeno their leader, prophesies and exculpates the flock from wrongdoing, while the sisters are presented as victims seeking just revenge. Aeneas, or Virgil his creator, wonders whether these sirens, basically innocent and harassed creatures, are "goddesses or filthy sea birds" (3, 256–270).

In the Hindu *Mahabharata,* (epic poem that dates back to the 5th or 4th century B.C.), we can already find some themes parallel with the medieval French Mélusine. The same phenomenon applies to the Rig Veda (hymns, c. 1500–1200 B.C.), wherein the nymph Urvasi must not be seen in the nude by her husband Pururavas. After he disobeys the prohibition, his wife flees forever from his side. In Syria, Dorkedo, the Fertility Mother, is a city builder identified with Venus or Astarte, although her body ends in a fish tail (Xenophon, *Anabasis,* history, 4th century B.C., 4–49). Eventually she reverts into a total fishlike state after having loved a young Syrian mortal (Lucian, *Peri tēs Syriēs theou* [*The Syrian Goddess*, satire, 2d. century A.D.]).

In Germanic and in Scandinavian mythology, as typified by the *Nibelungenlied* and the *Edda* (epic poems, c. 1200), one finds the "Meerfrauen," nixies, or Danube sirens. These are water spirits who were to be eventually transformed into the Wagnerian Rhine maidens at a much later date. They all belong to the fluvial and watery element; they are associated with gold and with hoard, and their character is somewhat ambivalent. In some cases, they fall victims to trickery, as connived by the knight Hagen, but in others, they are uncaring if not dangerous. In any case, they are devoid of moral character.

In late classicism, especially in the second century A.D., as featured in the treatise of Phlegon of Tralles, *Peri thaumasion (Mirabilia),* these semianimal female creatures become empuses, lamias, or vampires, all spectres who destroy men. Similar traits can be found in Celtic mythology where Cú Chulaínn is seduced by the wife of the Sea God Má Naán. The irresistible temptress can also be found in the much more ancient *Gilgamesh Epic* (c. 2000 B.C.) of Babylonia, where love is fraught with ambivalence, and the incestuous goddess is fatal to the young hero.

Biblical Mythology

In the Bible (Isa. 12:22, Vulgate), the prophet alludes to an imaginary species of serpent, a sort of winged adder. Shakespeare and Milton later borrowed this song of doom. In Genesis, Eve is closely associated with the Serpent, and so are countless other biblical characters such as Delilah, Potiphar's wife, and other seductresses who through their honeyed words and wiles would induce a naïve youth into sin. Saint Paul especially issued warnings to the faithful against the lures of the harlots.

The Medieval Period

The medieval siren blends her prehistorical roots with a Christian background in which the Crusades play an important part. The Mélusine character is the most international and pervasive. Although Jehan d'Arras selects Poitou as the locale of his novel, *Mélusine* (*Romance of Melusine,* c. 1390), one can find Oriental and pagan features borrowed from the Great Syrian Mother Dorkedo and Atargatis therein. In a more direct fashion the legend is connected with the traditions surrounding the House of Lusignan. Many elements are contained in it and echoes reverberate into the past. The very tale presents a variation of the Eros and Psyche theme. Mélusine herself displays elements of the Magna Mater of the Gauls, a giantess, a city builder, and finally a "fée-serpente." On the other hand, she is an exemplary Christian wife and mother. Yet despite these attributes, she too belongs to a hybrid race of semiaquatic and air-borne creatures. Her direct origin is Scottish. Her mother, Pressine, whose fate seems to foreshadow her daughter's, is met in typical fashion at a well, while she combs her hair and sings sweetly, by Brumblico, who marries her after he promises never to see his wife in the act of child-bearing or tending. The father infringes upon the taboo and is imprisoned in a mountain by his eldest daughter, Mélusine. The latter is thereupon set adrift and is promised a knightly husband. Like her mother who met Brumblico by a well, Mélusine meets Raimondin de Lusignan by a well. She also enthralls her would-be suitor by her voice and by her cascading locks, which she combs. She admonishes him of the taboo to which he must submit. Her husband-to-be must never behold her or seek her presence on any Saturday. Mélusine is a happy bride, a good stewardess to her husband, an indefatigable citadel and castle builder, and a good mother to twelve beautiful sons who all bear a demonic blemish of a feral nature. Urged by a jealous brother, the husband breaks into his wife's secret chamber on a Saturday and finds her thrashing about a well, endowed with a giant snake's tail in lieu of legs. At the discovery of her husband's betrayal of faith, Mélusine jumps off a window sill and transforms herself into a winged serpent, circling thrice around her former estate while uttering unearthly screams. She is never seen again, except by the youngest of her infants, whom she consoles stealthily by night in her former human shape.

This legend captured the medieval imagination and spread like wildfire. A French version in verse was composed by the troubadour Couldrette, who wrote *Li livres de Lusignan* in the fourteenth century. A similar fragment was created by the Swiss Thüring von Ringoltingen (*Die schöne Melusine,* 1456). Around 1500 there appeared an English translation of Jehan d'Arras' novel, while other texts quite close to the original appeared in Spanish, Dutch, Russian, and Polish. Of course, there are some local variations in details. Mélusine is Wanda, the Water Sprite for the Poles. She jumps into the Vistula to redeem her people, whereas her Russian counterpart, Meljuzini, in less beneficent fashion, surrounds the ships in an attempt to seduce and drown unwary sailors in her half-female half-fish form.

Actually, even before the Jehan d'Arras version gained popularity, similar themes appeared. For example, in Egenolf von Staufenberg's poem, *Peter von Staufenberg* (c. 1310), a beautiful woman protects a knight since his childhood and later gives him her love on condition that he must never marry another nor divulge his love secret. After breaking his promise in order to marry the king's daughter, the knight promptly dies. The folklore of many parts of the world abounds with similar themes that recur from India to Avalon and the Court of King Arthur's Knights. It resurfaces in Esthonia with only minor transpositions, such as the taboo applying to Thursday rather than Saturday. In the latter case the siren takes her lover underwater with her, while she is endowed with a fishlike appendage rather than a snake's.

The Renaissance through Romanticism

In his tragedy *Antony and Cleopatra* written in 1607, Shakespeare compares his heroine's fatal lures with the song of the sirens. She is associated with the adder. In 1671, in his dramatic poem *Samson Agonistes,* John Milton, in a similar vein, equates Delilah's deceitful blandishments with the serpent song as mentioned in the Book of Isaiah.

It is not surprising that this legendary theme suffered a temporary eclipse during the Age of Reason and the Enlightenment. In the work of F. Nodot, *Histoire de Mélusine* (1698), the theme is watered down to the level of a "roman galant." In 1757, the same theme is reduced to a parody in F. W. Zacharia's mock epic poem *Murner in der Hölle (Tabby in Elysium).* In a similar vein, Goethe's *Die neue Melusine (New Melusina,* story, 1817), hardly deserves consideration here, as it represents mainly a parody on the topic. Yet Goethe composed a more relevant poem, the ballad "Der Fischer," ("The Fisherman"), in 1779 wherein a siren drags a man down into the water so as to prevent him from beholding her bodily anomalies.

There is a marked recrudescence of interest in the Mélusine theme in the nineteenth century. L. Tieck wrote a story in 1800, *Sehr wunderbare Historie von der Melusina,* while Grillparzer composed in 1823 *Melusina,* an opera libretto set to music by K. Kreutzer in 1833. During the romantic period, there is also another manifestation of the siren image. This is first prevalent in German literature, although it soon spread to the rest of Europe. The German Friedrich de la Motte Fouqué (1777–1843) is the author of the first *Undine* (tale, 1811) whose repercussions were to ring for more than a century later in the very similar play by Giraudoux, *Ondine* (1939). In this fairy tale, the heroine is a water siren, but a new element has been introduced, as the siren can only attain a soul (and mortality) by marriage to a human who must remain faithful to his vows. A waterlord gives his baby daughter to a fisher couple to raise, so as to give her a chance to gain a soul. The knight Huldbrand, who courts Bertalda, meets Undine and marries her. She subsequently transforms herself from a carefree nixie or naiad into a loving spouse. Later her husband goes back to his former love, Bertalda, the human woman. Undine kills him with a kiss. E.T.A. Hoffmann borrowed this text to compose an opera, *Undine,* in 1816. A. Lortzing wrote his own opera on the same motif in 1845, yet added a happy ending. Several ballets were conceived on the theme.

In a more popular vein, H. C. Andersen's tale, "Den lille havfrue" ("The Little Sea Maid," 1837), is a variation on the same theme. In this case, the loving and girlish little siren is the victim of human deceit and indifference. The case is very different for the Loreleis that abound in the nineteenth century. As early as 1801, C. Brentano composed the ballad "Lore Lay," whose heroine Lore Lay, the mermaid, would like to die in order to put an end to the curse she presents to men. Heine's better-known poem "Die Loreley," ("The Loreley," written 1823), is again set on the Rhine. There the siren is perched on a rocky promontory and combs her golden tresses while singing her allurements to unwary sailors whose skiffs smash on the reef. Similar to such a malevolent spirit, are the Grimms' nixies. The first, tale 79, entitled "Die Wassernixe" ("The Nixie," 1812), is intended for children. It deals with an evil witch who carries children into a well. There is also version 181 for adults, "Die Nixe im Teich" ("The Nixie in the Pond," 1816). It deals with a treacherous water sprite who first tricks a baby away from a couple, then abducts the husband from the wife. Again the mermaid is shown combing her undulating hair. The sexual lure entraps the man from his earthly wife, who comes to his rescue. In all cases, treachery, danger, and oblivion play a key role in the drama. Whereas the Grimms' nixies are evil and cunning, Hans Christian Andersen's Little Sea Maid is pure and lovely. She sings like an angel but ends in a fishtail, to her grief and dismay. She is the real anti-Mélusine: a fish who sacrifices everything, even immortality, to become human and endowed with a soul. Here again hair and singing play a major part. Finally the siren reverts to water and ultimately she is metamorphosed into an air spirit. In Gerhart Hauptmann's play *Die versunkene Glocke, (The Sunken Bell,* 1896), the elf Rautendelein shows less angelic qualities.

Eduard Mörike displays a more comic vein in his short story "Historie von der schönen Lau," which is part of the collection *Das Stuttgarter Hutzelmännlein,* written in 1852. In this Swabian folktale, the nixie is beneficent in general and aids the humans who are kind to her, although she can play wicked tricks whenever provoked. Except for webbed fingers and toes, she is depicted as human in appearance and in character.

Later Literature

Maeterlinck's Mélisande (*Pelléas et Mélisande* [*Pelléas and Mélisande,* play, 1892]), whose very name echoes that of Mélusine, is seated at the edge of a well when Pelléas discovers her. She also projects her image in the watery mirror while she lets her unbound hair flow. In this case she incarnates the very image of the childlike and amoral blonde temptress. Modern literature abounds with female protagonists who are half human and half animal. To mention but a few, in Thomas Mann's *Joseph in Ägypten* (*Joseph in Egypt,* novel, 1936), Mut-em-enet, wife of the eunuch Petepre and would-be seducer of Joseph, is cast in the role of a vulture-woman (Mut means not only "Mother" but "vulture" in Egyptian). She is also considered to be like a water lily who holds her head up in clouds, while her roots are anchored in primeval slime. She too would tempt youthful Joseph by her honeyed blandishments in order to destroy him subsequently. Similar counterparts can be found in the works of Nikos Kazantzakis, who projects the Magna Mater Archetype in the form of a vulture and of a serpent in such novels as *Ho teleutaios peirasmos (The Last Temptation of Christ*, 1954), *Ho Christos Xanastaurōnetai (The Greek Passion*, 1951), and, others, where the sirenlike Magdalenes and seductive widows, ready to prey upon young men, keep recurring. These females represent a direct threat of sexual transgression and temptation for the spiritual heroes. Similar types abound in the works of Pär Lagerkvist, who presents the Magna Mater as part-human, part-snake in such novels as *Barabbas* (1950), *Sibyllan (The Sibyl*, 1956), *Pilgrim på havet (Pilgrim at Sea*, 1962), and *Det heliga landet (The Holy Land*, 1964). Tennessee Williams creates heroine Maggie as the *Cat on a Hot Tin Roof* (play, 1955); in this case the lure is of a more feline or sphinxlike nature.

In modern poetry the sirens play an important part. William Butler Yeats in "The Mermaid" (1928) depicts a creature who unwittingly but uncaringly drowns a swimming boy. Although her intent is not evil, her unconsciousness dooms her victim. In "La Loreley," a poem that is part of Apollinaire's *Alcools* (1913), the image of the Lorelei is revived. We can even find similar echoes ringing throughout the works of Haitian poet and novelist Jacques Roumain, who in his novels *Montagne ensorcelée* (1931) and *Gouverneurs de la rosée (Masters of the Dew*, 1944), presents, respectively, a snake-woman and a Loreleilike "Maîtresse Erzilée," who combs her long tresses while singing a song of perdition for the enraptured sailors, thus combining European, African, and Caribbean parallel mythological motifs.

To conclude, the siren is a projection of the male spirit who fears yet yearns for the infantile world of his first hopes and dreams. To him the female element is fraught with mystery, taboos, and prohibitions, and clad with theriomorphic and natural fantasies. Whereas a mature hero such as Ulysses may exorcise the fluid feminine and lunar element of the shimmering water mirage, lesser men fall prey to the soulless, primitive side of the demon issuing from the well of primordial unconsciousness. At times this well is fertile, sometimes it causes death or regurgitates monstrous nightmares. At any rate, it is common to all mankind. From the Harpies to Scylla, from Circe to Mélusine and to Undine, the siren is shifting and mellifluous as well as tentacular. Sometimes her song is melodious, sometimes it sounds raucous and threatening. She combines the beauty and the strength of the beast with the blandishments of the mother. One feature is common to all of these phases and faces: it is the harmony with the underground or underwater mysteries of nature.

See also: La Belle Dame sans Merci, Monsters.

Selected Bibliography

Barot, A. "Histoire de Mélusine." *L'ethnographie* 46 (1951): 6–45.

Kastner, Georges. *Les sirènes; essai sur les principaux mythes relatifs à l'incantation,*

les enchanteurs, la musique magique, le chant du cygne, etc. . . . Paris: G. Brandus
and S. Dufour, 1858.

O'Clery, Helen. *The Mermaid Reader and of Mermen, Nixies, Water-Nymphs, Sea Sirens,
Sea-Serpents, Sprites, and Kindred Creatures of the Deep.* New York: F. Watts,
1964.

Weicker, Georg. *Der Seelenvogel der alten Literatur und Kunst.* Leipzig: Teubner,
1902.

ADELE BLOCH

SOCIAL STATUS OF HERO

In its earliest manifestation—in the form of mythology or as part of primitive
worship—storytelling was about gods and a few human beings who were often
semidivine (the Greek meaning of "hero"). When literature proper begins, the
select circle is enlarged only slightly. For in a traditional society (e.g., Europe
during most periods down to the Renaissance), power gravitates to the monarchs,
aristocrats, and warriors, while people who deal with money or work with their
hands are ancillary. Literature reflects that social reality.

Antiquity and the Middle Ages

In Homer's epic poem *Ilias* (*Iliad,* c. 8th century B.C.), the only person representative of the vast majority of the population—people who work with their
hands—is Thersites; he appears long enough to say a few words and be thrashed
for the honor of it by Odysseus. The story is rather about Achilles, the premier
warrior of the age, a leader of his own tribe, son of a minor king, and semidivine
in nature. He is, however, not as important as Agamemnon, and indeed the
original clash is over their relative importance. In other words, the hero here is
a part of what sociologists or Marxists would call "the ruling circle." The same
applies to Homer's epic poem *Odysseia* (*Odyssey,* c. 8th century B.C.), the one
difference in status being that no divinity participated in the begetting of the
hero. In Aeschylus one hero is a divinity (Prometheus), and the *Oresteia* (trilogy
of plays, 458 B.C.), like Sophocles' Theban plays, is about a king and his
immediate family. The other Greek tragedies continue the norm. Dionysus is a
god; Hercules is semidivine; Philoctetes, Ajax, and Jason are leading warriors;
Antigone, Medea, Hippolytus, and Electra are children of kings.

Only in Sophocles' *Oidipous tyrannos* (*Oedipus Rex,* play, c. 429 B.C.) does
status become a central concern instead of a *donnée.* That work has been cited
by one critic as the original version in Europe of a theme that will become
prominent in the nineteenth-century novel—the Young Man from the Provinces
who succeeds in the metropolis. Oedipus is, of course, twice a prince; the son
of the royal couple in Thebes, he is raised as the son of the royal couple in
Corinth. After fleeing Corinth because of the troubling oracle, he comes to
Thebes, where he answers the riddle and slays thereby the sphinx. He is, in
effect, a nobody to whom the crown and the queen are gladly given as a reward

for saving the city and not for any putative royal blood in him. His multiple public selves are symptomatic of the crucial psychological and philosophical questions raised by the play. Who am I? He knows himself correctly to be a prince—albeit on the wrong assumptions—but he earns kingship by his own achievements: "I account myself a child of Fortune." Later, exercising his kingship by seeking to solve a major crime, he for a while even suspects, wrongly, that Jocasta fears she married a nobody. And indeed the solution of the crime brings with it the discovery that, though of royal Theban blood, he by his deeds had unwittingly made himself the meanest of men.

The main characters of the historians (Herodotus, Thucydides, Plutarch, Livy, Tacitus) are usually kings, princes, and generals, except for a rare interloper like Gyges. In Plato's dialogues, the leading interlocutors are philosophers, sophists (teachers), and wealthy men, but the central individual, Socrates, is of humble origins, being the son of a stonemason and a midwife. Like Oedipus, successful through the use of his wits, he is the first real self-made man in literature. That breach in literary decorum is enlarged in Aristophanes' contemporary comedies, perhaps because philosophy (the questioning of assumptions) and comedy (a vacation from all that is earnest) are less socially conservative branches of the Humanities. The heroes in most of Aristophanes' comedies are such average citizens as farmers, bourgeois wives, nondescript elderly men, a juryman, even a playwright (Euripides). Even when a god appears, things are different from tragedy: Dionysus in *Batrachoi (The Frogs*, 405 B.C.) is a poltroon and fool, not the fearsome, vindictive deity of Euripides' *Bakchai (The Bacchants,* c. 405 B.C.).

The plays of Plautus and Terence are mainly about middle-class men, their sons, and their intriguing slaves. As with Aristophanes, something of the flavor of the real quotidian life seeps into literature only in the comic genre. The epic of Virgil and the tragedies of Seneca remain the domain of gods, kings, and generals. In Lucian's less locale-bound type of comedy, the characters are often gods and mythological figures, albeit portrayed with terribly human foibles and defects. The protagonist of Apuleius' *Metamorphoses (The Golden Ass,* novel, c. 150) is a sociologically indefinite individual who falls in status all the way down to the subhuman level of asshood. After (and probably as a result of) adverse adventures, however, he undergoes a re-entry into humanity, becoming an initiate in a priestly caste that practices purity of life. The story echoes, or prepares for, the Christian thesis that before ascending one must descend. Petronius' *Satyricon* (A.D. 60), the first realistic novel, is another work that deviates from the norm; its hero is sociologically vague—an intellectual "drop out," someone Goliard-like or Villon-like living in a gray area where matters of intellect, sex, and crime mingle uneasily.

In the Old Testament, a kind of egalitarianism is at work in a noncomic context. God chooses to call upon individuals who are neither royal nor aristocratic. Noah and Abraham appear to have been, or become, affluent men, at best minor tribal chieftains. Job is a righteous, rich gentile. Moses, like Oedipus, is a leader with uncertain background—born to a Levite Jewish family, raised at the Egyptian court as a prince, and mysteriously gravitating back to the humble people he apparently sprang from. Saul and David are shepherds (though of affluent families) who go on to high status as kings. Even more than all these men, the prophets establish their importance not by their social origins but by becoming the vessels of God's message.

Developing this Hebraic motif, the New Testament makes a revolution in the presentation of the social status of the hero and of his milieu. It is still tied to pagan tradition by the suggestion that Jesus has at least one immortal parent. But novel is the idea that he is also a lowly carpenter. He somewhat resembles thereby Euripides' Dionysus (at first disguised and incarcerated in Thebes) and Sophocles' Oedipus (not known by the Thebans to be of their royal house). His apostles include a fisherman, a tentmaker, and others from an equally humble level of society who had been excluded from the precincts of serious high literature (and whose cultural enfranchisement Nietzsche was to decry). Because of the new Christian vision, the social status of the hero comes to be of little importance in a work like the *Confessiones* (*Confessions*, c. 397) of St. Augustine. Just as the Judeo-Christian sense of guilt or sin replaces the pagan sense of shame and peer judgment, so the moral state of the man—how he stands vis-à-vis God—is much more important than his status in society (a society barely perceived in this book). Moreover, the hero, the central persona who also happens to be writing the book, is a teacher of rhetoric and philosophy. This marks the first time—except in Plato (who does not narrate tales) and Aristophanes (who is a comedian)—that a professor rather than a god, king, prince, or general is at the heart of a serious story. And not the last, for one of the more famous, or notorious, medieval stories, Abélard's *Historia calamitatum* (c. 1134), also has such a protagonist.

A part of the institutionalized church, Abélard was a teacher of Christianized philosophy. Early medieval literature, however, either remains pagan (*Nibelungenlied*, epic poem, c. 1200, notably part 1), or is Christianized only superficially (*Beowulf*, epic poem, c. 8th century), or, though Christianized, contains values apparently remote from those of Jesus (*La chanson de Roland* [*Song of Roland*, epic poem, c. 1100]). The social status of the hero, therefore, remains what it had been in pagan antiquity. Beowulf is a warrior, nephew to a king, leader of a fighting band, and eventual king himself. Roland is a leading warrior, nephew to the king; the Cid Campeador is a victorious general; Siegfried is a prince, a leading warrior, and eventually a king; Hagen is a leading vassal and warrior. Parzival is the son of a knight and himself a leading warrior; Gawain is a premier knight and nephew to the king. Tristan alone introduces several new elements; in addition to being, as usual, a prominent warrior who is son of a prominent warrior, the hero is an exemplary—and yet illicit—lover and, what is sociologically more interesting, something of an artist. He is educated (rare for a knight then), plays an instrument, and brings his intellectual achievements to bear on his wooing.

The artistic dimension is also important in the delineation of the hero of that most medieval of works, Dante's epic poem *La divina commedia* (*The Divine Comedy,* c. 1320). The narrator is, on one level, everyman, and the journey in question is that of "nostra vita" ("our life"). But where the hero of *Everyman* (morality play, c. 1500) is so universal and abstract as to have no social status or vocation, this persona is highly individualized, with a personal name ("Dante" is used once), with a set of specific sins (an errancy caused in part by eros and pride), and with a personal spiritual guide or bearer of revelation (Beatrice). The hero's vocation is that of writer—the first major work with a writer as protagonist—one good enough to join in shop talk with the likes of Homer. He is also a prominent Florentine, promising enough to have the blessed Beatrice look after him and to have his worthy ancestor, Cacciaguida, a knight and crusader, make a long address to him filled with prophecies and exhortation. For the universe— if not his own society—is made to acknowledge Dante to be not just a writer but also a social critic, prophet, and visionary.

The frame story of Boccaccio's *Il decamerone* (*Decameron,* novellas, c. 1350) has as hero a group rather than an individual. They are young, attractive male and female scions of the lower aristocracy or leisured urban upper middle class who spend their time in games of love. Physical prowess is no more germane to social status here than in the *Divine Comedy, Confessions,* or Gospel; but its place is taken by Eros, not Agape. In the analogous work, the *Canterbury Tales* (c. 1380–1400), there is a knight, one indeed with a long list of campaign ribbons and newly returned from a campaign abroad. Yet the tale he tells is of love rather than of sword and gore. The other characters constitute a cross section of society, and the one who brings them together, the gregarious narrator, a certain Chaucer, is a minor character with indistinct social rank and vocation. Certainly he cannot be a writer, for he tells the worst story of all and is the only one in fact who has to be stopped mid-tale for reasons of sheer incompetence.

In the later Arthurian romances, including Ariosto, Tasso, and Spenser, the heroes are knights whose credentials as warriors must be matched by credentials as lovers, as if love had become a vocation, a status symbol, or a litmus test of masculinity and fulfillment. In fact, in the Petrarchan sonnet sequences, the persona is only a lover, with no vocation or status as knight, visionary, or anything other than poet of love.

The Renaissance and Neoclassical Periods

Juan Ruiz's *El libro de buen amor* (*The Book of Good Love,* poem, c. 1343) is somewhat unusual in having a priest as protagonist (and as would-be lover). In the anonymous tragicomedy, *Tragicomedia de Calisto y Melibea* (*Celestina,* 1499–1502), Calisto the lover seems to belong to a higher class than does his Melibea, whose father has wealth based on building and trade; and the person who shares the spotlight with them is the crone or matchmaker, someone rather like a pimp. Rabelais' (*Gargantua et Pantagruel* [*Gargantua and Pantagruel,* novels, 1532–1564]) main characters are two kings, but Panurge, who dominates the latter half of the work, is a déclassé character, like Petronius' Encolpius or like Villon. The hero, or at least the center, of Montaigne's essays, (1580–1588) with their autobiographical drift, is the author himself, a member of the lower aristocracy and for a while mayor of Bordeaux.

Shakespeare's milieu is almost entirely aristocratic. The late romances and the histories focus on royalty. The tragedies are about members of the royalty (Hamlet, Lear) or, especially, generals (Titus, Caesar, Othello, Macbeth, Antony, Coriolanus). The only exceptions are Timon, a wealthy citizen of Athens, and Romeo, who (with Juliet) seems to belong to the upper middle class and, like the characters in Boccaccio, has no other vocation than that of lover—though he proves to be, like Hamlet, an excellent fencer when tested by events. Prince Hal, Hamlet, and Antony are well-rounded Renaissance men, Hamlet being an intellectual and connoisseur to boot, as well as (like Beowulf, Roland, Gawain) nephew to the current king. In the major comedies, one hero is a warrior and lover (Benedick) and another mainly a lover (Orlando), but the central characters are often women: Rosalind, the daughter of a duke; Beatrice, niece to a governor; Helena, daughter of a physician; Isabella, a nun from an indistinct social background. Portia is a middle-class heiress in a play about a pair of wealthy merchants, Antonio and Shylock. Falstaff, part of the lower aristocracy, finds himself in the *Merry Wives of Windsor* (c. 1600) in a middle-class setting. Lower-class characters appear only on the periphery of the plays, only in comic contexts, and only speaking prose, for example, the gravediggers in *Hamlet* (c. 1600) or the "mechanicals" in *A Midsummer Night's Dream* (c. 1595).

Marlowe's *Dr. Faustus* (play, 1604) is a professor, like Augustine and Abélard. Dekker's *The Shoemaker's Holiday* (play, 1600) celebrates the ascendancy of the merchants and craftsmen. Some of the main characters in Jonson's finest comedies are servants (Mosca in *Volpone*, 1606, and Face in *The Alchemist*, 1610), a heritage of Latin comedy, with its sly, intriguing slaves and parasites. Webster's *Duchess of Malfi* (1613) is a sport in having a woman as a protagonist in tragedy, and, at that, a woman whose tragic fall is caused by something as domestic as remarrying against the wishes of her brothers and beneath her class. In thus moving in the direction of middle-class tragedy, the play represents an early departure from the heroic realm of Greek and Shakespearean tragedy, in which the flaws of the hero affect the realm. Beatrice Joanna in Middleton's *The Changeling* (play, 1622) is another (vaguely) aristocratic woman who is undone by domestic intrigues that reluctantly tie her amatorily to a social inferior, a servant in fact. Yet a third unusual domestic tragedy is Heywood's *A Woman Killed with Kindness* (1603).

Cervantes' *Don Quijote* (*Don Quixote*, novel, 1605, 1615) is about a character type that rarely appeared in literature, a knight in old age and retirement. The hero of Milton's *Paradise Lost* (poem, 1667), Adam, is an everyman character, more generalized than Dante and more individualized than Everyman. The subsidiary characters, despite their special theological positions, are familiar literary upper-class types. Jesus is the prince whose designation as heir apparent bestirs the leading general, Satan, into rebellion and treachery (rather as the "promotion" of Malcolm goads Macbeth or, on a lesser level, that of Cassio in part goads Iago). Milton's Samson (1671) is not only a Hercules-like biblical hero whose birth was the occasion of angelic revelation, a Beowulf-like savior of his people through martial prowess, but also a pious member of the abstinent Nazarite sect. The Jesus of *Paradise Regained* (poem, 1671) is interesting; a humble carpenter undergoes an identity crisis, from which he emerges, with the unwitting aid of Satan, with the discovery of his true status as divine or semidivine (or at least as someone with a divine mission that transcends his lowly origins)—an Oedipus Rex in reverse.

Most of the serious secular plays of Corneille and Racine, like many of Lope de Vega and Calderón, are about rulers, aristocrats, and warriors. Molière (fl. 1660s), specializing in comedy, treats of middle-class people. Orgon is upper middle class and Tartuffe is lumpencleric. Arnolphe is middle class in his anxieties over grooming a faithful wife, and Harpagon and Jordain have quintessentially bourgeois obsessions—money and status. (These are as yet, we should note, subjects for comedy, unlike in Arthur Miller's tragic *Death of a Salesman* [1949]). Only Alceste and Don Juan deviate; Alceste, whose social status is nebulous, acts like an aristocrat or at least lacks middle-class worries, while Don Juan is the archetype of one sort of aristocrat—atheist, articulate, libertine, irresponsible—exactly the sort of man that a cautious soul like Arnolphe was worried about.

The main characters of Restoration comedy are from the lower aristocracy or the leisured upper middle class, but their major interest is not the respectable, licit wooing that characterizes the young narrators in the *Decameron* and *Romeo and Juliet* (play, c. 1596), but seduction. That is the milieu also of Pope's *Rape of the Lock* (poem, 1712); in the salon of Hampton Court, the young people play cards and flirt during a "day" that begins at dusk, the very time when the day ends for hard-working middle-class men coming wearily home: "The merchant from the Exchange returns in peace, / And the long labours of the toilet cease."

Swift's Gulliver (1726) is at once a surgeon and a middle-class Everyman figure. In having gone to college, he belongs to the few privileged enough to have had any education, but the trimming college he attended, his being the third of five sons, even the associations of his name (gullible)—everything suggests middling status, "mediocrity," and "meanness" in the original sense of these words, the educated version of *l'homme moyen sensuel*. He is directly representative of his audience (as is the Modest Proposer, 1729) in a way in which the tragic heroes are not, and at key junctures that audience is alienated from him (and from the Proposer), at the very point where it is meant to sympathize with the tragic hero. Some of this also applies to Voltaire's Candide (novel, 1759)—even the overtones of the name are similar.

The rise of capitalism and its reenforcement by industrialism thrust a new man upon the stage of Europe. Reason and money, accompanying the businessman, the entrepeneur, and the newly rich, acted as social solvents that undermined social and political institutions based on blood, privilege, land, rank, tradition, mystiques. The change is reflected in the social status of the hero in literature. For one thing, the realistic novel becomes a dominant genre, and, with the rise of the novel, the protagonists more and more come from the lower middle or the working class. Defoe's *Moll Flanders* (1722) is born in Newgate prison. Richardson's Pamela (1740) is from the servant class (though both his Clarissa (1748) and her betrayer are high born). Fielding's Jonathan Wild (1743) is a scoundrel, but that is an ironic work. Joseph Andrews (1742) and Tom Jones (1749), like Oedipus or Milton's Jesus, do not know their true origins. Joseph is a servant and Tom is a foundling; both turn out to be son or nephew to a country squire (and Sophia is the daughter of one). While Tom eventually finds out who he is, Rameau's nephew (in Diderot's work of that name, 1762–1784), begins with clear biological lineage—he is related to a famous composer—but with social status which remains hazy to the end. Half looking back to the classical parasite and the medieval goliardic poet, half forward to the bohemian, the modern "intellectual," the minor or pseudo artist, he is the first of an important new kind of hero, the "anti-hero." A parallel figure is found in Goethe's Werther (1774), a sensitive middle-class youth in revolt against aristocratic pride and middle-class respectability.

The changing nature of the hero in the late eighteenth-century revolutionary period is also manifested in the plays of Beaumarchais, *Le barbier de Séville* (*The Barber of Seville*, 1775) and *Le mariage de Figaro* (*The Marriage of Figaro*, 1784), in which the aristocrat is morally and esthetically upstaged by the local barber and factotum. Yet another important change at this time takes place in England, where George Lillo's minor work, *The London Merchant* (1731)—the story of a young apprentice whose budding career as a merchant is ruined by a femme fatale—is of interest for being an early bourgeois tragedy. Goethe's Faust (play, 1808) is, as in Marlowe, a professor, but where the earlier Faust, in being something of a conjuror or magician, is mainly a figure out of fantasy, this Faust is more clearly a part of a realistic social setting, the son of a locally admired physician.

If the autobiography of Casanova dramatizes the life of someone whose parents were in the theater but whose ancestor was secretary to a king, those of Franklin, Rousseau, Restif, and (somewhat) Wordsworth give the nonfiction versions of the Young Man from the Provinces tale, the man of humble social origins who makes good in the metropolis. Byron's Childe Harold (narrative poem, 1812–1818) is the aristocrat on the Grand Tour, but, haunted by the ruins of the past and self-indulgently looking for the meaning of life, he is hardly your average aristocrat. His Don Juan (epic poem, 1819–1824) is an aristocrat on an unintentional Grand Tour in which detachment, casual love affairs, adventures, and joie de vivre have replaced the earlier posturing. The central characters of Balzac's novels are either aristocrats or wealthy middle-class types, and, while Stendhal's Fabrice is well connected with aristocrats, his Julien Sorel is the son of a carpenter. In Dickens, the march of progressive ideas can be gauged by the fact that many of his protagonists are of middle- or lower-class background, and the Young Man from the Provinces motif comes into its own in novels like *David Copperfield* (1850) and *Great Expectations* (1860–1861).

Gogol's "Shinel' '' ("The Overcoat," story, 1842), like Melville's *Bartleby* (novella, 1853), introduces something new in literature: an office worker, secretary or clerk, bureaucrat—Dickens' Wemmick, as it were, made the center of a pair of disturbing surrealistic or metaphysical tales. Elsewhere, Gogol likes to toy with the uncertainties of status. The main character of *Revizor* (*The Inspector General,* play, 1836) is an impecunious young gentleman taken by a town for an inspector, while Chichikov (*Mërtvye dushi* [*Dead Souls,* novel, 1842]) is apparently a petty official passing himself off as a landowner. The latter especially is somewhat like Rameau's nephew in being of indeterminate social background and parasitical life style. The leading characters in Turgenev's *Otŝy i deti* (*Fathers and Children,* novel, 1862) move in a world of middle-class landowners with liberal sympathies, but Bazarov, the son of a minor country physician in whose professional footsteps he hopes to follow, is a rebel, rationalist, individualist, nihilist. He is the first and perhaps still greatest portrait in literature of an important historical type—the revolutionary from a middle-class background. In Tolstoy's *Voĭna i mir* (*War and Peace,* novel, 1865–1869), Andrey is an aristocrat, a soldier who is the son of a general, while Pierre, as one of the richest men, has the leisure to seek the meaning of life. Natasha comes from the upper middle class Rostovs. In *Anna Karenina* (novel, 1877), the heroine, married to a member of the upper echelons of the civil service, has a prolonged affair with a young aristocrat. Concurrently, the rich landowner Levin marries the middle-class Kitty.

Dostoevsky's world is peopled mainly with middle-class characters (except for Myshkin and Stavrogin). Raskolnikov (*Prestuplenie i nakazanie* [*Crime and Punishment,* novel, 1866]) is the middle-class youth as impecunious college student. Pyotr Verhovenski (*Besi* [*The Possessed,* novel, 1871–1872]) is the pseudo-radical son of a liberal former professor. Old man Karamazov's (novel, 1880) sons may be the salt of the earth in their different ways, but he himself is a merchant of the most repulsive, sycophantic, lying, debauched sort. Truly unique, however, is the Underground Man (novel, 1864), part perverse Everyman, part sui generis animal in its lair; part parasite à la Chichikov or Rameau's nephew, part lower level bureaucrat à la Bartleby or the hero of Dostoevsky's earlier *Dvoĭnik* (*The Double,* novel, 1846); part bohemian, part insane; and all anti-hero (he, in fact, coins the term). One of the most individualized and complex characters in all literature, he nearly transcends questions of social origins and status.

Ibsen (fl. 1880–1900) deals almost exclusively with the middle class. Some protagonists are ministers (Brand, Rosmer). Some work hard to maintain gentility: Torvald, the rising functionary at the bank; Tesman, the pedantic professor married to the aristocratic Hedda; Hjalmar, the none too successful photographer.

Some are successful professionals: Stockman, the physician; Borkman, the banker; Solness, builder; Rubek, the sculptor; Peer Gynt, the tycoon and adventurer. Chekhov's plays (1895–1904) have, by contrast, no individual heroes, only groups of main characters. They are almost all from the landed middle class. Living in country manors, they grapple with a sense of futility and boredom. Vaguely threatened by new art, new politics, new money, they face extinction as a class. Some work too hard (Vanya and Sonya), most drift vocationally and emotionally. Lopakhin is one of the rising new breed. The son of a serf, he now buys the estate to which his father once belonged.

The Modern Era

The heroes of Kafka's two major novels seem to be professional men. Joseph K. (*Der Prozess* [*The Trial*, 1925]) is an executive at a bank, caught up in office politics with a rival, the Assistant Manager. K. (*Das Schloss* [*The Castle*, 1926]) claims to be a land surveyor—though whether he is what he claims and the significance of either the job or the claim are endlessly disputed.

If the eighteenth and nineteenth centuries saw the middle class rising to political and cultural prominence, the twentieth century has been, at least in rhetoric and aspirations, the age of the common man, of democracy in its etymological sense, of a liberalism defined as government interventionism on behalf of toiling masses rather than as unshackling of the bourgeoisie. Again the change is reflected in literature. If the later eighteenth and the nineteenth centuries see the rise of the middle-class hero in noncomic literature, the twentieth brings with it two new heroic types: the worker and the artist. The latter is like the former in the sense that he is alienated from money-making or money-worshipping society. The advent of the worker has not produced many works of the first water, but the artist is ubiquitous in major works. In D. H. Lawrence's *Sons and Lovers* (novel, 1913), in fact, the two new types merge in one person. Paul Morel is the offspring of that quintessential worker—the inarticulate coalminer—and of a sensitive, educated daughter of a clergyman. Though working in an office, he establishes his individuality by his painting, which has begun to win prizes. Joyce's Stephen Dedalus (*Portrait of the Artist*, 1916, and *Ulysses*, 1922 [novels]), the son of a pious mother and a witty but improvident father, is an intellectual and would-be artist seeking his vocation. Marcel, in Proust's *A la recherche du temps perdu* (*Remembrance of Things Past*, novels, 1913–1927) is the son of a government functionary with aristocratic connections; he establishes early his writing ability but, lacking the will and the subject matter to do something big, only belatedly finds his vocation.

Mann's protagonists are either the scions of upper middle-class, quasi-aristocratic families or they are artist types. *Buddenbrooks* (novel, 1901) traces through four generations the rise of the latter in the bosom of the former, while "Tonio Kröger" (story, 1903) shows the same change in one generation—Tonio is a writer, his father a grain merchant. If Tonio is beset by the sense of his deviation from the social norms, Aschenbach (*Der Tod in Venedig* [*Death in*

Venice, novelle, 1912]), coming from a prominent family with many commercial and military achievements, has suppressed such queasiness by bringing to his successful writing the puritanic spirit, the hard work, and the self-discipline of his family tradition. Hans Castorp (*Der Zauberberg* [*The Magic Mountain,* novel, 1924]) is yet another scion of a quasi-aristocratic family who drops out—this time not into creativity but into philosophic contemplation. And Felix Krull (1911, 1954), son of an unsuccessful wine merchant, turns into an artist of deception and roguery. Only Adrian Leverkühn (*Doktor Faustus,* novel, 1947), more successful as composer even than Kröger and Aschenbach as writers, comes from a humble (though intellectually sensitive) farming family; he proves to be as solitary and alienated a soul as the other two, with their more reputable social origins.

If, because of general growing introversion and because of his feelings of irrelevance to modern life, the artist has become one kind of paradigmatic hero for the modern writer, the lower middle-class salesman is another, perhaps because in modern capitalist society, with its cash nexus, the main activity is parting people from their money. Bloom (*Ulysses*) is a salesman in the field of advertising (itself a modern profession). He is one of the few people whose average workday is portrayed in a major modern novel, or indeed anywhere in literature. None too successful, he has had many other jobs and is an outsider in his own city of Dublin. Equally isolated is Kafka's Gregor Samsa ("Die Verwandlung" ["Metamorphosis," story, 1915]), a traveling salesman who, his father having (like Bloom's) failed in business and having become a mere doorman, has the responsibility of supporting the family. His work requires frequent travel by train, even as frequent travel by car is the lot of the hero of Arthur Miller's *Death of a Salesman,* a man who sees himself at the end of a career (abruptly terminated by his employer) with nothing to pass on to his sons—no values, money, achievement, dignity. Yet another salesman is Hickey or Hickman (O'Neill's *Iceman Cometh,* play, 1946), who now attempts his biggest selling job, not of a product but of a philosophy. He tries in vain to persuade a group of pipe dreamers and drop-outs to emerge from the saloon and grapple with reality. He turns out to have both done and not done himself what he urges on others. He was unable to master his own drinking habit, but he was able to kill his wife, whose chronic forgiving of his many relapses had driven his guilt feelings and self-loathing to the breaking point.

The names in question here —*Hick*man, *Lo*man—remind us that, as Miller expressed it ("Tragedy and the Common Man," 1949) the task of modern literature is to deal with the experience of the little man. Just as history books until the eighteenth century focused on kings, courtiers, and generals, and, since then, have become more concerned with forces and movements, with ignored people like peasants, blacks, women, the indigent, the insane, the incarcerated, so has the center of attention in literature shifted from the world shakers of Greek and Shakespearean tragedy to humble folk. The change is exemplified by two typical modern works, Beckett's *En attendant Godot* (*Waiting for Godot,* 1952) and Stoppard's *Rosencrantz and Guildenstern Are Dead* (1967). When Shakespeare wanted to plumb the human condition, he analyzed the challenges confronting a prince; Hamlet is also a Renaissance man, an attractive, witty intellectual who, though having everything one could want, still faces tragedy. The play therefore dramatizes a species of a fortiori reasoning. If Hamlet comes to grief, what of the rest of us? The modern writer finds such a perspective irrelevant. For him the essential dramatization of the plight of man (or at least of modern man) is not of the prince but of, as in Stoppard's play, two minor functionaries, or, as in many of Beckett's plays, two old people living in garbage pails. For not only are most of us minor functionaries in life, caught up in the detritus of existence, but even prominent men are now seen as the victims of abstract forces rather than as shapers of history. Modern literature therefore offers such unusual heroes—anti-heroes really—as down-at-the-heel clowns *(Waiting for Godot),* an idiot (Faulkner's *The Sound and the Fury,* novel, 1929), a putative half-caste who becomes an outcast (his *Light in August,* novel, 1932). The traditional view, in other words, assesses the human condition in terms of the best of which man—aided by birth, endowment, and luck—is capable, while the modern view assesses it in terms of the mediocre or even the worst. This is, after all, the Century of the Common Man.

See also: Birth of the Hero, Christian Hero, Comic Hero, Leader, Noble Criminal, Tragicomic Hero.

Selected Bibliography

Auerbach, Erich. *Mimesis: The Representation of Reality in Western Literature*. Trans. Willard R. Trask. Princeton, N.J.: Princeton University Press, 1953,

Burns, E., and I. Burns, eds. *The Sociology of Literature and Drama*. Baltimore: Penguin Books, 1973.

Spindler, Michael. *American Literature and Social Change*. Bloomington: Indiana University Press, 1983.

MANFRED WEIDHORN

SPY

Spies are found primarily in works of fiction created by the British in the twentieth century and developed further in other countries, mainly—but not exclusively—in America. These characters are agents of national governments who obtain secret military, economic, or political information vital to the interest of the agents' home countries. Conversely, agents may be engaged in counterespionage activities, apprehending spies from an adversary nation or organization, or preventing them from obtaining secret information from the agents' home countries. Spy fiction can be as guilty of sexual stereotyping as any other form of literature, but much of it does contain strong female characterization. The main characters within this type of literature, whether they are male or female, are driven by a variety of motives: patriotism, greed, personal gain, lust, revenge, coercion, or a need for adventure. Despite the presence of psychological motivation and character development, spy fiction depends heavily upon the action of the characters and descriptions of the craft of intelligence. Because spy fiction involves complex international intrigue and explication of the characters' adventures and motivation, its main medium has been the novel—with subsequent film adaptations and imitations—and it has been closely associated with popular literature.

Pretwentieth-Century Background

Napoleon once said that a well-placed spy was worth more to him than 20,000 troops, and military/political leaders long before and after him would not disagree with his maxim. Authors long before and after Napoleon also have known the value of weaving espionage activities into their mirrors of reality. Book 2 of Joshua relates the adventures of two spies who collaborate with the harlot Rahib to gain information that will help tumble the walls of Jericho. In Homer's epic poem *Ilias* 10 (*Iliad*, 8th century B.C.) wily Odysseus and his comrade Diomedes equip themselves to infiltrate Trojan territory to learn the exact strength of Hector's forces. While gathering this combat intelligence, they kill a number of the enemy, steal valuable livestock, and capture, interrogate, and kill the Trojan spy Dolon, who had been sent on a similar mission into the Achaean camp. The central part of Virgil's epic poem *Aeneis* 9 (*Aeneid,* 19 B.C.) focuses on the secret mission of Euralus and Nisus, who equip themselves to cross into the lines of the Rutulians, where they plan to gather military information valuable to their absent leader and friend Aeneas.

Twentieth-Century Development

These tales, however, are really stories within stories. With a few notable exceptions such as James Fenimore Cooper's *The Spy* (1821), a novel about the adventures of a rebel double agent during the American Revolution, espionage activities in fiction were merely colorful threads woven into the main fabric of the story. The spy novel as a distinct subgenre, which features the espionage or counterespionage activities of the main characters, is generally recognized as a twentieth-century British development. Rudyard Kipling's *Kim* (1901) could be considered the beginning of this modern literary phenomenon. Very popular in its time, the novel dealt with the adventures of an Irish orphan in India who is trained by the British Secret Service to gather secret intelligence for the good of the Empire. Although not a gentleman himself, Kipling's Kim plays "The Great Game" on behalf of a colonial power run by "gentlemen" who assumed that they possess the only correct definition of civilization and proper social order. But within the contemporary definition of the spy novel, it is Erskine Childers' *Riddle of the Sands* that claims distinction as the first spy thriller. Published in London in 1903, the book relates the adventures of two young Englishmen who stumble upon Imperial Germany's plans for the invasion of

Great Britain while sailing among the Frisian Islands near the coast of Northern Germany; it is an almost prophetic tale given later events of history.

Throughout the decade and into World War I, other spy novels such as William Le Queux's *The Czar's Spy* (1907) and *Revelations of the Secret Service* (1911), E. Phillips Oppenheim's *The Secret* (1907), and John Buchan's *The Thirty-Nine Steps* (1915) brought their authors considerable recognition. Similar to *Kim* and *Riddle of The Sands,* these works have been criticized as naïvely patriotic and ethnocentric because their protagonists represent all that is good about the British Empire and because their antagonists are dedicated to the destruction of this stable, albeit elitist, social order. Even Joseph Conrad, the master craftsman of English imaginative writing, used his skill to produce two spy novels. In both works, *The Secret Agent* (1907) and *Under Western Eyes* (1911), the main characters infiltrate anarchist organizations and suffer for their crusade against revolutionary disrupters of society. With the literary giant Conrad adding his contribution, the spy novel was becoming firmly entrenched as an established subgenre.

Historically, this literary development parallels occurrences in the world of international politics. Before the twentieth century, spies were viewed as sneaky, unwashed, ill-bred pariahs. Secret intelligence gathering by governments was extremely low-key, and, if governments had such organized activity, they officially ignored its existence. The turn of the century, bringing with it the fierce tensions among the great colonial powers, saw a change in that attitude. By sheer necessity organized intelligence gathering was developing greater sophistication and was openly sanctioned by government. A British gentleman who felt noblesse oblige could with dignity enter His (or Her) Majesty's Secret Service, and patriotic citizens of any other country could now with pride serve God, King, and Country as intelligence officers. In short, spying had become a quite socially acceptable profession, and the art of literature in turn had begun to mirror that reality.

Post-World War I

Between the world wars espionage fiction, often written by men and women who worked for British Intelligence, continued to reflect the crisis-ridden international arena and continued to attract readers. In the 1930s authors extended the scope of spy fiction by introducing suspense elements inherent in the long-established detective thriller. Graham Greene in 1936 published *A Gun for Sale* (*This Gun for Hire* in America), a gripping story about the alienated, deformed Simon Raven, who is contracted by a treacherous character named "Control" to assassinate a socialist foreign minister. Eric Ambler, a recognized master of the spy thriller, published five classic novels in two years: *Background to Danger* (1937), *Cause for Alarm* (1937), *Epitaph for a Spy* (1938), *A Coffin for Dimitrios* (1937), and *Journey into Fear* (1937). Ambler recalls that the detective thriller had become so terribly overworked that he was inspired to do something new; he intellectualized it ("An Interview with Eric Ambler," *Journal of Popular*

Culture 9 [1975]: 287–293). The world, like the characters in the detective mystery, had lost its sense of innocence, and Ambler says that he brought this sense of loss to his spy novels. No longer could gentlemen, typified by Buchan's upper-class establishment figures, play "The Great Game." Ambler's more common men and women did not have the luxury of clear-cut black versus white moral decisions; they had to choose among varying shades of gray. Similar to real men and women, they faced more difficult alternatives in a more complex world of amoral international intrigue. They forshadowed the semifictional situations of three decades later, for example, in James Grady's *Six Days of the Condor* (1974), where the protagonist must contend with perverted policy and tactics within his own "agency" or "company," situations where amorality had made the frighteningly easy transition to immorality in the name of national security.

As the 1930s ended, the world political situation was entering an extremely dark period, which offered fertile soil to the imaginative world of spy fiction. It was also at this approximate time that Americans, whose government possessed virtually no espionage apparatus, took notice of John P. Marquand's Mr. Moto series. However, the intrepid Japanese agent quickly fell from favor when J. Edgar Hoover's G-men turned their attention from chasing indigenous criminals to pursuing Japanese and Nazi spies. As America became more involved in the war, the counterespionage exploits of the FBI and the apparently romantic adventures of "Wild Bill" Donavan's OSS danced in the head of most patriotic citizens. For propaganda value the reporting of these deeds in books and periodicals, irregardless of fact, was understandably subtly encouraged by U.S. government officials.

Post-World War II

The end of World War II brought a new beginning to the world of espionage. Two new superpowers dominated global events, waging a so-called Cold War. On one side, the Soviet Union relied upon an international network of socialist sympathizers and twenty years of ruthless, experienced spying and counterspying. The United States on the other side made use of its vast financial and technological resources and borrowed heavily from the espionage expertise of the British. The Cold War drew very fuzzy and very complex battle lines. The right versus wrong struggle, which had become cloudy in the 1930s, became a bad versus worse situation in the late 1940s; black versus white drifted increasingly farther into choices among finer shades of gray. Tensions on a scale never before seen called for espionage with a degree of sophistication never before experienced, and spy fiction grew in proportional size and scope along with this grim reality.

Mass Appeal of Spy Novels

Ian Fleming's James Bond series is the prime example of the growth in popularity of spy fiction. The first of the novels, *Casino Royale,* which featured the playful but violent adventures of an archetypal cold warrior, appeared in 1953. By the mid-1960s fifty-five million copies of Fleming's James Bond novels had been sold (Mordecai Richler, ''James Bond Unmasked,'' in *Mass Culture Revisited*, ed. B. Rosenberg and D. White [1971]:341). The enormous popularity of this series illustrates a lingering problem associated with the spy novel—its close relationship to popular literature. The obvious rewards of a best seller entice authors who write poor quality novels, which are purchased by millions of nondiscriminating readers.

Whether Ian Fleming's novels are poor or not is a matter for critical opinion. Eric Ambler, for instance, believes that Fleming's books are well written, literate, and captivating (''An Interview,'' 291). Richler, however, thinks that Fleming was an ''appalling'' writer with limited powers of invention and a strong dependence on this strict formula: (1) Bond summoned by M; (2) Initial confrontation of Bond and villain; (3) Bond meets and seduces sexy woman; (4) Bond captured by villain; (5) Bond escapes and triumphs; and (6) Delayed tryst of Bond and sexy woman (''James Bond Unmasked,'' 341–343).

Both Ambler and Richler easily could find support for their divergent opinions. Ian Fleming's novels in fact often are the measure against which subsequent spy novels are judged. A sympathetic book reviewer might say that a certain work is as readable and as gripping as any James Bond novel. But novelists, who believe their work is of better quality and closer to reality, might deny their plots and characters any James Bond attributes. Ironically, real intelligence operations sometimes are compared in positive or negative terminology with the exploits of this fictional hero. However, in the realm of literary criticism, the James Bond series cannot be considered Matthew Arnold's touchstone. For example, Joseph Conrad's *Secret Agent*, written a half century before *Casino Royale*, contains a high seriousness comparable to the great author's other eminent works. John Le Carré's (David John Moore Cornwell) George Smiley trilogy (*Tinker, Tailor, Soldier, Spy*, 1974; *The Honourable Schoolboy*, 1977; and *Smiley's People*, 1979), written well after Bond had become a cult figure, shows an elaborate character development and a concern for the universal qualities of love, friendship, and loyalty attributable to much of great literature. Thus, espionage fiction is not in a position for praise or condemnation as an entire subgenre. Despite the existence and popularity of many works of bad quality, each spy novel, as with any form of literature from Homer to Hemingway, is open to critical judgment on its own individual merits.

The James Bond series did call attention to the mass appeal of the spy novel, and in doing so led to the creation of James Bond imitations such as Donald Hamilton's Matt Helm and Adam Hall's Quiller. Fleming's popularity also coincided with more intricate and less formulaic spy novel successes such as Len Deighton's *Funeral in Berlin* (1964), or Le Carré's *Spy Who Came in from the Cold* (1963), which portrayed a seedier, unromantic side of the intelligence profession. As the 1960s progressed, the spy novel captured a significant portion of the fiction market, and by the mid-1970s 25 percent of all books published in the United States were categorized as "thrillers" (Bruce Merry, *Anatomy of the Spy Thriller* [1977]:1).

Although common consensus and the sheer volume of popular interest attributed the creation and development of the spy novel to English and American literary circles, other nations have not ignored the subgenre. Espionage, after all, is a global phenomenon, and the novel in its mimetic form always uses the materials at hand. For example, widely popular authors such as Hans Helmut Kirst and Johannes Mario Simmel have written spy thrillers for their German-speaking readers, and Gérard de Villiers found success among French readers with his highly successful Prince Malko Linge series. This spy-hero, an Austrian nobleman, has very straightforward motivation. He needs money to repurchase his ancestral castle. But in order to do so, he works for the American CIA on very complicated cases. De Villiers appeals further to the healthy French sense of literary irony through Malko's extreme sophistication and abhorrence of violence, which is offset by the seedy intriguers and violent action with which he becomes involved.

Spy Novels as Fantasy

The growth of the spy novel, as we have seen, following closely the growth and development of the intelligence community, was steady but not sudden. The more that international events necessitated spy activity, the greater the world of literature mimicked the reality. Paradoxically, the spy novel, conceived in Britain and lovingly adopted in America and on the Continent, was nurtured by societies where spying has caused great harm ("An Interview," 291). Perhaps this explains why much of spy fiction directly contradicts intelligence gathering as it actually takes place. The lowest level clerk to the most senior control officer realize that intelligence work can be tedious, fragmented, and inconclusive. Dramatic breakthroughs are rare and usually result from either frustrating, hard work or chance occurrence.

Therefore, Allen Dulles, a former CIA Director, correctly labels spy fiction the modern literature of fantasy, the replacement for tales of cowboys, swashbucklers, and knights errant (Allen Dulles, ed., *Great Spy Stories from Fiction* [1969]: xi). With notable exceptions like George Smiley, the methodical, melancholy investigator, fictional spies like Bond and Malko appear as modern Galahads returning the Grail of truth, justice, and order to troubled twentieth-century Camelots. They are quite the opposite of real statesmen, scientists, and civil servants, who grapple for solutions to international tensions, a task painstakingly slow, full of frustrations, setbacks, and failure. The spies of literature rise above the nameless, colorless mass of apparently bumbling bureaucrats and cut to the core of global problems with the most simplistic methods.

But herein lies the difference between the art of literature and the fields of historiography, political science, and journalism. While spy literature might remain true to the technical craft of intelligence, it is the fantasy of the spy novel, the departure from grim, dull reality that attracts and maintains readers' attention. If readers wished to gain intellectual satisfaction only from the technical, political, or historical aspects of spy literature, they could find more accurate information in a declassified intelligence report or a journalistic exposé.

In spy fiction the "Director" or "Control" sends a famous agent dashing into a foreign country on a mission well known to the enemy. During the course of the assignment, the agent encounters dangerous but exciting adventures, and when the assignment is successfully completed, the agent is welcomed home by a gratified nation, to the dismay of the rivals. As it happens, however, no intelligence organization ever sends a well-known operative into a foreign country. This would inevitably result in the loss of an expensively trained agent and the failure of the mission. Real spying most often is performed by citizens of the foreign country. Working for money, revenge, sex, or ideology—usually in that order—operatives pass their information to case officers who direct them from diplomatically immune embassies or from safe locations across the national boundaries. A cardinal rule of intelligence gathering keeps all operatives and operations in a foreign country unknown, and in reality the greatest espionage successes seldom reach the public eye; it is more often the failures that are reported.

The Spy Novel As Modern Epic or Romance

Readers of spy literature are no different, however, from their ancestors, who listened in wonder to tales of Odysseus or King Arthur, because espionage fiction, as a literature of fantasy, does bear strong resemblance to ancient epics and medieval romances. Fictional spies are heroic figures who undertake a series of quests. Their prowess is fortified by twentieth-century armor and secular magic, that is, dazzling weaponry and technological equipment. Because spies are summoned by the will of the new god-kings—national leaders—they may engage in otherwise immoral acts, namely, theft, seduction, and murder (Merry, *Anatomy*, 218–223). Like chivalrous knights, they come to the aid and comfort of society in hours of need. Like bygone heroes, they are mortal, but they possess suprahuman powers. They stand alone, but only because they stand above the masses as exceptional individuals who represent the national character. Their quests take them to frightening and exotic lands, where strange people with strange customs speak strange languages. Instead of blood-thirsty Cyclopes and fire-eating dragons, they struggle against ruthless KGB agents or other enemies of peace and democracy. Their transportation is not on black ships, divine wings, or gallant steeds, but rather on supersonic airlines or luxurious private jets.

Contemporary spy fiction enables the ordinary salesclerk to dream of colorful Istanbul, just as the isolated peasant once listened in wonder to descriptions of Phaecia or Camelot. Modern readers in cozy houses and cramped apartments can experience the excitement of an international airport, where vicariously they can escape day-to-day existence and fly away to adventure. However, this clearly escapist literature often does come in an esoteric package. The better quality spy fiction demands from the reader at least a small understanding of power politics, international intrigue, modern technology, and military strategy. Also, spy heroes, with whom the reader relates, possess intellectual and other unusual skills that aid in their successful ventures. They speak foreign languages, quote literature, fly aircraft, practice Oriental martial arts, and generally are very sophisticated in the ways of the world. In this light fictional spies do reflect somewhat their real models, because intelligence organizations, especially British and American, initially recruited from the more educated elite of their respective societies.

Given its relatively short history, spy fiction has spawned a large number of recognized English language craftsmen such as Eric Ambler, John Le Carré, Len Deighton, Ian Fleming, Frederick Forsythe, Graham Greene, Helen MacInnes, and Alistair MacLean. These authors, in addition to producing a long list of classic thrillers, also have inspired a host of crude imitators. Only time and closer critical scrutiny will determine which twentieth-century classic spy thriller, if any, should enter a canon of great literature. Furthermore, whether spy fiction will keep its popular appeal depends purely on the caprice of the reading public. Nevertheless, it is certain that as long as intelligence communities serve world powers, imaginative literature will imitate the reality.

See also: Noble Criminal.

Selected Bibliography

Marchetti, Victor, and J. Marks. *The CIA and the Cult of Intelligence*. London: Cape, 1974.

Merry, Bruce. *Anatomy of the Spy Thriller*. Montreal: McGill-Queens University Press, 1977.

Orlov, Alexander. *Handbook of Intelligence and Guerilla Warfare*. Ann Arbor: University of Michigan Press, 1963.

Smith, Myron J. *Cloak and Dagger Bibliography*. Metuchen, N.J.: Scarecrow Press, 1976.

EDWARD J. DANIS

STUPIDITY

"Stupidity" is the lack of mental ability, understanding, or foresight that renders a person vulnerable to misfortune and the schemes of others. As a theme stupidity is usually presented in one of three ways, each with a long tradition. A treatment originating in the folk traditions of many cultures uses the stupidity of the antagonist as a foil for the cleverness of the protagonist. In such early versions, the emphasis is on the success of the hero, and the stupidity he overcomes is only described for the effect of comedy or suspense. This first treatment was later modified by satirists, who give much more emphasis to exposing the stupidity of the foils. A second treatment reverses the sympathies of the first, making the clever character the antagonist and following the fortunes of a less cerebral hero or heroine, who, of course, is described not as stupid but as innocent, guileless, loyal, or pious. These two treatments usually assign human traits differently, with the first more frequently assigning unselfish, humanitarian impulses to the clever (an attitude most frequently found in cultures that praise rationality and social responsibility), while the second sees rationality in conflict with the moral sense (an attitude of cultures that embrace romantic, individualistic, or spiritual ideals). But this division should not be overemphasized; as two such familiar tales as "Jack and the Beanstalk" and "Little Red Riding Hood" can show, most cultures are willing to accept both views of the battle between cleverness and stupidity.

A third treatment, with a tradition that goes back to the early religious writings of many cultures, refuses to assign stupidity to only a portion of mankind, but insists instead that stupidity—limited knowledge, limited understanding, limited foresight—is the human condition. This attitude lends itself to both deeply religious and highly skeptical versions, with such contrasting practitioners as Erasmus and Camus.

Antiquity

In Greek literature, the theme of cleverness and its antithesis, stupidity, first appears in the Homeric epic *Odysseia* (*Odyssey*, c. 8th century B.C.). Unlike Homer's *Ilias* (*Iliad*), which develops the themes of piety, valor, and revenge but pays little attention to the mental abilities of its characters, the *Odyssey*, with its greater use of folktale material, suggests that battles are sometimes won and catastrophes averted by setting traps for the stupid. It is no coincidence that the story of the Trojan horse, the scheme by which the Trojans are tricked into accepting into the city a gigantic structure concealing enemy forces, first appears in the *Odyssey*. Odysseus' valor is not enough to defeat such enemies as the one-eyed monster Polyphemos, but his cleverness is a more than adequate match for Polyphemus' stupidity, and he is able to blind the monster and escape. Odysseus' cleverness also helps him to escape the witch Circe, the enchantress Calypso, and the Sirens whose songs lead sailors to crash on the rocks. Odysseus' faithful wife Penelope holds off the stupid suitors who would marry her in her husband's absence by the ruse of secretly unraveling her weaving each night. Odysseus returns to reclaim his wife, kill all the suitors, and live out his years in peace. Although Odysseus is a mature soldier returning home rather than a younger brother seeking his fortune, the folktale pattern is quite evident, and the emphasis as always is that stupidity is a greater liability than poverty or lack of allies.

In his early formulation of Greek mythology, *Theogonia* (*Theogony*, poem), Hesiod (c. 8th century B.C.) first describes certain Greek notions of forbidden knowledge, the idea that humans are not only naturally ignorant in certain areas but are in danger of punishment if they attempt to overcome that ordained stupidity. The stories of Pandora, whose curiosity unleashed troubles into a world better ignorant of them, and of Prometheus, punished by the gods for providing humans with fire, are presented in Hesiod. He also describes the four ages of man, a world view of progressive degeneration in which, among other failures, humans grow more and more stupid as generations pass. This image of decay became a powerful tool for later writers, who view human mental deficiency as insurmountable.

Also widely influential are the depictions of forbidden knowledge in the Hebrew Old Testament. Most familiar is the story of the fall of Adam and Eve in Genesis. Their ingesting the fruit of the Tree of Knowledge of Good and Evil and being prevented from eating of the Tree of Life are probably elements from earlier folk mythology attempting to explain the human condition. Although cleverness is rewarded in such biblical heroes as Jacob, who tricks his father Isaac out of the blessing intended for his older brother Esau, independent thinking is more often associated with disobedience and punished, as is the case with Lot's wife, turned into a pillar of salt for curiosity about the fate of Sodom and Gomorrah. This insistence that God's inscrutability is not to be probed by humans is most clearly seen in the Book of Job, in which the voice of God, speaking from the whirlwind, insists that man is too limited in power and knowledge to do anything but accept the world as it is. A similar viewpoint—but without the internal endorsement of God Himself—is found in the later Book of Ecclesiastes, in which the speaker illustrates the futility of man's lot, including the impotence of human knowledge and reasoning.

Later Greek and Roman Literature

Although most Greek tragedies concern themselves with other themes, two deserve mention. Aeschylus' *Promētheus desmōtēs* (*Prometheus Bound,* mid-5th century B.C.), a play difficult to assess because its companion plays are missing, celebrates the hero's defiance of the gods' attempt to keep man in ignorance. In Sophocles' *Oedipus tyrannos* (*Oedipus Rex,* c. 429 B.C.), the hero's attempts to elude his fate by stratagems and his willingness to test his mental acuity, already demonstrated by solving the sphinx's riddle, by unraveling the identity of Laius' murderer ironically lead to his destruction. In the world that Sophocles depicts, mental ability cannot save a man from his god-ordained fate.

Although these tragedies and the Old Comedy dramas of Aristophanes are poles apart in tone and material, they share a conservative denial of the confidence in human mental potential being expressed by such contemporary philosophers as Socrates. Aristophanes attacks this view directly in such comedies as *Nephelai* (*The Clouds,* 423 B.C.), in which Socrates' instruction in philosophy is derided as a bag of oratorical tricks successful only in turning one kind of fool into another.

Later Greek comedy was more romantic, so it was not until the more farcical Roman comedy that stupidity re-emerged as a dramatic theme. Plautus capitalized on the stupidity of such of his characters as in the title role of *Miles gloriosus* (*The Braggart Soldier,* c. 204 B.C.), both by basing his plots on the ease with which they are gulled and by extensive use of dramatic irony, a technique developed by the Greeks that allows the audience to feel superior to certain characters because of its access to information they lack. Thus the stupidity of the characters is a feature of the play's structure as well as of its material.

The comedies of Terence are more sentimental than those of Plautus, but the ridicule of characters who can be outwitted by those cleverer than they continues. Frequently the mental agility is found in a slave, the ally of his young owner, and the stupidity resides in the parents who would thwart a romance. One such play is *Heauton-timorumenos* (*The Self-Punisher,* 163 B.C.). Because Roman comedy, especially that of Terence, was used extensively in later European education, the influence of these treatments was great.

The Roman verse satirists attacked stupidity less frequently than their Renaissance imitators, but Juvenal deserves mention. The corruption of the times of the later Roman emperors is his main subject, but in such of his satires as 3, 8, and 10, Juvenal clearly links human misery with human stupidity.

Folktales

Although many folktales are much older than the literature already discussed, early extant collections date mostly from the Middle Ages. One of the earliest is from India, the *Panchatantra* (*Five Books,* c. 300–500). The tales feature both animal and human adventures and frequently reward the clever in their battles with the stupid. The *Panchatantra* is considered a source and model for medieval European tales, especially those collected in the *Gesta Romanorum* (*Deeds of the Romans,* c. 13th century), which in turn was a source and model for Chaucer, Boccaccio, and others.

Not collected until about 1450, but reflecting situations in India and Baghdad before the eighth century, are the tales called *Alf Layla wa-layla* (*The Arabian Nights,* 8th to 17th centuries). Scheherazade, the vizier's daughter who is able to thwart her cruel husband's intentions by her storytelling, is herself a protagonist who wins through cleverness, as are Sinbad the Sailor, Aladdin, and many others.

The Middle Ages

In the gradual secularization of the liturgical drama in medieval Germany, France, and England, the popular playwrights sometimes capitalized on mental as well as spiritual limitations. The *Wiener Osterspiel* (*Vienna Easter Play,* 15th century) features a wily quack doctor who is outsmarted by his even wilier assistant. In the English *Second Shepherd's Play* (c. 1410) the would-be clever shepherd Mak is caught in his thievery by the other shepherds.

In the late Middle Ages mocking satire appeared in many different areas. Swindlers and dupes abound in such works as the Scandinavian *Bandamanna saga* (*The Confederates,* c. 13th century), in which the clever scalawag Ufeig saves his stuffier son, Odd, from his enemies by clever arguments and schemes; Adam de la Halle's *Le jeu de la feuillée* (*The Play of the Bower,* c. 1262), in which the dupe is a monk relieved of his relics; and the French fabliaux, verse tales by various authors in the twelfth through fourteenth centuries, which were imitated by writers in other countries. Less comic rationalistic examinations of contemporary ideals are found in part 2 of *Le roman de la rose* (*The Romance of the Rose,* c. 1275), in which author Jehan de Meung satirizes courtly love; and in Omar Khayyám's *Rubáiyát* (12th century) verses, in which the Persian poet considers the stupidity and futility of dependence on fame or Eternal Providence.

The Renaissance

The fourteenth, fifteenth, and sixteenth centuries show a renewed attack on the stupidity of man in general or individuals in particular. The comic tales of Geoffrey Chaucer (*Canterbury Tales,* 1380–1400) and Giovanni Boccaccio (*Il decamerone* [*The Decameron,* novellas, c. 1350]) are often reworkings of medieval fabliaux, preserving their clever heroes, who dupe the naïve to gain money or women. Sometimes these masters expose the shortcomings of the would-be clever; one of the most artful is Chaucer's *Pardoner's Tale,* in which the irony of the three revellers outwitting themselves in the Pardoner's story is mirrored in Chaucer's presentation of the Pardoner himself, unknowingly revealing his weaknesses to the audience. Chaucer thus transforms a fabliau form that separates the clever from the stupid into a critical assessment of the human condition.

Such reduction of all men to fools is the theme of two other seminal works of the Renaissance, Sebastian Brant's *Das Narrenschiff* (*Ship of Fools,* satire, 1494) and Erasmus' *Moriae encomium* (*Praise of Folly,* essay, 1511). For both men the final stupidity of all humans is their reluctance to avail themselves of the grace of God, freely offered through the church. What passes for cleverness in the world—learning, rhetorical skills, political power, material success—is stupidity from a cosmic view. Erasmus develops this theme by means of a discourse in which Folly herself claims to do just the opposite—to defend folly as the appropriate and desirable behavior for mankind.

The theme of Christopher Marlowe's *Doctor Faustus* (play, 1604) is quite similar. Faustus, a brilliant, learned man by worldly standards, ironically commits the most egregious folly—he makes a compact with Lucifer to trade his soul for twenty years of pleasure, power, and knowledge. The benefits prove illusory and the price much too high.

François Rabelais in his satires that detail the adventures and attitudes of the giants *Pantagruel* (1532) and *Gargantua* (1534), presents a portrait of society that views stupidity as one of the most characteristic human qualities. The stupidity, however, is of an exuberant, fantastic, and strangely attractive kind, and the shifting perspectives, torrential language, and marvelous invention suggest that Rabelais' satiric analysis of sixteenth-century society should not be emphasized more than his joyous acceptance of imperfect humanity.

The dramatist Lope de Vega satirized the follies of human society in such comedies as *La dama boba* (*The Stupid Lady,* 1613), in which the difference between a bluestocking and her stupid sister disappears after both are transformed by love.

Dramatic tragedies of the period explore the terrible results of a stupid decision or uncalculated action. William Shakespeare's *King Lear* (1605) explores the fate of a man who comes to awareness too late, awareness fostered by his own madness and his association with a fool and a feigned madman. Shakespeare's *Othello* (c. 1604) has connections with the fabliau and the morality play; it shows a man victimized in his innocence by Iago, more devil than trickster. *The Changeling* (1622) by Thomas Middleton and Thomas Rowley presents the repellent but fascinating Beatrice-Joanna, who assumes that her schemes can fulfill all her whims but who is out-tricked by her confederate, De Flores.

Stupidity is an even more frequent theme in late Renaissance comedy. Hans Sachs' farces, for example *Der fahrendt Schüler im Paradeis* (*The Wandering Student from Paradise,* c. 1550), often feature student heroes like those of the fabliaux who deftly exploit simpleminded villagers. In John Heywood's *John John the Husband, Tyb his Wife, and Sir John the Priest* (1533), the exploitation of the husband by the other two characters is not so deft, and he rebels. The Italian commedia dell'arte, or professional improvisational theater of the sixteenth and seventeenth centuries, was more romantic in its interests, but introduced many stock characters—the old man Pantalone, the comic scholar Dottore, the hothead Pulcinella—whose lack of understanding or misplaced self-confidence allowed for the humor of the Italian plays and also served as models for later comic characters created all over Europe. The stupid villagers of the farces, the fabliaux, and the commedia dell'arte are transformed in some of Shakespeare's comedies from objects of derision to standards of decency and justice without increasing their brainpower. The "rude mechanicals" of *A Midsummer Night's Dream* (c. 1595) and the Watch of *Much Ado about Nothing* (c. 1598) muddle their ways through life but help goodness to triumph at last.

Shakespeare's contemporary, Miguel de Cervantes, also links stupidity with goodness, although the world that the idealistic title character of *Don Quijote* (*Don Quixote,* novel, 1605, 1615) inhabits is not so easily redeemed. Don Quixote, intoxicated by the romance of chivalry, cannot separate illusion from reality. While Don Quixote is a satiric version of the knight of romance, his squire, Sancho Panza, is a reworking of a dull but loyal companion who serves as foil. Don Quixote's idealism and Sancho Panza's loyalty and final enthusiasm for their crusade prove more attractive than the crass and selfish individuals that defeat them.

The less sanguine Ben Jonson sees no such saving grace in fools. Almost all his comedies feature characters held up to ridicule for mental deficiencies. Jonson's humor theory of comedy, in which an exaggerated character trait or obsession governs a person's actions, is a development of classical and Italian comic theory. Frequently Jonson's tricksters gloat over their victims' stupidity too soon, only to be subsequently out-tricked themselves. The title character of *Volpone* (play, 1606) prevents his elaborate con-scheme against his would-be heirs from unraveling only to be double-crossed by his servant Mosca. The trio of con-artists in *The Alchemist* (play, 1610) are loyal to each other as long as the dupes fall easily, but when difficulties arise they also turn on each other. In Jonsonian comedy, there are different levels of stupidity. In a similar vein are such comedies as Thomas Middleton's *A Trick to Catch the Old One* (c. 1605) and Philip Massinger's *A New Way to Pay Old Debts* (c. 1625).

Plays of the later seventeenth century are more mannered and class conscious, but the stupidity of certain characters remains an important mainspring of the plots and an important source of satire for the playwrights. An important practitioner was Molière. In his *Tartuffe* (1664) the title character is an egotistical con-artist similar to Volpone in his overreaching, but different in that he plays not on his victims' greed but on their religious impulses. Although the audience laughs at the obtuseness of Tartuffe's victims, they are more appealing and Tartuffe more despicable than the parallel Jonson characters. The ending of *Volpone* celebrates the cleverness of Jonson himself; the exposure of Tartuffe presents a warning and a hope for Molière's society.

Johann Jacob Christoph von Grimmelhausen presents a character in his picaresque novel *Der abenteuerliche Simplicissimus* (*The Adventurous Simplicissimus,* 1669) that represents several different aspects of the stupidity theme. Simplicissimus begins as "ein reiner Tor," an innocent fool, but the harsh world of the Thirty Years War into which he is born transforms him into a sly buffoon. Finally, he renounces the folly and vanity of the world and withdraws in search of spiritual peace.

The Eighteenth Century

The Enlightenment of the eighteenth century produced a renewed attack on stupidity, particularly in England and France. The naïve hero of *Candide* (novel, 1759) by Voltaire finally overcomes his own stupidity to see the stupidity of others—particularly the followers of Leibnitz who try to deny the harshness of human existence. Human folly in religion and social institutions was Voltaire's enduring satiric target in all his works, especially *Essai sur les mœurs* (*Essay on Manners,* 1756) and *Dictionnaire philosophique* (*Philosophical Dictionary,* 1764).

Jonathan Swift shared Voltaire's mistrust of facile optimism; in *Gulliver's Travels* (satire, 1726) humans appear in various guises that emphasize their pettiness and short-sightedness. In book 4 the society of the Houyhnhnms, totally rational horses, runs smoothly but lacks warmth and compassion, and Gulliver's admiration for them is depicted as madness. Alexander Pope examines stupidity in many guises, most typically as it is found in would-be intellectuals and poets. *The Dunciad* (1728–1743) exposes the stupidity of his critics and rivals by blasting them in a mock-heroic poem that establishes Pope's claim to be the superior poet and intellect.

A more sanguine view of the human capacity for stupidity is found in the English novelists of the period. The stupid gentry, clergymen, and townspeople of Henry Fielding's *Tom Jones* (1749) cannot prevent the hero's success, while the more whimsical fools of Laurence Sterne's *Tristram Shandy* (1759–1767) are as attractive as the hero. To Fielding and Sterne, stupidity is a source not of grief but of amusement.

The Nineteenth Century

The romantic movement of nineteenth-century Europe glorified the innocence and purity of children and common people, seeing in them an attractive alternative to the sterile rationalism of the Enlightenment. The French precursor of nineteenth-century romanticism, Jean-Jacques Rousseau, argued in such works as *Emile* (novel, 1762) that a natural environment, away from the depraving tendencies of civilization, produces humans who are happy and good. A similar celebration of the naïve and noncerebral is seen in such poems of William Wordsworth as "We Are Seven" (1800), in which a little girl responds to love and family solidarity and rejects elementary arithmetic, and "Michael" (1800), which sympathetically presents a simple shepherd who loses his land and his son to the crafty and the wicked.

The revival of interest in the common man did not always present his misfortunes so complacently. Such novelists as Charles Dickens also believed that innocence and goodness most frequently reside in the humble, but he regretted rather than glorified their defeats. In Dickens' novels mental agility is usually associated with the exploitation of the weak and stupid, as seen in the crass millowners exposed in *Hard Times* (1854) or the equally crass legal system detailed in *Bleak House* (1853). The wily and materialistic village druggist of Gustave Flaubert's *Madame Bovary* (1856) succeeds, while the frivolous title character fails, but Flaubert presents him as no more attractive. Flaubert just before his death turned again to the subject of the obtuse folly of middle-class Frenchmen in the satire *Bouvard et Pécuchet* (*Bouvard and Pécuchet*, 1881).

Mark Twain, in his novels, sometimes slyly turns the tables on the Rousseau viewpoint, suggesting that city sophistication is a sham that can be penetrated by the occasional rural intellect whose apparent stupidity is really insight. In *The Innocents Abroad* (1869), a fictionalized version of Twain himself as tourist attempts to unmask the absurdities of European culture; in *The Tragedy of Pudd'nhead Wilson* (1894) and *A Connecticut Yankee in King Arthur's Court* (1889), the title characters take on this role.

Other nineteenth-century novelists rejected the innocence/evil dichotomy to reiterate the view that all humanity is flawed. Although usually more interested in sin than in stupidity, Nathaniel Hawthorne, Fyodor Dostoevsky, and Leo Tolstoy occasionally present intellectual achievements as a false hope for human redemption. Such dissimilar characters as Hawthorne's adulterous minister Arthur Dimmesdale (in *The Scarlet Letter*, 1850) Dostoevsky's radical murderer Raskolnikov (in *Prestuplenie i nakazanie* [*Crime and Punishment*, 1866]) and Tolstoy's social-climbing judge Ivan Ilyich (in *Smert' Ivana Il'icha* [*The Death of Ivan Ilyich*, story, 1886]) all learn that failure to humble oneself before the will of God is the final stupidity.

At the end of the nineteenth century the drama became again an important vehicle for the examination of stupidity in society. The problems examined in the plays of Henrik Ibsen are usually exacerbated by the stupidity, egotism, and hypocrisy of such authority figures as the tyrannical husband Torvald Helmer in *Et dukkehjem* (*A Doll's House*, 1879). In *Vildanden* (*The Wild Duck*, 1884), however, Ibsen suggests that total self-knowledge is also destructive, that humans deprived of all illusions, like the teenager Hedvig, cannot go on living. George Bernard Shaw, an admirer of Ibsen, is less solemn but equally serious in his attempt to re-examine contemporary values. Stupidity for Shaw is blind acceptance of outdated codes, and his protagonists are remarkably cerebral and free-spirited. The title character of *Major Barbara* (1905) thinks her way to a position distinct from the naïve pieties of the Salvation Army, the priggish codes of her aristocratic mother, and the contrary capitalism of her madcap father.

The Twentieth Century

Although all the treatments of stupidity have their counterparts in the twentieth century, the most characteristic is a deeply pessimistic acceptance of stupidity as the human condition. Franz Kafka shows in such novels as *Das Schloss* (*The Castle*, 1926) that humans can never understand the rules of the universe in which they are forced to live in isolation and despair. T. S. Eliot, in such poems as *The Waste Land* (1922) and *The Hollow Men* (1925), shows humans as so deficient in physical and mental strengths—and even in resolution—that they can have no real effect on the sterile, inhospitable world they inhabit.

The Italian playwright Luigi Pirandello questions not only human capabilities but the concept of human identity and the very existence of truth. Giving dramatic irony an ironic twist, Pirandello extends to the audience the confusions that kept earlier dramatic characters from discovering the truth. In *Cosi è se vi pare* (*It Is So, If You Think So,* 1917), Signora Ponzo may be her husband's first or second wife; elaborate arguments for many relationships appear, each of which is so plausible that the audience itself must admit to stupidity.

The existentialist philosopher Jean-Paul Sartre and two authors influenced by him, Albert Camus and Samuel Beckett, agree that human paralysis and impotence are pervasive. Sartre's *Huis clos* (*No Exit,* play, 1944) demonstrates his view that man makes his own life. The flawed humans who find themselves in hell in this play are stupid and selfish—and, according to Sartre, without excuses. Camus in such novels as *L'étranger* (*The Stranger,* 1942), the story of a pointless murder, insists on the inability of humans to understand or explain the universe or their role in it. Beckett also presents ineffectual humans unable to understand or make an impression on their world. The tramps of *En attendant Godot* (*Waiting for Godot,* play, 1952) are aware of their shortcomings as they wait for an answer that never comes.

Other twentieth-century authors present human stupidity less bleakly, focusing on the solidarity and spirit of human struggles to overcome and understand. William Faulkner's *The Sound and the Fury* (novel, 1929) reaffirms loyalty and endurance as qualities superior to man's questionable intellect. García Márquez in *Cien años de soledad* (*One Hundred Years of Solitude,* novel, 1967) celebrates the vitality of his ineffectual, confused, sensual South American peasants. For Faulkner and García Márquez, stupidity is the human condition, but humanity is not thus to be dismissed or despised.

See also: Fool.

Selected Bibliography

Tabori, Paul. *The Natural Science of Stupidity.* Philadelphia: Chilton, 1959.

ANITA LAWSON

SUBLIMITY

A sense of grandeur, awe, or loftiness; sometimes an emotional experience combining terror and delight describes "sublimity." Often distinguished from the more pleasing, subdued emotions evoked by beauty, sublimity may have as its root cause, as Edmund Burke suggested, pain or fear. Initially used in a classical rhetorical tradition to suggest a grandeur of style or expression, the sublime was subsequently applied to objects and scenes in nature. A topic of much debate among aestheticians during the eighteenth century, the concept of sublimity underwent painstaking definition and redefinition, asserting a wide and varied influence on neoclassical and romantic prose and poetry. When aestheticians ceased to find fascination in uncovering subtle modulations in sister categories like the beautiful and the picturesque, the sublime was often used to portray subjects that defied the restrictions of ordinary language, as well as the normal limits of the human imagination. In short, sublimity came to connote the ineffable.

Rhetorical Background

Often attributed to Cassius Longinus (c. 213–273), the treatise *Peri hypsous* (*On the Sublime*) was, in all likelihood, written in the first century. "Sublimity" (Gk. "hypsos"), as defined in this treatise, was roughly synonymous with excellence of expression. Its stylistic emphasis is obvious in the author's outlining of five sources of the sublime: grandeur of thought, inspired passion, effective figures, noble diction, and dignified composition. If sublimity later signified an appreciation of isolated moments of rapture or elevation, the author of *On the Sublime* was perhaps its first connoisseur. Occasionally he breaks free from his purely rhetorical emphasis to the deeper sources of literary greatness, as in his discussion of outstanding passages from Homer and the Book of Genesis. The rhetorical sublime was prominent up through the eighteenth century, Longinus receiving praise from Alexander Pope in his *Essay on Criticism* (poem, 1711). Boileau's *Art poétique* (*The Art of Poetry,* didactic poem, 1674), a revival of Longinus, was also influential in England.

Aesthetic Background

Interest in the sublimity of external nature developed out of a confluence of religious, scientific, and epistemological forces. Thomas Burnet's *The Sacred Theory of the Earth,* English translation of the first volume of *Telluris theoria sacra* (Latin, 1681; English, 1684) is often cited as the work that marks a major shift in the aesthetics of nature in English culture. Before Burnet, the concept of infinitude had a theological basis, and the term "sublime" was often associated with the numinous and the divine. To the Christian world before the seventeenth century, external nature manifested God's will and judgment. Hardly the sole context for an emerging aesthetics of nature, this theological dimension merged with growing interest in branches of natural history, geology, and astronomy to focus attention on the grand spectacles of the natural world, notably chasms, mountains, and gorges. Burnet, in favoring the unfamiliar and strange rather than the harmonious and orderly, established, in particular, a novel way of looking at mountains. In the jagged confusion of rocks and the obscure disorder of caverns, Burnet discerned a magnificence that haunted the imagination. Burnet's strong emotional response, originally derived from religious experience, assumed its place as a normal reaction to great events, superior works of art, and grand scenery. Response to the infinite, once reserved for God, angels, heavenly bodies, or mythological figures, acquired the more general meaning of emotional transport. This response to the vast, irregular, and energetic in nature was called the "sublime." As Marjorie Hope Nicolson has pointed out, the sense of sublimity in external nature, perhaps more than any other attitude, marks the difference between seventeenth- and eighteenth-century aesthetics.

In its response to mountains, Burnet's *Sacred Theory,* nevertheless, reiterated the conceptions of its predecessors by describing the so-called decay of nature. In a religious context, the world was seen as a massive ruin; the cursed earth was subject to the judgment of an awesome deity. While the emotional delight with which Burnet surveyed the mountainous ruins of the earth distinguished his response to nature, he could not unshackle the imagination from orthodox strictures because of the "decay of nature" theme.

The epistemology of John Locke (*An Essay Concerning Human Understanding,* 1690) provides the crucial linkage that furthered the cult of the natural sublime. The Lockean faculty of the imagination stood at a critical midpoint between immediate sense impressions and the faculty of understanding. The imagination remained sensitive to immediate impressions, but also possessed an organizing power to group them. Locke therefore placed new emphasis on the effects on the human imagination rather than on the qualities located inherently in external objects. Vision, in particular, monopolized mental activity with a resultant expanded interest in the beauties of landscape. With a premium placed on simple sensations, Locke contributed to an ongoing movement toward subjectivism, paradoxically occurring in an objective age of science. Like previous theories, Lockean epistemology took account of sense impressions, but unlike the old philosophy, which moved by analogy or ascent to higher spiritual realms, the age of Locke moved by breadth in its respect for the discreteness of immediate sense impressions. Lockean empiricism provided the epistemological support for the new vogue of the natural sublime. External space not only *reflected* the attributes of God but came to *share* the qualities of the deity. As the vast and empty spaces of the earth acquired a sacred character, a sense of nature's immensity ceased to be a mere metaphor for an incomprehensible spiritual realm and became an actual part of human experience. Lockean epistemology, in other words, transferred the concept of infinity from God to space. As this concept was extended to objects in the landscape that gave the impression of infinity, interest in the natural sublime increased.

Bearing indirect witness to Locke's impact, the title of Mark Akenside's poem *The Pleasures of Imagination* (1744) displays the cultivation of appreciative feelings derived from an experience of vastness: "What human heart / E'er doubts, before the transient and the minute, / To prize the vast, the stable, and sublime." Since imaginative gratification resulted not only from immediate sensations but also from secondary pleasures that flow from ideas of visible objects, opportunities existed for an explicitly *aesthetic* response to nature. The so-called sublime poem of the late seventeenth and eighteenth centuries—whose major practitioners were Gray, Collins, and Thomson—was richly adorned by a vocabulary of sense impressions resulting from a passionate encounter with the natural world. Equally as important as the lofty subject matter and cumulative phrasing of these poems were the emotional effects induced in the reader. Subjective effects became as important as subject matter, and literary impact derived as much from uplift to a sublime pitch of emotion as from expressed content. The sublime poem achieved respectability, and in some cases, even superseded old generic distinctions, such as the epic. With the categorizing tendency of the eighteenth century asserting itself, the sublime distinguished itself from other responses to nature.

The most famous manifestation of this tendency to categorize is Edmund Burke's *A Philosophical Enquiry into the Origin of our Ideas of the Sublime and Beautiful* (1757), perhaps the most influential aesthetic treatise of the eighteenth century. Notable for his emphasis on the psychological basis of human responses, Burke attempted to classify certain objects, such as oceans, precipices, and caverns, which evoke the sublime. He perhaps achieved greater notoriety for his claim that sublimity and beauty cannot be reconciled without detracting from their effects. Burke's contribution is most important, however, for his notion that pain, in its extremity, can be a source of the sublime. Since pain carries as a latent threat the extinction of life, Burke argued that the fear of death is the basis of the sublime. While Burke has received criticism for his somewhat primitive physiological analysis of this response, his inclusion of terror as a component of sublimity carries special significance.

Burke's *Philosophical Enquiry* asserted such a wide influence that it had an impact even on those who never read it. Burke's "delightful horror" stimulated the imaginations of poets and novelists not only during the eighteenth century but for many subsequent decades. Its influence on the Gothic novel was immense, as a survey of Ann Radcliffe's novels abundantly demonstrate (*A Sicilian Romance,* 1790; *The Romance of the Forest,* 1791; *The Mysteries of Udolpho,* 1794; and *The Italian,* 1797). Burke's treatise was attractive, partially because it provided an implicit challenge to the constraints of classical decorum in literature and the other arts. Before Burke, the response to the *sublime* was always teleologically informed, that is, an appeal to immensity was divinely sanctioned, morally oriented, or scientifically based. Burke opened the human sensibility to utter vastness because of his radical sensationist bias, his attention to immediate rather than final causes.

In the development of the sublime aesthetic, however, the opposite effect often became just as prominent. The prospect of emotional chaos through immediate sense impressions carried such ominous potency that it became easier to exploit rather than to endure novel emotional states. In much Gothic fiction—Radcliffe's novels are pertinent examples—the sublime served to indicate, by aesthetic distance, that particular characters did not face mortal danger. In addition, several of Burke's contemporaries and subsequent aestheticians acted to check the rampant emotionalism that the *Philosophical Enquiry* might have engendered. In negative reaction to the *work,* Burke's influence manifested itself as strongly as in its positive impact.

The most cogent qualification of Burkean aesthetics came from the so-called Common Sense school of philosophy. While most of the adherents of Common Sense agreed with Burke that literature functioned primarily to communicate emotion, their theories also acted as a check by keeping emotion within rational bounds. Dugald Stewart (*Philosophical Essays,* 1810), for example, stated that power supported the sensation of the sublime, but he kept that notion within the framework of final teleological causes. He made his ultimate appeal to the powers of God and showed that sublimity was the transference from objects of religious worship to things "analogous." In this limited sense, Stewart harked back to the religious matrix of the sublime. Lord Kames, in his *Elements of Criticism* (treatise, 1762), urged attention to the grand and elevating objects of nature. Finding them universally agreeable, he nevertheless warned that their appeal eluded rational scrutiny.

Archibald Alison provided the transition between the Common Sense philosophers and the early Romantics in his *Essays on the Nature and Principles of Taste* (treatise, 1790), which displays marked affinities with eighteenth-century rationalism but also lays the theoretical groundwork for the romantic glorification of the imagination. If aesthetic appreciation consisted merely of the receipt of sense impressions, Alison suggested, the role of the artist was narrowly circumscribed. If art is the reproduction of a limited group of impressions, then each artist would be reduplicating the work of his predecessors. A strict Lockean sensationalism, according to Alison, assumed that only a restricted set of forms could be beautiful, that art might be exhausted by a repetition of identical patterns.

Responding to this challenge, Alison emphasized a subjective "train of associations," locating the aesthetic effect in the mind of the perceiver. The response to a grand object was not located in external nature but in an emotive act, conditioned by a train of associations in the mind of the perceiver. Whereas pre-Lockean philosophy explained the relationship between a perceiver and the grand in nature by divine analogy, the associationists located this relationship in the psychology of the observer. The perceiver's aesthetic response to the natural sublime was influenced by mental associations induced by the observed object.

As the sublime aesthetic developed outside English culture, a further step in the direction of subjectivism was provided by German idealism. Most notably, Kant's *Kritik der Urteilskraft* (*The Critique of Judgment,* treatise, 1790) locates the sublime in man's imagination, not in nature. Kant, in one sense, extends Burke's claim that the sublime is a feeling of delightful horror. But while Burke's catalogue of sublime objects consisted of tumultuous seas, craggy precipices, and dark caverns, Kant confronted man with himself; in Robert Kiely's words (*The Romantic Novel in England,* 1972), man was limited by his senses but capable of imagining the limitless. Sublimity, Kant argued, could not be located in nature because the sublime response was the mental capacity to transcend the world of sensations. Discomfort results because sublime transport is impossible in the realm of sensations. Delight comes from the capacity to transcend the sensuous world by a leap of the imagination. Thus Kant and those he influenced, like Schiller and Coleridge, retained a measure of Burkean terror and delight. In fact, the visionary character of the sublime reaches its culmination in Kant's emphasis on the imagination's unlimited capacity.

Kant achieves further categorization in his distinction between the mathematical and the dynamic sublime. The former arises from the mental attempt to apprehend and comprehend increasingly extensive multitudes. The latter is aroused by confrontation with powerful natural forces that threaten to overwhelm man. Representative examples of the dynamic sublime include the boundless ocean in a tumultuous state, a lofty waterfall, or a mighty river. Kant argues that resistance to dynamic natural forces induces the imagination to transcend them and thus to render them insignificantly small by comparison with the imagination. The Kantian terms of the mathematical sublime—indicating immense size, a sense of the infinite, proportions beyond imaginable bounds—and the dynamic sublime—reflecting absolute power, overwhelming forces, and stormy tumult—provide convenient foci for discerning nuances among aesthetic categories.

Toward the Romantic Sublime

All these aesthetic assumptions were not confined to eighteenth-century treatises. The English poetic tradition found a standard of artistic sublimity in Milton's epic *Paradise Lost* (1667). In poem after poem—Thomas Gray's "The Progress of Poesy" (1757) and William Collins' "Ode on the Poetical Character" (1747) are two clear examples—Milton was glorified as the figure whose vision, execution, and lofty intellect led to genuine sublimity. In effect, the Miltonic became the true sublime. Byron's comments in the preface to his epic *Don Juan* (1819–1824) stand as a point of perspective in this tradition, this sustained bardolatry of the author of *Paradise Lost*: "If, fallen in evil days on evil tongues, / Milton appealed to the Avenger, Time, / If Time, the Avenger execrates his wrongs / And makes the word "Miltonic" mean "sublime." If Milton represented a worthy model in an epic mode, other poets attempted similar effects in descriptive verse. In the 1740s, three long poems appeared, all concerned with the *sublime*: James Thomson's *The Seasons* (1726–1730; enlarged, 1744; 1746), Akenside's *The Pleasures of Imagination,* and Edward Young's *Night Thoughts* (1742–1745). For Akenside, sublimity was equated with radiance, an awful light that brightened the path toward celestial truth. Perhaps owing to Milton's majestic descriptions of darkness, however, the sublime gradually developed into an aesthetic of obscurity. Thomson's "Spring" was lit by the tinctures of Beauty, but his other seasons fell under the pall of darkness: "Solemn and slow the shadows blacker fall / And all is awful listening gloom around." A climax in this ever-darkening treatment of nature came in Young's *Night Thoughts*. As his title suggests, the gentler tones of Beauty are scanted in favor of the obscurity of night, scenes laid in darkness and devoid of color.

Burke would codify the aesthetics of obscurity in his *Philosophical Enquiry* by stating: "Night increases our terror more perhaps than any thing else." With his stress on delightful terror, he would list among the sources of sublimity an entire array of "privations": "Vacuity, Darkness, Solitude, and Silence." By linking the extremes of terror and shadowy obscurity, Burke provided a bridge by which the neoclassical sublime could transform itself into a species of the romantic sensibility. German idealism had injected a stronger element of subjectivism into emerging aesthetic doctrine, but of equal importance, writers sought symbols that would represent the private, shadowy recesses of the human imagination. Among these conventional symbols of the human psyche, suitably tinged with Burkean obscurity, were caves, caverns, castles, palaces, vaults, passageways, ruins, towers, and blasted trees. The word "shadow" itself came to represent a hidden, buried layer of human consciousness. The continued emphasis on natural grandeur, vastness, and infinite greatness served the openness of purpose demanded by the sublime mode, but under the aegis of romantic individualism, an encapsulating tendency helped to focus on subjective emotional states.

Almost all the major romantic poets display an overt interest in the sublime. Wordsworth wrote an essay on sublimity (published posthumously), mentioned "that sense sublime" that interfuses all nature in "Tintern Abbey" (poem, 1798), and devoted several passages to the mixture of terror and beauty in *The Prelude* (philosophical poem, 1799–1805). Book 6 of *The Prelude,* in particular, contains a remarkable series of pairings in which tumult and peace, darkness and light, sublimity and beauty join in visionary coalescence. Coleridge's comments on the sublimity of architectural forms and literary greatness are sprinkled throughout his criticism. The convergence of terror and beauty in Keats's poetry (*Lamia, Hyperion,* and "La Belle Dame Sans Merci"; all 1820) suggests an indebtedness to Burkean aesthetics. The conventions of the sublime figure perhaps more pervasively in the poetry of Byron and Shelley. More specifically, these two Romantics display a fascination with the dynamics of ocean storms, a favorite subject in the tradition of sublimity that goes back to Longinus. Byron's famous stanza in *Childe Harold's Pilgrimage* (poem, 1812–1818), "Roll on, thou deep and dark blue Ocean" is an apt example of oceanic dynamism. Perhaps to an even greater degree than Byron, Shelley was preoccupied with the tumultuous sublimity of the ocean. In *Alastor* (poem, 1816), the poet is "rejoicing in the fearful war / Of wave running on wave, and Blast / Descending and black flood on whirlpool driven / With dark obliterating course." In "Ode to the West Wind" (poem, 1819), the speaker wishes for "A wave to pant beneath the power and share / The impulse of thy strength, only less free / Than thou, O uncontrollable!" Of particular moment to Shelley was the association of the ocean with death. The sea induced an impulse toward greatness at the same time it threatened like the grave, delight attended by terror. The association of the ocean with mortality is particularly evident in "Lines Written among the Euganean Hills" (1818), in which the speaker hopes for "One remembrance; more sublime / Than the tattered pall of time."

In addition to enhancing this fascination with oceanic power, the sublime helped to further the interest in ruins and caverns that occupied writers well into the nineteenth century. Awe before ruins prevails in the Coliseum section of *Childe Harold's Pilgrimage.* Caves, caverns, chasms, and craggy hills provide ubiquitous decor in Shelley's *Prometheus Unbound* (verse drama, 1820). The poet in *Alastor* flees before a storm and pursues "the windings of the cavern" and "huge caves / Scoop'd in the dark base of their aery rocks." The vast size of caves and caverns opened the soul to nature, but their immense antiquity and ruined forms suggested a complementary tendency toward circumscription. For the Romantics, the secret and awesome places of the earth served as symbols of the aspirations and limits of the human soul.

The American Sublime

Developed in an English and Continental context, the aesthetic of sublimity was transferred to America and given a distinctive native flavor. In the early half of the nineteenth century, editions of Kames's *Elements of Criticism,* Hugh Blair's *Lectures on Rhetoric and Belles-Lettres* (treatise, 1783), and Stewart's *Philosophical Essays* were required reading in American colleges and universities. German aesthetic thought, influenced by Kantian doctrines, was sifted to Americans through intermediaries such as Coleridge, Carlyle, and Madame de Staël. While puritanical restrictions thwarted some appreciative reaction to the romantic poets and Gothic novelists, several American authors responded sensitively to Byron, Shelley, and their contemporaries. The sublime developed a peculiarly native cast as a new element was added to the category: nationalism.

Landscape description served as more than a literary device; it became a pretext for defining the needs of a nation seeking self-definition. With the aesthetics of the prominent British treatise writers asserting influence, the sublime became an ornament of the nation's expansive geography. In the beauty and majesty of their landscape, Americans discerned reserves of that neoclassical desideratum, the sublime. In much writing of the early national period, authors assumed that scenic grandeur guaranteed sublimity of poetic vision. By extension, the purity of landscape would insure the robust development of the hardy American character. Because America, at the turn of the nineteenth century, had no well-defined literature it could call its own, it looked to the Augustan aestheticians for stimulation. To minds nurtured on Kames and Blair, the sublime became an apt vehicle for describing grand scenery. As Benjamin Spencer has noted, a concerted effort to transform Niagara into the quintessential American poem had begun.

William Bartram's *Travels* (1791) marks the first extensive use of the sublime in American letters. A naturalist rather than a professional *littérateur*, Bartram was "seduced by those sublime enchanting scenes of primitive nature" during his trip to Florida's Lake George. Likewise, in the Carolinas, Bartram "beheld with rapture and astonishment, a sublimely awful scene of power and magnificence, a world of mountains piled with mountains." Replete with references to the vastness of the American landscape, Bartram's *Travels* displays a religious rather than a purely aesthetic orientation, since he links natural grandeur to divine power. American scenery owes its majesty to "the supreme author of nature" whose "wisdom and power" manifest themselves in the wilderness.

The sublime appealed to naturalists and explorers like Bartram, but more often, the perceiver was a man of leisure and taste, a tourist who had developed an appreciation for landscape aided by sophistication and study. Thomas Jefferson's *Notes on the State of Virginia* (1784–1785) combined a well-developed sense of taste with nationalistic sentiments in its proud description of Virginia's Natural Bridge. Contributing to a debate on the relative merits of American and European scenery that would extend into the next century, Jefferson claimed that this scene was well worth the voyage across the Atlantic. He calls the Natural Bridge "the most sublime of nature's works," conceiving the scene with adroit attention to its aesthetic possibilities.

Travel and promotional literature did much to advertise the sublimity of American scenery, foreshadowing a gradual transition by which aesthetic categories became incorporated into fiction and poetry. Charles Brockden Brown's novels owe much to the aesthetics of obscurity, especially the wilderness scenes in *Edgar Huntly* (1799). Sensitive to the scarcity of antique associations and social shadings in America, other authors strove self-consciously to place native landscape in a theater of recognizable human events. James Fenimore Cooper's novels, most notably *The Leatherstocking Tales* (1823–1841) and *The Spy* (1821), exploit the categories of the sublime, the picturesque, and the beautiful. Similar aesthetic interests are found in the poems of William Cullen Bryant.

Washington Irving stressed the sublime aspects of American scenery in his nonfictional works *Astoria* (1836) and *A Tour on the Prairies* (1835), as well as manipulated similar pictorial techniques in *The Sketch Book* (tales, 1819–1820).

Other writers of the so-called American Renaissance exploited the sublime according to personal predilection. Hawthorne seems ambivalent about the powerful energies of sublimity in his sketch "My Visit to Niagara" (1835). Amidst the litany of superlatives used to describe the "salt-sea mastodon," the White Whale, Melville turned to the characteristics of the Burkean sublime in *Moby-Dick* (novel, 1851). In his portrayal of the many facets of wilderness life, Thoreau sometimes evoked the natural sublime, especially when nature assumed its wildest, most untamed character (*The Maine Woods,* 1864; *Cape Cod,* 1865). Ever conscious of locales where terror of the soul was regnant, Edgar Allan Poe linked the sensation of fear with spiritual transport, most notably in his sea tales ("MS. Found in a Bottle," 1833; *The Narrative of Arthur Gordon Pym,* 1838; and "A Descent into the Maelström," 1841).

The taste for expansive scenery had two outlets outside the specifically literary domain: interest in formal landscape gardens and patronage of so-called grand tours. In the 1830s and 1840s in America, travelers armed with Claude glasses and sketchbooks recorded their impressions of a whole range of "sublimities": mountains, rivers, caverns, gorges, and forests. The Catskills, Albany, West Point, and the Connecticut Oxbow were favorite locations for the American tour; they were native analogues to the attractions of European mountains and forests. These tours had a circular movement, since they usually commenced from a gardened estate, manor house, or cottage and plunged into the wilderness. The circular transit from domesticity to the wilds and back to civilization was achieved upon completion of the tour. The writings of major figures like Hawthorne, Melville, Poe, and Thoreau are not totally comprehensible unless viewed within the context of these tourist and travel books, a tradition that begins with Bartram and Timothy Dwight (*Travels in New England and New York,* 1821–1822) and continues up to Bryant's *Picturesque America* (descriptive prose, 1872) and Henry James's *The American Scene* (descriptive prose, 1907). John Wesley Powell's *Explorations of the Colorado River* (1875, 1895) stands at a point of perspective in this tradition, the awesome sublimity of the river representing the survival of the old aesthetics in the literature of official exploration. Wallace Stevens' poem "The American Sublime" (1936) provides a later gloss on these native writings, the grandeur of American scenery having been appropriated by a national officialdom.

The Decay of the Sublime

A general tendency of aesthetic thought in the nineteenth century was toward a blurring of the distinction between the sublime and the beautiful, which were held as rigid polarities by Burke and his followers. As the human imagination was called upon to respond to the grand and vast in so many different contexts—

in nature, architecture, painting, and literature—the sublime and beautiful, held in fixed contradistinction in the eighteenth century, more closely merged. Thus, as several scholars have claimed, exclusive interest in the aesthetic of sublimity waned after 1860. A new aesthetic category emerged, furthering the collapse of Burke's lucid bifurcation. The picturesque, as defined by the British aestheticians William Gilpin, Uvedale Price, and Humphry Repton, occupied a midpoint between the wild irregularity of sublimity and the graceful repose of beauty. Essentially appealing to the "painterly" eye of the perceiver, the picturesque was composition-oriented and stressed the manipulation of color, texture, and light.

In America the voices of the sublime were on the wane by the 1840s. The sublime had been exploited by those writers who sought to celebrate native scenery to fulfill the psychological needs of a country thirsting for greatness. In their respective turns, however, writers like Poe and Melville had dropped out of the chorus of sublime voices. The 1840s brought not only a flood of second-rate literature with chauvinistic overtones but also grandiose pictorial dramas like Thomas Cole's series of five allegorical scenes completed in 1836, *The Course of Empire*. Such displays were ill-suited to those writers whose taste did not run to oversized panoramas or gaudy spectacles. Melville turned away from the broad expanses of *Moby-Dick* to such intensely circumscribed tales as *Bartleby the Scrivener* (1853), and Poe forsook scenic grandeur to probe the subtle responses of individual minds under stress. By the latter part of the century, the critic Richard Dowling, sensing a transition in aesthetic taste, could lament the decay of the sublime ("The Decay of the Sublime," in *Ignorant Essays, 1888*).

In "Signs of the Times" (essay, 1829), Thomas Carlyle, questioning the late-romantic worship of power and grandeur, implied that Victorian moralism would feel uncomfortable with the untrammeled emotional excess of the romantic sublime. If taken as an index of broad cultural trends, Carlyle's comment was prophetic; nevertheless, the sublime continued to play a significant, if muted, role. Tennyson's "On Sublimity" (1827) functioned as an adolescent poetic exercise, but Ruskin's "On Water" in *Modern Painters* (prose, 1843–1860) enthusiastically endorsed the oceanic sublime. For Ruskin the paintings of J.M.W. Turner epitomized the wild energies of the dynamic sea. If less rhapsodic than Ruskin about the power inherent in natural phenomena, other Victorian authors described human responses that recall Burke's mixture of terror and delight. The neo-Gothic landscapes and wild emotions in Emily Brontë's *Wuthering Heights* (novel, 1847) and Charlotte Brontë's *Jane Eyre* (novel, 1847) suggest the sublime. Hardy's description of Egdon Heath in the first chapter of *The Return of the Native* (novel, 1878) introduces a contrast between orthodox and unparalleled beauty that recalls Burke's lucid dichotomy. Writers as different as George Eliot (*The Mill on the Floss*, 1860) and George Meredith (*The Ordeal of Richard Feverel*, 1859) evoke the wild energies of nature in their novels. The mixture of dark terror and holy dread in Hopkins' "The Wreck of the Deutschland'' (poem, 1875, published posthumously in 1918) also reflects a debt to a long-standing aesthetic tradition.

The critic Lionel Trilling has suggested that the sublime ''has much more bearing on our own literature than modern critics have recognized'' (''The Fate of Pleasure,'' in *Beyond Culture,* 1965). Perhaps the old-fashioned response to sublimity is not as far removed as some commentators have claimed from the sense of anxiety and anguish that permeates so much contemporary fiction. One significant difference between the old aesthetics and the new *Weltanschauung,* however, is readily apparent. Kant claimed that two things filled the mind with awe: the ''starry firmament'' above and the moral law within. Kant thus saw a happy coincidence between the laws of the universe and those of the human spirit. With its emphasis on nausea, forlornness, and alienation, much modern fiction seems to retain the sense of being dwarfed by immensity without the secure internal boundaries that distinguish Kantian doctrine. The literature of existentialism, in particular, seems to emphasize the puniness of man in the face of intractable forces.

Paradoxically, while some contemporaneous critics of Burke were concerned about the blindness of emotions in the sublime, its allegedly empty moral content, several modern writers have returned to the old aesthetics, finding a resource by which to resurrect moral and spiritual meaning. In his analysis of the *mysterium tremendum,* Rudolf Otto (*Das Heilige* [*The Idea of the Holy,* philosophy, 1917]) describes the feeling of holy dread as sublime. Different from fear but close enough to it to recall Burke's terror and delight, Otto's sublimity marks an encounter with the wholly other, a radical confrontation with powers outside the human person. Similarly, the novelist Iris Murdoch, in two essays (''The Sublime and the Beautiful Revisited'' and ''The Sublime and the Good,'' 1959), claims that great art grants a somber delight akin to our recognition of morality. For Murdoch, whose essays contain rich implications for the study of fiction, the sublime suggests a ''vast and varied reality,'' nearly infinite in its particularity, which draws us out of ourselves to witness the spectacle of human life.

Nonetheless, with elaborate spectacles having been appropriated by popular culture and the technological media, there seems less opportunity for serious literature to compete with such oversized effects. The old aesthetics of nature still appear in serious fiction, sometimes to evoke a bygone era (Wallace Stegner's novel, *Angle of Repose,* 1971). As an alternative, modern portrayals of wild nature, without explicitly mentioning aesthetic categories, may evoke that mixture of fear and exhilaration that recalls Burke's terror and delight (James Dickey, *Deliverance,* novel, 1970). Wallace Stevens' ironic and witty ''The American Sublime'' is perhaps more typical of modern treatments in its suggestion that authentic grandeur is often lost on the insensitive masses; the majority seems to mistake counterfeit forms, represented by the culture of officialdom, for the true sublime. Stevens furthermore suggests that genuine sublimity cannot be resurrected by renewed contact with traditional or conventional external sources: the sea or the landscape. Rather, to rediscover the sublime, one must return to immediate sensation; one must be, as it were, an empty spirit open to variety and immensity amidst infinite space. For Stevens, the sublime experience, in essence, enacts a process of self-discovery, conditioned by submission to "otherness" and enhanced by release of some part of the self that is given novel existence. In the poem, however, the tasteless form of an official statue overshadows the speaker's desire to "behold" something grander. The poem implicitly confirms Goethe's cryptic claim that the sublime, having been banished by quotidian and practical concerns, must, for its own survival, conceal itself and take refuge in other forms. In modern literature, sublimity survives, sometimes in deceptive guises. Stevens' poem and Goethe's claim give Thomas Mann's statement about modern art a telling credence. Art "has ceased to recognize the categories of the tragic and comic. . . . It sees life as tragi-comedy, with the result that the grotesque is its most genuine style—to the extent, indeed, that today that is the only guise in which the sublime may appear."

See also: Psychic Landscape, Travel.

Selected Bibliography

Hipple, Walter J. *The Beautiful, the Sublime, and the Picturesque in Eighteenth-Century British Aesthetic Theory*. Carbondale: Southern Illinois University Press, 1957.

Monk, Samuel Holt. *The Sublime: A Study of Critical Theories in Eighteenth-Century England*. New York: MLA, 1935.

Nicolson, Marjorie Hope. *Mountain Gloom and Mountain Glory: The Development of the Aesthetics of the Infinite*. Ithaca, N.Y.: Cornell University Press, 1959.

Tuveson, Ernest Lee. *The Imagination as a Means of Grace: Locke and the Aesthetics of Romanticism*. Berkeley: University of California Press, 1960.

KENT LJUNGQUIST

T
//

TERROR

The Oxford English Dictionary defines terror as "the state of being terrified or greatly frightened; intense fear, fright, or dread." Because many authors use the terms "terror" and "horror" interchangeably, and because many combine terror with horror, the two terms are often confused. Fear of an extraordinary intensity is the operating principle of terror. Fear is also a characteristic of horror, but with horror that fear becomes so dreadful as to result in loathing, abhorrence, or revulsion.

Some generalizations can be made about the ways that authors evoke terror and about the reasons they use it as a theme or motif in their works by examining the evolution of terror in literature. When characters are frightened by physical danger or death, by supernatural occurrences, or by their own excessive imaginations, they experience terror. Another type of terror results from a character's learning about his or her own guilt or about others' evil natures or criminal behavior. Some authors include terror in their works to illustrate a moral or a truth about human nature; some use it to cause the reader or audience to empathize with the hero or heroine. Still others use it to show the interrelatedness of emotions—the connection between pleasure and pain, melancholy and love. Finally, many authors, particularly of popular literature, use terror primarily for entertainment.

An eighteenth-century essay, "On the Pleasure Derived from Objects of Terror" (from *Miscellaneous Pieces in Prose* by John and Anna Laetitia Aikin— later Mrs. Barbauld—[London, 1773]), accounts for the popular appeal of some types of terror. The reader's love of a

strange and unexpected event awakens the mind, and keeps it on the stretch; and where the agency of invisible beings is introduced, of "forms unseen, and mightier far than we," our imagination, darting forth, explores with rapture the new world which is laid open to its view, and rejoices in the expansion of its powers. Passion and fancy co-operating elevate the soul to its highest pitch; and the pain of terror is lost in amazement.

Thus, because of the reader's fascination with curiosity and suspense, terror, which could be potentially painful, often becomes pleasurable instead. A primary ingredient of the Gothic novel, terror was in vogue in England from about 1775 through about 1815, but there has been in the popular fiction and film of the mid-twentieth century a revival of interest in terror.

Origin and Historical Background

Aristotle discusses "fear," which term appears to be synonymous with terror, in his *Rhētorikē technē* (*Rhetoric,* treatise, c. 360 B.C.):

Fear may be defined as a pain or disturbance due to a mental picture of some destructive or painful evil in the future. . . . From this definition it will follow that fear is caused by whatever we feel has great power of destroying us, or of harming us in ways that tend to cause us great pain. Hence the very indications of such things are terrible, making us feel that the terrible thing itself is close at hand.

In his *Peri poiētikēs* (*Poetics,* 4th century B.C.), Aristotle concludes that tragedy produces pleasure by arousing and then purging "fear and pity." Thus, feelings of pity or empathy for the hero or heroine, like curiosity and suspense, transform a potentially painful emotion into a pleasurable one, and terror becomes morally beneficial.

Antiquity and the Middle Ages

In Sophocles' play *Oidipous tyrannos* (*Oedipus Rex,* c. 429 B.C.), the plot structure that gradually leads to Oedipus terrifying discovery of the truth produces a kind of pleasure for the audience. Oedipus fled from Corinth because he feared the prophecy that he would murder his father and marry his mother; yet the dread aroused by the prophecy remained with him. Sophocles uses the theme of terror to illustrate the universal fears of being ruled by perverse fate and of acquiring knowledge of one's own guilt. Mortals have no need to fear when chance reigns supreme, Iocaste tells Oedipus; but when she finally realizes that prophecies are not worthless, she kills herself in despair. Despite Oedipus' fear that he is on the brink of "dreadful hearing," he demands the truth about his parentage. Finally, when the suspense is over, the blind Oedipus continues to arouse terror and pity: "Dreadful indeed for men to see. / Never have my [Choragos] own eyes / Looked on a sight so full of fear." The chorus wants to understand Oedipus' terrible fate, but terror that he reflects a universal fate prevents it. Sophocles concludes that mortals can not be happy until they die and can suffer no more.

The epic poem *Beowulf,* written in about the first half of the eighth century, treats the theme of terror quite differently. Succumbing to terror is a character flaw, something that an Anglo-Saxon hero must avoid; thus the reader feels no pity for characters' fears in *Beowulf.* The author affirms that to win fame, a hero must overcome terror and fight bravely. The Danes abandon Heorot because of their terror, and Unferth gives up his chances for winning fame because he is afraid of risking his life in the hellish lake where Grendel's mother lives. Even Grendel becomes "frightened in his spirit" when he feels Beowulf's strong grip. Beowulf, on the other hand, is not terrified by either Grendel or his mother; fear and Beowulf are strangers. In his last battle, Beowulf's heart is "heavy." Still he fights bravely against the monster-dragon. Beowulf's and Wiglaf's courage in the face of that awesome fire-breathing adversary is a contrast to the other Geatish warriors, who "crept to the wood, protected their lives" in terror. The shame they will suffer for their cowardice, Wiglaf tells them, will be worse than death.

The Renaissance

Terror in Shakespearean tragedy produces an effect similar to that of Greek tragedy; it produces pleasure by evoking pity for the tragic heroes as the audience watches them move (often, like Oedipus, blindly) to their destruction. Terror is particularly evident in *Hamlet* (c. 1600) and *Macbeth* (1605–1606); it functions in part to entertain, but it also has a thematic function. In both plays terror humanizes the tragic heroes. Facing terror demands greatness of spirit; however, becoming immune to it leads to different ends.

The appearance of the ghost at the beginning of *Hamlet* is at first startling. When Horatio notices the ghost's likeness to the dead king, he says, "it harrows me with fear and wonder." The reactions to the ghost then become more complex. Both Hamlet and Horatio respond to Elizabethan fears that supernatural apparitions may be demons in disguise. The audience pities Hamlet's indecision because, until Claudius reveals his guilt during "The Mouse-Trap" play, the audience, like Hamlet, is not sure if the ghost is "an honest" one.

Hamlet confronts yet another kind of fear in the play. The famous "To be or not to be" soliloquy, a philosophical discussion that addresses the terrors of death, evokes pity for Hamlet because of the universality of his emotion:

> . . . the dread of something after death,
> The undiscovered country, from whose bourn
> No traveler returns, puzzles the will,
> And makes us rather bear those ills we have,
> Than fly to others that we know not of?
> Thus conscience does make cowards of us all.

Hamlet rejects suicide and overcomes his terrors of death. The hardened, fearless Hamlet of act 5, though, goaded on by his desire for vengeance, like Oedipus, moves to his "destruction." Nevertheless, by overcoming terror, Hamlet gains self-knowledge and nobility. He is able to face the possibility of his death without fear and to accept the will of Providence: "The readiness is all. Since no man of aught he leaves knows, what is't to leave betimes? Let be."

Terror is even more evident in *Macbeth*. Excessively imaginative, Macbeth is particularly vulnerable to fears aroused by his imagination and by the super-natural. Like Hamlet's fears, Macbeth's are natural human emotions; unlike Hamlet, however, when Macbeth overcomes terror, he becomes a monster. That he is not terrified by the witches when he first meets them reflects the strength of his character at the beginning of the play; his conscience is still clear. As Macbeth degenerates from an ambitious, yet virtuous man who is "too full o' the milk of human kindness," toward becoming the "dead butcher," he gradually becomes more susceptible to terror. Ultimately, however, the process reverses and he grows impervious to fear. Before he kills Duncan, Macbeth is awed by the dagger he sees before him and frightened when "gouts of blood" appear on the handle and blade. When he does the deed, he hears a voice (either, like the dagger, imaginary or supernatural) cry, "Sleep no more! Macbeth does murder sleep." Terrified both by his guilt from the terrible crime he has committed and by the sight of his bloody hands (badges of that guilt), Macbeth refuses to return the daggers and to smear the grooms with blood. Every "noise appalls" him, he says, as he hears the knocking at the gate.

Macbeth reacts to Banquo's ghost ("the very painting" of his fear), which, unlike the ghost in Hamlet is seen only by him, with extraordinary terror:

> Avaunt! and quit my sight! let the earth hide thee!
> Thy bones are marrowless, thy blood is cold;
> Thou hast no speculation in those eyes
> Which thou dost glare with!
>
> . . .
>
> What man dare, I dare.
> Approach thou like the rugged Russian bear,
> The arm'd rhinoceros, or th' Hyrcan tiger;
> Take any shape but that, and my firm nerves
> Shall never tremble.

Macbeth's intense fear, which "unmans" him and exposes his guilt to his courtiers, evokes pity in the audience as the formerly strong and virtuous man becomes tormented by his guilt.

In act 4, Macbeth's behavior at the sight of the witches' final apparitions is strikingly different from his composure in act 1 and his guilty terror in act 3. The brave front he shows when he demands the witches speak to him changes as he is again terrified by the sight of Banquo's ghost: "Thou art too like the spirit of Banquo; down! . . . / Horrible sight! now, I see, 'tis true; / For the blood-boltered Banquo smiles upon me, / And points at them [apparitions of kings] for his." There is an important change in Macbeth's reaction; he is no longer fearful because his conscience is guilty, but rather because he realizes that Banquo's sons will indeed inherit the throne.

Finally, to the audience who suffered with Macbeth as his ambition and his wife's prodding turned his virtue to evil and his strength to lapses of weakness, his character at the end, devoid of terror, devoid of "the milk of human kindness" (even indifferent to the news of his wife's death), becomes truly tragic:

> I have almost forgot the taste of fears.
> The time has been, my senses would have cool'd
> To hear a night-shriek, and my fell of hair
> Would at a dismal treatise rouse and stir
> As life were in't. I have supp'd full with horrors;
> Direness, familiar to my slaughterous thoughts
> Cannot once start me.

Macbeth's lack of fear, then, is a sign of his total degeneration—of his spiritual death. He becomes the "dead butcher" even before Macduff beheads him.

Although John Milton uses "horror" and "terror" interchangeably in the first two books of his epic poem *Paradise Lost* (1667), before Adam's and Eve's falls, terror rather than horror prevails. Milton's earliest descriptions of Sin and Death are terrifying because they foreshadow the evils that will result from man's first disobedience. The allegorical figures also have another thematic function. Lust produces sin, and sin results in death. Sin is half-woman, half-serpent; barking hell-hounds, who were born after her son, Death, raped her, encircled her waist:

> These yelling monsters, that with ceaseless cry
> Surround me, as thou saw'st, hourly conceived
> And hourly born, with sorrow infinite
> To me, for, when they list, into the womb
> That bred them they return, and howl, and gnaw
> My bowels, their repast, then, bursting forth
> Afresh, with conscious terrors vex me round,
> That rest or intermission none I find.

Death is even more terrifying than Sin, his mother and paramour. When he was born and Sin cried out *"Death,"* "Hell trembled at the hideous name, and sighed / From all her caves, and back resounded *Death!*" His shape is indistinguishable: "black it stood as Night, / Fierce as ten Furies, terrible as Hell, / And shook a dreadful dart; what seemed his head / The likeness of a kingly crown had on." As his father, Satan, fearlessly speaks to "the grisly terror," Death's shape grows more dreadful and deformed, foreshadowing the horrors to come after the fall of man. But Milton's epic is not a tragedy. The mood of the conclusion is one of triumph. Michael tells Adam that Christ's resurrection "Shall bruise the head of Satan, crush his strength, / Defeating Sin and Death"; and Adam learns "that to obey is best, / And [to] love with fear the only God." Fear is ultimately important to Milton because it will produce obedience to God. The terrifying aspects of his unholy trinity (Satan, Sin, Death) encourage revulsion from the consummate evil they represent and with which they would blight the destiny of mankind.

The Eighteenth Century

With the publication of Horace Walpole's *The Castle of Otranto* in 1764, a host of Gothic novels flooded the English market to satisfy a growing popular taste for terror. These novels appealed directly to supernatural terror, imaginary fears, and prolonged suspense; and the majority included, in varying combinations, medieval castles, ruins, ghosts or other supernatural apparitions, banditti, and corrupt monks or nuns.

In his preface to the first edition of *Otranto,* Walpole said, "terror, the author's principal engine, prevents the story from ever languishing." The primary function of terror in *Otranto* is to entertain, but terror also serves to reinforce the guilt of the tyrannical Manfred, the chief character in the story. To the eighteenth-century reader, the supernatural occurrences of this Gothic tale were truly awesome. The portrait of Manfred's grandfather sighs; a giant foot, part of a leg, and a giant hand appear; a gigantic helmet falls inexplicably from the sky and crushes an innocent boy; blood drips from the nose of a statue; and Alfonso, the former lord of Otranto, appears as a vision and announces the true heir. When Manfred mistakes Theodore for Alfonso's ghost, however, the tyrant's reaction recalls Macbeth's guilty terror at Banquo's ghost; the terrors in Walpole's romance are not totally gratuitous.

Ann Radcliffe, who has been called the "Shakespeare of romance writers," uses terror differently. Although her heroes and heroines are extremely susceptible to fear and awe (sensations that are sometimes pleasurable to them and thus, illustrate the interrelatedness of emotions), Radcliffe's novels warn about the importance of reason and the dangers of uncontrolled passion. Although she regales her readers with terrors, her supernatural occurrences, unlike Walpole's, always have reasonable explanations. In *The Mysteries of Udolpho* (1794), Emily's father warns her to command her feelings rather than become a victim of them, yet most of Emily's terrors arise from her uncontrolled imagination. Nurtured by her excessive sensibility, she is bombarded by terrifying experiences. Suggestions of the supernatural (for example, the ghostly musician in Languedoc, the voice that calls out to Montoni, the spectral figures floating through the halls of Udolpho, and Ludovico's disappearance), even though they are later explained, continually open up for the reader the possibilities of the unknown and suggest intruders from another world.

The German *Schauerromane,* another important type of Gothic fiction, differs from the Radcliffean romance in its emphasis on horror rather than terror.

Versed in English Gothic fiction, American novelist Charles Brockden Brown also uses terror in his novels. In *Arthur Mervyn: or Memoirs of the Year 1793* (1799), he uses it somewhat differently from Walpole and Radcliffe. Originally an innocent country boy, Mervyn encounters terrors that provide him with insights into human nature. The evil Welbeck's story of all his villainies, for instance, astonishes Mervyn "by its novelty," and terrifies him "by its horror." (Here is a case of an author using the terms "terror" and "horror" interchangeably.) More important, however, by exposing the young hero to evil, Welbeck's narrative makes Mervyn even more determined to lead a virtuous life. Some of Brown's terrifying scenes nonetheless seem gratuitous, as for example, when

Mervyn is shocked first by the sight of Wallace and later Welbeck, both whom he had believed dead.

The Nineteenth Century

Jane Austen's *Northanger Abbey* (written in 1797 and 1798, but published in 1818), employs terror to satirize Gothic fiction, using *The Mysteries of Udolpho* as her principal model. Reality, Austen affirms, is more terrifying than the irrational. Her novel is symptomatic of the decline of popular taste for Gothic fiction—of the reaction of readers who had been satiated with supernatural occurrences, maidens in distress, and Gothic edifices with secret passages. Because Austen's heroine, Catherine Morland, has read so many Gothic romances, she has absurd expectations when she arrives at Northanger Abbey. She is frightened by a chest, which contains a bedspread, and by an ebony cabinet, whose "precious manuscript" is an inventory of linen and a washing bill. Her terrifying suspicions about General Tilney's murdering his wife (which make "her blood run cold") are similarly shattered. Catherine learns, however, that the General is indeed a "terrible" man, but only terrible in that he is a mundane, materialistic hypocrite, not a romantic, Gothic villain.

Despite the decline of public interest in Gothic fiction, an important Gothic novel, Mary Shelley's *Frankenstein* (1818), was published around the same time as Austen's parody. Shelley's novel is terrifying, but horror prevails it. In this same period terror also continued to be a motif in the works of Charles Robert Maturin, Sir Walter Scott, Edward Bulwer-Lytton, William Harrison Ainsworth, and Thomas Love Peacock. Poetry, however, dominated the romantic period in England.

More than the other romantic poets, Samuel Taylor Coleridge used supernatural terror in his works and thus reflected the romantic rebellion against eighteenth-century rationality. In his *Biographia Literaria* (1817) Coleridge states that in the poems he was to write for *Lyrical Ballads* (1798, with Wordsworth), "the incidents and agents were to be, in part at least, supernatural; and the excellence aimed at was to consist in the interesting of the affections by the dramatic truth of such emotions as would naturally accompany such situations, supposing them real." Thus, in "The Rime of the Ancient Mariner" (1798) and "Christabel" (1816) disbelief is suspended; and through the terrifying experiences of the Mariner and Christabel, Coleridge deals with the theme of crime and punishment.

Because he commits an irrational act, the mariner becomes the victim of a capricious universe. The poem suggests that even the most trivial violation of God's love will bring a terrifying, prolonged punishment. One of the most effective passages in the poem occurs when the mariner tells about the terror he felt even after the spell was snapped and he could remove his eyes from the dead men's:

> Like one, that on a lonesome road
> Doth walk in fear and dread,
> And having once turned round walks on;
> And turns no more his head;
> Because he knows, a frightful fiend
> Doth close behind him tread.

Christabel's guilt is more obscure than the Mariner's; as a result her punishment is more terrifying. "Christabel" suggests that human suffering does not always have rational explanations. The world of the "Ancient Mariner," where the fate of the crew is determined by a dice game, is much less frightening than that of "Christabel," where the innocent heroine mysteriously becomes Geraldine's victim. What the heroine sees when Geraldine exposes her breast is frightening, but it is even more dreadful when Christabel remembers the sight, yet can not speak of it:

> The vision of fear, the touch and pain!
> She shrunk and shuddered, and saw again—
>   . . .
> Again she saw that bosom old,
> Again she felt that bosom cold,
> And drew in her breath with a hissing sound . . .

Influenced by English Romantic poets (particularly Byron) and Gothic novelists, French writer Charles Nodier published his tale *Smarra, ou les démons de la nuit* in 1821. In it he uses the theme of terror to show the close relationship between the irrational dream world and the world of reality. A tale about vampirism in which the vampire is a supernatural, dreamlike being, "Smarra" explores the impact of the frightening dream world on the psyche of the dreamer. Lucius' terrifying nightmare, in which he is accused of murdering his friend, is condemned to death and beheaded, suggests the complexities of man's guilt.

Two major American authors of the early nineteenth century, Hawthorne and Poe, can be described as masters of terror. Nathaniel Hawthorne's works are terrifying both because of what they suggest rather than tell and because of the theme that prevails in most of them: "Evil is the nature of mankind." In the story "Young Goodman Brown" (1835), for example, more terrifying to the reader and the hero than the devil or than the witches' sabbath is young Goodman Brown's realization that "he was himself the chief horror of the scene, and [he] shrinks not from its other horrors. . . . The fiend in his own shape is less hideous than when he rages in the breast of man."

Edgar Allan Poe's works tend to be both horrifying and terrifying, but "The Tell-Tale Heart" (story, 1843) clearly exemplifies Poe's use of terror and its effects on the psyche. The narrator's terror is a fear of life itself. This fear is symbolized by the old man's "Evil Eye," which makes the narrator's "blood run cold" and so vexes him that he determines to kill to rid himself of the eye. When the old man groans in fear right before the narrator murders him, the killer recognizes the sound and identifies with the old man's terror: "Many a night, just at midnight, when all the world slept, it [the groan of terror] was welled up from my own bosom, deepening, with its dreadful echo, the terrors that distracted me." The murder then becomes a kind of suicide, the narrator's attempt to escape from his own distracting terrors. Later, though, terror serves a different function; the sound of the dead old man's heartbeat so terrifies the narrator that he confesses to the police. His fear, like Macbeth's, derives both from his guilty conscience and from his excessive imagination; he alone hears the heartbeat.

Motifs of terror, which permeate Charles Dickens' novels, function both to entertain and to inculcate morality. The interpolated tales in his first primarily comic novel, *Pickwick Papers* (1836–1837), for example, are, for the most part, Gothic episodes in which terror and horror become major themes. Like their eighteenth-century predecessors, they are thrilling; but they also foreshadow the pessimistic vision of the world that prevails in Dickens' later novels. Although terror is present in the earliest novels, for the most part it is formulaic. Good characters are terrified of evil ones, and ultimately good triumphs over evil. The diabolic Fagin and Quilp, for instance, terrify Oliver Twist and Little Nell, respectively (*Oliver Twist*, 1837–1838; and *The Old Curiosity Shop*, 1840).

Dickens' use of terror is more complex in *Great Expectations* (1860–1861). Through his various experiences with terror, the hero eventually understands his own guilt and then repents. Magwitch terrifies young Pip in the graveyard; but when he visits Pip in London and reveals that he is the snobbish young gentleman's benefactor, Pip experiences a different sort of terror, one mixed with horror, which makes him tremble: "The abhorrence in which I held the man, the dread I had of him, the repugnance with which I shrank from him, could not have been exceeded if he had been some terrible beast." Although Pip recalls his early fears of Magwitch's violence being directed toward him, he is horrified that he has become a gentleman with a convict's money rather than Miss Havisham's. At this point, in fact, good and evil become reversed. Magwitch (the Fagin-Quilp counterpart) is morally superior to the hero, Pip (the Oliver Twist-Little Nell counterpart). Finally, Pip is again terrified when his life is threatened by the evil Orlick. But, Pip says, "far more terrible than death was the dread of being misremembered after death." Thus, through Pip's later experience with terror, Dickens illustrates his hero's moral reformation—Pip's transformation from a selfish snob to a young man who has come to love his formerly repugnant convict-benefactor.

Like Poe, J. S. Le Fanu uses terror to show the potentially self-destructive psychological effects of fear in his short story "Green Tea" (1872). Mr. Jennings' story about the monkey whose mere presence first terrifies him and then begins to urge him "to crimes, to injure others, or myself," is indeed strange. The monkey becomes more aggressive and malicious until "it" causes Jennings to cut his throat. Le Fanu's story is more frightening because no one but Jennings sees the beast; and although Dr. Hesselius accounts for the "supernatural" by pointing out the green tea, which supposedly disturbed Jennings' equilibrium and allowed disembodied spirits to operate, the reader is left with a sensation of terror at the end because of the uncertainty. Was it the tea? Was the monkey a demon? Or was it Jennings' disturbed imagination?

French author Guy de Maupassant's "Le Horla" ("The Horla," 1887) has a similar theme. Excessive fear of the unknown can result in madness. The narrator's early terrors of impending doom increase until he is convinced that his soul is dominated by an occult being, the Horla, which jumped to land from a Brazilian ship. To escape his evil nemesis, the narrator burns down his home, only to conclude at the end that the Horla did not die and that he must then kill himself:

If he were not dead?—Perhaps time alone has power over that Invisible and Redoubtable Being. Why this transparent, unrecognizable body, this body belonging to a spirit, if it also has to fear ills, infirmities and premature destruction?

Premature destruction? All human terror springs from that! After man, the Horla. After him who can die every day, at any hour, at any moment, by any accident, came the one who would die only at his own proper hour, day, and minute, because he had touched the limits of his existence!

No—no—without any doubt—he is not dead—Then—then—I suppose I must kill myself!

Like Le Fanu's tale, Maupassant's is particularly frightening because the reader is never certain whether the Horla exists or whether it is the product of a madman's diseased imagination.

In a letter to W. D. Howells, Henry James called *The Turn of the Screw* (1898) "a little 'tale of terror.' " James uses terror to suggest the ambiguous nature of evil. His intent was to make the ghosts of Peter Quint and Miss Jessel more than ghosts—rather evil spirits trying to possess the souls of the children, Miles and Flora. But because the ghosts are only seen "for certain" by the governess, a young lady with a romantic imagination who thinks of Radcliffe's *Udolpho* and Brontë's *Jane Eyre* (novel, 1847) when she first sees Peter Quint, James leaves the reader with the same sort of uncertainty that Le Fanu and Maupasssant do. The ghosts "horrify" the governess; but to the reader, who is uncertain whether the narrator is reliable, the story is terrifying. Miles and Flora seem to be innocent and to be unaware of the appearances of the dead servants, despite the governess's insistence that the children are not. Unlike earlier Gothic novels, the story is more frightening because it does not rely on familiar stereotypes. The ghosts or evil spirits, for example, are after the children rather than the heroine. Watching her charges, the governess exclaims,

Oh yes, we may sit here and look at them, and they may show off to us there to their fill; but even when they pretend to be lost in their fairy-tale they're steeped in their vision of the dead restored to them. He's [Miles] not reading to her [Flora] . . . they're talking of *them*—they're talking horrors!

The governess claims that the spirits and the children (who see things "terrible" and "unguessable") are enough to make her mad but that she is certain she is not. However, because Mrs. Grose never sees the ghosts, it is ultimately ambiguous whether or not the governess is indeed mad. Are the ghosts real, or arc they products of her disordered imagination? Does she save Miles from demonic possession, or does she frighten him to death?

The Twentieth Century

In the modern age, world wars, concentration camps, nuclear power, assassinations, films, and television have saturated the public with more real terrors than the earlier Gothic novelists probably ever dreamed of. The renewed popularity of "escape" literature in this century seems to be both a reflection of the terrors of our age and an attempt to escape from them through mystery, fantasy, science fiction, Gothic romance, and so forth.

American author H. P. Lovecraft is a contemporary master of terror and horror. "The Colour out of Space" (1927) intriguingly combines science fiction, Gothic fiction, and vampire fiction to suggest the unknown terrors of outer space and of the possibility of destructive life on other planets. After a meteorite (the color out of space) falls out of the sky and lands next to the Gardner family's well, "stark terror seemed to cling round the Gardners and all they touched." The family members go mad and turn into "things," while the old farm house (built before 1670) crumbles to ruins. The meteorite behaves like a vampire "suckin' the life out of everything . . . an' it burns an' sucks . . . it come from some place whar things ain't as they is here." The ending is especially frightening because even though the meteorite, which gained strength from the family it destroyed, leaves earth, part of it still remains in the well.

As in Dickens' novels, motifs of terror permeate the works of the American master William Faulkner. His use of terror is especially shocking because he combines it with "realistic" contemporary life. Three short stories in his collection *These Thirteen* (1931) deal with the terrors of war and dying, of racism—of being "nothing but a nigger" in Mississippi, and of spinsterhood and loss of pride. In "Crevasse," for example, the hysterical refrain of the wounded man while he and the others are digging their way out of the pit, "A'm no dead!" reflects the terror of all the men of being buried alive, but more so of getting out of the pit and of returning to the war, while, in "That Evening Sun," Nancy's irrational, compulsive fear of Jesus, her husband, is metaphoric of her role as servant to whites, to her husband, and to her own passions. The depth of her terror is expressed when she makes "the sound . . . the sound that was singing and not unsinging."

In "A Rose for Emily," a Gothic tale of a woman who murdered her sweetheart when he planned to desert her, Faulkner creates terror through his tightly controlled narration of the events and through his realistic description. Miss Emily is not a romantic heroine; she is an old, obese, gray-haired, cantankerous woman who led an "ordinary" life for years after her lover "disappeared." When Miss Emily dies, the townspeople discover a skeleton in an upstairs bedroom:

For a long while we just stood there, looking down at the profound and fleshless grin. The body had apparently once lain in the attitude of an embrace, but now the long sleep that outlasts love, that conquers even the grimace of love, had cuckolded him. What was left of him, rotted beneath what was left of the nightshirt, had become inextricable from the bed in which he lay.

Even more terrifying than the discovery of the skeleton and of Miss Emily's crime is the discovery of her "relationship" with the rotted corpse. On the second pillow of the bed, beside the skeletal body, were the indentation of a head and a long strand of gray hair.

Terror is also a major characteristic of twentieth-century detective and escape fiction. In *Before the Fact* (1932) British author Francis Iles deals with the psychological effects of terror on the mind of a victim. When the heroine, Lina Aysgarth, realizes that her husband Johnnie plans to kill her, she alternates between hysteria and calmness. As long as she remains terrified of her husband, she has instinctive feelings of self-preservation. Eventually, however, the moments of "exquisite terror" disappear, and she sinks gradually "into apathy"— a kind of madness that drives her to become an "Accessory Before the Fact" to her own murder. Without terror, Iles says, we become passive victims who peacefully sit and wait for our deaths. Lina's final acceptance of being the rabbit to Johnnie's snake is more frightening to the reader than her husband's crimes.

British author Daphne Du Maurier's *Jamaica Inn* (1936), on the other hand, is an example of twentieth-century escape fiction in which terror functions primarily to entertain. Du Maurier's novel is a Gothic love story, similar to Radcliffe's romances, but set in modern times. The orphaned heroine is forced to live in the ruined Jamaica Inn (a replica of the Gothic castle) with her only relatives—her mousey aunt and her terrifying uncle by marriage, a drunken, murderous smuggler. She is first frightened by learning the truth about her uncle—how he wrecks ships to smuggle the goods; but even more dreadful for her is being kidnapped by the gang and then being forced to witness innocent victims drown when the pirates wreck a ship. Finally, she is terrified when she is captured by the real leader of the gang, the albino Vicar who she once believed to be her only friend. Du Maurier makes a few moralistic comments on the hypocrisy of religious institutions (through the heroine's disgust for the evil Vicar); but the villain is never depicted realistically enough to make the reader ever forget that the story is make-believe.

British author Richard Adams' contemporary novel, *The Girl in a Swing* (1980) is a different kind of love story. Because Adams blends the ordinary with the extraordinary, the terrors become much more real than they are in Du Maurier's novel. The terrifying events in *The Girl in a Swing* ultimately lead to the question: What actually is Truth? Adams suggests that there are no pat explanations to love, evil, or any of life's mysteries.

The hero, Alan Desland, is a cold, unattractive man whose only passions early in the novel are for porcelain and his ceramics business. Thus, his whirlwind romance with the beautiful and mysterious Kathë is startling. It becomes even more so when the terrors begin, which are ostensibly caused because Kathë murdered her daughter in order to marry Alan, and the child's ghost returns to haunt her mother. Although Adams provides rational explanations for nearly all the "supernatural" occurrences in the novel, he leaves the reader with more frightening questions than answers. The most terrifying questions involve who or what Kathë was. Was she merely an unusually beautiful woman who murdered her child and then suffered from guilt? Was she a demon in a different shape, who drew Alan into madness and damnation? Or was she, as Alan comes to believe, a pagan goddess—a supernatural being who used Alan for some sort of mysterious ritual? Because Alan is such an ordinary man, all explanations are frightening.

See also: Anxiety, Death and the Individual, Horror.

Selected Bibliography

Howells, Coral Ann. *Love, Mystery, and Misery: Feeling in Gothic Fiction.* London: Athlone Press, 1978.

Punter, David. *The Literature of Terror: A History of Gothic Fictions from 1765 to the Present Day.* New York: Longman, 1980.

Spector, Robert Donald. *The English Gothic: A Bibliographic Guide to Writers from Horace Walpole to Mary Shelley.* Westport, Connecticut: Greenwood Press, 1984.

Wilt, Judith. *Ghosts of the Gothic: Austen, Eliot, and Lawrence.* Princeton, New Jersey: Princeton University Press, 1980.

NATALIE SCHROEDER

THEATRICAL ABSURDITY

Absurdity is an underlying concept of farce and tragedy and, as such, it is as old as secular drama. Our existence is absurd because we are born without asking to be born, we die without seeking death. We live between birth and death trapped within our body and our reason, unable to conceive of a time in which we were not, or a time in which we will not be—for nothingness is very much like the concept of infinity: something we perceive only in so far as we cannot experience it. Thrust into life, armed with our senses, will, and reason, we feel ourselves to be potent beings. Yet our senses give the lie to our thought and our thought defies our senses. We never perceive anything completely. We are permitted to entertain committedly only one perspective of any object, fact, or situation: our own. We labor to achieve distinction and permanence only to find that our assessments are perspectively incomplete and therefore never wholly effective. All of our creations are doomed to decay as we ourselves are doomed to death. We create in order to identify ourselves in some semblance of permanence, but our creations become autonomous facts the instant we have created them and do not identify us except in so far as we pretend that they do. Therefore, the more we strive for definition and permanent distinction, the more absurd we are. Yet, the only value we can affirm with certainty is a self-defeating complex that we do not understand: our life. If we despair of definition, of ever achieving a sense of permanence, and we contemplate suicide, we are put in the absurd situation of sacrificing our only concrete value, life, for a dream of power and permanence that no man on this earth has ever experienced. On the other hand, if in despair we turn to religion or illusion of any sort, we betray and deny our only means of perception: our reason. If, in a transport of ecstacy, be it mystical or sensuous, we feel at one with power and permanence, we are forced to admit the illusionistic aspect of this transport and we must confess that our sense of power, permanence, and definition is achieved at the sacrifice of our reason. If it is impossible for us to act with complete efficacy, to perceive with complete accuracy, to create anything definite and lasting that expresses exactly our intentions, we must also remember that it is impossible for us to cease acting as long as we live. This then is the condition of man that we of the twentieth century call ''absurd.'' It is the same state of being that Aristotle labeled ''ignorance.'' It is this complex of self-defeating paradoxes, this even check and balance of power and impotence, knowledge and ignorance, attunement and alienation, that is the subject of playwrights of all ages who write about absurdity, no matter what form or style they may have chosen to express it.

The absurdist playwrights of today reflect the condition of absurdity through a variety of means which no longer adheres to the representational strictures of conventional farce or tragedy. Theirs is a wildly varied assortment of plays that defies generalization; it is best, therefore, to describe the practice of the absurdists by making a list of their major interpretative conventions:

1. A fondness for mixing or juxtaposing tragedy and farce, the serious and the comic. The works of Samuel Beckett such as *En attendant Godot (Waiting for Godot,* 1952) and *Fin de partie (Endgame,* 1957) best exemplify this admixture of the tragic and farcical.

2. A tendency toward didacticism emanating from their purpose to explain absurdity through dramatic example. Within a realistic approach to absurdity, Albert Camus' *Caligula* (1944) is interesting because the entire action is that of a man who feels compelled to teach Rome the meaning of absurdity. Any person who gives himself the task of reading in sequence three plays by Eugène Ionesco such as *La cantatrice chauve (The Bald Soprano,* 1950), *Les chaises (The Chairs,* 1952), and *La leçon (The Lesson,* 1951) will notice that the fun of the bizarrerie becomes more and more translucent, with each reading revealing the didactic intent of the plays. The bizarrerie is comparable to the orange juice with which mothers have tried for years to induce us to take our castor oil.

3. A delight in attacking all values and procedures that have in times past served to affirm human importance. Alfred Jarry's *Ubu roi* (1896) attacks all social systems of value, affirming solely the gratification of our personal desires with infantile

honesty and brutality. These assaults may be presented realistically and "personally" as they are in Samuel Beckett's *Krapp's Last Tape* (1958) or they may be carried out through fantastic actions such as those of *Strip-tease* (*Striptease*, 1961) by Sławomir Mrożek.

4. Concrete illogic presented solemnly as though it were logic. Lucky's speech in *Waiting for Godot* by Beckett or the Maid's speech in *The Bald Soprano* by Ionesco are among the most famous examples. However, exchanges such as those between the Lady and the Gentlemen in Ionesco's *La jeune fille à marier* (*A Maid to Marry*, 1953) are equally provocative in their plausible illogicality.

5. Humanity puppetized to emphasize its impotence and indefensible condition. The *Dumb Waiter* (1957) by Harold Pinter even suggests the metaphysical strings of a malevolent or idiotic deity in the cords of the dumb waiter. Beckett's early characters suffer a marionettish "thingification" of their bodies—in *Endgame* Clov cannot sit and Ham cannot stand; Nag and Nell pop out of their garbage pails like a senile Punch and Judy.

6. Language and argumentation emptied of meaning or "stuffed" with incongruous meaning. Mr. and Mrs. Martin in *The Bald Soprano* do a very thorough job of identifying each other by means of circumstantial evidence; their logic is obviated by the fact that they are man and wife and should not need this identification. In Beckett's *Krapp's Last Tape*, the word "spool" acquires almost magical proportions in its complex functions within the action: a) its utterance has become a sensuous experience for Krapp, the kind of thing that justifies his continued existence; b) it remains the word for the tapes on which Krapp has endeavored to engrave and entrap his life; c) it conveys a cyclical meaning that reflects the cycle of Krapp's life; d) its sound rhymes with "fool," "stool," and other relevant words—seldom has a word acquired such density within the context of any given play.

7. Nonsense spoken with great passion or portentiousness or perfectly intelligible language rendered meaningless. Lucky's speech in *Waiting for Godot* appears to be written in accessible language, but the syntax corrodes the meaning and no single phrase of it will relate adequately to produce comfortable meaning. However, in Beckett's *Play* (1963) we encounter perfectly intelligible soliloquies that are so chopped-up that they prove totally unintelligible at first hearing; it takes at least four readings of the play in order to insure intelligibility.

8. The physical world deliberately distorted so that natural laws are shown to be ineffective. Men are addressed as women (*A Maid to Marry*), characters become rhinoceroses (*Le rhinocéros* [*Rhinoceros*, 1960]), imaginary characters are given palpable form (the Orator in *The Chairs*)— Ionesco is by far the most skilled of the absurdist authors at this systematic distortion of nature.

9. Settings stripped of the reality that connects them to time and geography. Since absurd man is *dasein*, his rootlessness is reflected in the stage setting. *Waiting for Godot* occurs in a "thematic space"—its one identifying element, the tree, has its reality only as symbol (the one leaf). The space of Mrożek's *Striptease* is a prison-limbo which, as the play progresses, becomes an obvious analogue for the real world.

10. Man's physical surroundings take on a malevolent and animated rebelliousness. In *Waiting for Godot* shoes never fit, surroundings are so unqualified that it is impossible for the characters to take their bearings.

11. God is depicted as a perverse idiot or an infuriatingly elusive and unintelligible figure. *Waiting for Godot* can be described as a series of dramatic puns on the elusiveness and persistence of God. The creature that sends down orders in *The Dumb Waiter* is an odious god. The Hands in *Striptease* are more than just political powers, they are symbols of divinity.

12. Endings tend to be either abrupt assaults upon our expectations or to suggest a drifting continuation of the preceding action into an indefinite future. Both of these endings are intended to suggest the absurdist evaluation of human experience. Having repeated the entire play in *Play* Beckett gives us just the faintest hint or tease of a continuation of the action. *A Maid to Marry* is brought to a close by Ionesco with a sudden and unexpected non sequitur. We are told that Ionesco wanted to end the first production of *The Bald Soprano* by firing a machine gun over the heads of the audience. In one of Beckett's mimes the character gives up all action and rejects all stimuli . . . he just sits waiting for the future to corrode him.

Some absurdist plays merely proclaim the individual's discovery of absurdity. These works tend to be naïve and simplistic. Other plays begin to help the audience to come to terms with their own absurdity. It is in this last group that one detects a tendency to return to a more realistic representation of life. This more realistic effort to help us adjust to our absurdity is likely to express its action with some resonance of pathos and warmth. The more expressionistic and symbolic plays are constantly in danger of ratiocinational coldness.

It is not incorrect to say that the absurdists of today have employed the devices and conventions of expressionism, surrealism, and dadaism to dramatize philosophical doubts and ironies that once both troubled and informed the greatest works of tragedy and farce.

See also: Alienation, Existentialism, Nihilism, Tragicomic Hero.

Selected Bibliography

Esslin, Martin. *The Theatre of the Absurd*. 3d ed. New York: Penguin, 1980.

WILLIAM I. OLIVER

TIME

Like St. Augustine, we know what time is until we are asked to describe it. Time is perhaps the most elusive yet familiar phenomenon that we experience—familiar, as a perception immediately given to consciousness, yet elusive, for our descriptions are always limiting, whether they are experiential, scientific, or poetic. Time is experienced in two fundamental ways: as an endless flow, and as a succession of discrete moments and intervals. As the element within which natural events occur, the organic time of sun and stars gives us the complex, recurring patterns of the day, the season, and the year; and it yields a description of time as a circle. Yet time seems linear most of the time, stretching backward into the past and forward into the future—a description of time as a line that arises essentially from the Judaeo-Christian tradition in which specific and unique events are consequential and progressive. To complicate definition further, there is the objective time that charts change and difference, as well as subjective time-consciousness that affirms permanence and sameness. For science, time has been the "rate of change" in the sequential relations between entities or events, but ever since Zeno faced the artificial immobility of his arrow in flight, scientists have realized that their stabilizing manipulations end up absurdly denying the reality of time. They continue, however, to assign measure, order, and direction to time, while human consciousness continues to experience time as nonuniform, reversible, continuous, and durational; as unified and flowing through past, present, and future; as having, in eternity, a sacred and timeless double. The ancient estrangement between time in nature and time in human experience persists, and it yet remains for the sciences of man to account for the wide disparities between the personal, psychological experience of time and time's public validity as a structuring force in nature.

The descriptive difficulty for both human and physical time arises partially from the fact that time is not absolute but relative, interacting everywhere and at all moments with space. Piaget confirmed that the automatic association of time with space originates early in human childhood, and Einstein offered cosmic support for such a humanized time, insofar as time is a universal variable, relative to the spatial position and frame of reference of the observer. It is thus to be expected that our definitions of time will be contaminated by space, that our most celebrated definitions are wholly metaphorical, spatialized configurations for time—as in time as a line or circle, time as an arrow, a river, a journey. In eschewing imprecise metaphor for precise measurement, physics and astronomy have expanded their knowledge of time only by severely restricting it to a function in their formulations. Poets, philosophers, and humankind in general have been dissatisfied with time's mere quantification, yet their broader search for the qualities of time ultimately rests with metaphorical descriptions on the model of "Time is like—."

Early Time, Greek and Christian

When the pre-Socratic philosopher Heraclitus defined time as an everlasting flux, he did so in the memorable metaphor of the river that one cannot step into twice, a figure that has demonstrated its appeal through subsequent appropriations as diverse as those of Ovid, Marcus Aurelius, and Henry David Thoreau. To time as change, Heraclitus added the corollary of the world as chance ("Time is a child playing at draughts: the kingship is in the hands of the child"), a notion that had to await its full elaboration in twentieth-century quantum physics and microbiology. The more general propensity, however, has been to concede chaos as the pretemporal origin of things, and then to construe time as a vehicle of operations that confers order upon the flux. The Greeks proceeded from the insatiable, irrational pre-Olympian Kronos to the hierarchy and balance under

Zeus of the Olympian gods, assigning comprehensible human motive and consequence to the gods' actions and to their effects on the physical universe. The
Judaeo-Christian origin of the cosmos begins with the temporal division into
darkness and light, human beings originate in the timeless idyll of the Garden
of Eden, and thereafter Christian history is ordered into the Fall, Redemption,
and Apocalypse. Indeed, what Parmenides and the school of eleatic philosophers,
most notably Zeno, seized upon in Heraclitus was the faith that underlying an
apparently chaotic universe were changeless laws of change, which could be
computed and quantified.

Recognizing measurement as the means to render change relatively unprob-
lematic, Aristotle in his *Physikē akroasis* (*Physics*, essay, 4th century B.C.)
formulated the well-known definition of time as "the number of motion with
respect to earlier and later." Because not time itself but things in time are given
to perception, we construct time from the changes in states of objects as they
exist in space, and, in fact, we can only become aware of time through such
transience. Moreover, by grounding the human concept of cause and effect in
our prior perception of earlier and later, Aristotle can then effortlessly transport
scientific time to his *Peri poiētikēs* (*Poetics*, essay, 4th century B.C.) where he
introduces the standard typology, thereafter to dominate Western thought, of
time as a line. There, *mythos* or plot is "the soul of tragedy" and "the imitation
of the action" that is a unified whole with a beginning, middle, and end. Plot
presents to the human memory and intelligence a pattern of narrative and dramatic
events in which time is perceived as structuring mere sequence into a harmonious,
coherent unity, and evolving possibility into probability and finally into necessity.
Time will recur in the West as a theme for meditation by philosophers, as a
subject of study for psychologists and physicists, as a motif of lyrical poets—
but, especially in the West, Aristotelian time will provide the linear structure of
our narratives and our logic.

With Aristotle's mentor Plato, we gain a definition of time as "the moving
image of eternity," a definition that situates temporality as the imperfect, visible
approximation of a dimension of timelessness. In the *Timaios* (*Timaeus*, 4th
century B.C.), Plato's cosmological treatise, necessity is but errant cause, associated with accident and coincidence in a contingent universe, until it is partially
controlled by divine Reason; and man learns reason through learning time and
number as he observes the celestial order. Below the stars, however, the rest of
the visible world is but a fallen realm of becoming; and true being, therefore,
resides in a time without time, with neither beginning nor end. This changeless
eternity as a higher dimension of time will have a direct appeal for Aquinas and
the Christian theologians, and it will fascinate secular man with the possibility
of an aesthetic escape from prosaic time into privileged moments approximating
the timelessness of eternity.

For the medieval Christian, God guaranteed the continuity and duration within
existence, and the Christian life was perceived as a directional tending-in-time
toward God. Just as the Anglo-Saxon poets (c. 8th century) of *The Wanderer*

and *Beowulf* had appropriated from the Latin the *"ubi sunt?"* lament for a perfect time long past and irretrievable, so also the fourteenth-century medieval poet of *The Pearl* and W. Langland in his poem *Piers Plowman* (c. 1362–1387) yearned for the eschatological future and the millennial reunion with God. With its saints' days recurring year after liturgical year, the church calendar reinforced the abiding permanence of things intended by God in the endless patterns of cosmic time. The introduction of the mechanical clock drastically changed the daily life of medieval man, however, yoking him to the linear, countable time of hours, minutes, and seconds. This new experience of time—as mechanized, quantified, and removed from nature—led to philosophical inquiry into the source of the medieval confidence in a time that endures. St. Augustine became the first philosopher of subjective time when, in book II of the *Confessiones* (*Confessions*, c. 397–400), he produced the paradox of a time that "passes from that which does not exist, by way of that which lacks extension, into that which is no longer." Faith in a God-given continuity is severely tried in his conclusion that the present has no breadth, and that neither the past nor the future can exist outside of human expectation and memory. In Augustine's meditation we can clearly discern the seed of subjectivity that will blossom later into affirmations of a completely human source for our notions of continuity and duration. The flowering will include Kant's situating of time as a transcendental category of consciousness, William James's "saddleback" present, Bergson's *durée*, Proust's involuntary memory, and the stream of consciousness of modernist fiction.

The Renaissance, Reformation, and Seventeenth Century

For the man of the Renaissance, the habitual grace and continued creation with which a transcendent God sustained medieval man had given way. The divine Creator had become an indwelling, immanent force within a universe that tirelessly agitated and transformed things in their becoming. Cosmic mutability made the time of human life one of discrete, fleeting moments, always precarious without the divine guarantee of duration into the future, but nonetheless abundant in its burgeoning, creative potential. For some, the brevity of life and the finality of death was an exhortation to the enjoyment of present pleasures. The *carpe diem* ("seize the day") motif is prominent in the lyrics of the Cavalier poets; if Time is indeed a fleeting chariot, then Herrick's virgins would do well to make much of time. For others, the transitoriness of this life provided the occasion for contrast with the eternity of the Christian afterlife; and Christian poets, like Herbert and Spenser before him, caution their readers not to delay in performing good deeds within the brief and therefore precious span allotted them. Thus, the present, superabundant instant that yielded the self-affirming ecstasy of Descartes' *Cogito* also produced such sobering reflections as those of Shakespeare's Jaques: "And so, from hour to hour, we ripe and ripe, / And then, from hour to hour, we rot and rot."

For the Calvinist and Puritan, the independence of the moments of time was a source of much more portent agonies. Their single stability was the unknowable will of a predestining God, and only a personal act of absolute faith would connect the vicissitudinous instant to the eternal end of time. Moment to moment, but for the unascertainable mercy of the Redeemer, the abyss threatened. As Protestant allegory, Bunyan's *Pilgrim's Progress* (1678–1684) portrays the exile experienced by the Protestant in his uncharted way through life, a journeying through time fraught with contingencies and bereft of the divine stabilities and sureties that had previously upheld Dante's very Catholic *La divina commedia* (*Divine Comedy,* epic poem, c. 1320).

Increasingly, seventeenth-century minds were turning from the sacred to the profane, to determine whether they might be able to map a continuity and discern a direction for the secular, historical time of man. Bacon's ambition was that time might be ordered through our causal understanding of its events, and he worked hard to establish for civil history a continuity based upon causes and their effects through time. The long controversy among poets and literary critics in France and England concerning the relative superiority of the ancients and the moderns was, in effect, a concerted effort to confer upon time a gradient, to decide whether it flowed in the direction of descent or ascent, decay or progress.

The Eighteenth Century

The notion of the universe as a divinely ordered hierarchy of fixed, unchanging species probably contributed to the static and unhistorical sense of time that dominated the eighteenth century. Certainly, the Creator who had designed the Great Chain of Being was retired as a superfluous watchmaker by a Newtonian universe that was an efficient machine operating independently of any influence outside that of its own laws. Just as the calculus could yield a mechanistic explanation of process and change without reference to an originating First Cause, so could the eighteenth century organize its knowledge without recourse to history, causality, or the question of origins. In Pope and Johnson, as well as Leibniz, one discerns a peculiar rage for spatial synchronies—for taxonomies, proportion, degree, harmony—with no accompanying interest in questions of diachrony. The Enlightenment fought hard to enthrone Reason as the civilized substitute for the emotion and superstition of Hobbes's brutish man in nature; and the absolute distinction they made between animal and human nature must have helped them, in the light of their rational present, to ignore with good conscience an irrational past.

It is well known, of course, that the eighteenth century is not only the age of wit and judgment, but also the age of feeling—of sensibility, taste, pathos, sadism, and passionate eccentricity. The often desperate pursuit of the intensity and multiplicity of sensation, as a means of sustaining a continuity that might define a self, proceeds from the philosophical spatialization of those mental operations that had previously sustained temporal duration. When Locke and Hume identify the self merely as the locus of simple and separate impressions, which the mind organizes only through atemporal associations, then both self and thought become threatened with habitual fragmentation. Philosophy, consequently, becomes anecdotal, speculative, and versatile; and the fiction of the period emerges rich in colorful adventures and erratic encounters, although manifestly un-Aristotelian in structure. Its space is panoramic and its time is episodic—entirely appropriate to the century's fragmentation of durational ordering. The worldly Fortune of public time, rather than otherworldly Fate, governs the outcome of its resourceful, lively heroes and heroines. For the phenomenology of a private existence measured in ways commensurate with the succession of ideas in eighteenth-century minds, one reads the life and opinions of Sterne's *Tristram Shandy* (novel, 1759–1767), which are as scattered, digressive, and irresponsive to temporal continuities as the narrative that purports to record them. Never again will time be so overcome by space as it was in the enlightened mind of the eighteenth century.

The Nineteenth Century

Whether one labels it the age of Darwin, historicism, capitalism, or the novel, the nineteenth century is that epoch in which linear time achieved its ascendancy. Historicism in its different varieties solved the previous century's problem with distinct, unbridgeable moments of time by discovering the laws that conferred a continuous, unified structure upon all successions of temporal change. Evolutionary law organized the biological species into genealogies of descent, and the laws of history—whether evolutionary (Huxley, Spencer), dialectical (Hegel, Marx, Comte), or cyclical (Vico, Nietzsche, Spengler)—guaranteed a temporal order within the chaos of historical facts. All knowledge was integrated in its commitment to exploiting the continuities between past and present according to historical principles of interpretation, and explicit or implicit in these various historicisms was the notion of progress. Change could be challenging, for time had provided it with a sense and direction that was purposive, progressive, and productive. The world became a place of activity, strenuous living, and social utility, an arena where awards could be won through effort and striving. Faustian man treated his temporal moments as units of production and the time of his life as a commodity not to be wasted. The capitalist eager for earthly success, often cohabiting the same body with the Protestant avid for spiritual salvation, managed and used time by taking inventory of the past, setting goals for the future, and generally adjusting present means to ends.

In the nineteenth-century novel, which faithfully adhered to a literary mimesis of this linear reality, the line of life becomes the line of narration. The critic Edward Said (*Beginnings*, 1975) has described this imitation of the sequential form of time as "the dynastic principle of narrative, which is the marriage of promise to time in a spacious familial coherence." Significant form for the Victorian, American, and European novelists of the era entails the representation of those "fictions of concord," in Frank Kermode's phrase (*The Sense of an Ending*, 1967), that link cause to effect and motive to consequence between the terminals of human birth and death. The *Bildungsroman*, with its protagonist's progress from innocence to experience and from ignorance to knowledge, was the prototype for an entire genre in which, at story's end, time retrospectively conferred meaning upon the very processes of a life.

There were those, of course, who continued to lead spiritual or aesthetic lives, and sought to detach themselves from the tyranny of social time that was the motor of their century. Wordsworth's autobiographical poem *Prelude* (1799–1805) is a poignant testimony to the rarity of those epiphanic moments, the "spots of time," during which the poetic soul could personally experience the sacred. As "borrowers of eternity," Carlyle and Emerson attempted to envelop the temporal totality with literary philosophies of the "Everlasting Now" and the transcendental moment. But the strong currents of historical law, the secular substitute for timelessness, were not to be deterred in this strong century's acceptance of the opportunity and novelty that time held out to it.

Twentieth-Century Modernism

It is difficult for us now to recapture the metaphor of time as a cornucopia, when human reason seemed infinitely perfectible and when economic and technological advancements seemed unending. It is much easier for us to appreciate the negative reaction to this faith in progress, which had been communicated through various forms of pessimism (Schopenhauer, Tennyson, Hardy) in the nineteenth century. For twentieth-century man, time is indifferent or hostile to human work and values, it is constantly falling short of the ideal, and its single direction leads man to death. The time of the world is a source of suffering, anxiety, and despair.

Existential Time

Martin Heidegger is the philosopher of time's irreversible direction and of the anguish of man adrift within its contingency. In *Sein und Zeit* (*Being and Time*, 1927) he argues that in order to live fully and authentically the moments of his life, each man must face his own "being-towards-death"; everywhere, however, Heidegger uncovers inauthentic mass-man, anonymous, atomized, and alienated in relation to his own life. The literature of existentialism—which originates in the preceding century with Dostoevsky and the late Tolstoy and culminates in postwar France with Camus and Sartre—records over and over the *Angst* caused by time's inexorability and man's inability to act responsibly and decisively in the face of it. Even the Christian poet of our century, T. S. Eliot, will define time as "a drifting wreckage," and "no healer," and as redeemable only through a Christian resignation to our human condition. Powerless to narrate the past, live his present, or seize a future, existentialist man appears as a victim of the world. Kafka's protagonists wake up to catastrophic metamorphosis, arrest, or exile, while Camus' Meursault (*L'étranger* [*The Stranger*, novel, 1942]) is prosecuted by society, ultimately, because he couldn't remember whether his mother died yesterday or the day before. Sartre locates the *mauvaise foi* of the traditional novel in the stability of its characters and the determinacy of its plots. The philosophy of *L'être et le néant* (*Being and Nothingness,* treatise, 1943) receives literary expression in *La nausée* (*Nausea,* novel, 1938), in which Sartre's Roquentin, consistently refusing to transform reality's absurd contingency through the self-sustaining lies of conventional narrative, must drink the full horrors of an authentic life that lacks all potency and potentiality.

The Stream of Consciousness

Many modernist authors retreated from this harsh world-time to explore the private, interior time of human psychology. Their philosopher was Bergson, whose famous doctrine of *durée* and the "streaming of consciousness" attempted to free subjective time from the space of the world. Bergson situated the creative, dynamic source of man's free will in a primitive intuition of undivided duration, a voluntary psychological activity that initiates the unbounded flow of time through interpenetrating states of feeling, in a succession without distinction. Real time is not an empirical given that lends itself to rational, mechanistic explanation, but rather a structure of psychological association, a form dependent upon the human mind. Early novelists of the *monologue intérieur* were, in France, Edouard Dujardin (*Les lauriers sont coupés,* 1888); in Germany, Arthur Schnitzler (*Leutnant Gustl,* 1901); and in England, Dorothy Richardson and Virginia Woolf. But it became most influential after Joyce's *Ulysses* (novel, 1922), when it was employed by Faulkner, Robbe-Grillet, and Beckett. All of these authors inherit from Proust the relentless search for some principle of cohesive unity within the fluctuations of time, but not one achieves the magnificent retrievals of Proust's affective memory in *A la recherche du temps perdu* (*Remembrance of Things Past,* novels, 1913–1927). Faulkner's narrators, defective and mendacious in interesting ways, are nevertheless incapable of reconstructing story, life, or history; Robbe-Grillet's narrators shift in their subtle variations so unexpectedly that the contents of consciousness become undecidable, unless the reader consigns the protagonist to an explicit psychopathology; and Beckett's minds, with a barren precision that is the low-level order of habit, produce repetitive patterns and circular narratives, lacking in significant incident and closure. In Beckett's work one finds united the two major human responses to the dispiriting time of our century: existentialist despair and a retreat to the interior.

Sub Specie Aeternitas

Although the religious belief in the infinite time of eternity has steadily declined in our century, yet we still seek a release from the painful chronology of physical time, and often we find it in an aesthetic approximation of timelessness—time charged with significance, when the sacred seems to interrupt or withstand the profane. Hans Meyerhoff has enumerated the several contexts in which we experience within art and life the aspects of eternity. But whether these are the privileged moments of Joyce's and Eliot's epiphanies or the permanently intense *now* of a past retrieved by the privileged memory of Gide and Nabokov or the living in undying art of the decadents and imagists or the slow-time of Mann's *Der Zauberberg* (*The Magic Mountain,* novel, 1924) or the mystical union with the ineffable shared by Huxley and Hesse—twentieth-century man, upon sober reflection, admits that for timelessness there is no correlate in the objective time structure of nature, and no confirmation in his everyday reality.

Contemporary Literature

"Time in literature" has changed so drastically since Hans Meyerhoff wrote under that title in 1955 that, for explanation, one turns to the revolutions in contemporary science rather than to the traditionalist reflections of philosophy. Just as Einstein's theory of relativity, Heisenberg's uncertainty principle, and Gödel's theorem were construable as "anti-physics," so also does the aesthetically distinguished, contemporary novel appear to be an anti-novel. What experimentation in both fields questions is the received structure of time as a regulating and directional principle informing process. When parity falls and mirror events occur with no basis in real processes, or when time reversals fail and time's irreversible flow becomes the entropic price of complexity, or when space contraction and time dilation establish simultaneity as merely relative—then Nature's jokes affect the literary artist as well as the physicist.

Contemporary humankind seems to share a collective sense of living at the wrong end of time, in a world of aftermath where the present is *post*-everything; nevertheless, quantum theory carries on its quests, and literature, far from being exhausted, enters a new cycle of replenishment with the general extension of scientific knowledge to the layman. The time of science makes its initial appearance as a theme of distinguished fiction. Borges in his stories and essays, *Ficciones* (*Fictions,* 1945, 1956) and *Laberintos* (*Labyrinths,* 1962), Calvino in *Ti con zero* (*t-Zero,* stories, 1967), Vonnegut in *Slaughterhouse Five* (novel, 1969), and Pynchon in *Gravity's Rainbow* (novel, 1973) all directly confront the paradoxes of time as they presently exist in scientific investigation. Because narrative has been the literary form most dependent upon time for its inner form, the novel becomes the laboratory of an anti-creation, with its own assumptions, laws, and processes distinct from those of quotidian reality. Novelistic strategies of innovation produce plots that are circular, surrealistic, or practically non-existent; characters that assume pluralistic selves, talk like authorial puppets, or act like cartoons; language that breaks out of conventional patterning and signification in order to celebrate or question itself. Narrative, like physics, begins to perceive its own existence as problematic.

The novel, long associated with history in its content and historical narratives in its form, now uncovers new resources in themes of prehistory and in narrative forms that predate its own. Myth, fairy tale, fable, saga, and other popular subgenres are excavated and refurbished, generously accommodated

by an aesthetic mode of consciousness akin to the savage mind, which appre-
hends in the cyclical return of all things a circular unity in time that is undifferentiated, neutral, beyond good and evil. Employing myth as a "timeless
schema" for composition, the modernists—Mann, Joyce in *Ulysses,* Giraudoux, Anouilh—had chosen their mythic prototypes of human experience to
confer order upon, and express the ironies of, life in the twentieth century.
Postmodernist novelists, however, resist the clear division between myth and
history and are inspired instead by Joyce's *Finnegans Wake* (novel, 1939),
where Adam's story is subsumed by the resurrected giant from prehistory,
and all times are jumbled in an ever present *now* moved through by Everyman Earwicker. *Cien años de soledad* (*One Hundred Years of Solitude,*
novel, 1967) by García Márquez and *Terra nostra* (novel, 1975) by Carlos
Fuentes encompass all time, from creation to apocalypse, and testify to the
creative resources being tapped by artists not bound to the cultural time-consciousness of Europe. From within that culture, fictionists infected with the
same comic exuberance—Grass, Calvino, Barth, Pynchon—are liberating
their own history from its received interpretations and reconstructing it as
myth.

Confronted by Foucault confronted with Borges being confronted with the
Chinese encyclopedia, postmodernists gamble on the polysemous, pluralistic
harvests of alternative worlds; and the atemporal disorderliness of their art reflects a novel sense of the novelist's vocation, expressed by Lezama Lima as
"the happy humility of remaining in a labyrinth." Once time is dispensable,
so also is narration. But what modernist critics came to understand as the
novel of "spatial form" has escalated, since Dos Passos' novel-as-newspaper
(*U.S.A.,* trilogy of novels, 1938), into fictions organized according to the
low-level temporal order of the alphabet and the tape recorder, or the high-
level spatial disorders of film, dream, and hallucination; fictions that confuse
sequence and refuse closure within the oscillations mandated by adjacency,
juxtaposition, doubling, and repetition; fictions, in Roland Barthes' summation, that refuse "to secrete words within that great category of the continuous which is narrative." In refusing to connect, develop, run, or flow, the
contemporary novel negates our myth of life as an organic unity and refutes
our most cherished metaphors of time. Contemporary fiction is irreverent and
playful, but only as these are the attributes of a keen intelligence that is self-
reflexive as well as philosophically reflective; in reading our fictions, we discover there, as do all ages, the consciousness of our own culture, the key to
which remains the human sense of time.

See also: Existentialism, Science, Universe.

Selected Bibliography

Poulet, Georges. *Studies in Human Time*. Trans. Elliott Coleman. Baltimore: Johns
    Hopkins, 1956–1957.

Shallis, Michael. *On Time: An Investigation into Scientific Knowledge and Human Experience*. New York: Schocken, 1982.

Sherover, Charles M. *The Human Experience of Time: The Development of Its Philosophical Meaning*. New York: New York University Press, 1975.

Tobin, Patricia Drechsel. *Time and the Novel: The Genealogical Imperative*. Princeton, N.J.: Princeton University Press, 1978.

PATRICIA TOBIN

TOWER

Mankind always lives on the surface of the earth, even if that be low in a valley or high atop a mountain. That surface is therefore associated with normal quotidian existence, and departures from it have come to symbolize exotic experiences, feelings, ideas. Before the age of the submarine and the airplane (or the balloon), the only departures from the surface were the tower and the cave. Because of its darkness, the cave is the locus of the secretive, corporeal, infernal, subterrestrial, wild. The tower, reaching to the sky and embraced by light, betokens the intellectual, spiritual, reflective, pious, sacred. Either cave or tower may stand for solitude, ostracism, or individualism. Freudian theory would add another dimension by making much of the obvious sexual symbolism of either entity, especially when they appear together, but that theory is as yet only an ingenious surmise.

Antiquity

Cave and tower have their important moments in the Bible, both good and bad. The incest of Lot's daughters, no less than the preserving of David's life, takes place in a cave. Evil is again conspicuous in the tale of the Tower of Babel, a story that accounts for the multiplicity of languages in the world by ascribing that perceived flaw to human arrogance. The tower is a symbol of hubris in the strict original Greek sense of the term—the attempt to deny one's earthbound nature and to cross some invisible boundary between the human and the divine. A rabbinic interpretation is that the tower stands for the attempt to keep men centered on one spot, thereby flouting God's wish that they should be scattered on the face of the earth.

The Trojan ramparts in Homer's epic poem *Ilias* (*Iliad,* c. 8th century B.C.) have a towerlike part from which prominent persons view the battle and take note of heroic individuals. Early in the work, Helen's ascent there is the occasion for the famous murmuring of the old men admiring her beauty in spite of themselves, and, at the end of the work, Priam and Hecuba watch Hector's doomed fight with Achilles and the mutilation of their son's body. The tower here functions as a superior vantage point, a place where one can see the larger picture of reality, where prominent people approximate the olympian scope of the gods. Aeschylus' *Oresteia* (trilogy of plays, 458 B.C.) begins with a watchman on the roof of the palace, a towerlike place for receiving news from a network of hilltop bonfires signalling the fall of Troy. The tower is thus associated even more strongly with far-reaching vision, with the receipt of news of important events as soon as they occur. The trilogy that began with a tower ends with references to a cave, as the Furies, infernal inhabitants of various sacred caves, metamorphose into the Eumenides, deities newly become beneficent to Athens and in turn gratefully worshipped by its inhabitants. Aristophanes' plays *Nephelai* (*The Clouds*, 423 B.C.) and *Ornithes* (*The Birds*, 414 B.C.) do not in the strict sense have towers, but in the former, Socrates dwells in a sort of hammock in the sky, as part of the satire of his alleged pretentiousness and smug sense of superiority, and in the latter, the building of the cloudcuckooland suggests that ideal republics exist only in the sky.

Other important caves function (in Homer's *Odysseia* [*Odyssey*, epic poem, c. 8th century B.C.]) as the home of that primitive man, Polyphemus, and as the site of the afterworld, (in Plato) as the symbol of the unenlightened man, and (in Virgil) as a site of a tryst that, by obstructing a divine mission, echoes the Cyclopean and Platonic caves. All these associations come together in Dante's epic poem *La divina commedia* (*The Divine Comedy*, c. 1320), where Hell is again a cavelike place and contrasts with the towerlike Mount of Purgatory. In the courtly love transvaluation of Gottfried von Strassburg's *Tristan* (romance, c. 1210) the cave of the lovers, instead of having the pejorative associations of Homer, Plato, Virgil, is a beautiful refuge for beautiful people in a world hostile to love. Courtly love also shapes the didactic *Roman de la rose* (*Romance of the Rose*). In the allegorical language of Jehan de Meung's continuation of it (c. 1275), a figurative Tower of Shame (i.e., the woman's modesty or resistance) is overthrown by Venus' arrows of fire; as a result, the lover makes his way into the woman's body, which is described as a Tower of Ivory. In this hothouse atmosphere, the conjunction of penis and tower in the mind of the author need not be ruled out.

In Spenser and Bacon, caves have rich pejorative connotations, but the Cave of Montesinos in Cervantes' *Don Quijote* (*Don Quixote*, novel, 1605, 1615) becomes, in conjunction with an alleged wide view obtained from a flying horse, as one might get from the top of a tower, the occasion for a profound episte-mological parable.

Marlowe (*Doctor Faustus*, play, 1604) coined the immortal phrase "topless towers of Ilion." The tower here symbolizes urban splendor and imperial great-ness, and the toplessness—that is, the reaching so far into the sky that the end of the building cannot even be described (an effect readily found in modern cities when a low-flying cloud covers the upper reaches of a skyscraper)—perhaps harks back to the Tower of Babel and to the hubris and doom which overtook it, as was the case also with Troy. One of the most evocative tower references has nothing to do with religion or mythology. Montaigne (*Essais* [*Essays*, 1580–1588]), describing his early retirement from the active life, tells how his château or manor has a tower in which, atop a room he often uses to sleep alone in, is his study and library, a place of complete privacy and solitude. The tower thus symbolizes the philosopher's or contemplative man's vocation. By its height, its detachment from earthbound practical and political matters, and by its broad view of the horizon, it symbolizes the olympian grasp of the meaning of current events as well as of history and literature, a grasp made possible by the library's being at the top of the tower. It is as if from that vantage point, Montaigne can see some far-off military clash of Catholic and Protestant forces in the current French Civil War even as he sits at the window reading in a history book of some ancient war between fanatics. This dual larger vision enables him to apprehend the present in perspective, to see present and past as one, each shedding light on the other. Like God, he sees a reality in which time and space are erased and in which, everything being a part of recurring cycles and principles, nothing surprises or shocks.

In Calderón (*La vida es sueño* [*Life Is a Dream,* play, 1635]), a king tries to avoid a prophesied disaster by having his son brought up in complete isolation in a tower. Here the tower symbolizes something more usually symbolized by a cave—subjectivity, ignorance, a crippling isolation. When released under controlled circumstances, the prince behaves badly, but whether that is due to the fulfillment of the prophecy or to the counterproductiveness of the confinement that was meant to elude the prophecy is beyond human resolution. In Milton's early twin poems "L'Allegro" and "Il Penseroso" (1632), both cave and tower appear. The opening lines of "L'Allegro," dismissing melancholy, associate it with "Stygian caves forlorn," with "uncouth cell," and with horrid shapes and sights. A tower first conjures up medieval chivalric romances, being a place where a beautiful woman, "the cynosure of neighboring eyes," waits for her lover hero. Then the "towered cities" phrase suggests, like Marlowe's line, riches and worldliness. The poet indeed describes the excitements of the city that the towers symbolize: "the busy hum of men"; the congregating of prominent people ("Knights and Barons"); the holding of tourneys and the presence of many great ladies; the wedding celebrations and other festivals—though whether he witnesses all this or merely reads and thinks about them is not clear. Many items in "L'Allegro" are echoed in a more solemn key in "Il Penseroso"; so is it with the tower reference. In one of the greatest of all passages on the subject, the persona speaks of the tower as a "high lonely" place where he literally burns the midnight oil while the rest of mankind (like no doubt the disciples in Gethsemane—exhausted, lazy, weak, carnal) sleeps; he, through study there of Plato and related abstruse philosophers, leads the soul (temporarily) from the sublunary world into the realm of spirits, mysteries, heaven, and immortality. There also he confronts literature—through reading instead of theatergoing, tragedy instead of comedy, classics instead of English, ennobling works instead of entertainment. Milton's tower functions rather like Montaigne's, except that the Frenchman saw it as a locale for savoring history, good sense, good story, casual philosophy, and a sampling of current events, while the Englishman grappled there rather with serious study, mystical philosophy, strenuous spiritual climbing, eternal verities. What is for the earthbound Montaigne a vantage point for a better daytime view of this world ("I am never there at night") is for the religious Milton a launching pad for nighttime mental departure from this world to some higher reality. As one critic has pointed out, the tower not only stands for alertness and contemplation but also symbolizes the site of that contemplation—the head, the part of the body most remote from the earth and from earthly matters. The tower also thus symbolizes the mind of the platonic philosopher shutting out sense experience and seeking higher knowledge through reason, intuition, and mystical processes.

The Neoclassical to Modern Periods

In Thomas Gray's *Elegy Written in a Country Churchyard* (poem, 1750–1751), the "ivy mantled tower" in which an owl "complains" is part of the new preromantic picturesque scene painting even while looking back to Milton's tower with the cynosure. "Il Penseroso" is echoed in Gray's "Eton Ode" (1742–1747), where the "antique towers" partly suggest the city of learning and grandeur and partly—this is new—nostalgia for the hopes and innocence of one's youth. Wordsworth gets something of a towerlike effect in the Westminster Bridge sonnet, as the bridge, like a tower, enables him to see from afar the large city (including its "towers") in its entirety and with breathtaking effect. In Coleridge's "Kubla Khan" (poem, 1816), the conjunction of pleasure dome and caves is repeatedly made, perhaps suggesting the role of opposites in life—light and dark, sun and ice, height and depth. The pleasure dome itself is like a tower that repeats the perceived domelike shape of the sky and that symbolizes perhaps the comprehensive imagination of the poet. It also is antithetical to Montaigne's and especially Milton's towers. Instead of elevation, contemplation, and mystical flights, the object is apparently a deeper immersion in the natural, earthly realm, as the supreme worldly power (Kubla Khan) strives to reach the limits of delight available to man, with overtones of sensual Oriental notions of Paradise. In Shelley's poem "Ode to the West Wind" (1819), the tower has rich, exotic associations with dreams, history, the Mediterranean, and the imagery of tower and cave in fact abounds in romantic and symbolist poetry.

In Stendhal's two major novels, *Le rouge et le noir* (*The Red and the Black*, 1830) and *La chartreuse de Parme* (*The Charterhouse of Parma*, 1839), the imprisonment of the young heroes in towers symbolizes their quest for self-definition and their solitary struggle with an asphyxiating society; an autonomous individual is like a tower rising above the mass. One critic has aptly referred to the tower in these cases as "an exalted seed bed of the soul." One of the most famous uses of the tower as a symbol was made in passing by the French critic Sainte-Beuve (mid-19th century), who, in commenting on contemporaries, referred to the poet Alfred de Vigny as a reserved soul returning early in the day to his "ivory tower." The phrase (actually anticipated in a different sense in the Song of Songs) has been proverbial ever since. To the traditional Montaigne-

Milton symbol of retirement and contemplation, it adds the idea of devoting one's poetry to universal esthetic and philosophic matters rather than to current burning issues. It came to mean "art for art's sake" (itself an old phrase given new meaning), that is, a pure poetry uncontaminated by "messages," nostrums, reforms, or even themes or ideas. By contrast, in Browning's poem "Childe Roland to the Dark Tower Came" (1852–55)—based on a tower reference in *King Lear*—the "dark tower" appears to be emblematic of the goal of a journey, a place of initiation or achievement.

One work in which the tower is central is Ibsen's play *Bygmester Solness* (*The Master Builder*, 1892). The protagonist is just finishing a new home for himself but, because of his dead marriage and the numerous anxieties attendant upon a highly successful career, is ambivalent about moving into it. The troll-like young woman, Hilda, who enters his life and who charms him, coaxes him into climbing the tower of the new home. He had always feared heights and had once failed in a similar attempt to ascend. But now he makes the venture, and, just when he seems to have reached the top, he crashes to his death. The reasons for his perverse act are many. The young people, the next generation of architects whom he regarded as rivals, had come to see him fail, and he was intent on foiling them. In a life of successes, he felt the need to overcome his last obstacle and weakness, his acrophobia. As a type of the artist, he felt the need also, after having done everything else in his career and become disillusioned with each stage in turn, to meet some new challenge, to reach out for the infinite, even if it be life-threatening. The presence of young Hilda rejuvenated him and no doubt reminded him of that early failing. Erotically attracted to her, he wanted to impress her, to live up to her childlike dream of him and to at once recapture and improve his youthful self. Nor should one rule out a suicidal tendency on the part of someone who, having accomplished every worldly goal, had nothing left to live for except for vague yearnings toward Hilda and wild talk about building castles in the air for and with her. Given his competitive nature, his love of work and success, the idea of retirement is, as he makes clear, out of the question, and he will go down with a grand flourish rather than fade away into quiescence and senescence. This tower, harking back to the biblical Babel, embodies restless striving, Faustian unwillingness to accept human limitations, and, as a result, defeat and death.

Joyce's *Ulysses* (novel, 1922) begins in the Martello tower, one of a series of such relics on the British coastline from the Napoleonic Wars. That historical dimension is irrelevant, for the setting suggests rather Sainte-Beuve's Ivory Tower. Stephen Dedalus, who rents the tower, is a young intellectual intent on finding his vocation as a writer but too cerebral, narcissistic, and haughty. He lacks that contact with other people that constitutes the stuff of experience and the raw material for art. On the outskirts of the city, the solitary tower symbolizes Stephen's existence as a marginal man who is cut off from family, church, and the bourgeois society of Dublin no less than from experience and creativity. During the course of the day that the novel describes, he permanently leaves both his teaching job and the tower and encounters the warm human presence of Leopold Bloom. The novel thus dramatizes the artist's departure from the sterile art-for-art's-sake mode (a late nineteenth-century temptation or affliction here symbolized by the tower) as well as his replacing detachment with human contact and consequent future artistic achievement.

Joyce's compatriot, Yeats, published in 1928 *The Tower*, one of the major volumes of poems in this century. He had recently settled down in an isolated house with a tower, rather like Montaigne's. The poems, written mainly in the tower, "attribute to it most of the meanings attributed in the past to the Tower, ...and to its winding stair [the title of a volume of his poems of 1933] those attributed to the gyre or whorl." (In the lead poem, he assigned himself the task, rather like the persona in "Il Penseroso," of reading Plato and Plotinus.) The tower itself, "a permanent symbol of my work plainly visible to the passerby," is isolated amid the "indifferent multitude," threatened by the Irish Civil War (shades of Montaigne and Milton), and emblematic of his theory of the "rooting of mythology in the earth."

Cavelike places have rich meanings in Shaw's *Heartbreak House* (play, 1919) and Kafka's "Der Bau" ("The Burrow," story, c. 1924), but a tower is a compelling symbol in the latter's *Das Schloss* (*The Castle*, novel, 1926). The castle, which K. tries in vain to enter, reach, or at least communicate with, is a huddle of houses topped by an irregularly shaped tower. This structure, described as unimpressive, is yet, paradoxically, the seat of power and authority; and this power is inaccessible, indecipherable, apparently unjust, and often just plain shabby in its operation.

A classic example of a literary work in which a tower, though mainly in the background, takes on symbolic importance is Virginia Woolf's *To the Lighthouse* (1927). The significance of the tower varies with character and time. At first it is, overtly, the goal of an outing that the seven-year-old James desperately wants to take; he is prevented from doing so by adverse weather, which the father takes note of with insensitive bluntness. For the altruistic mother, the planned trip to the tower is the occasion for bringing clothes to the poor family that lives in it. The tower is thus the goal of human aspiration and idealism, whether in child or adult, whether involving curiosity and achievement for its own sake or acts of charity. Its upright, solid, phallic, and aspiring form is also to be associated with the philosopher-father, while its soft light is associated with the compassionate, protective mother.

A decade later, the trip that had been cancelled because of the weather is finally taken. But the mother has died in the meantime, and James, now an adolescent and without any more interest in the lighthouse, is much more concerned with resisting what he regards as the tyranny of the father. That tyranny takes the form of making the son accompany him to the tower even as it had long ago ironically taken the form of frustrating such a trip. The father sees the present trip as a memorial to his deeply missed wife, an act of homage expressed by continuing the tradition of taking clothes to the lighthouse keepers. During the passage across the sea, James takes over the steering and wins at long last some words of praise from his father, some recognition that he is a man and an equal. The trip to the tower has therefore become both a metaphor and a rite of passage, and the tower itself symbolizes every young person's goal of becoming a responsible, autonomous adult. When they reach their goal, James discovers that the tower, when seen from afar and as the object of desire, is not the same tower when seen from up close and as part of the palpable here and now. This discovery of perspectivism, subjectivity, and mutability as the cardinal principles of human existence defines, even more than do the act of steering and the garnering of praise, his becoming a mature, enlightened man. Such principles likewise characterize the tower itself and make it a much richer symbol than it would be if subjected to simplistic allegorization and this-equals-that exegesis. Most literary towers are more than the sum of their bricks.

See also: Cave.

Selected Bibliography

Bayard, J. P. *La symbolique du monde souterrain*. Paris: Payot, 1973.
Gilman, Stephen. *The Tower as Emblem*. Frankfurt: Klostermann, 1967.
Jobst, Werner. *Die Höhle im griechischen Theater*. Wien: Böhlau in Komm, 1970.

MANFRED WEIDHORN

TRAGICOMIC HERO

The tragicomic hero, who usually appears in literature of low mimetic and ironic modes, evinces both a tragic capacity for suffering, endurance, and self-discovery and a comic inability to transcend human finitude or to escape the mechanical repetition of physical existence. The tragicomic hero is, to use George Eliot's phrase from *Middlemarch* (novel, 1871–1872), a "mysterious mixture" (for example, of reason and instinct or of intellect and emotion) sometimes energized, sometimes enervated by the antithetical elements of self. Embodied in this figure is a vision of humankind as capable of noble aspiration but frustrated by an intractable or seemingly purposeless reality. In affective terms the tragicomic hero elicits both sympathy, as a representative of the universal human condition, and criticism, as a comically fallible or ineffectual character. Depending on whether pathos or irony is stressed, the tragicomic hero gravitates toward the sentimental protagonist of romance or melodrama, on the one hand, and toward the anti-heroic protagonist of satiric or dark humor, on the other hand.

The tragicomic hero is a modern phenomenon, emerging from the realism and naturalism of the nineteenth century. The realists' attempt to be true to "the way things are" leads both to a rejection of aesthetic formulae, such as comedy and tragedy, and to a realization that experience belies the unequivocality of purely tragic or comic characters. In general, three types of tragicomic heroes developed roughly chronologically between the mid-nineteenth and the mid-twentieth centuries. The first is the protagonist of mimetic literature, usually an ordinary individual, capable of action but suffering the defeats of quotidian experience. Comedy is largely a matter of the irony of hopes deflated by circumstance and character, tragedy a result of hopes deferred and activity frustrated. The second is the character of sensibility, emerging from fin-de-siècle aestheticism. Often the narrator of the work in which he appears, the hero endows tragic events with a sense of beneficent and resigned humor. While the hero is flawed and passive, these limitations are counterbalanced by a bittersweet recognition of life's joys and sorrows. The third is the stylized, expressionistic anti-hero of dark humor and the absurd. Laughter and pain are inseparable in the tragicomic protagonist, whose absurdly comic limitations express the tragedy of humanity isolated in and victimized by a world that can be neither understood nor controlled. The hero provokes what Samuel Beckett calls "the *risus purus*, . . . the laugh that laughs . . . at that which is unhappy."

Background in Antiquity and the Renaissance

Classical genre theory prohibited mixing comic and tragic elements within a single play—to say nothing of doing so within a single character. Although the debate on the decorum of mixed drama was to continue through the eighteenth century, the popularity of tragicomic literature was widespread. Renaissance apologists for the new *tragedia mista, Michspiel,* and *drame libre* drew upon the example of Euripides, whose plays *Kyklōps (Cyclops,* n.d.) and *Alkēstis Alcestis,* 438 B.C.) included high and low characters; the authority of Aristotle and Horace, whose aesthetic theories were construed to justify joining the elements of conventional tragedy and comedy; and the terminology of Plautus, who coined *tragicomoedia* to describe his *Amphitruo (Amphitryon,* c. 215–186 B.C.). The combination of the genres took several forms: first, mixing of tragic and comic characters and incidents in parallel but separate plots; second, resolving potentially tragic plots with happy endings (*tragedia de lieto fin*); and, third, using a double plot that rewards virtue and punishes vice. Foremost among the writers of mixed plays of the sixteenth and seventeenth centuries are Giraldi Cinthio in Italy, John Fletcher and Francis Beaumont in England, and Johann Christian Hallmann in Germany. In addition, pastoral tragicomedy became an important form, and Guarini's *Il pastor fido (The Faithful Shepherd,* 1590) was both the focal point of the critical controversy over the propriety of mixed genres and a forerunner of the plays of Alexandre Hardy, Jean de Mairet, Ben Jonson, Samuel Daniel, and E. C. Homburg. In the basically melodramatic romantic comedies of this period, as well as in the more sentimental comedies (*comédie larmoyante, weinerliches Lustspiel*) of the eighteenth century, tragic and comic elements remain discrete. Different characters fill the roles of the hero, villain, and clown; single tragicomic characters do not appear. While tragicomedy of the period admits a greater variety of characters and range of responses than (neo-)classical genres, it remains for the nineteenth century to synthesize those elements in a single figure.

Realism and the Tragicomic Hero

The earliest tragicomic heroes appear in the age of realism and of the novel (a genre defined by Ortega y Gasset "as a synthesis of comedy and tragedy"), when larger-than-life heroes and exaggerated comic caricatures alike seem false to the nature of quotidian experience. In these early stages, protagonists are typified by idealistic objectives that are painfully proven to be false, or at best partial. Thus, in George Eliot's *Middlemarch,* the idealism of Dorothea Brooke and Tertius Lydgate is out of place in provincial middle-class life. Their limited reintegration into the social order occurs only after a compromise of their ideals; their power to influence society is minimal. An even darker vision is presented by Gustave Flaubert in his novels *Madame Bovary* (1856) and *L'éducation sentimentale* (*The Sentimental Education,* 1869). Emma Bovary's romantic dreams and adolescent optimism are belied by the initially common and ultimately sordid facts of ordinary life. The term "tragicomedian" is used by George Meredith to define his characters for whom "the comic in their natures led by interplay to the tragic issue," and it accurately describes not only the protagonists of *The Tragic Comedians* (novel, 1880), but also Sir Willoughby Patterne and Diana Merion of *The Egoist* (novel, 1879) and *Diana of the Crossways* (novel, 1885). Generally in nineteenth-century fiction, characters are unaware of the purely comic elements of their plight, with a twofold result. First, ironic effects are muted (except in extreme forms of naturalism) and, second, audiences are invited to view characters from a superior vantage point, but more sympathetically than critically.

Twentieth-century tragicomedians continue this struggle against the limitations of self and society—an important figure in this regard being the clown, whose innocence both guarantees his victimization and raises him above his chaotic and cruel surroundings. In *Ulysses* (novel, 1922), James Joyce simultaneously invites and deflates comparisons of Leopold Bloom to Odysseus and Christ. By submitting to the insult and oppression of modern life, Bloom emerges as a humble but clownish hero. A similarly alienated innocent in the modern waste-land is Rabbit Angstrom, hero of John Updike's novels (*Rabbit, Run* [1960], *Rabbit Redux* [1971], and *Rabbit Is Rich* [1981]), whose tragicomic nature is defined early in his life by the prostitute who says: "in your stupid way you're still fighting." A darker vision emerges in Graham Greene, whose protagonists evince a greater degree of self-conscious, often self-directed humor. The whiskey priest in *The Power and the Glory* (novel, 1940), although crippled by alcohol and fear, remains true to his responsibilities, for which he is killed. By the time of *The Comedians* (novel, 1966), however, this martyrdom seems purposeless. The narrator Brown remains indifferent to the irrational violence of the world, insisting sardonically that he "belonged to the world of comedy and not of tragedy." This increasing, and increasingly dark, self-consciousness on the part of characters tends to deny audiences a superior perspective but also to moderate the harshness of the tragicomic vision by including them in it.

Tragicomedy is also an important element of the theater of this period, most notably in the plays of Henrik Ibsen. The eponymous Hedda Gabler (1890) is a victim of *bovarisme,* her romantic vision leading to Lövberg's grotesque death and culminating in her own. In *Vildanden (The Wild Duck,* 1884) Hjalmar Ekdal's comic short-sightedness produces a tragic end, yet poised between the blind idealism of Werle and the pragmatism of Relling, Ekdal embodies humankind's middle state. A more clearly comic and less naturalistic vision appears in Ireland in the plays of J. M. Synge, G. B. Shaw, and Sean O'Casey. Christy Mahon, in Synge's *The Playboy of the Western World* (1907), undergoes a transformation in a rural community's eyes from abject criminal to idolized hero, only to reject social norms and the concept of hero itself. Ironically, in that rejection he becomes the hero for which he had initially been mistaken. This pattern also appears in Shaw's *Pygmalion* (1913). A lower-class flower girl is transmogrified into a high-society puppet, only to reassert her human dignity. Eliza Dolittle, however, is trapped in an agonizing no-man's land between a squalid but honest street life to which she cannot return and a luxurious but false debutante's existence for which she is socially and financially unsuited. A similar tension is embodied in Mrs. Boyle of O'Casey's *Juno and the Paycock* (1924). On the one hand, the dimly perceived and imperfectly enacted ideals of her children lead only to defeated action; on the other hand, the false idealism of her husband is merely a rationale for inaction. While Ibsen's tragicomedians are caught in a naturalistic world that ultimately defeats them, the three Irish playwrights depict alternative tragicomic stances ranging from comic recovery (of Christy, not of his society) to tragic discovery (of Juno and her daughter Mary). The middle ground is represented by Eliza, who receives no answer to her question, "What am I fit for?"

Sensibility and the Tragicomic Hero

The tragicomedian of sensibility possesses an awareness of his plight that is generally denied the realistic/naturalistic character. The hero of aesthetic temperament cultivates a life of heightened consciousness, making his own interior life a work of art. But the activity of consciousness, which also invests ordinary experience with meaning, isolates the individual within himself. The title character of Walter Pater's *Marius the Epicurean: His Sensations and Ideas* (1885) is the prototype of the hero of refined sensibility. Only in death can he reconcile the opposed worlds of materialism and idealism, of flux and permanence. A common trope in this literature is the dramatic or novelistic structure of life itself. Cut off from the world, the post-Cartesian hero assumes a series of dramatic roles and personae, multiplying the self-conscious tragicomic effects. The "human comedy" takes on a tragic dimension with the recognition of the inevitability of the "final curtain." Thus, the appropriateness of Jaques' mordant conclusion in Shakespeare's *As You Like It* (play, c. 1599): "All the world's stage / And all the men and women merely players.'' The last of humankind's many roles is ''second childishness and mere oblivion / Sans teeth, sans eyes, sans taste, sans everything.''

In Marcel Proust's *A la recherche du temps perdu* (*Remembrance of Things Past*, novels, 1913–1927), the narrator Marcel cultivates a plaintive sensibility that is both a result of and responsible for his relationships with women: his mother, Swann's daughter, and Albertine. The irrationality and mutability of Eros typify life in general, which overwhelms the hypersensitive Marcel. Such is also the case for William Gerhardi's novelist-heroes. Andrei Andreiech (*Futility*, novel, 1922) describes life as ''melancholy, but strangely fascinating,'' an attitude of bemused detachment adopted even to his own protracted and ultimately unsuccessful courtship. The result is what Gerhardi calls ''humorous tragedy (that very adult compound of pathos and humour: the very spirit of an age which has outgrown Greek tragedy).'' Consciousness proves incapacitating—as is darkly shown by Thomas Mann's Aschenbach in *Der Tod in Venedig* (*Death in Venice*, novelle, 1912), who says, ''Knowledge is the abyss,'' and is comically illustrated by John Barth's Jacob Horner in *The End of the Road* (novel, 1958, rev. 1967). The protagonists of sensibility are as restricted by literary molds as other characters are by social constraints. Anton Chekhov provides a formula for tragicomic drama: ''a landscape . . . , lots of literary talk, little action, a ton of love.'' Characters in his plays are dwarfed by landscape— a lake in *Chaïka* (*The Seagull*, 1896), Moscow in *Tri sestry* (*The Three Sisters*, 1901), and the orchard in *Vishnëvyĭ sad* (*The Cherry Orchard*, 1904). These settings operate symbolically, not naturalistically. Characters project fears and longings onto place, creating an incapacitating emotional environment. Once again, a conventional element of comedy, unrequited love, is the index of the larger failure to act on vaguely formulated but endlessly discussed plans. The Prozorov family exemplifies this dilemma, and *The Three Sisters* ends with Masha's plaintive cry: ''maybe, if we wait longer, we shall find out why we live, why we suffer. . . . Oh, if we only knew, if only we knew!'' Edmond Rostand's *Cyrano de Bergerac* (play, 1897) adds a new element to the portrayal of the lyrical hero. Accentuating the tragicomic theme is the contrast between Cyrano's noble ideals and his comical appearance. Both motifs, waiting and physical grotesqueness, are exaggerated in the next stage of tragicomedy, but in these works they remain within the realm of plausibility. Thus audiences are less alienated or disturbed by the tragicomic heroes than engulfed in the mood of melancholy. Sympathetic responses are qualified by the incapacitating and comic extremes to which sensitivity is taken.

Absurdity and the Tragicomic Hero

Albert Camus writes in *Le mythe de Sisyphe* (*The Myth of Sisyphus*, essay, 1942) that the ''absurd is so solely by virtue of the disproportion between intention and reality. . . . The absurd is esentially a divorce. It lies in neither of the elements compared; it is born of their confrontation.'' This vision is shared by all tragicomedians; twentieth-century writers, however, are distinguished by their extreme and nonmimetic expression of it. While earlier tragicomic heroes are normal characters or characters self-consciously adopting literary poses, more recent tragicomedians find the modern experience so alienating that "normal" becomes a meaningless term and the borders between fact and fiction or between the prosaic and the fantastic are impossible to draw. This condition produces two types of tragicomic hero: first, characters, often exaggerated or grotesque, who are stylized expressions of the alienated human condition and, second, characters, more representational or realistic, who accept alienation and respond concretely to it. The first type is represented by the eponymous hero of *Watt* (1953), who is enmeshed in a domestic routine of "formal brilliance but indeterminable purport." His exhaustive attempts to impose meaning on experience through language and logic bring him no closer to understanding himself or his world. The expressionistic heroes of Franz Kafka—Gregor Samsa, transformed into an insect ("Die Verwandlung" ["Metamorphosis," story, 1915]); Joseph K., inexplicably arrested for unspecified crimes (*Der Prozess* [*The Trial*, novel, 1925]); and K., hoping to gain admittance to the castle (*Das Schloss* [*The Castle*, novel, 1926])—present a much more sardonically humorous picture of the inverse ratio between the need and the possibility of understanding. The second type is exemplified by Dr. Rieux of Camus' *La peste* (*The Plague*, novel, 1947) who, despite a sense of the ludicrousness of the attempt, works endlessly against an epidemic. Rieux, like the heroes of John Fowles and Saul Bellow, decides that, at the least, he will not contribute to suffering and, at the most, he might be able to alleviate it.

The tragicomic hero appears most frequently in the Theater of the Absurd. Eugène Ionesco, for example, writes that his plays depict "our tragicomic human condition, the malaise of being." Although the protagonist Bérenger is not consistent from play to play, he epitomizes the tragicomic hero. In *Tueur sans gages* (*The Killer*, 1958), he loses faith in the commonplace morality that makes life possible, ultimately accepting the inevitability of his own murder. In *Le rhinocéros* (*Rhinoceros*, 1960), Bérenger, although resisting the dehumanization by rhinoceritis that transforms others and exposes the conformity of modern life, is a reluctant hero who shares many of the traits of the way of life he rejects. Bérenger is a kind of Everyman, like Edward Albee's All-American boy (*The American Dream*, 1960), serving both to criticize the shallowness of modern-day society and to express the meaninglessness of human existence. Lacking the sense of order upon which it is usually based, tragedy is now inseparable from comedy. As Friedrich Dürrenmatt, whose play *Der Besuch der alten Dame* (*The Visit*, 1956) is subtitled a tragic comedy, insists, "We can produce the tragic out of comedy, bring it forth as a terrifying moment, as an abyss opening up . . . comedies from which the tragic arises."

While *Rhinoceros* exemplifies the use of grotesques, the motif of waiting dominates Beckett's *En attendant Godot* (*Waiting for Godot*, 1952) and Tom Stoppard's *Rosencrantz and Guildenstern Are Dead* (1967). The life/literature theme is exploited by Luigi Pirandello in *Sei personaggi in cerca d'autore* (*Six Characters in Search of an Author,* 1921). The play so confuses the identities of the actors and the roles played that distinguishing reality from make-believe is impossible. The effect of these plays is to deny audiences the comfort of conventional responses and to create a sense of unease and alienation that had heretofore been confined to the stage itself. For example, in *Mutter Courage und ihre Kinder* (*Mother Courage and Her Children,* 1939) and *Leben des Galilei* (*The Life of Galileo,* 1938) Brecht's protragonists deny unambiguous responses because they are characters of radical contradictions—courageous yet self-serving, dedicated to causes (survival and science, respectively) but at great cost to their families. Brecht, like Camus, pursues "that truly rending contradiction between experience and portrayal, empathy and demonstration, justification and criticism." Thus, as tragicomic heroes evolve through realism, sensibility, and absurdity, the superior vantage point of audiences erodes, until readers and viewers themselves become potential tragicomic heroes, experience the contradictions described by Brecht, and therein verify the inseparability of life and literature.

See also: Alienation, Anti-Hero, Birth of Hero, Comic Hero, Laughter, Social Status of Hero, Theatrical Absurdity.

Selected Bibliography

Guthke, Karl. *Modern Tragicomedy.* New York: Random House, 1966.
Hall, James. *The Tragicomedians.* Bloomington: Indiana University Press, 1963.
Herrick, Marvin. *Tragicomedy.* Urbana: University of Illinois Press, 1955.
Kenner, Hugh. *The Stoic Comedians.* London: W. H. Allen, 1964.

RANDALL CRAIG

TRAVEL

Under a variety of changing forms—the journey, the voyage, the pilgrimage—travel has functioned as one of the most fundamental, widespread, and perduring themes in world literature. Real or imaginary, actual or symbolic, fantastic, extraordinary, or burlesque, its modalities are legion, and it offers almost unlimited possibilities for development. Travel constitutes at once a genre in its own right, a formal element in the structure of a text, and a major or minor motif in innumerable works of fiction, poetry, or drama. It obviously figures most prominently as a theme in the minor genre of the travel narrative and in those forms that lend themselves most readily to being structured according to the pattern of the journey or the voyage—the epic, the romance, the novel. From antiquity on, however, it has been a standard topos for poets and philosophical essayists, and dramatists have made journeys in real space (e.g., *Le voyage de M. Perrichon* of Labiche and Martin [*M. Perrichon's Excursion,* 1860]) as well as symbolic and inward odysseys like Eugene O'Neill's *Long Day's Journey into Night* (1956) into major themes of their plays.

The essence of travel is displacement, a displacement "in time, in space, and in social hierarchy" (Lévi-Strauss), an estrangement from the protective environment of the familiar in order to discover the newness of oneself and of things. Its psycho-literary space lies in what Gabrielle Roy has called an endless tugging between at homeness and the infinite, in a ceaseless quest for an elsewhere, the objectification of which is forever changing (Golden Fleece, Mystic Isle, Holy Grail, Promised Land, the Road itself). It is the element of seeking that transforms the banal act of traversing space into an authentic act of traveling, the archetype of which is the journey to the Cosmic Center. So fundamental is the experience of the journey that the passage from life to death or the progression of the spirit through the various stages of virtue and knowledge are expressed in travel metaphors.

Because our conceptualization of travel is a direct function of our evolving notions of space, the development of travel as a theme has closely paralleled changes in our experience and consciousness of the universe. Early texts do not generally differentiate neatly between real and mythic space; but, as the contours of physical, fictive, psychic, or spiritual space have become more sharply defined, so too have distinctions in both the meaning and modalities of travel. Chronologically, the development of the theme falls into three broad periods: the closed space of antiquity and the Middle Ages; the discovery and mastery of physical space in the Renaissance and Enlightenment; and the shift from an objective to a subjective perception of space among romantic and postromantic travelers.

Travel is such a protean theme that numerous ancillary themes have crystallized around it and must figure, albeit incidentally, in any treatment of the subject: for example, adventure, discovery, escape, evasion, exoticism, flight, homecoming, insularity, labyrinth, *pícaro,* quest, speed, utopia. Because it encompasses so many modalities, however, certain very specific thematizations of travel—for example, descent into hell, cosmic travel, time travel, shipwreck—will be treated here only in passing.

Antiquity and the Middle Ages: Travel in Mythic and Real Space

All the primal travel patterns known to literature, whether they be defined in terms of their terrain (land journey, sea voyage, journeys of ascent and descent), their intentionality (quest, odyssey, pilgrimage, homecoming, home-founding journey), or by their consequences (journeys of initiation, rejuvenation, integration, transformation), are to be found in antiquity, where they were elaborated over the centuries in the writings of various cultures. Indeed, travel itself, in its most basic manifestation of the wandering, is part of humankind's fund of archetypal experiences. Rooted in a collective recollection of ancestral migrations in prehistoric times, the wandering is a recurrent motif in early texts, where it frequently takes on both a literal and a figurative sense. Abraham's odyssey from Ur to Canaan, the going-down to Egypt of Joseph and his brethren, Moses' forty-year trek in the desert following the Exodus are examples of great land journeys that memorialize the real displacements of a people as well as their progress toward greater spiritual consciousness. In their emphasis on its moral or symbolical dimensions, these biblical narratives exemplify a general tendency in earlier cultures to valorize the ideational over the phenomenological aspects of the journey, to consider travel more as an interior experience than as a means to acquiring historical or geographical data. As a result we find the journey figuring as a major motif in poetry and song, in sacred and mystical texts long before it became the staple of travel narrative. In fact, throughout antiquity and the Middle Ages, accounts of discovery and exploration or the peregrinations of the curious were consistently deemed less important than more transcendentally motivated displacements; and it is around representative forms of the latter type of travel that the theme is best studied in both periods: the journey of heroic quest, the epic sea voyage, the pilgrimage, and the allegorical and symbolic journey.

Journeys of Heroic Quest. The first fictional travelers are the legendary epic heroes who set out in search of adventure, love, and knowledge. In the Mesopotamian *Epic of Gilgamesh* (c. 2000 B.C.), the hero and his companion Enkidu embark on a series of perilous exploits, performing prodigious feats of strength, until they arouse divine wrath and the latter is slain by the goddess Enlil. At that point adventure becomes quest—that is to say, journeying is transformed into mission, or purposeful travel—as Gilgamesh goes in search of immortality, a journey of many stages and trials, through deserts, mountains, and dark ways, to the edge of the world, then across the waters of death to fetch the plant of eternal life; the quest fails, however, for, on the return journey, Gilgamesh loses his priceless find. Variations on the above pattern are standard fare in Indic, Iranian, and Graeco-Roman heroic literature, where adventure-seekers like Hercules, Perseus, and Theseus are obliged to travel hither and yon in carrying out their tasks. But it was medieval courtly romance that transformed wandering itself ("errance") into a truly seminal motif, as the apparently aimless setting-forth of the hero became an act fraught with hidden destiny, leading not only to an exploration of the mysterious by-ways of "aventure" but to a discovery of the true nature of the "erring" self. The journeys of the Arthurian knights-errant (Yvain, Lancelot, Galahad, Gawain, Tristan) to win the idealized woman's love; Parsifal's literal and spiritual itinerary in quest of the Grail; indeed, the real-life wanderings that were the theme of both the art and life of the peripatetic poet-scholars (the *vagantes*)— these are all manifestations of a teleologically conscious age's need to find meaning in movement.

The medieval epic too was centered on heroic travels in an idealized space; and great expeditions were a basic component of its structure even before the Crusades gave a new teleological focus to such undertakings, inspiring a vast body of works ranging from the twelfth-century *Pèlerinage de Charlemagne à Jérusalem et à Constantinople* (*Charlemagne's Pilgrimage to Jerusalem and Constantinople*) to Tasso's *Gerusalemme liberata* (1581). Finally, the chivalric novels of the late Middle Ages like *Amadís de Gaula* (*Amadis of Gaul*, compiled by Montalvo in 1508) helped to prolong well into the Renaissance and the baroque the vogue for fabulous journeys of heroic quest, until Cervantes' *Don Quijote* (*Don Quixote*, 1605, 1615) and its realistic progeny turned knight-errantry into parody. They survive, none the less, in much altered form, as a feature of the adventure novel and occasionally recapture some semblance of their original heroic quality in modern quest and fantasy literature.

The Voyage in Epic, Saga, and Romance. Originally a term to describe any passage by land or sea, the voyage will refer here specifically to a journey by water, occasionally by air, to distant places, real or imaginary. Grounded in myth and fact—for example, the voyage in the Ark of the survivors of the universal flood, early sea-faring expeditions of exploration and colonization—the voyage embodies more fully than any other mode the affective connotations of travel, witness, for example, the pervasive use of the nautical metaphor to represent the journey of life. Indeed, the voyage's expressive value made it one of ancient literature's primary motifs; and in the epic poems *Odysseia*, (*Odyssey*, c. 8th century B.C.), *Aeneis* (*Aeneid*, 19 B.C.), and *Argonautika* (*Argonauts*, 3d century B.C.) we find elaborated its three great archetypal patterns, namely, the restorative voyage of the hero; the unitive or home-founding voyage of the community of exiles; and the circular voyage of seekers after a sacred boon.

Although stories of fantastic sea travel are found in pre-Homeric texts like the Egyptian tale "The Shipwrecked Sailor" (early 2d millennium), the *Odyssey* is the first major work to figure around the voyage; its eponymic hero is the prototype of the intrepid voyager who leads his crew beyond the limits of geographically demarcated space into a mythic space inhabited by fabulous beings, from which he alone returns, a solitary witness to the fabled world he has visited. A multivalent voyage text, the *Odyssey* is made up of several archetypal journeys: the *Tēlemacheia* or the son's search for the father; the experiential and expiatory wanderings of the homeward-bound hero, or "odyssey" per se; the voyage to the abode of the dead; the homecoming. As one of literature's great traveler-types, the Odysseus-Ulysses figure often reappears in later works. Dante (*La divina commedia* [*The Divine Comedy*, epic, c. 1320]), for example, makes him a symbol of culpable daring, whose effort to navigate the uncharted South Atlantic ends in death (*Inferno* [*Hell*], 26, 55–142); whereas in the character of Leopold Bloom (*Ulysses*, novel, 1922) Joyce portrays an unheroic Odysseus who retraces through the maze of modern Dublin Homer's archetypal voyage with exemplary Dubliners assuming fabled roles.

With Virgil, on the contrary, whose own last sea crossing became a motif in Hermann Broch's novel *Der Tod des Vergil* (*The Death of Virgil*, 1945), the age-old voyage of colonization is endowed with patriotic and religious grandeur, for the *Aeneid* is not one man's voyage alone, but that of a whole people embarked on a sacred expedition to found the future imperial city. Unlike the *Odyssey*, the itinerary Aeneas followed in his seven years of wandering took place in a well-defined geographical and historical space, with each stage of the journey a conscious step toward a distant goal. A similar sense of purpose pervades the most celebrated voyage in antiquity, the expedition of the Argo in quest of the Golden Fleece, which was successively thematized in Pindar's *Pythia 6* (*Pythian Odes,* 462 B.C.), Apollonius of Rhodes's *Argonauts,* and Valerius Flaccus' poem *Argonautica* (c. A.D. 80–93). Based on an actual expedition to the Black Sea by the Minyans of Thessaly, it gradually incorporated into its structure a whole network of historical and legendary voyages to the north and west, with the vessel itself eventually assuming under Orphic influence a mystic character (e.g., the late poem *Argonautica Orphica,* c. A.D. 350). A recurrent motif in medieval and Renaissance literature, it has more recently been the subject of verse-epic (William Morris, *The Life and Death of Jason,* 1867) and of the historical novel (Robert Graves, *Hercules, My Shipmate,* 1945).

The *Argonauts* is an especially critical text in that it delineates the tripartite pattern basic to all future travel romance: the outbound voyage of hero and companions; the central episodes of initiation along a road of trial and testing; the ultimate return of the enlightened hero. That pattern, reworked in sundry ways, reappears in literature from the Hellenistic Age on, beginning with the Graeco-Oriental novel of love and adventure (e.g., the *Aithiopika* of Heliodorus [*An Aethiopian History,* 3d century]), which regularly uses the voyage and its attendant motifs—shipwreck, separation by pirates, and so on—as a conventional device. But the two most significant contributions of later antiquity to the motif lie in the production of that large body of fanciful popular travel writing dubbed by Tarn "the underside of geography," and in the creation, with Lucian's *Alēthēs historia* (*A True Story,* 2d century), of the satirical or burlesque voyage. The work of a widely travelled author, it lampooned voyage literature, both fictive and factual, from Homer to Herodotus, from the *Indika* (4th century B.C.) of Ctesias the Cnidian to the wonders recounted by Iambulus and his successors in the art of tall-story-telling, and has, since its re-emergence during the Renaissance, inspired latter-day Lucianic narrators like Rabelais and Swift to make the fantastic voyage a prime vehicle for satire.

Although indebted to late antiquity for various and sundry topics (e.g., the India of the Alexander Romances, the wonders beyond Thule of Antonius Diogenes), the medieval voyage narrative derived its most distinctive thematic strands from the indigenous travel lore of peoples outside the old Graeco-Roman orbit, in particular the Arabs, the Celts, and the different Germanic tribes. Indeed, the voyage motif found its richest expression during the Middle Ages in Anglo-Saxon literature (see, for example, the voyages of Ohthere and Wulfstan, the elegiac poems [c. 8th century] *The Seafarer* and *The Wanderer*); in Celtic narratives of travel to the Other World, notably the Irish *immram* or *navigatio;* in the Icelandic sagas of exploration, pillage, and pilgrimage; and in the fabulous adventures of Sindbad the Sailor. Each set of texts offers a distinct approach to the motif.

In the seven voyages of Sindbad (*Alf Layla wa-layla* [*The Arabian Nights,* 8th to 17th centuries]), echoes of the *Odyssey,* the Greek romances, and Persian compendia of *mirabilia* mingle with recollections of travel by explorers and traders in the wide reaches of the Indian Ocean, and Sindbad himself typifies the merchant-adventurer whose wealth and wisdom result from his having crossed the bar between real and fabulous space. Fantastic rather than mysterious or other-worldly, his voyages differ from those in Anglo-Saxon or Celtic literature, where sea travel readily takes on the mystic sense associated with journeys of initiation or transformation. That the eighth century *Seafarer,* for example, treats the voyage both as physical experience and as emblematic of the Christian pilgrim's journey of life points up how complex had become the motif in a culture where the voyage's figurative sense has not only been superimposed upon, but become one with its literal sense.

Nowhere is the multivalent sense of sea travel more apparent than in Celtic or Celtic-inspired voyage literature, where the mythico-historic sea journeys of pre-Christian times have evolved into the missionary and penitential voyages of the monks of the new dispensation. A text like the *Navigatio Sancti Brendani* (c. 8th-9th centuries), which is rooted in an actual voyage by Brendan, abbot of Clomfert, casts into Christian referential terms earlier forms of other-worldly sea travel—of the type perhaps reflected in the *Echtrae Brain* (*Voyage of Bran,* c. 7th century) or the *Immram Curaig Maíle Dúin* (*Voyage of Mael Dúin's Boat,* c. 8th century)—turning what had been an expedition to a pagan Elysium into a paradisiacal journey to the promised land of the saints. But so fundamental is the voyage to the Celtic mind-set that it is not limited to the specific mode of the *immrama;* and sea-crossings figure as a device in various genres, including texts of Celtic provenance in other vernaculars like the numerous articulations of the Tristan myth or certain *lais* of Marie de France (*Guigemanr*, c. 1170). As with analogous works in Anglo-Saxon or Germanic literature (e.g., the expeditions of Beowulf), voyaging is here an essential prelude to adventures by gods and men in a twilight zone astride real and mythic space.

By contrast, travel in the Norse sagas reflects actual voyages in an identifiable space-time frame: voyages of discovery and settlement to Iceland, Greenland, and Vinland by historical figures like Eric the Red and his sons; voyages of piety and study to Rome and other Continental centers of learning. As befitted sea-faring folk, the sagas stress the voyage's phenomenological aspects, particularly the arduous nature of sailing uncharted oceans. But, however important may be these various types of voyages in fictive, semifictive, or real space, the most significant development of the travel theme in medieval literature lies in its allegorical, symbolical, and spiritual dimensions, prototypes of which already exist in antiquity; for example, travel to the Other World; mystic journeys of ascent and descent; *itineraria* of the soul toward salvation.

Allegorical and Symbolical Travel. Journeys to the Other World occur under various guises in the sacred texts of many early cultures. In Hindu mythology, for example, we find the journey of the soul after death along one of two paths (*Deva-yana,* or way of the gods; *pitri-yana,* or way of the ancestors) depending on whether or not it has been liberated from manifest existence; in Egyptian sacred lore, the Night-Sea Crossing, or nocturnal journey of the sun from west to east, on the subterranean sea (the *Thuat*); in Jewish apocrypha, the celestial, infernal, and edenic journeys of Enoch, Moses, Elias, Sophonias; and in the fertility myths of the Near Eastern and Aegean world, the seasonal descent of the goddess into the underworld in search of her lover, later of the semideified hero (Dionysus, Hercules, Orpheus) to bring back from the dead the goddess-heroine (Semele, Alcestis, Eurydice). Such descents to the netherworld are the archetypes of the symbolic journeys of initiation that figure in Pythagorean and Platonic mythic thought, in the Hellenistic and Roman mystery cults, and in the allegorical tales and romances of later antiquity like Apuleius' *Metamorphoses* (*The Golden Ass*, c. A.D. 150), where a genial convergence of moral and physical space has turned what might have been no more than a curious traveler's proto-picaresque journey into a mystical itinerary of the soul.

Such journeying in moral and symbolic space is the hallmark of medieval literature. Already in antiquity a taut link between allegory and travel had been forged by Seneca and the Stoics, who compared the life of man to a journey, as well as by scholiasts and philosophers, who tended to interpret in symbolic terms voyages in physical space depicted in epic and romance: for example, Plotinus, who explained Odysseus' travels as the circular course of the soul back to its primal home. But it was the allegorical mode itself, so prevalent from the fifth century on, that favored the thematization of travel. The journey is the natural medium in which to cast allegorical narrative, since the movement of the inner life—be it spiritual, moral, intellectual, or affective—can be most effectively represented in processional forms, where the figure of *homo viator* or one of the hypostasized virtues (vices, natural forces), accompanied as a rule by various guides, traverses a symbolic landscape dotted with signposts pointing the way to enlightenment, fulfillment, salvation. Now that journey may be accomplished in a dream, on occasion a waking vision, as in Langland's poem *Piers Plowman* (c. 1362–1387); or it may take the form of a pilgrimage of life through a succession of way stations (e.g., Guillaume de Digulleville's *Pèlerinage de vie humaine* [*Pilgrimage of the Life of Man*, c. 1330]); involve mental or interior progress along a mystical path of knowing as with St. Bonaventure's *Itinerarium mentis ad Deum* (*The Journey of the Soul to God*, after 1255) and Walter Hilton's *Scale of Perfection* (late 14th century); or require passage through an elaborate cartography of the heart like the maze of trial and testing laid out in *Le roman de la rose* (*The Romance of the Rose*, didactic poem by Guillaume de Lorris [c. 1230] and Jehan de Meung [c. 1275]) and its Renaissance and baroque avatars.

The medieval predilection for situating all beings along a vertical axis according to which each entity occupies some place on an ontological or moral scale gave special prominence to journeys of ascent and descent; and numerous allegories use one or the other device in moving symbolic or hypostasized characters through successively higher or lower spheres. Frequently realized through the medium of a dream (e.g., Christine de Pisan's celestial journey in *Le livre du chemin de long estude* (poem, 1402), they fall into several categories depending on the journey's goal, the most significant of which are the paradisiacal and purgatorial voyages of the type described in Henry of Saltrey's *Tractatus* (c. 1185–1189) and those dream-journeys in search of Eden (e.g., Rutebeuf's *Voie de paradis,* late 13th century) that were a popular submotif of Christian travel lore as late as Columbus' time.

All these divergent strands come together in the *Divine Comedy,* a truly cosmic itinerary of the soul, in which the poet journeys first down to Hell, then through the bowels of the earth to the southern hemisphere, whence he ascends to the earthly paradise at the summit of Mount Purgatory, there to begin his celestial voyage through the nine heavens to the empyrean sphere of Paradise. Dante's poem is indeed a comprehensive travel text. When seen in terms of its individual parts, it represents a systematic articulation of medieval literature's major allegorical travel modes—journey of descent (*Inferno* [*Hell*]), journey of life (*Purgatorio* [*Purgatory*]), journey of ascent (*Paradiso* [*Paradise*]); taken in its totality, it marks the suprmme realization of that literature's single greatest theme, the spiritual pilgrimage, the origins of which predate Christianity itself.

The Motif of the Pilgrimage. "A very specialized journey, the destination of which was hallowed by religious and other associations," the pilgrimage has roots in Hindu, Arabian, Buddhist, Jewish, and other sacred lore—for example, Indra's injunction to Harischandra in the Aitareya Brāhmaṇa (c. 300–600 B.C.) to wander for his spiritual well-being; the primitive Arabian *hajj* or journey to sacred places, which anticipates by centuries the Islamic prescription of travel to Mecca; the practice inaugurated by the Emperor Asoka (3rd century B.C.) of visiting the various sites that mark the stages of the Buddha's spiritual progress; the obligation, incumbent on all who are able, to go up annually to Jerusalem for the great festivals; and so forth. That it eventually became one of world literature's great motifs is due, however, to the extraordinary development it received, over a thousand-year span, in the Christian West, where the conjunction of the Pauline metaphor that we are all aliens and sojourners on earth (Heb. 11:13–16) with the notion of a geo-spiritual center toward which all mankind gravitates gave, from the outset, special importance to the act of journeying in Christian thought and practice, with the result that both the interior pilgrimage, or itinerary of the soul, and actual pilgrimages to specific religious sites became major topoi for numerous writers working in a wide range of literary genres.

What distinguishes the pilgrimage from related subthemes generated by travel (the wandering, the quest, the odyssey) is the precise sense of mission associated with the pilgrim's progress, the unswerving conviction of the wayfarer that, as he passes through each stage on his journey, he approaches ever nearer to a fixed goal, the existence and authentic worth of which was predicated at the time of his setting forth. Pilgrimage is fundamentally centripetal travel, its destination a spiritual center localized and concretized in an historical setting, be it Jerusalem, Rome, or one of many saints' shrines like Canterbury or Saint James of Compostella. From the fifth through the fifteenth centuries, innumerable journeys to these prime goals of the Christian wayfarer took place, generating in their wake a copious pilgrimage literature—guide books to accompany the pilgrim on his way; *itineraria* (logbooks) that range in scope from brief notations of distances covered and places visited to elaborate journey narratives, by authentic as well as armchair pilgrims, whose unquestionably spiritual motivations do not preclude occasional manifestations of a traveler's natural curiosity about what is seen and heard along the way. Of varying degrees of literary and historical importance, they make up a vast corpus of writing, of which some of the more significant examples are the *Itinerarium Egeriae* (*Egeria's Diary of a Pilgrimage*, c. 400); the accounts of Willibald (8th century), Ingulphus (11th century), and William of Boldensele (14th century); and Wynkyn de Worde's *Information for Pilgrims unto the Holy Land* (1498).

But pilgrimage as actual physical travel constitutes only one aspect of theme; and, alongside the numerous accounts of real journeys to hallowed sites, there exists a plethora of texts using pilgrimage as a metaphor, a motif, a narrative frame. The Pauline metaphor, taken up by the Fathers and made the subject of theological commentary from Gregory the Great on, found its way into didactic and imaginative literature, both Latin and vernacular, manifesting itself in such diverse genres as scriptural glossing and sermon literature; the personal letter of friendship; and plays based on the biblical narrative of the journey to Emmaus (Luke, 24:13–35). Because the medieval mind conceived the trajectory of human life as a journey of the soul to the heavenly Jerusalem, the spiritual pilgrimage eventually permeated all literary modes in which some type of travel constituted the informing principle, most especially the literature of quest and the allegory, where the Senecan journey-of-life metaphor gradually became identified with the Christian wayfarer's progress toward his spiritual homeland.

Throughout the Middle Ages there was a steady interaction between real and figurative pilgrimage with the great literary manifestation of the motif occuring in the fourteenth and fifteenth centuries at a time when the vogue for going on pilgrimage was at its height, but when, paradoxically, the practice itself was under increasing criticism as its original wellsprings were contaminated by curiosity-seeking and a search for worldly diversion in travel. Four broad trends in the articulation of the motif stand out in the course of these centuries: (1) the interiorization of the act of pilgrimage in Lollard and other heterodox religious literature; (2) its employment as the narrative thread giving thematic unity to the great allegorical poems of the journey of life; (3) its function as the informing principle of certain morality plays like the *Castle of Perseverance* (15th century) and *Everyman* (c. 1500); and (4) its use both as outward and inward sign in realistic works like the *Canterbury Tales* (c. 1380–1400), where the physical act of pilgrimage provided the text with its basic narrative frame while the struggle of the individual pilgrim to accomplish the interior journey that alone gives meaning to his wayfaring constituted its underlying principle of composition. Taken together these various strands make up something of a composite pilgrimage topos that was passed on to later literary periods and which, in certain cultures like that of Puritan England, was ultimately to bear a rich harvest.

Despite all the contradictions inherent in the motif in these waning centuries of the Middle Ages, pilgrimage continued to be the dominant travel theme of the period; witness the unabated interest in spiritual wayfaring up to the time of the Reformation and the central role given to the Holy Land journey in the most popular of medieval travel books, *The Buke of John Maundeville* (also known as *The Travels of Sir John Mandeville*), that ingenious melange of fact and fancy written c. 1360 by a fireside pilgrim and read by all serious travelers well into the Renaissance. Indeed, by the end of the Middle Ages pilgrimage narratives made up such a sizable body of literature that, measured in quantitative terms alone, they constituted one of the two principal components—the other being the merchant-explorer's logbook—of that still vaguely defined subgenre, the *récit de voyage,* or travel narrative, which was only gradually to win for itself a niche in the canon of established literary forms.

Travel Narrative from Herodotus to Marco Polo. If the literature of travel as such produced few masterpieces during antiquity and the Middle Ages, that was probably due to the relatively low esteem in which travelers' reports were held in cultures that conceived the world of phenomena as but the visible manifestation of an immutable order, and the information furnished by voyagers as, perforce, but the rounding out of the contours of an already divinely fixed cartography. Travel narrative is a borderline genre that becomes true literature only when factual or purportedly factual reportage is filtered through the sensibility of a privileged observer, a situation all too infrequently realized before the Renaissance. There do, of course, exist from early times individual travelers' reports as well as accounts of far-reaching expeditions like that of Hanno the Carthaginian to the west coast of Africa (c. 525 B.C.); but the traveler-narrator probably first emerged as an autonomous literary personality in classical Greece, where the father of history, Herodotus, gave impetus to this genre as well with his tales of travel to the Near East recorded in the opening books of the *Historiai* (*History,* 5th century B.C.). Following his example, travel narrative in antiquity was generally incorporated into existing genres: accounts of military expeditions or the writings of naturalists, geographers, and cosmographers like Pliny the Elder, Strabo, and Ptolemy. A rare example of a pure travel book is Pausanias' *Periēgēsis tēs Hellados* (*Description of Greece,* 2d century A.D.). A manual for the curious cosmopolitan in search of antiquities, it was the first such type of writing to attain the status of a literary artifact and stands as the progenitor of that most prolific and perduring of marginal subgenres, the traveler's guide.

Significant prototypes of future *récits de voyage* are, nonetheless, to be found in antiquity, with the great land journey through perilous or unmapped regions serving as the shaping and directing principle of Xenophon's *Anabasis* (c. 386–377 B.C.) and missionary travel on behalf of the Gospel as the governing motif of Luke's Acts of the Apostles (1st century A.D.). Indeed, not only do the voyages of Saint Paul provide the narrative thread that ties together the diverse episodes of the latter half of the Book of Acts, but, more importantly, they objectify the itinerary of an idea from the frontiers of a universal state to its spiritual and material center. Initially, to give greater seriousness to their accounts, traveler-narrators had presented their material in the third person, but under the Empire the first-person journey narrative, either in prose or verse, became a conscious art form. Horace's satire "Iter Brundisinum" ("Journey to Brindisi," c. 37 B.C.) modeled after Gaius Lucilius' *Iter Siculum* (*Sicilian Journey*, 2d century B.C.), is especially noteworthy in this regard, for it marked a significant evolution of the travel theme into a vehicle for self-expression, as would, over the succeeding centuries, a number of medieval *itineraria* cast in the form of the personal letter, like that of the twelfth-century Norman ecclesiastic Baldric of Dol. But it was in the new genre of the spiritual autobiography that this development found its natural medium, and in Saint Augustine's *Confessiones* (*Confessions,* c. 397–400) travel motifs and metaphors were fully deployed for the first time to express the many contradictory movements of the agitated spirit in search of the rest that could only be found in God. Finally, antiquity must be credited with making the reliability of the travel reporter a topos in its own right, as accounts of visits to exotic places were questioned by skeptics like Aulus Gellius and Lucian.

There are a number of important trends in travel narrative during the Middle Ages both in Christendom as well as in Islamic and Far Eastern lands. Geographical exploration was the forte of Arab travelers who, from the eighth century on, left detailed descriptions of Islamic lands from the Indies to the Atlantic: al-Idrīsī (12th century); the Andalousian al-Bakrī with his account of travels in West Africa (1068); above all the great wanderer Ibn Battuta (c. 1324–1354), who journeyed through Arabia and Asia Minor, along the east coast of Africa, finally to Spain. From India and Persia, too, came significant travel journals along with collections of fantastic voyages by land, sea, and air; for example, Nāṣir-i *Kh*ushrau's *Safar-nāma* (*Book of Travels,* 11th century), Somadeva's *Kathāsaritsāgara* (*Ocean of the Rivers of Tales,* 1050).

It is Chinese travel narrative, however, with its cut-and-dry accounts of royal, administrative, diplomatic, missionary, and cultural journeys, that stands out for variety and scope in both subject matter and forms. Dating back to the tenth-century travels of the Emperor Mu in a half-mythic space of great deserts and mountains, it includes classics like Chang Ch'ien's narrative of a mission to the Yüeh-chih in Bactria and the Wu-sun in Ili Valley north of the Tarim Basin (139–126, 115 B.C.) as set down in the *Shih chi* (*Historical Records;* chaps. 116 and 123) of the Chinese Herodotus Ssu-ma Ch'ien (145?–90? B.C.), as well as accounts of pilgrimages to India by Buddhist monks such as Fa-hsien, the author of *Fa-kuo chi* (*Record of Buddhist Kingdoms,* 399–414), and Hsüan-tsang, whose relations of his sixteen years abroad, *Hsi-yü chi* (*Records of the Western Regions,* 648), became the basis for the most important Chinese novel figuring around a journey, Wu Ch'eng-en's (c. 1500–1580) fantastic tale, *Hsi-yü chï* (*The Journey to the West).* Like their Chinese counterparts, Korean and Japanese monks left accounts of their spiritual missions abroad; for example, the *Wang o-ch'ŏnchukkuk chŏn (Record of a Pilgrimage to Five Indian States),* a record of a journey to India between 723–727 by the Korean monk Hyech'o, and the *Nittō guhō junrei gyōki (Record of a Pilgrimage in Search of the Dharma,* 847), the diary by the Japanese monk Ennin. But it was in the domain of the personal travel diary that writers from both lands excelled. In China, Li Ao (died c. 844) and the neo-Confucianists of the T'ang dynasty set the model for successive generations of diarists of the Sung, Yüan, Ming, and Ch'ing dynasties with a first-person narrative that sought to capture both the phenomena of the journey and the perduring principles underlying travel. Similarly, in Japan, the earliest examples of the form—Ki no Tsurayuki's *Tosa nikki (The Tosa Diary,* 935), the anonymous *Kagerō nikki (The Gossamer Years,* c. 970–974), the *Tōkan kikō (Journey to the Eastern Barrier,* c. 1242) attributed to Kamo no Chōmei (c. 1156–1216), and the nun Abutsuni's *Izayoi nikki (Diary of the Waning Moon,* 1280)—anticipate the impressionistic verse-prose journeys of the seventeenth century haiku poet Matsuo Bashō. Finally, Korean literature offers an interesting example of the castaway's diary in *P'yohae rok (A Record of Drifting Across the Sea,* 1488) by Ch'oe Pu.

In the West, the fact that Christianity had early on developed a moral stance toward traveling proved to be a determining factor in European literature's articulation of the theme throughout the Middle Ages and beyond. From the time of the Fathers, theologians contrasted the monastic ideal of *stabilitas* with the passion for useless wandering stimulated by vain and often culpable curiosity. Indeed, the *curiosus,* whether on a real journey to learn the secrets of nature or engaged in symbolic travel through the arcane recesses of a library, was an object of suspicion and censure; witness the strictures of Saint Bernard against the "gyrovagi" and, later, Pascal's condemnation of man's need to find diversion in incessant movement. Nonetheless, Christianity must be credited with giving to travel a definite teleological sense, and the great medieval traveler-types— the pilgrim, the knight-errant, the crusader, and the missionary—set out on their voyages impelled, at least in principle, by transcendental goals to be attained at journey's end.

With the widening of physical and moral horizons, however, these ideals inevitably gave way to the traveler's innate spirit of inquisitiveness. The Crusades played a critical role here, heightening interest in the peoples and customs of the Near and Far East; and, from the thirteenth century on, there was a steady accumulation of travel records from missionaries, merchants, and diplomats to the Courts of the Mongols. Towering above them all was the *Divisament dou monde (The Book of Ser Marco Polo the Venetian,* c. 1298), a merchant-explorer's logbook transformed into a work of art by a writer of courtly literature, Rustichello of Pisa, who applied to the elaboration of an authentic journey narrative the techniques and devices of romance. How far, indeed, travel narrative was from emancipating itself from fiction is readily apparent in the most widely read of medieval books of travel, *The Buke of John Maundeville,* whose author borrowed freely both from genuine travel accounts as well as from compilations of legendary and fantastic lore to create a work that appealed to an age intent on learning more about the East while simultaneously gratifying its taste for marvelous tales of adventure. In certain texts intimations of a new awareness of the journey's role in the maturation of the individual traveler can be discerned, but even with a writer like Petrarch, who sensitively recorded his impressions of landscape on ascending Mount Ventoux, the approach ultimately remains anchored in a premodern concept of travel. Indeed, substantive changes in the nature and function of the voyage could only come about with a profound transformation in man's perception of the universe and of his place in it—a development that would have to await the discovery, at the end of the fifteenth century, of a hitherto unsuspected "fourth part of the world" in the great mythic sea surrounding the Afro-Eurasian land mass.

The Golden Age of the Travel Narrative: From the Renaissance Voyages of Discovery to the Eighteenth-Century "Bildungsreise"

The conquest of physical space, through voyages of discovery, exploration, and exploitation, has been a key factor in the making of the modern mind. The shift away from the medieval concept of a knowable world that was fixed and circumscribed to one whose boundaries are forever expanding had repercussions in all areas of human experience, no more so than in the domain of travel narrative, the nature and function of which changed radically in the period between 1500 and 1800. Beginning with the Renaissance, travel literature became more than a verification of received truths about exotic places; it constituted an essential step in mastering space through the mediation of the text. From Columbus's *Cartas de relación de la conquista del descubrimiento de América* (*Four Voyages to the New World,* 1492–1503), and Antonio Pigafetta's account of Magellan's circumnavigation of the globe (*Primo viaggio intorno al globo terracqueo . . . 1519–1522* [*First Voyage around the World,* 1536], to the eighteenth-century narratives of Bougainville, Cook, and the Forsters, there grew up a vast corpus of travelers' accounts detailing the progressive extension of man's control over the visible world. At once symptom and cause of profound epistemic change, they reflect the instauration of the new empirical method in which every journey, ideally, becomes the testing of a hypothesis, and each individual travel narrative the experiment's literate expression and verbal authentification. Toward the end of the period Samuel Johnson summed up the spirit of the entire age, when he noted that "the use of travelling is to regulate imagination by reality, and instead of thinking how things may be, to see them as they are" (Letter 326).

The slow but steady development of a rational, scientific, and pragmatic approach to the phenomenon of traveling had consequences both for travel narrative per se and for all literature figuring around the journey from the Renaissance through the end of the Enlightenment. The tendency, for example, to see the individual journey not in isolation but as part of a corporate enterprise to master space through a systematic accumulation of facts about unknown or imperfectly known lands led to the creation, from the mid-sixteenth century on, of great collections of travel literature—Giambattista Ramusio's *Navigationi e viaggi* (*The Navigations and Voyages*, 1550–1559); Richard Hakluyt's *The Principal Navigations, Traffics and Discoveries of the English Nation* (1589–1600), along with its continuation by Samuel Purchas in *Haklyutus Posthumus: or Purchas His Pilgrimes* (1625); Theodor de Bry's two major compendia, *Collectiones peregrinationum in Indiam orientalem et Indiam occidentalem* and the *Grands et petits voyages* (*Collections of Voyages; The Greater and Lesser Voyages*, 1590–1635)—a development that culminated in such eighteenth-century productions as the Abbé Prévost's *Histoire générale des voyages* (1746–1768) and Smollett's *A Compendium of Authentic and Entertaining Voyages* (1756). So prevalent was the vogue for systematization that, by century's end, even the great fictive journeys, past and present, had been gathered together in the thirty-nine volumes of Charles Garnier's *Voyages imaginaires, songes, visions, et romans cabalistiques* (1787–1795).

But the problem of disentangling fact from fancy, of distinguishing the veracious traveler from the travel liar, haunted anthologizers, critics, and readers in an age when the voyage was the most facile mode in which to cast one's narrative. Standards for travel reports were only gradually imposed by such bodies as the Royal Society and other scientific academies; and the task of separating the authentic travel book either from the fictive voyage closely modeled after it (e.g., Defoe's novel, *Robinson Crusoe*, 1719) or from the mendacious accounts of fireside travelers purporting to be true (e.g., William Symson's *A New Voyage to the East Indies*, 1715) tested even the most discriminating practitioners of the art; witness Samuel Johnson's and Horace Walpole's labeling as lies the reports of James Bruce's real though astounding experiences in Abyssinia. Indeed, Bruce's *Travels to Discover the Sources of the Nile* (1790) were subjected, even before their definitive publication, to parody by Erich Rudolph Raspe, the prevaricating purveyor of the most unabashedly fantastic of journeys, *Baron Münchhausen's Narrative of his Marvellous Travels and Campaigns in Russia* (1785).

None the less, the critical spirit that governed the writing of travel narrative effected the composition of imaginary journey forms as well; and, while the older mythological patterns continued to manifest themselves, the dominant modes were those in tune with the new empirical outlook: the philosophical and didactic, the moralistic and edifying, the satirical and burlesque type of travel text. Demystifying the journey led, perforce, to transformations in the persona of the voyager, as the three great archetypal traveler-figures inherited from antiquity and the Middle Ages—the heroic quester, the Odyssean adventurer, the pilgrim wayfarer—were gradually reduced to the more mundane dimensions of the peregrinating *pícaro*, the ubiquitous merchant-explorer, or the cosmopolitan grand tourist observer. Moreover, the successive cultivation of the humanistic, the pragmatic, and the philosophical voyage led to a rising consciousness of the meaning of travel. Renaissance essayists like Montaigne (*Essais* 3.9 [*Essays,* 1580–1588], "De la vanité" ["On Vanity"]) and Bacon (*Essays,* 18, "Of Travel," 1597–1625) laid the foundations for a philosophy of travel that reached fruition in the eighteenth century with a Charles de Brosses (*Lettres familières écrites d'Italie en 1739 et 1740,* 1798–1799) or a Samuel Johnson (e.g., *Idler* 97, 1758–1760). But it was, above all, the on-going dialogue between travel and other areas of human experience, the continuous interaction between travel-writing and imaginative literature, the gradual permeation of all belle-lettrist genres by the structures, motifs, and metaphors of the voyage that stamped these three centuries as the golden age of travel.

The development of the theme over this three-hundred-year span falls into two roughly equal periods. The first, from 1500 to 1660, encompassing the Renaissance and the age of the baroque, was marked by an infusion of new life into those literary forms that had traditionally given prominence to the travel theme and its subsidiary motifs—epic, heroic romance, and various allegorico-didactic modes; the second, from 1660 to 1800, witnessed the great vogue for prose literature figuring around a journey, a vogue fostered by ever-increasing opportunities for travel and characterized by a determined effort on the part of authors of travel-centered works to give greater verisimilitude to both authentic and imaginary voyage narratives. That the dividing line between the periods was marked by a perceptible change in reading habits was duly noted by contemporary writers like the poet and academician Chapelain (1595–1674). But whatever differences may have existed between the two periods—and they were substantial—the Renaissance and baroque experience of travel incontestably prepared the way for the flowering of the theme after 1660, and to that initial phase one must first turn to find mapped out the new directions it would subsequently take.

Renaissance and Baroque Travel Themes: Charting a New Course (1500– 1660). Although the period from 1660 on witnessed probably the most sustained development of travel-oriented writing known to literary history, the preceding century and a half must be reckoned as its true golden age, for it was during that period that the new discoveries impacted most forcefully and immediately on the imagination, helping to fuel the Renaissance of letters throughout Europe, especially in those countries directly involved with the business of exploration, and in those genres in which the European mind could best come to grips with the consequences of the great voyages: epic, romance, satire, and experimental essay.

As might be expected, the historical voyages of the Renaissance navigators found ready symbolical representation in the motif of the epic sea journey, of which Camões' *Os Lusíadas* (*The Lusiads,* 1572) was the supreme realization. Taking for his subject Vasco da Gama's voyage around the Cape of Good Hope to India in 1497–1498, Camões used both dream vision and prophecy to inscribe into his poem the exploits of several generations of Portuguese captains, traders, and colonizers in order to better capture the epic sweep of European man's extension of imperium over vast tracts of land and sea. Although Portuguese writers were especially prolific in the production of works growing out of this expansionist spirit—for example, Fernão Mendes Pinto's *Peregrinação* (*Adventurous Travels*, 1614); Sá de Menezes' heroic poem *Malaca conquistada* (*Conquest of Malacca*, 1634)—its effects were felt in almost every literature; and the voyage motif became the single most important vehicle for translating man's acquisition of power over material and spiritual realities. Both the compiler Hakluyt, celebrating the triumphs of English navigation, and Shakespeare's Prospero, who through sheer might of intellect controls the forces of nature on a fanciful island discovered through travel, identify in their different ways power with the voyage. So too, in general, do humanists like Ariosto and Rabelais, for whom it functioned simultaneously as an encomiastic device for translating into spatial terms contemporary progress in science and letters and as a vehicle for debunking such outdated travel modes as the Crusade and the pilgrimage. Indeed, as E. A. Chesney (*The Countervoyage of Rabelais and Ariosto*, 1982) has shown, their mock epics the *Orlando furioso* (1516) and the *Gargantua et Pantagruel* (*Gargantua and Pantagruel*, 1532–1564), are elaborately structured parodies in which Homeric and Lucianic voyage patterns have been combined in dizzying counterpoint with motifs gleaned from accounts of recent sea journeys and with themes generated by the epistemological quests of contemporary humanism.

The on-going interaction among fictive, authentic, and symbolical voyage writing gave new dimensions to the motif. In forms akin to the epic, like the romance and the heroic novel, writers such as Spenser (*The Faerie Queene*, 1590–1596), Sidney (*Arcadia*, 1590), or Gomberville (*Polexandre* [*The History of Polexander*, 1629–1638]) reinvigorated standard voyage patterns by situating their protagonists' fictive sea journeys in the new historico-mythic sea-space opened up since Columbus' day; while a Walter Raleigh and his counterparts in England and elsewhere, in an effort to embellish and magnify their discoveries, were fleshing-out the normally bare-bone narratives of explorers and navigators with the stuff of romance. Finally, as testimony to the pervasiveness of the voyage theme, symbolical and allegorical sea-journey motifs, like the late medieval topos of the *Ship of Fools* (see Brant's *Das Narrenschiff*, 1494), were woven into the basic texture of Renaissance and baroque writing, along with an associated field of traditional voyage-anchored metaphors suited to contextualizing the experience of a universe suddenly and headily set in motion.

As befitted an age in which all was in movement (Montaigne 3.2), travel themes served to express a wide range of activities both physical and mental. The motif of displacement for reasons of learning or employment or because of the uprooting effects of national and religious wars was translated into a variety of modes. To the existing body of tramp literature (*liber vagatorum*), dating back to the late Middle Ages (e.g., *Der Betler Orden*, printed 1509) was added the new current of picaresque fiction, for which the road narrative provided the essential structural and thematic underpinning. Regardless of whether the individual picaresque text emphasized roguery or formative experience, travel was essential to the unfolding of plot. In some, like *Lazarillo de Tormes* (novel, 1554), the journey represented no more than a ramble "through all the mazes of squalid beggery," as a later practitioner of the genre, Tobias Smollett (*Ferdinand Count Fathom,* novel, 1753), would remark; whereas in others, like Mateo Alemán's *Guzmán de Alfarache* (1599–1602) and its progeny in Spain and elsewhere, physical movement through a determined social and geographical space was accompanied by moral and spiritual progression on the *pícaro*'s part. The richest articulation of the picaresque mode as quest and pilgrimage is to be found, perhaps, in German literature, in Grimmelshausen's novel *Der abenteuerliche Simplicissimus* (*The Adventurous Simplicissimus*, 1669), where a search for both temporal and spiritual peace amid the devastations of the Thirty Years War involved its anti-hero Melchior Sternfels in far-flung travels that included holy-land journeying and subterranean voyaging. There is considerable variety in the tone and style of the early modern travel novel. English prose narrative of the Renaissance furnishes contrasting traveler-types in the persons of Lyly's Euphues, the cultured man who embarks on an aesthetic journey from Greece to England, and of Jack Wilton, the indigenous *pícaro* figure, who traverses the continent in Thomas Nashe's novel *The Unfortunate Traveller* (1593), experiencing everywhere the misfortunes of those who subject themselves to "the lottery of travel." So too does French mannerist fiction, with its idealized journeys inscribed in the heroic and pastoral mode set in contrapuntal rhythm to the burlesque road narratives of the comic or the bourgeois novels of a Sorel or a Furetière.

The road metaphor as an emblem of the journey of life was also a commonplace in poetry among both secular Renaissance poets like Herrera and Garcilaso de la Vega as well as among more spiritually minded writers like the La Ceppède of *Les théorèmes* (*The Theorems*, 1613–1621), who made the speaker in their poems a pilgrim and the journey inscribed therein a spiritual pilgrimage heavenward. Indeed, the outpouring of devotional prose and poetry in both Protestant and Counter-Reformation Europe resulted in a revitalization of such traditional motifs as the ascent of the soul to God and the interior journey of the purified spirit to the nuptial chamber of mystical union within. Similarly, Milton's epic of man's fall and redemption, *Paradise Lost* (1667) and *Paradise Regained* (1671), by the very nature of its subject, involved multiple journeys of ascent and descent, like the voyage of Satan through the spheres. In metaphysical and *précieux* literature, too, liberal use was made of travel metaphors and motifs. For example, the symbolical journey of the lover through the landscape of the heart was expressed in cartographical terms (see the *carte de tendre* in Madeleine de Scudéry's courtly novel *Clélie,* 1654–1660), as were the meanderings of the spirit in search of truth in many a mannerist and baroque poem. Finally, among allegorical travel motifs in a minor key, a noteworthy addition to the thematic repertory is to be found in the journey to Mount Parnassus (e.g., Cesare Caporali's poem *Viaggio di Parnaso,* 1582; Cervantes' poem *Viaje del Parnaso*

[*Journey to Parnassus*, 1614])—along with such later literary analogues thereof such as Bougeant's *Voyage merveilleux du Prince Fan-Férédin dans la Romancie* (*Prince Fan-Férédin's Marvelous Journey into the Realm of Romance*, 1735)— in which an author-critic employs travel structures to pass judgment on current literary fashion.

Of note, too, is the fact that certain journey themes found propitious ground for renewal in particularized religious and cultural settings. In Catholic lands, an extensive literature grew up around the travels of missionary orders charged with carrying the gospel to the peoples of the New World and of Asia (e.g., *The Jesuit Relations*); whereas in Protestant countries like seventeenth century Puritan England, whole groups of people found in the motif of the pilgrimage— with its emphasis on "arrival and the necessity of steady application or fortitude in overcoming obstacles" (J. Paul Hunter, *Occasional Form*, 1975—an appropriate symbolical form in which to express their spiritual and temporal travails. Enriched through association with analogous motifs like the progress, which stressed "growth and accumulation of judgment and skill" by the individual (Hunter), the pilgrimage became a major motif of nearly two centuries of English literature, serving not only as the dominant theme of such overtly religious texts as Bunyan's *Pilgrim's Progress* (prose allegory, 1678–1684) but as the informing principle of numerous profane texts by writers steeped in the Puritan tradition.

Finally, travel as education, as service, as pleasure was the theme of much authentic journey literature of the age—works like Montaigne's *Journal de voyage en Italie* (*Diary of a Journey to Italy*, 1580–1581 [publ. 1774]); the poet Samuel Twardowski's verse narrative of a Polish diplomatic mission to Istambul (*Przeważna legacja . . . [The Most Important Legation of Christopher Zbaraski*, 1633]); and the accounts of such representative figures of early English grand tourism as Thomas Coryat (*Crudities Hastily Gobled Up in Five Moneths Travells in France, Savoy, Italy, Rhetia*, 1611), James Howell (*Instructions for Forriene Travell*, 1642), and the diarist John Evelyn. By the 1660s the literary travelogue had attained sufficient status to have become a medium of creative expression for established writers. As new cultures were brought to light, the educative nature of travel through cross-cultural dialogue—what Montaigne called "frotter et limer notre cervelle contre celle d'autrui"—took on special importance. Indeed, from the Renaissance on began the systematic association of ethnography and cultural anthropology with the experience of traveling, out of which nexus has since emerged a whole current of critical commentary on voyage literature of sufficient breadth to constitute an autonomous subgenre in its own right, with a pantheon of masterpieces ranging from Diderot's *Supplément au voyage de Bougainville* (*Supplement to Bougainville's Voyage*, 1796) to Lévi-Strauss's *Tristes tropiques* (*World on the Wane*, 1955).

Yet, in spite of this seemingly all-pervasive stress on movement, there were throughout the period powerful countervailing tendencies at work. In fact, by the mid-seventeenth-century, the forces that since the early Renaissance had spawned so much travel-oriented literature seemed spent, and a renewed spirit of *stabilitas* was manifesting itself in the controlling mechanism of the emerging neoclassical aesthetics—witness the imprecations of a Pascal against vain quests for diversion. None the less, as the age of the baroque reached its apogee, signs of a new passage from stability to movement were evident in the accelerating shift in the weight of European power from south to north (*translatio imperii* motif) and in the concomitant transfer of intellectual and cultural hegemony (*translatio studii* motif) from Mediterranean to more northerly centers, thus setting the stage for an explosion of travel-centered writing in their literatures after 1660.

The Thematization of Travel: The Major Phase (1660–1800). Three aspects of the thematization of travel stand out in this period: (1) the creation of a substantial body of narrative literature figuring around a journey that can loosely be grouped under the rubric of travel fiction; (2) the phenomenal growth of the extraordinary voyage as a formal element in utopian and philosophical literature; and (3) the emergence of the autobiographical travel narrative as an autonomous subgenre. Although hard and fast lines of demarcation among these three basic groupings are sometimes difficult to establish and given works may fall under more than one category, they offer, none the less, a convenient system of classification at a time when the individual author often worked in overlapping areas (e.g., Tobias Smollett wrote both travel novels and authentic travel books) and when both generic blurring and generic cross-fertilization were commonplace.

TRAVEL FICTION. Of the different types of fiction from this period utilizing travel as a theme, there are four in which the journey is an indispensible formal element: (1) novels in the picaresque vein; (2) the philosophical tale; (3) the novel of education *(Bildungsroman* and *Erziehungsroman);* and (4) the Robinsoniad and other sea-novels.

True to the spirit of the times, eighteenth-century offshoots of picaresque fiction coupled travel and learning as a fundamental trait of the anti-hero's wanderings: "I have travelled over the greater part of Europe [and] I have learned that life is at best a paltry province," writes Smollett in *Peregrine Pickle* (novel, 1751). In general, however, those who travelled "the open and ironic road" (Fussell, *The Rhetorical World of Augustan Humanism,* 1965) found the journey more fruitful both materially and morally. Such was the experience of Lesage's novel *Gil Blas* (1717–1735), of Fielding's *Tom Jones* (novel, 1749), and of their peripatetic counterparts everywhere, whether their travels were over some known physical terrain, or whether they took place across a more abstract socio-economic space like that traversed by the peasant and/or roguish parvenus, both male and female, of a Defoe, a Marivaux, a Mouhy. While the journey would often seem to be only a device permitting the introduction of new characters, new milieux, new incidents, it was, in fact, the principal determinant of the fundamental rhythmic pattern of neopicaresque fiction, which is that of a perpetual alternance between motion and pause. But the most unique contribution to the travel theme of these eighteenth-century road narratives was their ongoing, intra-textual reflection on the journey motif itself, to the point of making the calling into question of the act of traveling the critical factor in the problematic of such anti-novels as Sterne's *Tristram Shandy* (1759–1767) and Diderot's *Jacques le fataliste* (*Jacques the Fatalist*, 1773).

The philosophical journey, which enjoyed its greatest vogue during the Enlightenment, is the natural outgrowth of the crosscultural dialogue to which the Renaissance voyages of discovery gave rise. Based on an expressed or understood comparison between two dissimilar cultures, it uses both subtle irony and blatant satire to criticize the religious, ethical, political, social, and economic structure of the writer's own nation. It takes two basic forms: foreign travelers may visit the writer's native land as in Montesquieu's *Lettres persanes* (*Persian Letters*, 1721); the writer, or his surrogate narrator, becomes the traveler in another country, real or fabulous, as in Swift's satire *Gulliver's Travels* (1726). Its most accomplished practitioner was Voltaire, himself a "philosophical traveler," whose *Lettres philosophiques* (*Philosophical Letters*, 1734) represented the culmination of some sixty years of anglophilia on the part of curious and/or disaffected Continental visitors to the British Isles, and whose philosophical tales, especially *Candide* (1759), embody a deft fusion of the twists and turns of the ironic road narrative with the disabused man's quest for wisdom and sanity.

Many philosophical journeys assumed a more lofty pose and became indistinguishable from the educational travel novel, a fertile subgenre that included both morally uplifting tales about the formation of a young prince in either classical antiquity (e.g., Fénelon's *Les aventures de Télémaque* [*The Adventures of Telemachus*, 1699) or some exotic site fashionable with eighteenth-century travel buffs (e.g., Johnson's *Rasselas*, 1759) as well as those archetypes of the modern *Bildungsroman*, Goethe's *Wilhelm Meisters Lehrjahre* (*Wilhelm Meister's Apprenticeship*, 1795–1796) and its sequel *Wilhelm Meisters Wanderjahre* (*Wilhelm Meister's Travels*, 1829). A place apart among pedagogical travel fiction must be reserved for the subtheme of the archaeological voyage, which drew upon such ancient models as Xenophon's *Kyrou paideia* (*Cyropaedia*, 4th century B.C.) and authentic narratives of eighteenth-century antiquarians to classical sites in Italy, Greece, and the Levant. French literature was particularly fertile in the production of such works, especially of the fictional educational journey to Greece, in which a young man, living on the margins of Hellenic civilization, is introduced to the cultural refinements of its literary, artistic, and philosophical centers. Major examples of this motif include the Chevalier de Ramsay's *Les voyages de Cyrus* (*The Journeys of Cyrus*, 1727), the abbé Terrasson's *Séthos* (*The Life of Sethos*, 1731), and the abbé Barthélémy's *Le voyage du jeune Anarcharsis en Grèce* (*The Journey of the Young Anarcharsis to Greece*, 1784). Finally, in addition to the classical *periplum* proper to the pedagogical novel, rococo and neoclassical travel fiction features perambulations of a galant, satirical, and didactic nature, of which German literature furnished notable examples in the works of Weise, Winckler, Schnabel, and Reuter.

The Enlightenment had its impact on the voyage theme as well. The eighteenth-century sea novel represents a reduction of the heroic voyage of myth and epic to the pragmatic dimensions of a more mercantile style of traveling in which the experimental and utilitarian nature of the voyage has equal billing with its more adventurous aspects. The Robinsoniad, whose proper subject is the desert-island castaway, is a variant thereon, and its archetype, Defoe's *Robinson Crusoe* (1719), combines all the drama proper to sea voyage literature with the didacticism and moralizing inherent both in the philosophical journey and in the wayward Puritan's pilgrimage back to economic prosperity and saving grace. The utopian strain endemic to the mode shows up in later Robinsoniads like Schnabel's *Die Insel Felsenburg* (*Felsenburg Island,* 1731–1743), thus bringing it within the orbit of the period's second major articulation of the travel theme, the extraordinary or fantastic voyage.

IMAGINARY AND EXTRAORDINARY VOYAGES: UTOPIAN AND FANTASTIC ODYSSEYS. For many critics (e.g., Atkinson, *The Extraordinary Voyage in French Literature,* 1920–1922; Trousson, *Voyages aux pays de nulle part,* 1975; etc.) the terms "imaginary" or "extraordinary" voyage are most often associated during this period with some sort of utopistic writing—with the former generally being used to describe travel to a fictitious society that, except for its distant location, is basically an idealized image of the voyager's own; the latter, travel either to a realm of fantastic beings and goings-on or to one that can only be reached by extraordinary (i.e., fantastic) means. Classifying a particular work as a utopia or as an imaginary voyage is a matter of proportion. A text is essentially utopian when the voyage functions only as a device; it becomes a true imaginary voyage where there is substantial development of the travel element and of its associated thematic field: estrangement, exoticism, evasion, adventure, storm, shipwreck. Depending on where the utopia is situated, the voyage may be transoceanic, extraterrestrial, or subterranean.

Most utopias lie at the end of a transoceanic voyage, on a fabulous continent or island, the prototype of which is the realm of Atlantis, which Plato had described in the fourth century B.C. dialogues *Timaios* (*Timaeus*) and *Kritias* (*Critias*), and which had already found imitators in antiquity. But the impetus for a systematic development of the concept of a utopian society and the consequent vogue for the voyage to the land of nowhere came only with the opening up, during the Renaissance, of hitherto uncharted sea routes leading to unsuspected continents, archipelagos, and isolated islands, where utopias could be conveniently located and discovered. Initially, the imaginary voyage aspect of the theme was downplayed, since the utopian isle was either posited from the outset as existing in fact (Thomas More, *Utopia,* 1516) or at least situated in a geographical area familiar to navigators (Tommaso Campanella, *La città del sole* [*The City of the Sun,* 1602]). With Bacon's *New Atlantis* (1627), however, the extraordinary voyage became an integral part of the utopian quest, since the island-state of Bensalem was only discovered by narration, and sea travel was predicated as essential to the ideal society's on-going pursuit of truth in whatever corner of the globe it was to be found. By the early 1700s the French utopists—

Gabriel de Foigny, Denis Vairasse, Simon Tyssot de Patot—had succeeded in making accounts of imaginary voyages more credible by bringing their narrative techniques into line with those used in authentic voyage literature. Finally, with the Enlightenment, the motif came full cycle as allegorizers and propagandizers turned sea travel to fabled lands into an uninspired didacticism, while satirists, in an effort to heighten the effect of their critiques, outdid such ancient writers as Iambulus and Theopompus in exaggerating the fantastic nature of both the utopian realm and the means of getting there.

If the search for a Northwest Passage through forbidding Arctic wastes or the quest for the semimythic austral continent of easy living in the Southern Hemisphere would ultimately give new life and grandeur to the extraordinary voyage, it was in the area of extraterrestrial and subterranean travel that the motif was destined to make its great strides. Both the extraterrestrial voyage and its burlesquing have a long history going back to Lucian; and, with the rise of modern astronomy during the Renaissance, the concept of cosmic travel took firm hold on the literary and philosophical imagination. While it is generally the earthling who voyages out into space, on occasion extraterrestrials may also visit this planet as in Swift's "Voyage to Laputa" (part 3 of *Gulliver's Travels),* or Voltaire's *Micromégas* (1752). Both the pioneering seventeenth-century space-journey texts—for example, Kepler's *Somnium* (1634), Cyrano de Bergerac's *Histoire comique des états et empires de la lune / du soleil (The Comical History of the States and Empires of the Moon / the Sun,* 1657, 1662)—and their eighteenth-century avatars were largely vehicles for philosophical speculation; none the less, as the notion of travel by air gained credibility, not only the fact of extraterrestrial voyaging but the means of accomplishing it became part of the warp and woof of the text.

The subterranean voyage, though also increasingly accomplished through credible and verifiable means, is rooted in the mythic journey of descent, and, as such, is a variation on the age-old voyage-of-initiation motif. Thus, in the *Anatomy of Melancholy* (essay, 1621), Robert Burton yearns for "a convenient place to go down with Orpheus, Ulysses, Lucian's Menippus . . . and see what is in the bowels of the earth"; while the Mummelsee episode in Grimmelshausen's *Simplicissimus* involves, as an essential feature of the picaresque hero's quest, a descent into watery depths. For his part, Athanasius Kircher (*Mundus subterraneus,* 1678) hypothesizes that a whole universe, comparable to that found by extraterrestrial travelers, exists beneath the surface of the earth, and Margaret Cavendish (*The Blazing World,* 1666), envisages a vast utopian city beneath the polar ice. All these strands of the motif come together in the masterpiece of eighteenth-century subterranean travel, Ludvig Holberg's novel *Nicolai Klimii iter subterraneum (A Journey to the World Underground,* 1741). Finally, in anticipation of Verne and Wells, the extraordinary voyage could also take the form of time travel, as a number of Enlightenment writers like Mercier (*L'an 2440* [*Memoirs of the Year 2500,* 1771]) turned to travel into the future via the dream in their search for new utopian sites.

AUTOBIOGRAPHICAL TRAVEL NARRATIVE: FROM EMPIRICAL JOURNEYS OF MORAL AND SOCIAL INQUIRY TO THE SENTIMENTAL "BILDUNGSREISE." The period from the mid-seventeenth to the end of the eighteenth century witnessed the coming to maturity of the autobiographical travel narrative as an autonomous literary genre. Under such variegated titles as *Account, Description, Journal, Journey, Observations, Letters, Views, Remarks, Relation, Sketch, Expedition, Tour, Travels, Voyages,* there arose a vast body of narrative detailing the visits of a wide spectrum of travelers—predominantly European, and with the heaviest contingent from the British Isles—to centers of interest, both famous and off the beaten track, in their own countries and in foreign lands. Written largely in prose, but with some notable examples in verse as well as in forms that alternate prose with poetry, these travel books reflect the aesthetic canons of their age, seeking both to instruct and to please the reader, while striving to maintain a balance between objective reportage and the narrative thread furnished by the personal experience of the journey. In point of view they range from the empirical journey of moral and social inquiry to the sentimental *Bildungsreise,* counting among their narrators most of the traveler types enumerated by Sterne in his *Sentimental Journey* (1768): Idle, Inquisitive, Lying, Proud, Vain, Splenetic, Delinquent, Felonious, Unfortunate, Innocent, Sentimental, and the Traveler of Necessity. Although the autobiographical travel narrative has affinities with the guidebook, it differs from the latter type of writing in that it stresses the individual traveler's perception of place rather than providing an impersonal catalogue of historical and topographical data, emphasizing, as Johnson remarked about Boswell's *Account of Corsica* (1768), "notions generated from within" rather than "notions borrowed from without." So popular was the form that its narrative and descriptive techniques were imitated both in armchair travelogues and in novels cast in the guise of travel books (e.g., Smollett's *The Expedition of Humphry Clinker,* 1771), until their use and abuse by a host of travel-scribblers made them an object of parody for ironists like Samuel Paterson *(Another Traveller,* 1767) and William Combe *(The Tour of Dr. Syntax in Search of the Picturesque,* verse, 1809–1812).

Of the various forms in which an author could cast a journey narrative, the two most consciously artful were the verse-prose diary, of which Japan furnished an outstanding example in the proto-impressionistic travel journals of Matsuo Bashō *(see* his *Oku no hosomichi [The Narrow Road to the Deep North,* 1691]); and the excursion poem—of the type represented, say, by Goldsmith's *The Traveller* (1765)—where the journey was at once an occasion for moralizing on the foibles of nations and a medium for thematizing the nascent vogue for the picturesque and the sentimental. But the dominant travel mode in the Age of Reason proved to be the pragmatic journey undertaken in the spirit of Lockean empiricism and utilizing either the logbook or the letter to record the traveler's observations and reflections. Although Continental literary travelers like de Brosses or J. G. Keyssler produced a number of such narratives, it was in eighteenth-century England where fictionalized and factual travel narrative were so closely intertwined that the form realized its greatest potential. Beginning with Addison's stylization of the grand tour in his *Remarks on Several Parts of Italy* (1705) and continuing well beyond mid-century, it numbered among its successes Defoe's historical-typographical *Tour Through the Whole Island of Great Britain* (1724–1727), Fielding's *The Journal of a Voyage to Lisbon* (1755), Smollett's splenetic *Travels Through France and Italy* (1766), and Johnson's *A Journey to the Western Islands of Scotland* (1775), giving way only in the late 1700s to more subjective modes, the extreme example of which would be Beckford's thematization of his Italian journey, *Dreams, Waking Thoughts, and Incidents* (1783).

Indeed, with the flowering of sensibility after 1760, there began a gradual shift toward subjectivizing travel narrative as writers stressed their emotional responses to awesome scenes of natural beauty or to poignant human situations. Rousseau and Sterne were most influential in effecting this change, with the former's glorification of traveling on foot in *Confessions* (1781–1788) and of the country stroll in *Rêveries du promeneur solitaire* (*Daydreams of a Solitary Stroller*, 1782) creating the vogue for the pedestrian tour, and the latter's *Sentimental Journey* giving a new orientation to the literary travelogue throughout Europe, German travelers like J. S. Jacobis (*Winterreise*, 1769), J. T. Hermes (*Sophiens Reise von Memel nach Sachsen*, 1770), and M. A. von Thümmel (*Reise in die mittäglichen Provinzen von Frankreich im Jahr 1785 bis 1786* [*Journey of Sentimental Travels in the Southern Provinces of France*, 1791– 1805]) were quick to adopt the new mode, but, as Reuell Wilson (*The Literary Travelogue*, 1973) has emphasized, it was in Russia that Sterne found his most creative disciples. Whether the journey be fictitious, as in Radishchev's *Puteshestvie iz Peterburga v Moskvu* (*Journey from Petersburg to Moscow*, 1790), or authentic, as with Karamzin's *Pis'ma russkogo puteshestvennika* (*Letters of a Russian Traveler*, 1789–1790), the procedure is the same: to make the journey a medium for objective reportage filtered through a lyrico-ironic sensibility or for developing a sustained polemic against political or social inequities. The Sternian travel memoir was a vehicle particularly well suited to the Russian scene, and the first third of the nineteenth century witnessed an outpouring of such works, culminating in Pushkin's factually grounded *Puteshestvie v Arzrum* (*Journey to Erzurum*, 1836) and in Aleksandr Vel'tman's voyage of the imagination, *Strannik* (1831–1832). Transmogrified, the sentimental-ironical journey became the dominant motive-principle of Gogol's *Mërtvye dushi* (*Dead Souls*, 1842), at once novel of manners and burlesque travel book.

Among Western European writers, the marriage of travel and feeling was reflected in several ways in the last decades of the eighteenth century: in the production of elegiacally tinged picturesque travelogues like Patrick Brydone's *A Tour Through Sicily and Malta* (1773); in pilgrimages by the tender-hearted to the tombs of Heloïse and Abélard or to Rousseau's resting-place at Ermenonville; in the valorization of foot-journeying by de Saussure (*Voyages dans les Alpes*, 1780–1796), Moritz (*Reisen eines Deutschen in England im Jahr 1782*

[*Journeys of a German in England,* 1783]), and Wordsworth (*Descriptive Sketches Taken during a Pedestrian Tour in the Alps,* poem, 1793); above all, in the creation of the archetypal journey of maturation of the aesthetic consciousness in Goethe's *Italienische Reise* (*The Italian Journey,* 1816–1817), the account of a tour through Italy by a privileged sensibility from September 1786 to May 1788 that became the guidebook for future literary travelers. Finally, in the century's closing years appeared that quintessential travelogue of the imagination, Xavier de Maistre's *Voyage autour de ma chambre* (*A Nocturnal Expedition round My Room,* 1794). A mental journey by an officer confined to his quarters for forty-two days, de Maistre's text stands astride two cultural epochs, for not only did it mark the extreme limit of eighteenth-century autobiographical travel narrative, but, by its redefinition of the relationship of the traveler to the experience of traversing space, it foreshadowed future developments in romantic and postromantic literature.

Variations on a Protean Theme: From Romanticism to the Present

It is the subjectivization of the traveler's sense of space and place and the consequent transformation of landscape into what Hopkins termed inscape that has determined the trajectory of the travel theme in nineteenth- and twentieth-century writing. Beginning with romanticism, there occurred a shift in emphasis away from an objectively knowable world of persons and places to the interior space of the traveler, with the result that journeys through real space have increasingly become analogues for the progress of the self through the recesses of consciousness. Thoreau, citing the seventeenth-century poet William Habington's admonition to "Direct your eye inward, . . . and be / Expert in home cosmography," defined the archetypal modern journey as an inward voyage of self-discovery and likened the contemporary traveler to a spiritual "Columbus to whole new continents within" (*Walden,* essays, 1854)—an apt analogy in that the mental traveler of Thoreau's day was inaugurating as great a revolution in the thematization of travel as had the Genoese navigator at the dawn of the age of discovery. But, if the great poetical voyages of romantic and later literature have essentially been journeys through the interior landscapes of the psyche, they are by no means limited to expressing symbolic passage through abstract space. On the contrary, the interiorization of travel has been accompanied by such fine tuning of the traveler's skill at rendering the phenomenological aspects of the journey that both the physical act of traveling as well as the manifold details of the individual journey have become integral components of the semiotic field of the text.

Although subjectivizing the journey constitutes the critical difference in the thematization of travel in modern times, there are three other important ways in which more recent articulations of the theme differ from those of earlier epochs. There is, first of all, the transformation of the traveler and of the nature and function of traveling. In place of the pragmatic journey of self-betterment that had been the hallmark of the eighteenth century, there has arisen a new form of travel aptly defined by Francis Steegmuller as "sensibility on tour." This shift in focus from the object of the voyage to the experience of the voyager-voyaging has resulted in a valorization of travel for its own sake, a phenomenon that, in turn, has generated that uniquely modern type of journey in which the place where one goes is infinitely less important than the fact of one's going ("For my part, I travel not to go anywhere but to go," R. L. Stevenson, *Travels with a Donkey in the Cévennes*, 1879); where simply to set out, to depart ("Les vrais voyageurs . . . partent / Pour partir" Baudelaire, "Le voyage," ["The Voyage," poem, 1857]) constitutes sufficient purpose in itself.

Secondly, there is the taut link that has been formed between travel and writing. Howell's observation that "we were all travellers before we were novellers" finds its echo across the decades in Michel Butor's reminder that "travel is writing, reading is travel." So much so that the lines of demarcation between travel writing per se and the belletristic use of travel themes have been blurred, when not completely erased, in much contemporary literature. Finally, a salient feature of the elaboration of the theme over the past two hundred years has been the reprise, renewal, and reinterpretation of all the major travel patterns known to world literature, along with their often skillful and ingenious recombinations into the complex patterns of the multi-journey text.

While these general lines of development are, on the whole, predicable of the thematization of travel throughout the modern period, so multiple have been the variations on this protean theme that its modalities are best understood if treated in terms of select categories that allow for the spelling out of generic, motif, national, and period differences.

Travel and the Release of the Romantic Imagination (1800–1850). Travel became the master theme of romantic literature reflecting not only the many personal peregrinations of individual authors through places both familiar and exotic, but even more their collective awareness of how archetypal journey patterns could serve to give form to the gropings of the modern consciousness. The prototype of the romantic journey is Chateaubriand's *René* (novel, 1802), where the hero's search for a cure for his ennui takes him through a new mythic space of alienation, ranging from the sterile city-scapes of Paris to a variety of emotively charged European landscapes (a turbulent Mount Etna, the stormy Scottish Highlands, melancholy Breton moors) and, ultimately, to the primitive forests of the New World. *René* epitomizes the work of a whole generation of authors in whose writing the restlessness of the romantic age translates into compulsive movement.

Whether in the form of actual or fanciful displacement, travel represents for the romantic consciousness not only a psycho-physical imperative to get out of oneself and of one's setting, but even more the liberating possibility of doing so. As much as an escape from an unsatisfying here and now as it is a flight to an elsewhere either in or out of this world, the romantic journey is a truly protean theme, capable of appearing under the guise of any number of historic travel-motif patterns, running the gamut from picturesque wandering amid conventionally poetical sites to voyages of the imagination that generate their own interior landscapes. How multivalent a theme was travel during romanticism and its immediate aftermath and how tangibly it could contribute to the molding of a literature are manifest in the richly variegated modes it assumed in nineteenth-century English verse.

Ranging from the inward-directed journeyings of Blake's "The Mental Traveller" (c. 1801–1803) or the allegorical voyages of Keats's Endymion (1818) and Hyperion (1820) to the reprise by Tennyson of a whole series of questing traveler-types from classical, medieval, and popular lore (e.g., Ulysses [dramatic monologue, 1842], "Sir Galahad" [poem, 1842]), English Romantic and Victorian poetry included in its thematic repertory such variants as Arnold's "The Scholar-Gypsy" (1853)—in which metaphors of roaming, rambling, and straying translate a profound sense of spiritual lostness—Browning's reworking of the night voyage as horrific journey in "Childe Roland to the Dark Tower Came" (1852–1855), and the elaboration of the motif of the haunted and hunted exile in both Coleridge's "The Wanderings of Cain" (1798) and Shelley's The Wandering Jew (1810). In fact, with certain English Romantics, the experience of travel and/or the revelations of travel books have determined the very structure of their major works. Wordsworth's poetical persona, whether he be the pedestrian tourist of An Evening Walk or of Descriptive Sketches (both 1793), or the pilgrim wanderer of the major poems, The Prelude (1799–1805) and The Excursion (1814), is fundamentally a bucolic traveler in search of "The Road that pointed towards the chosen Vale," where he may commune with Nature. And, as for Byron, his Childe Harold's Pilgrimage (1812–1818) is, in essence, a poetical travelogue by a romantic Grand Tourist whose journey has ended in sobering disillusionment; while his Don Juan (1819–1824) is an epic voyage by a mock-heroic traveler whose escapades take him from idyllic Mediterranean shores to stuffy English drawing-rooms.

But it is with Coleridge, whether he be on the road to Xanadu or on the tracks of Captain Cook, that one experiences most intensely the release of the imagination through travel. Indeed, his "Rime of the Ancient Mariner" (1798) is an exemplary journey text, an illustration of how fruitful can be the encounter of unfettered poetical fancy with a body of historical voyage literature as apposite for thematizing the dreams, aspirations, and restless drives of the romantic consciousness as were the narratives of late eighteenth-century South Sea and South Polar voyages of exploration. An event of great literary and artistic consequences—one which, even before 1800, had already triggered a sizable corpus of writing of both a documentary and creative nature especially in Germany (e.g., Georg Forster's Reise um der Welt, first published in English [1777] as Voyage Round the World)— Cook's voyages provided nineteenth-and twentieth-century poets, novelists, dramatists, and painters with an imaginary space as fertile as that revealed to earlier generations by the Renaissance voyages of discovery. As pervasive as has been the effect on literature of Cook's voyages (see, for example, Captain James Cook: Image and Impact, ed. by W. Veit,

1972), it is not in any one journey fable that the release of the imagination finds its prime objective correlative, but in the act of traveling itself, of which the two most overt manifestations were the reinvigoration of traditional motifs like the voyage, and the generation of a whole new thematic built around the dynamic modes of traveling being developed by modern science and industry.

The Voyage Motif in Nineteenth- and Twentieth-Century Literature. One measure of the creative impulse inherent in romanticism was the series of fictive, extraordinary, symbolist, and visionary voyages to which its release ultimately gave rise over a span of nearly two centuries. Major novels, tales, and short stories figuring around the voyage occur in American, British, and, to a lesser degree, French fiction, with Melville and Conrad furnishing the most significant examples of both the epic sweep and the metaphysical import of travel on the high seas. Whether it be in the form of an all-consuming quest across thousands of ocean leagues (Melville's novel *Moby-Dick,* 1851), or of man's struggle against the elemental sea (Conrad's *The End of the Tether,* 1900; *Typhoon,* 1903) their prose narratives restore the awesome grandeur of the mythic voyage to such familiar travel patterns as the New England whaling expedition and intercoastal shuttling along the South China Sea. Modern British colonial novelists and American neorealists have also made the voyage a locus of intense metaphysical drama and soul-searching. In *A High Wind in Jamaica* (1929), for example, Richard Hughes created a modern pirate's tale in which the awakening of an adolescent girl and her siblings to the presence of evil is developed synchronically with the progress of the voyage, while in *The Old Man and the Sea* (1952) Ernest Hemingway turned the narrative of a Caribbean fisherman's last outing into a spiritual journey in search of the meaning of life. In France, Claude Farrère and Pierre Loti have also treated the motif in a colonial setting, although the latter's most poignant thematization of the voyage remains his tragic tale of Breton fishermen working the Icelandic waters (*Pêcheur d'Islande* [*Iceland Fisherman,* 1886]). Finally, in a lighter vein, there is the subtheme of the transatlantic crossing, representative examples of which are Howells' *Their Silver Wedding Journey* (1899) and F. Scott Fitzgerald's short story, "The Rough Crossing" (1929).

Edgar Allan Poe and Jules Verne are the masters of the extraordinary voyage in the nineteenth century. Poe's tales contain examples of subterranean travel ("A Descent into the Maelström," 1841) and of transatlantic air travel ("The Balloon-Hoax," 1844), but his most sustained treatment of the extraordinary voyage is his only novel, *Narrative of Arthur Gordon Pym* (1838), a fantastic sea voyage to Antartica ending in a mystic vision on the edge of a colossal primordial cataract. Poe was a major influence on Jules Verne, who published his novels of submarine, subterranean, extraterrestrial, and otherwise unusual travel under the general rubric of *Les voyages extraordinaires* (1863–1904). The forerunner of the twentieth-century novel of time and space travel, in which extraordinary voyages to other epochs and to the far reaches of the cosmos are carried out through scientifically plausible means, Jules Verne represents—with his mixture of humor, adventure, and fabulous technology—the progression from myth to visionary fantasy in the elaboration of the voyage motif in science fiction.

But it is in the symbolist voyage of the latter half of the nineteenth century that the romantic travel impulse achieves its supreme objectification. Rooted in the poet's desire to flee from the philistine and materialistic world in which he lives to that ideal realm where "order, beauty, luxury, calm, and voluptuousness" reign (Baudelaire, "L'invitation au voyage" ["Invitation to the Voyage," poem, 1857]), it reaches its zenith of illusion and deception in the intoxicating voyage of Rimbaud's *Le bateau ivre (The Drunken Boat,* poem, 1871), with its fusion of real, surreal, and fantastic seascapes, to become a motif of anguished impotence in Mallarmé and his disciples. Its most sustained orchestration is probably to be found in a text that foreshadows its author's ultimate rejection of symbolism, André Gide's *Le voyage d'Urien (Urien's Voyage,* novel, 1893), where all the travel motifs developed by the symbolists have been incorporated into a voyage that, according to its envoi, never took place. Still, the grand vision of the symbolist voyage was to perdure into the twentieth century—for example, Claudel's play *Le livre de Christophe Colomb (The Book of Christopher Columbus,* 1930; and Yeats's "Sailing to Byzantium," poem, 1927)—and would continue to be a fertilizing motif for much subsequent verse.

Perduring Patterns in Changing Times (1800–1914): Life-Journey Novels, Utopian and Burlesque Voyages, Pilgrimages of Grace and Taste. Besides the great sea and space voyage, a number of basic travel themes reappear under various guises in much nineteenth- and twentieth-century writing, in particular the journey of life motif, the utopian and burlesque voyage, and the pilgrimage both real and metaphorical. In each instance perduring patterns have been shaped to fit changing literary currents.

The novel is the chief locus of these thematic clusters, most especially of the large body of life-journey fiction that derives either directly from the Goethean *Bildungsroman* (e.g., Carlyle's *Sartor Resartus,* 1833–1834) or from the converging strands of the eighteenth-century road narrative with such newer trends in memoir writing as those confessions of the young man from the provinces made fashionable by Rousseau. Indeed, the aspiring provincial's journey to the city in quest of his/her fortune became a major motif in realism and naturalism, as the physical space traversed came to symbolize the social and psychological distance covered by the parvenu in his rise to and often fall from fortune. Whether it be Julien Sorel's progression to Paris via the seminary at Besançon or Pip's going-up to London, movement through space is both sign and realization of a radical transformation in social status. But the motif of the journey of life in search of fortune and truth was not the property of any one literary movement; and, if it found its most natural expression in the apprenticeship novel, it was so in tune with the spirit of the age that it constitutes the ground work of most realistic fiction before World War I.

Not surprisingly, travel has also remained an integral component of nineteenth- and twentieth-century utopian novels, where some form of withdrawal from a society found wanting represents the first essential step toward the realization of the ideal community. The physical space separating the utopian from the nonutopian world varies with each writer. For the Hawthorne of *The Blithedale Romance* (1852) it is within easy reach of the mundane world from which the visionaries have withdrawn; for the Samuel Butler of *Erewhon* (1872) it lies literally over the range in a land already situated thousands of ocean miles from the quester's native country. When, however, the utopian society can only be reached through time travel (e.g., H. G. Wells, *The Time Machine,* 1895; *The Sleeper Awakes,* 1899; etc.), or, as will increasingly be the case, through cosmic travel, then the spatio-temporal gap between the two worlds takes on added significance, and the means of travel required to bridge it becomes a central motif of the text.

Burlesquing the journey, which had, in earlier times, taken the form of the mock-heroic voyage or the parody of picaresque and picturesque traveling, now focused on ordinary travelers in outlandish situations, such as Dickens' peripatetic Mr. Pickwick and his fellow-traveling clubmen of *The Posthumous Papers of the Pickwick Club* (1836–1837) or Labiche's beleaguered vacationer, M. Perrichon (play, 1860). Certain aspects of the American travel scene lend themselves easily to parody, and Mark Twain turned two such motifs into burlesque narratives: traveling the frontier in *Roughing It* (1872) and the ocean cruise as holy land pilgrimage in *The Innocents Abroad* (1869).

If the New World innocent on pilgrimage is essentially a comic type, nineteenth and twentieth-century literature also attests to both the perdurance of the religiously motivated pilgrimage to sacred places and to its transmutation into mission-conscious journeys to shrines hallowed by aesthetic, cultural, and nostalgic associations. The religious revival that occurred in reaction to the French Revolution created a propitious climate for Jerusalem-bound pilgrims of the highest literary caliber, and Chateaubriand's *Itinéraire de Paris à Jérusalem* (*Travels from Paris to Jerusalem,* 1811) inaugurated the modern journey to the physical and symbolical roots of the Christian faith. That his itinerary should take him first to Greece, then to Constantinople and Syria, indicates how multivalent is the modern pilgrimage text, encompassing both a curiosity about the hallowed sites of other creeds and a need to seek out the sacred founts of Western culture.

Perhaps because of its strong Puritan roots, American literature became particularly fertile ground for the pilgrimage motif. In the tales "The Canterbury Pilgrims" (1851) and "The Celestial Railroad" (1843), Hawthorne reworked the classic English pilgrimage texts of Chaucer and Bunyan, while a number of nineteenth-century irreverent American pilgrims like J. Ross Browne and the Melville of *Clarel* (poem, 1876) gave an ironic twist to Holy Land travel. But it is the cultural pilgrim's return eastward, "retracing the steps of the race" (Thoreau, "Walking," 1862), that constitutes American literature's most original contribution to the motif. Beginning with Washington Irving, the American writer's preoccupation with Old World culture—what Henry James called "a superstitious valuation of Europe''—led both the author and his/her characters on repeated pilgrimages to its physical and historical roots in England and on the Continent.

Finally, special historical circumstances can create a whole new pilgrimage motif (e.g., the expiatory journey, in the aftermath of World War II, to the sites of Nazi extermination camps or to Hiroshima) and even restore to an old motif something of its original sense in a modern context. Charles Péguy's efforts to reaffirm, in the years preceding World War I, France's national and religious roots were eventually concretized in his revitalization of the pilgrimage to the Virgin of Chartres, a pilgrimage he himself accomplished twice in 1912–1913, and which he thematized in his ''Présentation de la Beauce à Notre Dame de Chartres'' (''Presentation of the Beauce to Our Lady of Chartres,'' 1913), a text whose steady rhythms capture the pilgrims' march on foot to their predetermined goal.

The New Modalities of Traveling: The Valorization of Walking and "The Glory of Motion." Already in the eighteenth century the mode of traveling had become an autonomous subtheme, with the Rousseau of *Emile* (novel, 1762) manifesting such a predilection for walking over riding as to counsel his eponymic hero to take the postchaise only if his goal was simply to arrive at a certain destination, noting that should Emile wish to travel, he must go on foot. The first stirrings of the romantic sensibility had fueled popular interest in the pedestrian tour; and, with the advent of the modern naturist consciousness, walking took on the proportions of a major motif, as Rousseau's spiritual descendants built a whole literary ethos around the pursuit. In Europe, the Swiss pedagogue Rodolphe Töpffer elaborated the mode of the Alpine pedestrian journey by schoolboys in his *Voyages en zigzag* (1844) at approximately the same time as the American naturists were extolling the liberating effects of being afoot with one's vision both in town and in country. Thoreau, throughout his writings, but especially in the excursion essays like ''Walking,'' set forth a philosophy of foot travel befitting a transcendental Anteus who derived his moral force from persistent contact with the spirits of the Earth around his native Concord; while Whitman, ''afoot and lighthearted,'' celebrated in *Leaves of Grass* (poetry, 1855) the joys of taking ''to the open road.'' But it was in the work of Rimbaud, the quintessential ambulatory poet, whom Verlaine called ''the man with the soles of wind,'' that the aesthetics of walking reached maturity, as a whole cluster of positively charged neopagan values crystallized around the persona of the tramp-adventurer, and poetic creation itself came to be equated with the act of being afoot.

As a structural motif in literary texts, walking appears most frequently in the guise of the promenade, that intermediate mode of traveling which, as Jean Grenier has suggested, lies midway between going elsewhere and remaining at home (Nouvelle revue française, Nov. 1964). Its most common form, the stroll in the country, occurs as an incidental motif in any number of works, attaining its most imaginative thematization in Proust's novels *A la recherche du temps perdu* (*Remembrance of Things Past*, 1913–1927), especially in the opening volume, *Du côté de chez Swann* (*Swann's Way*, 1913), where the two country paths along which the narrator's family alternately orient their daily perambulations foreshadow the directional lines that will eventually define the entire novel's trajectory. But walking need not be limited to a nature-oriented thematic; and the urban promenade, whether it be the dominant theme of a work (e.g., Stendhal's *Promenades dans Rome* [*A Roman Journal*, 1829]), or one among several of its governing motifs—as is the case with such city-centered texts as Baudelaire's poems *Tableaux parisiens* (*Parisian Scenes*, 1861) or Joyce's *Ulysses* (novel, 1922)—has taken on increasing prominence in literature, as the endless and often fruitless ramblings of characters through the maze of the modern city have come to symbolize the bewildering criss-cross patterns of contemporary life.

If the valorization of walking has significantly impacted on the thematization of travel, the technological revolution in the means of transportation that has been going on since the early 1800s has had even more far-reaching consequences. The invention of new modes of locomotion has brought about a new relationship between travel and speed and a new conception of the traveler's perception of the space he traverses. Indeed, the journey by railroad, steamer, automobile, plane, and space craft has spawned a uniquely modern type of traveler, for whom, as Vigny had predicted in his poem "La maison du berger" ("The Shepherd's House," 1844), "distance and time have been conquered." Even before the full onslaught of rail travel, writers like Thomas de Quincey were celebrating the radical changes already inaugurated by the advent of the mail-coach, which had "through a velocity at that time unprecedented . . . revealed the glory of motion" (*The English Mail-Coach or the Glory of Motion*, 1849); and while a Vigny or a Ruskin might speak out against the triumph of graceless travel introduced by the steam engine, there were far more voices both in England and on the Continent to celebrate than to deplore the new poetry of speed. The literary-artistic movement that gave perhaps the greatest prominence to the aesthetics of speed and to the thematization of the modes of travel was futurism; and, in his *Manifesto* of 1909, Marinetti called on poets to sing the glories of the steamship, the locomotive, and the plane.

In certain instances a special relationship seems to have been readily established between the individual author and the mode of travel: Mark Twain and the river boat, Valéry Larbaud and the millionaire's private railway car, Blaise Cendrars and the transcontinental train, Saint-Exupéry and the commercial mail plane. Finally, as much as the individual author, a national literature may be identified with the thematization of the modes of locomotion. American literature seems unique in this respect both for the variety and the frequency of its use of the means of traveling as a theme—a phenomenon explicable in part by the imperative first to master its own transcontinental space, then to extend that mastery to both intercontinental and interplanetary space. Indeed, it is in that imperative to control one's national space that the travel theme takes on special relevance for certain literatures.

Mastering Space: The Impact of Travel on Various National Literatures. Increasingly, in the nineteenth and twentieth centuries, there has been an association of the travel theme with the literatures of certain countries where the sense of space is vast and where extensive journeying seems to have imposed itself by the very need of mastering that space. For a D. H. Lawrence, America's destiny ''is to go down the open road . . . accomplishing nothing save the journey, . . . accomplishing herself by the way.'' Indeed, the circumstances attendant upon her discovery, exploration, colonization, and expansion westward have made travel an integral part of the American experience, and her literature has in consequence developed a whole series of journey motifs connected with these successive phases of national self-realization. The sixteenth-century journeys of discovery and exploration, already important topics in colonial literature, became major themes for early nineteenth-century writers (e.g., Ph. Freneau, Washington Irving); and, with the progress of geographical, social, and cultural displacement, there developed—as various critics (e.g., Janis Stout, *The Journey Narrative in American Literature. Patterns and Departures,* 1983) have noted—two basic directional travel patterns: one, the westerly journey or journey out, a journey of migration, of setting forth, of home-founding, a journey of escape and quest, an essentially future-centered journey; the other, the easterly journey or journey back, an inward-looking and home-seeking journey, a journey to the historic past and a pilgrimage to both the native and European well-springs of the race, a journey of withdrawal, of retreat, of back-trailing, but also one of spiritual and cultural enrichment (the case of James, Adams, Wharton, etc.). These archetypal patterns, worked out in nineteenth-century literature, have perdured into late twentieth-century writing, with the endless and oftentimes aimless road narratives west alternating with seemingly more purposeful journeys east.

In Canada, where, since the earliest settlements, traveling into the wild has been a constant feature of life, there developed among Francophone authors a specialized motif, that of the long journey to both a real and a mythic *pays d'en-haut,* which, as Jack Warwick (*The Long Journey: Literary Themes of French Canada,* 1968) has shown, may take a variety of forms, depending on the motivations of the writer and his/her relationship to the societal superstructure: journeys of *rayonnement* or empire-building as in the case of Jos.-Ch. Taché and Alain Grandbois; magical journeys of quest like those of a Gabriel Sagard and an Alain Desrochers; journeys of regeneration with Roger Lemelin and Yves Thériault; finally, journeys of revolt, in the writings of Ringuet (Ph. Panneton), Langevin, and Gabrielle Roy. Anglophone Canadian writers, while cultivating similar themes—for example, John Buchan's novel *Sick Heart River* (1941) with its depiction of a quest for wholeness through the journey north—have also developed a body of verse focusing on the figure of the lone voyager and a fiction centered around pioneering on the western plains (Fr. Ph. Grove's *Over*

Prairie Trails, 1922). Among journey themes shared by Canadian and American writers there is gold-rush traveling which, in the works of a Tom MacInness, evolved into the broader thematic of bohemian vagabondage, as well as trans-continental traveling of a "beat" nature which finds expression in Jean-Jules Richard's *Journal d'un hobo* (1965).

But if North American writing seems to offer the greatest variety of journey structures generated by a people's need to come to grips with its national space, significant examples of the process do occur in other literatures. The motif of exploring the Australian heartland, for instance, has been thematized in Patrick White's *Voss* (novel, 1957); that of traversing the expanses of Russia, in Chekhov's narrative *Step'* (*The Steppe,* 1888); of navigating the Amazon, in José Eustasio Rivera's novel *La vorágine* (*The Whirlpool,* 1924). The Great Trek was a fertilizing element in South African writing, while Algerian literature in French furnishes an interesting variation on the great land journey motif in Louis Bertrand's novel *Le sang des races* (1899), a work depicting travel across the North African heartland by immigrant carters whose wagon trains supplied the distant towns and military outposts of the interior. Finally, contemporary writers everywhere have become prolific world-wide travelers, inscribing their mastery of intercontinental space in numerous journey narratives filled with personal and social commentary.

Evolving Patterns of Travel Narrative: Toward a New Objective Subjectivity. The evolution of the nineteenth- and twentieth-century autobiographical travel narrative closely parallels developments of the theme in other literary genres. As with romantic poetry and fiction, the great divide in travel narrative comes with the writer's new-found concern with subjectivizing landscape. Gérard de Nerval notes that "il y a eu des temps où l'impression de voyage n'existait pas [There have been periods when the impression of the journey did not exist]" (*Lettres d'Allemagne* [*Letters from Germany,* Sept. 1, 1838]), an observation that suggests both a new way of seeing things and a shift away from the voyage as pragmatic process toward travel as the very warp and woof of art. Albert Thibaudet ("Le genre littéraire du voyage," *Nouvelle revue française,* May 1912) has identified three major trends in the literary travel narrative since 1800: (1) the growth and development of the picturesque journey as travelers transposed their impressions of exotic scenes into colorful tableaux in the manner of Gautier; (2) the transformation of the gentleman's Grand Tour into the sensitive esthete's pilgrimage to places where religious, cultural, and historical associations have marked them as ever-worthy objectives of the traveler's efforts; and (3) the creation of the romantic or modern journey per se, in which travel is the expression of the identification of person with place, or, in Gide's phrase, the state of finding oneself interesting in a given locale. It is the emergence and gradual predominance of this third type of travel that stamps the modern journey narrative as a text of objective subjectivity.

What has characterized travel writing since 1800 is the sheer volume of journey narratives by both professional and amateur authors, ranging from accounts of voyages of exploration into still unknown regions to reports by the literati of their tours along the European cultural and the Afro-Asian exotic circuit. Although the variations on the journey narrative are legion, the explorer's logbook and the literary travelogue continue to constitute the basic forms of travel writing in the nineteenth and twentieth centuries; and however different may be the destinations (uncharted wastes, familiar scenes), motivations (evasion, adventure, quest, straightforward reportage), consequences (blazing new trails, revealing new sites and new selves) of a given journey, what the best examples of both forms have succeeded in capturing is a sense not only of individual passage but of privileged place.

Certain journey narratives of exploration—whether it be by reason of the exotic nature of the quest involved (e.g., the search for the sources of the Nile, the reporter Stanley's efforts to find the missionary-hero David Livingstone); or the sheer heroism inherent in the undertaking itself (e.g., expeditions by Nansen, Scott, Amundsen, Filchner to Arctic and Antarctic wastes); or because of the awesome array of scientific and technological skill required to bring the enterprise to fruition (e.g., travel to the moon, interplanetary and interstellar voyages)—have exercised on readers the same fascination as the adventure novel. Corresponding to the exotic journey to cultures far removed in space and time from the ordinary world of the traveler are those forays nearer to home undertaken by socially-conscious inquirers through the variegated strata that make up nineteenth- and twentieth-century Western society. The burgeoning metropolis spawned by the Industrial Revolution became a socio-economic new frontier that poets and novelists would explore with as much interest as the social historian. To depict his movements homeward through the slum quarters of London, for example, De Quincey *(Confessions of an English Opium Eater*, 1822) had employed elaborate metaphors drawn from voyage literature, portraying himself as "the discoverer of some of these Terrae incognitae," which he doubted "had yet been laid down in the modern charts of London."

The evolution, over the past two hundred years, of the belletristic writer into a world traveler has transformed the journey narrative into a multi-faceted literary mode bearing the imprint of individual, national, and period styles. Since 1800 the literary travelogue has steadily moved from the position of adjunct text to that of being an integral component of an author's total œuvre, functioning both as a crucible in which the raw stuff of literature takes fledgeling shape and as a versatile medium of creative expression and critical reflection. With German and French Romantics alike, travel writing represented an extension of the fundamental theme of their fiction and poetry, so much so that for a Gérard de Nerval actual physical travel—whether it happened to be a lengthy tour of the Near East (*Le voyage en Orient* [*The Oriental Journey*, 1843–1851]) or a simple excursion to the Valois country (*Promenades et souvenirs*, 1854–1855])—was only another stage in the poet's objectification of his interior voyage through the landscapes of the mind. In more recent times travel narrative has even become something of a surrogate text, especially for the novelist; witness the creation of the meta-travelogue by Butor, Theroux, Naipaul. By no means has the literary travelogue of the last two centuries been a standard text. Real national differences, for example, exist in the stylization of nineteenth-century travel writing, with German (Heine, Laube) and especially Russian travelers tending to give a strong didactic, ideological, and political coloration to their journey narratives, while their English and American counterparts aimed rather at fixing their impressions "in the vivid image and the very scene" (Henry James). Moreover, a perceptible shift in the orientation of the literary travelogue is discernible after 1890. Whereas the romantic and symbolist traveler had sought to subjectivize the experience of the journey, transposing his/her travel notes into prose poems of the road, the trajectory of travel writing since the turn of the present century can be defined as one of gradual passage from sensibility to social consciousness, as the journeys of the literati turned, more and more frequently, into critical confrontations with changing political and social realities. Illustrative in this regard is André Gide, whose earlier journeys had focused on the discovery of self through voluntary estrangement, but who subsequently reoriented his travel narratives toward a rigorous examination of both French colonialism (*Voyage au Congo* [*Journey to the Congo*, 1927]) and the Communist experiment in Russia (*Retour de l'U.R.S.S.* [*Back from the USSR*, 1936]). But the mutations of the journey narrative represent only one phase of the interaction of travel and writing in twentieth century literature, a subject that has assumed increasing importance with each succeeding generation of writers, and which, because of changing political, social, and aesthetic factors, is best treated in two distinct stages, the first encompassing the period from 1900 through the end of World War II, the second the years from 1945 to the present.

Journey Structures and Travel Metaphors in Modern Fiction and Poetry (1900–1945). The salient feature of the thematization of travel in modern fiction and poetry has been the interaction of the real and the imaginary voyage in the structuring of the literary work. A critical determinant in the composition of travel-oriented texts since romanticism, the dialectical interplay between the journey in real space and its mythic, symbolic, and metaphysical resonances in the imaginary space of the artist's creative consciousness became an even more significant factor in the aftermath of symbolism and with the breakthrough to modernism in the first decades of the twentieth century. The œuvre of André Gide (d. 1951) typifies the complexities of the modern author's relationship to the journey and the multifarious ways in which travel has been transposed into text. Not only did journeying constitute one of the basic polarities of his own life—the other being the familial hearth to which he always returned—but he made the very act of renouncing the voyage into a minor travel motif (*Le renoncement au voyage,* essay, 1906). Throughout his career he experimented with different categories of travel writing, periodically inscribing specific journeys into a variety of travelogue-modes; and his great turn-of-the-century North African voyages of transformation underwent successive stages of thematization in several distinct genres: prose poem (*Les nourritures terrestres* [*The Earthly*

Livelihoods, 1897]); novel (*L'immoraliste* [*The Immoralist*, 1902]); travel diary (*Amyntas*, 1906); spiritual autobiography (*Si le grain ne meurt* [*If It Die*, 1926]). Moreover, Gide's novels drew on biblical, classical, and symbolist travel myths for themes (*Le retour de l'enfant prodigue* [*The Return of the Prodigal Son*, 1907]; *Thésée* [*Theseus*, 1944]) and regularly employed the journey as sign and function of character development (e.g., Alissa's journey in *La porte étroite* [*Straight is the Gate*, 1909]). Finally, both the proto-surrealistic *Les caves du Vatican* (*The Vatican Cellars*, 1914) and the cubistic *Les faux-monnayeurs* (*The Counterfeiters*, 1925) are characterized by a multiplicity of fragmented journey patterns including a farcical variation on the pilgrimage-crusade motif in the former and the disjointed elements of a horrific journey into a new "heart of darkness" in the latter.

In large measure Gide's oeuvre mirrors the major trends of the theme's trajectory during the years preceding and following World War I—to wit, an increasing reliance on the journey for the elaboration of the literary text coupled with a radical fragmentation and recomposition of its traditional motif patterns. The proliferation of so many ordinary travel sequences in the popular cultural media (e.g., the chase in American Western and gangster fiction and cinema) spurred poets and mega-novelists everywhere toward a renewed allegorization of traveling in an effort to endow the modern journey with something of the unitive and regenerative qualities of archetypal voyage forms. A quest for wholeness amid growing spiritual and cultural fragmentation shows up, for instance, in two prewar French journey-texts: Alain Fournier's mystic adventure novel *Le grand Meaulnes* (*The Wanderer*, 1913) and Ernest Psichari's spiritual odyssey *Le voyage du centurion* (*A Soldier's Pilgrimage*, 1916); while the fiction, poetry, and poetical theater of the interwar years were marked by a reprise of some of the great travel myths as totalizing structural motifs: the odyssey in Joyce's *Ulysses*, the quest for the Grail in Eliot's poem *The Waste Land* (1922), the anabasis in Saint-John Perse's epic *Anabase* (1924), the voyage of the Ark in Obey's play *Noé* (*Noah*, 1931), the Renaissance voyages of discovery and conquest in Claudel's free-verse drama *Le soulier de satin* (*The Satin Slipper*, 1928–1929). The sources of the modern poem of the voyage are as many as they are varied. A D. H. Lawrence utilized the Etrusco-Egyptian journey-of-the-soul motif in "The Ship of Death" (1928), and Pound's verse was filled with fragments of voyage structures from Graeco-Roman, Chinese, Anglo-Saxon, and late medieval literature. Finally, Hart Crane's *The Bridge* (1930) typifies the travel poem of the interwar years with its weaving together of multiple journey motifs to present the artist's personal odyssey against the backcloth of a series of American historical voyages.

Under the dual impact of the modernist revolution in art and the general destabilization of political and social structures, travel themes reflected more and more the fractured order of things. World War I gave the lie to the grand illusions of "Belle Epoque" Europe, and in its after-shock there emerged the so-called lost generation, with the writer cast in the role of a cultural expatriate whose journeyings—whether real or fictionalized—most often represented a vain search for meaning in a world gone awry.

One consequence of the broken world of the twenties and the thirties was the re-emergence of certain elemental travel motifs like the wandering, which could now be projected on a global scale as a result of the universalization of travel. A case in point is Céline's pre-absurdist wanderer Bardamu who travels from World War I battlefields to tropical Africa, then on to the American megalopolis of Chicago, finally back to a sinister Parisian suburb in his "journey to the end of the night" (*Voyage au bout de la nuit,* novel, 1932). Céline's *Voyage,* with its steady drift into darkness, captured the spirit of the *avant-guerre* years and prepared the way for the horrific journeys about to be spawned by the cataclysm of a whole world at war. As with all wars (see such earlier texts as Zola's novel *La débâcle* [*The Downfall,* 1892]; Tennyson's *The Charge of the Light Brigade,* poem, 1855), the motif of movement in turmoil was an important component of the thematic cluster associated with World War II. Developed both in texts written during the war (e.g., Saint-Exupéry's autobiographical *Pilote de guerre* [*Flight to Arras,* 1942), and in works composed subsequently, it is a motif that can be expressed either on an individual or collective scale, either in the drama of a young boy sent into hiding and shunted from village to village in Eastern Poland (Jerzy Kosinski's novel *The Painted Bird,* 1965) or in the marches and countermarches of an army in rout (Claude Simon, *La route des Flandres* [*The Flanders Road,* novel, 1960]). Finally, it was again Céline who gave expression to one of the least noble of travel motifs associated with World War II, namely, the series of aimless displacements of collaborators obliged to find haven in the wake of collapsing fascist regimes (e.g., *D'un château l'autre* [*Castle to Castle,* novel, 1957].

The Travel Theme since 1945: New Directions of Reprise of Constants? Various factors have contributed to giving a particular coloration to the travel theme since 1945: (1) the pervasiveness of tourism and of a whole body of writing inspired by tourism ranging from the banal travelogue to satirical sketches of country-hopping excursionists like those in Mel Stuart's movie *If It's Tuesday, This Must Be Belgium* (1969); (2) the elaboration of a modern "exodus" literature reflecting the great migration of peoples triggered by the political and social changes that have occurred in the wake of World War II; (3) the spectacular realization of humanity's age-old yearning for extraterrestrial voyaging and the creation of a new mythic space for both science fiction and travel narrative; (4) the Beat Generation's journey out of society and the consequent neoprimitivistic nomadism pervading much of "beat" literature; and (5) the dissolution of traditional societal patterns and the concomitant loss of a clear directional purpose to human existence resulting in a shift away from travel as measured progress towards *traveling* as endless process—a phenomenon exemplified in the circuitous night-journeys of Beckett's absurdist protagonists or in the compulsive wandering of the anti-heroes of Kerouac's novel *On the Road* (1957).

Certain developments of the theme deserve particular comment. Science fiction has been especially fruitful in rejuvenating such archetypal travel motifs as the journey of initiation or the visionary voyage and has given new vitality to journeying in reduced or foreshortened space (e.g., Isaac Asimov's *Fantastic Voyage,* 1966, in which a team of doctors travel through a patient's bloodstream). The actualities of manned space travel have captured the attention of both novelists and mythographers, with Norman Mailer turning the first landing on the earth's satellite into a piece of imaginative literary reportage (*Of A Fire on the Moon,* 1970) and Joseph Campbell expounding on moon flight as a contemporary example of the outbound voyage that leads back into the psyche (*Myths To Live By,* 1972). On a more mundane level a critic like Janis Stout has identified a typically American variant on the motif of the circuitous journey in novels by a Philip Roth or a Larry McMurtry depicting the "endlessly looping circuit" of a baseball club around the league in the course of a playing season. Of further note in a period when, as Germaine Brée has observed ("The Ambiguous Voyage: Mode or Genre," *Genre,* 1968), "the voyage as principle for the elaboration of fiction is tending to become prevalent," there has been an increasingly sophisticated treatment of travel in the novel—a now classic example being Michel Butor's *La modification* (*Change of Heart,* 1957), a multi-voyage in space, time, memory, and consciousness, which features a sustained use of the journey as theme, framing device, and overall structuring principle. Butor's novel is a good example also of both the doubling of the physical by the mental journey, and of the readiness to experiment with the latter form of traveling as an autonomous thematic mode. Lastly, the facility with which we now traverse space has demystified the act of traveling and contributed to the demythologizing of the exotic journey in quest of the secrets of life. Indeed, the privileged vayage has spawned the anti-voyage, as in the novelist Muriel Cerf's travel narrative to the Far East, *L'antivoyage* (1974), a reprise of the stoical topos that traveling changes nothing and that the real journey is an inward-directed voyage that requires no special intinerary of locale and that can occur anywhere.

A number of recent trends can be cited as symptomatic of the perdurance, vitality, and potential for development of the travel theme: for example, Jean Grenier's attempt at a phenomenological analysis of the "Promenade" and the "Voyage" in two pioneering essays written in 1964 for the *Nouvelle revue française*; Michel Butor's call for the creation of the new discipline of "Iterology" or science of traveling ("Travel and Travel Writing," *Mosaic,* 1974); the founding in 1973 of the critical journal *Exploration* to probe the relationship between travel and literature, as well as the growing tendency of both literary and scholarly reviews to devote entire issues to creative and reflective pieces figuring around the voyage (see, for example, the *N.R.F.* for October 1974); the perceptible increase in university research on journey structures and the travel metaphor for understanding individual authors and literary periods by such scholars as Charles L. Batten, Jr., Laurel Braiswell, Ross Chambers, Charles N. Coe, Thomas Curley, Martin Day, Paul Fussell, J. Paul Hunter, Claude Pichois, J. Plessen, Warren Rice, Dan Vogel, Christian Zacher, and others; above all, the renewed interest in the travel book as an imaginary genre on the part of novelists like Butor (*Mobile. Etude pour une représentation des Etats-Unis* [*Mobile. Study for a Representation of the United States,* 1962]), V. S. Naipaul (*The Middle Passage,* 1962), and Paul Theroux (*The Old Patagonian Express. By Train through the Americas,* 1979), who see in its fluid thematic and structural patterns a means of reinvigorating narrative fiction. Finally, if humankind is inherently an unrepentant traveler, and if, as Northrop Frye has suggested, "the marvelous journey is the one formula that is never exhausted" (*Anatomy of Criticism,* 1957), then the travel theme can be expected to continue serving not only writers of romance but all poets, novelists, and dramatists who discern in the human condition an imperative to push ever forward the boundaries of consciousness.

See also: Escape, Mountaineering, Picaresque, *Pícaro* in American Literature, Science, Sublimity, Utopia.

Selected Bibliography

Adams, Percy G. *Travel Literature and the Evolution of the Novel.* Lexington: The University of Kentucky Press, 1983.

Amelinckx, Frans C., and Joyce N. Megay, eds. *Travel, Quest, and Pilgrimage as a Literary Theme: Studies in Honor of Reino Virtanen.* Manhattan, Kans.: Society of Spanish and Spanish-American Studies, 1978.

Blackstone, Bernard, *The Lost Travellers. A Romantic Theme with Variations.* London: Longmans, 1962.

Casson, Lionel. *Travel in the Ancient World.* London: Allen and Unwin, 1974.

Cox, Edward G. *A Reference Guide to the Literature of Travel,* 3 vols. 1935–1949. New York: Greenwood Press, 1969.

Dodd Philip, ed. *The Art of Travel. Essays on Travel Writing.* London: Frank Cass, 1982.

Gove, Philip B. *The Imaginary Voyage in Prose Fiction: A History of Its Criticism and a Guide for Its Study, with an Annotated Check List of 215 Imaginary Voyages from 1700 to 1800.* 1941. New York: Octagon Books, 1975.

Lowes, John Livingston. *The Road to Xanadu. A Study in the Ways of the Imagination.* 1927. Princeton, N.J.: Princeton University Press, 1985.

Michael, Maurice Albert, ed. *Traveller's Quest. Original Contributions towards a Philosophy of Travel.* 1950. Freeport, N.Y.: Books for Librairies Press, 1972.

Possin, Hans Joachim. *Reisen und Literatur: Das Thema des Reisens in der englischen Literatur des 18. Jahrhunderts.* Tübingen: Max Niemeyer, 1972.

Roppen, Georg, and Richard Sommer. *Strangers and Pilgrims. An Essay on the Metaphor of the Journey.* Norwegian Studies in English 11. New York: Humanities Press, 1964.

Versins, P. *Encyclopédie de l'utopie, des voyages extraordinaires, et de la science fiction.* 2d ed. Lausanne: Editions de l'Age d'Homme, 1984.

GEORGE E. GINGRAS

U
//

UNDERGROUND MAN

The term "Underground Man" (U.M.) to designate a specific type of literary protagonist is based on the narrator in Dostoevsky's *Zapiski iz podpol'ĩa* (*Notes from Underground,* novel, 1864); it was later expanded to include a variety of twentieth-century prototypes in Edward Abood's critical study, *Underground Man* (1973). U.M. is a modern skeptic who doubts himself into a corner. Isolated, disgusted with the imperfections in himself and the world, he nonetheless stops short of cynicism; for he is at heart a frustrated idealist. Insisting on his freedom at any cost, and unable to accept what does not satisfy his demanding intellect, he avoids commitment. Lacking conviction, he sees little significance or purpose in his actions. Isolated, he lacks the support of others. Thus he views his ego as a tenuous entity in an uncertain universe.

It seems curious that so contemporary a figure as U.M. should come almost full-blown out of a novel written in 1864. But the novel was completely new and prophetic. In a note on the first page Dostoevsky refers to U.M. as a character of the "recent past," a "representative of the current generation." So the author was not continuing in a literary tradition, but creating one.

Background in the Early Nineteenth Century

To be sure, there are antecedents for Dostoevsky's U.M. But because of his complex and contradictory make-up, it is not always certain what he takes from his predecessors and what he rejects. For example, he continually pokes fun at the romantic hero, what he gibingly refers to as "l'homme de la nature et de la vérité" [the man of nature and truth]. Yet his own sensibility and subjectivism can be traced to the Romantics, particularly the heroes of Pushkin and Lermontov, who are also alienated from society. For while he has much of their temperament, he is otherwise quite different. There is a heroic ideal behind the jaded posturings of a Pechorin or a Eugene Onegin; U.M.'s rebellion is accompanied by shame and anxiety. Whereas the former are motivated by a sense of pride and honor, however perverse, U.M. cannot believe strongly enough in anything, least of all the *point d'honneur*, to be able to act on it; or if he does act, his gesture is invariably gratuitous, unconnected to any principle or code of conduct. U.M.'s inertia suggests, rather, such nineteenth century Russian prototypes as Goncharov's Oblomov or Turgenev's (and later Chekhov's) Superfluous Men. But these characters are passive for different reasons. Oblomov, Rudin, and Pavel Kirsanof are vestiges of a dying, agrarian culture. Products of that culture, they still retain the values that characterize it, even though those values are obsolete. Essentially landed gentry and Slavophiles, they contrast sharply with city-bred U.M. Instead of in the open fields, he dwells in a nasty room, his "hole," which shelters him from the "yellow," "wet," and "dingy" snow of unfriendly St. Petersburg. Thus nature, if not hostile, is certainly no source of renewal, as it is for Turgenev's landlords. Secondly, being younger and more contemporary, he does not suffer from nostalgia for a vanishing era, and he has little kinship with the Slavophiles. In fact, despite his vehement rejection of nihilism, he comes directly out of that movement (as did Dostoevsky himself before Siberia).

Zapiski iz podpolīa is a direct rebuttal of Nikolai Chernyshevsky's *Chto delat'?* (*What Is to Be Done?*, novel, 1863), the epitome of nihilistic doctrine. Chernyshevsky envisions a socialistic utopia brought about through applied science (technology) and utilitarianism, the philosophy that urges us to seek our enlightened self-interest. According to Chernyshevsky, the universe, including man, is governed by the irrevocable "laws of nature." Once man recognizes these laws and the role they play in his life, he will, being rational, automatically conform to them. Man, in fact, will necessarily choose what is best for him.

U.M. scoffs at this contradictory notion of freedom because it limits man to rational choice. For him, true freedom allows no limits. Chernyshevsky postulates certain basic, unquestioned assumptions about man's nature and needs; for example, that he is a being who requires food and shelter. The function of reason is simply to draw the logical consequences from these assumptions. U.M., believing Chernyshevsky confuses "primary" with "secondary" causes, rejects these and all other so-called first causes as limits to rational inquiry. In a deleted passage from the first draft of the novel, U.M. suggests, in lieu of Chernyshevsky's materialism, Christ as a legitimate primary cause, but the passage was never restored.

In subsequent novels, Dostoevsky does offer the option of Christ to his underground protagonists; for example, Raskolnikov in *Prestuplenie i nakazanie* (*Crime and Punishment*, novel, 1866); but in the earlier novel, U.M. is denied any absolute foundation for action. Questioning everything, U.M.'s futile pursuit of a basic cause leads him into the infinite regress. Of course, since he is human, he must act, but his actions are without purpose or meaning, that is, they are absurd. They spring from impulse and caprice and, contrary to utilitarian theory, are not necessarily in his own self-interest. Yet while his actions are irrational, his thinking is not. He views the world as an intellectual, demanding logical explanations for everything, including his own and other people's irrational behavior. Consequently, he is an unrelenting critic of both himself and others. Consciousness being a key component of his make-up, he suffers considerable guilt and alienation.

U.M. prior to World War I

U.M. is a synthesis of several qualities; although subsequent nineteenth-century literary characters embody some of his traits, few if any (aside from characters in Dostoevsky's last novels) have all of them. In the period between the publication of *Zapiski iz podpol'ia* and World War I, U.M. appears in the limited dimension of the social rebel challenging conventional morality. Michel, in Gide's *L'immoraliste* (*The Immoralist,* novel, 1902), and Gustav, in Mann's *Der Tod in Venedig* (*Death in Venice,* novella, 1912), choosing in the spirit of Nietzsche Dionysus over Apollo, turn their backs on the Protestant North—with its work ethic, its constraining morality, and its stifling conventions—for the relatively free and hedonistic environment of Italy and North Africa, respectively. Their bold espousal of homosexuality marks the epitome of their revolt. Kurtz's exile, in Conrad's *Heart of Darkness* (novella, 1902), takes him to the African jungle where, in unleashing the beast in himself, he indicts the missionary zeal of nineteenth-century imperialism, along with Western man's claim to a higher order of development. Jude, in Hardy's *Jude the Obscure* (novel, 1896), shakes his bony fist at such institutions as the university and the church, dying a victim of social inequality and intolerance in Edwardian England. These protagonists resemble the naturalistic hero caught in the vortex of great social forces. Yet they differ from him, not so much in their attempt at active revolt, but in their self-consciousness and introspection. In the manner of U.M., they reflect on their plight, always searching for some personal meaning in it. And, like U.M., their rebellion invariably ends in decadence or defeat.

U.M. between World War I and World War II

The cataclysm of World War I saw a proliferation of underground characterizations in literature, as the "war to end wars" turned out to be a brutal sham. Writers who felt betrayed by the controlling forces in society—the government, the press, the pulpit, the educational establishment—rejected the values of their elders and joined the swelling ranks of the "lost generation." Many outstanding literary works of the century are essentially denunciations of the war and its aftermath. While these include notable poems and plays (T. S. Eliot's *The Waste Land,* poem, 1922; R. C. Sherriff's *Journey's End,* play, 1929), it is in the postwar novel that we find distinctive underground protagonists as such—Jake Barnes in Hemingway's *The Sun Also Rises* (1926), Harry Haller in Hesse's *Der Steppenwolf* (*Steppenwolf,* 1927), and Bardamu in Céline's *Voyage au bout de la nuit* (*Journey to the End of the Night,* 1932). Loveless and rootless, alienated from God, country, and society, they are certainly underground; but their skewed perspective has been colored by the war. Having been rendered impotent in battle, Jake Barnes is denied love and family, one sure way out of underground. Choosing exile in postwar Paris, he vainly attempts to ward off the horror of Nada (U.M.'s void) through a kind of existentialist epicureanism. The physical pleasure of the moment, pursued with aesthetic style, is the only reality he can be certain of besides his pain. Bardamu flees the battlefield only to find brutality, stupidity, and folly waiting for him at every turn in the postwar civilian world. His response is noncommitment and evasion. But years of living on the fringe eventually take their toll on him, as he slowly degenerates into a selfish cynic. The war and its aftermath have turned Harry Haller into an anti-social "steppenwolf." Older than either Barnes or Bardamu, he has his roots in the late nineteenth century, particularly German romanticism. Hence, while the war has shattered the Germany of his youth, it has not succeeded in obliterating a latent mysticism in Haller, which, as we shall see later, frees him from underground.

While each of these characters is critical of society, none of them seriously considers taking political action. However, many intellectuals at the end of the war did, turning to Russia and the Bolshevik Revolution. In addition to its promise of equality and justice, communism had a spiritual appeal for them. Instead of the traditional God, it offered them a more tangible absolute, to be experienced here and now, in action instead of in the tortured cubicle of one's own psyche. But they were soon disenchanted. Not only were they repelled by Russia's cynical pragmatism—the suppression of the kulaks, the Moscow Trials, the pact with Hitler—but they also found themselves incapable of that total denial of individuality and freedom of thought that the party demanded. Doubters such as U.M. quickly realized that it was no easier to believe in dialectical materialism and historical necessity than it was any other article of faith.

Out of the vast output of pro-Communist literature, much of it flatly doctrinaire, Andŕe Malraux's novel *La condition humaine* (*Man's Fate,* 1933) stands out for its portrayal of U.M. seeking regeneration in communism. The novel focuses mainly on Kyo and other young intellectuals during the Shanghai Insurrection of 1927. Born in an era of transition from feudalism to modernism, they are at first marginal characters despised by both their Western and Chinese masters. They seek in communism personal dignity and identity, as well as political freedom. As communists they create a kind of religious brotherhood, a community actively engaged in the pursuit of an ideal, which would have been unthinkable under the rule of Confucius or the Christian missionaries. Although they are physically defeated in the end, they die as martyrs believing even more intensely in their cause.

A major reason for the defeat of the Chinese Communists in the novel is the incompatability between them and the Soviet Communist Party, from whom they take their orders. The conflict between indvidual revolutionists and the Soviet Communist Party is a persistent theme in works critical of communism, such as Camus' *L'homme révolté* (*The Rebel,* essay, 1951), Orwell's *Homage to Catalonia* (history, 1938), Sartre's *Les mains sales* (*Dirty Hands,* play, 1948) and *The God That Failed* (autobiographical essay, ed. R. Crossman, 1949). But the classic in this vein is probably Arthur Koestler's *Darkness at Noon* (novel, 1941). Comrade Rubashov, who has spent most of his adult life carrying out party edicts, no matter how onerous, comes to recoil from his actions and the party's dictum that the "means justify the ends." Thus his progress is the reverse of Kyo's in *La condition humaine*. Shortly before his execution during the Moscow Trials, a longing for God (the "oceanic sense") does assert itself in him; but since he never puts it to the test, he dies in the limbo of Dostoevsky's U.M. (whom Koestler deliberately evokes).

Closely related to U.M.'s social alienation, and no less significant a theme in postwar literature, is his divorce from a safe and comfortable God. Writers such as T. S. Eliot in *The Waste Land* and Hesse in *Der Steppenwolf* begin at this point. But by the time we have got to Eliot's *Four Quartets* (poem, 1943) and the plays, Eliot has found his way out of the underground back to the church. Hesse leads Steppenwolf out of his labyrinth through Jungian analysis (with its emphasis on the transcendent Self) synthesized with Zen Buddhism and Taoism. In the works of these writers, the prodigal returns to the fold. For Kafka, Camus, and Sartre, on the other hand, the divorce is permanent.

Franz Kafka does not deny the existence of God; he only laments His total indifference and inaccessibility. His shadowy protagonists—Joseph K. in *Der Prozess* (*The Trial*, novel, 1925), K. in *Das Schloss* (*The Castle*, novel, 1926)— flounder about helplessly in a sinister maze. Clearly an omniscient and omnipotent power governs the world they move in, but it is whimsical, arbitrary, and elusive, making a mockery of the protagonists' feeble logic and frustrating them throughout (Joseph K. is literally destroyed).

Along with Dostoevsky, Kafka views the disappearance of God, as well as a purposeful universe, as cause for despair. Camus and Sartre, on the other hand, see God's disappearance as a liberation for man, permitting him to construct a positive humanism. Acknowledging a discord between consciousness and the objective world, both writers postulate a subjective, or psychological, freedom, in a world that is otherwise beyond their control. For Sartre's Existentialist this translates into action that is its own justification; for Camus' Absurd Man, it is passionate revolt against the Absurd, which governs the universe. Roquentin in Sartre's *La nausée* (*Nausea*, novel, 1938) is driven to the brink of madness when he realizes that raw nature (being-in-itself) defies rational classification and analysis and when he experiences it as an undifferentiated mass engulfing everything, including himself. Meursault in Camus' *L'étranger* (*The Stranger*, novel, 1942) has committed a murder that he does not understand and is sentenced to death for reasons that have nothing to do with his crime. It is only when both protagonists assert their own sense of self and inviolability, in spite of the Absurd, and give up trying to reduce reality to rational analysis, that they are able to find value.

U.M. after World War II

Concern with metaphysical absurdity is greatest, perhaps, in the two decades following World War II. Probably the starkest portrayal of U.M. in contemporary literature is to be found in the novels and plays of Jean Genet and Samuel Beckett. Denying any absolute basis for meaning, Genet depicts his fictional characters (and himself) as play-actors who do not believe in their roles (recalling Dostoevsky's U.M.). The roles themselves—hoodlum, faggot, prostitute—are in reaction to societal norms, which likewise derive their meaning from their opposites. The result is an endless circle. In *Notre-Dame des fleurs* (*Our Lady of the Flowers,* novel, 1943) the transvestite Divine and his/her cohorts find meaning only in the style and intensity (measured by the orgasm) with which they execute their roles, not from any conviction of the philosophical or moral rightness of their actions. Value, like the orgasm, is only momentary, the only enduring reality being the void.

Beckett's God, if He does exist, is a malicious pupeteer engineering the slow obliteration of man. In a typical work such as *Fin de partie* (*Endgame,* play, 1957) the characters, last survivors in a decaying universe, are underground simply because of the human condition. Having given up any hope for meaning or redemption, physically falling apart, cursing God and the destiny of man, they withdraw into themselves as if into a womb, awaiting oblivion.

In the writing of the sixties and the seventies, there is a noticeable shift from the pessimism of Beckett and Genet. Today, with the exception of Beckett, the curtain has essentially fallen on the theater of the absurd. The leap from underground to the establishment is conspicuous in the progression from Pinter's *The Birthday Party* (1958) and Albee's *Zoo Story* (1959) to practically all of the plays they have written since. Even the self-acclaimed absurdist Eugène Ionesco has transformed the nothingness of his earlier plays into a Buddhist Nirvana. Bérenger in *Le roi se meurt* (*Exit the King,* 1962) comes belatedly to an appreciation of the little things of life; yet the void engulfing the stage at the conclusion of that play is comforting alongside the macabre emptiness at the close of *Les chaises* (*The Chairs,* 1952), characteristic of his earlier drama.

While working in the absurdist tradition, contemporary authors lean more to the pragmatic humanism of Sartre and Camus than to Beckett's nihilism. They seek oases of meaning—love, community, living for its own sake—in an otherwise mad world. Introduced as early as *Dangling Man* (novel, 1944), the theme of affirmation becomes increasingly pronounced in Saul Bellow's novels. In *Herzog* (1964), for example, the battered protagonist could have stepped right out of the frenzied pages of Dostoevsky, except for the calm conclusion, in which Herzog resolves to give up his freneticism and return to Romona, his garden, and all the other "ordinary middling considerations" of his life.

Accommodation, if not outright reconciliation, also underscores the literature of social protest after World War II. Mao Tsetung and Ché Guevara doubtless have had a romantic appeal to college students, but with the equivocal exceptions of Brecht and Sartre, major postwar writers have reacted to communism. Kruschev's denunciation of Stalin, Russia's brutal suppression of revolt in East Europe, Solzhenitsyn's shocking revelations of the gulags have only confirmed Koestler's dark picture of communism (at least in Russia). The idealists of the twenties and thirties are viewed as naïve by their postwar successors, for example, Günter Grass in Germany, the angry young men in England, the beats and blacks in the United States. While Grass is a scathing critic of German society after the war, the dwarf in his *Die Blechtrommel (Tin Drum,* novel, 1959) is safely tucked away in an insane asylum at the end of the novel. For all of Jimmy Porter's rantings in Osborne's *Look Back in Anger* (play, 1956), he is content to cuddle up with his Alison at the final curtain; Osborne's anger, along with that of Kingsley Amis and the other young Englishmen, is short-lived. So is the *Howl* in Gingsberg's beat poem (1956). Despite their outcry, the beats avoid political action. Jack Kerouac's "dharma bums" (novel, 1960) seek instead momentary kicks in drugs, sex-on-the-run, and instant Zen. Their successors, the hippies, were somewhat more active politically; but the one notable writer that they did inspire, Ken Kesey, belongs in his advocacy of the counterculture to the beatnik tradition, and not the revolutionary movement.

A constant source of social critism is, of course, black literature. It took a brief radical turn in the sixties, as, for example, in Eldridge Cleaver's *Soul on Ice* (essay, 1968) or the poems and plays of Imamu Baraka (LeRoi Jones). For the most part, however, black writers, despite their rage, have urged evolution rather than revolution. For the black this means essentially accommodation to a hostile white society. James Baldwin, in *Notes of a Native Son* (essays, 1955) does advise blacks to fight prejudice, but he seems more intent on cautioning them against their own self-destructive hatred. The exhausted hero of Ralph Ellison's *Invisible Man* (novel, 1952) decides to leave his basement refuge and return aboveground. He goes back, not with Camus' scorn and attitude of revolt, but in a mellow mood of reconciliation. Resignation runs also through the writings of Richard Wright, from his early *The Man Who Lived Underground* (novella, 1942) to *The Outsider* (novel, 1953). *The Outsider* presents the black man in a metaphysical rather than political dimension. In a world devoid of God, all men, whatever their color, suffer from dread and loss of identity. Reasoning at first that because the world is absurd all things are permissible, the hero Cross Damon goes on a murderous rampage; but as he is dying he reverses his position. Like the Invisible Man, he renounces hate, concluding that the outsider must make peace with society and join the human community.

The evolution of U.M. is neatly epitomized in Richard Wright. He suffered the pain of the social outcast, the disillusionment of the ex-Communist, and the anguish of the Existentialist. Yet he did not succumb either to pessimism or the blandishments of religion. Nor did he seek solace in the counterculture or the black establishment, choosing instead exile on the Left Bank of Paris. Even in his existentialism he lacks the assurance and bravado of a Camus or Sartre.

See also: Absurd, Alienation, Cave, Existentialism, Nihilism.

Selected Bibliography

Abood, Edward F. *Underground Man.* San Francisco: Chandler & Sharp, 1973.
Barrett, William. *Irrational Man.* Garden City, N.Y.: Doubleday, 1958.

Esslin, Martin. *The Theatre of the Absurd*. Garden City, N.Y.: Doubleday, 1961.
Howe, Irving. *Politics and the Novel*. New York: Horizon Press, 1957.

EDWARD ABOOD

UNICORN

The main feature of this mythical quadruped is a large, single horn growing from its forehead. Details of the supposed appearance of the animal vary widely over the centuries and from place to place. The unicorn has other unusual physical characteristics and powers, which are also described in many different ways.

Ancient Greek and Roman writers reported that such animals as oxen, horses, wild donkeys, or antelopes may appear with only one horn. But these are referred to as exceptions, prodigies, or perhaps unusual variations that live in remote regions. There is no hint that these one-horned versions of common animals are thought to constitute a separate, independent species.

The Greek historian Ctesias, who was a physician at the court of Darius II of Persia, wrote a work on India (*Indika,* early 4th century B.C.), in which he included an account of certain wild asses that could be found in that country. His account marks an important stage in the development of the legend of the unicorn, as it is very detailed and apparently authoritative. The Indian wild asses, according to Ctesias, were as large as horses and sometimes larger. Their bodies were white, their heads purple, their eyes blue. On their forehead they had a sharp horn one cubit (about one-and-one-half feet) in length. The horn was white at the base, red at the top, and black in the middle. Drinking cups were made from this horn and whoever used them was protected from certain diseases and from poisons. This one-horned wild ass had ankle-bones, which made it exceptional among all other asses, wild or domestic, and also among all other single-hoofed animals. These ankle-bones were unusually beautiful, according to Ctesias, and, together with the horn, they were the main reason for hunting these wild asses, for the flesh was bitter and inedible. The animal was difficult to hunt because it was exceptionally swift and could outrun the horses of the hunters easily. The only time the animal could be caught was when it had its young with it. Then, if it could be surrounded, it would not run away and desert its offspring. Bows and arrows had to be used to subdue it, because it would not allow itself to be taken alive.

Aristotle, accepting this report by Ctesias, refers to the animal several times and expounds learnedly on the biological relationship between its single horn and single hoof. Other later writers of antiquity added the detail, among others, that to hunt the single-horned wild ass and to own drinking vessels made from the horn were rights reserved only to the most prominent people.

Roman writers repeated these accounts of a one-horned quadruped with some slight variations and additions. An account in Aelian of the rhinoceros, which he says was called *kartazōnos* among the Indians, gives some of the traits of the monoceros (unicorn) to the rhinoceros. The reports of the unicorn in the writers of antiquity are confined to historians or naturalists; the animal does not seem to have entered the literary or pictorial iconography of the ancient world.

The reports in the Greek authors had an unexpected influence. In the Old Testament there are seven references to an animal called in Hebrew *re'em*. (Num. 23:22; Deut. 33:17; Ps. 22:21; 29:6; 92:10; Isa. 34:7; Job 39:9–12). Modern scholars believe that this animal was a wild buffalo that was once native to the Middle East. In the translation of the Hebrew Bible into Greek (the Septuagint, 2d century B.C.), the word *re'em* is translated consistently as "monoceros" (single-horn), the translators presumably following the reports in such writers as Aristotle and Aelian. the monoceros of the Greek Bible became the *unicornis* (single-horn) of the Latin Vulgate, and from this word comes the word for unicorn in its various modern linguistic guises.

The authority of the Bible was by this process given to the existence of unicorns. Any animal mentioned in Holy Writ must be real. The commentators on the Bible, relying in medieval fashion on written sources, used the terms "monoceros," "rhinoceros," and "unicorn" almost interchangeably. Unicorn, however, prevailed, since Latin became the language of the church and of learning in the West.

In the passages in the Old Testament that mention the unicorn, the two features that are picked out are its horn and its strength. The horn appears to be the symbol of the animal's wildness and power. The allegorizing explanations of the meaning of the unicorn in the Bible referred most often to the horn, but the interpretations of it are by no means consistent. The unicorn itself in various church fathers and commentators might be seen as a symbol of Christ or of the Devil, of Christians or Jews, of worldly princes or the Apostles. The horn figures as the Cross of Christ, but the most frequent equivalence is between the unicorn and Christ Himself. He has the single horn or single power from His Father; He is the sole-begotten Son; His is the single kingdom; He is the single savior of the world. The variety and ingenuity of the exegeses of this kind are almost inexhaustible. The strength of the unicorn and its supposed physiological uniqueness are the points of most frequent comparison.

The ancient reports and the biblical references are two sources of the unicorn legend. A third and very important source was the widely circulated allegorizing bestiary called *Physiologos* (*Physiologus,* c. A.D. 2d century). Its account of the unicorn adds on to the other accounts the story of how it can be captured and also alters some details of the animal's appearance. The *Physiologus* says that the unicorn is a small animal, about the size of a goat, very lively and so strong that a hunter cannot capture it. It can be taken only by putting a virgin in its path. The unicorn will jump onto her lap, she suckles it and takes it to the "king in his palace." The motif of the fierce animal that can only be captured by a beautiful young woman can be traced back to Indian sources. It is not known how it came into the *Physiologus,* nor is the precise date of the first version of the book known. The Latin version (c. 4th century), however, had a long popularity and it was a decisive influence on the unicorn legend.

Medieval bestiaries, encyclopedias, and vernacular fable-books of all kinds elaborated the basic version of the capture of the unicorn. Christian allegorizing of the story saw the young woman who entraps the unicorn as the Virgin Mary; the unicorn, representing Christ, shows its love of virginity and chastity when it leaps into the virgin's lap and allows itself to be captured. That this love for meeker qualities conflicts with the description of the unicorn as a strong, wild animal is not uncharacteristic of the unpredictable elaboration of medieval allegorizing.

By the thirteenth century, the secular allegorizing of the basic unicorn-story in the *Physiologus* had become widespread in poetic and prose forms. The erotic potential of the capture is drawn out and the young woman becomes a beloved who captures and tames her lover. The unicorn thus becomes a figure in love poetry and in the symbolism of courtly love. It is a highly charged figure, carrying strong religious overtones along with the erotic content. Since the size, color, strength, and detailed physiology of the animal are matters of tradition and imagination, the iconography of the unicorn can be as inventive and as free as the literary tradition, and there is no doubt that they interacted.

In the medieval Alexander Romances, a unicorn with a precious stone growing at the base of its horn is sent as a gift to Alexander by an eastern queen. The association between precious stones, which the Middle Ages thought had curative properties, and the potent unicorn's horn, or alicorn, was a natural one. Although there are references throughout medieval and early Renaissance literature to the unicorn, the creature does not take a leading role in a single major narrative. Two typical uses of the unicorn may be cited. The heroine of *Le romans de la dame à la lycorne et du biau chevalier au lyon* (*The Romance of the Woman with the Unicorn and the Worthy Knight of the Lion,* early 14th century) is given a unicorn by the god of Love. The prose romance called *Le chevalier au papegaut* (*The Knight of the Parrot,* 14th century) contains an inset narrative in which a dwarf tells King Arthur of his adventures with a family of unicorns.

The efficacy of the unicorn's horn is almost as much a part of the lore as the animal itself. The touch of the horn into a spring or river would purify the waters of anything harmful. The other animals, wanting to take a drink, would wait for the unicorn to arrive and touch the surface of the water with the tip of his horn. Horns believed to be those of unicorns were part of royal and ecclesiastical treasures. Cups made from the horn were believed to neutralize poisons and so were useful to the powerful. Powdered unicorn horn was prescribed and sold for its curative properties until the nineteenth century, when it was finally declared to have no medical value.

Numerous representations of the beast were made from the Middle Ages onward. They occured first in illustrations of the *Physiologus* and other bestiaries.

Unicorns were also commonly shown in pictures of Paradise, where they were given a position more prominent than other animals because part of the lore about the unicorn was that it was the first animal created or the first animal named by Adam, a belief that would spring from the identification of the unicorn in the Bible as a symbol of Christ.

Skepticism about the truth of the existence of unicorns is detectable in the late Renaissance. Widening exploration outside of Europe led to the publication of many traveler's books in which the sighting or reporting of unicorns was frequent. Remote parts of Asia, Northern Europe, and Africa were places where travelers reported seeing or hearing about the animal. In the New World they were reported in Florida, Canada, and elsewhere. Often the evidence was not the animal itself, but a horn or a piece of a horn. Growth of scientific zoology led to attempts to rationalize the growth of the unicorn legend by finding its origin in the mistaken interpretation of the glimpse of unfamiliar or exotic species of wild animals on land or such sea-creatures as the narwhal in the ocean.

The heraldic use of the unicorn is very important. Two sets of tapestries associated with royalty have been widely illustrated and studied. The seven tapestries called *The Hunt of the Unicorn,* now in the Cloisters in New York City, are very popular and often reproduced. A set of six tapestries called *The Lady and the Unicorn* in the Cluny Museum in Paris is equally well known. These works date from the end of the fifteenth or the beginning of the sixteenth century and are the most spectacular examples of the popularity of the unicorn in European art. *The Hunt of the Unicorn* implies an elaborate allegorical narrative, which has been variously reconstructed and interpreted. These tapestries have supplied imagery in W. C. Williams' poem *Paterson* (1946–1958) and A. M. Lindbergh's *The Unicorn and Other Poems* (1956). A further important heraldic use is in the Royal Arms of England, where the unicorn appears with its traditional enemy, the lion, as supporter of the shield.

The appearances of the unicorn in modern literature are widely scattered. It has lost virtually all of its religious associations and tends to be used as a symbol of such abstractions as beauty, uniqueness, unattainability, and purity. It has taken a prominent place in the iconography of some types of children's literature, fantasy, and science fiction, where it often conveys a vaguely medievalizing atmosphere. Winged unicorns are a free modern invention, probably originating from a confused cross-breeding with Pegasus.

See also: Monsters, Werewolf.

Selected Bibliography

Beer, Robert Rudiger. *Unicorn. Myth and Reality.* Trans. Charles M. Stern. New York: Mason/Charter, 1977.

Brandenburg, H. "Einhorn." *Reallexicon für Antike und Christentum.* Stuttgart: Hiersemann, 1959. Bd. 4, coll. 840–862.

Freeman, Margaret B. *The Unicorn Tapestries*. New York: The Metropolitan Museum of Art, 1976.
Shepard, Odell. *The Lore of the Unicorn*. 1930. New York: Avenel Books, 1982.

HARRY G. EDINGER

UNIVERSE

The universe is the philosophical, scientific, religious, or literary concept of the heavenly bodies and the earth, their origin, their relations, their nature, and their buildup to a system. Concepts of the universe go beyond the realm of scientific astronomy since they involve individual attitudes of the authors, enthusiastic evaluations, ingenious conjectures, artistic dreams, and sometimes pure fancy. Elements of astrology come up occasionally. The evolution of this theme from Greek and Roman antiquity through early Christianity, the Middle Ages, the Renaissance, the seventeenth, eighteenth, nineteenth, and twentieth centuries represents typical expressions of these times and the various phases of the history of thought.

The Greek Cosmos

The first crystallization of Greek theories of the universe, Hesiod's *Theogonia* (*Theogony,* poetic treatise, c. 8th century B.C.), with its vision of spatial grandeur and its mingling of body and spirit, is highly characteristic of Hellenic metaphysics. After the appearance of the earth and of God Eros in the Void the rest of the Cosmos arose little by little by the process of procreation. The earth "gives birth" to the sky, and from the "embracement" of the earth and the sky is born the ocean. From the ocean emerge the rest of the Gods, who then multiply through sexual intercourse with one another.

The Pythagoreans (6th century B.C.) developed a concrete vision of the shape of the earth. At first they thought of it as a disc, later as a cylinder, and finally as a sphere. Around it were considered circling the spheres of the moon, of the sun, and of the planets. Above them the fixed stars were attached like nails to the crystalline sky. Following some Oriental influences, the planets were thought of as divinities marked by an unchanging regularity of motion around the earth. This is how the names of Mercury, Venus, Mars, Saturn, and Jupiter came about. The Pythagoreans invented an arithmetology, an arcane science that explains the universe by numbers.

The close relationship between the universe and human life established philosophically by the Pythagoreans received poetic qualifications in the Greek tragedy. The atmosphere of the genre is eminently cosmic. In Aeschylus' *Hiketides* (*The Suppliants,* 463 B.C.), the first Greek tragedy extant, the daughters of Danaus, after a trip taken over a large section of the then known world, raised their voices to metaphysical heights to invoke the help of Zeus. Sinister influences emanate from the universe in the Greek drama.

In Euripides' *Hekabē* (*Hecuba,* c. 424 B.C.), the wind that traverses the big spaces of the world and propels the boat of the Greeks, who are on their way home with their Trojan slaves, stops at the island of Thracia in order to reveal to Hecuba the murder of her son and give her an opportunity to wreak horrible vengeance. Several of Aristophanes' comedies, such as *Eirēnē* (*Peace,* 421 B.C.) and the *Nephelai* (*Clouds,* 423 B.C.), depict in their turn the universe. The chorus of the *Ornithes* (*Birds,* 414 B.C.) tells in a humorous yet moving tone the story of the creation in passages reminiscent of Hesiod's *Theogony.* The Greek amphitheater, being open to the skies, offers a fitting setting for these plays.

In contrast to Pherecydes, who believed in the existence of five cosmoi, Plato maintained that there was only a single one. It is the "most beautiful" and the "best," just as its author is the best of all creative agents, he says in his *Timaios* (*Timaeus,* dialogue, 4th century B.C.) As an expression of the divine concept, the "idea" as Plato calls it, the world is marked by perfection. It is a living substance and embraces within its immense volume all mortal and immortal beings. All heavenly bodies are divine and eternal and they move performing a round-dance. The earth is suspended in space and is divine in its turn. In the *Nomoi* (*Laws,* dialogue, c. 350 B.C.), the author speaks of the soul (*Psychē*) of the cosmos, the moving power of all bodies and the initiator of all cosmic metamorphoses. He does not believe that the earth was formed ex nihilo but that the act of creation was rather an organizational task. The Demiurge, as he called the principal divinity, made order in a world marked by utter confusion. With all objects set up at their proper place, the universe received the shape of a sphere, the most perfect of all possible shapes.

Although more rationalistic and absolute in his statements, Aristotle (*Peri ouranou* [*Skies,* treatise, 4th century B.C.]) follows in the footsteps of Plato, his master, in some of the essentials of his theories. He too believes in a single cosmos, its completeness, its possessing the highest aesthetic and ethical qualifications. World harmony reigns in the sky. The stars have souls and they are propelled by their own power. But Aristotle does not share Plato's ideas of the creation. The order of the cosmos, in his interpretation, has been and will remain the same for all eternity. Only the earthy section of the universe is unsteady and accidental. Beyond the material world there is neither place nor space and not even emptiness. It is the region of the divine spirit. Although eternally motionless, it is the "spirit of motion" and the substance of all things.

Early Predictions of Modern Theories

Epicurus (341–270 B.C.) and his followers believed that the world always was and always will be. The bodies existing in space consist of elements, so-called atoms, that are infinite in number and of an incomprehensibly large variety of shapes and occur in the infinity of the Void. Epicurean philosophy, somewhat more concerned with ethics than with physics, was widespread in antiquity and had many followers in the Western world. In Rome Lucretius (*De rerum natura* [*On the Nature of Things,* philosophical poem, 1st century B.C.]) and in France Pierre Gassendi (1596–1655) and Anatole France (1844–1924) adopted this philosophy.

On the basis of some hypotheses laid down by the Pythagoreans, Heraclides Ponticus (4th century B.C.), a follower of Plato, actually suggested that the earth was a planet. Aristarchus of Samos (3d century B.C.) set up for the first time the theory of the heliocentric system, in which the earth appeared to be a mere point in a universe of tremendous extension. According to the Heraclidistic system, every star appeared to be a little cosmos in its own right.

The Stoics in Greece and in Rome

The Hellenic theories on the universe reach a special and very articulate expression in the writings of the Stoics. The gods here are to a large extent identified with matter. In a special version of pantheism the early followers of this philosophical movement, Zeno, Cleanthes, and Chrysippos believed that the divine breath of life, the fiery pneuma, is marked by physical as well as psychic characteristics and that it operates all over the material world. They believed that an eternal "All-God" reigns in the cosmos. In its essentially philosophical context, the theme acquired emotional undertones and served as an inspiration to both pagan and Christian hymnic poetry. Epictetus, an outstanding figure in the history of the movement (*Egcheiridion* [*Arrian's Manual,* treatise, c. A.D. 130]), influences with his ethics and his cosmology Roman and Western thought. Cicero bears witness to a deep understanding of the Stoic doctrine of the universe in his *De natura deorum* (*The Nature of Gods,* treatise, 44 B.C.), in his *De republica,* (*Republic,* treatise, c. 50 B.C.), and his *De legibus* (*Laws,* treatise, c. 50 B.C.). In a Stoic frame of mind, Virgil speaks in his *Georgica* (*Georgics,* poem, 29 B.C.) and his *Aeneis* (*Aeneid,* epic poem, 19 B.C.) of the *mens divina* as the mover of *mundus,* the world. And Marcus Aurelius starts his *Ta eis eauton* (*Meditations,* treatise, c. 161–180) with a stoically inspired prayer. In it he calls the world a "state," a metaphor that has become a standard term in subsequent literature. From it arose the compound adjective "cosmopolitan," in which man's relation to the universe turns into a quasi-political tie.

Early Christianity

The belief of the Christians that the world was created by God ex nihilo and that it would dissolve again into nothingness is basic to a new concept of the universe. With stress laid on its inferiority to the spiritual, the temporal loses much of its former luster. Its decline is well expressed in the principles of moral conduct, the condemnation of "worldliness" as an evil, an obstacle on the road to salvation. Although essentially new, Greek influences make themselves felt in the notion of the cosmos. In his account of the creation, Minucius Felix (3d century A.D.) reverts to the Platonic and Stoic "All-God," a predecessor of the God of Christianity. Tertullian, in his *Apologeticus* (*Apologetics,* treatise, c.

197), insists that Christianity contradicts pagan philosophies, but sets up just the same Stoicism as a model of conduct. In his *De civitate Dei* (*The City of God*, treatise, 413–426) St. Augustine has been able to harmonize Christian ideological principles with Neoplatonic materials found in Plotinus, Porphyry, and Iamblichus. In the conception of the temporal, his aesthetics bypasses his ethics. While denouncing the sinfulness inherent in worldly living, he describes in glowing colors the beauty of the world and calls God an artist, predicting thereby a concept that will crystallize in the Renaissance.

The observation of the sky, although applied to traditional Greek astronomical notions, made some progress in these centuries. Ptolemy (fl.127–148), in his *Mathēmatikē syntaxis* (Almagestum, treatise) developed into a geometric scheme theories formed 600 years before him by Eudoxus of Cnidos and according to which the sun, the moon and the planets each partook of the superimposed motion of a set of ideal concentric spheres rotating in the several periods associated with the particular body concerned. His cosmology was accepted up to the Renaissance and led to poetic descriptions of the sky.

The Middle Ages

John Erigena, Anselm of Canterbury, Bernard de Tours, Alain de Lille, Albertus Magnus, Averroës, Francis of Assisi, Bernard de Clairvaux, and other great thinkers of the Middle Ages contributed to the philosophy and the image of the universe.

Characteristic of the period are the writings of Honorius Augustodunensis— his dialogue *Elucidarium* as well as his treatises *De philosophia mundi* and *De imagine mundi*. Written in the early twelfth century, these works were among the most wide-spread of the time, and they were even translated into several vernacular tongues. Influenced by Aristotle and Ptolemaeus and based more particularly on Pliny the Elder, Isidore of Seville and Baeda, these are independent and highly original pieces of writing.

The universe here forms a unity but is built up in a degree-wise manner. Beyond the firmament this author sees the world of the spheres, a region called *aqueum caelum*. Above it, the spiritual sky, the *paradisus paradisorum,* the residence of the blessed, is divided into nine orders that correspond to the nine orders of the angels. It is built of ether, the fifth and incorruptible element. With regard to the incorporeal aspects of the world, the *anima mundi,* the author calls them the *spiritus sanctus* (the Holy Spirit), *naturalis vigor* (the natural strength), or an *incorporea substantia* (an incorporeal substance) residing in bodily objects. Following in the footsteps of Ptolemy, Honorius thought that the harmony of the world materializes in music, the seven tones of the spheres, the model and origin of all music known on earth. The musical tones of the spheres depended on their visual distances to one another. The distance of the earth to the sun equals that of the sun to the firmament, which makes for a division of the physical world into two, each marked by three-and-a-half tonic lengths adding up to seven.

The Renaissance

The Renaissance was marked by a strong desire for intellectual and physical expansion. This led to territorial discoveries on the earth and in the skies. Astronomy, which lagged throughout the Middle Ages, becomes one of the most vital sciences of the period. Toscanelli, Fracastoro, Peter Bienewitz (Apianus), Georg Purbach, and Johannes Müller (Regiomontanus) are passionate observers of the sky and add considerably to the knowledge about it. New *mappae mundi* saw daylight and defined with a precision heretofore unknown the position of the stars. The increased preoccupation with the size of the world went hand in hand with a rise of its aesthetic evaluation. Pico della Mirandola, with his treatise *Oratio de hominis dignitate* (*Oration on the Dignity of Man,* treatise, 1486) calls God an artist and feels he created man to admire his work. In France Ronsard depicts the cosmos with a splendid imagery in his hymns.

It is within this general trend that the heliocentric system was discovered. It was altogether slow in coming and was preceded by the growing realization of the endlessness of the universe. Nicholas of Cusa, admitting to a *docta ignorantia* (*On Learned Ignorance,* 1440) pronounced God to be in the center as well as in the circumference of an endless cosmos. Copernicus' heliocentric theory *De revolutionibus orbium coelestium* (*On the Revolutions of Heavenly Bodies,* treatise, 1543), which came out shortly before the death of its author, was by no means readily accepted. The great astronomer, Tycho Brahe, refused to adhere to it. In 1633 Galileo had to abjure it before the Inquisition.

The Seventeenth Century

Galileo, constructor of the first telescope, discovered the existence of sun spots, the relief of the moon, the satellites of Jupiter, and the phases of Venus *Dialogo supra i due massimi sistemi del mondo* [*Dialogue Concerning the Two Chief World Systems,* treatise, 1632]). Kepler, correcting Copernicus, found that the planetary movements are elliptic and not circular. He also laid down principles that permitted Newton to establish the law of gravitation (*Tabulae rudolphinae* [*Rudolphine Tables,* treatise, 1627]).

Writers, philosophers, and scientists reacted in a variety of ways to these novelties. Gassendi modernized the theory of atomism. The conflict between science and religion took a dramatic turn with the execution of Giordano Bruno, who was forced to forswear before the Inquisition (1600) his philosophical tenets (*La cena delle ceneri* [*Ash Wednesday Supper,* treatise, 1584]). Combining the physical with the spiritual world, Spinoza draws parallels between the absolute perfection of God and the infinity of space (*Ethica ordine geometrico* [*Ethics of a Geometrical Order Demonstrated,* treatise, 1663–1677]).

From another point of view the simple visual pleasure found in the image of the universe gave room to anxiety at the realization of its endlessness and an inclination to stress its structure rather than its sensory appeal. The lyric enthusiasm of the sixteenth century at the sight of the cosmos has vanished. Pascal was filled with apprehension at the endlessly growing and diminishing objects of the world and felt man was lost between the infinite and nothingness (*Pensées* [*Thoughts,* essay, 1670]).

The Eighteenth Century

With his discovery of the rule of gravitation, Newton explained the mechanics of the motion of heavenly bodies, a step of tremendous importance made toward the knowledge of the universe (*Philosophiae naturalis principia mathematica* [*The Mathematics of Natural Philosophy,* treatise, 1685]). Newton's theories served as a basis for the philosophy of Kant (1770) and Laplace (1796). Earlier in the century Leibnitz had studied the harmony of the world in his *Monadologie* (*Monadology,* treatise, 1714). Having reached a new highlight, astronomy now tends to enter the belles lettres. The French writer Fontenelle compared, in the form of a polite conversation, the cosmos to an imagined marquise on a starlit night. The stars in his description seem to be moving about to the music of a minuet (*Entretiens sur la pluralité des mondes* [*Conversations on the Plurality of the Worlds,* treatise, 1686]). Voltaire, in a witty tale, has individuals come down to earth from a satellite of Sirius and from Saturn (*Micromégas,* 1752). In spite of stress laid on its physical manifestations, the spiritual universe is far from being absent in literature. In his search for truth, Goethe's Faust invokes the "spirit" of the universe and of the earth (*Faust,* tragedy, 1808).

The Nineteenth Century

Great progress now occurs in observational, dynamical astrononmy and astronomical spectroscopy. Following Laplace, P. G. Montecoulant modified and redefined the general theories of lunar and planetary motion. F. W. Bessel of Königsberg established a scientific procedure for the exact measurement of the true positions of stars in the sky (*Tabulae Regiomontanae* [*Refraction Tables,* treatise, 1830]). The feverish search for astrophysical realities led to assumptions that have been rejected by more modern science. Such was the suggestion that the world is in a continuous state of expansion.

On the literary level the general interest in astronomy materialized in exalted and in some cases disquieting concepts of the relation between man and the universe. The French preromantics J.- J. Rousseau and Chateaubriand had at times the strange sensation that their egos would disappear in the cosmos. In Germany, poets like Brentano, Schelling, Novalis, and Hölderlin speak of the mysterious rhythm that pulsates throughout the world and gives a magic sort of unity to the totality of all things. In some cases fancy predicts reality to come. Jules Verne, in an altogether well researched yet fantastic novel, describes a trip to the moon (*De la terre à la lune* [*From the Earth to the Moon,* 1865]).

The Twentieth Century

As a result of Einstein's essays (*The Meaning of Relativity,* 1921; *The Builders of the Universe,* 1932), unexpected progress was made, particularly in the United

States, in observational and dynamical astronomy. The concept of the universe remains in a state of flux with answers left open to numerous new problems. Einstein's finds on the curvature of space made the current theory on gravitation questionable. The so-called black holes, contracted stars that eventually disappear, cannot be completely explained by contemporary conceptions of the conservation of matter. Radio signals received from distant galaxies, theories on the creation of the world based on the belief of an explosion of a cosmic egg, space travel, actual trips taken to the moon, information received from unmanned orbital spacecrafts all fired the imagination of authors who wrote stories more or less relevant to actual science. In some of his imaginative and altogether well-documented romances, H. G. Wells dealt in this manner with the cosmos (*The First Men in the Moon*, novel, 1901; *Tales of Space and Time*, short stories, 1899). Carl Sagan's spirited popularizations of astronomy and numerous novels dealing with alternate possible universes fall into the domain of science fiction and are typical of the contemporary frame of mind.

See also: Demonic Music, Nihilism, Reason, Science, Time.

Selected Bibliography

Baudry, Jean. *Les problèmes de l'origine et de l'éternité du monde dans la philosophie grecque de Platon à l'ère chrétienne*. Paris: Société d'édition des Belles Lettres, 1931.

Ehrhardt, Arnold. *The Beginning. A Study in the Greek Philosophical Approach to the Concept of Creation from Anaximander to St. John*. New York: Barnes and Noble, 1968.

Kranz, Walter. *Kosmos*. Bonn: H. Bouvier, 1955–1957.

JOHN F. WINTER

UTOPIA

Before 1800

Few literary terms are as difficult to define as "utopia." However, even the most cursory survey of works that have been subsumed under this term will provide an explanation for this difficulty. For the most part, creators of utopian works have not been interested in producing purely literary—belles lettres—artifacts. They have tried to demonstrate—with a zeal for reform, as a means of escape, as an exercise in philosophical speculation, or purely for entertainment—what a better society than their own might be like. As a result, these works cover a wide range of practical and impractical, specific and dreamy, possible and impossible proposals. Dictionaries almost always define the term first as a place that does not exist; second, as a place of ideal perfection; and third, as some kind of impractical scheme for improving the world.

These definitions leave much to be desired. The first, while acknowledging its source in Sir Thomas More's Latin word, coined from Greek *ou* (no) and *topos* (place), fails to note More's own pun *ou* and *eu* (good). More, of course, contributed to the confusion both by writing to Erasmus on September 3, 1516, "Nusquamam nostram nusquam bene scriptam ad te mitto" ("I am sending you my nowhere, which is nowhere well written") and by including a prefatory poem that points out, "The Ancients called me Utopia or Nowhere because of my isolation. . . . Deservedly ought I to be called by the name of Eutopia or Happy Land." The second and third definitions, though biased in opposite directions, have in common the concept of something better than this world. Those who support the second definition will doubtless agree with the often-quoted words of Anatole France: "Without the Utopias of other times man would still live in caves, miserable and naked," and Oscar Wilde: "A map of the world that does not include Utopia is not worth even glancing at, for it leaves out the one country at which Humanity is always landing." Those who support the third definition will agree with Wordsworth: "Not in utopia, . . . But in this very world, . . . We find our happiness or not at all." Macaulay was even more vehement: "An acre of Middlesex is better than a principality in Utopia."

Utopian scholars are concerned with a wide range of possibilities, and their definitions are frequently no better than those found in ordinary dictionaries. Some proposed definitions are so broad that almost anything proposing a different society becomes utopian: the Declaration of Independence, the Weatherman Manifesto, the platform of a major political party, the teachings of major religions, a newspaper editorial, or an island vacation spot. Dozens of terms such as Arcadia, Perfect Moral Commonwealth, Lost Eden, Millennium, Kingdom of God on Earth, Hobo Heaven, the related genres of Fantastic Voyage, Robinsoniad, Science Fiction, Political Pamphlet, and Reform Platform, and the opposites of utopia—dystopia, anti-utopia, cacatopia, futopia, and satiric utopia— add to the confusion.

Nevertheless, from a literary point of view, most scholars agree that three major characteristics distinguish utopia from other literary forms: a utopia is fictional, it deals with a specific unit of society, and its basic theme is the political framework of that unit. Utopias vary in the degree of attention paid to each of these characteristics, but the work that does not pay some attention to all three is probably peripheral to the genre. Scholars need to consider other works and events, especially those nonfictional proposals for a better society and those practical attempts to form a more perfect society that are an important part of human history, but in any literary study the emphasis must be on writings that display these three basic characteristics.

The canon of utopias is still uncertain, and determining just what should be included in the study of utopia has been a major concern of scholars in recent years. Three recent bibliographies have been helpful in this respect. The first of these, Glenn Negley's *Utopian Literature, a Bibliography with a Supplementary Listing of Works Influential in Utopian Thought* (1977), lists and locates in major libraries some 1,600 works from the sixteenth century to the present. Lyman

Tower Sargent's *British and American Utopian Literature 1516–1975: An Annotated Bibliography* (1979) provides brief annotations of about 1,600 utopias published in English during this period, as well as a 125–page bibliography of secondary works on utopian literature. The most recent, Arthur O. Lewis' *Utopian Literature in The Pennsylvania State University Libraries: A Selected Bibliography* (1984) describes and annotates representative works from a major— over 2,000 volumes—utopian collection. All three include introductions valuable to the utopian scholar.

Prior to More the term "utopia" did not exist, but writings exemplifying utopian ideals have come down to us either in fragments or in references in the works of other classical writers. Homer's Phaeacia, Hesiod's Golden Age, Horace's Isles of the Blest, and the Hyperboreans, Meropians, Thulesians, and other, usually peripherally Mediterranean, exotic societies described in the Hellenistic romances all have something of the utopian ideal. Closely related to the medieval Land of Cockayne or the modern Hobo Heaven, these are basically agricultural lands where the crops grow with little help and the people are resultingly happier. More significantly, some of the most important lawgivers of Greece, Solon, Lycurgus, and Pythagoras, for example, described societies that inspired later utopian thought and are often included in the canon of utopias. However, the most important utopian writings of the classical world are those of Plato, Xenophon, and Zeno.

In his so-called Seventh Letter, written in his old age, Plato describes how, following the death of Socrates, he gave up politics and came to the belief that permeates his utopian works:

Finally I came to the conclusion that all existing states were badly governed, and that their constitutions were incapable of reform without drastic treatment and a great deal of good luck. I was forced, in fact, to the belief that the only hope of finding justice for society for the individual lay in true philosophy, and that mankind will have no respite from trouble until either real philosophers gain political power or politicians become by some miracle true philosophers.

In a broader sense of the term much of Plato's work is utopian but *Politeia (The Republic,* c. 380 B.C.) is most important in expressing the basic principle upon which the ideal state would be founded and in setting a pattern that has been followed by succeeding utopian writers to the present day. Plato begins by attempting to answer a moral question: What is the meaning of justice? In answering this question he looks at society as an analogue for the individual and describes a state made up of rulers, producers, and a professional army to protect them. The subject of most of this dialogue is the education, selection, organization, and responsibilities of the Guardians (rulers and soldiers), who make the just life possible for the largest class, the citizens (the slaves, as elsewhere in classical Greece, are not part of society). Plato's model is clearly the Sparta of Lycurgus rather than the Athens of Solon, and he is thus far more authoritarian than many modern utopian writers. Plato believed in the necessity of moral compulsion, laws, institutions, authority, and the regulation of all aspects of life. Such laws as would be needed would be proper laws because all members of society, especially the Guardians, would be properly educated, and proper education would necessarily lead to a good government and a just society. The Guardians hold property in common, permit no marriage, treat children as the children of all, and maintain absolute equality of men and women. There is an understanding that part of their job is to propagandize the rest of society into accepting their enlightened and beneficent rule by whatever propagandistic means might be necessary.

Three other works of Plato are closely related to *The Republic: Timaios (Timaeus,* 4th century B.C.), presented as a sequel to *The Republic,* introduces the myth of Atlantis and the defeat of that empire by ancient Athens; the fragmentary *Kritias (Critias,* 4th century B.C.), intended as a sequel to *Timaeus,* describes briefly the somewhat utopian governments of both Athens and Atlantis, and Plato's last work, apparently unfinished, is *Nomoi (The Laws,* c. 350 B.C.). *The Laws* is a work in which the dictatorial rule described in *The Republic* has given way to a constitutional government. The change in emphasis is brought about not because people would not agree to rule by philosopher-kings but because of the apparent impossibility of finding philosopher-kings who could rule as needed. It is more practical than *The Republic,* cast in the form of advice to a man who is to set up a new colony, and includes a careful description of what must be done to create a good, if not perfect, society. Plato's own attempt to put some of these principles into practice at Syracuse was unsuccessful. Nevertheless, despite attacks by others, including his own greatest pupil Aristotle, who, among other things, objected to communal property because he believed it would cause laziness and loss of benevolence, it is Plato's utopia against which all others must be measured.

Not much remains of Zeno's *Politeia (The Republic,* c. 300 B.C.), which is known chiefly from statements by Diogenes Laertius, Philodemus, and Chrysippos. Plutarch said that he wrote it "against Plato's Republic," but that, like Plato, he based his design for society on that of Lycurgus. Thus, the small city-state, ruled by the wise, would be an integral part of a world-state, based on reason and love. As in Plato, the ruling classes, at least, held property, wives, and children in common and regarded education as the means to virtue; interpretation of divine will seems to have been a major component of government. The idea of a brotherhood of humanity that appears to have motivated this ideal state is a strain not often absent from more recent proposals. It should be noted that the communal society advocated by Plato and Zeno was nothing new in Greek thought, as Aristophanes' attack a dozen years before Plato's *Republic* in *Ekklēsiazousai (Women in Parliament,* play, performed 392 B.C.) demonstrates.

Xenophon's *Kyrou paideia (The Education of Cyrus,* c. 368 B.C.) is in many ways a historical novel that includes a detailed discussion of the proper education of a wise and tolerant ruler. Especially in the seventeenth and eighteenth centuries this work became a model for utopian thinkers who believed that the way to the ideal state was through a wise monarch.

After the great days of the Greek lawgivers and utopian writers, there is a long near-silence in the field broken, in the Western world, only by minor works such as those of Marcus Aurelius, Lucian, the Hellenistic romances, and a few writings of the church fathers, these based largely on prophetic and apocalyptic works of Hebrew prophets such as Amos and Hosea. Two Eastern works deserving of mention, though perhaps peripheral to the tradition, are *Sukhāvatīv-yūha* (*Description of the Pure Land*, c.150), a Mahayana Buddhist version of a happy land, and T'ao Ch'ien's "T'ao-hua-yüan chi" (*The Peach Blossom Spring*, prose, c. 400), a brief glimpse of an earthly paradise that owes much to Taoist principles.

The place of Saint Augustine's *De civitate Dei* (*The City of God*, treatise, 413–426) is secure in the history of Western thought, and for some utopian scholars it is a part of the utopian canon. It has, of course, been the subject of much debate, especially in regard to whether Augustine was writing of a secular city to be established on earth or of a purely heavenly city to which mankind might aspire. From the utopian point of view it does not really matter, for this city, based on knowledge and love of God, is indeed the perfect society. Augustine's vision, especially in book 22, has provided a guide not only for succeeding theologians, believers, and reformers, but also—even if his city is not, strictly speaking, a utopia—for many thinkers from the Renaissance to the present time.

After Saint Augustine, the definition of utopia is often stretched to include such Christian visions as those of Joachim and such Judaic visions as those of both Maimonides and the cabbalists. Perhaps Ramón Lull's novel, *Blanquerna,* written in the late thirteenth century but not published until 1521, deserves to be included. But it is in the Renaissance that utopia as a literary form comes to full bloom, and its authors looked back, not to the Middle Ages, but to classical Greece. Thomas More's *Utopia* (1516) is an agricultural-based society of small cities, communal property, contempt for gold, and equality among the heads of the family units that form the basis of society. There is a hierarchy of pleasures, praise of honest work as essential to a moral society, and freedom of religion. There is much of Plato in More, but the pre-Christianity of his Utopians is close to many of the Christianized utopian visions that followed soon after.

Utopia was first written and widely disseminated in Latin, but translations into other languages were not long in coming: German (1524), Italian (1548), French (1550), English (1551), Dutch (1553), Spanish (1637). Imitations began to appear almost at once. In Italy, the road to utopian speculation had been paved by a number of architectural writers of the late fifteenth century. Plans for ideal, largely aristocratic cities, intended to create an environment in which man would become more virtuous, more harmonious, and more able to engage in that pursuit of duty which they perceived to be the essence of the good life, such as Leone

Battista Alberti's *De re aedificatoria* (*On Architecture*, 1485), Antonio Averlino's *Sforzinda* (*Treatise on Architecture*, 1461–1464), and Francesco di Giorgio Martini's *Trattato di architettura* (*Treatise on Architecture*, c. 1481), were an important influence on later utopian writers, many of whom drew upon their ideas in describing the ideal cities where their utopians would live. Sixteenth-century Italy also provides examples of utopian writing, broadly defined, of some significance both as influence on later writers and as evidence of the complex, political, and philosophical media from which the literary utopias sprang. Of these, mention should be made of Gasparo Contarini's *De magistratibus et republica Venetorum libri quinque* (*The Commonwealth and Government of Venice*, 1553) an encomium on the virtues of the Venetian form of government, and, like others of its kind, an inspiration, however wrongly interpreted, in the next century and a half for numerous proposals for improvement of the governments of Great Britain, France, and various German states.

The philosophically sophisticated Italian utopias such as Francesco Patrizi's *La città felice* (*The Happy City*, 1553) and Ludovico Agostini's *La repubblica immaginaria* (*The Imaginary Republic*, written about 1580, first published 1957) were little known until comparatively recently. For the most part, the Italian utopian writers took the side of Aristotle and his objection to the communistic proposals of Plato and More. Property and the right to hold it were essential to the development of a truly happy society. The most notable exception and, indeed, the most influential Italian utopia of the sixteenth century, Antonio Francesco Doni's *I mondi celesti, terresti, et infernali, de gli accademici Pellegrini* (*The Celestial, Earthly, and Infernal Worlds*, 1552–1553) went through numerous editions and several languages. In Doni's egalitarian society, there is no private ownership, citizens receive such goods as may be needed, and, since there is little desire for anything beyond the mere necessities of life, there is no need for intensive labor to obtain these necessities. There is a sense not found in More, whose influence is otherwise quite strong, that each human being will find a place in an ideal world and behave accordingly. Compared to many of his contemporaries, Doni was a free spirit and consequently often in difficulty with the church.

In the seventeenth century, utopian writings generally fall into two groups, those that attempt to reconcile the "truths" of science and religion and those that speak of a new social order either secular or millenarian. The former tended to attack the Aristotelian dogma and proposed that observable natural phenomena led to a true understanding of both nature and God. The most outstanding utopian works of this group are those of Tommaso Campanella, Francis Bacon, and Johann Valentin Andreae. These three, together with Samuel Hartlib, Samuel Gott, Giordano Bruno, Jan Amos Komenskij (Comenius), and numerous less well-known writers, are frequently referred to as pansophists because of their common desire to draw together the various branches of knowledge and to use this new synthesis as a means of propagating Christian beliefs that would be accepted as far truer than those of the medieval church.

The most influential of these works, Bacon's *New Atlantis: A Worke Unfinished* (1627; probably written some fifteen years earlier), portrays the imaginary island of Bensalem, a hierarchical society. The heart of Bensalem is the House of Salomon, a college for scientific research and application that much resembles the modern research institute. Knowledge, Bacon said, is power, and scientific knowledge is more likely to bring superior power than any other kind. The influence of this work in the development of modern Western technology is far out of proportion to its length and has made Bacon's name synonymous with that of the enemy among those modern thinkers who regard the technological road as the wrong one for humanity to have taken or to continue to follow. Almost as influential, Campanella's *Politicae civitas solis idea reipublicae philosophicae* (*The City of the Sun*, 1623, first written in 1602 in Italian as *La città del sole*) describes a hierarchical society in which all citizens belong to the state and must serve it as best they can. Each receives sufficient material goods to satisfy needs, but there is provision for those of greater merit to receive more. All authority is vested in the citizens who have won positions of leadership through merit. Compulsory education for both men and women places great emphasis on science and technology. The third of the three major utopias in this group, Andreae's *Reipublicae christianopolitanae descriptio* (*Christianapolis*, 1619), is the most overtly Christian of the three. A triumvirate—a judge, a priest, and a kind of college president or a dean—rule, and divine law, in the Lutheran interpretation, is the basis of all activity. Worship of God through cultivation of the Christian life and pursuit of knowledge creates good citizens, who in turn create a stable, obedient, society, presumably enduring forever under God's protection.

Other works that might be grouped as pansophist, though less well known, are worthy of note. Giordano Bruno's *Spaccio della bestia trionfante The Expulsion of the Triumphant Beast*, 1584) described a religious utopia, probably correctly assessed by the church as not basically Christian, set in a universe not merely the creation of divinity but of divinity immanent. As with many later utopians, Bruno's is one in which humanity has changed for the better and is thus able to accept this new, living universe. Comenius, like so many others of his group, wrote far more than he published, and most of his genuinely utopian writings were not published until 1966. Nevertheless, in many of the pedagogical works for which he is best known, Comenius described an educational system that would lead to a utopian society, and sections of the unpublished works were known to colleagues throughout Western Europe. Of his works published in the seventeenth century, *Labyrint světa a ráj srdce, to jest* (*The Labyrinth of the World and the Paradise of the Heart*, 1631) is the most utopian. In this fictional journey, reminiscent of *Pilgrim's Progress*, "genuine Christians" live safely in a kingdom of God on earth because they make the best use of earthly things but delight in the heavenly. Long attributed to John Milton, Samuel Gott's *Novae Solymae libri sex . . .* (*Nova Solyma, The Ideal City*, 1648) is a romance that owes something to Andreae but resembles Comenius in proposing a society in which proper religious and moral education will lead to a perfect Christian society. Although also much influenced by Andreae, Gabriel Plattes' *A Description of the Famous Kingdome of Macaria* (1641) is an example of the transition to more secular concerns. Among its characteristics, clearly intended as models for England, are a powerful judiciary, a 5 percent tax on all property to be used for public works, and ownership of land restricted to that which a man might improve. *Macaria,* which has only recently been demonstrated to have been written by Plattes rather than by still another close colleague of Comenius, Samuel Hartlib, is further evidence of the international character of the pansophist movement.

Representative of those concerned more with a new social order than with reconciling religion and science, James Harrington wrote dozens of utopian works, most of them political tracts, but his *The Commonwealth of Oceana* (1656) is a detailed and significant proposal intended to move England itself to such a society. There could be, he believed, no real political power without economic power, and abuse of all power must be prevented by appropriate governmental arrangements. In his rigidly stratified society, the amount of land that could be held by any one person was restricted, but only property owners could vote; he called for rotation of all elected officers and for separation of the judicial, executive, and legislative functions. His concern for religious liberty, the rule of law, and education is reflected not only in many succeeding utopias but also in the documents that are at the basis of many modern democratic governments. The makers of the American Constitution, for example, drew many of their ideas from his fictional treatment. Although it is not a true fictional utopia, Gerrard Winstanley's *The Law of Freedom in a Platform* (1652) is an important document, representative of many proposals for cooperative communal societies intended to hold mankind at a higher level of life while awaiting a Second Coming, that called for a reformed economic and democratic government. As in the case of Harrington, numerous later utopian documents show the influence of Winstanley.

The most interesting utopias of the late seventeenth century fall under the category often described as fantastic voyage. Expanding on the tradition of satirizing earthly society by portraying a more perfect society on the moon, Cyrano de Bergerac's *Histoire comique des états et empires de la lune* (*The Comical History of the States and Empires of the Moon,* 1657) and *Histoire comique des états et empires du soleil* (*The Comical History of the States and Empires of the Sun,* 1662) were obviously influenced by Campanella. Three such works are set in the then romantic and largely unknown part of the earth, the South Seas: Denis Vairasse's *L'histoire des Sevarambes* (*The History of the Sevarites or Sevarambi,* 1677, published in England in 1675 and quite possibly originally written in English), Gabriel de Foigny's *La terre australe connue (A New Discovery of Terra Incognita Australis,* 1676), and Simon Tyssot de Patot's *Voyages et avantures de Jaques Massé* (*The Travels and Adventures of James Massey,* 1710). Vairasse (or Veiras) describes a remarkably modern utopia founded in the fifteenth century by a Persian named Sevarias. This deistic, rationalistic, highly technological society, although an absolute monarchy, is devoted to individual freedom and equality. The king is elected democratically, but all property is vested in him, and he is held accountable for the welfare of all. Each citizen draws upon the common warehouses for whatever may be needed. Although there is compulsory military service, there is also universal education for both males and females and freedom to think and speak as one might wish. De Foigny's Australian society is a rationalistic, androgynous land of absolute equality based on the belief in the innate goodness of human nature. There is no need for government under such conditions, except that education, which lasts well into mid-life, is a community matter. Such perfect bliss bores the hero, who eventually escapes and returns to France. The best of several visits to utopias in far-off lands that Tyssot de Patot wrote is more concerned with the adventures of Massey than with the utopian aspects of the society he finds in a fertile, peaceful valley. This society uses better technology than Europe, especially in the expediting of trade. Except for a few special privileges for the king and permission for the higher classes to practice polygamy, all members of society appear to be treated alike.

In the voyage tradition, though set in the Mediterranean in classical times, *Les aventures de Télémaque* (*The Adventures of Telemachus,* 1699) was published without the knowledge of its author, the scholarly tutor to the duke of Burgundy, François de Salignac de La Mothe Fénelon. Although obviously intended to demonstrate moral virtues to the royal student by portraying an ideal kingdom where reason and justice could prevail, it was interpreted as a satire on the court of Louis XIV and led to Fénelon's banishment from the court. In his wanderings Telemachus finds two different utopias. In the kingdom of Salente there is a paternalistic government that regulates all matters; La Bétique, which has no government at all, is perhaps the best example of an arcadian or even an anarchistic utopia yet written. For Fénelon, monarchy was the ideal state, but his anarchistic arcadia has often been more popular with later writers. During the eighteenth century the fantastic voyage continued as a popular vehicle for utopian speculation, often with shipwreck on an island as an important feature. Thus, one of the most popular German novels of the period was Johann Gottfried Schnabel's long *Die Insel Felsenburg* (*Felsenburg Island,* 1732), in which the hero, forced from home by the Thirty Years' War, constructs an ideal state following his disastrous voyage.

Simon Berington's *The Adventures of Sig. Gaudentio di Lucca* (1737) claimed to be a translation from the Italian and was often attributed to Bishop George Berkeley, an attribution neither Berkeley nor Berington, himself an English Catholic priest, seems to have denied. The hero of this voyage describes the kingdom of Mezzorania in northern Africa during testimony before the Inquisition. Mezzorania's guiding principle is that nature is a source of all that is good and its people, refugees some 3,000 years earlier from invading armies and since then out of contact with the outside world and living in a natural environment, have been free to develop a natural religion and, consequently, a utopian society. Ludvig Holberg's *Nicolai Klimii iter subterraneum* (*A Journey to the World Underground,* novel, 1741) is still another imaginary voyage that takes place, in this case in the interior of the earth. The hero, Niels Klim, visits a number of different countries, including Patu, the ideal state, as well as other countries modeled on various terrestrial nations such as France and Russia. Klim's most interesting invention is the class of rational trees born with marks on their foreheads to indicate how long they will live. One group lives only four years and spends three of these preparing for death; others live to be 400, very seldom think of death, and lead lives of riotous activity. Many scholars have suggested the possible influence on Holberg of *Gulliver's Travels* (satire, 1726). Another work that may have been influenced by Swift is the Japanese scientist Hiraga Gennai's *Fūryū Shidōken den* (*The Gallant History of Shidōken,* 1763), which satirizes society in the lands of women, dwarfs, giants, and others. However, Holberg may not have known *Gulliver's Travels* at all, and Hiraga, who possibly knew a Dutch translation, may have been more influenced by Chinese fantastic voyages; the influence of Swift in both cases remains hypothetical. Certainly, the utopian connotations of Swift's work are less related to the fantastic voyage aspect than to his concern with the moral and social activities of human beings. If *Gulliver's Travels* is a utopian document, it is closer to the episode of the Troglodytes in letters 11–15 of Montesquieu's *Lettres persanes* (*Persian Letters,* 1721) than to the usual fantastic voyage. Montesquieu's short description of the rise and fall of the good society is perhaps the best single brief expression of the belief that man is naturally good and can, given the opportunity, bring about the perfect state. Although the earlier published letters suggest the downfall of the good society, a fragmentary sequel first published in 1899–1901 suggests a more optimistic view.

Perhaps the first Spanish utopia, *Descripción de la Sinapia, peninsula en la tierra austral* (*Description of Sinapia, Peninsula in the Southern Land;* author unknown; apparently written in the mid-eighteenth century, but not published until 1975), describes still another society founded in the unknown South Seas— a Christian, communistic society in which all governors, judges, and even clergymen are elected from a group who have prepared themselves for such positions by rigid learning beginning quite early in life. The influence of Plato, Campanella, Bacon, and More is clear, and, as in *Utopia,* the family is the basic social and political unit, with agriculture as the basis of economic life. Another communistic society governed by natural laws and without vice appears in a work by the French author known only as Morelly, *Naufrage des isles flottantes, ou Basiliade du célèbre Pilpai* (*The Basiliade: or the Book of Truth and Nature,* 1753), an allegorical poem expressing ideas much more carefully worked out later in Morelly's *Code de la nature* (*Nature's Code,* 1755).

Even the French theater did not escape the utopian ideal, for in at least three plays Marivaux produced satiric comedies of Europeans shipwrecked on strange islands with various kinds of utopian government. In *L'île des esclaves* (*The Isle of Slaves,* first performed in 1725), nobles and servants forced to exchange place with each other learn appropriate lessons and discover that social injustice can be cured because natural goodness is the creator of equality. In *L'île de la raison, ou les petits hommes* (*The Isle of Reason or the Little Men,* first performed in 1727) eight Europeans, including peasants and noblemen, are shipwrecked on an island where the reasonableness of a man's conduct determines his stature. The visitors are all reduced to small proportions, but the natives attempt, with limited success, to cure them of their disease. The point of the play is that where one is shown the unreasonableness of his views and wishes to improve himself, he can do so. Many social conventions—in this play the idea of marriage contracts is the chief example—are thus unnecessary among reasonable people. In *La colonie* (*The Colony;* this one-act version first published in 1750 is all that remains of a lost three-act version *La nouvelle colonie, ou la ligne des femmes,* first performed in 1799). Refugees landing on an island inhabited by hostile natives assume that men will have the prerogative of setting up a government, but in this plea for the equal rights of women the women have other ideas and set up their own. The play ends with their return to the protection of the men. Many of the social reforms suggested are far in advance of Marivaux's time.

One final example of the fantastic voyage is Restif de la Bretonne's *La découverte australe par un homme-volant, ou le Dédale français* (*The Southern Discovery of a Flying Man, or the New French Daedalus,* 1781). Among the several utopias depicted is Megapatagonia, once more set in Australia, which maintains itself as a society in which both men and women are able to carry out their very different destinies in harmony with what nature had intended through observance of five basic rules. Do unto others as you would have done to yourself; treat animals fairly and in a way that you would want a superior animal to act toward you; all property is the property of all; everyone works for the common good; everyone participates equally. Restif wrote numerous other utopian works including his five volume series *Idées singulières* (1769–1797). Several short pieces such as "Status du Bourg d'Oudun" (1776) and "Les vingt épouses des vingt associés" (1780) are nonfictional but in the tradition of the egalitarian utopia popular in eighteenth-century France.

The utopias of the Enlightenment are often distinguished and significant. While such fictional works as those previously mentioned are frequently more interesting reading, it should not be overlooked that most of the important philosophers and political thinkers of the eighteenth century also concerned themselves with possible utopian societies. Many, as in the case of Leibniz, Kant, and Priestley, approached utopia as a means of achieving universal peace. Others, like the encyclopedists, often worked for reform, which in the end might well have become utopia, as did Diderot; even Holbach's synagogue, the home of several encyclopedists, has on occasion been called a utopian community. Rousseau, especially in *Emile* (novel, 1762) and *Du contrat social* (*The Social Contract,* treatise, 1762) has had a lasting influence on utopian thought. Utopian ideals were promulgated by thinkers from a variety of occupations and points of view:

satirists (Voltaire), navigators (Bougainville), kings (Stanislas Leszczyński of Poland), libertines (the Marquis de Sade), radical communists (Babeuf and the Abbé Mably), and public servants (Turgot) who contributed to an even greater diversity of utopian proposals both literary and practical in the nineteenth century. Outside France the same demand for a return to natural law that drove Rousseau appeared in the Japanese Andō Shōeki's *Shizen shin'eidō* (*The Way of Achieving Natural Truth*, c. 1755,); Andō's natural society, it has been suggested, more closely resembles those of Winstanley and Harrington than that of Rousseau. Two other approaches, widely divergent but nevertheless in the eighteenth-century voyage traditions, are Thomas Spence's various versions of utopia that began with *A Supplement to the History of Robinson Crusoe* (1782) and reached its fullest statement in *The Constitution of a Perfect Commonwealth* (1798) and, in the early years of the nineteenth century, Li Ju-chen's *Ching-hua yüan* (*Flowers in the Mirror*, 1828, probably written 1810–1820), which presented a Chinese *Gulliver's Travels* through several utopian lands. By the middle of the nineteenth century, however, the emphasis, in fictional utopias at least, had shifted from the satiric jabs at present society so prominent in the fantastic voyage to a less-exciting but often more carefully thought-out statement both of needed reforms and of means to achieve them, if not in the present, then some time in the future.

After 1800

In one sense, the definition of utopia must necessarily shift with the circumstances. Despite attempts to maintain a purely literary perspective, the common confusion of utopian thought, utopian communities, and utopian fiction has frequently led to definitions that will not hold up under close scrutiny. Furthermore, many attempts to study specific utopias, in isolation, as a literary artifact only, have resulted in unprofitable investigations of works completely out of context with what has gone before and what has come after the work under consideration. It is much more useful to view the utopian effort of the nineteenth and twentieth centuries as representative of three major traditions: reform writings that often led to practical attempts to found utopian communities; literary utopias (some of which also led to attempts to found communities or reform society to conform with their ideals); and anti-utopias or dystopias, which rejected utopian ideals as paths to unacceptable future societies.

Although depiction of utopian societies existing in some remote as yet undiscovered part of the earth or, later, elsewhere in the universe continued as an important segment of the genre, one new characteristic of nineteenth-century utopia was its frequent location in the future, both immediate in the case of reformers wishing to put their principles into operation and distant in the case of those who offered only a glimpse of the completed new society. Perhaps the earliest significant example of these utopias of the future—euchronias, as they are sometimes designated—was Louis Sébastien Mercier's *L'an deux mille quatre cent quarante* (*Memoirs of the Year 2500* [sic], 1771). Like many of his predecessors in the Enlightenment, Mercier was certain that man and his society would ultimately be perfected through refinements in technology and in science and its universal highest language, mathematics. Similarly, Faddei Bulgarin, an officer in Napoleon's Polish Legion and later a conservative journalist in St. Petersburg, described a technologically advanced society in his short work, "Pravdopodobnyĭa nebylitsy, ili Stranstvovanie po svetu v dvadt̃s at' deviatom veke" ("Plausible Fantasies, or A Journey in the 29th Century," 1824). A product of the same intellectual atmosphere, the Marquis de Condorcet's non-fictional *Esquisse d'un tableau historique des progrès de l'esprit humain (Outline of a Historical View of the Progress of the Human Mind),* written in the midst of revolution and published posthumously (1795), supported the view that science would lead to human perfection, and this theme permeated utopian writing, fictional and nonfictional, for most of the following century. Condorcet's special sense that a study of history could serve as a scientific basis for progress was an added dimension that frequently gave way in later utopias to a Darwinian— or, better, Spencerian—reliance on survival of the fittest or to a Comtean belief in the answers of "social physics," but it continues to have its adherents even today.

Strictly speaking, Claude Henri de Saint-Simon, Charles Fourier, and Robert Owen did not write utopias, nor were their works describing their proposed utopian worlds especially literary in any but the lowest sense of that term. Nevertheless, the creators of utopia in the nineteenth and twentieth centuries drew heavily on their ideas in their own proposals.

Saint-Simon, a prolific writer whose belief that the ultimate perfectibility of humanity is demonstrated by history never varied despite other contradictory aspects of his work, is best known through the efforts of his disciples to interpret the master's work, a task begun before his death and continued for some years thereafter. A major document in this interpretation is *Doctrine de Saint-Simon* (1832), which maintained that brotherly love together with the application of science to political, social, and industrial progress in a hierarchical organization of the state led by those most qualified—industrialists, technocrats, and politicians—would bind society together. Yet in the interests of social harmony Saint-Simon's disciples permitted no dissent from the official doctrine of the state and thus advocated a totalitarian though benevolent government.

Charles Fourier frequently elaborated on his initial thesis, first stated in *Théorie des quatre mouvements (Theory of the Four Movements,* 1808), that the laws of social movement and "passionate attraction" he had discovered would lead to a genuine utopia—he used the word on several occasions. The society he proposed was based on laws of harmony that he believed would permit people to work joyfully and voluntarily, with much freer social and sexual relations, in a hierarchical society based on the organized unit that he titled the "phalanx." For him the successful society was necessarily agricultural, in large part because of the resultant harmonious association of humanity with nature, a necessary condition for a lasting better world.

Robert Owen, a successful manufacturer whose strong belief in good working conditions, benevolent leadership, and thorough education was described in some detail in *A New View of Society: Essays on the Principle of the Formation of the Human Character* (1813), favored development of small villages in which industrial activity would be balanced against the agricultural activity of the surrounding areas. Unlike Saint-Simon and Fourier, Owen personally led attempts to put into practice the ideas he described in his writing; although the most famous of these attempts at New Harmony, Indiana, was short-lived, the Owenite movement in England has continued to the present time.

Many later reformers who were attracted to the ideas of Saint-Simon, Fourier, and Owen not only wrote utopias but often tried to develop new communities based on them, especially in Europe and North America. One such follower of Fourier, Étienne Cabet, produced a dull but immensely popular novel, *Voyage en Icarie (Voyage to Icaria,* 1840), and, as early as 1847, began the first of several attempts to found Icaria within the boundaries of the United States. Cabet's society was based on personal equality, with all members united by the bonds of fraternity into a single family, and a democratic government, with all goods held as part of the common capital. Despite its democratic ideology, the Icarian communities were overregulated, with rules on every aspect of life, and the common agreement to abide by a kind of extension of the golden rule was not strong enough to prevent numerous quarrels and splits among Cabet's followers. Nevertheless, although the initial success of the Icarians at Nauvoo in Illinois was short-lived, in large part because of Cabet's insistence on his own superiority as administrator, spin-offs from the community lasted until the 1930s in California and Louisiana.

Representative of utopias that did not lead to actual experiments is Calvin Blanchard's *The Art of Real Pleasure. That New Pleasure, for Which an Imperial Reward was Offered* (1864), an incomplete utopia based in part on the work of Fourier as well as that of Comte and Feuerbach. Blanchard called for a religion of science as the basis of a utopian world in which the only purpose of government would be to satisfy all human desires and bring about "harmony and perfect, universal, and immutable, freedom." He emphasized the need for complete happiness for all, and, in his call for creation of beautiful surroundings, reflected a growing concern of utopian writers about the impact of environment on the human spirit.

Nikolai Chernyshevsky's *Chto delat'?* (*What Is to Be Done?,* novel, 1863) was written while the author was in prison, and its publication was obviously an oversight on the part of the authorities. The "new people" of the story are guided by the principle that self-interest and the common good are synonymous; for them cooperative labor arrangements somewhat after the model of Owen were the way to a more rational society. The future utopia is described in four dreams of the heroine; the fourth dream portrays the future as a rational, beautiful world organized in Fourier-like phalansteries in which women have achieved true equality. Dostoevsky's attack on this concept in *Zapiski iz podpol'ia* (*Notes from Underground,* novel, 1864) has received much greater attention and made

Chernyshevsky's noble vision much less influential than it might have been. The conflict between the rational, planned society and human irrationality—described by Dostoevsky as essential to being human—is at the heart of many later anti-utopian works. Valerii Briusov's "Respublika iuznogo kresta" ("The Republic of the Southern Cross," story, 1907) even portrays the perfect society destroyed by an unexplained epidemic of irrational behavior.

Edward Bellamy's *Looking Backward 2000–1887* (1888) is in many ways the most successful utopian novel ever published. A best-seller in its first year and immediately translated into numerous other languages, it has never been out of print. The Nationalist Club it inspired had significant influence on American politics during the rest of the century. At first glance Bellamy's ideas appear to have little in common with those of Saint-Simon, Fourier, and Owen, but they contain the same belief in the perfectibility of mankind, in peaceful rejection of competition in favor of a system of brotherhood and in technology as a means to a better life. Bellamy's model state-socialist utopia is brought about by the logical development of one great national trust from a consolidation of large private trusts. Efficient use of machinery and of human energy permits human nature, free of economic insecurity, to rise to higher moral heights and more significant intellectual pursuits.

Numerous other utopian works were published in the years immediately following publication of *Looking Backward,* some favoring, some opposing Bellamy's views. Although not directly responsive to Bellamy, one comparatively unknown work, Charles William Wooldridge's *Perfecting the Earth, a Piece of Possible History* (1902), solves the nation's problems through major technological advances and huge public works to create a cooperative commonwealth, a society that leaves men free to develop their best attributes in preparation for eternal life.

In spite of major differences in their ideas, Saint-Simon, Fourier, and Owen became a kind of trinity of what Marx and Engels were later to call the utopian socialists, and it was Marx and Engels who, though frequently building on the work of the trinity and in the case of Marx most especially on that of Owen, mounted the most significant attack on their ideas. From a literary point of view, these antagonisms make it almost impossible to distinguish the source of many later utopian writings. Perhaps the distinctions are unnecessary, for many, both among the utopian socialists and among the scientific socialists who followed Marx and Engels, supported some version of the slogan "From each according to his ability, to each according to his needs." The chief distinction between the two schools is in the tendency of utopian socialists to limit such needs and to rely on the agricultural society as the best road to utopia, while the scientific socialists tend to call for the most advanced technology to produce the greatest abundance so that ever-increasing needs might be met. The aim in both cases is human happiness through better organization of society and its means of production.

A case in point is that of the Austrian economist Theodor Hertzka. In *Freiland*

(Freeland, 1890) the voluntary associations of Fourier are clearly reflected, but at the same time, although he specifically disagreed with Karl Marx in most matters and said so in his introduction, Hertzka proposed that increasing technological competence would be a major factor in creating a society overflowing with all the material things, including previously unobtainable luxuries, that human beings could desire. He further proposed that land and all things necessary for production of goods would belong to the state, that each citizen would have equal rights in this common property, that wages would be paid according to the skill and merit of the individual, and that the state would care for those not able to earn their own way. Hertzka's vision of a free social order was enormously popular and led to attempts to establish communities in East Africa, England, and the United States. In *Altneuland (Old-New Land,* 1902) Hertzka's contemporary, the Austrian Zionist Theodor Herzl, similarly proposed a model state based on cooperative free labor and heavy emphasis on social planning and technology. Herzl's sources, too, were quite eclectic, and his utopia is well within the nineteenth-century tradition. Although the modern state of Israel has obviously modified some aspects of the proposal, his might be regarded as one of the most successful of utopian works, even though the state that came out of these proposals would hardly be regarded as utopian today.

In *Auf zwei Planeten* (1897; the English *Two Planets* is a translation of a 1948 abridgment by Erich Lasswitz), Kurd Lasswitz placed his utopia on Mars, as did many others in the nineteenth century. His Martians eventually assist the people of Earth in their movement toward utopia. Aleksandr Bogdanov's *Krasnaïa zvezda (Red Star,* 1908), subtitled *Utopi (Utopia),* described a Martian society built on Marxist principles, and, in the best nineteenth-century tradition, his visitor to Mars is given a tour of the various social institutions and technologically advanced factories upon which Martian civilization depends. To bring about this utopia on earth, revolution will be necessary. Half a century later, the revolution Bogdanov supported long since past, Ivan Antonovich Efremov described a future socialist earth in *Tumannost' Andromedy (Andromeda: A Space Age Tale,* 1958). Although the work is, for the most part, a space opera dealing with exploration and contact with another civilization, the socialist state has been brought about and humanity has been advanced to what Efremov regards as a utopian world.

Representative of works opposing the technologically dependent society of Bellamy is William Morris' *News from Nowhere; or, An Epoch of Rest* (1890). Morris, a socialist, believed that technology is beneficial when shared with everyone but that reliance on machinery tends to make men slaves of those very machines. Morris' agrarian, small-village society is devoted to the production of beauty through personal craftmanship, and behind-the-scenes heavy machinery has freed men from heavy labor and permitted them, accepting from technology only those limited goods that a simpler life style requires, to live a more human existence. Similar belief in the superior quality of life in a rural setting has been a major theme of later utopian works, among them Robert Graves, *Seven Days in New Crete* (1949), Ernest Callenbach, *Ecotopia* (1975), and Marge Piercy, *Woman on the Edge of Time* (1976). Samuel Butler's earlier satiric *Erewhon* (1872) had carried opposition to technology even further by describing a society in which all machines were banned.

In the enormous canon of H. G. Wells's writings are several utopian works, three of which are especially deserving of attention. In *A Modern Utopia* (1905), a work that shows traces of Plato, Comte, Bellamy, and especially Hertzka, Wells makes two significant points: that "no less than a planet will serve the purpose of a modern utopia," and that utopian possibilities are limited to what can be achieved by human beings working within the boundaries that nature places upon them. In his worldwide society, the Samurai, who resemble the guardians of Plato, control an efficient bureaucracy that provides for the well-being of all citizens within carefully prescribed limits. Significantly, Wells suggests that utopia is not static and that even the final world state toward which each generation moves ever closer will continue to develop after its creation. *Men Like Gods* (1923) accepts the premise that a change in human beings is necessary in order to bring about utopia and that the major change must be removal of the idea of competition from human thinking. *The Shape of Things to Come* (1933) suggests that after the chaos of worldwide conflict scientists and engineers will manage the world for the good of mankind. Although it occasionally appears that this new world is merely one of super gadgets, it is clearly in the tradition of the long-held belief that technology will bring about the utopian society.

The twentieth century utopian tradition has often been described, probably erroneously, as anti-utopian or, more specifically, dystopian. Certainly works objecting to utopian ideas as either unworkable or leading to a bad society have been prominent in the last half century. Thus H. G. Wells also wrote extensively in the anti-utopian genre and often adumbrated ideas found in later, better-known anti-utopian works. In *The Time Machine* (1895) he suggested that the current trend toward a technologically oriented materialistic society would result not in a utopia but in the destruction of all mankind. In *When the Sleeper Wakes* (1899) he attacked the overall monopoly advocated by Bellamy and others as a means to the good life and suggested that the result would be a heavily industrialized society in which a favored few might have access to the fruits of technological production but that most of mankind would be mere victims, subject to totalitarian control of all human activity. The Selenite society of *The First Men in the Moon* (1901) described the consequences of physical and psychological conditioning to create a kind of antlike society which, while using natural resources efficiently, would result in complete loss of individuality if adopted for mankind. At the end of his life *The Mind at the End of Its Tether* (1945) reflected his despair that mankind could never overcome the evil in human nature to reach utopia, and even *The Happy Turning* (1945), his last utopian work, proposed an arcadian, garden like state, rejecting the technology that he had once advocated as a means to utopia.

Probably the best and most influential anti-utopian fiction is Evgenii Zamiatin's *My (We,* novel, 1924). This work, still not published in the Soviet Union, has its literary antecedents in both Wells and Dostoevsky. In *We,* Zamiatin made the point that even the most revolutionary of human beings can be forced to accept a regimented life specified down to the smallest detail: identical dress, numbers rather than names, activities conducted according to a kind of railroad timetable, obedience to the leader in all things. If man requires irrationality, as suggested by Dostoevsky, that irrationality can and will be eradicated by an operation to remove that part of the brain which requires it. The United States will go on, but the individual has no importance; the planned utopia is really a dystopia that brings with it the loss of humanity.

The theme of humanity lost in the search for utopia is common to most twentieth-century anti-utopians, but the causes differ: too great reliance on machines and technology, as in E. M. Forster's short story "When the Machine Stops" (1908) and Jack Williamson's *The Humanoids* (1949); brainwashing, as in George Orwell's *Nineteen Eighty-Four* (1949); frontal lobtomy, as in *We* and Bernard Wolfe's *Limbo* (1952); genetic change, as in David M. Parry's *The Scarlet Empire* (1906) and Franz Werfel's *Stern der Ungeborenen (Star of the Unborn,* 1946); drugs, as in Frank Herbert's *The Santaroga Barrier* (1968). Aldous Huxley's *Brave New World* (1932), an ordered land of sophisticated playtime gadgets, genetic engineering, test-tube babies, rigidly stratified socio-intellectual classes, and happiness drugs, sums up the objection quite well in the hero's insistence on the right to the human "necessities" of disease, disorder, and unhappiness. Worthy of mention are short, satiric works by two Poles. Both in Sławomir Mrożek's play *Policja (Police,* 1958) and in Stanislaw Lem's short story "Altruizine," in *Cyberiada (The Cyberiad,* 1965) the expectation of a perfect society is shown to be unwarranted and laughable. Perhaps the most melancholy objection to the utopian ideal yet published is Jorges Luis Borges' short story "Utopia de un hombre questa cansado" ("Utopia of a Tired Man," 1975). Borges has made other ventures into the utopian world, but in this Latin-speaking land of no governments and no personal possessions, Mankind is deliberately forgetting its collective past and dying out. Even utopia achieved provides no true human happiness.

Most utopian works reflect those aspects of the writer's time that he found repugnant and which the utopia is designed to correct. Especially in recent times it is often those aspects that *she* found repugnant that appear in utopian fiction. Although many utopian writers of the past have suggested new, more significant roles for women, the twentieth-century feminist movement has found even these proposed changes less than welcome. Earlier, the comparatively few feminist writers of literary utopias (perhaps three dozen in the United States in the nineteenth century, for example) tended to reflect only a slight improvement in the relationship of women with the rest of society. Although reflecting a greater concern for women's needs, for the most part these works suggested only such palliatives as higher praise for the traditional female roles, institution of communal dining and centralized laundry facilities, and some hope that women's "gentler influence" might improve society. Men, even the utopians agreed, were naturally leaders and holders of property, and even where equality of leadership and the right to property were granted, it was assumed that something in the female nature would prevent women from usurping the traditional place of men. Thus Mary Griffith, in *Three Hundred Years Hence* (novella, 1836) wrote of a utopia brought about by the liberation of women. But having attained economic equality women have devoted themselves to changing men into more peaceful, healthful, happier beings, and men continue to control society. Women, said Griffith, have no desire for anything else. Mary E. Bradley's *Mizora: A Prophecy* (serial, 1880–1881; book, 1889), an otherwise uninspired work, expanded on the idea of Griffith that women hold the secret of creating a better world. Her world of high-level science and technology is a refined and beautiful utopia, but, having learned that life can be continued with no need for the male of the species, these women have eliminated men altogether. Charlotte Perkins Gilman's *Herland* (1915) described a remote valley that, all its men lost by accident centuries earlier, has maintained itself through parthenogenesis and created a beautiful, womanly, mothering society. The women of this society are most eager to have men introduced under appropriate conditions because their genes would improve the race. In *The Republic of the Future* (1887), Anna Bowman Dodd dissented from the view that women might lead the movement toward a better world. In this new socialist utopia the emancipation of women has led only to a dull, almost nonhuman life. There is no poverty, for machines do all the work, but time hangs heavy. *Mizora* had suggested that the all-female society would come about following a final war between men and women. In the much more recent, often puzzling, world of Monique Wittig's *Les Guérillères* (1969), there is an almost eternal war between men and women. Presumably, the conquering women, returning to a matriarchal, almost tribal society will create a more human world of peaceful, happy existence. Some militantly feminist writers have created feminist "utopian" worlds in which men have no place, as in Joanna Rush's *The Female Man* (1975), Suzy McKee Charnas' *Motherlines* (1978), and Sally Miller Gearhart's *The Wanderground: Stories of the Hill Women* (1978).

Although such views have had widespread influence in recent years, the best of the feminist utopias are those which posit what might be called an androgynous society, that is, a society in which there is no rigid assignment of human feelings or even characteristics on the basis of sex. Among the best of these are Ursula Le Guin's *The Dispossessed, An Ambiguous Utopia* (1974), Marge Piercy's *Woman on the Edge of Time*, and the continuing series of the South African writer, Doris Lessing, *Canopus in Argos: Archives* (1978—). It is perhaps worth noting that a similar society was the aim of the commissar of social welfare in the early days of the Bolshevik regime in Russia, Aleksandra Mikhailovna Kollontai. Both in political action and in her nonfictional writings, Kollontai worked toward a future in which both feminine and masculine aspects of human personality would be integrated in each individual. In the last two decades feminist thinkers throughout the world have become more and more vociferous in demanding that the better world, perhaps even the utopia of tomorrow, must have a different role for women than what has been true up until now. But thus far, for the most part, the literary statement of such principles has been by the English-speaking wing of the movement.

Eastern utopian thinkers have seldom written fictional utopian works. However, some mention must be made of two early twentieth-century Chinese utopian thinkers. The first of these, K'ang Yu-wei, had comparatively little knowledge of Western utopian thought, although he knew something of the social Darwinist movement. His utopian work, *Ta-t'ung shu* (*Book of Great Equality,* variously translated as *Grand Unity, One World,* etc., 1913–1935) is grounded in new readings of Confucianism. Reminiscent of Fourier in the specificity of his description of a worldwide utopia, K'ang described a democratic communal society in which what he called "boundaries" (barriers between men, between nations, between men and nature) would be eliminated. K'ang's contemporary, Liu Jen-hang, probably knew something of K'ang's work. His *Tung-fang ta-t'ung hsüeh-an* (*Preliminary Studies Concerning the Great Equality of the East,* 1926) clearly shows not only the influence of K'ang but also of many Western utopians whose works he knew either in English or in Japanese. For Liu the final order of society would be matriarchal, and science and technology would be major keys to the new, great world.

In the period between the two world wars, several significant utopian works appeared. The first of these, Gerhart Hauptmann's *Die Insel der grossen Mutter* (*The Island of the Great Mother,* 1925), is an almost poetic story of an ideal world. Following the shipwreck of a luxury liner on an unknown South Sea island, one hundred women and a twelve-year-old boy establish a matriarchal society, a paradise of natural existence. Male children are banished to the other side of the island, but when they reach adulthood they revolt and the temporary utopian society is ended by a return of the island to "civilization." J. D. Bernal's influential *The World, the Flesh, and the Devil* (1929) carried the idea of science as the key to utopia far beyond his predecessors. Man, he said, will alter both his environment by moving into space and his own body through speeding up evolution to achieve the ultimate mental perfection that must be the goal of all men. In James Hilton's *Lost Horizon* (1933) the leaders of the hidden utopian valley of Shangri-La have brought physical and mental abilities to a high level; they propose to wait out the coming storm of war in order to restore the postwar world to a more ideal state. The war had begun before publication of the most literate of modern utopias, Austin Tappan Wright's *Islandia* (1942). This long, thoughtful opus, edited from an enormous posthumous manuscript detailing all aspects of the utopian fantasy begun in the author's childhood, describes life on the unknown Karain continent at the turn of the century. In this nonurbanized, agricultural society, natural resources are used in a limited fashion, technology is at the pre-Industrial-Revolution level, and limited contact with the rest of the world is the key to maintenance of this almost idyllic civilization.

After World War II utopian writings continue to reflect the variety of views found in earlier examples. Thus, the postcatastrophe development of utopia suggested appears once more in Oskar Maria Graf's *Die Eroberung der Welt* (*The Conquest of the World*, 1948) written during the Second World War but optimistically suggesting that after the Third World War a humane, world government will be established. Robert Graves' *Seven Days in New Crete* also describes a world following major nuclear catastrophe, in which the future golden age is less technologically oriented and harmony is found in worship of nature and a matriarchal society. The behavioral psychologist B. F. Skinner's *Walden Two* (1948) is an agricultural, self-sufficient community based on the principles of behavioral engineering. Opponents have seen this approach as leading to loss of freedom and undesirable manipulation of human beings; others, subscribing, at least in part, to its principles, have made it a model for numerous communities, some of which have continued with some success to the present time. Starting from Marxism but moving well beyond in the hope of uniting traditional utopian proposals with future new systems, Ernst Bloch's *Das Prinzip Hoffnung* (*The Principle of Hope*, 1954–1959) is a lengthy treatise that conceives utopian thought as a means of exploring a wide range of human possibilities. Much earlier, August Cieszkowski's *Ojcze-Nasz* (*Our Father*, 1848, 1899–1906) had examined the Lord's Prayer as a blueprint for utopia, and, in that same hope of a twentieth-century version of the Kingdom of God, Paul Tillich's *Politische Bedeutung der Utopie im Leben der Völker* (*The Political Meaning of Utopia*, 1951), among others of his works, called for a union of secular and spiritual belief to overcome twentieth-century pessimism about Man's future. The city-planners put their faith in development of appropriate environments. An outstanding example is Konstantinos Doxiades, whose *Between Dystopia and Utopia* (1966) can stand for dozens of similar nonfictional calls for a physical, environmental thrust toward utopia.

The continuing view that utopia once achieved will lead to human existence at a higher intellectual or spiritual level, perhaps in a state no longer recognizable as human, is well represented in Hermann Hesse's *Das Glasperlenspiel* (*The Glass Bead Game* [*Magister Ludi*], 1943) and Arthur C. Clarke's *Childhood's End* (1953). In the former, the hero rejects his own utopian society's ideal of individual perfection and moves to another level of greater social consciousness; in the latter, visitors from space (whose previous visits have been the source of devil imagery) assist mankind to an earthly utopia from which the next generation evolves into beings at a higher level of consciousness. Aldous Huxley, whose fascination with utopian ideals has been best expressed in his anti-utopia *Brave New World*, produced one final utopian work, *Island* (1962). Acceptance of life as it is, as a means to perfection of the individual, leads to attainment of complete humanity. In the tradition of tantric Buddhism, people are thus free to act as they believe right, at all levels and in all areas of human activity. Hallucinogenic drugs assist in bringing about the beatific vision that is a goal of members of this society. That this beautiful experiment will be destroyed in the end by an oil-greedy neighbor does not detract from the power of the ideal Huxley has presented—although it must be admitted in somewhat less believable fictional form than his earlier anti-utopian works. In Robert Merle's *Malevil* (1972) a few survivors of nuclear war move swiftly back to an almost ideal society made possible in part because of the wisdom of the leader and in part by the high technology that is quickly restored. Here, too, the book ends with a suggestion that this new development will only lead to still another catastrophe.

Ernest Callenbach's *Ecotopia* can serve as an example of the many recent utopian works that make use of appropriate technology, environmental concern, natural recycling, decentralization, cooperation, and careful planning to produce a society perhaps not yet utopian but on its way. The Northwestern United States has seceded under control of an almost feminist political party that has adopted the small-is-beautiful view of the world. After nineteen years it presents a significant contrast to the United States, which has continued to develop as a high technology, urbanized, frantic land of shortages and ever-increasing government interference in the lives of its people.

Utopian thinkers of the nineteenth and twentieth centuries have expressed their ideas in a variety of forms, as suggested by the examples described here. The common theme is that human society can somehow be made better (even those who write dystopias do so because they dislike the direction in which society is moving). How this desirable end is to be achieved continues to be the subject of utopian discussion, more often than not to the detriment of the writer's literary aspirations. Nevertheless, such discussion lights the road to whatever Humanity's future may be, and it is likely that utopias will continue to provide useful additions to the literary scene in coming years.

See also: Arcadia, Beat Generation, Dystopias, Escape, Feminism, Language, Religion in Science-Fiction, Travel.

Selected Bibliography

Biesterfeld, Wolfgang. *Die literarische Utopie*. Stuttgart: Metzler, 1974.

Kateb, George. *Utopia and Its Enemies*. New York: Free Press of Glencoe, 1963.

Manuel, Frank, and Fritzie P. Manuel. *Utopian Thought in the Western World*. Cambridge, Mass.: Belknap Press, 1979.

Roemer, Kenneth M., ed. *America as Utopia, Collected Essays*. New York: B. Franklin, 1981.

Trousson, Raymond. *Voyage aux pays du nulle part, histoire littéraire de la pensée utopique*. 2d ed. Brussels: Editions de l'Université de Bruxelles, 1979.

ARTHUR O. LEWIS

V
//

VAMPIRISM

While not a true literary character until the advent of Continental and British romanticism, the vampire is as old as human superstition itself. Virtually every culture in the world has at its roots some folktales or legends relating to vampirism, and while the stories may differ in terms of content, they concur on a basic definition of the vampire: a reanimated corpse or malevolent spirit whose sole purpose is to destroy the living by absorbing the life force, whether it be in the form of blood or of psychic energy, or perhaps both. The true appeal of vampirism as a literary theme is perhaps best stated in the form of a question, one which Jonathan Harker poses about the real spiritual nature of his fearsome Transylvanian host, Count Dracula, in Bram Stoker's classic novel. "What manner of man is this," Harker asks, "or what manner of creature is it in the semblance of man?" *Dracula* (1897) is clearly the culmination of disparate strains of literary vampirism and remains to this day the work by which all vampire literature is measured, and rightly so. In Harker's inquiry is located the very essence of vampirism, a state that can be defined only in horrifyingly oxymoronic terms. The vampire is undead, which would logically imply that it is alive, but its true state defies any such logic. Harker's question remains basically an unanswerable one. The vampire is both man and creature, a dramatic ambiguity vampire literature explores and oftentimes attempts to resolve.

Locating the origin of the belief in vampires is almost an impossible task, but perhaps the best place to begin is in various religious books of the dead. Such books in Tibet and Egypt set forth a strong belief in a state occupying the realm between life and death, in which the soul, out of its torment, seeks to destroy the living, to bring other souls into its own state. In order to prevent this, these books of the dead prescribe elaborate burial procedures, all of which emphasize that the dead body should never be exposed to nature for any extended period or it will surely undergo some sort of transformation. Tales of reanimated corpses, inspired by the various taboos associated with the dead body, seem to have spread from the Orient and the Middle East to Greece, India, and Africa, where the notion of the corpse's insatiable thirst for human blood became increasingly important. However, it is in eastern Europe where vampire folklore was codified as a proto-literary narrative tradition, and, in fact, here is also found the very etymology of the word "vampire" itself.

In Transylvania, Rumania, Czechoslovakia, Serbia, and Bulgaria, the vampire became a literal presence. Thousands of vampire attacks were recorded between the fifteenth and nineteenth centuries (and in fact are still being recorded today), and with these attacks came innumerable definitions of the vampire through its various characteristics: its thirst for human blood, its shape-shifting powers, supernatural strength, confinement to nocturnal hours, its fear of Christian iconography, and, of course, its gruesome physical appearance, which is highlighted by abnormally long and sharp teeth to facilitate its tearing open its victim's throat. Accompanying these characteristics were various measures for preventing a vampire attack: garlic (because of its strong and offensive odor), wolfbane, the rosary, the crucifix, and mirrors (to reinforce for the vampire its damned state by not casting a reflection). Finally, this folklore supplied the conventional means of disposing of a vampire, with a stake driven through the heart and simultaneous decapitation, after which the body was burned and the mouth stuffed with garlic and thrown in running water or buried to prevent the spirit of the vampire from reclaiming the instrument of its destructive power—its mouth.

Vampirism, as defined by eastern European culture, is a relatively late addition to literature, but strains of it exist in some of the very earliest writings. In book 11 of Homer's epic *Odysseia* (*Odyssey*, c. 8th century B.C.), for example, one of Odysseus' many wanderings leads him to the land of the dead, or the Underworld, where he seeks Tiresias, the blind prophet, who holds valuable information that will enable Odysseus to lead his men back to Ithaca. In order to reach the prophet, however, Odysseus must first supplicate the spirits of the dead with a "drink offering." After digging a pit, Odysseus pours into it a mixture of honey, milk, water, and wine, but it is not until he adds the blood of several sheep that the dead emerge, and only after they have sated themselves do the spirits tell him where he may find Tiresias. A similar blood rite is depicted by Virgil in the *Aeneis* (*Aeneid*, epic poem, 19 B.C.), when in book 6 Aeneas descends to Hades in his journey to Rome. There he encounters souls attempting to appease the Furies by filling bowls with lamb's blood, which they offer to Hecate, the goddess of darkness.

Within the Greek and Roman epic traditions, blood is an all-powerful symbol for both the gods and man. In battle, blood is a necessary element in persuading the gods to show favor, as demonstrated by Agamemnon's required sacrifice of his daughter, Iphigenia, which allows the Greeks to set sail for Troy. Accounts of warriors drinking the blood of their slain enemies to increase their own strength and military prowess abound in the epic. The taint associated with such practices seems not to have existed before the rise of Christianity, which prohibits the drinking of blood, especially during the sacrificial rite. Deuteronomy 12:23–25 makes clear that ingestion of blood is clearly a violation of a taboo:

Only be sure that thou eat not the blood; for the blood is the life; and thou mayest not eat the life with the flesh. Thou shalt not eat it; thou shalt pour it upon the earth as water. Thou shalt not eat it; that it may go well with thee, and with thy children after thee, when thou shalt do that which is right in the sight of the Lord.

Of course, a major contradiction arises with the introduction of the Eucharist to Christian practice. When during the Last Supper, Christ commands his disciples to drink of the wine, he tells them they are actually drinking the blood he will soon shed for them. Even though the blood that is drunk during the ritual is purely symbolic, its power is not, for it contains the life, eternal life. Here, within this very cornerstone of Christianity, is located the pervasive spirit of evil in the vampire's literal interpretation of Christ's admonition; it drinks the blood for eternal life. This daring reversal of the Christian rite will provide writers of vampire literature with the powerful spirit of attraction and repulsion that accompanies the violation of any taboo, but especially the taboo of spilling and drinking blood.

One of the first and most blatant literary violators of the blood taboo is Lamia, a character in Greek mythology who has inspired the creation of innumerable female vampires. According to myth, Lamia was one of Zeus's many lovers, but one who unfortunately aroused Hera's most destructive jealousy. Out of spite, Hera cursed Lamia with madness, which intensified to such a degree that Lamia eventually killed and devoured her own children. Thereafter, she became one of the most feared "night monsters," who sustained herself on the blood of the young. The story is recounted by Philostratus in a tale about Mennipus and Apollonius included in his biography, *Ta es ton Tyanea Apollōnion* (*The Life of Apollonius of Tyana*, c. A.D. 120). In the story, "the lamia," as she came to be known, appears as a true vampire who with her beauty lures young men into the trap of marriage, after which she makes them her wedding feast. Mennipus is fortunate enough to escape this fate because of the intervention of Apollonius, the great philosopher and mystic, who drives away the lamia by confronting her with her true identity. A similar story is told by Phlegon of Tralles in "Phillinion," one of the many "Wondrous Things" that make up *Peri thaumasion* (*Mirabilia*, treatise, A.D. 2d century). Like the lamia, the female vampire who appears here is exceedingly lovely and attains easy admittance to her male prey's bedroom to destroy him in a moment of passion.

The Lamia myth receives an extensive treatment in Goethe's Gothic ballad, "Die Braut von Korinth" ("The Bride of Corinth," 1797), which re-introduces the female vampire to literature after a virtual 1,700–year absence. Even though cannibalistic monsters appear in much earlier literature (Grendel and his mother in the epic *Beowulf* [c. 8th century] being prime examples), vampirism as a fully developed theme did not come into currency until the beginnings of Continental and British romanticism, and Goethe's vampire ballad is one of the first literary works to concern itself wholly with the theme.

The motif of the dead lover returning from the grave is certainly not original with Goethe, but his blending of the motif with vampirism is. The young man in the poem who comes to Corinth in search of his bride meets her only in the darkest hours of the night when she appears, "veiled in white," in his bedroom. Initially, the girl seems quite weak, but soon she undergoes a dramatic transformation:

> Dully boomed the ghosting midnight hour;
> Only now her eyes take on a shine,
> Pallid lips of hers, now they devour,
> Gulping it, the bloody coloured wine,
> But of wheaten bread
> Offered by the lad
> Not a single crumb to take would deign.

Soon after, her "breathless kiss" arouses the boy's passion and during a moment of sexual frenzy, she sucks the blood from his heart. When her mother interrupts her ghastly feeding, the girl tells of her agony beyond the grave and begs her mother to remove her body from the tomb and to burn it, or else she will "with my fury tear young folk apart."

Of the many significant features of Goethe's poem, one is of special interest— the explicitly erotic treatment of the vampire attack, a secondary theme that will become more important in later vampire literature. And clearly this erotic impulse accounts in large part for the popularity of the female vampire among male writers, who express both a fascination with and a fear of the power of unrepressed female sexuality, an impulse Coleridge defines brilliantly in "Christabel" (1816). The poem introduces the vampire into English literature in the form of Geraldine, a virtual dynamo of destructive sexual energy. While her initial goal is to usher the naïve Christabel into the world of vampirism (Coleridge's vehicle for free sexual expression), her simultaneous purpose is to undercut the power of the patriarchy, represented in the poem by Sir Leoline, Christabel's father. By the time Geraldine completes her diabolical plan, Sir Leoline is virtually powerless even in his own castle. He can only have Geraldine escorted out, which leaves Christabel "O'er-mastered by the mighty spell" Geraldine has cast over her, the consequences of which Coleridge merely allows the reader to ponder.

While the poem is a resounding statement of the male attraction to and repulsion from female sexual energy, conceived in the form of vampirism, it also develops many of the conventions of vampire literature. Geraldine appears to Christabel in the forest as Christabel is fantasizing about her departed lover. Little does Christabel know that the "damsel bright / Drest in a silken robe of white" is actually a vampire. Because the castle has been blessed by the spirit of Christianity, Geraldine cannot enter it of her own volition; she must be carried inside, a motif that becomes a major element in later literature; that is, showing that a vampire must be invited in by the intended victim. Once inside the castle, Geraldine reacts violently to the mention of the name of the Virgin and to any form of Christian iconography. She also fears the family dog, who senses her true nature. The vampire attacks themselves, while not presented in any graphic form, are charged with obvious erotic overtones as Geraldine progressively absorbs Christabel's energy, making her a tool in her subversive plot to supplant male supremacy.

Keat's *Lamia* (poem, 1820) carries the attraction/repulsion theme even further by exploring the true nature of the female vampire, who first appears in the poem in her actual form—a snake. However, she is a snake of "dazzling hue," exhibiting a magnetic beauty amidst the ugliness of her form, a beauty that is externalized when Hermes transforms Lamia into physical form. Just as the beauty has been externalized, so the poisonous nature of her being has been internalized. Based on the Mennipus and Apollonius legend, Keats's poem delves deeply into the torment inherent in the life of the vampire as both a creature and a human. Lamia's love for the young Lycius is countered by her own attraction/repulsion exhibited by her need for the warm blood of her fiancé and her disgust over that need. Keats creates a sense of tragedy associated with the vampire that neither Goethe nor Coleridge had developed completely. When at the end of the poem, Lamia is exposed as a vampire, the truth kills her lover, who becomes a victim not of a direct vampire attack, but of the destructive potential of female sexuality, a theme Keats also explores in the ballad "La Belle Dame sans Merci," written in the same year as *Lamia*.

Perhaps the most romantic portrayal of the female vampire is found in Poe. In Poe's works, where the death of a beautiful woman is the greatest subject for literature, we find a number of vampiristic women. Madeline Usher, in "The Fall of the House of Usher" (1839), and Ligeia, in the story of the same name (1840), are but two of many of Poe's women who rise from the dead to wreak havoc on the surviving male lover. In "Berenice" (tale, 1840), the lover's fear of the return of the dead woman to carry out his destruction is so great that he opens her grave in order to remove her teeth, to make her powerless. As did his British counterparts, Poe develops such stories around the attraction/repulsion syndrome, or more appropriately, a sado-masochistic spirit that controls the male characters who appear to will the return of the dead woman as some form of death wish while they simultaneously fear that return. Yet, the attraction (or masochism) is the stronger of the two impulses, and Poe's men cannot suppress their desire to be dominated and destroyed by the sexual energy of women.

Willed female domination and vampiristic elements that make the domination even more pleasurable are a large part of the Marquis de Sade's hedonistic vision in novels such as *Justine* (1791), *Juliette* (1797), and *La philosophie dans le boudoir* (*The Philosophy of the Bedroom*, 1795). Similar decadent strains are found in tales such as Théophile Gautier's *La morte amoreuse* (*The Loving Dead*, 1836), in which a priest willingly exchanges his blood for sex with a female vampire, Clarimonde. Yet, the erotic vampire theme received its most explicit treatment in Sheridan Le Fanu's *Carmilla* (1872), a novella inspired by Coleridge's "Christabel." Employing the vampire story as a vehicle, Le Fanu systematically exposes the hypocrisy of sexual repression by demonstrating through Carmilla, the beautiful and seductive vampire, that true pleasure comes from free sexual exchange.

Le Fanu relies heavily on the setting and characters of "Christabel," relocating and renaming them in eastern Europe. Like Geraldine, Carmilla gains entrance to the world of the unsuspecting victims by invitation, in this case, to a party. Left by her "mother" in the care of Laura and her father, Carmilla soon charms both and becomes the friend and confidant of the sheltered Laura, who lives in a world of men and has yet to come to any understanding of herself as a woman. Carmilla's incessant attacks on Laura prove both a pleasurable and a painful method by which Laura slowly comes to see herself as a sexual being, an awareness she conveys by her choice of language in which to describe her feelings during the vampire attack:

Certain vague and strange sensations visited me in my sleep. The prevailing one was of that pleasant, peculiar cold thrill which we feel in bathing, when we move against the current of a river. This was soon accompanied by dreams that seemed interminable, and were so vague that I could never recollect their scenery or persons, or any one connected portion of their action. But they left an awful impression, and a sense of exhaustion, as if I had passed through a long period of great mental exertion and danger. . . . Sometimes there came a sensation as if a hand was drawn softly along my cheek and neck. Sometimes it was as if warm lips kissed me, longer and more lovingly as they reached my throat, but there the caress fixed itself. My heart beat faster, my breathing rose and fell rapidly and full drawn; a sobbing, that rose into a dreadful convulsion, in which my senses left me, and I became unconscious.

In this and similar passages in *Carmilla*, the eroticism linked to vampirism achieves its fullest statement to date, paving the way for the even more explicit language Bram Stoker would employ in *Dracula*.

After *Carmilla*, the female vampire gives way to the supremacy of the male vampire, yet she lives on in various manifestations in later literature. The misogynistic vision of Strindberg (1849–1912), for example, finds a fitting image of women in the form of the vampire, who seeks not to destroy men in any pleasurable fashion but in a sadistic battle of wills, and in Strindberg's plays she is more often successful than not. Eugene O'Neill (1888–1953) follows a similar view of women in drama, and often the battle for supremacy ends in the spiritual if not physical death of men. These are but two examples of the twentieth-century view of the female vampire, who serves as an expression of male fascination with and fear of the mysterious sexual nature of women.

The origin of vampirism as an instrument of male supremacy is relatively easy to trace. While elements of male vampirism are again evident in Sade's work, the appearance of John Stagg's ballad "The Vampyre" in 1810 introduces the male vampire in literature. Written partially as a treatise on vampirism, the ballad codifies the literary motifs that will develop the theme in later writing, most importantly the motif of death by the stake through the heart. Nine years later, John Polidori, Lord Byron's personal physician and friend, inspired by Stagg's poem, penned the first actual vampire novel, titling it simply *The Vampyre; A Tale*. This is a literary effort resulting from the famous evening in Geneva when Percy and Mary Shelley, Byron, and Polidori all agreed to write a ghost story, an agreement that also saw the publication of Mary Shelley's *Frankenstein* (1818).

Lord Ruthven, the vampire in Polidori's novel, is based on both Byron and his literary counterpart, the Byronic hero. In his introduction Polidori quotes extensively from Byron's poem, *The Giaour* (1813), in which the title character is cursed with the fate of the living dead:

> But first on earth, as Vampyre sent,
> Thy corse shall from its tomb rent;
> Then ghastly haunt the native place,
> And suck the blood of all thy race;
> There from thy daughter, sister, wife,
> At midnight drain the stream of life;
> Yet loathe the banquet which perforce
> Must feed thy living corse,
> Thy victims, ere yet they expire,
> Shall know the demon for their sire;
> As cursing thee, thou cursing them,
> Thy flowers are withered on the stem.

Ruthven, the nobleman with the "dead grey eye" and "deadly hue of his face," exemplifies the plight of the vampire as Byronic hero, who in gaining access to the highest circles of society, despises his existence and wishes all those around him dead, yet he also despises this attitude. As a counterpoint to his high social standing, Ruthven engages in a life of vice, in which he constantly seeks physical gratification of both his sexual and vampiristic needs. During Ruthven's attacks on women, Polidori catalogues the various attributes of the vampire, including his incredible strength, his hypnotic power over women, the marks of the teeth on the victims' throats, and the vampire's hatred of itself and its existence, which Ruthven quite accurately describes in the same terms that fit the Byronic hero: "I heed the death of my existence," he says, "as little as that of the passing day."

Even though Byron himself attempted to write a vampire novel in 1816, he was unable to sustain in prose what he had done in poetry. Nonetheless, he created heroes in such poems as *The Giaour* (1813), *Lara* (1814), and *Manfred* (1817), who were vastly influential in the development of the theme of male domination through vampirism. The "fatal embrace" of the Byronic hero and his yearning to die while living a life in which everything he touches withers and dies encapsulate the vampire as romantic hero, who like Byron's own vision of Prometheus, is half man-half diety, albeit in the case of the vampire, a Satanic deity. This form of existence in the Byronic vision is akin to that of the vampire, for as Manfred states at the end of Byron's closet drama:

> I linger yet with Nature, for the Night
> Hath been to me a more familiar face
> Than that of man; and in her starry shade
> Of dim and solitary loneliness,
> I learned the language of another world.

This form of immortality or deity is, as Byron writes, "the immortality of Hell." And it is precisely this form of immortality that makes the Byronic hero and the vampire fitting examples of the romantic spirit. Aware of a potential power within the self, both the Byronic hero and the vampire see only destruction as its result, yet it is the power itself that holds the attraction.

While the image of the male vampire as lethal lover undergoes various changes at the hands of writers such as Prosper Mérimée (*La Guzla* [*The Ghoul*, poems, 1827]), Nikolai Gogol ("Viĭ" ["Viy," 1835]), and Tolstoy ("Vampir" ["The Vampire," 1841]), vampirism did not provide commercial success for writers until well into the Victorian period in England, where the vampire tale became a bestseller, resulting in countless "shilling shockers" by hack writers, who stress the graphic bloodletting of the vampire attack. In the age of conservative morality and the Industrial Revolution, the vampire emerges as a reflection of both unrepressed sexuality and unrestrained aristocratic greed. The best and most influential of these commercial efforts was Thomas Peckett Prest's *Varney the Vampire, or The Feast of Blood* (1847). Through 868 pages of the original edition, Sir Francis Varney, a decadent nobleman, dominates and drains the blood of an entire family of aristocratic heritage, providing Prest with the means to attempt a rather unsophisticated form of social criticism, in which the vampire is linked to the cannibalistic urges of the upper class in their quest for power. Yet Prest also carries through the erotic impulse that apparently allows women to submit to the blatant form of sexual supremacy. While the novel ultimately is a badly written exercise in pure sensationalism, its impact was enormous and partly explains why late Victorian England was ready for the greatest vampire novel of them all.

Bram Stoker's *Dracula* is without doubt the boldest and most comprehensive treatment of vampirism. Count Dracula encompasses every characteristic of the vampire that had been established up to that time, while embodying new ones as well. He is a Victorian revision of the Byronic hero, whose tragedy gives him greatness, and like Sir Frances Varney, he is also a wealthy nobleman who literally devours the peasant class of his native Transylvania and then moves on to England for the same purpose. His supernatural power also establishes him as a dominator not only of women, but also virtually of all men, save one, Dr. Abraham Van Helsing, an interesting reincarnation of Apollonius, the great seer and interpreter. And perhaps the most effective element of the novel, an aspect that preceding vampire literature had never quite developed, is the inversion of

Christianity, which adds the true horror to the theme of vampirism. Dracula becomes, in essence, an embodiment of a Satanic Christ-figure, who in the world of the novel seems to hold as powerful a sway over human events as God does.

The life of vampirism is revealed as one of complete inversion, over which Dracula stands as lord. The ghastly baptism and Eucharist rituals he practices on both Lucy Westenra and Mina Harker are the boldest perversions of Christian practice, yet they are presented in such persuasively erotic terms that they almost become acceptable to the reader. Dracula is, of course, an inversion of the Victorian man, who is well-represented in the novel by Jonathan Harker, Arthur Holmwood, John Seward, and Van Helsing. Unlike his living counterparts, Dracula shows no restraint, and here lies the attraction women feel for him, as well as the repulsion men experience in his presence. He is pure, unbridled animal energy, and as such, he is clearly a threat to both sexes. By making women his victims, Dracula releases their suppressed sexual energies, thus in turn, posing a threat to men, who are entirely unaccustomed to aggressively sexual women. They find it both arousing and disgusting at the same time, as Harker reveals in his encounter with the female vampires in Dracula's castle.

In the repressed society of Victorian England, Dracula is perceived as an almost apocalyptic agent who seeks to destroy every social convention and moral conviction in his efforts to bring the outside world into his world of living death, where pleasure is momentary and torment eternal, a daring inversion of Christ's promise of eternal life through drinking his blood. Dracula reverses the emphasis, and by taking the blood for himself, leaves his victims in a state of eternal damnation, unless they are fortunate enough to be released by an all-knowing Van Helsing with a stake through the heart. Curiously though, Harker explains the motivation for killing Dracula not as one to redeem society or to reinforce the power of Christianity, but simply as the need to save one woman, Mina, his wife. The threat of released female power is far more dangerous to a patriarchal society than the actual vampire himself.

In the twentieth century, few attempts have been made to supplant *Dracula* as the definitive vampire novel. Writers such as F. Marion Crawford, H. P. Lovecraft, Algernon Blackwood, and M. R. James experimented with the theme, but provided few new insights. Recently, however, Stephen King successfully rejuvenated the vampire in *'Salem's Lot* (novel, 1975), importing it to the New England village, an archetype in itself, thanks primarily to the witchcraft crisis in seventeenth-century Salem, Massachusetts, and to Hawthorne's tireless analyses of the human evil that thrives in such villages. Interestingly, King drops the erotic overtones of vampirism that had done so much to develop the theme; instead, he concentrates on the element of social criticism, which Victorian vampire literature had also incorporated. Vampirism in King's novel becomes the way by which neighbor kills neighbor and friend destroys friend without moral impunity, releasing man's destructive capacity, which American law and culture have attempted to keep concealed.

Far more attractive to the modern writer is the theme of psychic vampirism, in which the attack is on the mind and not the body. This form of vampirism can be traced to the origins of literature itself, if literally interpreted as a struggle of wills. However, the earliest examples of it as a vampiristic act appear in nineteenth-century novels in the deeds of men such as Heathcliff in Emily Brontë's *Wuthering Heights* (1847), Vohles in Dickens' *Bleak House* (1853), and Hawthorne's Roger Chillingworth (*The Scarlet Letter,* 1850) and Judge Pyncheon (*House of the Seven Gables,* 1851). In Guy de Maupassant's story, "Le Horla" ("The Horla," 1887), the psychic vampire achieves a fame almost equal to its physical counterpart. A feverish narrator, reminiscent of many of those who people Poe's fiction, insists that some invisible agent is slowly draining away his energy, and in this awareness and in his attempts to destroy the force (which he comes to call "the Horla"), he goes mad and decides to take his own life rather than have it taken from him.

With few exceptions (Ray Bradbury's novel *Something Wicked This Way Comes* [1962] being one of them), psychic vampirism leads into the proliferation of science fiction, in which the vampire becomes an alien of some sort, and this of course, represents a totally different catalogue of themes, vampirism being only a minor one. Yet the traditional theme of vampirism continues to hold a special fascination, for it is certainly one of the strongest anti-social themes in all of literature, which makes it one of the most attractive. Vampirism's capacity to express fear, eroticism, the quest for sexual domination, social criticism, and a clear violation of basic taboos ensure its perpetual success. Like the vampire itself, the literary theme of vampirism never dies; it merely rests.

See also: Horror, Lesbianism, Monsters, Werewolf.

Selected Bibliography

Carter, Margaret L. *Shadows of a Shade: A Survey of Vampirism in Literature.* New York: Gordon Press, 1976.

Masters, Anthony. *The Natural History of the Vampire.* New York: G.P. Putnam's Sons, 1972.

Summers, Montague. *The Vampire: His Kith and Kin.* 1928. New York: New Hyde Park, 1960.

Wright, Dudley. *Vampires and Vampirism.* 1914. New York: Gordon Press, 1973.

GARY L. GREEN

W
//

WEREWOLF

A werewolf is a human being who has been transformed into a wolf. In animal form, the werewolf is generally depicted as a ravaging, ravenous killer; but world literature contains several examples of sympathetic, even heroic werewolves. The term is most likely a combination of the Old English words for "man" *(were,* cf. Latin *vir)* and "wolf" *(wulf).* The theme is also referred to as lycanthropy, from the Greek words for "human being" *(anthropos)* and "wolf" *(lukos).*

Lycanthropy is in fact but a specific aspect of the larger theme of metamorphosis. Wereanimals of many types occur in folklore and literature, from were-leopards to werecrocodiles. Several major works of world literature have as their subject the transformation of a human being into an animal. Apuleius' Latin prose romance *Metamorphoses (The Golden Ass,* c. 150) uses the theme of a man transformed into an ass as a basis for a philosphical inquiry into the vanity of the search for transitory pleasures and mundane knowledge. Franz Kafka, in his short story "Die Verwandlung" ("The Metamorphosis," 1915), uses the image of a man transformed into a beetle to dramatize, among other things, the pain of alienation.

It is the werewolf, however, that has held the greatest fascination for the Western imagination; and the metamorphosis from human being to wolf is treated often and with many variations in literature. The transformation may be temporary, may recur periodically, or may be permanent. When voluntary, the transformation usually involves knowledge of magic and a set of ritual actions. Involuntary transformation is most often the result of a curse or a magic spell; however, folklore abounds also in accidental causes, among which are sleeping outdoors under a full moon and eating the flesh of a rabid wolf.

Few recurring literary motifs have so readily discernible an underlying meaning as does that of lycanthropy. In essence, the metamorphosis of man into beast represents the triumph of our bestial nature over reason. Nor is the fascination with the wolf difficult to understand; for wolves have long been viewed as graphic symbols of unrestrained violence. The Western tradition, in particular, emphasizes the ferocity and ravenous hunger of that animal, two qualities that are stressed in many comparisons with men; for example, in the Bible the wicked princes of Jerusalem are likened to "wolves tearing the prey, destroying lives to get dishonest gain" (Ezek. 22:27). Boethius, whose *De consolatione philosophiae* (*The Consolation of Philosophy*. c. 524) was among the most widely read and influential books in the Middle Ages, argues that the sinful man, by yielding to bestial desires, forfeits his humanity, the greedy man being like a wolf. Lord Byron, in *Don Juan* (1819–1824) offers a poetic restatement of the same interpretation: "Lycanthropy/I comprehend, for without transformation/ Men become wolves on any slight occasion." The most famous psychiatric interpretation of lycanthropy is by Ernest Jones in *On the Nightmare* (1931). Jones sees the werewolf fantasy as arising from feelings of sexual jealousy and hostility and as being "throughout sadistic in nature." Finally, the concept may be related to a form of mental illness in which an individual believes that he/ she is in fact a wolf. This malady, known as "lycanthropia," is defined by Robert Burton in the *Anatomy of Melancholy* (1621) as "wolf-madness, when men run howling about graves and fields in the night, and will not be persuaded but that they are wolves."

The werewolf symbolizes, then, the capacity of human beings to behave as beasts, doing violence to society and themselves. The concept of metamorphosis dramatizes the divorce of the individual from a social context; the image of man as an animal can be seen as a representation of the failure to harmonize the rational and emotional elements of the human psyche.

Antiquity

Although werewolves are mentioned by several Greek writers, among them Plato and Herodotus, the first significant treatment of lycanthropy as a literary theme occurs in the *Metamorphoses* (epic poem, c. A.D. 2–17) by the Roman poet Ovid. He recounts the Greek myth of Lycaon, who was transformed by Jupiter into a wolf as fit punishment for his inhuman treatment of guests. Here can be seen already the use of the werewolf as a symbol for the loss of one's moral humanness. More elaborate is the werewolf story introduced by the Roman author Petronius into his *Satyricon* (novel, A.D. 60). Petronius' werewolf can transform himself at will. In his bestial shape, he wreaks havoc among sheep and cattle.

The Middle Ages

The Christian Middle Ages produced the finest literary treatments of lycanthropy. The medieval interest in werewolves has a theological basis. Since in medieval Christian theology sin must involve rational consent, evil deeds committed by a transformed human being would not be sinful. And what would happen to the soul of an individual who dies a werewolf? Among the Christian theologians to deal with werewolves and other wereanimals were St. Augustine and St. Thomas Aquinas, both of whom argue what became the orthodox position that the transformation of a human by magic or the devil cannot actually occur and therefore must be only an illusion. Belief in werewolves is, for the Christian, a sin.

Medieval narratives tend to take a sympathetic view of the werewolf and place less emphasis upon depiction of his animal savagery. Marie de France's lay, *Bisclavret* (c. 1170), concerns a gallant knight who, because of a curse upon his family, must spend three days of every week as a werewolf. When his faithless wife, whom he tells of his dilemma, steals his clothes while he is in his animal form, he is condemned to be a lycanthrope perpetually. However, captured by a king who is out hunting, he impresses his captor with his humanlike intelligence. Eventually, the werewolf regains his human form and returns to a life of chivalric adventure. The wife is properly punished. Marie employs the werewolf theme to portray human qualities. The "beast" is less feral than his greedy wife; and he regains his humanity through the sympathy and charity of the king (perhaps a symbol of divine grace), who looks beneath physical ugliness to see moral beauty in the wolf.

Three other medieval narratives include sympathetic werewolves. In the anonymous French narrative *Guillaume de Palerne* (c. 1195), the werewolf is in reality Alphonse, the rightful heir to the Spanish throne, who has been transformed through the evil magic of his stepmother. Even in his bestial form, Alphonse retains his human powers of reason and memory, and he too regains his humanness. Similarly, the Latin tale known as *Arthur and Gorlagon* (c. 1200) tells of a king who is turned into a wolf by the trickery of his faithless wife, but later saved by another king whom he impresses by his unbestial behavior. He too becomes a man again. Finally, Giraldus Cambrensis includes in his *Topographia hibernica* (*Topography of Ireland*, c. 1215) the story of a couple who is compelled to spend seven years as wolves. When the wife is dying, the husband goes to a startled priest to seek the last rites for her. Giraldus' tale uses the medieval theory of "illusory change"; for when the male werewolf rolls back a portion of his wife's animal skin, her human form is revealed beneath.

The Renaissance through the Eighteenth Century

The werewolf theme is by and large ignored in literature from the Middle Ages until the nineteenth century. Cervantes does make use of folklore about lycanthropy in *Los trabajos de Persiles y Sigismunda* (*Persiles and Sigismunda* novel, 1617); and a werewolf is a character in John Webster's *The Duchess of Malfi* (play, 1613). However, most mentions of lycanthropy in these centuries occur in legal and theological rather than literary texts. The inquisition, during which numerous individuals were convicted of being werewolves, is responsible for many of these accounts. Among the most influential discussions of werewolves are Francesco Guazzo's *Compendium maleficarum* (*Manual of Witches*, 1608) and Jean de Nynauld's *Lycanthropie* (1615).

The Nineteenth and Twentieth Centuries

The werewolf emerges again as a literary theme in the mid-nineteenth century. Lycanthropy became particularly common as a subject for short stories. No novel of exceptional literary merit was built on the theme. In Germany, the novel *Der Wärwolf* by Willibald Alexis (1848) was extremely popular, although now it is all but unknown. Typical of the treatment of lycanthropy in longer narratives is the melodramatic *Wagner, The Wehr-Wolf* (1857), by George W. M. Reynolds, which exploits the horrific but not the philosophic possibilities of the theme. A better but equally melodramatic novel is *Le meneur de loups* (*The Wolf Leader*, 1857), by Alexandre Dumas, père.

Among the major nineteenth- and early twentieth-century authors who based short stories on the werewolf theme are Algernon Blackwood, Guy de Maupassant, Rudyard Kipling, Saki (H.H. Munro), and Robert Louis Stevenson. In many respects the best nineteenth century werewolf tale is Maupassant's "Le loup," ("The White Wolf", 1882), a story of revenge that employs the image of the lycanthrope to portray man's inherent savagery. Beginning at the turn of the century, stories about female werewolves become more frequent; and it has been suggested that interest in this variation on the theme by male writers may be connected with the emergence of the women's suffrage movement. Among the best stories concerning a female werewolf is "The Were-Wolf" (1896), by Clemence Housman.

In the twentieth century, lycanthropy has remained a popular but artistically limited theme. Guy Endore's *The Werewolf of Paris* (1933) is widely regarded as the finest werewolf novel. Endore interweaves the story of the werewolf Bertrand Caillet (based on an historical figure) with the history of Paris in the late nineteenth century. Endore does more than exploit the theme for violence; for the bestiality of the werewolf pales in comparison with that of the untransformed humans responsible for the Communards' harsh rule and the horrors of the French bourgeois government's counterrevolution. The one major twentieth-century author to base a novel on the theme is Frank Norris. The protagonist in his first novel (published posthumously, 1914), *Vandover and the Brute,* believes himself to be a werewolf—a delusion identified within the narrative by the pseudo-medical term "lycanthropiamathesis." In the novel, which is a study of Vandover's moral degeneration, the werewolf theme serves as a symbolic representation of his inability to curb the animal—that is, sensual—element of his nature.

For the most part, in the twentieth century the werewolf theme has been largely ignored in serious literature, but has been a staple of mass entertainment. It has been especially popular as a subject for motion pictures; since 1941, for example, more than twenty-five movies have been based on the theme. Endore's novel has been adapted twice for the cinema: *The Werewolf of London* (1935) and *Curse of the Werewolf* (1961). Of the many cinematic versions, the most famous is *The Wolf Man* (1941). The films, like most literary versions, emphasize the werewolf primarily as the embodiment of savagery.

In contemporary American literature, the theme survives mainly as a stock element of popular novels and pulp fiction, where with rare exceptions the emphasis is upon ferocity and horror rather than the psychological implications of lycanthropy. Perhaps the best of the short stories from the pulp magazines is Bruce Elliott's "Wolves Don't Cry" (1954), a story that inverts the traditional theme by examining the reaction of a wolf that is suddenly transformed into a human being. Outside the pulp magazines, the finest twentieth-century short story about lycanthropy is undoubtedly "Lila, the Werewolf" (1974), by Peter S. Beagle, author of the highly praised fantasy novel *The Last Unicorn* (1968). The werewolf in Beagle's ironic tale is a woman, for whom the recurrent transformations into a wild beast are less annoying than her allergies. Beagle uses the reactions of Lila's befuddled lover to explore the nature of human relationships in a cynical urban society.

In general, the obvious symbolic value of the werewolf seems to have stunted its development as a literary theme. Most literary treatments are but variations on the idea of bestial violence freed from the restraints of reason and morality and exploit the horrific aspects of the concept without using it as the basis for more thoughtful investigation. Only a few works, such as *Bisclavret* and "Lila the Werewolf," have delved into the philosophical or psychological implications of the theme. The most compelling literary treatments of the metamorphosis theme are about, not a wolf, but an ass and a beetle.

See also: Monsters, Metamorphosis, Unicorn.

Selected Bibliography

Baring-Gould, Sabine. *The Book of Werewolves*. 1865. New York: Causeway Books, 1973.

Eisler, Robert, *Man into Wolf*. London: Routledge and Paul, 1951.

Summers, Montague. *The Werewolf*. London: K. Paul, Trench, Trubner, 1933.

Woodward, Ian. *The Werewolf Delusion*. New York: Paddington Press, 1979.

DENNIS M. KRATZ

CROSS-INDEX

//

The following list contains in alphabetical order, key words for terms used in entry titles as well as alternate or subsidiary terms. The terms on this list refer the reader to the appropriate entry or entries.

Absurd: Alienation, Existentialism, Nihilism, Theatrical Absurdity, Tragicomic Hero.
Actor: Role Playing.
Adolescense: Adolescence.
Adult: Adolescence.
Adultery: *Liebestod*, Secret Love, Sex, (Heterosexual, Erotic).
Adventure: Travel.
Afterlife: Afterlife, Descent into Hell.
Agnosticism: Epistemology.
Air: Demonic Musician and the Soulbird.
Alchemy: Alchemy
Alcoholism: Anxiety.
Alienation: Alienation, Anti-Hero, Anti-Semitism, Escape, Existentialism, Hermit, Trag-
    icomic Hero.
Amazon: Amazons.
Androgyny: Androgyny.
Angel: Incubus and Succubus, Daemon.
Animals: Bear; Butterflies; Dragons; Grotesque; Hunt; Lion; Monsters; Rat, Mouse; Un-
    icorn; Werewolf.
Anti-hero: Anti-Hero, Anti-Intellectualism, Nihilism, Picaresque, Scapegoat, Tragicomic
    Hero.
Anti-intellectualism: Anti-Intellectualism.
Anti-Semitism: Anti-Semitism.
Anti-utopia: Dystopias.
Anxiety: Anxiety, Dream, Existentialism.
Apocalypse: Apocalypse, Divine Tutor, Religion in Science Fiction.
Apology: Apology (Self-Defense of Satirists and Humorists).
Arcadia: Arcadia.
Aristocracy: Social Status of Hero.

Art: Artist in Literature through the Renaissance, Artist/Poet in Drama since the Renaissance, Cinema, Dance, Emblem, Hieroglyphics, Masque or Mask.

Artist: Artist in Literature through the Renaissance, Artist/Poet in Drama since the Renaissance, Literature within Literature.

Asceticism: Hermit.

Astrology: Universe.

Astronomy: Universe.

Atomic Age: Science.

Autobiography: Autobiographical Impulse, Literature within Literature.

Bandit: Noble Criminal.

Banker: Banker, Financier, and Usurer.

Banquet: Eating.

Bear: Bear.

Beast: Grotesque.

Beat: Beat Generation, Hippie.

Beauty: Sublimity.

Bird: Demonic Musician and the Soulbird.

Birth: Birth of the Hero.

Black: Underground Man.

Body: Crippling, Lameness, Vampirism.

Bourgeois: Banker, Financier, and Usurer.

Braggart soldier: Braggart.

Bridge: Afterlife.

Brother: Incest.

Business: Capitalism.

Butterflies: Butterflies.

Cabbalism: Alchemy.

Capitalism: Banker, Financier, and Usurer; Capitalism.

Castration: Lameness.

Cave: Cave, Tower.

Cavern; Labyrinth.

Chance: Fortune.

Charity: Christian Hero.

Child, Children: Adolescence, Family, Great Father, Marriage, Parents and Children, Search for Father.

Christianity: Anti-Semitism, Apocalypse, Christian Hero, Christianity Versus Christendom, Death and the Individual, Demonic Music, Descent into Hell, Divine Tutor, Dragons, Evil, Existentialism, Fool, Hermit, Pact with the Devil, Rebellion, Time, Universe, Vampirism.

Cinema: Cinema.

City: City, Retreat.

Civilization: Noble Savage.

Class: Peasant in Novels, Social Status of Hero.

Clergy: Christianity Versus Christendom.

Cleverness: Stupidity.

Clothing: Clothing.

Clown: Braggart, Fool.

Colonies: History in American Literature.

Comedy: Comedy (Comic Spirit).

Comic: Apology (Self-Defense of Satirists and Humorists), Comedy (Comic Spirit), Comic Hero, Laughter, Tragicomic Hero.

Commerce: Capitalism.

Communication: Dialogue, Language.

Communism: Underground Man.

Computer: Robots and Computers.

Confession: Autobiographical Impulse.

Confidence man: Picaresque, *Pícaro* in American Literature, The.

Contemplation: Retreat.

Conversation: Dialogue.

Conversion: Prostitute with a Good Heart.

Cosmos: City, Dance, Jealousy, Nature: *Naturae Cursus* and the State of Nature; Universe.

Countryside: Arcadia, Escape, Mountaineering, Noble Savage, Peasant in Novels, Psychic Landscape, Retreat.

Courtly love: Love Triangle, Secret Love.

Courtship: Dance.

Crime: Detective, Rape.

Criminal: Detective.

Cripple: Crippling, Dwarf, Fool, Lameness.

Daemon: Daemon.

Damnation: Pact with the Devil.

Dance: Dance, Dance of Death, Demonic Music.

Daughter: Incest, Parents and Children, Search for Father.

Death: Afterlife, Dance of Death, Death and the Individual, Demonic Musician and the Soulbird, Descent into Hell, Detective, Grotesque, Horror, *Liebestod*, Terror, Vampirism.

Deformity: Crippling, Dwarf, Lameness.

Deliquent: Picaresque.

Demon: Daemon, Demonic Music, Demonic Musician and the Soulbird, Grotesque, Incubus and Succubus, Pact with the Devil.

Destiny: Responsibility.

Detective: Detective.

Devil: Crippling; Daemon; Demonic Music; Demonic Musician and the Soulbird; Descent into Hell; Dragons; Evil; Grotesque; Incubus and Succubus; Lameness; Pact with the Devil; Rat, Mouse; Scatology; Shadow.

Dialogue: Dialogue.

Dictator: Leader.

Discrimination: Anti-Semitism.

Disguise: Androgyny, Lesbianism, Role Playing.

Don Juan: Libertine, Seduction.

Doom: Apocalypse.

Double: Personality (Double-Split-Multiple), Shadow.

Dragon: Dragons.

Dream: Dream, Incubus and Succubus.

Drugs: Beat Generation.

Dupe: Picaresque, Stupidity.

Friendship: Homosexuality, Lesbianism.

Frog: Rat, Mouse.

Future: Apocalypse, Dystopias.

Garden: Arcadia.

Ghost: Shadow.

God: Birth of the Hero, Death and the Individual, Divine Tutor, Evil, Existentialism, Language, Nature: *Naturae Cursus* and the State of Nature; Nihilism, Reason, Rebellion, Science, Theatrical Absurdity, Time, Underground Man.

Gods and Goddesses: Androgyny, Birth of the Hero, Butterflies, Descent into Hell, Divine Tutor, Dragons, Evil, Great Father, Jealousy, Lameness, Libertine, Love in Greek and Roman Literature, Metamorphosis, Monsters, Rape, Rebellion, Reason, Seduction, Vampirism.

Government: Nature: *Naturae Cursus* and the State of Nature.

Grace: Christian Hero.

Great Father: Great Father.

Great Mother: Cave.

Greed: Money.

Grotesque: Grotesque.

Grotto: Cave.

Guide: Afterlife, Demonic Musician and the Soulbird.

Hedonism: Sex (Heterosexual, Erotic).

Hell: Afterlife, Descent into Hell, Pact with the Devil.

Hermit: Hermit, Retreat.

Hero: Anti-Hero, Anxiety, Birth of the Hero, Braggart, Christian Hero, Comic Hero, Leader, Noble Criminal, Social Status of Hero, Spy, Tragicomic Hero.

Hieroglyphics: Hieroglyphics, Emblem.

Hippie: Beat Generation, Hippie.

History: History In American Literature.

Hobby: Butterflies, Mountaineering, Philately.

Homosexuality: Homosexuality.

Horror: Cave, Grotesque, Horror, Terror.

Hospitality: Hermit.

Human condition: Alienation, Anti-Semitism, Braggart, Comedy (Comic Spirit), Crippling, Dystopias, Evil, Existentialism, Incest, Lameness, Nature: *Naturae Cursus* and the State of Nature; Nihilism, Noble Savage, Peasant in Novels, Picaresque, *Pícaro* in American Literature, The, Rebellion, Social Status of Hero, Stupidity, Theatrical Absurdity, Time.

Human nature: Adolescence, Anti-Hero, Autobiographical Impulse, Comic Hero, Evil, Horror, Jealousy, Laughter, *Liebestod*, Money, Nature: *Naturae Cursus* and the State of Nature; Personality (Double-Split-Multiple), Picaresque, *Pícaro* in American Literature, The, Pride, Psychic Landscape, Reason, *Senex Amator*, Spy, Terror, Tragicomic Hero.

Humor: Laughter.

Hunt: Hunt.

Ideal: Utopia.

Identity: Name and Naming.

Image: Shadow.

Imagination: Sublimity.

Marriage: Escape, Feminism, Incest, Marriage, Secret Love.
Martyr: Christian Hero, Hermit, Scapegoat.
Marxism: Nihilism.
Mask: Grotesque, Masque or Mask, Role Playing.
Masque: Dance, Dance of Death, Dwarf, Emblem, Grotesque, Masque or Mask.
Mechanization: Crippling.
Melancholy: Melancholy.
Merchant: Banker, Financier, and Usurer.
Mermaid: Demonic Musician and the Soulbird, Siren.
Metamorphosis: Androgyny; Bear; Metamorphosis; Rat, Mouse; Werewolf.
Middle Class: Social Status of Hero.
Miles gloriosus: Braggart.
Mime: Fool.
Miracle: Birth of Hero.
Mirror: Mirror, Personality (Double-Split-Multiple), Shadow.
Miser: Money.
Mistress: La Belle Dame sans Merci, Love in Greek and Roman Literature.
Modesty: Clothing.
Money: Banker, Financier, and Usurer; Capitalism.
Monster: Birth of Hero, Cave, Demonic Musician and the Soulbird, Dragons, Grotesque, Horror, Lion, Monsters, Robots and Computers, Siren, Vampirism, Werewolf.
Mood: Melancholy.
Morality: Apology (Self-Defense of Satirists and Humorists).
Mother: Family, Incest, Oedipus Complex, Parents and Children, Psychoanalysis of the Self, Search for Father.
Mountain: Afterlife, Mountaineering, Psychic Landscape.
Moutaineering: Mountaineering.
Mouse: Rat, Mouse.
Movie: Cinema.
Multiple personality: Personality (Double-Split-Multiple).
Murder: Detective, Horror.
Muse: Artist in Literature through the Renaissance.
Music, Musician: Demonic Music, Demonic Musician and the Soulbird.
Mystic, Mysticism: Alchemy.
Name: Name and Naming.
Narcissicism: Mirror.
Native American: Noble Savage.
Nature: Arcadia, Butterflies, Mountaineering, Noble Savage, Psychic Landscape, Sublimity, Travel.
Nature (human): *See* Human Nature.
Nihilism: Existentialism, Nihilism.
Nobility: Social Status of Hero.
Noble savage: Noble Savage.
Nuclear age: Dystopias.
Obscenity: Apology (Self-Defense of Satirists and Humorists).
Oedipus complex: Odeipus Complex.
Old Age: Senex Amator.
Orality: Dialogue.

Outcast: Fool.
Outlaw: Noble Criminal.
Outsider: Picaresque.
Pacifism: Pacifism.
Pact: Pact with the Devil.
Paradise: Afterlife.
Parents: Family, Parents and Children, Search for Father.
Passion: Homosexuality, Jealousy, *Liebestod*, Love Triangle.
Pastoral: Arcadia, City, Noble Savage.
Peasant: Noble Savage, Peasant in Novels.
Perfection: Arcadia.
Performance: Dance.
Persecution: Anti-Semitism.
Personality: Personality (Double-Split-Multiple).
Philately: Philately.
Philosophy: Anti-Intellectualism, Dialogue, Epistemology, Evil, Existentialism, Hippie, Sublimity, Time, Universe.
Picaresque: Grotesque, Picaresque, *Pícaro* in American Literature, The.
Picaro: Anti-Hero, Picaresque, *Pícaro* in American Literature, The, Travel.
Picture: Emblem, Hieroglyphics.
Pilgrimage: Travel.
Plague: Dance of Death.
Poet: Artist in Literature through the Renaissance, Artist/Poet in Drama since the Renaissance, Literature within Literature.
Police: Detective.
Politics: Utopia.
Population: Dystopias.
Pornography: Sex (Heterosexual, Erotic).
Power: Leader.
Prey: Hunt.
Pride: Pride.
Priest: Christian Hero.
Prison: Escape, Pacifism.
Progress: Dystopias.
Prophecy: Apocalypse, Descent into Hell, Dream.
Prophet: Leader.
Psychic: Vampirism.
Psychic landscape: Psychic Landscape.
Psychoanalysis: Psychoanalysis of the Self.
Psychology: Personality (Double-Split-Mulitple).
Purgatory: Afterlife.
Queen: Leader.
Quest: Beat Generation, Search for Father, Travel.
Rape: Incest, Rape.
Rat: Rat, Mouse.
Reality: Epistemology.
Reason: Reason.
Rebellion: Alienation, Beat Generation, Rebellion.

Recluse: Hermit.

Recognition: Prostitute with a Good Heart, Search for Father.

Relativism: Epistemology.

Religion: Apocalypse, Christian Hero, Christianity Versus Christendom, Hippie, Religion in Science Fiction.

Rescue: Descent into Hell.

Responsibility: Responsibility.

Retreat: Retreat.

Revelation: Apocalypse.

Revenge: Horror.

Revolt: Nihilism.

Ridicule: Comic Hero.

Ritual: Dance.

River: Afterlife.

Robber: Noble Criminal.

Robot: Robots and Computers.

Rogue: Picaresque, *Pícaro* in American Literature, The.

Role Playing: *Pícaro* in American Literature, The, Role Playing.

Sacrifice: Great Father, Scapegoat.

Saint: Christian Hero, Dragons, Hermit.

Satire: Comedy (Comic Spirit).

Scapegoat: Fool, Scapegoat.

Scatology: Scatology.

Science, Scientist: Alchemy, Anti-Intellectualism, Dystopias, Religion in Science Fiction, Robots and Computers, Science, Time.

Sea: Travel.

Search for identity: Escape, *Pícaro* in American Literature, The.

Secret love: Love Triangle, Secret Love.

Seduction: La Belle Dame sans Merci, Libertine, Metamorphosis, Seduction, Sex (Heterosexual, Erotic).

Self: Adolescence, Alienation, Anti-Hero, Anxiety, Autobiographical Impulse, Dream, Dystopias, Epistemology, Existentialism, Incest, Leader, Literature within Literature, Oedipus Complex, Personality (Double-Split-Multiple), Psychoanalysis of the Self, Retreat, Role Playing.

Senex Amans: *Senex Amator*.

Serpent: Dragons, Siren.

Sex: Homosexuality, Incest, Incubus and Succubus, Lesbianism, Libertine, Seduction, Sex (Heterosexual, Erotic).

Sexuality: Androgyny, Feminism, Homosexuality, Lesbianism, Oedipus Complex, Sex (Heterosexual, Erotic).

Shadow: Shadow.

Shipwreck: Utopia.

Sin: Descent into Hell, Evil, Homosexuality, Pride, Scapegoat.

Siren: Demonic Musician and the Soulbird, Siren.

Sister: Incest.

Skeleton: Dance of Death.

Skepticism: Epistemology.

Snake: Androgyny.

INDEX

//

(Index includes authors and titles, including bibliographical references.)

ABOUT THE EDITORS AND CONTRIBUTORS

//

EDWARD F. ABOOD, Ph.D., is Professor of English at California State University, Los Angeles. He specializes in world literature. His publications include "Jung's Concept of Individuation in Hesse's *Steppenwolf*," *Underground Man*, and "Don Quixote in Search of a Self."

A. OWEN ALDRIDGE, Ph.D., is Professor Emeritus at the University of Illinois. In 1986–1987 he became Will and Ariel Durant Professor of Humanities at Saint Peter's College and in 1987 a Visiting Professor at the Pennsylvania State University. He has also taught at the Universities of Toulouse and Clermont-Ferrand in France, the University of Rio de Janeiro in Brazil, Nihon University in Japan, and the University of Kuwait. Aldridge is the founder and present editor of *Comparative Literature Studies* and past-president of the American Comparative Literature Association. He is the author of eight books in English and two others in Japanese translation. His most recent books are *The Reemergence of World Literature: A Study of Asia and the West* and *Early American Literature: A Comparatist Approach*. A collection of essays has just been published in his honor, *Deism, Masonry, and the Enlightenment: Essays Honoring Alfred Owen Aldridge*, ed. J. A. Leo Lemay.

JOSEPH R. ALFRED, Ph.D. in French, subsequently earned a master of divinity degree from the United Theological Seminary. Since being ordained, he has served in parish ministry positions in the United Church of Christ and has written a number of hymns, including "A Living Faith," which has been widely used.

MARGARET J. ALLEN, Ph.D., is Associate Professor of English at St. John's College, University of Manitoba. She specializes in Middle English literature. Her publications include "The Harlot and the Mourning Bride," in *The Practical Vision: Essays in English Literature in Honour of Flora Roy*, ed. Jane Campbell and James Doyle, and *Bestiary*.

PAUL F. ANGIOLILLO, Ph.D., Professor Emeritus of French and Italian at Dickinson College (Pennsylvania), is the author of numerous articles as well as *Armed Forces' Foreign Language Teaching* and *A Criminal as Hero: Angelo Duca*.

ARMIN ARNOLD, Dr. ès Lettres, Fellow of the Royal Society of Canada, is Auxiliary Professor at McGill University and Dozent (Höhere Wirtschafts- und Verwaltungsschule, Olten, Switzerland). His publications include *D. H. Lawrence and America, Heinrich Heine in England and America, James Joyce, G. B. Shaw, Die Literatur des Expressionismus, Friedrich Dürrenmatt, Prosa des Expressionismus, D. H. Lawrence,* and *Reclams Kriminalromanführer,* with J. Schmidt. He is editor of twenty books and three series of literary criticism.

DEBORAH AVERILL, Ph.D., is Associate Professor of English at Northampton County Area Community College, Bethlehem, Pennsylvania. Her publications include a book, *The Irish Short Story from George Moore to Frank O'Connor,* and several articles.

FRANCES K. BARASCH, Ph.D., is Professor of English at Baruch College of the City University of New York. She is author and editor of numerous articles and books, including an edition of Thomas Wright's *A History of Caricature and the Grotesque in Literature and Art; The Grotesque: A Study of Meanings;* and "The Grotesque as a Comic Genre."

PETER BARTA, Ph.D., is Assistant Professor of Russian at Texas Tech University. He is the author of "The 'Apollonian' and the 'Dionysian' in Andrei Bely's *Petersburg*"; "Childhood in the Autobiographical Novel: An Examination of Tolstoy's *Childhood,* Joyce's *A Portrait of the Artist as a Young Man* and Bely's *Kotik Letaev,*" in *Literary Interrelations: Ireland, England and the World,* ed. Wolfgang Zach and Heinz Kosok; and several articles forthcoming in the *Dictionary of Continental Women Writers.*

PAUL ALLEN BATES, Ph.D., is Professor Emeritus of English at Colorado State University. His publications include *Faust: Sources, Works, Criticism;* "Elements of Folk Literature and Humanism"; and others.

HAROLD L. BERGER, Ph.D., is Associate Professor of English Emeritus at the University of Connecticut. His publications include, among others, *Science Fiction and the New Dark Age;* "Emerson and Carlyle: The Dissenting Believers"; and "Recognition of Non-Conformity."

JEFFREY BERMAN, Ph.D., is Associate Professor of English at the State University of New York, Albany. He is the author of *Joseph Conrad: Writing as Rescue; The Talking Cure: Literary Representations of Psychoanalysis;* and numerous articles on literature and psychoanalysis.

MAYA C. BIJVOET, Ph.D., is Assistant Professor of French and German at the University of Colorado, Colorado Springs. She is the author of a forthcoming book *Liebestod: Its Function and Meaning,* as well as several articles on women writers.

ALEXANDER BLACKBURN, Ph.D., is Professor of English at the University of Colorado, Colorado Springs. He specializes in fiction writing, comparative literature, and Western American literature. He is editor of the *Writer's Forum* and author of many articles and books, including *The Myth of the Picaro: Continuity and Transformation of the Picaresque Novel, 1554–1954; The Cold War of Kitty Pentecost: A Novel*; and an edition, *The Interior Country: Stories of the Modern West*.

ADELE BLOCH, Ph.D., is Professor of Foreign Languages at the Brooklyn Center of Long Island University. Her publications include, among others, *"Don Juan* and *Dom Giovanni"*; *Molière and the Commonwealth of Letters: Patrimony and Prosperity"*; "Michel Butor and the Social Structure"; and "Mythological Syncretism in the Works of Four Modern Novelists."

STEVEN B. BOWMAN, Ph.D., is Associate Professor in the Judaic Studies Program at the University of Cincinnati. His main interests are the history of Jews and the Greeks through the ages, and Jerusalem. His publications include, among others, "Explaining Anti-Semitism"; *The Jews of Byzantium (1204–1453)*; and "Jews in War-Time Greece."

GERHARD BRAND, M.A., is Professor of English and Comparative Literature at California State University, Los Angeles. He has published on nineteenth- and twentieth-century French, German, and Russian literature.

ANDREW J. BURGESS, Ph.D., is Associate Professor of Philosophy and Chair of the Religious Studies Program at the University of New Mexico. He is the author of *Passion, "Knowing How," and Understanding: An Essay on the Concept of Faith*; "Science Fiction and Religion," in *Teaching Science Fiction: Education for Tomorrow*, ed. Jack Williamson; "The Concept of Eden," in *The Transcendent Adventure: Studies of Religion in Science Fiction/Fantasy*, ed. Robert Reilly (Greenwood Press); and others.

PAUL BURRELL, Ph.D., is Associate Professor of French at the University of Cincinnati. He is cotranslator of Jean Piaget's *Origin of the Idea of Chance in Children* and of Jacques Dubois and Groupe Mu's *A General Rhetoric*. He is author of, among others, "Pierre Bayle's *Dictionnaire historique et critique*," in *Notable Encyclopedias of XVIIth and XVIIIth Centuries: Nine Predecessors of the Encyclopédie*, ed. Frank A. Kafker.

ELLEN M. CALDWELL, Ph.D., is Assistant Professor of English at Kalamazoo College (Michigan) and specializes in Renaissance drama. Her publications include "The Rhetorics of Enthusiasm and of Restraint in Rolle's *The Form of Living* and *The Cloud of Unknowing"*; "Ellen Glasgow and the Southern Agrarians"; and "John Lyly's *Gallathea*: A New Rhetoric of Love for the Virgin Queen."

PAMELA CASWELL, A.B., is a fiction writer living in San Francisco.

NATHAN ANTHONY CERVO, Ph.D., is Professor in the Humanities Division of Franklin Pierce College (New Hampshire). He is associate editor of *The Pre-Raphaelite Review* and author of many articles in *Hopkins Quarterly, Explicator, The Arnoldian, Xavier Review*, and others.

HALE CHATFIELD, A.M., is Poet in Residence, Professor and Chairman, Department of English, Hiram College (Ohio). Founder and coeditor of the *Hiram Poetry Review*, he has published six volumes of poetry, a collection of short fiction, *Little Fictions, Loving Lies*, and a number of articles on literary criticism.

YING-YING CHIEN, Ph.D., is Assistant Professor of Foreign Languages and Literatures at the National Taiwan University, specializing in East-West comparative literature and women's studies.

MARY M. CHILDERS, Ph.D., is Visiting Assistant Professor of English at Dartmouth College. She has written several articles on the English novel and women's studies, including "Thomas Hardy, the Man Who 'Liked' Women"; "Women's Studies: Sinking and Swimming in the Mainstream"; and "Narrating Structures of Opportunity."

RANDALL CRAIG, Ph.D., is Assistant Professor of English at the State University of New York, Albany. His recent articles include "Reader-Response Criticism and Literary Realism," "Beckford's Inversion of Romance in *Vathek*," and "Plato's *Symposium* and the Tragicomic Novel." His book, *The Tragicomic Novel: Studies in a Fictional Mode from Meredith to Joyce*, is forthcoming.

KENNETH CRAVEN, Ph.D., former Assistant Professor of English at City College, City University of New York, has published in English and Russian letters of the Enlightenment.

EDWARD J. DANIS, Ph.D., is currently employed by the Division of Undergraduate Studies of the Pennsylvania State University and is affiliated with its Department of Comparative Literature. He is coediting the fourth volume of *Anglo-German and American-German Crosscurrents* and is the editor of the *Journal* of the National Academic Advising Association.

ROBERT CON DAVIS, Ph.D., is Associate Professor of English at the University of Oklahoma. He is the author of many articles and has edited several books on American literature and critical theory, including *The Fictional Father: Lacanian Readings of the Text*; *Lacan and Narration: The Psychoanalytic Difference in Narrative Theory*; and *Contemporary Literary Criticism: Modernism through Poststructuralism*.

DANIEL DERVIN, Ph.D., is Professor of English at Mary Washington College (Virginia). He is the author of numerous articles and books, including *Bernard Shaw: A Psychological Study*; *A "Strange Sapience:" The Creative Imagination of D. H. Lawrence*; and *Through a Freudian Lens Deeply: A Psychoanalysis of Cinema*.

NANCY GRAY DÍAZ, Ph.D., is Assistant Dean of the Faculty of Arts and Sciences, Rutgers–The State University, Newark. Her publications include "Imagery and the Theme of Perception: *L'éducation sentimentale* and *Nieblá*"; "El mexicano naufragado y la literatura 'pop': 'La fiesta brava' de José Emilio Pacheco"; and a forthcoming book, *The Radical Self: Metamorphosis to Animal Form in Modern Latin American Narrative*.

BERNARD F. DICK, Ph.D., is Professor of English and Comparative Literature at Fairleigh Dickinson University (Teaneck–Hackensack Campus). He has published widely in literary and film criticism. His books include *The Hellenism of Mary Renault*; *The Apostate Angel: A Critical Study of Gore Vidal*; *Anatomy of a Film*; *Billy Wilder*; *Hellman in Hollywood*; *The Star-Spangled Screen: The American World War II Film*; and *William Golding*.

MILAN V. DIMIČ Dip., is Professor of Comparative Literature at the University of Alberta. He is an expert in Romanticism and folk literature, coeditor of *Actes du septième congrès de l'association internationale de littérature comparée*, and the editor of the *Canadian Reivew of Comparative Literature/Revue de littérature comparée*.

BEVERLEY D. EDDY, Ph.D., is Associate Professor of German at Dickinson College (Pennsylvania). She specializes in nineteenth-century Danish and German literature. Her publications include *Abbeys, Ghosts, and Castles: A Guide to the Folk History of the Middle Rhine*; *Dracula. A Translation of the 1488 Nürnberg Edition with an Essay*; "Peter Nansen's Epistolary Fiction"; and others.

HARRY G. EDINGER, Ph.D., is Associate Professor of Classics at the University of British Columbia. He specializes in ancient drama and epic. His major publications include "The Lay of Demodocus in Context" and *Index Analyticus Graecitatis Aeschyleae*.

CHARLES ELKINS, Ph.D., is Professor of English and Associate Dean for the college of Arts and Sciences, Florida International University. Coeditor of *Science-Fiction Studies*, his recent essays include "George Orwell, 1903–1950," in *Science Fiction Writers: Critical Studies of the Major Authors from the Early Nineteenth Century to the Present Day*, ed. Everett Franklin Bleiler; "E. M. Forster's 'The Machine Stops': Liberal-Humanist Hostility to Technology," in *Clockwork Worlds: Mechanized Environments in SF*, ed. Richard D. Erlich et al. (Greenwood Press); and "An Approach to the Social Functions of Science-Fiction Narrative," in *The Scope of the Fantastic: Culture, Biography, Themes, Children's Literature*, ed. Robert A. Collins and Howard D. Pearce (Greenwood Press).

MARY J. ELKINS, Ph.D., is Associate Professor and Chair of the Department of English at Florida International University. Her recent articles include "Elizabeth Bishop and the Act of Seeing"; "Alenoushka's Return: Motifs and Movement in Margaret Drabble's *The Middle Ground*," in *Critical Essays on Margaret Drabble*, ed. Ellen Cronan Rose; and "*Dinner at the Homesick Restaurant*: Anne Tyler and the Faulkner Connection."

RICHARD FABRIZIO, Ph.D., is Associate Professor of English at Pace University (New York). Recent publications of his include "Moravia's *Il dio Kurt*: Sophocles and the Oedipus Theme in Italy" and "Wonderful No-Meaning: Language and the Psychopathology of the Family in Dickens' *Hard Times*."

LILLIAN FADERMAN, Ph.D., is Professor of English at the California State University, Fresno. She is the author of *Surpassing the Love of Men: Romantic Friendship and Love between Women from the Renaissance to the Present*; *Scotch Verdict: Miss Pirie and Miss Woods v. Dame Cumming Gordon*; and numerous articles on women's relationships.

MARIE-HENRIETTE FAILLIE, Ph.D., is Associate Professor of French at Hunter College of the City University of New York. Her major publications include *La femme et le code civil dans la* Comédie humaine *d'Honoré de Balzac* and *L'esprit et la lettre: la grammaire appliquée*, with Nadine Savage.

WENDY B. FARIS, Ph.D., is Associate Professor of English at the University of Texas, Arlington. Her publications include, among others, "Alejo Carpentier à la recherche du temps perdu," and *Labyrinths of Language: Symbolic Landscape and Narrative Design in Modern Fiction.*

IRÈNE FINEL-HONIGMAN, Ph.D., is Director of the French Language Program, Crédit Lyonnais Bank, New York. Among her publications are "The Orpheus and Eurydice Myth in Camus's *The Plague*," "American Misconceptions of French Feminism," and "A Historical Perspective of International Investors and Investments," in *The Handbook of International Investing*, ed. Carl R. Beidleman.

RICHARD F. FLECK, Ph.D., is Professor of English at the University of Wyoming. He specializes in nineteenth-century American literature and is the author of *Henry Thoreau and John Muir among the Indians*; the introduction to Thoreau's *The Maine Woods*; and numerous scholarly articles.

LESLIE D. FOSTER, Ph.D., is Professor of English at Northern Michigan University. His essays include "*Walden* and Its Audience: Troubled Sleep, and Religious and Other Awakenings"; "Maurya: Tragic Error and Limited Transcendence in *Riders to the Sea*"; and "The Implicit Poetics of Wallace Stevens' 'The Idea of Order at Key West.' "

ALMA S. FREEMAN, Ed.D., is Professor of English and Dean of University College, Alabama State University. Her publications include "The Androgynous Vision" with Nancy T. Bazin; *Black Culture and Black Identity: Albert Murray's* Train Whistle Guitar *and Ralph Ellison's* Invisible Man *in Alabama*; and "Zora Neale Hurston and Alice Walker: A Spirtual Kinship."

ELLIOT L. GILBERT, Ph.D., is Professor of English at the University of California, Davis. He edits the *California Quarterly* and is the author of numerous articles and stories. Among his published books are *The Good Kipling: Studies in the Short Story*; *The World of Mystery Fiction: A Guide*; and " '*O Beloved Kids': Rudyard Kipling's Letters to His Children.*"

GEORGE E. GINGRAS, Ph.D., is Associate Professor in the Department of Modern Languages at the Catholic University of America. He translated and annotated *Egeria: Diary of a Pilgrimage*; coedited the forthcoming *Tirso's Don Juan: The Metamorphosis of a Theme*; and is the author of several articles, including "Louis Bertrand and the Popularization of Patristics," in *Diakonia: Studies in Honor of Robert T. Meyer*, ed. Thomas Halton and Joseph Williman.

ROBERT E. GOODWIN, Ph.D., is Lecturer in Classics and Sanskrit at Brown University. He is the author of several conference papers on Sanskrit drama as well as a forthcoming article, "Kalidasa's Metadrama."

SARAH WEBSTER GOODWIN, Ph.D., is Assistant Professor of English at Skidmore College (New York). Her publications include "Circumscription and the Female in the Early Romantics," "Emma Bovary's Dance of Death," and the forthcoming *Kitsch and Culture: The Dance of Death in Nineteenth-Century Literature and Graphic Arts.*

GARY L. GREEN, Ph.D., is Assistant Professor of English at Youngstown State University (Ohio). He is the author of numerous conference papers on film and the coauthor of *Buster Keaton: A Bio-Bibliography* (forthcoming from Greenwood Press).

DONALD GREENE, Ph.D., is Bing Professor Emeritus of English at the University of Southern California. He is the author of numerous books and articles, including *The Politics of Samuel Johnson*; *The Age of Exuberance: Backgrounds to Eighteenth-Century English Literature*; and *Samuel Johnson*.

ANDREA HAMMER, Ph.D., is Assistant Professor of English at St. Mary's College of Maryland. She has published "Poetry and Family: An Interview with Karl Shapiro."

PETER L. HAYS, Ph.D., is Professor of English at the University of California, Davis. He is the author of *The Limping Hero: Grotesques in Literature* and of numerous articles, primarily in American literature and drama. Most recent are "Hemingway as *Auteur*" and "Pynchon's Cunning Lingual Novel: Communication in *Lot 49*."

MICHAEL HOLLAND, Ph.D., is Associate Professor of English at the California State University, Fullerton. He has published poetry and completed two novels.

EDWARD T. JONES, Ph.D., is Professor of English and Chairman of the Department of English and Speech at York College of Pennsylvania. He is the author of numerous articles as well as of *L. P. Hartley* and *Following Directions: A Study of Peter Brook*.

FRANÇOIS JOST earned doctorates from the Universities of Fribourg, Switzerland, and Paris. Professor of Comparative Literature and French at the University of Illinois, he has achieved worldwide recognition in these areas. Among his many books are *Alexandre Vinet, interprète de Pascal*; *Jean-Jacques Rousseau Suisse: Etude sur sa personnalité et sa pensée*; two volumes of *Essais de littérature comparée*; and *Introduction to Comparative Literature*.

NICOLAS KIESSLING, Ph.D., is Professor of English at Washington State University. He specializes in Medieval and Renaissance English literature and is coeditor of a forthcoming edition of Robert Burton's *The Anatomy of Melancholy*. His major publications include *The Incubus in English Literature: Provenance and Progeny* and *The Library of Robert Burton* (forthcoming).

SHOSHANA KNAPP, Ph.D., is Associate Professor of English at the Virginia Polytechnic and State University. She has published a number of articles, including "Tolstoj's Reading of George Eliot: Visions and Revisions"; "The Transformations of a Pinter Screenplay: Freedom and Calculators in *The French Lieutenant's Woman*"; and "George Eliot and W. S. Gilbert: *Silas Marner* into *Dan'l Druce*."

LESLEY C. KORDECKI, Ph.D., is Associate Professor and Chair of English at Barat College (Illinois). Her publications include "Prophecy, Dragons and Meaning in Malory," in *Proceedings of the Illinois Medieval Association*, ed. Roberta Bux Bosse; "Fables: The Moral of the Story," in *Teaching the Middle Ages II*, ed. Robert Graybill;

and "Twain's Critique of Malory's Romance: *Forma tractandi* and *A Connecticut Yankee.*"

DENNIS M. KRATZ, Ph.D., is Professor of Arts and Humanities at the University of Texas, Dallas, and coeditor of the journal *Translation Review*. His fields of interest include heroism, the fantastic, medieval literature, and translation. His major publications are *Mocking Epic: Waltharius, Alexandreis, and the Problem of Christian Heroism* and *Waltharius and Ruodlieb*.

JOHN R. KRUEGER, Ph.D., is now retired as Professor of Uralic and Altaic Studies at Indiana University. His numerous publications include *Chuvash Manual: Introduction, Grammar, Reader, and Vocabulary*; *The Bejewelled Summary of the Origin of Khans*; *Mongolian Epigraphical Dictionary in Reverse Listing*; and *Materials for an Oirat-Mongolian to English Citation Dictionary*.

JOSEPH LABAT, Ph.D., is Associate Professor of French at Washington State University. He is coeditor of *La France en mutation depuis 1955* and author of "La dialectique culturelle et le devenir de la France," and "Anthropologie et sartrisme."

ANITA LAWSON, Ph.D., is Professor of English and Director of the Honors Program at Murray State University (Kentucky). She is interested in the comic spirit wherever it appears, as in the subject of her biography, *Irvin S. Cobb*.

BARBARA FASS LEAVY, Ph.D., is Professor of English at Queens College, New York. She is the author, among others, of *La Belle Dame sans Merci and the Aesthetics of Romanticism* and "Christina Rossetti and St. Agnes' Eve," and coauthor of *Ibsen's Forsaken Merman: Folklore in the Late Plays*.

PETER H. LEE, Ph.D., is Professor of Korean and Comparative Literature at the University of California, Los Angeles. A Guggenheim Fellow, Lee participated in the National Academy of Sciences' Distinguished Scholar Exchange Program, lecturing on East Asian and comparative literature at Peking University. His publications include a translation of lives of eminent Korean monks; *Songs of Flying Dragons: A Critical Reading*; *Celebration of Continuity: Themes in Classic East Asian Poetry*; and anthologies of Korean literature, classical and modern.

SUZANNE J. LEPPE, after being awarded a Ph.D., chose a career in engineering. She is now an engineer at General Dynamics, while keeping up an interest in the relationship of music and film to literature. She is currently working on an advanced degree in computer science.

ARTHUR O. LEWIS, Ph.D., is Professor Emeritus of English and Associate Dean Emeritus, College of the Liberal Arts at Pennsylvania State University. He has written, edited, co-edited, and published extensively in American, compartive, and English literatures. His publications related to Utopian Studies include editing *Of Men and Machines*; *American Utopias*; *Utopian Literature* (reprint series); authoring *Utopian Literature in The Pennsylvania State University Libraries: A Selected Bibliography*; and coediting *Utopie per gli anni ottanta: Studi inderdisciplinari sui temi, la storia, i progetti*.

WILLIAM LITTLE, Ph.D., is Professor and Head, Foreign Languages Department, and Coordinator of the Humanities Program at the California Polytechnic State University, San Luis Obispo. His recent publications include "Notas sobre *Tres tristes tigres* de G. Cabrera Infante," "Varios aspectos de don Juan y el donjuanismo," and "The Don Juan Myth in Charles Baudelaire's *oeuvre*," forthcoming in *Simposio de Tirso do Molina*.

KENT LJUNGQUIST, Ph.D., is Professor of English at Worcester Polytechnic Institute (Massachusetts). He is the author of *The Grand and the Fair: Poe's Landscape Aesthetics and Pictorial Techniques* and coeditor of J. F. Cooper's *The Deerslayer*. He has published a number of articles on Poe, Cooper, Thoreau, and Frost, and was a contributor to *American Literary Magazines: The Eighteenth and Nineteenth Centuries*, ed. Edward E. Chielens (Greenwood Press).

APARAJITA MAZUMDER is a Ph.D. student in comparative literature at the University of Illinois.

LAURA JEHN MENIDES, Ph.D., is Associate Professor of English at the Worcester Polytechnic Institute (Massachusetts). She specializes in the relationship between history and literature, and in film studies. Her publications include "John Huston's *Wise Blood* and the Myth of the Sacred Quest"; "Choosing One's Place: Charles Olson, Worcester, and Gloucester"; and "There, but for the Grace of God, Go I: T. S. Eliot and William Carlos Williams on Poe," in *Poe and Our Times: Influences and Affinities*, ed. Benjamin Franklin Fisher IV.

M. J. MURATORE, Ph.D., is Assistant Professor of French at the University of Missouri, Columbia. Her most recent publications include "Theater as Theater: The Language of Cornelian Illusion"; "Racinian Stasis," in *Re-lectures raciniennes: Nouvelles approches du discours tragique*, ed. R. L. Barnett; and "Polyeucte, the Divine Comedian."

WILLIAM I. OLIVER, Ph.D., is Professor of Drama at the University of California, Berkeley. He is well known as a director and playwright (his *To Learn to Love* won the Stanley Award). He has translated many French, Latin American, and Spanish plays. He coedited *Modern Drama, Essays in Criticism* and edited *Voice of Change in the Spanish American Theater*.

ROSALIE OSMOND, Ph.D., former Assistant Professor at York University, Toronto, teaches in the Department of Extra-Mural Studies of the University of London. Her publications include "Body, Soul, and the Marriage Relationship: The History of an Analogy"; "Body and Soul Dialogues in the Seventeenth Century"; and "George Herbert: Richness in Austerity."

MICHAEL L. PERNA, Ph.D., is Assistant Professor of Spanish at Hunter College, City University of New York. He has contributed articles to the forthcoming *Twentieth Century Spanish Poets* volume of the *Dictionary of Literary Biography*.

JOHN ANDREW PYROS, Ph.D., is a former Assistant Professor of English at Cumberland County College (New Jersey), Southern University (Louisana), and Lincoln

University (Pennsylvania). His major publications are *Mike Gold: Dean of American Proletarian Writers* and *William Wantling: A Biography and Selected Works.*

CHARLES H. REEVES, Ph.D., is Professor Emeritus of Classics at Case Western Reserve University. Among his publications are "The Parados of the *Agamemnon*"; a translation of *Johannes Nider, "On the Contracts of Merchants"*; and "Love in Aeschylus: The Earlier Plays."

ELIZABETH S. ROGERS, Ph.D., is Professor of Spanish at Miami University (Ohio). Her recent articles include "*La jaula*: An Ortegan View of Mass-Man"; "Myth, Man, and Exile in *El retorno de Ulises* and *¿Por que corres, Ulises?*" and "Death and Rebirth as a Double Mythic Dimension in *La dama del alba.*"

DIETER J. ROLLFINKE, Ph.D., is Associate Professor of German and Chair of the Department of German and Russian at Dickinson College (Pennsylvania). His scholarly interests focus on modern German literature. He is coauthor of *The Call of Human Nature: The Role of Scatology in Modern German Literature.*

DANIEL RUSSELL, Ph.D., is Professor and Chairman of French and Italian at the University of Pittsburgh. Coeditor of the journal *Emblematica*, he has published numerous articles on emblems and all aspects of French Renaissance culture, as well as a book, *The Emblem and Device in France.*

JANA SAWICKI, Ph.D., is Associate Professor of Philosophy at the University of Maine. She is the author of many articles on Foucault, including "Foucault and Feminism: Toward a Politics of Difference"; "Heidegger and Foucault: Escaping Technological Nihilism" (forthcoming); and "Feminism and the Power of Foucauldran Discourse," in the forthcoming *After Foucault: Humanistic Knowledges, Postmodern Challenges*, ed. Jonathan Arac.

JOHN D. SCHAEFFER, Ph.D., is Associate Professor of English at Columbus College (Georgia). His speciality is the history of rhetoric. His articles include "Socratic Method in More's *Utopia*"; "Giambattista Vico's Rhetorical Model of the Mind: *Sensus Communis* in the *De nostri temporis studiorum ratione*"; and "From Wit to Narration: Vico's Theory of Metaphor in Its Rhetorical Context."

WINFRIED SCHLEINER, Ph.D., is Professor of English at the University of California, Davis. He has published *The Imagery of John Donne's Sermons* and numerous articles on English, American, and German literature, including "The Nexus of Witchcraft and Male Impotence in Renaissance Thought and Its Reflection in Mann's *Doctor Faustus*" and "Renaissance Exampla of Schizophrenia: The Cure by Charity in Luther and Cervantes."

NATALIE SCHROEDER, Ph.D., is Assistant Professor of English at the University of Mississippi. She has published a number of articles on the British novel and Victorian literature, including "The Oedipal Triangle in Pater's 'Hyppolytus Veiled,' " "Regina Maria Roche and the Early Nineteenth-Century Irish Regional Novelists," and "*Barnaby Rudge* and *Jack Sheppard*: Yet More 'Humbug' from a 'Jolter-Head.' "

JEAN-CHARLES SEIGNEURET, Ph.D., is Professor of French at the University of Cincinnati. He has published a number of articles on French literature, culture, and philology, as well as professional concerns. His books include *Le roman du comte d'Artois (XVe siècle)*; a translation with introduction and notes of Pierre de Larivey's *The Spirits, Four Renaissance French Plays*; and *La France en mutation depuis 1955*, which he coedited. In 1976 the French government conferred upon him the rank of *Chevalier* in the Order of the Academic Palms.

ARMAND E. SINGER, Ph.D., is Emeritus Professor of Romance Languages at West Virginia University. For the past thirty-five years he has been editor-in-chief of the *West Virginia University Philological Papers* and has published extensively. His books include *The Don Juan Theme, Versions and Criticism: A Bibliography*; *Paul Bourget*; and *Essays on the Literature of Mountaineering*, of which he was contributing editor.

MICHAEL SKAU, Ph.D., is Professor of English at the University of Nebraska, Omaha. His book, *Constantly Risking Absurdity*, is forthcoming. Among his articles are "The Central Verbal System: The Prose of William S. Burroughs" and "American Ethos: Richard Brautigan's *Trout Fishing in America*."

CHARLOTTE SPIVACK, Ph.D., is Professor of English at the University of Massachusetts, Amherst. She has published extensively. Her books include *Early English Drama from the Middle Ages to the Early Seventeenth Century*, with William Bracy; *George Chapman*; *The Comedy of Evil on Shakespeare's Stage*; *Ursula K. Le Guin*; and *Merlin's Daughters: Contemporary Women Writers of Fantasy* (Greenwood Press).

IRENE SUBOCZEWSKI, Ph.D., is Assistant Professor of English Studies at the University of the District of Columbia. She has published translations of Lithuanian poetry in *Contemporary East European Poetry: An Anthology*, ed. Emery George.

JON THIEM, Ph.D., is Associate Professor of English at Colorado State University. His major scholarly interests are Renaissance literature, translation, and the history of ideas. Among his essays are "The Library of Alexandria Burnt: Towards the History of a Symbol" and "Borges, Dante, and the Poetics of Total Vision" (forthcoming).

PATRICIA TOBIN, Ph.D., is Associate Professor of English at Rutgers University, New Brunswick, (New Jersey). She is the author of *Time and the Novel: The Genealogical Imperative*; "The Autumn of the Signifier: The Deconstructionist Moment of García Márquez"; and others.

STEPHEN JOHN TONSOR, Ph.D., is Professor of History at the University of Michigan. Associate Editor of *Modern Age*, he has published dozens of articles and books, including *National Socialism: Conservative Reaction or Nihilist Revolt?*; *Tradition and Reform in Education*; and "The Medieval Model of Social Reconstruction."

ROBERT M. TORRANCE, Ph.D., is Professor of Comparative Literature at the University of California, Davis. He has published widely. Among his principal publications are translations of Sophocles' *The Women of Trachis* and *Philoctetes*; *The Comic Hero*;

and *Ideal and Spleen: The Crisis of Transcendent Vision in Romantic, Symbolist, and Modern Poetry.*

HAROLD A. VEESER, Ph.D., is Assistant Professor of English at the Wichita State University. His publications include, among others, " 'That Dangerous Supplement,' *La Verdad Sospechosa* and the Literary Speech Situation," in *Things Done with Words: Speech Acts in Hispanic Drama*, ed. Elias L. Rivers; "Embarrassing the Signifier," in the forthcoming *Anatomy of a Bestseller*, ed. Thomas Inge; and "Moving Visions: The New Historicism of Edward W. Said" (forthcoming).

MICHÈLE E. VIALET, Ph.D., is Assistant Professor of French at the University of Cincinnati. She specializes in French seventeenth-century literature, literary theory, and Francophone studies. Her publications include *"Adolphe*: échec en amour ou temporisation" and *"Le roman bourgeois*: écriture de l'incohérence," in *Les contes de Perrault. La contestation et ses limites - Furetière. Actes de Banff - 1986*, ed. Michel Bareau et al.

PATRICIA S. WARRICK, Ph.D., is Professor of English at the University of Wisconsin, Fox Valley. She has written numerous articles and books on the subject of science fiction, including *The Cybernetic Imagination in Science Fiction* and *Mind in Motion: The Fiction of Philip K. Dick.*

MANFRED WEIDHORN, Ph.D., is Professor of English at Yeshiva University. He is the author of *Dreams in Seventeenth-Century English Literature*; *Richard Lovelace*; *Sword and Pen: A Survey of the Writings of Sir Winston Churchill*; *Sir Winston Churchill* as well as numerous essays and a biography of Napoleon for young adults.

FLORENCE M. WEINBERG, Ph.D., is Professor of Modern Languages and Classics at St. John Fisher College (New York). Her publications include *The Wine and the Will: Rabelais's Bacchic Christianity*; *Garantua in a Convex Mirror: Fischart's View of Rabelais*; *The Cave: The Evolution of a Metaphoric Field from Homer to Ariosto*; and numerous articles.

ULRICH WICKS, Ph.D., is Associate Professor of English at the University of Maine. He has published a number of essays on the picaresque. His most recent articles include "Borges, Bertolucci, and Metafiction," in *Narrative Strategies: Original Essays in Film and Prose Fiction*, ed. Syndy M. Conger and Janice R. Welsch; "Studying Film as Integrated Text"; and "Metafiction in *Don Quixote*: What is the Author Up To?" in *Approaches to Teaching Cervantes' Don Quixote*, ed. Richard Bjornson.

The late JOHN F. WINTER, Ph.D., was Professor Emeritus of French at the University of Cincinnati. He has published extensively on sixteenth- and seventeenth-century French literature, including "A Forerunner of Molière's *Misanthrope*"; "Visual Variety and Spatial Grandeur in Rabelais"; and *Visual Variety and Spatial Grandeur: A Study of the Transition from the Sixteenth to the Seventeenth Century in France.*

LOIS PARKINSON ZAMORA, Ph.D., is Associate Professor of English and Comparative Literature at the University of Houston. She has published a number of articles on contemporary North and South American fiction, has edited *The Apocalyptic Vision in America: Interdisciplinary Essays on Myth and Culture*, and is the author of the forthcoming book, *Last Words: Apocalyptic Ends and Endings in Contemporary U.S. and Latin American Fiction. Enclosed Garden*, a translation of the short fiction of contemporary Mexican writer Angelina Muñiz-Huberman, is also forthcoming.